How does context impact our growth and development? Do the places, sociocultural environments, and ways in which we were raised influence who we will become and how we will grow and change?

EXPLORE DEVELOPMENT THROUGH THE THEME OF CONTEXTS

A thoroughly integrated emphasis on the role of context in the lifespan and the diverse forms that context takes helps readers understand the wide range of dynamic influences that shape human development.

Lives in Context & **Cultural Influences on Development** boxes include compelling examples of contextual and cultural influences on development and highlight issues informed by lifespan research.

Dr. Kuther's Chalk Talks—brief, captivating videos—help students learn basic concepts outside the classroom, allowing class time to be spent on active learning, while follow-up questions stimulate critical thinking.

Lives in Context Video Cases explore the lives and contexts of individuals in every stage of the lifespan. Using audio narration, author Tara L. Kuther guides students beyond the book into homes, schools, and workplaces to help students master learning objectives through real-life examples and demonstrations.

EXPLORE DEVELOPMENT THROUGH APPLICATION

Applying Developmental Science boxes reflect the increasing relevance and influence of developmental science, providing students the opportunity to explore real-world questions on contemporary issues influencing our lives.

EXPLORE DEVELOPMENT THROUGH THE BRAIN

Lifespan Brain Development boxes apply research on neurological development to current topics.

EXPLORE DEVELOPMENT THROUGH HELPFUL LEARNING & STUDYING TOOLS

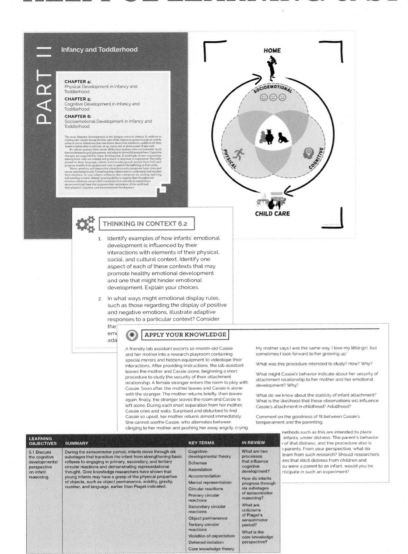

Concept Maps and learning objectives that introduce each text section anchor student learning goals while emphasizing key text concepts.

Thinking in Context critical thinking questions at the end of each section and boxed features encourage students to consider and apply theory and research to solve problems.

What Do You Think? questions at the end of every boxed feature challenge students to assess and evaluate the issues highlighted in that feature.

Chapter-ending **Apply Your Knowledge** case scenarios, followed by in-depth questions, help students apply their understanding of text concepts to particular situations or problems.

Visual Reviews reinforce the text's core themes at the chapter level in a memorable and visually appealing manner.

BRING DEVELOPMENT TO LIFE FOR YOUR STUDENTS

Combine **Lifespan Development, 2e** with Stephanie Wright's *Cases in Lifespan Development* to connect students to the process of development across the lifespan.

This package option offers twelve diverse, engrossing, and comprehensive cases through which students will view realistic and varied life outcomes across key developmental stages. The bundle includes the Kuther textbook and a print collection of 12 cases, which are also offered digitally with assessments in our **SAGE coursepacks**.

To Fred

LIFESPAN
DEVELOPMENT
LIVES IN CONTEXT SECOND EDITION

TARA L. KUTHER

Western Connecticut State University

Los Angeles | London | New Delhi
Singapore | Washington DC | Melbourne

FOR INFORMATION:

SAGE Publications, Inc.
2455 Teller Road
Thousand Oaks, California 91320
E-mail: order@sagepub.com

SAGE Publications Ltd.
1 Oliver's Yard
55 City Road
London, EC1Y 1SP
United Kingdom

SAGE Publications India Pvt. Ltd.
B 1/I 1 Mohan Cooperative Industrial Area
Mathura Road, New Delhi 110 044
India

SAGE Publications Asia-Pacific Pte. Ltd.
18 Cross Street #10-10/11/12
China Square Central
Singapore 048423

Printed in Canada.

Library of Congress Cataloging-in-Publication Data

Names: Kuther, Tara L., author.

Title: Lifespan development / Tara L. Kuther.

Description: Second Edition. | Thousand Oaks : SAGE, [2019] | Revised edition of the author's Lifespan development, [2017] | Includes bibliographical references and index.

Identifiers: LCCN 2018032303 | ISBN 9781544332284 (loose-leaf : alk. paper)

Subjects: LCSH: Developmental psychology. | Life cycle, Human.

Classification: LCC BF713 .K87 2019 | DDC 155—dc23 LC record available at https://lccn.loc.gov/2018032303

Acquisitions Editor: Lara Parra
Editorial Assistant: Drew Fabricius
Content Development Editors: Lucy Berbeo and Emma Newsom
Production Editor: Olivia Weber-Stenis
Copy Editor: Gillian Dickens
Typesetter: Hurix Digital
Proofreader: Sally Jaskold
Indexer: Sheila Bodell
Cover Designer: Gail Buschman
Marketing Manager: Katherine Hepburn

This book is printed on acid-free paper.

MIX
Paper from
responsible sources
FSC
www.fsc.org   FSC® C011825

19 20 21 22 23 10 9 8 7 6 5 4 3 2 1

BRIEF CONTENTS

CONTENTS

Hannah Gal/Science Source

John Cancalosi / Alamy Stock Photo

iStock/FatCamera

Blend Images - KidStock/ Brand X Pictures via Getty Images

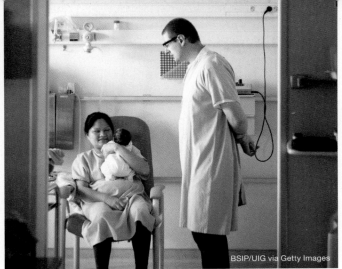

BSIP/UIG via Getty Images

ian west / Alamy Stock Photo

PART III

EARLY CHILDHOOD 188

CHAPTER 7: PHYSICAL AND COGNITIVE DEVELOPMENT IN EARLY CHILDHOOD 190

CHAPTER 8: SOCIOEMOTIONAL DEVELOPMENT IN EARLY CHILDHOOD 220

iStock/Dushyant Kumar Thakur

Olaf Doering / Alamy Stock Photo

Shoji Fujita/DigitalVision via Getty Images

AFP Contributor / AFP via Getty Images

Alys Tomlinson / Taxi / via Getty Images

TAO Images Limited / Alamy Stock Photo

Reuters/Noah Berger

Thomas Barwick/Taxi via Getty Images

CHAPTER 14: SOCIOEMOTIONAL DEVELOPMENT IN EMERGING AND EARLY ADULTHOOD 414

PART VII

MIDDLE ADULTHOOD 442

CHAPTER 15: PHYSICAL AND COGNITIVE DEVELOPMENT IN MIDDLE ADULTHOOD 444

Sonja Pacho/Corbis

Kirill Kukhmar\TASS via Getty Images

NurPhoto via Getty Images

Mario Tama/Getty Images News via Getty Images

PREFACE

Lifespan Development: Lives in Context has its origins in 20-plus years of class discussions about the nature of development in which my students have questioned, challenged, and inspired me. My goal in writing this text is to explain the sophisticated interactions that constitute development in a way that is comprehensive yet concise.

Lifespan Development: Lives in Context focuses on two key themes that promote understanding of how humans develop through the lifespan: the centrality of context and the applied value of developmental science. These two themes are highlighted throughout the text as well as in boxed features. This text also emphasizes cutting-edge research and a student-friendly writing style.

CONTEXTUAL PERSPECTIVE

Development does not occur in a vacuum but is a function of dynamic transactions among individuals, their biological makeup, and myriad contextual influences. We are all embedded in multiple interacting layers of context, including tangible and intangible circumstances that influence and are influenced by our development, such as family, ethnicity, culture, neighborhood, community, norms, values, and historical events. The contextual approach of *Lifespan Development: Lives in Context* emphasizes the intersection of context and diversity and the many forms that diversity takes (gender, race and ethnicity, socioeconomic status, etc.).

Lifespan Development: Lives in Context emphasizes how individual factors, combined with the places, sociocultural environments, and ways in which we are raised, influence who we become and how we grow and change throughout the lifespan. This theme is infused throughout the text and highlighted specifically in two types of boxed features that appear in each chapter: Lives in Context and Cultural Influences on Development. Examples of Lives in Context features include the effects of maternal depression on emotional development in infancy and toddlerhood, transgender children, and the effects of exposure to war and terrorism in childhood. The Cultural Influences on Development feature examines cultural perspectives on biological changes such as birth, menarche, menopause, and death. This feature also examines cultural influences on individuals' development and how they understand their world, such as language development, theory of mind, views of aging, and susceptibility to dementia.

EMPHASIS ON APPLICATION

The field of lifespan developmental science is unique because so much of its content has immediate relevance to our daily lives. Students may wonder this: Do the first 3 years shape the brain for a lifetime of experiences? Is learning more than one language beneficial to children? Do people's personalities change over their lifetimes? Do adults go through a midlife crisis? How common is dementia in older adulthood? Moreover, findings from lifespan developmental science have been applied to inform social policies that affect us all. *Lifespan Development: Lives in Context* engages students by exploring these and many more real-world questions. The emphasis on application is highlighted specifically in the Applying Developmental Science boxed feature, which examines applied and social policy topics such as the implications of the opioid crisis, whether video games cause aggression, antibullying legislation, age discrimination, and the issue of disclosing dementia diagnoses to patients.

CURRENT RESEARCH

The lifespan course comes with the challenge of covering the growing mass of research findings within the confines of a single semester. *Lifespan Development: Lives in Context* integrates carefully selected current research findings with the classic theory and research that remains an important foundation for today's most exciting scholarly work. I integrate cutting-edge and classic research to present a unified story of what is currently known in developmental science. For example, neuroscience and epigenetics are some of the most rapidly growing areas of developmental science research. These topics are reflected throughout the text and especially in the Brain and Biological Influences on Development feature, which examines topics such as pregnancy and the maternal brain, poverty and brain development, the effects of sleep on emotional regulation in young children and neurological functioning in adults, chronic traumatic encephalopathy in athletes, and whether age-related neurological changes increase older adults' risk for maltreatment.

ACCESSIBLE WRITING STYLE

Having taught at a regional public university for over 20 years, I write in a style intended to engage undergraduate readers like my own students. This text is intended to help them understand challenging concepts in language that will not overwhelm: I have avoided jargon but maintained the use of professional and research terms that students need to know in order to digest classic and current literature in the lifespan development field. I regularly use my own text in class, and my students' responses and learning guide my writing.

ORGANIZATION

Lifespan Development: Lives in Context is organized into 19 chronological chapters that depict the natural unfolding of development over the lifespan from genetic foundations, conception, and birth to older adulthood and the end of life. Chapters are grouped into nine thematic units that represent the major periods in the lifespan.

Part I, Foundations of Lifespan Human Development, includes Chapters 1, 2, and 3. Chapter 1 combines lifespan theory and research design within a single chapter. I chose this streamlined approach because, given limited class time, many instructors (including myself) do not cover stand-alone research chapters. The streamlined approach combines comprehensive coverage of methods of data collection, research design, developmental designs (such as sequential designs), and ethical issues in research with full coverage of the major theories in developmental psychology. Chapter 2 presents the biological foundations of development, including patterns of genetic inheritance, gene–environment interactions, and epigenetics. Chapter 3 describes prenatal development and birth.

Part II, Infancy and Toddlerhood, comprises three chapters because the rapid and dramatic transformations over the first years of life merit comprehensive discussion of the physical, cognitive, and socioemotional changes in stand-alone chapters (Chapters 4, 5, and 6).

Parts III through VIII contain two chapters each: physical and cognitive development as well as socioemotional development. Part III covers early childhood; Part IV, middle childhood; Part V, adolescence; Part VI, early adulthood; Part VII, middle adulthood; and Part VIII, late adulthood. Finally, Part IX (Chapter 19) presents death and dying, including the processes of death, how children and adults understand death, and coping with bereavement.

PEDAGOGY

My day-to-day experiences in the classroom have helped me to keep college students' interests and abilities at the forefront. Unlike many textbook authors, I teach four classes each semester at a comprehensive regional public university (and have done so since 1996). I taught my first online course in 2002. My daily exposure to multiple classes and many students helps keep me grounded in the ever-changing concerns and interests of college students. I teach a diverse group of students. Some live on campus, but most commute. Most of my students are ages 18 to 24, but my classes also include many so-called adult learners over the age of 24. Many are veterans, a rapidly increasing population at my institution. I have many opportunities to try new examples and activities. I believe that what works in my classroom will be helpful to readers and instructors. I use the pedagogical elements of *Lifespan Development: Lives in Context* in my own classes and modify them based on my experiences.

LEARNING OBJECTIVES AND SUMMARIES

Core learning objectives are listed at the beginning of each chapter. The end-of-chapter summary returns to each learning objective, recapping the key concepts presented in the chapter related to that objective. In the second edition, these objectives have been streamlined and reduced to highlight the most important content.

CRITICAL THINKING

Critical Thinking Questions: At the end of each main section within the chapter, these Thinking in Context critical thinking questions encourage readers to compare concepts, apply theoretical perspectives, and consider applications of research findings presented.

Boxed Features: Each boxed feature appears in every chapter and concludes with critical thinking questions that challenge students to assess and evaluate the issues highlighted in that feature. The boxed features exemplify the applied, contextual, and research-based theme of *Lifespan Development: Lives in Context*:

Lives in Context

Applying Developmental Science

Cultural Influences on Development

Brain and Biological Influences on Development

Case-Based Application: Each chapter closes with a case scenario, Apply Your Knowledge, followed by in-depth questions that require students to apply their understanding to address a particular situation or problem.

SUPPLEMENTS

Original Video

Lifespan Development in Context, Second Edition, is accompanied by a robust collection of **Lives in Context Video Cases** that demonstrate key concepts through real-life examples, as well as **Dr. Kuther's Chalk Talks**, a series of whiteboard-style videos carefully crafted to engage students with course content. All videos are accessible through the interactive eBook available to pair with the text.

For Instructors

SAGE edge is a robust online environment featuring an impressive array of tools and resources. At edge.sagepub.com/kuther2e, instructors using this book can access the password-protected customizable PowerPoint slides, along with an extensive Test Bank built on Bloom's taxonomy that features multiple-choice, true/false, essay, and short answer questions for each chapter. The instructor's manual is mapped to learning objectives and features lecture notes, discussion questions, chapter exercises, class assignments, and more.

For Students

Free resources are available at **http://edge.sagepub.com/kuther2e** to promote mastery of course material. Students are encouraged to access articles from award-winning **SAGE Journals**, listen to **podcasts**, and watch open-access **video resources**. Students can then practice with mobile-friendly **Flashcards** and **Quizzes** to find out what they've learned. The text can also be paired with an interactive eBook that offers one-click access to these study tools and to the book's **Original Video** package for a seamless learning experience.

WHAT'S NEW IN *LIFESPAN DEVELOPMENT: LIVES IN CONTEXT*, SECOND EDITION?

I approached writing the second edition of *Lifespan Development: Lives in Context* with three goals:

1. **Increase the coverage of context, including ethnic, cultural, and socioeconomic diversity.**

I addressed this goal by adding findings and sections covering contextual and cultural influences throughout each chapter. For example, the Cultural Influences on Development feature in each chapter speaks to the role of cultural factors in development.

2. **Update the text to include the most current research to date.**

Our knowledge of human development is rapidly expanding. My goal was to select, highlight, and integrate cutting-edge research findings with existing theory and research. The second edition includes over 1,400 references published since 2016, including nearly 900 published in 2017 and 2018.

3. **Streamline the text.**

My goal for this second edition was to paradoxically increase coverage of current research while increasing concision. This goal is influenced by my observations of my own students' use of this text. I approached this goal by carefully considering each section of each chapter and painstakingly paring down the verbiage and excess detail while retaining and enhancing the scientific basis for conclusions. As a result, each chapter is shorter with streamlined, but not reduced, coverage of the major findings in developmental science. I have also sharpened the chapter learning objectives and summaries.

Below I list the major revisions reflected in this second edition of *Lifespan Development: Lives in Context*. It is my hope that this volume will improve instructors' and students' experiences in and out of class—and that students will be inspired to apply the findings of developmental science to their lives.

Chapter 1

- Updated *What Is Lifespan Human Development?*, including *Development Is Multidimensional, Development Is Multidirectional, and Development Is Plastic*

- Added new coverage of age-graded influences, history-graded influences, and nonnormative influences to *Development Is Influenced by Multiple Contexts*

- Updated and revised *Cultural Influences on Development: Defining Culture*

- Updated *Basic Issues in Lifespan Human Development*, including *Continuities and Discontinuities in Development, Individuals Are Active in Development,* and *Nature and Nurture Influence Development*

- Updated coverage and evaluation of *Freud's Psychosexual Theory*

- Updated *Operant Conditioning, Piaget's Cognitive-Developmental Theory*, and *Information Processing Theory*

- Updated and expanded coverage of *Ethology and Evolutionary Developmental Theory*

- New *Applying Developmental Science: The Real-World Significance of Developmental Research*, highlighting the ethical issues that arise in developmental science and its implications for international policy

- New coverage of *Physiological Measures*

- New feature on *Brain and Biological Influences on Development: Methods of Studying the Brain*

- Added new research examples of *Experimental Research*

Chapter 2

- Updated coverage and streamlined *Cell Reproduction*

- Updated coverage of *Ethical and Policy Applications of Life Span Development: Prenatal Sex Selection* and retitled as *Applying Developmental Science: Prenatal Sex Selection*

- Updated coverage of *Genes Shared by Twins*

- Updated and extended coverage of *Dominant-Recessive Inheritance* to include additional information about sickle cell trait

- Updated and expanded coverage of *Genomic Imprinting*

- Updated coverage of *Dominant-Recessive Disorders*

- Updated and reorganized coverage of *X-Linked Disorders*

- Updated and expanded coverage of *Chromosomal Abnormalities*

- Updated coverage of *Mutation*

- New section: *Genetic Counseling* with new subsections on *Reproductive Technology* and *Adoption*

- Updated and expanded coverage of *Prenatal Testing* to include fetal MRI

- Updated and expanded coverage of *Prenatal Treatment of Genetic Disorders* to include fetoscopy

- Updated coverage of *Behavioral Genetics*, including *Genetic Influences on Personal Characteristics, Gene-Environment Interactions, Canalization*, and *Gene-Environment Correlations*

- Updated coverage of *Epigenetic Influences on Development* replaces *Epigenetic Framework*

- Updated *Applying Developmental Science: Altering the Epigenome* retitled as *Brain and Biological Influences on Development: Altering the Epigenome*

Chapter 3

- Updated coverage of *Prenatal Development*

- New coverage of *Contextual and Cultural Influences on Prenatal Care*

- New feature on *Brain and Biological Influences on Development: Pregnancy and the Maternal Brain*

- Updated coverage and reorganized *Principles of Teratology* section to combine *Developmental Delays* and *Sleeper Effects* as *Complicated Effects*

- Updated and reorganized *Types of Teratogens*

- Updated and retitled *Ethical and Policy Applications of Lifespan Development: Maternal Drug Use While Pregnant* as *Applying Developmental Science: Maternal Drug Use While Pregnant*

- Divided and expanded *Childbirth and the Newborn* into two sections

- New *Childbirth* section includes new coverage of *Medication During Delivery, Cesarean Delivery, Natural Childbirth*, and *Home Birth*

Chapter 4

- Updated coverage and streamlined presentation of *Growth Norms, Breastfeeding, Solid Food*, and *Malnutrition*

- Updated coverage and retitled *Ethical and Policy Applications of Life Span Development*

- Updated and streamlined coverage of *Failure to Thrive*

- Updated coverage of *Processes of Neural Development*

- New coverage of *The Cerebral Cortex*

- Updated coverage of *Experience and Brain Development*

- New coverage of *Sleep and Brain Development*

- Updated coverage of *Imitation* to address recent criticism

- Updated *Lives in Context: Pain and Neonatal Circumcision*

- Updated coverage of *Intermodal Perception* and expanded to include discussion of affordances

- Updated coverage and added new examples to *Motor Development During Infancy and Toddlerhood*

- New feature on *Brain and Biological Influences on Development: Hand Preference and Language Development in Infancy*

- Updated and expanded *Motor Development as a Dynamic System*

Chapter 5

- Updated and expanded coverage of *Deferred Imitation Tasks*

- Updated and expanded coverage of *Core Knowledge Theory: An Alternative Perspective*

- Updated coverage of *Organization of the Information Processing System, Attention,* and *Memory*

- Updated coverage of *Categorization* and retitled as *Infants' Thinking*

- New feature: *Brain and Biological Influences on Development: Poverty and Development*

- Updated *Information Processing Approach to Intelligence* with new examples and retitled as *Intelligence as Information Processing*

- Updated and expanded coverage of *Prelinguistic Communication* and *First Words* and *Learning Words: Semantic Growth*

- Updated coverage of *Learning Theory and Language Development* and *Nativist Theory and Language Development*

- Updated, reorganized, and expanded coverage of *Interactionist Perspective on Language Development*, including *Biological Contributions to Language Development* and *Contextual Contributions to Language Development*

- New feature: *Cultural Influences on Development: Culture and Language Development in Infancy*

Chapter 6

- Updated *Cultural Influences on Development: Father–Infant Interactions*, retitled from *Lives in Context: Attachment to Fathers*, and moved from later in the chapter

- Reorganized *Infants' Emotional Experiences*, creating sections with new coverage of *Basic Emotions* and *Self-Conscious Emotions*

- Updated and rewrote *Parental Interaction*, integrating *Interactive Play* and *Test of Wills*

- Updated and rewrote *Social Referencing*

- Updated and revised *Emotional Display Rules* and *Stranger Wariness*

- New *Lives in Context* feature on *Maternal Depression and Emotional Depression*, emphasizing the emotional effects of ongoing reciprocal interactions over infancy

- Updated *Styles of Temperament* and expanded to include Mary Rothbart's model

- New feature on *Brain and Biological Influences on Development: Trauma and Emotional Development*

- New coverage of *Cultural Differences in Temperament*

- Expanded *Bowlby's Ethological Perspective on Attachment* to include new coverage of *Infants' Signals and Adults' Responses* and *Secure Base, Separation Anxiety, and Internal Working Models*

- Updated coverage of *Attachment-Related Outcomes*

- Updated and expanded section on *Cultural Variations in Attachment Classifications*

- Reorganized and updated *Self-Concept and Self-Recognition* to distinguish *Self-Awareness* and *Emerging Self-Concept*

- Updated coverage of *Self-Control*

Chapter 7

- New feature on *Lives in Context: Picky Eating*

- Updated and reorganized coverage of *Brain Development in Early Childhood* and moved to *Physical Development in Early Childhood*

- Updated and revised coverage of *Gross Motor Skills* and *Fine Motor Skills*

- *Piaget's Cognitive-Developmental Theory: Preoperational Reasoning* reorganized to include *Characteristics of Preoperational Reasoning* and *Evaluating Preoperational Reasoning*

- Rewrote and added new coverage of *Vygotsky's Sociocultural Theory* and added *Guided Participation and Scaffolding, Zone of Proximal Development*, and *Evaluating Vygotsky's Sociocultural Theory*

- Revised coverage of *Attention*

- New coverage of *Working Memory and Executive Function*

- Updated and reorganized coverage of *Memory*

- New coverage of *Conceptions of Moral, Social, and Personal Issues*

- New feature on *Cultural Influences on Development: Culture and Theory of Mind*

- *Ethical and Policy Applications of Life Span Development: Project Head Start* integrated into *Early Childhood Education Interventions*

Chapter 8

- Updated coverage of *Psychosocial Development in Early Childhood*

- New *Cultural Influences on Development: Children's Participation in Household Work*

- Updated and rewritten coverage of *Self-Concept*

- New coverage of *Self-Esteem*

- Updated and reorganized *Empathy and Prosocial Behavior* to include sections on *Prosocial Behavior, Influences on Prosocial Behavior*, and *Aggression*

- Updated and expanded discussion of *Influences on Prosocial Behavior* to include *Biological Influences, Emotional Influences, Family Influences*, and *Contextual Influences*

- Updated and rewritten coverage of *Aggression*

- Updated coverage of *Culture, Context, and Parenting*

- Updated coverage of *Child Maltreatment*

- New coverage of *Gender Role Norms and Gender Stereotypes*

- Updated and rewritten coverage of *Contextual Explanations*

Chapter 9

- Updated and rewrote coverage of *Motor Development*

- New coverage of *Childhood Injuries*

- Updated coverage of *Obesity*

- Updated coverage of *Classification*

- Updated and revised organization of *Culture and Concrete Operational Reasoning*

- *Central Executive Function* updated and replaced with new coverage of *Working Memory and Executive Function in Children*

- Updated coverage of *Memory Strategies*

- Updated coverage of *Intelligence Tests* to include the WISC-V

- Updated coverage of *Individual and Group Differences in IQ*

- New coverage of *Contextual Influences on IQ*

- Updated coverage of *Multiple Intelligences*

- Revised and streamlined coverage of *Moral Reasoning: Piaget's Perspective*

- Updated and rewrote *Kohlberg's Theory of Moral Reasoning*, and retitled as *Children's Conceptions of Justice: Kohlberg's Cognitive-Developmental Perspective*

- Updated and revised coverage of *Distributive Justice Reasoning* and *Distinguishing Moral and Conventional Rules*

- Updated *Language Development* and revised *Vocabulary*

- Updated and reorganized coverage of *Reading and Mathematics*

- Updated coverage of *Transition to First Grade*

- Updated *Ethical and Policy Applications of Life Span Development: Grade Retention and Social Promotion* and retitled *Applying Developmental Science: Grade Retention and Social Promotion*

- New coverage of *Autistic Spectrum Disorder*

- Updated and streamlined coverage of *Attention-Deficit/Hyperactivity Disorder*

Chapter 10

- Updated and reorganized coverage of *Self-Concept*

- Updated and expanded coverage of *Self-Esteem* to include age differences and contextual and cultural influences

- New coverage of *Achievement Motivation* and *Contextual Influences on Achievement Attributions and Motivation*

- Updated and reorganized coverage of *Friendship*

- Updated coverage of *Popularity* and *Peer Rejection*

- Updated and reorganized *Bullying*, including *Children Who Bully* (retitled), *Victims of Bullying* (retitled), and *Intervening in Bullying*

- Updated *Ethical and Policy Applications of Life Span Development: Antibullying Legislation* and retitled as *Applying Developmental Science: Antibullying Legislation*

- Updated and streamlined coverage of *Parent–Child Relationships* and *Siblings*

- Updated coverage of *Cultural Influences on Development: China's One-Child Policy*

- Updated and streamlined coverage of *Same-Sex Parented Families, Single-Parent Families*, and *Cohabiting Families*

- Updated and retitled as *Divorce and Divorcing Families*

- Updated coverage of *Stepfamilies* and retitled as *Blended Families*

- Updated and rewrote coverage of *Common Fears and Anxiety*, retitling it as *School Refusal*

- Updated and reorganized *Child Sexual Abuse*

- Updated and rewrote coverage of *Resilience*

- Updated and rewrote *Lives in Context: Exposure to War and Terrorism and Children's Development*

Chapter 11

- Updated and integrated *Popular Views of Adolescence: Storm and Stress* into *Is Adolescence a Period of Storm and Stress?*

- Updated and streamlined coverage of *Adolescent Moodiness*

- Updated and reorganized coverage of *Puberty* into *Changes in Body Size and Shape, Sexual Characteristics*, and *Sexual Maturation*

- New *Cultural Influences on Development: Menarche Rituals of the !Xoo*

- Updated coverage of *Psychosocial Effects of Early and Late Puberty* and revised to *Psychosocial Effects of Pubertal Timing*, expanding coverage of context

- Updated *Puberty and Sleep Patterns*

- Updated and rewrote *Nutrition and Development*

- Updated *Brain Development in Adolescence* and expanded to include the dual-systems model

- Updated *Socioemotional Perception*

- Updated and rewrote *Risk Taking*

- Updated *Piaget's Cognitive-Developmental Theory* and *Information Processing Theory*

- Updated and streamlined *Implications of Adolescent Thinking*

- Updated, revised, and retitled *Ethical and Policy Applications of Lifespan Development: Legal Implications of Adolescent Decision Making* as *Applying Developmental Science: Legal Implications of Adolescent Decision Making*

- New *Lives in Context: Volunteer Work and Social Responsibility*

- Updated coverage of *School Transitions*

- Updated and expanded *Applying Developmental Science: School Dropout* and integrated it into the text

Chapter 12

- Updated and streamlined coverage of *Self-Concept* and *Self-Esteem*

- Updated and rewrote coverage of *Identity*, including *Identity Statuses, Influences on Identity Development, Outcomes Associated With Identity Development*, and *Ethnic Identity*

- New *Cultural Influences on Development: Cultural Views of Gender*

- Updated and rewrote coverage of *Parent–Adolescent Conflict*

- Updated and differentiated *Parenting Style and Monitoring* into separate sections, *Parenting* and *Parental Monitoring*

- Updated coverage of *Friendships* and *Cliques and Crowds*

- Updated and reorganized coverage of *Peer Conformity*

- Updated and rewrote coverage of *Dating*

- Updated *Sexuality* and *Influences on Sexual Activity,* combined into one section, *Sexuality*, and expanded to include topics such as ethnic differences, timing, sexting, and risk factors

- Updated and rewrote coverage of *Lesbian, Gay, Bisexual, and Transgender Adolescents*

- Updated and streamlined coverage of *Contraceptive Use, Sexually Transmitted Infections*, and *Adolescent Pregnancy*

- Updated and reorganized *Depression and Suicide, Eating Disorders*, and *Alcohol and Substance Use*

Chavpter 13

- New coverage of *Emerging Adulthood: Transition to Adulthood*

- New *Cultural Influences on Development: Emerging Adulthood and Culture*

- Updated and reorganized *Physical Development*, retitling it as *Physical Changes*

- New *Brain and Biological Influences on Development: Chronic Traumatic Encephalopathy in Athletes*

- Updated coverage of *Fertility and Reproductive Capacity*

- Updated coverage of *Overweight and Obesity* to include contextual influences on obesity

- Updated coverage of *Physical Activity*

- New coverage of *Sexual Activity*

- New coverage of *Sexual Coercion*

- Updated and reorganized coverage of *Substance Abuse,* including rewritten coverage of *Alcohol Use and Abuse* and *Marijuana*

- New *Applying Developmental Science: Marijuana Legalization*

- Updated coverage of *Epistemic Cognition* and reorganized into *Postformal Reasoning*

- New coverage of *Evaluating Cognitive-Developmental Approaches to Adult Development*

- Updated and streamlined coverage of *Developmental Impact of Attending College*

- New coverage of *First-Generation College Students*

- Updated and revised coverage of *Nontraditional College Students*

- Updated and streamlined coverage of *The Forgotten Third*

- Updated and revised *Stages of Vocational Development*, retitled as *Occupational Stages*

- Updated and expanded *Influences on Vocational* Choice to include SES and parental influence

- New coverage of *Transition to Work* and *Diversity in the Workplace*

- New coverage of *Work and Family*

Chapter 14

- Distinguished emerging adulthood and early adulthood throughout

- New coverage of *Identity Versus Role Confusion*

- *Lives in Context: Internet Dating* updated

- Updated and expanded coverage of *Friendship* and *Mate Selection*

- New *Brain and Biological Influences on Development: Your Brain on Love*

- Updated coverage of *Intimate Partner Violence*

- Updated coverage of *Singlehood, Cohabitation,* and *Same-Sex Marriage*

- Updated and reorganized coverage of the transition to marriage and marital success in *Marriage*

- Updated *Ethical and Policy Applications of Life Span Development: Same-Sex Marriage and the Law* and retitled as *Applying Developmental Science: The Legalization of Same-Sex Marriage*

- Updated and streamlined *Divorce*, integrating *Predicting Divorce* and *Consequences of Divorce*
- Updated *Becoming a Parent, Never-Married Single Parent, Same-Sex Parents*, and *Childlessness*
- New coverage of *Stepparents*

Chapter 15

- Updated and reorganized coverage of *Theories of Aging*, moved from Chapter 13
- Updated and organized coverage of *Reproductive Aging*
- Updated *Cultural Influences on Development: Cultural Perspectives on Menopause*
- Reorganized *Health in Middle Adulthood* to include *Common Illnesses, Stress*, and *Hardiness and Health*
- New coverage of *Sexual Activity*
- Updated *Appling Developmental Science: Hormone Replacement Therapy*
- Updated coverage of *Fluid and Crystallized Intelligence* and *Intelligence Over the Adult Years*
- New *Lives in Context* feature on *The Flynn Effect: Context and IQ*
- Updated coverage of *Attention, Memory*, and *Processing Speed*
- New *Brain and Biological Influences on Development: Sleep as a Brain Cleanser*
- Updated and streamlined coverage of *Expertise*

Chapter 16

- Updated coverage of *Erikson's Generativity Versus Stagnation* and the *Midlife Crisis*
- Reorganized and streamlined coverage of *Levinson's Seasons of Life*
- New *Brain and Biological Influences on Development: Mindfulness Meditation and the Brain*
- Updated *Self-Concept*, expanded coverage of *Subjective Age* and *Possible Selves*
- Updated and expanded coverage of *Gender Identity in Middle Adulthood*

- Updated and reorganized coverage of *Personality in Middle Adulthood*
- Updated and streamlined coverage of *Friendships*
- Updated and combined coverage of *Marriage* and *Divorce* into one comprehensive section
- Expanded coverage of *Parent–Child Relationships* into two sections: *Parents to Adult Children* and *Parents to Infants and Young Children*
- Updated *Grandparenthood* and *Lives in Context: Grandparents Raising Grandchildren*
- Updated coverage of *Caring for Aging Parents*
- Updated coverage of *Job Satisfaction*
- New coverage of *Planning for Retirement*

Chapter 17

- Integrated material from *Life Expectancy* into *Health in Late Adulthood*
- Updated and expanded coverage of *Brain Aging* (was titled *Nervous System*)
- New *Brain and Biological Influences on Development: Aerobic Exercise and the Brain*
- Reorganized material on sensory changes into *The Senses*, with updated coverage of *Vision* and *Hearing*
- New coverage of *Smell and Taste*
- Updated coverage of *Cardiovascular, Respiratory, and Immune Systems*
- New coverage of *Motor Aging*
- *Health and Disability in Late Adulthood* retitled as *Health in Late Adulthood*
- Updated coverage of *Nutrition* and *Exercise*
- Updated coverage of *Osteoporosis* and moved from Chapter 15
- Updated coverage of *Falls*
- Updated coverage of *Alzheimer's Disease, Vascular Dementia*, and *Parkinson's Disease*
- New *Cultural Influences on Development: Ethnicity and Alzheimer's Disease*
- New coverage of *Lewy Body Dementia*
- Updated and retitled *Reversible Dementia* as *Delirium*

- Reorganized *Cognitive Development in Late Adulthood* to include new coverage of *Attention* and expanded *Working Memory* to include *Context, Task Demands, and Memory Performance* and *Emotion and Working Memory*
- Updated coverage of *Age-Related Changes in Language* and retitled as *Aging and Language*
- Revised coverage of *Problem Solving and Wisdom*
- Updated coverage of *Cognitive Changes* and revised to *Influence on Cognitive Change in Adulthood*

Chapter 18

- Updated coverage of *Subjective Age* and *Reminiscence and Life Review*
- New *Cultural Influences on Development: Cultural Attitudes Toward Older Adults*
- Updated coverage of *Personality* and *Religiosity* and to *The Self in Late Adulthood*
- Reorganized and updated *Late Adulthood and Social Contexts* to include *Social Support in Older Adulthood, Aging in the Social World, Neighborhoods, Residential Communities, Nursing Homes,* and *Aging in Place*
- Updated and retitled *Residing at Home* as *Aging in Place*
- Updated coverage of *Friendships* and *Sibling Relationships*
- Updated and integrated coverage of *Marriage, Divorce,* and *Cohabitation*
- Updated *Sexuality* and *Elder Abuse*
- New *Brain and Biological Influences on Development: Neurological Risk for Financial Abuse*
- Updated and retitled *Ethical and Policy Applications of Lifespan Development: Social Security* as *Lives in Context: Social Security*
- Updated coverage of *Deciding to Retire, Transition to Retirement and Adjustment,* and *Influences on Retirement Adjustment*

New Chapter 19

- New coverage of death and dying

ACKNOWLEDGMENTS

Many have contributed to these books—and I am very grateful. I am fortunate to work with a talented team. I thank Marian Provenzano for feedback and editorial suggestions on this edition. I am appreciative to Nathan Davidson and Gail Buschman for sharing their expertise in design, photos, and figures. Sara Harris wears many hats and has provided invaluable support in constructing ancillaries, videos, and more. I thank Matthew Isaak for providing the student multimedia resources. Thanks to Rachel Flores for her assistance with the glossary and references. Thanks to Gillian Dickens for sharing her copyediting expertise. At SAGE, I thank Olivia Weber-Stenis for overseeing production, Sheryl Adams and Katherine Hepburn for their work in marketing, and Zach Valladon for his speedy email replies and work in securing and consolidating reviews. I am very grateful for Lucy Berbeo's exceptional project management skills, insight, and warmth (not to mention her lists!). Thanks to Lara Parra for her work as editor extraordinaire, leader, advocate, and friend. I thank my students for asking the questions and engaging in the discussions that inform these pages. I am especially appreciative of those who have shared their feedback and helped me to improve this book. Thank you to the many instructors who have reviewed and provided feedback on these chapters. Arielle Catalina Bliss provided a range of support throughout this project, for which I am grateful.

Finally, I thank my family, especially my parents, Phil and Irene Kuther, for their emotional support and wisdom. I am also grateful for the support of my Martell family, Fred and Joan, and Freddy and Julia. Most of all, I am thankful for the extraordinary patience, encouragement, and unwavering optimism of my husband, Fred. Without your love and support, none of this would be possible.

SAGE thanks the following expert reviewers, who provided detailed recommendations in their areas of expertise with a focus on multicultural and cross-cultural findings and diversity in development.

Cassendra Bergstrom completed her PhD in educational psychology at the University of Northern Colorado (UNC), where she is now an assistant professor. She held a postdoctoral research position working on a National Science Foundation grant through the Math and Science Teaching Institution, also at UNC. Dr. Bergstrom's research focuses on the intersection of motivation and learning environments, with a recent focus on equity. Her publications and presentations stem from research projects on the topics of transformative experience, goal orientation, and problem-based learning (PBL) environments. Dr. Bergstrom currently teaches undergraduate psychology courses, as well as graduate courses in educational psychology.

Jessamy Comer is a lecturer at Rochester Institute of Technology in Rochester, New York. She has been teaching developmental psychology for over a decade, as well as many other undergraduate and graduate courses. Her area of research interest and specialization is in parent–child relationships, particularly during adolescence. She earned her BA degree in psychology from Baylor University in Waco, Texas, and she earned her MA and PhD in developmental psychology from the University of Rochester in Rochester, New York. She is also a recipient of the Helen and Vincent Nowlis Award for Excellence in Teaching.

Kathy Erickson is a University of Arizona faculty member teaching in the human services and family studies departments. Professor Erickson earned a master's degree in holistic psychology, with an emphasis in mindfulness and addiction. She has an undergraduate degree in counseling with a minor in holistic education. For two decades, Kathy worked with adolescents in education and social services settings. She introduced students to biofeedback and mindfulness techniques to help them develop mechanisms to alleviate and manage stress. She is committed to the value of integrating mindfulness throughout all aspects of one's life as well as in the courses she teaches.

Flora Farago is an assistant professor of human development and family studies at Stephen F. Austin State University, with a background in developmental psychology and early childhood education. Her teaching and research interests center on children's prejudice and stereotype development, as well as antibias curricula surrounding race and gender. Dr. Farago is particularly interested in the link between research and community activism. She collaborates with colleagues and organizations nationally and internationally, including the Indigo Cultural Center, the Jirani Project, and the Girl Child Network, to promote racial and gender equity.

Merranda Romero Marín is an associate professor in the Department of Family and Consumer Science at New Mexico State University, where she teaches courses ranging from lifespan development to multicultural family life education and clinical courses in marriage and family therapy. Dr. Romero Marín is a licensed psychologist and a licensed marriage and family therapist specializing in the treatment of posttraumatic stress disorder (PTSD). Her areas of research include understanding the impact of poverty on children and family systems, the effects of trauma on family and community systems, multicultural counseling, and individual and family resilience.

Sarah Savoy is an associate professor of psychology at Stephen F. Austin State University, where she teaches courses in developmental, social, and health psychology. Dr. Savoy's research concerns topics such as social and cognitive processes that contribute to the development of disordered eating as well as stigma related to eating disorders and obesity.

Robert S. Weisskirch, MSW, PhD, is a professor of human development in the Liberal Studies Department at California State University, Monterey Bay. His research interests focus on language brokering, ethnic identity and acculturation, developmental perspectives on romantic relationships, how technology affects relationships (i.e., parent–adolescent relationships, sexting, and romantic relationships), and pedagogy of adolescent development. He received his PhD in human development from the University of California, Davis; a Master of Social Work from San Diego State University; and a Multiple Subjects Teaching Credential and BA in psychology from the University of California, Irvine.

SAGE wishes to thank the following reviewers for their valuable contributions to the development of this manuscript:

Marita Andreassen, Inland Norway University of Applied Sciences

Linda Aulgur, Westminster College

Stephen Baker, Saint Francis University

Jamie Borchardt, Tarleton State University

Ashley Cosentino, The Chicago School of Professional Psychology

Barry Davis, Augustana University

Christine Weinkauff Duranso, California State University–San Bernardino

Robert Gall, Grace University

Theresa Garfield, Texas A&M University–San Antonio

Jerry Green, Tarrant County College

Erin Harmeyer, Louisiana State University

Crystal Harris, Governors State University

Janice Hartgrove-Freile, Lone Star College

Jerry Haywood, Fort Valley State University

Jeff Kellogg, Marian University Indianapolis

Cynthia Jacox, Alamo College

Benjamin Jeppsen, University of Nevada, Reno

Lakitta Johnson, Jackson State University

Staci Simmelink Johnson, Walla Walla Community College

Cristina Jose-Kampfner, Eastern Michigan University

Nancy Lamphere, Caldwell Community College and Technical Institute

Robyn Long, Baker University

Robert Martinez, Alamo College

Robert Martinez, University of the Incarnate Word

Geraldine Lotze, Virginia Commonwealth University

Maribeth Palmer-King, SUNY Broome

Melanie Palomares, University of South Carolina

Kathy Phillippi-Immel, University of Wisconsin Colleges

Gary Popoli, Stevenson University

Martha Ravola, Alcorn University

Mary Schindler, Sonoma State University

Brittney Schrick, University of Arkansas Cooperative Extension Service

Patrick Smith, Virginia Community College

Brooke Spangler-Cropenbaker, Miami University

Tara Stoppa, Eastern University

Marcia Tipton, Milwaukee Area Technical College

Debra Tower, University of Oklahoma

Bridget Walsh, University of Arkansas Cooperative Extension Service

Shauna Nefos Webb, Milligan College

ABOUT THE AUTHOR

Tara L. Kuther is professor of psychology at Western Connecticut State University, where she has taught courses in child, adolescent, and adult development since 1996. She earned her BA in psychology from Western Connecticut State University and her MA and PhD in developmental psychology from Fordham University. Dr. Kuther is a fellow of the Society for the Teaching of Psychology (American Psychological Association, Division 2), has served in various capacities in the Society for the Teaching of Psychology and the Society for Research on Adolescence, and is the former chair of the Teaching Committee for the Society for Research in Child Development. Her research interests include social cognition and risky activity in adolescence and adulthood. In addition to the award-winning *Lifespan Development: Lives in Context*, Dr. Kuther has authored over a dozen books in developmental psychology and student development. She is interested in promoting undergraduate and graduate students' professional development and helping them navigate the challenges of pursuing undergraduate and graduate degrees in psychology.

PRACTICE AND APPLY WHAT YOU'VE LEARNED

▶ edge.sagepub.com/kuther2e

CHECK YOUR COMPREHENSION ON THE STUDY SITE WITH:

- **Diagnostic Quizzes** to identify opportunities for improvement.

- **Multimedia Resources** that explore chapter content using media and current events.

- **Journal Articles** that support and expand on chapter concepts.

PART I

Foundations of Lifespan Human Development

CHAPTER 1:
Understanding Human Development: Approaches and Theories

CHAPTER 2:
Biological and Environmental Foundations

CHAPTER 3:
The Prenatal Period, Birth, and the Newborn

Development is a lifelong process. We experience many dynamic changes in biological, cognitive, and socioemotional processes that interact over time. For example, brain development, a biological change, permits more sophisticated thinking, or cognitive development, which influences socioemotional development, including how children understand emotions and how they interact with other people.

All throughout life, we are embedded in multiple contexts that influence, and are influenced by, us. The specific contexts and the relative importance of each shift over time. In infancy, the family context is most pertinent because an infant spends all of its time with its caregivers. As the child develops and enters school, peer and school contexts become increasingly important. In adolescence and adulthood, the work context emerges.

All of the contexts in which we are embedded interact, influencing each other. Interactions at home with parents and siblings influence interactions at school and in the peer group. We are also embedded in a larger neighborhood context, with a more distal influence on us, through factors such as the availability of parks and playgrounds, after-school programs, and feelings of safety. We and our ever-changing contexts are also embedded in a culture that influences our values, attitudes, and beliefs throughout our lives.

Watch at
edge.sagepub.com/kuther2e

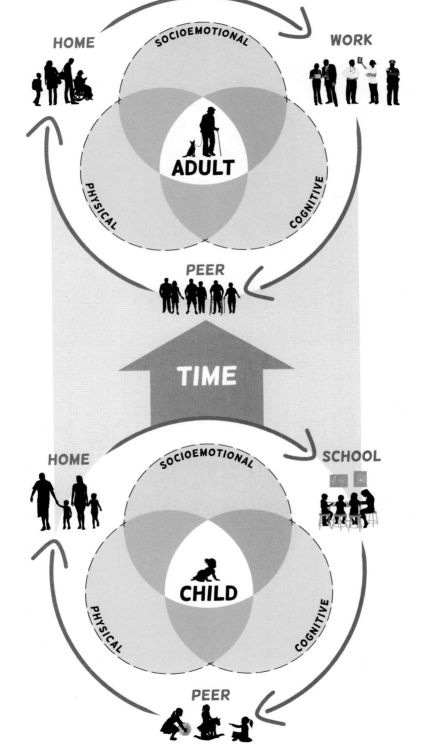

Images: ©iStock.com

1

Understanding Human Development

Approaches and Theories

Think back over your lifetime. How have you grown and changed through the years? Do your parents describe you as a happy baby? Were you fussy? Do you remember your first day of kindergarten? What are some of your most vivid childhood memories? Did you begin puberty early, late, or at about the same time as others your age? Were your adolescent years a stressful time? What types of changes do you expect to undergo in your adult years? Where will you live? Will you have a spouse? Will you have children? What career will you choose? How might these life choices and circumstances influence how you age and your perspective in older adulthood? Will your personality remain the same or change over time? In short, how will you change over the course of your lifespan?

Learning Objectives

1.1 Outline five principles of the lifespan developmental perspective.

1.2 Explain three theoretical controversies about human development.

1.3 Summarize five theoretical perspectives on human development.

1.4 Describe the methods and research designs used to study human development.

1.5 Discuss the ethical responsibilities of researchers to protect their participants.

Digital Resources

Connect: Poverty and Brain Development

▶ **Lives in Context Video 1.1:** Sociocultural Influences on Development: Desegregation

Watch: Nature and Nurture

Explore: Educational Aspirations of African American Adolescents

Listen: Childhood Exposure to Lead

▶ **Lives in Context Video 1.2:** Children of Katrina: Longitudinal Research

Explore: Voluntary Participation in HIV Research

WHAT IS LIFESPAN HUMAN DEVELOPMENT?

» LO 1.1 Outline five principles of the lifespan developmental perspective.

This is a book about **lifespan human development**—the ways in which people grow, change, and stay the same throughout their lives, from conception to death. When people use the term *development,* they often mean the transformation from infant to adult. However, development does not end with adulthood. We continue to change in predictable ways throughout our lifetime, even into old age. Developmental scientists study human development seeking to understand these lifetime patterns of change.

Table 1.1 illustrates the many phases of life through which we progress from conception to death. The phases may have different labels and different sets of developmental tasks, but all have value. The changes that we undergo during infancy, for instance, influence how we experience later changes, such as those during adolescence and beyond. Each phase of life is important and accompanied by its own demands and opportunities.

Change is perhaps the most obvious indicator of development. For example, the muscle strength and coordination needed to play sports increases over childhood and adolescence, peaks in early adulthood, and begins to decline thereafter, declining more rapidly from middle to late adulthood. However, there also are ways in which we change little over our lifetimes. Some personality traits, for example, are highly stable over the lifespan, so that we remain largely the "same person" into old age (Schwaba & Bleidorn, 2018; Wortman, Lucas, & Donnellan, 2012).

Lifespan human development can be described by several principles. As discussed in the following sections, development is (1) multidimensional, (2) multidirectional, (3) plastic, (4) influenced by multiple contexts, and (5) multidisciplinary (Baltes, Lindenberger, & Staudinger, 2006; Overton & Molenaar, 2015).

Development Is Multidimensional

Development is *multidimensional* and includes changes in the areas of physical, cognitive, and socioemotional development (Baltes et al., 2006). **Physical development** refers to body maturation and growth, such as body size, proportion, appearance, health, and perceptual abilities. **Cognitive development** refers to the maturation of thought processes and the tools that we use to obtain knowledge, become aware of the world around us, and solve problems. **Socioemotional development** includes changes in personality, emotions, views of oneself, social skills, and interpersonal relationships with family and friends. These areas of development overlap and interact. For example, brain maturation, a physical development, underlies advances in cognitive development, which might enable an adolescent to become better at understanding her best friend's point of view (Braams & Crone, 2017).

TABLE 1.1

Stages in Human Development

LIFE STAGE	APPROXIMATE AGE RANGE	DESCRIPTION
Prenatal	Conception to birth	Shortly after conception, a single-celled organism grows and multiplies. This is the period of the most rapid physical development as basic body structures and organs form, grow, and begin to function.
Infancy and toddlerhood	Birth to 2 years	The newborn is equipped with senses that help it to learn about the world. Physical growth occurs and motor, perceptual, and intellectual skills develop. Children show advances in language comprehension and use, problem solving, self-awareness, and emotional control. They become more independent and interested in interacting with other children and form bonds with parents and others.
Early childhood	2 to 6 years	Children grow steadily, their muscles strengthen, and they become better at coordinating their bodies. Memory, language, and imagination improve. Children become more independent and better able to regulate their emotions. Family remains children's primary social tie, but other children become more important and new ties to peers are established.
Middle childhood	6 to 11 years	Growth slows, but strength and athletic ability increase dramatically. Children show improvements in their ability to reason, remember, read, and use arithmetic. As children advance cognitively and gain social experience, they understand themselves in more complex ways compared with younger children. As friendships develop, peers and group memberships become more important.
Adolescence	11 to 18 years	Adolescents' bodies grow rapidly. They become physically and sexually mature. Although some immature thinking persists, adolescents can reason in sophisticated and adultlike ways. Adolescents are driven to learn about themselves and begin the process of discovering who they are, apart from their parents. Peer groups increase in importance.
Early adulthood	18 to 40 years	Physical condition peaks and then shows slight declines with time. Lifestyle choices play a large role in influencing health. Most young adults join the workforce, marry or establish a long-term bond with a spouse, and become parents. The timing of these transitions varies. Adolescents in Western industrialized societies often experience **emerging adulthood**, an extended transition to adulthood, spanning from ages 18 to 25, and as late as age 29.
Middle adulthood	40 to 65 years	In middle adulthood, people notice changes in their vision, hearing, physical stamina, and sexuality. Basic mental abilities, expertise, and practical problem-solving skills peak. Career changes and family transitions require that adults continue to refine their understandings of themselves. Adults help children to become independent, adapt to an empty nest, and assist elderly parents with their own health and personal needs.
Late adulthood	65 years and beyond	Most older adults remain healthy and active. Reaction time slows, and most older adults show a decline in some aspects of memory and intelligence, but an increase in expertise and wisdom compensates for losses. Most older adult friendships are old friendships, and these tend to be very close and a source of support. Adults adjust to retirement, changes in health, and personal losses (such as the death of a loved one), as well as search for meaning in their lives.
Death		Death itself is a process entailing the stopping of heartbeat, circulation, breathing, and brain activity. A person's death causes changes in his or her social context—family members and friends must adjust to and accept the loss.

In turn, she might become more empathetic and sensitive to her friend's needs and develop a more mature friendship, influencing her socioemotional development. Figure 1.1 illustrates how the three areas of development interact.

Development Is Multidirectional

Development is commonly described as a series of improvements in performance and functioning, but in fact development is *multidirectional,* meaning that it consists of both gains and losses, growth and decline, throughout the lifespan (Baltes et al., 2006; Overton & Molenaar, 2015). For example, infants are born with a stepping reflex, an innate involuntary response in which they make step-like movements when held upright over a horizontal surface (for more on infant reflexes, see Chapter 4). The stepping reflex disappears by about 2 months but reemerges as a voluntary action at 8 to 12 months

FIGURE 1.1

Multidimensional Nature of Development

Physical

Cognitive

Socioemotional

Advances in physical, cognitive, and socioemotional development interact, permitting children to play sports, learn more efficiently, and develop close friendships.

iStock/Essentials; iStock/Signature; Jupiter/Pixland/Thinkstock

of age as infants begin walking with support (Adolph & Franchak, 2017). Throughout life, there is a shifting balance between gains, improvements in performance (common early in life), and losses, declines in performance (common late in life) (Baltes et al., 2006). At all ages, however, individuals can compensate for losses by improving existing skills and developing new ones (Boker, 2013). The speed at which people think tends to slow in late adulthood, for example, but increases in knowledge and experience enable older adults to compensate for the loss of speed when completing everyday tasks (Hess, Leclerc, Swaim, & Weatherbee, 2009; Margrett, Allaire, Johnson, Daugherty, & Weatherbee, 2010). The brain naturally adapts to a lifetime of sensory experiences in order to portray the world around us efficiently and accurately as we age into older adulthood (Moran, Symmonds, Dolan, & Friston, 2014).

Development Is Plastic

Development is characterized by **plasticity:** It is malleable, or changeable. Frequently, the brain and body can compensate for illness and injury. In children who are injured and experience brain damage, for instance, other parts of the brain take on new functions. The plastic nature of human development allows people to modify their traits, capacities, and behavior throughout life (Baltes et al., 2006; Overton & Molenaar, 2015). For example, older adults who have experienced a decline in balance and muscle strength can regain and improve these capabilities through exercise (McAuley et al., 2013). Plasticity generally tends to decline as we age, but it does not disappear entirely. Short instruction, for instance, can enhance the memory capacities of very old adults but less so in younger adults (Brehmer, Westerberg, & Bäckman,

We are born with a stepping reflex, an innate involuntary response. When this infant is held under the arms in a standing position on a flat surface, his legs move in a stepping motion.
Phanie / Alamy Stock Photo

Some plasticity is retained throughout life. Practicing athletic activities can help older adults rebuild muscle and improve balance.
Reuters/Mariana Bazo

2012; Willis & Belleville, 2016). Plasticity makes it possible for individuals to adjust to change and to demonstrate **resilience**, the capacity to adapt effectively to adverse contexts and circumstances (Luthar et al., 2015; Masten, 2016).

Development Is Influenced by Multiple Contexts

Context refers to where and when a person develops. Context encompasses many aspects of the physical and social environment, such as family, neighborhood, country, and historical time period. It includes intangible factors, characteristics that are not visible to the naked eye, such as values, customs, ideals, and culture. (For more on the nature of cultural influences, see the accompanying feature Cultural Influences on Development: Defining Culture.) In order to understand a given individual's development, we must look to his or her context. For example, consider the context in which you were raised. Where did you grow up? City? Suburb? Rural area? What was your neighborhood like? Were you encouraged to be assertive and actively question the adults around you, or were you expected to be quiet and avoid confrontation? How large a part was religion in your family's life? How did religious values shape your parent's childrearing practices and your own values? How did your family's economic status affect your development? The multitude of contextual factors that interact over the life course can be organized into three categories: age-graded influences, history-graded influences, and nonnormative influences (Elder & George, 2016; Elder, Shanahan, & Jennings, 2016).

Age-graded influences are closely tied to chronological age and are largely predictable. Most individuals walk at about a year of age and reach puberty in early adolescence. Similarly, most women reach menopause in the late 40s or early 50s. Age-graded influences tend to be most influential early and late in life. Although these influences are often tied to biology, social milestones can also form age-graded influences. Most people in the United States enter school at about 5 years of age, graduate high school and enter college at about age 18, and retire during their 60s. Some age-graded influences are context dependent. For example, adolescents in suburban and rural contexts commonly get driver's licenses at age 16, but this may not be true of adolescents in urban settings where driving may be less common.

History-graded influences refer to how the time period in which we live and the unique historical circumstances of that time period affect our development. Examples of history-graded influences include wars, epidemics, advances in science and technology, and economic shifts such as periods of depression or prosperity (Baltes, 1987). Contextual influences tied to particular historical eras explain why a generation of people born at the same time, called a **cohort**, is similar in ways that people born at other times are different. For example, adults who came of age during the Great Depression and World War II are similar in some ways that make them different

---

Defining Culture

Cultural influences on development are illustrated by the many ethnic communities that comprise most U.S. cities. What subcultures and neighborhoods can you identify in your community?
Reuters/Lucy Nicholson

We are embedded in **culture,** a set of customs, knowledge, attitudes, and values that are shared by members of a group and are learned early in life

through interactions with group members (Markus & Kitayama, 1991). Early studies of culture and human development took the form of *cross-cultural research,* comparing individuals and groups from different cultures to examine how these universal processes worked in different contexts (Mistry & Dutta, 2015).

Most classic theories and research on human development are based on Western samples, and developmental researchers once believed that the processes of human development were universal. Yet research that defines normative development based on Western samples can lead to narrow views of human development that do not take into account the variety of contexts in which people live. At the extreme, differences in human development within other cultural groups might be viewed as abnormal (Cole & Packer, 2015).

Developmental norms vary by cultural context (Schweder et al., 1998). Biology and culture are inseparable, and the cultural context in which individuals live influences the timing and expression of many aspects of development

(Mistry, 2013). For example, the average age that infants begin to walk varies with cultural context. In Uganda, infants begin to walk at about 10 months of age, in France at about 15 months, and in the United States at about 12 months. These differences are influenced by parenting practices that vary by culture. African parents tend to handle infants in ways that stimulate walking, by playing games that allow infants to practice jumping and walking skills (Hopkins & Westra, 1989; Super, 1981).

There is a growing trend favoring *cultural research*, which examines how culture itself influences development, over cross-cultural research, which simply examines differences across cultures (Cole & Packer, 2015). Cultural research examines development and culture as fused entities that mutually interact, with culture inherent in all domains of development and a contributor to the context in which we are embedded, transmitting values, attitudes, and beliefs that shape our thoughts, beliefs, and behaviors (Mistry & Dutta, 2015). The shift toward cultural research permits the examination of the multiple subcultures that exist within a society (Oyserman, 2016, 2017). For example, North American culture is not homogeneous; many subcultures exist,

defined by factors such as ethnicity (e.g., African American, Asian American), religion (e.g., Christian, Muslim), geography (e.g., southern, midwestern), and others, as well as combinations of these factors. Current trends in cultural research document diversity and emphasize understanding how the historical, cultural, and subcultural contexts in which we live influence development throughout our lives.

What Do You Think?

1. How would you describe North American culture? Can you identify aspects of North American culture that describe most, if not all, people who live there? Are there aspects of culture in which people or subgroups of people differ?

2. What subcultures can you identify in your own neighborhood, state, or region of the country? What characterizes each of these subcultures?

3. Consider your own experience. With which culture or subculture do you identify? How much of a role do you think your cultural membership has had in your own development? ●

---

from later cohorts; they tend to have particularly strong views on the importance of the family, civic mindedness, and social connection (Rogler, 2002).

Take a moment to think about what role larger historical events have played in your development. For example, consider the costly and deadly 2017 Hurricanes Harvey, Irma, and Maria. The mass flooding destroyed homes and businesses in Texas, the southeastern United States, and Puerto Rico and killed thousands of people. Other examples of historical events include the terrorist attacks of September 11, 2001; the election of the first African American president of the United States in 2008; the school shooting in Newtown, Connecticut, in 2012; and the legalization of same-sex marriage in 2015. How have historical events influenced you and those around you? Can you identify ways in which, because of historical events, your cohort may differ from your parents' cohort?

Whereas age-graded and history-graded influences are common to all people or all members of a cohort, individuals also have experiences that are unique to them. *Nonnormative influences* are experiences or events that happen to a person or a few people. Examples of nonnormative influences include experiencing the death of a parent in childhood, widowhood in early adulthood, winning the lottery, or illness. Nonnormative events are not predictable and are not easily studied, as they are not experienced by most people—and the nature of nonnormative events varies widely. With age, nonnormative influences become more powerful determinants of development.

Developmental Science Is Multidisciplinary

Psychologists, sociologists, anthropologists, biologists, neuroscientists, and medical researchers all conduct research that is relevant to understanding aspects of human development. For example, consider cognitive development. Children's performance on cognitive measures, such as problem solving, are

 THINKING IN CONTEXT 1.1

1. Describe your own development. In what ways have you changed over your lifetime? What characteristics have remained the same?

2. Consider your own experience and provide examples from your life that illustrate the multidimensional nature of your own development. Can you do the same for multidirectionality and for plasticity? How has the context in which you were raised and live influenced your development?

3. Compare the historical context in which you, your parents, and your grandparents were raised. How did historical and societal influences affect your grandparents' development, their worldview, and their childrearing strategies? What about your parents? How might historical influences affect your own development, worldview, and perspective on parenting?

influenced by their physical health and nutrition (Anjos et al., 2013), interactions with peers (Holmes, Kim-Spoon, & Deater-Deckard, 2016), and neurological development (Ullman, Almeida, & Klingberg, 2014)—findings from the fields of medicine, psychology, and neuroscience, respectively. To understand how people develop at all periods in life, developmental scientists must combine insights from all of these disciplines.

BASIC ISSUES IN LIFESPAN HUMAN DEVELOPMENT

»» LO 1.2   Explain three theoretical controversies about human development.

Developmental scientists agree that people change throughout life and show increases in some capacities and decreases in others from conception to death. Yet they may sometimes disagree about how development proceeds, what specific changes occur, and what causes the changes. Developmental scientists' explanations of how people grow and change over their lives are influenced by their perspectives on three basic issues, or fundamental questions, about human development:

1. Do people change gradually often imperceptibly, over time, or is developmental change sudden and dramatic?

2. What role do people play in their own development—how much are they influenced by their surroundings, and how much do they influence their surroundings?

3. To what extent is development a function of inborn genetic characteristics, and to what extent is it affected by the environment in which individuals live?

The following sections examine each of these questions.

Continuities and Discontinuities in Development

Do children slowly grow into adults, steadily gaining more knowledge and experience and becoming better at reasoning? Or do they grow in spurts, showing sudden, large gains in knowledge and reasoning capacities? In other words, is developmental change **continuous**, characterized by slow and gradual change, or **discontinuous**, characterized by abrupt change? As shown in Figure 1.2, a discontinuous view of development emphasizes sudden transformation, whereas a continuous view emphasizes gradual and steady changes.

Scientists who argue that development is continuous point to slow and cumulative changes, such as a child slowly gaining experience, expanding his or her vocabulary, and learning strategies to become quicker at problem solving (Siegler, 2016). Similarly, they point out that middle-aged adults experience gradual losses of muscle and strength (Keller & Engelhardt, 2013).

The discontinuous view of development describes the changes we experience as large and abrupt, with individuals of various ages dramatically different from one another. For example, puberty transforms children's bodies into more adult-like adolescent bodies (Wolf & Long, 2016), infants' understanding and capacity for language is fundamentally different from that of school-aged children (Hoff, 2014), and children make leaps in their reasoning abilities over the course of childhood, such as from believing that robotic dogs and other inanimate objects are alive to understanding that life is a biological process (Beran, Ramirez-Serrano, Kuzyk, Fior, & Nugent, 2011; Zaitchik, Iqbal, & Carey, 2014).

It was once believed that development was either continuous or discontinuous—but not both. Today, developmental scientists agree that development includes both continuity and discontinuity (Lerner, Agans, DeSouza, & Hershberg, 2014). Whether a particular developmental change appears continuous or discontinuous depends in part on our point of view. For example, consider human growth. We often think of increases in height as involving a slow and steady process; each month, an infant is taller than the prior month, illustrating continuous change. However, as shown in Figure 1.3, when researchers measured infants' height every day, they discovered that infants have growth days and nongrowth days, days in which they show rapid change in height interspersed with days in which there is no change in height, illustrating discontinuous change (Lampl, Johnson, Frongillo, & Frongillo, 2001). In this example, monthly measurements of infant height suggest gradual increases, but daily measurements show spurts of growth, each lasting 24 hours or less. Thus, whether a given phenomenon, such as height, is described as continuous or discontinuous can vary. Most developmental scientists agree that some aspects of lifespan development are best described as continuous and others as discontinuous (Miller, 2016).

Individuals Are Active in Development

Do people have a role in influencing how they change over their lifetimes? That is, are people active in influencing their own development? Taking an active role means that they interact with and influence the world around them, create experiences

FIGURE 1.2

Continuous and Discontinuous Development

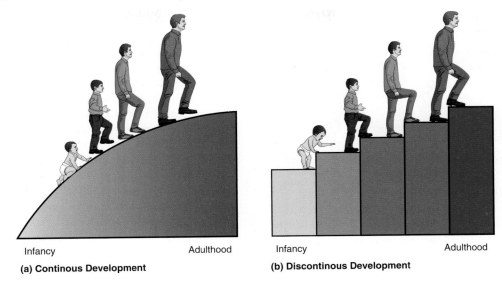

Infancy   Adulthood   Infancy   Adulthood
(a) Continous Development   **(b) Discontinous Development**

Source: Adapted from End of the Game (2014) Child Development 101, History and Theory, https://endofthegame.net/2014/04/15/child-development-101-history-and-theory/3/

FIGURE 1.3

Infant Growth: A Continuous or Discontinuous Process?

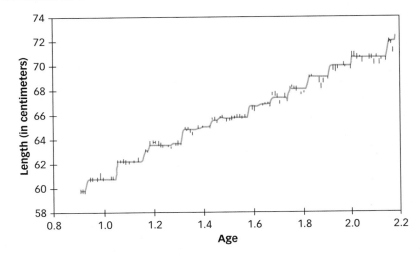

Infants' growth occurs in a random series of roughly 1-centimeter spurts in height that occur over 24 hours or less. The overall pattern of growth entails increases in height, but whether the growth appears to be continuous or discontinuous depends on our point of view.

Source: Figure 1 from Lampl, M., Veldhuis, J. D., & Johnson, M. L. (1992.) Saltation and stasis: A model of human growth. *Science*, 258, 801-803. With permission from AAAS.

that lead to developmental change, and thereby influence how they themselves change over the lifespan. Alternatively, if individuals take a passive role in their development, they are shaped by, but do not influence, the world around them.

The prevailing view among developmental scientists is that people are active contributors to their own development (Lerner et al., 2014). People are influenced by the physical and social contexts in which they live, but they also play a role in influencing their development by interacting with and changing those contexts (Elder et al., 2016). Even infants influence the world around them and construct their own development through their interactions. Consider an infant who smiles at each adult he sees; he influences his world because adults are likely to

It's easy to see how this baby can influence the world around her and construct her own development through her interactions. By smiling at each adult she sees, she influences her world because adults are likely to smile, use "baby talk," and play with her in response.

iStock/MartenBG

smile, use "baby talk," and play with him in response. The infant brings adults into close contact, making one-on-one interactions and creating opportunities for learning. By engaging the world around them, thinking, being curious, and interacting with people, objects, and the world around them, individuals of all ages are "manufacturers of their own development" (Flavell, 1992, p. 998).

Nature and Nurture Influence Development

Perhaps the most fundamental question about lifespan human development concerns why people change in predictable ways over the course of their lifetimes. The answer reflects perhaps the oldest and most heated debate within the field of human development: the **nature–nurture issue**. Is development caused by nature or nurture? Explanations that rely on nature point to inborn genetic traits (heredity), maturational processes, and evolution as causes of developmental change. For example, most infants take their first steps at roughly the same age, suggesting a maturational trend that supports the role of nature in development (Payne & Isaacs, 2016). An alternative explanation for developmental change is nurture, the view that individuals are molded by the physical and social environment in which they are raised, including the home, school, workplace, neighborhood, and society. From this perspective, although most begin to walk at about the same time, environmental conditions can speed up or slow down the process. Infants who experience malnutrition may walk later than well-nourished infants, and those who are given practice making stepping or jumping movements may walk earlier (Siekerman et al., 2015; Worobey, 2014). Although developmental scientists once attempted to determine whether development

depended on nature *or* nurture, most now agree that *both* nature and nurture are important contributors (Rutter, 2014; Sasaki & Kim, 2017). Thus, walking is heavily influenced by maturation (nature), but experiences and environmental conditions can influence the timing of a child's first steps (nurture). Today developmental scientists attempt to determine *how* nature and nurture interact and work together to influence how people grow and change throughout life (Bjorklund, 2018; Lickliter & Witherington, 2017).

To review, the three basic questions regarding lifespan human development are as follows:

1. Is developmental change gradual, showing continuity, or abrupt, illustrating discontinuity?

2. What role do people play in their own development—how much are they influenced by their surroundings and how much do they influence their surroundings?

3. To what extent is development a function of heredity, and to what extent is it a function of the environment in which individuals live?

Developmental scientists vary in their responses to these questions, as we will see throughout this book.

THINKING IN CONTEXT 1.2

1. Can you identify ways in which you have changed very gradually over the years? Were there other times in which you showed abrupt change, such as physical growth, strength and coordination, thinking abilities, or social skills? In other words, in what ways is your development characterized by continuity? Discontinuity?

2. What role did your physical and social environment play in your growth? In what ways, if any, did you take an active role in your own development?

3. How much of who you are today is a function of nature? Nurture?

THEORETICAL PERSPECTIVES ON HUMAN DEVELOPMENT

» LO 1.3   **Summarize five theoretical perspectives on human development.**

Over the past century, scientists have learned much about how individuals progress from infants, to children, to adolescents, and to adults, as well as how they change throughout adulthood. Developmental scientists explain their observations by constructing theories of human development. A **theory** is a way of organizing a set of observations or facts into a comprehensive explanation of how something works. Theories are important tools for compiling and interpreting the growing body of research in human development as well as determining gaps in our knowledge and making predictions about what is not yet known.

Effective theories generate specific **hypotheses**, or proposed explanations for a given phenomenon, that can be tested by research. It is important to note that this testing seeks to find flaws in the hypothesis—not to "prove" that it is flawless. A good theory is one that is *falsifiable,* or capable of generating hypotheses that can be tested and, potentially, refuted. As scientists conduct research and learn more about a topic, they modify their theories. Updated theories often give rise to new questions and new research studies, whose findings may further modify theories.

The great body of research findings in the field of lifespan human development has been organized into several theoretical perspectives. As the following sections illustrate, these theoretical perspectives vary greatly in how they account for the developmental changes that occur over the lifespan.

Psychoanalytic Theories

Are there powerful forces within us that make us behave as we do? Are we pushed by inner drives? **Psychoanalytic theories** describe development and behavior as a result of the interplay of inner drives, memories, and conflicts we are unaware of and cannot control. These inner forces influence our behavior throughout our lives. Freud and Erikson are two key psychoanalytic theorists whose theories remain influential today.

Freud's Psychosexual Theory

Sigmund Freud (1856–1939), a Viennese physician, is credited as the father of the psychoanalytic perspective. Freud believed that much of our behavior is driven by unconscious impulses that are outside of our awareness. As shown in Table 1.2, Freud believed we progress through a series of *psychosexual stages,* periods in which unconscious drives are focused on different parts of the body, making stimulation to those parts a source of pleasure. Freud explained that the task for parents is to strike a balance between overgratifying and undergratifying a child's desires at each stage to help the child develop a healthy personality with the capacity for mature relationships throughout life. Notably, Freud did not

Sigmund Freud (1856–1939), the father of the psychoanalytic perspective, believed that much of our behavior is driven by unconscious impulses.
Wikimedia

study children; his theory grew from his work with female psychotherapy patients (Crain, 2016).

In part because of its heavy emphasis on childhood sexuality, Freud's psychosexual stage framework, especially the phallic stage, is not widely accepted (Westen, 1998). Yet many of Freud's ideas have stood up well to the test of time and have permeated popular culture. These ideas include the notion of unconscious processes of which we are unaware, the importance of early family experience, and the role of emotions in development (Bargh, 2013). Another reason why Freud's theory tends to be unpopular with developmental scientists is that it cannot be directly tested and is therefore not supported by research (Miller, 2016). How are we to study unconscious drives, for instance, when we are not aware of them?

Erikson's Psychosocial Theory

Erik Erikson (1902–1994) was influenced by Freud, but he placed less emphasis on unconscious motivators of development and instead focused on the role of the social world, society, and culture. Erikson posed a lifespan theory of development, as shown in Table 1.3. According to this theory, individuals progress through eight *psychosocial stages* that include

TABLE 1.2

Freud's Psychosexual Stages

STAGE	APPROXIMATE AGE	DESCRIPTION
Oral	0 to 18 months	Basic drives focus on the mouth, tongue, and gums. Feeding and weaning influence personality development. Freud believed that failure to meet oral needs influences adult habits centering on the mouth, such as fingernail biting, overeating, smoking, or excessive drinking.
Anal	18 months to 3 years	Basic drives are oriented toward the anus, and toilet training is an important influence on personality development. If caregivers are too demanding, pushing the child before he or she is ready, or if caregivers are too lax, individuals may develop issues of control such as a need to impose extreme order and cleanliness on their environment or extreme messiness and disorder.
Phallic	3 to 6 years	In Freud's most controversial stage, basic drives shift to the genitals. The child develops a romantic desire for the opposite-sex parent and a sense of hostility and/or fear of the same-sex parent. The conflict between the child's desires and fears arouses anxiety and discomfort. It is resolved by pushing the desires into the unconscious and spending time with the same-sex parent and adopting his or her behaviors and roles, adopting societal expectations and values. Failure to resolve this conflict may result in guilt and a lack of conscience.
Latency	6 years to puberty	This is not a stage but a time of calm between stages when the child develops talents and skills and focuses on school, sports, and friendships.
Genital	Puberty to adulthood	With the physical changes of early adolescence, the basic drives again become oriented toward the genitals. The person becomes concerned with developing mature adult sexual interests and sexual satisfaction in adult relationships throughout life.

changes in how they understand and interact with others, as well as changes in how they understand themselves and their roles as members of society (Erikson, 1950) (see Table 1.3). Each stage presents a unique developmental task, which Erikson referred to as a crisis or conflict that must be resolved. How well individuals address the crisis determines their ability to deal with the demands made by the next stage of development.

Regardless of their success in resolving a crisis of a given stage, individuals are driven by biological maturation and social expectations to the next psychosocial stage. No crisis is ever fully resolved, and unresolved crises are revisited throughout life. Although Erikson believed that it is never too late to resolve a crisis, resolving a crisis from a previous stage may become more challenging over time as people focus on current demands and the crises of their current psychosocial stages.

Erikson's psychosocial theory is well regarded as one of the first lifespan views of development. He took a positive view of development and included the role of society and culture by basing his theory on a broad range of cases, including larger and more diverse samples of people than did Freud. Erikson's theory is criticized as difficult to test, but it has nonetheless sparked research on specific

Erik Erikson (1902–1994) posited that, throughout their lives, people progress through eight stages of psychosocial development.
Jon Erikson/Science Source

TABLE 1.3

Erikson's Psychosocial Stages of Development

STAGE	APPROXIMATE AGE	DESCRIPTION
Trust vs. mistrust	Birth to 1 year	Infants learn to trust that others will fulfill their basic needs (nourishment, warmth, comfort) or to lack confidence that their needs will be met.
Autonomy vs. shame and doubt	1 to 3 years	Toddlers learn to be self-sufficient and independent though toilet training, feeding, walking, talking, and exploring or to lack confidence in their own abilities and doubt themselves.
Initiative vs. guilt	3 to 6 years	Young children become inquisitive, ambitious, and eager for responsibility or experience overwhelming guilt for their curiosity and overstepping boundaries.
Industry vs. inferiority	6 to 12 years	Children learn to be hard working, competent, and productive by mastering new skills in school, friendships, and home life or experience difficulty, leading to feelings of inadequacy and incompetence.
Identity vs. role confusion	Puberty to early adulthood	Adolescents search for a sense of self by experimenting with roles. They also look for answers to the question, "Who am I?" in terms of career, sexual, and political roles or remain confused about who they are and their place in the world.
Intimacy vs. isolation	Early adulthood	Young adults seek companionship and a close relationship with another person or experience isolation and self-absorption through difficulty developing intimate relationships and sharing with others.
Generativity vs. stagnation	Middle adulthood	Adults contribute to, establish, and guide the next generation through work, creative activities, and parenting or stagnate, remaining emotionally impoverished and concerned about themselves.
Integrity vs. despair	Late adulthood	Older adults look back at life to make sense of it, accept mistakes, and view life as meaningful and productive or feel despair over goals never reached and fear of death.

stages, most notably on the development of identity during adolescence and the drive to guide youth and contribute to the next generation during middle adulthood (Crain, 2016). Erikson's lifespan theory of development holds implications for every period of life. We will revisit his theory throughout this book.

Behaviorist and Social Learning Theories

In response to psychoanalytic theorists' emphasis on the unconscious as an invisible influence on development and behavior, some scientists pointed to the importance of studying observable behavior rather than thoughts and emotion, which cannot be seen or objectively verified. Theorists who study **behaviorism** examine only behavior that can be observed and believe that all behavior is influenced by the physical and social environment. For example, consider this famous quote from John Watson (1925), a founder of behaviorism:

Give me a dozen healthy infants, well formed, and my own specified world to bring them up in and I'll guarantee to take any one at random and train him to become any type of specialist I might

select—doctor, lawyer, artist, merchant, chief, and yes, even beggar-man and thief, regardless of his talents, penchants, tendencies, abilities, vocations, and race of his ancestors. (p. 82)

By controlling an infant's physical and social environment, Watson believed he could control the child's destiny. Behaviorist theory is also known as *learning theory* because it emphasizes how people and animals learn new behaviors as a function of their environment. As discussed in the following sections, classical and operant conditioning are two forms of behaviorist learning; social learning integrates elements of behaviorist theory and information processing theories.

Classical Conditioning

Classical conditioning is a form of learning in which a person or animal comes to associate environmental stimuli with physiological responses. Ivan Pavlov (1849–1936), a Russian physiologist, discovered the principles of classical conditioning when he noticed that dogs naturally salivate when they taste food, but they also salivate in response to various sights and sounds that occur before they taste food, such

Ivan Pavlov (1849–1936) discovered classical conditioning when he noticed that dogs naturally salivate when they taste food, but they also salivate in response to various sights and sounds that they associate with food.
Sovfoto/Newscom

FIGURE 1.4

Classical Conditioning in a Newborn

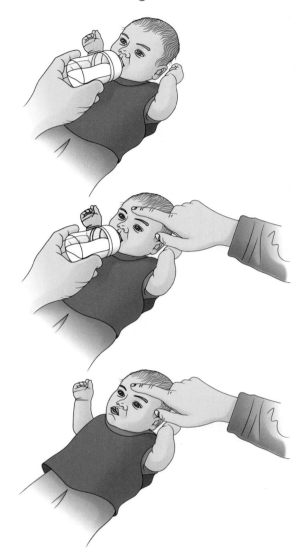

Classical conditioning has been observed in newborns, who naturally make sucking movements (unconditioned response) in response to sugar water (unconditioned stimulus). When stroking the forehead (neutral stimulus) is paired with sugar water, infants come to make sucking movements (conditioned response) in response to forehead strokes (conditioned stimulus).

as their bowl clattering or their owner opening the food cupboard. Pavlov tested his observation by pairing the sound of a tone with the dog's food; the dogs heard the tone, then received their food. Soon the tone itself began to elicit the dogs' salivation. Through classical conditioning, a neutral stimulus (in this example, the sound of the tone) comes to elicit a response originally produced by another stimulus (food). Classical conditioning has been observed in newborns, as shown in Figure 1.4. Many fears, as well as other emotional associations, are the result of classical conditioning. For example, some children may fear a trip to the doctor's office because they associate the doctor's office with the discomfort they felt upon receiving a vaccination shot. Classical conditioning applies to physiological and emotional responses only, yet it is a cornerstone of psychological theory. A second behaviorist theory accounts for voluntary, nonphysiological responses, as described in the following section.

Operant Conditioning

Perhaps it is human nature to notice that the consequences of our behavior influence our future behavior. A teenager who arrives home after curfew and is greeted with a severe scolding may be less likely to return home late in the future. An employer who brings coffee and muffins to her staff on Monday morning and then notices that her employees are in good spirits and productive may be more likely to bring them snacks in the future. These two examples illustrate the basic tenet of B. F. Skinner's (1905–1990) theory of **operant conditioning**, which holds that behavior becomes more or less probable depending on its consequences. According to Skinner, a behavior followed by a rewarding or pleasant outcome, called **reinforcement**, will be more likely to recur, but one followed by an aversive or unpleasant outcome, called **punishment**, will be less likely to recur.

Operant conditioning explains much about human behavior, including how we learn skills and habits. Behaviorist ideas about operant conditioning and the nature of human behavior are woven into the fabric of North American culture and are often applied to understand parenting and parent–child interactions (Troutman, 2015). Developmental scientists, however, tend to disagree with operant conditioning's emphasis on external events (reinforcing and punishing consequences) over internal events (thoughts and emotions) as influences on behavior (Crain, 2016). That is, controlling a child's environment can influence his or her development, but change can also occur through a child's own thoughts and actions. A child can devise new ideas and learn independently, consistent with the lifespan concept that individuals are active contributors to their development.

Social Learning Theory

Like behaviorists, Albert Bandura (1925–) believed that the physical and social environments are important, but he also advocated for the role of thought and emotion as contributors to development. According to Bandura's **social learning theory**, people actively process information—they think and they feel emotion—and their thoughts and feelings influence their behavior. The physical and social environment influences our behavior through their effect on our thoughts and emotions. For example, the teenager who

In a classic study conducted by Albert Bandura, children who observed an adult playing with a bobo doll toy roughly imitated those behaviors, suggesting that children learn through observation.
Albert Bandura

breaks his curfew and is met by upset parents may experience remorse, which may then make him less likely to come home late in the future. In this example, the social environment (a discussion with upset parents) influenced the teen's thoughts and emotions (feeling bad for upsetting his parents), which then influenced the teen's behavior (not breaking curfew in the future). In other words, our thoughts and emotions about the consequences of our behavior influence our future behavior. We do not need to experience punishment or reinforcement to change our behavior (Bandura, 2012). We can learn by thinking about the potential consequences of our actions.

One of Bandura's most enduring ideas about development is that people learn through observing and imitating others, which he referred to as **observational learning** (Bandura, 2010). This finding suggests that children who observe violence rewarded, such as a child grabbing (and successfully obtaining) another child's toy, may imitate what they see and use aggressive means to take other children's toys. People also learn by observing the consequences of others' actions. A child observer might be less likely to imitate a child who takes another child's toy if the aggressor is scolded by a teacher and placed in time-out. Observational learning is one of the most powerful ways in which we learn.

Bandura has also contributed to the field of lifespan human development through the concept of **reciprocal determinism**, according to which individuals and the environment interact and influence each other (Bandura, 2011). In contrast with behaviorist theorists, Bandura viewed individuals as active in their development rather than passively molded by their physical and social environments. Specifically, development is a result of interactions between the individual's characteristics, his or her behavior, and the physical and social environment (see Figure 1.5).

FIGURE 1.5

Bandura's Model of Reciprocal Determinism

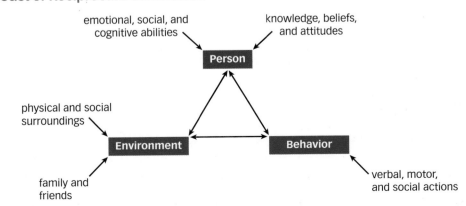

As an example, consider how a particular person's characteristics might influence that person's behavior and the surrounding social environment. Suppose Issac is an excitable person, which makes him quick to debate with others. This behavior, in turn, stimulates those around him to engage in debate. But suppose, too, that Issac's behavior (being quick to debate) does not result only from his personal characteristics (excitability). It is also influenced by the environment (e.g., being surrounded by smart people who enjoy debating), and it influences the environment (e.g., people who enjoy debating are more likely to talk to Issac, while people who avoid debating are less likely to talk to him). This is an example of the complex interplay among person, behavior, and physical and social environment that underlies much of what we will discuss throughout this book.

Behaviorist theories have made important contributions to understanding lifespan human development. Classical and operant conditioning and social learning are powerful means of explaining human behavior at all ages. Concepts such as observational learning, reinforcement, and punishment hold implications for parents, teachers, and anyone who works with people. Social learning theory and reciprocal determinism offer a more complex explanation for development and behavior than do behaviorist theories. We will revisit these concepts in later chapters.

Cognitive Theories

Cognitive theorists view cognition—thought—as essential to understanding people's functioning across the lifespan. In this section, we look at some of the ideas offered by cognitive-developmental theory and information processing theory.

Piaget's Cognitive-Developmental Theory

Swiss scholar Jean Piaget (1896–1980) was the first scientist to systematically examine infants' and children's thinking and reasoning. Piaget believed that to understand children, we must understand how they think, because thinking influences all behavior. Piaget's **cognitive-developmental theory** views children and adults as active explorers of their world, driven to learn by interacting with the world around them and organizing what they learn into **cognitive schemas**, or concepts, ideas, and ways of interacting with the world. Through these interactions, they construct and refine their own cognitive schemas, thereby contributing to their own cognitive development.

Piaget proposed that children's drive to explore and understand the world—to construct more sophisticated cognitive schemas—propels them through four stages of cognitive development, as shown in Table 1.4.

Jean Piaget (1896–1980) believed that children's drive to explore and understand the world around them propels them through four stages of cognitive development.
Bill Anderson / Science Source

Piaget's cognitive-developmental theory transformed the field of developmental psychology and remains one of the most widely cited developmental theories. It was the first to consider *how* infants and children think and to view people as active contributors to their development. In addition, Piaget's concept of cognitive stages and the suggestion that children's reasoning is limited by their stage has implications for education—specifically, the idea that effective instruction must match the child's developmental level.

Some critics of cognitive-developmental theory argue that Piaget focused too heavily on cognition and ignored emotional and social factors in development (Crain, 2016). Others believe that Piaget neglected the influence of contextual factors by assuming that cognitive-developmental stages are universal—that all individuals everywhere progress through the stages in a sequence that does not vary. Some cognitive theorists argue that cognitive development is not a discontinuous, stage-like process but instead is a continuous process (Birney & Sternberg, 2011), as described in the following section.

TABLE 1.4

Piaget's Stages of Cognitive Development

STAGE	APPROXIMATE AGE	DESCRIPTION
Sensorimotor	Birth to 2 years	Infants understand the world and think using only their senses and motor skills, by watching, listening, touching, and tasting.
Preoperations	2 to 6 years	Preschoolers explore the world using their own thoughts as guides and develop the language skills to communicate their thoughts to others. Despite these advances, their thinking is characterized by several errors in logic.
Concrete operations	7 to 11 years	School-aged children become able to solve everyday logical problems. Their thinking is not yet fully mature because they are able to apply their thinking only to problems that are tangible and tied to specific substances.
Formal operations	12 years to adulthood	Adolescents and adults can reason logically and abstractly about possibilities, imagined instances and events, and hypothetical concepts.

Information Processing Theory

A developmental scientist presents a 5-year-old child with a puzzle in which a dog, cat, and mouse must find their way to a bone, piece of fish, and hunk of cheese. To solve the puzzle, the child must move all three animals to the appropriate locations. How will the child approach this task? Which item will she move first? What steps will she take? What factors influence whether and how quickly a child completes this task? Finally, how does the 5-year-old child's process and performance differ from that of children older and younger than herself?

The problem described above illustrates the questions studied by developmental scientists who favor **information processing theory**, which posits that the mind works in ways similar to a computer in that information enters and then is manipulated, stored, recalled, and used to solve problems (Halford & Andrews, 2011). Unlike the theories we have discussed thus far, information processing theory is not one theory that is attributed to an individual theorist. Instead, there are many information processing theories, and each emphasizes a different aspect of thinking (Callaghan & Corbit, 2015; Müller, Kerns, Müller, & Kerns, 2015; Ristic & Enns, 2015). Some theories focus on how people perceive, focus on, and take in information. Others examine how people store information, create memories, and remember information. Still others examine problem solving—how people approach and solve problems in school, the workplace, and everyday life.

According to information processing theorists, we are born with the ability to process information. Our mental processes of noticing, taking in, manipulating, storing, and retrieving information do not show the radical changes associated with stage theories. Instead, development is continuous and entails changes in the efficiency and speed with which we think. Maturation of the brain and nervous system contributes to changes in our information processing abilities. We tend to become more efficient at attending to, storing, and processing information over the childhood years and to slow over the adult years (Luna, Marek, Larsen, Tervo-Clemmens, & Chahal, 2015). Experience and interaction with others also contribute by helping us learn new ways of managing and manipulating information. We naturally engage in information processing throughout our lives. We will discuss these changes and their implications for children, adolescents, and adults in later chapters.

Information processing theory offers a complex and detailed view of how we think, which permits scientists to make specific predictions about behavior and performance that can be tested in research studies. Indeed, information processing theory has generated a great many research studies and has garnered much empirical support (Halford & Andrews, 2011). Critics of the information processing perspective argue that a computer model cannot capture the complexity of the human mind and people's unique cognitive abilities. In addition, findings from laboratory research may not extend to everyday contexts in which people must adapt to changing circumstances and challenges to attention (Miller, 2016).

Contextual Theories

Contextual theories emphasize the role of the sociocultural context in development. People of all ages are immersed in their social contexts; they are inseparable from the cultural beliefs and societal, neighborhood, and familial contexts in which they live. The origins of sociocultural systems theory lie with two theorists, Lev Vygotsky and Urie Bronfenbrenner.

Vygotsky's Sociocultural Theory

Writing at the same time as Piaget, Russian scholar Lev Vygotsky (1896–1934) offered a different perspective on development that emphasized

Lev Vygotsky (1896–1934) emphasized the importance of culture in development. Children actively engage their social world, and the social world shapes development by transmitting culturally relevant ways of thinking and acting that guide children's thought and behavior.
Heritage/Corbis

the importance of culture. As we have discussed on page 8, *culture* refers to the beliefs, values, customs, and skills of a group; it is a product of people's interactions in everyday settings (Markus & Kitayama, 2010). Vygotsky's (1978) **sociocultural theory** examines how culture is transmitted from one generation to the next through social interaction. Children interact with adults and more experienced peers as they talk, play, and work alongside them. It is through these formal and informal social contacts that children learn about their culture and what it means to belong to it. By participating in cooperative dialogues and receiving guidance from adults and more expert peers, children adopt their culture's perspectives and practices, learning to think and behave as members of their society (Rogoff, 2016). Over time, they become able to apply these ways of thinking to guide their own actions, thus requiring less assistance from adults and peers (Rogoff, Moore, Correa-Chavez, & Dexter, 2014).

Vygotsky's sociocultural theory holds important implications for understanding cognitive development. Like Piaget, Vygotsky emphasized that children actively participate in their development by engaging with the world around them. However,

Vygotsky also viewed cognitive development as a social process that relies on interactions with adults, more mature peers, and other members of their culture. Vygotsky also argued that acquiring language is a particularly important milestone for children because it enables them to think in new ways and have more sophisticated dialogues with others, advancing their learning about culturally valued perspectives and activities. We will revisit Vygotsky's ideas about the roles of culture, language, and thought in Chapter 7.

Vygotsky's sociocultural theory is an important addition to the field of lifespan human development because it is the first theory to emphasize the role of the cultural context in influencing people's development throughout life. Critics argue that sociocultural theory overemphasizes the role of context, minimizes the role of individuals in their own development, and neglects the influence of genetic and biological factors (Crain, 2016). Another perspective on development, described next, refocuses attention on the individual in context.

Bronfenbrenner's Bioecological Systems Theory

Similar to other developmental theorists, Urie Bronfenbrenner (1917–2005) believed that we are active in our own development. Specifically, Bronfenbrenner's **bioecological systems theory** poses that development is a result of the ongoing interactions among biological, cognitive, and psychological changes within the person and his or her changing context (Bronfenbrenner & Morris, 2006). Bronfenbrenner proposed that all individuals are embedded in, or surrounded by, a series of contexts: home, school, neighborhood, culture, and society, as shown in Figure 1.6. The bioecological systems theory thus offers a comprehensive perspective on the role of context as an influence on development. As shown in Figure 1.6, contexts are organized into a series of systems in which individuals are embedded and that interact with one another and the person to influence development.

At the center of the bioecological model is the individual. The developing person's genetic, psychological, socioemotional, and personality traits interact, influencing each other. For example, physical development, such as brain maturation, may influence cognitive development, which in turn may influence social development, such as a child's understanding of friendship. Social development then may influence cognitive development, as children may learn activities or ideas from each other. In this way, the various forms of development interact. The individual interacts with the contexts in

FIGURE 1.6

Bronfenbrenner's Bioecological Systems Theory

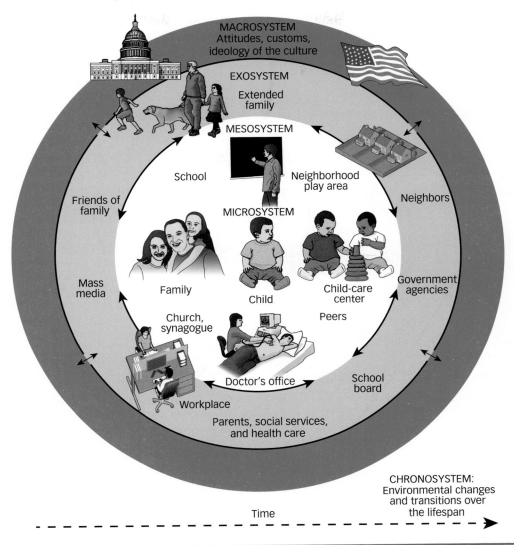

Source: Adapted from Bronfenbrenner and Morris (2006).

which he or she is embedded, influencing and being influenced by them (Bronfenbrenner & Morris, 2006).

The individual is embedded in the innermost level of context, the **microsystem**, which includes interactions with the immediate physical and social environment surrounding the person, such as family, peers, and school. Because the microsystem contains the developing person, it has an immediate and direct influence on his or her development. For example, peer relationships can influence a person's sense of self-esteem, social skills, and emotional development.

The next level, the **mesosystem**, refers to the relations and interactions among microsystems, or connections among contexts. For example, experiences in the home (one microsystem) influence those at school (another microsystem); parents who

encourage and provide support for reading will influence the child's experiences in the classroom. Like the microsystem, the mesosystem has a direct influence on the individual because he or she is a participant in it.

The **exosystem** consists of settings in which the individual is not a participant but that nevertheless influence him or her. For example, a child typically does not participate in a parent's work setting, yet the work setting has an indirect influence on the child because it affects the parent's mood. The availability of funding for schools, another exosystem factor, indirectly affects children by influencing the availability of classroom resources. The exosystem is an important contribution to our understanding of development because it shows us how the effects of outside factors trickle down and indirectly affect children and adults.

The **macrosystem** is the greater sociocultural context in which the microsystem, mesosystem, and exosystem are embedded. It includes cultural values, legal and political practices, and other elements of the society at large. The macrosystem indirectly influences the child because it affects each of the other contextual levels. For example, cultural beliefs about the value of education (macrosystem) influence funding decisions made at national and local levels (exosystem), as well as what happens in the classroom and in the home (mesosystem and microsystem). The accompanying Lives in Context feature illustrates how one element of the macrosystem, historical events, may influence development.

Sociohistorical Influences on Development

Sociohistorical influences, such as the Great Depression (1929–1939), contribute to cohort, or generational, differences in development.
Photo12/UIG via Getty Images

Historical events, such as wars, times of prosperity, economic and natural disasters, and periods of social unrest, are contextual influences that shape our world and our development. The effect of historical events on development depends in part on when they occur in a person's life (Elder et al., 2016).

The same historical event is experienced differently by successive cohorts, reflecting the fact that they are in different life stages, with different social roles, levels of maturity, and life experiences. For example, researchers examined the influence of the Great Depression (1929–1941) and World War II (1939–1945) on two cohorts of California-born Americans, followed from childhood to older adulthood, over a 70-year period (Elder & George, 2016).

These two cohorts offer striking examples of how sociohistorical context influences development.

The older Oakland cohort (born in 1920–1921) were children during the affluent 1920s, a time of economic growth in California, and they experienced a prosperous and relatively stress-free childhood. They entered adolescence during the Great Depression, a period of severe economic stress in which unemployment skyrocketed and people's savings were depleted. As adolescents during the Great Depression, the Oakland cohort tended to behave responsibly and assist their families in coping. The boys often assumed jobs outside the home to aid financially troubled families, which enhanced their social independence and reduced their exposure to family stress. However, girls spent more time at home caring for siblings and performing household chores, as many mothers worked outside the home; they were exposed to greater amounts of family stress and showed poorer adjustment than did the boys. The Oakland cohort completed high school just prior to the onset of World War II, and over time, nearly all of the young men entered the armed forces.

Unlike the Oakland cohort, individuals in the Berkeley Guidance Study (born in 1928–1929) experienced the Great Depression during their vulnerable early childhood years. The children thus experienced economic scarcity and family discord early in life, at a time when they were very dependent on family. The Berkeley cohort entered adolescence during World War II, a period of additional economic and emotional stress resulting from empty households (as both parents worked to support the war effort) and the military service and war trauma of older brothers. As adolescents, the Berkley boys experienced greater emotional difficulties, poorer attitudes toward school, and less hope, self-direction, and confidence about their future than did the boys in the Oakland cohort. Like the girls in the Oakland cohort, the Berkeley girls spent time at home. They experienced stress but showed better adjustment than the Oakland girls, who experienced multiple stressors and transitions of adolescence (such as puberty and changes in social roles) simultaneously with the onset of the Great Depression.

Although the Berkeley boys tended to be troubled in adolescence, they demonstrated resilience in adulthood, largely because of the influence of military service. Three quarters of the males in the Berkeley sample served in the military between 1945 and the end of the Korean War in the early 1950s. The most disadvantaged young men tended to join the military early, and early entry into the military predicted personal growth. Military service appeared to offer several opportunities, such as the chance to begin again and reconsider their lives, to travel, and to take advantage of the GI Bill of Rights, which enabled them to expand their education and acquire new skills after the war.

These two cohorts of young people offer striking examples of how sociohistorical context influences development. Context always plays a role in development—not only in times of social upheaval but every day and for every generation.

What Do You Think?

1. Consider the sociohistorical context in which you were raised. What historical and societal events may have influenced you? What events have shaped your generation's childhood and adolescence?

2. Consider the societal and cultural events that your parents may have experienced in childhood and adolescence. What technology was available? What historical events did they experience? What were the popular fads of their youth? What influence do you think these sociohistorical factors may have had on your parents' development? ●

A final element of the bioecological system is the **chronosystem**, which refers to how the bioecological system changes over time. As people grow and change, they take on and let go of various roles. For example, graduating from college, getting married, and becoming a parent involve changes in roles and shifts in microsystems. These shifts in contexts, called *ecological transitions,* occur throughout life.

Recently, the bioecological model has been criticized for its vague explanation of development, especially the role of culture (Vélez-Agosto, Soto-Crespo, Vizcarrondo-Oppenheimer, Vega-Molina, & García Coll, 2017). Situated in the macrosystem, culture is said to influence development through the interdependence of the systems. Yet current concep-tualizations of culture view it as all the processes used by people as they make meaning or think through interactions with group members (Mistry et al., 2016; Yoshikawa, Mistry, & Wang, 2016). Critics therefore argue that since culture is manifested in our daily activities, it is inherent in each bioecological level (Vélez-Agosto et al., 2017). A second criticism arises from the sheer complexity of the bioecological model and its attention to patterns and dynamic interactions. We can never measure and account for all of the potential individual and contextual influences on development at once, making it difficult to devise research studies to test the validity of the model. Proponents, however, argue that it is not necessary to test all of the model's components at once. Instead, smaller studies can examine each component over time (Jaeger, 2016; Tudge et al., 2016). In any case, bioecological theory remains an important contribution toward explaining developmental change across the lifespan and is a theory that we will consider throughout this book.

Shortly after birth, goslings imprint to their mothers, meaning that they bond to her and will follow her to ensure they will be fed and remain protected. Ethologists propose that animal and human caregiving behaviors have an evolutionary basis.
iStock/EmilyNorton

Ethology and Evolutionary Developmental Theory

What motivates parents of most species to care for their young? Some researchers argue that caregiving behaviors have an evolutionary basis. **Ethology** is the scientific study of the evolutionary basis of behavior (Bateson, 2015). In 1859, Charles Darwin proposed his theory of evolution, explaining that all species adapt and evolve over time. Specifically, traits that enable a species to adapt, thrive, and mate tend to be passed to succeeding generations because they improve the likelihood of the individual and species' survival. Several early theorists applied the concepts of evolution to behavior. Konrad Lorenz and Niko Tinbergen, two European zoologists, observed animal species in their natural environments and noticed patterns of behavior that appeared to be inborn, emerged early in life, and ensured the animals' survival. For example, shortly after birth, goslings imprint to their mothers, meaning that they bond to her and follow her. Imprinting aids the goslings' survival because it ensures that they stay close to their mother, get fed, and remain protected. In order for imprinting to occur, the mother goose must be present immediately after the goslings hatch; mothers instinctively stay close to the nest so that their young can imprint (Lorenz, 1952).

According to John Bowlby (1969), humans also display biologically preprogrammed behaviors that have survival value and promote development. For example, caregivers naturally respond to infants' cues. Crying, smiling, and grasping are inborn ways that infants get attention from caregivers, bring caregivers into physical contact, and ensure that they will be safe and cared for. Such behaviors have adaptive significance because they meet infants' needs and promote the formation of bonds with caregivers, ensuring that the caregivers will feel a strong desire and obligation to care for them (Bowlby, 1973). In this way, innate biological drives and behaviors work together with experience to influence adaptation and ultimately an individual's survival.

Another theory, **evolutionary developmental theory**, applies principles of evolution and scientific knowledge about the interactive influence of genetic and environmental mechanisms to understand the changes people undergo throughout their lives (Bjorklund, 2018; Witherington & Lickliter, 2016). You may have wondered, for example, whether you—your abilities, personality, and competencies—result from your genes or from the physical and social environment in which you were raised. Evolutionary developmental scientists explain that this is the wrong question to ask. From an evolutionary development perspective, genes and context interact in an ever-changing way so that it is impossible to isolate the contributions of each to development (Witherington & Lickliter, 2016) While all of our traits and characteristics are influenced by genes, contextual factors influence the expression of genetic instructions, as illustrated in Figure 1.7.

As an example, contextual factors such as gravity, light, temperature, and moisture even influence how genes are expressed and therefore how individuals develop (Meaney, 2017). For instance, in some reptiles, such as crocodiles, sex is determined by the temperature in which the organism develops. Eggs incubated at one range of temperatures produce male crocodiles and at another temperature produce female crocodiles (Pezaro, Doody, & Thompson, 2017).

According to evolutionary developmental theory, genetic factors and biological predispositions interact with the physical and social environment

to influence development, and Darwinian natural selection determines what genes and traits are passed on to the next generation (Bjorklund, 2018;

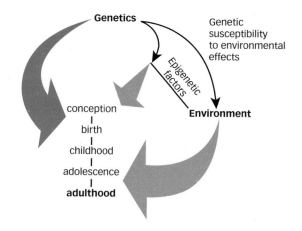

FIGURE 1.7

Interaction of Genetic and Environmental Factors

Development is influenced by the dynamic interplay of genetic and environmental factors. Genetic predispositions may influence how we experience environmental factors, and environmental factors may influence how genes are expressed.

Source: The Role of Genetic and Environmental Factors in the Development of Schizophrenia by Jonathan Picker, PhD, *Psychiatric Times*, August 01, 2005.

THINKING IN CONTEXT 1.3

Maria and Fernando have just given birth to their first child, a healthy baby boy. Like most new parents, Maria and Fernando are nervous and overwhelmed with their new responsibilities. Of utmost importance to them is that the baby develop a strong and secure bond to them. They want their baby to feel loved and to love them.

1. What advice would a psychoanalytic theorist give Maria and Fernando? Contrast psychoanalytic with behaviorist perspectives. How might a behaviorist theorist approach this question?

2. How might an evolutionary developmental theorist explain bonding between parents and infants? What advice might an evolutionary developmental theorist give to Maria and Fernando?

3. Considering bioecological systems theory, what microsystem and mesosystem factors influence the parent–child bond? What role might exosystem and macrosystem factors take?

TABLE 1.5

Comparing Theories of Human Development

	CONTINUITY VS. DISCONTINUITY	ACTIVE VS. PASSIVE INDIVIDUAL	NATURE VS. NURTURE
Freud's psychosexual theory	Discontinuous stages	Passive individuals motivated by inborn basic drives	Greater emphasis on nature: People are driven by inborn drives, but the extent to which the drives are satisfied influences developmental outcomes.
Erikson's psychosocial theory	Discontinuous stages	Active individuals interact with their social world to resolve psychosocial tasks.	Both nature and nurture: Biological and social forces propel people through the stages and social and psychosocial influences determine the outcome of each stage.
Behaviorist theory	Continuous process of learning new behaviors	Passive individuals are shaped by their environment.	Nurture: Environmental influences shape behavior.
Bandura's social learning theory	Continuous process of learning new behaviors	Individuals' characteristics and behavior interact with the environment.	Both nature and nurture: Inborn characteristics and the physical and social environment influence behavior.
Piaget's cognitive-developmental theory	Discontinuous stages but also continuous process of seeking equilibration	Active individuals interact with the world to create their own schemas.	Both nature and nurture: An innate drive to learn coupled with brain development leads people to interact with the world. Opportunities provided by the physical and social environment influence development.
Information processing theory	Continuous increase of skills and capacities	Active individuals attend to, process, and store information	Both nature and nurture: People are born with processing capacities that develop through maturation and environmental influences.
Vygotsky's sociocultural theory	Continuous interactions with others lead to developing new reasoning capacities and skills.	Active individuals interact with members of their culture.	Both nature and nurture: People learn through interactions with more skilled members of their culture; however, capacities are influenced by genes, brain development, and maturation.
Bronfenbrenner's bioecological systems theory	Continuous: People constantly change through their interactions with the contexts in which they are embedded.	Active individuals interact with their contexts, being influenced by their contexts but also determining what kinds of physical and social environments are created and how they change.	Both nature and nurture: People's inborn and biological characteristics interact with an ever changing context to influence behavior.
Ethology and evolutionary developmental theory	Both continuous and discontinuous: People gradually grow and change throughout life, but there are sensitive periods in which specific experiences and developments must occur.	Active individuals interact with their physical and social environment.	Both nature and nurture: Genetic programs and biological predispositions interact with the physical and social environment to influence development and Darwinian natural selection determines what genes and traits are passed on to the next generation.

Witherington & Lickliter, 2016). People are viewed as active in their development, influencing their contexts, responding to the demands for adaptation posed by their contexts, and constantly interacting with and adapting to the world around them. The relevance of both biological and contextual factors to human development is indisputable, and most developmental scientists appreciate the contributions of evolutionary developmental theory

(DelGiudice, 2018; Frankenhuis & Tiokhin, 2018; Legare, Clegg, & Wen, 2018). The ways in which biology and context interact and their influence on development change over the course of the lifetime, as we will discuss throughout this book.

The many theories of human development offer complementary and contrasting views of how we change throughout our lifetimes. Table 1.5 provides a comparison of theories of human development.

RESEARCH IN HUMAN DEVELOPMENT

» LO 1.4   Describe the methods and research designs used to study human development.

The many theories of lifespan human development differ in focus and explanation, but they all result from scientists' attempts to organize observations of people at all ages. Developmental scientists conduct research to gather information and answer questions about how people grow and change over their lives. They devise theories to organize what they learn from research and to suggest new hypotheses to test in research studies. In turn, research findings are used to modify theories. By conducting multiple studies over time, developmental scientists refine their theories about lifespan human development and determine new questions to ask.

The Scientific Method

Researchers employ the **scientific method**, a process of posing and answering questions by making careful and systematic observations and gathering information. The scientific method provides an organized way of formulating questions, finding answers, and communicating research discoveries. Its basic steps are as follows:

1. Identify the research question or problem to be studied and formulate the hypothesis, or proposed explanation, to be tested.

2. Gather information to address the research question.

3. Summarize the information gathered and determine whether the hypothesis is refuted, or shown to be false.

4. Interpret the summarized information, consider the findings in light of prior research studies, and share findings with the scientific community and world at large.

In practice, the scientific method usually does not proceed in such a straightforward, linear fashion. Frequently, research studies raise as many questions as they answer—and sometimes more. Unexpected findings can prompt new studies. For example, researchers may repeat an experiment (called a *replication*) to see whether the results are the same as previous ones. Sometimes analyses reveal flaws in data collection methods or research design, prompting a revised study. Experts may also disagree on the interpretation of a study. Researchers may then conduct new studies to test new hypotheses and shed more light on a given topic. For all of these reasons, scientists often say the scientific method is "messy."

Methods of Data Collection

The basic challenge that scientists face in conducting research is determining what information is important and how to gather it. Scientists use the term *data* to refer to the information they collect. How can we gather data about children, adolescents, and adults? Should we simply talk with our participants? Watch them as they progress through their days? Hook them up to machines that measure physiological activity such as heart rate or brain waves? Developmental scientists use a variety of different methods, or measures, to collect information.

Observational Measures

Observational measures are methods that scientists use to collect and organize information based on watching and monitoring people's behavior. Developmental scientists employ two types of observational measures: naturalistic observation and structured observation.

Scientists who use **naturalistic observation** observe and record behavior in natural, real-world settings. For example, Coplan, Ooi, and Nocita (2015) studied peer interaction patterns in children by observing 9- to 12-year-old children in the schoolyard during recess and lunch. They recorded the children's activity and interaction with peers and found that children who were consistently unengaged with peers tended to show high levels of problems, such as anxiety, depression, and loneliness, as reported by both the children and their mothers.

Sometimes the presence of an observer causes those being observed to behave in unnatural ways or ways that are not typical for them. This is known as *participant reactivity,* and it poses a challenge to gathering by naturalistic observation. One way of reducing the effect of observation is to conduct multiple observations so that the children get used to the observer and return to their normal behavior. Another promising method of minimizing participant

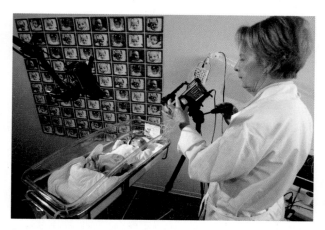

This researcher is using a video camera to observe and record the facial expressions a newborn baby makes while it sleeps.
Thierry Berrod, Mona Lisa Production / Science Source

reactivity is to use an electronically activated voice recorder (EAR) (Mehl, 2017). Participants carry the EAR as they go about their daily lives. The EAR captures segments of information over time: hours, days, or even weeks. It yields a log of people's activities as they naturally unfold. The EAR minimizes participant reactivity because the participant is unaware of exactly when the EAR is recording. For example, researchers who study child trauma use EAR to sample conversations between parents and children to understand how parent–child interactions influence children's adjustment and how the family environment can aid children's recovery from trauma (Alisic, Krishna, Robbins, & Mehl, 2016).

Naturalistic observation permits researchers to observe patterns of behavior in everyday settings, such as whether a particular event or behavior typically precedes another. Such observations can help researchers determine which behaviors are important to study in the first place. For example, a scientist who studies bullying by observing children's play may notice that some victims act aggressively *before* a bullying encounter (Kamper-DeMarco & Ostrov, 2017). The scientist may then decide to examine aggression in victims not only after a bullying incident but also beforehand. Naturalistic observation is a useful way of studying events and behaviors that are common. Some behaviors and events, however, are uncommon or are difficult to observe, such as physical aggression among adults, requiring a researcher to observe for very long periods of time to obtain data on the behavior of interest. For this reason, many researchers make structured observations.

Structured observation entails observing and recording behaviors displayed in a controlled environment, a situation constructed by the experimenter. For example, children might be observed in a laboratory setting as they play with another child or complete a puzzle-solving task. The challenges of identifying and categorizing which behaviors to record are similar to those involved in naturalistic observation. However, the laboratory environment permits researchers to exert more control over the situation than is possible in natural settings. In addition to cataloguing observable behaviors, some researchers use technology to measure biological functions such as heart rate, brain waves, and blood pressure. One challenge to conducting structured observations is that people do not always behave in laboratory settings as they do in real life.

Self-Report Measures

Interviews and questionnaires are known as self-report measures because the person under study answers questions about his or her experiences, attitudes, opinions, beliefs, and behavior. Interviews can take place in person, over the phone, or over the Internet.

The interviewer is asking this young boy about his own experiences, opinions, and behavior. Interviews and questionnaires are known as self-report measures.
Per-Anders Petterson/Corbis News/ Getty Images

One type of interview is the **open-ended interview**, in which a trained interviewer uses a conversational style that encourages the participant, or the person under study, to expand his or her responses. Interviewers may vary the order of questions, probe, and ask additional questions based on responses. The scientist begins with a question and then follows up with prompts to obtain a better view of the person's reasoning (Ginsburg, 1997). An example of this is the Piagetian Clinical Interview, which requires specialized training to administer. Consider this dialogue between Piaget and a 6-year-old child:

You know what a dream is?

When you are asleep and you see something

Where does it come from?

The sky

Can you see it?

No! Yes, when you're asleep

Could I see it if I was there?

No.

Why not?

Because it is in front of us…. When you are asleep you dream and you see them, but when you aren't asleep you don't see them.

(Piaget, 1929, p. 93)

Open-ended interviews permit participants to explain their thoughts thoroughly and in their own words. They also enable researchers to gather a large amount of information quickly. Open-ended interviews are very flexible as well. However, their flexibility poses a challenge: When questions are phrased differently for each person, responses may not capture real differences in how people think about a given topic and instead may reflect differences in how the questions were posed and followed up by the interviewer.

A **structured interview** poses the same set of questions to each participant in the same way. On one hand, structured interviews are less flexible than open-ended interviews. On the other hand, because all participants receive the same set of questions, differences in responses are more likely to reflect true differences among participants and not merely differences in the manner of interviewing. For example, Evans, Milanak, Medeiros, and Ross (2002) used a structured interview to examine American children's beliefs about magic. Children between the ages of 3 and 8 were asked the following set of questions: What is magic? Who can do magic?

> Is it possible to have special powers? Who has special powers?
>
> Does someone have to learn to do magic? Where have you seen magic? (p. 49)

After compiling and analyzing the children's responses as well as administering several cognitive tasks, the researchers concluded that even older children, who have the ability to think logically and perform concrete operations, may display magical beliefs.

To collect data from large samples of people, scientists may compile and use **questionnaires**, also called surveys, made up of sets of questions, typically multiple choice. Questionnaires can be administered in person, online, or by telephone, email, or postal mail. Questionnaires are popular data collection methods because they are easy to use and enable scientists to collect information from many people quickly and inexpensively. Scientists who conduct research on sensitive topics, such as sexual interest and experience, often use questionnaires because they can easily be administered anonymously, protecting participants' privacy. For example, the Monitoring the Future Study is an annual survey of 50,000 eighth-, tenth-, and twelfth-grade students that collects information about their behaviors, attitudes, and values concerning drug and alcohol use (Miech et al., 2017). The survey permits scientists to gather an enormous amount of data, yet its anonymity protects the adolescents from the consequences of sharing personal information that they might not otherwise reveal.

Despite their ease of use, self-report measures are not without challenges. Sometimes people give socially desirable answers: They respond in ways they would like themselves to be perceived or believe researchers desire. A college student completing a survey about cheating, for example, might sometimes look at nearby students' papers during examinations, but she might choose survey answers that do not reflect this behavior. Her answers might instead match the person she aspires to be or the behaviors she believes the world values—that is, someone who does not cheat on exams. Self-report data, then, may not always reflect people's true attitudes and behavior. Some argue that we are not always fully aware of our feelings and therefore cannot always provide useful insight into our own thoughts and behavior with the use of self-report measures (Newell & Shanks, 2014).

Physiological Measures

Physiological measures are increasingly used in developmental research because cognition, emotion, and behavior have physiological indicators. For example, when speaking in public, such as when you give a class presentation, do you feel your heart beat more rapidly or your palms grow sweaty? Increases in heart rate and perspiration are physiological measures of anxiety that might be measured by researchers. Other researchers might measure cortisol, a hormone triggered by the experience of stress (Simons, Cillessen, & de Weerth, 2017).

Some researchers measure eye movements or pupil dilation as indicators of attention and interest. For example, researchers who tracked participants' eye movements as they viewed Facebook feeds learned that people are naturally attracted to social and news posts that are rich with pictures and links, yet most people are unable to report what they have viewed, even immediately after viewing it (Vraga, Bode, & Troller-Renfree, 2016). A researcher who employs physiological measures might use an infant's pupil dilation as a measure of interest (Wetzel, Buttelmann, Schieler, & Widmann, 2016). An advantage of physiological measures is they do not rely on verbal reports and generally cannot be faked. A challenge to physiological measures is that, although physiological responses can be recorded, they may be difficult to interpret. For example, excitement and anger may both cause an increase in heart rate. Physiological measures of brain activity are a particularly promising source of data, as discussed in the Brain and Biological Influences on Development feature. Data collection methods are summarized in Table 1.6.

Research Designs

There are many steps in conducting research. In addition to determining the research question and deciding what information to collect, scientists must choose a research design—a technique for conducting the research study.

Case Study

A case study is an in-depth examination of a single person (or small group of individuals). It is conducted by gathering information from many sources, such as

TABLE 1.6

Data Collection Methods

	ADVANTAGE	DISADVANTAGE
Clinical interview	Gather a large amount of information quickly and inexpensively.	Nonstandardized questions. Characteristics of the interviewer may influence participant responses.
Structured interview	Permits gathering a large amount of information quickly and inexpensively.	Characteristics of the interviewer may influence participant responses.
Questionnaire	Permits collecting data from a large sample more quickly and inexpensively than by interview methods.	Some participants may respond in socially desirable or inaccurate ways.
Naturalistic observation	Gathers data on everyday behavior in a natural environment as behaviors occur.	The observer's presence may influence the participants' behavior. No control over the observational environment.
Structured observation	Observation in a controlled setting.	May not reflect real-life reactions and behavior.
Physiological measures	Assesses biological indicators and does not rely on participant report.	May be difficult to interpret.

through observations, interviews, and conversations with family, friends, and others who know the individual. A case study may include samples or interpretations of a person's writing, such as poetry or journal entries, artwork, and other creations. A case study provides a rich description of a person's life and influences on his or her development. It is often employed to study individuals who have unique and unusual experiences, abilities, or disorders. Conclusions drawn from a case study may shed light on an individual's development but may not be generalized or applied to others. Case studies can be a source of hypotheses to examine in large-scale research.

Correlational Research

Are children with high self-esteem more likely to excel at school? Are older adults with more friends happier than those with few? Are college students who work part-time less likely to graduate? All of these questions can be studied with **correlational research**, which permits researchers to examine relations among measured characteristics, behaviors, and events. For example, in one study, scientists examined the relationship between physical fitness and academic performance in middle school students and found that children with higher aerobic capacity scored higher on achievement tests than did children with poorer aerobic capacity (Bass, Brown, Laurson, & Coleman, 2013). Note that this correlation does not tell us *why* aerobic capacity was associated with academic achievement. Correlational research cannot answer this question because it simply describes relationships that exist among variables;

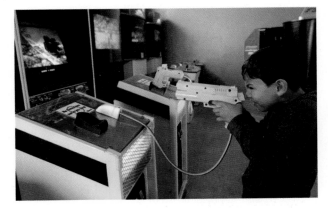

Researchers experimentally manipulate which children play with violent video games to determine their effect on behavior.
BSIP/UIG via Getty Images

it does not enable us to reach conclusions about the causes of those relationships. It is likely that other variables influence both a child's aerobic ability and achievement (e.g., health), but correlation does not enable us to determine the causes for behavior—for that we need an experiment.

Experimental Research

Scientists who seek to test hypotheses about *causal* relationships, such as whether media exposure influences behavior or whether hearing particular types of music influences mood, employ **experimental research**. An experiment is a procedure that uses control to determine causal relationships among variables. Specifically, one or more variables thought to influence a behavior of interest are changed, or manipulated, while other variables are held constant. Researchers can then examine how the changing variable influences the behavior under study. If the

BRAIN AND BIOLOGICAL INFLUENCES ON DEVELOPMENT

Methods of Studying the Brain

Modern brain imaging techniques enable us to measure brain activity as individuals think and solve problems.
Phanie / Alamy Stock Photo

What parts of the brain are active when we solve problems or feel emotions? How does the brain change with development? Until recently, the brain was a mystery. Over the past hundred years, researchers have devised several ways of studying brain activity that have increased our understanding of how the brain functions and how it develops.

The earliest instrument created to measure brain activity was the electroencephalogram, first used with humans in the 1920s (Collura, 1993). Electroencephalography (EEG) measures electrical activity patterns produced by the brain via electrodes placed on the scalp. Researchers study fluctuations in activity that occur when participants are presented with stimuli or when they sleep. EEG recordings measure electrical activity in the brain, but they do not provide information about the location of activity.

Not until the invention of positron emission tomography (PET) in the early 1950s did researchers obtain the first glimpse of the inner workings of the brain (Portnow, Vaillancourt, & Okun, 2013). Researchers inject a small dose of radioactive material into the participant's bloodstream and detected by the PET scan. The radioactive material enables researchers to monitor the flow of blood. Blood flows more readily to active areas of the brain, and the resulting images can illustrate what parts of the brain are active as participants view stimuli and solve problems. Developed in 1971, computerized tomography, known as the CT scan, produces X-ray images of brain structures (Cierniak, 2011). A movable X-ray unit rotates around a person's head as it records images of the brain (Herman, 2009). The images are then combined to make a three-dimensional picture of the person's brain, providing images of bone, brain vasculature, and tissue. CT scans can provide researchers with information about the density of brain structures to illustrate, for example, how the thickness of the cortex changes with development.

Functional magnetic resonance imaging (fMRI) measures brain activity by monitoring changes in blood flow in the brain (Bandettini, 2012). Developed in the 1990s, MRI machines house a powerful magnet that uses radio waves and to measure blood oxygen level. Active areas of the brain require more oxygen-rich blood. Like PET scans, fMRI enables researchers to determine what parts of the brain are active as individuals complete cognitive tasks. However, fMRI images are much more detailed than PET scans. An important advantage of fMRI over PET scans is that it does not rely on radioactive molecules, which can only be administered a few times before becoming unsafe.

Another imaging process, called diffusion tensor imaging (DTI), uses an MRI machine to track how water molecules move in and around the fibers connecting different parts of the brain (Soares, Marques, Alves, & Sousa, 2013). DTI gauges the thickness and density of the brain's connections, permitting researchers to measure the brain's white matter and determine changes that occur with development and with age-related illnesses, such as Alzheimer's disease.

What Do You Think?

If you were going to study the brain, which measure would you choose and why? What type of information would you obtain from your chosen measure? Identify a research question that your measure might help you answer. ●

behavior changes as the variable changes, this suggests that the variable caused the change in the behavior.

For example, Gentile, Bender, and Anderson (2017) examined the effect of playing violent video games on children's physiological stress and aggressive thoughts. Children were randomly assigned to play a violent video game (*Superman*) or a nonviolent video game (*Finding Nemo*) for 25 minutes in the researchers' lab. The researchers measured physiological stress as indicated by heart rate and cortisol levels before and after the children played the video game. Children also completed a word completion task that the researchers used to measure the frequency of aggressive thoughts. The researchers found that children who played violent video games showed higher levels of physiological stress and aggressive thoughts than did the children who played nonviolent video games. They concluded that the type of video game changed children's stress reactions and aggressive thoughts.

Let's take a closer look at the components of an experiment. Conducting an experiment requires choosing at least one **dependent variable**, the behavior under study (e.g., physiological stress—heart rate and cortisol—and aggressive thoughts) and one **independent variable**, the factor proposed to change the behavior under study (e.g., type of video game). The independent variable is manipulated or varied systematically by the researcher during the experiment (e.g., a child plays with a violent or a nonviolent video game). The dependent variable is expected to change as a result of varying the independent variable, and how it changes is thought to depend on how the independent variable is manipulated (e.g., physiological stress and aggressive thoughts vary in response to the type of video game).

In an experiment, the independent variable is administered to one or more *experimental groups,* or test groups. The *control group* is treated just like the experimental group except that it is not exposed to the independent variable. For example, in an experiment investigating whether particular types of music influence mood, the experimental group would experience a change in music (e.g., from "easy listening" to rock), whereas the control group would hear only one type of music (e.g., "easy listening"). **Random assignment**, whereby each participant has an equal chance of being assigned to the experimental or control group, is essential for ensuring that the groups are as equal as possible in all preexisting characteristics (e.g., age, ethnicity, and gender). Random assignment makes it less likely that any observed differences in the outcomes of the experimental and control groups are due to preexisting differences between the groups. After the independent variable is manipulated, if the experimental and control groups differ on the dependent variable, it is concluded that the independent variable *caused* the change in the dependent variable. That is, a cause-and-effect relationship has been demonstrated.

As another example, consider a study designed to examine whether massage therapy improves outcomes in preterm infants (infants who were born well before their due date) (Abdallah, Badr, & Hawwari, 2013). Infants housed in a neonatal unit were assigned to a massage group (independent variable), who were touched and their arms and legs moved for 10-minute periods once each day, or to a control group, which received no massage. Other than the massage/no-massage periods, the two groups of infants were cared for in the same way. Infants who were massaged scored lower on the measure of infant pain and discomfort (including indicators such as heart rate, oxygen saturation, and facial responses) at discharge (dependent variable). The researchers concluded that massage therapy reduces pain responses in preterm infants.

Developmental scientists conduct studies that use both correlational and experimental research. Studying development, however, requires that scientists pay close attention to age and how people change over time, which requires the use of specialized research designs, as described in the following sections.

Developmental Research Designs

Does personality change over the lifespan? Do children outgrow shyness? Are infants' bonds with their parents associated with their adult relationships? These challenging questions require that developmental scientists examine relationships among variables over time. The following sections discuss the designs that researchers use to learn about human development. As you learn about each design, consider how we might employ it to answer a question about development. For example, how does alcohol use among adolescents change from 6th grade through 12th grade?

Cross-Sectional Research Design

A **cross-sectional research study** compares groups of people of different ages at a single point in time. For example, to examine how alcohol use changes from 6th through 12th grade, a scientist might visit a school system in 2020 and administer a survey about alcohol use to students ages 12, 14, 16, and 18. By analyzing the survey, the scientist can describe age differences in alcohol use and identify how 12-year-olds differ from 18-year-olds. However, the results do not tell us whether the observed age differences in alcohol use reflect age-related or developmental change. In other words, we don't know whether the 12-year-olds will show the same patterns of alcohol use as the current 18-year-olds when they are 18, six years from now.

Cross-sectional research permits age comparisons, but participants differ not only in age but also in cohort, limiting the conclusions researchers can draw about development. Recall that a cohort is a group of people of the same age who are exposed to similar historical events and cultural and societal influences. The 12-year-olds and the 18-year-olds are different ages, but they are also in different cohorts, so the two groups may differ in reported alcohol use because of development (age-related changes) or cohort (group-related changes). For example, perhaps the 12-year-olds received a new early prevention program at school that was not available to the 18-year-olds when they were 12. The difference in alcohol use between 12-year-olds and 18-year-olds might then be related to the prevention program, not to age. Cross-sectional research is an important source of information about age differences, but it cannot provide information about age change.

Longitudinal Research Design

A **longitudinal research study** follows the same group of participants over many points in time. Returning to the previous example, to examine how alcohol use changes from 12 to 18 years of age, a developmental scientist using longitudinal research might administer a survey on alcohol use to 12-year-olds and then follow up 2 years later when they are 14, again when they are 16, and finally when they are 18. If a researcher began this study in 2020, the last round of data collection would not occur until 2026.

Longitudinal research provides information about age change because it follows people over time, enabling scientists to describe how the 12-year-olds' alcohol use changed as they progressed through adolescence. However, longitudinal research studies only one cohort, calling into question whether findings indicate developmental change or whether they are an artifact of the cohort under study. Was the group of 12-year-olds that the scientist chose to follow for 6 years somehow different from the cohorts or groups of students who came before or after? Because only one cohort is assessed, it is not possible to determine whether the observed changes are age-related changes or changes that are unique to the cohort examined.

Sequential Research Designs

A **sequential research design** combines the best features of cross-sectional and longitudinal research by assessing multiple cohorts over time, enabling scientists to make comparisons that disentangle the effects of cohort and age (see Table 1.7). Consider the alcohol use study once more. A sequential design would begin in 2020 with a survey to students ages 12, 14, 16, and 18. Two years later, in 2022, the initial sample is surveyed again; the 12-year-olds are now 14, the 14-year-olds are now 16, and the 16-year-olds are now 18. The 18-year-olds are now 20 and are not assessed because they have aged out of the study. Now a new group of 12-year-olds is surveyed. Two years later, in 2024, the participants are surveyed again, and so on.

A sequential design combines cross-sectional and longitudinal designs, permitting the researcher to study multiple cohorts over time.

The sequential design provides information about age, cohort, and age-related change. The cross-sectional data (comparisons of 12-, 14-, 16-, and 18-year-olds from a given year) permit comparisons among age groups. The longitudinal data (annual follow-up of participants ages 12 through 18) permit helps scientists separate cohort effects from

TABLE 1.7

Sequential Research Design

	2020	2022	2024	2026	2028
6th grade	A	E	F	G	H
8th grade	B	A	E	F	G
10th grade	C	B	A	E	F
12th grade	D	C	B	A	E

Source: Adapted from Kim & Böckenholt (2000) *Psychological Methods*, Vol 5(3). Sep 2000, 380–400.

TABLE 1.8

Comparing Research Designs

DESIGN	STRENGTHS	LIMITATIONS
RESEARCH DESIGNS		
Case study	Provides a rich description of an individual.	Conclusions may not be generalized to other individuals.
Correlational	Permits the analysis of relationships among variables as they exist in the real world.	Cannot determine cause-and-effect relations.
Experimental	Permits a determination of cause-and-effect relations.	Data collected from artificial environments may not represent behavior in real-world environments.
DEVELOPMENTAL RESEARCH DESIGNS		
Longitudinal	Permits the determination of age-related changes in a sample of participants assessed for a period of time.	Requires a great deal of time, resources, and expense. Participant attrition may limit conclusions. Cohort-related changes may limit the generalizability of conclusions.
Cross-sectional	More efficient and less costly than the longitudinal design. Permits the determination of age differences.	Does not permit inferences regarding age change. Confounds age and cohort.
Sequential	More efficient and less costly than the longitudinal model. Allows for both longitudinal and cross-sectional comparisons, which reveal age differences and age change, as well as cohort effects.	Time-consuming, expensive, and complicated in data collection and analysis.

age-related change. Because several cohorts are examined at once, the effect of cohort can be studied. The sequential design is complex, but it permits human development researchers to disentangle the effects of age and cohort, as well as answer questions about developmental change.

In summary, scientists use the scientific method to systematically ask and seek answers to questions about human development. Researchers' decisions about measures and research designs influence the information that they collect and the conclusions that they make about development. Researchers have responsibilities to conduct sound research and also to adhere to standards of ethical conduct in research, as the next section describes. See Table 1.8 for a comparison of research designs.

THINKING IN CONTEXT 1.4

Dorothy is interested in understanding smoking in middle school students. Specifically, she believes that low self-esteem causes students to smoke.

1. How might Dorothy gather information to address her hypothesis?

2. What kind of research design should Dorothy use? What are the advantages and disadvantages of this design?

3. What are some of the challenges of measuring behaviors such as smoking and internal characteristics such as self-esteem?

4. How can her study be improved to overcome the weaknesses you have identified?

RESEARCH ETHICS

» LO 1.5 Discuss the ethical responsibilities of researchers to protect their participants.

Suppose a researcher wanted to determine the effects of an illegal drug on pregnant women or the effects of malnutrition on kindergarteners. Would it be possible to design a study in which certain pregnant women were assigned to ingest the illegal drug? Or one in which certain kindergarteners were deprived of food? These studies violate the basic ethical principles that guide developmental scientists' work: (1) beneficence and nonmaleficence, (2) responsibility, (3) integrity, (4) justice, and (5) respect for autonomy (American Psychological Association, 2010).

Beneficence and nonmaleficence are the dual responsibilities to do good and to avoid doing harm. Researchers must protect and help the individuals,

families, and communities with which they work by maximizing the benefits and minimizing the potential harms of their work. Sometimes, though, researchers' desire to answer questions and solve problems may conflict with the need to protect the participants in research studies. For example, suppose a researcher studying adolescents learns that a participant is in jeopardy, whether engaging in health-compromising behaviors (e.g., cigarette smoking, unsafe driving, or unhealthy behavior), contemplating suicide, or engaging in illegal or harmful activities (e.g., drug addiction, stealing, or violence). Is the researcher responsible for helping the adolescent? If the researcher is studying a behavior that correlates with health-compromising behaviors, she might anticipate encountering participants who are in jeopardy. Researchers who study risky behaviors *expect* to encounter participants who engage in potentially dangerous activities. Helping the adolescent might involve removing him or her from the study and potentially compromising the study. In addition, adolescents generally expect that researchers will maintain confidentiality; violating their confidentiality may be harmful. Although current ethical guidelines address researchers' obligations to help and not harm, they leave a certain amount of judgment to the researcher regarding how to help and not harm participants and the conflicting duties to maintain confidentiality and disclose participant problems (Hiriscau, Stingelin-Giles, Stadler, Schmeck, & Reiter-Theil, 2014; Sharkey, Reed, & Felix, 2017).

A second principle that guides developmental scientists' work is that they must act responsibly by adhering to professional standards of conduct, clarifying their obligations and roles to others, and avoiding conflicts of interest. For example, a psychologist who conducts research with children and parents must clarify her role as scientist and not counselor and help her participants understand that she is simply gathering information from them rather than conducting therapy.

Researchers are responsible not only to their participants but also to society at large. In reporting results, researchers should be mindful of the social and political implications of their work (Society for Research in Child Development, 2007). Researchers must consider how their findings will be portrayed in the media, attempt to foresee ways in which their results may be misinterpreted, and correct any misinterpretations that occur. For example, one highly publicized study compiled the existing research literature examining college students who had become sexually involved with an adult prior to reaching the legal age of consent (Rind, Tromovitch, & Bauserman, 1998). After compiling the results of many research studies, the scientists determined that young people's coping and development varied depending on a number of factors within the individual, situation, and broader context; not all the young people appeared to be harmed, and those who were older when the relationship began often appeared well adjusted. These findings were misinterpreted by some organizations, media outlets, and politicians as suggesting that sexual involvement with minors was acceptable or even beneficial—clearly not the researchers' conclusions (Garrison & Kobor, 2002).

The principle of *integrity* requires that scientists be accurate, honest, and truthful in their work and make every effort to keep their promises to the people and communities with which they work. The principle of *justice* means that the benefits and risks of participation in research must be spread equitably across individuals and groups. Scientists must take care to ensure that all people have access to the contributions and benefits of research. For example, when research study suggests that an intervention is successful, the participants who did not receive it (those who were in the control group) must be given the opportunity to benefit from the intervention.

Perhaps the most important principle of research ethics is that scientists have a special obligation to respect participants' **autonomy**, their ability to make and implement decisions. Ethical codes of conduct require that researchers obtain from all participants their **informed consent**—their informed, rational, and voluntary agreement to participate. Researchers must provide participants with information about the research study, answer questions, help them to make their own decisions about whether to participate in the study, and ensure that they understand that they are free to decide not to participate in the research study and that they will not be penalized if they refuse.

Respecting people's autonomy also means protecting those who are not capable of making judgments and asserting themselves. Parents provide parental permission for their minor children to participate because researchers (and lawmakers) assume that minors are not able to meet the rational criteria of informed consent. Although children cannot provide informed consent, researchers respect their growing capacities for decision making in ways that are appropriate to their age by seeking *assent,* children's agreement to participate (Tait & Geisser, 2017). For a toddler or young child, obtaining assent may involve simply asking if he or she wants to play with the researcher (Brown, Harvey, Griffith, Arnold, & Halgin, 2017). With increasing cognitive and social development, children are better able to understand the nature of science and engage meaningfully in decisions about research participation. In short, discussions about research participation should be tailored to children's development, including offering more detailed information and seeking more comprehensive assent as children grow older (Kuther, 2003; Roth-Cline & Nelson, 2013). Moreover, seeking assent helps children learn how to make decisions and participate in decision making within safe contexts (Oulton et al., 2016).

Traumatic brain injury, dementia, mental illness, some physical illnesses, and advanced age can impair adults' capacities to provide informed consent (Prusaczyk, Cherney, Carpenter, & DuBois, 2017). In such cases, researchers seek assent by providing participants with meaningful information in a format that they can understand (as well as obtaining consent from a surrogate decision maker). Cognitive capacities can often fluctuate and, in the case of

---

TABLE 1.9

Rights of Research Participants

RIGHT	DESCRIPTION
Protection from harm	Research participants have the right to be protected from physical and psychological harm. Investigators must use the least stressful research procedure in testing hypotheses and, when in doubt, consult with others.
Informed consent	Participants have the right to be informed about the purpose of the research, expected duration, procedures, risks and benefits of participation, and any other aspects of the research that may influence their willingness to participate. When children are participants, a parent or guardian must provide informed consent on behalf of the child and the investigator should seek assent from the child.
Confidentiality	Participants have the right to privacy, to conceal their identity on all information and reports obtained in the course of research.
Information about the results	Participants have the right to be informed of the results of research in language that matches their level of understanding.
Treatment	If an experimental treatment under investigation is believed to be beneficial, participants in control groups have the right to obtain the beneficial treatment.

Sources: American Psychological Association (2010); Society for Research in Child Development (2007).

The Real-World Significance of Developmental Research

In September 2016, the United Nations adopted Sustainable Development Goals. The goals are a global consensus for supporting individuals in all countries. Goals include improving nutrition and health, ending poverty, promoting education, and achieving gender equality.
Randy Duchaine / Alamy Stock Photo

In its early years, the study of human development was based on laboratory research devoted to uncovering universal aspects of development by stripping away contextual influences. This basic research was designed to examine how development unfolds, with the assumption that development is a universal process with all people changing in similar ways and in similar timeframes. In the early 1980s, influenced by contextual theories (such as Bronfenbrenner's bioecological approach) and the growing assumption that people are active in their development (a cornerstone of lifespan developmental theory), developmental scientists began to examine developmental processes outside of the laboratory (Lerner, Johnson, & Buckingham, 2015). It quickly became apparent that there are a great many individual differences in development and that development varies with a myriad of contextual influences. The field of **applied developmental science** emerged, studying individuals within the contexts in which they live and applying research findings to improve people's lives.

Research in human development is now directed toward understanding social problems and issues of immediate social relevance, such as the capacities of preterm infants, children's ability to provide eyewitness testimony, adolescent sexual practices, and the impact of disability on the psychological and social adjustment of older adults and their adult children (Fisher, Busch-Rossnagel, Jopp, & Brown, 2013; Lerner, 2012). Applied developmental research often raises ethical questions. For example, sometimes seeking consent from parents may interfere with a researcher's goals or may pose risks to minor participants. For example, in one study, lesbian, gay, bisexual, or transgender (LGBT) adolescents believed that participating in research on sexuality and health is important for advancing science, yet indicated that they would not participate if guardian permission were required, citing negative parental attitudes or not being "out" about their LBGT identity (Macapagal, Coventry, Arbeit, Fisher, & Mustanski, 2017). As one 15-year-old bisexual participant explained,

> I believe it could harm some [teens] because the risk of being let out of the closet. I know some people whose family would not approve of any other sexuality [other than heterosexuality]. Such as my own, my mother would turn on me for not being her perfect image.

(Continued)

(Continued)

In response to these ethical challenges, researchers frequently obtain *passive consent* for conducting research on sensitive topics with adolescents. Passive consent procedures typically involve notifying parents about the research and requiring them to reply if they do *not* want their child to participate.

Applied developmental science is a multidisciplinary field that unites scientists from around the world to examine and contribute to policies on issues that affect children, adolescents, adults, and their families, such as health and health care delivery, violence, school failure. For example, they might study contextual influences such as the impact of environmental contaminants or poor access to clean water on development or the ways in which poverty influences children's development and economic status in adulthood (Aizer, 2017; Gauvain, 2018; Golinkoff, Hirsh-Pasek, Grob, & Schlesinger, 2017; Huston, 2018).

In September 2016, the member states of the United Nations defined and adopted Sustainable Development Goals, a global consensus on 17 goals for supporting individuals and ensuring equity and health in all countries (United Nations General Assembly, 2015). Sample goals include ending poverty in all its forms everywhere; improving nutrition, health, and well-being for all people; promoting education and lifelong learning opportunities; and achieving gender equality and empowering all women and girls. The goals are broad in scope, and reaching them will require the knowledge and skills of applied developmental scientist researchers and practitioners from many disciplines working in interdisciplinary teams (Gauvain, 2018).

What Do You Think?

What are some of the challenges of multi-disciplinary research? What concerns might a researcher face in studying problems such as risky behavior, child maltreatment, and school dropout? In your view, under what circumstances is passive consent acceptable, if ever? ●

traumatic brain injury patients, often improves (Triebel et al., 2014). Researchers must be prepared to tailor their explanations to the participant's fluctuating competence. Table 1.9 summarizes the rights of research participants.

Lifespan human development is a broad field of study that integrates theory and research from many disciplines to describe, predict, and explain how we grow and change throughout our lifetime. Developmental scientists apply their knowledge to identify, prevent, and solve problems and to improve opportunities for individuals, families, and communities. Throughout this book, you will learn the fundamentals of lifespan human development, including physical, cognitive, and socioemotional change, as well as the implications of developmental

science for social issues. We begin our journey in Chapter 2 by considering the role of genetics and environment in shaping who we become.

 THINKING IN CONTEXT 1.5

1. Suppose, as part of your research, you wanted to interview children at school. What ethical principles are most relevant to your work? Why? What challenges do you anticipate?

2. Consider collecting observations and interviews of older adults in a nursing home. What ethical issues can you anticipate? What principles are most pertinent?

 APPLY YOUR KNOWLEDGE

1. Steven enters the school psychologist's office with a frown, grumbling to himself. His teacher, Ms. Marta, has suggested that he visit the school psychologist for help understanding and treating his academic problems. Steven is a bright fifth grader, but he has great difficulties reading and his mathematics skills lag far behind his peers. Ms. Marta contacts Steven's mother, reassuring her that the school has excellent resources for diagnosing children's learning problems and special education professionals who can intervene and help children overcome learning difficulties.

The school psychologist interviews Steven's mother in order to compile a history of Steven's development. Through this interview, he learns that Steven suffered a great deal of trauma early in life; as an infant, he was physically abused by his biological mother, then taken away and placed in foster care. At age 3, he was adopted into a middle-class, suburban family with two older, nonadopted children.

As we have seen, each developmental theory has a unique emphasis. How might each theory address Steven's academic difficulties?

a. What factors would psychoanalytic theories point to in order to explain Steven's functioning?

b. How would cognitively oriented theories, such as Piaget's cognitive-developmental theory and information processing theory, account for and intervene with Steven's difficulties?

c. Identify contextual factors that may play a role in Steven's academic problems; from Bronfenbrenner's bioecological theory, what factors may be addressed?

2. Suppose you wanted to conduct research on academic achievement during elementary and middle school.

a. Identify a research question appropriate for a correlational research study.

b. How would you address that question with a cross-sectional research study? Longitudinal? Sequential?

c. What are the advantages and disadvantages of each type of study?

$SAGE edge™

Visit **edge.sagepub.com/kuther2e** to help you accomplish your coursework goals in an easy-to-use learning environment.

LEARNING OBJECTIVES	SUMMARY	KEY TERMS	IN REVIEW
1.1 Outline five principles of the lifespan developmental perspective.	Development is a lifelong process. It is multidimensional, multidirectional, plastic, influenced by the multiple contexts in which we are embedded, and multidisciplinary.	Lifespan human development Physical development Cognitive development Socioemotional development Emerging adulthood Plasticity Resilience Context Cohort Culture	What are five principles developmental scientists use to explain lifespan development?
1.2 Explain three theoretical controversies about human development.	Theories of human development can be compared with respect to their stance on the following questions. First, in what ways is developmental change continuous, characterized by slow and gradual change, or discontinuous, characterized by sudden and abrupt change? Second, to what extent do people play an active role in their own development, interacting with and influencing the world around them? Finally, is development caused by nature or nurture—heredity or the environment? Most developmental scientists agree that some aspects of development appear continuous and others discontinuous, that individuals are active in influencing their development, and that development reflects the interactions of nature and nurture.	Continuous development Discontinuous development Nature–nurture issue	What position do most contemporary developmental scientists take on each of the three theoretical controversies about human development?

| 1.3 Summarize five theoretical perspectives on human development. | Freud's psychosexual theory explains personality development as progressing through a series of psychosexual stages during childhood. Erikson's psychosocial theory suggests that individuals move through eight stages of psychosocial development across the lifespan, with each stage presenting a unique psychosocial task, or crisis. Behaviorist theory emphasizes environmental influences on behavior, specifically, classical conditioning and operant conditioning. In classical conditioning, neutral stimuli become associated with stimuli that elicit reflex responses. Operant conditioning emphasizes the role of environmental stimuli in shaping behavior through reinforcement and punishment. Bandura's social learning theory suggests that individuals and the environment interact and influence each other through reciprocal determinism. Piaget's cognitive-developmental theory explains that children actively interact with the world around them and that their cognition develops through four stages. Information processing theorists study the steps involved in cognition: perceiving and attending, representing, encoding, retrieving, and problem solving. Sociocultural systems theories look to the importance of context in shaping development. Vygotsky's sociocultural theory emphasizes interactions with members of our culture in influencing development. Bronfenbrenner's bioecological model explains development as a function of the ongoing reciprocal interaction among biological and psychological changes in the person and his or her changing context: the microsystem, mesosystem, exosystem, macrosystem, and chronosystem. Evolutionary developmental psychology integrates Darwinian principles of evolution and scientific knowledge about the interactive influence of genetic and environmental mechanisms. | Theory

Hypotheses

Psychoanalytic theories

Behaviorism

Classical conditioning

Operant conditioning

Reinforcement

Punishment

Social learning theory

Observational learning

Reciprocal determinism

Cognitive-developmental theory

Cognitive schemas

Information processing theory

Sociocultural theory

Bioecological systems theory

Microsystem

Mesosystem

Exosystem

Macrosystem

Chronosystem

Ethology

Evolutionary developmental theory | How do five major theoretical perspectives account for human development? |
| 1.4 Describe the methods and research designs used to study human development. | A case study is an in-depth examination of an individual. Interviews and questionnaires are called self-report measures because they ask the persons under study questions about their own experiences, attitudes, opinions, beliefs, and behavior. Observational measures are methods that scientists use to collect and organize information based on watching and monitoring people's behavior. Physiological measures gather the body's physiological responses as data. Scientists use correlational research to describe relations among measured characteristics, behaviors, and events. To test hypotheses about causal relationships among variables, scientists employ experimental research. Developmental designs include cross-sectional research, which compares groups of people at different ages simultaneously, and longitudinal research, which studies one group of participants at many points in time. Sequential designs combine the best features of cross-sectional and longitudinal designs by assessing multiple cohorts over time. | Scientific method

Naturalistic observation

Structured observation

Open-ended interview

Structured interview

Questionnaire

Correlational research

Experimental research

Dependent variable

Independent variable

Random assignment

Cross-sectional research study

Longitudinal research study

Sequential research design | What are methods used for collecting data and answering research questions?

What designs do researchers use to study development? |

1.5 Discuss the ethical responsibilities of researchers to protect their participants.	Researchers must maximize the benefits to research participants and minimize the harms, safeguarding participants' welfare. They must be accurate and honest in their work and respect participants' autonomy, including seeking informed consent and child assent throughout. In addition, the benefits and risks of participation in research must be spread equitably across individuals and groups.	Informed consent Autonomy Applied developmental science	What ethical responsibilities do researchers have to their participants?

2 Biological and Environmental Foundations

"Roger and Ricky couldn't be more different," marveled their mother. "People are surprised to find out they are brothers." Roger is tall and athletic, with blond hair and striking blue eyes. He spends most afternoons playing ball with his friends and often invites them home to play in the yard. Ricky, 2 years older than Roger, is much smaller, thin, and wiry. He wears thick glasses over his brown eyes that are nearly as dark as his hair. Unlike his brother, Ricky prefers solitary games and spends most afternoons at home playing video games, building model cars, and reading comic books. How can Roger and Ricky have the same parents and live in the same home yet differ markedly in appearance, personality, and preferences? In this chapter, we discuss the process of genetic inheritance and principles that can help us to understand how members of a family can share a great many similarities—and many differences.

Learning Objectives

2.1   Discuss the genetic foundations of development.

2.2   Identify examples of genetic disorders and chromosomal abnormalities.

2.3   Discuss the choices available to prospective parents in having healthy children.

2.4   Describe the interaction of heredity and environment, including behavioral genetics and the epigenetic framework.

Digital Resources

Explore: Genomic Imprinting and the Psychology of Music

▶ **Lives in Context Video 2.1:** Genetics and Pregnancy

Watch: Iceland's Down Syndrome Dilemma

Connect: Raising a Kid of a Different Race

▶ **Lives in Context Video 2.2:** Twins

Watch: Just Alike: Twins Separated at Birth

GENETIC FOUNDATIONS OF DEVELOPMENT

» LO 2.1   Discuss the genetic foundations of development.

Roger looks quite different from his older brother but shares so many characteristics with his father that most people comment on the strong physical resemblance. In other ways, however, Roger is more like his highly sociable mother. His older brother Ricky also shares similarities with each of his parents. Ricky resembles his mother and her brothers in his physical appearance, but he shares his father's quiet personality. Most of us learn early in life, and take it for granted, that children tend to resemble their parents. But to understand just how parents transmit their inborn characteristics and tendencies to their children, we must consider the human body at a molecular level.

Genetics

The human body is composed of trillions of units called cells. Within each cell is a nucleus that contains 23 matching pairs of rod-shaped structures called **chromosomes** (Plomin, DeFries, Knopik, & Neiderhiser, 2013). Each chromosome holds the basic units of heredity, known as genes, composed of stretches of **deoxyribonucleic acid (DNA)**, a complex molecule shaped like a twisted ladder or staircase. **Genes** are the blueprint for creating all of the traits that organisms carry. It is estimated that 20,000 to 25,000 genes reside within the chromosomes and influence all genetic characteristics (Finegold, 2017).

Much of our genetic material is not unique to humans. Every species has a different genome, yet we share genes with all organisms, from bacteria to primates. We share 99% of our DNA with our closest genetic relative, the chimpanzee. There is even less genetic variation among humans. People around the world share 99.7% of their genes (Lewis, 2017). Although all humans share the same basic genome, every person has a slightly different code, making him or her genetically distinct from other humans.

Cell Reproduction

Most cells in the human body reproduce through a process known as **mitosis** in which DNA replicates itself, permitting the duplication of chromosomes and ultimately the formation of new cells with identical genetic material (Sadler, 2015). The process of mitosis accounts for the replication of all body cells. However, sex cells reproduce in a different way, through **meiosis** (see Figure 2.1). First, the 46 chromosomes begin to replicate as in mitosis, duplicating themselves. But before the cell completes dividing, a critical process called crossing over takes place. Chromosome pairs align, and DNA segments cross over, moving from one member of the pair to the other. Crossing over creates unique combinations of genes (Sadler, 2015). The cell then continues to divide. As the new cells replicate, they create gametes, containing only 23 single, unpaired chromosomes. **Gametes** are the cells of sexual reproduction: sperm in males and ova in females. Ova and sperm join at fertilization to produce a fertilized egg, or **zygote**, with 46 chromosomes, forming 23 pairs with half from the biological mother and half from the biological father. Each gamete has a unique genetic profile. It is estimated that individuals can produce millions of versions of their own chromosomes (National Library of Medicine, 2017).

Sex Determination

The sex chromosomes determine whether a zygote will develop into a male or female. As shown in Figure 2.2, 22 of the 23 pairs of chromosomes are matched; they contain similar genes in almost identical positions and sequence, reflecting the distinct genetic blueprint of the biological mother and father. The 23rd pair are sex chromosomes that specify the biological sex of the individual. In females, sex chromosomes consist of two large X-shaped chromosomes (XX). Males' sex chromosomes consist of one large X-shaped chromosome and one much smaller Y-shaped chromosome (XY).

Because females have two X sex chromosomes, all ova contain one X sex chromosome. A male's sex chromosome pair includes both X and Y chromosomes;

FIGURE 2.2

Chromosomes

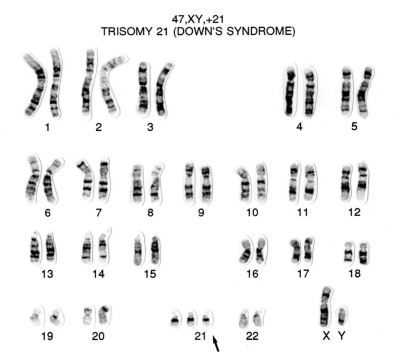

Source: U.S. National Library of Medicine.

FIGURE 2.1

Meiosis and Mitosis

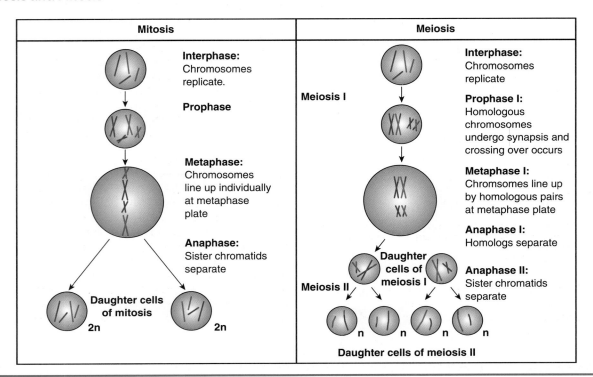

therefore, one half of the sperm males produce contain an X chromosome and one half contain a Y. The Y chromosome contains genetic instructions that will cause the fetus to develop male reproductive organs. Thus, whether the fetus develops into a boy or girl is determined by which sperm fertilizes the **ovum**. If the ovum is fertilized by a Y sperm, a male fetus will develop, and if the ovum is fertilized by an X sperm, a female fetus will form, as shown in Figure 2.3. (The introduction of sex selection methods has become more widely available, and some parents may seek to choose the sex of their child. For more on this topic, see the accompanying feature, Applying Developmental Science: Prenatal Sex Selection.)

Genes Shared by Twins

All biological siblings share the same parents, inheriting chromosomes from each. Despite this genetic similarity, siblings are often quite different from one another. Twins are siblings who share the same womb. Twins occur in about 1 out of every 33 births in the United States (Martin, Hamilton, Osterman, Driscoll, & Drake, 2018).

The majority of naturally conceived twins are **dizygotic (DZ) twins**, or fraternal twins, conceived

when a woman releases more than one ovum and each is fertilized by a different sperm. DZ twins share about one half of their genes, and like other

FIGURE 2.3

Sex Determination

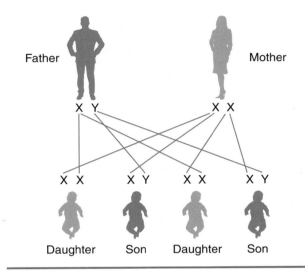

APPLYING DEVELOPMENTAL SCIENCE

Prenatal Sex Selection

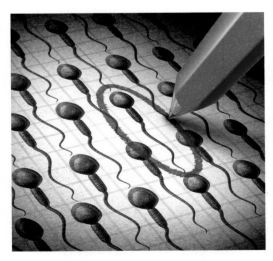

Sperm cells can be sorted by whether they carry the X or Y chromosome. Through in vitro fertlization a zygote with the desired sex is created.
Brain light / Alamy Stock Photo

Parents have long shown a preference for giving birth to a girl or boy, depending on circumstances such as cultural or religious traditions, the availability of

males or females to perform certain kinds of work important to the family or society, or the sex of the couple's other children. Yet, throughout human history until recently, the sex of an unborn child was a matter of hope, prayer, and folk rituals. It is only in the past generation that science has made it possible for parents to reliably choose the sex of their unborn child. The introduction of sex selection has been a boon to couples carrying a genetically transmitted disease (i.e., a disease carried on the sex chromosomes), enabling them to have a healthy baby of the sex unaffected by the disease they carried.

There are two methods of sex selection: preconception sperm sorting and preimplantation genetic diagnosis (PGD) (Bhatia, 2018). Preconception sperm sorting involves staining the sperm with a fluorescent dye and then leading them past a laser beam where the difference in DNA content between X- and Y-bearing sperm is visible. PGD creates zygotes within the laboratory by removing eggs from the woman and fertilizing them with sperm. This is known as in vitro (literally, "in glass") fertilization because fertilization takes place in a test tube, outside of the woman's body. After 3 days,

(Continued)

(Continued)

a cell from each blastula is extracted to examine the chromosomes and determine whether or not it contains a Y chromosome (i.e., whether it is female or male). The desired male or female embryos are then implanted into the woman's uterus. The second type of sex selection, sperm sorting, entails spinning sperm in a centrifuge to separate those that carry an X or a Y chromosome. Sperm with the desired chromosomes are then used to fertilize the ovum either vaginally or through in vitro fertilization.

As sex selection becomes more widely available, parents may seek to choose the sex of their child because of personal desires, such as to create family balance or to conform to cultural valuing of one sex over the other, rather than to avoid transmitting genetic disorders (Robertson & Hickman, 2013). Critics argue that sex selection can lead down a "slippery slope" of selecting for other characteristics—hair color, eye color, intelligence, and more (Dondorp et al., 2013). Might children born from gender selection be expected to act in certain sex-typical ways, and if they do not, might that disappoint parents? Others express concerns about societal sex ratio imbalances if sex selection becomes widely practiced (Colls et al., 2009; Robertson & Hickman, 2013). Such sex ratio imbalances favoring males have occurred in India and China because of female infanticide, gender-driven abortion, and China's one-child family policy (see the Cultural Influences on Development feature in Chapter 10 for more information; Bhatia, 2010; Ethics Committee of the American Society for Reproductive Medicine, 2001).

Should selecting an embryo's sex be a matter of parental choice? A review of 36 countries, including 25 in Europe, revealed that many had no policies regarding selection; those that did prohibited sex selection for nonmedical reasons (Darnovsky, 2009). The European Union bans socially, nontherapeutically motivated sex selection (Council of Europe, 1997). The United States does not have a formal policy regarding sex selection (Deeney, 2013). Sex selection remains hotly debated in medical journals, hospital and university ethics boards, and the public.

What Do You Think?

1. What do you think about parents choosing the sex of their children? In your view, under what conditions is sex selection acceptable?
2. If you were able to selectively reproduce other characteristics, apart from sex, what might you choose? Why or why not? ●

---

siblings, most fraternal twins differ in appearance, such as hair color, eye color, and height. In about half of fraternal twin pairs, one twin is a boy and the other a girl. DZ twins tend to run in families, suggesting a genetic component that controls the tendency for a woman to release more than one ovum each month. However, rates of DZ twins also increase with in vitro fertilization, maternal age, and each subsequent birth (Pison, Monden, & Smits, 2015).

Monozygotic (MZ) twins, or identical twins, originate from the same zygote, sharing the same genotype with identical instructions for all physical and psychological characteristics. MZ twins occur when the zygote splits into two distinct separate but identical zygotes that develop into two infants. It is estimated that MZ twins occur in 4 of every 1,000 U.S. births (American College of Obstetricians and Gynecologists & Society for Maternal-Fetal Medicine, 2014). The causes of MZ twinning are not well understood. Temperature fluctuations are associated with MZ births in animals, but it is unknown whether similar effects occur in humans (Aston, Peterson, & Carrell, 2008). In vitro fertilization and advanced

Monozygotic, or identical, twins share 100% of their DNA.
Ray Evans / Alamy Stock Photo

maternal age (35 and older) may increase the risk of MZ twins (Knopman et al., 2014).

Patterns of Genetic Inheritance

Although the differences among various members of a given family may appear haphazard, they are the result of a genetic blueprint unfolding. Researchers are just beginning to uncover the instructions contained in the human genome, but we have learned that traits and characteristics are inherited in predictable ways.

Dominant–Recessive Inheritance

Lynn has red hair while her brother, Jim, does not—and neither do their parents. How did Lynn end up with red hair? These outcomes can be explained by patterns of genetic inheritance, how the sets of genes from each parent interact. As we have discussed, each person has 23 pairs of chromosomes, one pair inherited from the mother and one from the father. The genes within each chromosome can be expressed in different forms, or **alleles**, that influence a variety of physical characteristics. When alleles of the pair of chromosomes are alike with regard to a specific characteristic, such as hair color, the person is said to be **homozygous** for the characteristic and will display the inherited trait. If they are different, the person is **heterozygous**, and the trait expressed will depend on the relations among the genes (Lewis, 2017). Some genes are passed through **dominant–recessive inheritance** in which some genes are *dominant* and are always expressed regardless of the gene they are paired with. Other genes are

recessive and will be expressed only if paired with another recessive gene. Lynn and Jim's parents are heterozygous for red hair; both have dark hair, but they each carry a recessive gene for red hair.

When an individual is heterozygous for a particular trait, the dominant gene is expressed, and the person becomes a **carrier** of the recessive gene. For example, consider Figure 2.4. Both parents have nonred hair. People with nonred hair may have homozygous or heterozygous genes for hair color because the gene for nonred hair (symbolized by N in Figure 2.4) is dominant over the gene for red hair (r). In other words, both a child who inherits a homozygous pair of dominant genes (NN) and one who inherits a heterozygous pair consisting of both a dominant and recessive gene (Nr) will have nonred hair, even though the two genotypes are different. Both parents are heterozygous for red hair (Nr). They each carry the gene for red hair and can pass it on to their offspring. Red hair can result only from having two recessive genes (rr); both parents must carry the recessive gene for red hair. Therefore, a child with red hair can be born to parents who have nonred hair if they both carry heterozygous genes for hair color. As shown in Table 2.1, several characteristics are passed through dominant–recessive inheritance.

FIGURE 2.4

Dominant-Recessive Inheritance

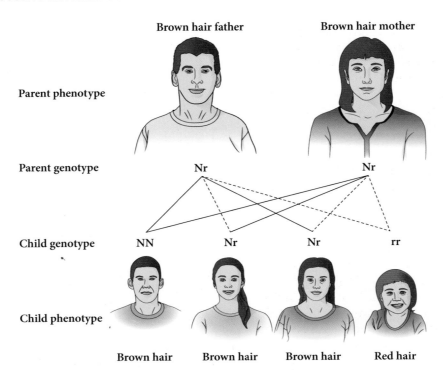

TABLE 2.1

Dominant and Recessive Characteristics

DOMINANT TRAIT	RECESSIVE TRAIT
Dark hair	Blond hair
Curly hair	Straight hair
Hair	Baldness
Nonred hair	Red hair
Facial dimples	No dimples
Brown eyes	Blue, green, hazel eyes
Second toe longer than big toe	Big toe longer than second toe
Type A blood	Type O blood
Type B blood	Type O blood
Rh-positive blood	Rh-negative blood
Normal color vision	Colorblindness

Sources: McKusick (1998); McKusick-Nathans Institute of Genetic Medicine (2017).

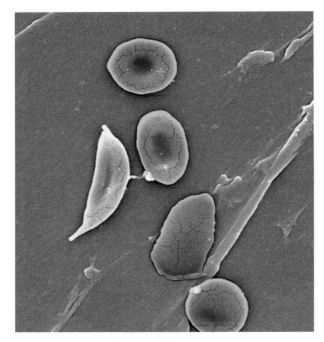

Recessive sickle cell alleles cause red blood cells to become crescent shaped and unable to distribute oxygen effectively throughout the circulatory system. Alleles for normal blood cells do not mask all of the characteristics of recessive sickle cell alleles, illustrating incomplete dominance.
Wikimedia

Incomplete Dominance

In most cases, dominant–recessive inheritance is an oversimplified explanation for patterns of genetic inheritance. **Incomplete dominance** is a genetic inheritance pattern in which both genes influence the characteristic (Finegold, 2017). For example, consider blood type. Neither the alleles for blood type A and B dominate each other. A heterozygous person with the alleles for blood type A and B will express both A and B alleles and have blood type AB.

A different type of inheritance pattern is seen when a person inherits heterozygous alleles in which one allele is stronger than the other yet does not completely dominate. In this situation, the stronger allele does not mask all of the effects of the weaker allele. Therefore, some, but not all, characteristics of the recessive allele appear. For example, the trait for developing normal blood cells does not completely mask the allele for developing sickle-shaped blood cells. About 5% of African American newborns (and relatively few Caucasians or Asian Americans) carry the recessive **sickle cell trait** (Ojodu, Hulihan, Pope, & Grant, 2014). Sickle cell alleles cause red blood cells to become crescent, or sickle, shaped. Cells that are sickle shaped cannot distribute oxygen effectively throughout the circulatory system (Ware, de Montalembert, Tshilolo, & Abboud, 2017). The average life expectancy for individuals with sickle cell anemia is 55 years in North America (Pecker & Little, 2018). Alleles for normal blood cells do not mask all of the characteristics of recessive sickle cell alleles, illustrating incomplete dominance. Sickle cell carriers do not develop full-blown sickle cell anemia (Chakravorty & Williams, 2015). Carriers of the trait for sickle cell anemia may function normally but may show some symptoms such as reduced oxygen distribution throughout the body and exhaustion after exercise. Only individuals who are homozygous for the recessive sickle cell trait develop sickle cell anemia.

Polygenic Inheritance

Whereas dominant–recessive and codominant–recessive patterns account for some genotypes, most traits are a function of the interaction of many genes, known as **polygenic inheritance**. Hereditary influences act in complex ways, and researchers cannot trace most characteristics to only one or two genes. Instead, polygenic traits are the result of interactions among many genes. Examples of polygenic traits include height, intelligence, personality, and susceptibility to certain forms of cancer (Bouchard, 2014; Kremen, Panizzon, & Cannon, 2016; Penke & Jokela, 2016). As the number of genes that contribute to a trait increases, so does the range of possible traits. Genetic propensities interact with environmental influences to produce a wide range of individual differences in human traits.

Genomic Imprinting

The principles of dominant–recessive and incomplete dominance inheritance can account for over 1,000 human traits (McKusick, 2007). However, a few traits are determined by a process known as **genomic imprinting**. Genomic imprinting refers to the instance in which the expression of a gene is determined by whether it is inherited from the mother or the father (Kelly & Spencer, 2017; National Library of Medicine, 2017). For example, consider two conditions that illustrate genomic imprinting: Prader-Willi syndrome and Angelman syndrome. Both syndromes are caused by an abnormality in the 15th chromosome (Kalsner & Chamberlain, 2015). As shown in Figure 2.5, if the abnormality is acquired by the father (illustrated in black), the individual—whether a daughter or son—will develop Prader-Willi syndrome, a set of specific physical and behavioral characteristics including obesity, insatiable hunger, short stature, motor slowness, and mild to moderate intellectual impairment (Butler, Manzardo, Heinemann, Loker, & Loker, 2016). If the abnormal chromosome 15 arises from the mother (shown in red), the individual—again, whether it is a daughter or a son—will develop Angelman syndrome, characterized by hyperactivity, thin body frame, seizures, disturbances in gait, and severe learning disabilities, including severe problems with speech (Buiting, Williams, & Horsthemke, 2016). Prader-Willi and Angelman syndromes are rare, occurring on average in 1 in 12,000 to 20,000 persons (Kalsner & Chamberlain, 2015; Spruyt, Braam, & Curfs, 2018). Patterns of genetic inheritance can be complex, yet they follow predictable principles. For a summary of patterns of genetic inheritance, refer to Table 2.2.

FIGURE 2.5

Genomic Imprinting

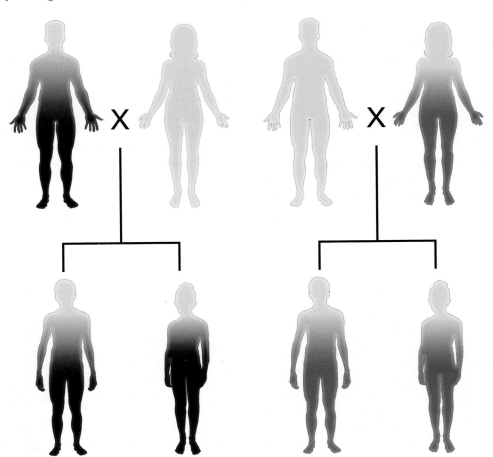

Source: C. Cristofre Martin, 1998.

THINKING IN CONTEXT 2.1

1. Why do twins occur? Consider the evolutionary developmental perspective discussed in Chapter 1. From an evolutionary developmental perspective, does twinning serve an adaptive purpose for our species? Why or why not?

2. Consider your own physical characteristics, such as hair and eye color. Are they indicative of recessive traits or dominant ones?

3. Do you think that you might be a carrier of recessive traits? Why or why not?

TABLE 2.2

Summary: Patterns of Genetic Inheritance

INHERITANCE PATTERN	DESCRIPTION
Dominant–recessive inheritance	Genes that are dominant are always expressed, regardless of the gene they are paired with, and recessive genes are expressed only if paired with another recessive gene.
Incomplete dominance	Both genes influence the characteristic, and aspects of both genes appear.
Polygenic inheritance	Polygenic traits are the result of interactions among many genes.
Genomic imprinting	The expression of a gene is determined by whether it is inherited from the mother or the father.

CHROMOSOMAL AND GENETIC PROBLEMS

» LO 2.2   Identify examples of genetic disorders and chromosomal abnormalities.

Many disorders are the result of genes passed through inheritance from one or both parents. Others are the result of variations in chromosomes. Fortunately, the vast majority of people —and animals, for that matter—inherit healthy genes. Many hereditary and chromosomal abnormalities can be diagnosed prenatally. Others are evident at birth or can be detected soon after an infant begins to develop. Still others reveal themselves only over a period of many years.

Genetic Disorders

Disorders and abnormalities that are inherited through the parents' genes include such well-known conditions as cystic fibrosis and sickle cell anemia,

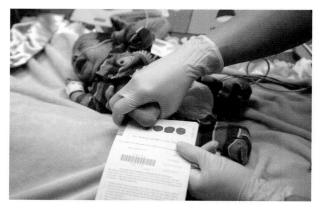

A blood sample to detect PKU is taken from this newborn. Phenylketonuria (PKU) is a genetic disorder in which the body lacks the enzyme that breaks down phenylalanine. Without treatment, the phenylalanine builds up to toxic levels and can damage the central nervous system.
Marmaduke St. John / Alamy Stock Photo

as well as others that are rare and, in some cases, never even noticed throughout the individual's life.

Dominant–Recessive Disorders

Recall that in dominant–recessive inheritance, dominant genes are always expressed regardless of the gene they are paired with and recessive genes are expressed only if paired with another recessive gene. Table 2.3 illustrates diseases that are inherited through dominant–recessive patterns. Few severe disorders are inherited through dominant inheritance because individuals who inherit the allele often do not survive long enough to reproduce and pass it to the next generation. One exception is Huntington disease, a fatal disease in which the central nervous system deteriorates (National Library of Medicine, 2017). Individuals with the Huntington allele develop normally in childhood, adolescence, and young adulthood. Symptoms of Huntington's disease do not appear until age 35 or later. By then, many individuals have already had children, and one half of them, on average, will inherit the dominant Huntington gene.

Phenylketonuria (PKU) is a common recessive disorder that prevents the body from producing an enzyme that breaks down phenylalanine, an amino acid, from proteins (Kahn et al., 2016; Romani et al., 2017). Without treatment, the phenylalanine builds up quickly to toxic levels that damage the central nervous system, contributing to intellectual developmental disability, once known as mental retardation, by 1 year of age. The United States and Canada require all newborns to be screened for PKU (Blau, Shen, & Carducci, 2014).

PKU illustrates how genes interact with the environment to produce developmental outcomes. Intellectual disability results from the interaction of the genetic predisposition and exposure to phenylalanine from the environment (Blau, 2016). Children with PKU

TABLE 2.3

Diseases Inherited Through Dominant–Recessive Inheritance

DISEASE	OCCURRENCE	MODE OF INHERITANCE	DESCRIPTION	TREATMENT
Huntington disease	1 in 20,000	Dominant	Degenerative brain disorder that affects muscular coordination and cognition	No cure; death usually occurs 10 to 20 years after onset
Cystic fibrosis	1 in 2,000 to 2,500	Recessive	An abnormally thick, sticky mucus clogs the lungs and digestive system, leading to respiratory infections and digestive difficulty	Bronchial drainage, diet, gene replacement therapy
Phenylketonuria (PKU)	1 in 10,000 to 15,000	Recessive	Inability to digest phenylalanine that, if untreated, results in neurological damage and death	Diet
Sickle cell anemia	1 in 500 African Americans	Recessive	Sickling of red blood cells leads to inefficient distribution of oxygen throughout the body that leads to organ damage and respiratory infections	No cure; blood transfusions, treat infections, bone marrow transplant; death by middle age
Tay-Sachs disease	1 in 3,600 to 4,000 descendants of Central and Eastern European Jews	Recessive	Degenerative brain disease	None; most die by 4 years of age

Sources: Kahn et al. (2016); McKusick-Nathans Institute of Genetic Medicine (2017).

can process only very small amounts of phenylalanine. If the disease is discovered, the infant is placed on a diet low in phenylalanine. Yet it is very difficult to remove nearly all phenylalanine from the diet. Individuals who maintain a strict diet usually attain average levels of intelligence, although tend to score lower than those without PKU (Jahja et al., 2017). Some cognitive and psychological problems may appear in childhood and persist into adulthood, particularly difficulty in attention and planning skills, emotional regulation, depression, and anxiety (Hawks, Strube, Johnson, Grange, & White, 2018; Jahja et al., 2017). The emotional and social challenges associated with PKU, such as the pressure of a strict diet and surveillance from parents, may worsen these symptoms, and dietary compliance tends to decline in adolescence (Medford, Hare, & Wittkowski, 2017).

X-Linked Disorders

A special instance of the dominant–recessive pattern occurs with genes that are located on the X chromosome (Shah, DeRemigis, Hageman, Sriram, & Waggoner, 2017). Recall that males (XY) have both an X and a Y chromosome. Some recessive genetic disorders, like the gene for red-green colorblindness, are carried on the X chromosome. Males are more likely to be affected by X-linked genetic disorders because they have only one X chromosome and therefore any genetic marks on their X chromosome are displayed. Females (XX) have two X chromosomes; a recessive gene located on one X chromosome will be masked by a dominant gene on the other X chromosome. Females are thereby less likely to display X-linked genetic disorders because both of their X chromosomes must carry the recessive genetic disorder for it to be displayed.

Fragile X syndrome is an example of a dominant–recessive disorder carried on the X chromosome (Hagerman et al., 2017). Because the gene is dominant, it need appear on only one X chromosome to be displayed. That means that fragile X syndrome occurs in both males and females. Males with fragile X syndrome typically have a long, narrow face; large ears; and large testes. Fragile X syndrome is the most common known inherited form of intellectual disability (Doherty & Scerif, 2017), and children with fragile X syndrome tend to show moderate to severe intellectual disability (Raspa, Wheeler, & Riley, 2017). Cardiac defects are common as well as several behavioral mannerisms, including poor eye contact and repetitive behaviors such as hand flapping, hand biting, and mimicking others, behaviors common in individuals with autistic spectrum disorders (Hagerman et al., 2017). Fragile X syndrome is often codiagnosed with autism, with estimates of 30% to 54% of boys and 16% to 20% of girls with fragile X syndrome meeting the diagnostic criteria for autism (Kaufmann et al., 2017). As carriers, females may show some characteristics of the disorder but tend to display levels of intelligence within the normal or near-normal range.

Hemophilia, a condition in which the blood does not clot normally, is another example of a recessive disease inherited through genes on the X chromosome (Shah et al., 2017). Daughters who inherit the gene for hemophilia typically do not show the disorder because the gene on their second X chromosome promotes normal blood clotting and is a dominant gene. Females, therefore, can carry the gene for hemophilia without exhibiting the disorder. A female carrier has a 50/50 chance of transmitting the gene to each child. Sons who inherit the gene will display the disorder because the Y chromosome does not have the corresponding genetic information to counter the gene. Daughters who inherit the gene, again, will be carriers (unless their second X chromosome also carries the gene).

Table 2.4 illustrates diseases acquired through X-linked inheritance.

Chromosomal Abnormalities

Chromosomal abnormalities are the result of errors during cell reproduction, meiosis or mitosis, or damage caused afterward. Occurring in about 1 of about every 1,500 births, the most widely known chromosome disorder is trisomy 21, more commonly called **Down syndrome**

(de Graaf, Buckley, Dever, & Skotko, 2017; Morrison & McMahon, 2018). Down syndrome occurs when a third chromosome appears alongside the 21st pair of

Down syndrome is the most common cause of intellectual disability. Interventions that encourage children to interact with their physical and social environment can promote motor, social, and emotional development.
Agencja Fotograficzna Caro / Alamy Stock Photo

TABLE 2.4

Diseases Acquired Through X-Linked Inheritance

SYNDROME/DISEASE	OCCURRENCE	DESCRIPTION	TREATMENT
Colorblindness	1 in 12 males	Difficulty distinguishing red from green; less common is difficulty distinguishing blue from green	No cure
Duchenne muscular dystrophy	1 in 3,500 males	Weakness and wasting of limb and trunk muscles; progresses slowly but will affect all voluntary muscles	Physical therapy, exercise, body braces; survival rare beyond late 20s
Fragile X syndrome	1 in 4,000 males and 1 in 8,000 females	Symptoms include cognitive impairment; attention problems; anxiety; unstable mood; long face; large ears; flat feet; and hyper-extensible joints, especially fingers	No cure
Hemophilia	1 in 3,000 to 7,000 males	Blood disorder in which the blood does not clot	Blood transfusions

Source: McKusick-Nathans Institute of Genetic Medicine (2017).

chromosomes. Down syndrome is associated with marked physical, health, and cognitive attributes, including a short, stocky build, and striking facial features mark the disorder, such as a round face, almond-shaped eyes, and a flattened nose, as shown in Figure 2.6 (Davis & Escobar, 2013; Kruszka et al., 2017). Children with Down syndrome tend to show delays in physical and motor development relative to other children and health problems, such as including congenital heart defects, vision impairments, poor hearing, and immune system deficiencies (Ram & Chinen, 2011; Zampieri et al., 2014). Down syndrome is the most common genetic cause of intellectual developmental disability (Vissers, Gilissen, & Veltman, 2016), but children's abilities vary. Generally, children with Down syndrome show greater strengths in nonverbal learning and memory relative to their verbal skills (Grieco, Pulsifer, Seligsohn, Skotko, & Schwartz, 2015). Expressive language is delayed relative to comprehension. Infants and children who participate in early intervention and receive sensitive caregiving and encouragement to explore their environment show positive outcomes, especially in the motor, social, and emotional areas of functioning (Næss, Nygaard, Ostad, Dolva, & Lyster, 2017; Wentz, 2017).

As recently as the early 1980s, individuals with Down syndrome lived to an average age of only 25. Advances in medicine have addressed many of the physical health problems associated with Down syndrome so that today, the average life expectancy is 60 years of age and many live into their 70s and beyond (Glasson, Dye, & Bittles, 2014; National Association for Down Syndrome, 2017). However, Down syndrome is associated with premature aging and an accelerated decline of cognitive functioning (Covelli, Raggi, Meucci, Paganelli, & Leonardi, 2016; Ghezzo et al., 2014). As more adults age with Down syndrome, we have discovered a link between Down syndrome and Alzheimer's disease, a brain degenerative disease that typically strikes in older adulthood (Hithersay, Hamburg, Knight, & Strydom, 2017; Wiseman et al., 2015). Individuals with Down syndrome are at risk to show signs of Alzheimer's disease very early relative to other adults. This is an example of how disorders and illnesses can be influenced by multiple genes and complex contextual interactions; in this case, Down syndrome and Alzheimer's disease share genetic markers (Lee, Chien, & Hwu, 2017).

Some chromosomal abnormalities concern the 23rd pair of chromosomes: the sex chromosomes. Given their different genetic makeup, sex chromosome abnormalities yield different effects in males and females. They are summarized in Table 2.5.

One of the most common sex chromosome abnormalities, with prevalence estimates between 1 in 500 and 1 in 1,000 males, is **Klinefelter syndrome**, in which males are born with an extra X chromosome (XXY; National Library of Medicine, 2017). Symptoms range in severity such that some males experience symptoms that impair daily life, and others may be unaware of the disorder until they are tested for infertility (Bird & Hurren, 2016; Wistuba, Brand, Zitzmann, & Damm, 2017). Severe symptoms include a high-pitched voice, feminine body shape, breast enlargement, and infertility. Many boys and men with Klinefelter syndrome have long legs, a tendency to be overweight, and language and short-term memory impairments that can cause difficulties in learning (Bonomi et al., 2017). As adults, men with Klinefelter syndrome are at risk for a variety of disorders that are more common in women, such as osteoporosis (Juul, Aksglaede, Bay, Grigor, & Skakkebæk, 2011).

A second type of sex chromosome abnormality experienced by men is XYY syndrome, or **Jacob's syndrome**, a condition that causes men to produce high levels of testosterone (Pappas, Migeon, Pappas, & Migeon, 2017). In adolescence, they tend to be slender and show severe acne and poor coordination, but most men with XYY syndrome are unaware that they have a chromosomal abnormality. The prevalence of XYY syndrome is uncertain given that most men go undiagnosed. Females are susceptible to a different set of sex chromosome abnormalities. About 1 in 1,000 females are born with three X chromosomes, known as triple X syndrome (Wigby et al., 2016). Women with triple X syndrome show an appearance within

FIGURE 2.6

Down Syndrome

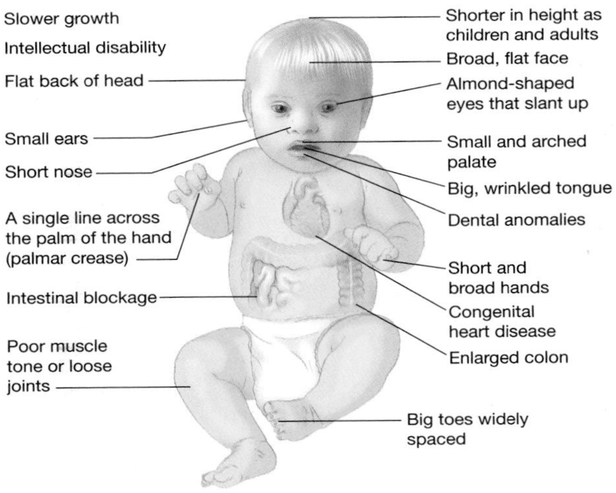

- Slower growth
- Intellectual disability
- Flat back of head
- Small ears
- Short nose
- A single line across the palm of the hand (palmar crease)
- Intestinal blockage
- Poor muscle tone or loose joints

- Shorter in height as children and adults
- Broad, flat face
- Almond-shaped eyes that slant up
- Small and arched palate
- Big, wrinkled tongue
- Dental anomalies
- Short and broad hands
- Congenital heart disease
- Enlarged colon
- Big toes widely spaced

TABLE 2.5

Sex Chromosome Abnormalities

FEMALE GENOTYPE	SYNDROME	DESCRIPTION	PREVALENCE
XO	Turner	As adults, they are short in stature, often have small jaws with extra folds of skin around their necks (webbing), lack prominent female secondary sex characteristics such as breasts, and show abnormal development of the ovaries. Elevated risk for thyroid disease, vision and hearing problems, heart defects, diabetes, and autoimmune disorders.	1 in 2,500 females
XXX	Triple X	Grow about an inch or so taller than average with unusually long legs and slender torsos and show normal development of sexual characteristics and fertility. Because many cases of triple X syndrome often go unnoticed, little is known about the syndrome.	Unknown

MALE GENOTYPE	SYNDROME	DESCRIPTION	PREVALENCE
XXY	Klinefelter	Symptoms range in severity from going unnoticed to severe symptoms such as a high-pitched voice, feminine body shape, breast enlargement, and infertility. Many boys and men with Klinefelter syndrome have long legs, a tendency to be overweight, and language and short-term memory impairments that can cause difficulties in learning.	1 in 500 to 1 in 1,000
XYY	XYY, Jacob's syndrome	Accompanied by high levels of testosterone.	Prevalence of XYY syndrome is uncertain as most men with XYY syndrome are unaware that they have a chromosomal abnormality.

Sources: Bardsley et al. (2013); Bird and Hurren (2016); Herlihy and McLachlan (2015); National Library of Medicine (2013); Pinsker (2012).

the norm. They tend to be about an inch or so taller than average with unusually long legs and slender torsos, as well as normal development of sexual characteristics and fertility. Some may show intelligence in the low range of normal with small learning difficulties. Because many cases of triple X syndrome often go unnoticed, little is known about the syndrome.

The sex chromosome abnormality known as **Turner syndrome** occurs when a female is born with only one X chromosome (National Library of Medicine, 2017). Girls with Turner syndrome show abnormal growth patterns. As adults, they are short in stature and often have small jaws with extra folds of skin around their necks (webbing) and lack prominent female secondary sex characteristics such as breasts. Their ovaries do not develop normally, and they do not ovulate (Culen, Ertl, Schubert, Bartha-Doering, & Haeusler, 2017). Girls with Turner syndrome are at risk for precocious puberty (in middle to late childhood), often with spontaneous onset instead of the gradual changes that typically accompany puberty (Improda et al.,

2012), as well as thyroid disease, vision and hearing problems, heart defects, diabetes, and autoimmune disorders. Current estimates of its frequency range from 1 in 2,500 worldwide (National Library of Medicine, 2017). If Turner syndrome is diagnosed early, regular injections of human growth hormones can increase stature, and hormones administered at puberty can result in some breast development and menstruation (Christopoulos, Deligeoroglou, Laggari, Christogiorgos, & Creatsas, 2008; Culen et al., 2017).

Mutation

Not all inborn characteristics are inherited. Some result from **mutations**, sudden changes and abnormalities in the structure of genes that occur spontaneously or may be induced by exposure to environmental toxins such as radiation and agricultural chemicals in food (Lewis, 2017). A mutation may involve only one gene or many. It is estimated that as many as one half of all conceptions include mutated chromosomes

Genes as Protective Factors in Development

Not all children exposed to adversity experience negative outcomes. Genes, such as MAOA, influence children's sensitivity to maltreatment.
iStock/fiorigianluigi

Children who are maltreated or abused by their parents are at risk for developing many problems, including aggression and violent tendencies. Yet not all children who are maltreated become violent adolescents and adults. Why? A classic study examined this question.

Caspi and colleagues (2002) followed a sample of males from birth until adulthood and observed that not all maltreated boys developed problems with violence. Only boys who carried a certain type of gene were at risk for becoming violent after experiencing maltreatment. Specifically, there are two versions of a gene that controls *monoamine oxidase A (MAOA)*, an enzyme that regulates specific chemicals in the brain; one produces high levels of the enzyme, and the other produces low levels. Boys who experienced abuse and other traumatic experiences were about twice as likely to develop problems with aggression, violence, and to even be convicted of a violent crime—but only if they carried the low-MAOA gene. Maltreated boys who carried the high-MAOA gene were no more likely to

become violent than nonmaltreated boys. In addition, the presence of the low-MAOA gene itself was not associated with violence. The low-MAOA gene predicted violence only for boys who experience abuse early in life. These findings have been replicated in another 30-year longitudinal study of boys (Fergusson, Boden, Horwood, Miller, & Kennedy, 2011) as well as a meta-analysis of 27 studies (Byrd & Manuck, 2014).

Similar findings of a MAOA gene × environment interaction in which low MAOA, but not high MAOA, predicts negative outcomes in response to childhood adversity has been extended to include other mental health outcomes such as antisocial personality disorder and depression (Beach et al., 2010; Cicchetti, Rogosch, & Sturge-Apple, 2007; Manuck & McCaffery, 2014; Nikulina, Widom, & Brzustowicz, 2012). Many of these studies have examined only males. Females show a more mixed pattern, with some studies showing that girls display the MAOA gene × environment interaction but to a much lesser extent than boys, whereas other studies suggest no relationship (Byrd & Manuck, 2014).

In addition, some genes might increase our sensitivity to, and the effectiveness of, environmental interventions (Bakermans-Kranenburg & van IJzendoorn, 2015; Chhangur et al., 2017). Just as we may adjust contextual factors to contribute to successful developmental outcomes and resilience, in the future we might learn how to "turn on" protective genes and "turn off" those that contribute to risk.

What Do You Think?

1. In your view, how important are genetic contributors to development?

2. If some genes may be protective in particular contexts, should scientists learn how to turn them on? Why or why not? What about genes that may be harmful in particular contexts? ●

(Plomin et al., 2013). Most mutations are fatal—the developing organism often dies very soon after conception, often before the woman knows she is pregnant (Sadler, 2015).

Sometimes mutations are beneficial. This is especially true if the mutation is induced by stressors in the environment and provides an adaptive advantage to the individual. For example, the sickle cell gene is a mutation that

originated in areas where malaria is widespread, such as Africa (Ware, de Montalembert, Tshilolo, & Abboud, 2017).

Children who inherited a single sickle cell allele were more resistant to malarial infection and more likely to survive and pass it along to their offspring (Croke et al., 2017; Gong, Parikh, Rosenthal, & Greenhouse, 2013). The sickle cell gene is not helpful in places of the world where malaria is not a risk.

The frequency of the gene is decreasing in areas of the world where malaria is uncommon. For example, only 8% of African Americans are carriers, compared with as much as 30% of Black Africans in some African countries (Maakaron & Taher, 2012). Therefore, the developmental implications of genotypes—and mutations—are context specific, posing benefits in some contexts and risks in others, as illustrated in the Lives in Context feature.

| **THINKING IN CONTEXT 2.2** |

1. Identify risk factors for genetic and chromosomal disorders. What can prospective parents do to minimize the risks? What specific advice do you give?

2. Discuss how PKU illustrates the following two themes in human development: (1) the role of nature and nurture in development and (2) interactions among domains of development.

REPRODUCTIVE CHOICES

» LO 2.3 Discuss the choices available to prospective parents in having healthy children.

The likelihood of genetic disorders often can be predicted before conception. Moreover, advances in technology permit abnormalities to be detected earlier than ever before. In this section, we start with a discussion of genetic counseling. We then consider why couples turn to reproductive technology methods such as artificial insemination, in vitro fertilization, and surrogacy. We also look at the option of adoption that prospective parents consider. Finally, we discuss the methods of prenatal diagnosis and the prenatal treatment of genetic disorders.

Genetic Counseling

The growing understanding of genetic inheritance has led many couples to wonder about their own genetic inheritance and what genes they will pass on to their children. Many prospective parents seek **genetic counseling** to determine the risk that their children will inherit genetic defects and chromosomal abnormalities (Ioannides, 2017; Uhlmann, Schuette, & Yashar, 2009). Candidates for genetic counseling include those whose relatives have a genetic condition, couples who have had difficulties bearing children, women over the age of 35, and couples from the same ethnic group. Genetic tests can also determine whether a couple's difficulty conceiving or recurrent miscarriages are

Parents meet with a genetic counselor to determine the risk that their children will inherit genetic defects and chromosomal abnormalities.
Michelle Del Guercio/Science Source

influenced by sperm chromosomal abnormalities in the male (Kohn, Kohn, Darilek, Ramasamy, & Lipshultz, 2016).

The genetic counselor interviews the couple to construct a family history of heritable disorders for both prospective parents. This service is particularly valuable when one or both prospective parents have relatives with inborn disorders. If a disorder is common in either parent's family or it appears that they are likely to carry a genetic disorder, genetic screening blood tests may be carried out on both parents to detect the presence of dominant and recessive genes and chromosomal abnormalities associated with various disorders. The tests determine whether each parent is a carrier for recessive disorders and estimate the likelihood that a child may be affected by a genetic disorder. The genetic counselor interprets the results and helps the parents understand genetic concepts by tailoring the explanation to match the parents' knowledge (Nance, 2017).

Once prospective parents learn about the risk of conceiving a child with a disorder, they can determine how to proceed—whether it is to conceive a child naturally or through the use of in vitro fertilization—after screening gametes for the disorders of concern. Given advances in our knowledge of genetic disorders and ability to screen for them, some argue that genetic counseling should be available to all prospective parents (Minkoff & Berkowitz, 2014). Others argue that abnormalities are rare and so few would be discovered that universal screening is of little utility (Larion, Warsof, Maher, Peleg, & Abuhamad, 2016). Whether to seek genetic counseling is a personal decision for prospective parents based on their history, view of their risks, and their values. Adults who carry significant risks of conceiving a child with a genetic disorder sometimes consider alternative methods of reproduction.

Reproductive Technology

Couples turn to reproductive technology for a variety of reasons. As noted, some couples at risk for bearing children with genetic or chromosomal abnormalities seek alternative methods of conception. About 15% of couples in the United States experience infertility, the inability to conceive (Thoma et al., 2013). About 35% of the time, factors within the male are identified as contributors to infertility (Centers for Disease Control and Prevention, 2017). In addition, single men and women, as well as gay and lesbian couples,

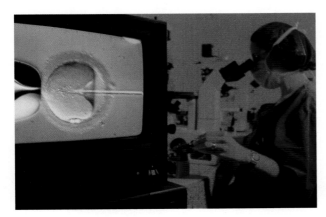

In vitro fertilization is a form of reproductive technology in which an ovum is fertilized outside of the womb.
Mauro Fermariello/Science Source

often opt to conceive with the use of reproductive technology.

Artificial insemination refers to the injection of sperm into a woman. The male partner's sperm may be used or, if the male experiences reproductive difficulties, a donor's sperm may be used. Artificial insemination through a donor also enables women without male partners, whether single or lesbian, to conceive.

Another common method, **in vitro fertilization**, introduced in the United States in 1981, permitted conception to occur outside of the womb. A woman is prescribed hormones that stimulate the maturation of several ova, which are surgically removed. The ova are placed in a dish and sperm are added. One or more ova are fertilized, and the resulting cell begins to divide. After several cell divisions, the cluster of cells is placed in the woman's uterus. If they implant into the uterus and begin to divide, a pregnancy has occurred.

The success rate of in vitro fertilization is about 50% and varies with the mother's age. For example, the success rate is 47% in 35-year-old women, 27% in 41- to 42-year-old women, and 16% in 43- to 44-year-old women. Artificial insemination contributed to 1.6% of all infants born in the United States in 2014 (Saswati et al., 2017). As shown in Figure 2.7, about 40% of in vitro cycles begun result in pregnancy.

FIGURE 2.7

Number of Outcomes of Assisted Reproductive Technology Procedures, by Type of Outcome— United States and Puerto Rico, 2014

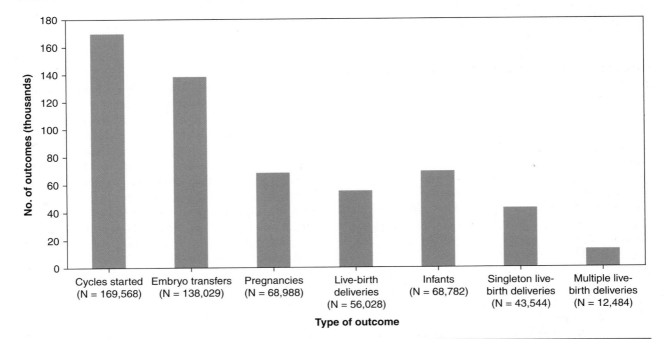

Source: Sunderam et al., 2017.

Infants conceived by artificial insemination are at higher risk of low birthweight (Fauser et al., 2014), although it has been suggested that it is because of maternal factors, such as advanced age, and not in vitro fertilization per se (Seggers et al., 2016). Infants conceived by artificial insemination show no differences in growth, health, development, and cognitive function relative to infants conceived naturally (Fauser et al., 2014). Because in vitro fertilization permits cells to be screened for genetic problems prior to implantation, in vitro infants are not at higher risk of birth defects (Fauser et al., 2014). However, about 40% of births from artificial insemination included more than one infant (38% twins and 2% triplets and higher). Multiple gestations increase risk for low birth weight, prematurity, and other poor outcomes (Sullivan-Pyke, Senapati, Mainigi, & Barnhart, 2017).

Surrogacy is an alternative form of reproduction in which a woman (the surrogate) is impregnated and carries a fetus to term and agrees to turn the baby over to a woman, man, or couple who will raise it. Single parents, same-sex couples, and couples in which one or both members are infertile may choose surrogacy. Sometimes the surrogate carries a zygote composed of one or both of the couple's gametes. Other times, the ova, sperm, or zygote are donated. Despite several highly publicized cases of surrogate mothers deciding not to relinquish the infant, most surrogacies are successful. In 2015, 2,807 babies were born through surrogacy in the United States, up from 738 in 2004, according to the American Society for Reproductive Medicine (Beitsch, 2017). Longitudinal research suggests no psychological differences at least through age 14 between children born through surrogacy compared with other methods (Golombok, 2013; Golombok, Ilioi, Blake, Roman, & Jadva, 2017). In addition, mothers of children who were the product of surrogates do not differ from those conceived using other methods and surrogate mothers show no negative effects (Jadva, Imrie, & Golombok, 2015; Söderström-Anttila et al., 2015). Finally, some argue that surrogacy may pose ethical issues. For example, women are often paid at least $30,000 to surrogate a fetus (Beitsch, 2017), creating financial incentives for surrogacy that may be difficult for low socioeconomic status women to resist.

Adoption

Another reproductive option for prospective parents is **adoption**. Adults who choose to adopt have similar motives for parenthood as those who raise biological children, such as valuing family ties, continuing a

Adults choose to adopt for a variety of reasons, such as infertility, the desire to raise a child with a same-sex partner, and to provide a home for a child in need.
iStock/CREATISTA

family line, feeling that parenting is a life task, and the desire for a nurturing relationship with a child (Jennings, Mellish, Tasker, Lamb, & Golombok, 2014; Malm & Welti, 2010). Heterosexual and same-sex adults report similar reasons for choosing adoption (Goldberg, Downing, & Moyer, 2012).

Adoptive children tend to be raised by parents with higher levels of education and income than other parents. This is partly due to self-selection and partly because of the screening that adoptive parents must go through before they are allowed to adopt. Adoptive children also tend to spend more time with their parents and have more educational resources than other children (Zill, 2015).

Yet adopted children show less engagement in class and tend to have more academic difficulties. Longitudinal research suggests that adoption is associated with lower academic attainment achievement across childhood, adolescence, and emerging adulthood compared with nonadopted comparison groups (Brown, Waters, & Shelton, 2017). Adopted children are also more likely than their nonadopted peers to show psychological problems and adjustment difficulties, in some cases persisting into adulthood (Brown et al., 2017; Grotevant & McDermott, 2014; Palacios & Brodzinsky, 2010).

Children's experiences prior to adoption and their developmental status at the time of adoption influence their outcomes (Balenzano, Coppola, Cassibba, & Moro, 2018). Children who experience neglect and fear and lack an early bond to a caregiver may experience difficulty regulating emotion and conflict. Biological mothers who choose to adopt may have experienced physical or mental health problems that interfered with their ability to care

Internationally Adopted Children

International adoption has become more common in the United States, and there are important challenges that adopted children and families face.
Thierry Esch/Paris Match via Getty Images

Over the past five decades, international adoption has become commonplace. In many countries throughout the world, children are reared in orphanages with substandard conditions—without adequate food, clothing, or shelter and with poorly trained caregivers. Such orphanages have been found in a number of countries, including China, Ethiopia, Ukraine, Congo, and Haiti, accounting for over two thirds of internationally adopted children (U.S. Department of State, 2014). Underfunded and understaffed orphanages often provide poor, nonnurturing care for children, increasing the risks for malnutrition, infections, physical handicaps, and growth retardation (The Leiden Conference on the Development and Care of Children Without Permanent Parents, 2012). With high infant-to-caregiver ratios, children available for adoption often spend a significant amount of time deprived of consistent human contact.

Few internationally adopted children enter the United States healthy and at age-appropriate developmental norms. Not surprisingly, the longer the children were institutionalized, the more developmental challenges they face (Jacobs, Miller, & Tirella, 2010). Physical growth stunting is directly associated with the length of institutionalization, but catch-up growth is commonly seen after adoption (Wilson & Weaver, 2009). As with growth, the time spent in an orphanage predicts the degree of developmental delay. Longer institutionalization is associated with delays in development of language, fine motor skills, social skills,

attention, and other cognitive skills (Mason & Narad, 2005; Wiik et al., 2011).

Speech and language delays are among the most consistent deficiencies experienced by internationally adopted children, especially those adopted after the age of 1 (Eigsti, Weitzman, Schuh, de Marchena, & Casey, 2011). However, more children reach normative age expectations 1 to 2 years postadoption (Glennen, 2014; Rakhlin et al., 2015). Generally, the younger the child is at adoption, the more quickly he or she will adapt to the new language and close any gaps in language delays (Mason & Narad, 2005). Some research suggests internationally adopted children are prone to long-term deficits in executive function likely due to neurological factors (Merz, Harlé, Noble, & McCall, 2016). The presence of a high-quality parent–child relationship promotes development of language, speech, or academic outcomes, and most children reach age-expected language levels (Glennen, 2014; Harwood, Feng, & Yu, 2013).

As adolescents, all children struggle to come to a sense of identity, to figure out who they are. This struggle may be especially challenging for internationally adopted children who may wonder about their native culture and homeland (Rosnati et al., 2015). Frequently, adolescents may want to discuss and learn more yet inhibit the desire to talk about this with parents (Garber & Grotevant, 2015). Parents who assume a multicultural perspective and provide opportunities for their children to learn about their birth culture support adopted children's development and promote healthy outcomes (Pinderhughes, Zhang, & Agerbak, 2015). Internationally adopted children seek to understand their birth culture and integrate their birth and adopted cultures into their sense of self (Grotevant, Lo, Fiorenzo, & Dunbar, 2017). A positive sense of ethnic identity is associated with positive outcomes such as self-esteem in international adoptees (Mohanty, 2015). Although there are individual differences in the degree of resilience and in functioning across developmental domains, adopted children overall show great developmental gains and resilience in physical, cognitive, and emotional development (Misca, 2014; Palacios, Román, Moreno, León, & Peñarrubia, 2014; Wilson & Weaver, 2009).

What Do You Think?

In your view, what are the most important challenges internationally adopted children and their families face? Identify sources and forms of support that might help adopted children and their parents. ●

and form a bond and might be passed on. In other cases, the child may have experienced neglect, deprivation, and trauma, which influence adjustment (Grotevant & McDermott, 2014). Many children adopted from international orphanages arrive with experiences that are harmful, as discussed in the accompanying Cultural Influences on Development feature, Internationally Adopted Children.

For many children, emotional differences are transitional. Research has suggested that most children show resilience in the years after adoption, but some issues continue (Palacios & Brodzinsky, 2010). Those who develop a close bond with adoptive parents tend to show better emotional understanding and regulation, social competence, and also self-esteem (Juffer & van IJzendoorn, 2007). This is true also of children who have experienced emotional

neglect, and those effects hold regardless of age of adoption (Barone, Lionetti, & Green, 2017).

Prenatal Diagnosis

Prenatal testing is recommended when genetic counseling has determined a risk for genetic abnormalities, when the woman is older than age 35, when both parents are members of an ethnicity at risk for particular genetic disorders, or when fetal development appears abnormal (Barlow-Stewart & Saleh, 2012). Technology has advanced rapidly, equipping professionals with an array of tools to assess the health of the fetus. Table 2.6 summarizes methods of prenatal diagnosis.

The most widespread and routine diagnostic procedure is **ultrasound**, in which high-frequency

TABLE 2.6

Methods of Prenatal Diagnosis

	EXPLANATION	ADVANTAGES	DISADVANTAGES
Ultrasound	High-frequency sound waves directed at the mother's abdomen provide clear images of the womb projected onto a video monitor.	Ultrasound enables physicians to observe the fetus, measure fetal growth, reveal the sex of the fetus, and determine physical abnormalities in the fetus.	Many abnormalities and deformities cannot be easily observed.
Amniocentesis	A small sample of the amniotic fluid that surrounds the fetus is extracted from the mother's uterus through a long, hollow needle inserted into the mother's abdomen. The amniotic fluid contains fetal cells. The fetal cells are grown in a laboratory dish to create enough cells for genetic analysis.	It permits a thorough analysis of the fetus's genotype. There is a near 100% diagnostic success rate.	Safe, but poses a greater risk to the fetus than ultrasound. If conducted before the 15th week of pregnancy, it may increase the risk of miscarriage.
Chorionic villus sampling (CVS)	Chorionic villus sampling requires studying a small amount of tissue from the chorion, part of the membrane surrounding the fetus, for the presence of chromosomal abnormalities. The tissue sample is obtained through a long needle inserted either abdominally or vaginally, depending on the location of the fetus.	It permits a thorough analysis of the fetus's genotype. CVS is relatively painless, and there is a 100% diagnostic success rate. Can be conducted earlier than amniocentesis, between 10 and 12 weeks.	It may pose a higher rate of spontaneous abortion and limb defects when conducted prior to 10 weeks' gestation.
Fetal MRI	Uses a magnetic scanner to record detailed images of fetal organs and structures.	Provides the most detailed and accurate images available.	It is expensive. At present, there is no evidence to suggest that it is harmful to the fetus.
Noninvasive prenatal testing (NIPT)	Cell-free fetal DNA are examined by drawing blood from the mother.	There is no risk to the fetus. It can diagnose several chromosomal abnormalities.	It cannot yet detect the full range of abnormalities. It may be less accurate than other methods. Researchers have identified the entire genome sequence using NIPT, suggesting that someday, NIPT may be as effective as other, more invasive techniques.

Sources: Akolekar, Beta, Picciarelli, Ogilvie, and D'Antonio (2015); Chan, Kwok, Choy, Leung, and Wang (2013); Gregg et al. (2013); Odibo (2015); Shahbazian, Barati, Arian, and Saadati (2012); Shim et al. (2014); Theodora et al. (2016).

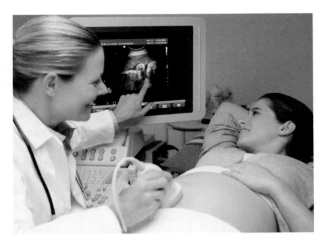

Ultrasound technology provides clear images of the womb, permitting physicians to observe the fetus, measure fetal growth, judge gestational age, reveal the sex of the fetus, detect multiple pregnancies, and determine physical abnormalities in the fetus.
iStock/Chris Ryan

sound waves directed at the mother's abdomen provide clear images of the womb represented on a video monitor. Ultrasound enables physicians to observe the fetus, measure fetal growth, judge gestational age, reveal the sex of the fetus, detect multiple pregnancies (twins, triplets, etc.), and determine physical abnormalities in the fetus. Many deformities can be observed, such as cardiac abnormalities, cleft palate, and microencephaly (small head size). At least 80% of women in the United States receive at least one prenatal ultrasound scan (Sadler, 2015). Three to four screenings over the duration of pregnancy are common to evaluate fetal development (Papp & Fekete, 2003). Repeated ultrasound of the fetus does not appear to affect growth and development (Stephenson, 2005).

Fetal MRI applies MRI technology to image the fetus's body and diagnose malformations (Griffiths et al., 2017). Most women will not have a fetal MRI. It is often used as a follow-up to ultrasound imaging to provide more detailed views of any suspected abnormalities (Milani et al., 2015). Fetal MRI can detect abnormalities throughout the body, including the central nervous system (Saleem, 2014). MRI in the obstetrical patient is safe for mother and fetus in the second and third trimesters but is expensive and has limited availability in some areas (Patenaude et al., 2014).

Amniocentesis is a prenatal diagnostic procedure in which a small sample of the amniotic fluid that surrounds the fetus is extracted from the mother's uterus through a long, hollow needle that is guided by ultrasound as it is inserted into the mother's abdomen (Odibo, 2015). The amniotic fluid contains fetal cells, which are grown in a laboratory dish to create enough cells for genetic

analysis. Genetic analysis is then performed to detect genetic and chromosomal anomalies and defects. Amniocentesis is less common than ultrasound, as it poses greater risk to the fetus. It is recommended for women aged 35 and over, especially if the woman and partner are both known carriers of genetic diseases (Vink & Quinn, 2018a). Usually amniocentesis is conducted between the 15th and 18th weeks of pregnancy. Conducted any earlier, an amniocentesis may increase the risk of miscarriage (Akolekar et al., 2015). Test results generally are available about 2 weeks after the procedure because it takes that long for the genetic material to grow and reproduce to the point where it can be analyzed.

Chorionic villus sampling (CVS) also samples genetic material and can be conducted earlier than amniocentesis, between 9 and 12 weeks of pregnancy (Vink & Quinn, 2018b). CVS requires studying a small amount of tissue from the chorion, part of the membrane surrounding the fetus. The tissue sample is obtained through a long needle inserted either abdominally or vaginally, depending on the location of the fetus. Results are typically available about 1 week following the procedure. CVS is relatively painless and, like amniocentesis, has a 100% diagnostic success rate. Generally, CVS poses few risks to the fetus (Shim et al., 2014). However, CVS should not be conducted prior to 10 weeks' gestation as some studies suggest an increased risk of limb defects and miscarriages (Shahbazian, Barati, Arian, & Saadati, 2012).

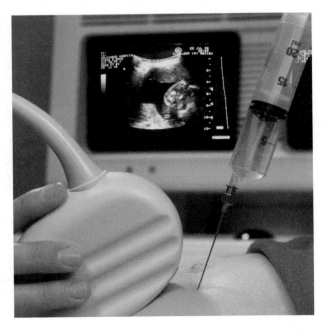

During amniocentesis, ultrasound is used to guide the insertion of a long, hollow needle into the mother's abdomen in order to extract a sample of the amniotic fluid that surrounds the fetus. The amniotic fluid contains fetal cells, which are grown in a laboratory dish and tested for genetic and chromosomal anomalies and defects.
Saturn Stills/Science Source

Noninvasive prenatal testing (NIPT) screens the mother's blood to detect chromosomal abnormalities. Cell-free fetal DNA (chromosome fragments that result in the breakdown of fetal cells) circulates in maternal blood in small concentrations that can be detected and studied by sampling the mother's blood (Warsof, Larion, & Abuhamad, 2015). Testing can be done after 10 weeks, typically between 10 and 22 weeks. Given that the test involves drawing blood from the mother, there is no risk to the fetus; however, NIPT cannot detect as many chromosomal abnormalities as amniocentesis or CVS and with less accuracy (Chan, Kwok, Choy, Leung, & Wang, 2013; National Coalition for Health Professional Education in Genetics, 2012). Researchers have identified the entire genome sequence using NIPT, suggesting that someday, NIPT may be as effective as other, more invasive techniques (Tabor et al., 2012). Pregnant women and their partners, in consultation with their obstetrician, should carefully weigh the risks and benefits of any procedure designed to monitor prenatal development.

Prenatal Treatment of Genetic Disorders

What happens when a genetic or chromosomal abnormality is found? Advances in genetics and in medicine have led to therapies that can be administered prenatally to reduce the effects of many genetic abnormalities. **Fetoscopy** is a technique that uses a small camera, inserted through a small incision on the mother's abdomen or cervix and placed into the *amniotic sac* that encases the fetus, to examine and perform procedures on the fetus during pregnancy. Risks of fetoscopy include infection, rupture of the amniotic sac, premature labor, and fetal death. However, when serious abnormalities are suspected, fetoscopy permits a visual assessment of the fetus, which aids in diagnosis and treatment. Hormones and other drugs, as well as blood transfusions, can be given to the fetus by inserting a needle into the uterus (Fox & Saade, 2012; Lindenburg, van Kamp, & Oepkes, 2014). Surgeons rely on the images provided by fetoscopy to surgically repair defects of the heart, lung, urinary tract, and other areas (Deprest et al., 2010; Sala et al., 2014).

In addition, researchers believe that one day, we may be able to treat many heritable disorders thorough genetic engineering, by synthesizing normal genes to replace defective ones. It may someday be possible to sample cells from an embryo, detect harmful genes and replace them with healthy ones, and then return the healthy cells to the embryo where they reproduce and correct the genetic defect (Coutelle & Waddington, 2012). This approach has been used to correct certain heritable disorders in animals and holds promise for treating humans.

THINKING IN CONTEXT 2.3

Suppose you are a 36-year-old woman pregnant with your first child. Considering the types of prenatal diagnostic testing described in this section, what would be the advantages and disadvantages of each? What factors would influence a health care provider's recommendations for prenatal testing?

HEREDITY AND ENVIRONMENT

» LO 2.4   Describe the interaction of heredity and environment, including behavioral genetics and the epigenetic framework.

We have learned a great deal about genetic inheritance. Most human traits, however, are influenced by a combination of genes working in concert with environmental influences. Our genes, inherited from our biological parents, consist of a complex blend of hereditary characteristics known as genotype. Our **genotype**, or genetic makeup, is a biological influence on all of our traits, from hair and eye color to personality, health, and behavior. However, our **phenotype**, the traits we ultimately show, such as our specific eye or hair color, is not determined by genotypes alone. Phenotypes are influenced by the interaction of genotypes and our experiences.

Behavioral Genetics

Behavioral genetics is the field of study that examines how genes and experience combine to influence the diversity of human traits, abilities, and behaviors (Krüger, Korsten, & Hoffman, 2017; Plomin et al., 2013). Genotypes alone do not determine people's traits, characteristics, or personalities; instead, development is the process by which our genetic inheritance (genotype) is expressed in observable characteristics and behaviors (phenotype). Behavioral geneticists recognize that even traits that have a strong genetic component, such as height, are modified by environmental influences (Dubois et al., 2012; Plomin, DeFries, Knopik, & Neiderhiser, 2016). Moreover, most human traits, such as intelligence, are influenced by multiple genes, and there are often multiple variants of each gene (Bouchard, 2014; Chabris, Lee, Cesarini, Benjamin, & Laibson, 2015; Knopik et al., 2017).

Methods of Behavioral Genetics

Behavioral geneticists devise ways of estimating the heritability of specific traits and behaviors. **Heritability** refers to the extent to which variation among people on a given characteristic is due to genetic differences. The remaining variation not due to genetic differences is instead a result of the environment and experiences. Heritability research therefore examines the contributions of the genotype but also provides information on the role of experience in determining phenotypes (Plomin et al., 2016). Behavioral geneticists assess the hereditary contributions to behavior by conducting selective breeding and family studies.

Using *selective breeding studies,* behavioral geneticists deliberately modify the genetic makeup of animals to examine the influence of heredity on attributes and behavior. For example, mice can be bred to very physically active or sedentary by mating highly active mice only with other highly active mice and, similarly, breeding mice with very low levels of activity with each other. Over subsequent generations, mice bred for high levels of activity become many times more active than those bred for low levels of activity (Knopik, Neiderhiser, DeFries, & Plomin, 2017). Selective breeding in rats, mice, and other animals such as chickens has revealed genetic contributions to many traits and characteristics, such as aggressiveness, emotionality, sex drive, and even maze learning (Plomin et al., 2016).

Behavioral geneticists conduct *family studies* to compare people who live together and share varying degrees of relatedness. Two kinds of family studies are common: twin studies and adoption studies (Koenen, Amstadter, & Nugent, 2012). *Twin studies* compare identical and fraternal twins to estimate how much of a trait or behavior is attributable to genes. If genes affect the attribute, identical twins should be more similar than fraternal twins because identical twins share 100% of their genes, whereas fraternal twins share about only 50%. *Adoption studies,* on the other hand, compare the degree of similarity between adopted children and their biological parents whose genes they share (50%) and their adoptive parents with whom they share no genes. If the adopted children share similarities with their biological parents, even though they were not raised by them, it suggests that the similarities are genetic.

Adoption studies also shed light on the extent to which attributes and behaviors are influenced by the environment. For example, the degree to which two genetically unrelated adopted children reared together are similar speaks to the role of environment. Comparisons of identical twins reared in the same home with those reared in different environments can also illustrate environmental contributions to phenotypes. If identical twins reared together are more similar than those reared apart, an environmental influence can be inferred.

Genetic Influences on Personal Characteristics

Research examining the contribution of genotype and environment to intellectual abilities has found a moderate role for heredity. Twin studies have shown that identical twins consistently have more highly correlated scores than do fraternal twins. For example, a classic study of intelligence in over 10,000 twin pairs showed a correlation of .86 for identical and .60 for fraternal twins (Plomin & Spinath, 2004). Table 2.7 summarizes the results of comparisons of intelligence scores from individuals who share different genetic relationships with each other. Note that correlations for all levels of kin are higher when they are reared together, supporting the role of environment. Average correlations also rise with increases in shared genes.

Genes contribute to many other traits, such as sociability, temperament, emotionality, and susceptibility to various illnesses such as obesity, heart disease and cancer, anxiety, poor mental health, and a propensity to be physically aggressive (Esposito et al., 2017; McRae et al., 2017; Ritz et al.,

TABLE 2.7

Average Correlation of Intelligence Scores From Family Studies for Related and Unrelated Kin Reared Together or Apart

	REARED TOGETHER	REARED APART
MZ twins (100% shared genes)	.86	.72
DZ twins (50% shared genes)	.60	.52
Siblings (50% shared genes)	.47	.24
Biological parent/child (50% shared genes)	.42	.22
Half-siblings (25% shared genes)	.31	—
Unrelated (adopted) siblings (0% shared genes)[a]	.34	—
Nonbiological parent/child (0% shared genes)[a]	.19	—

Source: Adapted from Bouchard and McGue (1981).

Note: MZ = monozygotic; DZ = dizygotic.

[a] Estimated correlation for individuals sharing neither genes nor environment = .0.

2017). Yet even traits that are thought to be heavily influenced by genetics can be modified by physical and social interventions. For example, growth, body weight, and body height are largely predicted by genetics, yet environmental circumstances and opportunities influence whether genetic potentials are realized (Dubois et al., 2012; Jelenkovic et al., 2016). Even identical twins who share 100% of their genes are not 100% alike. Those differences are due to the influence of environmental factors, which interact with genes in a variety of ways.

Gene–Environment Interactions

"You two are so different. Edward and Evan, are you sure you're twins?" kidded Aunt Joan. As fraternal twins, Edward and Evan share 50% of their genes and are reared in the same home. One might expect them to be quite similar, but their similar genes are not the whole story. Genes and the environment work together in complex ways to determine our characteristics, behavior, development, and health (Chabris et al., 2015; Ritz et al., 2017; Rutter, 2012). **Gene–environment interactions** refer to the dynamic interplay between our genes and our environment. Several principles illustrate these interactions.

Range of Reaction

Everyone has a different genetic makeup and therefore responds to the environment in a unique way. In addition, any one genotype can be expressed in a variety of phenotypes. There is a **range of reaction** (see Figure 2.8), a wide range of potential expressions of a genetic trait, depending on environmental opportunities and constraints (Gottlieb, 2000, 2007). For example, consider height. Height is largely a function of genetics, yet an individual may show a range of sizes depending on environment and behavior. Suppose that a child is born to two very tall parents. She may have the genes to be tall, but unless she has adequate nutrition, she will not fulfill her genetic potential for height. In societies in which nutrition has improved dramatically over a generation, it is common for children to tower over their parents. The enhanced environmental opportunities, in this case nutrition, enabled the children to fulfill their genetic potential for height. Therefore, a genotype sets boundaries on the range of possible phenotypes, but the phenotypes ultimately displayed vary in response to different environments (Manuck & McCaffery, 2014). In this way, genetics sets the range of development

---

FIGURE 2.8

Range of Reaction

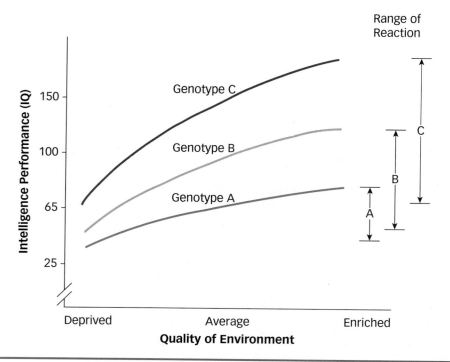

Source: Adapted from Gottlieb (2007).

outcomes and the environment influences where, within the range, that person will fall.

Canalization

Some traits illustrate a wide reaction range. Others are examples of **canalization**, in which heredity narrows the range of development to only one or a few outcomes. Canalized traits are biologically programmed, and only powerful environmental forces can change their developmental path (Flatt, 2005; Posadas & Carthew, 2014; Waddington, 1971). For example, infants follow an age-related sequence of motor development, from crawling, to walking, to running. Around the world, most infants walk at about 12 months of age. Generally, only extreme experiences or changes in the environment can prevent this developmental sequence from occurring. For example, children reared in impoverished international orphanages and exposed to extreme environmental deprivation demonstrated delayed motor development, with infants walking 5 months to a year later than expected (Chaibal, Bennett, Rattanathanthong, & Siritaratiwat, 2016; Miller, Tseng, Tirella, Chan, & Feig, 2008).

Motor development is not entirely canalized, however, because some minor changes in the environment can subtly alter its pace and timing. For example, practice facilitates stepping movements in young infants, prevents the disappearance of stepping movements in the early months of life, and leads to an earlier onset of walking (Adolph & Franchak, 2017; Ulrich, Lloyd, Tiernan, Looper, & Angulo-Barroso, 2008).

These observations demonstrate that even highly canalized traits, such as motor development, which largely unfolds via maturation, can be subtly influenced by contextual factors.

Gene–Environment Correlations

Heredity and environment are each powerful influences on development. Not only do they interact, but heredity and environmental factors also are often correlated with each other (Plomin et al., 2016; Scarr & McCartney, 1983). **Gene–environment correlation** refers to the idea that many of our traits are supported by both our genes and environment (Lynch, 2016). That is, genes give rise to behaviors, which are associated with the environment (Knafo & Jaffee, 2013). There are three types of gene–environment correlations—passive, reactive, and active—as shown in Figure 2.9.

FIGURE 2.9

Gene–Environment Correlation

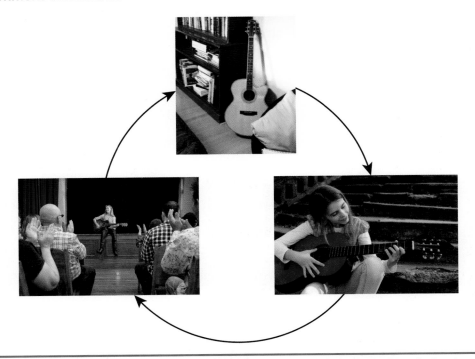

The availability of instruments in the home corresponds to the child's musical abilities, and she begins to play guitar (passive gene–environment correlation). As she plays guitar, she evokes positive responses in others, increasing her interest in music (evocative gene–environment correlation). Over time, she seeks opportunities to play, such as performing in front of an audience (niche-picking).

iStock/Essentials; iStock/Signature

Parents create homes that reflect their own genotypes. Because parents are genetically similar to their children, the homes that they create are not only in line with their own interests and preferences but also correspond with the child's genotype—an example of a *passive gene-environment correlation* (Wilkinson, Trzaskowski, Haworth, & Eley, 2013). For example, parents might provide genes that predispose a child to develop music ability and also provide a home environment that supports the development of music ability, such as by playing music in the home and owning musical instruments. This type of gene-environment correlation is seen early in life because children are reared in environments that are created by their parents, who share their genotype.

People naturally evoke responses from others and the environment, just as the environment and the actions of others evoke responses from the individual. In an *evocative gene-environment correlation,* a child's genetic traits (e.g., personality characteristics including openness to experience) influence the social and physical environment, which shape development in ways that support the genetic trait (Burt, 2009; Klahr, Thomas, Hopwood, Klump, & Burt, 2013). For example, active, happy infants tend to receive more adult attention than do passive or moody infants (Deater-Deckard & O'Connor, 2000), and even among infant twins reared in the same family, the more outgoing and happy twin receives more positive attention than does the more subdued twin (Deater-Deckard, 2001). Why? Babies who are cheerful and smile often influence their social world by evoking smiles from others, which in turn support the genetic tendency to be cheerful.

In this way, genotypes influence the physical and social environment to respond in ways that support the genotype. Children who engage in disruptive play tend to later experience problems with peers (Boivin et al., 2013). To return to the music example, a child with a genetic trait for music talent will evoke pleasurable responses (e.g., parental approval) when she plays music; this environmental support, in turn, encourages further development of the child's musical trait. In addition, some individuals may be more affected by environmental stimuli due to their genetic makeup (Belsky & Hartman, 2014).

Children also take a hands-on role in shaping their development. Recall from Chapter 1 that a major theme in understanding human development is the finding that individuals are active in their development; here we have an example of this pattern. As children grow older, they have increasing freedom in choosing their own activities and environments. An *active gene-environment correlation* occurs when the child actively creates experiences and environments that correspond to and influence his genetic predisposition. For example, the child with a genetic trait for interest and ability in music actively seeks experiences and environments that support that trait, such as friends with similar interests and after-school music classes. This tendency to actively seek out experiences and environments compatible and supportive of our genetic tendencies is called **niche-picking** (Corrigall & Schellenberg, 2015; Scarr & McCartney, 1983).

The strength of passive, evocative, and active gene-environment correlations changes with development, as shown in Figure 2.10 (Scarr, 1992). Passive gene-environment correlations are

---

FIGURE 2.10

Development Stage and Gene–Environment Correlations

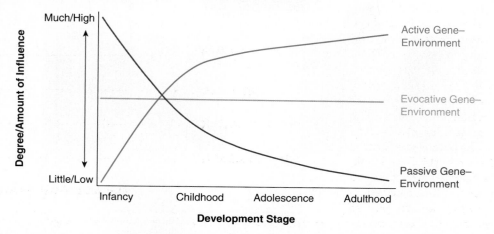

common at birth as caregivers determine infants' experiences. Correlations between their genotype and environment tend to occur because their environments are made by genetically similar parents. Evocative gene–environment correlations also occur from birth, as infants' inborn traits and tendencies influence others, evoking responses that support their own genetic predispositions. In contrast, active gene–environment correlations take place as children grow older and more independent. As they become increasingly capable of controlling parts of their environment, they engage in niche-picking by choosing their own interests and activities, actively shaping their own development. Niche-picking contributes to the differences we see in siblings, including fraternal twins, as they grow older. But identical twins tend to become more similar over time perhaps because they are increasingly able to select the environments that best fit their genetic propensities. As they age, identical twins—even those reared apart—become alike in attitudes, personality, cognitive ability, strength, mental health, and preferences, as well as select similar spouses and best friends (McGue & Christensen, 2013; Plomin et al., 2016; Plomin & Deary, 2015; Rushton & Bons, 2005).

Epigenetic Influences on Development

We have seen that development is influenced by the dynamic interaction of biological and contextual forces. Genes provide a blueprint for development, but phenotypic outcomes, individuals' characteristics, are not predetermined. Our genes are expressed as different phenotypes in different contexts or situations, known as **epigenetics** (Moore, 2017). The term *epigenetics* literally means "above the gene." The epigenome is a molecule that stretches along the length of DNA and provides instructions to genes, determining how they are expressed, whether they are turned on or off. Epigenetic mechanisms determine how genetic instructions are carried out to determine the phenotype (Lester, Conradt, & Marsit, 2016). At birth, each cell in our body turns on only a fraction of its genes. Genes continue to be turned on and off over the course of development and also in response

to the environment (Meaney, 2017). Environmental factors such as toxins, injuries, crowding, diet, and responsive parenting can influence the expression of genetic traits. In this way, even traits that are highly canalized can be influenced by the environment.

For example, consider brain development. Providing an infant with a healthy diet and opportunities to explore the world will support the development of brain cells, governed by genes that are switched on or off. Brain development influences motor development, further supporting the infant's exploration of the physical and social world, thereby promoting cognitive and social development. Active engagement with the world encourages connections among brain cells. Exposure to toxins or extreme trauma might suppress the activity of some genes, potentially influencing brain development and its cascading effects on motor, cognitive, and social development. In this way, an individual's neurological capacities are the result of epigenetic interactions among genes and contextual factors that determine his or her phenotype (Lerner & Overton, 2017). These complex interactions are illustrated in Figure 2.11 (Dodge & Rutter, 2011). Interactions between heredity and environment change throughout development as does the role we play in constructing environments that support our genotypes, influence our epigenome, and determine who we become (Lickliter & Witherington, 2017). For a striking example of epigenetics, see the Applying Developmental Science feature.

FIGURE 2.11

Epigenetic Framework

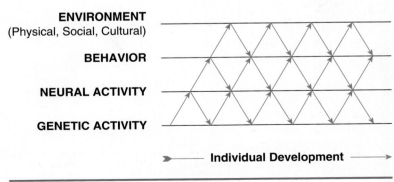

BIDIRECTIONAL INFLUENCES

ENVIRONMENT
(Physical, Social, Cultural)

BEHAVIOR

NEURAL ACTIVITY

GENETIC ACTIVITY

Individual Development

Source: Gottlieb (2007). With permission from John Wiley & Sons.

Altering the Epigenome

These two mice are genetically identical. Both carry the agouti gene but in the yellow mouse the agouti gene is turned on all the time. In the brown mouse it is turned off.
Wikimedia

One of the earliest examples of epigenetics is the case of agouti mice, which carry the agouti gene. Mice that carry the agouti gene have yellow fur, are extremely obese, are shaped much like a pincushion, and are prone to diabetes and cancer. When agouti mice breed, most of the offspring are identical to the parents—yellow, obese, and susceptible to life-shortening disease. However, a groundbreaking study showed that yellow agouti mice can produce offspring that look very different (Waterland & Jirtle, 2003). The mice in the photo above both carry the agouti gene, yet they look very different; the brown mouse is slender, is lean, and has a low risk of developing diabetes and cancer, living well into old age.

Why are these mice so different? Epigenetics. The epigenome carries the instructions that determine what each cell in your body will become, whether heart cell, muscle cell, or brain cell, for example. Those instructions are carried out by turning genes on and off.

In the case of the yellow and brown mice, the phenotype of the brown mice has been altered, but the DNA remains the same. Both carry the agouti gene, but in the yellow mouse, the agouti gene is turned on all the time. In the brown mouse, it is turned off. In 2003, Waterland and Jertle discovered that the agouti female's diet can determine her offspring's phenotype. In this study, female mice were fed foods containing chemicals that attach to a gene and turn it off. These chemical

clusters are found in many foods such as onions, garlic, beets, soy, and the nutrients in prenatal vitamins. Yellow agouti mothers fed extra nutrients passed along the agouti gene to their offspring, but it was turned off. The mice looked radically different from them (brown) and were healthier (lean, not susceptible to disease) even though they carried the same genes.

Another example supports the finding that the prenatal environment can alter the epigenome and influence the lifelong characteristics of offspring. Pregnant mice were exposed to a chemical (bisphenol-A or BPA, found in certain plastics). When female mice were fed BPA 2 weeks prior to conception, the number of offspring with the yellow obese coat color signaling an activated agouti gene increased (Dolinoy, 2008). When the pregnant mice were exposed to BPA plus nutritional supplementation (folic acid and an ingredient found in soy products), the offspring tended to be slender and have brown coats, signaling that the agouti gene was turned off. These findings suggest that the prenatal environment can influence the epigenome and thereby influence how genes are expressed—and that nutrition has the potential to buffer harm.

The most surprising finding emerging from studies of epigenetics, however, is that the epigenome can be influenced by the environment before birth and can be passed by males and females from one generation to the next without changing the DNA itself (Soubry, Hoyo, Jirtle, & Murphy, 2014; Szyf, 2015). This means that what you eat and do today could affect the epigenome—the development, characteristics, and health—of your children, grandchildren, and great-grandchildren (Bale, 2015; Vanhees, Vonhögen, van Schooten, & Godschalk, 2014).

What Do You Think?

1. Much of the research on epigenetics examines animals, but there is a growing body of work studying humans. In what ways, if any, might you expect research findings based on people to differ from the findings of animal research, described previously? Explain.

2. What might you do to "care for" your epigenome? Identify activities and behaviors that you think might affect the health of your genome today and tomorrow. ●

THINKING IN CONTEXT 2.4

To answer the following questions, begin by thinking about how your own development reflects interactions among your genes and sociocultural context. Then, describe a skill, ability, or hobby in which you excel.

1. How might a passive gene–environment correlation account for this ability? For example, in what ways has the context in which you were raised shaped this ability?

2. In what ways might this ability be influenced by an evocative genetic environment correlation?

3. Provide an example of how this ability might reflect an active gene–environment correlation.

4. Which genetic environment correlation do you think most accurately accounts for your skill, ability, or hobby?

5. How might you apply the epigenetic framework to account for your ability?

APPLY YOUR KNOWLEDGE

Strapped in and buckled in the rear seat of her mother's bicycle, 1-year-old Jenna patted her helmet as her mother zoomed along the bike path to the beach. There she giggled and kicked her legs as her mother whooshed her through the water. As a child, Jenna loved to be outside and especially in the water. Jenna practiced swimming at the local YMCA nearly every day and became quite skilled. Jenna's proud mother encouraged her daughter's athleticism by enrolling her in swim classes. As a teenager, Jenna decided that if she were going to become an exceptional swimmer, she would have to go to a summer swimming camp. She researched camps and asked her mother if she could attend. Jenna further honed her skills as a swimmer and won a college scholarship for swimming.

Many years later, Jenna was surprised to learn that she had a twin sister, Tasha. Separated at birth, Jenna and Tasha became aware of each other in their early 40s. Jenna was stunned yet couldn't wait to meet her twin sister. Upon meeting, Jenna and Tasha were surprised to find that they were not exactly the same. Whereas Jenna was athletic and lithe, Tasha was more sedentary and substantially heavier than Jenna. Unlike Jenna, Tasha grew up in a home far from the beach and with little access to

outdoor activities. Instead, Tasha's interest was writing. As a child, she'd write stories and share them with others. She sought out opportunities to write and chose a college with an exceptional writing program. Both Jenna and Tasha excelled in college, as they did throughout their education, and earned nearly identical scores on the SAT.

Jenna and Tasha look very similar. Even the most casual observer could easily tell that they are sisters as both have blond hair, blue eyes, and a similar facial structure. Tasha's skin, however, is more fair and unlined. Jenna's face is sprinkled with freckles and darker spots formed after many days spent swimming outside. Jenna and Tasha both are allergic to peanuts, and they both take medication for high blood pressure. The more that Jenna and Tasha get to know each other, the more similarities they find.

1. Considering Jenna and Tasha, provide examples of three types of gene–environment correlations: passive, evocative, and active.

2. Do you think Jenna and Tasha are monozygotic or dizygotic twins? Why or why not?

3. What role might epigenetic influences play in determining Jenna and Tasha's development?

$SAGE edge™

Visit **edge.sagepub.com/kuther2e** to help you accomplish your coursework goals in an easy-to-use learning environment.

LEARNING OBJECTIVES	SUMMARY	KEY TERMS	IN REVIEW
2.1 Discuss the genetic foundations of development.	Most cells in the human body reproduce through mitosis, but sex cells reproduce by meiosis, creating gametes with 23 single, unpaired chromosomes. Some genes are passed through dominant–recessive inheritance, in which some genes are dominant and will always be expressed regardless of the gene it is paired with. Other genes are recessive and will only be expressed if paired with another recessive gene.	Chromosomes Deoxyribonucleic acid (DNA) Genes Mitosis Meiosis Gamete	What are genes? How is sex determined? What percentage of genes are shared by twins?

	When a person is heterozygous for a particular trait, the dominant gene is expressed and the person remains a carrier of the recessive gene. Incomplete dominance is a genetic inheritance pattern in which both genes influence the characteristic. Polygenic traits are the result of interactions among many genes. Some traits are determined by genomic imprinting, determined by whether it is inherited by the mother or the father.	Zygote Ovum Dizygotic (DZ) twins Monozygotic (MZ) twins Alleles Homozygous Heterozygous Dominant-recessive inheritance Carrier Incomplete dominance Sickle cell trait Polygenic inheritance Genomic imprinting	What are dominant–recessive inheritance, incomplete dominance, genomic imprinting, and polygenic inheritance?
2.2 Identify examples of genetic disorders and chromosomal abnormalities.	PKU is a recessive disorder that occurs when both parents carry the allele. Disorders carried by dominant alleles, such as Huntington disease, are expressed when the individual has a single allele. Some recessive genetic disorders, like the gene for hemophilia, are carried on the X chromosome. Males are more likely to be affected by X-linked genetic disorders, such as hemophilia. Fragile X syndrome is an example of a dominant–recessive disorder carried on the X chromosome. Because the gene is dominant, it must appear on only one X chromosome to be displayed. Klinefelter syndrome occurs in males born with an extra X chromosome (XXY), and Jacob's syndrome occurs when males have an extra Y chromosome (XYY). Females are diagnosed with triple X syndrome when they are three X chromosomes and Turner syndrome when they are born with only one X chromosome. The most common chromosome disorder is trisomy 21, known as Down syndrome.	Phenylketonuria (PKU) Fragile X syndrome Hemophilia Down syndrome Klinefelter syndrome Jacob's syndrome Turner syndrome Mutations	Give an example of: a dominant recessive disorder, an X-linked disorder, and a chromosomal abnormality. What is a mutation?
2.3 Discuss the choices available to prospective parents in having healthy children.	Genetic counseling is a medical specialty that helps prospective parents determine the likelihood that their children will inherit genetic defects and chromosomal abnormalities. Some couples at risk for bearing children with genetic or chromosomal abnormalities seek alternative methods of conception such as artificial insemination, in vitro fertilization, and surrogacy. Others consider the option of adoption. Prenatal diagnosis is recommended when genetic testing has determined a risk for genetic abnormalities. Advances in genetics and in medicine have led to therapies that can be administered prenatally to reduce the effects of many genetic abnormalities.	Genetic counseling Artificial insemination In vitro fertilization Surrogacy Adoption Ultrasound Fetal MRI Amniocentesis Chorionic villus sampling (CVS) Noninvasive prenatal testing (NIPT) Fetoscopy	What is genetic counseling? What are the differences between artificial insemination, in vitro fertilization, surrogacy, and adoption? What are the five most common methods of prenatal diagnosis?

2.4 Describe the interaction of heredity and environment, including behavioral genetics and the epigenetic framework.	Behavioral genetics is the field of study that examines how genes and experience combine to influence the diversity of human traits, abilities, and behaviors. Heritability research examines the contributions of the genotype in determining phenotypes but also provides information on the role of experience through three types of studies: selective breeding studies, family studies, and adoption studies. Genetics contributes to many traits, such as intellectual ability, sociability, anxiety, agreeableness, activity level, obesity, and susceptibility to various illnesses. Passive, evocative, and active gene–environment correlations illustrate how traits often are supported by both our genes and environment. Reaction range refers to the idea that there is a wide range of potential expressions of a genetic trait, depending on environmental opportunities and constraints. Some traits illustrate canalization and require extreme changes in the environment to alter their course. The epigenetic framework is a model for understanding the dynamic ongoing interactions between heredity and environment whereby the epigenome's instructions to turn genes on and off throughout development are influenced by the environment.	Genotype Phenotype Behavioral genetics Heritability Gene–environment interactions Range of reaction Canalization Gene–environment correlation Niche-picking Epigenetics	What is behavioral genetics? What are three types of gene–environment correlations? What is the range of reaction? What is the epigenetic framework?

3

The Prenatal Period, Birth, and the Newborn

Looking down at his newborn daughter's face, Remmy said admiringly, "Carla looks just like you." His wife, Darla, replied, "That's what my mother said." "I'm in awe," said Remmy. "Less than a year ago we decided to start a family and now, seemingly overnight, here she is. It's magical—over a few short months, this little person popped into existence from pixie dust!" Darla laughed and protested, "My baby girl was never pixie dust!"

Remmy's silly observation describes the dramatic process of prenatal development. Over 9 months, a single cell transforms and grows into a **neonate**, a newborn. Every infant is born with a unique set of characteristics that reflect the genetic makeup of both parents. In this chapter, we discuss the process of how prenatal development unfolds, how a baby is born, and what the newborn baby is like.

Learning Objectives

3.1 Describe the three periods of prenatal development that begin with conception.

3.2 Identify how exposure to teratogens can influence the prenatal environment.

3.3 Explain the process of childbirth.

3.4 Discuss the neonate's physical capacities, including development in low-birthweight infants.

Digital Resources

Watch: Fetal Development: Ultrasound

▶ **Lives in Context Video 3.1:** Pregnancy and Ultrasound

Connect: Nevada Campaign Urges Marijuana Abstinence During Pregnancy

Explore: Gender and Childbirth Choices

▶ **Lives in Context Video 3.2:** The Process of Childbirth

Listen: Survival of Premature Babies

PRENATAL DEVELOPMENT

» LO 3.1 Describe the three periods of prenatal development that begin with conception.

Remarkably, a human infant progresses from fertilization to birth in just 266 days, or 38 weeks. Conception, the union of ovum and sperm, marks the beginning of prenatal development, the transformative process in which the fertilized ovum, known as a *zygote*, progresses through several periods of development, finally emerging from the womb as a neonate. Prenatal development takes place over several stages representing shifts in the developmental processes.

Conception

A woman can conceive only during a short window of time each month. About every 28 days, an ovum bursts from one of the ovaries into the long, thin fallopian tube that leads to the uterus; this event is known as ovulation (see Figure 3.1). The ovum is the largest cell in the human body, yet it is only 1/175th of an inch in diameter (about the size of the period at the end of this sentence). Over several days, the ovum travels down the fallopian tube while the corpus luteum, the spot on the ovary from which the ovum was released, secretes **hormones** that cause the lining of the uterus to thicken in preparation for the fertilized ovum (Sadler, 2015). If fertilization does not occur, the lining of the uterus is shed through menstruation about 2 weeks after ovulation.

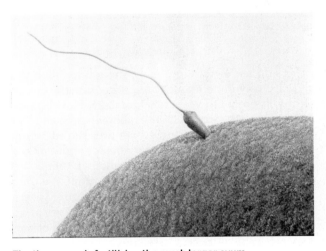

The tiny sperm is fertilizing the much larger ovum.
F. Leroy / Science Source

Conception, of course, also involves the male. Each day, a man's testes produce millions of sperm, which are composed of a pointed head packed with 23 chromosomes' worth of genetic material and a long tail. During ejaculation, about 360 million, and as many as 500 million, sperm are released, bathed in a protective fluid called semen (K. L. Moore & Persaud, 2016). After entering the female's vagina, the sperm's tail propels it through the cervix into the uterus and onward toward the ovum. Sperm must travel for about 6 hours to reach the fallopian tube, where an ovum may—or may not—be present. The journey is difficult: Some sperm get tangled up with other sperm, some travel up the wrong fallopian tube, and

FIGURE 3.1

Female Reproductive System

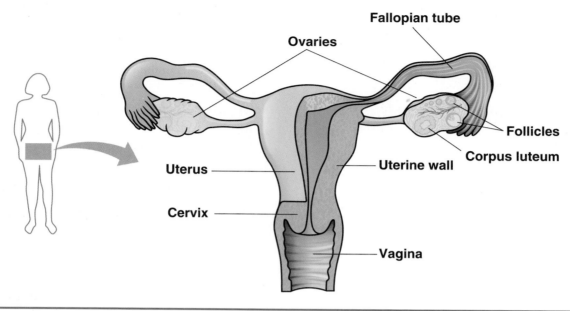

Source: Levine and Munsch (2010, p. 102).

others do not swim vigorously enough to reach the ovum. On average, about 300 sperm reach the ovum, if one is present (Webster, Morris, & Kevelighan, 2018). Those that travel up the fallopian tube can live up to 6 days, able to fertilize a yet unreleased ovum. The ovum, however, remains viable for about only a day after being released into the fallopian tube.

Both sperm and the woman's reproductive tract play a role in fertilization (Suarez, 2016). Sperm are guided by temperature, tracking the heat of an expectant ovum, as well as by chemical signal (Lottero-Leconte, Isidro Alonso, Castellano, & Perez Martinez, 2017). In the presence of an ovum, sperm become hyperactivated, they swim even more vigorously, and the sperm's head releases enzymes to help it penetrate the protective layers of the ovum (Bianchi & Wright, 2016). As soon as one sperm penetrates the ovum, a chemical reaction makes the ovum's membrane impermeable to other sperm. The sperm's tail falls off, and the genetic contents merge with that of the ovum.

At the moment of conception, the zygote contains 46 chromosomes, half from the ovum and half from the sperm. After fertilization, the zygote rapidly transforms into a multicelled organism. Prenatal development takes place over three developmental periods: (1) the germinal period, (2) the embryonic period, and (3) the fetal period.

Germinal Period (0 to 2 Weeks)

During the **germinal period,** also known as the period of the zygote, the newly created zygote

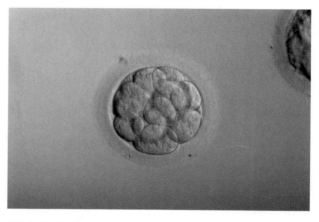

This ball of cells, known as a morula, is formed at about three days after conception. Each of these cells is identical. Differentiation has not yet begun.
Pascal Goetgheluck / Science Source

begins cell division as it travels down the fallopian tube, where fertilization took place, toward the uterus. About 30 hours after conception, the zygote then splits down the middle, forming two identical cells (Webster et al., 2018). This process is called cleavage, and it continues at a rapid pace. As shown in Figure 3.2, the two cells each split to form four cells, then eight, and so on. Each of the resulting cells is identical until about the third set of cell divisions. This process of cell division continues rapidly. Any of these cells may become a person (and sometimes do, in the case of monozygotic or identical twins).

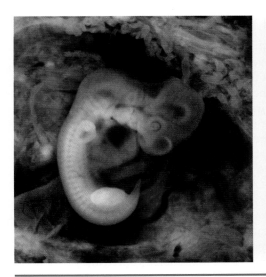
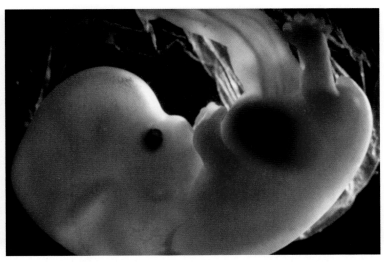

Development proceeds very quickly during the embryonic period. Note the dramatic changes from the fifth week (left) to the seventh week (right) of prenatal development.
Wikimedia / Petit Format / Science Source

FIGURE 3.2

Germinal Period

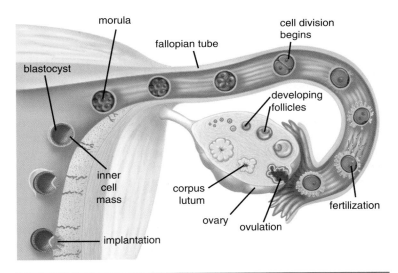

Source: Levine and Munsch (2010, p. 102).

Cell differentiation begins roughly 72 hours after fertilization when the organism consists of about 16 to 32 cells. Differentiation means that the cells begin to specialize and are no longer identical. By 4 days, the organism consists of about 60 to 70 cells formed into a hollow ball called a **blastocyst**, a fluid-filled sphere with cells forming a protective circle around an inner cluster of cells from which the embryo will develop.

Implantation, in which the blastocyst burrows into the wall of the uterus, begins at about day 6 and is complete by about day 11 (K. L. Moore & Persaud, 2016). By the end of the second week, when fully implanted into the uterine wall, the outer layer of the blastocyst begins to develop into part of the **placenta**, the principal organ of exchange between the mother and developing organism. The placenta will enable the exchange of nutrients, oxygen, and wastes via the umbilical cord. Also, during this stage, the developing organism is encased in amniotic fluid, providing temperature regulation, cushioning, and protection from shocks.

Embryonic Period (3 to 8 Weeks)

By the third week after conception, the developing organism—now called an *embryo*—begins a period of structural development during which the most rapid developments of the prenatal period take place. All of the organs and major body systems form during this **embryonic period**. The mass of cells composing the **embryonic disk** develops into layers, which will develop into all of the major organs of the body. The **ectoderm**, the upper layer, will become skin, nails, hair, teeth, sensory organs, and the nervous system. The **endoderm**, the lower layer, will become the digestive system, liver, lungs, pancreas, salivary glands, and respiratory system. The middle layer, the **mesoderm**, forms later and will become muscles, skeleton, circulatory system, and internal organs.

During the third week, at about 22 days after conception, the endoderm folds to form the **neural tube**, which will develop into the central nervous system (brain and spinal cord) (Webster et al., 2018).

Now the head can be distinguished. A blood vessel that will become the heart begins to pulse and blood begins to circulate throughout the body. During days 26 and 27, arm buds appear, followed by leg buds on days 28 through 30. At about this time, a tail-like appendage extends from the spine, disappearing at about 55 days after conception (Sadler, 2015). The brain develops rapidly and the head grows faster than the other parts of the body during the fifth week of development. The eyes, ears, nose, and mouth begin to form during the sixth week. Upper arms, forearms, palms, legs, and feet appear. The embryo shows reflex responses to touch.

During the seventh week, webbed fingers and toes are apparent; they separate completely by the end of the eighth week. A ridge called the indifferent gonad appears; it will develop into the male or female genitals, depending on the fetus's sex chromosomes (K. L. Moore & Persaud, 2016). The Y chromosome of the male embryo instructs it to secrete testosterone, causing the *indifferent gonad* to create testes. In female embryos, no testosterone is released, and the indifferent gonad produces ovaries. The sex organs take several weeks to develop. The external genital organs are not apparent until about 12 weeks.

At the end of the embryonic period, 8 weeks after conception, the embryo weighs about one seventh of an ounce and is 1 inch long. All of the basic organs and body parts have formed in a very rudimentary way. The embryo displays spontaneous reflexive movements, but it is still too small for the movements to be felt by the mother (Hepper, 2015). Serious defects that emerge during the embryonic period often cause a miscarriage, or spontaneous abortion (loss of the fetus); indeed, most miscarriages are the result of chromosomal abnormalities. The most severely defective organisms do not survive beyond the first trimester, or third month of pregnancy. It is estimated that up to 45% of all conceptions abort spontaneously, and most occur before the pregnancy is detected (Bienstock, Fox, & Wallach, 2015).

Fetal Period (9 Weeks to Birth)

During the **fetal period,** from the ninth week to birth, the organism, called a **fetus,** grows rapidly, and its organs become more complex and begin to function. The end of the third month marks the close of the first trimester, at which time all parts of the fetus's body can move spontaneously, the legs kick, and the fetus can suck its thumb (an involuntary reflex). By the end of the 12th week, the upper limbs have almost reached their final relative lengths, but the lower limbs are slightly shorter than their final relative lengths (Sadler, 2015).

Second Trimester (14 to 26 Weeks)

By the 14th week, at the start of the second trimester, limb movements are coordinated, but they will be too slight to be felt by the mother until about 17 to 20 weeks. The heartbeat gets stronger. Eyelids, eyebrows, fingernails, toenails, and tooth buds form. The first hair to appear is **lanugo,** a fine down-like hair that covers the fetus's body; it is gradually replaced by human hair. The skin is covered with a greasy material called the **vernix caseosa,** which protects the fetal skin from abrasions, chapping, and hardening that can occur with exposure to amniotic fluid (K. L. Moore & Persaud, 2016). At 21 weeks, rapid eye movements begin, signifying an important time of growth and development for the fetal brain. The brain begins to become more responsive. For example, startle responses have been reported at 22 to 23 weeks in response to sudden vibrations and noises (Hepper, 2015). During weeks 21 to 25, the fetus gains substantial weight, and its body proportions become more like those of a newborn infant. Growth of the fetal body begins to catch up to the head, yet the head remains disproportionately larger than the body at birth.

Third Trimester (27 to 40 Weeks; Seventh, Eighth, Ninth Months)

During the last 3 months of pregnancy, the fetal body grows substantially in weight and length; specifically, it typically gains over 5 pounds and grows 7 inches. At about 28 weeks after conception, brain development grows in leaps and bounds. The cerebral cortex develops convolutions and furrows, taking on the brain's characteristic wrinkly appearance (Andescavage et al., 2016). The fetal brain wave pattern shifts to include occasional bursts of activity, similar to the sleep-wake cycles of newborns. By 30 weeks, the pupils of the eyes dilate in response to light. At 35 weeks, the fetus has a firm hand grasp and spontaneously orients itself toward light.

During the third trimester, pregnant women and their caregivers are mindful that the baby may be born prematurely. Although the expected date of delivery is 266 days or 38 weeks from conception (40 weeks from the mother's last menstrual period), about 1 in every 10 American births is premature (Centers for Disease Control and Prevention, 2017b). The **age of viability**—the age at which advanced medical care permits a preterm newborn to survive outside the womb—begins at about 22 weeks after conception (Sadler, 2015). Infants born before 22 weeks rarely survive more than a few days, because their brain and lungs have not begun to function. Although a 23-week fetus born prematurely may survive in intensive care, its immature respiratory system places it at risk; only about one third of infants born at 23 weeks' gestation survive (Stoll et al., 2015). At about 26 weeks, the lungs become capable of breathing air and the premature infant stands a better chance of surviving if given intensive care. About 80% of infants born at 25 weeks survive, and 94% of those born at 27 weeks also survive. Premature birth has a variety of causes, including many environmental factors.

Contextual and Cultural Influences on Prenatal Care

Prenatal care, a set of services provided to improve pregnancy outcomes and engage the expectant mother, family members, and friends in health care decisions, is critical for the health of both mother and infant. About 26% of pregnant women in the United States do not seek prenatal care until after the first trimester; 6% seek prenatal care at the end of pregnancy or not at all (U.S. Department of Health and Human Services, 2014). Inadequate prenatal care is a risk factor for low-birthweight and preterm births as well as infant mortality during the first year (Partridge, Balayla, Holcroft, & Abenhaim, 2012). In addition, use of prenatal care predicts pediatric care throughout childhood, which serves as a foundation for health and development throughout the lifespan.

Why do women delay or avoid seeking prenatal care? A common reason is the lack of health insurance (Maupin et al., 2004). Although government-sponsored health care is available for the poorest mothers, many low-income mothers do not qualify

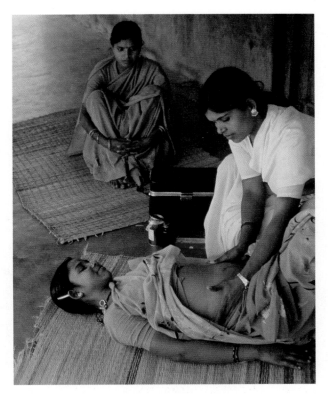

A rural health care worker in India gives prenatal care to a pregnant woman. Birth practices vary by culture.
S. Nagendra/Science Source

for care or lack information on how to take advantage of care that may be available. Figure 3.3 lists other barriers to seeking prenatal care, including difficulty in finding a doctor, lack of transportation, demands

FIGURE 3.3

Reasons for Delayed Prenatal Care Among Women, 2009–2010

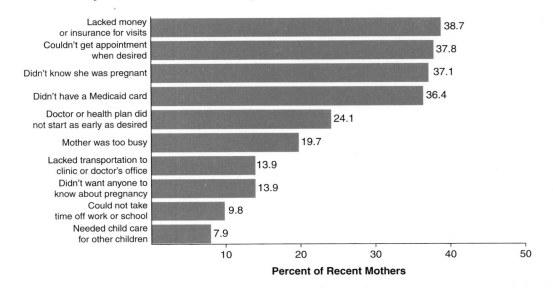

Reason	Percent of Recent Mothers
Lacked money or insurance for visits	38.7
Couldn't get appointment when desired	37.8
Didn't know she was pregnant	37.1
Didn't have a Medicaid card	36.4
Doctor or health plan did not start as early as desired	24.1
Mother was too busy	19.7
Lacked transportation to clinic or doctor's office	13.9
Didn't want anyone to know about pregnancy	13.9
Could not take time off work or school	9.8
Needed child care for other children	7.9

Source: U.S. Department of Health and Human Services et al., 2013.

of caring for young children, ambivalence about the pregnancy, depression, lack of education about the importance of prenatal care, lack of social support, poor prior experiences in the health care system, and family crises (Daniels, Noe, & Mayberry, 2006; Heaman et al., 2015; Mazul, Salm-Ward, & Ngui, 2016).

Moreover, there are significant ethnic and socioeconomic disparities in prenatal care. As shown in Figure 3.4, prenatal care is linked with maternal education. About 86% of women with a college degree obtain first-trimester care, compared with less than two thirds of women with less than a high school diploma

(U.S. Department of Health and Human Services, 2014). In addition, women of color are disproportionately less likely to receive prenatal care during the first trimester and are more likely to receive care beginning in the third trimester or no care (see Figure 3.5). Native Hawaiian and Native American women are least likely to obtain prenatal care during the first trimester, followed by Hispanic, African American, Asian American, and White American women (Hamilton, Martin, Osterman, Driscoll, & Rossen, 2017). In the most extreme case, only about half of Native Hawaiian or other Pacific Islander women obtain first-trimester care, and one in five obtains late or no prenatal care.

Ethnic differences are thought to be largely influenced by socioeconomic factors, as the ethnic groups least likely to seek early prenatal care are also the most economically disadvantaged members of society.

Although prenatal care predicts better birth outcomes, cultural factors also appear to protect some women and infants from the negative consequences of inadequate prenatal care. In a phenomenon termed the *Latino paradox*, Latina mothers, despite low rates of prenatal care, tend to experience low birthweight and mortality rates below national averages. These favorable birth outcomes are striking because of the strong and consistent association between socioeconomic status and birth outcomes and because Latinos as a group are among the most socioeconomically disadvantaged ethnic populations in the United States (McGlade, Saha, & Dahlstrom, 2004; Ruiz, Hamann, Mehl, & OConnor, 2016).

Several factors are thought to account for the Latino paradox, including strong cultural support for maternity, healthy traditional dietary practices, and the norm of selfless devotion to the maternal role (known as *marianismo*) (Fracasso & Busch-Rossnagel, 1992; McGlade et al., 2004). These protective cultural factors interact with strong social support networks and informal systems of health care among Latino women, in which women tend to take responsibility for the health needs of those beyond their nuclear households. Mothers benefit from the support of other family members such as sisters, aunts, and other extended family. In this

---

FIGURE 3.4

Timing of Prenatal Care Initiation, by Maternal Education, 2012

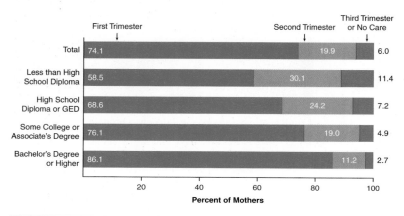

Source: U.S. Department of Health and Human Services et al., 2015.

FIGURE 3.5

Prenatal Care Beginning in the First Trimester and Late or No Care, by Race and Ethnicity, in the United States, 2016

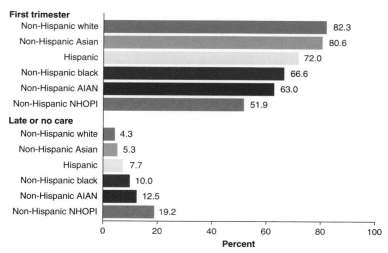

Source: Hamilton et al., 2017.

way, knowledge about health is passed down from generation to generation. There is a strong tradition of women helping other women in the community, and warm interpersonal relationships, known as *personalismo,* are highly valued (Fracasso & Busch-Rossnagel, 1992; McGlade et al., 2004).

Pregnancy and the Maternal Brain

Pregnancy is associated with neurological changes especially in the areas of the brain responsible for social cognition.
John Bavosi/Science Source

The developing embryo and fetus receive a great deal of research attention, but what does pregnancy mean for mothers' development? Women's bodies undergo a radical transformation during pregnancy. For example, the hormone progesterone increases up to 15-fold and is accompanied by a flood of estrogen that is greater than the lifelong exposure prior to pregnancy. Research has shown that hormonal shifts are associated with brain changes during puberty as well as later in life. Do the hormonal changes with pregnancy influence women's brain structure? Animal research suggests that pregnancy is accompanied by neurological changes, including changes in neural receptors, neuron generation, and gene expression, that are long-lasting (Kinsley & Amory-Meyer, 2011). It is likely that pregnancy is also associated with neural changes in humans, but there is little research to date (Hillerer, Jacobs, Fischer, & Aigner, 2014).

In a recent groundbreaking study, Elseine Hoekzema and colleagues (2017) conducted brain scans of women who were attempting to become pregnant for the first time as well as their partners. Women who became pregnant were scanned again after giving birth and at least 2 years later. The fathers and women who had not become pregnant were also assessed. The new mothers experienced reductions in the brain's gray matter, signifying increased neural efficiency in regions of the brain involved in social cognition, specifically, theory of mind, which enables us to sense another person's emotions and perspective (Schurz, Radua, Aichhorn, Richlan, & Perner, 2014). Theory of mind underlies a mother's ability to interpret her infant's mental states and is important for secure parent–infant attachment and for the development of the child's own social cognitive functions (Meins, Fernyhough, Fradley, & Tuckey, 2001). The changes in gray matter volume predicted mothers' attachment to their infants in the postpartum period, as indicated by mothers' increased neural activity in response to viewing photos of their infant compared with other infants. Other research suggests that pregnancy is associated with the enhanced ability to recognize faces, especially those displaying emotions (Pearson, Lightman, & Evans, 2009). Gestational alterations in the brain structures that are implicated in social processes may offer an adaptive advantage to mothers by facilitating their ability to recognize the needs of their children and to promote mother–infant bonding.

Moreover, similar to findings with animals (Kinsley & Amory-Meyer, 2011), Hoekzema and colleagues observed that the neural changes that accompanied pregnancy were long lasting, persisting 2 years after birth. The pregnancy-related neurological changes were so marked and predictable that all of the women could be classified as having undergone pregnancy or not on the basis of the volume changes in gray matter. Notably, fathers did *not* show a change in gray matter volume, suggesting that the neural effects of pregnancy are biological in nature rather than associated with the contextual changes that occur with the transition to parenthood.

What Do You Think?

What adaptive purpose might pregnancy-related neurological changes serve? ●

Although these cultural factors are thought to underlie the positive birth outcomes seen in Latino women, they appear to erode as Latino women acculturate to American society. The birth advantage has been found to decline in subsequent American-born generations. Recent findings have called the existence of the Latino paradox into question, as some samples have illustrated that the negative effects of socioeconomic disadvantage cannot be easily ameliorated by cultural supports (Hoggatt, Flores, Solorio, Wilhelm, & Ritz, 2012; Sanchez-Vaznaugh et al., 2016).

Our discussion thus far has emphasized fetal development; however, expectant mothers also experience radical physical changes during pregnancy. In addition to changes in body weight and shape, pregnancy is accompanied by changes in brain structure and function, as discussed in the Brain and Biological Influences on Development feature.

| THINKING IN CONTEXT 3.1 |

Petra noticed that her abdomen has not grown much since she became pregnant 3 months ago. She concluded that the fetus must not undergo significant development early in pregnancy. How would you respond to Petra?

ENVIRONMENTAL INFLUENCES ON PRENATAL DEVELOPMENT

» LO 3.2 **Identify how exposure to teratogens can influence the prenatal environment.**

As described, prenatal development unfolds along a programmed path. However, sometimes environmental factors can hinder prenatal development. A **teratogen** is an agent that causes damage to prenatal development, such as a disease, drug, or other environmental factor, producing a birth defect. The field of **teratology** attempts to find the causes of birth defects so that they may be avoided. Health care providers help pregnant women and those who intend to become pregnant to be aware of teratogens and avoid them, as much as possible, to maximize the likelihood of having a healthy baby.

Principles of Teratology

There are many ways in which teratogens may affect prenatal development, but it is not always easy to predict the harm caused by teratogens. Generally, the effects of exposure to teratogens on prenatal development vary depending on the following principles (K. S. Moore & Persaud, 2016; Sadler, 2015).

- **Critical Periods.** There are critical periods during prenatal development in which an embryo is more susceptible to damage from exposure to teratogens. The extent to which exposure to a teratogen disrupts prenatal development depends on the stage of prenatal development when exposure occurs. Generally, sensitivity to teratogens begins at about 3 weeks after conception (Webster et al., 2018). Structural defects occur when the embryo is exposed to a teratogen while that part of the body is developing. As shown in Figure 3.6, each organ of the body has a sensitive period in development during which it is most susceptible to damage from teratogens such as drugs, alcohol, and environmental contaminants. Once a body part is fully formed, it is less likely to be harmed by exposure to teratogens; however, some body parts, like the brain, remain vulnerable throughout pregnancy.

- **Dose.** The amount of exposure (i.e., dose level) to a teratogen influences its effects. Generally, the greater the dose, the more damage to development. However, teratogens also differ in their strength. Some teratogens, like alcohol, display a powerful dose–response relationship so that larger doses, or heavier and more frequent drinking, result in greater damage (Muggli et al., 2017).

- **Individual Differences.** Individuals vary in their susceptibility to particular teratogens based on the genetic makeup of both the organism and mother, as well as the quality of the prenatal environment.

- **Complicated Effects.** Different teratogens can cause the same birth defect, and a variety of birth defects can result from the same teratogen. Also, some teratogens have subtle effects that result in **developmental delays** that are not obvious at birth. For example, infants exposed prenatally to as little as an ounce of alcohol a day may display no obvious physical deformities at birth but later, as children, may demonstrate cognitive delays (Charness, Riley, & Sowell, 2016).

FIGURE 3.6

Sensitive Periods in Prenatal Development

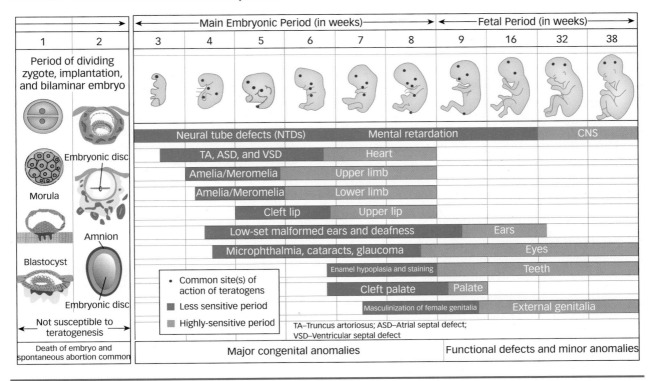

1	2	Main Embryonic Period (in weeks)						Fetal Period (in weeks)			
		3	4	5	6	7	8	9	16	32	38

Period of dividing zygote, implantation, and bilaminar embryo

Embryonic disc

Morula

Amnion

Blastocyst

Embryonic disc

Not susceptible to teratogenesis

Death of embryo and spontaneous abortion common

Neural tube defects (NTDs) | Mental retardation | CNS

TA, ASD, and VSD | Heart

Amelia/Meromelia | Upper limb

Amelia/Meromelia | Lower limb

Cleft lip | Upper lip

Low-set malformed ears and deafness | Ears

Microphthalmia, cataracts, glaucoma | Eyes

Enamel hypoplasia and staining | Teeth

Cleft palate | Palate

Masculinization of female genitalia | External genitalia

- Common site(s) of action of teratogens
- ■ Less sensitive period
- ■ Highly-sensitive period

TA–Truncus artoriosus; ASD–Atrial septal defect; VSD–Ventricular septal defect

Major congenital anomalies | Functional defects and minor anomalies

Source: Levine and Munsch (2010, p. 113).

Other teratogens display **sleeper effects**—effects that are not visible until many years later. For example, infants born to women who consumed diethylstilbestrol (DES), a hormone that was widely prescribed between 1945 and 1970 to prevent miscarriages, were born healthy but as adults were more likely to experience problems with their reproductive systems. Daughters born to mothers who took DES were more likely to develop a rare form of cervical cancer, have miscarriages, and give birth to infants who were premature or low birthweight (Conlon, 2017).

Types of Teratogens

Prenatal development can be influenced by many contextual factors, including maternal consumption of over-the-counter (OTC), prescription, and recreational drugs; illness; environmental factors; and more. Sometimes a pregnant woman and her doctor must make a difficult choice between forgoing a needed prescription drug and putting the fetus at risk. In those cases, the woman and

More than 90% of pregnant women take prescription or over-the-counter (OTC) medications. The findings regarding the teratogenic effects of drugs are mixed, with some studies suggesting potential harm and others suggesting no ill effects of a given drug.
Gary Friedman/Los Angeles Times via Getty Images

her doctor must weigh not just the benefits of the medication but also the potential harm from forgoing it compared with the risks to the fetus. Frequently, the risks are deemed as justified to protect the woman's mental and physical health.

And, in any case, a woman may not know she is pregnant until after the first few weeks of the embryonic stage are already past. Thus, in the real world, almost no pregnancy can be entirely free of exposure to teratogens. However, each year, about 97% of infants are born without defects (Centers for Disease Control and Prevention, 2017a).

Prescription and Nonprescription Drugs

More than 90% of pregnant women take prescription or OTC medications (Servey & Chang, 2014). Prescription drugs that can act as teratogens include antibiotics, certain hormones, antidepressants, anticonvulsants, and some acne drugs (Webster et al., 2018). In several cases, physicians have unwittingly prescribed drugs to ease pregnant women's discomfort that caused harm to the fetus. For example, in the late 1950s and early 1960s, many pregnant women were prescribed thalidomide to prevent morning sickness. However, it was found that taking thalidomide 4 to 6 weeks after conception (in some cases, even just one dose) caused deformities of the child's arms and legs, and, less frequently, damage to the ears, heart, kidneys, and genitals (Fraga et al., 2016). Isotretinoin, a form of vitamin A used to treat acne, is a potent teratogen associated with miscarriage as well as severe face, heart, and central nervous system abnormalities, as well as intellectual disability (Henry et al., 2016; Wilson, 2016). The teratogenic effect of isotretinoin is so severe that the U.S. Food and Drug Administration (2010) requires that women prescribed isotretinoin take physician-administered pregnancy tests for 2 months prior to beginning treatment and agree to use two methods of birth control and complete a monthly pregnancy test each month while taking it.

Nonprescription drugs, such as diet pills and cold medicine, can also cause harm, but research on OTC drugs lags far behind research on prescription drugs, and we know little about the teratogenic effect of many OTC drugs (Hussain & Ashmead, 2017). Frequently, findings regarding the teratogenic effects of drugs are mixed, with some studies suggesting potential harm and others suggesting no ill effects of a given drug. For example, some research suggests that high doses of the common painkiller aspirin may be associated with an increased risk of miscarriage and poor fetal growth (Elkarmi, Abu-Samak, & Al-Qaisi, 2007; Li, Liu, & Odouli, 2003). Yet low doses of aspirin may have benefits. Physicians commonly prescribe a low dose to prevent and treat preeclampsia and high blood pressure during pregnancy (Roberge, Bujold, & Nicolaides, 2017). Likewise, the most common OTC drug consumed during pregnancy, caffeine, found in coffee, tea, cola drinks, and chocolate, appears to be safe in low doses (200 milligrams or about one cup per day; March of Dimes, 2015). Heavy caffeine consumption, however, is associated with an increased risk for miscarriage and low birthweight (Chen et al., 2014, 2016).

Alcohol

An estimated 10% to 20% of Canadian and U.S. women report consuming alcohol during pregnancy (Alshaarawy, Breslau, & Anthony, 2016; Popova, Lange, Probst, Parunashvili, & Rehm, 2017).

Indeed, alcohol abuse during pregnancy has been identified as the leading cause of developmental disabilities (Webster et al., 2018). **Fetal alcohol spectrum disorders** refer to the continuum of effects of exposure to alcohol, which vary with the timing and amount of exposure (Hoyme et al., 2016). Fetal alcohol spectrum disorders are estimated to affect as many as 2% to 5% of younger schoolchildren in the United States and Western Europe (May et al., 2014). At the extreme end of the spectrum is **fetal alcohol syndrome (FAS),** a cluster of defects appearing after heavy prenatal exposure to alcohol. FAS is associated

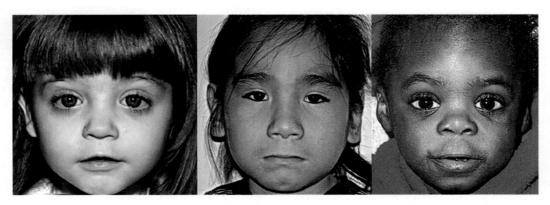

Fetal alcohol syndrome is associated with distinct facial characteristics, growth deficiencies, and deficits in intellectual development, language, motor coordination, and the combined abilities to plan, focus attention, and problem solve that persist throughout childhood and into adulthood.
Susan Astley, PhD, University of Washington

with a distinct pattern of facial characteristics (such as small head circumference, short nose, small eye opening, and small midface), pre- and postnatal growth deficiencies, and deficits in intellectual development, school achievement, memory, visuospatial skills, attention, language, problem solving, motor coordination, and the combined abilities to plan, focus attention, problem solve, and use goal-directed behavior (Gupta, Gupta, & Shirasaka, 2016; Wilhoit, Scott, & Simecka, 2017). The effects of exposure to alcohol within the womb persist throughout childhood and adolescence and are associated with cognitive, learning, and behavioral problems from childhood and adolescence through adulthood (Mamluk et al., 2016; Panczakiewicz et al., 2016; Rangmar et al., 2015).

Even moderate drinking is harmful as children may be born displaying some but not all of the problems of FAS, *fetal alcohol effects* (Hoyme et al., 2016). Consuming 7 to 14 drinks per week during pregnancy is associated with lower birth size, growth deficits through adolescence, and deficits in attention, memory, and cognitive development (Alati et al., 2013; Flak et al., 2014; Lundsberg et al., 2015). Even less than one drink per day has been associated with poor fetal growth and preterm delivery (Mamluk et al., 2017). Scientists have yet to determine if there is a safe level of drinking, but the only way to be certain of avoiding alcohol-related risks is to avoid alcohol during pregnancy altogether.

Cigarette Smoking

Every package of cigarettes sold in the United States includes a warning about the dangers of smoking while pregnant. Fetal deaths, premature births, and low birthweight are up to twice as frequent in mothers who are smokers than in those who do not smoke (Juárez & Merlo, 2013). Infants exposed to smoke while in the womb are prone to congenital heart defects, respiratory problems, and sudden infant death syndrome and, as children, show more behavior problems, have attention difficulties, and score lower on intelligence and achievement tests (He et al., 2017; Lee & Lupo, 2013; Sutin et al., 2017). Moreover, maternal smoking during pregnancy shows epigenetic effects on offspring, influencing predispositions to illness and disease in childhood, adolescence, and even middle adulthood (Joubert et al., 2016; Tehranifar et al., 2018). There is no safe level of smoking during pregnancy. Even babies born to light smokers (one to five cigarettes per day) show higher rates of low birthweight than do babies born to nonsmokers (Berlin, Golmard, Jacob, Tanguy, & Heishman, 2017; Tong, England, Rockhill, & D'Angelo, 2017). Quitting smoking before or during pregnancy reduces the risk of adverse pregnancy outcomes.

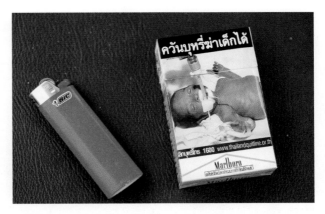

Smoking cigarettes during pregnancy is associated with adverse consequences.
iStock/Jan-Otto

Marijuana

The effects of marijuana on prenatal development are not well understood. Marijuana use during early pregnancy negatively affects fetal length and birthweight (Gunn et al., 2016). Prenatal exposure to marijuana is associated with impairments in attention, memory, and executive function as well as impulsivity in children, adolescents, and young adults (Grant, Petroff, Isoherranen, Stella, & Burbacher, 2018; Smith et al., 2016). Prenatal exposure to marijuana is associated with a thinner cortex, the outer layer of the brain, in late childhood, suggesting that there are long-term neurological effects (El Marroun et al., 2016). Researchers and health practitioners have thus concluded that it is important to educate the public about the impact of marijuana on pregnancy and to discourage the use of medical marijuana by pregnant women or women considering pregnancy (Chasnoff, 2017).

Cocaine and Heroin

Infants exposed to cocaine and heroin face special challenges, such as signs of addiction and withdrawal symptoms, including tremors, irritability, abnormal crying, disturbed sleep, and impaired motor control (Gupta, 2017; Raffaeli et al., 2017). Prenatal exposure to cocaine and heroin is associated with low birthweight, impaired motor skills, and reduced cortical and subcortical brain volume at birth and in infancy (Grewen et al., 2014; Warton et al., 2018). Exposure to these drugs during prenatal development influences brain development, particularly the regions associated with attention, arousal, and regulation (Bazinet, Squeglia, Riley, & Tapert, 2016; Levine & Woodward, 2018). For example, at 1 month after birth, babies who were exposed to cocaine have difficulty regulating their arousal states and show poor movement skills, poor reflexes, and greater excitability (Fallone et al., 2014).

Maternal Drug Use While Pregnant

Is maternal alcohol and substance use during pregnancy child abuse?
iStock/vchal

We have seen that exposure to teratogens such as drugs and alcohol adversely affects the developing fetus. Is maternal substance use fetal abuse? For many states, the answer is yes. Although laws are generally intended to promote health and protect fetuses, some developmental scientists and policy analysts argue that state laws are punitive as they potentially threaten women with involuntary treatment or protective custody during pregnancy (Seiler, 2016). As of 2017, 34 states had laws related to reporting of alcohol consumption during pregnancy (Alcohol Policy Information System, 2018). One half of states classify controlled substance use during pregnancy as child abuse, which may lead to removing the infant from parental custody or even terminating parental rights (Guttmacher Institute, 2018). In some cases, these consequences have been extended to include alcohol abuse and dependence (Paltrow & Flavin, 2013; Seiler, 2016).

Both the American College of Obstetricians and Gynecologists (2011) and the American Medical Association (2014) argue that criminal sanctions for maternal drug use are ineffective as they increase the risk of harm by discouraging prenatal and postnatal care and undermining the physician–patient relationship. Such policies can cause women to develop a mistrust in medical professionals that ultimately harms their care if they become reluctant to seek medical care for themselves and their children. Others argue that these policies are discriminatory toward women of color and those in low socioeconomic status brackets because low-income African American and Hispanic women are disproportionately tested and tried for substance use (Paltrow & Flavin, 2013). For example, a study of one California county with universal screening policies requiring drug and alcohol testing for all pregnant women found that, although Black and White women showed similar rates of drug and alcohol use, Black women were four times more likely than White women to be reported to child protective services after delivery (Roberts & Nuru-Jeter, 2012). Moreover, some experts argue that mandatory drug testing violates women's rights as they are treated differently under the law compared with men because of their sex and pregnancy status (Hui, Angelotta, & Fisher, 2017). Punitive approaches to maternal substance use that favor criminal charges over substance abuse treatment may pit the interdependent interests of the mother and fetus against each other. Some argue that there is no evidence that punitive measures improve maternal or fetal outcomes. Instead, fetal outcomes as supported by substance abuse treatment that rewards abstention, invests in family and community supports, and promotes contact with health care and social support services hold the most promise (Bada et al., 2012; Hui et al., 2017).

What Do You Think?

1. In your view, is substance use during pregnancy a form of abuse? Why or why not?

2. What do you think could be done to reduce the prevalence of substance use by pregnant women? ●

Although it was once believed that cocaine- and heroin-exposed infants would suffer lifelong cognitive deficits, research suggests more subtle effects (Behnke & Smith, 2013; Lambert & Bauer, 2012). Prenatal cocaine or heroin exposure has a small but lasting effect on attention and behavioral control, as well as language skills through late childhood (Singer, Minnes, Min, Lewis, & Short, 2015; Viteri et al., 2015). In adolescence, prenatal exposure to cocaine is associated with behavior problems and substance use (Min, Minnes, Yoon, Short, & Singer, 2014; Richardson, Goldschmidt, Larkby, & Day, 2015).

The challenge of determining the effects of prenatal exposure to cocaine and heroin is that most cocaine- and heroin-exposed infants were also exposed to other substances, including tobacco, alcohol, and marijuana, making it difficult to isolate the effect of each drug on prenatal development. We must be cautious in interpreting findings about illicit drug use and the effects on prenatal development because many other contextual factors often co-occur with parental substance use and also pose risks for development. These risks include poverty, malnutrition, inconsistent parenting, stress, and diminished parental responsiveness (Smith et al., 2016). For example, parents who abuse drugs tend to provide poorer quality care, a home environment less conducive to cognitive development, and parent–child interaction that is less sensitive and positive than the environments provided by other parents (Hatzis, Dawe, Harnett, & Barlow, 2017). Children raised by substance-abusing parents are at risk for being subjected to overly harsh discipline and lack of supervision as well as disruptions in care due to factors such as parental incarceration, inability to care for a child, and even death (e.g., from a drug overdose or violence).

At the same time, quality care can lessen the long-term impact of prenatal exposure to substances (Calhoun, Conner, Miller, & Messina, 2015). Some evidence suggests, for example, that developmental differences in exposed infants are reduced and often disappear when medical and environmental factors are considered (Behnke & Smith, 2013). Disentangling the long-term effects of prenatal exposure to substances, subsequent parenting, and contextual factors is challenging. Researchers and health care providers who construct interventions must address the contextual and parenting-related risk factors to improve the developmental outlook for children exposed to drugs prenatally. The accompanying Applying Developmental Science feature examines the difficulties of addressing maternal drug use in the legal system.

Maternal Illness

Depending on the type and when it occurs, an illness experienced by the mother during pregnancy can have devastating consequences for the developing fetus. For example, rubella (German measles) prior to the 11th week of pregnancy can cause a variety of defects, including blindness, deafness, heart defects, and brain damage, but after the first trimester, adverse consequences become less likely (Bouthry et al., 2014). Other illnesses have varying effects on the fetus. For example, chicken pox can produce birth defects affecting the arms, legs, eyes, and brain; mumps can increase the risk of miscarriage (Mehta, 2016; Webster et al., 2018). In addition to posing risks to development, some sexually transmitted infections (STIs), such as syphilis, can be transmitted to the fetus during pregnancy (Tsimis & Sheffield, 2017). Others, such as gonorrhea, genital herpes, and **human immunodeficiency virus (HIV)**, can be transmitted as the child passes through the birth canal during birth or through bodily fluids after birth. Since some diseases, such as mumps and rubella, can be prevented with vaccinations, it is important for women who are considering becoming pregnant to discuss their immunization status with their health care provider.

Some illnesses with teratogenic effects, such as the mosquito-borne Zika virus, are not well understood. Children born to women infected with the Zika virus are at greater risk of microencephaly, reduced head size (Prakalapakorn, Meaney-Delman, Honein, & Rasmussen, 2017). They may also show a pattern of defects now known as *congenital Zika syndrome*, which includes severe microcephaly characterized by partial skull collapse, damage to the back of the eye, and body deformities, including joints and muscles with restricted range of motion (Centers for Disease Control and Prevention, 2017c; D. L. Moore, 2017).

Environmental Hazards

Prenatal exposure to chemicals, radiation, air pollution, and extremes of heat and humidity can impair development. Infants prenatally exposed to heavy metals, such as lead and mercury, whether through ingestion or inhalation, score lower on tests of cognitive ability and intelligence, as well as have higher rates of childhood illness (Sadler, 2015; Vigeh, Yokoyama, Matsukawa, Shinohara, & Ohtani, 2014; Xie et al., 2013). Exposure to radiation can cause genetic mutations. Infants born to mothers pregnant during the atomic bomb explosions in Hiroshima and Nagasaki and after the nuclear power accident at Chernobyl displayed many physical deformities, mutations, and intellectual deficits. Prenatal exposure to radiation is associated

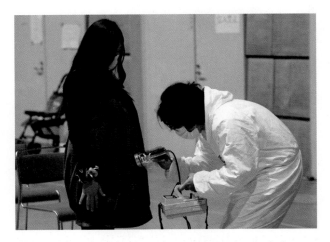

In April 2011, an earthquake and tsunami severly crippled a Japanese nuclear reactor. Hiromi Kobayashi, who was eight months pregnant, was tested for possible nuclear radiation exposure at an evacuation center.
Reuters/Kim Kyung Hoon

with Down syndrome, reduced head circumference, intellectual disability, reduced intelligence scores and school performance, and heightened risk for cancer (Chang, Lasley, Das, Mendonca, & Dynlacht, 2014). About 85% of the world's birth defects occur in developing countries, supporting the role of context in influencing prenatal development directly via environmental hazards but also indirectly through the opportunities and resources for education, health, and financial support (Weinhold, 2009).

Parental Characteristics and Behaviors

Teratogens—and the avoidance of them—are, of course, not the only determinants of how healthy a baby will be. A pregnant woman's characteristics, such as her age and her behavior during pregnancy, including nutrition and emotional well-being, also influence prenatal outcomes.

Nutrition. Nutrition plays a role in prenatal development both before and after conception. The quality of men's and women's diets influences the health of the sperm and egg (Sinclair & Watkins, 2013). Most women need to consume 2,200 to 2,900 calories per day to sustain a pregnancy (Kaiser, Allen, & American Dietetic Association, 2008). Yet about 41 million people in the United States (about 12% of households) reported food insecurity in 2016 (U.S. Department of Agriculture, 2017). That is, at least sometimes they lacked access to enough food for an active healthy lifestyle for all members of the household. About 795 million people of the 7.3 billion people in the world, or one in nine, suffer from chronic undernourishment, almost all of whom live in developing countries (World Hunger Education Service, 2017). Fetal malnutrition is associated with increased susceptibility to complex diseases in postnatal life (Chmurzynska, 2010). Dietary supplements can reduce many of the problems caused by maternal malnourishment, and infants who are malnourished can overcome some of the negative effects if they are raised in enriched environments. However, most children who are malnourished before birth remain malnourished; few have the opportunity to be raised in enriched environments after birth.

Some deficits resulting from an inadequate diet cannot be remedied. For example, inadequate consumption of folic acid (a B vitamin) very early in pregnancy can result in the formation of neural tube defects stemming from the failure of the neural tube to close. **Spina bifida** occurs when the lower part of the neural tube fails to close and spinal nerves begin to grow outside of the vertebrae, often resulting in paralysis. Surgery must be performed before or shortly after birth, but lost capacities cannot be restored (Adzick, 2013). Spina bifida is often accompanied by malformations in brain development and impaired cognitive development (Donnan et al., 2017). Another neural tube defect, **anencephaly**, occurs when the top part of the neural tube fails to close and all or part of the brain fails to develop, resulting in death shortly after birth. As researchers

Good nutrition is important for a healthy pregnancy.
iStock/becon

Some stress during pregnancy is normal, but exposure to chronic and severe stress during pregnancy poses risks including low birthweight, premature birth, and a longer postpartum hospital stay.
iStock/monkeybusinessimages

have learned and disseminated the knowledge that folic acid helps prevent these defects, the frequency of neural tube defects has declined to about 1 in 1,000 births (Viswanathan et al., 2017; Williams et al., 2015). However, in a national study of U.S. mothers, only 24% consumed the recommended dose of folic acid during pregnancy (Tinker, Cogswell, Devine, & Berry, 2010).

Emotional well-being. Although stress is inherently part of almost everyone's life, exposure to chronic and severe stress during pregnancy poses risks, including low birthweight, premature birth, and a longer postpartum hospital stay (Field, 2011; Schetter & Tanner, 2012). Maternal stress influences prenatal development because stress hormones cross the placenta, raising the fetus's heart rate and activity level. Long-term exposure to stress hormones in utero is associated with higher levels of stress hormones in newborns (Kapoor, Lubach, Ziegler, & Coe, 2016). As a result, the newborn may be more irritable and active than a low-stress infant and may have difficulties in sleep, digestion, and self-regulation (Davis, Glynn, Waffarn, & Sandman, 2011; Kingston, Tough, & Whitfield, 2012). Later in childhood, he or she may have symptoms of anxiety, attention-deficit hyperactivity disorder, and aggression (Glover, 2011). Prenatal stress may also have epigenetic effects on development, influencing stress responses throughout the lifespan (Van den Bergh et al., 2017). Stress in the home may make it difficult for parents to respond with warmth and sensitivity to an irritable infant (Crnic & Ross, 2017). Social support can mitigate the effects of stress on pregnancy and

infant care (Feldman, Dunkel-Schetter, Sandman, & Wadhwa, 2000; Ghosh, Wilhelm, Dunkel-Schetter, Lombardi, & Ritz, 2010).

Maternal age. U.S. women are becoming pregnant at later ages than ever before. As shown in Figure 3.7, since 1990, the pregnancy rate has increased for women ages 35 to 39 and 40 to 44 and decreased slightly for women in their 20s (Hamilton et al., 2017). Does maternal age matter? Women who give birth over the age of 35, and especially over 40, are at greater risk for pregnancy and birth complications, including miscarriage and stillbirth, than are younger women. They are more vulnerable to pregnancy-related illnesses such as hypertension and diabetes, and their pregnancies involve increased risks to the newborn, including low birthweight, preterm birth, respiratory problems, and related conditions requiring intensive neonatal care (Grotegut et al., 2014; Kenny et al., 2013; Khalil, Syngelaki, Maiz, Zinevich, & Nicolaides, 2013). The risk of having a child with Down syndrome also increases sharply with maternal age, especially after age 40 (Hazlett, Hammer, Hooper, & Kamphaus, 2011) (see Figure 3.8).

Although risks for complications rise linearly with each year (Yaniv et al., 2011), it is important to realize that the majority of women over age 35 give birth to healthy infants. Differences in context and behavior may compensate for some of the risks of advanced maternal age. For example, longer use of oral contraceptives is associated with a lower risk of giving birth to a child with Down syndrome (Nagy, Győrffy, Nagy, & Rigó, 2013).

FIGURE 3.7

Birth Rates, by Selected Age of Mother, United States, 1990–2016

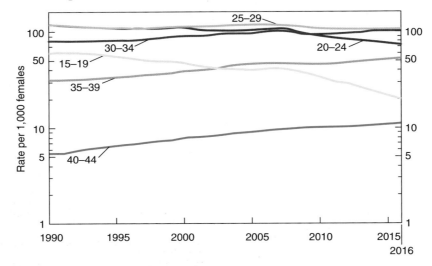

Source: Hamilton et al., 2017.

FIGURE 3.8

Maternal Age and Risk of Down Syndrome

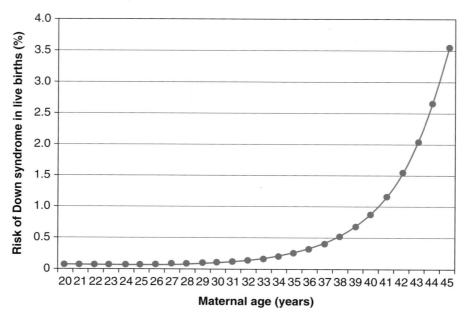

Although the risk for Down syndrome increases dramatically with maternal age, most infants are born healthy, regardless of maternal age.

Source: Reprinted with permission from Down Syndrome: Prenatal Risk Assessment and Diagnosis, August 15, 2000, Vol 62, No 4, *American Family Physician.* Copyright © 2000 American Academy of Family Physicians. All Rights Reserved.

THINKING IN CONTEXT 3.2

1. Referring to Bronfenbrenner's bioecological model (see Chapter 1), identify factors at each bioecological level that may influence development in the womb.

2. Imagine that you are a health care provider conferring with a woman who is contemplating becoming pregnant. Give some examples of specific advice you would offer to help her promote a healthy pregnancy and baby.

CHILDBIRTH

» LO 3.3   Explain the process of childbirth.

At about 40 weeks of pregnancy, or 38 weeks after conception, childbirth, also known as **labor,** begins.

Labor

Labor progresses in three stages. The first stage of labor, *dilation,* is the longest. It typically lasts 8 to 14 hours for a woman having her first child; for later-born children, the average is 3 to 8 hours. Labor begins when the mother experiences regular uterine contractions spaced at 10- to 15-minute intervals. Initial contractions may feel like a backache or

menstrual cramps or may be extremely sharp. The amniotic sac ("water") may rupture at any time during this stage. The contractions, which gradually become stronger and closer together, cause the cervix to dilate so that the fetus's head can pass through, as shown in Figure 3.9.

The second stage of labor, *delivery,* begins when the cervix is fully dilated to 10 cm and the fetus's head is positioned at the opening of the cervix—known as "crowning." It ends when the baby emerges completely from the mother's body. It is during this stage that the mother typically feels an urge to push or bear down with each contraction to assist the birth process. Delivery can take from 30 minutes to an hour and a half.

In the third stage of labor, the placenta separates from the uterine wall and is expelled by uterine contractions. This typically happens about 5 to 15 minutes after the baby has emerged, and the process can take up to a half hour.

Medication During Delivery

Medication is administered in over 80% of births in the United States (Declercq, Sakala, Corry, Applebaum, & Herrlich, 2014). Several drugs are used during labor, with varying effects. *Analgesics,* such as tranquilizers, may be used in small doses to relieve pain and to help the mother relax. These drugs pass through the placenta to the fetus and are associated

FIGURE 3.9

Stages of Labor

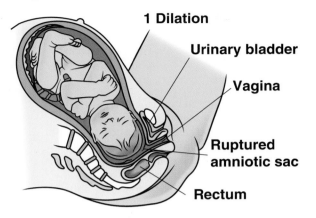

1 Dilation
- Urinary bladder
- Vagina
- Ruptured amniotic sac
- Rectum

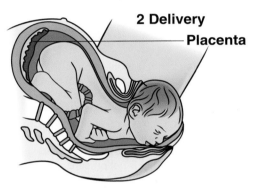

2 Delivery
- Placenta

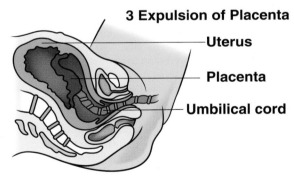

3 Expulsion of Placenta
- Uterus
- Placenta
- Umbilical cord

Source: Adapted from Gerard J. Tortora and Bryan H. Derrickson, 2009.

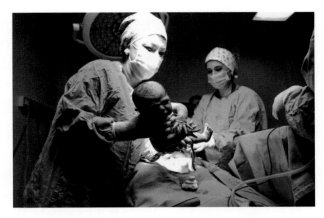

Childbirth, also known as labor and delivery, progresses in three stages.
Pacific Press/Sipa USA/Newscom

with decreases in heart rate and respiration (Hacker, Gambone, & Hobel, 2016). Newborns exposed to some medications show signs of sedation and difficulty regulating their temperature (Gabbe et al., 2016). *Anesthesia* is a painkiller that blocks sensations. General anesthesia (getting "knocked out") blocks consciousness entirely; it is no longer used because it is transmitted to the fetus and can slow labor and harm the fetus. Today, the most common anesthetic is an **epidural,** in which a regional anesthetic drug is administered to a small space between the vertebrae of the lower spine. The woman's lower body is numbed. There are several types of epidurals, with varying numbing effects ranging from immobilizing the lower body to numbing only the pelvic region, enabling the mother to move about (a so-called walking epidural). Epidurals, however, are associated with a longer delivery as they weaken uterine contractions and may increase the risk of a cesarean section, as discussed next (Gabbe et al., 2016; Herrera-Gómez et al., 2017).

Cesarean Delivery

Sometimes a vaginal birth is not possible because of concerns for the health or safety of the mother or fetus. For example, normally the baby's head is the first part of the body to exit the vagina. A baby facing feet-first is said to be in a **breech position,** which poses risks to the health of the baby. Sometimes the obstetrician can turn the baby so that it is head-first. In other cases, a **cesarean section,** or C-section, is common. A cesarean section is a surgical procedure that removes the fetus from the uterus through the abdomen. About 32% of U.S. births were by cesarean section in 2016 (Martin, Hamilton, Osterman, Driscoll, & Drake, 2018). Cesarean sections are performed when labor progresses too slowly, the fetus is in breech position or transverse position (crosswise in the uterus), the head is too large to pass through the pelvis, or the fetus or mother is in danger (Jha, Baliga, Kumar, Rangnekar, & Baliga, 2015; Visscher & Narendran, 2014). Babies delivered by cesarean are exposed to more maternal medication and secrete lower levels of the stress hormones that occur with vaginal birth that are needed to facilitate respiration, enhance circulation of blood to the brain, and help the infant adapt to the world outside of the womb. Interactions between mothers and infants, however, are similar for infants delivered vaginally and by cesarean section (Durik, Hyde, & Clark, 2000).

Cultural Differences in Childbirth

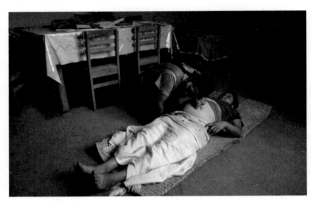

A midwife prepares a mother to give birth in her home. Birth practices vary by culture.
Stephanie Maze/Corbis

Societies vary in their customs and perceptions of childbirth, including the privacy afforded to giving birth and how newborns are integrated into the community. In the United States, birth is a private event that usually occurs in a hospital, attended by medical personnel and one or two family members. In most cases, the first-time mother has never witnessed a birth but is well educated and may have well-informed expectations. After birth, the mother and infant are often visited by family within designated hospital visiting hours; the newborn usually rooms with the mother all or part of the day.

In a small village in southern Italy, birth is a community event. It usually takes place in a hospital, attended by a midwife (Fogel, 2007; Schreiber, 1977). Just after birth, the midwife brings the mother's entire family (immediate and extended) to the mother's room and they take turns congratulating the mother and baby, kissing them. The family provides a party, including pastry and liqueurs. During labor and afterward, the mother is supported and visited by many of her friends and relatives to recognize the contribution that the mother has made to the community. The mother-in-law is an example of the social support system in place because a few days before and until about 1 month after the birth, she brings and feeds the mother ritual foods of broth, marsala, and fresh cheeses (Fogel, 2007; Schreiber, 1977).

In some other cultures, birth is an even more public process. The Jahara of South America give birth under a shelter in full view of everyone in the village (Fogel, 2007). On the Indonesian island of Bali, it is assumed that the husband, children, and other family will want to be present. The birth occurs in the home with the aid of a midwife and female relatives. As a result, Balinese women know what to expect in giving birth to their first child because they have been present at many births (Diener, 2000). The baby is immediately integrated into the family and community as

he or she is considered a reincarnated soul of an ancestor. Many kin are present to support the mother and baby since the child is considered to be related to many more people than its parents.

Childbirth is tied to social status in the Brong-Ahafo Region in Ghana. After a delivery, women achieve a higher social position and can then give advice to other women (Jansen, 2006). Home deliveries are highly valued. The more difficult the delivery and the less skilled assistance she receives, the more respect a woman attains, the higher her position will be, and the more influence she has on the childbirth decisions of other women, such as whether to give birth at home or in a medical setting and how to combine traditional and modern practices (Bazzano, Kirkwood, Tawiah-Agyemang, Owusu-Agyei, & Adongo, 2008).

Many cultures conduct rites that they believe protect newborns from evil and spirits. Among the Maya of the Yucatan region of Mexico, there are few changes in the expectant mother's surroundings; the Mayan woman lies in the same hammock in which she sleeps each night. The father-to-be is expected to be present during labor and birth to take an active role but also to witness the suffering that accompanies labor. If the father is not present and the child is stillborn, it is blamed on the father's absence. The pregnant woman's mother is present, often in the company of other females, including sisters, sisters-in-law, mothers-in-law, godmothers, and sometimes neighbors and close friends. The mother and child must remain inside the house for 1 week before returning to normal activity after birth because it is believed that the mother and newborn are susceptible to the influence of evil spirits from the bush (Gardiner & Kosmitzki, 2018).

A neighboring ethnic group, the Zinacanteco, place their newborns naked before a fire. The midwife who assisted the mother says prayers asking the gods to look kindly upon the infant. The infant is dressed in a long skirt made of heavy fabric extending beyond the feet; this garment is to be worn throughout the first year. The newborn is then wrapped in several layers of blankets, even covering the face, to protect against losing parts of the soul. These traditional practices are believed to protect the infant from illnesses as well as evil spirits (Brazelton, 1977; Fogel, 2007).

What Do You Think?

1. Which of these birthing customs most appeals to you? Why?

2. If you, a family member, or friend have given birth, describe the process. Where did the birth occur? Who witnessed it? What happened afterward? When did family and friends meet the baby? ●

Natural Childbirth

Natural childbirth is an approach to birth that reduces pain through the use of breathing and relaxation exercises. Natural childbirth methods emphasize preparation by educating mothers and their partners about childbirth, helping them to reduce their fear, and teaching them pain management techniques. Although most women use at least some medication in childbirth, many women adopt some natural childbirth methods.

The most widely known natural childbirth method—the Lamaze method—was created by a French obstetrician, Ferdinand Lamaze (1956). The Lamaze method entails teaching pregnant women about their bodies, including detailed anatomical information, with the intent of reducing anxiety and fear. When women know what to expect and learn a breathing technique to help them relax, they are better able to manage the pain of childbirth. The Lamaze method relies on the spouse or partner as coach, providing physical and emotional support and reminding her to use the breathing techniques.

In addition to the expectant mother's partner, a **doula** can be an important source of support. A doula is a caregiver who provides support to an expectant mother and her partner throughout the birth process (Kang, 2014). Doulas provide education about anatomy, delivery, and pain management practices, such as breathing. The doula is present during birth, whether at a hospital or other setting, and helps the woman carry out her birth plans. The presence of a doula is associated with less pain medication, fewer cesarean deliveries, and higher rates of satisfaction in new mothers (Gabbe et al., 2016; Kozhimannil et al., 2016).

Home Birth

Although common in nonindustrialized nations, home birth is rare, comprising 1.5% of all births in 2016 in the United States (MacDorman & Declercq, 2016). The remaining 98% of births occur in hospitals. Most home births are managed by a **midwife**, a health care professional, usually a nurse, who specializes in childbirth. Midwives provide health care throughout pregnancy and supervise home births. One review of 50 studies found that the use of midwives, whether as part of a home birthing plan or as part of a plan to birth in a hospital setting, is associated with reduced neonatal mortality, reduced preterm birth, fewer interventions, and more efficient use of medical resources (Renfrew et al., 2014).

Is a home birth safe? A healthy woman, who has received prenatal care and is not carrying twins, is unlikely to encounter problems requiring intervention—and may be a good candidate for a home birth (Wilbur, Little, & Szymanski, 2015). Although unpredictable events can occur and

immediate access to medical facilities can improve outcomes, studies from Europe indicate that home birth is not associated with greater risk of perinatal mortality. However, home birth is far more common in many European countries than the United States (20% in the Netherlands, 8% in the United Kingdom, and about 1% in the United States) (Brocklehurst et al., 2011; de Jonge et al., 2015). The few U.S. studies that have examined planned home birth compared with hospital birth have found no difference in neonatal deaths or Apgar scores, and women who have a planned home birth report high rates of satisfaction (Jouhki, Suominen, & Åstedt-Kurki, 2017; Zielinski, Ackerson, & Kane Low, 2015). Cultures vary in their approach to birth, as discussed in the Cultural Influences on Development feature.

THINKING IN CONTEXT 3.3

1. Given what you know, create a birth plan for a healthy woman in her 20s. Would you choose a hospital or home birth? Why? How would your plan address the expectant mother's need for pain relief?

2. If possible, ask adults of different generations, perhaps a parent or an aunt and a grandparent or family friend, about their birth experiences. How do these recollections compare with current birthing practices?

The Newborn

>> **LO 3.4**   **Discuss the neonate's physical capacities, including development in low-birthweight infants.**

The average newborn is about 20 inches long and weighs about 7½ pounds. Boys tend to be slightly longer and heavier than girls. Newborns have distinctive features, including a large head (about ¼ of body length) that is often long and misshapen from passing through the birth canal. The newborn's skull bones are not yet fused—and will not be until about 18 months of age—permitting the bones to move and the head to mold to the birth canal, easing its passage. A healthy newborn is red-skinned and wrinkly at birth; skin that is bluish in color indicates that the newborn has experienced oxygen deprivation. Some babies emerge covered with *lanugo,* the fuzzy hair that protects the skin in the womb; for other babies, the lanugo falls off prior to birth. The newborn's body is covered with *vernix caseosa,* a waxy substance that protects against infection; this dries up within the first few days. Although many hospital staff wash the vernix caseosa away after birth, research suggests that it is a naturally occurring barrier to infection and should be retained at birth (Jha et al., 2015).

Medical and Behavioral Assessment of Newborns

After birth, newborns are routinely screened with the **Apgar scale**, which provides a quick and easy overall assessment of the baby's immediate health. As shown in Table 3.1, the Apgar scale is composed of five subtests: appearance (color), pulse (heart rate), grimace (reflex irritability), activity (muscle tone), and respiration (breathing). The newborn is rated 0, 1, or 2 on each subscale for a maximum total score of 10. A score of 4 or lower means that the newborn is in serious condition and requires immediate medical attention. The rating is conducted twice, 1 minute after delivery and again 5 minutes after birth; this timing ensures that hospital staff will monitor the newborn over several minutes. Over 98% of all newborns in the United States achieve a 5-minute score of 7 to 10, indicating good health (Martin, Hamilton, Osterman, Curtin, & Mathews, 2013).

The **Brazelton Neonatal Behavioral Assessment Scale (NBAS)** is an neurobehavioral assessment commonly administered to newborns, especially those who are judged to be at risk (Bartram, Barlow, & Wolke, 2015). It is administered in the first few days after birth to assess the newborn's neurological competence as indicated by the responsiveness to the physical and social environment, perception, and motor skills such as activity level and the ability to bring a hand to the mouth (Nugent, 2013). The NBAS also assesses infants' attention and state changes, including excitability and ability to settle down after being upset. When parents observe and participate in their baby's NBAS screening, they learn about their newborn's perceptual and behavioral capacities and are better able to elicit gazes, quiet fussiness, and tend to be more responsive to their infants (Benzies et al., 2013).

The Newborn's Perceptual Capacities

Until recent decades, it was widely believed that the newborn was perceptually immature—blind and deaf at birth. Developmental researchers now know that the newborn is more perceptually competent than ever imagined. For example, both taste and smell are well developed at birth. Taste appears to function well before birth because research has shown that fetuses swallow sweetened amniotic fluid more quickly than bitter fluid (Ventura & Worobey, 2013). Newborns can discriminate smells and calm in response to the scent of amniotic fluid and other familiar smells (Neshat et al., 2016; Rotstein et al., 2015) The visual capacities of the newborn are more limited and focused primarily on the near environment. Newborn vision is blurry and best at about 18 inches away—the typical distance to a parent's face when holding the infant.

The most remarkable newborn capacities for perception and learning are auditory in nature. Pregnant women often report that they notice fetal movements in response to a loud sound like a car horn or a door slamming. The fetus responds to auditory stimulation as early as 23 to 25 weeks after conception (Hepper, 2015). By 32 to 34 weeks, the fetus responds to the mother's voice as indicated by a change in heart rate (Kisilevsky & Hains, 2011). Prior to birth, the fetus can discriminate voices and speech sounds (Granier-Deferre, Ribeiro, Jacquet, & Bassereau, 2011). At birth, newborns show preferences for speech sounds, their mother's voice, their native language, and even stories and music heard prenatally (Moon, Cooper, & Fifer, 1993). Moreover, from birth, the newborn is an active listener, paying attention to sounds and naturally taking advantage of opportunities to learn (Vouloumanos, Hauser, Werker, & Martin, 2010).

TABLE 3.1

Apgar Scale

INDICATOR	RATING (ABSENCE–PRESENCE)		
	0	1	2
Appearance (color)	Blue	Pink body, blue extremities	Pink
Pulse (heart rate)	Absent	Slow (below 100)	Rapid (over 100)
Grimace (reflex irritability)	No response	Grimace	Coughing, crying
Activity (muscle tone)	Limp	Weak and inactive	Active and strong
Respiration (breathing)	Absent	Irregular and slow	Crying, good

Source: Apgar (1953).

Newborn States of Arousal

Newborns display regular cycles of eating, elimination, and **states of arousal** or degrees of wakefulness. In a typical day, newborns move in and out of six infant states or levels of arousal, as shown in Table 3.2. Most newborns spend about 70% of their time sleeping and wake every 2 to 3 hours. These short stretches of sleep alternate with shorter periods of wakefulness that are primarily devoted to feeding. During the first month, infants often move rapidly from one state to another, dozing off during feeding, for example. Naps are punctuated by periods of drowsiness, alert and inalert activity, and crying.

Newborn sleep cycles are brief, lasting from 45 minutes to 2 to 3 hours, but similar to those of adults in that they consist of both REM sleep, or rapid eye movement (REM) sleep, and non-REM sleep (Korotchikova, Stevenson, Livingstone, Ryan, & Boylan, 2016). When a person is in REM sleep, the brain wave activity is remarkably similar to that of the waking state. The eyes move back and forth beneath closed lids; heart rate, blood pressure, and breathing are uneven; and there are slight body movements. It is sleep. Newborns spend about half of their sleep time in REM, but by ages 3 to 5, children spend about 15% to 20% of their sleep in REM, similar to adults (Grigg-Damberger & Wolfe, 2017; Kobayashi, Good, Mamiya, Skinner, & Garcia-Rill, 2004).

Why do newborns spend so much time in REM sleep? REM sleep is associated with dreaming in both children and adults. Neonates spend about 18 hours sleeping each day and therefore spend little time in the active alert state in which they get stimulation from the environment. REM is a way that the brain stimulates itself, which is important for the growth of the central nervous system (Grigg-Damberger & Wolfe, 2017). This view of REM sleep as serving a self-stimulation function is supported by findings that fetuses and preterm babies, who are even less able to take advantage of external stimulation than are newborns, spend even more time in REM sleep. In addition, neonates with low REM sleep activity tend to score lower on mental tests at 6 months of age (Arditi-Babchuk, Feldman, & Eidelman, 2009).

Low-Birthweight Infants: Preterm and Small-for-Date Babies

About 8% of infants born in the United States each year are low birthweight (Martin et al., 2013). Low-birthweight infants may be **preterm**, or premature (born before their due date), or **small for date**, who

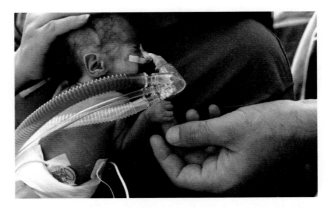

Low-birthweight infants require extensive care. They are at risk for poor developmental outcomes and even death.
Wikimedia

TABLE 3.2

Newborn States of Arousal

STATE	DESCRIPTION	DAILY DURATION IN NEWBORNS
Regular sleep	This is being fully asleep with little or no body movement. The eyes are closed with no eye movements. The face is relaxed, and breathing is slow and regular.	8–9 hours
Irregular sleep	Facial grimaces, limb movements, occasional stirring, and eye movement behind closed lids indicate rapid eye movement (REM) sleep. Breathing is irregular.	8–9 hours
Drowsiness	Falling asleep or waking up, eyes open and closed and have a glazed look. Breathing is even but faster than in regular sleep.	Varies
Quiet alertness	The eyes are open and attentive, exploring the world; the body is relatively inactive. Breathing is even.	2–3 hours
Waking activity	There are frequent bursts of uncoordinated activity. Breathing is irregular; the face may be relaxed or tense. Fussiness and crying may occur.	1–4 hours

Sources: Prechtl (1974); Wolff (1966).

are full term but have experienced slow growth and are smaller than expected for their gestational age. Infants are classified as **low birthweight** when they weigh less than 2,500 grams (5.5 pounds) at birth; **very low birthweight** refers to a weight less than 1,500 grams (3.5 pounds), and **extremely low birthweight** refers to a weight less than 750 grams (1 lb., 10 oz.). Infants who are born with low birthweight are at risk for a variety of developmental difficulties. Indeed, their very survival is far from certain; the Centers for Disease Control and Prevention lists prematurity and low birthweight among the leading causes of infant mortality, accounting for 35% of mortality cases in infancy (Mathews & MacDorman, 2013). Infants most at risk for developmental challenges, handicaps, and difficulty surviving are those with extremely low birthweight. As shown in Figure 3.10, women of color are disproportionately likely to give birth to low-birthweight infants. The socioeconomic inequalities that influence women's ability to seek early prenatal care also influence birth outcomes. Unfortunately, poor access to health care can prevent low-birthweight infants from getting the help that they need to overcome the formidable challenges ahead of them.

Low-birthweight infants are at a disadvantage when it comes to adapting to the world outside the womb. At birth, they often experience difficulty breathing and are likely to suffer from respiratory distress syndrome, in which the newborn breathes irregularly and at times may stop breathing. Low-birthweight infants have difficulty maintaining homeostasis, a balance in their biological functioning. Their survival depends on care in neonatal hospital units, where they are confined in isolettes that separate them from the world, regulating their body temperature, aiding their breathing with the use of respirators, and protecting them from infection. Many low-birthweight infants cannot yet suck from a bottle, so are fed intravenously.

The deficits that low-birthweight infants endure range from mild to severe and correspond closely to the infant's birthweight, with extremely low-birthweight infants suffering the greatest deficits (Hutchinson et al., 2013). Low-birthweight infants are at higher risk for poor growth, cerebral palsy, seizure disorders, neurological difficulties, respiratory problems, and illness (Adams-Chapman et al., 2013; Durkin et al., 2016; Miller et al., 2016). Higher rates of sensory, motor, and cognitive problems mean that low-birthweight children are more likely to require special education and display poor academic achievement in childhood, adolescence, and even adulthood (Eryigit Madzwamuse, Baumann, Jaekel, Bartmann, & Wolke, 2015; Hutchinson et al., 2013; MacKay, Smith, Dobbie, & Pell, 2010).

FIGURE 3.10

Very Low and Low Birthweight Rates, by Maternal Race/Ethnicity, 2015

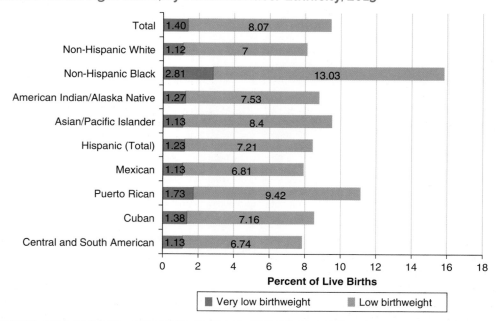

Source: Centers for Disease Control and Prevention, 2018.

HIV Infection in Newborns

Mother-to-child transmission of HIV has declined as scientists have learned more about HIV. However, it remains a worldwide problem especially in developing nations where cultural, economic, and hygienic reasons prevent mothers from seeking alternatives to breastfeeding, a primary cause of mother-to-child transmission of HIV.
Shutterstock/Honeyriko

The rate of mother-to-child transmission of HIV has dropped in recent years as scientists have learned more about HIV. The use of cesarean delivery as well as prescribing anti-HIV drugs to the mother during the second and third trimesters of pregnancy, as well as to the infant for the first 6 weeks of life, has reduced mother-to-child HIV transmission to less than 2% in the United States and Europe (from over 20%) (Torpey, Kabaso, et al., 2010). Aggressive treatment may further reduce the transmission of HIV to newborns, and research suggests that it may even induce remission (National Institute of Allergy and Infectious Diseases, 2014; Pollack & McNeil, 2013; Rainwater-Lovett, Luzuriaga, & Persaud, 2015). However, in developing countries, such interventions are widely unavailable. Worldwide, mother-to-child HIV transmission remains a serious issue. For example, in Zambia, 40,000 infants acquire HIV each year (Torpey, Kasonde, et al., 2010). Treating newborns is critical, although not always possible.

Worldwide, 20% to 30% of neonates with HIV develop AIDS during the first year of life and most die in infancy (United Nations Children's Fund, 2013).

Globally, breastfeeding accounts for 30% to 50% of HIV transmission in newborns (Sullivan, 2003; World Health Organization, 2011). The World Health Organization (2010) recommends providing women who test positive for HIV with information about how HIV may be transmitted to their infants and counseling them not to breastfeed. Yet cultural, economic, and hygienic reasons often prevent mothers in developing nations from seeking alternatives to breastfeeding. For example, the widespread lack of clean water in some countries makes the use of powdered formulas dangerous. Also, in some cultures, women who do not breastfeed may be ostracized from the community (Sullivan, 2003). Balancing cultural values with medical needs is a challenge.

Children with HIV are at high risk for a range of illnesses and health conditions, including chronic bacterial infections; disorders of the central nervous system, heart, gastrointestinal tract, lungs, kidneys, and skin; growth stunting; neurodevelopmental delays, including brain atrophy, which contribute to cognitive and motor impairment; and delays in reaching developmental milestones (Blanchette, Smith, Fernandes-Penney, King, & Read, 2001; Laughton, Cornell, Boivin, & Van Rie, 2013; Sherr, Mueller, & Varrall, 2009).

What Do You Think?

Imagine that you work as an HIV educator with women in an underdeveloped country. What challenges might you face in encouraging women to take steps to reduce the potential for HIV transmission to their infants? How might you help them? ●

Low-birthweight children often experience difficulty in self-regulation, poor social competence, and poor peer relationships, including peer rejection and victimization in adolescence (Georgsdottir, Haraldsson, & Dagbjartsson, 2013; Ritchie, Bora, & Woodward, 2015; Yau et al., 2013). As adults, low-birthweight individuals tend to be less socially engaged, show poor communication skills, and may score high on measures of anxiety (Eryigit Madzwamuse et al., 2015). Frequently, the risk factors for low birthweight, such as prenatal exposure to substances or maternal illness, also pose challenges for postnatal survival. The Lives in Context feature discusses HIV, a risk factor for neonate development.

Not only are low-birthweight infants at a physical disadvantage, but they often begin life at an emotional disadvantage because they are at risk for experiencing difficulties in their relationships with parents. Parenting a low-birthweight infant is stressful even in the best of circumstances (Howe, Sheu, Wang, & Hsu, 2014). Such infants tend to be easily overwhelmed by stimulation and difficult to soothe; they smile less and fuss more than their normal-weight counterparts, making caregivers feel unrewarded for their efforts. Often these infants are slow to initiate social interactions and do not attend to caregivers, looking away or otherwise resisting attempts to attract their attention (Eckerman, Hsu, Molitor, Leung, & Goldstein, 1999). Because low-birthweight infants often do not respond to attempts to solicit interaction, they can be frustrating to interact with, can be difficult to soothe, and are at risk for less secure attachment to their parents (Jean & Stack, 2012; Wolke, Eryigit-Madzwamuse, & Gutbrod, 2014). Research also indicates that they may experience higher rates of child abuse (Cicchetti & Toth, 2015).

Parental responses to having a low-birthweight infant influence the child's long-term health outcomes, independently of perinatal risk, suggesting that the parenting context is an important influence on infant health (Pierrehumbert, Nicole, Muller-Nix, Forcada-Guex, & Ansermet, 2003). When mothers have knowledge about child development and how to foster healthy development, are involved with their children, and create a stimulating home environment, low-birthweight infants tend to have good long-term outcomes (Benasich & Brooks-Gunn, 1996; Jones, Rowe, & Becker, 2009). For example, one study of low-birthweight children showed that those who experienced sensitive parenting showed faster improvements in executive function and were indistinguishable from their normal-weight peers by age 5; however, those who experienced below-average levels of sensitive parenting showed lasting deficits (Camerota, Willoughby, Cox, Greenberg, & the Family Life Project Investigators, 2015). Likewise, exposure to sensitive, positive parenting predicted low-birthweight children's catching up to their normal-birthweight peers at age 8 in academic achievement, but exposure to insensitive parenting predicted much poorer functioning (Jaekel, Pluess, Belsky, & Wolke, 2015). Longitudinal research has found that low-birthweight children raised in unstable, economically disadvantaged families tend to remain smaller in stature, experience more emotional problems, and show more long-term

deficits in intelligence and academic performance than do those raised in more advantaged homes (Taylor, Klein, Minich, & Hack, 2001).

Interventions to promote the development of low-birthweight children often emphasize helping parents learn coping strategies for interacting with their infants and managing parenting stress (Chang et al., 2015; Lau & Morse, 2003). Interventions focused on teaching parents how to massage and touch their infants in therapeutic ways as well as increase skin-to-skin contact with their infants are associated with better cognitive and neurodevelopmental outcomes at age 2 (Procianoy, Mendes, & Silveira, 2010). One intervention common in developing countries where mothers may not have access to hospitals is **kangaroo care,** in which the infant is placed vertically against the parent's chest, under the shirt, providing skin-to-skin contact (Charpak et al., 2005). As the parent goes about daily activities, the infant remains warm and close, hears the voice and heartbeat, smells the body, and feels constant skin-to-skin contact. Kangaroo care is so effective that the majority of hospitals in the United States offer kangaroo care to preterm infants. Babies who receive early and consistent kangaroo care grow more quickly, sleep better, score higher on measures of health, and show more cognitive gains throughout the first year of life (Boundy et al., 2015; Jefferies, 2012).

In summary, a remarkable amount of growth and development takes place between conception and birth. In 9 short months, the zygote transforms into a newborn. Although there are a variety of risks to health development within the womb,

THINKING IN CONTEXT 3.4

1. In what ways might newborns' perceptual capacities and states of arousal help them to adapt to life immediately after birth? Why is mature hearing, relative to vision, useful for infants? Do you think there is a benefit to shifting through several states of arousal?

2. Parental responses to having a low-birthweight infant influence the child's long-term health outcome. How might contextual factors influence parents' responses? What supports from the family, community, and broader society can aid parents in helping their low-birthweight infants adapt and develop healthily?

most newborns are healthy. Infants are born with a surprising array of competencies, such as well-developed hearing, taste, and smell. Additional physical, cognitive, and psychosocial capacities develop shortly after birth, as we will see in upcoming chapters.

 APPLY YOUR KNOWLEDGE

Dr. Preemie conducted a research study of the prevalence and correlates of drug use in college students. Because of the sensitive nature of the research topic, Dr. Preemie promised her participants confidentiality. Each college student who participated completed a set of surveys and an interview about his or her lifestyle and drug use habits. One participant, Carrie, revealed that she engages in moderate to heavy drug use (i.e., drinks two to four alcoholic beverages each day and smokes marijuana several times per week). During the interview, Carrie mentioned that she's feeling nauseous. Concerned, Dr. Preemie asked, "Do you want to stop the interview and go to the campus medical center?" "No," Carrie replied, "It's just morning sickness. I'm pregnant." "Oh," said Dr. Preemie, who nodded and continued with the interview.

Afterward, in her office, Dr. Preemie was torn and wondered to herself, "I'm worried about Carrie. Drugs and alcohol disrupt prenatal development, but I promised confidentiality. I can't tell anyone about this! Should I say something to Carrie? I'm supposed to be nonjudgmental!

Intervening might keep other students from participating in my research, for fear that I'd break my promises. I don't know what to do."

1. What are the effects of teratogens, like drugs and alcohol, on prenatal development?

2. Describe the course of prenatal development. How do the effects of exposure to teratogens change during prenatal development?

3. Consider the ethical principles discussed in Chapter 1. How might Dr. Preemie's obligations conflict? As a researcher, is she responsible to Carrie as a participant in her study who signed an informed consent form? Is Dr. Preemie responsible to the developing fetus? Why or why not? Do Dr. Preemie's actions have any ramifications for the other participants in her study? How might these responsibilities conflict?

4. What should Dr. Preemie do?

$SAGE edge™

Visit **edge.sagepub.com/kuther2e** to help you accomplish your coursework goals in an easy-to-use learning environment.

LEARNING OBJECTIVES	SUMMARY	KEY TERMS	IN REVIEW
3.1 Describe the three periods of prenatal development that begin with conception.	Conception occurs in the fallopian tube. During the germinal period, the zygote begins cell division and travels down the fallopian tube toward the uterus. During the embryonic period from weeks 2 to 8, the most rapid developments of the prenatal period take place. From 9 weeks until birth, the fetus grows rapidly, and the organs become more complex and begin to function.	Hormones Germinal period Cell differentiation Blastocyst Implantation Placenta Embryonic period Embryonic disk Ectoderm Endoderm Mesoderm Neural tube Fetal period Fetus Lanugo Vernix caseosa Age of viability Prenatal care	What are the three periods of prenatal development? What major milestones occur in each period? What are influences on prenatal care?

3.2 Identify how exposure to teratogens can influence the prenatal environment.	Teratogens include diseases, drugs, and other agents that influence the prenatal environment to disrupt development. Generally, the effects of exposure to teratogens on prenatal development vary depending on the stage of prenatal development and dose. There are individual differences in effects, different teratogens can cause the same birth defect, a variety of birth defects can result from the same teratogen, and some teratogens have subtle effects that result in developmental delays that are not obvious at birth or not visible until many years later. Prescription and nonprescription drugs, maternal illnesses, and smoking and alcohol use can harm the developing fetus. Prenatal development can also be harmed by factors in the environment.	Teratogen Teratology Developmental delays Sleeper effects Fetal alcohol spectrum disorders Fetal alcohol syndrome (FAS) Human immunodeficiency virus (HIV) Spina bifida Anencephaly	Define and provide three examples of teratogens. What are four principles that determine the effects of exposure to teratogens during prenatal development?
3.3 Explain the process of childbirth.	Childbirth progresses through three stages. The first stage of labor begins when the mother experiences regular uterine contractions that cause the cervix to dilate. During the second stage, the fetus passes through the birth canal. The placenta is passed during the third stage. Medication is used in most births, often in combination with breathing and relaxation techniques characteristic of natural births. About one third of U.S. births are by cesarean section.	Labor Epidural Breech position Cesarean section Doula Midwife	What are the three stages of childbirth? Describe characteristics of each stage. What are the differences among cesarean delivery, natural childbirth, and home birth?
3.4 Discuss the neonate's physical capacities, including development in low-birthweight infants.	Developmental researchers now know that the newborn is more perceptually competent than ever imagined. For example, both taste and smell are well developed at birth. However, the most well-developed sense is audition. Newborns display regular cycles of eating, elimination, and states of arousal or degrees of wakefulness, spending about 50% of their sleep time in REM, thought to permit the brain to stimulate itself. There are two types of low-birthweight infants, those who are preterm and those who are small for date. Low-birthweight infants struggle to survive. Low-birthweight infants experience higher rates of sensory, motor, and language problems; learning disabilities; behavior problems; and deficits in social skills into adolescence. The long-term outcomes of low birthweight vary considerably and depend on the environment in which the children are raised.	Apgar scale Brazelton Neonatal Behavioral Assessment Scale (NBAS) States of arousal Preterm Small for date Low birthweight Very low birthweight Extremely low birthweight Kangaroo care	How are neonates assessed at birth? Describe the neonate's perceptual capabilities. What are two types of low-birthweight infants? What factors determine long-term outcomes for low-birthweight babies?

PRACTICE AND APPLY WHAT YOU'VE LEARNED

▶ edge.sagepub.com/kuther2e

CHECK YOUR COMPREHENSION ON THE STUDY SITE WITH:

- **Diagnostic Quizzes** to identify opportunities for improvement.

- **Multimedia Resources** that explore chapter content using media and current events.

- **Journal Articles** that support and expand on chapter concepts.

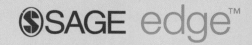

PART II

Infancy and Toddlerhood

CHAPTER 4:
Physical Development in Infancy and Toddlerhood

CHAPTER 5:
Cognitive Development in Infancy and Toddlerhood

CHAPTER 6:
Socioemotional Development in Infancy and Toddlerhood

The most dramatic developments in the lifespan occur in infancy. In addition to tripling their weight during the first year of life, infants progress through an orderly series of motor milestones that transforms them from newborns unable to lift their heads to babies able to roll over, sit up, crawl, and, at about a year of age, walk.

As infants practice their motor skills, they explore their environment, build their understanding of phenomena, and adapt to the world around them. Cognitive changes are supported by brain development. A multitude of new connections among brain cells are created and pruned in response to experience. Naturally primed to learn language, infants discriminate speech sounds from birth and progress steadily from gurgles and coos, to speech-like babbling, to first words.

Warm, sensitive, and responsive interactions with caregivers foster close and secure attachment bonds. Caregivers help infants learn to understand and regulate their emotions. In turn, infants influence their caregivers by smiling, reaching, and crawling to them. Infants' growing ability to express their thoughts and emotions advances parent–child communication and aids in sustaining a secure emotional base that supports their exploration of the world and their physical, cognitive, and socioemotional development.

DR. KUTHER'S
CHALK TALKS

Watch at
edge.sagepub.com/kuther2e

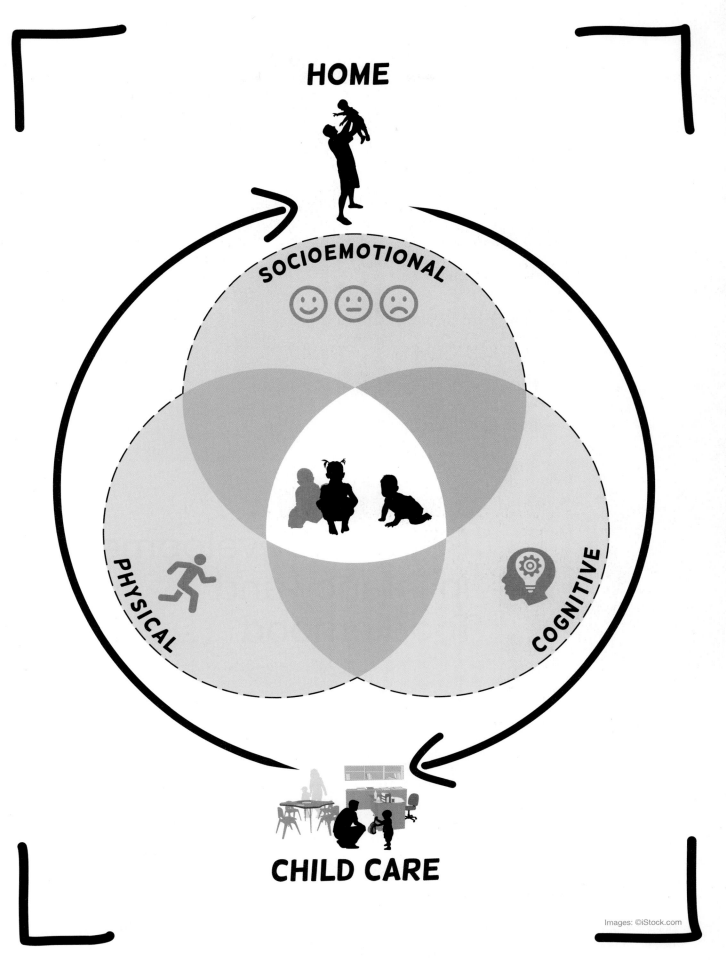

HOME

SOCIOEMOTIONAL

PHYSICAL

COGNITIVE

CHILD CARE

iStock/FatCa

4

Physical Development in Infancy and Toddlerhood

"You're such a big girl!" the pediatric nurse exclaimed as she weighed baby Regina. Regina's mother marveled at how much her daughter had grown during the first 6 months of her life—she had more than doubled her weight. Over 6 months, Regina has transformed from a newborn unable to raise her head into a baby who can sit up on her own. Her mother told the nurse, "She seems to like spending time on all fours. Maybe she's practicing and getting ready to crawl." The nurse smiled and said, "Start thinking about babyproofing your home because Regina will be crawling before you know it!" In

the next few months, Regina will crawl, pull herself up to stand, and eventually walk. Babies grow and change very quickly. In this chapter, we explore the physical changes that occur in a child's first 2 years of life. These first years are collectively called the developmental stage of infancy and toddlerhood. The term *toddler* refers to toddling, the unsteady gait of babies who are just learning to walk. During this stage, infants and toddlers experience advances in growth, perceptual capacities, and motor skills that enable them to interact with their world and learn in new ways.

Learning Objectives

4.1 Discuss growth and the role of nutrition in development during infancy and toddlerhood.

4.2 Summarize brain development during infancy and toddlerhood.

4.3 Compare infants' early learning capacities for habituation, classical conditioning, operant conditioning, and imitation.

4.4 Describe infants' developing sensory abilities.

4.5 Analyze the roles of maturation and contextual factors in infant and toddler motor development.

Digital Resources

Explore: Growth Among Infants and Preschoolers in India

▶ **Lives in Context Video 4.1:** Body Proportions in Infancy and Early Childhood

Listen: Play and Brain Development

Watch: The Little Albert Experiment

Listen: Babies and Sensory Experiences

Explore: A Multisensory Intervention for Preterm Infants

▶ **Lives in Context Video 4.2:** Motor Development in Infancy

BODY GROWTH AND NUTRITION IN INFANTS AND TODDLERS

» LO 4.1 Discuss growth and the role of nutrition in development during infancy and toddlerhood.

Perhaps the most obvious change that infants undergo during the first year of life is very rapid growth. Growth during the prenatal period and infancy proceeds in two systematic patterns. **Cephalocaudal development** refers to the principle that growth proceeds from the head downward. The head and upper regions of the body develop before the lower regions. For example, recall the fetus's disproportionately large head. During prenatal development, the head grows before the other body parts. Even at birth, the newborn's head is about one fourth the total body length, as shown in Figure 4.1. As the lower parts of the body develop, the head becomes more proportionate to the body. By 3 years of age, the child is less top-heavy. **Proximodistal development** refers to the principle that growth and development proceed from the center of the body outward. During prenatal development, the internal organs develop before the arms and legs. After birth, the trunk grows before the limbs and the limbs before the hands and feet.

Growth Norms

It is easy to observe that infants grow substantially larger and heavier over time—but there are many individual differences in growth. How can parents and caregivers tell if a child's growth is normal? By compiling information about the height and weight of large samples of children from diverse populations, researchers have determined growth norms. **Growth norms** are expectations for typical gains and variations in height and weight for children based on their chronological age and ethnic background.

In the first few days after birth, newborns shed excess fluid and typically lose 5% to 10% of their body weight. After this initial loss, however, infants gain weight quickly. Infants typically double their birth weight at about 4 months of age, triple it by 12 months, and quadruple it by 2.5 years (Kliegman et al., 2016). The average 3-year-old weighs about 31 pounds. Gains in height of 10 to 12 inches can be expected over the first year of life, making the average 1-year-old child about 30 inches tall. Most children grow about 5 inches during their second year of life and 3 to 4 inches during their third. To parents, growth may appear slow and steady, but research has shown that it often occurs in spurts in which an infant or toddler can grow up to one quarter of an inch overnight (Lampl, Johnson, & Frongillo, 2001). Infant growth appears to be tied to sleep as increased bouts of sleep predict small bursts of

FIGURE 4.1

Body Proportions Throughout Life

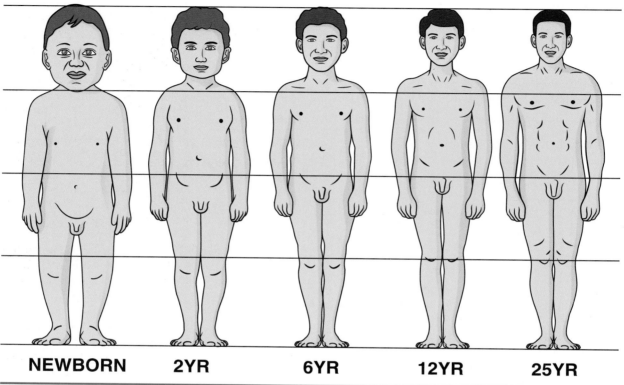

| NEWBORN | 2YR | 6YR | 12YR | 25YR |

Source: Huelke (1998).

growth (Lampl & Johnson, 2011). At about 2 years of age, both girls and boys have reached one half of their adult height (Kliegman et al., 2016).

Growth is largely maturational, but it can be influenced by health and environmental factors. Today's children grow taller and faster than ever before, and the average adult is taller today than a century ago. Increases in children's growth over the past century are influenced by contextual changes such as improved sanitation, nutrition, and access to medical care (Mummert, Schoen, & Lampl, 2018). Large gains have occurred in North America and Europe, followed by South Asia (NCD Risk Factor Collaboration, 2016). Although children of sub-Saharan Africa showed growth gains into the mid-1990s, mass poverty and starvation, poor infrastructure to provide clean water and sanitation, and exposure to the emotional and physical stresses of war and terror have affected growth (Simmons, 2015). Good nutrition is critical to healthy growth during infancy and toddlerhood. Many infants' first nutritional experiences are through breastmilk or formula.

Breastfeeding

The U.S. Department of Health and Human Services (2011) has recommended that mothers breastfeed their babies, and breastfeeding has increased in popularity in the United States in recent years. In 1990, about one half of mothers breastfed their babies, while about 83% breastfed in 2014 (Centers for Disease Control and Prevention, 2017). Over one half of women continue to breastfeed after 6 months and over one third at 12 months.

Breastfeeding practices vary by maternal age, education, and socioeconomic status (Hauck, Fenwick, Dhaliwal, & Butt, 2011). In the United States and the United Kingdom, for example, the lowest rates of breastfeeding are among low-income mothers, mothers who are young, and mothers with low levels of education. Researchers have observed that the employment settings of low-income mothers may offer few resources to support breastfeeding, such as private places for women to use breast pumps (Griffiths, Tate, & Lucy, 2007; Racine, Frick,

Breast-feeding is associated with many health benefits for infants and mothers, and provides opportunities for infant–mother bonding.
iStock/SelectStock

Guthrie, & Strobino, 2009). In contrast, women in developing countries who have low educational levels and are in the poorest social classes are *more* likely to breastfeed their children. Educated women of higher income brackets in these countries tend to shun breastfeeding, viewing it as an option primarily for poor women (Victora et al., 2016). Other factors affecting breastfeeding practices include ethnicity and social policies. In the United States, for instance, Hispanic mothers breastfeed at higher rates than non-Hispanic White mothers, who are more likely to breastfeed than non-Hispanic Black mothers (Centers for Disease Control and Prevention, 2013; Smith-Gagen, Hollen, Walker, Cook, & Yang, 2014). And unsurprisingly, countries where working women are allowed paid maternity leave for part or all of their infant's first year of life, such as Denmark, Norway, Sweden, and Australia, show very high breastfeeding rates of 94% and more (Hauck et al., 2011; Imdad, Yakoob, & Bhutta, 2011; Roelants, Hauspie, & Hoppenbrouwers, 2010).

Breastfeeding offers benefits for mothers and infants. Mothers who breastfeed have lower rates of diabetes, cardiovascular disease, and depression, and after they reach menopause, they are at lower risk for ovarian and breast cancer and bone fractures (Godfrey & Lawrence, 2010; Islami et al., 2015). A mother's milk is tailored to her infant and has the right amount of fat, sugar, water, and protein needed for the baby's growth and development. Most babies find it easier to digest breast milk than formula. In addition, breast milk contains immunizing agents that protect the infant against infections, and breastfed infants tend to experience lower rates of allergies and gastrointestinal symptoms as well as have fewer visits to physicians (Cabinian et al., 2016; Turfkruyer & Verhasselt, 2015). Breastfeeding for more than 6 months is associated with reduced risk of obesity and childhood cancer, especially lymphomas (Amitay, Dubnov Raz, & Keinan-Boker, 2016; Victora

et al., 2016). Recent research suggests that exclusively breastfeeding during the first 4 to 6 weeks of life may be associated with longer telomeres, protective caps on chromosomes that predict longevity, at age 4 and 5 (Wojcicki et al., 2016).

Research on the effects of breastfeeding on cognitive development yields mixed findings. In some studies, infants breastfed for more than 6 months perform better on tests of cognitive ability compared with their formula-fed counterparts (Kramer et al., 2008; Sloan, Stewart, & Dunne, 2010). Others suggest that the differences in test scores are influenced by the characteristics of mothers who breastfeed, such as higher levels of education and socioeconomic status (Der, Batty, & Deary, 2006; Schulze & Carlisle, 2010; Tanaka, Kon, Ohkawa, Yoshikawa, & Shimizu, 2009). Yet studies that control for maternal factors still support a cognitive advantage to breastfed infants (Sloan et al., 2010). The cognitive advantages may persist throughout childhood into adolescence. The duration of breastfeeding, specifically longer than 6 months, is associated with higher scores in language ability at ages 5 and 10 (Whitehouse, Robinson, Li, & Oddy, 2011) and intelligence in adolescence (Isaacs et al., 2010). Although breastfeeding appears to be associated with positive cognitive outcomes, it is important to recognize that differences in cognitive development between breastfed and formula-fed infants are small (Jenkins & Foster, 2014; Schulze & Carlisle, 2010).

Despite these benefits, many mothers choose not to breastfeed or are unable to breastfeed. Infant formula is a safe and healthy alternative to breast milk. While breastfeeding is recommended by pediatricians, formula feeding will not harm a baby. Formula production is monitored by the U.S. Food and Drug Administration. Most formulas are made from cow's milk, but soy-based alternatives exist for infants with allergies or parents who choose to raise their child vegetarian. Infants subsist on milk or formula alone for the first few months of life, after which other foods begin to be integrated into their diet.

Solid Food

Somewhere between 4 and 6 months of age, infants eat their first solid food—although "solid food" is actually a misnomer. The first food consumed is usually iron-fortified baby cereal mixed with breast milk or formula to make a very thin gruel. As babies get older, the amount of milk is reduced to make porridge of a thicker consistency. Now infants' diets begin to include other pureed foods, such as vegetables and fruits. The addition of pureed meats comes later. Infants do not necessarily like these new flavors and textures—many foods must be introduced over a dozen times before an infant will accept them.

Sometimes babies gain weight quickly and may appear chubby. Parents who feed their infants nutritious foods need not worry about increases in weight and should not restrict infants' caloric intake without consulting a pediatrician. Most chubby babies become thinner toddlers and young children as they learn to crawl, walk, run, and become more active. In addition, as infants' get better at manipulating their fingers (as discussed later in this chapter), they begin to feed themselves, which means meals may take more time and may reduce toddlers' food consumption.

However, many infants are not served nutritious foods. One recent study of 6- to 24-month-olds found that many were served fattening "junk" foods such as French fries, pizza, candy, and soda, and 20% of the infants had never consumed vegetables (Miles & Siega-Riz, 2017). Most infants are introduced to sweets early, and by 24 months, nearly two thirds consume cookies or candy in a given day (Deming et al., 2017). Rapid, excessive weight gain in infancy is associated with childhood obesity (Wang et al., 2016). Pediatricians suggest that parents consider their infants' growth in light of norms to determine whether intervention is needed. As shown in Figure 4.2,

about 5% of 12-month-old boys and girls weigh 26 pounds or more and are classified as obese (World Health Organization, 2009).

Malnutrition

Receiving adequate calories and nutrition is a challenge for many children, especially those in developing countries where chronic malnutrition is common. Malnutrition has devastating effects on physical growth, resulting in *growth stunting*. One in four children in the world suffer from growth stunting, the majority of whom live in developing countries. For example, growth stunting affects 43% of children in East African countries, 34% in West Africa, and 35% in South-Central Asia (de Onis & Branca, 2016). Infants who consume a diet that is chronically insufficient in calories, nutrients, and protein can develop **marasmus**, a wasting disease in which the body's fat and muscle are depleted (Kliegman et al., 2016). Growth stops, the body wastes away, the skin becomes wrinkly and aged looking, the abdomen shrinks, and the body takes on a hollow appearance. Another malnutritive disease is **kwashiorkor**, found in children who experience an insufficient intake of protein, which may occur when a child prematurely abandons breastfeeding, such as with the birth of a younger sibling. It is characterized by lethargy, wrinkled skin, and a fluid retention appearing as bloating and swelling of the stomach, face, legs, and arms. Because the vital organs of the body take all of the available nutrients, the other parts of the body deteriorate. Marasmus occurs most often in infants whereas kwashiorkor tends to occur in older infants and young children (Morley, 2016).

Malnutrition influences development in multiple ways. Malnourished children show cognitive deficits as well as impairments in motivation, curiosity, language, and the ability to effectively interact with the environment throughout childhood and adolescence and even into adulthood (Galler et al., 2012; Peter et al., 2016). Malnourishment damages neurons, as shown in Figure 4.3, and the resulting neurological and cognitive deficits from early malnutrition last. For example, among Ghannan children who survived a severe famine in 1983, those who were youngest at the time of the famine (under age 2) scored lower on cognitive measures throughout childhood and into adulthood than did those who were older (ages 6 to 8) (Ampaabeng & Tan, 2013). Malnutrition during the first year of life is associated with depression years later, when those children are 11 to 17 years old (Galler et al., 2010). Some of the damage caused by malnutrition can be reversed. For example, motor and mental development can be enhanced if nutrition is reinstated early. However, long-term difficulties in

---

FIGURE 4.2

Weight Norms for Infants and Toddlers

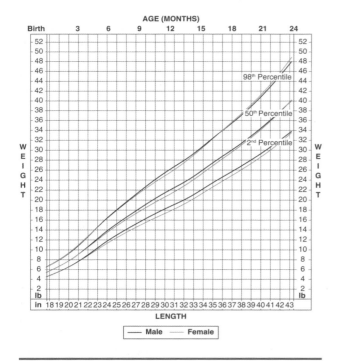

Source: Centers for Disease Control and Prevention, 2009.

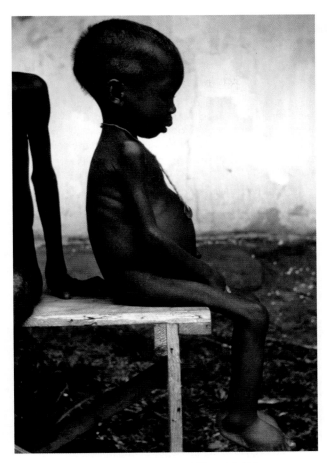

This child suffers from an extreme nutritional deficiency, kwashiorkor. Early treatment can reduce the deficits associated with kwashiorkor, but most children will not reach their full potential for height and growth.
Dr. Lyle Conrad - Centers for Disease Control and Prevention, Atlanta, Georgia, USA Public Health Image Library (PHIL); ID: 6901 http://phil.cdc.gov/

Effects of Malnourishment on Brain Development

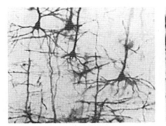

Source: De Onis and Branca, 2016, https://onlinelibrary.wiley.com/doi/epdf/10.1111/mcn.12231 licensed under CC BY 3.0 IGO, https://creativecommons.org/licenses/by/3.0/igo/legalcode

attention, learning, and intelligence often remain, even into middle adulthood (Kim, Fleisher, & Sun, 2017; Schoenmaker et al., 2015; Waber et al., 2014).

Although malnutrition is common in developing countries, it is also found in some of the world's wealthiest countries. Because of socioeconomic factors, many children in the United States and other developed countries are deprived of diets that support healthy growth. In 2015, about 13% (or 15.8 million) households were categorized as *food insecure*. That is, they lacked consistent access to food to support a healthy lifestyle for all family at some point during the year (Coleman-Jensen, Rabbitt, Gregory, & Singh, 2016). Low-income families may have difficulty providing children with the range of foods needed for healthy development. In the United States, we have linked inadequate nutrition with stunted growth, health problems, poor school performance, and poor relationships with peers (Abdelhadi et al., 2016; Alaimo, Olson, & Frongillo, 2001; Hampton, 2007).

In addition to providing adequate nutrition, the use of vaccines can promote the health of infants and young children, as noted in the Applying Developmental Science feature on vaccination.

Failure to Thrive

Individual differences are the norm when it comes to growth; children grow at different rates. However, some children show significantly slower growth than other children their age. Some infants display **failure to thrive**, a condition in which their weight is below the fifth percentile for their age, meaning that they weigh less than 95% of same-age children (S. Z. Cole & Lanham, 2011). Their caloric intake is insufficient to maintain growth (Larson-Nath & Biank, 2016). Children with failure to thrive may be irritable and emotional, lack age-appropriate social responses such as smiling and eye contact, and show delayed motor development. Untreated, failure to thrive is accompanied by delays in cognitive, verbal, and behavioral skills that make it difficult for the child to achieve success in school, home, and peer environments.

Failure to thrive can be caused by medical conditions., such as gastrointestinal and other health problems. Sometimes socioemotional and contextual factors contribute to failure to thrive, such as an insecure attachment to caregivers, parents with physical or mental health problems, emotional neglect and abuse, and, especially, living in poverty and experiencing contextual stressors such as violence within the community (Feigelman & Keane, 2017; Homan, 2016). Pediatricians typically treat failure to thrive by providing the child with the nutrients necessary to grow normally. They may also work with other health professionals such as psychologists and social workers to address underlying medical and psychosocial contributors (Feigelman & Keane, 2017). Although nutritional interventions can alleviate

Vaccination

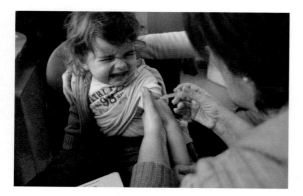

Vaccines protect children and communities from diseases that once spread quickly and killed thousands of people.
BSIP SA / Alamy Stock Photo

Over the past 60 years, childhood diseases such as measles, mumps, and whooping cough have declined dramatically because of widespread immunization of infants. A vaccine is a small dose of inactive virus that is injected into the body to stimulate the production of antibodies to guard against the disease. Vaccines control infectious diseases that once spread quickly and killed thousands of people.

Vaccines are administered early in life because many preventable diseases are more common in infants and young children. Vaccinations protect the child, as well as those in the child's community. An immunized person is less susceptible to a disease and less likely to transmit it to others. State laws require schoolchildren to be fully immunized, a requirement that has increased vaccination rates and prevented many diseases.

The Centers for Disease Control and Prevention (CDC) recommends that infants be vaccinated against most vaccine-preventable diseases by the time they are 2 years of age. Vaccination rates have increased markedly over the past 15 years. The proportion of children aged 19 to 35 months receiving the recommended series of vaccines increased from 69% to 83% between 1994 and 2004. However, the rate has stalled since, standing at 82% in 2013 (Child Trends Databank, 2015).

Why are nearly one fifth of children unvaccinated? One reason is that many families in the United States do not have access to the health care they need. Children in families with incomes below the poverty level are less likely to receive the combined series vaccination (Child Trends Databank, 2015). Many parents are unaware that children from low-income families who do not have medical insurance can receive vaccinations through the federal Vaccines for Children Program, begun in 1994. In addition, the vaccination schedule is complicated, with specific vaccines administered at specific times in development (Kurosky, Davis, & Krishnarajah, 2017).

Another, more troubling, reason for the stalled vaccination rate is the common misconception that vaccines are linked with autism. Some parents refuse to have their infants vaccinated due to this concern (Salmon, Dudley, Glanz, & Omer, 2015). Extensive research indicates that there is no association between vaccination and autism (Modabbernia, Velthorst, & Reichenberg, 2017; Taylor, Swerdfeger, & Eslick, 2014). Instead, children tend to receive vaccines at the age when some chronic illnesses and developmental disorders—such as autism—tend to emerge, but this correlation is not indicative of a cause-and-effect relationship. (Recall from Chapter 1 that correlational research documents phenomena that occur together but cannot demonstrate causation.) While specific causes of autism spectrum disorders have yet to be fully identified, we do know that autism has a strong genetic component and is also associated with both maternal and paternal age (B. K. Lee & McGrath, 2015; Waltes et al., 2014). Other parents report concerns about chemicals in vaccines and possible unforeseen future effects (Martin & Petrie, 2017). Longitudinal research has suggested no negative long-term effects of vaccines administered in infancy (Henry et al., 2018; Su et al., 2017; Wessel, 2017).

Even when children receive the full schedule of vaccinations, many do not receive them on the timetable recommended by the National Vaccine Advisory Committee. Vaccine timeliness is important because the efficacy of early and late vaccination is not always known and may vary by disease. When a child receives a vaccination may be just as important as whether the child receives it in promoting disease resistance.

What Do You Think?

1. What do you think about the use of vaccines?

2. In your view, what is the most important reason in favor of vaccinations?

3. Why do you think some parents object to their use? How might you respond to their objections? ●

many of the effects of malnutrition on physical development, some children might show long-term cognitive and psychosocial deficits.

We have seen that growth proceeds rapidly over the first 2 years of life and follows consistent patterns. Body growth is largely maturationally driven but also influenced by contextual factors. Whereas breastfeeding and introducing healthy solid foods can aid infants' growth, malnutrition and a poor diet can hinder infants' development with effects that can persist throughout childhood and even into adulthood.

THINKING IN CONTEXT 4.1

1. Why are marasmus and kwashiorkor uncommon in the United States? What contextual factors place children in developing nations at risk for these impairments?

2. How might you increase parents' knowledge about health topics such as breastfeeding or nutrition? If you were assigned to design such a program, what would you need to know to begin your design? How would you go about gathering information and ideas (see Chapter 1 for information about research design)?

BRAIN DEVELOPMENT DURING INFANCY AND TODDLERHOOD

» LO 4.2 **Summarize brain development during infancy and toddlerhood.**

All of the developments in infants' physical and mental capacities are influenced by the dramatic changes that occur in the brain. At birth, the brain is about 25% of its adult weight, and it grows rapidly throughout infancy, reaching about 70% of its adult weight by 2 years of age (Lyall et al., 2015). As the brain develops, it becomes larger and more complex.

Processes of Neural Development

The brain is made up of billions of cells called neurons. **Neurons** are specialized to communicate with one another to make it possible for people to sense the world, think, move their body, and carry out their lives. Brain development begins well before birth. **Neurogenesis**, the creation of new neurons, begins in the embryo's neural tube. We are born with more than 100 billion neurons, more than we will ever need—and more than we will ever have at any other time in our lives. Some of our neurons die, but neurogenesis continues throughout life, although at a much slower pace than during prenatal development (Stiles et al., 2015). As the brain develops, new neurons migrate along a network of glial cells, a second type of brain cell that tends to outnumber neurons (Gibb & Kovalchuk, 2018). **Glial cells** nourish neurons and move throughout the brain to provide a physical structure to the brain. As shown in Figure 4.4, neurons travel along glial cells to the location of the brain where they will function, often the outer layer of the brain, known as the **cortex**, and glial cells instruct neurons to form connections with other neurons (Kolb, Whishaw, & Tesky, 2016).

At birth, the neural networks of axons and dendrites are simple, with few connections, or **synapses**, between neurons (Kolb et al., 2016). Early in infancy, major growth takes place. Neurons and glial cells enlarge. As the dendrites grow and branch out, neurons form synapses and thereby increase connections with others, a process called **synaptogenesis**. Synaptogenesis peaks in different

FIGURE 4.4

Glial Cell-Neuron Relationship

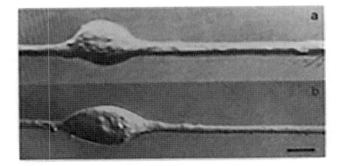
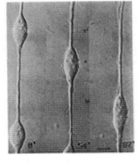
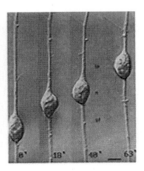

Neurons migrate along thin strands of glial cells.

Source: Gasser and Hatten (1990).

brain regions at different ages (Remer et al., 2017). The most active areas of synaptogenesis during the first 5 weeks of life are in the sensorimotor cortex and subcortical parts of the brain, which are responsible for respiration and other essential survival processes. The visual cortex develops very rapidly between 3 and 4 months and reaches peak density by 12 months of age. The prefrontal cortex—responsible for planning and higher thinking—develops more slowly and is not complete until early adulthood (Tamnes et al., 2017).

In response to exposure to stimulation from the outside world, the number of synapses initially rises meteorically in the first year of life, and the dendrites increase 500% by age 2 (Monk, Webb, & Nelson, 2001). By age 3, children have more synapses than at any other point in life, with at least 50% more synapses than in the adult brain. This explosion in connections in the early years of life means that the brain makes more connections than it needs, in preparation to receive any and all conceivable kinds of stimulation (Schuldiner & Yaron, 2015). Those connections that are used become stronger and more efficient, while those unused eventually shrink, atrophy, and disappear. This loss of unused neural connections is a process called **synaptic pruning**, which can improve the efficiency of neural communication by removing "clutter"—excess unused connections. Little-used synapses are pruned in response to experience, an important part of neurological development that leads to more efficient thought (Lyall et al., 2015). Another important process of brain development is **myelination**, in which glial cells produce and coat the axons of neurons with a fatty substance called myelin. Myelination contributes to advances in neural communication because axons coated with myelin transmit neural impulses more quickly than unmyelinated axons (Markant & Thomas, 2013). With increases in myelination, infants and children process information more quickly. Their thought and behavior becomes faster, more coordinated, and complex (Chevalier et al., 2015). Myelination proceeds most rapidly from birth to age 4, first in the sensory and motor cortex in infancy, and continues through childhood into adolescence and early adulthood (Qiu, Mori, & Miller, 2015).

The Cerebral Cortex

The brain comprises different structures with differing functions, located across four lobes. The

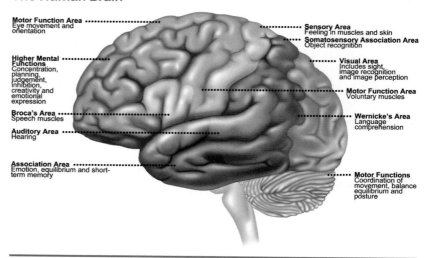

FIGURE 4.5

The Human Brain

various parts of the brain work together, but as shown in Figure 4.5, each lobe is specialized to a certain extent. In addition, the brain comprises two hemispheres that are joined by a thick band of neural fibers known as the corpus collosum. Although all four lobes appear on both hemispheres, the hemispheres are not identical. The right and left hemispheres are specialized for different functions, known as lateralization. For most people, language is governed by the left hemisphere. Each hemisphere of the brain (and the parts of the brain that comprise each hemisphere) is specialized for particular functions and becomes more specialized with experience. This process of the hemispheres becoming specialized to carry out different functions is called **lateralization** (Duboc, Dufourcq, Blader, & Roussigné, 2015).

Lateralization ("of the side" in Latin) begins before birth and is influenced both by genes and by early experiences (Young, 2016). For example, in the womb, most fetuses face toward the left, freeing the right side of the body, which permits more movement on that side and the development of greater control over the right side of the body (Previc, 1991). In newborns, the left hemisphere tends to have greater structural connectivity and efficiency than the right—more connections and pathways suggesting that they are better able to control the right side of their bodies (Ratnarajah et al., 2013). Newborns tend to have slightly better hearing from their right ear (Ari-Even Roth, Hildesheimer, Roziner, & Henkin, 2016). Infants generally display a hand preference, usually right, and their subsequent activity makes the hand more dominant because experience strengthens the hand and neural connections and improves agility. In this way, one hemisphere becomes stronger and more adept, a process known as **hemispheric dominance**. Most adults experience hemispheric dominance, usually with the left hemisphere dominating over the right, making about 90% of adults in Western countries right-handed (Duboc et al., 2015).

Although the left and right hemispheres are implicated for different functions, some researchers note that a strict right/spatial and left/language dichotomy is overly simplistic (Vilasboas, Herbet, & Duffau, 2017). Despite lateralization, the two hemispheres interact in a great many complex ways to enable us to think, move, create, and exercise our senses (Efron, 1990; Richmond, Johnson, Seal, Allen, & Whittle, 2016; Springer & Deutsch, 1998). Complex activities such as thinking and problem solving involve communication between both hemispheres of the brain (Turner, Marinsek, Ryhal, & Miller, 2015). The **corpus callosum**, a collection of 250 to 800 million neural fibers, connects the left and right hemispheres of the brain, permitting them to communicate and coordinate processing (Banich & Heller, 1998). During early childhood, the corpus callosum grows and begins to myelinate, permitting the two halves of the brain to communicate in more sophisticated and efficient ways and to act as one, enabling the child to execute large and fine motor activities such as catching and throwing a ball or tying shoelaces (Banich, 1998; Brown & Jernigan, 2012).

Experience and Brain Development

Stimulation and experience are key components needed to maximize neural connections and brain development throughout life, but especially in infancy. Much of what we know about brain development comes from studying animals. Animals raised in stimulating environments with many toys and companions to play with develop brains that are heavier and have more synapses than do those who grow up in standard laboratory conditions (Berardi, Sale, & Maffei, 2015). Likewise, when animals raised in stimulating environments are moved to unstimulating standard laboratory conditions, their brains lose neural connections. This is true for humans, too. Infants who are understimulated, such as those who experience child maltreatment or who are reared in deprivation, such as in poor understaffed orphanages in foreign countries, show deficits in brain volume as well as cognitive and perceptual deficiencies that may persist into adolescence (Hodel et al., 2015; C. A. Nelson et al., 2016; Sheridan & McLaughlin, 2014). In this way, infancy is said to be a *sensitive period* for brain development, a period in which experience had a particularly powerful role (Hensch, 2018).

The powerful role that experience plays in brain development can be categorized into two types. First, the brain depends on experiencing certain basic events and stimuli at key points in time to develop

The brain develops in response to experiences that are unique to each individual, such as playing with specific toys or participating in social interactions.
iStock/doble-d

normally (Bick & Nelson, 2017); this is referred to as **experience-expectant brain development**. Experience-expectant brain development is demonstrated in sensory deprivation research with animals. If animals are blindfolded and prevented from using their visual system for the first several weeks after birth, they never acquire normal vision because the connections among the neurons that transmit sensory information from the eyes to the visual cortex fail to develop; instead, they decay (DiPietro, 2000; Neville & Bavelier, 2001). If only one eye is prevented from seeing, the animal will be able to see well with one eye but will not develop *binocular vision,* the ability to focus two eyes together on a single object. Similarly, human infants born with a congenital cataract in one eye (an opaque clouding that blocks light from reaching the retina) will lose the capacity to process visual stimuli in the affected eye if they do not receive treatment. Even with treatment, subtle differences in facial processing may remain (Maurer, 2017). Deprivation of sound has similar effects on the auditory cortex (Mowery, Kotak, & Sanes, 2016). Brain organization depends on experiencing certain ordinary events early in life, such as opportunities to hear language, see the world, touch objects, and explore the environment

(Kolb, Mychasiuk, & Gibb, 2014; Maurer & Lewis, 2013). All infants around the world need these basic experiences to develop normally, and it is difficult to repair errors that are the result of severe deprivation and neglect (Berardi et al., 2015; McLaughlin, Sheridan, & Nelson, 2017).

A second type of development, **experience-dependent brain development**, refers to the growth that occurs in response to learning experiences (Bick & Nelson, 2017). For example, experiences such as learning to stack blocks or crawl on a slippery wood floor are unique to individual infants, and they influence what particular brain areas and functions are developed and reinforced. Experience-dependent development is the result of lifelong experiences that vary by individual based on contextual and cultural circumstances (Kolb et al., 2014; Stiles & Jernigan, 2010). Exposure to enriching experiences, such as interactive play with toy cars and other objects that move; hands-on play with blocks, balls, and cups; and stimulating face-to-face play can all enhance children's development (Kolb, 2018). For example, a longitudinal study that followed more than 350 infants from 5 to 24 months of age found that the quality of mother–infant interactions at 5 months predicted greater brain activity in the prefrontal cortex at 10 and 24 months of age, suggesting that parenting quality may contribute to brain development in infancy (Bernier, Calkins, & Bell, 2016). One the other hand, exposure to deprivation and trauma can have lasting negative effects on brain development (Harker, 2018).

Sleep and Brain Development

Whereas adults sleep approximately 8 hours each day, the typical neonate sleeps about 16 to 18 hours each day. Sleep declines steadily. Six-month-old infants sleep about 12 hours (Figueiredo, Dias,

One hypothesis for infants' increased time in sleep is that it provides stimulation and promotes brain development.
iStock/Imagesbybarbara

Pinto, & Field, 2016). Infant rats, rabbits, cats, and rhesus monkeys also sleep much longer than adults, suggesting that sleep serves a developmental function (Blumberg, Gall, & Todd, 2014). In adults, sleep is thought to permit the body to repair itself, as indicated by increased cell production and the removal of metabolic wastes during sleep (Tononi & Cirelli, 2014). Sleep is also associated with increases in connections among neurons (Krueger, Frank, Wisor, & Roy, 2016).

Sleep is associated with adult memory, improving the consolidation of memory, and sleep deficits are associated deficits in attention, memory, and learning (Chambers, 2017; Doyon, Gabitov, Vahdat, Lungu, & Boutin, 2018; R. M. C. Spencer, Walker, & Stickgold, 2017). REM sleep, rapid eye movement sleep, is thought to be particularly important for cognition. Adults' eyes flutter and move while in REM sleep, and dreaming occurs during REM sleep (Lewis, 2017). Infants spend about half of their sleep time in REM sleep, decreasing to about 20% in adulthood. Given that dreaming happens in REM, one hypothesis for infants' increased time in sleep is that it provides stimulation and promotes brain development (Friedrich, Wilhelm, Mölle, Born, & Friederici, 2017). Neonates with poor sleep patterns showed poor attention at 4 months and increased distractibility at 18 months of age (Geva, Yaron, & Kuint, 2016). In another study, infants assessed at 12 months of age and again at 3 to 4 years old showed that lower-quality sleep in infancy was associated with problems with attention and behavioral control in early childhood (Sadeh et al., 2015). Sleep also promotes physical growth and development (Tham, Schneider, & Broekman, 2017).

Sleeping serves a developmental function, yet young infants wake often. The typical newborn wakes every 2 hours to eat, and babies continue to require nighttime feedings until they are 4 or 5 months old. Cultures differ in infant sleep practices. For example, parents in the United States typically look forward to the time when their infant will sleep through the night, viewing the newborn's unpredictable sleep pattern as something to fix. In contrast, many European parents view newborn sleep as part of normal development and do not intervene to shape newborn sleep cycles. Children in Pacific-Asian countries tend to sleep an hour less than those in North America, Europe, and Australia (Galland, Taylor, Elder, & Herbison, 2012; Mindell, Sadeh, Wiegand, How, & Goh, 2010). Parental behavior influences infants' sleep patterns. Infants are more likely to continue waking overnight when

Co-Sleeping

While sharing a bedroom can enhance the infant–parent bond and make nighttime feedings easier, infants are safest in their own bassinets, such as this one, which is adapted to promote safe parent–infant contact.
Jennie Hart/Alamy

The practice of *co-sleeping*, which refers to the infant sharing a bed with the mother or with both parents, is common in many countries yet controversial in others. In Japan, China, Kenya, Bangladesh, and the Mayan peninsula of Mexico, co-sleeping in infancy and early childhood is the norm and is believed to enhance the child's sense of security and attachment to the mother (Morelli, Rogoff, Oppenheim, & Goldsmith, 1992; Super & Harkness, 1982; Xiao-na, Hui-shan, Li-jin, & Xi-cheng, 2010). In Latin America and Asia, infants are not usually expected to go to bed and sleep alone at a regular time each night. Instead, they are held until they fall asleep and then are placed in the parental bed (Lozoff, Wolf, & Davis, 1984). In contrast, in many industrialized countries, such as the United States and the United Kingdom, newborns are placed to sleep in their own bassinets, whether in their parents' room or in a separate nursery. In these countries, learning to sleep by oneself is viewed as fostering independence and the ability to self-regulate (Ball, Hooker, & Kelly, 1999; McKenna & Volpe, 2007). Parents' decisions of whether to co-sleep are influenced by their own values and beliefs, which are often shaped by the context in which they live.

Proponents of co-sleeping argue that it best meets the developmental needs of human newborns and aids in forming the attachment bond (McKenna, 2001). Infants who sleep with their mothers synchronize their sleep patterns with hers, permitting more awakenings for breastfeeding, yet lengthening the total time that infants sleep (Gettler & McKenna, 2011). Both mothers and babies benefit from skin-to-skin contact, as it enhances breast milk production, stabilizes infants' heart rate, increases the prevalence and duration of breastfeeding, and is associated with more positive mother–infant interactions (McKenna & Volpe, 2007; Taylor, Donovan, & Leavitt, 2008). Fathers report that they find co-sleeping rewarding rather than an intrusion on the marital bed (Ball, Hooker, & Kelly, 2000).

Pediatricians in Western nations tend to advise separate sleeping arrangements for parents and infants. Opponents of co-sleeping point to increased risk of accidental suffocation and an increased risk of SIDS (sudden infant death syndrome), especially among mothers who smoke (Mitchell, 2009). The American Academy of Pediatrics and the United Kingdom Department of Health have declared sharing a bed with an infant to be an unsafe practice; instead, they advise having infants sleep in a crib in the parents' room (Task Force on Sudden Infant Death Syndrome, 2016; U.K. Department of Health, 2005). Despite these warnings, co-sleeping has become more common among Western families. Some believe that co-sleeping can be safe if appropriate precautions are taken, such as using light bed coverings and a firm mattress and avoiding comforters and pillows (McKenna, 2001). The American Academy of Pediatrics (2016) advises that bedsharing should be abandoned in favor of room sharing, to provide the developmental advantages of co-sleeping and minimize the dangers.

What Do You Think?

1. In your view, what are the advantages and disadvantages of co-sleeping?
2. How might safety concerns of co-sleeping be addressed?
3. In what ways might parent–child sleeping arrangements influence emotional development? ●

their parents play with them during nighttime feedings, as stimulation and attention may reinforce nighttime waking (Sadeh et al., 2015). Cultures also have different practices around sleeping arrangements for infants, toddlers, and older children—including co-sleeping and bedsharing (see Cultural Influences on Development).

Brain development is a multifaceted process that is not is a result of maturational or environmental input alone. Brains do not develop normally in the absence of a basic genetic code or in the absence of essential environmental input. At all points in development, intrinsic and environmental factors interact to support the increasingly complex and elaborate structures and functions of the brain.

THINKING IN CONTEXT 4.2

1. How might contextual factors influence brain development? Consider infants raised in different contexts: urban, suburban, or rural contexts as well as with different family formations, such as single parent, two parent, only child, or multiple siblings. How might these differences influence brain development?

2. What would you tell a new parent about brain development? Why? What advice might you give new parents on how to promote brain development in their child over the first 3 years of life?

EARLY LEARNING CAPACITIES

» LO 4.3   Compare infants' early learning capacities for habituation, classical conditioning, operant conditioning, and imitation.

Can newborns learn? If we define learning as changing behavior in response to experience, certainly: Animals and even insects learn. Yet infants were once believed to be born incapable of sensing and understanding the physical world around them. Most new parents will quickly tell you that this is far from the truth. At birth, and even before, neonates can perceive their physical world and have powerful capacities for learning about it.

Habituation

Less than 1 day old, cradled next to his mother in the hospital maternity center, Tommy is already displaying the earliest form of learning. He no longer cries each time he hears the loud beep made by the machine that reads his mother's blood pressure. This type of learning is called **habituation**; it occurs when repeated exposure to a stimulus results in the gradual decline in the intensity, frequency, or duration of a response (see Figure 4.6). All animals and humans are programmed to learn. Even before birth, humans demonstrate habituation, as early as 22 to 24 weeks' gestation (Hepper, 2015). For example, 27- to 36-week-old fetuses demonstrate habituation to vibration as well as auditory stimuli, such as the sound of a tone. Initially, the fetus moves in response to the vibration, suggesting interest in a novel stimulus. After repeated stimulation, the fetus no longer responds to the stimulus, indicating that it has habituated to it (McCorry & Hepper, 2007; Muenssinger et al., 2013). Not only can the fetus habituate to stimuli but it can

FIGURE 4.6

Habituation

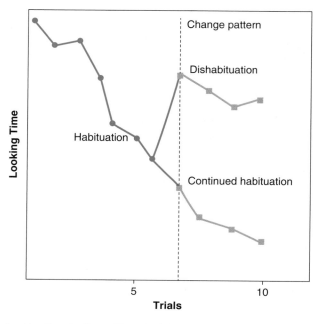

Looking time declines with each trial as the infant habituates to the pattern. Dishabituation, renewed interest, signifies that the infant detects a change in stimulus pattern.

Source: Visual development by Marcela Salamanca and Donald Kline, University of Calgary (http://psych.ucalgary.ca/PACE/VA-Lab/). Reprinted by permission of the authors.

recall a stimulus for at least 24 hours (van Heteren, Boekkooi, Jongsma, & Nijhuis, 2000).

Habituation improves with development. For example, the performance of fetuses on habituation tasks improves with gestational age (James, 2010). After birth, habituation is often measured by changes in an infant's heart rate and in attention or looking at a stimulus (Domsch, Thomas, & Lohaus, 2010). Younger infants require more time to habituate than older infants (Kavšek & Bornstein, 2010). Five- to 12-month-old babies habituate quickly—even after just a few seconds of sustained attention—and in some cases, they can recall the stimulus for weeks, such as recalling faces that they have encountered for brief periods of time (Richards, 1997).

Neural development, specifically development of the prefrontal cortex, is thought to underlie age-related gains in habituation skill (Nakano, Watanabe, Homae, & Taga, 2009). As the brain matures, infants process information more quickly and learn more about stimuli in fewer exposures. Younger infants and those with low birthweight require more time to habituate than do older and more fully developed infants (Kavšek & Bornstein, 2010; Krafchuk, Tronick, & Clifton, 1983; Rovee-Collier, 1987). Fetuses with more mature nervous systems require fewer trials to habituate than do those with less well-developed nervous systems, even at the same gestational age (Morokuma et al., 2004). Fetal habituation predicts measures of information processing ability at 6 months of age (Gaultney & Gingras, 2005).

There are also individual differences in habituation among healthy, developmentally normal infants. Some habituate quickly and recall what they have learned for a long time. Other infants require many more exposures to habituate and quickly forget what they have learned. The speed at which infants habituate is associated with cognitive development when they grow older. Infants who habituate quickly during the first 6 to 8 months of life tend to show more advanced capacities to learn and use language during the second year of life (Tamis-LeMonda, Song, & Bornstein, 1989). Rapid habituation is also associated with higher scores on intelligence tests in childhood (Kavšek, 2004). The problem-solving skills measured by intelligence tests tap information processing skills such as attention, processing speed, and memory—all of which influence the rate of habituation (McCall, 1994).

Innate learning capacities permit young infants to adapt quickly to the world, a skill essential for survival. Researchers use these capacities to study infant perception and cognition (Aslin, 2014). For example, to examine whether an infant can discriminate between two stimuli, a researcher presents one until the infant habituates to it. Then a second stimulus is presented. If dishabituation, or the recovery of attention, occurs, it indicates that the infant detects that the second stimulus is different from the first. If the infant does not react to the new stimulus by showing dishabituation, it is assumed that the infant does not perceive the difference between the two stimuli. The habituation method is very useful in studying infant perception and cognition and underlies many of the findings discussed later in this chapter.

Classical Conditioning

In addition to their capacity to learn by habituation, infants are born with a second powerful tool for learning. They can learn through association. Classical conditioning entails making an association between a neutral stimulus and an unconditioned stimulus that triggers an innate reaction. Eventually, the neutral stimulus (now conditioned stimulus) produces the same response as the unconditioned stimulus.

Newborns demonstrate classical conditioning. For example, when stroking the forehead was paired with tasting sugar water, 2-hour-old infants were conditioned to suck in response to having their heads stroked (Blass, Ganchrow, & Steiner, 1984). Similarly, Lipsitt and Kaye (1964) paired a tone with the presentation of a nipple to 2- and 3-day-old infants. Soon, the infants began to make sucking movements at the sound of the tone. Sleeping neonates can be conditioned to respond to a puff of air to the eye (Tarullo et al., 2016). Even premature infants can demonstrate associative learning, although at slower rates than full-term infants (Herbert, Eckerman, Goldstein, & Stanton, 2004). Research with chimpanzee fetuses has shown that they display classical conditioning before birth (Kawai, 2010). It is likely that the human fetus can as well. Although classical conditioning is innate, neurological damage can hinder infants' abilities to learn by association. Infants with fetal alcohol syndrome (FAS) require much more time than other infants to associate eye blinking with external stimuli, such as sounds (Cheng et al., 2016).

Newborns tend to require repeated exposures to conditioning stimuli because they process information slowly (Little, Lipsitt, & Rovee-Collier, 1984). As infants grow older, classical conditioning occurs more quickly and to a broader range of stimuli. For example, in a classic study, Watson and Raynor (1920) paired a white rat with a loud banging noise to evoke fear in an 11-month-old boy known as Little Albert. Repeated pairings of the white rat with the loud noise made Albert cry even when the rat was presented without the noise. In other words, Little Albert was conditioned to associate the neutral stimulus with the conditioned stimulus. Albert demonstrated fear in response to seeing the rat, indicating that emotional responses can be classically conditioned. Our capacities to learn through classical conditioning are evident at birth—and persist throughout life.

Operant Conditioning

At birth, babies can learn to engage in behaviors based on their consequences, known as operant conditioning. Behaviors increase when they are followed by reinforcement and decrease when they are followed by punishment. For example, newborns will change their rate of sucking on a pacifier, increasing or decreasing the rate of sucking, to hear a tape recording of their mother's voice, a reinforcer (Moon, Cooper, & Fifer, 1993). Other research shows that newborns will change their rate of sucking to see visual designs or hear human voices that they find pleasing (Floccia, Christophe, & Bertoncini, 1997). Premature infants and even third-trimester fetuses can be operantly conditioned (Thoman & Ingersoll, 1993). For example, a 35-week-old fetus will change its rate of kicking in response to hearing the father talk against the mother's abdomen (Dziewolska & Cautilli, 2006).

As infants develop, they process information more quickly and require fewer trials pairing behavior and consequence to demonstrate operant conditioning. It requires about 200 trials for 2-day-old infants to learn to turn their heads in response to a nippleful of milk, but 3-month-old infants require about 40 trials, and 5-month-olds require less than 30 trials (Papousek, 1967). Infants' early capacities for operant conditioning imply that they are active and responsive to their environments and adapt their behavior from birth.

Imitation

Toddler Tula puts a bowl on her head and pats it just as she watched her older sister do yesterday. Imitation is an important way in which children and adults learn. Can newborns imitate others? Believe it or not, some research suggests that newborns have a primitive ability to learn through imitation. In a classic study (see Figure 4.7), 2-day-old infants mimicked adult facial expressions, including sticking out the tongue, opening and closing the mouth, and sticking out the lower lip (Meltzoff & Moore, 1977). The prevalence and function of neonate imitation is debated (Suddendorf, Oostenbroek, Nielsen, & Slaughter, 2013). Some studies have failed to replicate this ability (Oostenbroek et al., 2016) and have suggested that tongue protruding simply reflects a general spontaneous newborn behavior (Keven & Akins, 2017), that it reflects arousal (Vincini, Jhang, Buder, & Gallagher, 2017), and that neonate imitation is not developmentally similar to later social imitation (Suddendorf et al., 2013). Others have confirmed that newborns from several ethnic groups and cultures display early capacities for imitation (Meltzoff & Kuhl, 1994; Nadel & Butterworth, 1999). In one study, newborns made corresponding mouth movements to both vowel and consonant vocal models; when the adult model made an *a* sound, newborns opened their mouths, and when the model made an *m* sound, newborns clutched their mouths (Chen, Striano, & Rakoczy, 2004). Studies that require infants to imitate several behaviors in response to different stimuli suggest that neonate imitation is not simply an arousal response (Nagy, Pilling, Orvos, & Molnar, 2013).

Newborns mimic facial expressions, but they are simply carrying out an innate program thought to be controlled by the mirror neuron system, located in the premotor cortex (Binder et al., 2017). The mirror neuron system, an inborn capacity to make associations and respond to the actions of others by mirroring their actions in our own neural circuits, is apparent in both newborn humans and monkeys (Cook, Bird, Catmur, Press, & Heyes, 2014; Olsen, 2006; Shaw & Czekóová, 2013). The ability to copy others' actions likely serves an evolutionarily adaptive purpose in humans, perhaps to aid the development of social communication (Tramacere,

FIGURE 4.7

Newborn Imitating Facial Expression

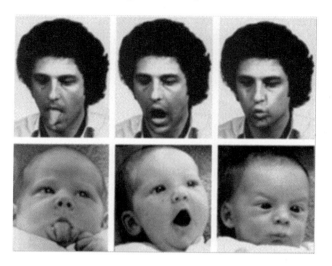

In this classic experiment Meltzoff and Moore demonstrated that neonates imitated the adults' facial expression more often than chance, suggesting that they are capable of facial imitation—a groundbreaking finding.

Source: Meltzoff and Moore (1977). Reprinted with permission of AAAS.

Pievani, & Ferrari, 2017). Newborns do not understand imitation; rather, the action of mirror neurons naturally syncs their body movements with the model. The regulatory mechanisms to inhibit imitative responding develop during infancy (Rizzolatti et al., 2008).

In summary, infants enter the world equipped with several basic learning capacities that permit them to learn even before birth. Newborns display classical and operant conditioning, imitation, and habituation, illustrating that they are wired to attend to their environment. Not only do infants display early competencies that permit them to learn quickly but they are also surprisingly adept at sensing and perceiving stimuli around them.

THINKING IN CONTEXT 4.3

1. What do early learning capacities mean for parenting? What information about habituation, conditioning, or imitation should parents be aware of, if any? Why?

2. How might these learning principles be applied to address childrearing issues, such as how to get infants to sleep through the night or how to introduce new foods?

SENSATION AND PERCEPTION DURING INFANCY AND TODDLERHOOD

» LO 4.4 Describe infants' developing sensory abilities.

Visiting the doctor's office for the first time in her young life, Kerry followed the doctor's finger with her eyes as he passed it over her face. "I think she sees it!" said her surprised mother. "She most certainly does," said the doctor. "Even as a newborn, your Kerry can sense the world. She can see, hear, and smell better than you know." Newborns can see, hear, smell, taste, and respond to touch, but it is unclear how infants perceive sensory stimuli. Developmental researchers draw a distinction between sensation and perception. **Sensation** occurs when our senses detect a stimulus. **Perception** refers to the sense our brain makes of the stimulus and our awareness of it. The newborn is equipped with a full range of senses, ready to experience the world.

Vision

It is impossible to know whether the fetus has a sense of vision, but the fetus responds to bright light directed at the mother's abdomen as early as 28 weeks' gestation (Johnson & Hannon, 2015). At birth, vision is the least developed sense, but it improves rapidly. Newborn visual acuity, or sharpness of vision, is approximately 20/400 (Farroni & Menon, 2008). Researchers study *visual acuity*, sharpness of vision or the ability to see, in infants with the use of preferential looking tasks designed to determine whether infants prefer to look at one stimulus or another. For example, consider an array of black and white stripes. As shown in Figure 4.8, an array with more stripes (and, therefore, many more narrow stripes) tends to appear gray rather than black and white because the pattern becomes more difficult to see as the stripes become narrower. Researchers determine infants' visual acuity by comparing infants' responses to stimuli with different frequencies of stripes because infants who are unable to detect the stripes lose interest in the stimulus and look away from it. Preferential looking studies show that infants reach adult levels of visual acuity between 6 months and 1 year of age (Mercuri, Baranello, Romeo, Cesarini, & Ricci, 2007). Improvement in vision is due to the increasing maturation of the structures of the eye and the visual cortex, the part of the brain that processes visual stimuli.

Newborns are born with preferences for particular visual stimuli. Newborns prefer to look at patterns, such as a few large squares, rather than a

FIGURE 4.8

Visual Acuity

Researchers and pediatricians use stimuli such as the Teller Acuity Cards illustrated here to determine what infants can see. Young infants attend to stimuli with wider lines and stop attending as the lines become smaller.

Source: Leat, Yadev, and Irving (2009).

FIGURE 4.9

Externality Effect and Face Perception

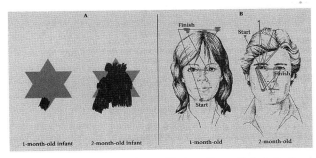

The externality effect refers to a particular pattern of infant visual processing. When presented with a complex stimulus, such as a face, infants under two months of age tend to scan along the outer contours, such as along the hairline. Older infants scan the internal features of complex images and faces, thereby processing the entire stimulus.

Source: Shaffer (2002, p. 190); adapted from Salapatek (1975).

plain stimulus such as a black or white oval shape (Fantz, 1961). Newborns also prefer to look at faces, and the preference for faces increases with age (Frank, Vul, & Johnson, 2009; Gliga, Elsabbagh, Andravizou, & Johnson, 2009). How infants explore visual stimuli changes with age (Colombo, Brez, & Curtindale, 2015). Until about 1 month of age, infants tend to scan along the outer perimeter of stimuli. For

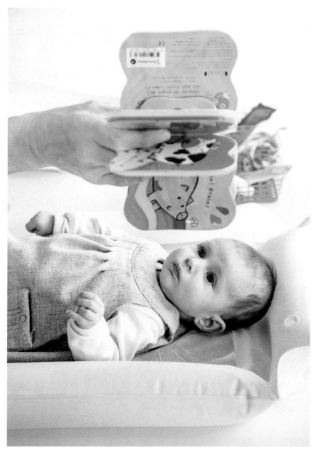

Newborns see color but they have trouble distinguishing among colors.
Phanie / Alamy Stock Photo

example, when presented with a face, the infant's gaze will scan along the hairline and not move to the eyes and mouth. By 6 to 7 weeks of age, infants study the eyes and mouth, which hold more information than the hairline, as shown in Figure 4.9 (Hunnius & Geuze, 2004). Similarly, the ability to follow an object's movement with the eyes, known as visual tracking, is very limited at birth but improves quickly. By 2 months of age, infants can follow a slow-moving object smoothly, and by 3 to 5 months, their eyes can dart ahead to keep pace with a fast-moving object (Agyei, van der Weel, & van der Meer, 2016; Richards & Holley, 1999). The parts of the brain that process motion in adults are operative in infants by 7 months of age (Weaver, Crespi, Tosetti, & Morrone, 2015).

Like other aspects of vision, color vision improves with age. Newborns see color, but they have trouble distinguishing among colors. That is, although they can see both red and green, they do not perceive red as different from green. Early visual experience with color is necessary for normal color perception to develop (Colombo et al., 2015; Sugita, 2004). Habituation studies show that by 1 month of age, infants can distinguish among red, green, and white (Teller, 1997). By 2 to 3 months of age, infants are as accurate as adults in discriminating the basic colors of red, yellow, and blue (Matlin & Foley, 1997; Teller, 1998). By 3 to 4 months of age, infants can distinguish many more colors as well as distinctions among closely related colors (Bornstein & Lamb, 1992; Haith, 1993). Seven-month-old infants detect color categories similar to those of adults; they can group slightly different shades (e.g., various shades of blue) into the same basic color categories as adults do (Clifford, Franklin, Davies, & Holmes, 2009).

Depth perception is the ability to perceive the distance of objects from each other and from ourselves. Depth perception is what permits infants to successfully reach for objects and, later, to crawl without bumping into furniture. By observing that newborns prefer to look at three-dimensional objects than two-dimensional figures, researchers have found that infants can perceive depth at birth (Slater, Rose, & Morison, 1984). Three- to 4-week-old infants blink their eyes when an object is moved toward their face, as if to hit them, suggesting that they are sensitive to depth cues (Kayed, Farstad, & van der Meer, 2008; Náñez & Yonas, 1994). Infants learn about depth by observing and experiencing motion.

A classic series of studies using an apparatus called the *visual cliff* demonstrated that crawling influences how infants perceive depth. The visual cliff, as shown in Figure 4.10, is a Plexiglas-covered table bisected by a plank so that one side is shallow, with a checkerboard pattern right under the glass, and the other side is deep, with the checkerboard pattern a few feet below the glass (E. J. Gibson & Walk, 1960). In this classic study, crawling babies readily moved from the plank to the shallow side but not to the deep side, even if coaxed by their mothers, suggesting that they perceive the difference in depth (Walk, 1968). The more crawling experience infants have, the more likely they are to refuse to cross the deep side of the visual cliff (Bertenthal, Campos, & Barrett, 1984).

Does this mean that babies cannot distinguish the shallow and deep sides of the visual cliff until they crawl? No, because even 3-month-old infants who are too young to crawl distinguish shallow from deep drops. When placed face down on the glass surface of the deep side of the visual cliff, 3-month-old infants became quieter and showed a decrease in heart rate compared with when they were placed on the shallow side of the cliff (Dahl et al., 2013). The young infants can distinguish the difference between shallow and deep drops but do not yet associate fear with deep drops.

As infants gain experience crawling, their perception of depth changes. Newly walking infants avoid the cliff's deep side even more consistently than do crawling infants (Dahl et al., 2013; Witherington, Campos, Anderson, Lejeune, & Seah, 2005). A new

FIGURE 4.10

Visual Cliff

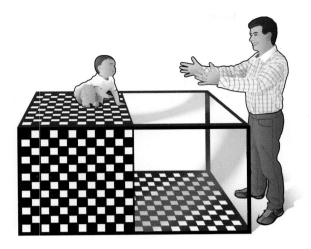

Three-month-old infants show a change in heart rate when placed face down on the glass surface of the deep side of the visual cliff, suggesting that they perceive depth, but do not fear it. Crawling babies, however, show a different response. In a classic study of visual perception, crawling babies moved to the shallow side of the visual cliff, even if called by their mothers. The more crawling experience infants had, the more likely they were to refuse to cross the deep side of the visual cliff.

Source: Levine and Munsch (2010).

perspective on the visual cliff studies argues that infants avoid the deep side of the cliff not out of fear but simply because they perceive that they are unable to successfully navigate the drop; fear might be conditioned through later experiences, but infants are not naturally fearful of heights (Adolph, Kretch, & LoBue, 2014).

Hearing

The capacity to hear develops in the womb; in fact, hearing is the most well-developed sense at birth. Newborns are able to hear about as well as adults (Northern et al., 2014). Shortly after birth, neonates can discriminate among sounds, such as tones (Hernandez-Pavon, Sosa, Lutter, Maier, & Wakai, 2008). By 3 days of age, infants will turn their head and eyes in the general direction of a sound, and this ability to localize sound improves over the first 6 months (Clifton, Rochat, Robin, & Berthier, 1994; Litovsky & Ashmead, 1997).

The process of learning language begins at birth, through listening. Newborns are attentive to voices and can detect their mothers' voices. Newborns only 1 day old prefer to hear speech sounds over similar-sounding nonspeech sounds (May, Gervain, Carreiras, & Werker, 2017). Newborns can perceive and discriminate nearly all sounds in human

languages, but from birth, they prefer to hear their native language (Kisilevsky, 2016). Brain activity in the temporal and left frontal cortex in response to auditory stimuli indicates that newborns can discriminate speech patterns, such as differences in cadence among languages, suggesting an early developing neurological specialization for language (Gervain, Macagno, Cogoi, Peña, & Mehler, 2008; Gervain & Mehler, 2010).

Touch

Compared with vision and hearing, we know much less about the sense of touch in infants. In early infancy, touch, especially with the mouth, is a critical means of learning about the world (Piaget, 1936/1952). The mouth is the first part of the body to show sensitivity to touch prenatally and remains one of the most sensitive areas to touch after birth.

Touch, specifically a caregiver's massage, can reduce stress responses in preterm and full-term neonates and is associated with weight gain in newborns (Diego et al., 2007; Hernandez-Reif, Diego, & Field, 2007). Skin-to-skin contact with a caregiver, as in kangaroo care (see Chapter 3), has an analgesic effect, reducing infants' pain response to being stuck with a needle for blood testing (de Sousa Freire, Santos Garcia, & Carvalho Lamy, 2008; Ferber & Makhoul, 2008). Although it was once believed that newborns were too immature to feel pain, we now know that the capacity to feel pain develops even before birth; by at least the 30th week of gestation, a fetus responds to a pain stimulus (Benatar & Benatar, 2003). The neonate's capacity to feel pain has influenced debates about infant circumcision, as discussed in the Lives in Context feature.

Smell and Taste

Smell and taste receptors functional in the fetus and preferences are well developed at birth (Bloomfield, Alexander, Muelbert, & Beker, 2017). Just hours after birth, newborns display facial expressions signifying disgust in response to odors of ammonia, fish, and other scents that adults find offensive (Steiner, 1979). Within the first days of life, newborns detect and recognize their mother's odor (Macfarlane, 1975; Porter, Varendi, Christensson, Porter, & Winberg, 1998; Schaal et al., 1980). Infants are calmed by their mother's scent. Newborns who smelled their mother's odor displayed less agitation during a heel-stick test and cried less afterward than infants presented with unfamiliar odors (Rattaz, Goubet, & Bullinger, 2005). Familiar scents are reinforcing and can reduce stress responses in infants (Goubet, Strasbaugh, & Chesney, 2007; Nishitani et al., 2009; Schaal, 2017).

Pain and Neonatal Circumcision

An eight-day-old Jewish boy is circumcised as part of a religious ceremony called a bris.
Dan Porges/Archive Photos/Getty Images

Neonatal **circumcision,** removal of the foreskin of the penis, is the oldest known planned surgery (Alanis & Lucidi, 2004). Although it is uncommon throughout much of the world, about three quarters of males in the United States are circumcised (Morris et al., 2016). As shown in Figure 4.11, there are regional differences, with nearly twice as many infant circumcisions in the Midwest as in the West (Owings, Uddin, & Williams, 2013). In recent years, circumcision has come under increasing scrutiny within the United States as some charge that it places the newborn under great distress and confers few medical benefits.

For decades, many scientists and physicians believed that newborns did not feel pain, leading many to perform circumcision without pain management. We now know that even the fetus feels pain (Benatar & Benatar, 2003). Newborns show many indicators of distress during circumcision, such as a high-pitched wail, flailing, grimacing, and dramatic rises in heart rate, blood pressure, palm sweating, pupil dilation, muscle tension, and cortisol levels (Paix & Peterson, 2012). Analgesia (pain relief in which the newborn remains conscious) is safe and effective in reducing the pain associated with circumcision (American Academy of Pediatrics, 1999). Treatment as simple as administering a sugar solution to infants aids in pain management (Matsuda, 2017).

The medical benefits of circumcision are debated (Beal, 2017; Freedman, 2016). Benefits include reduced risk of having urinary tract infections, developing penile cancer, and acquiring HIV (American Academy of Pediatrics Task Force on Circumcision Policy, 1999; American Medical Association, 1999; Morris et al., 2017). Some argue that these are relatively rare conditions and that

the evidence regarding HIV transmission comes from research with adult males in Africa. Whether the same effects apply to infants in Western industrialized countries is uncertain (Alanis & Lucidi, 2004). Moreover, behavior is a more important factor in preventing HIV infection than is circumcision.

In 1999, both the American Medical Association and American Academy of Pediatrics joined medical associations in Canada, Europe, and Australia in concluding that the benefits of circumcision are not large enough to recommend routine circumcision; instead, it is a parental decision. However, in 2012, the American Academy of Pediatrics (AAP) modified its view to note that although it is a parental decision, the benefits of circumcision justify providing access to the procedure (by insurance companies) to families who choose it. Critical physicians and representatives of medical associations in Canada, Australia, and several European countries counter that the revised recommendation was not based on medical evidence but instead reflected cultural bias on the part of the AAP to support social practices common in the United States (Frisch et al., 2013).

Regardless, formal recommendations by medical associations may ultimately have little sway on parents (Freedman, 2016). Education about the risks and benefits of circumcision, especially the controversy over the medical necessity of circumcision, generally does not influence parental decisions regarding circumcision (Binner,

FIGURE 4.11

Rates of Circumcision Performed, 1979–2010

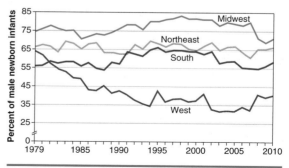

Source: Owings et al. (2013).

Notes: Rates represent circumcisions performed during the birth hospitalization. Circumcision is identified by International Classication of Diseases, Ninth Revision, Clinical Modication (ICD–9–CM) procedure code 64.0.

Mastrobattista, Day, Swaim, & Monga, 2003). Instead, it is tradition and culture, especially social factors such as religion, that influence parental decisions about circumcision. For example, in Jewish cultures, a boy is circumcised on the eighth day after birth in a ritual celebration known as a *bris*, in which the boy is welcomed as a member of the community. Parents' decisions are also influenced by social factors such as whether the father is circumcised and the desire that the child resemble his peers (Bo & Goldman, 2008). The decision is complicated, as parents weigh health risks and benefits with contextual factors such as religious and cultural beliefs, as well as personal desires, to determine what is best for their child.

What Do You Think?

1. In your view, what are the most important considerations in making a decision about whether to circumcise a newborn boy?
2. Imagine that you had a newborn boy. Would you choose to circumcise your son? Why or why not? ●

Infants show innate preferences for some tastes (Ross, 2017). For example, both bottle-fed and breastfed newborns prefer human milk—even milk from strangers—to formula (Marlier & Schaal, 2005). Newborns prefer sugar to other substances, and a small dose of sugar can serve as an anesthetic, distracting newborns from pain (Gradin, Eriksson, Schollin, Holmqvist, & Holstein, 2002). Experience can modify taste preferences, beginning before birth: Fetuses are exposed to flavors in amniotic fluid that influence their preferences after birth (Beauchamp & Mennella, 2011; Forestell, 2016). In one study, the type of formula fed to infants influenced their taste preferences at 4 to 5 years of age (Mennella & Beauchamp, 2002). Infants who were fed milk-based formulas and protein-based formulas were more likely to prefer sour flavors at 4 to 5 years of age compared with infants who were fed soy-based formulas, who, in turn, were more likely to prefer bitter flavors.

Intermodal Perception

All stimuli we encounter involve more than one type of sensory information. For example, we see a dog but we also hear its bark. Not only are infants able to sense in multiple modalities, but they are able to coordinate their senses. **Intermodal perception** is the process of combining information from more than one sensory system (Johnson & Hannon, 2015). Sensitivity to intermodal relations among stimuli is critical to perceptual development and learning—and this sensitivity emerges early in life (Lewkowicz, Leo, & Simion, 2010). That is, infants expect vision, auditory, and tactile information to occur together (Sai, 2005). For example, newborns turn their heads and eyes in the direction of a sound source, suggesting that they intuitively recognize that auditory and visual information co-occur and provide information about spatial location (Newell, 2004).

Newborns show a preference for viewing their mother's face at 72, 12, and even just 4 hours after birth (Pascalis, Dechonen, Morton, Duruelle, & Grenet, 1995). It was once believed that infants' preference for their mother's face was innate. Are infants born knowing their mother's face? In one study, neonates were able to visually recognize their mother's face only if the face was paired with their mother's voice at least once after birth (Sai, 2005). Thus, intermodal perception is evident at birth because neonates can coordinate auditory (voice) and visual stimuli (face) to recognize their mother. They quickly remember the association and demonstrate a preference for her face even when it is not paired with her voice.

Infants integrate touch and vision very early in life. In one classic study, 1-month-old infants were presented with a smooth-surfaced pacifier or one with nubs on it (see Figure 4.12). After exploring it with their mouths, the infants were shown two pacifiers—one smooth and one nubbed. The infants preferred to look at the shape they had sucked, suggesting that they could match tactile and visual stimuli (Meltzoff & Borton, 1979). In another example, 8- to 31-day-old infants fitted with special goggles were presented with a virtual object created by a shadow caster (Bower, Broughton, & Moore, 1970). The virtual object was an illusory object that could be seen by the infant but not touched. When the infant reached for the object, his or her hand felt nothing and flailed through the air. Infants exposed to the virtual object attempted to reach for it and became distressed when they did not feel it, suggesting that vision and touch are integrated and infants expect to feel objects that they can see and reach. Although young infants show impressive capacities to integrate visual and tactile information, these senses are not completely integrated at birth. Newborns can visually recognize an object previously held but not seen, but they cannot tactually recognize an object previously seen and not held, suggesting that intermodal relations among senses are not bidirectional at birth (Sann & Streri, 2007).

We have seen that individuals are embedded in and interact dynamically with their context. James and Eleanor Gibson studied perceptual development

FIGURE 4.12

Nubbed vs. Smooth Pacifier Used to Study Intermodal Perception

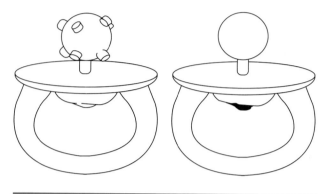

Source: Meltzoff and Borton, 1979.

from an ecological perspective, emphasizing that perception arises through interactions with the environment (Adolph & Kretch, 2015). Rather than collecting small pieces of sensory information and building a representation of the world, the Gibsons argued that the environment itself provides all the information needed and we perceive the environment directly, without constructing or manipulating sensory information.

Perception arises from action. Infants actively explore their environment with their eyes, moving their heads and, later, reaching their hands and, eventually, crawling. Perception provides the information infants need to traverse their environment. Through their exploration, infants perceive **affordances**—the nature, opportunities, and limits of objects (E. J. Gibson & Pick, 2000). The features of objects tell infants about their affordances, including their possibilities for action, such as whether an object is squeezable, mouthable, catchable, or reachable. Infants explore their environment, not randomly but rather systematically searching to discover the properties of the things around them (Savelsbergh, van der Kamp, & van Wermeskerken, 2013). From this perspective, perception arises from action, just as it influences action (J. Gibson, 1979). Exploration and discovery of affordances depends on infants' capacities for action, which is influenced by their development, genetics, and motivation. For example, a large pot might offer a 10-year-old the possibility of cooking because the child has developed this capacity and can perceive this affordance of the pot. An 18-month-old infant

may perceive very different affordances from the pot based on her capacities, such as a drum to bang or a bucket to fill. We naturally perceive affordances, such as knowing when a surface is safe for walking, by sensing information from the environment and coordinating it with our body sensations, such as our sense of balance (Kretch, Franchak, & Adolph, 2014). In this way, our perception of affordances, the opportunities for exploration, influences how we move and interact within our environments (Adolph & Kretch, 2015).

Newborns have remarkable capacities for sensing and perceiving stimuli. Their senses, although well developed at birth, improve rapidly over the first year of life. Moreover, capacities for intermodal perception mean that infants can combine information from various sensory modalities to construct a sophisticated and accurate picture of the world around them.

THINKING IN CONTEXT 4.4

1. How might infants' powerful sensory capacities prime them to learn how to think about their world? Learn language?

2. How might parents and caregivers design caregiving environments that are tailored to infants' early learning and sensory capacities and stimulate development? What advice would you give on how to design such an environment for a newborn? For a 6-month-old infant?

MOTOR DEVELOPMENT DURING INFANCY AND TODDLERHOOD

» LO 4.5   Analyze the roles of maturation and contextual factors in infant and toddler motor development.

Newborns are equipped to respond to the stimulation they encounter in the world. The earliest ways in which infants adapt are through the use of their reflexes, involuntary and automatic responses to stimuli such as touch, light, and sound. Each reflex has its own developmental course (Payne & Isaacs, 2016). Some disappear early in life and others persist throughout life, as shown in Table 4.1. Infants show individual differences in how reflexes are displayed, specifically the intensity of the response. Preterm newborns, for example, show reflexes suggesting a more immature neurological system than full-term newborns (Barros, Mitsuhiro, Chalem, Laranjeira, &

TABLE 4.1

Newborn Reflexes

NAME OF REFLEX	RESPONSE	DEVELOPMENTAL COURSE
Palmar grasp	Curling fingers around objects that touch the palm	Birth to about 4 months, when it is replaced by voluntary grasp
Rooting	Turning head and tongue toward stimulus when cheek is touched	Disappears over first few weeks of life and is replaced by voluntary head movement
Sucking	Sucking on objects placed into the mouth	Birth to about 6 months
Moro	Giving a startle response in reaction to loud noise or sudden change in the position of the head, resulting in throwing out arms, arching the back, and bringing the arms together as if to grasp something	Birth to about 5 to 7 months
Babinski	Fanning and curling the toes in response to stroking the bottom of the foot	Birth to about 8 to 12 months
Stepping	Making stepping movements as if to walk when held upright with feet touching a flat surface	Birth to about 2 to 3 months
Swimming	Holding breath and moving arms and legs, as if to swim, when placed in water	Birth to about 4 to 6 months

Guinsburg, 2011). The absence of reflexes, however, may signal neurological deficits.

Gross Motor Development

Gross motor development refers to the ability to control the large movements of the body, actions that help us move around in our environment. Like physical development, motor skills evolve in a predictable sequence. By the end of the first month of life, most infants can reach the first milestone, or achievement, in motor development: lifting their heads while lying on their stomachs. After lifting the head, infants progress through an orderly series of motor milestones: lifting the chest, reaching for objects, rolling over, and sitting up with support (see Table 4.2). Notice that these motor achievements reflect a cephalocaudal progression of motor control, proceeding from the head downward (Payne & Isaacs, 2016). Researchers have long believed that all motor control proceeds from the head downward, but we now know that motor development is more variable. Instead, some infants may sit up before they roll over or not crawl at all before they walk (Adolph & Robinson, 2015). Similarly, infants reach for toys with their feet weeks before they use their hands, suggesting that early leg movements can be precisely controlled, the development of skilled reaching need not involve lengthy practice, and early motor behavior does not necessarily follow a strict cephalocaudal pattern (Galloway & Thelen, 2004).

Success at initiating forward motion, or crawling (6–10 months), is particularly significant for both infants and parents. Infants vary in how they crawl

TABLE 4.2

Motor Milestones

AVERAGE AGE ACHIEVED	MOTOR SKILL
2 months	Lifts head Holds head steady when held upright
3 months	Pushes head and chest up with arms Rolls from stomach to back
4 months	Grasps cube
6 months	Sits without support
7 months	Rolls from back to stomach Attempts crawling Uses opposable thumb to grasp objects
8 months	Achieves sitting position alone Pulls to a stand
9 months	"Cruises" by holding on to furniture
10 months	Plays patty-cake
11 months	Stands alone
12 months	Walks alone
14 months	Builds tower of two cubes Scribbles
17 months	Walks up steps
18 months	Runs

(Adolph & Robinson, 2015). Some use their arms to pull and legs to push, some use only their arms or only their legs, and others scoot on their bottoms. Once infants can pull themselves upright while

By the end of the first month of life, most infants can lift their head while lying on their stomach.
iStock/aywan88

holding on to a chair or table, they begin "cruising," moving by holding on to furniture to maintain their balance while stepping sideways. In many Western industrialized countries, most infants walk alone by about 1 year of age.

Once babies can walk, their entire visual field changes. Whereas crawling babies are more likely to look at the floor as they move, walking babies gaze straight ahead at caregivers, walls, and toys (Kretch et al., 2014). Most beginning walkers, even through 19 months of age, tend to walk in shorts spurts, a few steps at a time, often ending in the middle of the floor (W. G. Cole, Robinson, & Adolph, 2016). Independent walking holds implications for cognitive, social, and emotional development, as it is associated not only with more attention and manipulation of objects but also with more sophisticated social interactions with caregivers, such as directing mothers' attention to particular objects and sharing. These behaviors, in turn, are associated with advanced language development relative to nonwalkers in both U.S. and Chinese infants (Ghassabian et al., 2016; He, Walle, & Campos, 2015).

Fine Motor Development

Fine motor development refers to the ability to control small movements of the fingers such as reaching and grasping. Voluntary reaching plays an important role in cognitive development because it provides new opportunities for interacting with the world. Like other motor skills, reaching and grasping begin as gross activity and are refined with time. Newborns begin by engaging in *prereaching*, swinging their arms and extending them toward nearby objects (Ennouri & Bloch, 1996; von Hofsten & Rönnqvist, 1993). Newborns use both arms equally and cannot control their arms and hands, so they rarely succeed in making contact with objects of interest (Lynch, Lee, Bhat, & Galloway, 2008). Prereaching stops at about 7 weeks of age.

Voluntary reaching appears at about 3 months of age and slowly improves in accuracy. At 5 months, infants can successfully reach for moving objects. By 7 months, the arms can reach independently, and infants are able to reach for an object with one arm rather than both (J. P. Spencer, Vereijken, Diedrich, & Thelen, 2000). By 10 months, infants can reach for moving objects that change direction (Fagard, Spelke, & von Hofsten, 2009). As they gain experience with reaching and acquiring objects, infants develop cognitively because they learn by exploring and playing with objects—and object preferences change with experience. In one study, 4- to 6-month-old infants with less reaching experience spent more time looking at and exploring larger objects, whereas 5- to 6-month-old infants with more reaching experience spent more time looking at and touching smaller objects. The older infants did this despite first looking at and touching the largest object (Libertus et al., 2013). With experience, infants' attention moves away from the motor skill (like the ability to coordinate their movement to hit a mobile), to the object (the mobile), as well as to the events that occur before and after acquiring the object (how the mobile swings and how grabbing it stops the swinging or how batting at it makes it swing faster). In this way, infants learn about cause and how to solve simple problems.

Biological and Contextual Determinants of Motor Development

Motor development illustrates the complex interactions that take place between maturation and contextual factors.

Biological Influences on Motor Development

Maturation plays a very strong role in motor development. Preterm infants reach motor milestones later than do full-term infants (Gabriel et al., 2009). Cross-cultural research also supports the role of maturation because around the world, infants display roughly the same sequence of motor milestones. Among some Native Americans and other ethnic groups around the world, it is common to follow the tradition of tightly swaddling infants to cradleboards and strapping the board to the mother's back during nearly all waking hours for the first 6 to 12 months of the child's life. Although this might lead one to expect that swaddled babies will not learn to walk as early as babies whose movements are unrestricted, studies of Hopi Indian infants have shown that swaddling has little impact on when Hopi infants initiate walking (Dennis & Dennis, 1991; Harriman & Lukosius, 1982). Such research suggests that walking is very much maturationally programmed. Other evidence for the maturational basis of motor development comes from twin studies. Identical twins, who share the same genes, have more similarities in the timing and pace of motor development than do fraternal twins,

Hand Preference and Language Development in Infancy

Infants who show an early preference for their right hand also show advanced language abilities at 2 months of age. It may be that infants with a dominant hand are better at stacking blocks and picking up other small objects and toys. These activites promote cognitive development, a contributor to language development.
iStock/ fatcamera

Are you a righty or a lefty? People—even infants—usually show a preference for the right hand over the left. In most people, handedness is lateralized to the left hemisphere (Annett, 2002). Language is also processed asymmetrically in the brain. For example, infants and adults tend to show activity in their left hemisphere in response to language (Dehaene-Lambertz, 2017), especially in response to their native language compared with nonnative language (Vannasing et al., 2016). Given that hand preference has been observed prenatally (Hepper, 2013), some researchers have begun to examine whether hand preference is an early indicator of hemispheric specialization and thereby language development. What is the relationship between handedness and language development? Does hand preference predict language development in infancy?

Although hand preferences have been observed in the womb, infants show individual differences. Some infants show consistent hand preferences across motor tasks and others show a more unstable pattern, switching

hands often (Cochet, 2012; Kotwica, Ferre, & Michel, 2008). Infants who consistently prefer the right hand demonstrate greater left hemispheric specialization than those without a consistent hand preference (E. L. Nelson, Campbell, & Michel, 2015). One longitudinal study followed infants at monthly intervals from 6 to 14 months and again from 18 to 24 months to examine the relationship of handedness and language development (E. L. Nelson, Campbell, & Michel, 2013). Although the infants did not differ on measures of cognition or general motor skills, infants who showed early preferences for their right hand also showed advanced language abilities at 2 months of age. A consistent right-hand preference during infancy suggested greater lateralization and activity in the left hemisphere, in regions long associated with language. It is important to note, however, that an early hand preference predicted *advanced* language skill, but children without a stable hand preference showed normative language development.

Why is having a consistent hand preference associated with advanced language acquisition? Perhaps infants who show a consistent hand preference are better at manipulating objects than those without a stable preference (Kotwica et al., 2008). Infants' skill in object manipulation is associated with cognition because it permits infants to examine objects in greater detail (Bruner, 1973). Fine motor skills enable infants to play in sophisticated ways, such as stacking blocks, picking up small objects, and filling cups and other containers—and then dumping out the contents. Infants with a dominant hand show greater skill in manipulating objects and using tools to carry out these tasks (Michel, Campbell, Marcinowski, Nelson, & Babik, 2016)—and each of these activities promotes cognitive development, a contributor to language development.

What Do You Think?

What might be the long-term implications for a consistent hand preference early in infancy? For language? Cognition? Motor skill? ●

who share half of their genes (Fogel, 2007; Wilson & Harpring, 1972). Samples of young children in the United States show no ethnic or socioeconomic status differences in gross motor skill such as running, hopping, kicking, and catching (Kit, Akinbami, Isfahani, & Ulrich, 2017).

Advancements in motor skill are influenced by body maturation and especially brain development. The pruning of unused synapses contributes to increases in motor speed and reaction time so that

11-year-old children tend to respond twice as quickly as 5-year-olds (Kail, 2003). Growth of the cerebellum (responsible for balance, coordination, and some aspects of emotion and reasoning) and myelination of its connections to the cortex contribute to advances in gross and fine motor skills and speed (Tiemeier et al., 2010). Brain development improves children's ability to inhibit actions, which enables children to carry out more sophisticated motor activities that require the use of one hand while controlling the

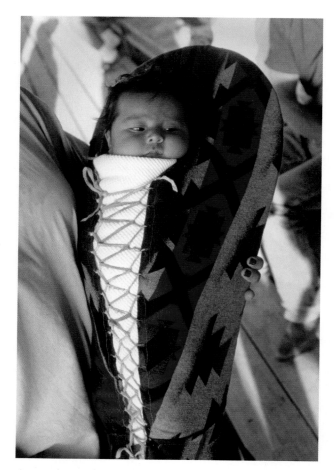

Although this infant spends most of his waking hours tightly swaddled to a cradleboard and carried on his mother's back, he will walk at about a year of age, similar to babies who are not swaddled.
Danita Delimont/Alamy Stock Photo

other, such as throwing a ball, or that require both hands to do different things, such as playing a musical instrument (Diamond, 2013). As infants and children gain experience coordinating their motor skills, activity in the areas of the brain responsible for motor skills becomes less diffuse and more focused, consistent with the lifespan principle that domains of development interact (Nishiyori, Bisconti, Meehan, & Ulrich, 2016).

Contextual Influences on Motor Development

Much of motor development is driven by maturation, yet opportunities to practice motor skills are also important. In a classic naturalistic study of institutionalized orphans in Iran who had spent their first 2 years of life lying on their backs in their cribs and were never placed in sitting positions or played with, none of the 1- to 2-year-old infants could walk, and fewer than half of them could sit up; the

researchers also found that most of the 3- to 4-year-olds could not walk well alone (Dennis, 1960). Recent research suggests that infants raised in orphanages score lower on measures of gross motor milestones at 4, 6, and 8 months of age and walk later compared with home-reared infants (Chaibal, Bennett, Rattanathanthong, & Siritaratiwat, 2016). While maturation is necessary for motor development, it is not sufficient; we must also have opportunities to practice our motor skills.

In fact, practice can enhance motor development (Lobo & Galloway, 2012). For example, when infants from 1 to 7 weeks of age practice stepping reflexes each day, they retain the movements and walk earlier than infants who receive no practice (Vereijken & Thelen, 1997; Zelazo, 1983). Even newborns show improvement in stepping after practicing on a treadmill (Siekerman et al., 2015). Practice in sitting has a similar effect (Zelazo, Zelazo, Cohen, & Zelazo, 1993). Even 1-month-old infants given postural training showed more advanced control of their heads and necks than other infants (H. Lee & Galloway, 2012). Similarly, infants who spend supervised playtime prone on their stomachs each day reach many motor milestones, including rolling over and crawling, earlier than do infants who spend little time on their stomachs (Fetters & Hsiang-han, 2007; Kuo, Liao, Chen, Hsieh, & Hwang, 2008). In one study, over a 2-week period, young infants received daily play experience with "sticky mittens"—Velcro-covered mitts that enabled them to independently pick up objects. These infants showed advances in their reaching behavior and greater visual exploration of objects, while a comparison group of young infants who passively watched an adult's actions on the objects showed no change (Libertus & Needham, 2010). Sticky mittens training in reaching at 3 months of age predicts object exploration at 15 months of age (Libertus, Joh, & Needham, 2016).

Practice contributes to cross-cultural differences in infant motor development. Different cultures provide infants with different experiences and opportunities for development. For example, in many cultures, including several in sub-Saharan Africa and in the West Indies, infants attain motor goals like sitting up and walking much earlier than do North American infants. Among the Kipsigi of Kenya, parents seat babies in holes dug in the ground and use rolled blankets to keep babies upright in the sitting position (Keller, 2003). The Kipsigis help their babies practice walking at 2 to 3 months of age by holding their hands, putting them on the floor, and moving them slowly forward. Notably, Kipsigi mothers do not encourage their infants to crawl; crawling is seen as dangerous as it exposes the child to dirt, insects, and the dangers of fire pits and roaming animals. Crawling is therefore virtually nonexistent in Kipsigi infants (Super & Harkness, 2015). Infants of many sub-Saharan villages, such as the !Kung San, Gusii, and Wolof, are also trained to sit using holes or containers for support and are often held upright and bounced up and down, a social interaction practice that contributes to earlier walking (Lohaus et al., 2011). Caregivers in some of these cultures further encourage walking by setting up two parallel bamboo poles that infants can hold onto with both hands, learning balance and stepping skills (Keller, 2003). Similarly, mothers in Jamaica and other parts of the West Indies use a formal handling routine to exercise their babies' muscles and help them to grow up strong and healthy (Dziewolska & Cautilli, 2006; Hopkins, 1991; Hopkins & Westra, 1989, 1990).

Infants' motor development varies with cultural styles of interaction, such as a Western cultural emphasis on individualism and Eastern cultural emphasis on collectivism. In one cross-cultural study comparing infants in Germany and in the Cambodian Nso culture, the Nso infants showed overall more rapid motor development. The Nso practice of close proximity, lots of close body contact, and less object play are related to the socialization goals of fostering relationships; they also provide infants with body stimulation that fosters gross motor skills. German mothers displayed a parenting style with less body contact but more face-to-face contact and object play, socialization practices that emphasize psychological autonomy but less gross motor exploration. However, the German infants learned how to roll from back to stomach earlier than the Nso infants, likely because Nso infants are rarely placed on their backs and instead are carried throughout the day (Lohaus et al., 2011).

Although practice can speed development and caregivers in many cultures provide their infants with opportunities for early practice of motor skills, sometimes survival and success require continued dependence on caregivers and delaying motor milestones. For example, crawling may not be encouraged in potentially dangerous environments, such as those with many insects, rodents, and/or reptiles on the ground. The nomadic Ache of eastern Paraguay discourage their infants from crawling or moving independently. Ache infants walk at 18 to 20 months, compared with the 12-month average of North American infants (Kaplan & Dove, 1987).

Even simple aspects of the childrearing context, such as choice of clothing, can influence motor development. In the 19th century, 40% of American infants skipped crawling, possibly because the long, flowing gowns they wore impeded movement on hands and knees (Trettien, 1990). One study of 13- and 19-month-old infants compared their gait while wearing a disposable diaper, a thicker cloth diaper, and no diaper (W. G. Cole, Lingeman, & Adolph, 2012). When naked, infants demonstrated the most sophisticated walking with fewer missteps and falls. While wearing a diaper, infants walked as poorly as they would have done several weeks earlier had they been walking naked. In sum, motor development is largely maturational, but subtle differences in context and cultural emphasis play a role in its timing.

Motor Development as a Dynamic System

Motor milestones, such as the ability to crawl, might look like isolated achievements, but they actually develop systematically and build on each other with each new skill preparing an infant to tackle the next (Thelen, 1995, 2000). According to **dynamic systems theory**, as shown in Figure 4.13, motor development reflects an interaction among developmental domains, maturation, and environment (Thelen, 1995, 2000). Simple motor skills are combined in increasingly complex ways, permitting advances in movement, including a wider range and more precise movements that enable babies to more effectively explore and control their environments. Separate abilities are blended together to provide more complex and effective ways of exploring and controlling the environment. For example, the abilities to sit upright, hold the head upright, match motor movements to vision, reach out an arm, and grasp are all combined into coordinated reaching movements to obtain a desired object (Corbetta & Snapp-Childs, 2009; J. P. Spencer et al., 2000). Motor skills become more specialized, coordinated, and precise with practice, permitting infants to reach for an object with one hand without needlessly flailing the other, for example (D'Souza, Cowie, Karmiloff-Smith, & Bremner, 2016).

Motor skills also reflect the interaction of multiple domains of development. All movement relies on the coordination of our senses and cognitive abilities to plan and predict actions. Sensory abilities such as binocular vision and the ability to direct gaze combine with exploratory hand and foot movements, designed to determine the opportunities a given surface provides for movement. For example, when 14-month-old infants were tested on a "bridge" of varying widths, they explored the bridge first with quick glances (Kretch & Adolph, 2017). When faced with an impossibly narrow width, infants with walking experience tended to engage in more

FIGURE 4.13

Dynamic Systems Theory

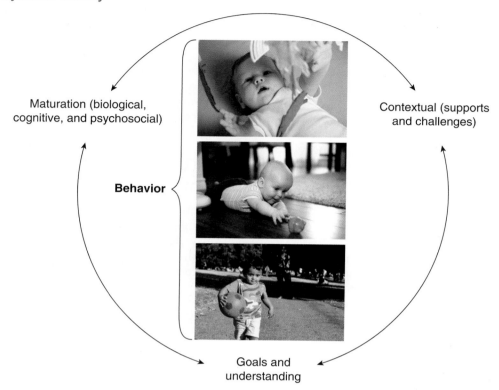

Maturation (biological, cognitive, and psychosocial)

Contextual (supports and challenges)

Behavior

Goals and understanding

The infant's abilities to reach out an arm, stretch, and grasp combine into coordinated reaching movements to obtain desired objects. Motor development progresses to sitting, crawling, walking, and eventually running, all reflections of infants' blending and coordinating abilities to achieve self-chosen goals, such as obtaining toys, and all tailored by environmental supports and challenges.

Source: ©iStockphoto.com/Essentials Collection; ©iStockphoto.com/Essentials Collection; © Can Stock Photo Inc./harishmarnad

extensive and time-consuming perceptual and motor exploration, such as touching with hands and feet, to determine whether to cross the bridge.

Motor development reflects goal-oriented behavior because it is initiated by the infant or child's desire to accomplish something, such as picking up a toy or moving to the other side of the room. Infants' abilities and their immediate environments (e.g., whether they are being held, lying in a crib, or lying freely on the floor) determine whether and how the goal can be achieved (J. P. Spencer et al., 2000). The infant tries out behaviors and persists at those that enable him or her to move closer to the goal, practicing and refining the behavior. For example, infants learn to walk by taking many steps and making many falls, but they persist even though, at the time, crawling is a much faster and more efficient means of transportation (Adolph et al., 2012). Why? Perhaps because upright posture leads to many more interesting sights, objects, and interactions. The upright infant can see more and do more, with two hands free to grasp objects, making walking a very desirable goal (Adolph & Tamis-LeMonda, 2014). New motor skills provide

new possibilities for exploration of the environment and new interactions with caregivers that influence opportunities. Differences in caregiver interactions and caregiving environments affect children's motor skills, the form they take, the ages of onset, and the overall developmental trend (Adolph & Franchak, 2017).

Social and cultural contexts contribute to our movements. Motor skills do not develop in isolation; rather, they are influenced by the physical and social context in which they occur. For example, a naturalistic study of video records of at-home interactions of mother–infant pairs from six countries revealed large differences in opportunities for infant sitting and infant performance (Karasik, Tamis-LeMonda, Adolph, & Bornstein, 2015). Infants from the United States, Argentina, South Korea, and Italy spent most of their sitting time in places that offered postural support, such as child furniture. In contrast, infants from Kenya and Cameroon, who spent most of their sitting time in places that offered little postural support, such as the ground of adult furniture, tended to show the longest bouts of independent sitting and at the earliest age. Cultural differences in daily activities influence motor skills across the lifespan. Long-distance running is part of daily life for Tarahumaran children, who routinely run 10 to 40 kilometers in a few hours and adults 150 to 300 kilometers in 24 to 48 hours (Adolph & Franchak, 2017). From childhood, East African females carry heavy loads balanced on their heads, altering their posture and gait to complete a contextually important activity.

Therefore, from a dynamic systems perspective, motor development is the result of several processes: central nervous system maturation, the infant's physical capacities, environmental supports, and the infant's desire to explore the world. It is learned by revising and combining abilities and skills to fit the infant's goals. In this way, motor development is highly individualized as each infant has goals and opportunities that are particular to his or her specific environment (Adolph & Franchak, 2017). For example, an infant might respond to slippery hardwood floors by crawling on her stomach rather than all fours or by shuffling her feet and hands

rather than raising each. Infants attain the same motor tasks, such as climbing down stairs, at about the same age, yet differ in how they approach the task. Some, for example, might turn around and back down, others descend on their bottoms, and others slide down face first (Berger, Theuring, & Adolph, 2007). By viewing motor development as dynamic systems of action produced by an infant's abilities, goal-directed behavior, and environmental supports and opportunities, we can account for the individual differences that we see in motor development.

THINKING IN CONTEXT 4.5

1. Carmen is concerned because her 14-month-old baby is not walking. All of the other babies she knows have walked by 12 months of age. What would you tell Carmen?

2. How might a fine motor skill, such as learning to use a spoon, reflect the interaction of maturation and sociocultural context?

APPLY YOUR KNOWLEDGE

Lena is 7 months old and lags behind in height and weight compared with other infants her age. Early in life, she showed normative growth, but her growth has since slowed. Recently, Lena's parents separated, and she and her mother moved to a new home. Her mother is 19 years old, does not have a high school degree, and had few job opportunities. She took the first job that panned out, despite its long hours. Lena was placed in child care. Her mother continued to breastfeed, despite its increasing difficulty given her new work schedule. Lena's mother insisted that Lena eat less solid food and baby food given her continued breastfeeding. Staff at the child care center approached Lena's mother to express their concern over Lena's lack of growth and development; she has not

begun crawling like other infants and tends to avoid eye contact with others.

1. What are normative patterns of growth for infants? Motor skills? How does Lena's development compare with these norms?

2. What are potential causes of or influences on the developmental difficulties Lena experiences? How might contextual factors influence Lena's development?

3. What are the child care staff's responsibilities?

4. What should the mother do? What treatment do you suggest?

Visit **edge.sagepub.com/kuther2e** to help you accomplish your coursework goals in an easy-to-use learning environment.

LEARNING OBJECTIVES	SUMMARY	KEY TERMS	IN REVIEW
4.1 Discuss growth and the role of nutrition in development during infancy and toddlerhood.	Growth proceeds from the head downward (cephalocaudal) and from the center of the body outward (proximodistal). Breastfeeding is associated with many benefits for mothers and infants. Malnourishment is associated with growth stunting and impaired learning, concentration, and language skills throughout childhood and adolescence. Severely malnourished children may suffer from diseases such as marasmus and kwashiorkor or, more common in the United States, failure to thrive. If nutrition is reinstated early, some of the damage caused by malnutrition can be reversed, but long-term cognitive difficulties often remain.	Cephalocaudal development Proximodistal development Growth norms Marasmus Kwashiorkor Failure to thrive	What are two patterns that describe growth in infancy and childhood? What are two types of malnutrition found primarily in developing nations? What is failure to thrive?
4.2 Summarize brain development during infancy and toddlerhood.	The brain develops through several processes: neurogenesis (the creation of neurons), synaptogenesis (the creation of synapses), pruning (reducing unused neural connections), and myelination (coating the axons with myelin to increase the speed of transmission). Experience shapes the brain structure. The brain produces an excess of connections among neurons during the first 3 years of life. Those connections that are used become stronger, and neural connections that are not used are pruned. Although infancy is a particularly important time for the formation and strengthening of synapses, experience shapes the brain structure at all ages of life.	Neurons Neurogenesis Glial cells Cortex Synapses Synaptogenesis Synaptic pruning Myelination Lateralization Hemispheric dominance Corpus callosum Experience-expectant brain development Experience-dependent brain development	Describe processes of neural development in infancy and toddlerhood. What is the cerebral cortex? What are examples of experience-expectant brain development and experience-dependent brain development?
4.3 Compare infants' early learning capacities for habituation, classical conditioning, operant conditioning, and imitation.	Innate learning capacities permit young infants to quickly adapt to the world. Habituation is a type of innate learning in which repeated exposure to a stimulus results in the gradual decline in the intensity, frequency, or duration of a response. In classical conditioning, an association is formed between a neutral stimulus and one that triggers an innate reaction. Infants also learn based on the consequences of the behaviors, whether they are followed by reinforcement or punishment, known as operant conditioning. Neonates mimic simple facial and finger expressions but do so without control. The regulatory mechanisms to inhibit imitative responding develop during infancy.	Habituation	Provide examples of how babies learn through: • habituation • classical conditioning • operant conditioning • imitation
4.4 Describe infants' developing sensory abilities.	Visual acuity, pattern perception, visual tracking, and color vision improve over the first few months of life. Neonates are sensitive to depth cues and young infants can distinguish depth, but crawling stimulates the perception of depth and the association of fear with sharp drops. Newborns can perceive and discriminate nearly all sounds in human languages, but from birth, they prefer to hear their native language. Intermodal perception is evident at birth as infants can combine information from more than one sensory system.	Sensation Perception Circumcision Intermodal perception Affordances	How does vision develop during infancy? Describe infants' abilities to smell and hear. What is intermodal perception? How does intermodal perception contribute to early learning?

4.5 Analyze the roles of maturation and contextual factors in infant and toddler motor development.	Infants are born with reflexes, each with its own developmental course. Gross and fine motor skills develop systematically and build on each other, with each new skill preparing the infant to tackle the next. Much of motor development is influenced by maturation, but infants benefit from opportunities to practice motor skills. Different cultures provide infants with different experiences and opportunities for practice, contributing to cross-cultural differences in motor development. Viewing motor development as dynamic systems of action produced by an infant's abilities, goal-directed behavior, and environmental supports and opportunities accounts for the individual differences that we see in motor development.	Gross motor development Fine motor development Dynamic systems theory	How do gross and fine motor development proceed in infancy and toddlerhood? What are examples of biological and contextual influences on motor development? What is dynamic systems theory?

5 Cognitive Development in Infancy and Toddlerhood

"Be careful with Baby Emily," Lila warned her 22-month-old son, Michael. "She's just 1 week old and very little. You were once little like her." "No," Michael said and giggled. "Big boy!" Michael picked up his teddy bear, cradled it like a baby, then held it to his chest rubbing its back, just like what he sees Mommy do with Baby Emily. In less than 2 years, Michael has transformed from a tiny infant, like Baby Emily, to a toddler who imitates what he sees and can verbally express his ideas. Like all newborns, Baby Emily is equipped with inborn sensory capacities and preferences that enable her to tune in to the world around her. Baby Emily's abilities to think, reason, problem solve, and interact with objects and people will change dramatically over the next 2 years. In this chapter, we will explore the cognitive developments that occur during infancy and toddlerhood.

Learning Objectives

5.1 Discuss the cognitive-developmental perspective on infant reasoning.

5.2 Describe the information processing system in infants.

5.3 Discuss individual differences in infant intelligence.

5.4 Summarize the patterns of language development during infancy and toddlerhood.

Digital Resources

Explore: Infants Know Poisonous Plants

▶ **Lives in Context Video 5.1:** Object Permanence

Connect: Why Is Categorization Important?

▶ **Lives in Context Video 5.2:** Infants, Young Children, and Technology

Listen: The Secret Language of Babies

Connect: Baby Talk Boosts Baby Brains

PIAGET'S COGNITIVE-DEVELOPMENTAL THEORY

>> **LO 5.1** **Discuss the cognitive-developmental perspective on infant reasoning.**

The first scientist to systematically examine children's thinking and reasoning, Swiss scholar Jean Piaget (1896–1980), believed that to understand children, we must understand how they think because thinking influences all of behavior. According to Piaget's cognitive-developmental theory, children and adults are active explorers who learn by interacting with the world, building their own understanding of everyday phenomena, and applying it to adapt to the world around them.

Processes of Development

According to Piaget (1952), children are active in their own development not simply because they engage other people but because they engage the world, adapting their ways of thinking in response to their experiences. Through these interactions, they organize what they learn to construct and refine their own cognitive schemas, or concepts, ideas, and ways of interacting with the world. The earliest schemas are inborn motor responses, such as the reflex response that causes infants to close their fingers around an object when it touches their

palm. As infants grow and develop, these early motor schemas are transformed into cognitive schemas, or thoughts and ideas. At every age, we rely on our schemas to make sense of the world, and our schemas are constantly adapting and developing in response to our experiences. Piaget also emphasized the importance of two developmental processes that enable us to cognitively adapt to our world: assimilation and accommodation.

Assimilation involves integrating a new experience into a preexisting schema. For example, suppose that 1-year-old Kelly uses the schema of "grab and shove into the mouth" to learn. He grabs and shoves his rattle into his mouth, learning about the rattle by using his preexisting schema. When Kelly comes across another object, such as Mommy's wristwatch, he transfers the schema to it—and assimilates the wristwatch by grabbing it and shoving it into his mouth. He develops an understanding of the new objects through assimilation, by fitting them into his preexisting schema.

Sometimes we encounter experiences or information that do not fit within an existing schema, so we must change the schema, adapting and modifying it in light of the new information. This process is called **accommodation.** For example, suppose Kelly encounters another object, a beach ball. He tries his schema of grab and shove, but the beach ball won't fit into his mouth; perhaps he cannot even grab it. He must adapt his schema or create a new one in order to incorporate the new information—

to learn about the beach ball. Kelly may squeeze and mouth the ball instead, accommodating or changing his schema to interact with the new object.

The processes of assimilation and accommodation enable people to adapt to their environment, absorbing the constant flux of information they encounter daily (see Figure 5.1). People—infants, children, and adults—constantly integrate new information into their schemas and continually encounter new information that requires them to modify their schemas. Piaget proposed that people naturally strive for *cognitive equilibrium*, a balance between the processes of assimilation and accommodation. When assimilation and accommodation are balanced, individuals are neither incorporating new information into their schemas nor changing their schemas in light of new information; instead, our schemas match the outside world and represent it clearly. But a state of cognitive equilibrium is rare and fleeting. More frequently, people experience a mismatch, or *disequilibrium*, between their schemas and the world.

Disequilibrium leads to cognitive growth because of the mismatch between schemas and reality. This mismatch leads to confusion and discomfort, which in turn motivate children to modify their cognitive schemas so that their view of the world matches reality. It is through assimilation and accommodation that this modification takes place so that cognitive equilibrium is restored. Children's drive for cognitive equilibrium is the basis for cognitive change, propelling them through the four stages of cognitive development proposed by Piaget (refer to Chapter 1). With each advancing stage, children create and use more sophisticated cognitive schemas, enabling them to think, reason, and understand their world in more complex ways.

Sensorimotor Substages

"There you go, little guy," Mateo's uncle says, placing a rattle within the infant's grasp. Six-month-old Mateo shakes the toy and puts it in his mouth, sucking on it. He then removes the rattle from his mouth and gives it a vigorous shake, dropping it to the ground. "Mateo! Where's your rattle?" asks his mother. "Whenever he drops his toy, he never looks for it," she explains to Nico's uncle, "not even when it's his favorite toy." Mateo displays sensorimotor thinking. During the sensorimotor stage, from birth to about 2 years old, infants learn about the world through their senses and motor skills. To think about an object, they must act on it by viewing it, listening to it, touching it, smelling it, and tasting it. Piaget (1952) believed that infants are not capable of **mental representation**—thinking about an object using mental pictures. They also lack the ability to remember and think about objects and events when they are not present. Instead, in order to think about an object, an infant must experience it through both the visual and tactile senses. The sensorimotor period of reasoning, as Piaget conceived of it, progresses through six substages in which cognition develops from reflexes to intentional action to symbolic representation.

Substage 1: Reflexes (Birth to 1 Month)

In the first substage, newborns use their reflexes, such as the sucking and palmar grasp reflexes, to react to stimuli. During the first month of life, infants use these reflexes to learn about their world, through the process of assimilation; they apply their sucking schema to assimilate information and learn about their environment. At about 1 month of age, newborns begin to accommodate, or modify, their sucking behaviors to specific objects, sucking differently in response to a bottle versus a pacifier. For example, they may modify their sucking schema when they encounter a pacifier, perhaps sucking less vigorously and without swallowing. During the first month of life, newborns strengthen and modify their original reflexive schemas to explore the world around them.

Substage 2: Primary Circular Reactions (1 to 4 Months)

During the second substage, infants begin to make accidental discoveries. Early cognitive

---

FIGURE 5.1

Assimilation and Accommodation

Assimilation   **Accommodation**

Bobby sees a cat that fits his schema for kitty (left). He has never seen a cat like this before (right). He must accommodate his schema for kitty to include a hairless cat.

Source: istock/GlobalP; istock/YouraPechkin

In the first substage (birth to 1 month), newborns use their reflexes to respond to stimuli. They strengthen and modify their reflexive schemas to explore the world around them.
iStock/Stefano Oppo

growth in the sensorimotor period comes through engaging in **circular reactions,** the repetition of an action and its response. Infants learn to repeat pleasurable or interesting events that originally occurred by chance. Between 1 and 4 months, infants engage in behaviors called **primary circular reactions,** which consist of repeating actions involving parts of the body that produce pleasurable or interesting results. A primary circular reaction begins by chance, as the infant produces a pleasurable sensation and learns to repeat the behavior to make the event happen again and experience the pleasurable effect again. For example, an infant flails her arms and accidentally puts her hand in her mouth. She is surprised at the outcome (her hand in her mouth) and tries to make it happen again. Therefore, the infant repeats the behavior to experience and explore her body.

In the second substage (1 to 4 months), infants discover that they can control their bodies and repeat the behavior to experience and explore their bodies.
iStock/W6

Substage 3: Secondary Circular Reactions (4 to 8 Months)

During the third sensorimotor substage, as infants' awareness extends further, they engage in **secondary circular reactions,** repetitions of actions that trigger responses in the external environment. Now the patterns of repetition are oriented toward making interesting events occur in the infant's environment. For example, the infant shakes a rattle to hear its noise or kicks his legs to move a mobile hanging over the crib. Secondary circular reactions indicate that infants' attention has expanded to include the environment outside their bodies and that they are beginning to understand that their actions cause results in the external world. In this way, infants discover new ways of interacting with their environments to continue experiencing sensations and events that they find pleasing.

During the third sensorimotor substage (4 to 8 months), infants' awareness extends to include objects. They repeat actions to view and experience their effects on objects.
iStock/FamVeld

Substage 4: Coordination of Secondary Circular Reactions (8 to 12 Months)

Unlike primary and secondary circular reactions, behaviors that are discovered by accident, the coordination of secondary circular reactions substage represents true means–end behavior and signifies the beginning of intentional behavior. During this substage, infants purposefully coordinate two secondary circular reactions and apply them in new situations to achieve a goal. For example, Piaget described how his son, Laurent, combined the two activities of knocking a barrier out of his way and grasping an object. When Piaget put a pillow in front of a matchbox that Laurent desired, the boy pushed the pillow aside and grabbed the box. In this way, Laurent integrated two secondary circular reactions to achieve a goal. Now planning and goal-directed behavior have emerged.

During the fourth substage (8 to 12 months) infants demonstrate object permanence, the understanding that objects exist outside of sensory awareness.
Doug Goodman / Science Source

During the fifth substage (12 to 18 months), infants begin to experiment with new behaviors to see the results.
iStock/MartinPrescott

One of the most important advances during the coordination of secondary circular reactions stage is **object permanence,** the understanding that objects continue to exist outside of sensory awareness (e.g., when they are no longer visible). According to Piaget, infants younger than 8 months of age do not yet have object permanence—out of sight is literally out of mind. An infant loses interest and stops reaching for or looking at a small toy after it is covered by a cloth. Not until 8 to 12 months, during the coordination of secondary circular reactions stage, will an infant search for hidden objects, thus displaying object permanence. This development is an important cognitive advance because it signifies a capacity for mental representation, or internal thought. The ability to think about an object internally is an important step toward learning language because language uses symbols: Sounds symbolize and stand for objects (e.g., infants must understand that the sound "ball" represents an object, a ball).

Stage 5: Tertiary Circular Reactions
(12 to 18 Months)

During the fifth substage, infants begin to experiment with new behaviors to see the results. Piaget described infants as "little scientists" during this period because they move from intentional behavior to systematic exploration. In what Piaget referred to as **tertiary circular reactions,** infants now engage in mini-experiments: active, purposeful, trial-and-error exploration to search for new discoveries. They vary their actions to see how the changes affect the outcomes. For example, many infants begin to experiment with gravity by dropping objects to the floor while sitting in a high chair. First an infant throws a ball and watches it bounce. Next a piece of paper floats slowly down. Then mommy's keys clatter to the floor. And so on. This purposeful exploration is how infants search for new discoveries and learn about the world. When presented with a problem, babies in the tertiary circular reactions substage engage in trial-and-error analyses, trying out behaviors until they find the best one to attain their goal. Figure 5.2 illustrates primary, secondary, and tertiary reactions.

Substage 6: Mental Representation
(18 to 24 Months)

The sixth sensorimotor substage marks a transition between the sensorimotor and preoperational reasoning stages. Between 18 and 24 months of age, infants develop *representational thought,* the ability to use symbols such as words and mental pictures to represent objects and actions in memory. In developing this ability, infants are freed from immediate experience: They can think about objects that they no longer see directly in front of them and can engage in deferred imitation, imitating actions of an absent model. Now, external physical exploration of the world gives way to internal mental exploration. Children can think through potential solutions and create new solutions without engaging in physical trial and error but simply by considering the potential solutions and their consequences. Table 5.1 summarizes the substages of sensorimotor reasoning.

Evaluating Sensorimotor Reasoning

Piaget's contributions to our understanding of cognitive development are vast and invaluable. He was the first to ask what develops during childhood

FIGURE 5.2

Primary, Secondary, and Tertiary Circular Reactions

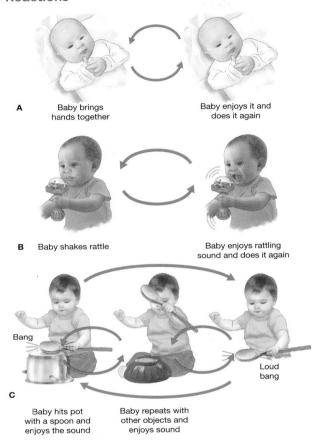

A   Baby brings hands together

Baby enjoys it and does it again

B   Baby shakes rattle

Baby enjoys rattling sound and does it again

Bang

Loud bang

C

Baby hits pot with a spoon and enjoys the sound

Baby repeats with other objects and enjoys sound

Source: Adapted from Papalia et al., 2001.

and how it occurs. Piaget recognized that motor action and cognition are inextricably linked, a view still accepted by today's developmental scientists (Libertus, Joh, & Needham, 2016).

Piaget's work has stimulated a great deal of research as developmental scientists have tested his theory. However, measuring the cognitive capabilities of infants and toddlers is very challenging because, unlike older children and adults, babies cannot fill out questionnaires or answer questions orally. Researchers have had to devise methods of measuring observable behavior that can provide clues to what an infant is thinking. For example, researchers measure infants' looking behavior by determining what infants look at and for how long. Using such methods, they have found support for some of Piaget's claims and evidence that challenges

others. One of the most contested aspects of Piaget's theory concerns his assumption that infants are not capable of mental representation until late in the sensorimotor period (Carey, Zaitchik, & Bascandziev, 2015). A growing body of research conducted with object permanence and imitation tasks suggests otherwise, as described in the following sections.

Violation-of-Expectation Tasks

Piaget's method of determining an infant's understanding of object permanence relied on the infant's ability to demonstrate it by uncovering a hidden object. Critics argue that many infants may understand that the object is hidden but lack the motor ability to coordinate their hands to physically demonstrate their understanding. Studying infants' looking behavior enables researchers to study object permanence in younger infants with undeveloped motor skills because it eliminates the need for infants to use motor activity to demonstrate their cognitive competence.

One such research design uses a **violation-of-expectation task**, a task in which a stimulus appears to violate physical laws (Hespos & Baillargeon, 2008). Specifically, in a violation-of-expectation task, an infant is shown two events: one that is labeled *expected* because it follows physical laws and a second that is called *unexpected* because it violates physical laws. If the infant looks longer at the unexpected event, it suggests that he or she is surprised by it, is aware of physical properties of objects, and can mentally represent them.

In a classic study, developmental researcher Renée Baillargeon (1987) used the violation-of-expectation method to study the mental representation capacities of very young infants. Infants were shown a drawbridge that rotated 180 degrees. Then the infants watched as a box was placed behind the drawbridge to impede its movement. Infants watched as either the drawbridge rotated and stopped upon hitting the box or did not stop and appeared to move through the box (an "impossible" event). As shown in Figure 5.3, 4½-month-old infants looked longer when the drawbridge appeared to move through the box (the "impossible" unexpected event) than when it stopped upon hitting the box. Baillargeon and colleagues interpreted infants' behavior as suggesting that the infants maintained a mental representation of the box, even though they could not see it, and therefore understood that the drawbridge could not move through the entire box.

TABLE 5.1		

Substages of Sensorimotor Reasoning

SUBSTAGE	MAJOR FEATURES	EXAMPLE
Reflexive activity (0–1 month)	Strengthens and adapts reflexes	Newborn shows a different sucking response to a nipple versus a pacifier.
Primary circular reactions (1–4 months)	Repeats motor actions that produce interesting outcomes that are centered toward the body	Infant bats mobile with arm and watches arm move.
Secondary circular reactions (4–8 months)	Repeats motor actions that produce interesting outcomes that are directed toward the environment	Infant bats mobile with his arm and watches the mobile move.
Coordination of secondary schemas (8–12 months)	Combines secondary circular reactions to achieve goals and solve problems; the beginnings of intentional behavior	Infant uses one hand to lift a bucket covering a ball and the other to grasp the ball. Infant uses both hands to pull a string attached to a ball and eventually reach the ball.
Tertiary circular reactions (12–18 months)	Experiments with different actions to achieve the same goal or observe the outcome and make new discoveries	Toddler hits a pot with a wooden spoon and listens to the sound, then hits other objects in the kitchen, such as the refrigerator, stove, or plates, to hear the sound that the spoon makes against the objects.
Mental representation (18–24 months)	Internal mental representation of objects and events; thinking to solve problems rather than relying on trial and error	When confronted with a problem, like a toy that is out of reach on the counter, the toddler considers possible solutions to a problem in his mind, decides on a solution, and implements it.

Other researchers counter that these results do not demonstrate object permanence but rather illustrate infants' preference for novelty or for greater movement (Bogartz, Shinskey, & Schilling, 2000; Heyes, 2014). For example, when the study was replicated without the box, 5-month-old infants looked longer at the full rotation, suggesting that infants looked at the unexpected event not because it violated physical laws but because it represented greater movement (Rivera, Wakely, & Langer, 1999). Nevertheless, studies that use simpler tasks have shown support for young infants' competence. Four- and 5-month-old infants will watch a ball roll behind a barrier, gazing to where they expect it to reappear (von Hofsten, Kochukhova, & Rosander, 2007). When 6-month-old infants are shown an object and the lights are then turned off, they will reach in the dark for the object (Shinskey, 2012), suggesting that they maintain a mental representation of the object and therefore have object permanence earlier than Piaget believed.

A-Not-B Tasks

Other critics of Piaget's views of infants' capacity for object permanence focus on an error that 8- to 12-month-old infants make, known as the *A-not-B*

error. The A-not-B error involves the following scenario: An infant is able to uncover a toy hidden behind a barrier. He then sees the toy moved from behind one barrier (Place A) to another (Place B), but he continues to look for the toy in Place A, even after watching it be moved to Place B (see Figure 5.4). Piaget believed that the infant incorrectly, but persistently, searches for the object in Place A because he lacks object permanence.

Some researchers, however, point out that infants look at Place B, the correct location, at the same time as they mistakenly reach for Place A, suggesting that they understand the correct location of the object (Place B) but cannot keep themselves from reaching for Place A because of neural and motor immaturity (Diamond, 1991). Other researchers propose that infants cannot restrain the impulse to repeat a behavior that was previously rewarded (Zelazo, Reznick, & Spinazzola, 1998). When looking-time procedures are used to study the A-not-B error (Ahmed & Ruffman, 1998), infants look longer when the impossible event occurs (when the toy is moved from Place A to Place B but is then found at Place A) than when the expected event occurs (when the toy is moved from Place A to Place B and is found at Place B). This suggests that infants have object permanence, but their motor skills prohibit

FIGURE 5.3

Object Permanence in Young Infants: Baillargeon's Drawbridge Study

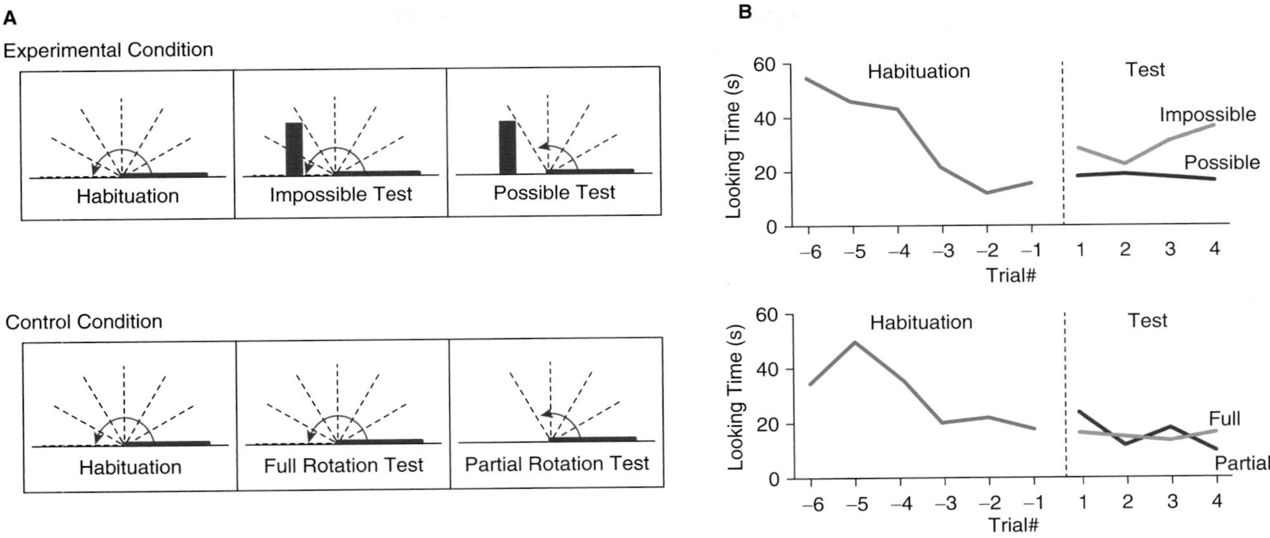

A

Experimental Condition

| Habituation | Impossible Test | Possible Test |

Control Condition

| Habituation | Full Rotation Test | Partial Rotation Test |

B

(Top graph: Looking Time (s) vs Trial#)
Habituation / Test
Impossible
Possible

(Bottom graph: Looking Time (s) vs Trial#)
Habituation / Test
Full
Partial

(A) Side view of habituation and test displays. Infants were habituated to a 180-degree drawbridge-like motion. (B) In the Experimental Condition, infants completed two types of test trials with a new object, a box. The Impossible Test involved the same full 180° rotation from habituation, but now the screen surprisingly passed through the box as it completed its rotation (with the box disappearing as it became obscured). The Possible Test involved a novel shorter rotation of screen up to the point where it would contact the box, where it stopped; this motion was "possible" in terms of solidity and object permanence. In the Control Condition, the screen rotations were identical, but no box was presented (such that both motions were equally possible). The results from the test phase are depicted in the right panels of (B). In the Experimental Condition, infants looked longer at the Impossible Test but not the Possible Test. However, in the Control Condition, no preference was observed. They looked equally at the full and partial rotation. These results suggest a violation of infants' expectations regarding object permanence.

Source: Turk-Browne et al., 2008.

FIGURE 5.4

A-Not-B Error

The infant continues to look for the ball under Place A despite having seen the ball moved to Place B.

them from demonstrating it in A-not-B tasks. One longitudinal study followed infants from 5 to 10 months of age and found that between 5 and 8 months, infants showed better performance on an A-not-B looking task than on a reaching task. Nine-

and 10-month-old infants performed equally well on A-not-B looking and reaching tasks (Cuevas & Bell, 2010). Age-related changes in performance on A-not-B and other object permanence tasks may be due to maturation of brain circuitry controlling motor skills and inhibition as well as advances in the ability to control attention (Cuevas & Bell, 2010; Marcovitch, Clearfield, Swingler, Calkins, & Bell, 2016).

Deferred Imitation Tasks

Another method of studying infants' capacities for mental representation relies on **deferred imitation,** the ability to repeat an act performed some time ago. Piaget (1962) believed that infants under 18 months cannot engage in deferred imitation because they lack mental representation abilities. Yet laboratory research on infant facial imitation has found that 6-week-old infants who watch an unfamiliar adult's facial expression will imitate it when they see the same adult the next day (Meltzoff & Moore, 1994). Six- and 9-month-old infants also display deferred imitation of unique actions performed with toys, such taking a puppet's glove off, shaking it to ring a bell inside, and replacing it over a 24-hour delay (Barr, Marrott, & Rovee-Collier, 2003).

When infants engage in deferred imitation, they act on the basis of stored representations of actions—memories—a contradiction of Piaget's beliefs about infants' capabilities (Jones & Herbert, 2006). Many researchers now suggest that deferred imitation, along with object permanence itself, is better viewed as a continuously developing ability rather than the stage-like shift in representational capacities that Piaget proposed (Miller, 2016).

For example, a 3-year longitudinal study of infants 12, 18, and 24 months old showed that performance on deferred imitation tasks improved throughout the second year of life (Kolling, Goertz, Stefanie, & Knopf, 2010). Between 12 and 18 months, infants remember modeled behaviors for several months and imitate peers as well as adults (Hayne, Boniface, & Barr, 2000). They also imitate across contexts, imitating behaviors that they learn in child care at home (Patel, Gaylord, & Fagen, 2013).

Increases in imitative capacity are observed with development up to 30 months of age. In addition, imitative capacity increases when shorter sequences of action are used, for example, a sequence of fewer than eight unique actions (Kolling, Goertz, Stefanie, & Knopf, 2010; Kressley-Mba et al., 2005). Furthermore, research following infants from 9 to 14 months of age suggests that individual differences in imitation are stable; children who show lower levels of imitation at 9 months of age continue to score lower on imitation at 14 months (Heimann & Meltzoff, 1996). These gradual changes suggest that infants and toddlers increase their representational capacities in a continuous developmental progression.

Core Knowledge Theory: An Alternative Perspective

Developmental psychologists generally agree with Piaget's description of infants as interacting with the world, actively taking in information, and constructing their own thinking. However, most researchers no longer agree with Piaget's belief that all knowledge begins with sensorimotor activity. Instead, infants are thought to have some innate, or inborn, cognitive capacities. Conservative theorists believe that infants are born with limited learning capacities such as a set of perceptual biases that cause them to attend to features of the environment that will help them to learn quickly (Bremner, Slater, & Johnson, 2015). Alternatively, the **core knowledge theory** proposes that infants are born with several innate

knowledge systems, or core domains of thought, that promote early rapid learning and adaptation (Spelke, 2016).

According to core knowledge theorists, infants learn so quickly and encounter such a great amount of sensory information that some prewired evolutionary understanding, including the early ability to learn rules, must be at work (Spelke, 2016). Using the violation-of-expectation method, core knowledge researchers have found that young infants have a grasp of the physical properties of objects, including the knowledge that objects do not disappear out of existence (permanence), cannot pass through another object (solidity), and will fall without support (gravity; Baillargeon, Scott, & Bian, 2016). Infants also display early knowledge that liquids are nonsolid substances able to pass through grids (Hespos, Ferry, Anderson, Hollenbeck, & Rips, 2016).

Infants are also thought to have early knowledge of numbers (Spelke, 2017). Five-month-old infants can discriminate between small and large numbers of items (Christodoulou, Lac, & Moore, 2017). Even newborns are sensitive to large differences in number, distinguishing nine items from three, for example, but newborns show difficulty distinguishing small numbers from each other (two vs. three items) (Coubart, Izard, Spelke, Marie, & Streri, 2014). Comparative research has shown that animals display these systems of knowledge early in life and without much experience (Piantadosi & Cantlon, 2017), suggesting that it is possible—and perhaps evolutionarily adaptive—for infants to quickly yet naturally construct an understanding of the world (Bjorklund, 2018). Increasingly, infants are viewed as statistical learners, able to quickly identify patterns in the world around them (Saffran & Kirkham, 2018).

Much core knowledge research employs the same looking paradigms described earlier, in which infants' visual preferences are measured as indictors of what they know, and this approach has come under criticism. Critics argue that it is unclear whether we can interpret looking in the same way in infants as in adults. Such measures demonstrate discrimination—that young infants can tell the difference between stimuli—yet perceiving the difference between two stimuli does not necessarily mean that infants understand *how* the two stimuli differ (Bremner et al., 2015). Others have suggested that infants are not detecting differences in number but rather differences in area (Mix, Huttenlocher, & Levine, 2002). For example, it may be that the infant differentiates nine items from three not because of the change in number but simply because nine items take up more space than three. More recent research has shown that 7-month-old infants can differentiate changes in number and area, are more sensitive to changes in number than area, and prefer to look at number changes than area changes (Libertus, Starr, & Brannon, 2014). Infants apply basic inferential mechanisms to quickly yet naturally construct an understanding of the world (Xu & Kushnir, 2013).

Overall, Piaget's theory has had a profound influence on how we view cognitive development. However, infants and toddlers are more cognitively competent than Piaget imagined, showing signs of representational ability and conceptual thought that he believed were not possible. Developmental scientists agree with Piaget that immature forms of cognition give way to more mature forms, that the individual is active in development, and that interaction with the environment is critical for cognitive growth. Today, electronic media are an important part of almost everyone's environment. Do infants interact with electronic media? The Lives in Context feature examines whether infants can learn from electronic media.

Baby Videos and Infant Learning

Infants and toddlers learn more from interaction with their parents and other caregivers than they do watching infant-directed educational content.
iStock/LucaLorenzelli

Infants and toddlers spend 1 to 2 hours a day engaged with screen media, including television and tablets, and are exposed to over 5 hours daily of background television intended for adults (Courage, 2017). Infant-directed videos and programming, which offer educational content embedded in an engaging video format, are often advertised as aids to babies' brain development, intelligence, and learning (Fenstermacher et al., 2010; Vaala & LaPierre, 2014). Most parents believe that age-appropriate videos can have a positive impact on early child development while providing good entertainment for babies and convenience for parents (Robb, Richert, & Wartella, 2009). Certainly, even very young infants attend to video material, as its movement, color, and rapid scene changes are attractive (Courage, 2017).

But do baby videos really aid development? Brain-building claims made by baby media manufacturers are not supported by longitudinal studies, which offer no evidence of long-term benefits of media use in early childhood (American Academy of Pediatrics Council on Communications and Media, 2016; Courage & Howe, 2010; Ferguson & Donnellan, 2014). For example, one study tested a popular DVD program that claims to help young infants learn to read. Ten- to 18-month-old infants who regularly watched the program for 7 months did not differ from other infants in intelligence, cognitive skills, reading skill, or word knowledge (Neuman, Kaefer, Pinkham, & Strouse, 2014). Baby videos are often advertised as aiding language development, yet several studies found that children under 2 years of age showed no learning of target words after viewing a language-learning DVD up to 20 times (DeLoache et al., 2010; Ferguson & Donnellan, 2014).

Infants learn more readily from people than from TV, a finding known as the **video deficit effect** (Anderson & Pempek, 2005). For example, when 12- to 18-month-old infants watched a best-selling DVD that labels household objects, the infants learned very little from it compared with what they learned though interaction with parents (DeLoache et al., 2010). Recently, the video deficit effect has been relabeled as a *transfer deficit* because infants are less able to transfer what they see on the screen to their own behavior than to transfer what they learn in active interactions with adults (Barr, 2010). The transfer deficit is reduced somewhat for older infants when their memory capacities are taken into account, that is, when content is repeated and verbal cues are added (Barr, 2013). When parents watch videos along with their infants and talk to them about the content, the infants spend more time looking at the screen, learn more from the media, and show greater knowledge of language as toddlers (Linebarger & Vaala, 2010). However, it is not clear that parent coviewing of media

(Continued)

(Continued)

provides a better alternative to learning than parent–infant interaction by itself (Courage, 2017).

Infants learn from contingent interactions with others—and baby videos do not provide contingent stimulation. Infants can, however, can learn from screens when contingent interactions with people are involved (McClure, Chentsova-Dutton, Holochwost, Parrott, & Barr, 2018). For example, 12- to 25-month-olds were presented with on-screen partners who taught novel words, actions, and patterns via real-time FaceTime conversations or prerecorded videos (Myers, LeWitt, Gallo, & Maselli, 2017). All of the infants were attentive and responsive, but only children in the FaceTime group responded to the partner in a time-synchronized manner. One week later, the children in the FaceTime group preferred and recognized their

partner, learned more novel patterns, and (among the older infants) learned more novel words. Although baby media will not transform babies into geniuses or even guarantee learning, babies can learn from real-time interactions with others—in person or on screen.

What Do You Think?

1. Imagine that you are a parent. What are some of the reasons why you might allow your young child to play with your mobile phone or tablet? In your view, what are some disadvantages to screen use by infants and toddlers?

2. How might you teach infants and toddlers how to learn from screens, such as from televisions, cell phones, and tablets? ●

THINKING IN CONTEXT 5.1

Identify a toy appropriate for an infant in the secondary circular reactions substage (e.g., a loud rattle or jingling set of toy keys).

1. Compare and contrast how infants in the secondary circular reactions substage and coordination of secondary schemas substage might play with the toy.

2. How might infants in the tertiary reactions substage play with it?

3. How might infants' play match their developing schemes?

4. Might parent–infant interactions, the home environment, and sociocultural context influence when infants develop object permanence? Why or why not?

5. Infants around the world delight in playing peekaboo. Compare and contrast how Piaget and core knowledge theorists might account for infants' attention and interest in the caregiver's disappearing and reappearing face.

INFORMATION PROCESSING THEORY

» LO 5.2   Describe the information processing system in infants.

Information processing theorists describe cognition as a set of interrelated components that permit people to process information—to notice, take in, manipulate, store, and retrieve it. Newborns are ready to learn and adapt to their world because they are born information processors.

Organization of the Information Processing System

According to information processing theory, the mind is composed of three mental stores: sensory memory, working memory, and long-term memory. From early infancy through late adulthood, information moves through these three stores, and we use them to manipulate and store information (see Figure 5.5).

Sensory memory is the first step in getting information into the mind; it holds incoming sensory information in its original form. For example, look at this page, then close your eyes. Did you "see" the page for a fraction of a second after you closed your eyes? That image, or *icon*, represents your sensory memory. Information fades from sensory memory quickly if it is not processed, even as quickly as fractions of a second. Newborn infants display sensory memory, but it is much shorter in duration than adults' memory (Cheour et al., 2002).

A great deal of information is taken in and rapidly moves through sensory memory. Not surprisingly, much of it is discarded. When we direct our attention to information, however, it passes to the next part of the information processing system, working memory.

Working memory holds and processes information that is being "worked on" in some way. Working memory consists of at least three components: a short-term store, a processing component, and a control mechanism (Baddeley, 2016). Just as your thoughts are constantly changing, so are the contents of working memory. We can hold only so much information in working memory, and we can hold it for only so long. Indeed, a core assumption of the information processing approach is the idea of limited capacity (Bjorklund & Myers, 2015; Oberauer, Farrell, Jarrold, & Lewandowsky, 2016). With development, we get better at retaining information in working memory and use it in more efficient ways.

Working memory is responsible for manipulating (considering, comprehending), encoding (transforming into a memory), and retrieving (recalling) information. All of your thoughts—that is, all conscious mental activities—occur within working memory. For example, reading this paragraph, remembering assignments, and considering how this material applies to your own experience taps your working memory.

An important part of working memory is the **central executive,** a control mechanism or processor that directs the flow of information and regulates cognitive activities such as attention, action, and problem solving (Just & Carpenter, 1992). The central executive determines what is important to attend to, combines new information with information already in working memory, and selects and applies strategies for manipulating the information in order to understand it, make decisions, and solve problems (Baddeley, 2012). Collectively, these cognitive activities are known as **executive function.**

As information is manipulated in working memory, it becomes more likely that it will enter long-term memory, the third mental store. **Long-term memory** is an unlimited store that holds information indefinitely. Information is not manipulated or processed in long-term memory; it is simply stored until it is retrieved to manipulate in working memory (e.g., in remembering events and thinking about them). As we develop, we amass a great deal of information in long-term memory, organize it in increasingly sophisticated ways, and encode and retrieve it more efficiently and with less effort.

We are born with the ability to take in, store, and manipulate information through our sensory, working, and long-term memory. The structure of the information processing system remains the same throughout the lifespan. With development, we get better at moving information through our cognitive system in ways that allow us to adapt to our world. We can process more information, retain more information, and do so more quickly and efficiently.

Attention

Attention refers to our ability to direct our awareness. The ability to focus and switch attention is critical for selecting information to process it in working memory and is influenced by neurological development, including advances in myelination (Qiu, Mori, & Miller, 2015). Important developments in attention occur over the course of infancy and continue throughout childhood.

Infant attention is often studied using the same methods used to learn about their visual perception. Preferential-looking procedures (measuring and comparing the length of time infants look at two

The toy keys have captured this infant's attention. Infants are more attentive to dynamic stimuli—stimuli that change over time—than to static, unchanging stimuli.
iStock/kamsta

FIGURE 5.5

Information Processing System

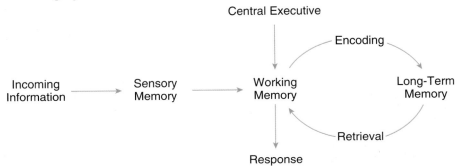

stimuli) and habituation procedures (measuring the length of time it takes infants to show a reduction in how long they look at a nonchanging stimulus) are used to study infants' attention to visual stimuli, such as geometric patterns (Ristic & Enns, 2015). Infants show more attentiveness to dynamic stimuli—stimuli that change over time—than to static, unchanging stimuli (Reynolds, Zhang, & Guy, 2013).

By around 10 weeks of age, infants show gains in attention. As infants' capacities for attention increase, so do their preferences for complex stimuli. For example, in one experiment, 3- to 13-month-old infants were shown displays that included a range of static and moving stimuli (Courage, Reynolds, & Richards, 2006). From about 6½ months of age, infants' looking time varied with stimulus complexity, decreasing for simple stimuli such as dot patterns, increasing slightly for complex stimuli such as faces, and increasing more for very complex stimuli such as video clips (Courage et al., 2006). Overall, looking time peaked at 14 weeks of age and dropped steadily, demonstrating infants' growing cognitive efficiency. As infants become more efficient at scanning and processing visual information, they require less exposure to stimuli to habituate.

Recently, researchers have begun using brain imaging techniques to measure infants' brain activity because the development of infant attention is thought to be closely related to neurological development in the areas underlying attentional control (Reynolds, 2015). In response to tasks that challenge attention, infants show activity in the frontal cortex (used for thinking and planning) that is diffuse (widely spread) at 5.5 months of age but more specific or localized by 7.5 months of age (Richards, 2010).

Memory

Habituation studies measuring looking time and brain activity demonstrate that neonates can recall visual and auditory stimuli (Muenssinger et al., 2013; Streri, Hevia, Izard, & Coubart, 2013). With age, infants require fewer trials or presentations to recall a stimulus and are able to retain material for progressively longer periods of time (Howe, 2015). Infants can also remember motor activities. In one study, 2- to 3-month-old infants were taught to kick their foot, which was tied to a mobile with a ribbon, to make the mobile move (as shown in Figure 5.6). One week later, when the infants were reattached to the mobile, they kicked vigorously, indicating their memory of the first occasion. The infants would kick even 4 weeks later if the experimenter gave the mobile a shake to remind them of its movement (Rovee-Collier & Bhatt, 1993).

Although infants have basic memory capacities common to children and adults, they are most likely to remember events that take place in familiar contexts and in which they are actively engaged (Rose, Feldman, Jankowski, & Van Rossem, 2011). Emotional engagement also enhances infants' memory. One method for testing the effect of emotional engagement on memory is the still-face interaction paradigm. In this experimental task, an infant interacts with an adult who first engages in normal social interaction and then suddenly lets his or her face become still and expressionless, not responsive to the infant's actions (Tronick, Als, Adamson, Wise, & Brazelton, 1978). Infants usually respond to the adult's still face with brief smiles followed by negative facial expressions, crying, looking away, thumb sucking, and other indications of emotional distress (Shapiro, Fagen, Prigot, Carroll, & Shalan, 1998; Weinberg & Tronick, 1994). In one study, 5-month-old infants who were exposed to the still face demonstrated recall over a year later, at 20 months of age, by looking less at the woman who had appeared in the earlier still-face paradigm than at two other women whom the infants had never previously seen (Bornstein, Arterberry, & Mash, 2004). In sum, memory improves over the course of infancy, but even young infants are likely to recall events that take place in familiar surroundings in which they are actively engaged and that are emotionally salient (Courage & Cowan, 2009; Learmonth et al., 2004).

Infants' Thinking

In infants' eyes, all of the world is new—"one great blooming, buzzing confusion," in the famous words of 19th-century psychologist William James (1890). How do infants think about and make sense of the world? As infants are bombarded with a multitude of stimuli, encountering countless new objects, people, and events, they form concepts by naturally grouping stimuli into classes or categories. **Categorization,** grouping different stimuli into a common class, is an adaptive mental process that allows for organized storage of information in memory, efficient retrieval of that information, and the capacity to respond with familiarity to new stimuli from a common class (Quinn, 2016). Infants naturally categorize information, just as older children and adults do (Rosenberg & Feigenson, 2013). Without the ability to categorize, we would have to respond anew to each novel stimulus we experience.

Just as in studying perception and attention, developmental researchers must rely on basic learning capacities, such as habituation, to study how infants categorize objects (Rigney & Wang, 2015). For example, infants are shown a series of stimuli belonging to one category (e.g., fruit: apples and

FIGURE 5.6

Rovee-Collier Ribbon Study

Young infants were taught to kick their foot to make an attached mobile move. When tested one week later the infants remembered and kicked their legs vigorously to make the mobile move.

Source: Nick Alexander; Levine and Munsch (2010).

oranges) and then are presented with a new stimulus of the same category (e.g., a pear or a lemon) and a stimulus of a different category (e.g., a cat or a horse). If an infant dishabituates or shows renewed interest by looking longer at the new stimulus (e.g., cat), it suggests that he or she perceives it as belonging to a different category from that of the previously encountered stimuli (Cohen & Cashon, 2006). Using this method, researchers have learned that 3-month-old infants categorize pictures of dogs and cats differently based on perceived differences in facial features (Quinn, Eimas, & Rosenkrantz, 1993).

Infants' earliest categories are based on the perceived similarity of objects (Rakison & Butterworth, 1998). By 4 months, infants can form categories based on perceptual properties, grouping objects that are similar in appearance, including shape, size, and color (Quinn, 2016). As early as 7 months of age, infants use conceptual categories

based on perceived function and behavior (Mandler, 2004). Moreover, patterns in 6- to 7-month-old infants' brain waves correspond to their identification of novel and familiar categories (Quinn, Doran, Reiss, & Hoffman, 2010). Seven- to 12-month-old infants use many categories to organize objects, such as food, furniture, birds, animals, vehicles, kitchen utensils, and more, based on both perceptual similarity and perceived function and behavior (Bornstein & Arterberry, 2010; Mandler & McDonough, 1998; Oakes, 2010).

Researchers also use sequential touching tasks to study the conceptual categories that older infants create (Perry, 2015). Infants are presented with a collection of objects from two categories (e.g., four animals and four vehicles) and their patterns of touching are recorded. If the infants recognize a categorical distinction among the objects, they touch those from within a category in succession more than would be expected by chance. Research using sequential touching procedures has shown that 12- to 30-month-old toddlers organize objects first at a global level and then at more specific levels. They categorize at more inclusive levels (e.g., animals or vehicles) before less inclusive levels (e.g., types of animals or types of vehicles) and before even less inclusive levels (e.g., specific animals or vehicles) (Bornstein & Arterberry, 2010). Infants' and toddlers' everyday experiences and exploration contribute to their growing capacity to recognize commonalities among objects, group them in meaningful ways, and use these concepts to think and solve problems.

Recognizing categories is a way of organizing information that allows for more efficient thinking, including storage and retrieval of information in memory. Therefore, advances in categorization are critical to cognitive development. The cognitive abilities that underlie categorization also influence language development as words represent categories, ways of organizing ideas and things. In the Applying Developmental Science feature, we look at the baby signing movement, which proposes that infants can apply gestures as symbols in order to communicate.

As shown in Table 5.2, information processing capacities, such as attention, memory, and categorization skill, show continuous change over the first 3 years of life (Rose, Feldman, & Jankowski, 2009). Infants get better at attending to the world around them, remembering what they encounter, and organizing and making sense of what they learn. Infants' emerging cognitive capacities influence all aspects of their development and functioning, including intelligence. Cognitive development is also influenced by the contexts in which infants and children live.

Baby Signing

Although signing may not accelerate language development, it offers opportunities for parent-infant interaction and play.
AP/Justin Hayworth

Few things are as frustrating for a parent as trying to decipher their baby's cry. What does she need? Is she hungry? Cold? Does she have a wet diaper? Is she hurt? Imagine how nice it would be if infants could communicate their needs! Is baby signing the answer?

The baby signing movement promotes early communication between infants and parents by teaching infants to communicate with symbolic gestures. The assumption behind baby signing is that the cognitive and gross motor skills needed for signing develop before the relatively fine motor control of the mouth, tongue, and breath needed to articulate speech (Goodwyn & Acredolo, 1998). The roots of baby signing lie in research conducted by Linda Acredolo and Susan Goodwyn. Their research has shown that babies readily acquire symbolic gestures when exposed to the enhanced gestural training that they refer to as baby signs (Acredolo, Goodwyn, & Abrams, 2009). They propose that the rewards of baby signing include larger and more expressive vocabulary, advanced mental development, improved parent–child relationships, and fewer tantrums and behavior problems (Acredolo & Goodwyn, 1988; Goodwyn & Acredolo, 1998). Based on their findings, Acredolo and Goodwyn created a signing program for infants with videos, classes, books, and cue cards (Acredolo et al., 2009). Parents who read about the benefits of teaching signs to their infants often embrace the practice. Numerous companies have been created to promote and sell baby signing materials. Most advertise benefits such as facilitating spoken language, reducing tantrums, and increasing IQ.

It is generally recognized that gesture and language are linked and that babies naturally make early gestures that precede their use of language (Iverson & Goldin-Meadow, 2005). Sensitive responses from caregivers tend to result in more pointing and

gesturing from infants, suggesting that gestures are a form of communication (Vallotton, Decker, Kwon, Wang, & Chang, 2017). But is baby signing effective in accelerating language and cognitive development? One review of 33 websites associated with various baby signing products revealed that all promoters claimed benefits such as faster language development, and many claimed to foster cognitive and emotional development, including higher IQs, improvements in parent–child interactions, and fewer child tantrums. Yet almost none provided evidence to support these claims. Those that did referred to case studies (such as Acredolo & Goodwyn, 1985) and opinion articles rather than experiments (Nelson, White, & Grewe, 2012). A review of research studies examining the outcomes of baby signing programs found that although some of the studies suggested some benefits, nearly all contained methodological weaknesses such as a lack of control groups or no random assignment. It was concluded that evidence to support these claims was insufficient (Johnston, 2005).

More recently, a longitudinal study tested the effects of baby signing products. Infants were followed from 8 months of age until 20 months of age (Kirk, Howlett, Pine, & Fletcher, 2013). Babies were randomly assigned to one of three conditions: baby sign training, verbal training (i.e., mothers modeled words without signs), and nonintervention. At 20 months of age, the language development was similar for all babies, regardless of intervention. Encouraging gestures did not result in higher scores on language measures, providing no support for the claims of baby signing proponents.

Nevertheless, many parents report that baby signing has improved their child's ability to communicate, cognitive ability, and overall parent–infant interactions (Doherty-Sneddon, 2008; Mueller & Sepulveda, 2014). For example, although U.K. infants enrolled in a baby signing class showed no differences in language development compared with their nonsigning peers, mothers who enrolled their infants in the baby signing class tended to use more mental terms and refer to thinking ("You want the toy, huh?") in their infant-directed interactions (Zammit & Atkinson, 2017). Baby signing may not have research support for accelerating language development, but if it promotes frequent parent–infant interaction, does not rush or pressure infants, and is helpful in parents' estimation, there is no reason to discourage its use.

What Do You Think?

Should we encourage parents to teach their babies how to sign? Why or why not? ●

TABLE 5.2

Changes in Information Processing Skills During Infancy

ABILITY	DESCRIPTION
Attention	• Attention increases steadily over infancy. • From birth, infants attend more to dynamic than static stimuli. • During the second half of their first year, infants attend more to complex stimuli such as faces and video clips. • Attention is linked with diffuse frontal lobe activity in young infants and localized frontal lobe activity by 7.5 months of age. • Individual differences appear at all ages and are stable over time. • Attention is associated with performance on visual recognition memory tasks.
Memory	• Memory improves with age. • Three-month-old infants can remember a visual stimulus for 24 hours. • By the end of the first year, infants can remember a visual stimulus for several days or even weeks. • Infants are most likely to remember events in familiar, engaging, and emotionally salient contexts.
Categorization	• Infants first categorize objects based on perceived similarity. • By 4 months, infants can form categories based on perceptual properties such as shape, size, and color. • By 6 to 7 months of age, infants' brain waves correspond to their identification of novel and familiar categories. • Seven- to 12-month-old infants can organize objects such as food, furniture, animals, and kitchen utensils, based on perceived function and behavior. • Twelve- to 30-month-old infants categorize objects first at a global level and then at more specific levels. • Infants categorize objects at more global and inclusive levels (such as motor vehicles) before more specific and less inclusive levels (such as cars, trucks, construction equipment). • The use of categories improves memory efficiency.

THINKING IN CONTEXT 5.2

1. What kinds of toys and activities would you recommend to caregivers who want to entertain infants while helping them develop skills in attention, memory, or categorization?

2. Recall from Chapter 1 that an important theme of development is that it is influenced by multiple contexts. How might contextual influences, such as family, neighborhood, sociocultural context, and even cohort or generation, influence attention, memory, categorization, and/or other aspects of cognition?

3. What are some of the challenges in studying how infants think and what they know? How have researchers addressed these issues? Can you identify criticisms to information processing researchers' methods, findings, or conclusions?

INDIVIDUAL DIFFERENCES IN INFANT INTELLIGENCE

» LO 5.3   Discuss individual differences in infant intelligence.

At its simplest, **intelligence** refers to an individual's ability to adapt to the world. Of course, different people have different levels of intelligence—an example of the concept of individual differences or variation from one individual to another. Intelligence tests are used to measure these differences; they include questions that measure memory, pattern recognition, verbal knowledge, quantitative abilities, and logical reasoning. Measuring intelligence in infancy is challenging because, as noted earlier, infants cannot answer questions. Instead, researchers who study infant intelligence rely on an assortment of nonverbal tasks—the same kinds of methods that are used to study cognitive development. There are two general approaches to studying intelligence in infancy. As discussed next, the testing approach emphasizes standardized tests that compare infants with age-based norms. A second approach, the information processing approach, examines specific processing skills.

Testing Approach to Intelligence

At 3 months of age, Baby Lourdes can lift and support her upper body with her arms when on her stomach. She grabs and shakes toys with her hands and enjoys playing with other people. Lourdes's pediatrician tells her parents that her development is right on track for babies her age and that she shows typical levels of infant intelligence. Standardized tests permit the pediatrician to determine Lourdes's development relative to other infants her age.

The most often used standardized measure of infant intelligence is the Bayley Scales of Infant Development III (BSID-III), commonly called "Bayley-III" (see Figure 5.7). This test is appropriate for infants from 1 month through 42 months of age (Bayley, 1969, 2005). The Bayley-III consists of five scales: three consisting of infant responses and two of parent responses. The Motor Scale measures gross and fine motor skills, such as grasping objects, drinking from a cup, sitting, and climbing stairs. The Cognitive Scale includes items such as attending to a stimulus or searching for a hidden toy. The Language Scale examines comprehension and production of language, such as following directions and naming objects. The Social-Emotional Scale is derived from parental reports regarding behavior such as the infant's responsiveness and play activity. Finally, the Adaptive Behavior Scale is based on parental reports of the infant's ability to adapt in everyday situations, including the infant's ability to communicate, regulate his or her emotions, and display certain behavior.

The Bayley-III provides a comprehensive profile of an infant's current functioning, but the performance of infants often varies considerably from one testing session to another (Bornstein, Slater, Brown, Roberts, & Barrett, 1997). Scores vary with infants' states of arousal and motivation. This suggests that pediatricians and parents must exert great care in interpreting scores—particularly poor scores—because an infant's performance may be influenced by factors other than developmental functioning. Alternatively, some researchers have argued that perhaps the variability in Bayley-III scores from one occasion to another suggests that intelligence itself is variable in infancy (Bornstein et al., 1997). Regardless, the low test–retest reliability (see Chapter 1) means that infants who perform poorly on the Bayley-III should be tested more than once.

Although Bayley-III scores offer a comprehensive profile of an infant's abilities, scores do not predict performance on intelligence tests in childhood (dos Santos, de Kieviet, Königs, van Elburg, & Oosterlaan, 2013; Rose & Feldman, 1995). Even Nancy Bayley, who invented the Bayley Scales, noted in a longitudinal study (1949) that infant performance was not related to intelligence scores at age 18. Why is infant intelligence relatively unrelated to later intelligence? Consider what is measured by infant tests: perception and motor skills, responsiveness, and language skills. The abilities to grasp an object, crawl up stairs, or search for a hidden toy—items that appear on the Bayley-III—are not measured by childhood intelligence tests. Instead, intelligence tests administered in childhood examine more complex and abstract abilities such as verbal reasoning, verbal comprehension, and problem solving.

FIGURE 5.7

Bayley-III Scales (BSID-III)

Infant assessment tests, such as the BSID-III, examine cognitive, language, social-emotional, and motor abilities, such as infants' skill in manipulating objects.

Source: Cliff Moore / Science Source

If the Bayley-III does not predict later intelligence, why administer it? Infants whose performance is poor relative to age norms may suffer from serious developmental problems that can be addressed. The intellectual abilities measured by the Bayley-III are critical indicators of neurological health and are useful for charting developmental paths, diagnosing neurological disorders, and detecting intellectual disabilities in infants and toddlers. Thus, the Bayley-III is primarily used as a screening tool to identify infants who can benefit from medical and developmental intervention. As discussed in the accompanying Brain and Biological Influences on Development feature, contextual conditions, especially exposure to poverty, can place some infants and children at risk for poor cognitive development and lower IQ.

Intelligence as Information Processing

The challenge in determining whether intelligence in infancy predicts performance in childhood and beyond rests in identifying measures that evaluate cognitive functioning from infancy through childhood. Information processing abilities, such as those related to attention, working memory, and processing speed, underlie performance in all cognitive tasks, including intelligence tests, and are therefore important indicators of intellectual ability that are evident at birth and persist for a lifetime (Baddeley, 2016; Müller & Kerns, 2015; Ristic & Enns, 2015).

Individuals who process information more efficiently are thought to acquire knowledge more quickly. This is true for infants as well as for older

BRAIN AND BIOLOGICAL INFLUENCES ON DEVELOPMENT

Poverty and Development

Poverty has a detrimental effect on children's development and is associated with deficits in memory and learning, cognitive control, and emotional processing. Chronic poverty is especially damaging because the neurological and cognitive deficits accumulate over childhood.
Mario Tama/Getty Images

Forty-five percent of U.S. children under 3 years of age (including two thirds of Black, Hispanic, and Native American children) live in low-income families (income less than $48,000 per year for a family of four), and 23% live in poor families (income less than $24,000) (Koball & Jiang, 2018) (see Table 5.8). In 2013, the American Academy of Pediatrics added child poverty to its Agenda for Children in recognition of poverty's broad and enduring effects on child health and development

(American Academy of Pediatrics, 2017). Infants and children from poor families experience higher rates of malnutrition, growth stunting, and susceptibility to illness than do their peers (Yoshikawa, Aber, & Beardslee, 2012).

Exposure to chronic long-term poverty has negative effects on brain growth and is associated with lower volumes in parts of the brain associated with memory and learning, cognitive control, and emotional processing (Johnson, Riis, & Noble, 2016; Ursache & Noble, 2016). For example, a longitudinal study of 77 children from birth to age 4 revealed a link between poverty and lower gray matter volume especially in the frontal and parietal regions associated with executive function (Hanson et al., 2013). In another study, 5-week-old infants in low socioeconomic status (SES) homes tended to have smaller brain volumes than other infants, suggesting that poverty may influence biological and cognitive development during the first few weeks of life or earlier (Betancourt et al., 2016).

The effects of socioeconomic status on development vary. SES is more closely related with brain structure and cognition in children from poor homes than high SES homes (Hair, Hanson, Wolfe, Pollak, & Knight, 2015; Noble et al., 2015). That is, the detrimental effect of low SES contexts is a greater influence on children's development than the positive effect of high SES contexts. Chronic poverty is especially damaging because the neurological and cognitive deficits accumulate over childhood (Dickerson & Popli, 2016). One way in which poverty affects development

FIGURE 5.8

Percentage of Children in Low-Income and Poor Families by Race/Ethnicity, 2016

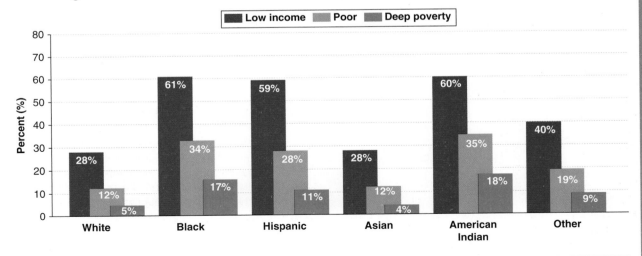

Source: Koball & Jiang (2018).

(Continued)

(Continued)

is through the quality of parent–infant interactions and infants' exposure to language (Hackman, Gallop, Evans, & Farah, 2015). Infants in higher SES homes are talked to more and the speech they hear is often more stimulating and supportive of language development than is the case in lower SES homes (Fernald, Marchman, & Weisleder, 2013; Sheridan, Sarsour, Jutte, D'Esposito, & Boyce, 2012).

Poverty is also thought to affect children's outcomes indirectly by contributing to household chaos, a combination of household instability and disorder (Berry et al., 2016). Children reared in economic uncertainty are more likely to experience disruptions in home settings and relationships through household moves and adults moving in and out of the home (Pascoe, Wood, Duffee, & Kuo, 2016). Impoverished environments often include household crowding, lack of structure, and excessive ambient noise in the home or neighborhood (Evans & Kim, 2013). Infants and children reared in environments of household chaos may be overwhelmed by stimulation combined with little developmentally appropriate

support with negative effects for cognitive development. The effects of a chaotic home environment begin early. For example, a chaotic environment has been shown to negatively affect visual processing speed for complex stimuli in 5.5-month-old infants (Tomalski et al., 2017). Poverty has early effects on children's brain development that increase over time with lifelong implications for cognitive and language development.

What Do You Think?

1. Infants and children reared in poverty face many contextual risks to development. Their contexts may also offer opportunities for resilience. Identify factors within the family and home that can promote the development of infants and children who are exposed to poverty.

2. How might the extended family, neighborhood, and community help to buffer the effects of challenging environments on development? ●

---

children and adults. Indeed, information processing capacities in infancy, such as attention, memory, and processing speed, have been shown to predict cognitive ability and intelligence through late adolescence.

Information processing abilities can be assessed in simple ways that allow us to study intelligence in infants who are too young to tell us what they think and understand. For example, infants' visual reaction time (how quickly they look when shown a stimulus) and preference for novelty (the degree to which they prefer new stimuli over familiar ones) are indicators of attention, memory, and processing speed and have been shown to predict intelligence in childhood and adolescence (Fagan, 2011). Habituation tasks also provide information about the efficiency of information processing because they indicate how quickly an infant learns: Infants who learn quickly look away from an unchanging stimulus (or habituate) rapidly. Longitudinal studies suggest that infants who are fast habituators score higher on measures of intelligence in childhood and adolescence than do those who are slower habituators (Kavšek, 2013; Rose, Feldman, & Jankowski, 2012). One study demonstrated that, compared with average and slow habituators, infants who were fast habituators had higher IQs and higher educational achievement when they were followed up 20 years later in emerging adulthood.

Many other studies confirm that infant information processing abilities are associated with measures of intelligence throughout life.

For example, working memory and visuospatial short-term memory in infancy are associated with IQ in fourth- and fifth-grade children (Giofrè, Mammarella, & Cornoldi, 2013). Working memory and processing speed are also associated with intelligence in children and adults (Redick, Unsworth, Kelly, & Engle, 2012; Rose, Feldman, Jankowski, & Van Rossem, 2012; Sheppard, 2008). Information processing skills in infancy are effective predictors of intelligence in childhood; however, these findings are generally the result of laboratory research. Although pediatricians might test an infant's attention and habituation as part of an examination, there is no standardized information processing test of intelligence to apply to infants comparable to the Bayley-III.

 THINKING IN CONTEXT 5.3

1. Thinking back to the continuity–discontinuity theme of development (see Chapter 1), would you say that intelligence represents an example of continuous or discontinuous change? Explain your answer.

2. Why is infant intelligence a poor predictor of later intelligence?

3. How might contextual factors, such as home environment and experiences, influence the skills measured by infant intelligence tests such as the Bayley-III?

LANGUAGE DEVELOPMENT IN INFANCY AND TODDLERHOOD

» LO 5.4 **Summarize the patterns of language development during infancy and toddlerhood.**

"You just love to hear Mommy talk, don't you?" Velma asked as newborn Jayson stared up at her. Can Jayson attend to his mother? Is Jayson interested in his mother's speech? As described in Chapter 4, hearing emerges well before birth, and evidence suggests that newborns can recall sounds heard in the womb (Dirix, Nijhuis, Jongsma, & Hornstra, 2009). Developing the ability to use language is a critical step in infancy and toddlerhood; it has important implications for the child's cognitive, social, and emotional development. Gaining the ability to use words to represent objects, experience, thoughts, and feelings permits children to think and to communicate with others in increasingly flexible and adaptive ways.

Early Preferences for Speech Sounds

Newborn infants are primed to learn language. Recall from Chapter 4 that neonates naturally attend to speech and prefer to hear human speech sounds, especially their native language, as well as stories and sounds that they heard prenatally (May, Gervain, Carreiras, & Werker, 2018). Infants naturally notice the complex patterns of sounds around them and organize sounds into meaningful units. They recognize frequently heard words, such as their names. By 4½ months of age, infants will turn their heads to hear their own names but not to hear other names, even when the other names have a similar sound pattern (e.g., Annie and Johnny) (Mandel, Jusczyk, & Pisoni, 1995). At 6 months of age, infants pay particular attention to vowel sounds and, at 9 months, consonants (Kuhl, 2015).

Although infants can perceive and discriminate sounds that comprise all human languages at birth, their developing capacities and preferences are influenced by context (Hoff, 2015). For example, the Japanese language does not discriminate between the consonant sounds of "r" in *rip* and "l" in *lip*. Japanese adults who are learning English find it very difficult to discriminate between the English pronunciations of these "r" and "l" sounds, yet up until about 6 to 8 months of age, Japanese and U.S. infants are equally able to distinguish these sounds. By 10 to 12 months, however, discrimination of "r" and "l" improves for U.S. infants and declines for Japanese infants. This likely occurs because U.S. infants hear these sounds often, whereas Japanese infants do not (Kuhl et al., 2006). As they are exposed to their native language, they become more attuned to the sounds (and distinctions between sounds) that are meaningful in their own language and less able to distinguish speech sounds that are not used in that language (Werker, Yeung, & Yoshida, 2012). Native-language discrimination ability between 6 and 7 months predicts the rate of language growth between 11 and 30 months (Kuhl, 2015).

Infants' speech discrimination abilities remain malleable in response to the social context (Kuhl, 2016). In one study, Kuhl and her colleagues exposed 9-month-old English-learning American infants to 12 live interaction sessions with an adult speaker of Mandarin Chinese over the course of 4 to 5 weeks (Kuhl, Tsao, & Liu, 2003). After the sessions, the infants were tested on a Mandarin phonetic contrast that does not occur in English. The infants discriminated the contrast as well as same-aged Mandarin-learning infants and retained the contrast for several days. The relevance of context is also illustrated by the infants' loss of the ability to discriminate the Mandarin contrast several days after training, presumably in the absence of ongoing exposure to the Mandarin language (Fitneva & Matsui, 2015).

Social interaction is vital to language learning. In the study just described, the English-learning infants did not learn the Mandarin phonetic contrast when they were exposed to it only by audio or video. Live interaction may have increased infants' motivation to learn by increasing their attention and arousal. Or perhaps live interaction provides specific information that fosters learning, like the speaker's eye gaze and pointing coupled with interactive contingency (Kuhl et al., 2003).

In addition, social input, such as the quality of mother–infant interactions, plays a critical role in determining the timing of infants' narrowing of speech sound discrimination. Specifically, infants who experience high-quality interactions with their mothers, characterized by frequent speech, show a narrowing earlier, as early as 6 months of age (Elsabbagh et al., 2013).

Prelinguistic Communication

At birth, crying is the infant's only means of communication. Infants soon learn to make many more sounds, like gurgles, grunts, and squeals. Between 2 and 3 months of age, infants begin **cooing,** making deliberate vowel sounds like "ahhhh," "ohhhh," and "eeeee." Infants' first coos sound like one long vowel. These vocal sounds are a form of vocal play; they are likely to be heard when babies are awake, alert, and contented. At the cooing stage, infants already use pauses that are consistent with the turn-taking pattern of spoken conversations. With age, the quality of coos changes to include different vowel-like sounds and

Babies learn language by hearing others speak and by modifying their babbling in response to caregiver interactions.
Eric Scouten / Alamy Stock Photo

combinations of vowel-like sounds (Owens, 2016). **Babbling,** repeating strings of consonants and vowels such as "ba-ba-ba" and "ma-ma-ma," begins to appear at about 6 months of age.

At first, babbling is universal. All babies do it, and the sounds they make are similar no matter what language their parents speak or in what part of the world they are raised. However, infants soon become sensitive to the ambient language around them, and it influences their vocalizations (Chen & Kent, 2010). In one study, French adults listened to the babbling of a French 8-month-old and a second 8-month-old from either an Arabic-speaking or a Cantonese-speaking family. Nearly three quarters of the time, the adults correctly indicated which baby in the pair was French (Boysson-Bardies et al., 1984). By the end of the first year, infants' babbling sounds more like real speech as they begin to vary the pitch of their speech in ways that reflect the inflections of their native languages (Andruski, Casielles, & Nathan, 2013). For example, in spoken English, declarative sentences are characterized by pitch that falls toward the end of the sentence, whereas in questions, the pitch rises at the end of the sentence. Older babies' babbling mirrors these patterns when they are raised by English-speaking parents, while babies reared with Japanese or French as their native languages show intonation patterns similar to those of the respective languages (Levitt et al., 1992). Longitudinal observations of infants raised in Catalan-speaking environments likewise show that their babbling shifts to mirror intonations in native speech (Esteve-Gilbert et al., 2013).

Language acquisition, as mentioned, is a socially interactive process: Babies learn by hearing others speak and by noticing the reactions that their vocalizations evoke in caregivers (Hoff, 2015; Kuhl, 2016). Social interaction elicits cooing, and infants modify their babbling in response to caregiver interactions (Tamis-LeMonda, Kuchirko, & Song,

2014). For example, when mothers of 9½-month-old infants speak in response to their infants' babbling, infants restructure their babbling, changing the phonological pattern of sounds in response to their mothers' speech (Goldstein & Schwade, 2008). Babbling repertoires reflect infants' developing morphology and are a foundation for word learning (Ramsdell, Oller, Buder, Ethington, & Chorna, 2012). Language development follows a predictable pattern.

First Words

Eleven-month-old William was wide eyed as his father handed him a ball and said, "Ball!" "Ba!" said William. William now understands many words and is beginning to try to utter them. Throughout language development, babies' *receptive language* (what they can understand) exceeds their *productive language* (what they can produce themselves; Tamis-Lemonda & Bornstein, 2015). That is, infants understand more words than they can use. Research suggests that infants may understand some commonly spoken words as early as 6 to 9 months of age, long before they are able to speak (Bergelson & Swingley, 2012; Dehaene-Lambertz & Spelke, 2015).

At about 1 year of age, the average infant speaks his or her first word. At first, infants use one-word expressions, called **holophrases,** to express complete thoughts. A first word might be a complete word or a syllable. Usually, the word has more than one meaning, depending on the context in which it is used. For example, "Da" might mean, "I want that," "There's Daddy!" or "What's that?" Caregivers usually hear and understand first words before other adults do. The first words that infants use are those that they hear often or are meaningful for them, such as their own name, the word *no*, or the word for their caregiver. Infants reared in English-speaking homes tend to use nouns first, as they are most concrete and easily understood (Waxman et al., 2013). For example, the word *dog* refers to a concrete thing—an animal—and is easier to understand than a verb, such as *goes*. In contrast, infants reared in homes in which Mandarin Chinese, Korean, or Japanese is spoken tend to learn verbs very early in their development in response to the greater emphasis on verbs in their native languages (Waxman et al., 2013).

Regardless of what language a child speaks, early words tend to be used in the following ways (MacWhinney, MacWhinney, & Brian, 2015; Owens, 2016):

- Request or state the existence or location of an object or person by naming it (car, dog, outside).

- Request or describe the recurrence of an event or receipt of an object (again, more).

- Describe actions (eat, fall, ride).
- Ask questions (what? that?).
- Attribute a property to an object (hot, big).
- Mark social situations, events, and actions (no, bye).

Learning Words: Semantic Growth

"I can't believe how quickly Matthew picks up new words. It's time for us to be more careful about what we say around him," warned Elana. Her husband agreed, "He's only 2 years old and he has quite a vocabulary. Who would think that he'd learn so many words so quickly?" By 13 months of age, children begin to quickly learn the meaning of new words and understand that words correspond to particular things or events (Woodward, Markman, & Fitzsimmons, 1994). Most infants of Matthew's age expand their vocabularies rapidly, often to the surprise of their parents. Infants learn new words through **fast mapping,** a process of quickly acquiring and retaining a word after hearing it applied a few times (Kan & Kohnert, 2008; Marinellie & Kneile, 2012). At 18 months, infants are more likely to learn a new word if both they and the speaker are attending to the new object when the speaker introduces the new word (Baldwin et al., 1996). Two-year-olds have been shown to be able to learn a word even after a single brief exposure under ambiguous conditions (Spiegel & Halberda, 2011) or after overhearing a speaker use the word when talking to someone else (Akhtar, Jipson, & Callanan, 2001). Between 24 and 30 months, infants can learn new words even when their attention is distracted by other objects or events (Moore, Angelopoulos, & Bennett, 1999).

Fast mapping improves with age and accounts for the **naming explosion,** or *vocabulary spurt*—a period of rapid vocabulary learning that occurs between 16 and 24 months of age (Owens, 2016). During this period, infants apply their word-learning strategies to learn multiple words of varying difficulty seemingly at once. Within weeks, a toddler may increase her vocabulary from 50 words to over 400 (Bates, Bretherton, & Snyder, 1988). As shown in Figure 5.9, however, infants vary in the speed of word acquisition, with some showing a rapid increase in vocabulary before others (Samuelson & McMurray, 2017). In addition, although fast mapping helps young children learn many new words, their own speech lags behind what they can understand because young children have difficulty retrieving words from memory (McMurray, 2007). The speed at which young children acquire words during the vocabulary spurt predicts the size of their vocabulary as preschoolers at 54 months of age (Rowe, 2012). That is, children who rapidly expand their knowledge of words during the vocabulary spurt tend to have larger vocabularies in preschool than their peers who acquire new words at a slower pace.

As children learn words, we see two interesting kinds of mistakes that tell us about how words are acquired (Gershkoff-Stowe, 2002). **Underextension** refers to applying a word more narrowly than it is usually applied so that the word's use is restricted to a single object. For example, *cup* might refer to Daddy's cup but not to the general class of cups. Later, the opposite tendency appears. **Overextension** refers to

---

FIGURE 5.9

Number of Words Known as a Function of Time for Individual Children

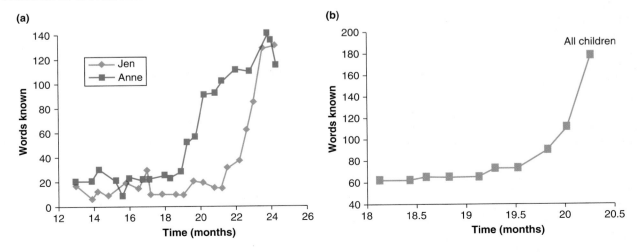

Source: Samuelson & McMurray 2017.

applying a word too broadly. *Cow* might refer to cows, sheep, horses, and all farm animals. Overextension suggests that the child has learned that a word can signify a whole class of objects. As children develop a larger vocabulary and get feedback on their speech, they demonstrate fewer errors of overextension and underextension (Brooks & Kempe, 2014).

Two-Word Utterances

At about 21 months of age, or usually about 8 to 12 months after they say their first word, most children compose their first simple two-word sentences, such as "Kitty come," or "Mommy milk." **Telegraphic speech,** like a telegram, includes only a few essential words. Like other milestones in language development, telegraphic speech is universal among toddlers. Children around the world use two-word phrases to express themselves.

Language development follows a predictable path, as shown in Table 5.3. Between 20 and 30 months of age, children begin to follow the rules for forming sentences in a given language. Soon they become more comfortable with using plurals, past tense, articles (such as *a* and *the*), prepositions (such as *in* and *on*), and conjunctions (such as *and* and *but*). By 2½ years of age, children demonstrate an awareness of the communicative purpose of speech and the importance of being understood (Owens, 2016). In one experiment, 2½-year-old children asked an adult to hand them a toy. A child was more likely to repeat and clarify the request for the toy when the adult's verbal response indicated misunderstanding of the child's request ("Did you say to put the toy on the shelf?") than when the adult appeared to understand the request, regardless of whether the adult gave the child the toy (Shwe & Markman, 1997).

TABLE 5.3	

Language Milestones

AGE	LANGUAGE SKILL
2–3 months	Cooing
6 months	Babbling
1 year	First word Holophrases
16–24 months	Vocabulary spurt Learn new words by fast mapping Underextension Overextension
21 months	Telegraphic speech
21–30 months	Syntax

Theories of Language Development

Over the first 2 years of life, children transform from wailing newborns who communicate their needs through cries to toddlers who can use words to articulate their needs, desires, and thoughts. Developmental scientists have offered several explanations for infants' rapid acquisition of language. Some explanations emphasize the role of the environment in accounting for language, whereas others emphasize biological factors.

Learning Theory and Language Development

Baby Howie gurgles, "Babababa!" His parents encourage him excitedly, "Say bottle; ba-ba!" Howie squeals, "Babababa!" "Yes! You want your ba-ba!" Parents play an important role in language development. They provide specific instruction and communicate excitement about their infants' developing competence, encouraging infants to practice new language skills. Learning theorist B. F. Skinner (1957) proposed that language, just like all other behaviors, is learned through operant conditioning: reinforcement and punishment. From birth, infants make sounds at random. Caregivers respond to infants' early utterances with interest and attention, imitating and reinforcing their verbal behavior (Pelaez, Virues-Ortega, & Gewirtz, 2011; Petursdottir & Mellor, 2017). Infants repeat the sounds. Caregivers then reward sounds that resemble adult speech with attention, smiles, and affection. Infants imitate sounds that adults make and repeat sounds that are reinforced. From this perspective, imitation and reinforcement shape children's language development. The quantity and quality of the parents' verbal interactions with the child and responses to the child's communication attempts influence the child's rate of language development (Hoff, 2015).

In the view of learning theorists, then, infants learn by observing the world around them and adults encourage and reinforce their language learning. However, critics point out that learning theory cannot account for all of language development because it cannot account for the unique utterances and errors that young children make (Berwick, Chomsky, & Piattelli-Palmarini, 2013). Word combinations are complex and varied—they cannot be acquired solely by imitation and reinforcement. Toddlers often put words together in ways that they likely have never heard (e.g., "Mommy milk"). Young children make grammatical errors, such as "mouses" instead of "mice" or "goed" instead of "went," that cannot be the result of imitation. If language is learned through imitation, how do young children make grammatical errors that they have never heard spoken? Young children repeat things that they hear (sometimes to parents' chagrin!), but they also construct new phrases and utterances that are unique. Reinforcement from parents and caregivers is powerful encouragement for children, but language development cannot be completely explained by learning theory alone. Despite wide variations in circumstances, living situations, and contexts, infants around the world achieve language milestones at about the same ages, suggesting a biological component to language development.

Nativist Theory and Language Development

Nativist theorist Noam Chomsky (Chomsky, 1959, 2017) argued that language use comprises behavior that is too complex to be learned so early and quickly via conditioning alone. Chomsky noted that all young children grasp the essentials of **grammar,** the rules of language, at an early age and that the languages of the world have many similarities. The human brain thus has an innate capacity to learn language. Specifically, Chomsky believed that infants are born with a **language acquisition device (LAD),** an innate facilitator of language that permits infants to quickly and efficiently analyze everyday speech and determine its rules, regardless of whether their native language is English, German, Chinese, or Urdu (Yang, Crain, Berwick, Chomsky, & Bolhuis, 2017). The LAD has an innate storehouse of rules, **universal grammar,** that apply to all human languages. When infants hear language spoken, they naturally notice its linguistic properties, and they acquire the language. Language, therefore, is a biologically driven cognitive mechanism of brain development that is triggered by exposure to language (Friederici, 2017).

The nativist perspective can account for children's unique utterances and the unusual grammatical mistakes they make in speaking because children are biologically primed to learn language and do not rely on learning. However, like learning theory, the nativist perspective offers an incomplete account of language development. Specifically, Chomsky's nativist perspective does not explain the process of language development and how it occurs (Ibbotson & Tomasello, 2016). Researchers have not identified the language acquisition device or universal grammar that Chomsky thought underlies all languages. In addition, there are more individual differences in language learning and in languages than Chomsky proposed (Dąbrowska, 2015). Moreover, language does not emerge in a finished form. Instead, children learn to string words together over time based on their experiences as well on as trial and error (Tomasello, 2012). Finally, it appears that language learning does not occur as quickly or effortlessly as Chomsky described (Miller, 2016).

Interactionist Perspective on Language Development

From an interactionist view, language development is a complex process reflecting the dynamic interplay of two factors: children's biological capacities and the social context in which they are reared. A newborn's ability to discriminate a wide variety of speech sounds and to prefer human speech over recorded sounds—as well as to prefer the sounds and patterns of their native language over those of other languages—suggests an inborn sensitivity to language. Yet the language that an infant learns and the pace of learning are influenced by environmental factors. Let's explore biological and contextual contributors to language.

Biological Contributions to Language Development. Evolutionary theorists explain language as having evolved as a function of natural selection. Language gave some of our early human ancestors an advantage in survival and reproduction over those who did not have language (Berwick & Chomsky, 2016; Hauser et al., 2014). Specifically, language evolved as an adaptation that fulfilled early humans' need to communicate information that was more complex than could be conveyed by simple calls and hoots (Tamariz & Kirby, 2016). Language may have emerged with increases in the size of human communities and the corresponding complexity of social dynamics, as well as humans' increasingly large, more sophisticated brains (Aiello & Dunbar, 1993; Turnbull & Justice, 2016).

The brain specifically is wired for language at birth. Speech sounds produce more activity in the left hemisphere of newborns' brains, while nonspeech sounds elicit more activity in the right hemisphere (Vannasing et al., 2016). Three-month-old infants show functional neural activity in response to language that is similar but less refined, focused, and organized than that of adults (Dehaene-Lambertz, 2017). Adult language, too, is largely governed by the left hemisphere, and cortical activity in language areas increases from infancy through adulthood (Paquette et al., 2015). Two areas in the left hemisphere of the brain are vital for language and distinguish humans from other primates: Broca's and Wernicke's areas (Friederici, 2017). **Broca's area** controls the ability to use language for expression. Damage to this area inhibits the ability to speak fluently, leading to errors in the production of language. **Wernicke's area** is responsible for language comprehension. Damage to Wernicke's area impairs the ability to understand the speech

Through infant-directed speech, adults attract infants' attention by using shorter words and sentences, higher and more varied pitch, repetition, and a slower rate. Infants prefer listening to infant-directed speech, and infant-directed speech appears cross culturally.
Ali Russell/Alamy

of others and sometimes affects the ability to speak coherently.

Although the brain plays a crucial role in language capacities, it cannot completely account for language development. For example, recent research has identified multiple genes associated with language development that work together in an epigenetic fashion, influenced by environmental factors (Dediu & Christiansen, 2016; Fisher, 2017). In addition, experience influences the brain architecture that supports language development (Westermann, 2016). For example, we have seen that infants' ability to detect sounds not used in their native language declines throughout the first year of life, suggesting that contextual factors—specifically, exposure to the native language—influence older infants' sensitivity to speech sounds (Posner, 2001; Sansavini, Bertoncini, & Giovanelli, 1997). At the same time, information processing factors largely dependent on neurological development, such as attention and memory, affect how infants comprehend and respond to social interaction and other contextual influences on language development (Perszyk & Waxman,

2018). For example, the statistical learning abilities that enable infants to see patterns and learn quickly are also associated with rapid language learning (Lany, Shoaib, Thompson, & Estes, 2018).

Contextual Contributions to Language Development. Language development occurs in a social context. Most adults naturally speak to young infants in a sing-song way that attracts their attention. Infant-directed speech, or "motherese," uses repetition, short words and sentences, high and varied pitch, and long pauses (Thiessen, Hill, & Saffran, 2005). Infants prefer listening to infant-directed speech than to typical adult speech, and they prefer adults who use infant-directed speech (Schachner & Hannon, 2011). EEG recordings show that babies demonstrate more neural activity in response to infant-directed speech than adult speech, suggesting that they are better able to attend to it and distinguish the sounds (Peter, Kalashnikova, Santos, & Burnham, 2016). Infant-directed speech exaggerates sounds, helping infants hear and distinguish sounds, and enables them to map sounds to meanings (Estes & Hurley, 2012; Kitamura & Burnham, 2003; Thiessen et al., 2005). In one study, 7- and 8-month-old infants were more likely to learn words presented by infant-directed speech than those presented through adult-directed speech (Singh, Nestor, Parikh, & Yull, 2009).

When babies begin to engage in **canonical babbling,** a type of babbling with well-formed syllables that sounds remarkably like language, parents, regardless of socioeconomic status, ethnicity, and home environment, tune in and treat the vocalizations in a new way (Oller, Eilers, & Basinger, 2001). Because the utterances sound like words, parents help infants to associate the word-like utterances with objects and events, encouraging vocabulary development.

Parental responsiveness to infants' vocalizations predicts the size of infants' vocabularies, the diversity of infants' communications, and the timing of language milestones (Tamis-LeMonda et al., 2014). One study showed that infants of highly responsive mothers achieved language milestones such as first words, vocabulary spurt, and telegraphic speech at 9 to 13 months of age, which was 4 to 6 months earlier than infants of low-responsive mothers (Tamis-LeMonda, Bornstein, & Baumwell, 2001). Fathers' responsiveness to their 2- and 3-year-olds predicted toddlers' cognitive and language abilities (Tamis-LeMonda, Shannon, Cabrera, & Lamb, 2004). Parental responsiveness is also associated with the language skills of adopted children, supporting the contextual influence of parents.

Babies learn language by interacting with more mature, expert speakers who can speak at their developmental level. Parents often adjust their infant-directed speech to match infants' linguistic needs by, for example, using longer and more complicated words and sentences as infants' comprehension increases (Englund & Behne, 2006; Sundberg, 1998). Even as infants learn speech, they continue to display preferences for some features of infant-directed speech. A study of 12- and 16-month-old infants indicated that they preferred the high pitch and pitch variability of infant-directed speech but not the shorter utterances or simplified syntax (Segal & Newman, 2015).

The quality of language input from parents and the number of words children hear is related to their vocabulary size at age 2 (Hoff et al., 2002). Children whose mothers address a great deal of speech to them develop vocabulary more rapidly, are faster at processing words they know, and are faster at producing speech than children whose mothers speak to them less often (Hurtado, Marchman, & Fernald, 2008; Weisleder & Fernald, 2013). The number of words and different grammatical structures used in maternal speech, as well as grammatical complexity, predict the size of children's vocabulary and understanding of grammar (Hadley, Rispoli, Fitzgerald, & Bahnsen, 2011; Huttenlocher, Waterfall, Vasilyeva, Vevea, & Hedges, 2010).

Although parents do not reliably reinforce correct grammar, they tend to communicate in ways that tell young children when they have made errors and show how to correct them (Saxton, 1997). Adults often respond to children's utterances with **expansions,** which are enriched versions of the children's statements. For example, if a child says, "bottle fall," the parent might respond, "Yes, the bottle fell off the table." Adults also tend to **recast** children's sentences into new grammatical forms. For example, "Kitty go," might be recast into, "Where is the kitty going?" When children use grammatically correct statements, parents maintain and extend the conversation (Bohannon & Stanowicz, 1988). When adults recast and expand young children's speech, the children tend to acquire grammatical rules more quickly and score higher on tests of expressive language ability than when parents rely less on these conversational techniques (Abraham, Crais, & Vernon-Feagans, 2013; Bohannon, Padgett, Nelson, & Mark, 1996).

Therefore, the interactionist perspective on language development points to the dynamic and reciprocal influence of biology and context. Infants are equipped with biological propensities and information processing capacities that permit them to perceive and analyze speech and learn to speak. Infants are motivated to communicate with others, and language is a tool for communication. Interactions with others provide important learning experiences, which help infants expand their language capacities and learn to think in ways similar to members of their culture (Fitneva & Matsui, 2015). The accompanying feature, Cultural Influences on Development, discusses cultural differences in infant-directed speech. Theories of language development are summarized in Table 5.4.

TABLE 5.4

Theories of Language Development

THEORY	DESCRIPTION
Learning theory	Language is learned through reinforcement, punishment, and imitation. The quantity and quality of the parents' verbal interactions with the child and responses to the child's communication attempts influence the child's rate of language development. Learning theory cannot account for the unique utterances and errors that young children make.
Nativist theory	Despite wide variations in circumstances, living situations, and contexts, infants around the world achieve language milestones at about the same time. An inborn language acquisition device (LAD) equipped with universal grammar permits infants to quickly and efficiently analyze everyday speech and determine its rules. Researchers have not identified the LAD or universal grammar Chomsky thought underlies all languages. Language does not emerge in a finished form. Instead, children learn to string words together over time based on their experiences and trial and error.
Interactionist theory	Infants have an inborn sensitivity to language and discriminate a wide variety of speech sounds, including those that adults can no longer distinguish. Exposure to language influences infants' sensitivity to speech sounds, and the ability to detect sounds not used in their native language declines throughout the first year of life. Language acquisition occurs in a social context. Babies learn language by interacting with more mature, expert speakers who can speak at their developmental level.

Culture and Language Development in Infancy

Parents from different cultures vary in how often they respond to their infants, but parental response patterns that are warm, consistent, and contingent on infant actions predict positive language development in infants across cultures.
Spencer Robertson/Newscom

Infant-directed speech has been documented in many languages and cultures (Bryant, Liénard, & Barrett, 2012; Kuhl et al., 1997). Comparisons of mothers from Fiji, Kenya, and the United States show the use of high-pitched speech, which is characteristic of infant-directed speech, with infants (Broesch & Bryant, 2015). The pattern of infant-directed speech is similar across cultures such that adults can discriminate it from adult-directed speech even while listening to a language they do not speak. For example, when adults in the Turkana region of northwestern Kenya listened to speech produced in English by American mothers, they were able to discriminate between infant-directed and adult-directed speech, suggesting that infant-directed speech is recognizable to adults of many cultures (Bryant, Liénard, & Barrett, 2012). Despite this, adults of different cultures vary in their interactions with infants.

Cultures differ in the use of infant-directed speech. For example, in Samoa, infants are not addressed directly

by caregivers until they begin to crawl. Parents tend to interpret their vocalizations as indicators of physiological state rather than as attempts to communicate. Because of the status hierarchy in Samoa, child-directed speech is uncommon in adults because it would reflect someone of higher status (i.e., an adult) adjusting his or her speech to someone of lower status (Ochs & Schieffein, 1984). Instead, older children are tasked with responding to infants' utterances, and it is largely older children who talk with infants (Lieven & Stoll, 2010). Similarly, the Kaluli of Papua New Guinea do not engage in infant-directed speech (Fitneva & Matsui, 2015). Infants are held oriented outward rather than toward the mother. When infants are addressed by others, the mother speaks for the infant in a high-pitched voice but does not use simplified language. Only when children themselves begin to talk do parents start talking to them, and then they focus on teaching them what to say (Ochs & Schieffein, 1984).

Although parents from different cultures vary in how often they respond to their infants, parental response patterns that are warm, consistent, and contingent on infant actions are associated with positive language development in infants across cultures (Tamis-LeMonda et al., 2014). For example, in a study of six cultural communities, mothers from Berlin and Los Angeles were more likely to respond to infant nondistress vocalizations and gazes than were mothers from Beijing and Delhi, as well as Nso mothers from various cities in Cameroon. In contrast, Nso mothers responded more often to infant touch than did mothers from other cultures. Although parental responsiveness may look different and take different forms across cultures, its benefits generalize across families from varying cultural communities and socioeconomic strata (Rodriguez & Tamis-LeMonda, 2011).

Culture even shapes the types of words that infants learn. In Asian cultures such as those of Japan, China, and Korea that stress interpersonal harmony, children tend to acquire verbs and social words much more quickly than do North American toddlers (Gopnik & Choi, 1995; Tardif et al., 2008). In another study, U.S. mothers responded to infant object play more than social play, whereas Japanese mothers responded more to social play (Tamis-LeMonda, Bornstein, Cyphers, Toda, & Ogino, 1992). For example, North American infants' first words tend to include more referential language, or naming words such as *ball*, *dog*, *cup*, and the like, while Japanese infants tend to use more expressive language, or words that are used mainly in social interaction, such as *please* and *want* (Fernald & Morikawa, 1993). Italian-, Spanish-, French-, Dutch-,

Hebrew-, and English-speaking infants tend to display a preference for using more nouns than verbs (Bassano, 2000; Bornstein et al., 2004; de Houwer & Gillis, 1998; Maital, Dromi, Sagi, & Bornstein, 2000; Tardif, Shatz, & Naigles, 1997). Cultures vary in common practices and contexts of infant-directed communication, yet all infants learn language, supporting the powerful role of maturation.

What Do You Think?

What might influence the cultural differences in which parents interact with infants and thereby influence language development? Consider physical surroundings, resources, and a culture's economy. How might outside factors influence parent–child interactions that support language development? ●

Infancy represents an important time for development that illustrates the interaction of biology, maturation, and the sociocultural context. Infants are equipped with early and rapidly emerging capacities to move and control their bodies, sense the world around them, and learn and think. However, interactions with their sociocultural context strengthen and modify infants' capacities in every domain of development. In turn, babies' actions influence elements of their sociocultural context. Infants' active role in their own cognitive development cannot be denied. Infants also play an active role in their socioemotional development, as discussed in Chapter 6.

THINKING IN CONTEXT 5.4

1. What role do other domains of development hold in influencing infants' language development? Consider motor development, perception, and cognition. How might advances in these domains influence infants' emerging language abilities?

2. Referring to Bronfenbrenner's bioecological model (see Chapter 1), identify factors that influence language acquisition. Specifically, identify examples of macrosystem and mesosystem factors that might play a role in language. How might the exosystem influence language acquisition? Macrosystem?

APPLY YOUR KNOWLEDGE

Researchers use a variety of methods to study infant cognition:

- In one experiment, an infant looks longer at an expected, seemingly impossible event that occurs: A board appears to move through a box.

- An infant is shown a toy, then the overhead lights are turned off, hiding the toy from his sight. The infant successfully reaches for the toy.

- An infant watches as a researcher covers a toy with a blanket. The infant reaches for the blanket and uncovers the toy.

- An infant watches as a researcher covers a toy with a blanket several times. The infant successfully reaches for the toy every time. Next, the researcher

places the toy under a different blanket, adjacent to the first hiding space. The infant reaches in the first place and is unsuccessful in finding the toy.

1. What do these tasks measure? What do the infants' responses demonstrate?

2. What Piagetian substage do each of these infants show?

3. How might changes in information processing skills contribute to these developments?

4. Are infants' responses to these tasks indicators of intelligence in infants? Why or why not?

$SAGE edge™

Visit **edge.sagepub.com/kuther2e** to help you accomplish your coursework goals in an easy-to-use learning environment.

LEARNING OBJECTIVES	SUMMARY	KEY TERMS	IN REVIEW
5.1 Discuss the cognitive-developmental perspective on infant reasoning.	During the sensorimotor period, infants move through six substages that transition the infant from strengthening basic reflexes to engaging in primary, secondary, and tertiary circular reactions and demonstrating representational thought. Core knowledge researchers have shown that young infants may have a grasp of the physical properties of objects, such as object permanence, solidity, gravity, number, and language, earlier than Piaget indicated.	Assimilation Accommodation Mental representation Circular reactions Primary circular reactions Secondary circular reactions Object permanence Tertiary circular reactions Violation-of-expectation task Deferred imitation	What are two processes that influence cognitive development? How do infants progress through six substages of sensorimotor reasoning? What are criticisms of Piaget's sensorimotor period? What is the core knowledge perspective?
5.2 Describe the information processing system in infants.	According to information processing theory, we are born with a functioning information processing system comprising sensory memory, working memory (which includes a short-term store, a processing component, and the central executive), and long-term memory. Young infants require a long time to habituate to stimuli and will look longer at stimuli than older infants. By 3 months of age, infants can remember a visual stimulus for 24 hours and for several days or even weeks by the end of the first year of life. Infants' earliest categories are based on the perceived similarity of objects. As early as 7 months of age, infants use conceptual categories based on perceived function and behavior. Seven- to 12-month-old infants use many categories to organize objects, such as food, furniture, birds, animals, vehicles, kitchen utensils, and more. Twelve- to 30-month-old infants categorize objects first at a global level and then at more specific levels.	Video deficit effect Sensory memory Working memory Central executive Executive function Long-term memory Attention Categorization	How is the information processing system organized? Describe developmental changes in attention, memory, and thinking during infancy.
5.3 Discuss individual differences in infant intelligence.	The most commonly used measure of infant intelligence is the BSID-III, or Bayley-III, appropriate for infants from 2 months through 30 months of age. The intellectual abilities measured by the Bayley-III are critical indicators of neurological health and are useful for charting developmental paths, diagnosing neurological disorders, and detecting mental retardation very early in life but are not closely related with childhood intelligence. New approaches look to information processing as an indicator of intellectual skill.	Intelligence	Describe the most often used standardized measure of infant intelligence. How useful are infant intelligence tests for predicting developmental outcomes? What is the information processing approach to intelligence?

| 5.4 Summarize the patterns of language development during infancy and toddlerhood. | Newborns are able to hear all of the sounds of which the human voice is capable, but by 10 to 12 months, their ability to perceive nonnative sound declines. Infants begin cooing by 3 months and babbling at about 6 months of age. At first, babbling is universal, but with exposure to speech, babbling sounds more like the infant's native language. Fast mapping helps young children learn many new words, but their own speech lags behind what they can understand, and they display underextension and overextension errors. At about 21 months of age, most children compose their first simple two-word sentences, telegraphic speech. Learning theory poses that language is learned through operant conditioning. Nativist theorists pose that the human brain has an innate capacity to learn language. An interactionist perspective integrates nature and nurture, noting that we have innate perceptual biases for discriminating and listening to language, and the brain is wired for language at birth. At the same time, language acquisition occurs in a social context in which adults use infant-directed speech to catch the infant's attention and facilitate language development by responding in ways that foster language learning, such as by using expansions and recasts. | Cooing

Babbling

Holophrases

Fast mapping

Naming explosion

Underextension

Overextension

Telegraphic speech

Grammar

Language acquisition device (LAD)

Universal grammar

Broca's area

Wernicke's area

Canonical babbling

Expansions

Recast | Describe the process of language development through infancy and toddlerhood.

How do learning theory and nativist theory explain language development?

Provide examples to illustrate the interactionist approach to language development. |

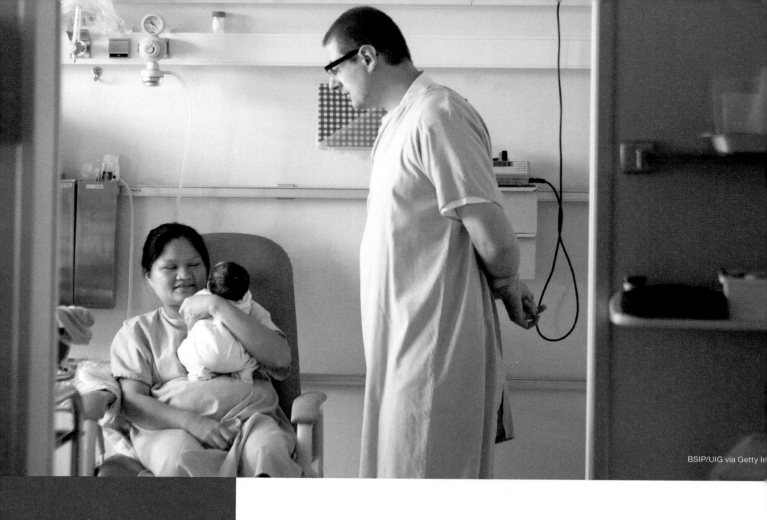

6 Socioemotional Development in Infancy and Toddlerhood

As a newborn, Terrence expressed distress by spreading his arms, kicking his legs, and crying. When he did this, his mother or father would scoop him up and hold him, trying to comfort him. Terrence quickly began to prefer interacting with attentive adults who cared for him. Soon Baby Terrence began to smile and gurgle when held. In turn, Terrence's parents played with him and were delighted to see his animated, excited responses. As a toddler, his emerging language skills enabled Terrence to express his needs in words. He quickly learned that words are powerful tools that can convey emotions ("I love you, Mommy"). Without realizing it, Terrence used words to help him manage strong emotions and difficult situations. For example, he distracted himself from stressful stimuli, like the neighbor's scary dog, by singing to himself. Terrence could express his ideas and feelings to everyone around him, making for new and more complex relationships with his parents and siblings.

Learning Objectives

6.1 Summarize the psychosocial tasks of infancy and toddlerhood.

6.2 Describe emotional development in infancy and identify contextual and cultural influences on emotional development in infants and toddlers.

6.3 Identify the styles and stability of temperament, including the role of goodness of fit in infant development.

6.4 Describe how attachment develops in infancy and toddlerhood.

6.5 Differentiate the roles of self-concept, self-recognition, and self-control in infant development.

Digital Resources

Listen: Erikson's 8 Stages

▶ **Lives in Context Video 6.1:** Transition to Parenthood

Watch: Infant Emotion

Explore: Infant Temperament Across Cultures

Watch: The Strange Situation

▶ **Lives in Context Video 6.2:** Parent and Infant Psychotherapy

Explore: Culture and Self-Recognition

As Terrence illustrates, in the first 2 years of life, babies learn new ways of expressing their emotions. They become capable of new and more complex emotions and develop a greater sense of self-understanding, social awareness, and self-management. These abilities influence their interactions with others and their emerging social relationships. These processes collectively are referred to as socioemotional development. In this chapter, we examine the processes of socioemotional development in infancy and toddlerhood.

PSYCHOSOCIAL DEVELOPMENT IN INFANCY AND TODDLERHOOD

»LO 6.1 Summarize the psychosocial tasks of infancy and toddlerhood.

According to Erik Erikson (1950), as we travel through the lifespan, we proceed through a series of psychosocial crises, or developmental tasks. As discussed in Chapter 1, how well each crisis is resolved influences psychological development and how the individual approaches the next crisis or developmental task. Erikson believed that infants and toddlers progress through two psychosocial stages that influence their personality development: **trust versus mistrust** and **autonomy versus shame and doubt.**

Trust Versus Mistrust

From the day she was born, each time Erin cried, her mother or father would come to her bassinet and hold her, check her diaper, and feed her if necessary. Soon, Erin developed the basic expectation that her parents would meet her needs. According to Erikson (1950), developing a sense of trust versus mistrust is the first developmental task of life. Infants must develop a view of the world as a safe place where their basic needs will be met. Throughout the first year of life, infants depend on their caregivers for food, warmth, and affection. If parents and caregivers attend to the infant's physical and emotional needs and consistently fulfill them, the infant will develop a basic sense of trust in her caregivers and, by extension, in the world in general.

However, if caregivers are neglectful or inconsistent in meeting the infant's needs, he will

Toddlers take pride in completing this task—tooth brushing—all by himself, developing a sense of autonomy.
iStock/dszc

develop a sense of mistrust, feeling that he cannot count on others for love, affection, or the fulfillment of other basic human needs. The sense of trust or mistrust developed in infancy influences how people approach the subsequent stages of development. Specifically, when interaction with adults around them inspires trust and security, babies are more likely to feel comfortable exploring the world, which enhances their learning, social development, and emotional development.

Autonomy Versus Shame and Doubt

Two-and-a-half-year-old Sarah is an active child who vigorously explores her environment, tests new toys, and attempts to learn about the world on her own. At dinnertime, she wants to feed herself and gets angry when her parents try to feed her. Each morning, she takes pleasure in attempting to dress herself and expresses frustration when her mother helps. Erin is progressing through the second stage in Erikson's scheme of psychosocial development—autonomy

---

CULTURAL INFLUENCES ON DEVELOPMENT

 ## Father–Infant Interactions

Fathers tend to have different interaction styles than mothers. Father–infant interaction tends to be play-oriented. This is true of fathers in Western contexts as well as those in non-Western contexts, such as the Kadazan of Malaysia and Aka and Bofi of Central Africa
Gerard Fritz/Science Source

We know a great deal about the influence of mother–infant relationships on infant attachment and adjustment, but infants also develop attachments to their fathers (Lickenbrock & Braungart-Rieker, 2015). At birth, fathers interact with their newborns much like mothers do. They provide similar levels of care by cradling the newborn and performing tasks like diaper changing, bathing, and feeding the newborn (Combs-Orme & Renkert, 2009). This is true of fathers in Western contexts as well as those in non-Western contexts, such as the Kadazan

of Malaysia and Aka and Bofi of Central Africa (Hewlett & MacFarlan, 2010; Tamis-LeMonda, Kahana-Kalman, & Yoshikawa, 2009; Ziarat Hossain, Roopnarine, Ismail, Hashmi, & Sombuling, 2007).

Early in an infant's life, however, fathers and mothers develop different play and communicative styles. Fathers tend to be more stimulating while mothers are more soothing (Feldman, 2003; Grossmann et al., 2002). Father–infant play is more physical and play oriented compared with the social exchanges centered on mutual gaze and vocalization that is characteristic of mother–infant play (Feldman, 2003). Fathers tend to engage in more unpredictable rough-and-tumble play that is often met with more positive reactions and arousal from infants; when young children have a choice of an adult play partner, they tend to choose their fathers (Feldman, 2003; Lamb & Lewis, 2016).

Differences in mothers' and fathers' interaction styles appear in many cultures, including France, Switzerland, Italy, and India, as well as among White non-Hispanic, African American, and Hispanic American families in the United States (Best, House, Barnard, & Spicker, 1994; Roopnarine, Talukder, Jain, Joshi, & Srivastav, 1992; Zirat Hossain, Field, Pickens, Malphurs, & Del Valle, 1997). However, interaction styles differ more in some cultures than in others. For example, German, Swedish, and Israeli kibbutzim fathers, as well as fathers in the Aka ethnic group of Africa's western Congo basin, are not more playful than mothers (Frodi, Lamb, Hwang, & Frodi, 1983;

Hewlett, 2008; Hewlett et al., 1998; Sagi et al., 1985). Furthermore, across cultures, most of the differences between mothers and fathers are not large (Lamb & Lewis, 2016).

Father–child interaction is associated with social competence, independence, and cognitive development in children (Sethna et al., 2016). Rough-and-tumble play contributes to advances in emotional and behavioral regulation in children (Flanders, Leo, Paquette, Pihl, & Séguin, 2009). Fathers provide opportunities for babies to practice arousal management by providing high-intensity stimulation and excitement, like tickling, chasing, and laughing. Fathers who are sensitive, supportive, and appropriately challenging during play promote secure bonds with their children (Grossmann et al., 2002; Lickenbrock & Braungart-Rieker, 2015). When fathers are involved in the caregiving of their infants, their children

are more likely to enjoy a warm relationship with their father as they grow older, carry out responsibilities, follow parents' directions, and be well adjusted. Similar to findings with mothers, sensitive parenting on the part of fathers predicts secure attachments with their children through age 3 (Brown, Mangelsdorf, & Neff, 2012; Lucassen et al., 2011). The positive social, emotional, and cognitive effects of father–child interaction continue from infancy into childhood and adolescence (Sarkadi, Kristiansson, Oberklaid, & Bremberg, 2008).

What Do You Think?

1. What are some of the challenges of studying father–child relationships? How might researchers address these challenges?

2. Why do you think fathers are more likely to be "play mates" than mothers? ●

---

versus shame and doubt—which is concerned with establishing a sense of autonomy, or the feeling that one can make choices and direct oneself.

Toddlers walk on their own, express their own ideas and needs, and become more independent. Their developmental task is to learn to do things for themselves and feel confident in their ability to maneuver in their environment. According to Erikson (1950), if parents encourage the toddler's initiative and allow him to explore, experiment, make mistakes, and test limits, the toddler will develop autonomy, self-reliance, self-control, and confidence. If parents are overprotective or disapprove of the child's struggle for independence, the child may begin to doubt his abilities to do things by himself, may feel ashamed of his desire for autonomy, may passively observe, and may not develop a sense of independence and self-reliance.

Both trust and autonomy develop out of warm and sensitive parenting and developmentally appropriate expectations for exploration and behavioral control throughout infancy and toddlerhood. Without a secure sense of trust in caregivers, toddlers will struggle to establish and maintain close relationships with others and will find it challenging to develop autonomy. Adjustment difficulties are more likely when children do not develop a sense of individuality and confidence in their own abilities to meet new challenges. Much of the research on parenting examines mothers, but infants' interaction relationships with fathers also predict autonomy and social competence. This is true across cultures and the accompanying feature, Cultural Influences on Development, looks at father–infant interactions.

THINKING IN CONTEXT 6.1

1. How do contextual factors, such as those that accompany being raised in an inner city, suburban neighborhood, rural environment, or nomadic society, influence how infants approach the psychosocial tasks of infancy—developing a sense of trust and autonomy? Would you expect infants in each of these contexts to demonstrate trust and autonomy in similar ways? Why or why not?

2. What kinds of behaviors on the part of parents promote a sense of trust in infants? Do trust-promoting activities, such as attentiveness and cuddling, also foster a sense of autonomy in infants? Why or why not?

EMOTIONAL DEVELOPMENT IN INFANCY AND TODDLERHOOD

» LO 6.2   **Describe emotional development in infancy and identify contextual and cultural influences on emotional development in infants and toddlers.**

What emotions do infants feel? Infants cannot describe their experiences and feelings, which makes studying infants' emotional development quite challenging. How do you determine what another person is feeling? Most people show their emotions on their faces, such as by smiling or frowning. If we use facial expressions as a guide to what emotions

Even young infants exhibit a wide range of emotions. Observation of newborn facial expressions suggests that newborns experience interest, distress, disgust, and happiness or contentment. Between 2 and 7 months of age, they begin to display other emotions, such as anger, sadness, surprise, and fear.
iStock/jjustas

TABLE 6.1	
Milestones in Emotional Development	

APPROXIMATE AGE	MILESTONE
Birth	Basic emotions Discriminates mother
2–3 months	Social smile Distinguishes happiness, anger, surprise, and sadness
6–8 months	Fear, stranger anxiety, and separation protest occur
7–12 months	Social referencing
18–24 months	Self-conscious emotions appear. Develops vocabulary for talking about emotions

infants might feel, the first and most reliable emotion that newborns show is distress. They cry, wail, and flail their arms and bodies, alerting caregivers to their need for attention. Newborns also show interest with wide-eyed gazes when something catches their attention, and they smile when they are happy.

Infants' Emotional Experience

Are we born with the ability to feel emotions? No one knows for sure, but observation of newborn facial expressions suggests that newborns experience interest, distress, disgust, and happiness or contentment (Izard, Woodburn, & Finlon, 2010). Of course, we do not know whether internal emotional states accompany these facial expressions, but infants' facial expressions are remarkably similar to those of adults (Sullivan & Lewis, 2003).

Basic Emotions

Basic emotions, also known as primary emotions (happiness, sadness, interest, surprise, fear, anger, and disgust), are universal, experienced by people around the world (Cordaro et al., 2018; Lench, Baldwin, An, & Garrison, 2018). Basic emotions emerge in all infants at about the same ages and are seen and interpreted similarly in all cultures that have been studied, suggesting that they are inborn (Izard et al., 2010). Between 2 and 7 months of age, infants begin to display anger, sadness, joy, surprise, and fear (Bennett, Bendersky, & Lewis, 2005).

Research with adults suggests that emotions are the result of interactions among richly connected,

subcortical brain structures, including the brainstem and the limbic system, as well as parts of the cerebral cortex (Celeghin, Diano, Bagnis, Viola, & Tamietto, 2017; Kragel & LaBar, 2016). These structures develop prenatally and are present in animals, suggesting that emotions serve a biological purpose, are crucial to survival, and are likely experienced by infants (Rolls, 2017; Turner, 2014).

Emotions develop in predictable ways, as shown in Table 6.1. As mentioned, basic emotions are assumed to be inborn. During the first few months of life, however, the ways that primary emotions are displayed and the conditions that elicit them change. For example, in adults, smiling indicates happiness. Newborns smile, and smiling is one of the most important emotional expressions in infancy. Newborn smiles are reflexive, involuntary, and linked with shifts in arousal state (e.g., going from being asleep to drowsy wakefulness), and they occur frequently during periods of rapid eye movement (REM) sleep (Kawakami et al., 2008). At about 3 weeks, infants smile while awake and alert and in response to familiarity—familiar sounds, voices, and tastes (Sroufe & Waters, 1976).

During the second month of life, as infants' vision improves, they smile more in response to visual stimuli—sights that catch their attention, such as bright objects coming into view (Sroufe, 1997). The **social smile** emerges between 6 and 10 weeks of age (Lewis, Hitchcock, & Sullivan, 2004). The social smile, which occurs in response to familiar people, is an important milestone in infant development because it shows social engagement (Messinger & Fogel, 2007). The social smile plays a large role in initiating and maintaining social interactions between infants and adults, especially by enhancing caregiver–child bonding. Parents are enthralled when their baby shows delight in seeing them, and the parents' happy response encourages their baby to smile even more (Beebe et al., 2016).

Smiling is one of the most important emotional expressions in infancy because it plays a role in initiating and maintaining social interactions between infants and adults.
iStock/quavondo

As infants grow, laughs begin to accompany their smiles, and they laugh more often and at more things. Infants may show clear expressions of joy and intense happiness as early as 2½ months of age while playing with a parent and at 3 to 4 months of age in response to stimuli that they find highly arousing (Bornstein & Lamb, 2011). At 6 months of age, an infant might laugh at unusual sounds or sights, such as when Mommy puts a bowl on her head or makes a funny face. Laughing at unusual events illustrates the baby's increasing cognitive competence as he or she knows what to expect and is surprised when something unexpected occurs. By a year of age, infants can smile deliberately to engage an adult.

Negative emotions change over time as well. Distress is evident at birth when newborns experience the discomfort of hunger, a heel prick, or a chilly temperature. Anger appears at about 6 months of age and develops rapidly, becoming more complex in terms of elicitors and responses (Lemerise & Dodge, 2008). Initially, physical restrictions such as being restrained in a high chair or when being dressed can elicit anger. The inability to carry out a desired act, such as unsuccessfully reaching to obtain a desired toy, can also provoke frustration and anger (Sullivan & Lewis, 2003). Between 8 and 20 months of age, infants gradually become more reactive, and anger is more easily aroused (Braungart-Rieker, Hill-Soderlund, & Karrass, 2010). They become aware of the actions of others, so that anger can be elicited by others' behavior. For example, an infant may become upset when Mommy goes to the door to leave or when Grandma takes out the towels in preparation for bath time. During the second year of life, temper tantrums become common when the toddler's attempts at autonomy are thwarted and he or she experiences frustration or stress. The anger escalates with the child's stress level (Potegal, Robison, Anderson, Jordan, & Shapiro, 2007). Some toddlers show extreme tantrums, lie on the floor, scream, and jerk their arms and legs. Other children's tantrums are more subtle. They may whine, mope, and stick out their lower lip.

Self-Conscious Emotions

Emotional development is an orderly process in which complex emotions build on the foundation of simple emotions. The development of **self-conscious emotions,** or secondary emotions—such as empathy, pride, embarrassment, shame, and guilt—depends on cognitive development, as well as an awareness of self. Self-conscious emotions do not begin to emerge until about 15 to 18 months, and they largely develop during the second and third years of life (Goodvin, Thompson, & Winer, 2015). To experience self-conscious emotions, toddlers must be able to have a sense of self, observe themselves and others, be aware of standards and rules, and compare their behavior with those standards (Lewis, 2016). Feelings of pride, for example, arise from accomplishing a personally meaningful goal, whereas guilt derives from realizing that one has violated a standard of conduct. Parental evaluations are the initial basis for many secondary emotions (Stipek, 1995).

Emotion Regulation

As children become aware of social standards and rules, **emotion regulation**—the ability to control their emotions—becomes important. How do infants regulate emotions? Very young infants have been observed to manage negative emotions by sucking vigorously on objects or turning their bodies away from distressing stimuli (Mangelsdorf, Shapiro, & Marzolf, 1995).

Smiling is also thought to serve a purpose in regulating emotions, as it allows the infant to control aspects of a situation without losing touch with it. When an infant gets excited and smiles, she looks away briefly. This may be a way of breaking herself away from the stimulus and allowing her to regroup, preventing overstimulation. Smiling is associated with a decline in heart rate, suggesting that it is a relaxation response to decrease an infant's level of arousal.

Whereas 6-month-old infants are more likely to use gaze aversion and fussing as primary emotion regulatory strategies, 12-month-old infants are more likely to use self-soothing (e.g., thumb sucking, rocking themselves) and distraction (chewing on objects, playing with toys). By 18 months of age, toddlers actively attempt to change the distressing situation, such as by moving away from upsetting stimuli, and begin to use distraction, such as by playing with toys or talking (Crockenberg & Leerkes, 2004; Feldman, Dollberg, & Nadam, 2011).

After 18 months of age, toddlers' vocabulary for talking about feelings develops rapidly, and their ability to tell caregivers how they feel presents new opportunities for emotion regulation (Bretherton, Fritz, Zahn-Waxler, & Ridgeway, 1986). Vocabulary predicts self-regulation abilities in 24-month-old infants (Vallotton & Ayoub, 2011). In one longitudinal study of children from 18 to 48 months, toddlers with better language skill tended to engage in more support seeking and distracted themselves more, which was linked with showing less anger at 48 months (Roben, Cole, & Armstrong, 2013). Researchers have also found that infants' abilities to self-regulate at 15 months predict executive functioning at 4 years (Ursache, Blair, Stifter, Voegtline, & The Family Life Project Investigators, 2013).

Responsive parenting helps infants learn to manage their emotions and self-regulate.
iStock/AleksandarNakic

Social Interaction and Emotional Development

Infants and young children often need outside assistance in regulating their emotions. Warm and supportive interactions with parents and other caregivers can help infants understand their emotions and learn how to manage them.

Parental Interaction

Responsive parenting that is attuned to infants' needs helps infants develop skills in emotion regulation, especially in managing negative emotions like anxiety, as well as their physiological correlates, such as accelerated heart rate (Feldman et al., 2011). For example, sensitive responses coupled with soft vocalizations aid 3-month-old infants in regulating distress (Spinelli & Mesman, 2018). Likewise, when mothers responded promptly to their 2-month-old infants' cries, these same infants, at 4 months of age, cried for shorter durations, were better able to manage their emotions, and stopped crying more quickly than other infants (Jahromi & Stifter, 2007).

Parents help their infants learn to manage emotions through a variety of strategies, including direct intervention, modeling, selective reinforcement, control of the environment, verbal instruction, and touch (Waters, West, Karnilowicz, & Mendes, 2017). These strategies change as the infants grow older. For example, touching becomes a less common regulatory strategy with age, whereas vocalizing and distracting techniques increase (Meléndez, 2005). When mothers provide guidance in helping infants regulate their emotions, the infants tend to engage in distraction and mother-oriented strategies, such as seeking help, during frustrating events.

Parent–infant interactions undergo continuous transformations as infants develop. For example,

infants' growing motor skills influence their interactions with parents, as well as their socioemotional development. Crawling, creeping, and walking introduce new challenges to parent–infant interaction and socioemotional growth (Adolph & Franchak, 2017). As crawling begins, parents and caregivers respond with happiness and pride, positive emotions that encourage infants' exploration. As infants gain motor competence, they wander further from parents (Thurman & Corbetta, 2017). Crawling increases a toddler's capability to attain goals—a capability that, while often satisfying to the toddler, may involve hazards.

As infants become more mobile, emotional outbursts become more common. Parents report that advances in locomotion are accompanied by increased frustration as toddlers attempt to move in ways that often exceed their abilities or are not permitted by parents (Clearfield, 2011; Pemberton Roben et al., 2012). When mothers recognize the dangers posed to toddlers by objects such as houseplants, vases, and electrical appliances, they sharply increase their expressions of anger and fear, often leading to fear and frustration in their toddlers. At this stage, parents actively monitor toddlers' whereabouts, protect them from dangerous situations, and expect them to comply—a dynamic that is often a struggle, amounting to a test of wills. At the same time, these struggles help the child to begin to develop a grasp of mental states in others that are different from his or her own.

Changes in emotional expression and regulation are dynamic because the changing child influences the changing parent. In particular, mothers and infants systematically influence and regulate each other's emotions and behaviors. Mothers regulate infant emotional states by interpreting their emotional signals, providing appropriate arousal, and reciprocating and reinforcing infant reactions. Infants regulate their mother's emotions through their receptivity to her initiations and stimulation and by responding to her emotions (Bornstein, Hahn, Suwalsky, & Haynes, 2011; Bornstein, Suwalsky, & Breakstone, 2012). By experiencing a range of emotional interactions—times when their emotions mirror those of their caregivers and times when their emotions are different from those of their caregivers—infants learn how to transform negative emotions into neutral or positive emotions and regulate their own emotional states (Guo, Leu, Barnard, Thompson, & Spieker, 2015).

Social Referencing

Early in life, the ability emerges to discriminate facial expressions that indicate emotion. In one study, 2-day-old infants initially did not show a preference for a happy or disgust face, but after being habituated to either a happy or disgust face, they successfully discriminated between the two, suggesting an early sensitivity to dynamic-faced expressing emotions (Addabbo, Longhi, Marchis, Tagliabue, & Turati, 2018). Likewise, newborns are able to discriminate happy faces from fearful ones (Farroni, Menon, Rigato, & Johnson, 2007). It is thought that infants are innately prepared to attend to facial displays of emotion, because such displays are biologically significant and the ability to recognize them is important for human survival (Leppanen, 2011). Between 2 and 4 months of age, infants can distinguish emotional expressions, including happiness as opposed to anger, surprise, and sadness (Bornstein, Arterberry, & Lamb, 2013). Infants 6½ months old can identify and match happy, angry, and sad emotions portrayed on faces but also body movements indicating emotion (Hock et al., 2017).

Beyond recognizing the emotional expressions of others, infants also respond to them. Between 6 and 10 months of age, infants begin to use **social referencing,** looking to caregivers' or other adults' emotional expressions to find clues for how to interpret ambiguous events, which influences their emotional responses and subsequent actions (Walle, Reschke, & Knothe, 2017). For example, when a toddler grabs the sofa to pull herself up, turns, and tumbles over as she takes a step, she will look to her caregiver to determine how to interpret her fall. If the caregiver has a fearful facial expression, the infant is likely to be fearful also, but if the caregiver smiles, the infant will probably remain calm and return to attempts at walking. The use of social referencing is one way that infants demonstrate their understanding that others experience their own emotions and thoughts.

Older infants tend to show a negativity bias when it comes to social referencing. That is, they attend to and follow social referencing cues more closely when the cues indicate negative attitudes toward an object, compared with neutral or happy attitudes (Vaish, Grossmann, & Woodward, 2008).

In addition, infants may be more influenced by the vocal information conveyed in emotional messages than the facial expressions themselves, especially within the context of fearful messages (Biro, Alink, van IJzendoorn, & Bakermans-Kranenburg, 2014).

How infants employ social referencing changes with development. Ten-month-old infants show selective social referencing. They monitor the caregiver's attention and do not engage in social referencing when the adult is not attending or engaged (Stenberg, 2017). At 12 months, infants use referential cues such as the caregiver's body posture, gaze, and voice direction to determine to what objects caregivers' emotional responses refer (Brooks & Meltzoff, 2008). Twelve-month-old infants are more likely to use a caregiver's cues as guides in ambivalent situations when the caregiver responds promptly to the infants' behavior (Stenberg, 2017). In sum, social referencing reflects infants' growing understanding of the emotional states of others; it signifies that infants can observe, interpret, and use emotional information from others to form their own interpretation and response to events.

Cultural Influences on Emotional Development

As we've already seen, emotional development does not occur in a vacuum. Contextual factors, such as culture, influence how infants interpret and express emotions, as well as what emotions they feel. In this section, we explore the role of context in shaping children's knowledge about the appropriate display of emotions, as well as the degree to which children experience a fear common in infancy: stranger wariness.

Emotional Display Rules

Every society has a set of **emotional display rules** that specify the circumstances under which various emotions should or should not be expressed (Safdar et al., 2009). We learn these rules very early in life through interactions with others. Every interaction between parent and infant is shaped by the culture in which they live, which influences their emotional expressions (Bornstein, Arterberry, & Lamb, 2013). When North American mothers play with their 7-month-old babies, for instance, they tend to model positive emotions, restricting their own emotional displays to show joy, interest, and surprise (Malatesta & Haviland, 1982). They also are more attentive to infants' expression of positive emotions, such as interest or surprise, and respond less to negative emotions (Broesch, Rochat, Olah, Broesch, & Henrich, 2016). Thus, babies are socialized to respond and display their emotions in socially acceptable ways.

In some cultures infants cry very little, perhaps because they are in constant contact with their mothers.
Pavel Gospodinov/Design Pics/Corbis

Which emotions are considered acceptable, as well as how they should be expressed, differ by culture and context. North American parents tickle and stimulate their babies, encouraging squeals of pleasure. The Gusii and Aka people of Central Africa prefer to keep babies calm and quiet; they engage in little face-to-face play (Hewlett, Lamb, Shannon, Leyendecker, & Scholmerich, 1998; LeVine et al., 1994). These differences communicate cultural expectations about emotions (Halberstadt & Lozada, 2011). North American infants learn to express positive emotions, and Central African babies learn to restrain strong emotions.

Similarly, cultures often have particular beliefs about how much responsiveness is appropriate when babies cry and fuss, as well as expectations about infants' abilities to regulate their own emotions (Halberstadt & Lozada, 2011). The !Kung hunter-gatherers of Botswana, Africa, respond to babies' cries nearly immediately (within 10 seconds), whereas Western mothers tend to wait a considerably longer period of time before responding to infants' cries (e.g., 10 minutes) (Barr, Konner, Bakeman, & Adamson, 1991). Fijian

mothers tend to be more responsive than U.S. mothers to negative facial expressions in their infants (Broesch et al., 2016). Gusii mothers believe that constant holding, feeding, and physical care are essential for keeping an infant calm, which in turn protects the infant from harm and disease; therefore, like !Kung mothers, Gusii mothers respond immediately to their babies' cries (LeVine et al., 1994). Non-Western infants are thought to cry very little because they are carried often (Bleah & Ellett, 2010). In one study, infants born to parents who were recent immigrants from Africa cried less than U.S. infants, illustrating the role of culture in influencing infant cries (Bleah & Ellett, 2010). Caregivers' responses to infant cries influence infants' capacity for self-regulation and responses to stress. Babies who receive more responsive and immediate caregiving when distressed show lower rates of persistent crying, spend more time in happy and calm states, and cry less overall as they approach their first birthday (Axia & Weisner, 2002; Papoušek & Papoušek, 1990).

Stranger Wariness

Many infants around the world display **stranger wariness** (also known as *stranger anxiety*), a fear of unfamiliar people. Whether infants show stranger wariness depends on the infants' overall temperament, their past experience, and the situation in which they meet a stranger (Goodvin, Thompson, & Winer, 2015). In many, but not all, cultures, stranger wariness emerges at about 6 months and increases throughout the first year of life, beginning to decrease after about 15 months of age (Bornstein et al., 2013; Sroufe, 1977).

Recent research has suggested that the pattern of stranger wariness varies among infants. Some show rapid increases and others show slow increases in stranger wariness; once wariness

As attachments form, infants become more wary and display "stranger anxiety" when in the presence of unfamilar people. In many, but not all cultures, stranger wariness emerges at about 6 months and increases throughout the first year of life.
YOSHIKAZU TSUNO/AFP/Getty Images

has been established, some infants show steady decline and others show more rapid changes. Twin studies suggest that these patterns are influenced by genetics, because the patterns of change are more similar among monozygotic twins (identical twins who share 100% of their genes) than dizygotic twins (fraternal twins who share 50% of their genes) twins (Brooker et al., 2013).

Among North American infants, stranger wariness is so common that parents and caregivers generally expect it. However, infants of the Efe people of Zaire, Africa, show little stranger wariness. This is likely related to the Efe collective caregiving system, in which Efe babies are passed from one adult to another, relatives and nonrelatives alike (Tronick, Morelli, & Ivey, 1992), and the infants form relationships with the many people who care for them (Meehan & Hawks, 2013). In contrast, babies reared in Israeli kibbutzim (cooperative agricultural settlements that tend to be isolated and subjected to terrorist attacks) tend

to demonstrate widespread wariness of strangers. By the end of the first year, when infants look to others for cues about how to respond emotionally, kibbutz babies display far greater anxiety than babies reared in Israeli cities (Saarni, Mumme, & Campos, 1998). In this way, stranger wariness may be adaptive, modifying infants' drive to explore in light of contextual circumstances (Easterbrooks, Bartlett, Beeghly, & Thompson, 2012).

Stranger wariness illustrates the dynamic interactions among the individual and context. The infant's tendencies toward social interaction and past experience with strangers are important, of course, but so is the mother's anxiety. Infants whose mothers report greater stress reactivity, who experience more anxiety and negative affect in response to stress, show higher rates of stranger wariness (Brooker et al., 2013; Waters et al., 2014). Characteristics of the stranger (e.g., his or her height), the familiarity of the setting, and how quickly the stranger approaches influence how the infant appraises the situation.

Maternal Depression and Emotional Development

Depression is characterized by a lack of emotion and a preoccupation with the self that makes it challenging for depressed mothers to care for their infants and recognize their infants' needs.
iStock/monkeybusinessimages

Challenging home contexts pose risks to infants' emotional development. One such challenge may come from maternal depression. Depression is not simply sadness; rather, it is characterized by a lack of emotion and a preoccupation with the self that makes it challenging for depressed mothers to care for their infants and recognize their infants' needs. Although

both mothers and fathers can become depressed, with negative implications for their children, most of the research on parental depression examines mothers. Mothers who are depressed tend to view their infants differently than nondepressed mothers and independent observers (Newland, Parade, Dickstein, & Seifer, 2016). Mothers who are diagnosed with depression are more likely to identify negative emotions (i.e., sadness) than positive emotions (i.e., happiness) in infant faces (Webb & Ayers, 2015). When depressed and nondepressed mothers were shown images of their own and unfamiliar infants' joy and distress faces, mothers with depression showed blunted brain activity in response to their own infants' joy and distress faces, suggesting muted responses to infants' emotional cues (Laurent & Ablow, 2013). Depressed women tend to disengage faster from positive and negative infant emotional expressions (Webb & Ayers, 2015). Therefore, challenging behaviors, such as fussiness and crying, and difficult temperaments tend to elicit more negative responses from depressed mothers (Newland et al., 2016).

In practice, mothers who are depressed tend to be less responsive to their babies, show less affection, use more negative forms of touch, and show more negative emotions and behaviors such as withdrawal, intrusiveness, hostility, coerciveness,

(Continued)

(Continued)

and insensitivity (Jennings et al., 2008). Given the poor parent–child interaction styles that accompany maternal depression, it may not be surprising that infants of depressed mothers show a variety of negative outcomes, including overall distress, withdrawn behavior, poor social engagement, and difficulty regulating emotions (Granat, Gadassi, Gilboa-Schechtman, & Feldman, 2017; Leventon & Bauer, 2013). They tend to show greater physiological arousal in response to stressors and are more likely to show a stress response when faced with socioemotional challenges. These infants have difficulty regulating emotion and are at risk for later problems (Suurland et al., 2017). They often show poor attentiveness, limited capacity to interact with objects and people, and difficulty reading and understanding others' emotions (Lyubchik & Schlosser, 2010). In addition, they are more likely to show deficits in cognitive development, language development, and insecure attachment in infancy and childhood (Liu et al., 2017; Prenoveau et al., 2017).

The ongoing reciprocal interactions between mothers and infants account for the long-term negative effects of maternal depression (Granat et al., 2017). In one study, maternal depressive symptoms 9 months after giving birth predicted infants' negative reactions to maternal behavior at 18 months of age and, in turn, higher levels of depressive symptoms on the part of mothers when the children reached 27 months of age (Roben et al., 2015). Similarly, in a sample of infants studied from 4 to 18 months of age, family factors such as maternal depression and the mother's experience of relationship stress were associated with the

infants' developing strong negative emotions early in infancy, which compromised their emotion regulation capacities (Bridgett et al., 2009). Declines in infants' regulatory control were in turn associated with negative parenting in toddlerhood, because parents and children interact and influence each other reciprocally.

Depression can be treated with therapy with or without the accompaniment of antidepressant medication (Hollon et al., 2016). For example, cognitive behavior therapy is particularly successful at treating depression as it teaches depressed individuals to recognize the connections among situations, thoughts, feelings, and behaviors; to examine the accuracy of their beliefs; and to consider alternative explanations (Sockol, 2015). Brief psychotherapy has been shown to be successful in improving maternal depressive symptoms and function (Swartz et al., 2016). Experts argue that in addition to treating maternal depression, parenting interventions are particularly important in helping children of depressed mothers (Goodman & Garber, 2017). Interventions that teach parents how to interact with their children will foster the parent–child relationships that promote healthy development (Dempsey, McQuillin, Butler, & Axelrad, 2016; Messer et al., 2018).

What Do You Think?

In your view, how can we best support mothers? If you were to create a program to help prevent depression or to help depressed mothers, what might you include? ●

Infants are more open when the stranger is sensitive to the infant's signals and approaches at the infant's pace (Mangelsdorf, 1992).

To sum up, over the first few months of life, infants display the full range of basic emotions. As their cognitive and social capabilities develop, they are able to experience complex social emotions, such as embarrassment. The social world plays a role in emotional development. Adults interact with infants, provide opportunities to observe and practice emotional expressions, and assist in regulating emotions. Much of emotional development is the result of the interplay of infants' emerging capacities and the contexts in which they are raised, especially the emotional contexts within the home. The accompanying Lives in Context feature discusses the challenges maternal depression poses for emotional development.

THINKING IN CONTEXT 6.2

1. Identify examples of how infants' emotional development is influenced by their interactions with elements of their physical, social, and cultural context. Identify one aspect of each of these contexts that may promote healthy emotional development and one that might hinder emotional development. Explain your choices.

2. In what ways might emotional display rules, such as those regarding the display of positive and negative emotions, illustrate adaptive responses to a particular context? Consider the context in which you were raised. What emotional displays do you think are most adaptive for infants?

TEMPERAMENT IN INFANCY AND TODDLERHOOD

» LO 6.3 **Identify the styles and stability of temperament, including the role of goodness of fit in infant development.**

"Joshua is such an easygoing baby!" gushed his babysitter. "He eats everything, barely cries, and falls asleep without a fuss. I wish all my babies were like him." The babysitter is referring to Joshua's temperament. **Temperament,** the characteristic way in which an individual approaches and reacts to people and situations, is thought to be one of the basic building blocks of emotion and personality. Temperament has strong biological determinants; behavior genetics research has shown genetic bases for temperament (Saudino & Micalizzi, 2015). Yet the expression of temperament reflects reciprocal interactions among genetic predispositions, maturation, and experience (Goodvin et al., 2015; Rothbart, 2011). Every infant behaves in a characteristic, predictable style that is influenced by his or her inborn tendencies toward arousal and stimulation as well as by experiences with adults and contexts. In other words, every infant displays a particular temperament style.

Styles of Temperament

Begun in 1956, the New York Longitudinal Study followed 133 infants into adulthood. Early in life, the infants in the study demonstrated differences several characteristics that are thought to capture the essence of temperament (Thomas & Chess, 1977; Thomas, Chess, & Birch, 1970). For example, infants differ in activity level; some wriggle, kick their legs, wave their arms, and move around a great deal, whereas others tend to be more still and stay in one place. Some infants have predictable patterns of eating and sleeping, and others are not predictable. Infants also differ in the intensity of their reactions, their tendency to approach or withdraw from new things, and their distractibility. Some aspects of infant temperament, particularly activity level, irritability, attention, and sociability or approach-withdrawal, show stability for months and years at a time and in some cases even into adulthood (Lemery-Chalfant, Kao, Swann, & Goldsmith, 2013; Papageorgiou et al., 2014). Thomas and Chess classified infant temperament into three profiles (Thomas & Chess, 1977; Thomas et al., 1970).

- **Easy temperament:** Easy babies are often in a positive mood, even-tempered, open, adaptable, regular, and predictable in biological functioning. They establish regular feeding and sleeping schedules easily.

- **Difficult temperament:** Difficult babies are active, irritable, and irregular in biological rhythms. They are slow to adapt to changes in routine or new situations, react vigorously to change, and have trouble adjusting to new routines.

- **Slow-to-warm-up temperament:** Just as it sounds, slow-to-warm-up babies tend to be inactive, moody, and slow to adapt to new situations and people. They react to new situations with mild irritability but adjust more quickly than do infants with difficult temperaments.

Although it may seem as if all babies could be easily classified, about one third of the infants in the New York Longitudinal Study did not fit squarely into any of the three categories but displayed a mix of characteristics, such as eating and sleeping regularly but being slow to warm up to new situations (Thomas & Chess, 1977; Thomas et al., 1970).

Another influential model of temperament, by Mary Rothbart, includes three dimensions (Rothbart, 2011; Rothbart & Bates, 2007):

- **Extraversion/surgency:** the tendency toward positive emotions. Infants who are high in extraversion/surgency approach experiences with confidence, energy, and positivity, as indicated by smiles, laughter, and approach-oriented behaviors.

- **Negative affectivity:** the tendency toward negative emotions, such as sadness, fear, distress, and irritability.

- **Effortful control:** the degree to which one can focus attention, shift attention, and inhibit responses in order to manage arousal. Infants who are high in effortful control are able to regulate their arousal and soothe themselves.

From this perspective, temperament reflects how easily we become emotionally aroused or our reactivity to stimuli, as well as how well we are able to control our emotional arousal (Rothbart, 2011). Some infants and children are better able to distract themselves, focus their attention, and inhibit impulses than others. The ability to self-regulate and manage emotions and impulses is associated with positive long-term adjustment, including academic achievement, social competence, and resistance to stress, in both Chinese and North American samples (Chen & Schmidt, 2015).

Infant temperament tends to be stable over the first year of life but less so than childhood temperament, which can show stability over years, even into adulthood (Bornstein et al., 2015). In infancy, temperament is especially open to environmental influences, such as interactions with others (Gartstein, Putnam, Aron, & Rothbart, 2016). Young infants' temperament can change with experience, neural development, and sensitive caregiving (e.g., helping babies regulate their negative emotions) (Jonas et al., 2015; Thompson et al., 2013). As infants gain experience and learn how to regulate their states and emotions, those who are cranky and difficult may become less so. By the second year of life, styles of responding to situations and people are better established, and temperament becomes more stable. Temperament at age 3 remains stable, predicting temperament at age 6 and personality traits at age 26 (Dyson et al., 2015).

Context and Goodness of Fit

Like all aspects of development, temperament is influenced by reciprocal reactions among individuals and their contexts. An important influence on socioemotional development is the **goodness of fit** between the child's temperament and the environment around him or her, especially the parents' temperaments and childrearing methods (Chess & Thomas, 1991). Infants are at particular risk for poor outcomes when their temperaments show poor goodness of fit to the settings in which they live (Rothbart & Bates, 1998). For example, if an infant who is fussy, difficult, and slow to adapt to new situations is raised by a patient and sensitive caregiver who provides time for him or her to adapt to new routines, the infant may become less cranky and more flexible over time. The infant may adapt her temperament style to match her context so that later in childhood, she may no longer be classified as difficult and no longer display behavioral problems (J. Bates, Pettit, Dodge, & Ridge, 1998). If, on the other hand, a child with a difficult temperament is reared by a parent who is insensitive, coercive, and difficult in temperament, the child may not learn how to regulate her emotions and may have behavioral problems and adjustment difficulties that worsen with age, even into early adolescence and beyond (Pluess, Birkbeck, & Belsky, 2010). Accordingly, when children are placed in low-quality caregiving environments, those with difficult temperaments respond more negatively and show more behavior problems than do those with easy temperaments (Poehlmann et al., 2011).

An infant's temperament may be stable over time because certain temperamental qualities evoke certain reactions from others, promoting goodness of fit. Easy babies usually get the most positive reactions from others, whereas babies with a difficult temperament receive mixed reactions (Chess &

Thomas, 1991). For example, an "easy" baby tends to smile often, eliciting smiles and positive interactions from others, which in turn reinforce the baby's "easy" temperamental qualities (Planalp, Van Hulle, Lemery-Chalfant, & Goldsmith, 2017). Conversely, a "difficult" baby may evoke more frustration and negativity from caregivers as they try unsuccessfully to soothe the baby's fussing. Researchers found that mothers who view their 6-month-old infants as difficult may be less emotionally available to them (Kim & Teti, 2014). Babies' emotionality and negative emotions predict maternal perceptions of parenting stress and poor parenting (Oddi, Murdock, Vadnais, Bridgett, & Gartstein, 2013; Paulussen-Hoogeboom, Stams, Hermanns, & Peetsma, 2007). Goodness of fit at 4 and 8 months of age predicts a close bond with caregivers at 15 months (Seifer et al., 2014).

Temperament can also be related to mothers' own temperament, as well as their expectations about their infants and their ability to parent (Grady & Karraker, 2017). In one study, mothers who, *prior to giving birth,* considered themselves less well equipped to care for their infants were found to be more likely to have infants who showed negative aspects of temperament, such as fussiness, irritability, and difficulty being soothed (Verhage, Oosterman, & Schuengel, 2013). This suggests that perceptions of parenting may shape views of infant temperament—and thereby shape temperament itself. In other research, 3 months after giving birth, new mothers' feelings of competence were positively associated with infant temperament. Mothers' beliefs about their ability to nurture are shaped by the interaction between their infants' traits and their own parenting self-efficacy, as well as their opportunities for developing successful caregiving routines (Verhage et al., 2013). This contextual dynamic has been found to hold true across cultures. Both British and Pakistani mothers in the United Kingdom reported fewer problems with their infants' temperaments at 6 months of age when the mothers had a greater sense of parenting efficacy and displayed more warm and less hostile parenting styles (Prady, Kiernan, Fairley, Wilson, & Wright, 2014).

As mentioned earlier, socioemotional development is a dynamic process in which infants' behavior and temperament styles influence the family processes that shape their development. Sensitive and patient caregiving is not always easy with a challenging child, and adults' own temperamental styles influence their caregiving. A poor fit between the caregiver's and infant's temperament can make an infant more fussy and cranky. When a difficult infant is paired with a parent with a similar temperament—one who is impatient, irritable, and forceful—behavioral problems in childhood and adolescence are likely (Chess &

Thomas, 1984; Rubin, Hastings, Chen, Stewart, & McNichol, 1998).

The most adaptive matches between infant temperament and context can sometimes be surprising. Consider the Maasai, an African semi-nomadic ethnic group. In times of drought, when the environment becomes extremely hostile, herds of cattle and goats die, and infant mortality rises substantially. Under these challenging conditions, infants with difficult temperaments tend to survive at higher rates than do those with easy temperaments.

Infants who cry and are demanding are attended to, are fed more, and are in better physical condition than easy babies, who tend to cry less and therefore are assumed to be content (Gardiner & Kosmitzki, 2018). Thus, the Maasai infants with difficult temperaments demonstrate higher rates of survival because their temperaments better fit the demands of the hostile context in which they are raised. Early experience can influence emotional development through biological means, as described in the Brain and Biological Influences on Development feature.

Trauma and Emotional Development

Experiencing adversity early in life may have epigenetic effects on the genes that regulate responses to stress. The caregiving environment also influences the developing stress response system and can buffer the negative effects of trauma.
iStock/jhandersen

Can infants remember early life experiences? Does exposure to adversity, such as maltreatment, poverty, and violence, influence infants' development? Very young infants likely do not recall specific experiences and events, but early exposure to trauma may affect infants' development in ways that can last a lifetime. For example, maladaptive contexts may pose risks of physical harm to children, directly influencing neurological development. However, trauma also poses invisible long-term risks to children's emotional development and mental health (Blair, 2010).

How does early trauma effect emotional development? The experience of early social adversity may have epigenetic effects on the genes that regulate the endocrine system, which controls hormone production and release at all ages in life (Conradt, 2017). Infancy may be a particularly plastic time in development with heightened potential for lifelong epigenetic changes that may sensitize responses to stress throughout the lifespan

(Laurent, Harold, Leve, Shelton, & Van Goozen, 2016). For example, research with adults reveals that childhood maltreatment is associated with an increased stress reactivity in adulthood (Turecki & Meaney, 2016).

However, not all infants respond to early life stress with heightened reactivity. Some infants exposed to trauma show lower levels of stress hormones and reduced reactivity to stress (Turecki & Meaney, 2016). The timing and intensity of adversity influences developmental outcomes. Exposure to particularly intense chronic stress early in development can lead to hyperactive stress responses that may be followed by blunted responses (Laurent et al., 2016). Blunted responses may reflect adaptations to chronically stressful situations. Unpredictable stressors, on the other hand, may lead to heightened stress reactivity as the individual adapts to volatile and unexpected situations (Blair, 2010). Both heightened and blunted stress responses may be adaptive attempts to optimize survival in nonoptimal caregiving environments, yet these adaptations may carry behavioral costs, such as heightened distress when confronted with stress and longer term anxiety and depressive symptoms, which negatively affect developmental trajectories (Laurent et al., 2016).

Early life stress poses risks to emotional development, but the caregiving environment also influences the developing stress response system. For example, maternal presence buffers and regulates infants' hormonal and behavioral responses to threats (Howell et al., 2017). Sensitive mothers tend to have infants who display better self-regulation during stressful events; intrusive mothers tend to have the opposite effect (Enlow et al., 2014). Warm parenting within a predictable stimulating environment with supportive adults and family can help infants develop the self-regulation skills to adapt to adverse contexts (Blair, 2010). Unfortunately, trauma often disrupts the caregiving system, making adaptation quite difficult. ●

Cultural Differences in Temperament

Researchers have observed consistent cultural differences in temperament that are rooted in cultural norms for how individuals are perceived. Japanese mothers, for example, view their infants as interdependent beings who must learn the importance of relationships and connections with others (Rothbaum, Weisz, Pott, Miyake, & Morelli, 2000). North American mothers, on the other hand, view their task as shaping babies into autonomous beings (Kojima, 1986). Whereas Japanese mothers tend to interact with their babies in soothing ways, discouraging strong emotions, North American mothers are active and stimulating (Rothbaum et al., 2000). Differences in temperament result, such that Japanese infants tend to be more passive, less irritable and vocal, and more easily soothed when upset than North American infants (Kojima, 1986; Lewis, Ramsay, & Kawakami, 1993; Rothbaum et al., 2000). Culture influences the behaviors that parents view as desirable and the means that parents use to socialize their infants (Chen & Schmidt, 2015; Kagan, 2013). Culture, therefore, plays a role in how emotional development—in this case, temperament—unfolds.

Asian cultures often prioritize low arousal and emotionality and socialize infants in line with these values. Chinese American, Japanese American, and Hmong children tend to display lower levels of irritability, exhibit less physical activity, and engage in more self-quieting and self-control than do European American children (Friedlmeier, Çorapçi, & Benga, 2015; Super & Harkness, 2010). Similarly, a recent comparison of toddlers from Chile, South Korea, Poland, and the United States showed that the South Korean toddlers scored highest on measures of control (Krassner et al., 2016).

If infants from Asian cultures engage in more self-soothing, are they more temperamentally resistant to stress? One study examined levels of the hormone cortisol in infants receiving an inoculation (Lewis et al., 1993). Cortisol, which is released as part of the fight-or-flight response, is often used as a marker of stress. Four-month-old Japanese infants showed a pronounced cortisol response, suggesting that they were experiencing great stress, coupled with little crying. The U.S. infants, on the other hand, displayed intense behavioral reactions to the pain and took longer to calm down, yet they displayed a lower cortisol response. In other words, although the Japanese babies appeared quiet and calm, they were more physiologically stressed than the U.S. infants. It seems that cultural views of the nature of arousal and emotional regulation influence parenting behaviors and ultimately infants' responses to stressors (Friedlmeier et al., 2015).

Culture plays a role in emotional development. Japanese mothers tend to encourage their infants to develop close ties and depend on their assistance whereas North American mothers tend to emphasize autonomy.
Asahi Shimbun/Getty

In summary, we have seen that the cultures in which we are immersed influence how we interpret stimuli and respond to the world, including how we manifest stress. Culture also influences attachment.

THINKING IN CONTEXT 6.3

1. In your view, is it possible for an infant with a difficult temperament to grow into a young child with an easy temperament? Why or why not?

2. Under what conditions might a child with an easy temperament become difficult?

ATTACHMENT IN INFANCY AND TODDLERHOOD

» LO 6.4   Describe how attachment develops in infancy and toddlerhood.

Raj gurgles and cries out while lying in his crib. As his mother enters the room, he squeals excitedly. Raj's mother smiles as she reaches into the crib, and Raj giggles with delight as she picks him up. Raj and his mother have formed an important emotional bond, called attachment. **Attachment** refers to a lasting emotional tie between two people who each strive to maintain closeness to the other and act to ensure that the relationship continues.

Attachment relationships serve as an important backdrop for emotional and social development. Our earliest attachments are with our primary caregivers, most often our mothers. It was once thought that feeding determined patterns of attachment. Freud, for example, emphasized the role of feeding and successful weaning on infants' personality and well-being. Behaviorist theorists explain attachment as the result of the infants associating their mothers with food, a powerful reinforcer that satisfies a biological need. Certainly, feeding is important for infants' health and well-being and offers opportunities for the close contact needed to develop attachment bonds, but feeding itself does not determine attachment. In one famous study, baby rhesus monkeys were reared with two inanimate surrogate "mothers": one made of wire mesh and a second covered with terrycloth (see Figure 6.1). The baby monkeys clung to the terrycloth mother despite being fed only by the wire mother, suggesting that attachment bonds are not based on feeding but rather on contact comfort (Harlow & Zimmerman, 1959). So how does an attachment form, and what is its purpose?

Bowlby's Ethological Perspective on Attachment

John Bowlby, a British psychiatrist, posed that early family experiences influence emotional disturbances not through feeding practices, conditioning, or psychoanalytic drives but via inborn tendencies to form close relationships. Specifically, Bowlby (1969, 1988) developed a theory of attachment that characterizes it as an adaptive behavior that evolved because it contributed to the survival of the human

---

FIGURE 6.1

Harlow's Study: Contact Comfort and the Attachment Bond

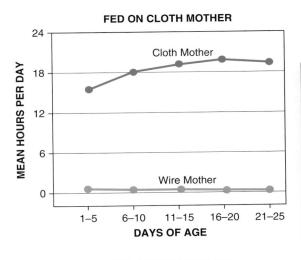

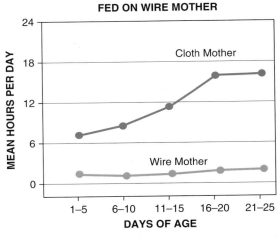

This infant monkey preferred to cling to the cloth-covered mother even if fed by the wire mother. Harlow concluded that attachment is based on contact comfort rather than feeding.

Source: Harlow, H. F. (1958); Photo Researchers Inc.

species. Inspired by ethology, particularly by Lorenz's work on the imprinting of geese (see Chapter 1) and by observations of interactions of monkeys, Bowlby posited that humans are biologically driven to form attachment bonds with other humans. An attachment bond between caregivers and infants ensures that the two will remain in close proximity, thereby aiding the survival of the infant and, ultimately, the species. From this perspective, caregiving responses are inherited and are triggered by the presence of infants and young children.

Infants' Signals and Adults' Responses

From birth, babies develop a repertoire of behavior signals to which adults naturally attend and respond, such as smiling, cooing, and clinging. Crying is a particularly effective signal because it conveys negative emotion that adults can judge reliably, and it motivates adults to relieve the infants' distress. Adults are innately drawn to infants, find infants' signals irresistible, and respond in kind. For example, one recent study found that nearly 700 mothers in 11 countries (Argentina, Belgium, Brazil, Cameroon, France, Kenya, Israel, Italy, Japan, South Korea, and the United States) tended to respond to their infants' cries and distress by picking up, holding, and talking to their infants (Bornstein et al., 2017). Infants' behaviors, immature appearance, and even smell draw adults' responses (Kringelbach, Stark, Alexander, Bornstein, & Stein, 2016). Infants, in turn, are attracted to caregivers who respond consistently and appropriately to their signals. During the first months of life, infants rely on caregivers to regulate their states and emotions—to soothe them when they are distressed and help them establish and maintain an alert state (Thompson, 2013). Attachment behaviors provide comfort and security to infants because they bring babies close to adults who can protect them.

Magnetic resonance imaging (MRI) scans support a biological component to attachment as first-time mothers show specific patterns of brain activity in response to infants. Mothers' brains light up with activity when they see their own infants' faces, and areas of the brain that are associated with rewards are activated specifically in response to happy, but not sad, infant faces (Strathearn, Jian, Fonagy, & Montague, 2008). In response to their infants' cries, U.S., Chinese, and Italian mothers show brain activity in regions associated with auditory processing, emotion, and the intention to move and speak, suggesting automatic responses to infant expressions of distress (Bornstein et al., 2017).

Phases of Attachment

Bowlby proposed that attachment formation progresses through several developmental phases

during infancy, from innate behaviors that bring the caregiver into contact to a mutual attachment relationship. With each phase, infants' behavior becomes increasingly organized, adaptable, and intentional.

Phase 1: Preattachment—Indiscriminate Social Responsiveness (Birth to 2 Months): Infants instinctively elicit caregiving responses from caregivers by crying, smiling, and making eye contact with adults. Infants respond to any caregiver who reacts to their signals, whether parent, grandparent, child care provider, or sibling.

Phase 2: Early Attachments—Discriminating Sociability (2 Through 6-7 Months): When caregivers are sensitive and consistent in responding to babies' signals, babies learn to associate their caregivers with the relief of distress, forming the basis for an initial bond. Babies begin to discriminate among adults and prefer familiar people. They direct their responses toward a particular adult or adults who are best able to soothe them.

Phase 3: Attachments (7-24 Months): Infants develop attachments to specific caregivers who attend, accurately interpret, and consistently respond to their signals. Infants can gain proximity to caregivers through their own motor efforts, such as crawling.

Phase 4: Reciprocal Relationships (24-30 Months and Onward): With advances in cognitive and language development, children can engage in interactions with their primary caregiver as partners, taking turns and initiating interactions within the attachment relationship. They begin to understand others' emotions and goals and apply this understanding through strategies such as social referencing.

Secure Base, Separation Anxiety, and Internal Working Models

The formation of an attachment bond is crucial for infants' development because it enables infants to begin to explore the world, using their attachment figure as a **secure base,** or foundation, to return to when frightened. When infants are securely attached to their caregivers, they feel confident to explore the world and to learn by doing so. As clear attachments form, starting at about 7 months, infants are likely to experience **separation anxiety** (sometimes called *separation protest*), a reaction to separations from an attachment figure that is characterized by distress and crying (Lamb & Lewis, 2015). Infants may follow, cling to, and climb on their caregivers in an attempt to keep them near.

Separation anxiety tends to increase between 8 and 15 months of age, and then it declines. This pattern appears across many cultures and environments as varied as those of the United States, Israeli kibbutzim, and !Kung hunter-gatherer groups in Africa (Kagan et al., 1994). It is the formation of the attachment bond that makes separation anxiety possible, because infants must feel connected to their caregivers in order to feel distress in the caregivers' absence. Separation anxiety declines as infants develop reciprocal relationships with caregivers, increasingly use them as secure bases, and can understand and predict parents' patterns of separation and return, reducing their confusion and distress.

The attachment bond developed during infancy and toddlerhood influences personality development because it comes to be represented as an **internal working model,** which includes the children's expectations about whether they are worthy of love, whether their attachment figures will be available during times of distress, and how they will be treated. The internal working model influences the development of self-concept, or sense of self, in infancy and becomes a guide to later relationships throughout life (Bretherton & Munholland, 2016).

Ainsworth's Strange Situation and Attachment Classifications

Virtually all infants form an attachment to their parents, but Canadian psychologist Mary Salter Ainsworth proposed that infants differ in **security of attachment**—the extent to which they feel that parents can reliably meet their needs. Like Bowlby, Ainsworth believed that infants must develop a dependence on parents, viewing them as a metaphorical secure base, in order to feel comfortable exploring the world (Salter, 1940). To examine attachment, Mary Ainsworth developed the **Strange Situation,** a structured observational procedure that reveals the security of attachment when the infant is placed under stress. As shown in Table 6.2, the Strange Situation is a heavily structured observation task consisting of eight 3-minute-long episodes. In each segment, the infant is with the parent (typically the mother), with a stranger, with both, or alone. Observations center on the infant's exploration of the room, his or her reaction when the mother leaves the room, and, especially, his or her responses during reunions, when the mother returns.

On the basis of responses to the Strange Situation, infants are classified into one of several attachment types (Ainsworth, Blehar, Waters, & Wall, 1978).

Mary Ainsworth (1913-1999) believed that infants differ in the security of attachment. She created the Strange Situation to measure infants' security of attachment.
JHU Sheridan Libraries/Gado/Getty Images

TABLE 6.2

The Strange Situation

EVENT	ATTACHMENT BEHAVIOR OBSERVED
Experimenter introduces mother and infant to playroom and leaves	
Infant plays with toys and parent is seated	Mother as secure base
Stranger enters, talks with caregiver, and approaches infant	Reaction to unfamiliar adult
Mother leaves room; stranger responds to baby if upset	Reaction to separation from mother
Mother returns and greets infant	Reaction to reunion
Mother leaves room	Reaction to separation from mother
Stranger enters room and offers comfort to infant	Reaction to stranger and ability to be soothed by stranger
Mother returns and greets infant. Tries to interest the infant in toys.	Reaction to reunion

- **Secure Attachment:** The securely attached infant uses the parent as a secure base, exploring the environment and playing with toys in the presence of the parent, but regularly checking in (e.g., by looking at the parent or bringing toys). The infant shows mild distress when the parent leaves. On the parent's return, the infant greets the parent enthusiastically, seeks comfort, and then returns to individual play. About two thirds of North American infants who complete the

Strange Situation are classified as securely attached (Lamb & Lewis, 2015).

- **Insecure-Avoidant Attachment:** Infants who display an insecure-avoidant attachment show little interest in the mother and busily explore the room during the Strange Situation. The infant is not distressed when the mother leaves and may react to the stranger in similar ways as to the mother. The infant ignores or avoids the mother on return or shows subtle signs of avoidance, such as failing to greet her or turning away from her. About 15% of samples of North American infants' responses to the Strange Situation reflect this style of attachment (Lamb & Lewis, 2015).

- **Insecure-Resistant Attachment:** Infants with an insecure-resistant attachment show a mixed pattern of responses to the mother. The infant remains preoccupied with the mother throughout the procedure, seeking proximity and contact, clinging even before the separation. When the mother leaves, the infant is distressed and cannot be comforted. During reunions, the infant's behavior suggests resistance, anger, and distress. The infant might seek proximity to the mother and cling to her while simultaneously pushing her away, hitting, or kicking. About 10% of North American infants tested in the Strange Situation fall into this category (Lamb & Lewis, 2015).

- **Insecure-Disorganized Attachment:** A fourth category was added later to account for the small set of infants (10% or below) who show inconsistent, contradictory behavior in then Strange Situation. The infant with insecure-disorganized attachment shows a conflict between approaching and fleeing the caregiver, suggesting fear (Main & Solomon, 1986). Infants showing insecure-disorganized attachment experience the greatest insecurity, appearing disoriented and confused. They may cry unexpectedly and may show a flat, depressed emotion and extreme avoidance or fearfulness of the caregiver.

Attachment-Related Outcomes

Secure parent–child attachments are associated with positive socioemotional development in infancy, childhood, and adolescence. Preschool and school-age children who were securely attached as infants tend to be more curious, empathetic, self-confident, and socially competent, and they will have more positive interactions and close friendships with peers (Groh, Fearon, van IJzendoorn, Bakermans-Kranenburg, & Roisman, 2017; Veríssimo, Santos, Fernandes, Shin, & Vaughn, 2014). The advantages of secure attachment continue into adolescence. Adolescents who were securely attached in infancy and early childhood are more socially competent, tend to be better at making and keeping friends and functioning in a social group, and demonstrate greater emotional health, self-esteem, ego resiliency, and peer competence (Boldt, Kochanska, Yoon, & Koenig Nordling, 2014; Sroufe, 2016; Stern & Cassidy, 2018).

In contrast, insecure attachment in infancy, particularly disorganized attachment, is associated with long-term negative outcomes, including poor peer relationships, poor social competence, and higher rates of antisocial behavior, depression, and anxiety from childhood into adulthood (Groh et al., 2017; Kochanska & Kim, 2013; Wolke, Eryigit-Madzwamuse, & Gutbrod, 2014). Insecure attachments tend to correlate with difficult life circumstances and contexts, such as parental problems, low socioeconomic status (SES), and environmental stress, that persist throughout childhood and beyond, influencing the continuity of poor outcomes (Granqvist et al., 2017). One longitudinal study suggested that infants with an insecure disorganized attachment at 12 and 18 months of age were, as adults, more likely to have children with insecure disorganized attachment, suggesting the possibility of intergenerational transmission of insecure attachment (and associated negative outcomes) (Raby, Steele, Carlson, & Sroufe, 2015). Conversely, attachment is not set in stone. Quality parent–child interactions can at least partially make up for poor interactions early in life. Children with insecure attachments in infancy who experience subsequent sensitive parenting show more positive social and behavioral outcomes in childhood and adolescence than do those who receive continuous care of poor quality (Sroufe, 2016). In addition, infants can form attachments to multiple caregivers with secure attachments, perhaps buffering the negative effects of insecure attachments (Boldt et al., 2014).

Influences on Attachment

The most important determinant of infant attachment is the caregiver's ability to consistently and sensitively respond to the child's signals (Ainsworth et al., 1978; Behrens, Parker, & Haltigan, 2011). Infants become securely attached to mothers who are sensitive and offer high-quality responses to their signals, who accept their role as caregiver, who are accessible and cooperative with infants, who are

The most important determinant of infant attachment is the caregiver's ability to consistently and sensitively respond to the child's signals
iStock/aywan88

not distracted by their own thoughts and needs, and who feel a sense of efficacy (Gartstein & Iverson, 2014). Mothers of securely attached infants provide stimulation and warmth and consistently synchronize or match their interactions with their infants' needs (Beebe et al., 2010). Secure mother–infant dyads show more positive interactions and fewer negative interactions compared with insecure dyads (Guo et al., 2015). The goodness of fit between the infant and parent's temperament influences attachment, supporting the role of reciprocal interactions in attachment (Seifer et al., 2014).

Infants who are insecurely attached have mothers who tend to be more rigid, unresponsive, inconsistent, and demanding (Gartstein & Iverson, 2014). The insecure-avoidant attachment pattern is associated with parental unavailability or rejection. Insecure-resistant attachment is associated with inconsistent and unresponsive parenting. Parents may respond inconsistently, offering overstimulating and intrusive caregiving at times and unresponsive care that is not attentive to the infant's signals at other times. Frightening parental behavior (at the extreme, child abuse) is thought to play a role in insecure disorganized attachment (Duschinsky, 2015). Disorganized attachment is more common among infants who have been abused or raised in particularly poor caregiving environments; however, disorganized attachment itself is not an indicator of abuse (Granqvist et al., 2017; Lamb & Lewis, 2015).

Parent–infant interactions and relationships are influenced by many contextual factors. For example, conflict among parents is associated with lower levels of attachment security (Tan, McIntosh, Kothe, Opie, & Olsson, 2018). Insecure attachment responses may therefore represent adaptive responses to poor caregiving environments (Weinfield, Sroufe, Egeland, & Carlson, 2008). For example, not relying on an unsupportive parent (such as by developing an insecure-avoidant attachment) may represent a good

strategy for infants. Toddlers who show an avoidant attachment tend to rely on self-regulated coping rather than turning to others, perhaps an adaptive response to an emotionally absent parent (Zimmer-Gembeck et al., 2017).

Stability of Attachment

Attachment patterns tend to be stable over infancy and early childhood, especially when securely attached infants receive continuous responsive care (Ding, Xu, Wang, Li, & Wang, 2014; Marvin, Britner, & Russell, 2016). The continuity of care influences the stability of attachment. For example, negative experiences can disrupt secure attachment. The loss of a parent, parental divorce, a parent's psychiatric disorder, and physical abuse, as well as changes in family stressors, adaptive processes, and living conditions, can transform a secure attachment into an insecure attachment pattern later in childhood or adolescence (Feeney & Monin, 2016; Lyons-Ruth & Jacobvitz, 2016).

Contextual factors such as low SES, family and community stressors, and the availability of supports influence the stability of attachment through their effect on parents' emotional and physical resources and the quality of parent–infant interactions. (Booth-LaForce et al., 2014; Thompson, 2016; Van Ryzin, Carlson, & Sroufe, 2011). Securely attached infants reared in contexts that pose risks to development are at risk to develop insecure attachments, whereas risky contexts tend to stabilize insecure attachment over time (Pinquart, Feußner, & Ahnert, 2013). An insecure attachment between child and parent can be overcome by changing maladaptive interaction patterns, increasing sensitivity on the part of the parent, and fostering consistent and developmentally appropriate responses to children's behaviors. Pediatricians, counselors, and social workers can help parents identify and change ineffective parenting behaviors to improve parent–child interaction patterns.

Although most research on attachment has focused on the mother–infant bond, we know that infants form multiple attachments (Dagan & Sagi-Schwartz, 2018). Consider the Efe foragers of the Democratic Republic of Congo, in which infants are cared for by many people, as adults' availability varies with their hunting and gathering duties (Morelli, 2015). Efe infants experience frequent changes in residence and camp, exposure to many adults, and frequent interactions with multiple caregivers. It is estimated that the Efe infant will typically come into contact with 9 to 14 and as many as 20 people within a 2-hour period. Efe infants are reared in an intensely social community and develop many trusting relationships—many attachments to many people (Morelli, 2015). On a smaller scale,

Western infants also develop multiple attachments to mothers, fathers, family members, and caregivers. Multiple attachment relationships offer important developmental opportunities. For example, an infant's

secure attachment relationship with a father can compensate for the negative effects of an insecure attachment to a mother (Dagan & Sagi-Schwartz, 2018; Grazyna Kochanska & Kim, 2013; Oldt et al., 2014).

APPLYING DEVELOPMENTAL SCIENCE

 # Infant Child Care

High-quality child care is associated with gains in cognitive and language development over the first 3 years of life.
age fotostock / Alamy Stock Photo

In the United States, more than half of all mothers of infants under 1 year old, and over two thirds of mothers of children under 6, are employed (U.S. Bureau of Labor Statistics, 2016). The infants and young children of working mothers are cared for in a variety of settings: in center-based care, in the home of someone other than a relative, or with a relative such as a father, grandparent, or older sibling (Federal Interagency Forum on Child and Family Statistics, 2014). A common misconception is that nonfamilial center-based care is damaging to children's development and places children at risk for insecure attachment. However, this belief is not supported by research. What are the effects of nonparental care?

One of the best sources of information about the effects of nonparental care is a longitudinal study of over 1,300 children conducted by the National Institute of Child Health and Development (NICHD). This study found infants' developmental outcomes are influenced more by characteristics of the family, such as parenting, maternal education, and maternal sensitivity, than by the type of child care (Axe, 2007; Dehaan, 2006). Center-based care did not predispose infants to forming insecure attachments (Belsky, 2005; Harrison & Ungerer, 2002). Some research suggests that center-based care is associated with more

disobedience and aggression but is accompanied by greater sociability (Jacob, 2009). Other work suggests that behavior problems may be more common in low-quality care but do not appear in high-quality care (Gialamas, Mittinty, Sawyer, Zubrick, & Lynch, 2014; Huston, Bobbitt, & Bentley, 2015).

Quality of child care matters. Infants and young children exposed to poor-quality child care score lower on measures of cognitive and social competence, regardless of demographic variables such as parental education and socioeconomic status (NICHD Early Child Care Research Network, 2005). In contrast, high-quality child care that includes specific efforts to stimulate children is associated with gains in cognitive and language development over the first 3 years of life and can even compensate for lower-quality and chaotic home environments (Berry et al., 2016; Gialamas et al., 2014; Mortensen & Barnett, 2015; Watamura, Phillips, Morrissey, McCartney, & Bub, 2011).

Child care quality has long-term effects as well. A recent study of Dutch infants showed that high-quality care, defined as providing high levels of emotional and behavioral support, predicted children's social competence a year later; specifically, children who spent at least 3.5 days a week in care showed lower levels of behavioral problems (Broekhuizen, van Aken, Dubas, & Leseman, 2018). Longitudinal research in Sweden showed that older children and adolescents who had received high-quality care as infants and toddlers scored higher on measures of cognitive, emotional, and social competence later in childhood (Andersson, 1989; Broberg, Wessels, Lamb, & Hwang, 1997). In addition, a longitudinal analysis of over 1,200 children from the NICHD study revealed that the quality of care predicted academic grades and behavioral adjustment at the end of high school, at age 15 and 18, as well as admission to more selective colleges (Vandell, Belsky, Burchinal, Steinberg, & Vandergrift, 2010; Vandell, Burchinal, & Pierce, 2016).

The challenge is that high-quality child care is expensive. In 2016, the annual cost of center-based care in the United States ranged from about $6,000 in Arkansas to $16,000 in Washington, D.C. (Schulte & Durana, 2016). In some countries, such as Sweden, Norway, and Finland, child care is heavily subsidized by the government (Gothe-Snape, 2017). In the United States, however, it remains a private responsibility. The few public subsidies for child care available in the United States are tied to economic need and are mainly targeted at low-income families who receive other forms of public assistance.

What Do You Think?

1. Consider your own experience with child care, either as a child or parent. Can you identify examples of high-quality care? Can you identify ways to improve the quality of care?
2. Assume that you are a parent seeking child care for your own child or that you were providing advice to a parent. What are indicators of quality care? What would you look for? ●

It is important that infants develop attachments with some caregivers—but which caregivers, whether mothers, fathers, or other responsive adults, matters less than the bond itself. Many infants are cared for by multiple adults in child care settings. The accompanying Applied Developmental Science feature discusses how the quality of infant child care affects developmental outcomes.

Cultural Variations in Attachment Classifications

Attachment occurs in all cultures, but whether the Strange Situation is applicable across cultural contexts is a matter of debate. Research has shown that infants in many countries, including Germany, Holland, Japan, and the United States, approach the Strange Situation in similar ways (Sagi, Van IJzendoorn, & Koren-Karie, 1991). In addition, the patterns of attachment identified by Ainsworth occur in a wide variety of cultures in North America, Europe, Asia, Africa, and the Middle East (Bornstein et al., 2013; Cassibba, Sette, Bakermans-Kranenburg, & IJzendoorn, 2013; Huang, Lewin, Mitchell, & Zhang, 2012; Jin, Jacobvitz, Hazen, & Jung, 2012; Thompson, 2013).

Nevertheless, there are differences. For example, insecure-avoidant attachments are more common in Western European countries, and insecure-resistant attachments are more prevalent in Japan and Israel (Van IJzendoorn & Kroonenberg, 1988). This pattern may result from the fact that Western cultures tend to emphasize individuality and independence, whereas Eastern cultures are more likely to emphasize the importance of relationships and connections with others. Individualist and collectivist cultural perspectives interpret children's development in different ways; Western parents might interpret insecure-resistant behavior as clingy, whereas Asian parents might interpret it as successful bonding (Gardiner & Kosmitzki, 2018).

Dogon infants from Mali, West Africa, show rates of secure attachment that are similar to those of Western infants, but the avoidant attachment style is not observed in samples of Dogon infants because infants are in constant proximity to mothers who respond to infant distress promptly and feed infants on demand.
Danita Delimont / Alamy Stock Photo

Many Japanese and Israeli infants become highly distressed during the Strange Situation and show high rates of insecure resistance. Resistance in Japanese samples of infants can be attributed to cultural childrearing practices that foster mother–infant closeness and physical intimacy that leave infants unprepared for the separation episodes; the Strange Situation may be so stressful for them that they resist comforting (Takahashi, 1990). In other words, the Strange Situation may not accurately measure the attachment of these infants. Similarly, infants who are raised in small, close-knit Israeli kibbutz communities do not encounter strangers in their day-to-day lives, so the introduction of a stranger in the Strange Situation procedure can be overly challenging for them. At the same time, kibbutz-reared infants spend much of their time with their peers and caregivers and see their parents infrequently and therefore may prefer to be comforted by people other than their parents (Sagi et al., 1985).

Dogon infants from Mali, West Africa, show rates of secure attachment that are similar to those of Western infants, but the avoidant attachment style is not observed in samples of Dogon infants (McMahan True, Pisani, & Oumar, 2001). Dogon infant care practices diminish the likelihood of avoidant attachment because the infant is in constant proximity to the mother. Infant distress is promptly answered with feeding and infants feed on demand, so mothers cannot behave in ways that would foster avoidant attachment.

As shown in Figure 6.2, although secure attachment is most common, the prevalence of other attachment styles varies internationally. The behaviors that characterize sensitive caregiving vary with culturally specific socialization goals, values, and beliefs of the parents, family, and community (Mesman, van IJzendoorn, & Sagi-Schwartz, 2016). For example, Puerto Rican mothers often use more physical control in interactions with infants, such as picking up crawling infants and placing them in desired locations, over the first year of life than do European American mothers. They actively structure interactions in ways consistent with long-term socialization goals oriented toward calm, attentive, and obedient children. Typically, attachment theory

conceptualizes this type of control as insensitive, yet physical control is associated with secure attachment status at 12 months in Puerto Rican infants (but not White non-Hispanic infants) (Carlson & Harwood, 2003; Harwood, Scholmerich, Schulze, & Gonzalez, 1999). Similarly, German mothers operate according to the shared cultural belief that infants should become independent at an early age and should learn that they cannot rely on the mother's comfort at all times. German mothers may seem unresponsive to their children's crying, yet they are demonstrating sensitive childrearing within their context (Grossmann, Spangler, Suess, & Unzner, 1985). In other words, the behaviors that reflect sensitive caregiving vary with culture because they are adaptations to different circumstances (Rothbaum et al., 2000).

In summary, attachment is an adaptive process in which infants and caregivers become attuned to each other and develop an enduring bond. Infants become attached to caregivers—mothers, fathers, and other adults—who are sensitive to their needs. Secure attachment in infancy is associated with emotional and social competence in infancy, early childhood, and even later childhood and adolescence. The attachment bond formed in infancy, whether

FIGURE 6.2

Cross-Cultural Variations in Attachment

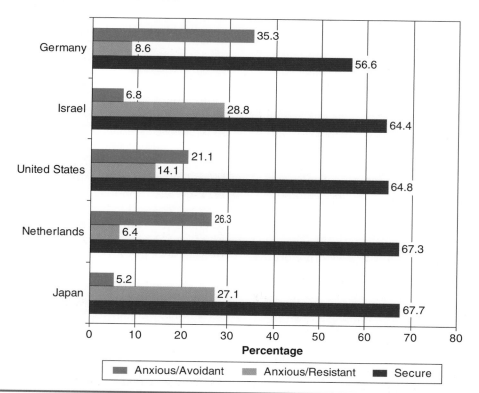

Source: Adapted from Van IJzendoorn & Kroonenberg, 1988.

secure or insecure, influences the child's developing internal working model of self and thereby his or her self-concept, as described in the next section.

THINKING IN CONTEXT 6.4

1. Children reared in impoverished orphanages are at risk of receiving little attention from adults and experiencing few meaningful interactions with caregivers. What might this experience mean for the development of attachment? What outcomes and behaviors might you expect from children reared under such conditions? In your view, what can be done to help such children?

2. How does an infant's emotional capacities, coupled with the goodness of fit between her temperament and that of her parent, influence attachment outcomes?

THE SELF IN INFANCY AND TODDLERHOOD

>> LO 6.5 **Differentiate the roles of self-concept, self-recognition, and self-control in infant development.**

What do babies know about themselves? When do they begin to know that they have a "self"—that they are separate from the people and things that surround them? We have discussed the challenges that researchers who study infants face. Infants cannot tell us what they perceive, think, or feel. Instead, researchers must devise ways of inferring infants' states, feelings, and thoughts. As you might imagine, this makes it very challenging to study infants' conceptions of self, as well as their awareness and understanding of themselves.

Self-Awareness

Maya, 4 months of age, delights in seeing that she can make the mobile above her crib move by kicking her feet. Her understanding that she can influence her world suggests that she has a sense of herself as different from her environment (Rochat, 1998). Before infants can take responsibility for their own actions, they must begin to see themselves as physically separate from the world around them.

Some developmental researchers believe that infants are born with a capacity to distinguish the self from the surrounding environment (Meltzoff, 1990). Newborns show distress at hearing a recording of another infant's cries but do not show distress at hearing their own cries, suggesting that they

can distinguish other infants' cries from their own and thereby have a primitive notion of self (Dondi, Simion, & Caltran, 1999). Newborns' facial imitation, that is, their ability to view another person's facial expression and produce it (see Chapter 4), may also suggest a primitive awareness of self and others (Meltzoff, 2007; Rochat, 2013). It is unclear, however, whether these findings suggest that newborns have self-awareness because infants cannot tell us what they know.

Others argue that an awareness of oneself is not innate but emerges by 3 months of age (Neisser, 1993). Some researchers believe that this emergence is indicated by infants' awareness of the consequences of their own actions on others (Langfur, 2013). As infants interact with people and objects, they learn that their behaviors have effects. With this awareness, they begin to experiment to see how their behaviors influence the world around them, begin to differentiate themselves from their environments, and develop a sense of self (Bigelow, 2017).

Self-Recognition

How do we know whether self-awareness is innate or develops in the early months of life? One way of

This toddler recognizes herself in the mirror, as shown by her touching the rouge mark on her face.
Thierry Berrod/Mona Lisa/Science Source

studying self-awareness in infants is to examine infants' reactions to viewing themselves in a mirror. **Self-recognition,** the ability to recognize or identify the self, is assessed by the "rouge test." In this experiment, a dab of rouge or lipstick is applied to an infant's nose without the infant's awareness—for example, under the pretext of wiping his or her face. The infant is then placed in front of a mirror (Bard, Todd, Bernier, Love, & Leavens, 2006). Whether the infant recognizes himself or herself in the mirror depends on cognitive development, especially the ability to engage in mental representation and hold images in one's mind. Infants must be able to retain a memory of their own image in order to display self-recognition in the mirror task. If the infant has an internal representation of her face and recognizes the infant in the mirror as herself, she will notice the dab of rouge and reach for her own nose.

Mirror recognition develops gradually and systematically (Brandl, 2018). From 3 months of age, infants pay attention and react positively to their mirror image, and by 8 to 9 months of age, they show awareness of the tandem movement of the mirror image with themselves and play with the image, treating it as if it is another baby (Bullock & Lutkenhaus, 1990). Some 15- to 17-month-old infants show signs of self-recognition, but it is not until 18 to 24 months that most infants demonstrate self-recognition by touching their nose when they notice the rouge mark in the mirror (Cicchetti, Rogosch, Toth, & Spagnola, 1997). Does experience with mirrors influence how infants respond to the rouge test? Interestingly, infants from nomadic tribes with no experience with mirrors demonstrate self-recognition at the same ages as infants reared in surroundings with mirrors (Priel & deSchonen, 1986). This suggests that extensive experience with a mirror is not needed to demonstrate self-recognition in the mirror task. In addition, research with Canadian toddlers shows that their performance on the mirror task is unrelated to their experience with mirrors in the home (Courage, Edison, & Howe, 2004).

Mirror recognition is not the only indicator of a sense of self—and may not be the earliest indicator. A recent study suggests that self-recognition may develop before infants can succeed on the mirror task (Stapel, van Wijk, Bekkering, & Hunnius, 2017). Eighteen-month-old infants viewed photographs of their own face, the face of an unfamiliar infant, the face of their caregiver, and the face of an unfamiliar caregiver while their brain activity was registered via electroencephalography (EEG). The infants showed more brain activity in response to their own face, suggesting self-recognition, yet only half of these infants succeeded on the mirror task.

By 18 to 24 months of age, children begin to recognize themselves in pictures and refer to themselves in the pictures as "me" or by their first names (Lewis & Brooks-Gunn, 1979). One study of 20- to 25-month-old toddlers showed that 63% could pick themselves out when they were presented with pictures of themselves and two similar children (Bullock & Lutkenhaus, 1990). By 30 months of age, nearly all of the children could pick out their own picture.

With advances in self-awareness, toddlers begin to experience more complex emotions, including self-conscious emotions, such as embarrassment, shame, guilt, jealousy, and pride (Lewis & Carmody, 2008). An understanding of self is needed before children can be aware of being the focus of attention and feel embarrassment, identify with others' concerns and feel shame, or desire what someone else has and feel jealousy toward that person. In a study of 15- to 24-month-old infants, only those who recognized themselves in the mirror looked embarrassed when an adult gave them overwhelming praise. They smiled, looked away, and covered their faces with their hands. The infants who did not recognize themselves in the mirror did not show embarrassment (Lewis, 2011). A developing sense of self and the self-conscious emotions that accompany it lead toddlers to have more complex social interactions with caregivers and others, all of which contribute to the development of self-concept.

Emerging Self-Concept

In toddlerhood, between 18 and 30 months of age, children's sense of self-awareness expands beyond self-recognition to include a **categorical self,** a self-description based on broad categories such as sex, age, and physical characteristics (Stipek, Gralinski, & Kopp, 1990). Toddlers describe themselves as "big," "strong," "girl/boy," and "baby/big kid." Children use their categorical self as a guide to behavior. For example, once toddlers label themselves by gender, they spend more time playing with toys stereotyped for their own gender. Applying the categorical self as a guide to behavior illustrates toddlers' advancing capacities for self-control.

At about the same time as toddlers display the categorical self, they begin to show another indicator of their growing self-understanding. As toddlers become proficient with language and their vocabulary expands, they begin to use many personal pronouns and adjectives, such as "I," "me," and "mine," suggesting a sense of self in relation to others (E. Bates, 1990). Claims of possession emerge by about 21 months and illustrate children's clear

TABLE 6.3

The Developing Self

CONCEPT	DESCRIPTION	EMERGENCE
Self-concept	Self-description and thoughts about the self	Begins as a sense of awareness in the early months of life
Self-awareness	Awareness of the self as separate from the environment	Innate or develops in the early months of life
Self-recognition	The ability to recognize or identify the self; typically tested in mirror recognition tasks	18–24 months
Categorical self	Self-description based on broad categories such as sex, age, and physical characteristics; indicates the emergence of self-concept	18–30 months

Source: Adapted from Butterworth (1992).

representation of "I" versus other (L. E. Levine, 1983), a milestone in self-definition and the beginnings of self-concept (Rochat, 2010).

Self-Control

Self-awareness and the emerging self-concept permit self-control, as one must be aware of oneself as separate from others to comply with requests and modify behavior in accordance with caregivers' demands. In order to engage in self-control, the infant must be able to attend to a caregiver's instructions, shift his or her attention from an attractive stimulus or task, and inhibit a behavior. Cortical development, specifically development of the frontal lobes, is responsible for this ability (Posner & Rothbart, 2018). Between 12 and 18 months, infants begin to demonstrate self-control by their awareness of, and compliance to, caregivers' simple requests (Kaler & Kopp, 1990).

Although toddlers are known for asserting their autonomy, such as by saying no and not complying with a caregiver's directive, compliance is much more common (Kochanska, 2000). Paradoxically, when parents encourage autonomous, exploratory, behavior, their children are more likely to show compliance to parental instructions in toddlerhood through early childhood (Laurin & Joussemet, 2017). Secure attachment relationships and warm parenting are associated with effortful control, likely as securely attached infants feel comfortable exploring their environment, which promotes autonomy (Pallini et al., 2018). Toddlers' capacities for self-control improve rapidly. For example, delay of gratification tasks suggest that between 18 and 36 months, toddlers become better able to control their impulses and wait before eating a treat or playing with a toy (Białecka-Pikul, Byczewska-Konieczny, Kosno, Białek, & Stępień-Nycz, 2018; Cheng, Lu, Archer, & Wang, 2018).

Infants make great strides in socioemotional development over the first 2 years of life, as summarized in Table 6.3. Infants' advances in emotional expression and regulation represent the interaction of biological predispositions, such as inborn capacities for basic emotions and temperament, and experience—particularly parent–child interactions—the contexts in which they are raised, and the goodness of fit between infants' needs and what their contexts provide. Infants' gains in emotional and social development and a growing sense of self form a socioemotional foundation for the physical and cognitive changes that they will experience in the early childhood years.

THINKING IN CONTEXT 6.5

1. Provide examples of how a Western emphasis on autonomy and independence might influence infants' and toddlers' sense of self, such as self-awareness, self-recognition, self-concept, and/or self-control.

2. How might non-Western cultural views that emphasize collectivism and interdependence influence infants' and toddlers' developing sense of self? Provide examples.

3. Compare Western and non-Western influences on infants' and toddlers' sense of self.

APPLY YOUR KNOWLEDGE

A friendly lab assistant escorts 12-month-old Cassie and her mother into a research playroom containing special mirrors and hidden equipment to videotape their interactions. After providing instructions, the lab assistant leaves the mother and Cassie alone, beginning a short procedure to study the security of their attachment relationship. A female stranger enters the room to play with Cassie. Soon after, the mother leaves and Cassie is alone with the stranger. The mother returns briefly, then leaves again; finally, the stranger leaves the room and Cassie is left alone. During each short separation from her mother, Cassie cries and wails. Surprised and disturbed to find Cassie so upset, her mother returns almost immediately. She cannot soothe Cassie, who alternates between clinging to her mother and pushing her away angrily, crying all the time.

"Is Cassie upset today?" asks the lab assistant.

"No, she's always this way," her mother smiled softly, "My Cassie is quite a handful. She's what my mother calls spirited. She's unpredictable and strong-willed. She'll eat and nap when she's ready—and that changes all the time.

My mother says I was the same way. I love my little girl, but sometimes I look forward to her growing up."

What was this procedure intended to study? How? Why?

What might Cassie's behavior indicate about her security of attachment relationship to her mother and her emotional development? Why?

What do we know about the stability of infant attachment? What is the likelihood that these observations will influence Cassie's attachment in childhood? Adulthood?

Comment on the goodness of fit between Cassie's temperament and the parenting.

Laboratory methods such as this are intended to place participants, infants, under distress. The parent's behavior is the source of that distress, and the procedure also is distressful to parents. From your perspective, what do researchers learn from such research? Should researchers use procedures that elicit distress from children and parents? If you were a parent to an infant, would you be willing to participate in such an experiment?

$SAGE edge™

Visit **edge.sagepub.com/kuther2e** to help you accomplish your coursework goals in an easy-to-use learning environment.

LEARNING OBJECTIVES	SUMMARY	KEY TERMS	IN REVIEW
6.1 Summarize the psychosocial tasks of infancy and toddlerhood.	The psychosocial task of infancy is to develop a sense of trust. If parents and caregivers are sensitive to the infant's physical and emotional needs and consistently fulfill them, the infant will develop a basic sense of trust in his or her caregivers and the world. The task for toddlers is to learn to do things for themselves and feel confident in their ability to maneuver themselves in their environment. Psychosocial development is supported by warm and sensitive parenting and developmentally appropriate expectations for exploration and behavioral control.	Trust versus mistrust Autonomy versus shame and doubt	What are the two psychosocial tasks of infancy and toddlerhood, according to Erikson's theory? How can parents promote positive psychosocial development during infancy and toddlerhood?
6.2 Describe emotional development in infancy and identify contextual and cultural influences on emotional development in infants and toddlers.	Newborns display some basic emotions, such as interest, distress, and disgust. Self-conscious emotions, such as empathy, embarrassment, shame, and guilt, depend on cognitive development, as well as an awareness of self, and do not emerge until about late infancy. With development, infants use different and more effective strategies for regulating their emotions. At about 6 months old, infants begin to use social referencing. Social referencing occurs in ambiguous situations, provides children with guidance in how to interpret the event, and influences their emotional responses and subsequent actions. Parents socialize infants to respond to and display their emotions in socially acceptable ways. The emotions that are considered acceptable, as well as ways of expressing them, differ by culture and context.	Basic emotions Social smile Self-conscious emotions Emotion regulation Social referencing Emotional display rules Stranger wariness	What are examples of basic and self-conscious emotions? How do infants regulate their emotions? How do social interactions influence emotional development? Describe cultural influences on emotional development.

6.3 Identify the styles and stability of temperament, including the role of goodness of fit in infant development.	Temperament, the characteristic way in which an individual approaches and reacts to people and situations, has a biological basis. Children are classified into three temperament styles: easy, slow to warm up, and difficult. Temperament is influenced by the interaction of genetic predispositions, maturation, and experience. Temperament tends to be stable, but there are developmental and individual differences. An important influence on socioemotional development is the goodness of fit between the child's temperament and the environment around him or her, especially the parent's temperament and childrearing methods.	Temperament Easy temperament Difficult temperament Slow-to-warm-up temperament Goodness of fit	What is temperament? What are three temperament styles? What are three dimensions of temperament? How stable is temperament? How does goodness of fit influence emotional development? What are cultural differences in temperament?
6.4 Describe how attachment develops in infancy and toddlerhood.	From an ethological perspective, attachment is an adaptive behavior that evolved because it ensures that the infant and caregiver will remain in close proximity, aiding the survival of the infant. The Strange Situation is a structured observational procedure that reveals the security of attachment; infants are classified as securely attached or insecurely attached (insecure -avoidant, insecure -resistant, or disorganized -disoriented). Secure attachments in infancy are associated with social competence and socioemotional health. Attachment patterns are seen in a wide variety of cultures around the world, but the behaviors that make up sensitive caregiving vary depending on the socialization goals, values, and beliefs of the family and community, which may vary by culture. Generally, infants become securely or insecurely attached to caregivers based on the caregiver's ability to respond sensitively to the child's signals. Mothers who consistently provide stimulation, warmth, and emotional support tend to have securely attached infants.	Attachment Secure base Separation anxiety Internal working model Security of attachment Strange Situation Secure attachment Insecure-avoidant attachment Insecure-resistant attachment Insecure-disorganized attachment	What is attachment? How do researchers measure infant attachment? What are four patterns of infant attachment? Describe cultural influences on attachment. What are ways of promoting a secure parent -child attachment bond?
6.5 Differentiate the roles of self-concept, self-recognition, and self-control in infant development.	The earliest notion of self-concept, self-awareness, is evident in a primitive fashion at 3 months of age. Self-recognition, as indicated by mirror self-recognition, develops gradually and systematically in infants, but it is not until 18 to 24 months that a majority of infants demonstrate self-recognition in the mirror test. Once children have a sense of self, they can experience more complex emotions, such as self-conscious emotions. Self-awareness permits self-control as one must be aware of oneself as an agent apart from others to comply with requests and modify behavior in accord with caregivers' demands.	Self-recognition Categorical self	What is self-concept and when does it first emerge? How does self-control develop?

PART III

Early Childhood

CHAPTER 7:
Physical and Cognitive Development in Early Childhood

CHAPTER 8:
Socioemotional Development in Early Childhood

In early childhood, advances in physical, cognitive, and socioemotional development permit young children to interact with their social world in new ways. With improvements in strength and motor skills, children engage their peers in rough-and-tumble play—games involving chasing, jumping, and play fighting.

Advances in cognitive development help children to become better at attending, planning, and remembering. A developing understanding of the mind helps young children become aware of other perspectives and engage in sociodramatic play—acting out roles, stories, and themes as they pretend to be mothers, astronauts, and cartoon characters.

Interactions with parents are especially important in fostering development. Children respond best to parenting that is warm and sensitive yet firm, relying on discussion and reasoning as discipline tools. Nursery school and preschool programs offer new opportunities to interact with adults and other children. Young children learn how to make and keep playmates, join groups, and manage conflict. In cooperative play, children learn to work with friends to achieve a common goal, express ideas, be assertive, and regulate emotions. Through interactions within the home, school, and peer contexts, young children come to view their worlds and themselves in new ways, providing opportunities to advance physical, cognitive, and socioemotional development.

DR. KUTHER'S CHALK TALKS

Watch at
edge.sagepub.com/kuther2e

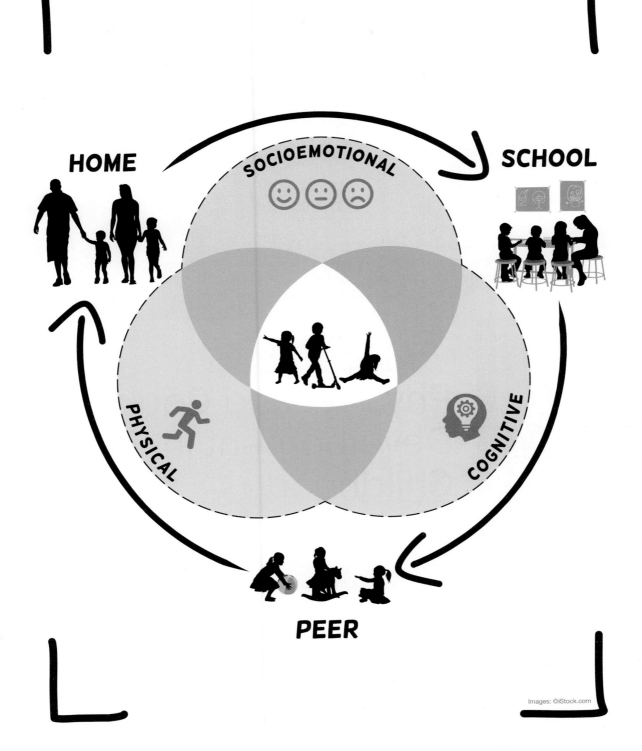

HOME

SCHOOL

SOCIOEMOTIONAL

PHYSICAL

COGNITIVE

PEER

Images: ©iStock.com

7 Physical and Cognitive Development in Early Childhood

George's parents watched with pride as their 4-year-old son kicked the soccer ball to the other children. George has grown from a bowlegged, round-tummied, and top-heavy toddler into a strong, well-coordinated young child. His body slimmed, grew taller, and reshaped into proportions similar to that of an adult. As a toddler, he often stumbled and fell, but George can now run, skip, and throw a ball. He has also gained better control over his fingers; he can draw recognizable pictures of objects, animals, and people. As his vocabulary and language skills have grown, George has become more adept at communicating his ideas and needs.

How do these developments take place? In this chapter, we examine the many changes that children undergo in physical and motor development as well as how their thinking and language skills change.

Learning Objectives

7.1 Discuss physical development in early childhood.

7.2 Compare Piaget's cognitive-developmental and Vygotsky's sociocultural theories on cognitive development in early childhood.

7.3 Describe information processing abilities during early childhood.

7.4 Summarize young children's advances in language development.

7.5 Contrast social learning and cognitive-developmental perspectives on moral development in early childhood.

7.6 Identify and explain various approaches to early childhood education.

Digital Resources

Watch: Physical Development in Childhood

▶ **Lives in Context Video 7.1:** Fostering Gross Motor Skills in Early Childhood

Watch: Preoperational Thinking: Egocentrism

Connect: Children's Lying: A Good Sign?

▶ **Lives in Context Video 7.2:** False Belief

Listen: Private Speech

▶ **Lives in Context Video 7.3:** Children's Understanding of Language

Explore: When the Spirit Is Willing But the Flesh Is Weak

Watch: A Multiple-Intelligences School

PHYSICAL DEVELOPMENT IN EARLY CHILDHOOD

» LO 7.1   Discuss physical development in early childhood.

George's abilities to run, skip, and manipulate his fingers to create objects with Play-Doh illustrate the many ways that children learn to control their bodies. George is also growing bigger and stronger day by day, although the speed of growth is not as dramatic as when he was younger. His pediatrician assures his parents that this is normal and counsels them about healthy dietary choices now that George has become a picky eater.

Growth

As compared with the first 2 years of life, growth slows during early childhood. From ages 2 through 6, the average child grows 2 to 3 inches taller and gains nearly 5 pounds in weight each year. The typical 6-year-old child weighs about 45 pounds and is about 46 inches tall.

Biological factors play a large role in physical development. Children's height and rate of growth are closely related to that of their parents (Kliegman et al., 2016). Genes influence the rate of growth by stipulating the amount of hormones to be released. Hormones are chemicals that are produced and secreted into the bloodstream by glands. One hormone, growth hormone, is secreted from birth and influences the growth of nearly all parts of the body. Children with growth hormone deficiencies show slowed growth, but growth hormone supplements can stimulate growth when needed (Stagi, Scalini, Farello, & Verrotti, 2017).

Ethnic differences in patterns of growth appear in developed nations such as England, France, Canada, Australia, and the United States (Natale & Rajagopalan, 2014). Generally, children of African descent tend to be tallest, followed by children of European descent, then Asian, then Latino. However, there are many individual differences. Even within a given culture, some families are much taller than others (Stulp & Barrett, 2016). It is difficult to assess ethnic differences in growth patterns of children in developing nations because malnutrition and growth stunting are common (de Onis & Branca, 2016). In addition, there is little research examining normative patterns of development in developing countries.

Nutrition

From ages 2 to 6, young children's appetites continue to decline as compared with infants and toddlers. This decline is normal and occurs as growth slows. At around age 3, it is not uncommon for children to go through a fussy eating phase where previously tolerated food is no longer accepted and it is hard to introduce new food (Fildes et al., 2014). From an evolutionary perspective, young children's common dislike of new foods, picky eating, may be adaptive because it encourages them to eat familiar and safe

 ## Picky Eating

Many parents pressure children to eat, but picky eating is a common phase with no effect on growth in most children.
Shutterstock/Robert Kneschke

Picky eating is common in early childhood. Estimates of picky eating vary widely, but it is highest (14%–50%) in preschool children and tends to decline with time (C. M. Taylor, Wernimont, Northstone, & Emmett, 2015). Parents of picky eaters report that their children consume a limited variety of foods, require foods to be prepared in specific ways, express strong likes and dislikes, and throw tantrums over feeding. Children who are picky eaters are likely to consume fewer calories, fruits and vegetables, and vitamins and minerals than other children. This behavior often raises parental concerns about nutrition (Berger, Hohman, Marini, Savage, & Birch, 2016). Pediatricians tend to view picky eating as a passing phase, often to the frustration of parents.

The overall incidence of picky eating declines with time, but for some children, it is chronic, lasting for several years. Persistent picky eating poses risks for poor growth (C. M. Taylor et al., 2015). One longitudinal study of Dutch children assessed at 1.5, 3, and 6 years of age suggested that persistent picky eating was associated with symptoms common to developmental problems such as attention-deficit disorder, autism, and oppositional defiant disorder at age 7 (Cardona Cano et al., 2016). Another study found that sensory sensitivity predicted picky eating at age 4 and at age 6 (Steinsbekk, Bonneville-Roussy, Fildes, Llewellyn, & Wichstrøm, 2017). Children who are more sensitive to touch in general are also more sensitive to the tactile sensation of food in their mouths, whether the food is crispy or slimy, thick or with bits, for example (Nederkoorn, Jansen, & Havermans, 2015). They then reject foods of a particular texture. Likewise, children with a difficult temperament at 1.5 years of age are more likely to be picky eaters 2 years later (Hafstad, Abebe, Torgersen, & von Soest, 2013).

Persistent picky eating illustrates the dynamic interaction of developmental domains. Physical and emotional factors, such as sensory sensitivity and temperament, can place children at risk for picky eating, which in turn influences physical development. Moreover, picky eating tends to elicit parental pressure to eat, which is associated with continued pickiness, suggesting that picky eating is sustained through bidirectional parent–child interactions (Jansen et al., 2017). Interventions for picky eating can help children learn to tolerate tactile sensations and help parents to understand that parental responses to pickiness can influence children's behavior and sustain picky eating (K. Walton, Kuczynski, Haycraft, Breen, & Haines, 2017).

In most cases, picky eating is a normative phase in preschool, with no significant effect on growth (Jansen et al., 2017). Regardless, picky eating is an important concern for parents and may remain so through much of childhood.

What Do You Think?

1. Were you a picky eater? Do you know a child with picky eating habits? What factors do you think influence picky eating, in general?

2. What would you tell a parent of a preschooler with picky eating habits? ●

Young children require a healthy diet, which can be accompanied by an occasional junk food splurge.
Israel images / Alamy Stock Photo

foods rather than novel and potentially toxic foods (Lam, 2015). The Lives in Context feature examines picky eating in childhood.

Young children require a healthy diet, with the same foods that adults need. Most children in developed nations eat enough, and often excessive, calories, but their diets are often insufficient in vitamins and minerals, such as Vitamin D, calcium, and potassium (Hess & Slavin, 2014). In one study of 96 child care centers, 90% served high-sugar or high-salt food or did not serve whole grains in a day's meals (Benjamin Neelon, Vaughn, Ball, McWilliams, & Ward, 2012). Replacement of current snack choices with nutrient-dense foods could lower the risk of nutrient deficiencies and help lower excess nutrient consumption. Increased consumption of low-sugar dairy foods, such as yogurt, could increase intake of important micronutrients without contributing to dietary excesses.

Brain Development

Early childhood is a period of rapid brain growth. The increase in synapses and connections among brain regions helps the brain to reach 90% of its adult weight by age 5 (Dubois et al., 2013). In early childhood, the greatest increases in cortical surface area are in the frontal and temporal cortex, which play a role in thinking, memory, language, and planning (Gilmore, Knickmeyer, & Gao, 2018). Children's brains tend to grow in spurts, with very rapid periods of growth followed by little growth or even reductions in volume with synaptic pruning (see Chapter 4) (Jernigan & Stiles, 2017). Little-used synapses are pruned in response to experience, an important part of neurological development that leads to more efficient thought.

The natural forming and pruning of synapses enables the human brain to demonstrate *plasticity*, the ability of the brain to change its organization and function in response to experience (Stiles, 2017). Young children who were given training in music demonstrated structural brain changes over a period of 15 months that correspond with increases in music and auditory skills (Hyde et al., 2009). Plasticity enables the young child's brain to reorganize itself in response to injury in ways that the adult's brain cannot. Adults who suffered brain injuries during infancy or early childhood often have fewer cognitive difficulties than do adults who were injured later in life.

Yet the immature young brain, while offering opportunities for plasticity, is also uniquely sensitive to injury. If a part of the brain is damaged at a critical point in development, functions linked to that region will be irreversibly impaired. Generally speaking, plasticity is greatest when neurons are forming many synapses, and it declines with pruning (Stiles, 2017). However, brain injuries sustained before age 2 and, in some cases, 3 can result in more global, severe, and long-lasting deficits than do those sustained later in childhood (V. A. Anderson et al., 2014), suggesting that a reserve of neurons is needed for the brain to show plasticity. Overall, the degree to which individuals recover from an injury depends on the injury, its nature and severity, age, experiences after the injury, and contextual factors supporting recovery, such as interventions (Bryck & Fisher, 2012).

Lateralization, the process of the hemispheres becoming specialized to carry out different functions, continues through early childhood and is associated with children's development (Duboc, Dufourcq, Blader, & Roussigné, 2015). For example, language tends to be lateralized to the left hemisphere in adults, and lateralization predicts children's language skills. Young children who show better performance on language tasks use more pathways in the left hemisphere and fewer in the right than those who are less skilled in language tasks (M. Walton, Dewey, & Lebel, 2018).

Myelination contributes to many of the changes that we see in children's capacities. As the neuron's axons become coated with fatty myelin, children's thinking becomes faster, more coordinated, and complex. Myelination aids quick, complex communication between neurons and makes coordinated behaviors possible (Chevalier et al., 2015). Patterns of myelination correspond with the onset and refinement of cognitive functions and behaviors (Dean et al., 2014). Myelination proceeds most rapidly from birth to age 4, first in the sensory and motor cortex, and then spreads to other cortical areas through childhood into adolescence and early adulthood (Qiu, Mori, & Miller, 2015).

Motor Development

The refinement of motor skills that use the large muscles of the body—as well as those that require hand–eye coordination and precise hand movements—is an important developmental task of early childhood. In this section, we describe the typical sequence of development of gross and fine motor skills.

Gross Motor Skills

Between the ages of 3 and 6, children become physically stronger, with increases in bone and muscle strength as well as lung capacity. Children make gains in coordination as the parts of the brain responsible for sensory and motor skills develop, permitting them to play harder and engage in more complicated play activities that include running, jumping, and climbing. Coordinating complex movements, like those entailed in riding a bicycle, is challenging for young children as it requires controlling multiple limbs, balancing, and more. As they grow and gain competence in their motor skills, young children become even more coordinated and begin to show interest in skipping and balancing. They enjoy playing games that involve feats of coordination, such as running while kicking a ball. By age 5, most North American children can throw and catch a ball, climb a ladder, and ride a tricycle. Some 5-year-olds can even skate or ride a bicycle (Gabbard, 2012).

Young children's motor abilities are also influenced by their context. For example, young children of some nations can swim in rough ocean waves that many adults of other nations would not attempt. Advances in gross motor skills help children move about and develop a sense of mastery of their environment, but it is fine motor skills that permit young children to take responsibility for their own care.

Fine Motor Skills

As children grow older, their fine motor skills improve. The ability to button a shirt, pour milk into a glass, assemble puzzles, and draw pictures all involve eye–hand and small muscle coordination. As children get better at these skills, they are able to become more independent and do more for themselves. Young children become better at grasping eating utensils and become more self-sufficient at feeding. Many fine motor skills are very difficult for young children because they involve both hands and both sides of the brain. Tying a shoelace is a complex act requiring attention, memory for an intricate series of hand movements, and the dexterity to perform them. Although preschoolers struggle

Climbing requires strength, coordination, and balance.
Michele Oenbrink / Alamy Stock Photo

with this task, by 5 to 6 years of age, most children can tie their shoes (Payne, Isaacs, & Larry, 2016). Recent research suggests that children's fine motor ability influences cognition—specifically, their ability to use their fingers to aid in counting predicts their mathematical skills (Fischer, Suggate, Schmirl, & Stoeger, 2018).

Young children's emerging fine motor skills enable them to draw using large crayons and, eventually, pencils. Drawing reflects the interaction of developmental domains: physical (fine motor control) and cognitive (planning skills, spatial understanding, and the recognition that pictures can symbolize objects, people, and events) (Yamagata, 2007). Although toddlers simply scribble when given a crayon, by 3 years of age, children's scribbles become more controlled, often recognizable, pictures. A human figure is often drawn as a tadpole-like figure with a circle for the head with eyes and sometimes a smiley mouth and then a line or two beneath to represent the rest of the body. Tadpole-like forms are characteristic of young children's art in all cultures (Cox, 1993). Most 3-year-olds can draw circles, squares, rectangles, triangles, crosses, and Xs and they begin to combine shapes into more complex designs. Between 3 and 4, young children begin to understand the representational function of drawings, and even when drawings appear to be nothing more than scribbles, young children often label them as representing a particular object and remember the label. In one study, children were asked to draw a balloon and a lollipop. The drawings looked the same to adults, but the children were adamant about which was which (Bloom, 2000), suggesting that it is important to ask a child what his or her drawing is rather than guess, because children's creations reflect their perspectives. Between ages 4 and 5, children's drawings loosely begin to depict actual objects, demonstrating the convergence of fine motor skills and the cognitive development of representational ability. As shown in Figure 7.1,

human figures typically include a torso, arms, legs, faces, and soon hands. As cognitive and fine motor skills improve, children create more sophisticated drawings of the human form. Table 7.1 summarizes milestones of gross and fine motor skill development in young children.

THINKING IN CONTEXT 7.1

1. Children who suffer brain injuries often regain some, and sometimes all, of their capacities. How might you explain this, given what you have learned about brain development?

2. How might contextual factors such as neighborhood, family, school, and culture influence the development of motor skills?

FIGURE 7.1

A Typical 2- to 3-Year-Old's Drawing of a Person

Source: Claire Marley, 2009.

COGNITIVE-DEVELOPMENTAL AND SOCIOCULTURAL REASONING IN EARLY CHILDHOOD

» LO 7.2 Compare Piaget's cognitive-developmental and Vygotsky's sociocultural theories on cognitive development in early childhood.

Four-year-old Timothy stands up on his toes and releases his parachute toy, letting the action figure dangle from a parachute drift a few feet from him and collapse on the floor. "I'm going to go up high and make it faster," he says, imagining standing on the sofa and making the toy sail far into the

TABLE 7.1

Gross and Fine Motor Skill Development in Early Childhood

AGE	GROSS MOTOR SKILL	FINE MOTOR SKILL
2–3 years	Walks more smoothly, runs but cannot turn or stop suddenly, jumps, throws a ball with a rigid body and catches by trapping ball against chest, rides push toys using feet	Unzips large zippers, puts on and removes some clothing, uses a spoon
3–4 years	Runs, ascends stairs alternating feet, jumps 15 to 24 inches, hops, pedals and steers a tricycle	Serves food, can work large buttons, copies vertical line and circle, uses scissors
4–5 years	Runs more smoothly with control over stopping and turning, descends stairs alternating feet, jumps 24 to 33 inches, skips, throws ball by rotating the body and transferring weight to one foot, catches ball with hands, rides tricycle and steers effectively	Uses scissors to cut along a line, uses fork effectively, copies simple shapes and some letters
5–6 years	Runs more quickly, skips more effectively, throws and catches a ball like older children, makes a running jump of 28 to 36 inches, rides bicycle with training wheels	Ties shoes, uses knife to cut soft food, copies numbers and simple words

clouds. He stands on the sofa and releases the toy, which sails a bit further this time. "Next time he'll jump out of the plane even higher!" Timothy thinks, excitedly. His friend Isaiah calls out, "Let's make him land on the moon! He can meet space people!"

Timothy and Isaiah can plan, think of solutions to problems, and use language to communicate their ideas. They learn through play by interacting with people and objects around them. From the cognitive-developmental perspective, young children's thought progresses from the sensory and motor schemes of infancy to more sophisticated representational thought.

Piaget's Cognitive-Developmental Theory: Preoperational Reasoning

According to Piaget, preoperational reasoning appears in young children from about ages 2 to 6. **Preoperational reasoning** is characterized by a dramatic leap in the use of symbolic thinking that permits young children to use language, interact with others, and play using their own thoughts and imaginations to guide their behavior. It is symbolic thought that enables Timothy and Isaiah to use language to communicate their thoughts and desires—and it is also what allows them to send their toy on a mission to the moon to visit with pretend space people.

Characteristics of Preoperational Reasoning

Young children in the preoperational stage show impressive advances in representational thinking, but they are unable to grasp logic and cannot understand complex relationships. Children who show preoperational reasoning tend to make several common errors, including egocentrism, animism, centration, and irreversibility.

Egocentrism. "See my picture?" Ricardo asks as he holds up a blank sheet of paper. Mr. Seris answers, "You can see your picture, but I can't. Turn your page around so that I can see your picture. There it is! It's beautiful," he proclaims after Ricardo flips the piece of paper, permitting him to see his drawing. Ricardo did not realize that even though he could see his drawing, Mr. Seris could not. Ricardo displays **egocentrism,** the inability to take another person's point of view or perspective. The egocentric child views the world from his or her own perspective, assuming that other people share her feelings, knowledge, and even physical view of the world.

A classic task used to illustrate preoperational children's egocentrism is the **three-mountain task.** As shown in Figure 7.2, the child sits at a table facing three large mountains. A teddy bear is placed in a chair across the table from the child. The child is asked how the mountains look to the teddy bear. Piaget found that young children in the preoperational stage demonstrated egocentrism because they described the scene from their own perspective rather than the teddy bear's. They did not understand that the teddy bear would have a different view of the mountains (Piaget & Inhelder, 1967).

Animism. Egocentric thinking can also take the form of **animism,** the belief that inanimate objects

FIGURE 7.2

The Three-Mountains Task

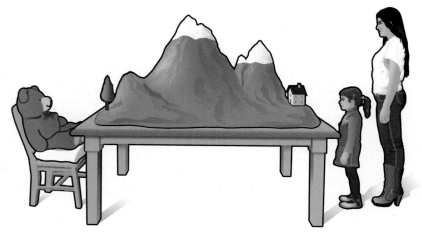

Children who display preoperational reasoning cannot describe the scene depicted in the three-mountains task from the point of view of the teddy bear.

are alive and have feelings and intentions. "It's raining because the sun is sad and it is crying," 3-year-old Melinda explains. Children accept their own explanations for phenomena as they are unable to consider another viewpoint or alternative reason.

Centration. Preoperational children exhibit **centration**, the tendency to focus on one part of a stimulus or situation and exclude all others. For example, a boy may believe that if he wears a dress, he will become a girl. He focuses entirely on the appearance (the dress) rather than the other characteristics that make him a boy.

Centration is illustrated by a classic task that requires the preoperational child to distinguish what something appears to be from what it really is, the **appearance–reality distinction.** In a classic study illustrating this effect, DeVries (1969) presented 3- to 6-year-old children with a cat named Maynard (see Figure 7.3). The children were permitted to pet Maynard. Then, while his head and shoulders were hidden behind a screen (and his back and tail were still visible), a dog mask was placed onto Maynard's head. The children were then asked, "What kind of animal is it now?" "Does it bark or meow?" Three-year-old children, despite Maynard's body and tail being visible during the transformation, replied that he was now a dog. Six-year-old children were able to distinguish Maynard's appearance from reality and explained that he only *looked* like a dog.

One reason that 3-year-old children fail appearance–reality tasks is because they are not yet capable of effective dual encoding, the ability to mentally represent an object in more than one way at a time (Flavell, Green, & Flavell, 1986). For example, young children are not able to understand that a scale model (like a doll house) can be both an object (something to play with) and a symbol (of an actual house) (MacConnell & Daehler, 2004).

Irreversibility. "You ruined it!" cried Johnson after his older sister, Monique, placed a triangular block atop the tower of blocks he had just built. "No, I just put a triangle there to show it was the top and finish it," she explains. "No!" insists Johnson. "OK, I'll take it off," says Monique. "See? Now it's just how you left it." "No. It's ruined," Johnson sighs. Johnson continued to be upset after his sister removed the triangular block, not realizing that by removing the block, she has restored the block structure to its original state. Young children's thinking is characterized by irreversibility, meaning that they do not understand that reversing a process can often undo it and restore the original state.

Preoperational children's irreversible thinking is illustrated by their performance on tasks that measure **conservation,** the understanding that the physical quantity of a substance, such as number, mass, or volume, remains the same even when its appearance changes. For example, a child is shown two identical glasses. The same amount of liquid is poured into each glass. After the child agrees that the two glasses contain the same amount of water, the liquid from one glass is poured into a taller, narrower glass and the child is asked whether one glass contains more liquid than the other. Young

---

FIGURE 7.3

Appearance vs. Reality: Is It a Cat or Dog?

Young children did not understand that Maynard the cat remained a cat despite wearing a dog mask and looking like a dog.

Source: DeVries, R. 1969. Constancy of generic identity in the years three to six. *Monographs of the Society for Research in Child Development,* 34(3, serial no 127), May. With permission from Blackwell Publishing

FIGURE 7.4

Additional Conservation Problems

Conservation Task	Original Presentation	Transformation
Number	Are there the same number of pennies in each row?	Now are there the same number of pennies in each row, or does one row have more?
Mass	Is there the same amount of clay in each ball?	Now does each piece have the same amount of clay, or does one have more?
Liquid	Is there the same amount of water in each glass?	Now does each glass have the same amount of water, or does one have more?

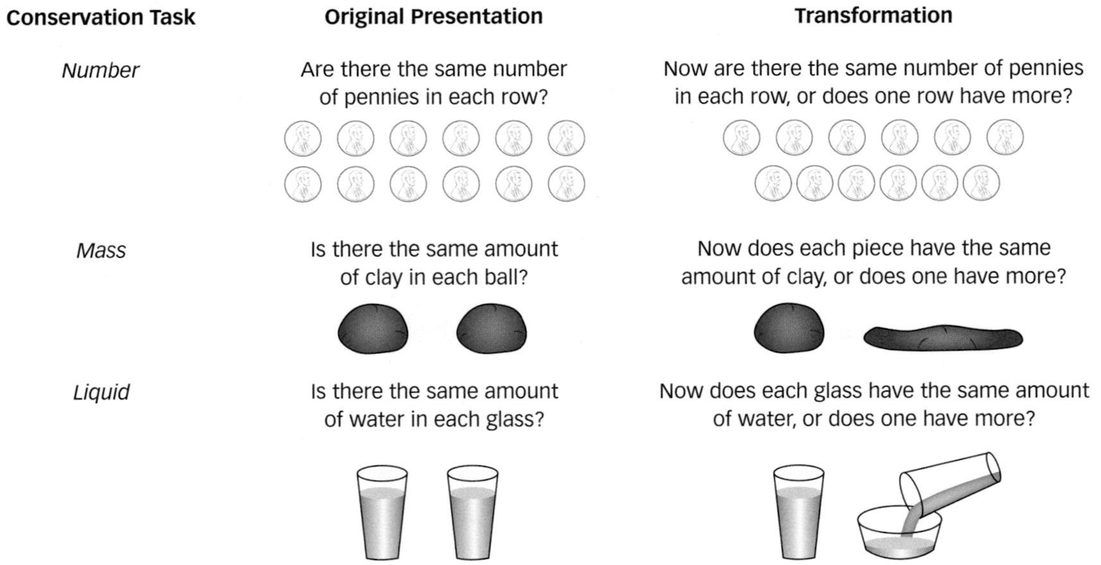

children in the preoperational stage reply that the taller narrower glass contains more liquid. Why? It has a higher liquid level than the shorter, wider glass has. They center on the appearance of the liquid without realizing that the process can be reversed by pouring the liquid back into the shorter, wider glass. They focus on the height of the water, ignoring other aspects such as the change in width, not understanding that it is still the same water. Figure 7.4 illustrates other types of conservation problems.

Characteristics of preoperational children's reasoning are summarized in Table 7.2.

TABLE 7.2

Characteristics of Preoperational Children's Reasoning

CHARAC-TERISTIC	DESCRIPTION
Egocentrism	The inability to take another person's point of view or perspective
Animism	The belief that inanimate objects are alive and have feelings and intentions
Centration	Tendency to focus attention on one part of a stimulus or situation and exclude all others
Irreversibility	Failure to understand that reversing a process can often undo a process and restore the original state

Evaluating Preoperational Reasoning

Research with young children has suggested that Piaget's tests of preoperational thinking underestimated young children. Success on Piaget's tasks appears to depend more on the child's language abilities than his or her actions. As we discussed earlier, to be successful at the three-mountain task, the child must not only understand how the mounds look from the other side of the table but also must be able to communicate that understanding. Appearance reality tasks require not simply an understanding of dual representation but the ability to express it. However, if the task is nonverbal, such as requiring reaching for an object rather than talking about it, even 3-year-old children can distinguish appearance from reality (Sapp, Lee, & Muir, 2000).

Research Findings on Egocentrism and Animism. Simple tasks demonstrate that young children are less egocentric than Piaget posited. When a 3-year-old child is shown a card that depicts a dog on one side and a cat on another, and the card is held up between the researcher who can see the cat and the child who can see the dog, the child correctly responds that the researcher can see the cat (Flavell, Everett, Croft, & Flavell, 1981). When the task is relevant to children's everyday lives (i.e., hiding), their performance suggests that they are not as egocentric as Piaget posited (Newcombe & Huttenlocher, 1992). Other research suggests that 3- to 5-year-old children can learn perspective-taking skills through training and retain their perspective-taking abilities 6 months later (Mori & Cigala, 2016).

Likewise, 3-year-old children do not tend to describe inanimate objects with lifelike qualities, even when the object is a robot that can move (Jipson, Gülgöz, & Gelman, 2016). Most 4-year-old children understand that animals grow, and even plants grow, but objects do not (Backschneider, Shatz, & Gelman, 1993). Sometimes, however, young children provide animistic responses. Gjersoe, Hall, and Hood (2015) suggest an emotional component to animistic beliefs. They found that 3-year-olds attribute mental states to toys to which they are emotionally attached but not to other favorite toys, even those with which they frequently engage in imaginary play. Finally, children show individual differences in their expressions of animism and reasoning about living things, and these differences are linked with aspects of cognitive development such as memory, working memory, and inhibition (Zaitchik, Iqbal, & Carey, 2014).

Research Findings on Reversibility and the Appearance–Reality Distinction. Although young children typically perform poorly on conservation tasks, 4-year-old children can be taught to conserve, suggesting that children's difficulties with reversibility and conservation tasks can be overcome (Gallagher, 2008). In addition, making the task relevant improves children's performance. For example, when children are asked to play a trick on someone (i.e., "let's pretend that this sponge is a rock and tell Anne that it is a rock when it really is a sponge") or choose an object that can be used to clean spilled water, many choose the sponge, illustrating that they can form a dual representation of the sponge as an object that looks like a rock (Sapp, Lee, & Muir, 2000). Three-year-old children can shift between describing the real and fake or imagined aspects of an object or situation. In addition, they can describe misleading appearances and functions of objects in response to natural conversational prompts, as compared with the more formal language in the typical prompts used in traditional appearance–reality tasks (e.g., "What is it really and truly?") (Deák, 2006). In sum, preschoolers show an understanding of the appearance–reality distinction, and it develops throughout childhood (Woolley & Ghossainy, 2013).

Vygotsky's Sociocultural Theory

Russian psychologist Lev Vygotsky emphasized the influence of culture on children's thinking. Specifically, he proposed that cognitive development is influenced by differences in the ways particular cultures and societies approach problems. Vygotsky's sociocultural perspective asserts that we are embedded in a context that shapes how we think and who we become. Much

Children learn culturally valued skills by interacting with and helping skilled partners.
John Scofield/ Contributor via Getty Images

of children's learning comes not from working alone but from collaborating with others.

Specifically, Vygotsky argues that mental activity is influenced by culture, specifically, cultural tools that are shared by members of a culture (Robbins, 2005; Vygotsky, 1978). Cultural tools include physical items such as computers, pencils, and paper but also ways of thinking about phenomena, including how to approach math and scientific problems. Spoken language is a vital cultural tool of thought. Children learn how to use the tools of their culture by interacting with skilled partners who provide guidance. For example, suppose a child wanted to bake cookies for the first time. Rather than send the child into the kitchen alone, we would probably accompany the child and provide the tools needed to accomplish the task, such as the ingredients, a rolling pin to roll the dough, cookie cutters, and a baking sheet. We would probably show the child how to use each tool, such as how to roll out the dough, and watch as he or she does it, scaffolding his or her learning. With interaction and experience, the child adopts and internalizes the tools and knowledge, becoming able to apply it independently. Both the learner and teacher contribute mutually (Rogoff, 2015). Vygotsky argued that in this way, culturally valued ways of thinking and problem solving get passed on to children.

Guided Participation and Scaffolding

Children learn through social experience, by interacting with more experienced partners who provide assistance in completing tasks. Children learn through **guided participation** (also known as an *apprenticeship in thinking*), a form of sensitive teaching in which the partner is attuned to the needs of the child and helps him or her to accomplish more than the child could do alone (Rogoff, 2014). As novices, children learn from more skilled, or expert, partners by observing them and asking questions. In this way, children are apprentices, learning how others approach problems. The expert partner provides **scaffolding** that permits the child to bridge the gap between his or her current competence level and the task at hand (Mermelshtine, 2017). For example, consider a child working on a jigsaw puzzle. She is stumped, unable to complete it on her own. Suppose a more skilled partner, such as an adult, sibling, or another child who has more experience with puzzles, provides a little bit of assistance, a scaffold. The expert partner might point to an empty space on the puzzle and encourage the child to find a piece that fits that spot. If the child remains stumped, the partner might point out a piece or rotate it to help the child see the relationship. The partner acts to motivate the child and provide support to help the child finish the puzzle, emphasizing that they are working together. The child novice and expert partner interact to accomplish the goal and the expert adjusts his or her responses to meet the needs of the child.

Scaffolding occurs in formal educational settings, but also informally, any time a partner adjusts his or her interactional style to fit the needs of a child and guide the child to complete a task that he or she could not complete alone (Rogoff, Callanan, Gutiérrez, & Erickson, 2016). Mothers vary their scaffolding behaviors in response to children's attempts at tasks. For example, they spontaneously use different behaviors depending on the child's attention skills, using more verbal engagement, strategic questions, verbal hints, and verbal prompts when children show difficulty paying attention during a task (Robinson, Burns, & Davis, 2009). Moreover, maternal reading, scaffolding, and verbal guidance are associated with 2- to 4-year-olds' capacities for cognitive control and planning (Moriguchi, 2014). Parents and child care providers often provide this informal instruction, but anyone who is more skilled at a given task, including older siblings and peers, can promote children's cognitive development (Rogoff et al., 2016). Collaboration with more skilled peers improves performance on cognitive tasks such as card-sorting tasks, Piagetian tasks, planning, and academic tasks (Sills, Rowse, & Emerson, 2016).

Zone of Proximal Development

As Vygotsky (1978) explained, "What the child can do in cooperation today, he can do alone tomorrow." Effective scaffolding works within the **zone of proximal development,** the gap between the child's competence level—what he can accomplish independently—and what he can do with assistance of a skilled partner. With time, the child internalizes the scaffolding lesson and learns to accomplish the task on her own—and her zone of proximal development shifts, as shown in Figure 7.5. Adults tend to naturally provide children with instruction

Parents' guidance acts as a scaffold within the zone of proximal development to help children accomplish challenging tasks. Soon children become able to complete the task independently.
iStock/XiXinXing

within the zone of proximal development (Rogoff, 2014). For example, adults reading a book to a child tend to point to items, label and describe characters' emotional states, explain, ask questions, listen, and respond sensitively, helping the child understand challenging material that is just beyond what the child can understand on his or her own (Silva, Strasser, & Cain, 2014).

The quality of scaffolding influences children's development. In one study of preschool teachers and children, the degree to which the adult matched the child's needs for help in playing predicted more autonomous play on the part of children over a 6-month period (Trawick-Smith & Dziurgot, 2011). Adults may act intentionally to encourage and support children's learning (Zuckerman, 2007). For example, one study of parents and young children visiting a science museum found that when parents provided specific guidance in considering a conservation of volume problem, such as discussing the size of the containers, asking "how" and "why" questions, and talking about simple math, children were more likely to give correct responses to scientific reasoning problems, including those

FIGURE 7.5

Zone of Proximal Development

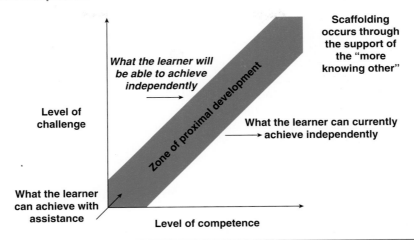

Source: Vygotsky's Zone of Proximal Development, https://lmrtriads.wikispaces.com/Zone+of+Proximal+Development *licensed under CC BY-SA 3.0* https://creativecommons.org/licenses/by-sa/3.0/

involving conservation (Vandermaas-Peeler, Massey, & Kendall, 2016).

Parents and preschool teachers can take advantage of the social nature of learning by assigning children tasks that they can accomplish with some assistance, providing just enough help so that children learn to complete the tasks independently. This helps to create learning environments that stimulate children to complete more challenging tasks on their own (Wass & Golding, 2014). Through guided play, teachers can develop play environments and settings with materials that encourage exploration and guide children with comments, encouraging them to explore, question, or extend their interests (Bodrova & Leong, 2018).

Evaluating Vygotsky's Sociocultural Theory

Although relatively unknown until recent decades, Vygotsky's ideas about the sociocultural nature of cognitive development have influenced prominent theories of development, such as Bronfenbrenner's bioecological theory (Bronfenbrenner, 1979). They have been applied in educational settings, supporting the use of assisted discovery, guiding children's learning, and cooperative learning with peers.

Similar to Piaget, Vygotsky's theory has been criticized for a lack of precision. The mechanisms or processes underlying the social transmission of thought are not described (Göncü & Gauvain, 2012). Moreover, constructs such as the zone of proximal development are not easily testable (Wertsch, 1998). In addition, underlying cognitive capacities, such as attention and memory, are not addressed. It is understandable, however, that Vygotsky's theory is

incomplete, as he died of tuberculosis at the age of 37. We can only speculate about how his ideas might have evolved over a longer lifetime. Nevertheless, Vygotsky provided a new framework for understanding development as a process of transmitting culturally valued tools that influence how we look at the world, think, and approach problems.

THINKING IN CONTEXT 7.2

1. Contrast Vygotsky and Piaget's theories of cognitive development.

2. Do you think that young children can be taught to respond correctly to conservation problems? Why or why not? Should they?

3. What cultural tools have you adopted? How have interactions with others influenced your cognitive development?

4. How might Vygotsky's ideas be applied to children's learning at home and in the classroom? Give some examples.

INFORMATION PROCESSING IN EARLY CHILDHOOD

» LO 7.3   Describe information processing abilities during early childhood.

From an information processing perspective, cognitive development entails developing mental strategies to guide one's thinking and use one's cognitive resources more effectively. In early childhood, children become more efficient at attending, encoding and retrieving memories, and problem solving.

Attention

Early childhood is accompanied by dramatic improvements in attention, particularly **sustained attention,** the ability to remain focused on a stimulus for an extended period of time (Rueda, 2013). Young children often struggle with selective attention. **Selective attention** refers to the ability to systematically deploy one's attention, focusing on relevant information and ignoring distractors. Young children do not search thoroughly when asked to compare detailed pictures and explain what's missing from one. They have trouble focusing on one stimulus and switching their attention to compare it with other stimuli (Hanania & Smith, 2010). For example, young children who sort cards according to one dimension such as color may later be unable to successfully switch to different sorting criteria (Honomichl & Zhe, 2011). Young children's selective attention at age 2.5 predicts working memory and response inhibition at age 3 (Veer, Luyten, Mulder, van Tuijl, & Sleegers, 2017).

Working Memory and Executive Function

Young children simply get better at thinking. Recall from Chapter 5 that working memory is where all thinking or information processing takes place. Working memory consists of a short-term store (*short-term memory*), a processor, and a control mechanism known as the central executive, responsible for executive function (Baddeley, 2016; Miyake & Friedman, 2012). Children get better at holding information in working memory, manipulating it, inhibiting irrelevant stimuli, and planning, which allows them to set and achieve goals (Carlson, Zelazo, & Faja, 2013).

Short-term memory is commonly assessed by a memory span task in which individuals are asked to recall a series of unrelated items (such as numbers) presented at a rate of about 1 per second. The greatest lifetime improvements on memory span tasks occur in early childhood. In a classic study, 2- to 3-year-old children could recall about two digits, increasing to about five items at age 7, but only increasing another two digits, to seven, by early adulthood (Bjorklund & Myers, 2015).

As their short-term memory increases, young children are able to manipulate more information in working memory and become better at planning, considering the steps needed to complete a particular act and carrying them out to achieve a goal (Rueda, 2013). Preschoolers can create and abide by a plan to complete tasks that are familiar and not too complex, such as systematically searching for a lost object in a yard (Wellman, Somerville, & Haake, 1979). But they have difficulty with more complex tasks. Young children have difficulty deciding where to begin and how to proceed to complete a task in an orderly way (Ristic & Enns, 2015). When they plan, young children often skip important steps. One reason why young children get better at attention, memory, and cognitive tasks is because they get better at inhibiting impulses to engage in task-irrelevant actions and can keep focused on a task.

Long-Term Memory

Young children's memory for events and information acquired during events, **episodic memory,** expands rapidly (Roediger & Marsh, 2003; Tulving, 2002). For example, a researcher might study episodic memory by asking a child, "Where did you go on vacation?" or "Remember the pictures I showed you yesterday?" Most laboratory studies of memory examine episodic memory, including memory for specific information, for scripts, and for personal experiences.

Memory for Information

Shana turns over one card and exclaims, "I've seen this one before. I know where it is!" She quickly selects its duplicate by turning over a second card from an array of cards. Shana recognizes a card she has seen before and recalls its location. Children's memory for specific information, such as the location of items, lists of words or numbers, and directions, can be studied using tasks that examine recognition memory and recall memory. **Recognition memory,** the ability to recognize a stimulus one has encountered before, is nearly perfect in 4- and 5-year-old children, but they are much less proficient in **recall memory,** the ability to generate a memory of a stimulus encountered before without seeing it again (Myers & Perlmutter, 2014).

Why do young children perform so poorly in recall tasks? Young children are not very effective at using **memory strategies,** cognitive activities that make us more likely to remember. For example, rehearsal, repeating items over and over, is a strategy that older children and adults use to recall lists of stimuli. Children do not spontaneously and reliably apply rehearsal until after the first grade (Bjorklund & Myers, 2015). Preschool-age children can be taught strategies, but they generally do not transfer their learning and apply it to new tasks (Titz & Karbach, 2014). This utilization deficiency seems to occur because of their limited working memories and difficulty inhibiting irrelevant stimuli. They cannot apply the strategy at the same time as they have to retain both the material to be learned and the strategy to be used. Instead, new information competes with the information the child is attempting to recall (Aslan & Bäuml, 2010). Overall, advances in executive function, working memory, and attention predict strategy use (Stone, Blumberg, Blair, & Cancelli, 2016).

However, young children do not always show more poor performance relative to adults. In one study, parents read a novel rhyming verse and a word list as their 4-year-old children's bedtime story on 10 consecutive days. When asked to recall the verse, the 4-year-old children outperformed their parents and a set of young adults who also listened to the verse (Király, Takács, Kaldy, & Blaser, 2017). The children and adults did not differ in the ability to recall the gist of the verse. Unlike adults, young children are immersed in a culture of verse and rely on oral transmission of information, likely underlying their skill relative to adults.

Memory for Scripts

Young children remember familiar repeated everyday experiences, like the process of eating dinner, taking a bath, or going to nursery school or preschool, as **scripts,** or descriptions of what occurs in a particular situation. When young children begin to use scripts, they remember only the main details. A 3-year-old might describe a trip to a restaurant as follows: "You go in, eat, then pay." These early scripts include only a few acts but usually are recalled in the correct order (Bauer, 1996). As children grow older and gain cognitive competence, scripts become more elaborate. Consider a 5-year-old child's explanation of a trip to a restaurant: "You go in, you can sit at a booth or a table, then you tell the waitress what you want, you eat, if you want dessert, you can have some, then you go pay, and go home" (Hudson, Fivush, & Kuebli, 1992). Scripts are an organizational tool that help children

understand and remember repeated events and help them to predict future events. However, scripts may inhibit memory for new details. For example, in one laboratory study, children were presented with a script of the same series of events repeated in order multiple times as well as a single alternative event. Preschoolers were less likely than older children to spontaneously recall and provide a detailed account of the event (Brubacher, Glisic, Roberts, & Powell, 2011).

Autobiographical Memory

Autobiographical memory refers to memory of personally meaningful events that took place at a specific time and place in one's past (Bauer, 2015). Autobiographical memory emerges as children become proficient in language and executive function and develops steadily from 3 to 6 years of age (Nieto, Ros, Ricarte, & Latorre, 2018). Young children report fewer memories for specific events than do older children and adults (Baker-Ward, Gordon, Ornstein, Larus, & Clubb, 1993). But by age 3, they are able to retrieve and report specific memories, especially those that have personal significance, are repeated, or are highly stressful (Nuttall, Valentino, Comas, McNeill, & Stey, 2014). For example, in one study, children who were at least 26 months old at the time of an accidental injury and visit to the emergency room accurately recalled the details of these experiences even after a 2-year delay (Goodman, Rudy, Bottoms, & Aman, 1990). Eight-year-old children have been found to accurately remember events that occurred when they were as young as 3½ years of age (Goodman & Aman, 1990).

Events that are unique or new, such as a trip to the circus, are better recalled; 3-year-old children will recall them for a year or longer (Fivush, Hudson, & Nelson, 1983). Frequent events, however, tend to blur together. Young children are better at remembering things they did than things they simply watched. For example, one study examined 5-year-old children's recall of an event they observed, were told about, or experienced. A few days later, the children who actually experienced the event were more likely to recall details in a more accurate and organized way and to require fewer prompts (Murachver, Pipe, Gordon, Owens, & Fivush, 1996).

The way adults talk with the child about a shared experience can influence how well the child will remember it (Haden & Fivush, 1996). Parents with an elaborative conversational style discuss new aspects of an experience, provide more information to guide a child through a mutually rewarding conversation, and affirm the child's responses. They may ask questions, expand children's responses, and help the child tell their story. Three-year-olds of parents who use an elaborative style engage in

This child demonstrates a script as she explains the process of going to a restaurant and ordering from a menu.
Inti St Clair/Blend/Newscom

Children's Suggestibility

Repeated questioning about an event that may or may not have happened may increase suggestibility in children.
Gordon Scammell / Alamy Stock Photo

The accuracy of children's memory, especially their vulnerability to suggestion, is an important topic because children as young as 3 years have been called upon to relate their memories of events that they have experienced or witnessed, including abuse, maltreatment, and domestic violence (Pantell & Committee on Psychosocial Aspects of Child and Family Health, 2017). Young children can recall much about their experiences, often material that is relevant and accurate (Cauffman, Shulman, Bechtold, & Steinberg, 2015). How suggestible are young children? Can we trust their memories?

Research suggests that repeated questioning may increase suggestibility in children (La Rooy, Lamb, & Pipe, 2011). For example, in one study, preschoolers were questioned every week about events that had either happened or not happened to them; by the 11th week, nearly two thirds of the children falsely reported having experienced an event (Ceci, Huffman, Smith, & Loftus, 1994). Preschool-age children may be more vulnerable to suggestion than school-age children or adults (Brown & Lamb, 2015). When children were asked if they could remember several events, including a fictitious instance of getting their finger caught in a mousetrap, almost none of them initially recalled these events. However, after repeated suggestive questioning, more than half of 3- and 4-year-olds and two fifths of 5- and 6-year-olds said they recalled these events—often vividly (Poole & White, 1991, 1993).

Young children's natural trust in others may enhance their suggestibility. In one study, 3-year-olds who received misleading verbal and visual information from an experimenter about a sticker's location continued to search in the wrong, suggested location despite no success (Jaswal, 2010). In another study, 3- to 5-year-old children watched as an adult hid a toy in one location, then told the children that the toy was in a different location. When retrieving the toy, 4- and 5-year-olds relied on what they had seen and disregarded the adult's false statements, but 3-year-olds deferred to what the adult had said, despite what they had directly observed (Ma & Ganea, 2010).

In some cases, children can resist suggestion. For example, in one study, 4- and 7-year-old children either played games with an adult confederate (e.g., dressing up in costumes, playing tickle, being photographed) or merely watched the games (Ceci & Bruck, 1998). Eleven days later, each child was interviewed by an adult who included misleading questions that were often followed up with suggestions relevant to child abuse. Even the 4-year-olds resisted the false suggestions about child abuse. Children also vary. Some children are better able to resist social pressure and suggestive questioning than others (Uhl, Camilletti, Scullin, & Wood, 2016).

Children are more vulnerable than adults, but adults are not entirely resistant to suggestion. For example, recent research suggests that in some situations, adults are *more* likely than children to make quick associations between suggestive details about unexperienced events and prior experiences, making them more vulnerable to suggestion (Otgaar, Howe, Merckelbach, & Muris, 2018). Like children, adults who are exposed to information that is misleading or inconsistent with their experiences are more likely to perform poorly during memory interviews—and repeated questioning has a similar effect on performance (Wysman, Scoboria, Gawrylowicz, & Memon, 2014).

What Do You Think?

Suppose you need to question a preschool child about an event. How would you maximize your likelihood of the child's giving an accurate account of what occurred? ●

longer conversations about events, remember more details, and tend to remember the events better at ages 5 and 6 (Fivush, 2011).

Young children can have largely accurate memories, but they can also tell tall tales, make errors, and succumb to misleading questions. Children's ability to remember events can be influenced by information and experiences that may interfere with their memories. These can include conversations with parents and adults, exposure to media, and sometimes intentional suggestions directed at changing the child's view of what transpired. Children's vulnerability to suggestion is discussed in Applying Developmental Science.

Theory of Mind

Over the childhood years, thinking becomes more complex. In particular, children become increasingly aware of the process of thinking and of their own thoughts. **Theory of mind** refers to children's awareness of their own and other people's mental processes. This awareness of the mind can be considered under the broader concept of **metacognition,** knowledge of how the mind works and the ability to control the mind (Lockl & Schneider, 2007). Let's explore these concepts.

Young children's theory of mind grows and changes between the ages of 2 and 5 (Bower, 1993; Flavell, Green, & Flavell, 1995; Wellman, 2017). For example, 3-year-old children understand the difference between thinking about a cookie and having a cookie. They know that having a cookie means that one can touch, eat, or share it, while thinking about a cookie does not permit such actions (Astington, 1993). Young children also understand that a child who wants a cookie will be happy upon receiving one and sad upon not having one (Moses, Coon, & Wusinich, 2000). Similarly, they understand that a child who believes he is having hot oatmeal for breakfast will be surprised upon receiving cold spaghetti (Wellman & Banerjee, 1991). Theory of mind is commonly assessed by examining children's abilities to understand that people can hold different beliefs about an object or event.

Culture shapes children's thinking. Samoan and Vanuatu cultures deemphasize internal mental states as explanations for behavior. Children are not exposed to discussions about the mind and they get little experience considering other people's thoughts.
age fotostock / Alamy Stock Photo

False Belief

Young children do not yet understand people can hold different beliefs and that some may be incorrect. Three-year-old children tend to perform poorly on **false-belief tasks,** tasks that require them to understand that someone can have an incorrect belief. In a classic false-belief task, children who are presented with a Band-Aid box that contains pencils rather than Band-Aids will show surprise but tend to believe that other children will share their knowledge and expect the Band-Aid box to hold pencils (Flavell, 1993), similar to Figure 7.6. The children do not yet understand that the other children hold different, false beliefs. In addition, the children will claim that they knew all along that the Band-Aid box contained pencils (Birch, 2005). They confuse their present knowledge with their memories for prior knowledge and have difficulty remembering ever having believed something that contradicts their current view (Bernstein, Atance, Meltzoff, & Loftus, 2007).

Some researchers, however, assert that young children are much more competent than they appear. Research with infants using preferential looking and habituation tasks has suggested an understanding of false belief as early as 15 months of age (Scott & Baillargeon, 2017). Similar to arguments regarding object permanence in infancy and egocentrism in early childhood (see Chapter 5), it

---

FIGURE 7.6

False-Belief Task

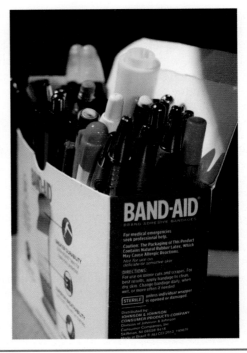

Source: Nathan Davidson

may be that children understand the concept (that another person will understand that the Band-Aid box contains bandages, not pencils) but may have difficulty communicating their understanding to the researcher (Helming, Strickland, & Jacob, 2014). Yet many researchers counter that false-belief findings with infants reflect perceptual preferences, that is, a desire to look at one object over another, not theory of mind (Heyes, 2014). Indeed, the research to date suggests that theory of mind as evidenced by false-belief tasks emerges at about 3 years of age and shifts reliably between 3 and 4 years of age (Grosse Wiesmann, Friederici, Singer, & Steinbeis, 2017). By age 3, children can understand that two people can believe different things (Rakoczy, Warneken, & Tomasello, 2007). Four-year-old children can understand that people who are presented with different versions of the same event develop different beliefs (Eisbach, 2004). By age 4 or 5, children become aware that they and other people can hold false beliefs (Moses et al., 2000).

Advanced cognition is needed for children to learn abstract concepts such as belief. Performance on false-belief tasks, such as the Band-Aid task, is associated with measures of executive function, the abilities that enable complex cognitive functions such as planning, decision making, and goal setting (Doenyas, Yavuz, & Selcuk, 2018; Sabbagh, Xu, Carlson, Moses, & Lee, 2006). Advances in executive functioning facilitate children's abilities to reflect on and learn from experience and promote development of theory of mind (Benson, Sabbagh, Carlson, & Zelazo, 2013). For example, one longitudinal study following children from ages 2 to 4 found that advances in executive functioning predicted children's performance on false-belief tasks (Hughes & Ensor, 2007). Children's performance on false-belief tasks is closely related with language development and competence in sustaining conversations (Hughes & Devine, 2015).

Context and Theory of Mind

The contexts in which children are embedded contribute to their developing understanding of the mind. Children in many countries, including Canada, India, Thailand, Norway, China, and the United States, show the onset and development of theory of mind between the ages of 3 and 5 (Callaghan et al., 2005; Wellman, Fang, & Peterson, 2011). However, social and contextual factors may influence the specific pattern of theory of mind development. North American and Chinese children develop theory of mind in early childhood, but along different paths (Wellman, 2017). Chinese culture emphasizes collectivism, commonality, and interdependence among community members. Chinese parents'

comments to children tend to refer to knowing and shared knowledge that community members must learn. U.S. parents emphasize Western values such as individuality and independence. They comment more on thinking, including differences in thoughts among individuals. U.S. children, and other children from individualist cultures, develop an understanding of beliefs before knowledge. Chinese children tend to show the reverse pattern: an early understanding of the knowledge aspect of theory of mind and later come to understand beliefs (Wellman, 2017). Children from Iran and Turkey follow a similar pattern in theory of mind development (Shahaeian, Peterson, Slaughter, & Wellman, 2011).

Everyday conversations aid children in developing a theory of mind because such conversations tend to center on and provide examples of mental states and their relation with behavior. When parents and other adults speak with children about mental states, emotions, and behaviors, as well as discuss causes and consequences, children develop a more sophisticated understanding of other people's perspectives (Devine & Hughes, 2018; Pavarini, Hollanda Souza, & Hawk, 2012). In addition, siblings provide young children with opportunities for social interaction, pretend play, and practice with deception. Children with siblings perform better on false-belief tests than do only children (McAlister & Peterson, 2013). Success in false-belief attribution tasks is most frequent in children who are the most active in shared pretend play (Schwebel, Rosen, & Singer, 1999).

Children's interactions with people in their immediate contexts can also influence the development of theory of mind. Children can be trained in perspective taking. For example, when children are presented with a series of objects that look like a certain thing but are actually something else (candle and apple) and are shown the appearance and real states of the objects, along with explanation, 3-year-olds showed improvements on false-belief tasks (Lohmann & Tomasello, 2003). Discussion emphasizing the existence of a variety of possible perspectives in relation to an object can improve performance in false-belief tasks—dialogue can facilitate the development of theory of mind (Bernard & Deleau, 2007). Other studies have engaged North American and European children in discussion about the thoughts, beliefs, and desires of characters in stories, especially stories in which characters play tricks to surprise or deceive one another. Children who receive the training improved their performance in subsequent false-belief tasks (Liu, Wellman, Tardif, & Sabbagh, 2008; Milligan, Astington, & Dack, 2007; Slaughter & Perez-Zapata, 2014). Similarly, conversation about deceptive objects (e.g., a pen that looked like a flower) also improves performance on false-belief tasks (Lohmann & Tomasello, 2003).

Metacognition

Theory of mind is a precursor to the development of metacognition (Lecce, Demicheli, Zocchi, & Palladino, 2015). Young children know that the mind is where thinking takes place. Between 3 and 5, children come to understand that they can know something that others do not (essential for success on false-belief tasks), that their thoughts cannot be observed, and that there are individual differences in mental states (Pillow, 2008). They begin to understand that someone can think of one thing while doing something else, that a person whose eyes and ears are covered can think, and that thinking is different from talking, touching, and knowing (Flavell et al., 1995). However, young children's understanding of the mind is far from complete. Three- and four-year-old children do not understand that we think even when we are inactive. They look for visible indicators of thinking—perhaps one reason why teachers of young children refer to "putting on your thinking cap"—and assume their absence indicates the absence of thought. It is not until middle childhood that children understand that the mind is always active (Flavell, 1999). Likewise, preschoolers tend to think of the mind as simply a container for items, but older children tend to see the mind as an active constructor of knowledge that receives, processes, and transforms information (Chandler & Carpendale, 1998).

Young children show limited knowledge of memory functions, contributing to their poor performance on memory tasks. Four-year-olds recognize that increasing the number of items on a list makes recall more difficult and that longer retention intervals increase the likelihood of forgetting (Pillow, 2008). But they know little about the effectiveness of deliberate memory strategies. For example, whereas 6- and 7-year-olds demonstrated an understanding of the role of deliberate practice in memory and practiced without being prompted, 5-year-olds showed an understanding of deliberate practice and some capacity to practice, but 4-year-olds showed neither of these capabilities (Brinums, Imuta, & Suddendorf, 2018). The advances that take place in information processing during early childhood are summarized in Table 7.3.

THINKING IN CONTEXT 7.3

1. What are the practical implications of young children's capacities for attention and memory?

2. In what ways might brain development account for cognitive changes that we see in early childhood such as increases in information processing capacity and changes in reasoning?

3. Recall from Chapter 1 that development is influenced by multiple contexts. How might contextual influences—family, neighborhood, sociocultural context, and even cohort or generation—influence aspects of cognitive development, such as autobiographical memory or theory of mind?

TABLE 7.3

Development of Information Processing Skills During Early Childhood

SKILL	DESCRIPTION
Attention	Young children are better able to focus and sustain their attention to complete tasks but have difficulty with complex tasks that require them to switch their attention among stimuli.
Memory	Young children's limited capacity to store and manipulate information in working memory influences their performance on memory and problem-solving tasks. Young children show advances in recognition memory and the ability to use scripts, but recall memory lags behind because they are not able to effectively use memory strategies. They often can be taught memory strategies but do not spontaneously apply them in new situations. Episodic memory emerges in early childhood, but the extent and quality of memories increase with age.
Theory of mind	Theory of mind refers to children's awareness of their own and other people's mental processes. When researchers use vocabulary that children are familiar with, observe them in everyday activities, and use concrete examples and simple problems such as those involving belief and surprise, it is clear that young children's understanding of the mind grows and changes between the ages of 2 and 5.
Metacognition	In early childhood theory of mind, an awareness of one's own and others' minds emerges. Young children demonstrate a growing ability for metacognition, understanding the mind. However, young children's abilities are limited, and they tend to fail false-belief and appearance–reality tasks, suggesting that their abilities to understand the mind and predict what other people are thinking are limited.

LANGUAGE DEVELOPMENT IN EARLY CHILDHOOD

» LO 7.4   Summarize young children's advances in language development.

Toddlers transitioning from infancy to early childhood tend to use telegraphic speech. They learn to use multiple elements of speech, such as plurals, adjectives, and the past tense. Children's vocabulary and grammar become dramatically more complex during early childhood, enabling them to communicate, but also think, in new ways.

Vocabulary

At 2 years of age, the average child knows about 500 words; vocabulary acquisition continues at a rapid pace. The average 3-year-old child has a vocabulary of 900 to 1,000 words. By 6 years of age, most children have a vocabulary of about 14,000 words, which means that the average child learns a new word every 1 to 2 hours, every day (Owens, 2015). How is language learned so quickly? Children continue to use fast mapping (see Chapter 5) as a strategy to enable them to learn the meaning of a new word after hearing it once or twice based on contextual association and understanding (Kucker, McMurray, & Samuelson, 2015). Fast mapping improves with age.

Children learn words that they hear often, that label things and events that interest them, and that they encounter in contexts that are meaningful to them (Harris et al., 2011). Preschoolers can learn words from watching videos with both human and robot speakers, but they learn more quickly in response to human speakers (Moriguchi, Kanda, Ishiguro, Shimada, & Itakura, 2011), especially when the speaker responds to them, such as through videoconferencing (e.g., Skype) (Roseberry et al., 2014). Children learn best in interactive contexts with parents, teachers, siblings, and peers that entail turn-taking, joint attention, and scaffolding experiences that provide hints to the meaning of new words (MacWhinney, 2015).

Another strategy that children use to increase their vocabulary is **logical extension.** When learning a word, children extend it to other objects in the same category. For example, when learning that a dog with spots is called a Dalmatian, a child may refer to a Dalmatian bunny (a white bunny with black spots) or a Dalmatian horse. Children tend to make words their own and apply them to all situations they want to talk about (Behrend, Scofield, & Kleinknecht, 2001). At about age 3, children demonstrate the **mutual exclusivity assumption** in learning new words: They assume that objects have only one label or name. According to mutual exclusivity, a

At around 5 years of age, many children can infer the meanings of words given the context. They can quickly understand and apply most words they hear.
RayArt Graphics / Alamy Stock Photo

new word is assumed to be a label for an unfamiliar object, not a synonym or second label for a familiar object (Markman, Wasow, & Hansen, 2003). In one study, young children were shown one familiar object and one unfamiliar object. They were told, "Show me the X," where X is a nonsense syllable. The children reached for the unfamiliar object, suggesting that they expect new words to label new objects rather than acting as synonyms (Markman & Wachtel, 1988). Similarly, young children use the mutual exclusivity assumption to learn the names of parts of objects, such as the brim of a hat, the cab of a truck, or a bird's beak (Hansen & Markman, 2009).

By 5 years of age, many children can quickly understand and apply most words that they hear. If a word is used in context or explained with examples, most 5-year-olds can learn it. Preschoolers learn words by making inferences given the context—and inferential learning is associated with better retention than learning by direct instruction (Zosh, Brinster, & Halberda, 2013). Certain classes of words are challenging for young children. For example, they have difficulty understanding that words that express comparisons—tall and short or high and low—are relative in nature and are used in comparing one object to another. Thus, the context defines their meaning, such that calling an object tall is often meant in relation to another object that is short. Children may erroneously interpret *tall* as referring to all tall things and therefore miss the relative nature of the term (Ryalls, 2000). Children also have difficulty with words that express relative place and time, such as *here, there, now, yesterday,* and *tomorrow.* Despite these errors, children make great advances in vocabulary, learning thousands of words each year.

Early Grammar

Young children quickly learn to combine words into sentences in increasingly sophisticated ways that follow the complex rules of grammar (de Villiers & de Villiers, 2014). Three-year-old children tend to use plurals, possessives, and past tense (Park, Yelland, Taffe, & Gray, 2012). They also tend to understand the use of pronouns such as *I, you,* and *we.* Similar to telegraphic speech, their sentences are short, leaving out words like *a* and *the.* However, their speech is more sophisticated than telegraphic speech because some pronouns, adjectives, and prepositions are included. Four- and 5-year-olds use four- to five-word sentences and can express declarative, interrogative, and imperative sentences (Turnbull & Justice, 2016). Context influences the acquisition of syntax. Four-year-old children will use more complex sentences with multiple clauses, such as "I'm resting because I'm tired," if their parents use such sentences (Huttenlocher, Vasilyeva, Cymerman, & Levine, 2002). Parental conversations and support for language learning are associated with faster and more correct language use (MacWhinney, 2015). Children often use run-on sentences, in which ideas and sentences are strung together.

"See? I goed on the slide!" called out Leona. **Overregularization errors** such as Leona's are very common in young children. They occur because young children are still learning exceptions to grammatical rules. Overregularization errors are grammatical mistakes that young children make because they are applying grammatical rules too stringently (Marcus, 2000). For example, to create a plural noun, the rule is to add *s* to the word. However, there are many exceptions to this rule. Overregularization is expressed when children refer to *foots, gooses, tooths,* and *mouses,* which illustrates that the child understands and is applying the rules. Adult speakers find this usage awkward, but it is actually a sign of the child's increasing grammatical sophistication. And despite all of the common errors young children make, one study of 3-year-olds showed that nearly three quarters of their utterances were grammatically correct. The most common error was in making tenses (e.g., *eat/eated, fall/falled*) (Eisenberg, Guo, & Germezia, 2012). By the end of the preschool years, most children use grammar rules appropriately and confidently.

Private Speech

As Leroy played alone in the corner of the living room, he pretended to drive his toy car up a mountain and said to himself, "It's a high mountain. Got to push it all the way up. Oh no! Out of gas. Now they will have to stay here." Young children like Leroy often talk aloud to themselves, with no apparent intent to communicate with others. This self-talk, called **private speech,** accounts for 20% to 50% of the utterances of children ages 4 to 10 (Berk, 1986).

Private speech serves developmental functions. It is thinking, personal speech that guides behavior (Vygotsky & Minick, 1987).

Private speech plays a role in self-regulation, which refers to the ability to control one's impulses and appropriately direct behavior; this increases during the preschool years (Berk & Garvin, 1984). Children use private speech to plan strategies, solve problems, and regulate themselves so that they can achieve goals. Children are more likely to use private speech while working on challenging tasks and attempting to solve problems, especially when they encounter obstacles or do not have adult supervision (Winsler, Fernyhough, & Montero, 2009). As children grow older, they use private speech more effectively to accomplish tasks. Children who use private speech during a challenging activity are more attentive and involved and show better performance than children who do not (Alarcón-Rubio, Sánchez-Medina, & Prieto-García, 2014). For example, in one study, 4- and 5-year-old children completed a complex multistep planning task over six sessions. Children who used on-task private speech showed dramatic improvements between consecutive sessions (Benigno, Byrd, McNamara, Berg, & Farrar, 2011).

During elementary school, children's private speech becomes a whisper or a silent moving of the lips (Manfra & Winsler, 2006). Private speech is the child's thinking and eventually becomes internalized as *inner speech,* or word-based internal thought, a silent internal dialogue that individuals use every day to regulate and organize behavior (Al-Namlah, Meins, & Fernyhough, 2012).

However, there is some evidence that private speech may not be as private as suggested. That is, private speech often occurs in the presence of others. When children ages 2½ to 5 years completed a challenging task in the presence of an experimenter who sat a few feet behind the child, not interacting, or alone, the children engaged in more private speech in the presence of a listener than they did when alone (McGonigle-Chalmers, Slater, & Smith, 2014). This suggests that private speech may have social value and may not be simply a tool for self-regulation.

Although Vygotsky considered the use of private speech a universal developmental milestone, further research suggests that there are individual differences, with some children using private speech little or not at all (Berk, 1992). Preschool girls tend to use more mature forms of private speech than boys. The same is true of middle-income children as compared with low-income children (Berk, 1986). This pattern corresponds to the children's relative abilities in language use. Talkative children use more private speech than do quiet children (McGonigle-Chalmers et al., 2014). Bright children tend to use private speech earlier, and children with learning disabilities tend to continue its use later in development (Berk, 1992). One of the educational implications of private speech is that parents and teachers must understand that talking to oneself or inaudible muttering is not misbehavior but, rather, indicates an effort to complete a difficult task or self-regulate behavior.

Finally, young children's transition from audible private speech to internalization accompanies advances in theory of mind, an awareness of how the mind works, and they are better able to consider other people's perspectives, which helps them become more effective in communicating their ideas (de Villiers & de Villiers, 2014). Preschoolers who are aware of their own private speech are better at using language to communicate their needs, use more private speech, and display more understanding of deception than those who are less aware of their use of private speech (Manfra & Winsler, 2006).

> ### THINKING IN CONTEXT 7.4
>
> 1. How might advances in language development influence other domains of development, such as social or cognitive development?
>
> 2. Given what we know about private speech, what advice do you give to parents and teachers?

MORAL DEVELOPMENT IN EARLY CHILDHOOD

» LO 7.5 **Contrast social learning and cognitive-developmental perspectives on moral development in early childhood.**

Young children's cognitive capacities and skills in theory of mind influence moral reasoning, how they view and make judgments in their social world (Skitka, Bauman, & Mullen, 2016). Two-year-old children classify behavior as good or bad. They respond with distress when viewing or experiencing aggressive or potentially harmful actions (Kochanska, Casey, & Fukumoto, 1995). By age 3, children judge a child who knocks another child off a swing intentionally as worse than one who does so accidentally (Yuill & Perner, 1988). Four-year-old children can understand the difference between truth and lies (Bussey, 1992). By age 5, children are aware of many moral rules, such as those regarding lying and stealing. They also demonstrate conceptions of justice or fairness (e.g., "It's my turn," "Hers is bigger," "It's not fair!"). How do these capacities develop?

There are many perspectives on moral development, as discussed in later chapters. Here we consider two classic views of moral development: social learning theory and cognitive-developmental theory. Both consider a young child's moral values and behavior as first influenced by outside factors. With development, moral values become internalized and moral behavior becomes guided by inner standards.

Social Learning Theory

Social learning theory views all behavior, including moral behavior, as acquired through reinforcement and modeling (Bandura, 1977; Grusec, 1992). Bandura and McDonald (1963) demonstrated that the moral judgments of young children could be modified through a training procedure involving social reinforcement and modeling. Parents and others naturally dole out reinforcement and punishment that shapes the child's behavior. Modeling also plays a role in children's moral development. Adults and other children serve as models for the child, demonstrating appropriate (and sometimes not!) actions and verbalizations. When children observe a model touching a forbidden toy, they are more likely to touch the toy. Some research suggests that children who observe a model resisting temptation are less likely to do so themselves (Rosenkoetter, 1973). However, models are more effective at encouraging rather than inhibiting behavior that violates a rule or expectation. Children are more likely to follow a model's transgressions rather than his or her appropriate behavior.

Children are more likely to imitate behavior when the model is competent and powerful (Bandura, 1977). They are also more likely to imitate a model that is perceived as warm and responsive rather than cold and distant (Yarrow, Scott, & Waxler, 1973). Over the course of early childhood, children develop internalized standards of conduct based on reinforcements, punishments, and observations of models (Bandura, 1986; Mussen & Eisenberg-Berg, 1977). Those adopted standards and moral values are then internalized and used by children as guides for behavior (Grusec & Goodnow, 1994). In this way, children's behavior is shaped to conform with the rules of society.

Cognitive-Developmental Theory

The cognitive-developmental perspective views moral development through a cognitive lens and examines reasoning about moral issues: Is it ever right to steal even if it would help another person? Is lying ever acceptable? Similar to cognitive development, children are active in constructing their own moral understanding through social experiences with adults and peers (Smetana, 1995; Smetana & Braeges, 1990). Young children's reasoning about moral problems changes with development as they construct concepts about justice and fairness from their interactions in the world (Gibbs, 1991, 2003).

Heteronomous Morality

Cognitive-developmental theorist Jean Piaget (Piaget, 1932) studied children's moral development—specifically, how children understand rules. He observed children playing marbles, a common game played in every schoolyard during Piaget's time, and asked them questions about the rules. What are the rules to the game? Where do the rules come from? Have they always been the same? Can they be changed? Piaget found that preschool-age children's play was not guided by rules. The youngest children engaged in solitary play without regard for rules, tossing the marbles about in random ways. Piaget posited that moral thinking develops in stages similar to those in his theory of cognition.

By 6 years of age, children enter the first stage of Piaget's theory of morality, **heteronomous morality** (also known as the *morality of constraint*). In this stage, as children first become aware of rules, they view them as sacred and unalterable. For example, the children interviewed by Piaget believed that people have always played marbles in the same way and that the rules cannot be changed. At this stage, moral behavior is behavior that is consistent with the rules set by authority figures. Young children see rules, even those created in play, as sacred, absolute, and unchangeable; they see behavior as either right or wrong; and they view the violation of rules as meriting punishment regardless of intent (DeVries & Zan, 2003; Nobes & Pawson, 2003). Young children

By 6 years of age, children become aware of rules, and they view them as sacred and unalterable. Children interviewed by Piaget believed that marbles are always played in the same way and that the rules cannot be changed. In the heteronomous stage, children believe that moral behavior is behavior that is consistent with the rules set by authority figures.
iStock/Yamtono_Sardi

may proclaim, without question, that there is only one way to play softball: As their coach advocates, the youngest children must be first to bat. Preschoolers will hold to this rule, explaining that it is simply the "right way" to play.

Preconventional Reasoning

Lawrence Kohlberg (1969, 1976) investigated moral development by posing hypothetical dilemmas about justice, fairness, and rights that place obedience to authority and law in conflict with helping someone. For example, is stealing ever permissible—even in order to help someone? Individuals' responses change with development; moral reasoning progresses through a universal order of stages representing qualitative changes in conceptions of justice. Young children who display cognitive reasoning at the preoperational stage are at the lowest level of Kohlberg's scheme: **preconventional reasoning.** Similar to Piaget, Kohlberg argued that young children's behavior is governed by self-interest, avoiding punishment and gaining rewards. "Good" or moral behavior is a response to external pressure. Young children have not internalized societal norms, and their behavior is motivated by desires rather than internalized principles. We will examine Kohlberg's perspective in greater detail when we discuss later childhood. Similar to cognitive development, children are active in constructing their own moral understanding through social experiences with adults and peers (Smetana, 1995; Smetana & Braeges, 1990).

Conceptions of Moral, Social, and Personal Issues

Social experiences—disputes with siblings over toys, for example—help young children develop conceptions about justice and fairness (Killen & Nucci, 1995). As early as 3 years of age, children can differentiate between moral imperatives, which concern people's rights and welfare, and social conventions, or social customs (Smetana & Braeges, 1990). For example, they judge stealing an apple, a moral violation, more harshly than violating a social convention, such as eating with one's fingers (Smetana, 1995; Turiel, 1998). In one study, 3- and 4½-year-old children viewed an interchange in which one puppet struggled to achieve a goal, was helped by a second puppet, and was violently hindered by a third puppet. When asked to distribute biscuits, the 4½-year-olds but not 3-year-olds were more likely to give more biscuits to the helper than the hinderer puppet. Most explained the unequal distribution by referring to the helper's prosocial behavior or the hinderer's antisocial behavior (Kenward & Dahl, 2011). In addition to moral and conventional issues,

Culture and Theory of Mind

As children develop, they show improvements in theory of mind and get better at taking other people's perspectives and communicating with them. Cultural differences in social norms might influence children's emerging understanding of the mind. Collectivist cultures emphasize the community, whereas individualist cultures focus on the needs of the individual. These differing perspectives may influence how children come to understand mental states as well as their ability to take their perspectives (Taumoepeau, 2015). For example, children from Japan tend to show delayed development on false-belief tasks compared with Western children (Wellman, Cross, & Watson, 2001). When researchers probed children's understanding of the false-belief task by asking them to explain why the actor searched in the wrong location for his chocolate, Japanese children failed to use thoughts as explanations. Instead of giving explanations associated with mental states, such as, "He didn't know it was moved," Japanese children provided justifications that referenced the physical situation (e.g., "The chocolate is now in a different place") or interpersonal factors (e.g., "He promised to do so"). The findings suggest a cultural difference in mind reading, whereby Japanese children who are raised with collectivist values focus less on an actor's mental states and more on his physical and social situation when answering questions about his behavior.

Culture shapes children's thinking. A study of 8-year-old children from Peru used a culturally appropriate version of the Band-Aid box task in which a sugar bowl contained tiny potatoes (Vinden, 1996). At first the children believed the bowl contained sugar. After learning that it contained potatoes, they answered typical false-belief questions incorrectly, predicting that others would respond that the bowl contained potatoes. Even at age 8, well after Western children succeed on similar tasks, the Peruvian children responded incorrectly, unable to explain why others might initially believe that the bowl contained sugar and be surprised to learn otherwise. One explanation is that the children in this study were raised in an isolated farming village where farmers worked from dawn to dusk and there was no reason or time for deception (Vinden, 1996). The Peruvian children's culture did not include ideas such as false belief, or deceiving others, as their day-to-day world was concerned more with tangible activities and things rather than considerations of people's thoughts.

Other research with Samoan and Vanuatu children of the South Pacific has confirmed the relevance of culture on theory of mind. Samoan children ages 3 to 14 years showed delayed development in theory of mind and a prolonged transition to succeeding on theory of mind tasks relative to Western samples (Dixson, Komugabe-Dixson, Dixson, & Low, 2018; Mayer & Träuble, 2015). Samoan and Vanuatu children's slow progression on theory of mind tasks is consistent with the Pacific Island doctrine of opacity of mind (Slaughter & Perez-Zapata, 2014). Samoan and Vanuatu cultures deemphasize internal mental states as explanations for behavior. Samoan and Vanuatu children, therefore, are not exposed to discussions about the mind. They get little experience considering other people's thoughts. Research with English-speaking Western samples has shown that conversations about people's thoughts predict children's understanding of false beliefs (Slaughter, Peterson, & Mackintosh, 2007). Therefore, Samoan and Vanuatu children's delayed success on false-belief tasks is likely a result of their culture's views. In support of this idea is a study of Pacific families living in New Zealand, in which mothers with a stronger Pacific cultural identity referred to beliefs less often when talking to their children than mothers whose Pacific identities were weaker (Slaughter & Perez-Zapata, 2014; Taumoepeau, 2015). Samoan and Vanuatu children may be relatively slow to attribute false beliefs because they take longer to recognize that such beliefs exist relative to cultures where minds are less opaque. Interestingly, however, Vanuatu children's performance varied by context. Vanuatu children who lived in towns showed more advanced performance than those who lived in rural settings, suggesting that the social contexts within a given cultural setting also influence how children come to understand the nature of people's thoughts (Dixson et al., 2018).

What Do You Think?

1. Is the development of theory of mind universally important? That is, is theory of mind important in all cultures? How might context determine the relevance of theory of mind?

2. How does theory of mind contribute to moral reasoning and behavior? ●

between ages 3 and 5, children come to differentiate personal issues, matters of personal choice that do not violate rights, across home and school settings (Turiel & Nucci, 2017). Individuals, including preschoolers, believe that they have control over matters of personal choice, unlike moral issues whose violations are inherently wrong.

Cross-cultural research suggests that children in diverse cultures in Europe, Africa, Asia, Southeast Asia, and North and South America differentiate moral, social conventional, and personal issues (Killen, McGlothlin, & Lee-Kim, 2002; Turiel, 1998; Yau & Smetana, 2003). However, cultural differences in socialization contribute to children's conceptions.

For example, a study of Chinese children ages 3 to 4 and 5 to 6 showed that, similar to Western children, the Chinese children overwhelmingly considered personal issues as permissible and up to the child, rather than the adults. The children's consideration of moral transgressions varied. The Chinese children tended to focus on the intrinsic consequences of the acts for others' welfare and fairness, as compared with the emphasis on avoiding punishment common in Western samples of preschoolers (Yau & Smetana, 2003). These differences are consistent with cultural preferences for collectivism and individualism. Whereas Western parents tend to emphasize individuality and independence, Chinese parents tend to emphasize children's obligations to the family and community (Chao, 1995; Yau & Smetana, 2003). One study of 4-year-old Chinese children and their mothers showed that mothers consistently drew children's attention to transgressions, emphasizing the consequences for others. The children learned quickly and were able to spontaneously discuss their mothers' examples and strategies, as well as reenact them in their own interactions, and their explanations reflected their own understanding of rules and expectations in their own terms, rather than reflecting simple memorization (Wang, Bernas, & Eberhard, 2008).

How adults discuss moral issues, such as truth telling, harm, and property rights, influences how children come to understand these issues. When adults discuss moral issues in ways that are sensitive to the child's developmental needs, children develop more sophisticated conceptions of morality and advance in their moral reasoning (Janssens & Dekovic, 1997; Walker & Taylor, 1991). As we have seen, there are cultural differences in how people think about moral and conversational issues—and these conceptualizations are communicated, internalized, and transformed by children as they construct their own concepts about morality. Culture also influences how we think about others and our ability to take their perspectives, as discussed in the Cultural Influences on Development feature.

EARLY CHILDHOOD EDUCATION

>> LO 7.6 **Identify and explain various approaches to early childhood education.**

Many children attend kindergarten prior to entering elementary school, but only 15 states require children to complete kindergarten (Education Commission of the States, 2014). Early education is important for children's cognitive, social, and emotional development. Preschool programs provide educational experiences for children ages 2 to 5.

Child-Centered and Academically Centered Preschool Programs

There are two general approaches to early childhood education. **Academically centered preschool programs** emphasize providing children with structured learning environments in which teachers deliver direct instruction on letters, numbers, shapes, and academic skills. **Child-centered preschool programs** take a constructivist approach that encourages children to actively build their own understanding of the world through observing, interacting with objects and people, and engaging in a variety of activities that allow them to manipulate materials and interact with teachers and peers (Kostelnik, Soderman, Whiren, & Rupiper, 2015). Children learn by doing, through play, and learn to problem solve, get along with others, communicate, and self-regulate.

Montessori schools, first created in the early 1900s by the Italian physician and educator Maria

THINKING IN CONTEXT 7.5

1. Evaluate the social learning and cognitive-developmental perspectives on moral development. What are the strengths and weaknesses of each? In your view, is one better able to account for moral development than another? Why or why not?

2. How might cultural values influence moral development? Is moral development culture free (i.e., is it an area in which people around the world show the same developmental progression)? Why or why not?

In this Montessori classroom, children explore and play together.
AP Photo/Lori Wolfe

Brain-Based Education

Effective instruction emphasizes active learning through creative play, artwork, physical activity, and social play.
Washington Post/Getty

Children play an active role in their own cognitive development by interacting with the world. Some educators advocate for brain-based education that capitalizes on children's natural inclinations toward active learning. Brain-based education views learning as multidimensional, including more than academics. In its simplest sense, brain-based education encourages children to develop all aspects of their brains, tapping physical, musical, creative, cognitive, and other abilities. Given that the brain changes with experience, enriched everyday experiences such as learning a musical instrument, role-playing, and expanding vocabulary may alter children's brains.

Neurological researchers, however, are critical of some popular brain-based educational approaches, such as those that emphasize teaching different parts of the brain separately (Howard-Jones, 2014). For example, a common brain-based education instructional strategy is to teach for the left or right lateralized brain. The "left brain" is said to be the "logical" hemisphere, concerned with language and analysis, while the "right brain" is said to be the "intuitive" hemisphere concerned with spatial patterns and creativity (Sousa, 2001). Brain-based learning theorists may then encourage teachers to teach specific hemispheres during adapted lessons. To teach to the left hemisphere, teachers have students engage in reading and writing, while right hemisphere–oriented lessons have students create visual representations of concepts (Sousa, 2001).

Brain researchers, however, are sharply critical of left/right brain teaching because, although the brain is lateralized, it functions as a whole (Howard-Jones, 2014). Language and spatial information—and, for that matter, most other abilities—are processed differently but simultaneously by the two hemispheres (Corballis, Lalueza-Fox, Orlando, Enard, & Green, 2014). It is highly improbable, then, that any given lesson, regardless of analytic or spatial type, can stimulate activation of only one hemisphere.

For this reason, some experts argue that the leap from neurological research to the classroom is large and not supported (Alferink & Farmer-Dougan, 2010). For many researchers, the problem of brain-based education is its reliance on the brain itself and in its oversimplification of complex theories and research (Alferink & Farmer-Dougan, 2010; Busso & Pollack, 2014). Although we have learned much, brain research is in its infancy. Researchers do not know enough about how the brain functions and learns to draw direct inferences about teaching (Bruer, 2008). For example, MRI research illuminates patterns of brain activity, but researchers do not yet conclusively know what those patterns mean or if those patterns of brain activity have implications for behavior (Willis, 2007). Applying these findings to inform education is premature. Many researchers, therefore, find it problematic to state that teaching strategies should be derived from brain research—at least not yet.

On the positive side, however, brain-based education emphasizes active learning. Teachers who foster active learning encourage students to become engaged and participate in their own learning, such as being creative in artwork, physical activity, and story making (Bruer, 2008). Active learning is an important educational strategy. Although many developmental researchers argue that the neurological science behind brain-based education is questionable, the active learning practices that comprise many brain-based learning activities advance children's learning.

What Do You Think?

1. Identify an advantage and a disadvantage to brain-based education.

2. In your view, should preschools emphasize teaching specifically to a specific part of the brain, such as the left or right hemisphere? ●

Montessori (1870–1952), exemplify the child-centered approach, in which children are viewed as active constructors of their own development and are given freedom in choosing their activities.

Teachers act as facilitators, providing a range of activities and materials, demonstrating ways of exploring them, and providing help when the child asks. The Montessori approach is credited with fostering independence, self-regulation, and cognitive and problem-solving skills.

In contrast, problems have been documented with rigid teacher-directed academic programs. Children immersed in such programs sometimes show signs of stress such as rocking, may have less confidence in their skills, and may avoid challenging tasks compared with children who are immersed in more active forms of play-based learning (Stipek, Feiler, Daniels, & Milburn, 1995). Such programs are also negatively associated with reading skills in first grade (Lerkkanen et al., 2016).

Instead of a purely academic approach, many practitioners advocate for a developmentally appropriate practice, which tailors instruction to the age of the child, recognizing individual differences and the need for hands-on active teaching methods (Kostelnik et al., 2015). Teachers provide educational support in the form of learning goals, instructional support, and feedback, but they also emphasize emotional support and help children learn to manage their own behavior (S. Anderson & Phillips, 2017). Moreover, teachers are provided with explicit instruction in how to teach and the teaching strategies needed to support young children's literacy, language, math, social, and self-regulatory development (Markowitz, Bassok, & Hamre, 2018). Responsive child-centered teaching is associated with higher reading and math scores during first grade (Lerkkanen et al., 2016).

Effective early childhood educational practice is influenced by cultural values (Gordon & Browne, 2016). In the United States, a society that emphasizes individuality, a child-centered approach in which children are given freedom of choice is associated with the most positive outcomes (Marcon, 1999). Yet in Japan, the most effective preschools tend to foster collectivist values and are society centered with an emphasis on social and classroom routines, skills, and promoting group harmony (Holloway, 1999; Nagayama & Gilliard, 2005). Japanese preschools prepare children for their roles in society and provide formal instruction in academic areas as well as art, swordsmanship, gymnastics, tea ceremonies, and Japanese dance. Much instruction is teacher directed, and children are instructed to sit, observe, and listen. Teachers are warm but address the group as a whole rather than individuals. This structured approach is associated with positive outcomes in Japanese children (Holloway, 1999; Nagayama & Gilliard, 2005), illustrating the role of culture in influencing outcomes of early childhood education. Even within a given country such as the United States, there exist many ethnicities and corresponding cultures, such as those of Native Americans and Mexican Americans. In each case, instruction that is informed by an understanding of children's home and community culture fosters a sense of academic belongingness that ultimately influences academic achievement (Gilliard & Moore, 2007; Gordon & Browne, 2016).

In Western countries, children spend most of their day at school and, aside from household chores such as picking up their toys or cleaning their dinner plates, work is not a part of the typical Western child's day. Most children are segregated from adult work and know little about their parents' workplace. Some educators advocate for applying neuroscience findings to improve early childhood education, as discussed in the Brain and Biological Influences on Development feature.

Early Childhood Education Interventions

Recognizing that young children's developmental needs extend beyond education, one of the most successful early childhood education and intervention programs in the United States, **Project Head Start,** was created by the federal government to provide economically disadvantaged children with nutritional, health, and educational services during their early childhood years, prior to kindergarten (Ramey & Ramey, 1998). Parents of Head Start children also receive assistance, such as education about child development, vocational services, and programs addressing their emotional and social needs (Zigler & Styfco, 2004).

Over the past four decades, a great deal of research has been conducted on the effectiveness of Head Start. The most common finding is that Head Start improves cognitive performance, with gains in IQ and achievement scores in elementary school (Zhai, Brooks-Gunn, & Waldfogel, 2011). Compared with children who do not participate in Head Start, those who do so have greater parental involvement in school, show higher math achievement scores in middle school, are less likely to be held back a grade or have problems with chronic absenteeism

Children who attend Head Start programs have early educational experiences that improve cognitive and social skills and prepare them for kindergarten and elementary school.
David Joles/Zuma/Corbis

in middle school, and are more likely to graduate from high school (Duncan, Ludwig, & Magnuson, 2007; Joo, 2010; Phillips, Gormley, & Anderson, 2016). Head Start is associated with other long-lasting social and physical effects, such as gains in social competence and health-related outcomes, including immunizations (Huston, 2008). Yet some research has suggested that the cognitive effects of Head Start may fade over time such that, by late childhood, Head Start participants perform similarly to control group low socioeconomic status children who have not participated in Head Start (U.S. Department of Health and Human Services & Administration for Children and Families, 2010). Early intervention may not compensate for the pervasive and long-lasting effects of poverty-stricken neighborhoods and inadequate public schools (Schnur & Belanger, 2000; Welshman, 2010). At the same time, long-term advantageous effects of attending Head Start include higher graduation rates and lower rates of adolescent pregnancy and criminality for low-income children who attend Head Start compared with their control group peers (Duncan & Magnuson, 2013). Despite these findings, only about one third of poor children are enrolled in Head Start, and this proportion has shrunk over the past decade, as shown in Figure 7.7.

Additional evidence for the effectiveness of early childhood education interventions comes from the Carolina Abecedarian Project and the Perry Preschool Project, carried out in the 1960s and 1970s. Both of these programs enrolled children from families with incomes below the poverty line and emphasized the provision of stimulating preschool experiences to promote motor, language, and social skills as well as cognitive skills, including literacy and math. Special emphasis was placed on rich, responsive adult–child verbal communication as well as nutrition and health services. Children in these programs achieved higher reading and math scores in elementary school than their nonenrolled peers (Campbell & Ramey, 1994). As adolescents, they showed higher rates of high school graduation and college enrollment, as well as lower rates of substance abuse and pregnancy (Campbell, Ramey, Pungello, Sparling, & Miller-Johnson, 2002; Muennig et al., 2011). At ages 30 and 40, early intervention participants showed higher levels of education and income (Campbell et al., 2012; Schweinhart et al., 2005).

The success of early education intervention programs has influenced a movement in the United States toward comprehensive prekindergarten (pre-K). Young children who participate in high-quality pre-K programs enter school with greater readiness to learn and score higher on reading and math tests than their peers (Gormley, Phillips, Adelstein, & Shaw, 2010). About one half of states offer some form of state-funded pre-K without income restrictions (Barnett, Carolan, Squires, Clarke Brown, & Horowitz,

---

FIGURE 7.7

Number of Children (in Thousands) Enrolled in Head Start and Early Head Start, and Children Enrolled as a Percentage of Children in Poverty, 2006–2014

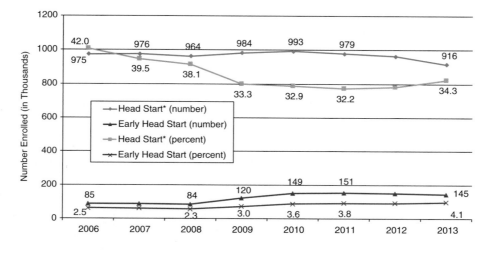

Source: Child Trends Databank (2015).

2015). A few states, including Oklahoma, Georgia, and Florida, provide universal pre-K to all children, and many more states are moving in this direction (Williams, 2015). Beginning in the fall of 2017, New York City initiated a city-funded "3-K for all" program of free full-day preschool to all 3-year-olds (K. Taylor, 2017). Although some research suggests that half-day and more intense full-day programs do not differ in academic and social outcomes, full-day preschool incorporates the benefit of free child care to working parents that is likely of higher quality than they might have otherwise been able to afford (Leow & Wen, 2017). Funding public preschool programs is daunting, but the potential rewards are tremendous.

THINKING IN CONTEXT 7.6

1. Why do you think the gains in cognitive and achievement scores shown by children in Head Start fade over time? From your perspective, what can be done to improve such outcomes?

2. Consider early childhood interventions such as Head Start from the perspective of bioecological theory. Identify factors at the microsystem, mesosystem, and exosystem that programs may address to promote children's development.

 ## APPLY YOUR KNOWLEDGE

Researchers who study deception in children must find unique ways of determining when young children are capable of lying. In one study (Saarni, 1984), children were given a desirable toy and promised that they would receive another. Instead, they received an undesirable gift that was not a toy. The child's facial expressions, nonverbal behavior, and emotional displays were recorded. The researchers were interested in when children would begin to mask their feelings and lie about the desirability of the gift. In another study (Lewis, Stanger, & Sullivan, 1989), young children were left alone in a laboratory environment, told by the researcher not to peek at a toy in the researcher's absence, and later questioned about whether they had peeked at the toy. Other studies (Polak & Harris, 1999) entailed the researcher telling children not to touch the toy and later questioning them about whether they had touched the toy in the researcher's absence.

1. How does cognitive development influence children's ability to deceive?

2. What emotional capacities does lying require?

3. When would you expect young children to become capable of lying? Why?

4. Do you think moral reasoning is related to lying?

5. What are ethical issues entailed in research on deception in children? How might considerations of children's feelings of guilt, shame, or frustration and their developing capacities for self-regulation inform this question?

Visit **edge.sagepub.com/kuther2e** to help you accomplish your coursework goals in an easy-to-use learning environment.

LEARNING OBJECTIVES	SUMMARY	KEY TERMS	IN REVIEW
7.1 Discuss physical development in early childhood.	Growth slows during early childhood. Ethnic differences in patterns of growth are apparent in most Western countries, but there are many individual differences. Young children make great advances in gross motor skills, becoming stronger and more coordinated, permitting them to play harder and engage in more complicated play activities. Fine motor skills permit young children to take responsibility for their own care. Myelination permits quick and complex communication between neurons, leading children's thinking to become faster, more coordinated, and sophisticated.		How do biological factors contribute to growth patterns in early childhood? What changes in the brain occur in early childhood? What gross and fine motor skills emerge in early childhood?

7.2 Compare Piaget's cognitive-developmental and Vygotsky's sociocultural theories on cognitive development in early childhood.	Piaget explained that children in the preoperational stage of reasoning are able to think using mental symbols, but their thinking is limited because they cannot grasp logic. Simplified and nonverbal tasks demonstrate that young children are more cognitively advanced and less egocentric than Piaget posed. From Vygotsky's sociocultural perspective, children's learning occurs through guided participation, scaffolding within the zone of proximal development. With time, the child internalizes the lesson and learns to accomplish the task on his or her own. According to Vygotsky, cognitive development and learning entails active internalization of elements of context.	Preoperational reasoning Egocentrism Three-mountain task Animism Centration Appearance–reality distinction Irreversibility Conservation Guided participation Scaffolding Zone of proximal development	What are characteristics of preoperational reasoning? What are criticisms of Piaget's explanation of thinking in early childhood? Provide an example of scaffolding and the zone of proximal development. What is a criticism of Vygotsky's theory?
7.3 Describe information processing abilities during early childhood.	The ability to sustain attention improves in early childhood through the preschool years. Episodic memory also improves steadily, but young children's limited working memory makes it difficult for them to use memory strategies. Autobiographical memory develops steadily and is accompanied by increases in the length, richness, and complexity of recall memory. Advances in theory of mind enable children to understand that people can believe different things, that beliefs can be inaccurate, and that sometimes people act on the basis of false beliefs. Children thereby become able to lie or use deception in play.	Sustained attention Selective attention Episodic memory Recognition memory Recall memory Memory strategies Scripts Autobiographical memory Theory of mind Metacognition False-belief tasks	How do attention and working memory change in early childhood? What are ways in which episodic memory changes? What is theory of mind and what influences its development?
7.4 Summarize young children's advances in language development.	Young children quickly move from telegraphic speech to combining words into sentences in increasingly sophisticated ways, using multiple elements of speech, such as plurals, adjectives, and the past tense. Parental conversations and support for language learning are associated with faster and more correct language use. At the end of the preschool years, most children use main grammar rules appropriately and confidently.	Logical extension Mutual exclusivity assumption Overregularization errors Private speech	What strategies do children use to increase their vocabulary? Provide an example of overregularization. What is private speech, and how does it contribute to improvements in self-regulation?
7.5 Contrast social learning and cognitive-developmental perspectives on moral development in early childhood.	Social learning theory explains that children develop internalized standards of conduct based on reinforcements and punishments as well as observing others and considering their explanations for behavior. The cognitive-developmental perspective examines reasoning about moral issues, specifically concerns of justice. Kohlberg explained that young children display preconventional moral reasoning, motivated by self-interest. As early as 3 years of age, children in diverse cultures can differentiate between moral concerns from social conventions, or social customs. Social experiences with parents, caregivers, siblings, and peers help young children develop conceptions about justice and fairness.	Heteronomous morality Preconventional reasoning	How does social learning theory explain the development of moral behavior in children? How does the cognitive-developmental perspective account for moral development? Compare heteronomous morality and preconventional reasoning.

| 7.6 Identify and explain various approaches to early childhood education. | Child-centered preschool programs encourage children to manipulate materials, interact with teachers and peers, and learn by doing, through play. Academically oriented preschool programs provide children with structured learning environments through which they learn letters, numbers, shapes, and academic skills via drills and formal lessons. Effective early childhood education is influenced by cultural values. | Academically centered preschool programs

Child-centered preschool programs

Project Head Start | Compare two common approaches to preschool education.

What is Project Head Start?

What are characteristics of successful early intervention programs? |

iStock/Dushyant Kumar

8 Socioemotional Development in Early Childhood

"I'm not a baby anymore. I use my words to do things," 4-year-old Daniel explained to his grandmother. His mother agreed. "Daniel is good at expressing his wants and needs. He doesn't cry as easily as he did when he was younger. My baby is quickly growing into a big boy." Early childhood is a time of transition from the dependence of infancy and toddlerhood to the increasing capacities for autonomy and emotional regulation characteristic of childhood. How do young children learn to understand and control their emotions? Do they experience the same complex emotions that older children and adolescents experience? What is the role of parents in children's emotional and social development? What is the function of play in development? In this chapter, we explore children's experience and understanding of their social and emotional world and how socioemotional development changes over the early childhood years.

Learning Objectives

8.1 Discuss young children's emerging sense of initiative, self-concept, and self-esteem.

8.2 Summarize the development of emotional understanding, regulation, and behavior in early childhood.

8.3 Identify four parenting styles and their associations with child outcomes.

8.4 Compare biological, cognitive, and contextual theoretical explanations of gender role development.

8.5 Explain the function of play and the form it takes during early childhood.

Digital Resources

Explore: Praising Children

Listen: Emotion Regulation in Children

Connect: Parenting Style and Success
▶ **Lives in Context Video 8.1:** Parenting and Discipline

Explore: Gender Cognition in Transgender Children
▶ **Lives in Context Video 8.2:** Gender Schemas and Play Preferences
Explore: Prescribing Play

EMERGING SENSE OF SELF

» LO 8.1   Discuss young children's emerging sense of initiative, self-concept, and self-esteem.

When assigned a task, such as dusting off a bookcase shelf, 3-year-old Shawna calls out, "I'll do it!" After completing the task, she proudly proclaims, "I did it!" The autonomy that Shawna developed during the toddler years has prepared her to master the psychosocial task of the preschool years: developing a sense of initiative (Erikson, 1950).

Psychosocial Development in Early Childhood

During Erikson's third psychosocial stage, **initiative versus guilt,** young children develop a sense of purpose and take pride in their accomplishments. As they develop a sense of initiative, young children make plans, tackle new tasks, set goals (e.g., climbing a tree, writing their name, counting to 10), and work to achieve them, persisting enthusiastically in tasks, whether physical or social, even when frustrated (Lambert & Kelley, 2011).

Much of the work of this stage occurs through play. During play, young children experiment and practice new skills in a safe context and learn to work cooperatively with other children to achieve common goals. Children in all societies practice adult roles in play, such as mother, father, doctor, teacher, and police officer (Gaskins, 2014). For example, Hopi Indian children pretend to be hunters and potters, and the Baka of West Africa pretend to be hut builders and spear makers (Roopnarine, Lasker, Sacks, & Stores, 1998). The sense of pride that children feel from accomplishment fuels their play and fosters curiosity. Children become motivated to concentrate, persist, and try new experiences, such as climbing to the top of the monkey bars. Through play, children also learn how to manage their emotions and develop self-regulation skills (Goldstein & Lerner, 2018). Cultures differ in their expectations for children and the opportunities by which children can develop a sense of initiative and pride, as discussed in the Cultural Influences on Development feature.

During early childhood, children come to identify with their parents and internalize parental rules. Young children feel guilt when they fail to uphold rules and when they fail to achieve a goal. If parents are controlling—not permitting children to carry out their sense of purpose—or are highly punitive, critical, or threatening, children may not develop high standards and the initiative to meet them. Instead, children may be paralyzed by guilt and worry about their inability to measure up to parental expectations. They may develop an overly critical conscience and be less motivated to exert the effort to master new tasks.

Children who develop a sense of initiative demonstrate independence and act purposefully.

Children's Participation in Household Work

Societies differ along many dimensions that have implications for children's socioemotional development. Children in collectivist societies that foster group orientation tend to show more other-oriented behavior than do children in more individualist societies. For example, Israeli children from kibbutz communities, which typically emphasize communal living and high cooperation to meet shared goals, have been shown to display more prosocial, cooperative, and otherwise other-oriented behaviors compared with their urban-dwelling peers.

In a groundbreaking study of children in six cultures, Whiting and Whiting (1975) observed that children's prosocial behavior varied with culture. Children in Mexico and the Philippines were more often observed offering help and support (e.g., by offering food, toys, and information) than were children in Okinawa, India, and the United States. Children in rural Kenya, the most traditional society of those studied, demonstrated the most pronounced levels of helpful behavior. The differences in prosocial behavior are influenced by cultural and contextual differences, such as the tendency for people to live together in extended families. The most prosocial children lived in cultures where the female role was important to the family's economic well-being, and children were assigned chores and responsibilities at an early age and were expected to contribute to the family's well-being.

Cultures vary widely in the degree to which children are expected to aid the family by participating in household and economic work—activities that offer opportunities for prosocial development (Lancy, 2008; Ochs & Izquierdo, 2009). Although Western industrialized societies tend to conceptualize childhood as an innocent, playful period free from labor, children in many societies participate extensively in household and economic labor. In these societies, adults naturally scale down responsibilities to match children's developmental stage and capabilities (Lancy, 2008). Participation in work often begins by children simply being present and watching adults' activities (Paradise & Rogoff, 2009). Young children and toddlers might perform simple tasks in close proximity to adults and later on their own (Ochs & Izquierdo, 2009). For example, Tarong parents express strong expectations for prosocial behavior and expect children as young as 3 or 4 years of age to contribute to household and wage labor by performing simple tasks such as pushing a baby's hammock or helping string tobacco leaves (Guzman, Do, & Kok, 2014). Alternatively, children might engage in work alongside adults but be expected to produce less, as in the case of Mikea children in Madagascar who forage for edibles as part of adult groups but are not expected to accomplish the same level of success (Tucker & Young, 2005). Compared with able-bodied adults, children might gather younger tubers that are easier to dig for or gather and carry fewer nuts and fruits. Older Tarong children, at 6 or 7 years of age, are expected to participate in more sophisticated ways, such as tending to animals or helping to gather weeds, prepare food, or clean the home (Guzman et al., 2014). From these examples, we can see that cultures and economic environments vary dramatically in their expectations for children's behavior, with implications for their development.

What Do You Think?

1. In your view, what role does participation in household work or responsibility play in prosocial development?

2. To what extent and in what ways should parents and other adults require children to participate in household work? What expectations are appropriate, in your view? ●

Participating in household work is one way in which children develop initiative, a sense of purpose and pride in their accomplishments.
iStock/Rawpixel

Their success in taking initiative and the feeling of competence and pride that accompanies it contribute to young children's developing sense of self.

Self-Concept

Three- and 4-year-old children tend to understand and describe themselves concretely, using observable descriptors including appearance, general abilities, favorite activities, possessions, and simple psychological traits (Harter, 2012). For example, Wanda explains, "I'm 4 years old. I have black hair. I'm happy, my doggie is white, and I have a television in my room. I can run really fast. Watch me!" Wanda's self-description, her **self-concept,** is typical of children her age. Soon children begin to include emotions and attitudes in their self-descriptions, such as "I'm sad when my friends can't play," suggesting an emerging awareness of their internal characteristics (R. A. Thompson & Virmani, 2010).

Children's conceptions of themselves are influenced by their interactions with parents and the cultural context in which they are raised. In one study, preschool through second-grade U.S. and Chinese children were asked to recount autobiographical events and describe themselves in response to open-ended questions (Q. Wang, 2004). The U.S. children often provided detailed accounts of their experiences. They focused on their own roles, preferences, and feelings and described their personal attributes and inner traits positively. In contrast, Chinese children provided relatively skeletal accounts of past experiences that focused on social interactions and daily routines. They often described themselves in neutral or modest tones, referring to social roles and context-specific personal characteristics. These differences are consistent with cultural values of independence in the United States and collectivism in China. In another study, U.S. preschool children reported feeling more sadness and shame in response to failure and more pride in response to success than did Japanese preschool children (Lewis, Takai-Kawakami, Kawakami, & Sullivan, 2010). The Japanese preschool children displayed few negative emotions in response to failure but showed self-conscious embarrassment in response to success. Culture, then, influences how children come to define and understand themselves and even the emotions with which they self-identify (R. A. Thompson & Virmani, 2010).

Self-Esteem

Young children tend to evaluate themselves positively. That is, they generally have a high sense of **self-esteem.** For example, 3-year-old Dorian exclaims, "I'm the smartest! I know all my ABCs! Listen! A, B, C, F, G, L, M!" Like Dorian, many young children are excited but also unrealistically positive about their abilities, underestimating the difficulty of tasks and believing that they will always be successful (Harter, 2012). Preschoolers often fail to recognize deficits in their abilities and tend to view their performance favorably, even when it is not up to par (Boseovski, 2010). Even after failing at a task several times, they often continue to believe that the next try will bring success.

Young children's overly optimistic perspective on their skills can be attributed to their cognitive development, attachment with caregivers, and the overwhelmingly positive feedback they usually receive when they attempt a task (Goodvin, Meyer, Thompson, & Hayes, 2008). These unrealistically positive expectations serve a developmental purpose: They contribute to young children's growing sense of initiative and aid them in learning new skills. Young children maintain their positive views about themselves because they do not yet engage in **social comparison.** In other words, they do not compare their performance with that of other children. With advances in cognition and social experience, children begin to learn their relative strengths and weaknesses, and their self-evaluations become more realistic (Rochat, 2013). Between ages 4 and 7, children's self-evaluations become linked with their performance. For example, in one study, children's self-evaluations declined when they failed tasks assigned by an adult as well as those they perceived as important (Cimpian, Hammond, Mazza, & Corry, 2017). Sensitive parenting that supports children's attempts at difficult tasks emphasizes the value of effort and helps children identify and take pride in success that promotes self-esteem.

> **THINKING IN CONTEXT 8.1**
>
> Recall from Chapter 1 that individuals are active in their development, influencing the world around them. How might children's psychosocial development and their emerging sense of self illustrate this principle of lifespan development?

EMOTIONAL DEVELOPMENT IN EARLY CHLIDHOOD

» LO 8.2 Summarize the development of emotional understanding, regulation, and behavior in early childhood.

Young children's advances in cognitive development and growing sense of self influence the emotions they show and the contexts in which they display these emotions. Moreover, young children come to understand people and social relationships in more complex ways, leading to new opportunities for emotional development. Emotional development includes an increasing awareness and management of emotion, as well as an ability to recognize others' emotions and infer causes and consequences of others' emotions (Camras & Halberstadt, 2017).

Emotional Understanding

Donald begins to cry as his mother leaves, dropping him off at preschool. Watching Donald, Amber explains to her mother, "Donald is sad because he misses his mommy," and she brings Donald a toy. "Don't be sad," she says. By 3 to 4 years of age, children recognize and name emotions based on their expressive cues. By age 4, children begin to understand that external factors (such as losing a toy) can affect emotion and can predict a peer's emotion and behavior (such as feeling sad and crying or feeling angry and hitting things) (Goodvin, Thompson, & Winer, 2015).

The emergence of theory of mind has profound implications for emotional development. As children begin to take other people's perspectives, they can apply their understanding of emotions to understand and help others, such as recognizing that a sibling is sad and offering a hug. Children's growing understanding of the mind leads them to appreciate the role of internal factors, such as desires, on emotion and behavior (Wellman, 2017). By age 5, most children understand that desire can motivate emotion, and many understand that people's emotional reactions to an event can vary based on their desires.

Theory of mind influences the development and expression of self-conscious emotions, such as pride and guilt. Self-conscious emotions emerge as children become aware of rules and standards that define socially appropriate behavior and that others have expectations for their behavior (Muris & Meesters, 2014). For example, in response to success, children's joy may be accompanied by the self-conscious emotion of pride. Likewise, shame results from recognizing that poor outcomes are the result of their behavior.

Interactions with others play an important role in advancing children's understanding of emotions. When parents talk to their preschoolers about emotions and explain their own and their children's emotions, the children are better able to evaluate and label others' emotions (Camras & Halberstadt, 2017). Preschool teachers also engage in emotion coaching, helping young children to understand the emotions they feel and see in others (Silkenbeumer, Schiller, & Kärtner, 2018). Young children often discuss emotional experiences with parents and peers. They also often enact emotions in pretend sociodramatic play, providing experience and practice in understanding emotions and their influence on social interactions (Goodvin et al., 2015). Pretend play with siblings and peers gives children practice in acting out feelings, considering others' perspectives, and implementing self-control, improving the children's understanding of emotion (Hoffmann & Russ, 2012). In one study, preschoolers' engagement in sociodramatic play predicted their expressiveness, knowledge, and regulation of emotion 1 year later (Lindsey & Colwell, 2013). Children's interactions with siblings offer important opportunities to practice identifying emotions, decoding the causes

of emotions, anticipating the emotional responses of others, and using their emotional understanding to influence their relationships and affect the behavior of others (Kramer, 2014).

Emotion Regulation

Over the course of childhood, children make great strides in regulating their emotions and become better able to manage how they experience and display emotions. Advances in emotion regulation are influenced by cognition, executive function, theory of mind, and language development. By age 4, children can explain simple strategies for reducing emotional arousal, such as limiting sensory input (covering their eyes), talking to themselves ("It's not scary"), or changing their goals ("I want to play blocks," after having been excluded by children who were playing another game) (R. A. Thompson & Goodvin, 2007). Emotion regulation strategies are a response to emotions, change with age, and also influence children's emotional experience (Eisenberg, Spinrad, & Knafo-Noam, 2015).

Parents remain important resources for emotional management in childhood. Mothers' emotional awareness and management skills influence children's emotional regulation skills (Crespo, Trentacosta, Aikins, & Wargo-Aikins, 2017). Parents who are responsive when children are distressed, who frame experiences for children (e.g., by acting cheery during a trip to the doctor), and who explain expectations and strategies for emotional management both model and foster emotion regulation (Sala, Pons, & Molina, 2014). In contrast, dismissive or hostile reactions to children's emotions prevent them from learning how to manage and not be overwhelmed by their emotions (Zeman, Cassano, & Adrian, 2013). Emotion regulation skill is associated with both social competence and overall adjustment (Deneault & Ricard, 2013). Children who are able to direct their attention and distract themselves when distressed or frustrated become well-behaved students and are well liked by peers (McClelland & Cameron, 2011). Emotional regulation is also influenced by physical functioning. The Brain and Biological Influences on Development feature examines the role of sleep in emotional regulation.

Empathy and Prosocial Behavior

In early childhood, young children develop the cognitive and language skills that permit them to reflect on emotions, talk about emotions, and convey feelings of **empathy,** the ability to understand someone's feelings (Stern & Cassidy, 2018). Empathy stems from the perspective-taking ability that emerges with theory of mind. The child must

Sleep and Emotional Regulation in Young Children

Sleep plays an important role in development throughout infancy, childhood, and adolescence and remains important in adulthood (Gómez & Edgin, 2015). We sleep most as infants, and sleep duration naturally declines about 20% from infancy into early childhood (Honaker & Meltzer, 2014). Most young children sleep 10 to 11 hours each night (Magee, Gordon, & Caputi, 2014).

A minority of children (less than 10%) show persistent sleep problems, such as awakening often, difficulty falling asleep, and poor sleep duration (Magee et al., 2014). Sleep problems pose risks to young children's development. For example, when preschoolers who nap during the day are deprived of their usual naptime, they show poorer cognitive and emotion processing and poor self-control (Berger, Miller, Seifer, Cares, & Lebourgeois, 2012; A. L. Miller, Seifer, Crossin, & Lebourgeois, 2015). Persistent sleep deficits are linked with cognitive and neurological difficulties, including problems with attention, working memory, and slower processing speed (Schumacher et al., 2017).

Sleep is influential to young children's socioemotional functioning. Poor sleep is associated with anxiety, depression, hyperactivity, and impulsivity (Keefe-Cooperman & Brady-Amoon, 2014). Persistent sleep problems and insufficient sleep in early childhood may have consequences that continue into the school-age years and beyond, posing long-term risks to development (Schumacher et al., 2017).

Poor sleep may have a cascading effect on development through its influence on brain function. For example, sleep deprivation affects the neural connectivity between the prefrontal cortex and the limbic system, responsible for emotion, resulting in overreactive and exaggerated emotional responses to positive and negative stimuli (Magee et al., 2014). Poor sleep is associated with impaired behavioral and emotional self-regulation

in young children, which can manifest as anxiety, depression, and impulsivity (Vaughn, Elmore-Staton, Shin, & El-Sheikh, 2015). These emotional problems can, in turn, interfere with sleep in a perpetual cycle with increasing negative effects for young children.

One longitudinal study of over 5,000 Australian children followed from infancy through age 9 suggested that sleep problems predicted deficits in emotional regulation across childhood, which in turn affected children's ability to regulate their attention and contributed to ongoing sleep problems (Magee et al., 2014). Children experiencing difficulty with emotional regulation may be preoccupied with attempts to regulate their emotional system, resulting in limited capacity to focus their attention, with implications for learning and social interactions. When children are unable to control their emotions and attention, they are unprepared to cope with social interactions and everyday frustrations—and will have difficulty learning in and out of school.

Parents can promote good sleep habits through the use of a bedtime routine, including a consistent bedtime (before 9:00 p.m.) and nightly bedtime reading (Mindell, Meltzer, Carskadon, & Chervin, 2009). In addition, young children should refrain from caffeinated products, sleep in a room without a television, and avoid the use of computer screens before bed.

What Do You Think?

1. Did you have a sleep routine as a child? How might a routine help children develop good sleep habits?

2. Do you currently have a sleep routine? Think about your nightly routine. In what ways does it prepare you for sleep? Can it be improved?

3. Should adults have bedtime routines similar to young children? Why or why not? ●

imagine another's perspective in order to understand how that person feels (Eisenberg, Spinrad, & Knafo-Noam, 2015). A secure attachment to a caregiver helps children develop the emotional understanding and regulation skills on which empathy depends (Ştefan & Avram, 2018).

Empathy influences how young children make judgments in their social world. Children who score higher on measures of empathy tend to rate moral transgressions involving physical and psychological harm as more serious and are more likely to rate unfairness as more deserving of punishment than other children (Ball, Smetana, & Sturge-Apple,

2017). Children who feel empathy for another person often are primed to engage in **prosocial behavior,** voluntary behavior intended to benefit another (Eisenberg, Spinrad, & Knafo-Noam, 2015). However, sometimes feelings of empathy for distressed others can result in personal distress, leading the child to focus on relieving his or her own distress rather than helping the person in need.

Prosocial Behavior

When does prosocial behavior emerge? A series of research studies using the violation-of-expectation

One example of prosocial behavior is sharing. Sharing becomes more equitable and complex with development.
iStock/FatCamera

method (see Chapter 5) have suggested that infants as young as 3 months may possess simple conceptions of prosocial behavior, such as preferring to look at characters that help rather than hinder others (Van de Vondervoort & Hamlin, 2016). For toddlers as young as 18 months, prosocial behavior is simple, such as the tendency to help adults, even unfamiliar experimenters, by picking up markers that have fallen (R. A. Thompson & Newton, 2013). Between 18 and 24 months of age, toddlers show increasingly prosocial responses to others' emotional and physical distress, but their responses are limited to their own perspective. That is, they tend to offer the aid that they themselves would prefer, such as bringing their own mother to help a distressed peer (Hepach, Vaish, & Tomasello, 2012). Although toddlers are capable of prosocial responding to distressed others, spontaneous prosocial behavior not prompted by adults is rare in toddlerhood (Eisenberg et al., 2015).

At 3½ years of age, children show more complex forms of *instrumental assistance,* or tangible help. Compared to 18-month-old children, 3½-year-olds are more likely to help an adult by bringing a needed object, to do so autonomously without the adult's specific request, and to select an object appropriate to the adult's need (Svetlova, Nichols, & Brownell, 2010). Young children may engage in prosocial behavior for egocentric motives, such as the desire for praise and to avoid punishment and disapproval. With development, children become less egocentric and more aware of others' perspectives. Their prosocial behavior becomes motivated by empathy as well as internalized societal values for good behavior (Eisenberg, Spinrad, & Morris, 2013).

In addition to helping, children display prosocial behavior by sharing. Children's views of sharing change over time. Three-year-old children conceptualize fair sharing as strict equality—for example, each child should get the same amount of candy, no matter what (Damon, 1977; Enright

et al., 1984). Using nonverbal measures, researchers have shown that 3-year-old children identify and react negatively to unfair distributions of stickers, especially if they receive fewer than another child (LoBue, Nishida, Chiong, DeLoache, & Haidt, 2011). Despite endorsing norms of sharing, behavioral studies show that 3-year-old children tend to favor themselves but become more likely to share with age (Smith, Blake, & Harris, 2013). However, sharing is influenced by context. For example, after working together actively to obtain rewards in a collaboration task, most 3-year-old children share equally with a peer (Warneken, Lohse, Melis, & Tomasello, 2011).

Between 3 and 5 years of age, young children show selectivity in sharing. Four- and 5-year-olds believe in an obligation to share, but they often allocate rewards based on observable characteristics, such as age, size, or other obvious physical characteristics (e.g., "The oldest should get more candy"). Often these decisions are based on personal desires and characteristics that adults would deem irrelevant, such as, "Girls should get more because they're girls!" When told that they must make an unequal distribution, 5-year-olds tend to share more with others whom they expect will reciprocate and more with friends than with peers they dislike (Paulus & Moore, 2014). Young children share more with children and adults who show prosocial behaviors such as sharing and helping others (Kuhlmeier, Dunfield, & O'Neill, 2014).

Early childhood prosocial behavior is associated with positive peer relationships, mental health, and social competence in preschool and beyond (Malti & Dys, 2018). Prosocial children tend to show low levels of aggressive and problem behaviors. They tend to be successful in school and score high on measures of vocabulary, reading, and language—perhaps because prosocial children are friendly and engage in interaction with teacher and peers (Eisenberg et al., 2015).

Influences on Prosocial Behavior

Prosocial behavior is influenced by many interacting factors, including biology and genes, family contexts, the larger social context, and the development of reasoning skills. Let's explore each of these influences.

Biological Influences. Genetic factors are thought to contribute to individual differences in prosocial behavior (Waldman et al., 2011). Twin studies, for example, have revealed that adult identical twins show more similar reports of prosocial behavior than do their fraternal twin peers (Knafo-Noam, Uzefovsky, Israel, Davidov, & Zahn-Waxler, 2015). Several genes have been implicated in prosocial

Twins tend to show similar patterns of sharing.
iStock/35007

tendencies, including one that influences the hormone oxytocin, which is associated with attachment and other socioemotional behaviors (Carter, 2014). A child's inborn temperament influences how the child regulates emotion, which is related to feelings of empathy for a distressed child or adult and, in turn, whether empathetic feelings result in personal distress or prosocial behavior (Eisenberg et al., 2015). Children who are unable to successfully regulate their emotions tend to react to distressed others with heightened physiological arousal, including increases in heart rate and brain activity in regions known to process negative emotions, suggesting a feeling of being overwhelmed that can interfere with prosocial responding (J. G. Miller, 2018).

Emotional Influences. Self-conscious emotions, such as guilt and pride, influence prosocial behavior. For example, in response to guilt, 2- and 3-year-olds are motivated to repair damage that they have caused (Vaish, 2018). When 3- and 4-year-old children feel pride in response to an achievement, they are more likely to offer spontaneous help to a person in need (Ross, 2017). Self-conscious emotions and the self-evaluations inherent in them might motivate prosocial behavior in an attempt to maintain an ideal self.

Family Influences. Rich interactions with parents engage the emotions, cognitions, and behaviors critical to prosocial responding (Brownell, 2016). The secure attachment that accompanies warm, sensitive parenting aids in the development of emotional regulation, a predictor of empathy and prosocial responding (Spinrad & Gal, 2018). Parents of prosocial children draw attention to models of prosocial behavior in peers and in media, such as in storybooks, movies, and television programs. As suggested earlier, parents may also describe feelings and model sympathetic concern and the use of language to discuss feelings. Young children whose parents do these things are more likely to use words to describe their thoughts and emotions and attempt to understand others' emotional states (Z. E. Taylor et al., 2013).

Parents also actively encourage prosocial behavior by including young children in their household and caregiving activities (Dahl, 2015). Parents' encouragement of children's participation in household cleanup routines predicts children's willingness to help another adult in a new context (Hammond & Carpendale, 2015). Children's prosocial behavior emerges out of prosocial activity shared with adults, and parental encouragement promotes its development (Brownell, 2016).

At the same time as parents influence children, children play a role in their own development by influencing their parents. One study that followed children from 4½ years of age through sixth grade found that maternal sensitivity influenced children's prosocial behavior and that prosocial behavior, in turn, predicted mothers' subsequent sensitivity, suggesting that mothers and children influence each other (Newton, Laible, Carlo, Steele, & McGinley, 2014). Children who are kind, compassionate, and helpful elicit responsive and warm parenting from their mothers.

Siblings offer opportunities to learn and practice helping and other prosocial behavior. Older siblings who display positive emotional responsiveness promote preschoolers' emotional and social competence. Researchers have observed that children with siblings tend to develop a theory of mind earlier than those without siblings (Kramer, 2014). As we have seen, the perspective-taking and cognitive skills that comprise theory of mind promote emotional understanding and prosocial behavior.

Contextual Influences. The broader social world also influences the development of prosocial behavior. Collectivist cultures, in which people live with extended families, work is shared, and the maintenance of positive relationships with others is emphasized, tend to promote prosocial values and behavior more so than do cultures that emphasize the individual, as is common in most Western cultures (Eisenberg et al., 2015). One study of mother–child dyads in Japan and the United States found that the Japanese mothers of 4-year-old children tended to emphasize mutuality in their interactions, stressing the relationship (e.g., "This puzzle is difficult for us. Let's see if we can solve it."). In contrast, the U.S. mothers tended to emphasize individuality (e.g., "This puzzle is hard for you, isn't it? Let's see you try again.") (Dennis, Cole, Zahn-Waxler, & Mizuta, 2002). These different styles influence how children display empathy, whether as sharing another's emotion or simply understanding another's emotion.

These cultural differences extend to children's reasons for sharing. When Filipino and American fifth graders were presented with hypothetical scenarios that required them to determine how resources should be shared, both the Filipino and American children preferred equal division of the resources regardless of merit or need (Carson & Banuazizi, 2008). However, the children offered different explanations of their choices. U.S. children emphasized that the characters in the scenario preformed equally and therefore deserved equal amounts of the resources, reflecting U.S. culture's emphasis on individuality and merit. Filipino children, on the other hand, tended to be more concerned with the interpersonal and emotional consequences of an unequal distribution, in line with their culture's emphasis on the collective and the importance of interpersonal relationships (Carson & Banuazizi, 2008). Norms and expectations for children vary dramatically with culture.

Aggression

Although their capacities for empathy and prosocial responses increase, young children commonly show **aggressive behavior,** behavior that harms or violates the rights of others. Most infants and children engage in some physically aggressive behaviors—hitting, biting, or kicking—some of the time (Tremblay et al., 2004). Some aggression is normal and not an indicator of poor adjustment.

The most common form of aggression seen in infancy and early childhood is **instrumental aggression,** aggression used to achieve a goal, such as obtaining a toy. Instrumental aggression is often displayed as physical aggression (Hay, Hurst, Waters, & Chadwick, 2011). For example, a child who grabs a crayon out of another child's hand is often motivated to obtain the crayon, not to hurt the other child. In addition to toys, preschool children often battle over space ("I was sitting there!"). Instrumental aggression increases from toddlerhood into early childhood, around age 4, as children begin to play with other children and act in their own interests. Indeed, instrumental aggression usually occurs during play. It is often displayed by sociable and confident preschoolers, suggesting that it is a normal aspect of development.

By ages 4 to 5, most children develop the self-control to resist aggressive impulses and the language skills to express their needs. Now physical aggression declines and verbal aggression becomes more frequent (Eisner & Malti, 2015). Verbal aggression is a form of **relational aggression,** intended to harm others' social relationships (Ostrov & Godleski, 2010). In preschool and elementary school, relational aggression often takes the form of name calling and excluding peers from play (Pellegrini & Roseth, 2006).

Most children learn to inhibit aggressive impulses; however, a small minority of children show high levels of aggression (e.g., repeated hitting, kicking, biting) that increase during childhood (Tremblay, 2014). Young children who show high levels of aggression are more likely to have experienced coercive parenting, family dysfunction, and low income; they are also more likely to have mothers with a history of antisocial behavior and early childbearing (F. Wang, Christ, Mills-Koonce, Garrett-Peters, & Cox, 2013). Children who do not develop the impulse control and self-management skills to inhibit their aggressive responses may continue and escalate aggressive behavior over the childhood years and show poor social and academic outcomes during the school age years and beyond (Gower, Lingras, Mathieson, Kawabata, & Crick, 2014).

THINKING IN CONTEXT 8.2

1. How do children learn strategies for self-control? How might parents, child care providers, and preschool teachers help children understand and learn to regulate their emotions?

2. What role might peers and siblings play in helping children learn to manage their impulses?

3. How might the development of prosocial and aggressive behavior reflect the interaction of nature (biology) and nurture (context)? In your view, does either hold more weight? Why or why not?

In the preschool years, children may engage in instrumental aggression when they want to obtain an object, such as the toy in this picture.
iStock/Zabavna

PARENTING

» LO 8.3   Identify four parenting styles and their associations with child outcomes.

The relationship that develops between parents and children has a tremendous influence on children's social and emotional development. **Parenting style** is the emotional climate of the parent–child relationship—the degree of warmth, support, and boundaries that parents provide. Parenting style influences parents' efficacy, their relationship with their children, and their children's development.

Parenting Styles

Parenting styles are displayed as enduring sets of parenting behaviors that occur across situations to form childrearing climates. These behaviors combine warmth and acceptance with limits and rule setting in various degrees. In a classic series of studies, Diana Baumrind (1971, 2013) examined 103 preschoolers and their families through interviews, home observations, and other measures. She identified several parenting styles and their effects on children (see Table 8.1, Figure 8.1).

Authoritarian Parenting

In Baumrind's classification, parents who use an **authoritarian parenting style** emphasize behavioral control and obedience over warmth. Children are to conform to parental rules without or question, simply "because I say so." Violations are often accompanied by forceful punishment, such as yelling, threatening, or spanking. Parents with an authoritarian style are less supportive and warm and more detached, perhaps even appearing cold.

Children raised by authoritarian parents tend to be withdrawn, mistrustful, anxious, and angry (Rose, Roman, Mwaba, & Ismail, 2018). They show more behavioral problems than other children, both as preschoolers and as adolescents (Baumrind, Larzelere, & Owens, 2010). Children reared in authoritarian homes tend to be disruptive in their interactions with peers and react with hostility in response to frustrating peer interactions (Gagnon et al., 2013). A recent meta-analysis of over 1,400 studies concluded that harsh parenting and psychological control show the strongest associations with behavior problems in childhood and adolescence (Pinquart, 2017). Moreover, parents and children influence each other. As parenting becomes more harsh, children tend to display more behavior problems, which may

---

TABLE 8.1

Parenting Styles

PARENTING STYLE	WARMTH	CONTROL
Authoritative	High	Firm, consistent, coupled with discussion
Authoritarian	Low	High, emphasizing control and punishment without discussion or explanation
Permissive	High	Low
Indifferent	Low	Low

FIGURE 8.1

Parenting Styles

Parenting style is an important influence on development. Authoritarian parenting emphasizes rigid strictness over warmth. Uninvolved parenting can make children feel invisible. Extreme forms of uninvolved parenting constitute neglect.

Source: iStock/Signature

Physical Punishment

Time-out removes the child from overstimulating situations and stops inappropriate behaviors without humiliating him or her. Time-out is effective when it is accompanied by explanation and a warm parent–child relationship.
Cynthia Dopkin/Science Source

Physical punishment—spanking—is against the law in over 50 countries (Grogan-Kaylor, Ma, & Graham-Bermann, 2018), yet hotly contested in many countries. For example, parents in many places within Asia, Africa, the Middle East, and North and South America report that spanking is acceptable, appropriate, and sometimes necessary (Hicks-Pass, 2009; Oveisi et al., 2010). In the United States, the majority of adults report that they were spanked as children without harm, and 80% of a sample of U.S. parents report spanking their young children (Gershoff, 2013). Why the controversy on spanking if it occurs in most cultures?

Research suggests that physical punishment tends to increase compliance only temporarily. Furthermore, physical punishment is associated with behavior problems at ages 1 and 3 and continued

behavior problems at age 5 (Choe, Olson, & Sameroff, 2013; Lee, Altschul, & Gershoff, 2013). Physical punishment is also damaging to the parent–child relationship. When a parent loses self-control and yells, screams, or hits a child, the child may feel helpless, become fearful of the parent, avoid him or her, and become passive. Parental use of spanking is associated with internalizing problems (such as anxiety and depression), externalizing problems (such as aggression), impaired cognitive ability, and low self-esteem in childhood and adolescence and mental health problems and antisocial behavior in adulthood (Balan, Dobrean, Roman, & Balazsi, 2017; Coley, Kull, & Carrano, 2014; Gershoff & Grogan-Kaylor, 2016).

Moreover, physical punishment can foster the very behavior that parents seek to stop. Parents often punish children for aggressive behavior, yet physical punishment models the use of aggression as an effective way of resolving conflict and other problems, teaching children that might makes right (D'Souza, Russell, Wood, Signal, & Elder, 2016). In one recent study, parents who reported using physical discipline were nearly three times as likely to report aggressive behaviors like hitting and kicking in their young children than parents who did not use physical discipline (R. Thompson et al., 2017). In addition, physical punishment tends to become less effective with repeated use and as children grow older (AAP Committee on Psychosocial Aspects of Child and Family Health, 1998). For example, the use of spanking is impractical with teenagers.

What can parents do about their children's undesirable behavior? Is punishment ever permissible and effective? While physical punishment is not generally effective, noncorporal punishment can be effective, in small doses and within specific contexts. Running into the street or touching a hot stove, for example, are behaviors that are dangerous to children or to others. These behaviors must be stopped immediately to prevent injury. To be effective, punishment should occur immediately after the dangerous behavior, be applied consistently, and be clearly connected to the behavior. The purpose of such punishment is to keep the child from engaging in the dangerous behavior, to make him or her comply but not to feel guilt. Time-out, which entails removing a child from the situation and from social contact for a short period of time, is often effective in reducing inappropriate behavior (Morawska & Sanders, 2011). Effective punishment is administered calmly, privately, and within the context of a warm parent–child relationship, and it is accompanied by an explanation so that the child understands the reason for the punishment (Baumrind, 2013).

What Do You Think?

1. Under what circumstances do you think it is appropriate to punish a child? Identify two examples of nonphysical punishment.

2. Considering operant conditioning (review learning theory in Chapter 1), how might you use reinforcement to shape a child's behavior?

3. Suppose that a child receives a punishment, such as time-out, yet continues to repeat the behavior that was punished. Considering operant conditioning, why might the child continue to engage in the forbidden behavior? ●

increase negative interactions with parents. The Applying Developmental Science feature examines the effects of one type of negative parent–child interaction, physical punishment, on children.

Permissive Parenting

Permissive parents are warm and accepting, even indulgent. They emphasize self-expression and have few rules and behavioral expectations for their children. When rules are set, they often are not enforced or are enforced inconsistently. Parents with a **permissive parenting style** often allow children to monitor their own behavior. Autonomy is not granted gradually and in developmentally appropriate ways in permissive households. Instead, children are permitted to make their own decisions at any early age, often before they are able. For example, children may decide their own bedtime or monitor their own screen time. Many children lack the self-regulation capacities to appropriately limit their activity. Preschoolers raised by permissive parents tend to be more socioemotionally immature and show little self-control and self-regulatory capacity compared with their peers (Piotrowski, Lapierre, & Linebarger, 2013). They often tend to be impulsive, rebellious, and bossy, and they show less task persistence, low levels of school achievement, and more behavior problems (Jewell, Krohn, Scott, Carlton, & Meinz, 2008). In short, a permissive parenting style interferes with the development of self-regulatory skills that are needed to develop academic and behavioral competence in childhood and adolescence (Hoeve, Dubas, Gerris, van der Laan, & Smeenk, 2011).

Uninvolved Parenting

Parents with an **uninvolved parenting style** focus on their own needs rather than those of their children. Parents who are under stress, emotionally detached, or depressed often lack time or energy to devote to their children, putting them at risk for an uninvolved parenting style (Baumrind, 2012). Uninvolved parents provide little support or warmth, exert little control, and fail to recognize their children's need for affection and direction. At the extreme, uninvolved parenting is neglectful and a form of child maltreatment. Uninvolved parenting can have negative consequences for all forms of children's development—cognitive, emotional, social, and even physical. For example, young children reared in neglectful homes show less knowledge about emotions than do children raised with other parenting styles (Sullivan, Carmody, & Lewis, 2010).

Authoritative Parenting

The most positive developmental outcomes are associated with what Baumrind termed the **authoritative parenting style.** Authoritative parents are warm and sensitive to children's needs but also are firm in their expectations that children conform to appropriate standards of behavior. While exerting firm, reasonable control, they engage their children in discussions about standards and grant them developmentally appropriate levels of autonomy, permitting decision making that is appropriate to the children's abilities (Baumrind, 2013). When a rule is violated, authoritative parents explain what the children did wrong and impose limited, developmentally appropriate punishments that are closely connected to the misdeed. Authoritative parents value and foster children's individuality. They encourage their children to have their own interests, opinions, and decisions, but ultimately, they control the children's behavior.

Authoritative parents tend to use **inductive discipline** strategies, methods that rely on reasoning

(AAP Committee on Psychosocial Aspects of Child and Family Health, 1998). Examples of inductive methods include helping children find and use words to express their feelings. Another inductive method is to provide children with choices (e.g., peas or carrots), permitting them to feel some control over the situation and be empowered. Parents who use inductive techniques model effective conflict resolution and help children to become aware of the consequences of their actions (Choe et al., 2013). Children are more likely to comply with rules that they understand.

Children of authoritative parents display confidence, self-esteem, social skills, curiosity, and high academic achievement, and they score higher on measures of executive functioning; these positive effects persist throughout childhood into adolescence (Fay-Stammbach, Hawes, & Meredith, 2014; Sosic-Vasic et al., 2017). Parents in a given household often share a common parenting style, but when they do not, the presence of authoritative parenting in at least one parent buffers the negative outcomes associated with the other style and predicts positive adjustment (Hoeve et al., 2011; McKinney & Renk, 2011).

Culture, Context, and Parenting

The strategies parents use to control children's behavior vary with the parent's and child's personalities, the age of the child, the parent–child relationship, and cultural customs and expectations. One concern that researchers have regarding discussions of discipline is that there is not just one effective way to parent. Instead, there are many cultural variations in parenting, and the effectiveness of disciplinary techniques may differ by cultural context (Cauce, 2008).

Expectations for behavior as well as methods of discipline vary with culture. North American parents permit and encourage children to express emotions, including anger, while Japanese parents encourage children to refrain from displaying strong emotions. In one cross-cultural experiment, U.S. preschoolers exposed to situations designed to elicit stress and anger demonstrated more aggressive behaviors than did Japanese children (Zahn-Waxler, Friedman, Cole, Mizuta, & Hiruma, 1996). In comparison with North American mothers, Japanese mothers are more likely to use reasoning, empathy, and disapproval to discipline their children. Such techniques are effective for Japanese mothers because of the strong mother–child relationship and collectivist values that are prevalent in Japan, illustrating the importance of relationships in that culture (Rothbaum, Pott, Azuma, Miyake, & Weisz, 2000).

Chinese parents tend to describe their parenting as relatively controlling and not emphasizing individuality and choice (Chao, 2001). They are

No-nonsense parenting is characterized by vigilant, strict control as well as warmth. African American children often report viewing this style as indicative of parental concern about their welfare and, unlike authoritarian parenting, this style is associated with positive outcomes—especially within challenging community contexts.
JGI/Jamie Grill/Blend/Newscom

directive and view exerting control as a way of teaching children self-control and encouraging high achievement (Huntsinger, Jose, & Larson, 1998). Yet most Chinese parents couple the emphasis on control with warmth (Xu et al., 2005). The combination of warmth and control is linked with cognitive and social competence. As in North American samples, however, excessive control without warmth is associated with depression, social difficulties, and poor academic achievement in Chinese children (Cheah, Leung, Tahseen, & Schultz, 2009).

Is strict control always harmful to North American children? Researchers have identified a disciplinary style common in African American families that combines strict parental control with affection (Tamis-LeMonda, Briggs, McClowry, & Snow, 2009). Sometimes referred to as "no-nonsense parenting," this style stresses obedience and views strict control as important in helping children develop self-control and attentiveness. African American parents who use controlling strategies tend to raise children who are more cognitively mature and socially competent than their peers who are being raised in other ways. This difference is particularly apparent in children reared in low-income homes and communities, where vigilant, strict parenting enhances children's safety (Weis & Toolis, 2010). Whereas physical discipline is associated with behavioral problems in European American children, it appears to protect some African American children from conduct problems in adolescence (Lansford, Deater-Deckard, Dodge, Bates, & Pettit, 2004). The warmth and affection buffer some of the negative consequences of strictness (McLoyd & Smith, 2002; Stacks, Oshio, Gerard, & Roe, 2009). Children's perception of parental discipline and intention is important in determining its effect. Children evaluate parental behavior in light of their culture and the emotional tone of the relationship. African American and low-income children reared in homes with strict but warm parents often see this style of discipline as indicative of concern about their well-being (Lee et al., 2016).

In the United States, it is often difficult to disentangle the effects of culture and neighborhood context on parenting behaviors because African American families are disproportionately represented in disadvantaged neighborhoods. Does strict discipline embody cultural beliefs about parenting? Or is it a response to raising children in a disadvantaged environment (Murry, Brody, Simons, Cutrona, & Gibbons, 2008)? Parental perceptions of danger and their own distress influence how they parent (Cuellar, Jones, & Sterrett, 2013). Parenting behaviors, including discipline, must be considered within a cultural and environmental context, as parenting is "not one size fits all" (Sorkhabi, 2005).

Child Maltreatment

According to the Child Abuse Prevention and Treatment Act, **child maltreatment**, also known as **child abuse,** is any intentional harm to a minor (an individual under 18 years of age), including actions that harm the child physically, emotionally, sexually, and through neglect (U.S. Department of Health and Human Services, 2016). Many children experience more than one form of abuse.

- Physical abuse refers to any intentional physical injury to the child and can include striking, kicking, burning, or biting the child, or any other action that results in a physical impairment of the child.

- Sexual abuse, more common among older children, refers to engaging in any sexual activity, coerced or persuaded, with a child. It also includes inappropriate touching or comments.

- Neglect occurs when a child is deprived of adequate food, clothing, shelter, or medical care.

Each year, there are over 700,000 confirmed cases of abuse or neglect in the United States (U.S. Department of Health and Human Services, 2016). Child maltreatment results in over 1,500 fatalities per year, about three quarters in children younger than 3 years. Parents are the most common perpetrators (in over 80% of cases, on average), with relatives other than parents and unmarried partners of parents constituting an additional 10% of perpetrators (U.S. Department of Health and Human Services, 2016). It is estimated that about 27% of children under the age of 17 have experienced sexual abuse (Kim, Wildeman, Jonson-Reid, & Drake, 2017). Sexual abuse may occur at any time during infancy, childhood, or adolescence, but it is most often reported in early and middle childhood, with about half of cases occurring between ages 4 and 12 (U.S. Department of Health and Human Services, 2013). Although these statistics are alarming, they underestimate the incidence of abuse because many children experience maltreatment that is not reported. Moreover, abuse often is not a one-time event; some children experience maltreatment that persists for years.

Effects of Child Maltreatment

The physical effects of physical maltreatment are immediate, ranging from bruises to broken bones to internal bleeding and more. Some physical effects are long lasting. Child abuse can impair brain development and functioning through physical damage, such as that caused by shaking an infant. Physical harm and prolonged stress can alter the course of brain development, increasing the child's risk for attention-deficit/hyperactivity disorder (ADHD), emotional regulation problems, conduct disorder, and learning and memory difficulties (Cicchetti & Toth, 2015; Hein & Monk, 2017). Maltreated children may display symptoms of **posttraumatic stress disorder (PTSD),** an anxiety disorder that occurs after experiencing a traumatic event and includes flashbacks, nightmares, and feelings of helplessness (Maniglio, 2013).

It follows that child maltreatment and its neurological and emotional consequences may negatively affect cognitive development (Font & Berger, 2014). Preschool children who are abused score lower on measures of school readiness and problem solving. Children who are abused experience difficulty understanding and completing day-to-day schoolwork and demonstrate serious learning difficulties, often resulting in academic failure (Widom, 2014). Teachers report maltreated children as inattentive, uninvolved, passive, and angry, as well as lacking in creativity, initiative, persistence, and confidence.

Maltreatment has negative effects on children. The socioemotional effects are especially daunting and long lasting.
iStock/Giulio Fornasar

The socioemotional effects of child maltreatment are especially daunting and long lasting. Young children who are abused tend to have poor coping skills, low self-esteem, and difficulty regulating their emotions and impulses, and they show more negative affect, such as anger and frustration, and less positive affect than other children (Barth et al., 2007). They tend to have difficulty understanding their own and other people's emotions and often have difficulty making and maintaining friendships (Cicchetti & Banny, 2014).

Children and adolescents who are abused also are at risk for a range of psychological disorders. These include anxiety, eating, and depressive disorders, as well as behavioral problems in adolescence, such as delinquency, teen pregnancy, illicit drug use, and risky behavior (Carlson, Oshri, & Kwon, 2015; Cecil, Viding, Fearon, Glaser, & McCrory, 2017; Jones et al., 2013).

Risk Factors for Child Maltreatment

Risk factors for child abuse exist at all ecological levels: the child, parent, community, and society, as

---

FIGURE 8.2

Bioecological Perspective of Risk Factors for Child Maltreatment

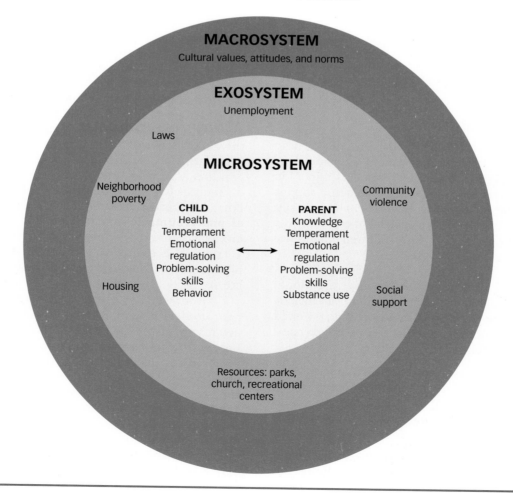

shown in Figure 8.2 (Cicchetti, 2016). Certain child characteristics have been found to increase the risk or potential for maltreatment. Children with special needs, such as those with physical and mental disabilities, preterm birth status, or serious illness, require a great deal of care that can overwhelm or frustrate caregivers, placing such children at risk of maltreatment. Similarly, children who are temperamentally difficult, inattentive, or overactive or have other developmental problems are also at risk because they are especially taxing for parents (Font & Berger, 2014).

Parents who engage in child maltreatment tend to perceive their child as stubborn and noncompliant and tend to evaluate the child's misdeeds as worse than they are, leading them to use strict and physical methods of discipline (Casanueva et al., 2010). They often lack knowledge about child development and have unrealistic expectations for their children. They may be less skilled in recognizing emotions displayed on their children's faces; find it difficult to recognize, manage, and express their own feelings appropriately; and have poor impulse control, coping, and problem-solving skills (Wagner et al., 2015). Abuse is more common in homes characterized by poverty, marital instability, and drug and alcohol abuse (Cicchetti & Toth, 2015). Children who are raised in homes in which adults come and go—repeated marriages, separations, and revolving romantic partners—are at higher risk of sexual abuse. However, sexual abuse also occurs in intact middle-class families. In these families, children's victimization often remains undetected and unreported (Hinkelman & Bruno, 2008).

Community factors, such as inadequate housing, community violence, and poverty, place children at risk for abuse (Cuartas, 2018; Widom, 2014). Neighborhoods with few community-level support resources, such as parks, child care centers, preschool programs, recreation centers, and churches, increase the likelihood of child maltreatment (Molnar et al., 2016). In contrast, neighborhoods with a low turnover of residents, a sense of community, and connections among neighbors support parents and protect against child maltreatment (van Dijken, Stams, & de Winter, 2016).

At the societal level, several factors contribute to the problem of child abuse. Legal definitions of violence and abuse and political or religious views that value independence, privacy, and noninterference in families may influence the prevalence of child abuse within a given society (Tzeng, Jackson, & Karlson, 1991). Social acceptance of violence—for example, as expressed in video games, music lyrics, and television and films—can send the message that violence is an acceptable method of managing conflict. Overall, there are many complex influences on child maltreatment.

Along with recognizing risk factors, it is important to be aware of signs that abuse may be taking place. Table 8.2 provides a nonexhaustive list of signs of

---

TABLE 8.2

Signs of Child Abuse and Neglect

The Child

- Exhibits extremes in behavior, such as overly compliant or demanding behavior, extreme passivity, withdrawal, or aggression.
- Has not received help for physical or medical problems (e.g., dental care, eyeglasses, immunizations) brought to the parents' attention.
- Has difficulty concentrating or learning problems that appear to be without cause.
- Is very watchful, as if waiting for something bad to happen.
- Frequently lacks adult supervision.
- Has unexplained burns, bruises, broken bones, or black eyes.
- Is absent from school often, especially with fading bruises upon return.
- Is reluctant to be around a particular person or shrinks at the approach of a parent or adult.
- Reports injury by a parent or another adult caregiver.
- Lacks sufficient clothing for the weather.
- Is delayed in physical or emotional development.
- States that there is no one at home to provide care.

The Parent

- Shows indifference and little concern for the child.
- Denies problems at home.
- Blames problems on the child.
- Refers to the child as bad or worthless or berates the child.
- Has demands that are too high for the child to achieve.
- Offers conflicting, unconvincing, or no explanation for the child's injury.
- Uses harsh physical discipline with the child or suggests that caregivers use harsh physical discipline if the child misbehaves.
- Is abusing alcohol or other drugs.

Source: Adapted from Child Welfare Information Gateway (2013).

abuse. Not all children who display one or more of the signs on this list have experienced maltreatment, but each sign is significant enough to merit attention. All U.S. states and the District of Columbia identify **mandated reporters,** individuals who are legally obligated to report suspected child maltreatment to the appropriate agency, such as child protective services, a law enforcement agency, or a state's child abuse reporting hotline (Child Welfare Information Gateway, 2013). Individuals designated as mandatory reporters typically have frequent contact with children: teachers, principals, and other school personnel; child care providers; physicians, nurses, and other health care workers; counselors, therapists, and other mental health professionals; and law enforcement officers. Of course, anyone can, and is encouraged to, report suspected maltreatment of a child.

THINKING IN CONTEXT 8.3

1. What factors might influence whether a parent adopts an authoritative style of parenting? How might contextual factors, including family, work, community, culture, and society, along with prior experience, influence parenting style?

2. What challenges do parents face in modifying their parenting styles as children age?

3. Child abuse is a problem with a complex set of influences at multiple bioecological levels. The most effective prevention and intervention programs target risk and protective factors in the child, parent, and community. Referring to the bioecological model, discuss factors at each bioecological level that might be incorporated into prevention and intervention programs to prevent child abuse and promote positive outcomes.

GENDER STEREOTYPES, GENDER DIFFERENCES, AND GENDER DEVELOPMENT

» LO 8.4   Compare biological, cognitive, and contextual theoretical explanations of gender role development.

Many people use the terms *sex* and *gender* interchangeably, but to developmental scientists, sex and gender have distinct meanings. Sex is biological and determined by genes—specifically, by the presence of a Y chromosome in the 23rd pair of chromosomes—and is indicated by the genitals. **Gender,** on the other hand, is social: It is determined by socialization and the roles that the individual adopts. One way to think about it—perhaps an irreverent way—is that sex refers to what is "between one's legs," whereas gender refers to what is "between one's ears."

Gender Role Norms and Gender Stereotypes

Most societies have **gender role norms,** normative expectations for males and females that are applied to everyday behavior. Many such norms derive from women's traditional role as child bearer and caregiver (Best & Bush, 2016). Nurturing the young and forming close family bonds requires emotional regulation skills and sensitivity to others. Expressive traits such as kindness, creativity, gentleness, and cooperation are key characteristics of the feminine gender role, as are physical traits such as being soft, small, and graceful (Bem, 1974). In contrast, the traditional masculine gender role entails instrumental agency—acting on the world to fulfill the role of provider and protector of the family—as well as physical characteristics such as being strong, powerful, and large. Instrumental traits include dominance, independence, and competitiveness. Gender role norms are seen in most cultures. For example, adults in 30 countries generally agree on the instrumental and expressive traits thought to characterize males and females, respectively (Guimond, Chatard, & Lorenzi-Cioldi, 2013; Lockenhoff et al., 2014).

Most people naturally expect that men and women will behave differently according to their society's gender roles. These expectations sometimes reflect **gender stereotypes,** broad generalized judgments of the activities, attitudes, skills, and characteristics deemed appropriate for males or females in a given culture. Gender stereotypes are exaggerated beliefs about what males and females should and should not do. Children show gender stereotypes as early as age 2, and stereotype knowledge increases during the preschool years as children acquire gender role norms, a process called **gender typing** (Liben, Bigler, & Hilliard, 2013). By 5 or 6 years of age, children have extensive knowledge of the activities and interests stereotyped for males and females (Blakemore, Berenbaum, & Liben, 2009). They express this knowledge as rigid rules about the behavior appropriate for boys and girls (Baker, Tisak, & Tisak, 2016). Preschoolers tend to expect males to be independent, forceful, and competitive and females to be warm, nurturing, and expressive (Martin et al., 2013). They also tend to show positive same-gender and negative other-gender attitudes (Halim, Ruble, Tamis-LeMonda, Shrout, & Amodio, 2017).

Stereotypes influence children's preferences and views of their own abilities. For example, by age 6, girls are less likely than boys to believe that members of their gender are "really, really smart." Also at age 6, girls begin to avoid activities said to be for children who are "really, really smart," lump more boys into the "really, really smart" category, and steer themselves away from games intended for the "really, really smart" (Bian, Leslie, & Cimpian, 2017). Gender stereotypes appear in many countries but vary in intensity. For example, in one study of children in 25 countries, high rates of gender stereotyping and stereotyped beliefs were observed in Pakistan, New Zealand, and England, whereas stereotypes were very low in Brazil, Taiwan, Germany, and France (Williams & Best, 1982).

Sex Differences

Despite common views, boys and girls are more alike than different (Leaper, 2013). The largest sex difference is in socioemotional functioning. From an early age, girls are better able to manage and express their emotions than boys. For example, at 6 months of age, males have more difficulty at regulating their emotions in frustrating or ambiguous situations than girls (Weinberg, Tronick, Cohn, & Olson, 1999). In infancy, childhood, and adolescence, girls are more accurate at identifying facial expressions, such as happy or sad, than boys (A. E. Thompson & Voyer, 2014). While girls tend to express happiness and sadness more often than boys, boys express more anger (Chaplin & Aldao, 2013). Girls also express shame and guilt, complex emotions that rely on cognitive and social development, more often than boys (Else-Quest, Higgins, Allison, & Morton, 2012).

Gender differences in aggression have been observed as early as 17 months of age, with boys showing more aggression (Hyde, 2014). Beginning at preschool age, boys tend to exhibit more physical and verbal aggression, whereas girls tend to demonstrate more relational aggression—excluding a peer from social activities, withdrawing friendship, spreading rumors, or humiliating the person (Ostrov & Godleski, 2010). Boys and girls also differ in inhibitory control, from as early as 3 months of age (Else-Quest, Hyde, Goldsmith, & Van Hulle, 2006). Differences in activity and the ability to restrain impulses likely play a role in sex differences in aggression. Although intelligence tests show no differences between boys and girls, girls tend to do better at verbal and mathematical computation tasks as well as those requiring fine motor skills (D. I. Miller & Halpern, 2014). Boys tend to perform better on a specific type of spatial reasoning task—mental rotation, or the ability to recognize a stimulus that is rotated in space (Hines, 2015). Even as infants, boys are more likely than girls to recognize stimuli that have been rotated (P. C. Quinn & Liben, 2014). Yet sex differences are not apparent on other spatial tasks (Hyde, 2016).

In all, as suggested earlier, there are few differences between boys and girls. In addition, there is a great deal of variability within each sex—more so than between the sexes. In other words, there is a greater number and variety of differences among boys than between boys and girls.

Theoretical Perspectives on Gender Role Development

Three-year-old Camila calls out, "I want the pink dress, just like a princess." Demarco pushes his truck and proclaims, "This monster truck is going to drive over the battlefield." Ask any adult, and they will likely tell you that boys and girls are very different. Yet we have seen that boys and girls show few reliable developmental differences. Nevertheless, boys and girls do, on average, adopt different gender roles. How do we explain the acquisition of gender roles? Several theoretical perspectives offer explanations of gender typing. Some lean more toward nature-oriented or biological explanations. Others use cognitive explanations, and still others turn to contextual explanations. A sufficient explanation of gender development integrates aspects of each theory.

Biological Explanations

Because most cultures have similar gender roles, sex differences may be a function of biology. Biological explanations point to the role of evolution and look to differences in biological structures, especially the brain, as well as hormones as contributors to sex differences in psychological and behavioral functioning (Hines, 2015).

From an evolutionary perspective, males adapted to become aggressive and competitive because these traits were advantageous in securing a mate and thereby passing along their genetic inheritance (Côté, 2009). Females became more nurturing, as it was adaptive to care for the young to ensure that their genes survived to be passed along to the next generation. Studies show that most mammalian species demonstrate a preference for same-sex playmates, males are more active and aggressive, and females are more nurturing (de Waal, 1993). These findings suggest that such gender differences in behavior are adaptive across species, including our own.

Gender differences begin at conception with the union of sex chromosomes, either XX (female) or XY (male; recall from Chapter 2). Genetic information on the Y chromosome leads to the formation of testes.

The subsequent production of testosterone results in the formation of the male genitals and reproductive system. Estrogens in the absence of testosterone lead to the formation of the female reproductive system (Sadler, 2015). In animals, testosterone produced prenatally influences neural survival and neural connectivity, leading to subtle sex differences in brain structure and function (Nugent & McCarthy, 2011).

Hormonal differences have effects on behavior as well. Animal and human studies have demonstrated that exposure to relatively high levels of testosterone promotes male-typical behavior development. When females are exposed to male sex hormones prenatally (e.g., in the case of congenital adrenal hyperplasia, a genetic disorder that causes excess androgen production beginning prenatally), they show more active play and fewer caregiving activities in early childhood compared with their female peers (Hines et al., 2016). Testosterone is linked with aggression. Higher levels of testosterone, prenatally and after birth, can account for boys' tendency to be more aggressive than girls. Hormonally influenced differences in behavioral styles then influence play styles; children choose to play with children who have similar styles, resulting in a preference for same-sex playmates (Berenbaum, 2018). In this way, biological factors influence the behaviors that are associated with gender roles. Other explanations for gender role development rely on understanding children's thinking, as described in the next section.

Cognitive Explanations

From the cognitive-developmental perspective, children's understanding of gender is constructed in the same manner as their understanding of the world: by interacting with people and things and thinking about their experiences. Infants as young as 3 to 4 months of age distinguish between female and male faces, as shown by habituation and preferential looking studies (P. C. Quinn, Yahr, Kuhn, Slater, & Pascalis, 2002). By 10 months of age, infants are able to form stereotypic associations between faces of women and men and gender-typed objects (scarf, hammer), suggesting that they have the capacity to form primitive stereotypes (Levy & Haaf, 1994). Most children develop the ability to label gender groups and to use gender labels in their speech between 18 and 24 months (Martin & Ruble, 2010).

Gender identity, awareness of whether one is a boy or a girl, occurs at about age 2 (Bussey, 2013). Once children label themselves as male or female, they classify the world around them, as well as their own behaviors, according to those labels (e.g., like me, not like me) (Kohlberg, 1966). In this way, children construct their own understandings of what it means to be a boy or a girl and thereby begin to acquire gender roles. By 2 to 2½ years of age, once children have established gender identity, they show more interest in gender-appropriate toys (e.g., dolls for girls, cars for boys) and a preference for playing with children of their own sex (Zosuls et al., 2009).

Recently, increased attention has been drawn to **transgender** children—those who do not identify with their biological sex but instead adopt an opposite-sex identity. Although there is much to learn, a recent study compared transgender and gender-conforming children on cognitive measures of gender preferences (Olson, Key, & Eaton, 2015). Transgender children showed a clear preference for peers and objects endorsed by peers who shared their expressed gender, as well as an explicit and implicit identity that aligned with their expressed gender. Their implicit preferences were indistinguishable from those of other children, when matched by gender identity. The prevalence of transgender identity is not well documented, but it appears to be rare. About .5% to 1% of the population of adults identify themselves as transgender (Conron, Scott, Stowell, & Landers, 2012; Gates, 2011), although the true figure may be higher. The vast majority of children adopt a gender identity that is congruent with their biological sex. The Lives in Context feature provides additional information about transgender children and adolescents.

Between ages 3 and 5, children show an increase in stereotype knowledge, evaluate their own gender more positively, and tend to show more rigid sex-typed behaviors (Halim et al., 2013). For example, in one study of diverse children from Mexican, Chinese, Dominican, and African American ethnic backgrounds, gender stereotypes held at age 4 predicted positive attitudes about their gender and more gender-stereotyped behavior at age 5 (Halim et al., 2017).

Three-year-old children associate gender with external behaviors and traits, but they do not yet understand gender as a biological construct. Young children tend to focus on appearance and therefore tend to believe that wearing a dress, for example, can change a child from boy to girl. Only toward later in childhood, when children come to understand Piagetian conservation tasks, do they come to realize that a boy will always be a boy, even if he grows long hair and wears a skirt, and that a girl will remain a girl no matter what she wears or which activities she chooses.

Gender constancy refers to the child's understanding that gender does not change—that he or she will always be the same regardless of appearance, activities, or attitudes (Kohlberg, 1966). Initially, gender constancy may further gender typing, as children become more aware of and pay more attention to gender norms (Arthur, Bigler, & Ruble, 2009). For example, the more positively

Transgender Children

Josie Romero is a transgender child who was born a boy called Joey Romero.
Barcroft/Barcroft Media/Getty Images

By 2 years of age, most children label themselves as boy or girl. This early sense of gender identity tends to intensify with development. However, a small minority of children experience incongruence between their gender identity and their biological sex. That is, some boys feel that they are really girls, and some girls feel that they are really boys. Although transgender individuals have a gender identity that does not fully correspond with their biological sex, their gender development is quite similar to that of other children. For example, like gender-typical children, transgender children show preferences for peers, toys, and clothing typically associated with their expressed gender, choose stereotypically gendered outfits, and say that they are more similar to children of their expressed gender than to children of the other gender (Fast & Olson, 2018).

Parents, peers, and teachers tend to discourage gender nonconformity in children, especially boys who show interest in girls' activities and toys (Halpern & Perry-Jenkins, 2016; Martin et al., 2013). Transgender children resist such pressure, insisting on their true gender identity. While in the past parents may have ignored children's wishes or outright prohibited them from adopting a transgender identity, some parents today adopt a different approach, permitting their children to "socially transition" to the gender identity that feels right to them. This type of social transitioning is reversible and nonmedical. It may entail changing the pronoun used to describe a child, the child's name, and the child's appearance, including hair and clothing. In this way, children are raised according to their gender identity rather than their biological sex.

Whether or not parents should support children's desire to live presenting as their gender identity is hotly debated (Steensma & Cohen-Kettenis, 2011; Zucker, Wood, Singh, & Bradley, 2012). The few studies that have examined transgender children have found that children who have not socially transitioned reported increased rates of anxiety and depression, with more than 50% of older children in some samples falling in the clinical range of internalizing symptoms (Ryan, Russell, Huebner, Diaz, & Sanchez, 2010; Simons, Schrager, Clark, Belzer, & Olson, 2013). In contrast, studies of transitioned transgender children suggest levels of depression and anxiety similar to gender-consistent children and overall norms (Olson, Durwood, DeMeules, & McLaughlin, 2016). There is growing evidence that social support is linked to better mental health outcomes among transgender adolescents and adults (Durwood, McLaughlin, & Olson, 2017). These findings suggest that social transitions in children, indicating parents' affirmation and support, may be associated with positive mental health in transgender children (Fuss, Auer, & Briken, 2015; Ryan et al., 2010). A sense of acceptance and the ability to live as one's perceived gender may buffer stresses that tend to accompany gender nonconformity.

In contrast to social transition, biological transition is a medical process. It typically involves both developmental changes, induced by means of hormone therapy, and permanent changes to the external genitals, accomplished by means of gender reassignment surgery. Older children who identify as transgender, in consultation with their parents and pediatrician, may take medication to delay the onset of puberty and the reproductive maturation that goes with it. Postponing puberty provides children with additional time to socially transition, decide whether biological transition is the right decision for them, and make a mature, informed choice.

What Do You Think?

1. What challenges might children with an incongruent gender identity face, and how might these challenges change with age?

2. What advice do you give to a parent who is concerned about gender-atypical behavior, such as a boy who is interested in playing with dolls or a girl who wishes to play with trucks and dress like a superhero? ●

children view their own gender and the more they understand that gender categories remain stable over time, the more likely girls are to insist on wearing dresses, and the more likely boys are to refuse to wear anything with a hint of femininity (Halim et al., 2014). When children develop positive other-gender attitudes, they tend to show less gender rigidity and less gender-stereotyped behavior (Halim et al., 2017). A full understanding of gender constancy includes the awareness that a person's sex is a biological characteristic, which typically occurs by about 7 years of age (Halim, 2016). Children with a more mature grasp of gender constancy may be less afraid to engage in cross-gender-typed activities than they had been previously because they understand that despite their engagement in cross-gender-typed activities, their gender will still remain the same (Halim et al., 2017).

Once children develop the ability to label their sex, they begin to form a **gender schema,** a concept or a mental structure that organizes gender-related information and embodies their understanding of what it means to be a male or female. Gender schema theory is a cognitive explanation of gender role development that emphasizes cognitive processing and environmental influences (Canevello, 2016; Weisgram, 2016). A child's gender schema becomes an organizing principle, and children notice more differences between males and females, such as preferred clothes, toys, and activities. Children also notice that their culture classifies males and females as different and encompassing different roles. Children then use their gender schemas as guides for their behavior and attitudes, and gender typing occurs. For example, when given gender-neutral toys, children first try to figure out whether they are boys' or girls' toys before deciding whether to play with them (C. F. Miller et al., 2006). When told that an attractive toy is for the opposite sex, children will avoid playing with it and expect same-sex peers to avoid it as well. Young children play with peers who engage in similar levels of gender-typed activities (e.g., playing dress-up, playing with tools) and, over time, engage in increasingly similar levels of gender-typed activities, contributing to sex segregation in children's play groups (Martin et al., 2013).

Gender schemas are such an important organizing principle that they can influence children's memory. For example, preschool children tend to notice and recall information that is consistent with their gender schemas (Liben et al., 2013). Children who see others behaving in gender-inconsistent ways, such as a boy baking cookies or a girl playing with toy trucks, often will misrecall the event, distorting it in ways that are gender consistent. They may not even recall gender-inconsistent information (Signorella & Liben, 1984). Not until around age 8 do children notice and recall information that contradicts their gender schemas. Yet even elementary school children have been shown to misrecall gender-inconsistent story information (Frawley, 2008). Clearly, children's knowledge and beliefs about gender and gender roles influence their own gender role and behavior. However, the world around the child also holds implications for gender role development. Terms that pertain to gender role development are summarized in Table 8.3.

Contextual Explanations

A contextual approach to understanding gender development emphasizes social learning and the influence of the sociocultural context in which children are raised. According to this approach, gender typing occurs through socialization, through

TABLE 8.3

Gender Role Development: Terms

TERM	DEFINITION
Gender differences	Psychological or behavioral differences between males and females
Gender constancy	The understanding that gender remains the same throughout life, despite superficial changes in appearance or attitude
Gender identity	A person's awareness of being a male or female
Gender role	The behaviors and attitudes deemed appropriate for a given gender
Gender schema	A mental structure that organizes gender-related information
Gender stability	The understanding that gender generally does not change over time; however, superficial changes in appearance might bring a change in gender
Gender typing	The process of acquiring gender roles

a children's interpretation of the world around them, influenced by parents, peers, teachers, and culture. Social learning theory emphasizes the importance of models in acquiring gender-typical behavior (Bandura & Bussey, 2004). Children observe models—typically the same-sex parent, but also peers, other adults, and even characters in stories and television programs. They use models as guides to their own behavior, resulting in gender-typed behavior. Feedback from others serves as reinforcement. Sometimes parents or other adults will directly teach a child about gender-appropriate behavior or provide positive reinforcement for behaving in sex-consistent ways: Boys get approval for building bridges and running fast, whereas girls get approval for preparing a make-believe meal or keeping a pretty dress neat. Each of these contextual factors also influences the cognitive components of gender, such as gender schema.

Parents often have different expectations for boys and girls and encourage their children to play with gender-appropriate toys.
iStock/gregoryelang

Parents. Boys and girls have different social experiences from birth (Martin & Ruble, 2010). Parents perceive sons and daughters differently and have different expectations for them. For example, parents often describe competition, achievement, and activity as important for sons and warmth, politeness, and closely supervised activities as important for daughters. Many parents encourage their children to play with gender-appropriate toys. Boys tend to receive toys that emphasize action and competition, such as cars, trains, and sports equipment, and girls tend to receive toys that focus on cooperation, nurturance, and physical attractiveness, such as baby dolls, Easy-Bake Ovens, and play makeup (Hanish et al., 2013). In one study, 3- and 5-year-old children were asked to identify "girl toys" and "boy toys" and then asked to predict parents' reactions to their preferences about gender-specific toys and behaviors (Freeman, 2007). Children predicted that parents would approve of their playing with gender-stereotyped toys and disapprove of choices to play with cross-gender toys.

Gender-consistent behavior is socially regulated through approval. Parents tend to encourage boys' independent play, demands for attention, and even attempts to take toys from other children, whereas parents tend to direct girls' play, provide assistance, refer to emotions, and encourage girls to participate in household tasks (Hines, 2015). Girls are often reinforced for behavior emphasizing closeness and dependency. Children internalize expectations about gender-related behavior and tend to feel good about themselves when their behavior is in accord with their internal standards and experience negative feelings when their behavior is not (Leaper, 2013).

Boys tend to be more strongly gender socialized than girls. Parents, especially fathers, tend to show more discomfort with sex-atypical behavior in boys (e.g., playing with dolls) than girls (e.g., playing with

trucks) (Basow, 2008). Fathers play an important role in influencing gender typing. A study of preschool children in England and Hungary revealed that children whose fathers did more housework and child care tended to demonstrate less awareness of gender stereotypes and less gender-typed play (Turner & Gervai, 1995). Dutch fathers with strong stereotypical gender role attitudes tended to use more physical control strategies with their 3-year-old boys than with girls, whereas fathers with counter-stereotypical attitudes used more physical control with girls; this differential treatment predicted gender differences in aggression 1 year later (Endendijk et al., 2017).

Peers. The peer group also serves as a powerful influence on gender typing in young children. As early as age 3, peers reinforce gender-typed behavior with praise, imitation, or participation. They criticize cross-gender activities and show more disapproval of boys who engage in gender-inappropriate behavior than of girls who are tomboys (Hanish et al., 2013). Among older children, gender-atypical behavior is associated with exclusion and peer victimization (Zosuls, Andrews, Martin, England, & Field, 2016).

Girls and boys show different play styles. Boys use more commands, threats, and force; girls use more gentle tactics, such as persuasion, acceptance, and verbal requests, which are effective with other girls but ignored by boys (Leaper, 2013). Girls, therefore, may find interacting with boys unpleasant, as boys pay little attention to their attempts at interaction and are generally nonresponsive. Differences in play styles influence boys' and girls' choices of play partners and contribute to sex segregation (Martin, Fabes, Hanish, Leonard, & Dinella, 2011). Peer and parental attitudes tend to be similar and reinforce each other, as both are part of a larger sociocultural system of socialization agents (Bandura & Bussey, 2004).

Media. Children's television and G-rated movies tend to depict the world as gender stereotyped, and these media depictions can promote gender-typed behavior in children. Typical children's media display more male than female characters, with male characters in action roles such as officers or soldiers in the military and female characters as more likely to have domestic roles and be in romantic relationships (England, Descartes, & Collier-Meek, 2011). Television commercials advertising toys tend to illustrate only one gender or the other, depending on the toy (Kahlenberg & Hein, 2010). In support of television's influence on gender typing, several Canadian towns that gained access to television for the first time showed a marked increase in children's gender-stereotyped attitudes 2 years after gaining access to television (Kimball, 1986).

One study of 4- and 5-year-old children found that nearly all had viewed media featuring Disney princess heroines, and two thirds of girls played with Disney princess toys at least once a week as compared with only 4% of the boys. Engagement with Disney princess toys and media was associated with more female gender-stereotypical behavior in girls 1 year later, even after controlling for initial levels of gender-stereotypical behavior (Coyne, Linder, Rasmussen, Nelson, & Birkbeck, 2016). Overall, there have been traditionally more male than female characters in children's literature, and female characters often need help while male characters tend to provide help (Evans, 1998). Coloring books display similar patterns, with more male than female characters, and male characters are depicted as older, stronger, more powerful, and more active than female characters (e.g., as superheroes vs. princesses) (Fitzpatrick &

Societal forces, such as children's television and movies, tend to depict the world as gender stereotyped.
United Archives GmbH / Alamy Stock Photo

McPherson, 2010). Even cereal boxes depict twice as many male as female characters (Black, Marola, Littman, Chrisler, & Neace, 2009).

Culture. The larger culture and its many aspects also influence gender typing, as most cultures emphasize gender differences. Some societies closely link activities and dress with gender; girls and boys may attend sex-segregated schools, wear contrasting types of school uniforms, and never interact (Beal, 1994). Societies vary in the types of behavior that are considered appropriate for men and women. For example, farming is a task for women in many parts of the world, but in North America, it is men who are traditionally in charge of farming tasks. The exact behaviors may vary across societies, but all societies have values regarding gender-appropriate behavior for males and females, and all societies transmit these values to young children. Table 8.4 summarizes perspectives on gender role development.

TABLE 8.4

Perspectives on Gender Role Development

Biological	Describes gender role development in evolutionary and biological terms. Males adapted to become more aggressive and competitive and females more nurturing as it ensured that their genes were passed to the next generation. Gender differences may also be explained by subtle differences in brain structure as well as differences in hormones.
Cognitive	The emergence of gender identity leads children to classify the world around them according to gender labels, and they begin to show more interest in gender-appropriate toys. Children show an increase in stereotype knowledge, evaluate their own gender more positively, and demonstrate rigidity of gender-related beliefs. Gender constancy furthers gender typing as children attend more to norms of their sex. According to gender schema theory, once children can label their sex, their gender schema forms and becomes an organizing principle. Children notice differences between males and females in preferred clothes, toys, and activities, as well as how their culture classifies males and females as different and encompassing different roles. Children then use their gender schemas as guides for their behavior and attitudes, and gender typing occurs.
Contextual	Contextual explanations rely on social learning and the influence of the sociocultural context in which children are raised. Males and females have different social experiences from birth. Gender typing occurs through socialization, through a child's interpretation of the world around him or her, and modeling and reinforcement from parents, peers, and teachers.

THINKING IN CONTEXT 8.4

1. How might contextual factors contribute to the sex differences that we see, for example, in socioemotional development? How might parents, teachers, peers, and environments influence sex differences?

2. Why do rigid views of gender roles increase and peak in childhood and then decline? Why do children view gender in extremely strict terms, and why do their views change?

PLAY AND PEER RELATIONSHIPS IN EARLY CHILDHOOD

»» LO 8.5   Explain the function of play and the form it takes during early childhood.

In early childhood, the social world expands to include peers. "Let's be pirates!" declared Ramon. "Okay. Here's my sword," Billy said as he held up the plastic wiffleball bat. Ramon and Billy ran to the playhouse at the end of the yard. "There's the boat. Let's get them!" Billy cried as he chased after his sister. Billy explained, "You're on the boat, and we're pirates coming to get you." "I'll run!" she said. Their grandmother watched from the porch as the children created stories, acted them out together, and climbed on every available surface. Play offers important learning opportunities for young children. Play contributes to physical, cognitive, emotional, and social development. Children learn how to use their muscles, control their bodies, coordinate their senses, and learn new motor skills. Play helps children to perspective take and understand other children's viewpoints, manage challenging situations, regulate emotions, practice creativity, learn to express their thoughts and desires, and problem solve (Coplan & Arbeau, 2009).

Types of Play

All children play, but the form that play takes varies with development (Lillard, 2015). At about age 2, play takes simple forms, such as bouncing a ball and trying to catch it or rolling a toy car as far as possible. Toddlers usually play independently. Piaget (1962) explained play as an important way in which children of all ages contribute to their own knowledge by actively exploring the world around them. By 5 years of age, children develop more sophisticated ways of interacting with play partners. Their cognitive capacities (such as their growing theory of mind) and emotional capacities (their ability to regulate their emotions) enable them to join peer groups more easily,

manage conflict more effectively, and select and keep playmates. Playing with other children may push them to learn to take the perspective of others and develop less egocentric ways of thinking (Piaget, 1962).

Young children's play develops over a series of steps that take place over the ages of 2 through 5 (Parten, 1932). Toddlers' play is characterized by *nonsocial activity,* including inactivity, onlooker behavior, and solitary play. *Parallel play* then emerges, in which children play alongside each other but do not interact. Play shifts to include social interaction in *associative play,* in which children play alongside each other but exchange toys and talk about each other's activities. Finally, *cooperative play* represents the most advanced form of play because children play together and work toward a common goal, such as building a bridge or engaging in make-believe play. These forms of play emerge in order but are not a strict developmental sequence because later behaviors do not replace earlier ones (Yaoying & Xu, 2010). For example, nonsocial play declines with age but still occurs in preschoolers and may take up to a third of kindergarteners' playtime (Dyer & Moneta, 2006).

Play and Children's Development

All children engage in **rough-and-tumble play,** which includes running, climbing, chasing, jumping, and play fighting. Children's rough-and-tumble play is seen around the world and can be distinguished from aggression by the presence of a play face, smiling, and laughing (Reed & Brown, 2001). Rough-and-tumble play is carefully orchestrated. It requires self-control, emotional regulation, and social skills. Children learn how to assert themselves, interact with other children, and engage in physical play without hurting the other child (Ginsburg, 2007). Rough-and-tumble play exercises children's gross motor skills and helps them to develop muscle strength and control. Both boys and girls engage in rough-and-tumble play, but boys do so at much

Rough-and-tumble play, which includes running, climbing, chasing, jumping, and play fighting, is seen around the world.
iStock/yellowsarah

This child is pretending to be an astronaut. She is involved in sociodramatic play and is learning to act out a role.
iStock/Choreograph

higher rates. For example, in one observation of preschool children, about 80% of the instances of rough-and-tumble play occurred in boys (Tannock, 2011). Research with animals has shown that rough-and-tumble play elicits positive affect that buffers the effects of stress, suggesting that it promotes resilience (Burgdorf, Kroes, & Moskal, 2017).

Young children also engage in **sociodramatic play,** taking on roles and acting out stories and themes (Lillard, 2015). By pretending to be mothers, astronauts, cartoon characters, and other personae, children learn how to explain their ideas and emotions; practice regulating emotions as they pretend to be sad, angry, or afraid; and develop a sense of self-concept as they differentiate themselves from the roles they play (Coplan & Arbeau, 2009). Sociodramatic play begins in toddlerhood, when a 2-year-old feeds or punishes a stuffed animal (Frahsek, Mack, Mack, Pfalz-Blezinger, & Knopf, 2010). It becomes more frequent and more complex from ages 3 to 6, often with intricate storylines (Rubin, Bukowski, & Bowker, 2015). Both boys and girls engage in sociodramatic play, with girls engaging in more such play than boys. Sociodramatic play offers important opportunities for development as children learn through social interactions. Children model higher level thinking and interaction skills, scaffold less skilled peers, and help them to reach their potential (Vygotsky, 1978). Sociodramatic play helps children explore social rules and conventions, promotes language skills, and is associated with social competence (Gioia & Tobin, 2010; Newton & Jenvey, 2011).

Although children around the world play, peer activities take different forms in different cultures. Children in collectivist societies tend to play games that emphasize cooperation. For example, children in India often engage in sociodramatic play that involves acting in unison coupled with close physical contact. In a game called *bhajtto*, for instance, the children imaginatively enact a script about going to the market, pretending to cut and share a vegetable, and touching each other's elbows and hands (Roopnarine, Hossain, Gill, & Brophy, 1994). In contrast, children from Western cultures that tend to emphasize the rights of the individual are inclined to play competitive games such as follow the leader, hide and seek, and duck, duck, goose! Play, like other aspects of development, is shaped by the context in which it occurs.

Peer Relationships

The earliest friendships emerge through children's play. Most young children can name a friend (M. Quinn & Hennessy, 2010). Young children generally understand friends as companions who live nearby and share toys and expectations for play. Friends are a source of amusement and excitement. Friends share with each other, imitate each other, and initiate social interactions with each other (van Hoogdalem, Singer, Eek, & Heesbeen, 2013). As children enter preschool, they spend more time interacting with peers, especially same-sex peers. Although researchers emphasize the proximity and play dimensions of young children's friendships, some research suggests that preschool friendships can be characterized by emotional qualities such as support and closeness, and high-quality friendships are more likely to endure over the school year (Sebanc, Kearns, Hernandez, & Galvin, 2007). Through peer interactions, young children gain social competence, communication, and emotional regulation skills that permit them to have more complicated—and rewarding—relationships in later childhood and adolescence.

Imaginary Companions

"You stay here, and I'll get the cookies," Katie told her friend Madison. "Does Madison want cookies too?" asked Mommy. "Of course!" replied Katie as she placed two cookies at a place setting in front of an empty chair. Imaginary companions or friends are common in early childhood, as early as ages 2 to 3, and occur in about 40% of young children (M. Taylor, Shawber, & Mannering, 2009). According to parents' reports, there is no clear triggering event that marks the emergence of most imaginary companions (M. Taylor et al., 2009). Children appear to come up with them on their own. Imaginary companions often represent extensions of real people known to the child, especially those who the child admires or characters from stories, television, or movies. Imaginary companions are usually human, although they may take the form of animals, aliens, and monsters (Gleason, Sebanc, & Hartup, 2000). The sense of what an invisible friend looks like is stable and can be retained for years.

Relationships with imaginary friends appear to resemble those with real friends and provide

Imaginary friends are common in early childhood and are indicative of a child's creativity and imagination.
Kansas City Star/Tribune/Getty

similar benefits, especially companionship (Gleason & Kalpidou, 2014). Children create realistic relationships with their imaginary companions that include pretend conflicts, feeling angry with them, and finding them unavailable to play (M. Taylor, 1999). Their similarity with real friends has sometimes caused concern in parents and professionals who fear that children create imaginary companions because they are lonely and have no playmates. However, research suggests that children with pretend friends are particularly sociable by nature and do not differ from other children in terms of the number of playmates or peer acceptance (Gleason & Kalpidou, 2014). In fact, children with imaginary companions are better at communicating with peers than are children without imaginary companions (Roby & Kidd, 2008). One study of 5-year-olds found that those with imaginary friends were better able to understand and talk about mental characteristics in actual friends (Davis, Meins, & Fernyhough, 2014).

Imaginary companions may be a marker for creativity. Children who create imaginary companions are more likely to report vivid imagery and elaborate storylines in daydreams, dreams, and pretend games (Bouldin, 2006; Trionfi & Reese, 2009). Perhaps imaginary companions and the mental gymnastics that create and sustain them indicate psychosocial health rather than deficits.

THINKING IN CONTEXT 8.5

1. Do you agree or disagree with this statement: Styles of play are universal and unfold with biological development. Explain your perspective.

2. What role do you think peers have in young children's development? Why?

APPLY YOUR KNOWLEDGE

Four-year-old Tony is an active, curious preschooler. His mother says that he "plays hard." Tony says that he wants to be the best, climb the highest, and run the fastest. When asked how high he can jump, Tony raises his arm to his shoulder. When given the chance to show his skills, Tony is never able to jump that high, but he's certain that he will on his next try.

Tony says that his father is the best father in the whole wide world because Daddy is big and strong. He wants to be just like Daddy when he grows up. He and Daddy do all kinds of "boy things," as Mommy calls it. Mommy bought Tony a special doll for boys, named My Buddy, but Daddy said that dolls are for girls. Tony doesn't want to be a girl. He thinks Daddy is smart and fun. Tony especially likes it when they wrestle on the floor each night. He and Daddy watch TV together. Tony also watches TV most afternoons while he waits for Daddy to come home from work. Tony's favorite shows are crime-fighting cartoons, but he also likes to watch wrestling.

Mommy often scolds Tony for playing too roughly with other children. She used to put Tony in time-out for 5 minutes when he misbehaved, but that did not decrease Tony's roughhousing and misbehaving. One time, when he hurt his cousin with his roughhousing, Tony's mother gave him a spanking to show him what it feels like and stop his behavior. She was so overcome with frustration over not being able to stop Tony's roughhousing that she didn't know what else to do. Tony's father says that rough play simply is what boys do. He tells Tony to be gentler with other children.

1. Discuss Tony's developing sense of initiative and self-concept.

2. Is Tony's play style developmentally appropriate? Why or why not? When is rough play excessive?

3. Tony's father discourages him from engaging in behavior atypical for his sex whereas his mother is concerned about helping Tony avoid becoming sex typed. What would you tell Tony's

parents about gender role development? What can Tony's mother do to reduce sex typing?

4. Assess Tony's risk for developing aggressive behavior. What aspects of his environment influence how likely he is to behave aggressively?

5. How does discipline factor into Tony's developing sense of self-regulation and impulse control? How might the various forms of discipline that Tony's parents use influence his development? Offer advice to Tony's parents.

$SAGE edge™

Visit **edge.sagepub.com/kuther2e** to help you accomplish your coursework goals in an easy-to-use learning environment.

LEARNING OBJECTIVES	SUMMARY	KEY TERMS	IN REVIEW
8.1 Discuss young children's emerging sense of initiative, self-concept, and self-esteem.	Young children's psychosocial task is to develop a sense of initiative over guilt, a sense of purpose and pride in their accomplishments. Young children tend to understand and describe themselves concretely. They have unrealistically positive views about their abilities and do not yet engage in social comparison. As children gain life experience and develop cognitively, their self-evaluations become more realistic and correlated with skills, accomplishments, evaluations by others, and other external indicators of competence.	Initiative versus guilt Self-concept Self-esteem Social comparison	According to Erikson, what are the benefits of developing a sense of initiative in early childhood? Contrast self-esteem with self-concept in early childhood. What contextual factors contribute to children's conceptions of themselves?
8.2 Summarize the development of emotional understanding, regulation, and behavior in early childhood.	Theory of mind influences the development and expression of self-conscious emotions, such as pride and guilt. Young children become better able to understand their own and others' emotions. Young preschoolers tend to engage in prosocial behavior for egocentric motives, to gain praise and avoid punishment. With development, children become less egocentric and their prosocial behavior becomes motivated by empathy and internalized societal perspectives of good behavior. Parents of prosocial children model prosocial behavior and empathetic concern. Aggression, especially instrumental aggression, is common in early childhood. All children will sometimes hit, fight, kick, and take other children's toys. By age 4, most children have developed the self-control to express their desires and to wait for what they want, moving from using physical aggression to expressing desires with words.	Empathy Prosocial behavior Aggressive behavior Instrumental aggression Relational aggression	What influences children's ability to understand and control their emotions? What individual and contextual factors influence the development of empathy and prosocial behavior? What is the most common form of aggression in early childhood, and how does this typically change?
8.3 Identify four parenting styles and their associations with child outcomes.	Parenting styles are enduring sets of parenting behaviors. Authoritarian parents emphasize control and obedience over warmth and raise children who tend to be withdrawn, are often mistrustful and anxious, and often tend to react to frustrating interactions with peers with hostility. Parents who are permissive are warm and accepting but have few rules and expectations for children, resulting in children with little self-control and who are immature, impulsive, and rebellious. Uninvolved parents provide little support or warmth and little control, with negative consequences for all forms of development. Authoritative parents are warm and sensitive to children's needs but also are firm in their expectations that children conform to appropriate standards of behavior. They are supportive and loving but have standards that they maintain firmly.	Parenting style Authoritarian parenting style Permissive parenting style Authoritative parenting style Uninvolved parenting style Inductive discipline Child maltreatment Child abuse Posttraumatic stress disorder (PTSD) Mandated reporter	Discuss characteristics and outcomes associated with four parenting styles. How do parenting styles differ by culture? What are the effects of child maltreatment? What are risks for child maltreatment?

	Children of authoritative parents are confident and cooperative, and they have self-control, self-esteem, social skills, and high academic achievement; these positive effects persist throughout childhood into adolescence. Parenting behaviors must be considered within their cultural context as parenting is not one size fits all.		
8.4 Compare biological, cognitive, and contextual theoretical explanations of gender role development.	Gender roles appear in all societies. Young children acquire gender roles early in life. Biological explanations of gender development cite evolutionary perspectives and look to differences in biological structures, especially the brain, as well as hormones such as testosterone as contributors to sex differences in psychological and behavioral functioning. Cognitive-developmental perspectives on gender development posit that children's understanding of gender is constructed in the same manner as their understanding of the world, by interacting with the world and thinking about their experiences. Cognitive explanations of gender development focus on the gender schema as a guide for their behavior and attitudes. Contextual explanations of gender development emphasize socialization.	Gender Gender role norms Gender stereotypes Gender typing Gender identity Transgender Gender constancy Gender schema	What are gender role norms, gender stereotyping, and gender typing? What sex differences exist between boys and girls? How do gender identity, gender constancy, and gender schema explain gender development? How do peers, media, and culture contribute to gender role development?
8.5 Explain the function of play and the form it takes during early childhood.	Play contributes to all aspects of development. All children play, but the form that play takes varies with development. Types of play include parallel, associative, cooperative, and sociodramatic play. Although all children around the world play, peer activities take different forms by culture.	Rough-and-tumble play Sociodramatic play	Identify types of play in early childhood. What are the benefits of rough-and-tumble play and sociodramatic play? How do peer interactions change in early childhood?

PART IV

Middle Childhood

CHAPTER 9:
Physical and Cognitive Development in Middle Childhood

CHAPTER 10:
Socioemotional Development in Middle Childhood

Middle childhood entails steady advances in physical, cognitive, and socioemotional functioning. With increases in body size, strength, and agility, children are better able to participate in sports and athletic activities. As children enter school, improvements in information-processing abilities underlie advances in academic tasks such as reading and mathematics. Children become better able to control their attention, take in information, and use their understanding of how the mind works to retain information more effectively. Now children can incorporate feedback about their abilities from parents, teachers, and peers to view themselves in more complex and organized ways.

Relationships with parents shift over the school years as children become more independent. Parents adapt by communicating expectations, monitoring, and permitting children to make more decisions. Like younger children, school-age children respond best to warm, responsive, and firm parenting. As children transition to first grade, the school context rises in importance. Similar to parent–child relationships, high-quality, responsive, and positive interactions with teachers aid children's adjustment. Children also experience changes within the peer context. Friendships evolve to emphasize responsivity, trust, intimacy, and loyalty. Children tend to have fewer but closer friends and friendship influences their adjustment and well-being. During elementary school, the home, school, and peer contexts influence interactions among physical, cognitive, and socioemotional domains of development.

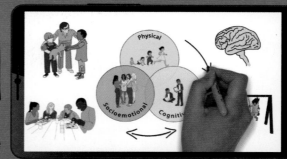

DR. KUTHER'S
CHALK TALKS

Watch at
edge.sagepub.com/kuther2e

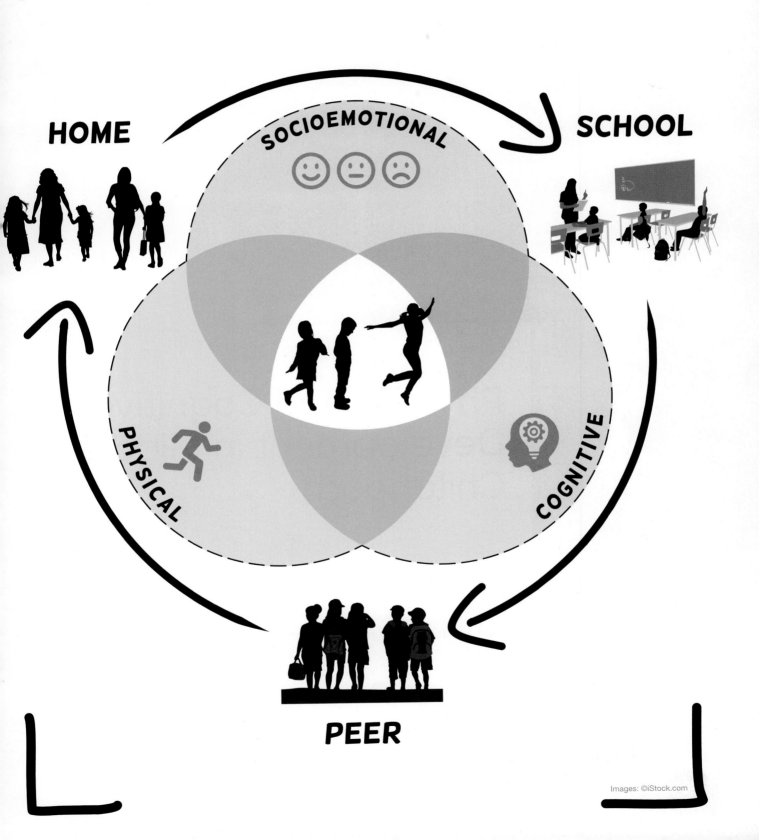

HOME

SCHOOL

SOCIOEMOTIONAL

PHYSICAL

COGNITIVE

PEER

Images: ©iStock.com

9

Physical and Cognitive Development in Middle Childhood

"I scored a goal today!" 8-year-old Christina exclaimed. Now that she can run faster and kick a ball farther than ever before, Christina enjoys playing on her elementary school soccer team and is becoming more skilled in the sport. Christina hopes to attend soccer camp this summer. Not only does she like playing soccer but she also likes learning about her favorite soccer players and memorizing game-related statistics. Advances in cognition have led Christina to enjoy other hobbies that require concentration and planning, such as making complex collages and playing video games with intricate plots. An increasingly sophisticated vocabulary, emerging social reasoning skills, and an ability to understand other people's perspectives aid Christina in expressing herself and communicating her needs. Is Christina a typical school-age child? In this chapter, we examine the physical and cognitive changes that children undergo in middle childhood, from about ages 6 to 11.

Learning Objectives

9.1 Identify patterns of physical and motor development during middle childhood and common health issues facing school-age children.

9.2 Discuss school-age children's capacities for reasoning and processing information.

9.3 Summarize views of intelligence, including the uses, correlates, and criticisms of intelligence tests.

9.4 Examine patterns of moral development during middle childhood.

9.5 Summarize language development during middle childhood.

9.6 Discuss children's learning at school.

Digital Resources

Explore: Attachment Insecurity and High-Calorie Food Consumption

Watch: Information Processing Theory

▶ **Lives in Context Video 9.1:** Piaget's Conservation Tasks

▶ **Lives in Context Video 9.2:** Executive Function

Listen: The IQ Test Wars

Explore: Moral Reasoning and Aggression

Explore: What's Worth Talking About?

Connect: Black Teachers Improve Lives for Black Students

PHYSICAL AND MOTOR DEVELOPMENT IN MIDDLE CHILDHOOD

>> **LO 9.1 Identify patterns of physical and motor development during middle childhood and common health issues facing school-age children.**

In middle childhood, physical development is more subtle and continuous than earlier in life. School-age children's bodies gradually get bigger, and they show advances in gross and fine motor development and coordination.

Body Growth

Growth slows considerably in middle childhood. Despite a slower growth rate, though, gradual day-to-day increases in height and weight add up quickly and can seem to sneak up on a child. In middle childhood, children grow 2 to 3 inches and gain 5 to 8 pounds per year, so that the average 10-year-old child weighs about 70 pounds and is about 4½ feet tall. In late childhood, at about age 9, girls begin a period of rapid growth that will continue into adolescence. During this time, girls gain about 10 pounds a year, becoming taller and heavier than same-age boys. As we will discuss in Chapter 11, not until early adolescence, at about age 12, do boys enter a similar period of rapid growth. As children grow taller, their body proportions become more like those of adults, slimmer and with longer limbs.

Genes and nutrition influence the rate of children's growth. African American children grow faster and are taller and heavier than White children of the same age. For example, 6-year-old African American girls tend to have greater muscle and bone mass than White or Mexican American girls their age (Ellis, Abrams, & Wong, 1997). Children who enter middle childhood with stunted growth and nutritional deficits often do not catch up. Instead, stunting often continues and worsens in middle childhood, especially if children remain in the same environments that caused malnourishment (Kitsao-Wekulo et al., 2013). For example, growth stunting in children in sub-Saharan Africa tends to persist and worsen throughout the school years (Senbanjo, Oshikoya, Odusanya, & Njokanma, 2011). Children who enter middle childhood with stunted growth are likely to experience a variety of problems, including cognitive deficits, aggression, behavior problems, and a greater risk of chronic illnesses and other health problems (Hoddinott, Alderman, Behrman, Haddad, & Horton, 2013).

Motor Development

Like growth, motor development advances gradually throughout childhood. Motor skills from birth to age 4 predict school-age children's motor abilities (Piek,

FIGURE 9.1

Gross Motor Skills

In middle childhood gross motor skills combine and become more complex, permitting faster running, higher jumping, and greater coordination, such as the ability to balance on a balance beam.

canstock/sergeevspb; canstock/kzenon; Comstock/Stockbyte/Thinkstock

Dawson, Smith, & Gasson, 2008). During the school-age years, the gross motor skills developed in early childhood refine and combine into more complex abilities, such as running and turning to dodge a ball, walking heel to toe down the length of a balance beam and turning around, or creating elaborate jump rope routines that include twisting, turning, and hopping (Gabbard, 2018). Increases in body size and strength contribute to advances in motor skills, which are accompanied by advances in flexibility, balance, agility, and strength. Now children can bend their bodies to do a somersault or carry out a dance routine, balance to jump rope, demonstrate agility to run and change speed and direction rapidly, and have the strength to jump higher and throw a ball farther than ever before, as shown in Figure 9.1.

Children also show advances in fine motor control that allow them to develop new interests. School-age children build model cars, braid friendship bracelets, and learn to play musical instruments—all tasks that depend on fine motor control. Fine motor development is particularly important for penmanship. Most 6-year-old children can write the alphabet, their names, and numbers in large print, making strokes with their entire arm. With development, children become able to use their wrists and fingers to write. Uppercase letters are usually mastered first; the lowercase alphabet requires smaller movements of the hand that require much practice. By third grade, most children can write in cursive. Girls tend to outperform boys in fine motor skills (Junaid & Fellowes, 2006). Success

in fine motor skills, particularly writing skills, may influence academic skills. Children who write with ease may be better able to express themselves in writing, for example.

Motor skill advances are influenced by body maturation and brain development. The pruning of unused synapses contributes to increases in motor speed and reaction time so that 11-year-old children tend to respond twice as quickly as 5-year-old children (Gabbard, 2018). Growth of the cerebellum (responsible for balance, coordination, and some aspects of emotion and reasoning) and myelination of its connections to the cortex contribute to advances in gross and fine motor skills and speed (Tiemeier et al., 2010). Brain development improves children's ability to inhibit actions, which enables children to carry out more sophisticated motor activities that require the use of one hand while controlling the other, such as throwing a ball, or that require the hands to do different things, such as playing an instrument (Diamond, 2013).

Contextual influences, such as nutrition, opportunities to practice motor skills, and health, also influence motor development. For example, children in different contexts have different opportunities to practice motor skills through vigorous physical play and other activities (Laukkanen, Pesola, Havu, Sääkslahti, & Finni, 2014). In addition, motor development has long-term implications for other domains of development. In one study, children's motor development and activity at age 8 predicted measures of cognitive development and academic

FIGURE 9.2

Death Rates for Children Ages 1 to 19 (deaths per 100,000) in the United States, 1980–2014

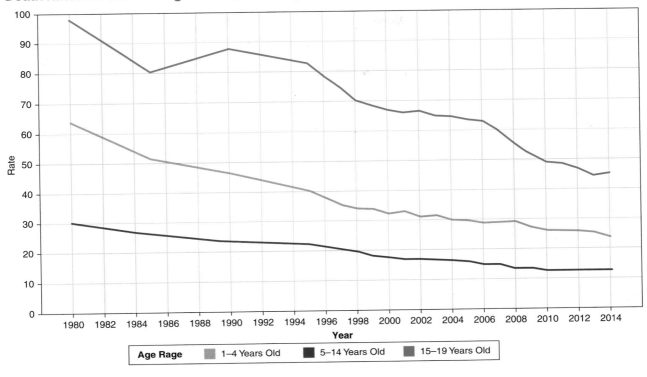

Source: Child Trends Databank (2016).

achievement 8 years later, at age 16 (Kantomaa et al., 2013). The ability to explore the world and play influences opportunities to interact and play with other children and thereby affects social and cognitive development.

Common Health Issues in Middle Childhood

Middle childhood generally is a healthy time. As shown in Figure 9.2, childhood mortality declines after infancy. In addition, mortality across childhood has declined over the past four decades (Child Trends Databank, 2016). However, children from low socioeconomic status (SES) homes have higher rates of mortality than do other children because of poor access to health care, poor nutrition, and stressful home and neighborhood environments (Baker, Currie, & Schwandt, 2017).

Childhood Injuries

Unintentional injuries from accidents are the most common cause of death in children and adolescents in the United States, causing about one in five deaths (Dellinger & Gilchrist, 2018; Xu, Murphy, Kochanek,

& Bastian, 2016). Motor vehicle accidents are the most frequent cause of fatal injuries in children ages 5 to 19 (Safe Kids Worldwide, 2015). Many more children incur nonfatal injuries. Rates for nonfatal injuries vary dramatically with age and are highest in infancy and adolescence, ages 15 to 19 (Child Trends Databank, 2014). At all ages, males experience more injuries than females, likely due to their higher levels of activity and risk taking. The most common types of injuries also vary with age, as shown in Figure 9.3. Falls are the most common source of injuries in children under age 9; from age 10 to 14, children are equally likely to be injured by a fall or being struck by an object or person (Child Trends Databank, 2014). Adolescents are the most likely to be injured by being struck by an object or person.

A variety of individual and contextual influences place children at risk of injury. Poor parental and adult supervision is closely associated with childhood injury (Ablewhite et al., 2015). Children's risk of injury rises when their parents report feeling little control over their behavior (Acar et al., 2015). Some parents hold the belief that injuries are an inevitable part of child development and may therefore provide less supervision and intervention (Ablewhite et al., 2015). Children who are impulsive, overactive, and

FIGURE 9.3

Nonfatal Injuries Treated in Emergency Rooms, Leading Causes by Age Group, 2013

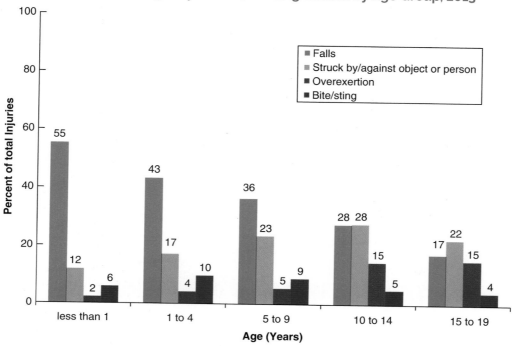

Source: Child Trends Databank (2014).

difficult, as well as those diagnosed with attention-deficit/hyperactivity disorder (ADHD), experience higher rates of unintentional injuries (Acar et al., 2015; Lange et al., 2016). Childhood injury is also associated with parental distraction, such as by talking to another parent or mobile phone use (Huynh, Demeter, Burke, & Upperman, 2017). Parents who work long hours or multiple jobs and who live in challenging environments may find it difficult to keep tabs on their children or may feel overwhelmed.

Neighborhood disadvantage, specifically low SES and lack of resources, is associated with higher rates of injuries and bone fractures in children in the United States, Canada, and the United Kingdom (McClure, Kegler, Davey, & Clay, 2015; McDonell, 2014). Disadvantaged neighborhoods may also contribute to children's injuries due to factors that increase overall injury risk, such as poor maintenance of streets and sidewalks and poor design or maintenance of housing and playgrounds. In addition to having fewer opportunities to be active, children in disadvantaged neighborhoods often have inadequate access to sources of healthy nutrition; this combination of circumstances can interfere with the development of healthy, strong bodies.

Just as there are multiple contextual factors that place children at risk of injury, there are many opportunities for preventing and reducing childhood injuries. Parenting interventions that improve supervision and monitoring, teach parents about risks to safety, and model safe practices can help parents reduce injuries in their children (Kendrick, Barlow, Hampshire, Stewart-Brown, & Polnay, 2008). School programs can help students learn and practice

Unintentional injuries from accidents are the most common cause of death in children and adolescents in the United States.
iStock/Steve Debenport

safety skills. At the community level, installing and maintaining safe playground equipment and protected floor surfaces can reduce the injuries that accompany falls. Disadvantaged communities, however, may lack the funding to provide safe play spaces, placing residing children at risk.

Childhood Obesity

Obesity is a serious health problem for children today. Health care professionals determine whether someone's weight is in the healthy range by examining **body mass index (BMI),** calculated as weight in kilograms divided by height in meters squared (kg/m2; World Health Organization, 2009). **Obesity** is defined as having BMI at or above the 95th percentile for height and age, as indicated by the 2000 Centers for Disease Control and Prevention (CDC) growth charts (Reilly, 2007). More than 17% of school-age children are classified as obese, as shown in Figure 9.4 (Ogden, Carroll, Fryar, & Flegal, 2015).

Rising rates of overweight and obesity among children and adolescents are a problem not only in the United States but also in all other developed nations, including Australia, Canada, Denmark, Finland, Germany, Great Britain, Ireland, Japan, Hong Kong, and New Zealand (de Onis, Blössner, & Borghi, 2010; Janssen et al., 2005; Lobstein et al., 2015; Wang & Lim, 2012). Obesity is also becoming more common in developing nations, such as India, Pakistan, and China, as they adopt Western-style diets higher in meats, fats, and refined foods and as they show the increased snacking and decreased physical activity linked with watching television (Afshin, Reitsma, & Murray, 2017).

Heredity plays a strong role in obesity, but contextual factors also place individuals at risk for obesity and interact with biology to determine whether genetic predispositions to weight gain are fulfilled (Albuquerque, Nóbrega, Manco, & Padez, 2017; Goodarzi, 2018). For example, children in low SES homes are at higher risk for obesity than their peers who live in high SES homes (Chung et al., 2016). The effects of SES may interact with individuals' genetic predispositions. For example, in one study, children who were carriers of a particular allele of the *OXTR* gene had greater BMI when reared in low SES environments but had the lowest BMI when reared in high SES homes (Bush et al., 2017). Community-level influences on obesity include the lack of safe playgrounds with equipment that encourages activity and even the proximity of fast-food restaurants to schools (Alviola, Nayga, Thomsen, Danforth, & Smartt, 2014; Black, Menzel, & Bungum, 2015; Fan & Jin, 2014).

U.S. children who eat an evening meal with parents are less likely to be overweight than other children (Horning et al., 2017) and are less likely to be overweight as young adults (Berge et al., 2015). These

FIGURE 9.4

Prevalence of Obesity Among Youth Aged 2 to 19 Years, by Sex and Age: United States, 2011–2014

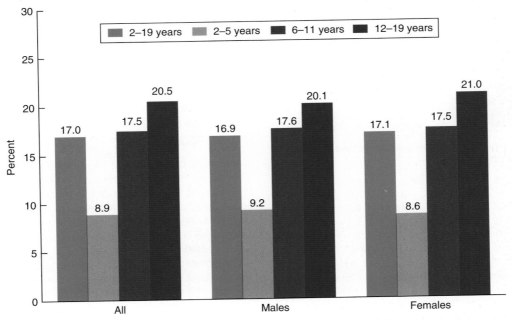

Source: Ogden et al., 2015.

children tend to have more healthy diets that include more fruits and vegetables and less fried foods and soft drinks. The frequency of family dinnertimes drops sharply between ages 9 and 14, however, and family dinners have become less common in recent decades (Fink, Racine, Mueffelmann, Dean, & Herman-Smith, 2014). Screen time—time spent in front of a television, computer, or electronic device screen—is a sedentary activity that places children at risk for obesity (Mitchell, Rodriguez, Schmitz, & Audrain-McGovern, 2013). Screen time increases with age (Rideout, 2013). Conversely, screen time and media consumption, especially exposure to media

depictions of unrealistically thin celebrities, predict **body image dissatisfaction**—dissatisfaction with one's physical appearance as shown by a discrepancy between one's ideal body figure and actual body figure (Slater & Tiggemann, 2016). Body image dissatisfaction can be seen as early as the preschool years and rises over the course of childhood. This is discussed in the Lives in Context box, Body Image Dissatisfaction.

Child and adolescent obesity is associated with short- and long-term health problems, including heart disease, high blood pressure, orthopedic problems, and diabetes (Pulgarón, 2013). Obese children and

---

Body Image Dissatisfaction

Body image dissatisfaction is often first seen in girls during middle childhood.
Peter Dazeley/Getty

"See how my stomach sticks out?" asked Amanda. "I have to wear baggy tops to hide it. I want to wear cropped tops like that one," Amanda said, pointing to a page in a magazine. "But I'm too fat." "Me too," said her best friend, Betsy. At 9 years of age, Amanda and Betsy display signs of body image dissatisfaction.

Up to half of elementary schoolchildren (6–12 years) are dissatisfied with some aspect of their body and shape (Dion et al., 2016; Smolak, 2011).

Perhaps it is not surprising, then, that dieting behaviors often begin in childhood, and about half of 8- to 10-year-old children report dieting at least some of the time (Dohnt & Tiggemann, 2005). Body image dissatisfaction is associated with poor self-esteem, depression, unhealthy eating and exercise behaviors, and inadequate weight gain in childhood (Dion et al., 2016; Duchin et al., 2015). Although less well researched, boys also are vulnerable to body dissatisfaction, often desiring a taller and more muscular physique (Costa, Silva, Alvarenga, & de Assis Guedes de Vasconcelos, 2016).

Peer interactions play a role in body image dissatisfaction. Girls often bond over "fat talk," criticizing their bodies (McVey, Levine, Piran, & Ferguson, 2013). Many school-age girls believe that being thin would make them more likable by their peers and less likely to be teased (Michael et al., 2014). Girls with a higher BMI report experiencing more teasing and bullying, which in turn is associated with body dissatisfaction (McVey et al., 2013; Williams et al., 2013). Even without being teased, simply having a higher BMI relative to peers predicts present body image concerns and those 1 year later in 9- to 12-year-old girls (L. Clark & Tiggemann, 2008).

Individuals' perceptions of body ideals and their own bodies are influenced by multiple contextual factors. Exposure to media images of thin models has often been associated with dieting awareness, weight concerns, and body dissatisfaction in girls and women (E. H. Evans, Tovée, Boothroyd, & Drewett, 2013; Gattario, Frisén, & Anderson-Fye, 2014). The influence of the media is perhaps best illustrated by longitudinal studies of teenagers in the Pacific island nation of Fiji before and after television became widely available in the islands. Disordered eating attitudes and behaviors arose after the introduction of television (Dasen, 1994). With the emergence of U.S. television programming, girls from rural Fiji reported comparing their bodies unfavorably to those of the program characters (Becker, Keel, Anderson-Fye, & Thomas, 2004).

School-based programs aim to educate students about body image using strategies such as lessons, group discussions, and role play as well as encouraging supportive peer groups (McCabe, Connaughton, Tatangelo, Mellor, & Busija, 2017; O'Dea & Yager, 2011). Improving media literacy is an important focus of many programs. The programs may include lessons about advertising, the homogeneity of body shapes shown on television and magazines, and the airbrushing of photos (Richardson, Paxton, & Thomson, 2009). For example,

as part of a 2011 governmental initiative in British schools, Britney Spears allowed pre-airbrushed images of herself in a bikini to be shown alongside the airbrushed ones for children aged 10 to 11 to show how media might try to alter and improve images (Gattario et al., 2014). Effective programs emphasize providing children with alternative ways of thinking about beauty and body ideals (Gattario et al., 2014).

What Do You Think?

Would you expect boys and girls to react to body image dissatisfaction in similar ways? Why or why not? ●

---

adolescents are at risk for peer rejection, depression, low self-esteem, and body dissatisfaction (Harrist et al., 2016; Pulgarón, 2013; Quek, Tam, Zhang, & Ho, 2017). The majority of obese youngsters do not outgrow obesity but instead become obese adults (Simmonds, 2016).

Physical activity affects body weight, and it tends to decline beginning in middle childhood, about age 7 (Farooq et al., 2018). It is estimated that only about 10% of 12- to 15-year-olds are at least moderately active for 60 minutes per day on at least 5 days per week, in accord with recommended guidelines (Kann et al., 2014). Programs that effectively reduce obesity in children and adolescents target their screen time and increase their physical activity and time spent outdoors. In addition, successful programs teach

children about nutrition and help them to reduce their consumption of high-calorie foods and increase their consumption of fruits and vegetables (Kumar & Kelly, 2017; Lobstein et al., 2015).

COGNITIVE DEVELOPMENT IN MIDDLE CHLDHOOD

>> LO 9.2 **Discuss school-age children's capacities for reasoning and processing information.**

We have seen that children make impressive gains in physical development, becoming bigger, stronger, and capable of a broader range of motor activities. Their leaps in cognitive development are even more impressive. Children's capacities to take in, process, and retain information all increase dramatically. They grasp the world around them in new, more adultlike ways and become capable of thinking logically, although their reasoning remains different from that of adults. Children become faster, more efficient thinkers, and they develop more sophisticated perspectives on the nature of knowledge and how the mind works.

Piaget's Cognitive-Developmental Theory: Concrete Operational Reasoning

When children enter Piaget's **concrete operational stage of reasoning,** at about age 6 or 7, they become able to use logic to solve problems but are still unable to apply logic to abstract and hypothetical situations. Older children's newly developed ability

---

⚙️ **THINKING IN CONTEXT 9.1**

1. Consider your own physical development and health in childhood and today. How have biological factors contributed to your development? What experiences have influenced you? Consider your context. What factors in the home, school, peer, and neighborhood contexts have influenced your physical development and health?

2. Obesity, body image, and dieting in school-age children reflect the interaction of contextual and developmental factors. If you were to design a prevention or intervention program, what developmental factors would you include? How might you incorporate contextual factors like home, peers, school, neighborhood, and culture into your program?

for logical thinking enables them to reason about physical quantities and is evident in their skills for conservation and classification.

Classification

What hobbies did you enjoy as a child? Did you collect and trade coins, stamps, rocks, or baseball cards? School-age children develop interests and hobbies that require advanced thinking skills, such as the ability to compare multiple items across several dimensions. **Classification** is the ability to understand hierarchies, to simultaneously consider relations between a general category and more specific subcategories. Several types of classification skills emerge during the concrete operational stage: transitive inference, seriation, and class inclusion.

The ability to infer the relationship between two objects by understanding each object's relationship to a third is called **transitive inference.** For example, present a child with three sticks: A, B, and C. She is shown that Stick A is longer than Stick B and Stick B is longer than Stick C. The concrete operational child does not need to physically compare Sticks A and C to know that Stick A is longer than the Stick C. She uses the information given about the two sticks to infer their relative lengths (Wright & Smailes, 2015). Transitive inference emerges earlier than other concrete operational skills. By about 5 years of age, children are able to infer that A is longer than C (Goodwin & Johnson-Laird, 2008).

Seriation is the ability to order objects in a series according to a physical dimension such as height, weight, or color. For example, ask a child to arrange a handful of sticks in order by length, from shortest to longest. Four- to five-year-old children can pick out the smallest and largest stick but will arrange the others haphazardly. Six- to seven-year-old children, on the other hand, arrange the sticks by picking out the smallest, and next smallest, and so on (Inhelder & Piaget, 1964).

Class inclusion involves understanding hierarchical relationships among items. For example, suppose that a child is shown a bunch of flowers, seven daisies and two roses. She is told that there are nine flowers; seven are called daisies and two are called roses. The child is then asked, "Are there more daisies or flowers?" Preoperational children will answer that there are more daisies, as they do not understand that daisies are a subclass of flowers. By age 5, children have some knowledge of classification hierarchies and may grasp that daisies are flowers but still not fully understand and apply classification hierarchies to correctly solve the problem (Deneault & Ricard, 2006). By about age 8, children not only can classify objects, in this case flowers, but also can make quantitative judgments and respond that there

are more flowers than daisies (Borst, Poirel, Pineau, Cassotti, & Houdé, 2013).

Children's ability and interest in hierarchical classification becomes apparent in middle childhood when they begin to collect items and spend hours sorting their collections along various dimensions. For example, one day Susan sorts her rock collection by geographic location (e.g., the part of the world in which it is most commonly found), with subcategories based on hardness and color. She might then reorganize her rocks based on other characteristics, such as age or composition.

Conservation

In a classic conservation problem, a child is shown two identical balls of clay and watches while the experimenter rolls one ball into a long hotdog shape. When asked which piece contains more clay, a child who reasons at the preoperational stage will say that the hotdog shape contains more clay because it is longer. Eight-year-old Julio, in contrast, notices that the ball shape is shorter than the hotdog shape, but it is also thicker. He knows that the two shapes contain the same amount of clay. At the concrete operational stage of reasoning, Julio understands that certain characteristics of an object do not change despite superficial changes to the object's appearance. An understanding of reversibility—that an object can be returned to its original state—means Julio realizes that the hotdog-shaped clay can be reformed into its original ball shape.

Most children solve this conservation problem of substance by age 7 or 8. At about age 9 or 10, children also correctly solve conservation of weight tasks (after presenting two equal-sized balls of clay and rolling one into a hotdog shape, "Which is heavier, the hotdog or the ball?"). Conservation of volume tasks (after placing the hotdog- and ball-shaped clay in glasses of liquid: "Which displaces more liquid?") are solved last, at about age 12. The ability to conserve develops slowly, and children show inconsistencies in their ability to solve different types of conservation problems.

Recent theorists link children's success on conservation tasks with the development of information processing capacities, such as working memory and the ability to control impulses (Borst et al., 2013). In response to conservation of number tasks, for example, older children show more activity in parts of the temporal and prefrontal cortex as well as other parts of the brain associated with working memory, inhibitory control, and executive control (Houdé et al., 2011; Poirel et al., 2012). With practice, the cognitive abilities tested in Piagetian tasks become automatic and require less attention and fewer processing resources, enabling children to think in more complex ways (Case, 1999). For example, once a child solves a conservation task, the problem becomes routine and requires less attention and mental resources than before, enabling the child to tackle more complex problems.

Culture and Concrete Operational Reasoning

Piaget emphasized the universal nature of cognitive development, assuming that all children around the world progressed through the same stages. Today's researchers, however, find that the cultural context in which children are immersed plays a critical role in development (Goodnow, Lawrence, Goodnow, & Lawrence, 2015). Studies of children in non-Western cultures suggest that they achieve conservation and other concrete operational tasks later than children from Western cultures. However, cultural differences in children's performance on tasks that measure concrete operational reasoning may be influenced by methodology (e.g., how questions are asked and the cultural identity of the experimenter) rather than children's abilities (Gauvain, Perez, Gauvain, & Perez, 2015). For instance, when 10- and 11-year-old Canadian Micmac Indian children were tested in English on conservation problems (substance, weight, and volume), they performed worse than 10- to 11-year-old White English-speaking children. But when tested in their native language, by researchers from their own culture, the children performed as well as the English-speaking children (Collette & Van der Linden, 2002).

Children around the world demonstrate concrete operational reasoning, but experience, specific cultural practices, and education play a role in how it is displayed (Manoach et al., 1997). Children are more likely to display logical reasoning when considering substances with which they are familiar. Mexican children who make pottery understand at an early age that clay remains the same when its shape is changed. They demonstrate conservation of substance earlier than other forms of conservation (Fry & Hale, 1996) and earlier than children who do not make pottery (Hitch, Towse, & Hutton, 2001; Leather & Henry, 1994).

Despite having never attended school and scoring low on measures of mathematics achievement, many 6- to 15-year-old children living in the streets of Brazil demonstrate sophisticated logical and computational reasoning. Why? These children sell items such as fruit and candy to earn their living. In addition to pricing their products, collecting money, making change, and giving discounts, the children must adjust prices daily to account for changes in demand, overhead, and the rate of inflation (Gathercole, Pickering, Ambridge, & Wearing, 2004). Researchers found that these children's competence in mathematics was influenced by experience, situational demands, and learning from others. Nevertheless, schooling also matters; children with some schooling were more adept at these tasks than were unschooled children (Siegel, 1994).

Schooling influences the rate at which principles are understood. For example, children who have been in school longer tend to do better on transitive inference tasks than same-age children with less schooling (Artman & Cahan, 1993). Likewise, Zimbabwean children's understanding of conservation is influenced by academic experience, age, and family socioeconomic status (Mpofu & Vijver, 2000). Japanese children's understanding of mathematical concepts tends to follow a path consistent with Piaget's maturational view, but other mathematical concepts are understood because of formal instruction, supportive of Vygotsky's principle of scaffolding (see Chapter 7).

School-age children's emerging capacities for reasoning influence their understanding of a variety of phenomena, including their conceptions of illness. We explore this concept more in the accompanying box, Cultural Influences on Development: Children's Understanding of Illness.

Information Processing

"If you're finished, put your head down on your desk and rest for a moment," Mrs. McCalvert advised. She was surprised to see that three quarters of her students immediately put their heads down. "They are getting quicker and quicker," she thought to herself. Information processing theorists would agree with Mrs. McCalvert's observation, because the information processing perspective describes development as entailing changes in the efficiency of cognition rather than qualitative changes in

These school-age children can process and retain information more accurately and quickly than younger children.
iStock/JohnnyGreig

Children's Understanding of Illness

Older children can hold both biological and cultural explanations about the causes of illness.
Reuters/ Ilya Naymushin

Cognitive development influences how children understand biology, their bodies, and the causes of illness. For example, young children tend to attribute contagious illnesses such as colds, coughs, and stomachaches to immanent justice—the belief that illness is caused by misdeeds and naughtiness (Myant & Williams, 2005). Other nonbiological explanations (e.g., magic or fate) are also common. As children advance in cognitive maturity, they develop more mature conceptions of illness, distinguish specific symptoms and diseases, and appreciate the biological causes of illness and contagiousness (Mouratidi, Bonoti, & Leondari, 2016).

Beliefs about biology and the causes of illness may vary by cultural setting. Research has suggested that nonbiological explanations of illness are common in adults from non-Western societies. For example, Murdock (1980) examined evidence from 139 nonindustrial societies around the world and found that most emphasized nonbiological causes of illness. Among the Zande of southern Sudan, for example, illness is thought to be caused by jealous or angry neighbors practicing witchcraft (T. Allen, 2007).

Cultural differences in beliefs about the causes of illness may arise from exposure to different explanations for illness. For example, most children in the United States are exposed to a germ and infection model of illness. Young children show a simple understanding of germs, and older children develop a more elaborate understanding. Children growing up in China have traditionally been exposed to Chinese medicine, which concerns the balance of yin and yang; breaking the balance is thought to lead to illness. In recent decades, however, Chinese children have been increasingly

exposed to Western medicine. With age and the cognitive development that accompanies it, Chinese children tend to integrate these two perspectives, emphasizing biological causes but also referring to concepts from traditional Chinese medicine (Zhu, Liu, & Tardif, 2009).

When exposed to biological concepts of illness, children of all cultures tend to incorporate them into their understanding. For example, one study of 5- to 15-year-old children and adults from Sesotho-speaking South African communities showed that the participants, who were exposed to Western medicine, most commonly endorsed biological explanations for illness but also often endorsed witchcraft (Legare & Gelman, 2008). Both natural and supernatural explanations were viewed as complementary. Likewise, comparisons of older children, adolescents, and adults from Tanna and Vanatu, remote islands off the coast of Malaysia, find that as individuals are confronted with scientific understandings of the world, they integrate scientific explanations with preexisting supernatural and other kinds of natural (e.g., folk-biological) explanations (Watson-Jones, Busch, & Legare, 2015). Tanna and Vanatu children endorsed biological just as frequently as supernatural explanations, but adolescents and adults most commonly endorsed biological explanations.

With age and across cultural groups, when individuals are exposed to biological explanations of illness, such explanations tend to be most frequently endorsed (Legare, Evans, Rosengren, & Harris, 2012). Moreover, the coexistence of biological and nonbiological reasoning about causes of illness is not confined to specific cultures. For example, in the United States and other industrialized societies, many alternative medicine practitioners attribute illness to negative thinking and other psychological problems. U.S. children and adults tend to retain some supernatural explanations alongside biological explanations (Legare et al., 2012). Among people in all cultures, diverse, culturally constructed belief systems about illness coexist with factual understanding and explanations of illness change with development.

What Do You Think?

1. How does our knowledge of individuals' understanding of illness compare with Piaget's cognitive-developmental theory?

2. Consider your own views and experience. Do you remember "catching a cold" when you were a child? What did that mean to you? ●

reasoning. School-age children can take in more information, process it more accurately and quickly, and retain it more effectively than younger children. They are better able to determine what information is important, attend to it, and use their understanding of how memory works to choose among strategies to retain information more effectively.

Working Memory and Executive Function

Children's working memory expands rapidly but is more limited than that of adults. By 8 years of age, children on average recall about half as many items as adults (Kharitonova, Winter, & Sheridan, 2015). Steady increases in working memory and executive function continue throughout childhood and are responsible for the cognitive changes seen during childhood. Advanced executive function capacities enable older children to control their attention and deploy it selectively, focusing on the relevant information and ignoring other information, compared with younger children, who are easily distracted and fidget (Ristic & Enns, 2015). Children not only get better at attending to and manipulating information, but they get better at storing it in long-term memory, organizing it in more sophisticated ways and encoding and retrieving it more efficiently and with less effort.

Improvements in memory, attention, and processing speed are possible because of brain development, particularly myelination and pruning in the prefrontal cortex and corpus callosum (Crone & Steinbeis, 2017; Perone, Almy, & Zelazo, 2018). Between ages 3 and 7, children show increasing prefrontal cortex engagement while completing tasks that measure working memory (Perlman, Huppert, & Luna, 2016). Neural systems for visuospatial working memory, auditory working memory, and response inhibition differentiate into separate parts to enable faster and more efficient processing of these critical cognitive functions (Crone & Steinbeis, 2017; Tsujimoto, Kuwajima, & Sawaguchi, 2007). Older children are quicker at matching pictures and recalling spatial information than younger children, and they show more activity in the frontal regions of the brain compared with younger children (Farber & Beteleva, 2011). Development of the prefrontal cortex leads to advances in response inhibition, the ability to withhold a behavioral response inappropriate in the current context. These advances improve children's capacity for self-regulation, controlling their thoughts and behavior. Advances in working memory and executive function are associated with language, reading, writing, and mathematics skills (Berninger, Abbott, Cook, & Nagy, 2017; Peng et al., 2018).

Age changes in performance on working memory tasks are also influenced by context. For example, the amount of schooling is a better predictor of working memory in Australian school children than chronological age (Roberts et al., 2015). High-quality relations with teachers are associated with higher scores on working memory tasks during elementary school (de Wilde, Koot, & van Lier, 2016).

Metacognition and Metamemory

Whereas young children tend to see the mind as a static container for information, older children view the mind in more sophisticated terms, as an active manipulator of information. Development of the prefrontal cortex influences children's growing capacities for metacognition. Children become mindful of their thinking and better able to consider the requirements of a task, determine how to tackle it, and monitor, evaluate, and adjust their activity to complete the task (Ardila, 2013).

Metamemory, an aspect of metacognition, includes the understanding of one's memory and the ability to use strategies to enhance it. Metamemory improves steadily throughout the elementary school years and contributes to advances in memory (Cottini, Basso, & Palladino, 2018; Schneider & Ornstein, 2015). Kindergarten and first-grade children understand that forgetting occurs with time and studying improves memory, but not until they are age 8 or 9 can children accurately evaluate their knowledge and apply it to learn more effectively. Older children perform better on cognitive tasks because they can evaluate the task; determine how to approach it given their cognitive resources, attention span, motivation, and knowledge; and choose and monitor the use of memory strategies that will permit them to successfully store and retrieve needed information (Schneider & Pressley, 2013). These abilities improve with neural maturation and experience.

Memory Strategies

Advances in executive function, working memory, and attention enable children to use memory strategies—cognitive activities ("tricks") that make them more likely to remember (Coughlin, Leckey, & Ghetti, 2018). Common memory strategies include rehearsal, organization, and elaboration. **Rehearsal** refers to systematically repeating information in order to retain it in working memory. A child may say a phone number over and over so that he does not forget it before writing it down. Children do not spontaneously and reliably apply rehearsal until after the first grade (Miller, McCulloch, & Jarrold, 2015; Morey, Mareva, Lelonkiewicz, & Chevalier, 2018). Shortly after rehearsal appears, children start to use **organization,** categorizing or chunking items to remember by grouping it by theme or type, such as animals, flowers, and furniture. When memorizing a list of words, a child might organize them into meaningful groups, or chunks—foods, animals, objects, and so forth. Growth in working memory is partially attributed to an increase in the number of chunks children can retain with age (Cowan et al., 2010). A third strategy, **elaboration,** entails creating an imagined scene or story to link the material to be remembered. To remember to buy bread, milk, and butter, for example, a child might imagine a slice of buttered bread balancing on a glass of milk. It is not until the later school years that children use elaboration without prompting and apply it to a variety of tasks (Schneider & Ornstein, 2015). As metacognition and metamemory skills, and the executive function that underlies these abilities, improve, children get better at choosing, using, and combining memory strategies, and their recall improves dramatically (Stone, Blumberg, Blair, & Cancelli, 2016). For example, fifth-grade students who use more complex memory strategies are more successful in delayed recall tasks in which they are asked to read a passage and then recall it after a delay (Jonsson, Wiklund-Hörnqvist, Nyroos, & Börjesson, 2014).

Context and Cognition

As children go about their daily lives, they acquire increasing amounts of information, which they naturally organize in meaningful ways. As children learn more about a topic, their knowledge structures become more elaborate and organized, while the information becomes more familiar and meaningful. It is easier to recall new information about topics with which we are already familiar, and existing knowledge about a topic makes it easier to learn more about that topic (Ericsson & Moxley, 2013). During middle childhood, children develop vast knowledge bases and organize information into elaborate hierarchical networks that enable them to apply strategies in more complex ways and remember more material than ever before—and more easily than ever before. For example, fourth-grade students who are experts at soccer show better recall of a list of soccer-related items than do students who are soccer novices, although the groups of children do not differ on the non-soccer-related items (Schneider & Bjorklund, 1992). The soccer experts tend to organize the lists of soccer items into categories; their knowledge helps them to organize the soccer-related information with little effort, using fewer resources on organization and permitting the use of more working memory for problem solving and reasoning. Novices, in contrast, lack a knowledge

base to aid their attempts at organization. Children's experiences, then, influence their memory, thinking, and reasoning.

The strategies that children use to tackle cognitive tasks vary with culture. In fact, daily tasks themselves vary with our cultural context. Children in Western cultures receive lots of experience with tasks that require them to recall bits of information, leading them to develop considerable expertise in the use of memory strategies such as rehearsal, organization, and elaboration. In contrast, research shows that people in non-Western cultures with no formal schooling do not use or benefit from instruction in memory strategies such as rehearsal (Rogoff & Chavajay, 1995). Instead, they refine memory skills that are adaptive to their way of life. For example, they may rely on spatial cues for memory, such as when recalling items within a three-dimensional miniature scene. Australian aboriginal and Guatemalan Mayan children perform better at these tasks than do children from Western cultures (Rogoff & Waddell, 1982). Culture and contextual demands influence the cognitive strategies that we learn and prefer, as well as how we use our information processing system to gather, manipulate, and store knowledge. Children of all cultures amass a great deal of information, and as they get older, they organize it in more sophisticated ways and encode and retrieve it more efficiently and with less effort.

THINKING IN CONTEXT 9.2

1. Physical and motor development have clear implications for cognitive development during infancy. Is the same true in middle childhood? In what ways might cognition be influenced by physical and motor development in school-age children?

2. How might your surroundings—culture, neighborhood, home, and school—have influenced specific aspects of your thinking, such as what strategies you use and your capacities for metacognition? Provide an example of how your context influenced your cognitive development.

INTELLIGENCE

» LO 9.3   **Summarize views of intelligence, including the uses, correlates, and criticisms of intelligence tests.**

At its simplest, intelligence refers to an individual's ability to adapt to the world in which he or she lives (Sternberg, 2014). Individuals differ in intelligence, an example of the lifespan concept of individual differences. There are many ways of defining and measuring intelligence. Intelligence is most commonly assessed through the use of **intelligence tests (IQ tests),** which measure intellectual aptitude, an individual's capacity to learn.

Intelligence Tests

Individually administered intelligence tests are conducted in a one-on-one setting by professionally trained examiners. The most widely used, individually administered measures of intelligence today are a set of tests constructed by David Wechsler, who viewed intelligence as "the global capacity of a person to act purposefully, to think rationally, and to deal effectively with his environment" (Wechsler, 1944, p. 3). The Wechsler Intelligence Scale for Children (WISC-V), appropriate for children ages 6 through 16, is the most widely used individually administered intelligence test for children. In addition to the

Intelligence tests are often administered individually, one-on-one.
BSIP/Universal/Getty

WISC, there are Wechsler tests for preschoolers (the Wechsler Preschool and Primary Scale of Intelligence, or WPPSI) and adults (the Wechsler Adult Intelligence Scale, or WAIS).

The WISC-V is composed of 10 subtests that comprise an overall measure of IQ as well as five indexes: verbal comprehension, visual spatial, fluid reasoning, working memory, and processing speed (Wechsler, 2014). The WISC tests verbal abilities that tap vocabulary and knowledge and factual information that is influenced by culture. It also tests nonverbal abilities, such as tasks that require the child to arrange materials such as blocks and pictures, that are thought to be less influenced by culture. The nonverbal subtests require little language proficiency, which enables children with speech disorders and those who do not speak English to be fairly assessed. Supplemental subtests are included to aid examiners in further assessing a child's capacities in a given area. Table 9.1 presents the subtests and sample items that comprise the WISC-V. By carefully examining a child's pattern of subtest scores, a professional can determine whether a child has specific learning needs, whether gifted or challenged (Flanagan & Alfonso, 2017).

The WISC is standardized on samples of children who are geographically and ethnically representative of the total population of the United States, creating norms that permit comparisons among children who are similar in age and ethnic background (Sattler, 2014). In Canada, an adapted WISC, standardized with children representative of the Canadian population, is available in English and French (Wechsler, 2014). The WISC has been adapted and used in many other countries, including the United Kingdom, Greece, Japan, Taiwan, Sweden, Lithuania, Slovenia, Germany, Austria, Switzerland,

TABLE 9.1

Sample Items From the Five Wechsler Intelligence Scale for Children (WISC-V)

WISC-V INDEX	SAMPLE ITEM
Verbal Comprehension Index (VCI)	Vocabulary: What does *amphibian* mean?
Visual Spatial Index (VSI)	Block design: In this timed task, children are shown a design composed of red-and-white bocks, are given a set of blocks, and are asked to put together the block in order to copy the design.
Fluid Reasoning Index (FRI)	Matrix reasoning: Children are shown an array of pictures with one missing. They must select the picture that completes the array.
Working Memory Index (WMI)	Digit span: Children are read lists of numbers and asked to repeat them as heard or in reverse order.
Processing Speed Index (PSI)	Coding: In this timed task, children are shown a code that converts numbers into symbols and are asked to transcribe lists of numbers into code.

France, and the Netherlands (Georgas, Weiss, van de Vijver, & Saklofske, 2003).

IQ scores are a strong predictor of academic achievement. Children with high IQs tend to earn higher-than-average grades at school and are more likely to stay in school (Mackintosh, 2011). School, in turn, provides children with exposure to information and ways of thinking that are valued by the majority culture and reflected in IQ tests. Same-age children with more years of schooling tend to have higher IQs than their less educated peers (Cliffordson & Gustafsson, 2008), and correlations between IQ and school achievement tests tend to increase with age (Sternberg, Grigorenko, & Bundy, 2001), suggesting that schooling is also an influence on IQ.

Individual and Group Differences in IQ

A consistent and controversial finding in the intelligence literature is that African American children as a group tend to score 10 to 15 points below non-Hispanic White Americans on standardized IQ tests (Rindermann & Thompson, 2013). The IQ scores of Hispanic children as a group tend to fall between those of children of African American and non-Hispanic White descent, and the scores of Asian American children tend to fall at the same level or slightly higher than those of non-Hispanic White children (Neisser et al., 1996; Nisbett et al., 2013). It is important to remember, however, that emphasizing differences between groups overlooks important facts. For one thing, individuals of all races and ethnicities show a wide range of functioning, from severely disabled to exceptionally gifted. In addition, the IQ scores of children of all races and ethnicities overlap. For example, at least 20% of African American children score higher on IQ than all other children, whether African American or non-Hispanic White (Rindermann & Thompson, 2013). Because there are more differences among African American children and among non-Hispanic White children than between the two groups, many researchers conclude that group comparisons are meaningless (Daley & Onwuegbuzie, 2011).

Contextual Influences on IQ

Like all facets of development, intelligence is influenced by dynamic interactions among genetic or biological factors and context. Heredity is thought to play a role in intelligence, but to date, researchers have not identified any specific genes that are responsible for IQ (Franić et al., 2015). Genes likely do not act independently but instead in conjunction with the environment (Dubois et al., 2012; Plomin,

DeFries, Knopik, & Neiderhiser, 2016). Perhaps most telling is that the heritability of IQ tends to vary with context.

Genes appear to play a large role in determining IQ scores of children from high SES homes but play less of a role in determining IQ scores for children in low SES homes (Nisbett et al., 2013). Because high SES homes tend to provide consistent support, such as cognitive stimulation, to help children achieve their genetic potential, differences in IQ among children reared in high SES homes are more likely due to genetics. Children from impoverished homes, however, often lack consistent access to the basic support needed for intellectual development, such as nutrition, health care, and stimulating environments and activities. In these cases, IQ scores are often heavily influenced by the context and opportunities that children have experienced (Nisbett et al., 2013). African American children are disproportionately likely to live in poverty, and impoverished children's IQ scores tend to be more influenced by the disadvantaged contexts in which they are immersed than by the genes with which they are born. Likewise, children who are adopted from low SES homes into higher SES homes typically score 12 points or higher on IQ tests than siblings who are raised by birth parents or adopted into lower SES homes (Duyme, Dumaret, & Tomkiewicz, 1999).

Socioeconomic status contributes to IQ through differences in culture, nutrition, living conditions, school resources, intellectual stimulation, and life circumstances such as the experience of discrimination. Any or all of these factors can influence cognitive and psychosocial factors related to IQ, such as motivation, self-concept, and academic achievement (Plomin & Deary, 2015). Education plays a particularly important role in IQ. As noted earlier, school provides children with exposure to information and ways of thinking that are valued by the majority culture and reflected in IQ tests. IQ rises with each year spent in school, improves during the school year—which runs from October to April in the United States—and drops over the summer vacation (Huttenlocher, Levine, & Vevea, 1998). The seasonal drop in IQ scores each summer is larger for children from low SES homes (Nisbett et al., 2013).

Some experts argue that IQ tests tap the thinking style and language of the majority culture (Heath, 1989; Helms, 1992). Language difficulties also may explain some group differences. For example, Latino and Native American children tend to do better on nonverbal tasks than ones that require the use of language (Neisser et al., 1996). However, even nonverbal sorting tasks can be influenced by culture. When presented with a series of cards depicting objects and activities and told to sort the cards into meaningful categories, children from Western cultures tend to sort the cards by category, putting bird and dog in the same category of animal. Children of the Kpelle tribe in Nigeria instead sort the cards by function, placing bird with fly, for example, because birds fly (Sternberg, 1985). Learning experiences and opportunities influence children's scores on nonverbal tasks. For example, performance on spatial reasoning tasks is associated with experience with spatially oriented video games (Subrahmanyam & Greenfield, 1996).

Finally, sociohistorical context influences intelligence. Since the 1930s, some researchers have noted that intelligence scores increase with each generation (Lynn, 2013). Over the past 60 years, intelligence scores have increased by about 9 points for measures of general knowledge and 15 points for nonverbal measures of fluid reasoning with each generation (Flynn, 1987, 1998). Referred to as the **Flynn effect,** this generational increase in IQ is thought to be a function of contextual factors—specifically, changes in education and environmental stimulation that improve children's reasoning and problem-solving skills (Flynn & Weiss, 2007). Each generation of children is exposed to more information and ideas than the generation before, and this exposure likely influences thinking itself (te Nijenhuis, 2013).

Alternative Views of Intelligence

Arguments about the cultural bias of IQ tests have led some researchers to reconsider what it means to be intelligent. Howard Gardner and Robert Sternberg propose that intelligence entails more than academics. Their theories link intelligence to everyday problems and situations.

Multiple Intelligences

A skilled dancer, a champion athlete, an award-winning musician, and an excellent communicator all have talents that are not measured by traditional IQ tests. According to Howard Gardner (2017), intelligence is the ability to solve problems or create culturally valued products. Specifically, Gardner's **multiple intelligence theory** proposes at least eight independent kinds of intelligence, shown in Table 9.2. Multiple intelligence theory expands the use of the term *intelligence* to refer to skills not usually considered intelligence by experts and has led to a great deal of debate among intelligence theorists and researchers (Kaufman, Kaufman, & Plucker, 2013).

According to multiple intelligence theory, each person has a unique pattern of intellectual strengths and weaknesses. A person may be gifted in dance (bodily-kinesthetic intelligence), communication (verbal-linguistic intelligence), or music (musical intelligence), yet score low on traditional measures of IQ. Each form of intelligence is thought to be biologically based, and each develops on a different timetable (Gardner, 2017). Assessing multiple intelligences requires observing the products of each form of intelligence (e.g., how well a child can learn a tune, navigate an unfamiliar area, or learn dance steps), which at best is a lengthy proposition and at worst is nearly impossible (Barnett, Ceci, & Williams, 2006). However, through extended observations, an examiner can identify patterns of strengths and weaknesses in individuals and help them understand and achieve their potential (Gardner, 2016).

The theory of multiple intelligences is an optimistic perspective that allows everyone to be intelligent in his or her own way, viewing intelligence as broader than book-learning and academic skills.

TABLE 9.2

Multiple Intelligences

INTELLIGENCE	DESCRIPTION
Verbal-linguistic intelligence	Ability to understand and use the meanings and subtleties of words ("word smarts")
Logical-mathematical intelligence	Ability to manipulate logic and numbers to solve problems ("number smarts")
Spatial intelligence	Ability to perceive the visual-spatial world accurately, navigate an environment, and judge spatial relationships ("spatial smarts")
Bodily-kinesthetic intelligence	Ability to move the body skillfully ("body smarts")
Musical intelligence	Ability to perceive and create patterns of pitch and melody ("music smarts")
Interpersonal intelligence	Ability to understand and communicate with others ("people smarts")
Intrapersonal intelligence	Ability to understand the self and regulate emotions ("self-smarts")
Naturalist intelligence	Ability to distinguish and classify elements of nature: animals, minerals, and plants ("nature smarts")

Source: Gardner, 2017.

If intelligence is multidimensional, as Gardner suggests, perhaps school curricula should target the many forms that intelligence may take and help students to develop a range of talents (Gardner, 2013). Although the theory of multiple intelligences has been criticized as not being grounded in research (Waterhouse, 2006), neuroscientists have noted that each type of intelligence corresponds to specific neurological processes (Shearer & Karanian, 2017). The theory of multiple intelligences draws attention to the fact that IQ tests measure a specific set of mental abilities and ignore others.

Triarchic Theory of Intelligence

Jason Bourne, hero of the popular spy-action novel and movie series *The Bourne Trilogy*, is highly adaptive. He can quickly gather information, such as a villain's plot, process it, and devise a plan. He adapts his plan on the fly as the situation changes and thinks creatively in order to escape seemingly impossible situations—traps, car chases, and other dangerous scenarios. Certainly Jason Bourne is a fictional character, but he illustrates another view of intelligence, articulated by Robert Sternberg. According to Sternberg (1985), intelligence is a set of mental abilities that permits individuals to adapt to any context and to select and modify the sociocultural contexts in which they live and behave. Sternberg's **triarchic theory of intelligence** poses three forms of intelligence: analytical, creative, and practical (Sternberg, 2011) (see Figure 9.5). Individuals may have strengths in any or all of them.

Analytical intelligence refers to information processing capacities, such as how efficiently people acquire knowledge, process information, engage in metacognition, and generate and apply strategies to solve problems—much like Bourne's ability to process information quickly and consider different solutions. *Creative intelligence* taps insight and the ability to deal with novelty. People who are high in

creative intelligence, like Bourne, respond to new tasks quickly and efficiently. They learn easily, compare information with what is already known, come up with new ways of organizing information, and display original thinking. *Applied intelligence* influences how people deal with their surroundings: how well they evaluate their environment, selecting and modifying it, and adapting it to fit their own needs and external demands—similar to Bourne's ability to modify his plans on the fly, using whatever resources are available. Intelligent people apply their analytical, creative, and applied abilities to suit the setting and problems at hand (Sternberg, 2011). Some situations require careful analysis, others the ability to think creatively, and yet others the ability to solve problems quickly in everyday settings. Many situations tap more than one form of intelligence.

Traditional IQ tests measure analytical ability, which is thought to be associated with school success. However, IQ tests do not measure creative and practical intelligence, which predict success outside of school. Some people are successful in everyday settings but less so in school settings and therefore may obtain low scores on traditional IQ tests despite being successful in their careers and personal lives. In this way, traditional IQ tests can underestimate the intellectual strengths of some children.

Cultures vary in the specific skills thought to constitute intelligence, but the three mental abilities that underlie intelligent behavior—analytic, creative, and applied intelligence—are recognized across cultures. Still, the relative importance ascribed to each may differ (Sternberg & Grigorenko, 2008). In Western cultures, the intelligent person is one who invests a great deal of effort into learning, enjoys it, and enthusiastically seeks opportunities for lifelong learning. In contrast, other cultures emphasize applied intelligence. For example, the Chinese Taoist tradition emphasizes the importance of humility, freedom from conventional standards of judgment, and awareness of the self and the outside world (Yang & Sternberg, 1997). In many African cultures, conceptions of intelligence revolve around the skills that maintain harmonious interpersonal relations (Ruzgis & Grigorenko, 1994). Chewa adults in Zambia emphasize social responsibilities, cooperativeness, obedience, and respectfulness as being important to intelligence. Likewise, Kenyan parents emphasize responsible participation in family and social life (Serpell, 1974; Serpell & Jere-Folotiya, 2008; Super & Harkness, 1982).

Views of intelligence even vary within a given context (Sternberg, 2014). For example, when parents were asked of the characteristics of an intelligent child in the first grade of elementary school, White American parents emphasized cognitive capacities. Parents who were immigrants from Cambodia, the Philippines, Vietnam, and Mexico, on the other hand,

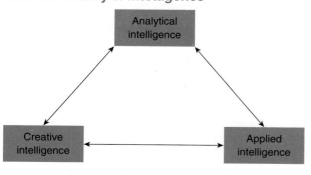

FIGURE 9.5

Triarchic Theory of Intelligence

pointed to motivation, self-management, and social skills (Okagaki & Sternberg, 1993), suggesting that characteristics valued as intelligent vary across cultures and that children within the same context may be immersed in different cultures (Sternberg, 2014). Once again, we see the complexity of context and culture as influences on development.

⚙️ **THINKING IN CONTEXT 9.3**

1. How do you define intelligence? From your perspective, what has influenced your own intelligence, as you have defined it? How does your view compare with the views that we have discussed?

2. How might definitions and views of intelligence differ across contexts—different socioeconomic levels, different neighborhoods, or different cultures, such as Western and non-Western?

MORAL DEVELOPMENT IN MIDDLE CHILDHOOD

» LO 9.4   Examine patterns of moral development during middle childhood.

The development of moral reasoning is influenced by childhood advances in cognitive development, social experience, and opportunities to consider issues of fairness. Specifically, children's reasoning about justice changes in middle childhood.

Moral Reasoning: Piaget's Theory

As elementary school children spend more time with peers and become better at taking their friends' perspectives, their understanding of rules becomes more flexible. Recall from Chapter 7 that according to Piaget (1932), young children view rules rigidly. Piaget referred to this stage as heteronomous morality. In middle childhood, at about age 7, children enter the second stage of Piaget's scheme, **autonomous morality** (also known as the *morality of cooperation*). Now children begin to see rules as products of group agreement and tools to improve cooperation. For example, older children are likely to recognize that the teacher's rule that the youngest children must be the first to bat at the piñata at a children's party is a way to help the youngest children, who are less likely to be successful. Some children might agree that the rule promotes fairness, while others might argue to abandon the rule as it gives younger children an unfair advantage. At this stage, children view a need for agreement on rules and consequences for violations. Piaget's theory of moral reasoning inspired Lawrence Kohlberg, who created perhaps the most well-known theory of moral reasoning.

Children's Conceptions of Justice: Kohlberg's Cognitive-Developmental Perspective

Kohlberg (1976) proposed that moral reasoning reflects cognitive development and is organized into stages and levels. Each level of moral reasoning is composed of two stages. Beginning in early childhood and persisting until about age 9, children demonstrate what Kohlberg called preconventional reasoning. Similar to Piaget, Kohlberg argued that young children's behavior is governed by self-interest, the desire to gain rewards and avoid punishments ("Don't steal because you don't want to go to jail"). Moral behavior is a response to external pressure, and children's reasoning illustrates their difficulty in taking another person's perspective. Instead, young children's moral reasoning is motivated by their desires. The preconventional level comprises two stages, in which children move from avoiding punishment as a motivator of moral judgments (Stage 1) to self-interest, rewards, and concern about what others can do for them (Stage 2).

At about age 9 or 10, children transition to the second level of Kohlberg's scheme, **conventional moral reasoning.** Children are now able to take others' perspectives and are motivated by reciprocity, seeking to be accepted and avoid disapproval. Rules maintain relationships. At Stage 3, children uphold rules in order to please others, gain affection, and be a good person—honest, caring, and nice. The Golden Rule motivates their behavior: "Do unto others as you would have them do unto you." At Stage 4, which emerges in adolescence, perspective taking expands beyond individuals to include society's rules. Adolescents accept rules as a tool to maintain social order and believe that everyone has a duty to uphold the rules. Reasoning is no longer influenced by relationships and a desire to be a good person. Instead, rules are universal and must be enforced for everyone. Many people demonstrate conventional reasoning throughout their lives. Not everyone develops the third and final level of reasoning, postconventional reasoning, discussed in Chapter 11. Preconventional and conventional moral reasoning are compared in Table 9.3.

Moral development is influenced by how parents and caregivers discuss moral issues, such as those involving telling the truth, harming others, and respecting property rights (Malti & Latzko,

TABLE 9.3

Moral Development in Middle Childhood: Comparison of Piaget and Kohlberg's Theories

	PIAGET'S STAGES		KOHLBERG'S LEVELS[a]	
	STAGE 1: MORALITY OF CONSTRAINT	STAGE 2: MORALITY OF COOPERATION	LEVEL 1: PRECON-VENTIONAL MORAL REASONING	LEVEL 2: CONVEN-TIONAL MORAL REASONING
Cognitive-developmental stage	Preoperational	Concrete operational	Preoperational	Concrete operational
Perspective	Individualistic. Children cannot take the perspective of others; they assume that everyone sees the world as they do.	Multiple. Children can take the perspective of others; they see that more than one point of view is possible and that others do not necessarily view issues as they do.	Individualistic. Children cannot take the perspective of others; they focus on their own needs.	Community. Children take the perspective of the community at large; there is an emphasis on societal rules and welfare.
View of justice	Absolute. Children see acts as either right or wrong, with no shades of gray. The wrongness of an act is defined by punishment.	Relative. Children see that there is often more than one point of view. Acts are seen as right or wrong regardless of punishment.	Absolute. Acts are either right or wrong, defined by punishment and rewards.	Absolute. Right or wrong acts are defined by social approval.
Understanding of rules	Rules are unalterable and sacred.	Rules are created by people and can be changed if it suits people's needs.	Rules are unalterable and imposed by authority figures.	Rules are unalterable and act to uphold the community.
Reason for compliance with rules	Rules are obeyed out of a sense of obligation to conform to authority and to avoid punishment.	Rules perceived as just are obeyed for their own sake rather than under threat of punishment.	Rules are followed in order to gain rewards and avoid punishment.	Rules are followed out of a sense of duty, in order to please others and gain social approval, which is more important than other rewards.

Sources: Adapted from Hoffman (1970); Kohlberg (1981); Piaget (1932).

[a]Each level comprises two stages. Level 3, Postconventional Moral Reasoning, is discussed in Chapter 11.

2010). Reasoning advances when children have opportunities to engage in discussions that are characterized by mutual perspective taking and opportunities to discuss different points of view. When children encounter reasoning that is slightly more advanced than their own, they may be prompted to reconsider their own thinking and advance their reasoning. Parents who are warm and engage their children in discussion, listen with sensitivity, and use humor promote the development of moral reasoning (Carlo, Mestre, Samper, Tur, & Armenta, 2011; Killen & Smetana, 2015).

Distributive Justice Reasoning

Every day, children are confronted with moral issues of distributive justice—how to divide goods fairly (Damon, 1977, 1988). For example, how should a candy bar be divided among three siblings? Does age matter? Height? Hunger? How much the child likes chocolate?

As with moral reasoning, children progress from self-serving reasons for sharing, expressed in early childhood (e.g., "I get more candy because I want it" or "I share candy so that Mikey will play with me"), to more sophisticated and mature conceptions of distributive justice in middle childhood (Damon, 1977). At about 7 years of age, children take merit into account and believe that extra candy should go to the child who has excelled or worked especially hard. At around 8 years of age, children can act on the basis of benevolence, believing that others at a disadvantage should get special consideration. For example, extra candy should go to the child who does not get picked to play on a sports team or a child who is excluded from an activity. Between ages 8 and 10, children come to understand that people can have different yet equally valid reasons for claiming a reward. They begin to reflect on the need to balance competing claims, such as those of merit and need (Smith & Warneken, 2016). Older children also tend to differentiate among their relationships, which may influence their judgments. For example, older children often see relationships with acquaintances as relationships of mutual exchange (e.g., you scratch my back and I'll scratch yours), whereas relationships with their best friends might be seen as communal and reciprocal; decisions may be guided by concern for the other and a desire to maintain the relationship (Frederickson & Simmonds, 2008). Preadolescents and young adolescents try to coordinate claims of merit, need, and equality and provide increasingly sophisticated answers that often cannot be expressed in a single sentence (Damon, 1980).

Culture subtly influences children's ideas about distributive justice. Research with young children from rural and urban areas of China, Peru, Fiji, United States, Brazil, and Tibet showed a similar pattern of development from self-interest to increasing fairness (Robbins, Starr, & Rochat, 2016; Rochat et al., 2009). Cultures varied in the magnitude of young children's self-interest. Children reared in small-scale urban and traditional societies thought to promote more collective values showed less self-interest and more fairness. When Filipino and American fifth graders were presented with hypothetical scenarios that required that they distribute resources, both the Filipino and American children preferred equal division of the resources regardless of merit or need, but the children offered different explanations of their choices that are based in differences in Filipino and U.S. culture (Carson & Banuazizi, 2008). U.S. children emphasized that the characters in the scenario preformed equally and therefore deserved equal amounts of the resources, reflecting U.S. culture's emphasis on individuality and merit. Filipino children, on the other hand, tended to be more concerned with the interpersonal and emotional consequences of an unequal distribution, in line with their culture's emphasis on the collective and the importance of interpersonal relationships (Carson & Banuazizi, 2008).

Distinguishing Moral and Conventional Rules

Like younger children, school-age children distinguish between moral and conventional rules, judging moral rules as more absolute than conventional rules (see Chapter 7) (Turiel & Nucci, 2017). Moral rules are seen as less violable, less contingent on authority, and less alterable than social conventions (Smetana, Jambon, & Ball, 2014). Children anticipate feeling positive emotions after following moral rules and are likely to label violations

As children grow older they are more likely to view relational aggression as morally wrong and comparable to physical aggression.
iStock/LSOphoto

of moral rules as disgusting (Danovitch & Bloom, 2009). With advances in cognitive development, children can consider multiple perspectives and become better able to consider the situation and weigh a variety of variables in making decisions. They discriminate social conventions that have a purpose from those with no obvious purpose. Social conventions that serve a purpose, such as preventing injuries (e.g., not running indoors), are evaluated as more important and more similar to moral issues than social conventions with no obvious purpose (e.g., avoiding a section of the school yard despite no apparent danger) (Smetana et al., 2014). School-age children also consider intent and context. For example, Canadian 8- to 10-year-old children understood that a flag serves as a powerful symbol of a country and its values—and that burning it purposefully is worse than accidentally burning it. The 10-year-old children also understood that flag burning is an example of freedom of expression and can be used to express disapproval of a country or its activities. They agreed that if a person were in a country that is unjust, burning its flag would be acceptable (Helwig & Prencipe, 1999).

School-age children also distinguish among moral issues. For example, elementary school children judged bullying as wrong independent of rules and more wrong than other moral issues, such as lapses in truth-telling—and both were judged more wrong than etiquette transgressions (Thornberg, Thornberg, Alamaa, & Daud, 2016). School-age children become increasingly able to demonstrate nuanced judgments in response to complex moral dilemmas. For example, 5- to 11-year-old children become increasingly tolerant of necessary harm— that is, violating moral rules in order to prevent injury to others (Jambon & Smetana, 2014).

Children develop and hone their understanding of morality through social interaction, at home, at

Moral Development and the Brain

Morality is multidimensional, influenced by cognition as well as by quick intuitive emotional responses (De Neys & Glumicic, 2008; Greene & Haidt, 2002; Haidt, 2008). Moral decisions are frequently described as gut reactions. How is morality represented in the brain?

Most of the research on the neural correlates of morality is conducted with adults. These studies suggest that activity in the frontal cortex, especially the ventromedial prefrontal cortex (vmPFC), is central to making moral decisions (Prehn et al., 2008; Young & Koenigs, 2008). The vmPFC plays a role in planning, responding to decision uncertainty, response inhibition, and directing the emotions that arise while solving moral problems. Increased vmPFC activity is observed in response to deliberating over more severe relative to less severe moral transgressions (Luo et al., 2006). Longitudinal research suggests that the vmPFC increases in thickness from childhood into adolescence, and the thickening is associated with increased capacities for introspection, which has implications for moral reasoning (Fandakova et al., 2017).

In one study, children and adults (ages 4–37) responded to scenarios depicting intentional versus accidental actions that caused harm or damage to people or objects (Decety, Michalska, & Kinzler, 2012). Both children and adults judged intentional harm as wrong. With age, participants showed greater activity in the vmPFC in response to intentional harm to people. They also showed greater connectivity between the vmPFC and

the amygdala, a part of the brain responsible for emotion (Jung et al., 2016), suggesting that, with age, cognitive and emotional processing of moral problems becomes increasingly coordinated. In support, other research has shown that adults who score high on moral reasoning tasks tend to show greater functional connectivity between the vmPFC and the amygdala (Jung et al., 2016). Moreover, connections between the vmPFC and amygdala increase with age (Decety et al., 2012). It is thought that the amygdala triggers automatic emotional responses to stimuli (Everitt, Cardinal, Parkinson, & Robbins, 2003). The vmPFC integrates this information to evaluate the problem and determine responses.

Moral development is complex, and the emotional and cognitive processes that comprise it are influenced by many brain regions that interact. Morality is supported not by a single brain circuitry or structure but by a multiplicity of circuits that overlap with other general complex processes (Decety et al., 2012).

What Do You Think?

1. What might the neurological basis of morality mean for the nature–nurture question?

2. What role do you think context plays in children's moral reasoning?

3. How do you reconcile findings supporting biological and contextual influences on moral development? ●

THINKING IN CONTEXT 9.4

1. Theories of moral reasoning emphasize cognition. In what ways might children's decisions about right and wrong reflect other factors, such as physical maturation or socioemotional development?

2. How might exosystem and macrosystem factors (recall Bronfenbrenner's bioecological model) influence children's views of right and wrong?

school, and with peers. Children regularly encounter moral and conventional issues, such as lying to a friend, not completing homework, or violating a household rule. Everyday social interactions can advance moral reasoning. When children engage in issue-focused discussions involving reasoning that is slightly more advanced than their own, it may

prompt them to reconsider their own thinking. As a result, they often internalize the new reasoning, advancing their moral thinking to a new level. Moral development is also thought to be influenced by brain development, as discussed in the Brain and Biological Influences on Development feature.

LANGUAGE DEVELOPMENT IN MIDDLE CHIDHOOD

» LO 9.5   Summarize language development during middle childhood.

School-age children expand their vocabulary and develop a more complex understanding of grammar, rules that permit combining words to express ideas and feelings. Children's understanding of pragmatics, how language is used in everyday contexts, grows and becomes more sophisticated during middle childhood.

Vocabulary

School-age children's increases in vocabulary are not as noticeable to parents as the changes that occurred in infancy and early childhood. Nevertheless, 6-year-old children's vocabularies expand by four times by the end of the elementary school years and six times by the end of formal schooling (E. V. Clark, 2017).

Children learn that many words can describe a given action, but the words often differ slightly in meaning (e.g., walk, stride, hike, march, tread, strut, and meander) (Hoff, 2014). They become more selective in their use of words, choosing the right word to meet their needs. As their vocabularies grow, children learn that some words can have more than one meaning, such as *run* ("The jogger runs down the street," "The clock runs fast," etc.). They begin to appreciate that some words have psychological meanings as well as physical ones (e.g., a person can be smooth and a surface can be smooth). This understanding that words can be used in more than one way leads 8- to 10-year-old children to understand similes and metaphors (e.g., a person can be described as "cold as ice" or "sharp as a tack") (Katz, 2017).

Everyday experiences shape our vocabulary, how we think, and how we speak. Words are often acquired incidentally from writing and verbal contexts rather than through explicit vocabulary instruction (Owens, 2016). Some complex words, such as scientific terms, require the acquisition of conceptual knowledge over repeated exposure in different contexts. One study examined 4- to 10-year-old children's knowledge of two scientific terms, *eclipse* and *comet*, before and after the natural occurrence of a solar eclipse. Two weeks after the solar eclipse and without additional instruction, the children showed improvement in their knowledge of eclipses but not comets; older and younger children did not differ in their knowledge (Best, Dockrell, & Braisby, 2006).

Children's vocabulary expands and becomes more complex during the school years.
iStock/FangXiaNuo

Grammar

Older children become increasingly aware of and knowledgeable about the nature and qualities of language, known as metalinguistic awareness (Simard & Gutiérrez, 2018). Language arts classes in elementary school teach children about the parts of language and the syntax of sentences, aiding children as they further develop their ability to think about their use of language.

By 8 years of age, children can analyze the grammatical acceptability of their utterances and spontaneously self-correct many of their errors (Hanley, Cortis, Budd, & Nozari, 2016).

In middle childhood, schoolchildren become better able to understand complex grammatical structures. They begin to use the passive voice ("The dog is being fed"), complex constructions such as the use of the auxiliary *have* ("I have already fed the dog"), and conditional sentences ("If I had been home earlier, I would have fed the dog") (E. V. Clark, 2017). Despite these advances, school-age children often have difficulty understanding spoken sentences of which the meaning depends on subtle shifts in intonation (Turnbull & Justice, 2016). An example can be found in the sentence, "John gave a lollipop to David, and he gave one to Bob." With the emphasis placed on "and," the sentence can be taken to mean that John gave a lollipop to both David and Bob, whereas if the emphasis is on "he," the sentence can be assumed to mean that John gave a lollipop to David, and David gave one to Bob.

Experience with language and exposure to complex constructions influence grammatical development. For example, most English-speaking children find passive-voice sentences (such as "The boy was struck by the car") difficult to understand and therefore master passive-voice sentences later than other structures (Armon-Lotem et al., 2016). In contrast, the Inuit children of Arctic Canada hear and speak the Inuktitut language, which emphasizes full passives; they produce passive-voice sentences in their language sooner than do children from other cultures (S. E. M. Allen & Crago, 1996). The culture and language systems in which children are immersed influence their use of language and, ultimately, the ways in which they communicate. Throughout middle childhood, sentence structure and use of grammar become more sophisticated, children become better at communicating their ideas, and their understanding of pragmatics improves.

Pragmatics

Pragmatics refers to the practical application of language to communicate (Owens, 2016). With age and advances in perspective-taking skills that come with cognitive development, children are more likely to change their speech in response to the needs of listeners. For example, when faced with an adult who will not give them a desired object, 9-year-old children are more polite in restating their request than are 5-year-old children (Ninio, 2014). Similarly, 10-year-old Marques asks to share a cookie with his friend ("Yo! Gimme a cookie!") using very different language and intonation than he does when asking his grandmother for a cookie ("May I please have a cookie?"). Children speak to adults differently than to other children, and they speak differently on the playground than in class or at home. In addition, older children begin to understand that there is often a distinction between what people say and what they mean.

One example of pragmatics that develops in middle childhood is the use of *irony*, choosing a word or expression that conveys the opposite of its literal meaning. Many contextual, linguistic, and developmental factors influence the processing and comprehension of irony, such as the ability to interpret intonation and facial expressions as well as the capacity to evaluate how well a statement matches the situation (Pexman, 2014). Children at the ages of 5 to 6 become capable of recognizing irony when they are able to understand that a speaker might believe something different from what has been said. Yet most children at this age tend to interpret irony as sincere, relying on the person's statement and disregarding other cues in the story, such as intonation and gestures. Cognitive development permits children to detect the discrepancy between what the speaker says and what he or she believes. Children's ability to understand ironic remarks continues to develop through middle childhood, and by age 8, children can recognize and use irony (Glenwright & Pexman, 2010). However, even in adolescence, the understanding of irony is still developing; children as old as 13 do not reliably distinguish irony, intended to joke or mock, from deception, intended to conceal information (Filippova & Astington, 2008).

THINKING IN CONTEXT 9.5

1. Recall from Chapter 1 that development is characterized by continuities and discontinuities. How might you characterize language development? Is it continuous or discontinuous? Why?

2. In what ways does language development illustrate the interaction of developmental and contextual factors? Give some examples related to school-age children's language development.

LEARNING AND SCHOOLING IN MIDDLE CHLDHOOD

» LO 9.6   Discuss children's learning at school.

Schoolchildren's growing cognitive abilities enable them to learn in more sophisticated ways. However, their understanding of logic is concrete, oriented toward the tangible. Effective instruction helps older children grasp complex ideas by identifying connections between new material and prior knowledge, building on what they already know, and keeping pace with their growing abilities. During the school years, older children become proficient at reading, writing, and mathematics.

Reading and Mathematics

Cognitive development, especially advances in executive functioning and working memory, contribute to advances in math achievement and reading comprehension in elementary school (Cormier, McGrew, Bulut, & Funamoto, 2017). Schooling plays a key role in aiding children in mastering reading and math.

In past generations, most children were taught to read via **phonics instruction,** lessons and drills that emphasized learning the patterns of sound combinations in words. Children learned the sounds of each letter, memorized language rules, and sounded out words (Brady, 2011). In the late 1980s, the whole-language approach to reading instruction was introduced. In this approach, literacy is viewed as an extension of language, and children learn to read and write through trial-and-error discovery that is similar to how they learn to speak—without drills or learning phonics. The emphasis on children as active constructors of knowledge is appealing and in line with cognitive-developmental theory. Today, the whole-language approach is still in widespread use, and many teachers are not trained in phonics instruction. However, the research comparing the two approaches has offered little support for whole-language claims and overwhelming support for the efficacy of phonics training in improving children's reading skills (Cunningham, 2013).

A substantial number of U.S. children are poor readers and thereby at risk for poor academic achievement. In 2015, about one third of fourth-grade students were unable to meet basic standards for reading at their grade level (National Center for Education Statistics, 2017a). Early reading deficits influence all areas of academic competence (math, writing, science, etc.), and children who experience

Advances in cognitive development underlie older children's achievements in math, reading, and other academic skills.
iStock/Choreograph

early difficulties in reading often remain behind (Hong & Yu, 2007). Children's attitudes, interests, and motivation in reading and writing tend to decline over the school years, and the drop occurs more rapidly in worse readers (Wigfield, Gladstone, & Turci, 2016). Deficits in reading skill are associated with social adjustment problems, and this association increases over time. For example, poor reading achievement in preschool and third grade predicts behavioral problems in first grade and fifth grade (Guo, Sun, Breit-Smith, Morrison, & Connor, 2015). Children with poor reading skills tend to have poor vocabularies, which may make it more difficult for them to successfully interact with peers (Benner, Nelson, & Epstein, 2002).

Similar to reading, in past generations, math was taught through rote learning activities such as drills, memorization of number facts (e.g., multiplication tables), and completion of workbooks. Many children found these methods boring or restrictive; they learned to dislike math and did not perform well. In 1989, the National Council of Teachers of Mathematics modified the national mathematics curriculum to emphasize mathematical concepts and problem solving, estimating, and probability; teachers were to encourage student interaction and social involvement in solving math problems. The emphasis changed from product—getting correct answers quickly—to process—learning how to understand and execute the steps in getting an answer. Teachers often use strategies that involve manipulatives, opportunities for students to interact physically with objects to learn target information, rather than relying solely on abstraction. Such strategies have been shown to be effective in enhancing problem solving and retention (Carbonneau, Marley, & Selig, 2013).

In contrast with research findings about the whole-language approach to reading, changes in the mathematics curriculum are supported by student achievement, as fourth-grade students' mathematical skills have improved over the past two decades. Between 1990 and 2015, the proportion of fourth-grade students performing at or above the proficient level increased from 13% to 40%, and the proportion that could not do math at their grade level fell from 50% in 1990 to 18% in 2015 (National Center for Education Statistics, 2017a). Although these represent important gains, the 18% statistic means that nearly one in five U.S. schoolchildren is still deficient in math skills, suggesting that there is more work to be done. The past decade has seen new educational initiatives that emphasize math and reading instruction coupled with frequent assessments of student achievement to ensure that progress is made and children do not fall through the cracks. What should educators do when children fail to meet academic standards for promotion to the next grade level? See the accompanying box, Applying Developmental Science: Grade Retention, for more discussion on this topic.

Bilingualism and Learning a Second Language

It is estimated that more than 50% of the world's children are exposed to more than one language (Grosjean, 2010). An estimated 350 languages, including 150 native North American languages, are spoken in U.S. homes (U.S. Bureau of the Census, 2015).

Simultaneous Bilingualism

Children who are exposed to two languages from birth are referred to as simultaneous bilinguals, or bilingual first-language learners (Genesee, 2006). Infants who are exposed to two languages build distinct language systems from birth and by 1 year of age show understanding of the phonetic categories for both languages (MacWhinney, 2015). The rate of acquisition for two languages, like that for one language, depends on the quantity and quality of the input in each language (Hoff & Core, 2015). Because children who are exposed to two languages will tend to hear less of either language than their monolingual peers, their rate of growth in each language tends to be slower than those who are exposed to and acquire a single language. Bilingual children tend to lag behind monolingual children in vocabulary and grammar in each language (Hindman & Wasik, 2015). However, bilingual children's combined vocabularies for both languages tend to be similar in size to the vocabulary of monolingual children (Bosch & Ramon-Casas, 2014). The gap in language development between monolingual and bilingual children narrows with age, and bilingual children

Grade Retention

Providing students and families with a variety of academic and support resources to promote student achievement may be more effective than the practice of grade retention.
Dennis MacDonald / Alamy Stock Photo

Today, at least 16 U.S. states require students who fall a grade behind in reading achievement to be retained, or "left back" (Jacob, 2016). About 10% of U.S. children are retained in a grade at least once between kindergarten and eighth grade (National Center for Education Statistics, 2017b). In addition to state-mandated retention due to low achievement scores, students are retained for other reasons, such as frequent unexcused absences, social and cognitive immaturity, and the belief that an

extra year of schooling will produce successful academic and socioemotional outcomes. African American and Hispanic students as well as students from poor households are disproportionately likely to be retained compared with European American students and those from middle and high socioeconomic status homes (National Center for Education Statistics, 2017b; Warren & Saliba, 2012).

Does grade retention work? In some cases, retention can be a wakeup call to children and parents. Some students show an improvement in grades and are less likely to take remedial courses (Schwerdt, West, & Winters, 2017). However, the cumulative evidence published to date shows that students who are retained in school, even in the first 2 years of elementary school, do not fare as well as promoted students. They later show poor performance in reading, mathematics, and language; poor school attendance; and more emotional and social difficulties. They also report a greater dislike for school than do their peers who were promoted (Ehmke, Drechsel, & Carstensen, 2010; Wu, West, & Hughes, 2010). Retained students are more likely to drop out of high school by age 16 (Hughes, Cao, West, Allee Smith, & Cerda, 2017). One 14-year longitudinal study confirmed the relation of retention and high school dropout; African American and Hispanic girls were most at risk for dropout

---

TABLE 9.4

National Association of School Psychologists' Recommendations to Enhance Academic Achievement and Reduce Retention and Social Promotion

TARGET	ACTION
Parental involvement	Encourage frequent contact with teachers and supervision of students' homework.
Instruction	Adopt age-appropriate and culturally sensitive instructional strategies. Systematically and continuously assess instructional strategies and effectiveness and modify instructional efforts in response. Implement effective early reading programs. Offer extended year, extended day, and summer school programs to develop and promote academic skills.
Student academic support	Use student support teams to identify students with specific learning or behavior problems, design interventions to address those problems, and evaluate the effectiveness of those interventions. Provide appropriate education services for children with educational disabilities, including collaboration between regular, remedial, and special education professionals.
Student psychosocial support	Create and implement school-based mental health programs that identify students in need of assistance and devise ways of aiding students. Use effective behavior management and cognitive behavior modification strategies to reduce classroom behavior problems. Establish full-service schools to organize educational, social, and health services to meet the diverse needs of at-risk students.

(Hughes et al., 2017). Dropping out of high school has long-term negative effects on postsecondary education, career, and income.

As shown in Table 9.4, the National Association of School Psychologists (2003) recommends providing students and families with a variety of academic and support resources to promote student achievement and address school failure. Promoting students to the next grade, paired with interventions that target a student's specific needs in class and at home, can help students achieve at grade level and beyond (Jimerson & Renshaw, 2012).

What Do You Think?

Under what conditions might the issue of grade retention arise? Should students be "left back"? Why or why not? ●

---

tend to catch up to monolingual peers by the age of 10 years (Hoff, Rumiche, Burridge, Ribot, & Welsh, 2014).

Second Language Learning

About 22% of school-age children in the United States speak a language other than English at home (Annie E. Casey Foundation, 2017). Of these, about one in five struggle with speaking English at school (Federal Interagency Forum on Child and Family Statistics, 2017). How should children be taught a new language? In the United States, English as a Second Language (ESL) is most often taught to children by English **immersion,** which places foreign-language-speaking children in English-speaking classes, requiring them to learn English and course content at the same time. Some studies suggest that immersion is associated with a loss in children's native language use (Baus, Costa, & Carreiras, 2013).

Another approach is **dual-language learning** (also called two-way immersion), in which English-speaking and non-English-speaking students learn together in both languages and both languages are valued equally. Advocates of dual-language learning argue that bringing a child's native language into the classroom sends children the message that their cultural heritage is respected and strengthens their cultural identity and self-esteem. Children exposed to dual-language immersion tend to retain their native language while learning the new language (Castro, Páez, Dickinson, & Frede, 2011). Longitudinal research with U.S. samples suggests that dual-language immersion approaches, which encourage students to retain their native language while learning English, are more effective than immersion approaches at promoting successful learning of English as well as overall academic achievement (Relji, Ferring, & Martin, 2015). Approaches to second language learning remain hotly debated, however.

Learning a second language during childhood often affects proficiency in the first or native language. The first language may be lost or the second language may become dominant, used more

In dual language learning, two languages are used for instruction. English-speaking and non-English-speaking students are taught in their native language and a second, new language.
AP Photo/Paul T. Erickson

often (Hoff, 2015). In one study of Chinese immigrant children in New York City, children who were under the age of 9 when they immigrated reported preferring English to Mandarin 1 year later and were more proficient in English 3 years later than children who were older than 9 at the time of immigration (Jia & Aaronson, 2003). Why the difference? The younger children became friends with children who spoke English and spent more time interacting with peers who spoke English than the older children. Peers and the surrounding community influence bilingual children's language acquisition and use, and the language that is used most becomes dominant.

A similar switch in language preference and dominance has been shown in a study of children in Southern California who first learned Spanish at home and then began to learn English at school at 5 years of age (Kohnert & Bates, 2002). The children improved their proficiency in both Spanish and English but made faster progress in English, so that by middle childhood, they were more proficient in English. Children who are living in the United States or another English-speaking country and are Spanish-English bilingual at 2 years of age often become English dominant by age 4. As a result, many adults who grew up in Spanish-speaking homes retain little ability to speak Spanish (Hoff et al., 2014).

The ability to speak more than one language is associated with many cognitive skills. Individuals who have mastered two or more languages have higher scores on measures of memory, selective attention, analytical reasoning, concept formation, and cognitive flexibility (Bialystok, 2015). Bilingual children tend to score higher on measures of executive function, particularly the ability to control attention and ignore misleading information (Barac & Bialystok, 2012; Barac, Bialystok, Castro, & Sanchez, 2014). These effects emerge slowly over the course of several years. For example, one study of second- and fifth-grade students showed improvements over a 5-year span in tasks such as verbal fluency and executive control (Bialystok, Peets, & Moreno, 2014). Moreover, when children are able to speak, read, and write in two languages, they are more cognitively and socially flexible and can participate in both cultures.

Transition to First Grade

Most children go to kindergarten before entering first grade, and many go to preschool before kindergarten. Despite some experience with the educational system, children usually feel a mixture of excitement and anxiety upon entering first grade. For most children and parents, first grade holds symbolic value as the threshold to elementary school and older childhood.

Easing children's transition to first grade is important because adjustment and behavior during the first year of elementary school influence teachers' perceptions as well as children's views of themselves, their academic performance, and class involvement (Zafiropoulou, Sotiriou, & Mitsiouli, 2007). Teachers play an important role in aiding children's adjustment to first grade. They provide both instructional and emotional support: For example, they attend to students' interests, promote initiative, provide appropriately challenging learning opportunities, and encourage positive social relationships (Cadima, Doumen, Verschueren, & Buyse, 2015). These forms of support help children develop not only academic skills but also social skills, such as self-control and the ability to follow directions (Lerkkanen et al., 2016).

High-quality, sensitive, responsive, and positive interactions with teachers are associated with greater student motivation and academic achievement and fewer problems with anxiety and poor behavior throughout elementary school (Maldonado-Carreño & Votruba-Drzal, 2011; Van Craeyevelt, Verschueren, Vancraeyveldt, Wouters, & Colpin, 2017). Conversely, teacher–child conflict is associated with aggression, poor social competence, and underachievement throughout elementary school (Runions et al., 2014; Spilt, Hughes, Wu, & Kwok, 2012; White, 2013).

First grade serves as a foundation for a child's educational career because the school curriculum of each grade builds on prior grades. Starting in first grade, reading and math skills build step by step each year, so that doing well in one year helps children perform well the next year (Entwisle, Alexander, & Steffel Olson, 2005). Early academic deficiencies often persist through the school years, and children may fall further behind with each successive year in school. In addition, children's performance in each grade is documented into a cumulative file that follows them from year to year, influencing teachers' perceptions and expectations of them, which, in turn, influences their educational success.

Educating Children With Special Needs

School systems must meet the needs of a diverse population of children, many with special educational needs. Children with intellectual and learning disabilities require assistance to help them overcome obstacles to learning.

Intellectual Disability

Formerly known as mental retardation, **intellectual disability** is a condition in which a child or teenager (under age 18) shows significant deficits in cognition (as defined by an IQ below 70) and in age-appropriate adaptive skills to such a degree that he or she requires ongoing support to adapt to everyday living (American Psychiatric Association, 2013). Difficulty in adaptation—the inability to appropriately modify one's behavior in light of situational demands—is essential to a diagnosis of intellectual disability (American Association on Intellectual and Developmental Disabilities, 2010). About 1% to 2% of people in the United States are diagnosed with intellectual disability (McKenzie, Milton, Smith, & Ouellette-Kuntz, 2016).

An individual with intellectual disability shows delayed development—that is, the pattern and sequence follow a typical order but at a slower rate and with limitations with respect to the final level of achievement. Children with intellectually disability are usually slower to use words and speak in complete sentences, their social development is sometimes delayed, and they may be slow to learn to dress and feed themselves. They tend to experience more behavioral problems, such as explosive outbursts, temper tantrums, and physically aggressive or self-injurious behavior, because their ability to communicate, understand, and control their emotional impulses and frustrations is impaired (Shea, 2012).

Special education classrooms that practice inclusion integrate all children into a regular classroom with additional teachers and educational support that is tailored to learning disabled students' special needs. Students with learning disabilities learn more and demonstrate more social advancement in inclusion settings.
Robin Nelson/Zuma/Corbis

There are many causes of intellectual disability. It is estimated that genetic causes may be responsible for approximately one fourth to one half of identified intellectual disability cases (Srour & Shevell, 2014). Other biological influences include Down syndrome, metabolic disorders such as phenylketonuria, and mutations. Contextual factors include neglect, childbirth trauma, and factors associated with poverty, such as lack of access to health care and poor nutrition (Heikura et al., 2008; Schalock, 2015). Furthermore, many cases of intellectual disability have no identifiable cause.

Autistic Spectrum Disorder

Autistic spectrum disorder (ASD) is a family of neurodevelopmental disorders that range in severity and are characterized by deficits in social communication and a tendency to engage in repetitive behaviors (Hall, 2018). About 1 in 68 U.S. children are diagnosed with ASD, with males about four times as likely to be diagnosed than females (Masi, DeMayo, Glozier, & Guastella, 2017). The social and communication impairments vary widely from minor difficulties in social comprehension and perspective taking to the inability to use nonverbal or spoken language. A common characteristic of ASD is repetitive behavior, such as rocking, hand-flapping, twirling, and repeating sounds, words, or phrases. Some children with ASD experience sensory dysfunction, feeling visual, auditory, and tactile stimulation as intense and even painful.

There is evidence for a hereditary influence on ASD, but it is likely the result of multiple interacting genes rather than a single gene (Sandin et al., 2017). Moreover, epigenetics likely plays a role (Eshraghi et al., 2018). Some research has suggested that prenatal exposure to toxins, particularly mercury and lead,

maternal infections, advanced parental age, and traumatic birth complications, may heighten the risk of ASD (Modabbernia, Velthorst, & Reichenberg, 2017).

Some children with ASD are intellectually disabled; others show average or above-average intelligence (Hall, 2018). Children with ASD often show difficulties with working memory, requiring additional time to process information (Wang et al., 2017). They may benefit from instruction that emphasizes modeling, hands-on activities, and concrete examples and teaches skills for generalizing learning from one setting or problem to another (Lewis, Wheeler, & Carter, 2017).

Attention-Deficit/Hyperactivity Disorder

Attention-deficit/hyperactivity disorder (ADHD) is the most commonly diagnosed disorder in children, diagnosed in about 10% of schoolchildren in the United States (Visser et al., 2014). ADHD is a neurodevelopmental disorder characterized by persistent difficulties with attention and/or hyperactivity/impulsivity that interferes with performance and behavior in school and daily life (Hinshaw, 2018). Difficulty with attention and distractibility may manifest such as failing to attend to details, making careless mistakes, not appearing to listen when spoken to directly, not following through on instructions, or difficulty organizing tasks or activities. Impulsivity may include frequent fidgeting, squirming in seat, and leaving seat in class; often running or climbing in situations where it is not appropriate; talking excessively, often blurting out an answer before a question is completed; and having trouble waiting a turn. While most children show one or two symptoms of inattention or hyperactivity at some point in their development, a diagnosis of ADHD requires consistent display of a minimum number of specific symptoms over a 6-month period, and the symptoms must interfere with behavior in daily life (Hinshaw, 2018).

ADHD has biological causes and is nearly 80% heritable (Aguiar, Eubig, & Schantz, 2010; Schachar, 2014). Research studying identical twins who are not concordant for ADHD has suggested a role for epigenetics in determining the degree to which genetic propensities are expressed (Chen et al., 2018). Environmental influences on ADHD include premature birth, maternal smoking, drug and alcohol use, lead exposure, and brain injuries (Tarver, Daley, & Sayal, 2014; Thapar, Cooper, Eyre, & Langley, 2013).

Stimulant medication is the most common treatment for ADHD. Stimulant medication increases activity in the parts of the brain that are responsible for attention, self-control, and behavior inhibition (Hawk et al., 2018). Behavioral interventions can help children learn strategies to manage impulses and hyperactivity, direct their attention, and monitor their behavior (S. W. Evans, Owens, Wymbs, & Ray, 2018).

Learning Disabilities

Learning disabilities are diagnosed in children who demonstrate a measurable discrepancy between aptitude and achievement in a particular academic area given their age, intelligence, and amount of schooling (American Psychiatric Association, 2013). Children with learning disabilities have difficulty with academic achievement despite having normal intelligence and sensory function. **Developmental dyslexia** is the most commonly diagnosed learning disability. Children with dyslexia demonstrate age-inappropriate difficulty in matching letters to sounds and difficulty with word recognition and spelling despite adequate instruction and intelligence and intact sensory abilities (Peterson & Pennington, 2012; Ramus, 2014). Dyslexia is estimated to affect 5% to nearly 18% of the school population, boys and girls equally.

Dyslexia is influenced by genetics (Carrion-Castillo, Franke, & Fisher, 2013). Children with dyslexia have a neurologically based difficulty in processing speech sounds. During speech tasks, they use different regions of the brain than other children, and they are unable to recognize that words consist of small units of sound, strung together and represented visually by letters (Lonigan, 2015; Schurz et al., 2015). Abnormalities in the brain areas responsible for reading can be seen in 11-year-olds with dyslexia but not in young children who have not been exposed to reading, suggesting that the brain abnormalities associated with dyslexia occur after reading commences (K. A. Clark et al., 2014). Successful interventions include not only training in phonics but also supporting emerging skills by linking letters, sounds, and words through writing and reading from developmentally appropriate texts (Snowling, 2013).

Another common learning disability is **dyscalculia,** mathematics disability. Children with dyscalculia are slow in learning mathematical concepts such as counting, addition, and subtraction and have a poor understanding of these concepts (Gilmore, McCarthy, & Spelke, 2010; Kucian & von Aster, 2015). In early elementary school, they may use relatively ineffective strategies for solving math problems, such as using their fingers to add large sums. Dyscalculia is thought to affect about 5% of students and is not well understood (Kaufmann et al., 2013; Rapin, 2016). Research suggests that it is influenced by brain functioning and difficulty with working memory and executive function, specifically visuospatial short-term memory and inhibitory function (Menon, 2016; Watson & Gable, 2013). Children with dyscalculia are usually given intensive practice to help them understand numbers, but there is much to learn about this disorder (Bryant et al., 2016; Fuchs, Malone, Schumacher, Namkung, & Wang, 2017).

Special Education

In the United States and Canada, legislation mandates that children with disabilities are to be placed in the "least restrictive" environment, or classrooms that are as similar as possible to classrooms for children without learning disabilities. Whenever possible, children are to be educated in the general classroom, with their peers, for all or part of the day. This is known as mainstreaming. Classes that practice mainstreaming have teachers who are sensitive to the special needs of students with learning disabilities and provide additional instruction and extra time for them to complete assignments. The assumption is that when children are placed in regular classrooms with peers of all abilities, they are better prepared to function in society. Some mainstreamed children benefit academically and socially, but others do not. Children's responses to mainstreaming vary with the severity of their disabilities as well as the quality and quantity of support provided in the classroom (Lewis et al., 2017).

Mainstreaming works best when children receive instruction in a resource room that meets their specialized needs for part of the school day and the regular classroom for the rest of the school day.

THINKING IN CONTEXT 9.6

1. What are some of the socioemotional challenges that a child learning a second language might face? Consider the child's emotions, social relationships, and sense of self. How might the cognitive task of learning a second language influence (and be influenced by) socioemotional factors?

2. What do you remember of your experiences in first grade—your teacher, your classmates, how you spent your days? In your view, what is the purpose of first grade? What kinds of learning experiences are most important for children to have when they start school?

3. Suppose you were tasked with creating a class environment that would address the needs of children with intellectual disabilities and learning disabilities as well as children without disabilities. What would your environment include? What are some of the challenges in creating such an environment?

Children with learning disabilities report preferring combining time in the regular classroom with time in a resource room that is equipped with a teacher who is trained to meet their special learning needs (Vaughn & Klingner, 1998). Interaction with peers and cooperative learning assignments that require children to work together to achieve academic goals help students with learning disabilities learn social skills and form friendships with peers.

A more recent approach to special education is inclusion, which refers to including children with learning disabilities in the regular classroom but providing them with a teacher or paraprofessional specially trained to meet their needs (Mastropieri & Scruggs, 2017). Inclusion is different from mainstreaming in that it entails additional educational support tailored to the learning disabled students' special needs. With an inclusion arrangement, students with learning disabilities are placed in the regular classroom, but for part of the day, they are taught separately in a resource room (Salend, 2015). Some argue that students' move from the regular classroom to resource room is disruptive to other children (Ainscow & Messiou, 2018). Around the world, children learn strategies to succeed despite their limitations, but the disabilities themselves and the academic and social challenges posed by them do not disappear. Parents and teachers are most helpful when they understand that learning disabilities are not a matter of intelligence or laziness but rather a function of brain differences and when they help children to learn to monitor their behavior.

 ## APPLY YOUR KNOWLEDGE

Dashawn sighs as he reads the next question. "Hmmm, which one of the following words best match the word *cup*," he reads to himself, "*wall, table, saucer,* or *window*?" Dashawn isn't sure what a saucer is. He concludes, "It must be *table*—you put a cup on a table." Dashawn finds that there are a lot of words he doesn't know on this test, like *regatta,* and situations that didn't make a lot of sense to him, like examples that refer to gardening and playing tennis. "Boy, this is a long test," he mutters to himself.

The next day, Dashawn takes a deep breath and begins his tumbling routine, hurtling his way down the mat, completing a series of forward flips and finishing with a back flip. "Fantastic!" shouts Coach Dawkins, "We should work on your timing, but keep it up and you'll be on your way to winning the state championship."

Later that week, Coach Dawkins arrives at the elementary school conference room to meet with the school's student troubleshooting team. The principal, school psychologist, and Dashawn's teacher are in attendance. The school psychologist, Dr. Martinez, begins, "I've brought us together to talk about Dashawn. I'm concerned that he may have special learning needs. His intelligence test scores show a large discrepancy in his performance on verbal and nonverbal test items. I'd like to learn more about your experiences with Dashawn before I contact his parents." As they speak, Dr. Martinez takes notes and creates a profile of Dashawn. Coach Dawkins explains that Dashawn is the most talented gymnast he's coached in his entire career. Dashawn's teacher agrees that he's a hard worker, sociable, and well liked by his classmates. His teacher explains that Dashawn's performance in math is in line with his classmates, but he is a bit behind in English. Dashawn is not the most talented student in class, but he seems to be a quick learner—when he's not fidgeting or requesting to go to the restroom way more often than necessary for a 9-year-old. Dr. Martinez concludes that Dashawn's IQ test scores may not indicate serious cognitive and academic problems, but he decides to monitor Dashawn's progress and discuss his concerns with Dashawn's parents.

1. Identify reasons why Dashawn might be unfamiliar with some words and terms used in the intelligence test. How might tests be modified to be fair to children of all backgrounds? What do you recommend?

2. Why might have Dashawn scored higher on the performance scale than the verbal scale? Discuss developmental reasons that might underlie his performance. Are there other possible reasons?

3. How might Dashawn's performance be explained using multiple intelligence theory? The triarchic theory of intelligence?

Visit **edge.sagepub.com/kuther2e** to help you accomplish your coursework goals in an easy-to-use learning environment.

LEARNING OBJECTIVES	SUMMARY	KEY TERMS	IN REVIEW
9.1 Identify patterns of physical and motor development during middle childhood and common health issues facing school-age children.	During middle childhood, growth in height and weight slows, and children demonstrate increases in strength, speed, reaction time, flexibility, balance, and coordination. Advances in growth and motor development are influenced by genetic and contextual factors. Middle childhood is a time of health, but injuries and obesity pose risks to children. Childhood obesity is associated with short- and long-term physical and psychological health problems, and most children do not grow out of obesity but instead become obese adults. Programs that are effective at reducing childhood obesity decrease children's television and video game use, increase their physical activity, and teach children about nutrition.	Body mass index (BMI) Obesity Body image dissatisfaction	How do body growth and motor skills advance in middle childhood? What are biological and contextual influences on growth and motor skills? What are the most common health issues facing school-age children?
9.2 Discuss school-age children's capacities for reasoning and processing information.	At about age 7, children enter the concrete operational state of reasoning, permitting them to use mental operations to solve problems and think logically, and to demonstrate several different kinds of classification skills and make advances in solving conservation tasks. Concrete operational reasoning is found in children around the world; however, experience, specific cultural practices, and education play a role in development. Brain maturation leads to improvements in executive functioning and attention, memory, response inhibition, and processing speed. As children's understanding of their own thinking and memory increases, they get better at selecting and using mnemonic strategies and become more planful.	Concrete operational stage of reasoning Classification Transitive inference Seriation Class inclusion Metamemory Rehearsal Organization Elaboration	What abilities mark the concrete operational reasoning? How do changes in working memory, executive function, and metacognition influence children's thinking and memory? What is the role of context and experience in cognitive development in middle childhood?
9.3 Summarize views of intelligence, including the uses, correlates, and criticisms of intelligence tests.	IQ tests measure intellectual aptitude and are often used to identify children with special educational needs. IQ predicts school achievement, how long a child will stay in school, and career attainment in adulthood. Persistent group differences are found in IQ scores, but contextual factors, such as socioeconomic status, living conditions, school resources, culture, and life circumstances, are thought to account for group differences. Multiple intelligence theory and the triarchic theory of intelligence conceptualize intelligence as entailing a more broad range of skills than those measured by IQ tests.	Intelligence tests (IQ tests) Flynn effect Multiple intelligence theory Triarchic theory of intelligence	What is intelligence? What is the most common IQ test, and how does it define intelligence? What are contextual influences on IQ scores? What are two alternative theories of intelligence?
9.4 Examine patterns of moral development during middle childhood.	Until about age 9, children demonstrate preconventional reasoning in Kohlberg's theory of moral development, moving from concern with punishment as a motivator of moral judgments (Stage 1) to self-interest and concern about what others can do for them (Stage 2). In late childhood, children advance to conventional moral reasoning in which they internalize the norms and standards of authority figures, becoming concerned with pleasing others (Stage 3) and maintaining social order (Stage 4). School-age children's views of fairness become more sophisticated, and they become more likely to consider the situation and weigh a variety of variables in making decisions.	Autonomous morality Conventional moral reasoning	What is autonomous morality? What is conventional moral reasoning? What is distributive justice reasoning? How do children distinguish between moral and conventional rules? What factors influence moral development?

9.5 Summarize language development during middle childhood.	Vocabulary expands fourfold during the elementary school years. School-age children learn words through contextual cues and by comparing complex words with simpler words. Understanding of complex grammatical structures, syntax, and pragmatics improves in middle childhood with experience with language and exposure to complex constructions, and children become better communicators.	Pragmatics	What advances in vocabulary and grammar take place during middle childhood? Provide an example illustrating the development of pragmatics.
9.6 Discuss children's learning at school.	Phonics methods are highly effective in teaching reading, yet most schools employ the whole-language approach, and a substantial number of U.S. children are poor readers. U.S. students' mathematical skills have improved over the past two decades, yet nearly one in five U.S. schoolchildren is deficient in math skills. Fluency in two languages is associated with higher scores on measures of selective attention, executive function, analytical reasoning, concept formation, and cognitive flexibility. Bilingual approaches to language learning are more effective than immersion approaches at teaching language and promoting academic achievement in children. In the United States and Canada, legislation mandates that, whenever possible, children with intellectual and learning disabilities are to be mainstreamed and educated in the general classroom, with their peers, for all or part of the day. However, the effectiveness of mainstreaming varies with the severity of the disability as well as the quality and quantity of support provided in the classroom.	Phonics instruction Immersion Dual-language learning Intellectual disability Autistic spectrum disorder Attention-deficit/hyperactivity disorder Developmental dyslexia Dyscalculia	What approaches are used to teach reading and mathematics? What are two approaches to teaching English language learners? What are common disabilities that are aided by special education? What are methods for educating children with special needs?

10 Socioemotional Development in Middle Childhood

Unlike his little brother, who will play with any child available, Tishaun is choosy about his friends. He meets with the same group of neighborhood boys each afternoon to play basketball in his driveway. Tishaun especially likes playing basketball with his friends because he's much better than them. Tishaun is proud that his gym teacher suggested that he try out for the school's basketball team. He also performs well in class, is a good student, gets along with others, and is well liked by his classmates. Tishuan has successfully navigated many of the socioemotional tasks of middle childhood. He has come to understand himself in more sophisticated ways, and he has established good relationships with his parents and peers. In this chapter, we examine ways in which family and peer contexts shape school-age children's socioemotional development.

Learning Objectives

10.1 Describe school-age children's self-conceptions and motivation.

10.2 Examine the roles of friendship, peer acceptance, and peer victimization in school-age children's adjustment.

10.3 Discuss family relationships in middle childhood and the influence of family structure on adjustment.

10.4 Analyze the role of resilience in promoting adjustment to adversity, including characteristics of children and contexts that promote resilience.

Digital Resources

Watch: Kids Need Structure

Listen: Social Bullying

Explore: Poverty Among Grandmother-Headed Families

▶ **Lives in Context Video 10.1:** Divorce: Parent's Perspective

▶ **Lives in Context Video 10.2:** Blended Families

Watch: 7 Characteristics of Resilient Children

PSYCHOSOCIAL DEVELOPMENT IN MIDDLE CHILDHOOD

>> **LO 10.1 Describe school-age children's self-conceptions and motivation.**

Middle childhood, ages 6 to 11, represents an important transition in children's conceptions of themselves and their abilities. According to Erik Erikson (1950), school-age children face the psychosocial crisis of **industry versus inferiority**. They must develop a sense of competence rather than feel inadequate. Children must learn and master skills that are valued in their society, such as reading, mathematics, writing, and using computers. Success at even simple culturally valued tasks influences children's feelings of competence and curiosity as well as their motivation to persist and succeed in all of the contexts in which they are embedded. Six-year-old Kia tied her shoelace and smiled to herself. "It's easy now. I'm really good at tying my shoelaces—much better than my little brother." When children are unable to succeed or when they receive consistently negative feedback from parents or teachers, they may lose confidence in their ability to succeed and be productive at valued tasks. Children's sense of industry influences their self-concept, self-esteem, and readiness to face the physical, cognitive, and social challenges of middle childhood.

Self-Concept

In middle childhood, children's emerging cognitive capacities enable them to think about themselves in new, more complex ways and develop more sophisticated and comprehensive self-concepts (Goodvin, Thompson, & Winer, 2015). Self-concept shifts from concrete descriptions of behavior to trait-like psychological constructs (e.g., popular, smart, good looking). For example, consider this school-age child's self-description: "I'm pretty popular. . . . That's because I'm nice to people and helpful and can keep secrets. Mostly I am nice to my friends, although if I get in a bad mood I sometimes say something that can be a little mean" (Harter, 2012b, p. 59). Like most older children, this child's self-concept focuses on competencies and personality traits rather than specific behaviors.

Older children include both positive and negative traits, unlike younger children who tend to describe themselves in all-or-none terms. Through interactions with parents, teachers, and peers, children learn more about themselves (Pesu, Viljaranta, & Aunola, 2016). Older children come to understand that their traits can vary with the context—for example, that a person can be nice or mean, depending on the situation. Brain development contributes to self-concept. When processing information about the self, children use many more areas of the brain than do adults, suggesting that, with development, processing becomes more efficient and self-concept becomes

Self-Concept and the Brain

Self-concept shifts over childhood from all or none trait descriptions in early childhood to complex integrations of psychological traits in middle to late childhood. By about 9 years of age, children describe and evaluate themselves across a range of domains, such as academic, athletic, and social competence (Harter, 2012b). Advances in perspective taking and social comparison abilities contribute to the development of self-concept from childhood through adolescence and adulthood. What happens in the brain during self-reflection? How does neural development contribute to the changing sense of self?

Research with adults has shown that several areas of the brain are active during self-reflection tasks, especially the medial prefrontal cortex (mPFC) (Northoff & Hayes, 2011). The mPFC is one of the last parts of the brain to develop, undergoing significant change into adulthood (Blakemore, 2012). Neuroimaging studies have shown developmental differences in this region that correlate with the emerging sense of self (Mills, Lalonde, Clasen, Giedd, & Blakemore, 2014; Pfeifer & Peake, 2012). For example, mPFC activity increases from childhood into adolescence in response to self-knowledge and evaluation tasks (Mills, Goddings, Clasen, Giedd, & Blakemore, 2014). In one longitudinal study, children engaged in a self-evaluation task at age 10 and again at 13 in which they judged their own social skills and those of a familiar fictional character (e.g., Harry Potter) (Pfeifer et al., 2013). With age, the children showed greater activity in the mPFC during self-evaluations than other-evaluations and overall mPFC activity increased from age 10 to 13.

Children and adults also show different patterns of mPFC activity in response to self-knowledge and evaluation tasks (Mills, Goddings, et al., 2014). For example, 10-year-old children and adults completed a self-knowledge task in which they judged whether phrases such as "I like to read just for fun" better described either themselves or a familiar fictional character (Pfeifer, Lieberman, & Dapretto, 2007). The children showed more activity in the mPFC when retrieving information about themselves. In addition, mPFC activity was more diffuse, spread out across a larger region, in children as compared to adults, suggesting that the task required greater neural resources in children. Children's increased mPFC activity indicates that they were actively processing the task, engaging in self-reflection. In addition, the adults showed more activity in the lateral temporal cortex (LTC), which is associated with semantic memory (Cabeza & Nyberg, 2000). The lower levels of mPFC activity and higher LTC activity in adults suggest that the adults engaged in less active processing and instead relied on memory to complete the task, perhaps because they have more extensive knowledge about themselves (Pfeifer et al., 2007). That is, the task was easier for adults. In the children, however, greater involvement of the mPFC and relatively less activation of semantic knowledge stores in the LTC imply that they actively constructed their self-descriptive attributes, evaluating themselves and creating self-descriptions as they completed the task. As children learn more about themselves, they rely on memory, freeing neural resources for more complex reflections about the self and others.

What Do You Think?

1. What might contribute to children's performance on self-knowledge tasks?

2. What can we do to improve children's knowledge about themselves? ●

---

more complex and differentiated (Pfeifer & Peake, 2012). As self-concept differentiates, children develop a physical self-concept (referring to physical attributes and attractiveness), academic self-concept (school performance), athletic self-concept (physical skills), social self-concept (social relationships with peers and others), and beliefs about behavioral conduct (whether they can behave appropriately) (Harter, 2012a). The Brain and Biological Influences on Development feature discusses the neurological correlates of self-concept.

Self-Esteem

Whereas preschoolers tend to have unrealistically positive self-evaluations, school-age children's sense of self-esteem becomes more realistic (Boseovski, 2010). Older children's growing ability to take other people's perspectives enables them to consider their abilities more objectively. Children evaluate their characteristics, abilities, and performance in comparison with peers, which influences their overall sense of competence (Harter, 2012b). Children also receive feedback about their abilities from parents, teachers, and peers, and this affects their self-esteem (Hart, Atkins, & Tursi, 2006). Perceived disapproval by peers, for example, is associated with declines in self-esteem (Thomaes et al., 2010). Although children learn about their abilities through their interactions with parents, teachers, and peers, children whose self-evaluations depend on approval from others tend to have low self-esteem (J. S. B. Moore & Smith, 2018). Children with low self-esteem tend to emphasize their weaknesses and downplay their strengths, evaluating their abilities inaccurately.

From late childhood into adolescence, beliefs about the self become more closely related to behavior (Davis-Kean, Jager, & Andrew Collins, 2009). Self-esteem is influenced by children's self-evaluations as well as by the importance they assign to the particular ability being evaluated. This is illustrated by a child's comment, "Even though I'm not doing well in those subjects, I still like myself as a person, because Math and Science just aren't that important to me. How I look and how popular I am are more important" (Harter, 2012b, p. 95). Children tend to report feeling most interested in activities in which they perform well and areas that they view as their strengths (Denissen, Zarrett, & Eccles, 2007).

Positive parent–child interactions and a secure attachment to parents predict a positive sense of self-esteem throughout childhood (Sroufe, 2016). Self-esteem is nurtured by parental warmth. Warm parents express positive emotions and acceptance and foster in their child the feeling that he or she matters. Children internalize the view of themselves as worthy individuals, and this internalized view is at the core of self-esteem (Brummelman, 2018). The home environment influences self-esteem throughout the lifespan. For example, in one longitudinal study, the quality of the early home environment through the first 6 years of life predicted self-esteem at age 8 through early adulthood, age 28 (Orth, 2017).

Children's ratings of self-esteem vary with ethnic, contextual, and cultural factors. For example, many African American children experience adverse contextual conditions such as poverty, unsafe neighborhoods, ongoing stressors, and the experience of racism and discrimination. As a result, African American children may score lower on measures of self-esteem than White and Hispanic children (Kenny & McEachern, 2009). Despite the fact that their academic achievement is in general higher than that of North American children, Chinese and Japanese children tend to score lower in self-esteem. One reason may be that competition is high and Asian children experience great pressure to achieve (Stevenson, Lee, & Mu, 2000). In addition, Asian cultures emphasize collectivism, social harmony, and modesty, and they do not encourage children to use social comparison to enhance their self-esteem (Toyama, 2001). Instead, children are encouraged to praise others, including their peers, while minimizing attention to themselves in order to foster and maintain relationships (Falbo, Poston, Triscari, & Zhang, 1997).

The cultural emphasis on individuality characteristic of North America contributes to children's high self-esteem. However, when parents overvalue their children's attributes, overpraise their performance, and overencourage them to stand out from others, children may develop a sense of narcissism, viewing themselves as superior to others (Brummelman, 2018). Children's self-esteem is best fostered within the context of warm and accepting parent–child interactions, parental encouragement for realistic and meaningful goals, and praise that is connected to children's performance.

Achievement Motivation

Children's sense of industry and emerging sense of self influences their **achievement motivation,** the willingness to persist at challenging tasks and meet high standards of accomplishment (Wigfield et al., 2015). How children explain their own successes and failures is important for sustaining motivation and ultimately influencing their own achievement. Some children gravitate toward internal attributions, emphasizing their own role in the outcome, such as through ability or choice of study techniques. Other children rely on external, uncontrollable attributions, such as luck, to explain their performance.

In addition to attributing success or failure to internal or external causes, children also vary in their **mindset,** the degree to which they believe that their abilities and characteristics are modifiable (Dweck, 2017). Some show a *growth mindset,* viewing their skills and characteristics as malleable or changeable. In contrast, others show a *fixed mindset,* believing that their characteristics are enduring and unchangeable.

Children who adopt internal explanations and a growth mindset tend to have a strong **mastery orientation,** a belief that success stems from trying hard and that failures are influenced by factors that can be controlled, like effort (Haimovitz & Dweck, 2017). When faced with challenges, children who

Some children respond to success and failure in maladaptive ways. Children who attribute success to factors such as luck and failure to factors such as ability are at risk to develop a learned helplessness orientation.
iStock/FatCamera

are mastery oriented focus on changing or adapting their behavior (Muenks, Wigfield, & Eccles, 2018). They are able to bounce back from failure and take steps, such as learning study strategies to improve their exam scores, to improve their performance.

Other children respond to success and failure in maladaptive ways, by attributing success to external factors such as luck and attributing failure to internal factors such as ability. Some children adopt a **learned helplessness orientation,** characterized by a fixed mindset and the attribution of poor performance to internal factors. Children who show learned helplessness are overwhelmed by challenges, are overly self-critical, feel incompetent, and avoid challenging tasks (Yeager & Dweck, 2012). A learned helplessness orientation can perpetuate poor performance. For example, students in fourth through sixth grades who were self-critical viewed their abilities as fixed, rated their own competence as lower, knew less about study strategies, avoided challenges, and performed more poorly at school than their non-self-critical peers (Pomerantz & Saxon, 2001). Poor performance, in turn, can confirm children's negative views of their ability and their sense of helplessness.

Contextual Influences on Achievement Attributions and Motivation

Our views about our abilities and our explanations for our successes and failures are influenced by our interactions with the people around us. The contexts in which we are immersed, including factors such as parents and teachers, socioeconomic status, and culture, also play a role in shaping our views of our abilities.

Parents

Parents influence children's achievement through their own beliefs and attitudes about ability. Children raised by parents with a fixed view of abilities tend to view their own ability as fixed and unchangeable and are more likely to show a learned helplessness orientation (Pomerantz & Dong, 2006). When parents believe that ability cannot be changed, they tend to provide few opportunities for children to improve and may ignore positive changes that children show. In addition, failing to provide opportunities to problem solve or intervening when a child tries a challenging task may inhibit children's desire to succeed and may foster helplessness (Orkin, May, & Wolf, 2017).

Parenting styles also have an effect. Warm and supportive parenting can help children to recognize their worth and appreciate their own competence.

Warm and supportive parenting that fosters autonomy can help children to recognize their worth, appreciate their own competence, and develop a mastery orientation.
iStock/JohnnyGreig

Authoritative parents who promote their children's autonomy, encourage their children to explore their environment, and permit them to take an active role in solving their own problems foster a mastery orientation (Raftery, Grolnick, & Flamm, 2012). In contrast, excessive control and harsh criticism can damage children's motivation.

Parents also influence children through the home context they provide. Socioeconomic status (SES) influences children's motivation through the availability of opportunities and resources and through parents' behavior. Research has shown that children who grow up in high SES families are more likely than their middle or low SES peers to show a greater mastery orientation and higher levels of achievement motivation, as well as better academic performance and greater involvement in organized activities after school (Wigfield et al., 2015). Children require not only opportunities to try new things but also parents who are aware of and able to take advantage of opportunities (Archer et al., 2012; Simpkins, Delgado, Price, Quach, & Starbuck, 2013). Parents in low SES families often work jobs that involve long hours, rotating and nonstandard shifts, and high physical demands. As a result, many low SES parents lack the energy and time to devote to children, and they may be unaware of opportunities or unable to take advantage of them (Parra-Cardona, Cordova, Holtrop, Villarruel, & Wieling, 2008).

Teachers

Like parents, teachers support a mastery orientation in students when they are warm and helpful and when they attribute children's failure to lack of effort (Wentzel, 2002). Students who believe that their teachers provide a positive learning environment tend to work harder in class and show higher achievement than students who lack this belief (Wigfield, Muenks, & Rosenzweig, 2015). When students view their teachers as unsupportive, they are more likely to attribute their performance to external factors, such as luck or the teacher, and to withdraw from class participation. As students' achievement declines, they further doubt their abilities, creating a vicious cycle between helpless attributions and poor achievement. Teachers who relate failure back to their students' effort, are supportive of their students, and stress learning goals over performance goals are more likely to have mastery-oriented students (Meece, Anderman, & Anderman, 2006).

Cultural Influences

Children and adolescents of many cultures point to family as an important influence on achievement. Internal attributions for success tend to be more common in Westerners and may be less common among people of other cultural backgrounds (Reyna, 2008). In one study, students from the Pacific islands (e.g., Samoa and Tonga) rated family, teacher, luck, and friends as more important for their best marks than did European, Asian, or Māori (indigenous) students (McClure et al., 2011). Moreover, Māori and other Pacific Islander students were less likely to adopt internal attributions (e.g., ability, effort) for their best and worst marks compared with European and Asian students.

Parents in many Asian countries tend to hold a growth mindset and to view the application of effort as a moral responsibility (Pomerantz, Ng, Cheung, & Qu, 2014). Parents in many Asian cultures tend to focus more on children's failure in order to encourage them to make corrections. North American parents, on the other hand, tend to pay attention to children's success and its relevance for self-esteem. For example, when U.S. and Chinese mothers watched their fourth- and fifth-grade students solve a puzzle, the U.S. mothers offered more praise after the child succeeded, but the Chinese mothers tended to point out poor performance and offer task-oriented statements to make the child try harder (e.g., "You only got 7 of 10"). After the mothers left the room, the children continued to play, and the Chinese children showed greater improvements in performance than the U.S. children (Ng, Pomerantz, & Lam, 2007).

Cultures also vary in the use and perception of criticism and praise. Students from some cultures may feel uncomfortable with praise because it singles them out from the group and, by implication, elevates them above their peers (Markus & Kitayama, 1991). Some students may be more motivated by critical feedback because their goal is to meet the expectations of their teachers and/or family (Pomerantz et al., 2014).

THINKING IN CONTEXT 10.1

1. In what ways do schoolchildren's developing self-concept influence their relationships with peers? In turn, how do peer interactions and relationships influence children's development?

2. Can self-esteem be too high? Considering influences on healthy self-esteem, what might cause excessively high, unhealthy self-esteem?

3. As a fourth-grade teacher, what can you do to promote students' academic achievement and academic motivation, as well as help them develop positive views of their own abilities?

PEER RELATIONSHIPS IN MIDDLE CHILDHOOD

» LO 10.2 **Examine the roles of friendship, peer acceptance, and peer victimization in school-age children's adjustment.**

As older children's self-concepts expand and they become better able to understand and appreciate others' perspectives, peer relationships become more complex. Older children spend more time with peers and place more importance on those relationships than do younger children (Schneider, 2016). Most school-age children have multiple friendships and are part of a peer group in school and, increasingly, out of school. Friendship and peer acceptance become important influences on adjustment.

Friends are an important source of companionship, support, and fun in middle childhood.
Jeffrey Greenberg/UIG via Getty Images

Friendship

Friendships serve important developmental purposes throughout the lifespan. They are a source of companionship, stimulation, and affection. Friends provide each other with tangible and emotional support. They are also a source of social comparison, permitting children to judge their competence relative to peers (Erdley & Day, 2017). At all times in life, friendships are rooted in similarity. Children tend to choose friends who share interests, play preferences, and personality characteristics (Laursen, 2017). Friends also show similarities in cognitive ability and intelligence, likely because these characteristics influence the capacity to take other people's perspectives and thus reciprocate (Boutwell, Meldrum, & Petkovsek, 2017; Ilmarinen, Vainikainen, Verkasalo, & Lönnqvist, 2017). In addition, friends tend to share demographics, such as gender, race, and ethnicity (Rubin, Coplan, et al., 2015). For example, in one study of 6- to 12-year-old U.S. children of Cambodian, Dominican, and Portuguese heritage, children became more proud of their heritage as they grew older and in turn showed a greater preference to form friendships within their ethnic group (Marks, Szalacha, Lamarre, Boyd, & Coll, 2007).

Contextual characteristics, such as the ethnic diversity of a neighborhood or school, also influence children's choices of friends within and outside of their own ethnic group. In schools that are ethnically, racially, and socioeconomically diverse, children are more likely to report having at least one close friend of another race (Iqbal, Neal, & Vincent, 2017; McGlothlin & Killen, 2006). School-age girls may be more likely to have ethnically diverse social networks and cross-race friendships than boys (Lee, Howes, & Chamberlain, 2007). Once established, cross-race friendships are similar to same-race friendships with regard to intimacy, companionship, and security (McDonald et al., 2013). Compared to children who do not have friends of other races, children in cross-race friendships tend to show a lower tolerance for excluding others (Killen, Kelly, Richardson, Crystal, & Ruck, 2010) and are less prone to peer victimization (Kawabata & Crick, 2011). They also tend to feel socially and emotionally safer and less vulnerable at school (Graham, Munniksma, & Juvonen, 2014; Munniksma & Juvonen, 2012).

In middle childhood, friendship transforms into a reciprocal relationship in which children are responsive to each other's needs and trust each other. Shared values and rules become important components to friendship by 9 to 10 years of age (Rubin, Bukowski, & Bowker, 2015). In middle to late childhood, friends are expected to be loyal and stick up for each other. Violations of trust, such as divulging secrets, breaking promises, and not helping a friend in need, can break up a friendship.

Because of their more complex perspectives on friendship, school-age children tend to name only a handful of friends, as compared with preschoolers, who say that they have lots of friends. "I know a lot of kids and am inviting them all to my birthday party," explained 9-year-old Shana, "but only a few are really my friends. I don't tell them everything. I only tell everything to my best friend. Only she knows that I like Nicky." As Shana illustrates, with age, children differentiate among best friends, good friends, and casual friends, depending on how much time they spend together and how much they share with one another (Rubin, Bukowski, et al., 2015). Older children, especially girls, tend to have fewer, but closer, friends, and by age 10, most children report having a best friend (Erdley & Day, 2017).

Friendships tend to remain stable from middle childhood into adolescence, especially among children whose friendships are high in relationship quality, characterized by sharing, mutual perspective taking, and compromise (Poulin & Chan, 2010). Nevertheless, because friendship is based largely on similar characteristics, proximity, and opportunities for interaction, friendships may come and go as children develop new interests, competencies, and values (Laursen, 2017). They may also end as children progress into new contexts, as when they change schools or move to a different neighborhood (Troutman & Fletcher, 2010). Older children become more upset at losing a friend and find making friends more challenging than do young children (Hartup, 2006).

Friendship dissolution may have serious consequences for children who are unable to replace the friendship. Some children who experience disruption and loss of close friendships have problems with depression, loneliness, guilt, anger, anxiety, and acting-out behaviors, yet children with psychosocial problems are also at risk to experience friendship loss and, in turn, show poor adjustment

Not all children have a best friend. Lacking close friendships is not indicative of maladjustment especially if children experience other close relationships.
Daniel Atkin / Alamy Stock Photo

(Rubin, Bukowski, et al., 2015). Many children replace "lost" friendships with "new" friendships. In one study of fifth graders, losing a friend was associated with adjustment difficulties only when the lost friendship was not replaced by a new friendship. For these children, the lost and new friendships were largely interchangeable (Wojslawowicz Bowker, Rubin, Burgess, Booth-Laforce, & Rose-Krasnor, 2006). For many children, the importance of stable best friendships during middle childhood may have less to do with the relationship's length and more to do with simply having a "buddy" by one's side who can provide companionship, recreation, validation, caring, help, and guidance.

Can a child be happy without friends or without a best friend? An estimated 15% to 20% of children are chronically friendless or consistently without a mutual best friend (Rubin, Bukowski, et al., 2015). Children without friends tend to report feeling more lonely than other children, especially when they desire friends. Friendless children may lack social skills or might direct their friendship toward children who are unlikely to reciprocate (Bowker et al., 2010). Some research suggests that young elementary schoolchildren without friends score lower on measures of theory of mind, suggesting that they are not cognitively prepared to take another person's perspective, a skill critical to making friends (Fink, Begeer, Peterson, Slaughter, & de Rosnay, 2015). Lacking a best friend itself is not necessarily harmful or indicative of problems or loneliness (Klima & Repetti, 2008). Some children simply prefer solitude; their preference for alone time is not driven by anxiety or fear (Coplan, Ooi, & Nocita, 2015). Although lacking close friends is not associated with maladjustment, social acceptance by the peer group influences children's adjustment, as discussed next.

Peer Acceptance, Popularity, and Rejection

Mykelle announced to her mother, "I heard from the last kid! Everyone in class is coming to my birthday party!" "Fantastic!" her mother replied. "Now I have to figure out how to fit 25 of your friends into our house." **Peer acceptance,** the degree to which a child is viewed as a worthy social partner by his or her peers, becomes increasingly important in middle childhood. Peer evaluations become vital sources of self-validation, self-esteem, and confidence (LaFontana & Cillessen, 2010). Some children stand out from their peers as exceptionally well liked or exceptionally disliked.

Popularity

Children who are valued by their peers are said to be popular. **Popular children** tend to have a variety of positive characteristics, including helpfulness, trustworthiness, assertiveness, and prosocial habits (Kornbluh & Neal, 2016). They are skilled in emotional regulation and social information processing (van den Berg, Deutz, Smeekens, & Cillessen, 2017). That is, popular children are good at reading social situations, problem solving, self-disclosure, and conflict resolution (Blandon, Calkins, Grimm, Keane, & O'Brien, 2010). For example, theory of mind predicts popularity throughout childhood (Slaughter, Imuta, Peterson, & Henry, 2015). Positive social competencies and prosocial behaviors are cyclical; children who excel at social interaction continue to do so, their peers tend to reciprocate, and positive effects on peer relationships increase (Laible, McGinley, Carlo, Augustine, & Murphy, 2014).

A minority of popular children do not show the prosocial and empathetic characteristics typical of popular children. Often labeled by peers and teachers as tough, these children are socially skilled yet show antisocial and aggressive behavior (Shi & Xie, 2012). Aggressive popular children show social competencies similar to prosocial popular children, yet also share many characteristics of children who are rejected by their peers (Kornbluh & Neal, 2016; Marks, 2017).

Peer Rejection

Children who experience **peer rejection** tend to be disliked and shunned by their peers. Children who have poor communication, language, emotional control, and social information processing skills are at risk for peer rejection (Bierman, Kalvin, & Heinrichs, 2015; Menting, van Lier, & Koot, 2011). For example, kindergarteners who had difficulty controlling their emotions were more likely than their more skilled peers to experience peer rejection through seventh grade (Bierman et al., 2014). Boys and girls with behavior problems are at risk for peer rejection—and peer rejection, in turn, is associated with increases in behavior problems throughout elementary school as well as rule breaking in adolescence (Ettekal & Ladd, 2015). Rejected children show two patterns of behavior, characterized by either aggression or withdrawal.

Mrs. Connelly turned to a fellow teacher and sighed. "Poor Monica. She tries to force her way into games, like knocking Jamie out of the way to take her spot in line for jump rope. No wonder the other children don't like her." *Aggressive-rejected* children like Monica are confrontational, hostile toward other children, impulsive, and hyperactive. They enter peer groups in destructive ways that disrupt the group's interaction or activity and direct attention to themselves. Aggressive-rejected children tend to have difficulty taking the perspective of others, and they tend to react aggressively to slights by peers, quickly assuming hostile intentions (Fite, Hendrickson, Rubens, Gabrielli, & Evans, 2013; Laible et al., 2014). Children whose parents show little warmth and use coercive discipline and threats are likely to threaten other children, have poor social skills, show aggressive behavior, and are more likely to be rejected by other children (Lansford, 2014).

Other rejected children are socially withdrawn, passive, timid, anxious, and socially awkward. *Withdrawn-rejected* children tend to isolate themselves from peers, rarely initiate contact with peers, and speak less frequently than their peers (Rubin, Coplan, & Bowker, 2009). They tend to spend most of their time playing alone and on the periphery of the social scene, often because of shyness or social anxiety. When socially withdrawn children experience peer rejection, they tend to become more withdrawn and even more disliked by their peers (Coplan et al., 2013). Despite this, socially withdrawn children are just as likely to have a best friend as other children (Rubin, Wojslawowicz, Rose-Krasnor, Booth-LaForce, & Burgess, 2006).

Both aggressive-rejected and withdrawn-rejected children are similar in that they misinterpret other children's behaviors and motives, have trouble understanding and regulating their emotions, are poor listeners, and are less socially competent than other children (Ladd & Kochenderfer-Ladd, 2016). Peer rejection further hinders social development by depriving children of opportunities to learn and practice social skills such as interacting with other children, resolving conflict, and regulating emotions. Peer rejection is associated with short- and long-term problems, such as loneliness, anxiety, depression, low self-esteem, low academic achievement, and, in adolescence, delinquency and school dropout (Cooley & Fite, 2016; Menting, Koot, & van Lier, 2014; Schwartz, Lansford, Dodge, Pettit, & Bates, 2015). Chronic peer rejection is associated with high levels of activity in regions of the brain linked with detecting and experiencing the emotional distress caused by social exclusion. Moreover, the experience of chronic rejection in childhood is associated with heightened neural responses to exclusion in adolescence (Will, van Lier, Crone, & Güroğlu, 2016). Table 10.1 summarizes characteristics associated with popular children and those who are rejected.

Bullying

Bullying, also known as **peer victimization,** refers to an ongoing interaction in which a child repeatedly attempts to inflict physical, verbal, or social harm on another child by, for example, hitting, kicking, name-calling, teasing, shunning, or humiliating the other child (Olweus, 2013). Bullying is a problem for school-age children in many countries. Estimated rates of bullying and victimization range from 15%

Children who show physical forms of bullying are often reared in homes with poor supervision, coercive control, and physical discipline.
iStock/fstop123

to 25% of children in Australia, Austria, England, Finland, Germany, Norway, and the United States (Zych, Farrington, Llorent, & Ttofi, 2017). Physical bullying is most common in childhood, and verbal/relational forms of bullying rise in childhood and remain common in adolescence (Finkelhor, Ormrod, & Turner, 2009). **Cyberbullying** is a type of relational bullying carried out by electronic means by text or electronic communication and social media (Vaillancourt, Faris, & Mishna, 2017). Cyberbullying tends to accompany other types of bullying rather than occur independently (Waasdorp & Bradshaw, 2015).

Children Who Bully

Boys who bully tend to be above average in size, use physical aggression, and target both boys and girls. Girls who bully tend to be verbally assertive, target other girls, and use verbal or psychological methods of bullying that threaten relationships (Murray-Close, Nelson, Ostrov, Casas, & Crick, 2016). These latter methods, known as *relational aggression,* include ridiculing, embarrassing, and spreading rumors. Boys and girls who bully tend to be impulsive and domineering, and they show little anxiety or insecurity in peer contexts. Bullying can be motivated by the pursuit of high status and a powerful dominant position in the peer group (Thomas, Connor, & Scott, 2017). Relationally aggressive children, including bullies, are frequently perceived by peers as cool, powerful, and popular; bullying can be helpful in maintaining prestige. Indirect forms of bullying, such as relational bullying, require social skills, which contribute to the relational bully's high social status among peers (Juvonen & Graham, 2014). In support of this, many bullies report making friends easily and receive similar levels of support from their classmates as other children (Menesini & Salmivalli, 2017).

TABLE 10.1

Characteristics of Popular and Rejected Children

	CHARACTERISTIC	OUTCOMES
Popular children	• Helpful, trustworthy, assertive • Cognitively skilled and achievement oriented • Socially skilled, able to self-disclose and provide emotional support • Good social problem-solving skills and conflict resolution skills • Prosocial orientation • Assume others have good intentions • A minority are also antisocial and aggressive. They interact with others in a hostile way, using physical or relational aggression, and are likely to bully other children.	Positive characteristics are strengthened though experience and peer approval. Positive peer evaluations are sources of self-validation, self-esteem, confidence, and attention from peers, and they influence adjustment. Without intervention, the minority of popular adolescents who are aggressive are likely to continue patterns of physical or relational aggression in response to peer approval and acceptance.
Aggressive-rejected children	• Confrontational, hostile toward other children • Impulsive and hyperactive • Difficulty with emotional regulation • Difficulty taking others' perspectives • Assume that their peers are out to get them • Poor social skills • Misinterpret other children's behaviors and motives	Similar outcomes for both types of rejected children Negative characteristics are strengthened. Few opportunities to learn and practice social skills, conflict resolution, and emotional regulation Anxiety, depression, and low self-esteem Behavior problems Poor academic achievement Increased physical and relational aggression over time Withdrawal and loneliness
Withdrawn-rejected children	• Passive, timid, and socially awkward • Socially withdrawn, isolate themselves from others • Anxious • Poor social skills • Fear being disliked by peers • Misinterpret other children's behaviors and motives	

Children who show physically aggressive forms of bullying often demonstrate hyperactive behavior, have poor school achievement, perceive less support from teachers than do other children, and may show higher rates of depression than other children (Turcotte Benedict, Vivier, & Gjelsvik, 2015). Bullies are more likely to experience inconsistent, hostile, and rejecting parenting. Parents of bullies are more likely to provide poor supervision, prefer coercive control and physical discipline, and tend to be permissive toward aggressive behavior, even teaching their children to strike back at perceived provocation (Gómez-Ortiz, Romera, & Ortega-Ruiz, 2016; Rajendran, Kruszewski, & Halperin, 2016).

Rates of bullying may vary with the sociocultural context. One study of Puerto Rican children living in the South Bronx, New York, and San Juan, Puerto Rico, showed that children were more likely to bully others when they were part of a minority group on the mainland than when they were living in their home culture in Puerto Rico (Morcillo et al., 2015). Mainland children who were more acculturated, or acclimated to U.S. culture, engaged in more bullying than did their less acculturated peers. The longer the children lived on the mainland, the greater the demands of navigating cross-cultural worlds. Bullying may be a response to the distress of navigating cross-cultural worlds or a response to perceived discrimination.

Victims of Bullying

Bullies report choosing their victims because they do not like them, often because the victims are perceived as different, as more quiet and cautious than other children (Juvonen & Graham, 2014). Victims of bullying are likely to be inhibited, frail in appearance, and younger than their peers. They often experience intrusive parenting, overprotectiveness, and criticism from parents, which increases their vulnerability to bullying (Menesini & Salmivalli, 2017). Perhaps not surprisingly, children who are bullied often report feeling lonely and less happy at school and having fewer good friends than their classmates (Reavis, Keane, & Calkins, 2010).

Many victim characteristics, including nonassertive styles of interacting with peers, shyness, passivity, and social withdrawal, as well as anxiety, depression, and poor emotional control, are present before the child becomes a target of peer victimization and are amplified by victimization (Perren, Ettekal, & Ladd, 2013). Much of the long-term stability of peer victimization and its negative effects can be explained by the dynamic interactions between **risk factors** for victimization and the effects of victimization (Shetgiri, Lin, & Flores, 2013). Risk factors are circumstances that increase the likelihood of negative outcomes and, in extreme cases, can impede development.

Although children respond in various ways to bullying, avoidance behaviors (such as not going to school and refusing to go certain places) are common (Waasdorp & Bradshaw, 2011). Victims of bullying may respond to victimization in ways that reinforce bullies by becoming defensive, crying, and giving into bullies' demands. Not all victims of bullying are passive and withdrawn, however. Older children who experience frequent victimization may respond with more intense feelings of anger and greater desires to retaliate, making them more likely to show *reactive aggression,* an aggressive response to an insult, confrontation, or frustration (Arseneault, 2018).

Some aggressive-rejected children become provocative victims or **bully-victims** (Hymel & Swearer, 2015). Bully-victims share characteristics of both bullies and victims but function more poorly than either. For example, bully-victims tend to show high levels of anxiety and depression, as well as low rates of social acceptance and self-esteem common to victims, but they also show more aggression, impulsivity, and poor self-control than do other victims (Swearer & Hymel, 2015; van Dijk, Poorthuis, & Malti, 2017). Children who are bully-victims have difficulties managing emotions that may increase their risk for reactive aggression and acting out behaviors that invite aggressive exchanges with others. These characteristics lead children who are both bullies and victims to have problems in peer relationships. Bully-victims often are among the most disliked members of a classroom (Arseneault, 2018).

Physical and relational bullying have negative emotional and academic consequences that appear as early as in kindergarten and persist over the childhood and adolescent years, often well after the bullying ends (S. E. Moore et al., 2017). For example, children who were bully-victims were more likely to experience anxiety and depression in late adolescence and in early adulthood—and even into middle adulthood (Evans-Lacko et al., 2017; McDougall & Vaillancourt, 2015). Like other forms of bullying, cyberbullying is associated with anxiety, depression, academic problems, and behavioral problems (Hamm et al., 2015; Vaillancourt et al., 2017). Cyberbullying may be more damaging, as it not only co-occurs with other types of bullying but also is more difficult for victims to avoid (Kowalski, Giumetti, Schroeder, & Lattanner, 2014). Cyberbullying can occur at any time of the day or any day of the week, and the victim need not be present. Victims of cyberbullying are also less likely to report their abuse or to seek help than victims of traditional bullying (Mishna, Cook, Gadalla, Daciuk, & Solomon, 2010).

Furthermore, the meaning and implications of bullying may vary with context. For example, relational bullying may be more emotionally damaging to children reared in collectivist cultures that highly value relationships. Accordingly, one comparison of Japanese and U.S. fourth graders showed more depression in Japanese victims (Kawabata, Crick, & Hamaguchi, 2010).

Intervening in Bullying

Table 10.2 summarizes interventions to combat bullying; such interventions address victims, bullies, and schools (Hutson, Kelly, & Militello, 2018; Nese, Horner, Dickey, Stiller, & Tomlanovich, 2014). Interventions focusing on victims seek to change victims' negative perceptions of themselves by helping them to acquire the skills needed to maintain relationships with peers and teaching them to respond to bullying in ways that do not reinforce their attackers (Olweus & Limber, 2010). Successful interventions stress that victimized children are not to blame for the abuse. Helping victims of bullying is not enough, though—perpetrators of bullying also need help. Parents and teachers should help bullies learn to identify, understand, and manage their and other people's emotions, as well as direct anger in safe and appropriate ways (Hutson et al., 2018). Teachers need to be aware of bullying and willing to intervene (Espelage, Low, & Jimerson, 2014). In addition, bystanders—children who watch episodes of bullying but do not act—reinforce bullies' behaviors and increase bullying (Kärnä, Voeten, Poskiparta, & Salmivalli, 2010; Salmivalli, 2014). Class norms can influence whether bystanders intervene (Pozzoli, Gini, & Vieno, 2012). So can advice from parents (Grassetti et al., 2018). Classmates can be encouraged to support one another when bullying events occur: Rather than being bystanders or egging the bully

TABLE 10.2

Bullying Risks and Interventions

		BULLYING RISK FACTOR	BULLYING INTERVENTION
Child	Victim	Physically weak Younger than peers Anxious, insecure, low self-esteem, dependent Quiet, cautious, withdrawn Little prosocial behavior Poor emotional control Loneliness Unhappiness at school Few good friends than peers	Teach assertiveness skills. Teach children alternative responses to bullying. Teach anxiety and emotional management as well as social and coping skills.
	Bully	Above average in size More physically and verbally assertive Impulsive Domineering, hostile toward peers Little anxiety or insecurity in peer contexts Makes friends easily Hyperactive behavior Academic difficulties Poor emotional control	Teach alternatives to violence. Help children develop empathy. Teach emotional management and coping skills to reduce impulsive behavior.
Parent	Victim	Intrusive, overprotective, and/or critical parenting	Teach authoritative parenting skills. Encourage parents to aid children in being independent and developing coping skills.
	Bully	Hostile and rejecting parenting Use of physical punishment Models aggressive behavior Permissive, inconsistent response to aggressive bullying behavior	Teach authoritative parenting skills. Parent with sensitivity and consistency. Model nonaggressive behavior, interpersonal interactions, and conflict management strategies. Provide positive feedback to children for appropriate social behaviors. Use alternatives to physical punishment.
School		Groups students by physical characteristics such as height Policies that discourage reporting bullying incidents Teachers and administrators who ignore bullying Environment of negative feedback and negative attention	Stress that victims are not to blame. Teach social skills and conflict management. Promote a positive school climate that encourages students to feel good about themselves. Encourage fair discipline that is not punitive. Train teachers to identify and respond to potentially damaging victimization. Teachers use positive feedback and modeling to address appropriate social interactions. School personnel never ignore bullying behaviors. Encourage classmates to support one another and, rather than simply watch bullying events occur, tell a teacher, and refuse to watch or encourage the bully. Review and modify school practices with an eye toward identifying how school procedures may contribute to bullying.

Antibullying Legislation

School policies that emphasize community, such as proclaiming school as a no-bullying zone and encouraging bystanders to intervene, are effective in reducing peer victimization.
Jim West/Alamy

Schools are responsible for children's physical well-being, but how far does that responsibility extend? What is the role of schools in addressing peer victimization? In a landmark case, the mother of fifth grader LaShonda Davis filed a suit against the Monroe County (Georgia) Board after the school failed to intervene during the months in which her daughter was the victim of severe harassment, often sexual, by a fellow student. The 1999 decision in *Davis v. Monroe County Board of Education* ruled that sexual harassment by peers violates Title IX of the Equal Opportunity in Education Act of 1972, which stipulates that "no person in the United States shall, on the basis of sex, be excluded from participation in, be denied the benefits of, or be subjected to discrimination under any education program or activity receiving Federal financial assistance." The court deemed that sexual harassment in the school setting violates students' rights to education.

Davis v. Monroe applies specifically to peer-to-peer sexual harassment, but researchers and legislators look to this ruling as an important precedent for antibullying legislation because bullying violates students' rights.

In recognition of the pervasiveness and severity of bullying, every state in the United States includes specific bully-related policies in their public school laws (U.S. Department of Health and Human Services, 2017). Antibullying laws do not criminalize bullying itself but stipulate that school districts take action to prevent or intervene when bullying occurs (Hinduja & Patchin, 2015). School boards are charged with establishing antibullying policies (Cornell & Limber, 2015).

Most developmental researchers agree that a model bullying law should include, at minimum, the following: a clear definition of bullying, explicit articulation of a bullying prohibition, implementation of prevention and treatment programs, and acknowledgment of the association between bullying and public health risks (Limber & Small, 2003; Srabstein et al., 2008). State antibullying laws vary dramatically but, as a whole, are associated with a 7% to 13% reduction in school violence and in reports of bullying (Nikolaou, 2017; Sabia & Bass, 2017).

The Safe Schools Improvement Act, proposed in 2013 and reintroduced to Congress in 2017, is legislation that would require states to collect and report information on the incidence of bullying and harassment. It would also permit schools to use federal grants to prevent and respond to incidents of bullying and harassment, require schools to provide annual reports of bullying prevalence and policies, and establish grievance procedures for students and parents to register complaints regarding such conduct. Although not yet passed by Congress, the Safe Schools Improvement Act sets an important precedent by acknowledging the relevance of peer victimization to children's everyday lives.

What Do You Think?

1. What role should schools take in addressing bullying?

2. Did your school draw attention to bullying and have rules or policies about bullying? ●

on, they can tell a teacher, refuse to watch, and even, if safe, encourage bullies to stop.

Bullying is not simply a child-to-child problem, and it requires more than a child-centered solution. Stopping bullying requires awareness and change within the school. Schools must review and modify practices with an eye toward identifying how class environment and procedures may maintain or increase bullying (Fink, Patalay,

Sharpe, & Wolpert, 2018; Nese et al., 2014). In recognition of the pervasiveness and severity of bullying, specific bully-related policies are included in public school laws in most states. Addressing the problem of bullying requires that children, teachers, and parents voice concerns about bullying; schools develop policies against bullying; teachers supervise and monitor children during lunch and recess times; and parents learn how to identify and change victims' and bullies' behaviors. The Applying Developmental Science feature discusses antibullying legislation.

> **THINKING IN CONTEXT 10.2**
>
> 1. Considering Bronfenbrenner's bioecological theory from Chapter 1, what microsystem factors (such as personal characteristics), mesosystem factors (such as family and school), and exosystem factors (such as neighborhood) might lead a child to be popular or unpopular with peers? Which factors are most important, in your view?
>
> 2. As a parent, what might you to do lower the likelihood that your child might become a bully or a victim of bullying?

FAMILIES IN MIDDLE CHILDHOOD

» LO 10.3 **Discuss family relationships in middle childhood and the influence of family structure on adjustment.**

Children are embedded in families that play an important role in their development. Children's relationships with parents and siblings are dynamic and reciprocal. Children influence and are influenced by every member of their family. Families may take many forms, as described in the following sections.

Parent–Child Relationships

As school-age children become more independent, they spend less time with their parents but remain close to their parents. Parents and school-age children tend to spend their time together engaging in task-oriented activities, such as doing homework, preparing meals, cleaning, and shopping. Interactions with parents help children practice, rehearse, and refine skills that are important for peer relationships. The parent–child relationship transforms as parents adapt their parenting styles to match their children's increased ability to reason and desire for independence. Parents tend to use less direct management and instead begin to share power—for example, by guiding and monitoring children's behavior from a distance, communicating expectations, and allowing children to be in charge of moment-to-moment decision making (Lamb & Lewis, 2015). Parents increasingly use reasoning and inductive techniques of discipline, such as pointing out the consequences of a child's behavior,

explaining how a child affects others, and appealing to the child's self-esteem and sense of values. Children who are securely attached to parents tend to develop positive emotion regulation skills that aid them in home, peer, and school contexts (Brumariu, 2015).

As in many aspects of development, continuity is typical in parenting and parent–child relationships (Bradley, Iida, Pennar, Owen, & Vandell, 2017). Patterns of harsh verbal discipline (yelling, threatening, punishment, shaming) and insensitive parenting established in early childhood tend to persist in middle childhood (Bradley & Corwyn, 2008; Lansford, Staples, Bates, Pettit, & Dodge, 2013). In turn, harsh parenting styles and poor-quality parent–child relationships in middle childhood tend to worsen and are associated with poor adjustment, antisocial activity, and delinquency into adolescence (Hakvoort, Bos, van Balen, & Hermanns, 2010; Keijsers, Loeber, Branje, & Meeus, 2011; Koehn & Kerns, 2018).

Siblings

Nearly 80% of children in the United States have at least one sibling (Gao, 2015). (In contrast, China has many one-child families, as discussed in the Cultural Influences on Development feature.) By middle childhood, children spend more time with siblings than with parents (Dunn, 2002). Siblings are an important influence on each other's development. Through interactions with siblings, children learn relationship skills such as conflict resolution (McHale, Updegraff, & Whiteman, 2012). They learn that relationships continue even through arguments and anger. Siblings offer each other social support and assistance with academic, family, and peer challenges (Gass, Jenkins, & Dunn, 2007). They help each other manage stressful life events and reduce the anxiety and depressive symptoms

Siblings who usually offer each other social support and assistance can sometimes come in conflict.
JGI/Jamie Grill Blend Images/Newscom

that often accompany them (Ji-Yeon, McHale, Crouter, & Osgood, 2007).

Sibling relationships are also often characterized by patterns of ambivalence and conflict, however (Kramer, 2010). Sibling rivalry tends to rise in middle childhood as children increasingly engage in social comparison. Parents, teachers, peers, other family members—and children themselves—naturally compare siblings' characteristics, interests, and accomplishments (McHale et al., 2012). Children who feel that a sibling receives more affection, approval, or resources from parents may feel resentful, which may harm the sibling relationship. Some fighting and violence are common among siblings. In one

---

China's One-Child Policy

China promoted the one-child policy as the key to greater resources and opportunities for families.
Imagine China/Newscom

In response to a rapidly growing population that posed social, economic, and environmental problems, the People's Republic of China implemented a policy in 1979 designed to curb population growth. Known as the **one-child policy,** it restricted the number of children married couples could have to one. The one-child policy was most strictly implemented in urban areas (McLoughlin, 2005). Couples in rural areas, especially those who require assistance to manage farms, could request permission for two children if the first child was a girl and the couple waited 4 to 5 years between births (Yang, 2007).

At the core of the one-child policy was a set of incentives, as well as penalties for infractions (McLoughlin, 2005). Penalties included stiff fines, reductions in health care and educational opportunities, and even job demotion or job loss. Incentives focused on health and education resources. The official slogan of the one-child-policy was *you sheng you yu* ("give birth to fewer children, but give them better care and education"; Yang, 2007). In exchange for limiting parents' childbearing, the Chinese government provided greater opportunities and resources at the national, community, and household levels for only children. The one-child policy was intended to give Chinese school-age only children advantages over those with siblings—specifically, more attention and resources.

Early research in the 1980s suggested that Chinese only children scored higher on measures of mathematics and verbal achievement but displayed more egocentrism, uncooperativeness, and difficulty managing emotions and impulses, as well as less sharing, respect of elders, and prosocial behavior than school-age children with siblings (Falbo et al., 1997; McLoughlin, 2005). Later research, however, suggested that Chinese only children scored higher than those with siblings on measures of IQ but did not differ on psychosocial measures such as dependence, helping behaviors, independence, aggression, friendliness, curiosity, self-confidence, peer relationships, social competence, and academic achievement (Chen, Rubin, & Li, 1994; Guo, Yang, Liu, & Song, 2005; Wang et al., 2000).

The one-child policy may have contributed to a gender imbalance in China. Given Chinese culture's tradition of valuing of boys, the one-child policy was implicated in high rates of female infanticide and sex-selective abortions, leading to a significant gender imbalance (Mosher, 2006). A population survey of more than 4.5 million Chinese children and teens found that the male to female ratio was 126:100 overall, with several provinces showing ratios of over 130:100 (Zhu, Lu, & Hesketh, 2009). Among second births, the ratio was as high as 149:100, with ratios of over 160:100 in nine provinces (Zhu et al., 2009). A rapidly aging population, coupled with a much smaller workforce, has recently prompted a change in the one-child policy. In 2015, China ended the policy, and now couples may apply to have two children (Buckley, 2015). Initially, fewer couples than expected applied to have a second child, leading to speculation that the one-child policy may have changed perceived norms on family size (Holliday, 2014). However, births in China increased nearly 8% between 2015 and 2016, suggesting that the change is effective (Levenson, 2017).

What Do You Think?

1. Why do you think fewer Chinese couples than expected initially applied to have a second child? What might have caused the subsequent increase?

2. Do you think the increase in births will continue? Why or why not? ●

Same-sex parents show similar levels of parenting competence but often experience greater well-being as compared with heterosexual parents.
Shih Weber/Newscom

study, nearly three quarters of families reported physical violence between siblings, and over 40% of children had been kicked, bitten, or punched by a sibling within the past year (Feinberg, Solmeyer, & McHale, 2012). Sibling conflict is associated with poor adjustment, peer aggression, and antisocial behaviors (Buist & Vermande, 2014).

Same-Sex Parented Families

In the early 1990s, a children's book titled *Heather Has Two Mommies* was a source of great controversy, as politicians and organizations opposed to lesbian, gay, bisexual, or transgender (LGBT) rights sought to ban it from libraries and schools. Today, children like the fictional Heather are not so unusual. An estimated 37% of LGBT-identified adults have a child at some time in their lives (Gates, 2013). Most children raised by LGBT parents are the biological children of these parents, as shown in Figure 10.1. However, LGBT parents are more likely to adopt children than are heterosexual parents (10% and 3%, respectively). As a result of *Obergefell v. Hodges*, the landmark 2015 U.S. Supreme Court ruling that legalized same-sex marriage nationwide, every state permits joint adoption by married couples, regardless of sexual orientation.

More than three decades of research conducted in the United States, the United Kingdom, Belgium, and the Netherlands has failed to reveal important differences in the adjustment or development of children and adolescents reared by same-sex couples compared with those reared by other couples (Fedewa, Black, & Ahn, 2014; Patterson, 2017; Perrin & Siegel, 2013). Specifically, children and adolescents raised by lesbian mothers or gay fathers do not differ from other children on measures of emotional development, such as empathy and emotional regulation (Bos, Knox,

van Rijn-van Gelderen, & Gartrell, 2016; Farr, 2017). Instead, some studies have suggested that children raised by gay and lesbian parents may score higher in some aspects of social and academic competence, as well as show fewer social and behavioral problems and lower levels of aggression, than other children (Golombok et al., 2014, 2018; Miller, Kors, & Macfie, 2017). Moreover, children raised by lesbian mothers and gay fathers show similar patterns of gender identity and gender role development as children raised by heterosexual parents—they are not more likely to identify as gay or lesbian in adulthood (Fedewa et al., 2014; Tasker & Patterson, 2007). Researchers have concluded that a family's social and economic resources, the strength of the relationships among members of the family, and the presence of stigma are far more important variables than parental gender or sexual orientation in affecting children's development and well-being (Farr, 2017; Perrin & Siegel, 2013).

Single-Parent Families

Over one quarter of U.S. children under age 18 live with a single parent, most commonly with their mother (Child Trends Databank, 2015). Figure 10.2 shows the various living arrangements

FIGURE 10.1

Relationship of Children to Parent(s) in Same-Sex Households in the United States, 2011

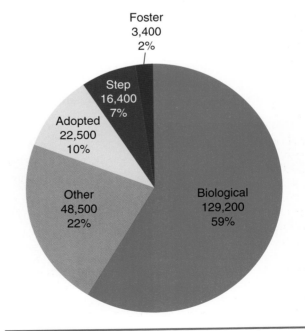

Source: 2011 American Community Survey, as published in Gates, G. J. (2013). *LGBT Parenting in the United States.* Los Angeles, CA: The Williams Institute..

FIGURE 10.2

Living Arrangements of Children Under 18, 1970–2014

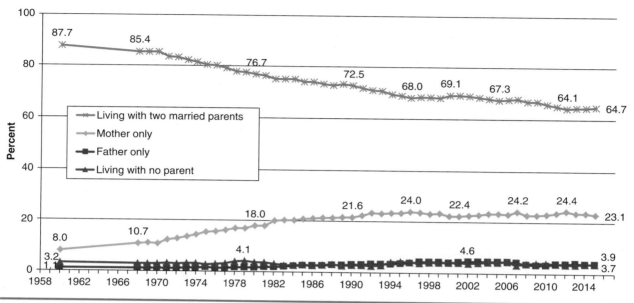

Source: Child Trends Databank, 2015.

for households with children (Child Trends Databank, 2015). African American children are disproportionally likely to live in a single-parent home (Figure 10.3); 49% of African American children live with their mother alone, compared with 26% of Hispanic, 15% of non-Hispanic White, and 11% of Asian American children.

Single-parent families may be created through divorce or death, or the single parent may never have married. In any case, children in such families tend to show more physical and mental health problems, poorer academic achievement, less social competence, and more behavior problems than do children in intact two-parent families (Taylor & Conger, 2017; Waldfogel, Craigie, & Brooks-Gunn, 2010). However, it is important to recognize that these effects tend to be small; the vast majority of children raised in one-parent homes are well adjusted (Lamb, 2012). Moreover, there are more differences among children in single-parent homes than between children in single-parent homes and two-parent homes. Children reared by parents who are single by choice tend to experience few adjustment problems; children of divorced parents tend to experience more difficulties due to the many transitions that accompany divorce, discussed later in this chapter (Golombok, & Tasker, 2015).

Children in single-mother homes, regardless of ethnicity, are disproportionately likely to live in poverty (Damaske, Bratter, & Frech, 2017). About one third of children raised in single-mother homes live in poverty, compared with 16% of children in single-father homes and less than 6% of children in homes of married couples (DeNavas-Walt & Proctor, 2014). Low socioeconomic status poses risks for academic, social, and behavioral problems. Economic disadvantage affects children in a myriad of ways, from having less money for books, clothes, and extracurricular activities to living in poorer school districts and neighborhoods. In addition, families headed by single mothers often experience many transitions, as single mothers tend to change jobs and homes more frequently than other mothers. Each transition poses

Around 25% of children under age 18 live with a single parent, most commonly with their mother. Children raised in one-parent households are generally well-adjusted.
ANDREW HOLBROOKE/Corbis via Getty Images

FIGURE 10.3

Living Arrangements of Children, by Race and Hispanic Origin, 2015

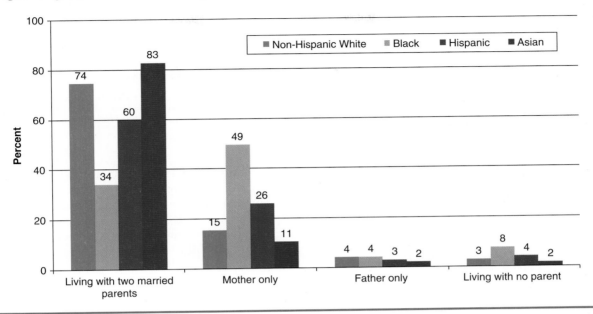

Source: Child Trends Databank, 2015.

challenges to children's adjustment (Evans, Li, & Whipple, 2013). In addition, single mothers report more depression and psychological problems than married mothers and, when depressed, undoubtedly function less well as parents (Reising et al., 2013; Waldfogel et al., 2010).

The vast majority of what we know about single-parent families comes from studying mothers. About one fourth of single-parent households are headed by men, however (Livingston, 2013). Single fathers are more likely than mothers to live with a partner and tend to have higher household incomes, both of which are associated with positive child outcomes. In fact, many of the differences associated with family structure are reduced or disappear when researchers take socioeconomic status into account, suggesting that differences in child well-being across family types are strongly influenced by family income, access to resources, and the stresses that accompany economic difficulties (Ryan, Claessens, & Markowitz, 2015).

Parenting success, then, is influenced by access to economic and social resources (Taylor & Conger, 2017). The level of social support afforded single mothers influences their abilities to provide emotional support for their children and implement effective parenting strategies. In African American communities, for example, single mothers are often integrated within their community, providing their children with opportunities to interact with many caring adult family members and friends of the family; thus, children are raised as members of a larger African American community (Jayakody & Kalil, 2002). Often, an adult male, such as an uncle or grandfather, takes on a fathering role, helping a child build competence and develop a relationship with a caring adult (Hill, Bush, & Roosa, 2003). In such families, grandmothers often are highly involved, warm, and helpful, taking on important support roles. In one study of U.K. single-parent homes, grandmothers served parental roles and aided their children much as would partners (Harper & Ruicheva, 2010). When children are close to highly involved extended family members, they develop family bonds and a sense of family honor that guides them and encourages them to succeed; this tends to hold true of all children, regardless of family structure (Jaeger, 2012).

Cohabiting Families

There are many kinds of families, and not all are formed through marriage. An estimated 40% of children will spend some time in a cohabiting-parent family before they reach age 12 (Manning, 2015). Children of unmarried cohabiting parents who have close caring relationships with them and whose union is stable develop as well as their counterparts whose parents' marriage is stable (Rose-Greenland & Smock, 2013).

Unmarried cohabiting couples tend to have less stable relationships than married couples, however (Manning, 2015). For example, about one third of cohabiting couples break up within 3 years (Copen, Daniels, & Mosher, 2013). In contrast, about two thirds of first marriages are intact after 10 years (Goodwin, Mosher, & Chandra, 2010). Children living in cohabiting households are much more likely to experience their parents' separation, conflict in the home, and transitions in family life than are children of married parents, all of which influence adjustment (Rose-Greenland & Smock, 2013).

Differences in socioeconomic status have an effect on the development of children of cohabiting parents, just as they do on other children's development. On average, children raised in cohabiting-parent families experience economic situations that are better than those of many children in single-parent families (e.g., higher parental education and family earnings) but more economically stressful than those reared by married parents (e.g., greater poverty and food insecurity) (Manning, 2015). About 20% of children living in cohabiting families are poor, compared with about 10% of children from two-parent married households and nearly 40% of children in single-parent households (Kennedy & Fitch, 2012).

The effect of cohabitation on children may vary with contextual norms. Consensual unions and childbearing within cohabiting unions are more common among minority families (Kennedy & Bumpass, 2008). Black and Hispanic children thus spend more time in cohabiting-parent unions than do White children. In addition, the difference in economic advantage between marriage and cohabitation is smaller for cohabiting Black and Hispanic families than for White families, perhaps partially accounting for minority children's more positive outcomes (Manning & Brown, 2006; Osborne, Manning, & Smock, 2007).

Divorced and Divorcing Families

Since 1960, divorce rates have tripled in many industrialized nations. Although the divorce rate in the United States is high relative to that in many countries, it has declined over the past three decades from its peak of 5.3 per 1,000 in the total population in 1981 to 3.2 in 2014 (National Center for Health Statistics, 2015). About 40% of marriages in the United States end in divorce within 15 years (Copen et al., 2012).

For many decades, it was assumed that divorce caused significant and irreparable harm to children. Most researchers today take a neutral stance, viewing divorce as a common transition that many children experience and that poses some

Divorce tends to be preceded by a period of parental conflict and uncertainty, and the tension may continue for several years after the divorce, with implications for children's emotional and psychological health.
iStock/Kerkez

challenges to adjustment. Research has suggested that divorce has some negative effects on children's adjustment, such as internalizing and externalizing problems, but the effects are small, vary by particular outcome, are often transient, and do not apply to all children uniformly (Amato & Anthony, 2014; Weaver & Schofield, 2014). Variations in child, parent, and family characteristics and contexts influence children's adjustment to parental divorce, but most children show improved adjustment within 2 years after the divorce, suggesting that the majority of children of divorce are resilient (Lamb, 2012). What initially appear to be effects of divorce are likely to be a complex combination of parent, child, and contextual factors that precede and follow the divorce in conjunction with the divorce itself (Amato & Anthony, 2014; Bennett, 2006).

Divorce triggers a reconfiguration of family roles, and parenting responsibilities shift disproportionately onto the resident parent. After divorce, children are typically raised by their mothers and experience a drop in income that influences their access to resources and opportunities, such as after-school programs and activities (Bratberg & Tjøtta, 2008). Single-parent-headed households often move to more affordable housing, causing additional changes in children's school, community, and circle of friends, reducing children's access to social support and opportunities to play with friends. Custodial parents might also increase the hours they work, leading to less contact with their children. These changes contribute to inconsistencies in family routines, activities, and parental monitoring prior to, during, and after the divorce. High-quality family relationships, including positive interactions with the noncustodial parent and low levels of parent–parent conflict, can buffer children against these stressors (Bastaits & Mortelmans, 2016; Weaver & Schofield, 2015).

Divorce tends to be preceded by a period of uncertainty and tension, often characterized by increases in conflict between parents that may continue for several years after the divorce (Amato, 2010). In fact, harmful family processes, such as parental conflict, poor parent–child interactions, and ineffective parenting strategies, may precede parental divorce by as much as 8 to 12 years (Drapeau, Gagne, Saint-Jacques, Lepine, & Ivers, 2009; Potter, 2010). These processes understandably take a toll on children's emotional and psychological health. Chronic exposure to parental conflict is associated with increased physiological arousal, an elevated stress response, and poorer adjustment (Davidson, O'Hara, & Beck, 2014; Davies & Martin, 2014). In turn, children's difficulties adapting, such as behavior problems, can increase parental conflict (Drapeau et al., 2009). Longitudinal research following children of married parents has found that children whose parents later divorce show many of the problems typical of children of divorce, such as anxiety, depression, delinquency, and poor academics, long before the divorce takes place (Strohschein, 2005). However, not all parents display high levels of conflict. When researchers take into account the quality of parenting and children's exposure to conflict, the link between parental divorce and children's adjustment lessens, suggesting that parenting strategies and relationships are more important influences on children's adjustment than divorce (Bing, Nelson, & Wesolowski, 2009; Whiteside & Becker, 2000).

Blended Families

About 15% of U.S. children live in a **blended family:** a family composed of a biological parent and a nonrelated adult, most commonly a mother and stepfather (Pew Research Center, 2015). Blended families, also sometimes referred to as *stepfamilies* or *reconstituted families,* present children with new challenges and adjustments, as the multiple transitions entailed by divorce and remarriage are stressful. It is often difficult for blended families to integrate and balance the many relationships among custodial, noncustodial, and stepparents, in addition to grandparents and extended family members (Nixon, Hadfield, Nixon, & Hadfield, 2016). As stepfamilies become more complex, that is, as the number of biologically and nonbiologically related individuals in the family increases, so do challenges to children's adjustment (Brown, Manning, & Stykes, 2015).

Age influences adaptation to a blended family. School-age children and adolescents tend to display more difficulties in adjusting to remarriage than do younger children (Ganong, Coleman, & Russell, 2015). Although adjusting to being part of a blended family may pose challenges, most children reared in stepfamilies do not differ from those raised in single-parent families in terms of cognitive, academic, and social outcomes (Ganong & Coleman, 2017). Many are similar to children in first-marriage families. Indeed, entering a stepfamily is associated with improved adjustment, especially when it results in an increase in family income (Ryan et al., 2015). Overall, blended families adapt more easily and children show better adjustment when stepparents build a warm friendship with the child and adopt their new roles slowly rather than rushing or forcing relationships (Doodson & Morley, 2006).

 THINKING IN CONTEXT 10.3

1. How might children's relationships with their family influence their relationships with peers? How are interactions and relationships with family members, such as siblings, similar to and different from those with peers?

2. Eight-year-old Sam's parents have announced that they plan to divorce. What are the major challenges facing Sam? What reactions and effects do you expect the divorce to have on Sam? How do you think Sam will adjust to a new living situation or a parent's remarriage?

COMMON SOCIOEMOTIONAL AND DEVELOPMENTAL PROBLEMS IN MIDDLE CHILDHOOD

» LO 10.4 **Analyze the role of resilience in promoting adjustment to adversity, including characteristics of children and contexts that promote resilience.**

Fear is a common problem of childhood. With cognitive and socioemotional development, as well as experience, fear tends to become less frequent and less intense but also expands to include wider contexts, such as the neighborhood, the country, and the world (Burnham, 2009). Older children may worry about parents' health, wars, natural disasters, illnesses such as AIDS, and terrorist attacks (Burnham, Lomax, & Hooper, 2012; Smith & Moyer-Gusé, 2006). Children who express many worries and anxieties tend to have lower self-confidence and perceived control than other children (Parkinson & Creswell, 2011). Many children's anxiety centers on school.

School Refusal

Some children's anxiety manifests as school refusal, the refusal to attend school or to stay in school (Elliott & Place, 2018). Children who refuse school often display physical complaints, such as dizziness, nausea, and stomachaches. These physical symptoms often disappear when they are allowed to stay home (Kearney, Diliberto, Kearney, & Diliberto, 2013). Nearly one third of school-age children in the United States refuse school at some point in their education, but only about 2% of children refuse school regularly (Maynard et al., 2015). School refusal can occur throughout the school years. However, it is more common from 5 to 6 years of age and 10 to 11 years of age, during transitions to elementary school, from elementary to middle or junior high school, and from childhood to adolescence (Melvin & Tonge, 2012). In some cases, school refusal is a response to media coverage of school shootings and other cases of extreme, but rare, school violence (Inglés, Gonzálvez-Maciá, García-Fernández, Vicent, & Martínez-Monteagudo, 2015).

Certain characteristics, such as shyness and behavioral inhibition, fear of failure, and low feelings of control, put children at risk for school refusal (Kearney, Diliberto, Kearney, & Diliberto, 2013). Children who refuse school may experience many psychological problems, such as excessive worrying, social anxiety, depressive symptoms, fatigue, and clinginess to parents. About half of children who chronically refuse to attend school suffer from anxiety disorders (Maynard et al., 2015). Poor relationships with peers place children at risk for school refusal; in turn, not attending school results in further relationship problems with peers (Havik, Bru, & Ertesvåg, 2015). Indeed, each risk factor for school refusal also places children at risk for poor adjustment to multiple school absences (Havik et al., 2015). School refusal may be more common during family transitions such as separations and divorce or may accompany family stressors such as mental health problems in parents (Kearney et al., 2013). Finally, children who display school refusal often fear a particular aspect of school, such as attending gym class, and the fears are often realistic, such as fear of a school bully, a harsh teacher, or intense pressures to achieve from parents or teachers (Havik, Bru, & Ertesvåg, 2013).

Treating school refusal requires teaching the child to cope with challenging situations and emotions, for example, by providing training in social skills, emotional regulation, and problem solving (Maric, Heyne, MacKinnon, van Widenfelt, & Westenberg, 2013; Maynard et al., 2018). Support from parents and teachers is essential. Most important, children must return to,

Child sexual abuse is most common in middle childhood. Sexual abuse often is not a one-time event; some children experience sexual abuse that persists for years.
iStock/ambrozinio

and remain in, school and use their new strategies and supports to manage and overcome their discomfort and fear.

Child Sexual Abuse

Sexual abuse refers to inappropriate touching, comments, or sexual activity, coerced or persuaded with a child. Once considered rare, child sexual abuse is now understood as a widespread problem around the world (Hillis, Mercy, Amobi, & Kress, 2016). It is estimated that about one quarter to one third of U.S. children under the age of 17 have experienced sexual abuse (Finkelhor, Shattuck, Turner, & Hamby, 2014). Many cases are unreported as many children do not disclose abuse (Leclerc & Wortley, 2015). Although both boys and girls are victims of sexual abuse, girls are more often victimized. Sexual abuse may occur at any time during infancy, childhood, or adolescence, but it is most often reported in middle childhood, with about half of cases occurring between ages 4 and 12 (U.S. Department of Health and Human Services, 2018). Older children are more likely to disclose sexual abuse, whereas sexual abuse of young children is most likely discovered accidentally, through eyewitness detection or in response to questions (Alaggia, Collin-Vézina, & Lateef, 2018). Although, as mentioned, girls are more often victims of sexual abuse, boys are much less likely to report abuse, perhaps because of internalized gender stereotypes about masculinity and perceived weakness associated with victimization (Gagnier & Collin-Vézina, 2016). It is often difficult for children who are sexually abused to cope and heal because sexual abuse often is not a one-time event; some children experience sexual abuse that persists for years.

Reported cases of child sexual abuse are more common in homes characterized by poverty, food and housing insecurity, marital instability, and drug and alcohol abuse (Berger, Font, Slack, & Waldfogel, 2017; Kim, Drake, & Jonson-Reid, 2018; U.S. Department of Health and Human Services, 2018). Children who are raised in homes in which adults come and go—repeated marriages, separations, and revolving romantic partners—are at higher risk of sexual abuse. However, sexual abuse also occurs in intact families and at all socioeconomic levels. Some researchers argue that maltreatment is more likely to be discovered in children of disadvantaged families than in children at higher socioeconomic levels, because disadvantaged children are likelier to come into contact with social services, such as when parents seek welfare and other forms of financial assistance or when parental substance use is discovered.

Perpetrators of sexual abuse are most often males whom the child knows, trusts, and has frequent contact with, such as parents, stepparents, and live-in boyfriends; stepfathers are likelier than fathers to be perpetrators (U.S. Department of Health and Human Services, 2018). Most sexual assaults occur in the home of the victim or the perpetrator, not in dark alleys or during abduction by a stranger (Kenny, 2018). Children comply with the abuser for a variety of reasons. Some are bribed by gifts or privileges and are told that they are special and that the activity is a secret that they share. Others are intimidated and threatened by physical harm and reprisal for noncompliance or for telling another adult.

Both boys and girls show similar emotional responses to sexual abuse, including symptoms of anxiety and depression and behavioral responses such as social withdrawal, aggression, sleep disturbances, poor academic achievement, and risky behaviors (Maikovich-Fong & Jaffee, 2010; Pérez-Fuentes et al., 2013). Childhood sexual abuse is associated with mental and behavioral health problems in adolescence and adulthood, including depression, anxiety, antisocial behavior, substance dependence, and suicide attempts (Maniglio, 2011, 2013; Pérez-González, Guilera, Pereda, & Jarne, 2017).

Moreover, the chronic trauma of sexual abuse is thought to alter neuron functioning in brain areas responsible for emotion regulation in adulthood, a physiological risk for mental health problems, difficulties managing stress, and an increased prevalence of disease (Nemeroff, 2016). Lifelong physical health issues associated with sexual victimization in childhood include gastrointestinal distress, reproductive problems, generalized pain, and overall poor health (Fergusson, McLeod, & Horwood, 2013; Herrenkohl, Hong, Klika, Herrenkohl, & Russo, 2013). As adolescents and adults, victims of sexual abuse are also likely to show sexual problems such as risky and unprotected sexual activity, avoidance of sex, and sexual anxiety and guilt (Homma, Wang, Saewyc, & Kishor, 2012; Jones et al., 2013). Sexual abuse victims of all ages are at risk to display symptoms of posttraumatic stress disorder (PTSD), an anxiety disorder includes flashbacks, nightmares, and feelings of helplessness (Kenny, 2018). Note, though, that not all children who experience traumatic events such as sexual abuse experience dire outcomes. Some children function well and even thrive despite adversity, as we will see later in this chapter.

Prevention and early identification of sexual abuse are essential. When abuse is identified and stopped early, children display more positive adjustment (Fryda & Hulme, 2015). Effective prevention and early identification of sexual abuse rely on training parents and teachers to recognize the signs of abuse and report suspicions to law enforcement and child protection agencies. As noted in Chapter 8, teachers and other professionals who come into contact with children are mandated reporters, legally obligated to report suspicions to authorities. Children tend to experience fewer long-term consequences of abuse if the child's account is believed, the abuse is stopped, and the home environment is structured, stable, and nurturing (Kenny, 2018). In addition to targeting parents, caregivers, and other adults, effective prevention programs educate children about their bodies and their right to not be touched. When children are exposed to school-based education programs that help them learn how to recognize inappropriate touches, they are more apt to report them to teachers and other adults (Brassard & Fiorvanti, 2015). Table 10.3 summarizes characteristics of effective sexual abuse prevention programs.

Resilience in Middle Childhood

Best friends Jane and Margarita walk to school together every day, partly because they live next door to each other, but also in response to several neighborhood shootings and the growing problem

TABLE 10.3

Characteristics of Effective Child Sexual Abuse Prevention Programs

CHARACTERISTIC	DESCRIPTION
Early identification	Train parents and teachers to recognize the risk factors and early signs of sexual abuse and report suspicions to law enforcement and child protection agencies.
Educate children	Educate children in a developmentally appropriate way about their bodies and their rights to not be touched. Provide children with the vocabulary to describe their bodies. Help children learn how to recognize inappropriate touches and learn what to do if touched.
Engage parents	Educate parents and assist them in discussing sexual abuse prevention with their children. Encourage them to support school efforts by discussing school activities.
Repeat exposure	Repeatedly expose children to the material in school and at home via homework and discussions with parents.
Strengthen parenting and families	Provide parents with support, parenting education, and other resources to help them improve the bond with their child, reducing children's attention-seeking behaviors.

of violence in their community. The contexts in which children are embedded pose both opportunities and risks for development. Recall that risk factors are associated with a higher likelihood of negative outcomes. In contrast, contexts also include **protective factors,** which may reduce or protect the child from the poor outcomes associated with adverse circumstances.

In Jane and Margarita's case, one contextual risk factor is neighborhood violence. Other contextual risk factors include child maltreatment, parental mental health problems, poverty, homelessness, and war (Luthar et al., 2015; Masten, Cicchetti, Masten, & Cicchetti, 2016). Risk factors are cumulative; the more risks children face, the more difficult it is for them to adjust (Ungar, 2015). For example, children exposed to war in Bosnia showed higher rates of PTSD and mental health and learning problems the more they witnessed the atrocities of war, such as death, violence, and forced displacement (Layne et al., 2008). (Children who are exposed to violence in their communities and the violence of war are at a particular risk, as discussed in this chapter's Lives in Context feature.) In all contexts, poor responses to adversity include psychological, behavioral, and health problems, including anxiety, depression, frequent illnesses and hospitalizations, poor academic achievement, and delinquent activity (Cutuli et al., 2017).

Culture can influence how risk and protective factors manifest. In one striking example, over 5,000 Aboriginal children who participated in the Western Australian Aboriginal Child Health Survey showed that risk factors such as harsh parenting, family violence, and caregiver unemployment cumulatively predicted children's problems (Hopkins, Taylor, D'Antoine, & Zubrick, 2012). And for these children, living in a high-SES neighborhood and demonstrating more knowledge of their culture were associated with *lower* levels of resilience to adversity. These unusual results were explained by the context. About 90% of Aboriginal people lived in lower-SES neighborhoods. Growing up in a more economically advantaged community may separate a child from social supports and expose the child to prejudice. Likewise, children's knowledge of their culture when they are members of a minority group and are ostracized from their community may create heightened sensitivity to oppression and lead to higher levels of depression and delinquency.

Even children from Western cultures show a range of outcomes in response to adversity. For example, like many of her classmates, Jane worries about her and her family's safety. Jane sometimes feels paralyzed by her fear and finds it hard to concentrate in class. She performs poorly in reading and math. Margarita also worries about her family and her own safety, but she can put her worries aside to focus on the teacher's lesson and earns As on many of her assignments. Margarita displays resilience, the ability to respond or perform positively in the face of adversity, to achieve despite the presence of disadvantages, or to significantly exceed expectations given poor home, school, and community circumstances (Masten, 2016). Characteristics of resilient children are displayed in Figure 10.4.

Despite experiencing a variety of intense stressors, some children display little trauma and are able to manage their anxiety to succeed at home and school, showing high self-esteem, low levels of

FIGURE 10.4

Characteristics of Resilient Children, as Reported by Their Parents

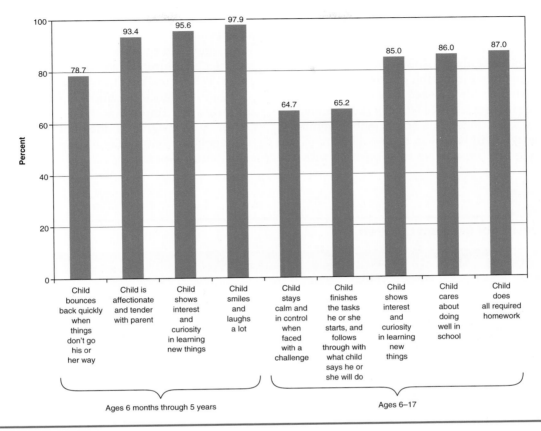

Source: Child Trends (2013).

depression, and few behavioral problems (Cicchetti, 2016; Pérez-González et al., 2017). Adaptation to adversity is a dynamic process involving interactions among a child's developmental capacities and his or her changing context, which includes both risk factors and protective factors. Protective factors may help shield children from risk factors, buffering the poor outcomes that accompany adverse circumstances and contexts. For example, Margarita often attends an after-school program, where she learned to play basketball and use a computer. She has a close relationship with her mother and uncle, who visits each week to accompany them to church. Each of these factors—school and community connections, warm relationships with adults, routines, and church attendance—is a protective factor that promotes adjustment and can reduce the negative outcomes associated with adversity (Masten & Monn, 2015; Ungar, 2015).

Protective factors may arise from within the child, from the family or extended family, and from the community (Pérez-González et al., 2017; Traub & Boynton-Jarrett, 2017). Resilient children tend to have personal characteristics that protect them from

adversity and help them learn from experience, such as an easy temperament, a sense of competence, self-control, good information processing and problem-solving skills, friendliness, and empathy (Afifi & MacMillan, 2011; Domhardt, Münzer, Fegert,

Children's adjustment is influenced by the balance of risk and protective factors they experience. The more risks children face, such as residing in poor and dangerous communities, the more likely they are to experience difficulties with adjustment and development.
Chris Hondros/Newsmakers

& Goldbeck, 2015; Marriott, Hamilton-Giachritsis, & Harrop, 2014). A fundamental characteristic is that they are successful in regulating their emotions and behavior (Eisenberg et al., 2010). Resilient individuals also have a proactive orientation, take initiative, believe in their own effectiveness, and have a positive sense of self (Luthar et al., 2015; Pérez-González et al., 2017). Avenues for fostering resilience include promoting children's strengths and bolstering children's executive function skills, self-appraisals, and sense of efficacy (Ellis, Bianchi, Griskevicius, & Frankenhuis, 2017; Traub & Boynton-Jarrett, 2017). Children who are resilient tend to have strong and supportive relationships with at least one parent, caregiver, or adult who provides warm guidance and firm support (Domhardt et al., 2015; Labella, Narayan, McCormick, Desjardins, & Masten, 2018). Effective supports for children at risk target parents' mental health and self-care skills, aid parents in establishing routines, promote parenting skills, and help parents understand the impact of trauma on children (Masten & Monn, 2015; Ungar, 2015). Table 10.4 illustrates characteristics that promote resilience in children. Resilient children illustrate an important finding: Exposure to adversity in childhood does not necessarily lead to maladjustment; many children thrive despite challenging experiences.

TABLE 10.4

Characteristics of Resilient Children

INDIVIDUAL COMPETENCIES	FAMILY COMPETENCIES AND CHARACTERISTICS	SCHOOL AND COMMUNITY CHARACTERISTICS
Coping skills	Close relationships with parents and caregivers	Access to local churches
Easy temperament	Organized home	After-school programs
Emotional regulation abilities	Parental involvement in children's education	Availability of emergency services
Good cognitive abilities	Positive family climate	Mentoring programs and opportunities to form relationships with adults
Intelligence	Postsecondary education of parents	Health care availability
Positive outlook	Provision of support	Instruction in conflict management
Positive self-concept	Religiosity and engagement with the church	Opportunity to develop and practice leadership skills
Religiosity	Socioeconomic advantage	Peer programs, such as big brother/big sister programs
Self-efficacy (feeling of control over one's destiny)	Warm but assertive parenting	Programs to assist developing self-management skills
Talents valued by others		Public safety
		Support networks outside of the family, such as supportive adults and peers
		Ties to prosocial organizations
		Well-funded schools with highly qualified teachers
		Youth programs

Sources: Anderson Moore et al., 2017; Child Trends, 2013; Lippman et al., 2014.

THINKING IN CONTEXT 10.4

Risk and protective factors illustrate the dynamic interactions among individuals and their contexts.

1. What factors within children might influence their capacity to adjust to adversity? Identify individual characteristics that may act as risk and protective factors for adjustment to challenging circumstances.

2. What contextual factors might influence children's capacity to adjust to adversity—that is, identify risk and protective factors within the contexts in which children are raised.

3. Do you think the same risk and protective factors influence adjustment to different challenges, such as fear of school, adaptation to parental divorce, or the experience of child maltreatment? Or do the factors that promote adaptation vary by the type of adversity? What do you think? Why?

Exposure to War and Terrorism and Children's Development

Children exposed to war and terrorism experience multiple devastating losses of life, homes, and even entire communities.
Pacific Press/LightRocket/Getty Images

Acts of war and terror affect children, families, and communities, with dire consequences for children's development. Living through chronic, unexpected bouts of terror and trauma, such as listening to bomb blasts, fleeing a home and community in search of safety, and losing loved ones to military service, confinement, or death, disrupts the contextual and social fabric of children's and families' lives (Masten, Narayan, Silverman, & Osofsky, 2015; Werner, 2012). Traumatic experiences may be particularly challenging for school-age children, as they are able to understand the gravity of the situation but have not yet developed the emotion regulation, abstract reasoning, and psychosocial maturity to process such events (Saraiya, Garakani, & Billick, 2013). Children exposed to acts of terror may show anxiety and symptoms of PTSD, fear of being alone, safety concerns, and behavior problems, such as aggression (Huesmann et al., 2016; Slone & Mann, 2016).

Parents influence how children process and adapt to trauma. Parents' ability to regulate their own experience of trauma and manage their stress and emotions influences children's adjustment (Halevi, Djalovski, Vengrober, & Feldman, 2016). The economic and physical hardships that accompany war can interfere with parents' ability to meet children's basic needs for food, shelter, and safety. Distress can contribute to harsh parenting and community insecurity can result in increased parental control (Sim, Fazel, Bowes, & Gardner, 2018). Parents face many challenges, but those who are able to instill a sense of warmth and security are best able to support their children's needs and promote resilience (Saraiya et al., 2013).

It is important to note, however, that many children show resilience. For example, one study of Palestinian children exposed to the 2008–2009 War on Gaza found that about three quarters of the children showed some recovery from PTSD symptoms (Punamäki, Palosaari, Diab, Peltonen, & Qouta, 2014). Likewise, one comprehensive review showed that most child survivors of war who participated in long-term follow-up studies showed no enduring patterns of emotional distress or poor psychosocial outcomes (Werner, 2012).

Nevertheless, exposure to war and ongoing, unpredictable terrorism is challenging for all children. The loss of a sense of safety and the familiar environment and routines of school, social networks, and patterns of family life poses risks for adjustment (Cummings, Goeke-Morey, Merrilees, Taylor, & Shirlow, 2014; Masten et al., 2015). Interventions to assist children promote children's attachment with parents and caregivers by ensuring that children stay physically and emotionally close to their parents. In addition to having their physical needs met, children must have opportunities to express ideas and feelings directly and through play, such as drawing, storytelling, drama, and games. Establishing routines is an important way of instilling a sense of security. No intervention can erase the effects of exposure to the trauma of war and terror, but interventions can help to bolster the factors that promote resilience to adversity.

What Do You Think?

Consider the problem of war or terrorism from the standpoint of Bronfenbrenner's bioecological theory. Identify factors within the microsystem that may help children adjust to experiencing terror. What factors might make it more challenging for children to adjust? What about mesosystem factors? Exosystem? Macrosystem? ●

APPLY YOUR KNOWLEDGE

Interested in peer dynamics, Professor Peer administered a survey to Ms. Holman's third-grade class. The survey asked students to list the three students they like most and the three students they like least. After the children completed the survey, the bell rang, and it was time for lunch. Students filed out into the hallway, chattering excitedly to each other. The next day as students played outside, waiting for the school day to begin, Ms. Holman notices that one student, Riley, who has always been somewhat withdrawn, is surrounded by a crowd of students. Ms. Holman moves toward the group and sees that the crowd of children is watching two students interact: Joey is pushing Riley and calling him names. Joey has always been boisterous and physical with other students, Ms. Holman recalls. After Ms. Holman breaks up the crowd, the students enter school and the school day begins.

In class, when Ms. Holman calls on Riley, he's slow to respond, as usual, given his shyness. When he speaks, the other students make coughing noises and giggle. At lunch, Riley is again surrounded by other students. This time, Ms. Holman scolds not only Joey but also

Mikey and Jose for teasing Riley. She worries that these negative peer experiences will make Riley become more withdrawn and that Riley will become even more prone to peer victimization.

1. How likely are Ms. Holman's worries?

2. What characteristics place children at risk for victimization by peers? What role do psychological factors and relationships with parents and peers play? What characteristics place students at risk of bullying other children?

3. How does victimization by peers influence psychological development and social relationships?

4. Consider Professor Peer's survey, which asked children to think of the students they most liked and most disliked. What role might have Professor Peer's survey played in influencing children's interactions? Do researchers have special responsibilities when they administer peer nomination measures such as this?

$SAGE edge™

Visit **edge.sagepub.com/kuther2e** to help you accomplish your coursework goals in an easy-to-use learning environment.

LEARNING OBJECTIVES	SUMMARY	KEY TERMS	IN REVIEW
10.1 Describe school-age children's self-conceptions and motivation.	School-age children's conceptions of themselves become more sophisticated, organized, and accurate. They incorporate feedback about their abilities from parents, teachers, and peers as well as engage in social comparison to derive a sense of self-esteem. Children differ in mindset as well as with regard to whether they attribute their performance to internal or external causes. A mastery orientation is associated with academic success. A learned helplessness orientation is associated with poor performance. Parents and teachers who are warm and supporting promote a mastery orientation.	Industry versus inferiority Achievement motivation Mindset Mastery orientation Learned helplessness orientation	What is the psychosocial task of middle childhood? How do self-concept and self-esteem change in middle childhood? What is achievement motivation and how is it influenced by context? Differentiate among mindset, mastery orientation, and learned helplessness orientation.
10.2 Examine the roles of friendship, peer acceptance, and peer victimization in school-age children's adjustment.	In middle childhood, friendship becomes a reciprocal relationship characterized by intimacy, loyalty, and commitment. Friendships offer opportunities for children to learn relationship skills and influence children's adjustment. Peer acceptance is a source of self-validation and self-esteem. Popular children tend to be helpful, trustworthy, and bright; they are skilled in self-regulation and conflict resolution. Aggressive-rejected and withdrawn-rejected children show poor emotion regulation skills and are at risk for short- and long-term problems. Children who bully tend to be physically and verbally assertive and impulsive, whereas bullied children are more likely to be inhibited, be anxious, and have low self-esteem and poor social and emotional regulation skills. School procedures can play a role in both increasing and decreasing the prevalence of bullying.	Peer acceptance Popular children Peer rejection Peer victimization Cyberbullying Risk factors Bully-victims	How are children's friendships associated with adjustment? What are characteristics of popular and rejected children? Describe common characteristics of bullies and victims of bullying. What are features of effective bullying interventions?

| 10.3 Discuss family relationships in middle childhood and the influence of family structure on adjustment. | Parents tend to adapt to children's growing independence by guiding and monitoring behavior from a distance, communicating expectations, using reasoning, and permitting children to be in charge of moment-to-moment decision making. Decades of research has failed to reveal important differences in the adjustment or development of children and adolescents reared by same-sex parents. Children's adjustment is influenced by socioeconomic status and family conflict, characteristics that vary with family structure. Divorce has some negative effects on children's adjustment, but the effects are small, vary by particular outcome, and do not apply to all children. Many of children's emotional, psychological, and behavioral problems stem from exposure to parental conflict before and after the divorce. Most children show improved adjustment within 2 years after the divorce. | One-child policy

Blended family | How do parent–child interactions shift over middle childhood?

What are some of the correlates of being raised by gay or lesbian parents? Single parents or cohabitating parents? Divorced parents, in a blended family? |
| 10.4 Analyze the role of resilience in promoting adjustment to adversity, including characteristics of children and contexts that promote resilience. | A common fear that develops in middle childhood concerns school and shows itself in school refusal, refusing to attend school. Child sexual abuse poses serious risks to children's physical, psychological, and emotional health and adjustment. Some children show resilience despite experiencing adversity.
Resilient children have personal characteristics that aid them in managing adversity and learning from their experiences. They also benefit from protective influences within their context, such as supportive relationships with caring adults, that help them to cope and adjust to adverse circumstances. | Protective factors | What is school refusal?

What are risk factors and outcomes associated with child sexual abuse?

What is resilience?

What are examples of risk and protective factors within the individual, family, and community? |

CHAPTER 11:
Physical and Cognitive Development in Adolescence

CHAPTER 12:
Socioemotional Development in Adolescence

Although a hallmark of adolescence, the process of biological maturation known as puberty often begins in late childhood. Physical developments include rapid growth, changes in body shape and composition, and, most notably, the ability to reproduce. Puberty also plays a role in neurological development, including changes that increase the speed and efficiency of information processing and contribute to the development of abstract thinking. Adolescents apply these new abilities to think about themselves and begin to construct a sense of identity.

Parents foster autonomy in their children through warm and firm parenting that is accompanied by monitoring. Although adolescent–parent conflict peaks in middle adolescence, it typically consists of small arguments over mundane issues. The peer context ascends in importance as friendship cliques emerge. By mid-adolescence, cliques include both boys and girls, creating opportunities for dating. The tendency to conform to peers peaks in middle adolescence but usually pertains to day-to-day issues such as clothing choices or whether to attend a party.

Adolescents are immersed in a school context that influences them through its match to their developmental needs. Finally, many adolescents experience a part-time work context that generally does not increase responsibility but will not cause harm. Over the adolescent years, the contexts in which young people participate grow in size and continue to interact, influencing their physical, cognitive, and socioemotional development.

DR. KUTHER'S
CHALK TALKS

Watch at
edge.sagepub.com/kuther2e

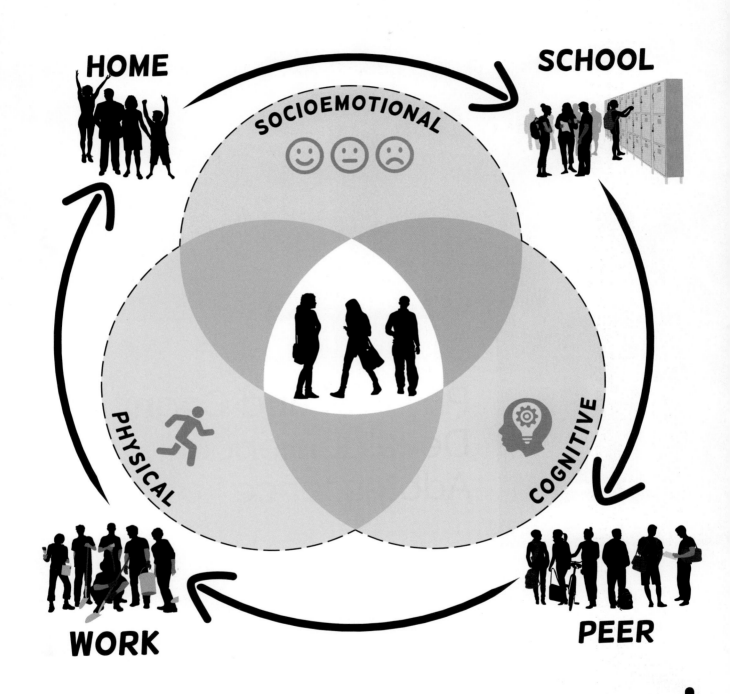

HOME

SCHOOL

SOCIOEMOTIONAL

PHYSICAL

COGNITIVE

WORK

PEER

Images: ©iStock.com

11

Physical and Cognitive Development in Adolescence

Part of the challenges young people and adults face occur because adolescence spans a great many years—longer than ever before. In earlier historical periods as well as in most nonindustrialized societies today, childhood was followed nearly immediately by the assumption of adult roles, such as worker, spouse, and parent (Schlegel, 2008; Steinberg & Lerner, 2004). In industrialized societies, becoming an adult usually entails seeking employment, which requires increasing levels of education and vocational training. Therefore, the passage to adulthood is more gradual in industrialized societies, making it a lengthy transition with a great many changes. Because of this, adolescence in industrialized societies is best understood as entailing three phases: early adolescence (11 to 14 years), middle adolescence (14 to 16 years), and late adolescence (16 to 18 years). In addition, many adolescents experience an extended transition to adulthood known as emerging adulthood (age 18 to about age 25) (Arnett, 2015).

Learning Objectives

11.1 Evaluate the storm and stress perspective on adolescence in light of research evidence.

11.2 Summarize the physical changes that occur with puberty and the correlates of pubertal timing.

11.3 Discuss brain development during adolescence and its effect on behavior.

11.4 Identify ways in which thinking changes in adolescence and how these changes are reflected in adolescent decision making and behavior.

11.5 Discuss moral development and influences on moral reasoning.

11.6 Describe the challenges that school transitions pose for adolescents and the role of parents in academic achievement.

Digital Resources

Listen: Teenage Mood Swings

Explore: Attachment, Stress, and Menarche

Watch: The Teen Brain: A Work in Progress

Connect: Adolescent Thinking: Risk-Taking or Exploration?

▶ **Lives in Context Video 11.1:** Coming of Age: Bat Mitzvah

Connect: Moral Development in Adolescence

Explore: Dropout Prevention for Students With Disabilities

▶ **Lives in Context Video 11.2:** Transition to Middle School

CONCEPTIONS OF ADOLESCENCE

» LO 11.1 Evaluate the storm and stress perspective on adolescence in light of research evidence.

Marissa raced into the house, threw her books on the table, and stormed off to her room, slamming the door. A moment later, the sounds of her stereo blasted and filled the house with a pulsing beat. Most adults are quick to dismiss Marissa's behavior as typical of adolescents, that adolescents naturally experience unexpected, intense, and volatile shifts in moods. Are adolescents naturally moody?

Is Adolescence a Period of Storm and Stress?

In his 1904 book *Adolescence,* G. Stanley Hall, known as the father of adolescence, defined it as a period of "storm and stress." He believed that puberty, the biological transition to adulthood often viewed as the beginning of adolescence, triggered a universal, inevitable, and extreme upheaval. He based his theory on then-popular Lamarckian evolutionary theory, which held that memories and acquired characteristics can be inherited from generation to generation and that the development of the individual mirrors that of the human species as a whole. Hall explained that adolescents' extreme volatility is inherited and reflects a time in human history that was very active and challenging, specifically, the birth of civilization. Therefore, intense turmoil, such as serious depression, severe troubles with parents, and extreme delinquent activity, was to be expected and was a sign of normal healthy development, triggered by puberty.

We now know that memories are not passed genetically from generation to generation; Lamarckian views have long been debunked in favor of Darwinian evolution. Despite this, Hall's storm and stress view of the nature of adolescence remains popular (Hollenstein & Lougheed, 2013). For example, teachers and parents tend to agree with statements like the following: "Adolescence is a difficult time of life" and adolescents "will be

G. Stanley Hall (1846–1924) believed that adolescence is a period of turmoil, or storm and stress.
Wikimedia

more difficult to get along with" (Hines & Paulson, 2006). Likewise, adolescents and emerging adults tend to endorse storm and stress notions, and such beliefs can create self-fulfilling prophecies, whereby adolescents' expectations influence their behavior (Buchanan & Bruton, 2016). However, expectations for adolescent behavior are culture bound. For example, U.S. adolescents were more likely than Chinese adolescents to report that adolescence is a time of decreased family responsibility and heightened school disengagement and peer orientation; these beliefs predicted a rise in disengagement from school in U.S. youth over the seventh and eighth grades (Qu, Pomerantz, Wang, Cheung, & Cimpian, 2016).

Research is largely at odds with the storm and stress view because extreme turmoil is not normal or healthy (Buchanan & Bruton, 2016). Without a doubt, adolescents engage in risk behavior, such as delinquent activity and extreme sports. However, for the majority of adolescents, risk behaviors are mild and temporary, and most do not experience serious problems (Boyer & Byrnes, 2016; Lerner et al., 2015). Although adolescence may be stressful for some teens, it does not typically present developmental problems. Furthermore, problems that do occur are neither inevitable nor universal (Hollenstein & Lougheed, 2013). For example, in a classic study, adolescents from 10 countries were interviewed (Australia,

Bangladesh, Germany, Hungary, Israel, Italy, Japan, Taiwan, Turkey, and the United States; Offer, Ostrov, Howard, & Atkinson, 1988). Most reported that they were usually happy, felt that they got along with their parents, and felt good about their progress toward adulthood. Although puberty and biological changes undoubtedly influence adolescents' experiences, contextual influences also play a role.

Adolescent Moodiness

We have seen that the classic storm and stress view of adolescence is not supported by research (Buchanan & Bruton, 2016). Yet the classic view that puberty is inextricably linked with adolescent moods, leading adolescents to experience unexpected, intense, and volatile shifts in emotion, is common to portrayals of adolescence. Adolescents do, in fact, tend to experience more mood shifts than adults; however, the source of the changes in adolescents' mood and behavior is complex and not simply a function of puberty. High and rapidly shifting levels of puberty-related hormones are associated with depression, irritability, and aggression in boys and girls. However, it is only early in puberty that hormones rapidly increase and fluctuate enough to cause such erratic and powerful shifts in adolescents' emotions and behaviors (Buchanan & Bruton, 2016). Researchers have found that the relationship between pubertal hormones and adolescent mood is weak and inconsistent (Balzer, Duke, Hawke, & Steinbeck, 2015; Duke, Balzer, & Steinbeck, 2014).

Contextual factors play an important role in adolescents' emotional experience. In a series of studies, adolescents and adults carried pagers, were beeped randomly throughout the day, and were asked to report what they were doing, who they were with, and how they felt (Larson & Csikszentmihalyi, 2014). This method, known as the *experience sampling method*, gives researchers a window into people's days. In accord with common views, adolescents' moods overall were less stable than

Most adolescescent moodiness is not the result of puberty.
iStock/pixelheadphoto

those of adults. They experienced wider and quicker mood changes. Contrary to popular views, though, the changes were unrelated to puberty, stress, a lack of personal control, or poor psychological adjustment (Larson, Csikszentmihalyi, & Graef, 2014). Instead, adolescents' mood swings varied with the context, and adolescents reported moving from one context to another, such as from school to work to family to peers, more often than did adults (Noë et al., 2017).

Adolescents' mood shifts are also influenced by changes in psychological and social factors that accompany situational changes. Rather than representing turmoil, wide mood swings appear to occur naturally with the many situational changes and shifts in peer settings that occur throughout adolescents' days and weeks. Peers play a role in adolescents' varying mood states. In one study, fifth graders who experienced more peer problems at school showed a shift toward more negative mood and lowered self-esteem over the course of the school day (Reynolds & Repetti, 2008). Adolescents' moods are also influenced by their activities and the degree to which adolescents perceive the activity as important to them and a personal choice (Weinstein & Mermelstein, 2007). Adolescents seek independence and decision-making control. When they feel that they have chosen an activity, such as reading, resting, partying, and engaging in extracurricular activities, they are likely to report more positive affect and greater enjoyment of the activity (Weinstein & Mermelstein, 2007). Mood changes do not occur in a vacuum but are influenced by adolescents' interactions with their contexts and their own perceptions.

In sum, developmental scientists today reject the notion that adolescence is a period of extreme storm and stress, replacing this idea with a more nuanced view that adolescence is a time of change characterized by individual differences in how this change is experienced. The danger of the storm and stress view lies in that it may influence expectations for adolescent behavior, creating self-fulfilling prophecies that subtly influence how adolescents

are treated. For example, believing that adolescents are moody and prone to problems can lead a parent to unwittingly become more easily angered, reduce attempts to interact with the teen, or become overly restrictive or permissive, perhaps increasing the likelihood of problems. Parents' expectations for underage substance use and risk taking, for example, predict adolescents' behavior (Lamb & Crano, 2014; Loeb, Hessel, & Allen, 2016). The beliefs we hold about adolescence and what we believe is normal for adolescents can profoundly affect adolescents' development.

PHYSICAL DEVELOPMENT IN ADOLESCENCE

» LO 11.2 **Summarize the physical changes that occur with puberty and the correlates of pubertal timing.**

The dramatic changes that adolescents' bodies undergo are often considered the hallmark of adolescence. **Puberty** is the biological transition to adulthood, in which adolescents mature physically and become capable of reproduction. The physical changes of puberty are accompanied by social changes. As adolescents appear more mature, they are treated more like adults. The physical changes serve as a signal to others of entry into a new life stage and convey personal and social meaning about new roles, expectations, and status.

Puberty

In late childhood, by age 8, the brain signals the endocrine system to gradually increase the release of hormones that trigger the onset of puberty (Berenbaum, Beltz, & Corley, 2015). Levels of **testosterone,** a hormone responsible for male sex characteristics, and **estrogen,** responsible for female sex characteristics, increase in both boys and girls but in different ratios. Testosterone is produced at a much higher rate in boys than girls, and estrogen is produced at a much higher rate in girls than boys, leading to different patterns in reproductive development. With increases in testosterone, at about 10 years of age, many children begin feeling a sense of sexual attraction (Best & Fortenberry, 2013).

Note that puberty is not an event. Rather, it is a process that takes about 4 years for boys and girls to complete but can vary dramatically from 1 to 7 years (Mendle, 2014). Puberty entails the development of reproductive capacity and influences a great variety of physical changes—not simply those typically associated with sexual maturity, such as changes in body size, shape, and function.

⚙ **THINKING IN CONTEXT 11.1**

1. In your view, is adolescence best characterized by continuity or discontinuity (recall from Chapter 1)? Compare your view with Hall's as well as with contemporary research findings.

2. Identify contextual factors that might make young people more or less likely to experience adolescence as a period of storm and stress.

Changes in Body Size and Shape

As a child, Sharene was always the same height as most of her classmates and never the tallest child in class. But when the students lined up for their fifth-grade class photograph, Sharene was surprised to find herself in the very center of the portrait, as the tallest child. As shown in Table 11.1, the first outward sign of puberty is the **adolescent growth spurt**, a rapid gain in height and weight that generally begins in girls at about age 10 (as early as age 7 and as late as 14) and in boys at about age 12 (as early as age 9 and as late as 16) (Tinggaard et al., 2012). Girls begin

Young adolescents' physical maturation varies dramatically by individual.
Bob Daemmrich / Alamy Stock Photo

TABLE 11.1

Sequence of Physical Changes With Puberty

BOYS		
CHARACTERISTIC	**MEAN AGE**	**RANGE**
Growth spurt begins	12.5	10.5–16
Testes and scrotum grow larger	11	9.5–13.5
Pubic hair appears	12	10–15
Penis growth begins	12	11–14.5
Spermarche	13	12–16
Peak height spurt	14	12.5–15.5
Peak weight spurt	14	12.5–15.5
Voice lowers	14	11.5–15.5
Facial and underarm hair begins	14	12.5–15.5
Penis and testes growth completed	14.5	12.5–16
Peak strength spurt	15	13–17
Adult stature	15.5	13.5–18
Pubic hair growth completed	15.5	14–18

GIRLS		
CHARACTERISTIC	**MEAN AGE**	**RANGE**
Breast growth begins	10	7–13
Growth spurt begins	10	8–14
Pubic hair appears	10.5	7–14
Peak strength spurt	11.5	9.5–14
Peak height spurt	11.5	10–13.5
Peak weight spurt	12.5	10–14
Menarche	12.5	10–16
Adult stature	13	10–16
Pubic hair growth completed	14.5	14–15
Breast growth completed	15	10–18

Sources: Bundak et al. (2007); Herman-Giddens (2006); Wu et al. (2002).

their growth spurt about 2 years before boys, so 10- to 13-year-old girls tend to be taller, heavier, and stronger than boys their age. By starting their growth spurts 2 years later than girls, boys begin with an extra 2 years of prepubertal growth on which the adolescent growth spurt builds, leading boys to end up taller than girls (Yousefi et al., 2013). The pattern and pace of growth are similar across most children (Sanders et al., 2017). On average, the growth spurt lasts about 2 years, but growth in height continues at a more gradual pace, ending by about 16 in girls and 18 in boys. Adolescents gain a total of about 10 inches in height.

Boys and girls gain fat and muscle but in different ratios. Girls gain more fat overall, particularly on their legs and hips, so that fat comes to comprise one fourth of their body weight—nearly twice as much as boys. Boys gain more muscle than do girls, especially in their upper bodies, doubling their arm strength between ages 13 and 18 (Payne & Isaacs, 2016). Bone density increases in both boys and girls, and the respiratory and cardiovascular systems mature. Boys become much better at taking in and using oxygen as their hearts and lungs grow larger and function more effectively and the number of red blood cells increases (Sadler, 2017). Consequently, once puberty has begun, boys consistently outperform girls in athletics (Tønnessen, Svendsen, Olsen, Guttormsen, & Haugen, 2015).

Sexual Characteristics

Puberty is most frequently associated with the development of **secondary sex characteristics,** body changes that indicate physical maturation but are not directly related to fertility. Examples of secondary sex characteristics include breast development, deepening of the voice, growth of body hair, and changes in the skin.

Rapid increases in estrogen cause the budding of breasts, which tends to accompany the growth spurt in girls as the first signs of puberty (Emmanuel & Bokor, 2017). Testosterone causes boys' voices to deepen, causing them to occasionally lose control over their voices and emit unpredictably high squeaks (Hodges-Simeon, Gurven, Cárdenas, & Gaulin, 2013). Girls' voices also deepen, but the change is slight and not as noticeable as in boys. Oil and sweat glands become more active, resulting in body odor and acne (Sadler, 2017). Hair on the head, arms, and legs becomes darker, and pubic hair begins to grow, first as straight and downy, and later becomes coarse.

Sexual Maturation

The reproductive organs are known as **primary sex characteristics.** In females, primary sex characteristics include the ovaries, fallopian tubes, uterus, and vagina. In males, they include the penis, testes, scrotum, seminal vesicles, and prostate gland. During puberty, the reproductive organs grow larger and mature.

In girls, sexual maturity is marked by the onset of menstruation, the monthly shedding of the uterine lining, which has thickened in preparation for the implantation of a fertilized egg. **Menarche**, the first menstruation, occurs toward the end of puberty, yet most children and adults view it as a critical marker of puberty because it occurs suddenly and is memorable (Brooks-Gunn & Ruble, 2013). In North America, the average European American girl experiences menarche shortly before turning 13 and the average African American girl shortly after turning 12 (Emmanuel & Bokor, 2017). Generally, African American girls tend to be heavier and enter puberty about a year earlier, reaching pubertal milestones such as the growth spurt and menarche earlier than

---

Menarche Rituals of the !Xoo

In many cultures, menarche is accompanied by rituals that mark it as a rite of passage to adulthood. For example, the !Xoo of Zutshwa in Botswana expect girls upon experiencing their first menses to immediately run from others and to hide in the bush (Nhlekisana, 2017). Soon the older women of the community search for the girl. The women carry the girl home so that her feet do not touch the ground and she is secluded in a private hut for 1 month. During their seclusion, !Xoo girls learn about the taboos associated with menstruation. For example, it is thought that a menstruating woman should not come into contact with anything that grows. Walking about the community or coming into contact with animals while menstruating, for example, is believed to cause drought or sickness (Nhlekisana, 2017).

While in seclusion, the girl is told not to look outside or make eye contact with others and she must sit with her back against the wall. She is cared for by her mother or grandmother, who feeds her, bathes her, and changes the grass that she lies on. The girl is instructed not to touch anything and not to move. She is given a twig to use to scratch her body when it itches but otherwise she may not touch herself. The girl is given meat and roots mixed with medicine believed to strengthen her and reduce the length of her menstruation (Marshall, 1999). She does not touch food with her hands but is fed by her caretaker.

During the month of seclusion, the girl is given instructions and advice in preparation for her new role in the community (Munthali & Zulu, 2007). She is trained in the moral and practical responsibilities of being a wife and child bearer, such as matters concerning womanhood, domestic and agricultural activities, reproduction, and behavior toward men (Denbow, James, & Thebe, 2006). The training is accompanied by singing and dancing.

After the !Xoo girl has been secluded for a month, arrangements for her emergence and reincorporation into the society are made. She is smeared with a reddish powder called *letsoku*. The *letsoku* symbolizes fertility and is intended to make the girl more attractive. Patterns are drawn on her face using white makeup. The girl is adorned with necklaces, armbands, and head bands made from ostrich shells. Her feet are washed with powdered seeds thought to give her freedom to walk safely.

Finally, the girl is accompanied around the community, including the fields and water well. After sunset, she carries a stick to each hut and lights it using the fire burning in each household, offering protection to each household and integrating the girl into the community (Nhlekisana, 2017).

What Do You Think?

1. What purpose does a ritual such as this serve the girl, her family, and the community?

2. What rituals and activities mark menarche in Western girls? ●

other girls (Emmanuel & Bokor, 2017). Frequently, during the first few months after menarche, menstruation takes place without ovulation, the ovaries' release of an ovum (Lacroix & Whitten, 2017). This period of temporary sterility is variable—it is unpredictable and does not apply to all girls. Many cultures mark menarche as a rite of passage, as discussed in the Cultural Influences on Development feature.

In boys, the first primary sex characteristic to emerge is the growth of the testes, the glands that produce sperm (Sadler, 2017). At about age 13, boys demonstrate a principal sign of sexual maturation: the first ejaculation, known as **spermarche** (Tomova, Lalabonova, Robeva, & Kumanov, 2011). The first ejaculations contain few living sperm. Many boys experience their first ejaculations as nocturnal emissions, or wet dreams: involuntary ejaculations that are sometimes accompanied by erotic dreams.

What does menarche mean to girls? How girls experience menarche is influenced by their knowledge about menstruation as well as their expectations (Brooke-Gunn & Ruble, 2013). Generations ago, as girls received little to no information about menarche, they tended to be surprised by it, viewed it negatively, and were often afraid of it (Costos, Ackerman, & Paradis, 2002). Today, girls are often surprised by menarche, but girls in more developed countries are not frightened, because they have been informed about puberty by health education classes and parents who are more willing to talk about pubertal development than parents in prior generations (Stidham-Hall, Moreau, & Trussell, 2012). However, the extent to which adolescents participate in discussions about menarche and sexuality varies by context and culture. Many girls in developing countries, for example, are uninformed and unprepared for menarche (Chandra-Mouli & Patel, 2017). For example, a study of 12- to 16-year-old Bangladeshi girls revealed that they generally were not informed about menarche, and over two thirds reacted with fear (Bosch, Hutter, & van Ginneken, 2008). Girls who did get information may have obtained it from mothers and other female family members who lacked adequate understanding of pubertal processes. In some cultures, girls can be excluded from interaction with others, including attending school, when they are menstruating (Chandra-Mouli & Patel, 2017). Girls who view menstruation negatively may be at risk to experience menstruation negatively, with more menstrual symptoms and distress (Rembeck, Möller, & Gunnarsson, 2006), but experience can alter girls' views on menstruation.

We know less about boys' experience of puberty because they lack easily determined objective markers, such as menarche (Herman-Giddens et al., 2012). Some studies of small groups of adolescent boys have suggested that most boys

react positively to first ejaculation, although many experience uneasiness and confusion, especially if they are uninformed about this pubertal change (Frankel, 2002; Stein & Reiser, 1994). Boys who know about ejaculation beforehand are more likely to show positive reactions, such as feeling pleasure, happiness, and pride. Unfortunately, many boys report that health education classes and parents generally do not discuss ejaculation (Omar et al., 2003; Stein & Reiser, 1994). Parents sometimes report discomfort talking with their sons about reproductive development, particularly ejaculation, because of the close link with sexual desire, sexuality, and masturbation (Frankel, 2002). Perhaps because of its sexual nature, boys are less likely to tell a friend about spermarche than are girls to discuss their own reproductive development (Downs & Fuller, 1991).

Individual Differences in the Timing of Pubertal Maturation

Casual observations of adolescents reveal that, although most tend to show similar levels of physical maturation, some vary substantially. For example, some 14-year-old adolescents have adultlike bodies, girls with more developed breasts and hips and boys with more facial hair and broader shoulders than their peers. Other 14-year-old adolescents might be just beginning the pubertal transformation. What determines the beginning of puberty?

The timing of puberty reflects the interaction of biological and contextual influences. Without question, genes play a role in pubertal timing (Tu et al., 2015). For example, identical twins experience menarche more closely in time than fraternal twins (Kretsch, Mendle, & Harden, 2016). But puberty is influenced by more than genes. It is also influenced by health and nutrition.

The onset of puberty is triggered by achieving a critical level of body weight, as an accumulation of leptin, a protein found in fat, may trigger the brain and endocrine system to increase the production and release of hormones (Elias, 2012; Sanchez-Garrido & Tena-Sempere, 2013). Girls with a greater body mass index (BMI) mature earlier than do other their peers, and girls who have a low percentage of body fat, whether from athletic training or severe dieting, often experience menarche late relative to other girls (Tomova, 2016). In one study of girls in 34 countries, obesity predicted early puberty (Currie et al., 2012). In contrast, extreme malnutrition can prevent the accumulation of adequate fat stores needed to support pubertal development so that menarche is delayed. In many parts of Africa, for example, menarche does not occur until ages 14 to 17, several years later than in Western nations (Tunau, Adamu, Hassan, Ahmed, & Ekele, 2012). Weight also affects the onset and tempo of puberty in boys, but less so than in girls (Tomova, Robeva, & Kumanov, 2015).

Adolescents' social contexts, especially exposure to stress, also influence pubertal timing. In fact, stress affects hormone production throughout the lifespan; it can trigger irregular ovulation and menstruation in females and reduce sperm production in males (Toufexis, Rivarola, Lara, & Viau, 2014). Severe stress, such as the experience of sexual abuse and maltreatment, can speed the onset of menarche (Noll et al., 2017). Similarly, poor family relationships, harsh parenting, family stress and conflict, parents' marital conflict, and anxiety are associated with early menarche in North American and European girls (Graber, Nichols, & Brooks-Gunn, 2010; Rickard, Frankenhuis, & Nettle, 2014). In industrialized countries such as the United States, Canada, and New Zealand, girls who are raised by single mothers experience puberty earlier than those raised in two-parent homes (Mendle et al., 2006). In addition, the absence of a biological father and the presence in the home of a biological unrelated male, such as a stepfather or a mother's live-in boyfriend, are associated with earlier onset of menarche (Deardorff et al., 2011; Webster, Graber, Gesselman, Crosier, & Schember, 2014). Animal studies show a similar trend: The presence of a biologically related male delays reproductive maturation and functioning while the presence of unrelated males speeds female reproductive maturation (Neberich, Penke, Lehnart, & Asendorpf, 2010). Father absence may hold similar implications for boys' pubertal development, speeding it; however, there is much less research on boys' development (Sheppard & Sear, 2012).

Contextual factors outside the home also influence pubertal timing. Adolescents who live in similar contextual conditions, especially those of socioeconomic advantage, reach menarche at about the same age, despite having different genetic backgrounds (Obeidallah, Brennan, Brooks-Gunn, & Earls, 2004). Low socioeconomic status is associated with early pubertal onset in the United States, Canada, and the United Kingdom and may account for some of the ethnic differences in pubertal timing (Kelly, Zilanawala, Sacker, Hiatt, & Viner, 2017; Sun, Mensah, Azzopardi, Patton, & Wake, 2017). For example, African American and Latina girls tend to reach menarche before White girls but are also disproportionately likely to live in low socioeconomic status (SES) homes and neighborhoods. Ethnic differences in the timing of menarche are reduced or even disappear when researchers control for the influence of socioeconomic status (Deardorff, Abrams, Ekwaru, & Rehkopf, 2014; Obeidallah, Brennan, Brooks-Gunn, Kindlon, & Earls, 2000).

The influence of contextual conditions and physical health in triggering puberty is thought to underlie the **secular trend,** or the lowering of the average age of puberty with each generation from prehistoric to the present times (Papadimitriou, 2016a) (Figure 11.1). Through the 18th century in Europe,

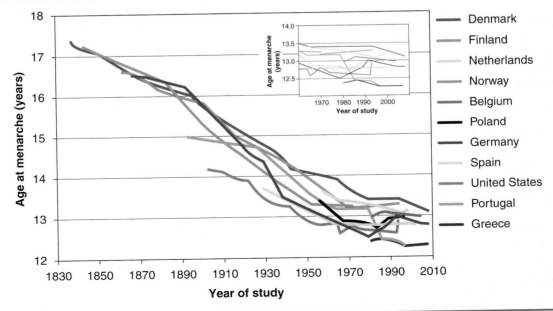

FIGURE 11.1

Secular Trend in Girls' Pubertal Development, 1830–2010

Source: Sørensen et al. (2012). With permission from Karger Publishers.

puberty occurred as late as age 17; between 1860 and 1970, the age of menarche declined by about 3 to 4 months per decade (Tanner, 1990). Boys in the United States and Canada begin puberty at least 1 to 1½ years earlier today than in the 1960s (Herman-Giddens, 2006; Herman-Giddens et al., 2012). The secular trend parallels increases in the standard of living and average BMI among children in Western countries and is especially influenced by the growing problem of childhood obesity (Biro, Greenspan, & Galvez, 2012). There are some indications that it has slowed or stopped in most industrialized nations (Kleanthous, Dermitzaki, Papadimitriou, Papaevangelou, & Papadimitriou, 2017; Papadimitriou, 2016b). Nevertheless, the secular trend poses challenges for young people and parents because the biological entry to adolescence is lowering at the same time as the passage to adulthood is lengthening, making the period of adolescence longer than ever before.

Psychosocial Effects of Pubertal Timing

Most adolescents experience puberty at about the same time, but some adolescents' bodies change much earlier or later than their peers. Adolescents who mature off-time relative to their peers are often treated differently by adults and peers, with consequences for their development. For example, adolescents who look older than their years are more likely to be treated in ways similar to older adolescents, which adolescents may perceive as stressful (Rudolph, Troop-Gordon, Lambert, & Natsuaki, 2014). Early maturation, in particular, poses challenges for both girls' and boys' adaptation (Stroud & Davila, 2016; Ullsperger & Nikolas, 2017).

Girls who mature early relative to peers tend to feel less positive about their bodies, physical appearance, and menstruation itself, and they show higher rates of depression, anxiety, and low self-esteem than do girls who mature on time or late (Benoit, Lacourse, & Claes, 2013; Stojković, 2013). Early maturing girls tend to date earlier than their peers, are at higher risk of dating violence, and experience more sexual harassment than their peers (Baams, Dubas, Overbeek, & van Aken, 2015; F. R. Chen, Rothman, & Jaffee, 2017; Skoog & Bayram Özdemir, 2016). Interestingly, girls' view of their own early pubertal timing, whether they view themselves as maturing much earlier than their peers, is often only loosely related to their actual development (Dorn & Biro, 2011) yet is often a better predictor of girls' age at first intercourse, sexual risk taking, substance use, depression, and anxiety than actual pubertal development (Moore, Harden, & Mendle, 2014; Stojković, 2013).

In males, earlier timing of puberty historically has been viewed as advantageous because it conveys physical advantages for athletic activities. There is less research on boys than on girls, but it appears that early maturing boys also experience some internalizing and externalizing symptoms (Rudolph et al., 2014; Stroud & Davila, 2016).

Around the world, early maturing boys and girls show higher rates of risky activity, including smoking, abusing alcohol and substances, and displaying aggressive behavior than do same-age peers (Biehl, Natsuaki, & Ge, 2007; Mrug et al., 2014; Schelleman-Offermans, Knibbe, & Kuntsche, 2013; Skoog & Stattin, 2014). Although all early maturing adolescents tend to experience more problems, early maturing girls are at higher risk for early sexual activity, as well as alcohol and substance use and abuse than boys (Ullsperger & Nikolas, 2017).

Contextual factors are thought to amplify the effects of early pubertal timing on behavior (Natsuaki, Samuels, & Leve, 2015; Seaton & Carter, 2018). Some of the problems that early maturing boys and girls experience arise because they tend to seek relationships with older peers who are more similar to them in physical maturity than their classmates (Kretsch, Mendle, Cance, & Harden, 2016). Spending time with older peers makes early maturing adolescents, especially girls, more likely to engage in age-inappropriate behaviors, such as early sexual activity and risky sexual activity (Baams et al., 2015; Moore et al., 2014).

The school context may also influence the effects of pubertal timing. For example, in one study, elementary school teachers shown drawings of girls at varying stages of pubertal development expected early developing girls to have more academic and social problems relative to other girls (Carter, Mustafaa, & Leath, 2018). In addition, they expected Black early developers to experience more problems than White early developers, possibly suggesting that race and ethnicity may influence how early puberty is experienced by girls. Other research also suggests that racial identity can influence the effects of pubertal timing. In one study of Black adolescents, early maturing girls were more likely to experience depressive symptoms when they attended mixed-race schools and believed that others held Blacks in poor regard (Seaton & Carter, 2018). The stress that accompanies perceived discrimination may pose serious risks to adaptation. In contrast, and perhaps surprisingly, a strong sense of racial identity was associated with increased depressive symptoms among late-maturing Black girls who attended schools with a mixed-race population. Late-maturing Black girls who identify with their race may value the earlier maturation common to Black girls and may feel dissatisfied with their bodies. Pubertal development influences girls' sense of self and may interact with their other self-relevant beliefs—as well as the social and racial contexts in which they are immersed—to influence their responses (Seaton & Carter, 2018).

Puberty and Sleep Patterns

Classes begin at 7:35 a.m., way too early for Raul, who yawns and stretches as he sits down at his desk. Raul did not go to bed until about 1:00 a.m. His mother shouted and shouted for him to get up this morning. He had barely enough time to put on clothes and brush his teeth before heading to school. Grumpy, Raul pulls out his notebook and tries to pay attention to his geometry teacher, but it is hard to focus with his headache.

Raul is not alone in feeling tired and irritable. From ages 13 to 19, the average hours of sleep reported by adolescents in Western countries, such as the United States and Germany, decreased from about 8 hours to 7 hours, with greater reductions in sleep with each year (Carskadon, 2009; Loessl et al., 2008). Yet researchers estimate that adolescents need about 9 hours of sleep each night to support healthy development.

A less well-known effect of puberty is a change in adolescents' sleep patterns and preferred sleep schedule, known as a **delayed phase preference** (Carskadon, 2009; Crowley, Acebo, & Carskadon, 2007). Delayed phase preference is triggered by a change in the nightly release of a hormone that influences sleep called melatonin. The rise in melatonin that accompanies the onset of sleep occurs, on average, about 2 hours later among adolescents who have experienced puberty as compared with those who have not begun puberty (Carskadon, Acebo, & Jenni, 2004). When adolescents are allowed to regulate their own sleep schedule, they tend to go to bed at about 1:00 a.m. and sleep until about 10:00 a.m. (Colrain & Baker, 2011). Adolescents naturally feel awake when it is time to go to sleep and groggy when it is time to wake for school in the morning. As a result, adolescents stay up later, miss out on sleep, and report sleepiness (Carskadon et al., 2004; Loessl et al., 2008). This tendency for adolescents to go to bed later is influenced by puberty, but it also has increased over the past three decades, along with the increased availability of television and electronic media that compete with sleep for adolescents' time (Bartel, Gradisar, & Williamson, 2015; Carskadon & Tarokh, 2014). Most adolescents have electronic devices such as cellphones, video games, and computers, and many report using electronic devices in bed. Greater bedtime devise

use is associated with less sleep (Vernon, Modecki, & Barber, 2018).

Poor sleep in adolescence is associated with anxiety, irritability, and depression (Fuligni, Arruda, Krull, & Gonzales, 2018; Wong & Brower, 2012). It increases the probability of health problems, including illnesses, obesity, and accidents (Darchia & Cervena, 2014; Mitchell, Rodriguez, Schmitz, & Audrain-McGovern, 2013b). Poor sleep duration predicts less engagement in extracurricular school activities and declines in academic performance (Fuligni et al., 2018; Minges & Redeker, 2016). Sleep problems are also associated with risky behaviors, including cigarette smoking and other substance use (Pieters et al., 2015; Telzer, Fuligni, Lieberman, & Galván, 2013; Wong et al., 2015) and predict the onset of heavy drinking and marijuana use up to 5 years later (Miller, Janssen, & Jackson, 2017; Nguyen-Louie et al., 2018).

Most middle and high schools start earlier than elementary school, often to allot time for after-school sports and activities. Earlier school starting times are associated with less total sleep, and students generally do not make up for lost sleep on the weekends (Paksarian, Rudolph, He, & Merikangas, 2015). For example, one comparison of middle school students who attended an early starting school (7:15 a.m.) and a later starting school (8:37 a.m.) found that students who attended the early starting school obtained about ¾ of an hour less sleep each night, or about 3½ hours less each week (Wolfson, Spaulding, Dandrow, & Baroni, 2007). After the students had been on their early or late school schedules for over 6 months, those who attended school early were tardy four times more often, and had more absences and worse grades, than the students who attended the school with the later starting time. Similar findings were apparent in another study that examined the effects of starting school 30 minutes later (i.e., from 8:00 a.m. to 8:30 a.m.). In other research, 3 months after a 50-minute delay in school start time, students reported getting 30 minutes more sleep each night and showed significant improvements in measures of adolescent alertness, mood, and health (Owens, Belon, & Moss, 2010; Owens, Dearth-Wesley, Herman, Oakes, & Whitaker, 2017).

Sleep matters, and perhaps some of the moodiness characteristic of the stereotypical adolescent is related to changes in sleep patterns. In 2017, the American Academy of Sleep Medicine (AASM) (Watson et al., 2017) issued a policy statement calling on communities, school boards, and educational institutions to implement start times of 8:30 a.m. or later for middle schools and high schools to ensure that every student arrives at school healthy, awake, alert, and ready to learn.

Good nutrition is essential to support adolescents' growth, yet young people's diets tend to worsen as they enter adolescence.
iStock/p_ponomareva

Nutrition and Development

As boys and girls enter the growth spurt, their bodies demand more calories. Good nutrition is essential to support adolescents' growth, yet young people's diets tend to worsen as they enter adolescence (Frazier-Wood, Banfield, Liu, Davis, & Chang, 2015). Adolescents tend to consume only about half of the U.S. recommendations for vegetables, whole grains, and fruits (Banfield, Liu, Davis, Chang, & Frazier-Wood, 2016). In addition, adolescents tend increase their consumption of fast food and snacks, are more likely to skip meals, and drink less milk (Stang & Stotmeister, 2017; Vikraman, Fryar, & Ogden, 2015). When a fast-food restaurant is near school, students in the United States, United Kingdom, Australia, and Finland show more irregular eating habits, greater consumption of fast food, and higher rates of overweight and obesity (Alviola, Nayga, Thomsen, Danforth, & Smartt, 2014; Janssen, Davies, Richardson, & Stevenson, 2018; Virtanen et al., 2015).

Family meals are an important way of establishing healthy eating habits. Young people who participate in family meals tend to have healthier eating habits 5 to 10 years later, as young adults (Berge et al., 2015; Burgess-Champoux, Larson, Neumark-Sztainer, Hannan, & Story, 2009). Family meals are associated with higher fruit and vegetable intake and lower BMI (Berge, Jin, Hannan, & Neumark-Sztainer, 2013; Watts, Loth, Berge, Larson, & Neumark-Sztainer, 2017).

Lack of exercise is a contributor to overweight and obesity during adolescence. Although some teens engage in competitive sports, average levels of physical activity decrease throughout adolescence, and many adolescents engage in no regular exercise or activity (Dumith, Gigante, Domingues, & Kohl, 2011; Farooq et al., 2018). Moreover, it is estimated that American adolescents spend over 11 hours each day in front of a screen viewing television and other media, playing games, and participating in social media (American Academy of Pediatrics

THINKING IN CONTEXT 11.2

1. Many adults hold misconceptions about puberty and its meaning for adolescents. Consider your own views and those of your friends and family. Identify two misconceptions, explain why they are incorrect, and offer accurate alternatives.

2. In what ways might the changing sociocultural context contribute to the secular trend and the collection of psychosocial characteristics that most adults view as "typical" of adolescents?

3. How might the dramatic physical changes that adolescents undergo—and the accompanying reactions from others—influence other aspects of development, such as social or emotional development?

& American Academy of Pediatrics Council on Communications and Media, 2013; Rideout, 2010). Samples of adolescents in the United States, United Kingdom, and Canada have linked screen time with unhealthy eating, obesity, and self-rated poor health (Herman, Hopman, & Sabiston, 2015; Mitchell, Rodriguez, Schmitz, & Audrain-McGovern, 2013a; Pearson et al., 2017).

Adolescents of low socioeconomic status are more likely to be sedentary and obese; this holds true for adolescents from a variety of countries, such as Canada, England, Finland, France, Czechoslovakia, Australia, and the United States (Frederick, Snellman, & Putnam, 2014; Hardy et al., 2017; Sigmund et al., 2018; J. L. Wang, Jackson, Zhang, & Su, 2012; Y. Wang & Lim, 2012). Research with American youth suggests a complex relation between socioeconomic status and obesity. One longitudinal study of over 4,800 U.S. children—10 and 11 years old—showed that those with the highest socioeconomic status were less likely to be obese than their peers in fifth and seventh

Screen time increases during adolescence, posing challenges to health.
Robert Alexander/Getty Images

grades (Fradkin et al., 2015). However, when ethnicity was considered, this pattern was confirmed for Latino and White adolescents not but Black adolescents. Likewise, the protective effect of daily physical activity was associated with reduced obesity only among Latino and White males in seventh grade, not fifth graders, females, or Black adolescents (Fradkin, Wallander, Elliott, Cuccaro, & Schuster, 2014). Thus, the health advantage associated with higher parental education and income may not apply consistently to boys and girls across all ethnic groups. Influences on young people's health, such as socioeconomic status, must be considered within the context of the broader social and physical environments in which youth live (Schreier & Chen, 2013).

BRAIN DEVELOPMENT IN ADOLESCENCE

» LO 11.3 Discuss brain development during adolescence and its effect on behavior.

Advances in neuroimaging have revealed dramatic changes in brain structure and functioning during adolescence (Morris, Squeglia, Jacobus, & Silk, 2018). The increase in sex hormones with puberty triggers a variety of neurological developments, including a second burst of synaptogenesis, resulting in a rapid increase of connections among neurons (Sisk, 2017). The volume of the cerebral cortex increases, peaking at about 10½ years of age in girls and 14½ in boys (Giedd et al., 2009). Connections between the prefrontal cortex and various brain regions strengthen, permitting rapid communication, enhanced cognitive functioning, and greater emotional and behavioral control (Fuhrmann, Knoll, & Blakemore, 2015). Synaptic pruning in response to experience occurs at an accelerated rate during adolescence and emerging adulthood (Giedd, 2018). Synaptic pruning decreases the volume of gray matter; thins and molds the prefrontal cortex, which is responsible for rational thought and executive function; and results in markedly more efficient cognition and neural functioning (Zhou, Lebel, Treit, Evans, & Beaulieu, 2015).

As shown in Figure 11.2, myelination continues through adolescence into emerging adulthood and leads to steady increases in the brain's white matter, especially in the prefrontal cortex and the corpus callosum, which increases up to 20% in size, speeding communication between the right and left hemispheres (Lebel & Deoni, 2018). Over the course of adolescence, adolescents' brains become larger, faster, and more efficient (Richmond, Johnson, Seal, Allen, & Whittle, 2016). However, different parts of the brain develop at different times, leaving adolescents with somewhat lopsided functioning for a time. The prefrontal cortex requires the most time to develop, continuing maturation into emerging adulthood.

According to the **dual-systems model,** the limbic system, responsible for emotion (Figure 11.3), undergoes a burst of development well ahead of the prefrontal cortex, responsible for judgment, and this difference in development can account for many "typical" adolescent behaviors (Shulman et al., 2016). Full development is achieved only when the prefrontal cortex catches up. These changes influence adolescents' thought and behavior in a myriad of ways.

FIGURE 11.2

Developmental Changes in Gray and White Matter Across Adolescence

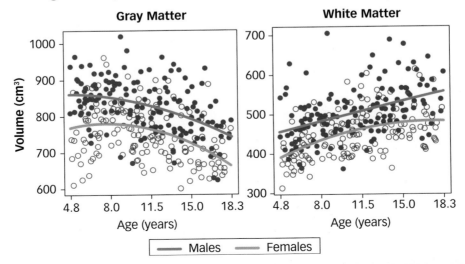

Socioemotional Perception

Parents often wonder whether they are speaking in a foreign language when their teens unexpectedly

FIGURE 11.3

Dual-Systems Model: Limbic System and Prefrontal Cortex

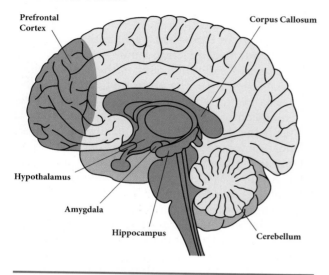

break off a conversation and storm away or when conflict arises over seemingly innocuous events. However, in a way, parents are speaking in a foreign language because adolescents' brains do not always lead them to accurately assess situations. Adolescents have difficulty identifying emotions depicted in facial expressions. In studies where both adults and adolescents are shown photographs of people's faces depicting fear, adults correctly identify the emotion shown in the photograph, but many of the adolescents incorrectly identify the emotion as anger (Yurgelun-Todd, 2007). Performance on tasks measuring sensitivity to facial expressions improves steadily during the first decade of life but dips in early adolescence, increasing in late adolescence into emerging adulthood (Motta-Mena & Scherf, 2017). Why? Blame the brain.

Functional magnetic resonance imaging (fMRI) scans indicate that when adults view facial expressions, both their **limbic system** (the part of the brain known as the seat of emotion) and prefrontal cortex are active. Scans of adolescents' brains, however, reveal a highly active limbic system but relatively inactive prefrontal cortex relative to adults, suggesting that adolescents experience emotional activation with relatively little executive processing in response to facial

FIGURE 11.4

Adolescents' and Adults' Processing of Fearful Faces

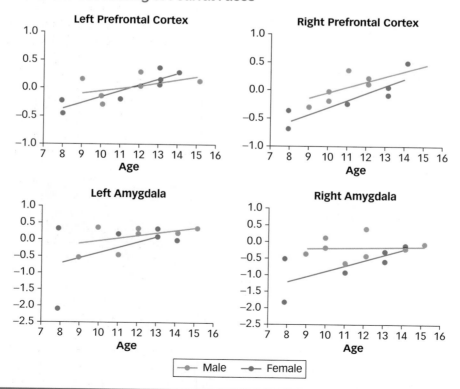

Source: Yurgelun-Todd (2007)

stimuli indicating fear (Yurgelun-Todd, 2007). Pubertal hormones cause a burst of development in the limbic system in early adolescence, well ahead of the parts of the brain responsible for executive control (Sisk, 2017). Adolescents experience heightened emotional reactivity, influencing their responses to emotionally charged stimuli, such as facial expressions of fear or anger.

Research with people ages 7 to 37 reveals developmental changes in brain activation with facial processing with activity in parts of the frontal cortex increasing over childhood, then decreasing in early adolescence, followed by an increase in late adolescence through emerging adulthood (Cohen Kadosh, Johnson, Dick, Cohen Kadosh, & Blakemore, 2013). In another study, older children and adolescents viewed images of fearful and happy faces while undergoing fMRI. As shown in Figure 11.4, in response to fearful stimuli, girls showed increases in bilateral prefrontal activity through mid-adolescence, but in males, age-related increases in brain activity were limited to the right prefrontal cortex (Yurgelun-Todd & Killgore, 2006). Given that girls begin puberty 2 years before boys, a lag in prefrontal maturation is expected.

Brain structure influences affective responses and interactions with others. For example, one part of the limbic system, the amygdala, is implicated in aggression. When faced with emotionally arousing contexts and stimuli, adolescents tend to show exaggerated amygdala activity relative to adults and fewer functional connections between the prefrontal cortex and amygdala, suggesting that adolescents experience more emotional arousal yet less cortical processing and control than adults (Blakemore & Mills, 2014). The ability to control responses to emotionally triggering stimuli develops independently and after the ability to reason about neutral stimuli (Aïte et al., 2018). Generally, amygdala volume increases more in adolescent males than females (Dumontheil, 2016). It seems that adolescents are wired to experience strong emotional reactions and to misidentify emotions in others' facial expressions, which can make communication and social interactions difficult.

Risk Taking

Most adults look back on their own adolescence and recall engaging in activities that included an element of risk or were even outright dangerous, such as racing bikes off ramps to soar through the air or driving at fast speeds. Risk taking and adolescence go hand in hand, and the brain plays a large part in such behavior. In early adolescence, the balance of neurotransmitters shifts. At 9 to 10 years of age, the prefrontal cortex and limbic system experience a marked shift in levels of serotonin and

Adolescents are neurologically primed to engage in risky behaviors.
iStock/Meinzahn

dopamine, neurotransmitters that are associated with impulsivity, novelty seeking, and reward salience (Luna, Marek, Larsen, Tervo-Clemmens, & Chahal, 2015; Mills, Goddings, Clasen, Giedd, & Blakemore, 2014). Sensitivity to rewards peaks at the same time as adolescents experience difficulty with response inhibition, the ability to control a response. A heightened response to motivational cues coupled with immature behavioral control results in a bias toward immediate goals rather than long-term consequences (van Duijvenvoorde, Peters, Braams, & Crone, 2016). As a result, risky situations, those that entail an element of danger, become enticing and experienced as thrills (Spielberg, Olino, Forbes, & Dahl, 2014). Adolescents may find themselves drawn to extreme sports, for example, enjoying the high and element of the unknown when they direct their skateboard into the air for a daring turn. These same mechanisms, adolescents' attraction to novelty and enhanced sensitivity to immediate rewards, serve to increase their vulnerability to the lure of drugs and alcohol (Bava & Tapert, 2010; Geier, 2013). The Brain and Biological Influences on Development feature examines the effects of substances on the brain.

Developmental shifts in risky behavior are common among adolescents around the world (Duell et al., 2018). For example, one study examined adolescents in 11 countries in Africa, Asia, Europe,

Substance Use and the Brain

Experimentation with alcohol and marijuana is a common form of risk taking during adolescence. How do alcohol and substance use affect the developing brain?

Alcohol use is associated with changes in the structure and function of the adolescent brain. Compared with those who do not use alcohol, adolescents who drink alcohol moderately show smaller brain volumes and gray matter density in areas responsible for executive control, including parts of the temporal and parietal lobes, and, especially, the frontal cortex (Cservenka & Brumback, 2017; Müller-Oehring et al., 2018). Executive control is responsible for higher-level cognitive functions such as planning, directing attention, and decision making. It also controls response inhibition, the ability to resist temptation, such as the rewards that come with risky but exciting activities, including drinking.

There is a strong dose–response relationship: Greater consumption of alcohol predicts decreased brain volume and less white matter integrity (Cservenka & Brumback, 2017; Silveri, Dager, Cohen-Gilbert, & Sneider, 2016). The effects of adolescent alcohol use on brain function may be long lasting because alcohol use is associated with impaired neurogenesis and long-term reductions in synaptic connections and memory in animals (Spear, 2018; Tapia-Rojas et al., 2017). Yet there is room for optimism because some research has shown that the adolescent brain can increase in volume and show improved executive function when alcohol use is discontinued (Lisdahl, Gilbart, Wright, & Shollenbarger, 2013). The extent and limits of this rebound effect are unclear.

Whereas regular alcohol use is associated predominantly with deficits in attention and executive function, regular marijuana use is associated with a broad set of neurocognitive deficits in attention, learning and memory, processing speed, visuospatial functioning, and executive control (Lisdahl et al., 2013; Meruelo, Castro, Cota, & Tapert, 2017). Like alcohol use, regular marijuana use is associated with brain alterations, including reduced brain and gray matter volumes in the frontal lobe, followed by the parietal and temporal lobes (Lopez-Larson et al., 2012; Takagi, Youssef, & Lorenzetti, 2016). Early onset of marijuana use, before age 18 and especially prior to age 16, is associated with more severe neurocognitive consequences, including learning, memory, and executive function (Lubman, Cheetham, & Yücel, 2015; Silveri et al., 2016). One study suggests that cognitive function improved after 3 weeks of abstention, but attention deficits remained (Hanson et al., 2010). It is unknown whether abstinence over a long period is associated with a rebound in function. Other research suggests that attention, verbal and working memory, and processing speed remain impaired up to 2 months later (Hanson, Thayer, & Tapert, 2014; Winward, Hanson, Tapert, & Brown, 2014). Given the plasticity of the brain, some recovery of neurological function after abstention is expected, but the degree of recovery is not clear (Meruelo et al., 2017).

Alcohol and marijuana use tend to co-occur, making it difficult to disentangle the independent effects of each. Regardless, the literature to date suggests that, although normative, alcohol and marijuana use pose serious risks to neurological development in adolescence.

What Do You Think?

1. How might findings about the effects of alcohol and marijuana on brain development be applied to prevent or change adolescent behavior?

2. Identify challenges that might arise in applying these findings as well as ways of countering challenges. ●

---

and the Americas and found that sensation seeking increased in preadolescence, peaked at around age 19, and declined thereafter (Steinberg et al., 2018). Risky activity is thought to decline in late adolescence in part because of increases in adolescents' self-regulatory capacities and the capacities for long-term planning that accompany maturation of the frontal cortex (Dumontheil, 2016). However, the balance between frontal and limbic activity and fine-tuning of behavioral control continues into emerging adulthood (Giedd, 2018).

Contextual factors, such as adult supervision, exposure to stressors, and impoverished communities, influence adolescents' brain development and hence their propensities for risk taking (Scott, Duell, & Steinberg, 2018; Smith, Chein, & Steinberg, 2013; Tottenham & Galván, 2016). For example, one study of Australian adolescents revealed that neighborhood socioeconomic disadvantage was associated with altered brain development from early to late adolescence (Whittle et al., 2017). Positive parenting reduced the effects of family and neighborhood disadvantage, supporting the role of contextual factors as influences—risk and protective factors—for neural development. This conclusion is supported by other research suggesting that parenting influences the neural circuitry governing emotion (Morris, Criss, Silk, & Houltberg, 2017).

ADOLESCENT COGNITIVE DEVELOPMENT

» **LO 11.4** **Identify ways in which thinking changes in adolescence and how these changes are reflected in adolescent decision making and behavior.**

At 14, Eric spends much of his time learning about astronomy. He wonders about the existence of dark matter—cosmological matter that cannot be observed but is inferred by its gravitational pull on objects like planets and even galaxies. Eric reads blogs written by astronomers and has started his own blog where he comments on the best websites for teenagers who are interested in learning about the galaxy. Eric's newfound ability and interest in considering complex abstract phenomena illustrates the ways in which adolescents' thinking departs from children's. As with earlier periods, the cognitive-developmental perspective on cognition describes adolescence as entailing a transformation in thought. The information processing perspective, on the other hand, explains cognitive development in adolescence as a continuation, growth, and refinement of capacities and skills developed in childhood.

Piaget's Cognitive-Developmental Theory: Formal Operational Reasoning

In early adolescence, at about 11 years of age, individuals may enter the final stage of Piaget's scheme of cognitive development: formal operations. **Formal operational reasoning** entails the ability to think abstractly, logically, and systematically (Inhelder & Piaget, 1958). Children in the concrete operational stage reason about specific *things*—that is, concepts that exist in reality, such as problems concerning how to equitably divide a bowl of

pudding into five servings. Adolescents in the formal operational stage, however, reason about *ideas*, possibilities that do not exist in reality and that may have no tangible substance, such as whether it is possible to love equitably—to distribute love equally among several targets. Adolescents become capable of reasoning about their own thinking and even positing their own existence. Alejandro, for instance, wonders, "I'm thinking about my thinking . . . and I'm thinking about thinking about how I think. Now, how do I know that I am real? Am I just a thought?" The ability to think about possibilities beyond the here and now permits adolescents to plan about the future, make inferences from available information, and consider ways of solving potential but not yet real problems.

Formal operational thought enables adolescents to engage in **hypothetical–deductive reasoning**, or the ability to consider problems,

FIGURE 11.5

Measuring Formal Operations: The Pendulum Task

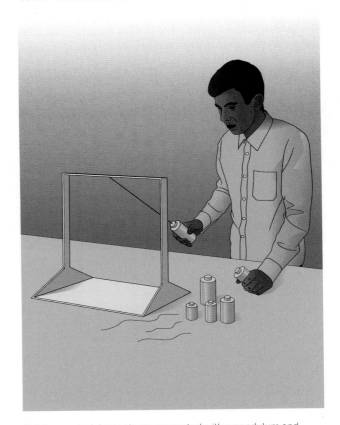

Children and adolescents are presented with a pendulum and are asked what determines the speed with which the pendulum swings. They are given materials and told that there are four variables to consider: (1) length of string (short, medium, long), (2) weight (light, medium, heavy), (3) height at which the weight is dropped, and (4) force with which the weight is dropped.

generate and systematically test hypotheses, and draw conclusions. Piaget's pendulum task (Figure 11.5) tests children and adolescents' abilities to use scientific reasoning to solve a problem with multiple possible solutions. Adolescents displaying formal operational reasoning develop hypotheses and systematically test them. For example, in the pendulum task, they change one variable while holding the others constant (e.g., trying each of the lengths of string while keeping the weight, height, and force the same). Concrete operational children, on the other hand, do not proceed systematically in a way that permits them to solve the pendulum problem; they fail to disentangle the variables and do not take into account nontangible variables such as height and force. For example, concrete operational children might test a short string with a heavy weight, then try a long string and short weight. Solving the pendulum problem requires the scientific reasoning capacities that come with formal operational reasoning.

Piaget believed that cognitive development is a universal process, yet the reality is that people vary. For example, most adolescents do not display formal operational thinking, and many adults, presumably capable of abstract reasoning, fail hypothetical-deductive tasks (Kuhn, 2013). Does this mean that they cannot think abstractly? Likely not. Piaget (1972) explained that opportunities to use formal operational reasoning influence its development. Individuals in the formal operational stage, unlike children in other stages, reason at the most advanced levels when considering material with which they have the greatest experience. For example, completing college courses is associated with gains in propositional and statistical thought, cognitive skills tapped in Piagetian tasks (Kuhn, 2012; Lehman & Nisbett, 1990). Ultimately, the appearance of formal operational reasoning is not consistent across people or across intellectual domains but instead varies with situation, task, context, and motivation (Birney & Sternberg, 2011; Labouvie-Vief, 2015; Marti & Rodríguez, 2012). Moreover, formal operational reasoning does not suddenly appear in early adolescence. Instead, cognitive change occurs gradually from childhood on, with gains in knowledge, experience, and information processing capacity (Keating, 2012; Moshman & Moshman, 2011).

Information Processing Theory

In the view of information processing theorists, improvements in information processing capacities—such as attention, memory, knowledge base, and speed—enable adolescents to think faster, more efficiently, and more complexly than ever

before. Specifically, brain development influences adolescents' growing capacities for executive function, permitting greater cognitive control and regulation of attention, thinking, and problem solving (Carlson, Zelazo, & Faja, 2013; Crone, Peters, & Steinbeis, 2018), as described in the following sections.

Attention, Response Inhibition, and Working Memory

Increased capacities for attention, response inhibition, and working memory are due to advances in executive function, influenced by brain development (Müller & Kerns, 2015). Adolescents become able to control attention and deploy it selectively, focusing on stimuli deemed important while tuning out others and remaining focused even as task demands change. Increases in attention permit material to be held in working memory while new material is taken in and processed (Barrouillet, Gavens, Vergauwe, Gaillard, & Camos, 2009). For example, at age 13, Julia is able to tune out the background noise in class to listen to her teacher, determine what is important, and take notes, remembering what she's writing while listening to her teacher. She can shift her attention to take notes from movies shown in class and can remain focused when the class format changes to discussion.

As we gain increasing control over our cognitive systems, we also become better at response inhibition, which allows us to keep responding or activating cognitive operations in response to a stimulus (Carlson et al., 2013). The ability to control and inhibit responses emerges in infancy, and advances through childhood, but shows substantial gains in adolescence and increases into adulthood (Crone et al., 2018; Zhai et al., 2015). Advances in response inhibition enable adolescents to adapt their responses to the situation. They can inhibit

Advances in cognitive abilities such as executive function contribute to adolescents' increasing ability to attend in class and grasp sophisticated material.
iStock/diego_cervo

well-earned responses when they are inappropriate to the situation (Luna, Paulsen, Padmanabhan, & Geier, 2013). For example, Robin is now able to keep herself from raising her hand in response to the teacher's question, telling herself, "I need to give other students a chance, too." However, the neurological changes that underlie response inhibition continue to develop into the 20s, and still-immature capacities for response inhibition are thought to underlie the risk-taking behavior common in adolescence (Luna et al., 2013; Peeters et al., 2015). In addition, the development of executive function is influenced by socioeconomic status, suggesting that adolescents in low-SES homes and neighborhoods may experience greater challenges in developing the cognitive control capacities needed for good decision making (Lawson, Hook, & Farah, 2018).

Working memory reaches adultlike levels by about age 19 (Luna, Garver, Urban, Lazar, & Sweeney, 2004). Combined with a growing knowledge base and increased strategy use, advances in working memory result in more sophisticated, efficient, and quick thinking and learning. Now adolescents can retain more information at once, better relate new information to what is already known, and combine information in more complex ways, underlying adolescents' increasing capacities for metacognition (Weil et al., 2013).

Metacognition and Scientific Reasoning

Recall from Chapter 7 that metacognition refers to knowledge of how the mind works and the ability to control the mind. As metacognition develops through middle adolescence, teenagers are better able to be planful about their cognitive system—how they take in, manipulate, and store information (Ardila, 2013; van der Stel & Veenman, 2013). They are better able to understand how they learn and remember and to choose and deploy strategies that enhance the representation, storage, and

retrieval of information. Eleventh grader Travis explains, "Studying for a biology exam is really different than studying for a history exam. In biology, I visualize the material, but when I study for history, I make up stories to help me remember it all." Travis illustrates the metacognitive skills that emerge in adolescence because he is able to evaluate his understanding, and he adjusts his strategies to the content that helps him learn best. Adolescents' abilities to apply metacognition in real-world settings continue to develop into late adolescence and early adulthood.

Metacognition plays an important role in scientific reasoning because it is by experimenting with and reflecting on cognitive strategies that adolescents begin to appreciate logic, which they increasingly apply to situations (Ardila, 2013; van der Stel & Veenman, 2013). As adolescents become able to reason about reasoning, they show improvements in manipulating abstract mental representations and engaging in the hypothetical–deductive reasoning that is characteristic of scientific reasoning (Kuhn, 2013).

Although adolescents show advances in scientific reasoning, their reasoning tends to emphasize single solutions to problems. In one study, sixth-grade students were presented with a detailed pictorial and written information about variables that were explained to have either a causal or noncausal influence on a hypothetical problem, the likelihood of an avalanche occurring. The students were given information about five variables and consistently chose only one as the probable cause, but their choice varied across trials. For example, a pair of students chose snow pollution as a cause of an avalanche, referring to the written materials, "Because it shows the snow pollution is high; snow is what causes an avalanche." Yet for a second prediction, the student pair turned to another single variable, slope angle, explaining, "Slope angle is an important part of how snow falls." In a third prediction, they turned to yet another single factor, wind speed: "We chose the wind speed because it affects how fast the snow falls" (Kuhn, Pease, & Wirkala, 2009, p. 439). Although adolescents can demonstrate scientific thinking, many tend to consistently prefer single-factor solutions to the multivariate solutions that tend to characterize complex real-life problems. They remain unable to coordinate the effects of multiple casual influences on outcomes (Kuhn, 2012). For many young people, the more complex reasoning required to consider multiple influences at once as well as a more sophisticated understanding of the nature of knowledge and scientific phenomena arises in emerging adulthood and early adulthood, as discussed in Chapter 13.

Advanced capacities for attention make adolescents better able to concentrate and study.
APTony Gutierrez

Implications of Adolescent Thinking

Adolescents' emerging abilities to reason influence how they view the world and themselves. However, abstract thought develops gradually. Teenagers are prone to errors in reasoning and lapses in judgment, as evidenced by the emergence of adolescent egocentrism and changes in decision-making ability.

Adolescent Egocentrism

One consequence of adolescents' advances in reasoning and metacognition is that they often direct their new abstract abilities toward themselves. Adolescents are egocentric and have difficulty with perspective taking, specifically with separating their own and others' perspectives. **Adolescent egocentrism** is manifested in two phenomena: the **imaginary audience** and the **personal fable** (Elkind & Bowen, 1979).

The imaginary audience is just that: Adolescents misdirect their own preoccupation about themselves toward others and assume that they are the focus of others' attention (Elkind & Bowen, 1979). The imaginary audience fuels adolescents' concerns with their appearance and can make the slightest criticism sting painfully, as teens are convinced that all eyes are on them. The imaginary audience contributes to the heightened self-consciousness characteristic of adolescence (Albert, Elkind, & Ginsberg, 2007).

Adolescents' preoccupation with themselves also leads them to believe that they are special, unique, and invulnerable—a perspective known as the personal fable (Elkind & Bowen, 1979). They believe that their emotions, the highs of happiness and depths of despair that they feel, are different from and more intense than other people's emotions and that others simply do not understand. The invulnerability aspect of the personal fable, coupled with brain development that predisposes adolescents to seek risks, leads them to believe that they are immune to the negative consequences of such risky activities as drug use, delinquency, and unsafe sex (Alberts, Elkind, & Ginsberg, 2007).

Both the imaginary audience and the personal fable are thought to increase in early adolescence, peak in middle adolescence, and decline in late adolescence (Elkind & Bowen, 1979). Recent research suggests that adolescent egocentrism may persist into late adolescence and beyond (Schwartz, Maynard, & Uzelac, 2008). Indeed, according to recent research, adolescents and adults show similar levels of egocentrism (Rai, Mitchell, Kadar, & Mackenzie, 2016). Moreover, for many adolescents (and adults), the audience is not imaginary. When posting to social media, many adolescents painstakingly consider their audience and play to them by sharing content to appear interesting, well liked, and attractive (Yau & Reich, 2018).

Decision Making

Adolescents are faced with a variety of decisions each day, ranging from the mundane, such as when to clean their rooms and how to spend an afternoon, to decisions that are important to their health, well-being, and future, such as which friendships to foster, whether to drink or smoke, what classes to take in school, and whether and where to go to college. With age and experience, adolescents take on increasing decision-making responsibility.

Researchers who study decision making from a cognitive perspective explain decision making as a rational process in which, when faced with a decision, people follow several steps. They first identify decision options and then identify the potential positive and negative consequences for each option (i.e., the pros and cons). They estimate how likely each potential outcome is, rate how desirable each outcome is, and finally combine all of this information to make a decision (Furby & Beyth-Marom, 1992). Under laboratory conditions, adolescents are capable of demonstrating rational decision making that is in line with their goals and is comparable to that of adults (Reyna & Rivers, 2008). In practice, however, decision making is more complex and is influenced by situational, emotional, and developmental factors.

Adolescents tend to place more importance on the potential benefits of decisions (e.g., social status, pleasure) than on the potential costs or risks (e.g., physical harm, short- and long-term health issues) (Javadi, Schmidt, & Smolka, 2014; Shulman & Cauffman, 2013). In the presence of rewards, adolescents show heightened activity in the brain systems that support reward processing and reduced activity in the areas responsible for inhibitory control, as compared with adults (Paulsen, Hallquist, Geier, & Luna, 2014; Smith, Steinberg, Strang, & Chein, 2015). Adolescents are more susceptible to risk taking in situations of heightened emotional arousal (Figner, Mackinlay, Wilkening, & Weber, 2009; Mills, Goddings, Clasen, Giedd, & Blakemore, 2014). In emotionally arousing situations, adolescents often act impulsively, seemingly without thought, and their decisions often are influenced by affective motivators such as the desire for pleasure, relaxation, stimulation, and excitement (Mills et al., 2014; van Duijvenvoorde et al., 2015).

Everyday decisions have personal relevance, require quick thinking, are emotional, and often are made in the presence and influence of others. Recall that the prefrontal cortex, responsible for executive functioning and decision making, is the last part of the brain to reach full maturity, lagging far behind the limbic system, responsible for emotion. Adolescents often feel strong emotions and impulses that they may be unable to regulate (Cohen & Casey, 2017). Therefore, laboratory studies of decision making are less useful in understanding how young people compare with adults when they must make choices that are important or occur in stressful situations in which they must rely on experience, knowledge, and intuition (Steinberg, 2013). When faced with unfamiliar, emotionally charged situations, spur-of-the moment decisions, pressures to conform, poor self-control, and risk and benefit estimates that favor good short-term and bad long-term outcomes, adolescents tend to reason more poorly than adults (Albert, Chein, & Steinberg, 2013; Breiner et al., 2018). Figure 11.6 illustrates the many influences on adolescent decision making. The Applying Developmental Science feature discusses the legal implications of how adult and adolescent decision making differ.

Although many adults display faulty decision making, adolescents are in greater need of protection from their poor decisions, because the consequences of their bad decisions—such as accepting a ride from a friend who has been drinking—are potentially more serious and long lasting. Adult guidance can aid adolescents in learning how to make good decisions. Such guidance may involve discussing how to consider options, including the pros and cons of each and the likelihood of each, and how to weigh information to come to a decision. In addition, experience in making decisions and learning from successes and failures, coupled with developments in cognition, self-control, and emotional regulation, lead to adolescent decision making that is more reflective, confident, and successful.

FIGURE 11.6

Influences on Adolescent Decisions

Brain Development
Increases in cortical volume and white matter

Decreases in gray matter

Rapid limbic system development in early adolescence

Prefrontal cortex matures slowly throughout adolescence into young adulthood

Shifts in levels of neurotransmitters in early adolescence

Cognitive Development
Advances in attention, memory, processing speed, and strategy repertoire and use

Abstract thinking

Scientific reasoning

Metacognition and metamemory

Executive functioning

Adolescent Decision-Making and Behavior
Difficulty reading other people and identifying their emotions

Emotionally charged responses before reasoning

Advances in planning abilities

Increasingly able to identify and weigh options and consider multiple sources of information

Impulsivity and novelty seeking, but over time, improvements in response inhibition

---

APPLYING DEVELOPMENTAL SCIENCE

 # Legal Implications of Adolescent Decision Making

Developmental scientists' work is often called upon to inform legal issues and influence social policy, as illustrated by a series of Supreme Court cases that examined whether minors should be subject to the same punishments as adults.

The landmark case *Roper v. Simmons*, decided by the Court in 2005, examined whether adolescents should be sentenced to the death penalty. At the time, 21 states permitted the death penalty for adolescents under the age of 18, and most of them permitted it at the age of 16 (Steinberg & Scott, 2003). As the case moved to the Supreme Court,

developmental scientists collaborated with the American Psychological Association to submit an amicus curiae ("friend of the court") brief to inform the justices about developmental research relevant to the case, specifically, research on adolescent judgment and decision making.

The brief explained that adolescents' developmental immaturity makes them less culpable for crimes and justifies a more lenient punishment than that of adults—but still holds that they are actors who retain responsibility for the crime (Cauffman & Steinberg, 2012; Steinberg & Scott, 2003).

(Continued)

(Continued)

Neurological and psychosocial factors play a prominent role in adolescent decision making and behavior, suggesting that courts should treat adolescents differently than adults.
AP Photo/W.A. Bridges Jr.

Research conducted over the past 15 years has supported the brief's conclusion. For example, neurological research suggests that adolescents tend to feel strong emotions and impulses that they may have difficulty controlling (Steinberg, 2017). Adolescents, especially males, react impulsively to threat cues more than do adults or children, even when instructed not to respond (Dreyfuss et al., 2014).

In addition to neurological development, psychosocial development—specifically, susceptibility to peer influence and future orientation—plays a prominent role in adolescent decision making and behavior (Albert et al., 2013). When adolescents make decisions in response to hypothetical dilemmas in which they must choose between engaging in an antisocial behavior suggested by friends and a prosocial one,

their choices suggest that susceptibility to peer influence increases between childhood and early adolescence, peaking around age 14 and declining slowly during high school (Allen & Antonishak, 2008). Not only are adolescents' decisions more likely to be influenced by peers, but simply thinking about peer evaluation increases risky behavior. Moreover, the presence of peers can increase risky behavior even when the probability of a negative outcome is high (Centifanti, Modecki, MacLellan, & Gowling, 2016; Smith, Rosenbaum, Botdorf, Steinberg, & Chein, 2018). Adolescents also have a poor sense of future orientation, envisioning themselves in the future, which is associated with participation in risky activities (P. Chen & Vazsonyi, 2013). Difficulty envisioning the future coupled with the influence of strong emotions, susceptibility to peers, and poor self-control can compromise adolescents' decision-making ability.

Adolescents and adults weigh the costs and benefits involved in making decisions differently. To the extent that teens are less psychosocially mature than adults, their decisions are likely to be inferior to those of adults, even if they score similarly to adults on cognitive measures (Cauffman & Steinberg, 2012; Modecki, 2014). Therefore, the amicus curiae brief prepared for *Roper v. Simmons* concluded that adolescents' developmental immaturity makes them less culpable for crimes and justifies a more lenient punishment than that for adults—but still holds that they are actors who retain responsibility for the crime (Cauffman & Steinberg, 2012; Steinberg, 2017).

In the case of *Roper v. Simmons*, the Supreme Court ruled against capital punishment for minors on the basis of their lack of maturity and susceptibility to peer influence. In 2010 and 2012, based on a similar rationale, in *Florida v. Graham, Miller v. Alabama, and Jackson v. Hobbs*, the Supreme Court ruled that minors cannot be sentenced to life in prison without parole.

What Do You Think?

1. To what degree do you think adolescents should be culpable for criminal offenses they commit?
2. Do you agree with the Supreme Court decisions against the death penalty or life in prison without parole for adolescents? Why or why not?
3. Do you advocate using developmental science research to make policy decisions such as this? Why or why not? ●

THINKING IN CONTEXT 11.4

1. What do teachers and parents need to know about cognitive development in adolescence?

2. Compare cognitive explanations of adolescent egocentrism and risk behavior with neurological explanations, such as the dual-systems model.

3. Describe some ways in which adolescent decision making is a product of interactions among puberty, brain development, cognitive growth, and contextual influences such as parents, peers, and community.

ADOLESCENT MORAL DEVELOPMENT

» LO 11.5 Discuss moral development and influences on moral reasoning.

Adolescents' newfound abilities for abstract reasoning lead them to approach problems in different ways, consider multiple perspectives, and delight in the process of thinking itself. It is these cognitive advances that enable adolescents to demonstrate the final and most sophisticated form of reasoning described in Lawrence Kohlberg's theory of moral reasoning: postconventional moral reasoning.

Postconventional Moral Reasoning

Much of Kohlberg's theory was based on longitudinal research with a group of boys, ages 10, 13, and 16, who were periodically interviewed over three decades (Kohlberg, 1969). Kohlberg discovered that the boys' reasoning progressed through sequential stages and in a predictable order. Kohlberg measured moral reasoning by presenting individuals with hypothetical dilemmas such as the following:

Near death, a woman with cancer learns of a drug that may save her. The woman's husband, Heinz, approaches the druggist who created the drug, but the druggist refuses to sell the drug for anything less than $2,000. After borrowing from everyone he knows, Heinz has only scraped together $1,000. Heinz asks the druggist to let him have the drug for $1,000 and he will pay him the rest later. The druggist says that it is his right to make money from the drug he developed and refuses to sell it to Heinz. Desperate for the drug, Heinz breaks into the druggist's store and steals the drug. Should Heinz have done that? Why or why not? (Kohlberg, 1969)

The Heinz dilemma is the most popular example of the hypothetical conflicts that Kohlberg used to study moral development. These problems examine how people make decisions when fairness and people's rights are pitted against obedience to authority and law. Participants' explanations of how they arrived at their decisions reveal developmental shifts through three broad levels of reasoning that correspond to cognitive development.

Recall from Chapter 7 that young children reason at the preconventional level. Their decisions are influenced by self-interest, the desire to gain rewards and avoid punishments. As noted in Chapter 9, school-age children's moral decisions tend to be socially driven. Conventional moral reasoning entails internalizing the norms and standards of authority figures, in a desire to be accepted (Stage 3) and to maintain social order (Stage 4).

Not until adolescence, according to Kohlberg, do people become capable of demonstrating the most advanced moral thinking, postconventional moral reasoning, which entails autonomous decision making from moral principles that value respect for individual rights above all else. Postconventional moral thinkers recognize that their self-chosen principles of fairness and justice may sometimes conflict with the law. At Stage 5, Social Contract Orientation, individuals view laws and rules as flexible and part of the social contract or agreement meant to further human interests. Laws and rules are to be followed as they bring good to people, but laws can be changed if they are inconsistent with the needs and rights of the majority. Sometimes, if laws are unjust—if they harm more people than they protect—they can be broken. Stage 6, Universal Ethical Principles, represents the most advanced moral reasoning, defined by abstract ethical principles that are universal, valid for all people regardless of law, such as equality and respect for human dignity.

A great deal of research has confirmed that individuals proceed through the first four stages of moral reasoning in a slow, gradual, and predictable fashion (Boom, Wouters, & Keller, 2007; Dawson, 2002). Specifically, reasoning at the preconventional level decreases by early adolescence. Conventional reasoning, Stage 3, increases through middle adolescence, and Stage 4 reasoning increases in middle to late adolescence and becomes typical of most individuals by early adulthood. Research suggests that few people advance beyond Stage 4 moral reasoning. Postconventional reasoning is rare and appears as Stage 5 reasoning (Kohlberg, Levine, & Hewer, 1983). The existence of Stage 6, the hypothesized, most advanced type of moral reasoning, is supported only by case-based anecdotal evidence. Kohlberg himself questioned the validity of Stage 6, dropped it from the stage scheme, but later included Stage 6 again because it represented an end goal state to which human development strives (Kohlberg & Ryncarz, 1990).

Kohlberg's theory of moral reasoning has led to four decades of research. Most of the research conducted has examined the role of social interaction in promoting development, the role of gender and culture, and the link between reasoning and behavior.

Social Interaction and Moral Reasoning

Moral development occurs within parent, peer, and school contexts and is influenced by social development. Social interactions offer important opportunities for the development of moral reasoning. High-quality parent–child relationships predict advanced moral reasoning (Malti & Latzko, 2010). Reasoning advances when adolescents have opportunities to engage in discussions that are characterized by mutual perspective taking. Engaging adolescents in discussion about personal experiences, local issues, and media events—while presenting alternative points of view and asking questions—advances reasoning. For example, a parent might ask, "Why do you think he did that? Was there something else that he could have done? How do you think other people interpret his actions?" Issue-focused discussions that present adolescents with reasoning that is slightly more advanced than their own prompts them to compare their reasoning with the new reasoning and often internalize the new reasoning, advancing their moral reasoning to a new level.

Parents who engage their children in discussion, listen with sensitivity, ask for children's input, praise them, engage them with questioning, and use humor promote the development of moral reasoning (Carlo, Mestre, Samper, Tur, & Armenta, 2011). Likewise, interactions with peers in which adolescents confront one another with differing perspectives and engage each other with in-depth discussions promote the development of moral reasoning (Power, Higgins, & Kohlberg, 1989). Adolescents who report having more close friendships in which they engage in deep conversations tend to show more advanced moral reasoning than do teens who have little social contact (Schonert-Reichl, 1999). They also report

feeling positive emotions when they make unselfish moral decisions (Malti, Keller, & Buchmann, 2013). Moral reasoning is inherently social. Some have argued, however, that the social basis of morality means that men and women should reason in very different ways.

Gender and Moral Reasoning

A popular criticism of Kohlberg's theory of moral reasoning arises because his initial research was conducted with all-male samples. Early research that studied both males and females suggested gender differences in moral reasoning, with males typically showing Stage 4 reasoning, characterized by concerns about law and order, and females showing Stage 3 reasoning, characterized by concerns about maintaining relationships (Poppen, 1974). Carol Gilligan (1982) argued that Kohlberg's theory neglected a distinctively female mode of moral reasoning, a **care orientation,** which is characterized by empathy, a desire to maintain relationships, and a responsibility not to cause harm. As Gilligan explains, the care orientation contrasts with the distinctively male mode of moral reasoning, a **justice orientation,** which is based on the abstract principles of fairness and individualism captured by Kohlberg. Care and justice represent frameworks modified by experience that influence how people interpret and resolve moral problems.

Although most people are capable of raising both justice and care concerns in describing moral dilemmas, Gilligan argued that care reasoning was thought to be used predominantly by females and justice reasoning by males (Gilligan & Attanucci, 1988). In agreement with Gilligan, most researchers acknowledge that more than one mode of moral reasoning exists (Kohlberg et al., 1983) but instead argue that moral orientations are not linked with gender (Knox, Fagley, & Miller, 2004). Male and female adolescents and adults display similar reasoning that combines concerns of justice (e.g., being fair) with those of care (e.g., being supportive and helpful), and when there are sex differences, they are very small (Jaffee & Hyde, 2000; Weisz & Black, 2002). The most mature forms of moral reasoning incorporate both justice and care concerns. Moral maturity tends to be accompanied by a sense of social responsibility, as discussed in the Lives in Context feature.

Culture and Moral Reasoning

Cross-cultural studies of Kohlberg's theory show that the sequence appears in all cultures but that people in non-Western cultures rarely score above Stage 3 (Gibbs, Basinger, Grime, & Snarey, 2007). Like cognitive capacities, morality and appropriate

Volunteer Work and Social Responsibility

In adolescence, moral development often includes a sense of social responsibility, a personal commitment to contribute to community and society (Wray-Lake & Syvertsen, 2011). Social responsibility values predict a variety of prosocial civic behaviors such as volunteering, voting, political activism, and environmental conservation (Caprara, Schwartz, Capanna, Vecchione, & Barbaranelli, 2006; Hart, Donnelly, Youniss, & Atkins, 2007; Pratt, Hunsberger, Pancer, & Alisat, 2003).

How does social responsibility develop? Surprisingly, prosocial behavior, voluntarily helping others, tends to plateau or even dip from late childhood into middle adolescence (Eisenberg et al., 2005; Smetana et al., 2009). The physical and cognitive transitions of adolescence draw adolescents' attention to themselves, and most adolescents tend to prioritize personal issues over social and moral concerns (M. T. Wang & Dishion, 2012). For example, a 3-year study following elementary, middle, and high school students ages 9 to 18 found that social responsibility decreased from ages 9 to 16 before leveling off in later adolescence (Wray-Lake, Syvertsen, & Flanagan, 2016). Connections to family, peers, school, and community contributed dynamically to advances in social responsibility. Parents with an authoritative style often model social responsibility values, and their behavior influences children and adolescents. Adolescents who participate in community service tend to have parents who volunteer and talk about volunteering and giving (Ottoni-Wilhelm, Estell, & Perdue, 2014). When parents recruit their children into community service, it transmits prosocial values, including the meaning of service and its effect on others (White & Mistry, 2016). Parental encouragement and modeling of volunteer work predict sympathy, feeling compassion for another

person, and adolescents' volunteer work (McGinley, Lipperman-Kreda, Byrnes, & Carlo, 2010; van Goethem, van Hoof, van Aken, Orobio de Castro, & Raaijmakers, 2014).

Volunteerism itself predicts social responsibility. When youth volunteer and engage in service learning, they demonstrate increases in prosocial attitudes toward others, as well as social responsibility and civic values (Conway, Amel, & Gerwien, 2009; van Goethem et al., 2014). Volunteerism and social responsibility values interact. Community service offers adolescents opportunities to better understand themselves as they interact with a heterogeneous group of people in their community who likely differ from them in age, ethnicity, religion, or social class (Flanagan, Kim, Collura, & Kopish, 2015; Yates & Youniss, 1996). Community service holds the potential to enhance sensitivity toward others. Compared to their nonvolunteer peers, early adolescents who do community volunteer work are more likely to see similarities between themselves and disadvantaged groups, less likely to stereotype outgroups, and more likely to believe that people are capable of change (Flanagan et al., 2015; Karafantis & Levy, 2004). In addition, volunteering during adolescence predicts voting, volunteering, and joining community organizations in adulthood (Hart, Donnelly, Youniss, & Atkins, 2007; McFarland & Thomas, 2006).

What Do You Think?

1. What are some of the potential barriers to engaging in volunteer work during adolescence? How can adolescents overcome those barriers?

2. Do you engage in volunteer work? What does it mean to you? ●

---

responses to ethical dilemmas are defined by each society and its cultural perspectives. Whereas Western cultures tend to emphasize the rights of the individual (justice-based reasoning), non-Western cultures tend to value collectivism, focusing on human interdependence (care-based reasoning). Individuals in collectivist cultures tend to define moral dilemmas in terms of the responsibility to the entire community rather than simply to the individual (Miller, 2018). Such emphasis on the needs of others is characteristic of Stage 3 in Kohlberg's scheme. However, because moral values are relative to the cultural context, Stage 3 reasoning is an advanced

form of reasoning in collectivist cultures, because it embodies what is most valued in these cultures, concepts such as interdependence and relationships.

Despite cross-cultural differences, individuals in many cultures show similarities in reasoning. For example, one study examined Chinese and Canadian 12- to 19-year-old adolescents' views of the fairness of various forms of democratic and nondemocratic government (Helwig, Arnold, Tan, & Boyd, 2007). Adolescents from both China and Canada preferred democratic forms of government and appealed to fundamental democratic justice principles such as representation, voice, and majority rule to support their judgments, suggesting that adolescents in collectivist cultures are able to reason with justice principles in particular contexts. In addition, similar age-related patterns in judgments and reasoning were found across cultures and across diverse regions within China. It appears that the development of moral reasoning progresses in a similar pattern across cultures. People of different cultures are able to reason using both care and justice orientations even though cultures tend to vary in the weight they assign moral orientations, emphasizing one over another.

Moral Reasoning and Behavior

Moral reasoning explains how people think about issues of justice, but reasoning is only moderately related to behavior (Colby & Damon, 1992). People often behave in ways they know they should not. For example, an adolescent who explains that stealing and cheating are wrong may slip a pack of gum into her pocket and leave a store without paying or may peek at a classmate's paper during an exam. Like

Most people at least sometimes behave in ways they know they shouldn't.
iStock/FatCamera

other decisions, ethical conflicts experienced in real life are complex, accompanied by intense emotions, social obligations, and practical considerations, which lead people to act in ways that contradict their judgments (Walker, 2004).

With advances in moral reasoning, adolescents often begin to coordinate moral, conventional, and personal concepts and are more likely to act in ways that are in line with their beliefs (Smetana, Jambon, & Ball, 2013). For example, adolescents who demonstrate higher levels of moral reasoning are more likely to share with and help others and are less likely to engage in antisocial behaviors such as cheating, aggression, or delinquency (Brugman, 2010; Comunian & Gielen, 2000). Although adolescents who show low levels of moral reasoning are thought to be at greater risk for delinquency,

Adolescents who demonstrate higher levels of moral reasoning are more likely to act prosocially by sharing, helping others, and engaging in service, such as these adolescents.
iStock/mixetto

findings are mixed in this area. Some studies find that low levels of reasoning predict delinquency, and others show no relationship (Leenders & Brugman, 2005; Tarry & Emler, 2007). Perhaps the degree to which moral reasoning is associated with behavior varies with whether adolescents perceive the behavior, as an issue regarding morality, social convention, or personal choice (Berkowitz & Begun, 1994; Brugman, 2010). Adolescents, particularly early adolescents, tend to overwhelmingly label behaviors as personal issues. Adolescents' moral development influences behaviors they label as moral decisions but not those viewed as social conventions or personal issues. Adolescents who engage in delinquency are more likely than other adolescents to view delinquent behaviors as issues of social convention or personal choice rather than moral issues, suggesting that their level of moral maturity is not an influence on their delinquent behavior because they do not label the behavior as entailing a moral decision (Kuther & Higgins-D'Alessandro, 2000; Leenders & Brugman, 2005). A variety of factors influence the development of moral reasoning and how adolescents view and behave in their world.

THINKING IN CONTEXT 11.5

1. Based on Kohlberg's theory, do you think morality can be taught?

2. What role, if any, might contextual factors such as socioeconomic status, community, and interactions with parents and peers play in moral development?

3. Do you think the average person can reach the highest level of Kohlberg's scheme? Why or why not?

SCHOOLS AND ACADEMIC FUNCTIONING IN ADOLESCENCE

» LO 11.6 Describe the challenges that school transitions pose for adolescents and the role of parents in academic achievement.

Apart from the home context, school is the most relevant and immediate context in which adolescents live. Most adolescents transition from an elementary school to a middle school (typically, 6th, 7th, and 8th grade) or junior high school (7th, 8th, and 9th grades) and then to a high school (9th through 12th grades).

School Transitions

Change, although often exciting, can cause stress to individuals of all ages. Many students find the transition to a new school, whether middle school or high school, a challenge. Academic motivation and achievement often suffer during school transitions (Booth & Gerard, 2014; Felmlee, McMillan, Inara Rodis, & Osgood, 2018). Many students may feel more lonely and anxious, and they may report depressive symptoms (Benner, Boyle, & Bakhtiari, 2017; Coelho, Marchante, & Jimerson, 2017). For most students, these adjustment difficulties are temporary, and their achievement recovers within 1 to 2 years as they adapt to their new schools (Crosnoe, Benner, Crosnoe, & Benner, 2015). However, students who perceive the school transition as more stressful tend to show greater drops in motivation and academic achievement and less connectedness to school that persists well beyond the school transition (Goldstein, Boxer, & Rudolph, 2015).

School transitions tend to coincide with many developmental and contextual changes. Many young people experience puberty during the transition to middle school. Changing thought capacities, self-perceptions, and relationships as well as new responsibilities and opportunities for independence pose challenges. As friendships become more important, school transitions can disrupt them by dividing friends into different schools. All of these simultaneous changes mean that many adolescents experience school transitions as stressful.

The school environment, teachers, and standards change with each transition. With each transition, adolescents must meet more stringent academic standards, and evaluation becomes more frequent and formal than in elementary school. At the same time, many students feel that they receive less support from teachers (Mueller & Anderman, 2010). Students commonly report feeling less connected to middle school teachers than elementary school teachers and view their middle school teachers as less friendly, supportive, and fair (Way, Reddy, & Rhodes, 2007). High school students often report that they receive less personal attention from teachers, more class lectures, fewer hands-on demonstration activities, and fewer opportunities to participate in class discussions and group decision making than they did in middle school (Gentle-Genitty, 2009; Seidman, Aber, & French, 2004). At the same time, teachers' sense of efficacy, their belief in their abilities as teachers, declines with each grade into secondary school (Eccles & Roeser, 2015). Teachers' sense of competence predicts high expectations for students, which in turn predicts student success. This decline is greater for teachers who educate high proportions of poor and minority children (Cooper, Kurtz-Costes, & Rowley, 2010), adding to the challenges that at-risk students face. As a result, middle school classrooms tend to be characterized by a greater emphasis on teacher control and offer fewer opportunities for student decision making and autonomy (Eccles & Roeser, 2015).

According to researcher Jacqueline Eccles, negative effects of school transitions occur when there is little stage–environment fit. That is, adolescents experience difficulties when there is a poor match between their developmental needs and what the school environment affords in its organization and characteristics (Eccles & Roeser, 2011). Teachers become more stringent, less personal, and more directive at the same time as young people value independence. Adolescents need more guidance and assistance with academic, social, and mental health issues just as teachers report feeling less responsibility for students' problems. The mismatch of adolescents' changing developmental needs and school resources contributes to declines in academic performance, motivation, and overall functioning (Booth & Gerard, 2014). Vulnerable students, such as those from low-income families or those who require special education services, tend to show a larger interruption in academic achievement (Akos, Rose, & Orthner, 2014).

Some adolescents face greater risks with school transitions than others. Changes in school demographics, particularly a mismatch between the ethnic composition of elementary and middle school, or middle school and high school, can pose challenges to adolescents' adjustment (Douglass, Yip, & Shelton, 2014). One study of over 900 entering high school students found that students who experienced more ethnic incongruence from middle to high school, a mismatch in demographics, reported declining feelings of connectedness to school over time and increasing worries about their academic success (Benner & Graham, 2009).

Students who moved to high schools with fewer students who were ethnically similar to themselves were most likely to experience a disconnect, as were African American male students. This is of particular concern because African American adolescents tend to experience more risk factors to academic achievement, have more difficulties in school transitions, and are more likely to fall behind during school transitions than adolescents of other ethnicities (Burchinal, Roberts, Zeisel, Hennon, & Hooper, 2006). Similarly, Latino students tend to be more sensitive to changes in the school climate and experience school transitions as more challenging than do non-Hispanic White students (Espinoza & Juvonen, 2011). Recent research suggests that students of all ethnicities—African American, Latino, Asian, and White adolescents—fare best in diverse schools with ethnic groups of relatively equal size (Juvonen, Kogachi, & Graham, 2018). Students in diverse schools reported feeling safer, less victimized, and less lonely; perceived teachers as more fair; and reported more favorable attitudes toward students of other ethnicities.

The best student outcomes occur when schools closely match adolescents' developmental needs. Small, tight-knit middle schools may reduce the alienation that some students experience during the middle school transition (Crosnoe, Benner, Crosnoe, & Benner, 2015). Small schools may also foster strong teacher–student relationships through more opportunities for teachers to interact with a smaller student base. Close relationships may help teachers feel comfortable providing opportunities for adolescents to have autonomy in classroom interactions and assignments while providing strong support. Adolescents who report high levels of teacher support and feel connected to their schools tend to show better academic achievement and better emotional health, including lower rates of depressive and anxiety symptoms (Kidger, Araya, Donovan, & Gunnell, 2012).

Adolescents' success in navigating school transitions is also influenced by their experiences outside of school. Adolescents are most vulnerable to the negative effects of school transitions when they lack the social and emotional resources to cope with multiple stressors. Young people who report feeling supported by their families and having many friends are less bothered by day-to-day stressors and experience school transitions with few problems (Kingery, Erdley, & Marshall, 2011; Rueger, Chen, Jenkins, & Choe, 2014). Finally, as in other aspects of development, expectations matter. Adolescents who expect a positive transition to secondary school are more likely to report experiencing a positive experience and are at lower risk of school dropout (Waters, Lester, & Cross, 2014).

School Dropout

School dropout rates in the United States have reached historic lows, with dramatic decreases for African American adolescents and especially Hispanic adolescents (see Figure 11.7). Nevertheless, each year, about 6% of high school students drop out of school (National Center for Educational Statistics, 2017). Students of low socioeconomic status are at high risk of school dropout, and minority and immigrant students are particularly vulnerable.

Students with behavior and substance use problems are most at risk for school dropout, but many who drop out simply have academic problems, skip classes with increasing frequency, and disengage emotionally and behaviorally (Bowers & Sprott, 2012; Henry, Knight, & Thornberry, 2012; M. T. Wang & Fredricks, 2014). Lack of parental involvement places students at risk for school dropout—and when parents respond to poor grades with anger and punishment, this can further reduce adolescents' academic motivation and feelings of connectedness to school (Alivernini & Lucidi, 2011). Many of the unfavorable characteristics that students report of their high schools predict dropout: large schools, few opportunities to form personal relationships with teachers or to speak out in class, poor emotional and academic support from teachers, and poor peer relationships and bullying (Freeman & Simonsen, 2015; Frostad, Pijl, & Mjaavatn, 2014; Jia, Konold, & Cornell, 2016).

Although dropout is often the result of extended difficulties, there are multiple paths to drop out. Many students show few problems until a particularly disruptive event or situation, such as severe peer victimization, health problems, family instability, or long work hours, impairs their coping skills (Dupere et al., 2015). For example, a study comparing Canadian students who were recent dropouts, at-risk students who remained in school, and average students found

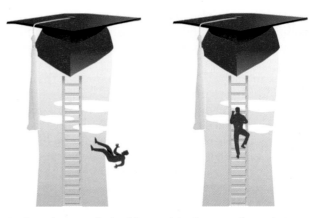

Students drop out of school for a variety of reasons. Some show an extended history of problems. Others experience a disruptive event or situation that impairs their coping skills and leads to dropout.
The Fresno Bee/MCT via Getty Images

FIGURE 11.7

School Dropout Rates Among Youth Ages 16 to 24 in the United States, 2000–2015

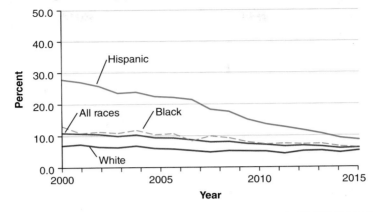

Source: U.S. Department of Education, National Center for Education Statistics, 2017.

that dropouts were over three times more likely to have experienced recent acute stressors, suggesting that it may be these acute stressors that place students at increased risk for dropout, over and above existing contextual risks (Dupéré et al., 2018).

As adults, high school dropouts experience higher rates of unemployment and, when hired, earn less than high school graduates throughout adulthood. Young people who have dropped out of school have the option of taking a high school equivalency test, the General Educational Development exam (GED). The GED was developed in the late 1940s to certify that returning World War II veterans who had left high school to serve in the military were ready for college or the labor market. Although passing the GED exam can signify that a young person has accumulated the knowledge entailed in earning a high school diploma, GED holders do not fare as well as regular high school graduates in the labor market, and they tend to get much less postsecondary education (Tyler & Lofstrom, 2009).

Parenting and Academic Competence

Close parent–adolescent relationships serve as an important buffer to academic motivation and performance from childhood through adolescence for young people at all socioeconomic levels (Dotterer, Lowe, & McHale, 2014). As in other areas of development, both the overly harsh parenting characterized by the authoritarian parenting style and the lax, permissive parenting style are associated with poor academic performance. Likewise, adolescents reared by uninvolved parents tend to show the

poorest school grades (Gonzalez & Wolters, 2006; Heaven & Ciarrochi, 2008). Authoritative parenting, in contrast, is associated with academic achievement in adolescents around the world, including Argentina, Australia, Canada, China, Hong Kong, Iran, Pakistan, Scotland, and the United States (Assadi et al., 2007; Garg, Levin, Urajnik, & Kauppi, 2005; Gonzalez & Wolters, 2006; Spera, 2005).

When parents use the authoritative style, they are open to discussion, involve their adolescents in joint decision making, and firmly but fairly monitor their adolescents' behavior and set limits. This style of parenting helps adolescents feel valued, respected, and encouraged to think for themselves (Dornbusch, Ritter, Mont-Reynaud, & Chen, 1990; Spera, 2005). Adolescents are learning to regulate their emotions and behavior and to set, work toward, and achieve educational goals (Aunola

Authoritative parenting is associated with academic achievement in adolescents around the world.
iStock/monkeybusinessimages

& Stattin, 2000; Moilanen, Rasmussen, & Padilla-Walker, 2015). Authoritative parenting supports these developments.

Just as in elementary school, parents can promote high academic achievement in middle and high school students by being active and involved—for example, by knowing their teens' teachers, monitoring progress, ensuring that their teens are taking challenging and appropriate classes, and expressing high expectations (Benner, 2011; Karbach, Gottschling, Spengler, Hegewald, & Spinath, 2013; M. T. Wang, Hill, & Hofkens, 2014). Parent–school involvement in 8th grade has been shown to predict 10th-grade students' grade point average regardless of socioeconomic status, previous academic achievement, and ethnicity (Keith et al., 1998). By being involved in the school, parents communicate the importance of education; they also model academic engagement and problem solving.

THINKING IN CONTEXT 11.6

1. Discuss the ways in which the fit between a young person's needs—personal and developmental—and the opportunities and supports provided to her within the school system influence her academic adjustment and likelihood of completing high school.

2. How might factors outside of school and in the home, peer network, community, and society contribute?

3. What can be done to help students stay in school and graduate from high school?

 APPLY YOUR KNOWLEDGE

At 14, Kendra had her very first alcoholic drink when her friends took her to a party hosted by Dylan, a high school senior. Soon Kendra and Dylan began dating. Kendra had always felt especially self-conscious about her body, as she had started needing a bra at age 10, and by age 13, she had sometimes been mistaken for an adult. She thought of herself as "too big," but Dylan insisted her body was "smokin'." With Dylan, Kendra began drinking regularly at parties as she found it eased her nerves and helped her feel more comfortable interacting with the older kids. After a few drinks, she would feel comfortable enough to take off her sweatshirt and show off her tank top. Dylan also introduced Kendra to marijuana, which she preferred over alcohol because it made it easy to forget her self-consciousness. Being high on marijuana made goofing around like her friends much more fun. One night they climbed the fence surrounding the high school and spray-painted the windows black. Another time, they sneaked onto a local golf course and went skinny-dipping in the pond. However, a neighbor called the police, and Kendra, Dylan, and their friends were arrested for trespassing and possession of alcohol and drugs.

1. What might you discern about Kendra's physical development, relative to her peers? What role might physical development play in Kendra's behavior?

2. How might neurological development account for some of Kendra's behavior?

3. What role might cognitive factors, such as cognitive development, adolescent egocentrism, and decision capacities, play?

4. Does moral development have a role in Kendra's behavior? Why or why not?

⑤SAGE edge™

Visit **edge.sagepub.com/kuther2e** to help you accomplish your coursework goals in an easy-to-use learning environment.

LEARNING OBJECTIVES	SUMMARY	KEY TERMS	IN REVIEW
11.1 Evaluate the storm and stress perspective on adolescence in light of research evidence.	G. Stanley Hall theorized that adolescence entails a universal and inevitable upheaval triggered by puberty. Although the basis of Hall's argument has been debunked, his storm and stress view remains popular. Developmental scientists today reject the notion that adolescence is a period of extreme storm and stress, replacing it with a more nuanced view that adolescence is a time of change characterized by individual differences in how this change is experienced.		How did G. Stanley Hall describe adolescence? What does contemporary research reveal about the accuracy of the storm and stress perspective? Describe influences on adolescents' moods.
11.2 Summarize the physical changes that occur with puberty and the correlates of pubertal timing.	The most noticeable signs of pubertal maturation are the growth spurt and the development of secondary sex characteristics, such as breast development, deepening of the voice, growth of body hair, and changes in the skin. During puberty, the primary sex characteristics, the reproductive organs, grow larger and mature, and adolescents become capable of reproduction. Pubertal timing is influenced by genetic and contextual factors. Early maturation poses challenges for both boys and girls, with more dramatic effects for girls. The consequences of early and late maturation differ dramatically for girls and boys.	Puberty Testosterone Estrogen Adolescent growth spurt Secondary sex characteristics Primary sex characteristics Menarche Spermarche Secular trend Delayed phase preference	Give examples of primary and secondary sex characteristics. What influences pubertal timing? Describe effects of experiencing puberty early or late relative to peers. How does puberty influence sleep?
11.3 Discuss brain development during adolescence and its effect on behavior.	Changes in the volume of the cortex, interconnections among neurons, and myelination influence the speed and efficiency of thought and the capacity for executive function. According to the dual-systems model, the limbic system undergoes a burst of development well ahead of the prefrontal cortex, and this difference in development can account for many "typical" adolescent behaviors. Changes in the balance of neurotransmitters that are associated with impulsivity and reward salience shift influencing adolescent engagement in risky behavior.	Dual-systems model Limbic system	What key changes in brain development occur in adolescence? What is the dual-process model? How does the dual-systems model account for adolescent behavior?
11.4 Identify ways in which thinking changes in adolescence and how these changes are reflected in adolescent decision making and behavior.	Adolescents become capable of formal operational reasoning permitting hypothetical–deductive reasoning and the use of propositional logic. Research suggests that formal operational reasoning does not suddenly appear in early adolescence, but instead, cognitive change occurs gradually from childhood on. Adolescents' advances in cognition are the result of improvements in information processing capacities, such as attention, memory, knowledge base, response inhibition, strategy use, speed, and metacognition.	Formal operational reasoning Hypothetical–deductive reasoning Adolescent egocentrism Imaginary audience Personal fable	What is formal operational reasoning, and how has it been criticized? How do attention, working memory, and metacognition contribute to advances in adolescent thinking? How does adolescent egocentrism develop? Compare adolescent and adult decision making.
11.5 Discuss moral development and influences on moral reasoning.	In adolescence, we become capable of demonstrating postconventional reasoning. Research has confirmed that individuals proceed through the first four stages of moral reasoning in a slow, gradual, and predictable fashion, but few people advance beyond Stage 4 moral reasoning. Social interactions offer important opportunities for the development of moral reasoning. Moral reasoning is only moderately related with behavior. Cross-cultural studies of Kohlberg's theory show that the sequence appears in all cultures but that cultures differ in the degree to which they value the individual or the collective.	Care orientation Justice orientation	What is postconventional moral reasoning? How do social contexts contribute to moral development? How does culture influence moral reasoning? How well does moral reasoning predict moral behavior?

| 11.6 Describe the challenges that school transitions pose for adolescents and the role of parents in academic achievement. | Many students experience school transitions as stressful, and academic motivation and achievement often decline. Poor stage–environment fit—the mismatch of adolescents' changing developmental needs with school resources—contributes to the challenges of school transitions. Authoritative parenting, parent involvement in the school, and close parent–adolescent relationships are important buffers to academic motivation and performance from childhood through adolescence for young people at all socioeconomic levels. | | What are some common challenges associated with school transitions?

How can parents and teachers promote adjustment?

What are risk factors for school dropout?

How can parents promote academic motivation and performance? |

PRACTICE AND APPLY WHAT YOU'VE LEARNED

▶ edge.sagepub.com/kuther2e

CHECK YOUR COMPREHENSION ON THE STUDY SITE WITH:

- **Diagnostic Quizzes** to identify opportunities for improvement.

- **Multimedia Resources** that explore chapter content using media and current events.

- **Journal Articles** that support and expand on chapter concepts.

Alys Tomlinson / Taxi / via Getty Im

12 Socioemotional Development in Adolescence

"I'm a walking contradiction," declares 15-year-old Casey. "I'm shy but also outgoing, kind but sometimes I want to be mean. I don't know what I want to do with my life. I'd like to go away to college, but I don't want to leave my friends. I think protecting the environment is important, and I want to make a difference in the world. But what does that mean for me? I guess I'm still figuring myself out," Casey concludes. She

has summed up much of the socioemotional task of adolescence: figuring yourself out. Specifically, adolescents construct a sense of self and identity, an understanding of who they are and who they hope to be. Adolescents' attempts at self-definition and discovery are influenced by their relationships with parents and peers, relationships that become more complex during the adolescent years.

Learning Objectives

12.1 Summarize the processes by which self-concept, self-esteem, and identity change during adolescence.

12.2 Discuss the nature of parent–child relationships in adolescence.

12.3 Examine the developmental progression of peer relations in adolescence.

12.4 Analyze patterns of adolescent sexual activity, including sexual orientation.

12.5 Identify common psychological and behavioral problems in adolescence.

Digital Resources

Explore: The Male Adolescent Identity Crisis

Watch: Family Conflict and Puberty

Connect: Teens and Peer Pressure
▶ **Lives in Context Video 12.1:** Friendships

Watch: Abstinence-Only Education
▶ **Lives in Context Video 12.2:** Transgender Youth

Explore: Parenting Style and Delinquency

PSYCHOSOCIAL DEVELOPMENT: THE CHANGING SELF

» LO 12.1 Summarize the processes by which self-concept, self-esteem, and identity change during adolescence.

Adolescents spend a great deal of time reflecting on themselves and engaging in introspective activities, such as writing in journals, composing poetry, and posting messages, photos, and videos about their lives on social media. These activities might seem self-indulgent, but they are a means of working on an important developmental task: forming a sense of self. During adolescence, we undergo advances in self-concept and identity.

Self-Concept

A more complex, differentiated, and organized self-concept emerges in adolescence (Harter, 2012a). Adolescents use multiple, abstract, and complex labels to describe themselves (e.g., witty, intelligent). As young people recognize that their feelings, attitudes, and behaviors may change with the situation, they begin to use qualifiers in their self-descriptions

(e.g., "I'm sort of shy"). Adolescents' awareness of the situational variability in their psychological and behavioral qualities is evident in statements such as, "I'm assertive in class, speaking out and debating my classmates, but I'm quieter with my friends. I don't want to stir up trouble." Many young adolescents find these inconsistencies confusing and wonder who they really are, contributing to their challenge of forming a balanced and consistent sense of self.

Adolescents' views of themselves reflect but also influence their behavior. For example, young adolescents' academic self-concept predicts their academic achievement in middle adolescence (Preckel, Niepel, Schneider, & Brunner, 2013). Adolescents identify a self that they aspire to be, the *ideal self,* which is characterized by traits that they value. Adjustment is influenced by the match between the *actual self*—the adolescents' personal characteristics—and their aspirational, ideal self. Mismatches between ideal and actual selves are associated with poor school grades, low self-esteem, and symptoms of depression (Ferguson, Hafen, & Laursen, 2010; Stevens, Lovejoy, & Pittman, 2014). In addition, adolescents who show poor stability or consistency in their self-descriptions tend to experience higher rates of depressive and anxiety symptoms throughout adolescence (Van Dijk et al., 2014).

Self-Esteem

The overall evaluation of self-worth, known as **global self-esteem,** tends to decline at about 11 years of age, reaching its lowest point at about 12 or 13 years of age, and then rises (Orth, 2017). This pattern is true for both boys and girls, with girls tending to show lower self-esteem (von Soest, Wichstrøm, & Kvalem, 2016). Declines in global self-esteem are likely due to the multiple transitions that young adolescents undergo, such as body changes and the emotions that accompany those changes, as well as adolescents' self-comparisons to their peers (Schaffhuser, Allemand, & Schwarz, 2017). Although school transitions are often associated with temporary declines in self-esteem, most adolescents view themselves more positively as they progress from early adolescence through the high school years (von Soest et al., 2016). For example, comparisons of adolescents in Grades 8, 10, and 12 reveal higher ratings of self-esteem with age for European American, African American, Asian American, and Latino youth (Bachman, O'Malley, Freedman-Doan, Trzesniewski, & Donnellan, 2011). Self-esteem tends to rise again from late adolescence and emerging adulthood through middle adulthood (Bleidorn et al., 2016).

As self-conceptions become more differentiated, so do self-evaluations. Adolescents describe and evaluate themselves overall, as well as in specific areas, such as academics, athletic ability, and social competence (Harter, 2012b). Adolescents develop a positive sense of self-esteem when they evaluate themselves favorably in the areas that they view as important. For example, sports accomplishments are more closely associated with physical self-esteem in adolescent athletes, who tend to highly value physical athleticism. Nonathletes tend to place less importance on athleticism (Wagnsson, Lindwall, & Gustafsson, 2014). Similarly, adolescents with high academic self-esteem tend to spend more time and effort on schoolwork, view academics as

more important, and continue to demonstrate high academic achievement (Preckel et al., 2013).

Whereas favorable self-evaluations are associated with positive adjustment and sociability in adolescents of all socioeconomic status and ethnic groups, persistently low self-esteem is associated with adjustment difficulties that can continue throughout the lifespan (Orth, 2017). For example, one longitudinal study assessed self-esteem annually in over 1,500 adolescents ages 12 to 16 years and found that both level and change in self-esteem predicted depression at age 16 and also two decades later, at age 35 (Steiger, Allemand, Robins, & Fend, 2014). Those who entered adolescence with low self-esteem and whose global or domain-specific self-esteem declined further during the adolescent years were more likely to show depression two decades later.

High-quality parent–adolescent relationships, characterized by an authoritative parenting style, are associated with greater self-worth and better adjustment in adolescents from the Netherlands, China, Australia, Germany, Italy, and the United States (Harris et al., 2015; Miconi, Moscardino, Ronconi, & Altoè, 2017; M.-T. Wang & Sheikh-Khalil, 2016; Wouters, Doumen, Germeijs, Colpin, & Verschueren, 2013). In contrast, parent–adolescent conflict and parental feedback that is critical, inconsistent, and not contingent on behavior predict the development of poor self-esteem (M.-T. Wang et al., 2016).

Peer acceptance can buffer the negative effects of a distant relationship with parents (Birkeland, Breivik, & Wold, 2014). Adolescents who feel supported and well liked by peers tend to show high self-esteem (Vanhalst, Luyckx, Scholte, Engels, & Goossens, 2013). Positive attachments to peers predict self-esteem in adolescence and emerging adulthood and may have long-lasting effects on self-evaluations (Sánchez-Queija, Oliva, & Parra, 2017). For example, a longitudinal study that spanned two decades showed that perceived peer approval predicted self-esteem in early adolescence, and adolescent self-esteem predicted self-esteem in adulthood, at age 35 (Gruenenfelder-Steiger, Harris, & Fend, 2016).

Identity

As adolescents come to understand their characteristics, they begin to construct an **identity,** a sense of self that is coherent and consistent over time (Erikson, 1950). According to Erikson, to establish a sense of identity, individuals must consider their past and future and determine a sense of their values, beliefs, and goals with regard to vocation, politics, religion, and sexuality. **Identity achievement** represents the successful resolution of this process,

After a drop in early adolescence, self-esteem tends to rise from middle to late adolescence.
iStock/Rawpixel

Some adolescents learn about different religions and explore their religious beliefs as part of their identity search.
iStock/FatCamera

establishing a coherent sense of self after exploring a range of possibilities.

Adolescents are best positioned to construct an identity when they experience what Erikson referred to as a **psychosocial moratorium,** which is a timeout period that gives adolescents the opportunity to explore possibilities of whom they might become. A psychosocial moratorium provides more freedom and independence than childhood but is without the full responsibilities of adulthood. Adolescents might sample careers, consider becoming an actor one week and a lawyer the next, or explore personalities and desires. Some adolescents examine their religion more closely and consider their own beliefs, perhaps learning about other religions. Young people who successfully engage in this process emerge with a sense of identity—an understanding of who they are and where they are going. The unsuccessful resolution of the identity search is confusion, in which one withdraws from the world, isolating oneself from loved ones, parents, and peers. Erikson's ideas about identity have influenced thinking in this area for the past half century, and researchers have devised ways of measuring identity, permitting his ideas to be tested.

Identity Statuses

"Wearing black again?" Rose sighs. Her daughter, Stephanie, retorts, "How can anyone wear too much black?" Rose wonders where last year's preppy girl went and hopes that Stephanie will lose interest in wearing goth attire. Stephanie's changing styles of dress reflect her struggle with figuring out who she is—her identity. Researchers classify individuals' progress in identity development into four categories known as **identity status,** the degree to which individuals have explored possible selves and whether they have committed to specific beliefs and goals (Marcia, 1966).

Table 12.1 summarizes four identity statuses, or categories, describing a person's identity development. The least mature status is **identity diffusion** (not having explored or committed to a sense of self), characterized by pervasive uncertainty with little motive for resolution (Berzonsky & Kuk, 2000; Boyes & Chandler, 1992). Individuals who are in the **identity foreclosed** status have prematurely chosen an identity without having engaged in exploration; they tend to be inflexible and view the world in black and white, right and wrong terms. The *moratorium status* involves an active exploration of ideas and a sense of openness to possibilities, coupled with some uncertainty. As the uncertainty is experienced as discomfort, young people are highly motivated to seek resolution and reduce the discomfort. The fourth category, **identity achievement status**, requires that individuals construct a sense of self through reflection, critical examination, and exploring or trying out new ideas and belief systems and that they have formed a commitment to a particular set of ideas, values, and beliefs.

Researchers assess identity status by administering interview and survey measures (Årseth, Kroger, Martinussen, & Marcia, 2009). Young people typically shift among identity statuses over the adolescent years, but the specific pattern of identity development varies among adolescents (Meeus, 2011). The most common shifts in identity status are from the least mature statuses, identity diffusion and identity foreclosure, to the most mature statuses, moratorium and achievement, in middle and late adolescence (Al-Owidha, Green, & Kroger, 2009; Yip, 2014). The overall proportion of young people in the moratorium status tends to increase during adolescence, peaking at about age 19 and declining over emerging adulthood as young people gradually commit to identities (Kroger, Martinussen, & Marcia, 2010). People form a sense of identity in many different realms within both the ideological (i.e., occupation, religion, and politics) and interpersonal domains (i.e., friendships and dating) (Grotevant, Thorbecke, & Meyer, 1982). Many adolescents experience daily shifts in identity certainty that accompany shifts in circumstances and moods (Becht et al., 2016).

Although Erikson emphasized identity development as a task for adolescence, researchers today believe that emerging adulthood, particularly the college years, is an important time for identity development (Arnett, 2015). As we will discuss in Chapter 13, the cognitive development that most emerging adults experience in college enables them to consider themselves and their roles in new ways, which contributes to a more complex integrated sense of self. Exposure to new environments and diverse

TABLE 12.1

Identity Status

		COMMITMENT	
		PRESENT	**ABSENT**
EXPLORATION	**PRESENT**	**Identity Achievement** **Description:** Has committed to an identity after exploring multiple possibilities **Characteristics:** Active problem-solving style, high self-esteem, feelings of control, high moral reasoning, and positive views of work and school	**Moratorium** **Description:** Has not committed to an identity but is exploring alternatives **Characteristics:** Information-seeking, active problem-solving style, open to experience, anxiety, experimentation with alcohol or substance use
	ABSENT	**Identity Foreclosure** **Description:** Has committed to an identity without having explored multiple possibilities **Characteristics:** Avoid reflecting on their identity choice, not open to new information, especially if contradicts their position, rigid and inflexible	**Identity Diffusion** **Description:** Has neither committed to an identity nor explored alternatives **Characteristics:** Avoidance; tend to not solve personal problems in favor of letting issues decide themselves, academic difficulties, apathy, and alcohol and substance use

students, coupled with increased independence, makes the college years key for identity development. Identity is revisited and reconstructed again and again (Crocetti, 2017). Identity development continues after college. Most theorists view it as a lifelong task.

Influences on Identity Development

Just as authoritative parenting fosters the development of positive self-concept and self-esteem, it also is associated with identity achievement. When parents provide a sense of security along with autonomy, adolescents tend to explore, much as toddlers do, by using their parents as a secure base (Schwartz, Luyckx, & Crocetti, 2015; Schwartz, Zamboanga, Luyckx, Meca, & Ritchie, 2013). Adolescents who feel connected to their parents, supported, and accepted by them but who also feel that they are free and encouraged to develop and voice their own views are more likely to engage in the exploration necessary to advance to the moratorium and achieved status. In turn, as adolescents commit to identities, their relationships with parents and siblings tend to improve (Crocetti, Branje, Rubini, Koot, & Meeus, 2017). The degree of freedom that adolescents are afforded for exploration varies with family and community contextual factors, such as socioeconomic status. Adolescents from high socioeconomic status homes may have fewer responsibilities to work outside the home, may reside in communities with more extracurricular opportunities, and may be more likely to attend postsecondary education than their peers from low socioeconomic homes—all factors that support the

exploration needed for identity achievement (Kroger, 2015; Spencer, Swanson, & Harpalani, 2015).

Peers also influence identity development as they serve as a mirror in which adolescents view their emerging identities, an audience to which they relay their self-narratives (McAdams & Zapata-Gietl, 2015). When adolescents feel supported and respected by peers, they feel more comfortable exploring identity alternatives (Ragelienė, 2016). As with parents, conflict with peers harms identity development as adolescents often feel less free to explore identity alternatives and lack a supportive peer group to offer input on identity alternatives, which holds negative implications for identity development, such as identity foreclosure or diffusion (S. P. Hall & Brassard, 2008).

Outcomes Associated With Identity Development

Identity achievement is associated with high self-esteem, a mature sense of self, feelings of control, high moral reasoning, and positive views of work and school (Jespersen, Kroger, & Martinussen, 2013; Spencer et al., 2015). In contrast, young people in the moratorium status often feel puzzled by the many choices before them (Lillevoll, Kroger, & Martinussen, 2013). Sorting through and determining commitments in the educational and relationship domains is stressful and is associated with negative mood and, at its extreme, can be paralyzing and curtail identity exploration (Crocetti, Klimstra, Keijsers, Hale Iii, & Meeus, 2009; Klimstra et al., 2016). Young people who show identity foreclosure tend to take a rigid and inflexible stance.

Unopen to new experiences, they avoid reflecting on their identity choice and reject information that may contradict their position.

Finally, while it is developmentally appropriate for early adolescents to have neither explored nor committed to a sense of identity, by late adolescence, identity diffusion is uncommon and has been considered indicative of maladjustment (Kroger et al., 2010). Young people in identity diffusion keep life on hold; they don't seek the meaning-making experiences needed to form a sense of identity (Carlsson, Wängqvist, & Frisén, 2016). Young people who show identity diffusion tend to use a cognitive style that is characterized by avoidance. Academic difficulties, general apathy, organization and time management problems, and alcohol and substance abuse are associated with identity diffusion and often precede it (Crocetti, Klimstra, Hale, Koot, & Meeus, 2013; Laghi, Baiocco, Lonigro, & Baumgartner, 2013).

Ethnic Identity

An important aspect of identity is **ethnic identity,** or a sense of membership to an ethnic group, including the attitudes, values, and culture associated with that group (whether Latino, Asian American, African American, White, etc.) (Phinney & Ong, 2007; Rivas-Drake et al., 2014; Umaña-Taylor et al., 2014). Some researchers instead refer to *ethnic-racial identity*, which includes both the aspect of identity that is based on one's ethnic heritage and the aspect based on one's racial group in a specific sociohistorical context (Umaña-Taylor, 2016). Ethnic identity emerges when children begin to identify and categorize themselves and others according to ethnic and racial labels.

Like other aspects of identity, the process of ethnic identity development involves exploring one's sense of self and internalizing values from one's ethnic group (Hughes, Del Toro, & Way, 2017).

Adolescents can develop a strong sense of ethnic identity by learning about their cultural heritage, including the language, customs, and shared history.
David McNew/Getty Images

Adolescents might explore their ethnic identity by learning about the cultural practices associated with their ethnicity by reading, attending cultural events, and talking to members of their culture (Romero, Edwards, Fryberg, & Orduña, 2014). As adolescents develop a sense of belonging to their cultural community, they may become committed to an ethnic identity. However, negative ethnic and racial stereotypes, discrimination, and inequality often pose challenges to developing a positive sense of ethnic identity development (McLean, Syed, Way, & Rogers, 2015).

Adolescents from a variety of racial and ethnic groups, both native born and immigrant, often report experiences of discrimination that are associated with low self-esteem, depression, poor social competence, and behavior problems (Mrick & Mrtorell, 2011; Rivas-Drake et al., 2014). Some ethnic minority adolescents perceive discrimination in the classroom, such as feeling that their teachers call on them less or grade or discipline them more harshly than other students. Discrimination at school has negative consequences for grades, academic self-concept, and school engagement, as well as adjustment and ethnic identity (Dotterer, McHale, & Crouter, 2009; Galliher, Jones, & Dahl, 2011). Minority adolescents often must manage confusing messages to embrace their heritage while confronting discrimination, making the path to exploring and achieving ethnic identity challenging and painful (McLean, Syed, Way, & Rogers, 2015).

A strong positive sense of ethnic identity can reduce the magnitude of the effects of racial discrimination on self-concept, academic achievement, and problem behaviors among African American, Latino, and multiracial adolescents, as well as act as a buffer to stress, including discrimination stress (Douglass & Umaña-Taylor, 2016; Romero et al., 2014; Zapolski, Fisher, Banks, Hensel, & Barnes-Najor, 2017). Adolescents who have achieved a strong sense of ethnic identity tend to have high self-esteem, optimism, and effective coping strategies, and they view their ethnicity positively (Douglass & Umaña-Taylor, 2017; Gonzales-Backen, Bámaca-Colbert, & Allen, 2016; J. L. Williams, Aiyer, Durkee, & Tolan, 2014). Ethnic identity is an important contributor to well-being. Adolescents from Mexican, Chinese, Latino, African American, and European heritage and with a strong sense of ethnic identity tend to show better adjustment and coping skills as well as having fewer academic, emotional, and behavior problems than do those who do not or only weakly identify with ethnicity (Miller-Cotto & Byrnes, 2016; Mrick & Mrtorell, 2011; Umaña-Taylor, 2016).

What fosters ethnic identity development? The exploration and commitment process that is key to identity achievement also underlies establishment of a sense of ethnic identity (Yip, 2014). The family is a particularly important context for ethnic identity formation, as close and warm relationships with parents are associated with more well-developed ethnic identities (Umaña-Taylor et al., 2014). Parents who provide positive ethnic socialization messages promote ethnic identity (Douglass & Umaña-Taylor, 2016). In contrast, adolescents who perceive excessive parental pressure and restrictions might respond with rebellion and rejection of ethnic heritage. Adolescents who learn about their culture, such as values, attitudes, language, and traditions, and regularly interact with parents and peers as members of a cultural community are more likely to construct a favorable ethnic identity (Romero et al., 2014; R. M. B. White, Knight, Jensen, & Gonzales, 2018). For example, ethnic identity is positively associated with an adolescent's proficiency in speaking his or her heritage language (Oh & Fuligni, 2010).

Similar to other aspects of development, perception matters. Adolescents' perception of their ethnic socialization—their view of the degree to which they adopt the customs and values of their culture—predicts ethnic identity rather than simply following their parents' views (Hughes, Hagelskamp, Way, & Foust, 2009). Likewise, among African American adolescents, high levels of peer acceptance and popularity among African American peers are associated with a strong sense of ethnic identity (Rivas-Drake et al., 2014; Rock, Cole, Houshyar, Lythcott, & Prinstein, 2011). Adolescents' perceptions of their ethnicity and ethnic groups are influenced by multiple layers of a dynamic ecological system, including families, schools, and peers, as well as the political social and economic climate (Way, Santos, Niwa, & Kim-Gervey, 2008).

Ethnic identity continues to influence adjustment in adulthood (Syed et al., 2013). Ethnic identity becomes integrated with and interacts with other domains of identity, such as gender, career, and relationship, to create a coherent overall identity (Umaña-Taylor et al., 2014).

The accompanying Cultural Influences on Development feature discusses the element of gender and the stereotypes that appear in all cultures.

CULTURAL INFLUENCES ON DEVELOPMENT

 ## Cultural Views of Gender

Most cultures specify gender roles for men and women. What are the expectations for men and women in your culture?
iStock/fstop123

Gender stereotypes appear in all cultures, but they vary in intensity, prominence, and developmental trajectory (Guimond, Chatard, & Lorenzi-Cioldi, 2013; Kapadia & Gala, 2015). For example, longitudinal research with African American youth found that young girls and boys show knowledge of gender stereotypes, but from ages 9 to 15, they show declines in traditional gender attitudes that level off through age 18 (Lam, Stanik, & McHale, 2017). Traditional attitudes in mothers, but not fathers, predict stereotyped attitudes in children. European American

youth show a similar pattern. Yet the magnitude of change may vary with ethnicity. Research has suggested that African American men and women are equally likely to endorse typically masculine traits as compared with European Americans, in which males are more likely to describe themselves with masculine traits than are women (A. C. Harris, 1996).

In Mexican American families, the traditional role of the female is to care for the children and take care of the home and males are expected to provide for the family (Cauce & Domenech-Rodríguez, 2002). These differences are related to the concept of machismo, which incorporates many traditional expectations of the male gender role, such as being unemotional, strong, authoritative, and aggressive. Yet gender differences in Mexican American males and females may be declining as women are increasingly providing for the family by working outside the home as well as sharing in decision making in the family. As families become more acculturated to the United States, Mexican American mothers and fathers tend to endorse more gender-egalitarian attitudes, reporting attitudes favoring similar treatment of boys and girls (Leaper & Valin, 1996).

One longitudinal study examined the role of acculturation in Mexican American adolescents' views of gender roles. Mexican American adolescents born in Mexico and the United States were followed from ages 13 to 20 (Updegraff et al., 2014). Among the adolescents born in Mexico, girls showed declines in traditional attitudes from early to late adolescence, but males' attitudes were stable over time. U.S.-born males and females did not differ in their traditional gender attitude trajectories, with both declining over time. Mexico-born adolescents' likely greater exposure to Mexican culture, wherein attitudes about men's and women's roles are generally quite traditional, may influence their views of gender roles (Cauce & Domenech-Rodríguez, 2002). Yet in this study, only Mexico-born males maintained their traditional gender role attitudes across adolescence (Updegraff et al., 2014). In addition, the differences in Mexico-born males' versus females' trajectories suggested that males may be less influenced by acculturation processes,

which are expected to lead to less traditional gender role attitudes. One possibility is that traditional gender role values in Mexican American families are advantageous for males, as Latino culture traditionally awards status and privilege (e.g., freedom to spend time outside the home) and fewer responsibilities (e.g., less involvement in housework) for adolescent and young adult males (Raffaelli & Ontai, 2004).

What Do You Think?

What gender-related values are evident within your culture or context, such as race, ethnicity, religion, or even neighborhood or part of the world? What are the accepted roles for men and women? Are gender roles changing over time in your context? ●

THINKING IN CONTEXT 12.1

1. An important theme of development is that domains or types of development interact and influence each other. How might this hold true for the development of a sense of self and identity? How might other areas of development influence how adolescents view themselves? For example, consider aspects of physical development, such as puberty, and cognitive development, such as reasoning.

2. Identify contextual influences on the development of a sense of self and identity. In what ways do interactions with contextual influences, such as parents, peers, school, community, and societal forces, shape adolescents' emerging sense of self?

3. Consider your own sense of ethnic identity. Is ethnicity an important part of your sense of self? Why or why not? Have you experienced shifts in your experience of ethnicity from childhood to adulthood?

ADOLESCENTS AND THEIR FAMILIES

» LO 12.2 Discuss the nature of parent–child relationships in adolescence.

From middle childhood into adolescence, parents must adapt their parenting strategies to children's increased ability to reason and their desire for independence. Adolescence marks a change in parent–child relationships. As they advance cognitively and develop a more complicated sense of self, adolescents strive for autonomy, the ability

to make and carry out their own decisions, and they decreasingly rely on parents. Physically, adolescents appear more mature. They also can demonstrate better self-understanding and more rational decision making and problem solving, creating a foundation for parents to treat adolescents less like children and grant them more decision-making responsibility. The parenting challenge of adolescence is to offer increasing opportunities for adolescents to develop and practice autonomy while providing protection from danger and the consequences of poor decisions (Kobak, Abbott, Zisk, & Bounoua, 2017). Parents may doubt their own importance to their adolescent children, but a large body of research shows that parents play a critical role in adolescent development alongside that of peers.

Parent–Adolescent Conflict

Julio's mother orders, "Clean your room," but Julio snaps back, "It's my room. I can have it my way!" Conflict between parents and adolescents tends to rise in early adolescence as adolescents begin to seek autonomy and begin to recognize that their parents are fallible and are capable of good and bad decisions. Conflict peaks in middle adolescence and declines from middle to late adolescence and emerging adulthood as young people become more independent and begin to better understand their parents as people (Branje, Laursen, & Collins, 2013). For example, in one longitudinal study, about 14% of participants reported turbulent relationships with parents characterized by low support and high conflict in early adolescence (age 12), rising to 29% at about age 16 and declining to 10% by around age 20 (Hadiwijaya, Klimstra, Vermunt, Branje, & Meeus, 2017). Most teenagers had the same type of relationship with their parents throughout

Parent-child conflict tends to peak in middle adolescence but it is usually over mundane issues, such as housework. Most adolescents report having warm and supportive relationships with their parents.
iStock/Sunlight19

adolescence. Although conflict rises during early adolescence, the majority of adolescents and parents continue to have warm, close, communicative relationships characterized by love and respect.

Parent-adolescent conflict is generally innocuous bickering over mundane matters: small arguments over the details of life, such as household responsibilities, privileges, relationships, curfews, cleaning of the adolescent's bedroom, choices of media, or music volume (Van Doorn, Branje, & Meeus, 2011). Conflicts over religious, political, or social issues occur less frequently, as do conflicts concerning other potentially sensitive topics (e.g., substance use, dating, sexual relationships) (Renk, Liljequist, Simpson, & Phares, 2005). Adolescents report having three or four conflicts or disagreements with parents over the course of a typical day, but they also report having one or two conflicts with friends (Adams & Laursen, 2007).

Severe parent-adolescent conflict occurs in some families. Like many aspects of development, there tends to be continuity in parenting and parent-child relationships (Huey, Hiatt, Laursen, Burk, & Rubin, 2017). Patterns of harsh verbal discipline (yelling, threatening, punishment, shaming) and insensitive parenting established in early childhood tend to persist and worsen in middle childhood and adolescence (Lansford, Staples, Bates, Pettit, & Dodge, 2013). Frequent arguments charged with negative emotion are harmful to adolescents (Huey et al., 2017). In adolescents of all ethnicities—African American, Latino, Asian, and White—parent-adolescent conflict is associated with internalizing problems such as depression, externalizing problems such as aggression and delinquency, and social problems such as social withdrawal and poor conflict resolution with peers, poor school achievement, and, among girls, early

sexual activity (Hofer et al., 2013; Moreno, Janssen, Cox, Colby, & Jackson, 2017; Skinner & McHale, 2016; Weymouth, Buehler, Zhou, & Henson, 2016).

Some conflict is conducive to adolescent development, helping adolescents learn to regulate emotions and resolve conflicts (Branje, 2018). Developmentally supportive conflict is coupled with acceptance, respect, and autonomy support.

Parenting

Parenting plays a large role in the development of autonomy during adolescence. As Romana explains, "My parents have rules. I hate some of those rules. But I know that my parents will always be there for me. If I needed to, I could tell them anything. They might be mad, but they'll always help me." Romana describes the most positive form of parenting, authoritative parenting. Recall from Chapter 8 that authoritative parenting is characterized by warmth, support, and limits. Across ethnic and socioeconomic groups, and in countries around the world, multiple studies have found that authoritative parenting fosters autonomy, self-reliance, self-esteem, a positive view of the value of work, and academic competence in adolescents (Bornstein & Putnick, 2018; McKinney & Renk, 2011; Uji, Sakamoto, Adachi, & Kitamura, 2013). Parental support and acceptance, as characterized by authoritative parenting, are associated with reduced levels of depression, psychological disorders, and behavior problems (Pinquart, 2017). Authoritative parents' use of open discussion, joint decision making, and firm but fair limit setting helps adolescents feel valued, respected, and encouraged to think for themselves. Parents in a given household often share a common parenting style, but when they do not, the presence of authoritative parenting in at least one parent buffers the negative outcomes associated with the other style and predicts positive adjustment (Hoeve, Dubas, Gerris, van der Laan, & Smeenk, 2011). Generally, emotional support by parents tends to increase and psychological control continues to decline during emerging adulthood (Desjardins & Leadbeater, 2017).

In contrast, authoritarian parenting, which emphasizes psychological control and punishment (e.g., "my way or the highway"), is much less successful in promoting healthy adjustment (Milevsky, 2016). Psychological control inhibits the development of autonomy and has been found to be linked with low self-esteem, depression, low academic competence, and antisocial behavior in adolescence through early adulthood in young people from Africa, Asia, Europe, the Middle East, and the Americas (Bornstein & Putnick, 2018; Griffith & Grolnick, 2013;

Lansford, Laird, Pettit, Bates, & Dodge, 2014; Uji et al., 2013). Moreover, it is adolescents' perceptions of negative or controlling parenting behavior, not parents' own views, that predict behavior problems (Dimler, Natsuaki, Hastings, Zahn-Waxler, & Klimes-Dougan, 2017). Finally, similar to findings with children, as discussed in Chapter 8, adolescents reared in permissive homes are more likely to show immaturity, have difficulty with self-control, and conform to peers (Hoeve et al., 2011).

Parental Monitoring

One way in which parents balance autonomy granting with protection is through parental monitoring, being aware of their teens' whereabouts and companions. **Parental monitoring** is associated with overall well-being in adolescents, including academic achievement, delayed sexual initiation, and low levels of substance use and delinquent activity in youth of all ethnicities (Ethier, Harper, Hoo, & Dittus, 2016; Lopez-Tamayo, LaVome Robinson, Lambert, Jason, & Ialongo, 2016; Malczyk & Lawson, 2017). Effective parental monitoring is accompanied by warmth and is balanced with respect for adolescents' autonomy and privacy. When parents monitor too closely, such that adolescents feel they are intrusive, adolescents are likely to conceal their activities from their parents and continue to do so at least 1 year later (Rote & Smetana, 2016).

Adolescents' views of the warmth and control provided by their parents are linked with their psychological adjustment, including conduct, emotional symptoms, and peer relations (Maynard & Harding, 2010). What is considered effective parental monitoring changes as adolescents grow older. From middle to late adolescence, parental knowledge declines as adolescents establish a private sphere and disclose less as parents exert less control (Masche, 2010; Wang, Dishion, Stormshak, & Willett, 2011). Overall, parenting entails a delicate balance of warmth and support, monitoring, and limit setting and enforcement—no easy task indeed.

THINKING IN CONTEXT 12.2

1. In what ways might physical and cognitive development influence adolescents' interactions with their parents and, especially, parent–adolescent conflict?

2. Compare and contrast popular views of parent–child relationships in adolescence with the research on parenting style and parental monitoring.

ADOLESCENTS AND THEIR PEERS

» LO 12.3 Examine the developmental progression of peer relations in adolescence.

The most easily recognizable influence on adolescents, and that which gets the most attention from adults and the media, is the peer group. Each week, adolescents spend up to one third of their waking, nonschool hours with friends (Hartup & Stevens, 1997).

Friendships

The typical adolescent has four to six close friends (French & Cheung, 2018). Adolescent friendships are characterized by intimacy, self-disclosure, trust, and loyalty (Bowker & Ramsay, 2016). Adolescents expect their friends to be there for them, stand up for them, and not share their secrets or harm them.

Most adolescents report having several close friendships that are characterized by trust, intimacy, loyalty, and companionship.
mauritius images GmbH / Alamy Stock Photo

Adolescent friendships tend to include cooperation, sharing, intimacy, and affirmation, which reflect their emerging capacities for perspective taking, social sensitivity, empathy, and social skills (Poulin & Chan, 2010).

Adolescent boys get together for activities, usually sports and competitive games, and tend to be more social and vocal in groups as compared with one-on-one situations. Boys tend to excel at being fun companions, coping with a friend who violates an expectation, and sustaining friendships within the context of having other friends (Rose & Asher, 2017). In contrast, most girls tend to prefer one-on-one interactions and often spend their time together talking, sharing thoughts and feelings, and supporting each other. Overall, girls' friendships tend to be shorter in duration, but characterized by more closeness, than are those of boys (Erdley & Day, 2017). High-quality friendships characterized by sharing, intimacy, and open communication tend to endure over time (Hiatt, Laursen, Mooney, & Rubin, 2015). Among early adolescents, it is estimated that one third to one half of friendships are unstable, with young people regularly losing friends and making new friendships (Poulin & Chan, 2010). After early adolescence, friendships become more stable, with young people retaining the majority of their friendships over the course of a school year.

As in childhood, similarity characterizes adolescent friendships. Friends tend to be similar in demographics, such as age, ethnicity, and socioeconomic status (Bowker & Ramsay, 2016). Close friends and best friends tend to be similar in orientation toward risky activity, such as willingness to try drugs and engage in delinquency and dangerous behaviors such as unprotected sex (de Water, Burk, Cillessen, & Scheres, 2016; Hiatt, Laursen, Stattin, & Kerr, 2017; Scalco, Trucco, Coffman, & Colder, 2015). Adolescent friends tend to share interests, such as tastes in music; they are also similar in academic achievement, educational aspirations, and political beliefs; and they show similar trends in psychosocial development, such as identity status (Markiewicz & Doyle, 2016; Shin & Ryan, 2014). Through interaction, friends tend to become even more similar to each other (Scalco et al., 2015). An important predictor of friendship stability in adolescence is similarity. In one study, adolescent friend *dyads,* or pairs, who differed in peer acceptance, physical aggression, and school competence in seventh grade were more likely to dissolve their friendship during high school than were dyads who were more similar (Hartl, Laursen, & Cillessen, 2015).

Sometimes, however, middle and older adolescents choose friends who are different from them, which encourages them to consider new perspectives. Cross-ethnic friendships, for example, are less common than same-ethnic friendships but are associated with unique benefits. Adolescent members of cross-ethnic friendships show decreases in racial prejudice over time (Titzmann, Brenick, & Silbereisen, 2015). Ethnic minority adolescents with cross-ethnic friends perceive less discrimination, vulnerability, and relational victimization and show higher rates of self-esteem and well-being over time than those without cross-ethnic friends (Bagci, Rutland, Kumashiro, Smith, & Blumberg, 2014; Graham, Munniksma, & Juvonen, 2014; Kawabata & Crick, 2011).

Close and stable friendships aid adolescents in their social adjustment (French & Cheung, 2018). By communicating with others and forming mutually self-disclosing supportive relationships, adolescents develop perspective taking, empathy, self-concept, and a sense of identity. Friends who are supportive and empathetic encourage prosocial behavior, promote psychological health, reduce the risk of delinquency, and help adolescents manage stress, such as the challenges of school transitions (Hiatt et al., 2015; Wentzel, 2014). Friendship continues to have positive benefits, and the nature of friendship continues to change in emerging adulthood and early adulthood (Miething, Almquist, Edling, Rydgren, & Rostila, 2017), as discussed in Chapter 14.

Cliques and Crowds

Each day after school, Paul, Manny, and Jose go with Pete to Pete's house where they apply what they learn in their automotive class to work on each other's cars and, together, restore a classic car. During adolescence, one-on-one friendships tend to expand into tightly knit peer groups of anywhere from three to about nine but most commonly around five members who are close friends. These close-knit, friendship-based groups are known as **cliques**. Paul, Manny, Jose, and Pete have formed a clique. Like most close friends, members of cliques tend to share similarities such as demographics and attitudes (Lansford et al., 2009). The norms of expected behavior and values that govern cliques derive from interactions among the group members. For example, a norm of spending time exercising together and snacking afterward, as well as valuing health and avoiding smoking, alcohol, and drugs, may emerge in a clique whose members are athletes. Belonging to a peer group provides adolescents with a sense of inclusion, worth, support, and companionship (Ellis & Zarbatany, 2017).

In early adolescence, cliques tend to be sex segregated, with some composed of boys and others composed of girls. Girls' groups tend to be smaller than boys' groups, but both are similarly tight knit (Gest, Davidson, Rulison, Moody, & Welsh, 2007). By mid-adolescence, cliques become mixed and form the basis for dating. A mixed-sex group of friends provides opportunities for adolescents to learn how to interact with others of the opposite sex in a safe,

In early adolescence same-sex cliques are most common. Cliques of boys and girls tend to merge in middle adolescence, creating larger integrated groups.
mauritius images GmbH / Alamy Stock Photo

nonromantic context (Connolly, Craig, Goldberg, & Pepler, 2004). By late adolescence, especially after high school graduation, mixed-sex cliques tend to split up as adolescents enter college, the workforce, and other post–high school activities (Connolly & Craig, 1999).

In contrast with cliques, which are an expansion of intimate friendships, **crowds** are larger and looser groups based on shared characteristics, interests, and reputation. Rather than voluntarily "joining," adolescents are sorted into crowds by their peers. Common categories of peer groups found in Western nations include populars/elites (high in social status), athletes/jocks (athletically oriented), academics/brains (academically oriented), and partiers (highly social; care little about academics). Other types of crowds include nonconformists (unconventional in dress and music), deviants (defiant; engage in delinquent activity), and normals (not clearly distinct on any particular trait) (Delsing, ter Bogt, Engels, & Meeus, 2007; Sussman, Pokhrel, Ashmore, & Brown, 2007; Verkooijen, de Vries, & Nielsen, 2007). Populars and jocks are generally rated by adolescents as higher in social status than brains and partiers (Helms et al., 2014).

Crowd membership is based on an adolescent's image or reputation among peers (Cross & Fletcher, 2009). Members of a crowd may or may not interact with one another; however, because of similarities in appearance, activities, and perceived attitudes, their peers consider them members of the same group (Verkooijen et al., 2007). Crowds differentiate young people on the basis of behaviors such as sexual activity, academic achievement, psychiatric symptoms, and health risks such as alcohol and substance use (Jordan et al., 2018). Some adolescents may use a particular crowd as a reference group and model their behavior and appearance accordingly, but adolescents do not always accurately perceive their own crowd status (Verkooijen et al., 2007). In one study, about one half of students placed

themselves in a crowd different from that assigned by peers—generally most tended to label themselves as *normals* or as not having a crowd. Only about 20% of adolescents classified in the low-status crowds, such as *brains,* agreed with their peers on their crowd status (Brown, Bank, & Steinberg, 2008). Adolescents who did not perceive themselves as part of a low-status crowd showed higher self-esteem than did adolescents who agreed with their crowd placement.

In middle adolescence, as their cognitive and classification capacities increase, adolescents begin to classify their peers in more complex ways and hybrid crowds emerge, such as *popular-jocks* and *partier-jocks.* As with cliques, crowds decline in late adolescence, especially after young people leave high school. However, recent research suggests that college students self-identify into crowds along four dimensions: social, scholastic, athletic, and counterculture, with social and counterculture affiliation predicting drug use (Hopmeyer & Medovoy, 2017). In contrast, the most social affiliation adolescent samples, populars, tend to engage in relatively few risk behaviors (Jordan et al., 2018), suggesting that norms regarding substance use may shift from adolescence into emerging adulthood.

Peer Conformity

"Look at these shoes. They're red. Cool, huh?" asks Jamaica's mother. "No—I want the black ones," Jamaica replies. "But honey, these are so different from what everyone else has, you'll really stand out." Jamaica shakes her head. "I don't want to stand out. The shoes need to be black. That's what everyone wears." Jamaica's insistence on wearing the black shoes that all of her friends own illustrates her desire to conform to peer norms about dressing. The pressure to conform to peers rises in early adolescence, peaks at about age 14, and declines through age 18 and after (see Figure 12.1; Steinberg & Monahan, 2007).

Most adolescents perceive pressure to conform to peer norms for both positive and, in this example, negative behavior.
iStock/sturti

FIGURE 12.1

Age Differences in Resistance to Peer Influence

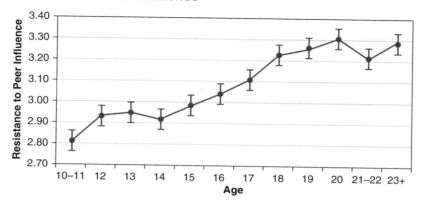

Source: Obtained with permission from Steinberg and Monahan (2007, p. 1536).

Most adolescents experience pressure to conform to peer norms. Peers tend to exert pressure to conform to day-to-day activities and personal choices such as appearance (clothing, hairstyle, makeup) and music. Adults tend to view peer pressure as a negative influence on adolescents, influencing them to behave in socially undesirable and even harmful ways. Adolescents' reporting of risky behavior such as smoking and unsafe sexual activity correlates with their peers' behaviors (Choukas-Bradley, Giletta, Widman, Cohen, & Prinstein, 2014; van de Bongardt, Reitz, Sandfort, & Deković, 2014).

It is not simply peer behavior that influences adolescent behavior, but it is adolescents' perceptions of peer behavior, as well as beliefs about peers' activity, that predict engaging in risky activities such as smoking, alcohol use, and marijuana use (Duan, Chou, Andreeva, & Pentz, 2009). In addition, adolescents naturally engage in more risk in the presence of peers, even without encouragement (van Hoorn, Crone, & van Leijenhorst, 2017). Young people vary in how they perceive and respond to peer pressure based on factors such as age, personal characteristics, and context, such as the presence of norms. Adolescents are especially vulnerable to the negative effects of peer pressure during transitions such as entering a new school and undergoing puberty (Brechwald & Prinstein, 2011) and when they are uncertain of their status in the peer group (Ellis & Zarbatany, 2017). Adolescents are more likely to conform to best friends' behavior when they share a high-quality and satisfying relationship (Hiatt et al., 2017).

Yet peer pressure is not always negative. Youths also report pressure from their friends to engage in prosocial and positive behaviors such as getting good grades, performing well athletically, getting along with parents, and avoiding smoking (Berndt & Murphy, 2002; Brown et al., 1986, 2008; Wentzel, 2014). For example, research with youths from Singapore demonstrates that peers exerted pressure on one another to conform to family and academic responsibilities—values that are particularly prized in Singapore culture (Sim & Koh, 2003). In laboratory experiments, U.S. adolescents were likely to show prosocial behavior, such as sharing coins with others, after believing that anonymous peers approved of their prosocial actions (van Hoorn, van Dijk, Meuwese, Rieffe, & Crone, 2016).

Dating

Establishing romantic relationships, dating, is part of the adolescent experience. Many young people have been involved in at least one romantic relationship by middle adolescence, and by age 18, most young people have some dating experience. By late adolescence, the majority of adolescents have been in an ongoing romantic relationship with one person (O'Sullivan, Cheng, Harris, & Brooks-Gunn, 2007).

Dating typically begins through the intermingling of mixed-sex peer groups and progresses to group dating and then one-on-one dating and romantic

Romantic relationships are common in adolescence
iStock/wundervisuals

relationships (Connolly, Nguyen, Pepler, Craig, & Jiang, 2013). Adolescents with larger social networks and greater access to opposite-sex peers date more than those who are less social. However, some research suggests that adolescents date outside of their friendship networks and that preexisting friendships are not likely to transform into romantic relationships (Kreager, Molloy, Moody, & Feinberg, 2016). Like friendship, romantic partners tend to share similarities, such as in academic achievement (Giordano, Phelps, Manning, & Longmore, 2008).

Adolescents' capacity for romantic intimacy develops slowly and is influenced by the quality of their experiences with intimacy in friendships and their attachments to parents (van de Bongardt, Yu, Deković, & Meeus, 2015). Specifically, one longitudinal study showed that attachment to parents and friendship quality at 10 years of age predicted being in a relationship and relationship quality at ages 12 and 15 (Kochendorfer & Kerns, 2017). Through romantic relationships, adolescents can learn to share, be sensitive to others' needs, and develop the capacity for intimacy. Close romantic relationships provide opportunities to develop and practice sensitivity, cooperation, empathy, and social support, as well as to aid in identity development.

In middle and late adolescence, romantic relationships are associated with positive self-concept, expectations for success in relationships, fewer feelings of alienation, and good physical and mental health (Connolly & McIsaac, 2011). However, early dating relative to peers is associated with higher rates of alcohol and substance use, smoking delinquency, and low academic competence over the adolescent years, as well as long-term depression, especially in early maturing girls (Connolly et al., 2013; Furman & Collibee, 2014).

Adolescent romantic relationships can have consequences for functioning later in life. For example, in one longitudinal study, high-quality romantic relationships at age 17 were associated with fewer externalizing problems, such as substance use and antisocial behavior, in early adulthood at ages 25 to 27 (Kansky & Allen, 2018). Poor relationships, however, predicted increased levels of anxiety and depression in early adulthood. Causality cannot be assumed. It is likely that interpersonal and developmental characteristics that led to poor relationships in adolescence also influenced poor functioning in adulthood. Romantic experiences in adolescence are often continuous with romantic experiences in adulthood, suggesting that building romantic relationships is an important developmental task for adolescents (Collins et al., 2009). Adolescents who date fewer partners and experience better-quality dating relationships in middle adolescence tend to demonstrate smoother partner interactions and relationship processes in young adulthood (e.g., negotiating conflict, appropriate caregiving) as compared with their peers who are more indiscriminate in their choice of dates (Madsen & Collins, 2011).

Dating violence, the actual or threatened physical or sexual violence or psychological abuse directed toward a current or former boyfriend, girlfriend, or dating partner, is surprisingly prevalent during adolescence. Like adult domestic violence, adolescent dating violence occurs in youth of all socioeconomic, ethnic, and religious groups (Herrman, 2009). This behavior is discussed in Lives in Context.

LIVES IN CONTEXT

 ## Adolescent Dating Violence

Many adolescents find themselves in abusive relationships, but dating violence is less likely to be reported than adult domestic violence.
iStock/stock-eye

On average, about 20% of high school students have experienced physical violence, and 9% sexual violence, within a dating relationship (Wincentak, Connolly, & Card, 2017). Both males and females perpetrate dating violence at roughly equal rates and within the context of relationships of mutual partner aggression in which both partners perpetrate and sustain the aggression (Sears, Sandra Byers, & Lisa Price, 2007; T. S. Williams, Connolly, Pepler, Laporte, & Craig, 2008). Girls are more likely to inflict psychological abuse and minor physical abuse (slapping, throwing objects, pinching), and boys are more likely to inflict more severe types of physical abuse, such as punching, as well as sexual abuse, making girls more likely to suffer physical wounds than boys. Physical violence tends to occur

(Continued)

(Continued)

alongside other problematic relationship dynamics and behaviors such as verbal conflict, jealousy, and accusations of "cheating" (Giordano, Soto, Manning, & Longmore, 2010).

Risk factors for engaging in dating violence include difficulty with anger management, poor interpersonal skills, early involvement with antisocial peers, a history of problematic relationships with parents and peers, exposure to family violence and community violence, and child maltreatment (Foshee et al., 2014, 2015; Vagi et al., 2013). Many of the risk factors for dating victimization are also outcomes of dating violence, such as depression, anxiety, negative interactions with family and friends, low self-esteem, and substance use (Exner-Cortens, Eckenrode, & Rothman, 2013; Niolon et al., 2015). Victims of dating violence in adolescence are more likely to experience intimate partner violence in adulthood.

Adolescent dating violence is less likely to be reported than adult domestic violence. Only about 1 in 11 cases is reported to adults or authorities (Herrman, 2009). In addition, only one third of adolescents report that they would intervene if they became aware of a peer's involvement in dating violence, predominately believing that dating violence is the couple's own private business (Weisz & Black, 2008). Encouraging close relationships with parents is an important way of preventing dating violence because adolescents learn about romantic relationships by observing and reflecting on the behaviors of others. Adolescent girls who are close with their parents are more likely to recognize unhealthy relationships, are less likely to be victimized by dating violence, and are more likely to seek help (Leadbeater, Banister, Ellis, & Yeung, 2008).

Developmental interventions to address adolescent dating violence are often housed within high schools. Interventions have been successful in increasing teens' awareness of dating violence, helping them to identify violence, and shifting teens' attitudes to be less supportive of violence in dating relationships (Fellmeth, Heffernan, Nurse, Habibula, & Sethi, 2013). However, school-based programs are generally not successful at reducing the incidence of violence in adolescents' dating relationships (De La Rue, Polanin, Espelage, & Pigott, 2017). It is likely that adolescents must learn skills to change their behavior. Successful interventions help adolescents build skills in regulating their emotions, communicating effectively, and resolving conflicts (Rizzo et al., 2018; Smith-Darden, Kernsmith, Reidy, & Cortina, 2017).

What Do You Think?

1. From your perspective, how prevalent is dating violence in adolescence?

2. Why do you think it occurs?

3. Why is it underreported?

4. What can be done to reduce dating violence and help victims of dating violence? ●

THINKING IN CONTEXT 12.3

1. Researchers who study peer relationships in adolescence might argue that cliques get a bad rap because common views portray cliques as harmful to adolescents. Compare the research on cliques with common views about cliques.

2. How might relationships with peers such as friends or dates vary by context? Consider an adolescent from an inner-city neighborhood and another from a rural community. In what ways might their peer interactions and relationships be similar? Different? Compare these adolescents with one from an affluent suburban community. How might contextual factors influence adolescents' peer relationships?

ADOLESCENT SEXUALITY

» LO 12.4 Analyze patterns of adolescent sexual activity, including sexual orientation.

An important dimension of socioemotional development during adolescence is sexual development, a task that entails integrating physical, cognitive, and social domains of functioning. Sexuality encompasses feelings about oneself, appraisals of the self, attitudes, and behaviors (McClelland & Tolman, 2014). With the hormonal changes of puberty, both boys and girls experience an increase in sex drive and sexual interest (Fortenberry, 2013). Social context influences how biological urges are channeled into behavior and adolescents' conceptions of sexuality.

Sexual Activity

Researchers believe that sexual behaviors tend to progress from hand-holding to kissing, to touching through clothes and under clothes, to oral sex and then to genital intercourse. However, research on adolescent sexuality tends to focus on intercourse, leaving gaps in our knowledge about the range of sexual activity milestones young people experience (Diamond & Savin-Williams, 2009). Adolescents are about as likely to engage in oral sex as vaginal intercourse (Casey Copen, Chandra, & Martinez, 2012; Lefkowitz, Vasilenko, & Leavitt, 2016). Male and female high school students show similar rates of receiving oral sex (49% and 45% of males and females, respectively) (Child Trends Databank, 2015). Oral sex does not seem to be a substitute for vaginal sex, as the majority of over 12,000 adolescents in one sample initiated oral sex after first experiencing vaginal intercourse, and about one half initiated oral sex a year or more after the onset of vaginal sex (Haydon, Herring, Prinstein, & Halpern, 2012).

Many adults are surprised to learn that the overall rate of sexual intercourse among U.S. high school students has declined from 54% in 1991 to 47% in 2013 (Kaiser Family Foundation, 2014). Overall rates of sexual activity are similar internationally, with comparable declines in recent years (Guttmacher Institute, 2014). Most young people have sexual intercourse for the first time at about age 17 (Figure 12.2) (Finer & Philbin, 2013; Guttmacher Institute, 2014). About one third of high school students report being sexually active, defined as within the previous 3 months. As shown in Figure 12.3, African American high school students are more likely to report being sexually active compared to White and Hispanic students (Child Trends Databank, 2017).

Ethnic differences in sexual activity are intertwined with the socioeconomic and contextual factors that accompany ethnicity. Early sexual activity and greater sexual experience are more common in adolescents reared in stressful contexts, such as low socioeconomic status homes and poverty-stricken and dangerous neighborhoods where community ties are weak (Carlson, McNulty, Bellair, & Watts, 2014; Warner, 2018). For example, in one study of middle school students, experiencing a direct threat of violence in the school or community predicted early sexual initiation (Coyle, Guinosso, Glassman, Anderson, & Wilson, 2017). In addition, ethnic differences in rates of pubertal maturation, with African American girls experiencing puberty earlier than other girls, influence sexual activity, as early maturation is a risk factor for early sexual activity (Carlson et al., 2014; Moore, Harden, & Mendle, 2014).

Although sexual activity is normative in late adolescence, early sexual activity, prior to age 15, is associated with problem behaviors, including alcohol and substance use, poor academic achievement, and delinquent activity, as well as having a larger number of sex partners relative to peers (McLeod & Knight, 2010). Yet a recent study suggests that the negative effects of early sexual initiation may be temporary. The researchers found that sexual initiation was associated with internalizing symptoms, such as anxiety and depression, for girls who initiated sexual activity prior to age 15, but not with boys or with teens who initiated sexual activity later. Moreover, 1 year later, there was no difference in internalizing

---

FIGURE 12.2

Sexual Initiation During Adolescence

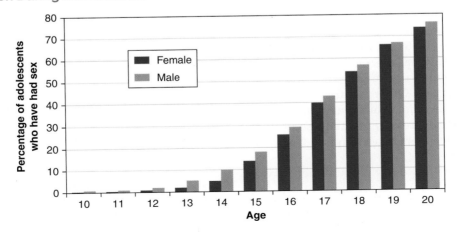

Source: Guttmacher Institute. (May 2014). American teens' sexual and reproductive health fact sheet. New York: Guttmacher Institute, http://www.guttmacher.org/pubs/FB-ATSRH.html

FIGURE 12.3

Percentage of Students in Grades 9 through 12 Who Report They Are Sexually Active, by Race and Hispanic Origin: 1991–2015

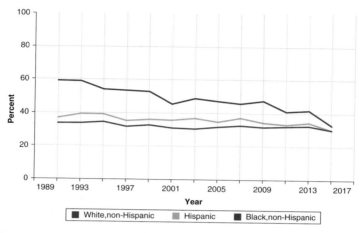

Source: Child Trends Databank, 2017.

symptoms between early and on-time sexually initiating girls, suggesting that early sexual initiation may not produce lasting detriments to girls' mental health (Wesche, Kreager, Lefkowitz, & Siennick, 2017).

In recent years, parents and health professionals have become increasingly concerned about adolescents' use of technology as tools for sexual exploration and expression. Sexting, the exchange of explicit sexual messages or images via mobile phone, is increasingly common among adolescents. Females and older youth are more likely to share sexual photos than males and younger youth. Several studies have found that sexting is associated with sexual activity, especially risky sexual activity, in adolescents as young as 13 (Rice et al., 2012; Romo et al., 2017; Ybarra & Mitchell, 2014). A sample of 1,100 Czech adolescents aged 10 to 18 suggested that sexting may be a precursor to offline sexual activity (Ševčíková, Blinka, & Daneback, 2018). One study of over 17,000 adolescents aged 11 to 16 from 25 European countries revealed that sexting was associated with emotional problems and alcohol use in girls and boys of all ages (Ševčíková, 2016). Other research supports the link between sexting and adolescent problems such as substance use, depression, and low self-esteem as compared with peers (Van Ouytsel, Van Gool, Ponnet, & Walrave, 2014).

Risk factors for early sexual activity in U.S. teens are early pubertal maturation, poor parental monitoring, and poor parent–adolescent communication (McClelland & Tolman, 2014; Negriff, Susman, & Trickett, 2011). In one study of nearly 15,000 adolescents, those who perceived that their parents made more warnings emphasizing the negative consequences of sex tended to accumulate more sexual partners (Coley, Lombardi, Lynch, Mahalik, & Sims, 2013).

Perhaps youth who feel bombarded with parental warnings resist or react against such warnings. Authoritative parenting, regularly shared family activities (e.g., outings, game nights, or shared dinners), parental monitoring, and parental knowledge are associated with lower rates of sexual activity (Dittus et al., 2015; Huang, Murphy, & Hser, 2011). Having sexually active peers and perceiving positive attitudes about sex among schoolmates predict initiation and greater levels of sexual activity and a greater number of sexual partners (Coley et al., 2013; Moore et al., 2014; C. N. White & Warner, 2015). In addition, adolescents' perceptions of the sexual norms in their neighborhood, as well as siblings' sexual activity, are associated with age of initiation, casual sex, and the number of sexual partners, even after controlling for neighborhood demographic risk factors (Almy et al., 2016; Warner, Giordano, Manning, & Longmore, 2011).

Lesbian, Gay, Bisexual, and Transgender Adolescents

Adolescents are driven to understand the sexual feelings they experience, and their emerging sexual orientation becomes an important contributor to their sense of self (McClelland & Tolman, 2014). **Sexual orientation** is an enduring pattern of emotional, romantic, and sexual attraction to opposite-sex partners (heterosexual), same-sex partners (gay or lesbian), or partners of both sexes (bisexual) (Greenberg, 2017). Adolescents who identify as

BRAIN AND BIOLOGICAL INFLUENCES ON DEVELOPMENT

Peer Interaction and the Brain

Peer interactions, both in person and via social media, are neurologically rewarding, which can lead to compulsive behavior, such as repeatedly checking and updating social media.
iStock/ViewApart

Adolescents spend much of their time with friends, and peer interactions become highly motivating. Adolescents' strong desire to spend time with and earn the approval of peers is accompanied by distinct patterns of neurological activity. For example, in one study, adolescents completed a risky driving task alone or in the presence of peers (Chein, Albert, O'Brien, Uckert, & Steinberg, 2011). The presence of peers was associated with increases in both risk taking and activity in the nucleus accumbens (NAcc), a subcortical structure that is part of the limbic system, a collection of brain structures that is implicated in emotion. The NAcc contains the brain's reward circuitry, playing a critical role in the experience of reward and pleasure, including social rewards and positive feedback, and in motivating goal-directed behavior (Fareri & Delgado, 2014). The NAcc shows greater responsivity to reward during the second decade of life, peaking in mid-to-late adolescence (Braams, van Duijvenvoorde, Peper, & Crone, 2015).

A great deal of adolescents' peer interaction occurs online, via social media designed for mobile devices, such as Instagram and Snapchat (Lenhart, Purcell, Smith, & Zickuhr, 2010). Social and emotional processes typical of adolescence, such as peer influence, are also enacted on social media. For example, Smith, Chein, and Steinberg (2014) demonstrated increased NAcc activation and risky activity in a gambling task when adolescents believed that they were interacting with and being observed by an anonymous peer, suggesting that peer influence and its neurological correlates may also occur online. In addition, the level of NAcc response to positive social feedback has been linked to intensity of social media use (Meshi, Morawetz, & Heekeren, 2013), suggesting that social media interactions may also be neurologically rewarding.

A recent study examined whether peer influence processes occur online and whether the effects of peer processes can be observed in the brain (Sherman, Payton, Hernandez, Greenfield, & Dapretto, 2016). Adolescents were recruited to participate in an "internal social network" that simulated Instagram, a popular photo-sharing tool. Participants submitted their own Instagram photos and viewed both their own and other photos that they believed belonged to other members of the social network. The researchers manipulated how many likes accompanied each photo. Adolescents were more likely to like photographs they believed to be popular (those that were assigned many likes), and neural responses differed as a function of photograph popularity. When adolescents' own photographs received many likes (vs. few), they showed significantly greater activation of the NAcc, suggesting that likes may be experienced as rewarding and may motivate online behavior and continued use of social media. These findings are supported by prior research linking NAcc response to social evaluation and the role of the NAcc in reward and reinforcement (Meshi et al., 2013).

A follow-up study compared high school and college students on the Instagram-like social network task to determine whether peer influence and its neurological correlates are particularly high in adolescence as compared with emerging adulthood (Sherman, Greenfield, Hernandez, & Dapretto, 2018). Both high school and college students were more likely to like popular photographs than unpopular photographs and showed greater NAcc activation in response to popular photographs, especially when viewing their own images. Among high school students, the NAcc response when viewing their own photos with many likes over few increased with age, but no age differences emerged among college students. Prior research suggests that both peer influence and NAcc sensitivity to rewarding stimuli increase in adolescence and peak at around ages 16 to 17 (Braams et al., 2015; Steinberg & Monahan, 2007). However, high school and college students did not differ in overall NAcc activation. It appears that peer influence remains important in college, with similar neural correlates, suggesting a gradual path for social and neurological development from adolescence through emerging adulthood.

What Do You Think?

1. Why might adolescents find engaging in social media rewarding? What are the potential rewards? How might the rewards influence adolescents' behavior?

2. How might individuals' experience of social media and its effects change as they progress into and through adulthood? ●

Gender is central to a sense of identity.
DEREK R. HENKLE/AFP/Getty Images

transgender do not identify with their biological sex but instead adopt a different-gender identity (Diamond et al., 2015). Gender identity is distinct from sexual orientation. That is, a transgender identity does not signify sexual orientation, whether one is gay, lesbian, or bisexual (Bosse & Chiodo, 2016). However, research on the intersection of transgender identity and sexual orientation is rare. Consequently many researchers study transgender adolescents alongside LGB adolescents (Galupo, Davis, Grynkiewicz, & Mitchell, 2014). Wherever possible, the following discussion distinguishes LGB and transgender adolescents.

Similar to other aspects of identity development, many youth enter a period of questioning in which they are uncertain of their sexuality and attempt to determine their true orientation by exploring and considering alternatives (Saewyc, 2011). After a period of questioning and exploration, adolescents may commit to a sexual orientation and integrate their sexuality into their overall sense of identity. This process is not unique to LGB, sometimes referred to as *sexual minority,* adolescents. Many adolescents, regardless of orientation, explore sexuality as part of identity development. The final stage of **sexual identity** development, acceptance and disclosure, may occur in adolescence but often occurs in emerging adulthood and afterward (Savin-Williams & Ream, 2007). However, adoption of a sexual orientation is not a linear process.

Many researchers today view sexual orientation as a dynamic spectrum, ranging from exclusive opposite-sex attraction and relations to exclusive same-sex attraction and relations, with multiple sexual orientations in between (Bailey et al., 2016; Savin-Williams, 2016). Many people are attracted to both sexes and attractions varying over time. For example, one longitudinal study followed nearly 14,000 youth from ages 12 to 33 and found three general patterns of sexual attraction: heterosexual (88%), mostly heterosexual (10%), and LGB (2%)

(Calzo, Masyn, Austin, Jun, & Corliss, 2017). Sexual attraction does not always match behavior; many people experience attractions that they do not act on. In addition, a small minority of people report an asexual orientation, feeling no sexual attraction whatsoever (Greaves et al., 2017; Van Houdenhove, Gijs, T'Sjoen, & Enzlin, 2015).

Moreover, reporting of same-sex attraction and behavior among adolescents and emerging adults is not stable. Longitudinal data with over 10,000 seventh- to twelfth-grade students over a 6-year period revealed some migration over time in both directions—from opposite-sex attraction and behavior to same-sex attraction and behavior and vice versa (Saewyc, 2011). However, stability develops over time. Over 12,000 emerging adults (ages 18–24) surveyed over a 6-year period revealed that stability of sexual orientation was more common than change, especially among emerging adults who identified strongly as heterosexual or homosexual (as compared with bisexual, which was the most unstable category) (Savin-Williams, Joyner, & Rieger, 2012).

In North America and many other developed countries, young people are disclosing their sexual orientation—"coming out" as gay or lesbian—at earlier ages than in prior generations, likely due to an increasingly inviting, positive cultural context for LGB young people (Calzo, Antonucci, Mays, & Cochran, 2011; Floyd & Bakeman, 2006; Lucassen et al., 2015). Research suggests that some sexual minority youth may disclose their sexuality starting at around age 14 or 15, yet many wait until late adolescence or emerging adulthood (Calzo et al., 2017; Savin-Williams & Ream, 2003). Young people most commonly disclose first to a best friend; parents are often last, as many young people report that they want to be absolutely certain of their sexuality before they initiate this significant disclosure (Cohen & Savin-Williams, 1996). Adolescents who anticipate negative responses from parents are less likely to disclose their sexual orientation; to avoid disclosure, LGBT youth may become emotionally distant from their parents and friends (Ueno, 2005). Despite stereotypes, adolescents who come out to a parent are rarely met with ongoing condemnation, severe negative response, or expulsion (Savin-Williams, Dubé, & Dube, 1998). Many receive responses that range from neutral to positive (Samarova, Shilo, & Diamond, 2014).

Constructing an identity as a young person who is lesbian, gay, bisexual, or transgender can be complicated by the prejudice and discrimination that many LGBT youth experience in their schools and communities. LGBT adolescents experience more harassment and victimization by peers and report a more hostile peer environment than their heterosexual peers (Robinson & Espelage, 2013). Perceived discrimination and victimization by peers contribute to LGBT adolescents' increased risk for psychological and behavioral problems, such as depression, self-harm, suicide, running away, poor academic performance, substance use, and risky sexual practices (Collier, van Beusekom, Bos, & Sandfort, 2013; Haas et al., 2011; Plöderl et al., 2013).

Within the school setting, the presence of gay–straight alliances (GSAs) is an important source of support and education for students and helps sexual minority students connect with peers, reduces hopelessness, and is associated with lower suicide attempts (Davis, Royne Stafford, & Pullig, 2014). Schools that have GSAs show lower rates of student truancy, smoking, drinking, suicide attempts, and casual sex than do those in schools without GSAs, with this difference being more sizable for LGBT than heterosexual youth (Poteat, Sinclair, DiGiovanni, Koenig, & Russell, 2013). Perceived GSA support predicts greater well-being in racial and ethnic minority students, regardless of sexual orientation (Poteat et al., 2015). In addition to GSAs, LGBT adolescents often turn to the Internet as a source of information and exploration of their sexual orientation by learning about sexual orientation, communicating with other LGBT people, and finding support from others (Harper, Serrano, Bruce, & Bauermeister, 2016).

Support from parents and peers can buffer the negative effects of stigmatization and victimization for LGBT individuals (Birkett, Newcomb, & Mustanski, 2015). For example, one study of a national sample of over 7,800 LGBT secondary school students revealed that adolescents who had come "out" were more likely to experience peer victimization but also reported higher self-esteem and fewer depressive symptoms than their "closeted" peers (Kosciw, Palmer, & Kull, 2015). Thus, being out may reflect, as well as promote, resilience within this population.

Contraceptive Use

Adolescent contraceptive use is at an all-time high, yet only about three quarters of sexually active 15- to 19-year-olds report using contraception during first intercourse (Kaiser Family Foundation, 2014). Two thirds of sexually active adolescents report the condom as the method used during the most recent sexual intercourse and the method used at first intercourse (Guttmacher Institute, 2014). Many adolescents use contraceptives only sporadically and not consistently (Pazol et al., 2015). Common reasons given for not using contraceptives include not planning to have sex, the belief that pregnancy is unlikely, and difficulty communicating and negotiating the use of condoms (Johnson, Sieving, Pettingell, & McRee, 2015).

Authoritative parenting and open discussions about sex and contraception are associated with increased contraceptive use (Bersamin et al., 2008; Malcolm et al., 2013). However, the influence of parental communication is complicated. Research with Scottish adolescents suggests that teens' perceptions of comfort talking about sex with their parents are unrelated to adolescents' sexual behavior or contraceptive use (Wight, Williamson, & Henderson, 2006). Instead, it is adolescents' knowledge that is important. Boys and girls with more reproductive knowledge report greater use of contraceptives and more consistent use of contraceptives (Jaramillo, Buhi, Elder, & Corliss, 2017; S. Ryan, Franzetta, & Manlove, 2007). Unfortunately, many adolescents are not knowledgeable about sex and contraception or lack access to contraceptives.

Sexually Transmitted Infections

With sexual activity comes the risk of transmitting or acquiring sexually transmitted infections (STIs), infections passed from one individual to another through sexual contact. STIs may be caused by viruses, bacteria, or parasites. In 2015, STIs—specifically, cases of chlamydia, gonorrhea, and syphilis—reached an all-time high in the United States (Centers for Disease Control and Prevention, 2016a). Although they represent only 25% of the sexually active population, 15- to 24-year-olds account for one half to two thirds of all STI diagnoses, depending on illness, each year. Untreated STIs can result in sterility and serious, even life-threatening, illnesses such as cancer. Despite the high risk for acquiring STIs among youth, only one third of adolescent girls and less than half (45%) of young women ages 19 to 25 report that they have discussed STIs with their health care providers (Kaiser Family Foundation, 2014).

Human papillomavirus (HPV) is the most common STI diagnosed in people of all ages. There are several types of HPV, and some can cause cancer in different areas of the body—most commonly cervical cancer in women (McQuillan, Kruszon-Moran, Markowitz, Unger, & Paulose-Ram, 2017). HPV vaccines are available, and the U.S. Centers for Disease Control and Prevention recommends HPV vaccinations for males and females starting at age 11. In 2015, 63% of females aged 13 to 17 had received one or more doses of the vaccine against HPV, and 42% had completed the recommended regimen of three doses as compared with 50% and 28% for males, respectively (Reagan-Steiner et al., 2016). Some believe that HPV vaccination rates are low, compared to other vaccinations, because of the erroneous belief that giving the vaccine might condone sexual activity (Holman et al., 2014).

The most serious sexually transmitted infection is human immunodeficiency virus (HIV), which causes acquired immune deficiency syndrome (AIDS). Adolescents and emerging adults aged 13 to 24 represented one in five of new HIV/AIDS diagnoses in 2015. Symptoms of AIDS, specifically a weakening of the immune system, occur about 8 to 10 years after infection with HIV. Among men, HIV is most often spread through same-sex activity, specifically anal intercourse (48%), injection drug use (25%), heterosexual contact (18%), and other sources, including multiple risk factors and contaminated blood transfusions (Centers for Disease Control and Prevention, 2015). The leading sources of HIV exposure for women are heterosexual contact (84%) and injection drug use (16%). Worldwide, heterosexual contact is the most common source of HIV infection.

Although most adolescents (about 85% of high school students) receive education and demonstrate basic knowledge about HIV/AIDS, many underestimate their own risks, know little about other STIs, and are not knowledgeable about how to protect themselves from STIs (Kann et al., 2014). The three ways to avoid STIs are to abstain from sex; to be in a long-term, mutually monogamous relationship with a partner who has been tested and does not have any STIs; or to use condoms consistently and correctly.

Adolescent Pregnancy

In 2014, the birth rate among 15- to 19-year-old girls in the United States was 24.2 per 1,000 girls, down from a high of 117 per 1,000 in 1990 (Centers for Disease Control and Prevention, 2016b). The decline in adolescent birth rates can be attributed to an increase in contraceptive use (Lindberg, Santelli, & Desai, 2016). However, many adolescents use contraceptives only

Adolescent mothers and their children face many risks to development, but educational, economic, and social supports can improve outcomes.
ZUMA Press, Inc. / Alamy Stock Photo

sporadically and not consistently (Pazol et al., 2015). Over the past two decades adolescent pregnancy has declined in most industrialized nations, as shown in Figure 12.4. Yet despite overall declines, the United States continues to have one of the highest teen birth rates in the developed world (Sedgh, Finer, Bankole, Eilers, & Singh, 2015). In addition, as shown in Figure 12.5, ethnic and socioeconomic disparities place vulnerable teens at heightened risk for pregnancy. Hispanic, African American, and American Indian/ Alaska Native adolescents, as well as those from low socioeconomic status homes and communities—both rural and urban—have the highest adolescent birth rates in the United States (Burrus, 2018).

The risks for adolescent pregnancy (see Figure 12.6) are much the same as for early sexual activity. Girls who experience menarche early, relative to peers, are at risk as this early maturation predicts early sexual behavior and, in turn, pregnancy (De Genna, Larkby, & Cornelius, 2011). Similarly, poor academic achievement, delinquency, substance use, depression, and affiliation with deviant peers are risk factors for early sexual activity and adolescent pregnancy (Carlson et al., 2014; Fortenberry, 2013). Low socioeconomic status homes, poor neighborhoods, and low levels of parental warmth and monitoring influence early sexual activity and the risk for adolescent pregnancy. In addition, the presence of family members, especially parents and siblings, who are adolescent parents is associated with a high risk of adolescent pregnancy (East, Reyes, & Horn, 2007). Involved and firm parenting during early adolescence can buffer the effects of multiple home and community risk factors on the likelihood of early sexual activity and adolescent pregnancy (East, Khoo, Reyes, & Coughlin, 2006).

Adolescent mothers are less likely than their peers to achieve many of the typical markers of adulthood on time, such as completing high school, entering a stable marriage, and becoming financially and residentially independent (Taylor, 2009). Lack of resources such as child care, housing, and financial support is associated with poor educational outcomes; adolescents with child care and financial resources tend to show higher educational attainment (Casares, Lahiff, Eskenazi, & Halpern-Felsher, 2010). Although adolescent pregnancy is associated with negative outcomes, the risk factors for adolescent pregnancy are also those that place youth at risk for negative adult outcomes in general, such as extreme poverty, family instability, and few educational and community supports (Oxford et al., 2005). It is therefore difficult to determine the degree to which outcomes are caused by adolescent pregnancy itself or the contextual conditions that are associated with it. Adolescent fathers are similar to adolescent mothers in that they are more likely than their peers to have poor academic performance, higher school

FIGURE 12.4

Changes in Adolescent Pregnancy Rates, 1995–2011

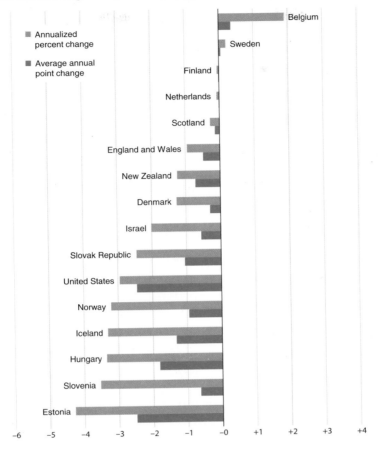

- Annualized percent change
- Average annual point change

Belgium, Sweden, Finland, Netherlands, Scotland, England and Wales, New Zealand, Denmark, Israel, Slovak Republic, United States, Norway, Iceland, Hungary, Slovenia, Estonia

–6   –5   –4   –3   –2   –1   –0   +1   +2   +3   +4

Source: Sedgh et al., 2015. © Society for Adolescent Health and Medicine. Published by Elsevier Inc.

FIGURE 12.5

Birth Rates for Adolescents Aged 15 to 19, 1960–2014

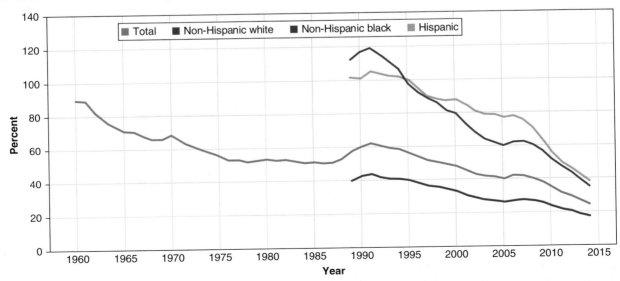

■ Total   ■ Non-Hispanic white   ■ Non-Hispanic black   ■ Hispanic

Source: Child Trends Databank (2016).

FIGURE 12.6

Influences on Adolescent Pregnancy

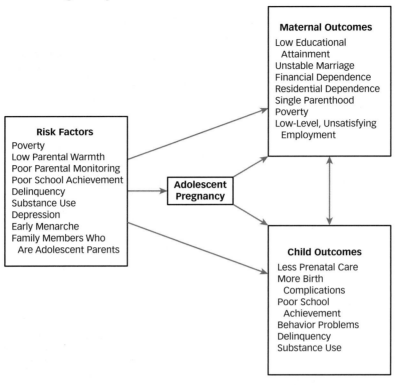

Risk factors for adolescent pregnancy also influence how adolescents adjust to parenthood, their long-term outcomes, and their children's outcomes. Protective factors—such as warm relationships with parents and other caring adults, parental monitoring, coping skills, and access to health care—promote positive adjustment in the face of risk and influence the outcomes of adolescent pregnancy for mothers and children.

dropout rates, finite financial resources, and lowered income potential (Kiselica & Kiselica, 2014).

Infants born to adolescent mothers are at risk for preterm birth and low birth weight (Jeha, Usta, Ghulmiyyah, & Nassar, 2015). Children of adolescent mothers tend to be at risk for a variety of negative developmental outcomes such as conduct and emotional problems, developmental delays, and poor academic achievement (Rafferty, Griffin, & Lodise, 2011; Tang, Davis-Kean, Chen, & Sexton, 2016). These outcomes are influenced by the characteristics of adolescents who are likely to become mothers, as well as the consequences of having a child at a young age (e.g., low level of maternal education, low socioeconomic status, frequent caretaker and residence changes, poor parenting) (De Genna et al., 2011; Rafferty et al., 2011). However, there is variability in outcomes. Many children of adolescent mothers demonstrate resilience and adjustment despite these risks (Levine, Emery, & Pollack, 2007). Positive adjustment is predicted by secure attachment, low maternal depressive symptoms, and positive

parenting on the part of the mother, characterized by warmth, discussion, and stimulation.

Adolescent parents can be effective if provided with supports—economic, educational, and social. Effective supports for adolescent parents include access to health care and affordable child care, encouragement to stay in school, and training in vocational skills, parenting skills, and coping skills (Easterbrooks, Chaudhuri, Bartlett, & Copeman, 2011). Social support predicts increased parenting self-efficacy and parental satisfaction (Angley, Divney, Magriples, & Kershaw, 2015; Umaña-Taylor, Guimond, Updegraff, & Jahromi, 2013). Relationships with adults who are close, are supportive, and provide guidance predict completing high school. Adolescent parents who share caregiving with their mothers or other adults learn as apprentices and become increasingly competent at parenting over time (Oberlander, Black, & Starr, 2007). Adolescent parents also benefit from relationships with adults who are sensitive not only to their needs as parents but also to their own developmental needs for autonomy and support.

THINKING IN CONTEXT 12.4

1. Identify influences on adolescent sexual activity (e.g., intercourse, oral sex, contraceptive use) at each of Bronfenbrenner's bioecological levels. How might interventions apply this information to reduce sexual activity and increase safe sex practices among adolescents?

2. It is a common belief that today's adolescents are more sexually active at younger ages than ever before. How would you respond to that statement, based on what you know about adolescent sexuality?

3. Given what is known about child development, specifically infant and young children's developmental needs, as well as what is known about parenting and its influence on developmental outcomes, what supports do adolescent parents need to become effective parents?

PROBLEMS IN ADOLESCENCE

» LO 12.5 Identify common psychological and behavioral problems in adolescence.

Most young people traverse the adolescent years without adversity, but about one in five teenagers experiences serious problems that pose risks to their health and development (Lerner & Israeloff, 2007). Common problems during adolescence include eating disorders, substance abuse, depression, and delinquency.

Depression and Suicide

The most common psychological problem experienced by adolescents is depression. Although about one third of adolescents report sometimes feeling hopeless (Kann et al., 2014), only 2% to 8% experience chronic depression that persists over months and years (Substance Abuse and Mental Health Services Administration, 2013). Depression is characterized by feelings of sadness, hopelessness, and frustration; changes in sleep and eating habits; problems with concentration; loss of interest in activities; and loss of energy and motivation. Rates of depression rise in early adolescence, and lifelong sex differences emerge, with girls reporting depression twice as often as boys (Thapar, Collishaw, Pine, & Thapar, 2012).

Genetic factors play a role in depression as they influence the brain regions responsible for emotional regulation and stress responses as well as the production of neurotransmitters (Maughan, Collishaw, & Stringaris, 2013). Longitudinal research demonstrates a role for epigenetics in depression during adolescence. For example, in one study, boys with a specific neurotransmitter allele showed severe symptoms of depression in the presence of poor family support but showed positive outcomes in the presence of high family support (Li, Berk, & Lee, 2013). The allele may increase reactivity to both negative and positive family influences, serving as a risk factor in an unsupportive family context but a protective factor when coupled with family support.

Contextual factors, such as the extended experience of stress, also influence depression. The longitudinal effects of stressful life events on depression are buffered by parent–child closeness and worsened by parental depression (Ge, Natsuaki, Neiderhiser, & Reiss, 2009; Natsuaki et al., 2014). Cultural factors also play a role in influencing adolescents' susceptibility to depression. Some adolescents find a discrepancy between their level of acculturation and that of their first-generation immigrant parents as stressful. Poor parental acculturation is linked with adolescent depression when adolescent–parent relationships are poor (Kim, Qi, Jing, Xuan, & Ui Jeong, 2009). For example, in one study, Chinese immigrant parents whose level of acculturation differed from their adolescent children tended to show more unsupportive parenting practices and the adolescents reported greater feelings of alienation (Kim, Chen, Wang, Shen, & Orozco-Lapray, 2013). Likewise, Vietnamese fathers who were less acculturated to the United States used more authoritarian parenting methods that fit their society, but their adolescents tended to experience more depression (Nguyen, Kim, Weiss, Ngo, & Lau, 2018). Latino adolescents who experienced a discrepancy in acculturation as compared with their parents also were at risk for depression (Howell et al., 2017; Nair, Roche, & White, 2018). As young people acculturate, they may challenge traditional attitudes and beliefs of their immigrant parents, leading to greater family conflict and emotional distress.

Intense and long-lasting depression can lead to thoughts of suicide. Suicide is among the top three causes of death for adolescents and emerging adults in many Western countries, including the United States, Canada, United Kingdom, and Australia (Australian Institute of Health and Welfare, 2016; Centers for Disease Control and Prevention, 2017; Office for National Statistics, 2015; Statistics Canada, 2015). Figure 12.7 (page 370) illustrates international differences in suicide rates. Large gender differences exist in suicide. Although females display higher rates of depression and make more suicide attempts, males are four times more likely to succeed in committing suicide (Xu, Kochanek, Murphy, & Arias, 2014). Girls tend to choose suicide methods that are slow and passive and that they are likely to be revived from, such as overdoses of pills. Boys tend to choose methods that are quick and irreversible, such as firearms. The methods correspond to gender roles that expect males to be active, decisive, aggressive, and less open to discussing emotions than females (Canetto & Sakinofsky, 1998; Hepper, Dornan, & Lynch, 2012). Some adolescents engage in nonsuicidal self-injury behaviors such as cutting. For more on these behaviors, see the accompanying feature on Applying Developmental Science.

LGBT youth, especially male and bisexual youth, experience an exceptionally high risk for suicide, with three to four times as many attempts as other youth (Grossman, Park, & Russell, 2016; Miranda-Mendizábal et al., 2017; Pompili et al., 2014). LGBT

APPLYING DEVELOPMENTAL SCIENCE

Self-Harm: Nonsuicidal Self-Injury

Common reasons that adolescents self-harm include anxiety, depression, feeling alone, anger, and self-dislike.
iStock/gawrav

Brianna closed the door to her room, rolled up her shirtsleeve, and looked down at the scarred and healing gashes in her arm before reaching for a new razor blade. Brianna engages in **self-harm**, self-injurious behavior. Although self-harm may indicate serious psychological disorders, it is also fairly common among adolescents in Western countries, with lifetime prevalence rates of 13% to 23% of adolescents in the United States, Canada, Australia, and Western Europe (Klemera, Brooks, Chester, Magnusson, & Spencer, 2017; Muehlenkamp, Claes, Havertape, & Plener, 2012). Rates may be even higher because most self-harming adolescents do not seek help or medical attention for their injuries (B. Hall & Place, 2010). Most adolescents who engage in self-harm behaviors do so a few times, and most do not show recurring self-harm.

Self-harm behaviors, particularly cutting, tend to emerge between ages 12 and 15, on average at about age 13 (Bjärehed, Wångby-Lundh, & Lundh, 2012). Girls are more likely than boys to report harming themselves, most commonly by cutting, but also hitting, biting, or burning, but there are no differences on the basis of ethnicity or socioeconomic status (Klemera et al., 2017; Nock, Prinstein, & Sterba, 2009). Some research has linked self-injurious behavior with impulsivity, perhaps accounting for the onset in early adolescence, when impulsivity tends to rise (Lockwood, Daley, Townsend, & Sayal, 2017; Stanford, Jones, & Hudson, 2017). Psychological and behavioral difficulties such as anxiety, depression, antisocial behavior, and poor problem-solving skills are also associated with self-harm (Bjärehed et al., 2012; S. K. Marshall, Tilton-Weaver, & Stattin, 2013). Adolescents who self-harm tend to report being more confused about their emotions, experiencing difficulty recognizing and responding to them and more reluctance to express their feelings and thoughts to others (Bjärehed et al., 2012; Nock et al., 2009). Common reasons that adolescents endorse for self-harm include depression, feeling alone, anger, self-dislike, and inadequacy.

Social problems and a difficulty forming close relationships are common among adolescents who self-harm (Ross, Heath, & Toste, 2009). Social risk factors include high family conflict, poor parent–adolescent communication, low levels of support, and intense conflict with peers and bullying (Claes, Luyckx, Baetens, Van de Ven, & Witteman, 2015; Fisher et al., 2012; Giletta, Burk, Scholte, Engels, & Prinstein, 2013). Yet positive parental involvement and support and close friendships can buffer adolescents against social risks for self-harm (Klemera et al., 2017).

Adolescents who repeatedly engage in cutting and other acts of self-harm tend to report that the act relieves emotional pain, reducing negative emotions (Scoliers et al., 2009; Selby, Nock, & Kranzler, 2014). Interestingly, self-harming adolescents tend to show little or no pain during the harm episode (Nock et al., 2009). Instead, the act of cutting or other self-harming behavior produces a sense of relief and satisfaction for adolescents who repeatedly self-harm. Soon, they tend to value self-harm as an effective way of relieving anxiety and negative emotions, making it a difficult habit to break (Madge et al., 2008; Selby et al., 2014).

The fifth edition of the *Diagnostic and Statistical Manual of Mental Disorders,* or *DSM–5* (American Psychiatric Association, 2013), includes a diagnosis for severe self-harm: nonsuicidal self-injury—self-injurious behavior that occurs with the expectation of relief from a negative feeling—to solve an interpersonal problem, or to feel better, and interpersonal difficulty and negative feelings of thoughts, premeditation, or rumination on nonsuicidal self-injury. Many adolescents who self-harm receive treatment similar to other internalizing disorders, including a combination of medication, therapy, and behavioral treatment. However, repeated self-harming behaviors are difficult to treat because the relief they produce is very reinforcing to adolescents, making psychologists and other treatment providers' work very challenging (Bentley, Nock, & Barlow, 2014; Nock, 2009).

What Do You Think?

1. Why might some adolescents find that "feeling bad" makes them "feel good"?

2. What role might brain development or contextual factors such as parents and peers contribute to the increase in cutting and other self-harm behaviors that many experience in adolescence? ●

Adolescents who feel isolated from peers or experience bullying are at greater risk for depression and suicide.
iStock/ljubaphoto

adolescents who attempt suicide often list family conflict, peer rejection, and inner conflict about their sexuality as influences on their attempts (Liu & Mustanski, 2012; Mustanski & Liu, 2013; Russell & Fish, 2016). Adolescents are more likely to attempt suicide following a friend's attempt (Nanayakkara, Misch, Chang, & Henry, 2013). Some adolescents who commit suicide first express their depression and frustration through antisocial activity such as bullying, fighting, stealing, substance abuse, and risk taking (Fergusson, Woodward, & Horwood, 2000). Peer victimization is a risk factor for suicide attempts (Bauman, Toomey, & Walker, 2013); another risk factor is a high level of anxiety (Hill, Castellanos, & Pettit, 2011).

Preventing suicide relies on recognizing and treating depression and symptoms of suicide. Frequently, however, adolescents who attempt suicide show warning signs beforehand, as listed in Table 12.2. After a suicide, family, friends, and schoolmates of the adolescent require immediate support and assistance in working through their grief and anger. The availability of support and counseling to all adolescents within the school and community after a suicide is important because adolescent suicides can occur in clusters, increasing the risk of suicide among adolescents in the community (Haw, Hawton, Niedzwiedz, & Platt, 2013).

Eating Disorders

Adolescents' rapidly changing physique leads many to become dissatisfied with their body image, which may place them at risk for eating disorders (Benowitz-Fredericks, Garcia, Massey, Vasagar, & Borzekowski, 2012). Core features of eating disorders are negative body image (overvaluing thinness, weight, or shape), obsession with weight control, and extreme weight control behaviors (Bruni & Dei, 2018).

Two eating disorders, **anorexia nervosa** and **bulimia nervosa,** entail excessive concern about body weight and attempts to lose weight, but they differ by means. Young people who suffer from anorexia nervosa starve themselves in an attempt to achieve thinness, maintaining a weight that is substantially lower than expected for height and age (American Psychiatric Association, 2013). Girls with

TABLE 12.2

Suicide Warning Signs

Any of the following behaviors can serve as a warning sign of increased suicide risk.

Change in eating and sleeping habits

Withdrawal from friends, family, and regular activities

Violent actions, rebellious behavior, or running away

Drug and alcohol use, especially changes in use

Unusual neglect of personal appearance

Marked personality change

Persistent boredom, difficulty concentrating, or a decline in the quality of schoolwork

Frequent complaints about physical symptoms, such as stomachaches, headaches, and fatigue

Loss of interest in pleasurable activities

Complaints of being a bad person or feeling rotten inside

Verbal hints with statements such as the following: "I won't be a problem for you much longer." "Nothing matters." "It's no use." "I won't see you again."

Affairs are in order—for example, giving away favorite possessions, cleaning his or her room, and throwing away important belongings

Suddenly cheerful after a period of depression

Signs of psychosis (hallucinations or bizarre thoughts)

Most important: Stating "I want to kill myself," or "I'm going to commit suicide."

Source: Adapted from American Academy of Child and Adolescent Psychiatry (2008).

FIGURE 12.7

International Suicide Rates for Adolescents, Age 15-19

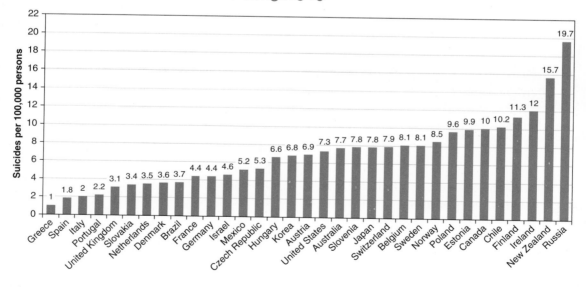

Source: McLoughlin et al. (2015).

anorexia nervosa avoid eating even when hungry, and many exercise vigorously to increase their weight loss. Anorexia nervosa affects about 2% of girls 19 and under; however, many more girls show poor eating behaviors characteristic of anorexia nervosa (Smink, van Hoeken, Oldehinkel, & Hoek, 2014). Bulimia nervosa is characterized by recurrent episodes of binge eating—consuming an abnormally large amount of food (thousands of calories) in a single sitting coupled with a feeling of being out

Adolescents with eating disorders often have a distorted and negative view of their bodies coupled with an obsession with weight control and extreme weight-control behaviors.
The Kansas City Star/MCT via Getty Images

of control—followed by purging, inappropriate behavior designed to compensate for the binge, such as vomiting, excessive exercise, or use of laxatives (American Psychiatric Association, 2013). Bulimia nervosa is more common than anorexia nervosa, affecting between 1% and 5% of females across Western Europe and the United States (Smink et al., 2014), and it is thought to be underdiagnosed.

Anorexia nervosa and bulimia nervosa are dangerous to young people's health (Bruni & Dei, 2018). Girls with anorexia nervosa may lose one quarter to one half of their body weight. The starvation characteristic of anorexia nervosa has serious health consequences, such as loss of bone mass causing brittle and easily broken bones, kidney failure, shrinkage of the heart, brain damage, and even death in as many as 16% of cases of anorexia nervosa. Side effects of bulimia nervosa include nutritional deficiencies, sores, ulcers, and even holes and cancers in the mouth and esophagus caused by repeated exposure to stomach acids.

Both anorexia nervosa and bulimia nervosa occur more often in both members of identical twins than fraternal twins, indicating a genetic basis (Strober, Freeman, Lampert, Diamond, & Kaye, 2014). Eating disorders are much more prevalent in females than males (Raevuori, Keski-Rahkonen, & Hoek, 2014). Adolescents who develop eating disorders tend to have problems with impulse control and anxiety (Haleem, 2012). Anorexia nervosa is associated with perfectionism and strict regulation of eating, and thus it may be viewed as a way to exert control and reduce negative mood states (Kaye, Wierenga, Bailer,

Simmons, & Bischoff-Grethe, 2013). Eating disorders are associated with altered neural activity in several limbic system structures and parts of the prefrontal cortex, responsible for aspects of emotion, rewards, and decision making (Fuglset, Landrø, Reas, & Rø, 2016).

Eating disorders occur in all ethnic and socioeconomic groups in Western countries and are increasingly common in Asian and Arab cultures (Isomaa, Isomaa, Marttunen, Kaltiala-Heino, & Björkqvist, 2009; Keski-Rahkonen & Mustelin, 2016; Pike, Hoek, & Dunne, 2014; Thomas et al., 2015). Girls who compete in sports and activities that idealize lean figures, such as ballet, figure skating, and gymnastics, are at higher risk for developing eating disorders than are other girls (Nordin, Harris, & Cumming, 2003; Voelker, Gould, & Reel, 2014). In the United States, White and Latina girls, especially those of higher socioeconomic status, are at higher risk for low body image and eating disorders than are Black girls, who may be protected by cultural and media portrayals of African American women that value voluptuous figures (Nishina, Ammon, Bellmore, & Graham, 2006; Smink, van Hoeken, & Hoek, 2013; Striegel-Moore & Bulik, 2007). Some researchers suggest, however, that ethnic differences in eating disorders are not as large as they appear. Instead, eating disorders may exist in Latina and Black girls but remain undetected and undiagnosed because of barriers to diagnosis and treatment (Wilson, Grilo, & Vitousek, 2007).

Eating disorders are difficult to treat. In one study of over 2,500 adolescents, 82% of those diagnosed with an eating disorder showed symptoms 5 years later (Ackard, Fulkerson, & Neumark-Sztainer, 2011). Anorexia nervosa and bulimia nervosa are treated in similar ways but show different success rates. Standard treatment for eating disorders includes hospitalization (if needed) to remedy malnutrition and ensure weight gain, antianxiety or antidepressant medications, and individual and family therapy (Hail & Le Grange, 2018; Herpertz-Dahlmann, 2017). Unfortunately, girls with anorexia nervosa tend to deny that there is a problem as they are unable to objectively perceive their bodies. As a result, only about 50% of girls with anorexia nervosa make a full recovery, and anorexia nervosa has the highest mortality rate of all mental disorders (Smink et al., 2013). Bulimia nervosa tends to be more amenable to treatment because girls with bulimia nervosa tend to acknowledge that their behavior is not healthy; however, relapse is common (Herpertz-Dahlmann, 2017).

Alcohol and Substance Use

Nearly half of U.S. teens have tried an illicit drug and two thirds have tried alcohol by the time they leave high school, as shown in Table 12.3. Experimentation

Most adolescents experiment with alcohol and some try other substances.
iStock/KatarzynaBialasiewicz

TABLE 12.3

Substance Use in U.S. Adolescents—2017

		LIFETIME PREVA-LENCE, %	30-DAY PREVA-LENCE, %
Cigarettes			
	8th grade	9.4	1.9
	10th grade	15.9	5.0
	12th grade	26.6	9.7
Any vaping			
	8th grade	18.5	6.6
	10th grade	30.9	13.1
	12th grade	35.8	16.6
Alcohol			
	8th grade	23.1	8.0
	10th grade	42.2	19.7
	12th grade	61.5	33.2
Been drunk			
	8th grade	9.2	12.2
	10th grade	25.1	8.9
	12th grade	45.3	19.1
Marijuana			
	8th grade	13.5	5.5
	10th grade	30.7	15.7
	12th grade	45.0	22.9
Other illicit drugs			
	8th grade	9.3	2.7
	10th grade	13.7	4.5
	12th grade	19.5	6.3

Source: Adapted from Johnston et al. (2018).
Note: Vaping includes vaping nicotine, marijuana, and flavoring.

with alcohol, tobacco, and marijuana use, that is, "trying out" these substances, is so common that it may be considered normative for North American adolescents. Rates of experimentation rise during the adolescent years into emerging adulthood (Miech et al., 2017). Perhaps surprising to some adults is that a limited amount of experimentation with drugs and alcohol is common in well-adjusted middle and older adolescents and associated with psychosocial health and well-being (Mason & Spoth, 2011). Why? Alcohol and substance use may serve a developmental function in middle and late adolescence, such as a way of asserting independence and autonomy from parents, sustaining peer relationships, and learning about oneself (Englund et al., 2013; Rulison, Patrick, & Maggs, 2015). Notice, however, that many more adolescents have tried a given substance ("experimented" with it) than use it regularly.

Many adolescents first try alcohol in high school and show steady increases in use throughout the high school years. Marijuana is used nearly as often as alcohol. As we will see in Chapter 14, alcohol and marijuana use tends to peak in emerging adulthood and then declines (Miech et al., 2017). Although most adolescents experiment with alcohol, tobacco, and marijuana, without incident, there are short-term dangers of alcohol and substance use, such as overdose, accidents, and motor impairment as well as long-term dangers of dependence and abuse.

Adolescents are particularly vulnerable to alcohol abuse because they show reduced sensitivity to the effects of alcohol that serve as cues in adults to limit their intake, such as motor impairment, sedation, social impairment, and quietness or distress (Spear, 2011). They develop a tolerance and are at risk for developing dependence for alcohol more quickly than adults (Simons, Wills, & Neal, 2014). Alcohol use in adolescence, even moderate use, is associated with damage to the brain, including reduced volume in the prefrontal cortex and hippocampus (Silveri,

Dager, Cohen-Gilbert, & Sneider, 2016; Squeglia et al., 2015). Heavy drinking is associated with reduced frontal cortex response during working memory tasks, slower information processing, and reductions in attention, visuospatial functioning, and problem solving (Carbia et al., 2017; Feldstein Ewing, Sakhardande, & Blakemore, 2014). Executive function, working memory, and learning suffer—and adolescents become less well able to regulate their behavior. At the same time, some research suggests that preexisting individual differences, such as poor functioning in tests of inhibition and working memory, smaller gray and white matter volume, and altered brain activation, are not only influenced by substance use but also place adolescents at risk for heavy substance use (Brumback et al., 2016; Squeglia & Gray, 2016).

Alcohol and substance use and abuse are associated with negative consequences that can interfere with adolescents' development, such as unwanted sexual encounters and risky sexual activity. Risks and negative consequences of alcohol and substance use include academic problems, social problems, aggression and victimization, unintentional injuries, anxiety, depression, car crashes, and suicide (E. J. Marshall, 2014).

Adolescents at risk to abuse alcohol and substances tend to begin drinking earlier than their peers (Palmer et al., 2009). Adolescents are at reduced risk of developing alcohol and substance abuse problems if their parents are involved, warm, supportive, and aware of their children's whereabouts and friends. Low socioeconomic status, family members with poor mental health, drug abuse within the family and community, and disadvantaged neighborhoods increase the risk of alcohol abuse in adolescence (Chaplin et al., 2012; Trucco, Colder, Wieczorek, Lengua, & Hawk, 2014). In turn, adolescents who have mental health problems, difficulty with self-regulation, or are victims of physical or sexual abuse are at higher risk of alcohol and drug abuse than their peers. However, perhaps the most direct influences on adolescents are their peers' drinking or substance abuse behavior, their perceptions of peer support for such use, and their access to alcohol and substances (Brooks-Russell, Simons-Morton, Haynie, Farhat, & Wang, 2014).

Because adolescent alcohol and substance use is a complex problem with multiple influences, prevention and treatment programs must be multipronged. Effective prevention and intervention programs target parents by encouraging that they be warm and supportive, set rules, and be aware of their children's activities. Effective alcohol and substance abuse prevention and treatment programs educate adolescents about the health risks of substance use and that, contrary to depictions in the media and society, substance use is not socially acceptable. Such programs teach adolescents how to resist pressure from peers, how to refuse offers, and how to build their coping and self-regulatory skills (Windle & Zucker, 2010).

Delinquency

"Have you got it?" asked Corey. "Here it is—right from Ms. Scarcela's mailbox!" Adam announced as he dropped the stolen item on the floor in front of his friends. During adolescence, young people

Most adolescents engage in at least one delinquent act, such as vandalism. Delinquency tends to rise in early adolescence, peak in middle adolescence, and decline in late adolescence.
iStock/Syldavia

experiment with new ideas, activities, and limits. For many adolescents, like Adam, experimentation takes the form of delinquent activity. Nearly all young people engage in at least one *delinquent* or illegal act, such as stealing, during the adolescent years, without coming into police contact (Flannery, Hussey, & Jefferis, 2005). In one study, boys admitted to engaging in, on average, three serious delinquent acts and girls reported one serious delinquent act between ages 10 and 20, yet nearly none of the adolescents had been arrested (Fergusson & Horwood, 2002).

Adolescents account for 8% of police arrests in the United States (Federal Bureau of Investigation, 2015). Males are about four times as likely to be arrested as females. African American youth are disproportionately likely to be arrested as compared with European American and Latino youth, who are similar in their likelihood of arrest; Asian American youth are least likely to be arrested (Andersen, 2015; Federal Bureau of Investigation, 2015). Adolescents' own reports, however, tend to suggest few to no gender or ethnic differences in delinquent activity (Rutter, Giller, & Hagell, 1998). Differences in arrest rates may be influenced by the tendency for police to arrest and charge ethnic minority youths in low socioeconomic status (SES) communities more often than European American and Asian American youth in higher SES communities (Rutter et al., 1998).

Most delinquent acts are limited to the adolescent years and do not continue into adulthood (Piquero & Moffitt, 2013). Antisocial behavior tends to increase during puberty and is sustained by affiliation with similar peers. With advances in cognition, moral reasoning, emotional regulation, social skills, and empathy, antisocial activity declines (Monahan, Steinberg, Cauffman, & Mulvey, 2013). That is, most adolescents tend to show an increase in delinquent activity in early adolescence that continues into middle adolescence and then declines in late adolescence. Although mild delinquency is common and not necessarily cause for concern, about one quarter of violent offenses in the United States, including murder, rape, robbery, and aggravated assault, are conducted by adolescents (Office of Juvenile Justice and Delinquency Prevention, 2014). Adolescents who engage in serious crime are at risk to become repeat offenders who continue criminal activity into adulthood. Yet most young people whose delinquent activity persists and evolves into a life of crime show multiple problem behaviors that begin in childhood (Farrington & Loeber, 2000), and they typically have their first contacts with the criminal justice system by age 12 or earlier (Baglivio, Jackowski, Greenwald, & Howell, 2014).

When biological and individual risk factors are coupled with challenging home and community environments, the risk for childhood onset of serious antisocial behavior that persists into adulthood increases (Dishion & Patterson, 2016). Parenting that is inconsistent, highly controlling and/or negligent, accompanied by harsh punishment, and/or low in monitoring can worsen impulsive, defiant, and aggressive tendencies in children and adolescents (Chen, Voisin, & Jacobson, 2013; Harris-McKoy & Cui, 2012).

Contextual factors in the community also matter. Communities of pervasive poverty are characterized by limited educational, recreational, and employment activities, coupled with access to drugs and firearms, opportunities to witness and be victimized by violence, and offers of protection and companionship by gangs that engage in criminal acts—all of which contribute to the onset of antisocial behavior (Chen et al., 2013). Exposure to high levels of community violence predicts delinquent activity (Jain & Cohen, 2013). Low-income communities tend to have schools that struggle to meet students' educational and developmental needs, with crowding, limited resources, and overtaxed teachers (Flannery et al., 2005). Young people who experience individual, home, community, and school risk factors for antisocial behavior tend to associate with similarly troubled peers, a pattern that tends to increase

delinquent activity as well as chronic delinquency (Evans, Simons, & Simons, 2014).

Preventing and intervening in delinquency requires examining individual, family, and community factors. Training parents in discipline, communication, and monitoring fosters healthy parent–child relationships, which buffers young people who are at risk for delinquency (Bowman, Prelow, & Weaver, 2007). High-quality teachers, teacher support, resources, and economic aid foster an educational environment that protects young people from risks for antisocial behavior. A 3-year longitudinal study following adolescents of low-income single mothers transitioning off welfare showed that involvement in school activities protects adolescents from some of the negative effects of low-income contexts and is associated with lower levels of delinquency over time (Mahatmya & Lohman, 2011). Economic, social, and employment resources empower communities to create environments that reduce criminal activity by all age groups and promote the development of children and adolescents.

THINKING IN CONTEXT 12.5

1. How do adolescents' physical, cognitive, and social characteristics influence their likelihood of developing an eating disorder such as anorexia nervosa or bulimia nervosa? How might context influence treatment options?

2. How might adults distinguish normative from atypical delinquent activity? For example, a rise in some delinquent activities is somewhat normative during adolescence and will decline in late adolescence, and sometimes the activity continues and increases.

3. Are there dangers in taking the perspective that some alcohol and substance use is common and simply a part of growing up? How should parents, teachers, and professionals respond to adolescent alcohol and substance use?

APPLY YOUR KNOWLEDGE

At 16, John recently had his very first alcoholic drink while at a party hosted by his best friend. Since then, John has begun drinking at parties every few weeks, although he usually stops after a couple of beers. Afterward, he always catches a ride with a friend or a taxi. Big for his age, John is popular in school and has many opportunities to socialize.

Even so, he only goes out once a week or so because his football schedule keeps him busy, and he works hard to maintain at least a B+ average.

Tim, also 16, has at least one beer nearly every day—often more than one. He explains that parents, school, work, and simply meeting expectations are overwhelming and frustrating. Drinking is calming, a refuge from the stress of everyday life. Last year, Tim's best friend brought marijuana to a party, and Tim found that it was even better than alcohol; marijuana made him feel free. Tim smokes marijuana whenever he can, which is not often given that it is much more expensive than alcohol. Lately, Tim has found that alcohol doesn't seem to make him feel as relaxed as it once did, so he's begun trying to obtain marijuana as often as possible. Sometimes Tim steals money—from his mother, job, even teachers—to fund a fun night out.

1. What experience does the average adolescent have with substances such as alcohol and marijuana? What is normative, statistically?

2. Describe correlates of substance use in adolescence. How do John's and Tim's experiences compare with that of the typical adolescent?

3. Many aspects of development offer insights into adolescent risk behavior, such as substance use, delinquency, and sexual activity. How might changing relationships with parents, including monitoring, parenting styles, and conflict, contribute to adolescent risk behavior? What role might relationships and interactions with peers take?

$SAGE edge™

Visit **edge.sagepub.com/kuther2e** to help you accomplish your coursework goals in an easy-to-use learning environment.

LEARNING OBJECTIVES	SUMMARY	KEY TERMS	IN REVIEW
12.1 Summarize the processes by which self-concept, self-esteem, and identity change during adolescence.	With cognitive advances, adolescents begin to use more abstract and complex labels to describe and evaluate themselves. Positive self-esteem predicts adjustment and sociability in adolescents of all socioeconomic status and ethnic groups. Adolescents must construct an identity that is coherent and consistent over time. Authoritative parenting and close relationships with peers encourage adolescents to explore identity alternatives. Identity achievement is associated with multiple positive outcomes.	Global self-esteem Identity Identity achievement Psychosocial moratorium Identity status Identity diffusion Identity foreclosed Identity achievement status Ethnic identity	How does self-concept and self-concept change during adolescence? What is identity and what are outcomes associated with four identity statuses? What is ethnic identity? What are influences on identity development?
12.2 Discuss the nature of parent–child relationships in adolescence.	Conflict between parents and adolescents rises in early adolescence and peaks in middle adolescence but takes the form of small arguments over minor details. Authoritative parenting fosters autonomy, self-esteem, and academic competence in adolescents. Authoritarian parenting inhibits the development of autonomy and is linked with poor adjustment. Parental monitoring promotes well-being and is a protective factor against risky behavior.	Parental monitoring	What are examples of typical parent–adolescent conflict? What parenting style is most effective with adolescents? How does parental monitoring contribute to positive development in adolescence?
12.3 Examine the developmental progression of peer relations in adolescence.	In adolescence, friendships are characterized by intimacy, loyalty, self-disclosure, and trust and promote positive adjustment. In early adolescence, cliques emerge and, by mid-adolescence, begin to include both boys and girls, creating opportunities for dating. Dating typically begins through the intermingling of mixed-sex peer groups, progresses to group dating, and then goes to one-on-one dating and romantic relationships. Both cliques and crowds, larger reputation-based groups, tend to decline in late adolescence. Susceptibility to peer conformity for both positive and negative behaviors tends to rise in early adolescence, peaks in middle adolescence, and declines thereafter.	Cliques Crowds Dating violence	What are characteristics of adolescent friendships? What purposes do cliques and crowds serve in adolescence? To what extent do most adolescents perceive peer pressure? How does dating typically progress in adolescence?

12.4 Analyze patterns of adolescent sexual activity, including sexual orientation.	Sexual activity among U.S. adolescents has declined over the past few decades. Risk factors for early sexual activity include early pubertal maturation, poor parental communication and monitoring, sexually active peers, risky behaviors, and stressful homes and neighborhoods. Despite a decline since 1990, the United States has one of the highest teen pregnancy rates in the developed world. Adolescent mothers are less likely to achieve many of the typical markers of adulthood. Children born to adolescent mothers are at greater risk for academic and behavioral problems.	Sexual orientation Sexual identity	When does sexual activity typically begin? How might contextual factors influence young people's exploration and expression of sexual orientation? What are risk factors and outcomes for adolescent pregnancy?
12.5 Identify common psychological and behavioral problems in adolescence.	Several problems tend to rise during adolescence: depression, eating disorders, substance use, and delinquency. Girls tend to show higher rates of depression and eating disorders. Alcohol and substance use rises for both boys and girls during the adolescent years through emerging adulthood. They may serve developmental functions but are associated with short- and long-term effects, such as accidents, academic problems, risks for dependence and abuse, and impaired neurological development. Nearly all adolescents engage in at least one delinquent activity, and overall rates of delinquency rise in early adolescence and decline in late adolescence.	Self-harm Anorexia nervosa Bulimia nervosa	What factors contribute to depression and suicide in adolescence? Distinguish between anorexia nervosa and bulimia nervosa. Discuss characteristics and outcomes associated with adolescent alcohol and substance abuse. What are some common patterns of adolescence delinquency? What are characteristics of chronic offenders?

PRACTICE AND APPLY WHAT YOU'VE LEARNED

▶ edge.sagepub.com/kuther2e

CHECK YOUR COMPREHENSION ON THE STUDY SITE WITH:

- **Diagnostic Quizzes** to identify opportunities for improvement.

- **Multimedia Resources** that explore chapter content using media and current events.

- **Journal Articles** that support and expand on chapter concepts.

PART VI

Emerging and Early Adulthood

CHAPTER 13:
Physical and Cognitive Development in Emerging and Early Adulthood

CHAPTER 14:
Socioemotional Development in Emerging and Early Adulthood

Early adulthood is a period of gaining and sustaining. After completing secondary school, many young people experience a gradual transition to adulthood known as emerging adulthood, which may extend into the mid-20s. The adoption of adult roles marks the end of emerging adulthood.

Once physical maturity is reached, aging begins. Physical changes are gradual. Most go unnoticed. Cognitive advances continue as young adults become able to appreciate multiple viewpoints, arguments, and contradictions. Socioemotional advances help young adults integrate cognition with emotion, regulate intense emotions, and think logically about complicated everyday situations. Developing a sense of identity, a commitment to a sense of self, values, and goals, prepares young adults for establishing intimate relationships.

Cohabitation is common, and most adults marry by the end of early adulthood. Marital success is predicted by maturity, realistic expectations, joint conflict resolution, and respect. Most adults become parents and often are surprised by the wide range of emotions that accompany their new baby and set of responsibilities. As the home context ascends in salience, the number of friends and time spent with them declines. The work context becomes prominent as young adults form occupational goals, settle into careers, and monitor their progress, changing their goals in light of their experiences, abilities, and interests. The school context remains relevant for many young adults. Nontraditional students balance work, family, and school but benefit from a more complex knowledge base and an emphasis on applying what they learn to their lives. Overall, contexts shift in salience during emerging and early adulthood but continue to interact and influence all domains of development.

Watch at
edge.sagepub.com/kuther2e

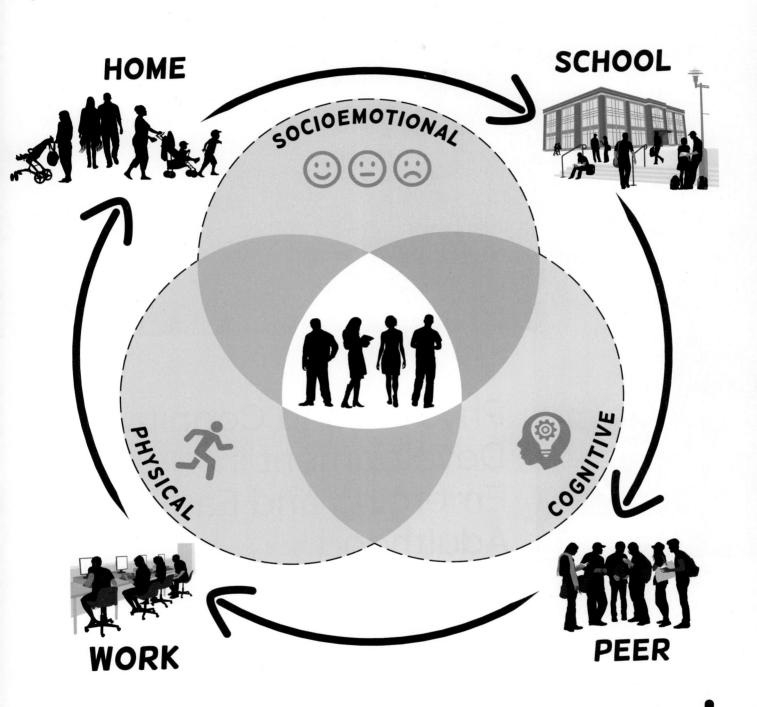

HOME

SCHOOL

SOCIOEMOTIONAL

PHYSICAL

COGNITIVE

WORK

PEER

Images: ©iStock.com

13

Physical and Cognitive Development in Emerging and Early Adulthood

As he drives to school, Regan recites definitions and concepts for his biology exam. At 19 years of age, Regan has just entered his second year of college. Like many emerging adults, Regan is still trying to figure out what career is for him. The first in his family to attend college, he feels a sense of responsibility to succeed, but he also finds it difficult to balance his schoolwork with his part-time job. As he progresses through college, Regan becomes better at planning his schedule and juggling his many responsibilities. He feels more comfortable weighing his options and choosing a major and career path. Regan feels that he is physically stronger than ever before, and he wonders how his body will change and how his life will unfold in the coming years.

Learning Objectives

13.1 Describe the features and characteristics of emerging adulthood.

13.2 Summarize the physical developments of emerging and early adulthood.

13.3 Analyze physical and sexual health issues in emerging and early adulthood.

13.4 Compare postformal reasoning, pragmatic thought, and cognitive-affective complexity.

13.5 Explain how attending college influences young adults' development, and identify challenges faced by first-generation and nontraditional students.

13.6 Discuss vocational choice and the transition to work.

Digital Resources

Listen: What Is Adulthood?

Listen: Sperm Counts Plummet in Western Men

Explore: Mental Health and Substance Use Problems in Emerging Adulthood

Watch: Postformal Thought

Watch: Coping With College

▶ **Lives in Context Video 13.1:** Emerging Adulthood: Choosing a Major

Connect: Holland Occupational Themes

▶ **Lives in Context Video 13.2:** Balancing College and Career in Emerging Adulthood

Regan is making the transition to adulthood, known as emerging adulthood (which extends from the end of secondary school, about age 18, to the assumption of adult roles at about age 25). Over the two decades spanning emerging adulthood and early adulthood (about ages 25–40), individuals experience many, often subtle, physical changes, as well as changes in the way they think and view the world around them. The distinction between emerging adulthood and early adulthood is new, often not agreed upon (Arnett, 2014; Côté, 2014; Syed, 2016). Therefore, the term *emerging adult* will refer to individuals age 25 and under (unless otherwise specified), and *young adult* will refer to all individuals under age 40, including emerging adults (unless otherwise specified).

EMERGING ADULTHOOD: TRANSITION TO ADULTHOOD

» **LO 13.1 Describe the features and characteristics of emerging adulthood.**

Much as adolescence is believed to be a social construction, a result of societal changes that separated adolescents from adults, developmental

scientists have posed that recent social changes have prolonged the transition to adulthood, creating the new period of emerging adulthood (Arnett, 2016). With more high school graduates entering college than ever before, the traditional markers of adulthood, such as completing one's education, entering a career, establishing a residence, becoming financially independent, marrying, and forming a family, are delayed relative to prior generations. As adolescents enter this stage, at about 18, they are generally dependent on their parents and perhaps beginning to explore romantic relationships. In the mid-20s, at the end of emerging adulthood, most live independently and have identified romantic and career paths. In the interim, young people in emerging adulthood occupy an "in-between" status in which they are no longer adolescents but have not yet assumed the roles that comprise adulthood. How young people traverse this stage, and how long it takes, is a result of the interaction of the individual's capacities and the context in which he or she lives—family, social, economic, and community resources (D. Wood et al., 2018).

Markers of Emerging Adulthood

Several characteristics mark emerging adulthood as a distinct period in life. First, it is a time of instability, arguably the most unstable period in life (Arnett,

Žukauskienė, & Sugimura, 2014). There is greater diversity in lifestyles in emerging adulthood than other periods of life. People aged 18 to 25 have the highest rates of residential change of any age group, shifting among residences and living situations. For example, some emerging adults live with their parents, and others live in college dormitories or in apartments with roommates or with spouses or alone. Changes in romantic relationships are also frequent, and as discussed in Chapter 13, most emerging adults experience several job changes. The instability is often challenging, posing risks to mental health (Tanner, 2016). More than half of emerging adults often experience anxiety, and a third report often feeling depressed.

Second, emerging adulthood is the primary time for identity exploration (Lapsley & Hardy, 2017). Although we may begin the identity search process in adolescence, as described in Chapter 12, it is not until emerging adulthood that most individuals have the opportunity to sample opportunities and life options. No longer under parental restrictions and without the full range of adult responsibilities, emerging adults are able to fully engage in the exploration that comprises identity development (D. Wood et al., 2018). As they explore alternatives, emerging adults often make changes in educational paths, romantic partners, and jobs. With identity exploration comes risk taking, such as increased substance use (Andrews & Westling, 2016). The identity search is exciting but also often confusing, especially for emerging adults who find themselves unable to make choices about which paths to explore or who feel that the choices they would like to make in love relationships and work are unattainable (Arnett et al., 2014).

Third, emerging adults often report feeling a sense of being in between neither adolescents nor adults. Emerging adults tend to view becoming an adult as independent of traditional markers of adulthood, such as marriage, and instead based on personal characteristics such as accepting responsibility for themselves and becoming financially independent (Sharon, 2016). Although most emerging adults do not identify role transitions, such as marriage and parenthood, as necessary for people to be considered adults, young people who have experienced these role transitions are more likely to see themselves as adult than are those who have not completed similar role transitions. As young people make progress toward resolving their identity, they are more likely to perceive themselves as adults (Schwartz, Zamboanga, Luyckx, Meca, & Ritchie, 2013). In addition, with increasing age, emerging adults are more likely to view themselves as full-fledged adults. For example, only about one third of 18- to 21-year-olds report that they consider themselves adults, as compared with over half of 22- to 25-year-olds and over two thirds of 26- to 29-year-olds (Arnett & Schwab, 2012).

Finally, although emerging adults experience many transitions, instability, and mixed emotions, most have a sense of optimism. For example, in one study of over 1,000 adults ages 18 to 29 years in the United States, 89% agreed with the statement, "I am confident that eventually I will get what I want out of life," and over 75% agreed with the statement, "I believe that, overall, my life will be better than my parents' lives have been" (Arnett & Schwab, 2012). Optimism is an important psychological resource during a turbulent time. Indeed, progress in identity development and success in completing the tasks of emerging adulthood are associated with psychosocial development. Self-esteem rises steadily from late adolescence through the mid-20s (Chung et al., 2014). Depressive symptoms decline, and well-being increases as young people make advances in emotional regulation, especially the ability to regulate intense emotions such as anger (Galambos, Barker, & Krahn, 2006; Zimmermann & Iwanski, 2014). Emerging adults adopt adult roles at different times, as shown in Figure 13.1.

Contextual Nature of Emerging Adulthood

Emerging adulthood is thought to be a response to larger societal changes in Western societies, such as increased education and later onset of marriage and parenthood. However, emerging adulthood is not universal (Syed, 2016). Transitions do not occur at the same pace or in the same order for everyone. Young people vary with regard to when they enter careers, when they marry, and when they become parents (Eisenberg, Spry, & Patton, 2015).

Most research on emerging adulthood has sampled college students, potentially yielding a narrow view of this period in life (Hendry & Kloep, 2010; Mitchell & Syed, 2015). College enrollment often delays residential and financial independence, as most college students tend to depend on parents for financial and often residential support. Indeed, Jeffrey Arnett (2016a) describes college as an essential playground for emerging adults, a temporary safe haven where they can explore possibilities in love, work, and worldviews without many of the responsibilities of adult life. Thus, emerging adulthood may be interwoven with socioeconomic status (du Bois-Reymond, 2016).

In contrast to college students, young people who are employed are more likely to be financially self-supporting and to live in a residence independent of parents, markers of adulthood. Young people who drop out of high school, experience early parenthood, begin working at a job immediately after high school, or live in low socioeconomic status (SES) homes and communities may experience only a limited

FIGURE 13.1

Percentage of Individuals Aged 18 to 27 Displaying Markers of Adulthood

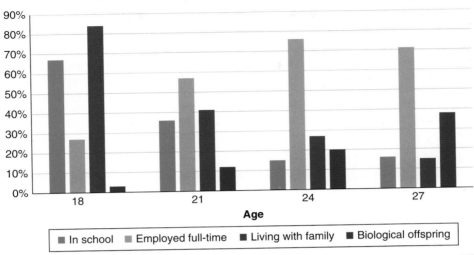

Source: Adapted from Cohen et al. (2003).

period of emerging adulthood or may not experience emerging adulthood at all (du Bois-Reymond, 2016; Maggs, Jager, Patrick, & Schulenberg, 2012).

Emerging adulthood may be extended into the late 20s for young people who obtain advanced training, such as attending medical school or law school, which delays entry into career, other adult roles, and financial independence. Some theorists therefore argue that emerging adulthood is not a life stage—it does not exist everywhere and for everyone—but is simply an indicator of medium to high socioeconomic status and the educational and career opportunities that accompany such status (Côté, 2014; Syed, 2016). Given that ethnicity is often interwoven with socioeconomic status, people of color may be less likely to experience emerging adulthood (du Bois-Reymond, 2016; Syed & Mitchell, 2014).

As discussed in the Cultural Influences on Development feature, culture may play a role in the experience of emerging adulthood. Although emerging adulthood is not universal, it has been observed among young people in many cultures, including many countries in North and South America, Northern and Eastern Europe, Israel, China, and Japan (Arnett et al., 2014; Arnett & Padilla-Walker, 2015; Nelson, 2009; Sirsch, Dreher, Mayr, & Willinger, 2009; Swanson, 2016). Each of these cultures endorses some similar criteria for adulthood as well as criteria that are unique. For example, each culture rates accepting responsibility for the consequences of one's actions as the most important criterion for adulthood, but other important criteria vary by culture (Nelson & Luster, 2015). North American emerging adults also rate making independent decisions and becoming financially independent as criteria for adulthood. In

Argentina, young people rated the capacity to care for young children as the second most important criterion for women (Facio & Micocci, 2003). Israeli young adults listed being able to withstand pressure as a required attribute for adulthood (Mayseless & Scharf, 2003), whereas Romanian young people reported norm compliance as an indicator of adulthood (Nelson, 2009). Chinese emerging adults rated learning to have good control of your emotions as being necessary for adulthood (Nelson, Badger, & Wu, 2004). Yet none of these criteria were rated as necessary for adulthood by North Americans (Arnett, 2003). It appears that emerging adulthood, the extended transition from adolescence to adulthood, often occurs in Western industrialized cultures. However, the specific features and characteristics with which young people define *adulthood* vary by culture and likely within cultures accompanying ethnic and socioeconomic differences (du Bois-Reymond, 2015; Syed & Mitchell, 2014). The extended transition to adulthood—and the contexts that support it—holds implications for physical and cognitive development.

THINKING IN CONTEXT 13.1

1. In what ways is emerging adulthood socially constructed, a product of contextual factors?

2. Did you experience, or are you currently in, emerging adulthood?

3. In your view, what is the most important or identifiable marker of emerging adulthood? Why?

CULTURAL INFLUENCES ON DEVELOPMENT

Emerging Adulthood and Culture

Emerging adulthood has been recognized in young people of many countries. However, the theory of emerging adulthood is based on samples of youth from Western countries, especially the United States. For example, one recent analysis found that three quarters of studies on emerging adulthood published between 2013 and 2015 examined U.S. samples (Ravert, Stoddard, & Donnellan, 2018). Findings obtained with Western samples cannot necessarily be generalized to people in other parts of the world.

The problem of relying and overgeneralizing findings of Western samples is not unique to research on emerging adulthood. In fact, the majority of research published tends to sample people from the English-speaking world or from Western Europe, with little representation from Latin America, Asia, Africa, or the Middle East. Henrich, Heine, and Norenzayan (2010) refer to the majority of research samples published in international journals as "Western, Educated, Industrialized, Rich, and Democratic" (WEIRD). Worldwide, few people are categorized as WEIRD, yet findings from WEIRD samples are treated as applicable to the rest of the world. The majority of studies of emerging adulthood are conducted in Western nations without attention to whether the features that mark emerging adulthood generalize to non-Western contexts.

Frequently in non-Western cultures, entry to adulthood is marked by rituals and is the same for everyone. For example, isolated hunter-gatherer communities tend to have scripted roles, responsibilities, and trajectories. Young people in these communities likely do not take time to decide what to do with their lives, engage in social experimentation, and find themselves (Schwartz, 2016). Instead, they adopt the roles ascribed to them and aid their communities. Emerging adulthood likely does not exist in these communities.

But as countries become developed, the transition to adulthood begins to lengthen. A comparison of Chinese and U.S. students (ages 18–25) found that two thirds of the Chinese students reported feeling that they have reached adulthood, as compared with about one quarter of the U.S. students (Badger, Nelson, & Barry, 2006). In one study of 18- to 26-year-old college students and nonstudents from a rural village in India, the majority viewed themselves as adults and believed that others viewed them as adults, contrary to predictions related to emerging adulthood (Seiter & Nelson, 2011). The college students, however, reported higher levels of optimism characteristic of emerging adulthood than did those who did not attend college.

With economic development often comes shifts in attitudes that may contribute to emerging adulthood (Arnett, Žukauskienė, & Sugimura, 2014). For example, over the past 40 years, Japan has undergone social and economic changes. In the latter half of the past century, after World War II, Japan's economy grew. By the 1980s, Japan became one of the most developed countries in the world. Traditionally, Japan has a collectivistic society in which individual and group goals are interdependent and social relationships are generally prioritized over individual needs and desires (Markus & Kitayama, 2010). Although traditional values of social harmony and obligations remain important, an emphasis on individuality has emerged (Hamamura, 2012), leading some to refer to Japanese culture as "individualistic collectivism" (Matsumoto, 2002). Young people are more able to choose their own life paths than were previous generations of Japanese adolescents and young adults, consistent with a defining marker of emerging adulthood (Sugimura, Yamazaki, Phinney, & Takeo, 2009). In addition, arranged marriages, accounting for 50% of all Japanese marriages in the 1950s, are now uncommon, accounting for about 5% of new marriages (Arnett et al., 2014). Whereas emerging adulthood may have been less applicable or may not have existed in Japan three decades ago, it is likely important now.

What Do You Think?

1.   Is valuing individualism central to the existence of emerging adulthood?

2.   Why effect might ethnicity, socioeconomic status, and culture have on whether an individual experiences emerging adulthood? Why? ●

PHYSICAL DEVELOPMENT IN EMERGING AND EARLY ADULTHOOD

»» LO 13.2   Summarize the physical developments of emerging and early adulthood.

All of the organs and body systems, including digestive, respiratory, circulatory, and reproductive systems, peak in functioning from emerging adulthood into early adulthood. We may not think of young adults as aging, but the biological fact is that once individuals are physically mature with growth and physical development at adult levels, **senescence**—a pattern of gradual age-related declines in physical functioning—begins (Spini, Jopp, Pin, & Stringhini, 2016). Measurable age-related changes in functioning occur by about age 30, but most people do not notice these until middle adulthood. Aging entails gradual changes in appearance, strength, body proportions, and fertility.

Similar to development throughout infancy, childhood, and adolescence, development in early adulthood is multidimensional and multidirectional. Different parts of the body age at different rates, and development comprises both gains and losses in strength, endurance, and motor skill. Age and physical development are closely related in childhood, but the link is much weaker in adulthood. Young adults display a wide range of individual differences in physical functioning and aging due to differences in genetics, context, and experience, including health, socioeconomic status, and behaviors such as smoking, exercise, and diet (Bonnie, Stroud, & Breiner, 2015; Federal Interagency Forum on Child and Family Statistics, 2014). For example, lung efficiency declines with age, but it drops 5% faster per decade for smokers as compared with nonsmokers (De Martinis & Timiras, 2003). In addition, organs vary in their rate of decline (McDonald, 2014); in one individual, for example, the digestive system may show signs of aging earlier than the cardiovascular system, while it may be the other way around for another individual.

Physical Changes

Age-related changes in the skin are gradual, predictable, and unavoidable, and they begin in emerging adulthood, at about age 20. The connective tissue gradually thins, resulting in less elastic skin and some visible wrinkles around the eyes by age 30 (Tobin, 2017). The skin becomes drier as oil glands become less active. Most adults in their 30s notice lines developing on their foreheads, and by the 40s, these lines are accompanied by crow's feet around the eyes and lines around the mouth—markers of four decades of smiles, frowns, laughter, and other emotions. However, the rate of skin aging is influenced by exposure to the elements, such as sun, heat, cold, and pollution. Exposure to the sun is thought to be the most dramatic contributor to skin aging, responsible for about 80% of skin changes and the leading cause of skin cancer (Flament, Bazin, & Piot, 2013). The use of sunscreen has been shown to retard skin aging (Hughes, Williams, Baker, & Green, 2013). Although more apparent in middle age, by age 30, some individuals begin to notice gray hairs, as the hair follicle cells that produce pigment, or color, become less abundant. Men who are prone to hereditary baldness typically begin balding in their 30s.

Physiological function, including muscle development and strength, tends to improve throughout the 20s, peaking at about age 30 (Kenney, Wilmore, & Costill, 2015). Adults' performance on activities that require body coordination and bursts of strength, such as sprinting and playing basketball,

tend to peak in the early 20s, whereas those that require endurance, such as distance running, peak in the early 30s and show declines after age 40. Muscle strength, as measured by the maximum force with which one can throw a ball, for example, shows a gradual decline beginning at about age 30 but is generally not noticeable to most people until middle age (Payne & Isaacs, 2016). Although physical abilities show a predictable pattern of change, adults vary in the rate of change in their performance. Physical activity plays a large role in maintaining weight, muscle mass, and endurance throughout adulthood. Athletes involved in contact sports may be at risk to develop a neurodegenerative disease known as CTE. We look at those risk factors in the accompanying Brain and Biological Influences on Development feature.

Fertility and Reproductive Capacity

Martina holds her newborn close to her while chatting with her family who has come to visit her in the maternity ward. At 32 years of age, Martina is older than the average first-time mother; most women are in their 20s when they give birth to their first child. However, as shown in Figure 13.2, births to women in their 30s and 40s have increased substantially

FIGURE 13.2

Birth Rates, by Age of Mother: United States, 1990–2015

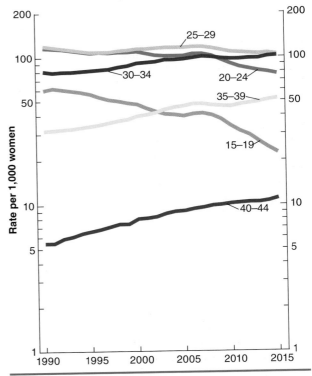

Source: Martin et al. (2017).

Note: Rates are plotted on a logarithmic scale.

Chronic Traumatic Encephalopathy in Athletes

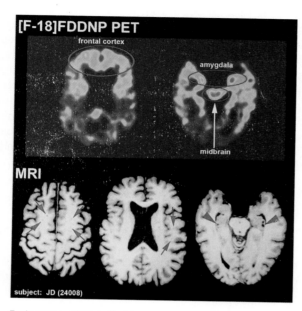

Brain scans of NFL hall of famer Joe DeLamielleure illustrate the extensive neurodegeneration that comprises CTE.
Jeff Siner/Charlotte Observer/MCT

Recently, professional sports have come under scrutiny for the dangers posed to athletes. Many sports, like soccer, hockey, and football, involve player-on-player or player-equipment collisions in which injuries, such as concussions, are common. A concussion is a brain injury. Athletes who experience multiple concussions, that is, repeated mild traumatic brain injury, are at risk to develop a progressive form of neurodegeneration known as chronic traumatic encephalopathy (CTE).

First identified in boxers, CTE is associated with symptoms of irritability, impulsivity, aggression, depression, short-term memory loss, and heightened suicidality, typically appearing 8 to 10 years after the disease onset. As CTE advances, dementia appears. Gait and speech abnormalities are common, and in the late stages, CTE may be mistaken for Alzheimer's disease. CTE has been identified in football, hockey, wrestling, and rugby players and may accompany exposure to blast or concussive injury associated with military service.

To date, research on CTE has centered on American football players. In a critical 2013 study, Ann McKee and colleagues conducted postmortem evaluations of 85 brains from former athletes and military veterans or civilians with a history of repetitive mild traumatic brain

injury, as well as 18 "control" brains from individuals without a history of mild traumatic brain injury. The results were striking: 80% of the individuals with a history of repetitive mild traumatic brain injury showed CTE symptoms (McKee et al., 2013). Thirty-four of the 35 former professional American football players showed CTE symptoms. Among the 5 hockey players studied, only 1 showed no disease. Athletes who experience traumatic head injuries are at risk for CTE. Football received a lot of attention as the sample of athletes was largely football players—and the football players were overwhelmingly diagnosed with CTE.

More recent research has confirmed the link. Ann McKee and colleagues (Mez et al., 2017) studied a sample of 202 deceased individuals from a brain donation program who played American football at all levels: high school, college, semiprofessional, and professional. CTE was diagnosed in 177 of the brains (88%), including 110 of 111 former National Football League players (99%). CTE appears to be strongly linked with head trauma experienced by participating in football as 48 of 53 college players, 9 of 14 semiprofessional players, and 7 of 8 Canadian Football League players were diagnosed with CTE. Football poses risks, but the risk of CTE is not limited to football.

An important caveat to this research is that CTE can be diagnosed definitively only postmortem. In these studies, the researchers examined donated brains. Many of the brains were donated by players for testing as they suspected that they had the disease while still alive. The sample is therefore skewed, but the results clearly indicate an association between the head trauma that often accompanies participating in football and CTE. In 2013, 4,500 retired National Football League (NFL) players filed a lawsuit against the league, claiming that the NFL concealed information about the dangers of head trauma, resulting in a $765 million settlement (Belson, 2013). The National Hockey League (NHL) is facing a similar lawsuit from hockey players (McIndoe, 2017). In 2016, NFL and NHL issued new protocols for identifying and evaluating concussions to better protect players (Flynn, 2016; NHL Public Relations, 2016).

What Do You Think?

1. To what degree do you think organizations such as the NFL and NHL are responsible for player injuries?

2. What can be done to reduce the risks of CTE?

3. Identify risk factors of emerging and early adults for CTE. ●

FIGURE 13.3

Mean Age at First Birth, by Race and Hispanic Origin of Mother: United States, 2000 and 2014

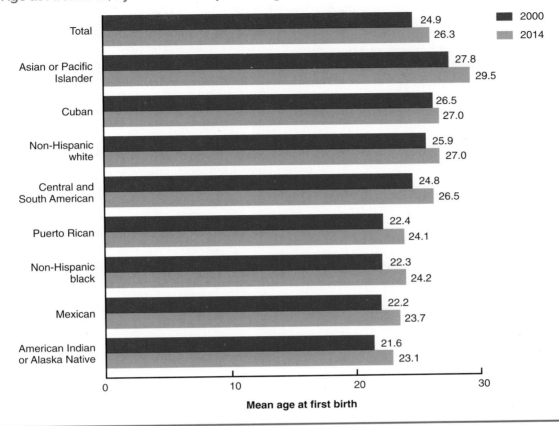

Source: Mathews, 2016.

since the early 1990s (J. A. Martin, Hamilton, & Osterman, 2017). As shown in Figure 13.3, the average age at first birth has increased for U.S. women of all ethnicities, ranging from 0.5 years for Cuban mothers to 1.9 years for non-Hispanic Black mothers (Matthews & Hamilton, 2016). The increase in maternal age is thought to be a result of the decline in adolescent pregnancy. Many young adults wait to have children until they have completed their education and established their careers. The maturity and financial stability that accompany the 30s can make for better parents. However, reproductive capacity peaks in the 20s and declines with age, increasing the risk for women in their mid-to-late 30s of experiencing difficulty conceiving (Jasienska, Bribiescas, Furberg, Helle, & Núñez-de la Mora, 2017).

As women's reproductive systems age, changes occur in the quality of ova and in the rate of ovulation. Although women are born with about 400,000 ova, they decay with age and chromosomal anomalies accumulate, increasing

the risk of pregnancy loss, or miscarriage (Bentov, Yavorska, Esfandiari, Jurisicova, & Casper, 2011). A common cause of female infertility is the failure to ovulate, to release an ovum into the fallopian tube. With advancing age, ovulation becomes less regular. A variety of factors also can prevent ovulation; some are treatable or preventable, such as drug and alcohol abuse, environmental toxins, obesity, and being underweight. Illnesses that affect the reproductive system, such as ovarian cancer and ovarian cysts, can also make it difficult or impossible to conceive. In addition, dwindling reserves of ova can prevent conception because it is thought that the body requires a minimum level of ova reserves in order to ovulate (Martins & Jokubkiene, 2017). However, the exact minimum is unknown and, like other aspects of physical development, may vary with genetic and contextual factors (Schuh-Huerta et al., 2012).

Men's rate of change in reproductive capacity is significantly different from that of women;

most men remain able to conceive into older adulthood. In young men, sperm can be affected by anything that interferes with the functioning of the body, such as fever, stress, drug abuse, alcoholism, radiation, and environmental toxins (Li, Lin, Li, & Cao, 2011). Exposure to these factors can reduce the number of sperm or affect their physical structure, activity, and motility. In this way, lifestyle and contextual factors contribute to young men's fertility. In addition, the number and quality of sperm produced decline in middle adulthood, beginning at about age 40 (Brahem, Mehdi, Elghezal, & Saad, 2011; Johnson, Dunleavy, Gemmell, & Nakagawa, 2015).

 THINKING IN CONTEXT 13.2

1. Recall that development is characterized by continuities and discontinuities (see Chapter 1). Identify aspects of physical development that illustrate continuity and others that illustrate discontinuity in emerging and early adulthood.

2. What are some of the personal and emotional implications of the timing of physical and reproductive change for early adults?

HEALTH, FITNESS, AND WELLNESS IN EMERGING AND EARLY ADULTHOOD

» **LO 13.3**   **Analyze physical and sexual health issues in emerging and early adulthood.**

Generally speaking, early adulthood is a time of good physical health. Few deaths among emerging and young adults are the result of illness. Instead, the leading cause of death in U.S. young adults through age 35 is unintentional injury, followed by homicide and suicide, and then cancer and heart disease (Centers for Disease Control and Prevention, 2017b). The most common fatal injuries among emerging and young adults are motor vehicle accidents and drug overdose, with accidents most common in adults under age 25 and overdoses in adults ages 25 to 34 (Centers for Disease Control and Prevention, 2017a). At all ages in life, socioeconomic status is linked with health through its influence on environmental factors (e.g., exposure to crowding, stress, and pollution), health-enhancing factors (e.g., exercise, diet, and social support), and health risks (e.g., obesity and substance abuse) (Cornman, Glei, Goldman, Ryff, & Weinstein, 2015).

Overweight and Obesity

During his first year of college, Byron welcomed the ability to make choices about food and plan his own meals. Without his health-conscious mother's input, he was able to munch on fried chicken wings whenever he wanted. By his senior year of college, Byron was 45 pounds overweight. The absence of parental controls, access to an abundance of food, being busy, and stresses associated with life transitions (such as to college and career) make it difficult for emerging adults to eat healthily. Obesity, defined as a body mass index (BMI) of 30 or above, and overweight (BMI greater than 25) have increased substantially in recent decades. Over three quarters of American adults over the age of 20 are overweight (33%) or obese (45%) (Fryar, Carroll, & Ogden, 2016). As shown in Figure 13.4, young adult men and women show similar rates of obesity (34.8% and 36.4%, respectively) (Hales, Carroll, Fryar, & Ogden, 2017). Obesity increases from early to middle adulthood for all adults, with females showing a small increase over men.

Adult obesity is influenced by heredity, but today's global obesity epidemic has stronger ties to environmental pressures than genetic factors (Giskes, van Lenthe, Avendano-Pabon, & Brug, 2011). Physical labor is less a part of the lifestyle in industrialized nations than ever before. Individuals in developing nations become less active with gains in technology. Food has become more abundant in Western countries, especially sugary, fatty, and processed foods. Increasingly, people in low- and middle-income countries consume Western diets (Ford, Patel, & Narayan, 2017). With age, it becomes more difficult to avoid overeating because caloric needs drop between the ages of 25 and 50, and the metabolic rate, the amount of energy the body uses at rest, gradually falls as muscle cells decline in number and size (Roberts & Rosenberg, 2006). Sedentary lifestyles, desk jobs, and especially the number of hours spent viewing television are closely associated with obesity (Heinonen et al., 2013).

Contextual factors, such as a sense of neighborhood safety, may encourage or deter engaging in outside physical activities, such as building a running habit (Gordon, 2017; Lakerveld & Mackenbach, 2017). Low-income communities tend to have fewer chain supermarkets and grocery stores but have more convenience stores and fast-food restaurants, offering high-calorie food items (Larson, Story, & Nelson, 2009). Financial disparities contribute to obesity as a healthier diet (e.g., a Mediterranean-type diet rich in fruit, vegetables, fish, and nuts) is at least 50% more expensive than a much less healthy diet (e.g., a diet rich in processed foods, meats, and refined grains) (Rao, Afshin, Singh, & Mozaffarian, 2013).

FIGURE 13.4

Prevalence of Obesity Among Adults Aged 20 and Older, by Sex and Age: United States, 2015–2016

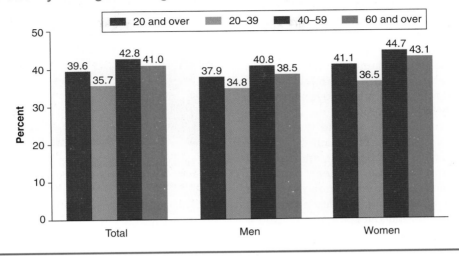

Legend: ■ 20 and over ■ 20–39 ■ 40–59 ■ 60 and over

Total: 39.6, 35.7, 42.8, 41.0
Men: 37.9, 34.8, 40.8, 38.5
Women: 41.1, 36.5, 44.7, 43.1

Source: Hales, 2017.

Obesity is a serious health risk, associated with a range of health problems and illnesses such as high blood pressure, stroke, circulatory problems, diabetes, digestive disorders, arthritis, cancer, and, ultimately, early death (Cheng, Medlow, & Steinbeck, 2016; Tchernof & Després, 2013). Moreover, weight gain throughout early adulthood predicts illnesses such as cardiovascular disease and cancer as well as death in middle adulthood (Zheng et al., 2017). Obese adults often experience weight-related bias and discrimination as negative attitudes about obese persons abound (Nutter, Russell-Mayhew, Arthur, & Ellard, 2018). Obese adults may experience more difficulty finding mates, rental apartments, and jobs than do nonobese adults (Puhl, Heuer, & Brownell, 2011). Adults' perceptions and experience of bias predict mental health problems, such as depression (E. Robinson, Sutin, & Daly, 2017).

Health outcomes improve with even moderate weight loss (Orzano & Scott, 2004). Successful long-term weight loss, however, is challenging, as indicated by the vast array of "quick" weight loss programs advertised in the media. Successful weight loss is most often a result of lifestyle changes, such as regular moderate exercise coupled with a nutritionally balanced diet low in calories and fat (Nicklas, Huskey, Davis, & Wee, 2012; Nurkkala et al., 2015). Effective weight loss interventions emphasize behaviors and encourage individuals to keep accurate records of what they eat and analyze eating patterns in their food choices (MacLean et al., 2015). Since many people overeat as a reaction to stress, training in problem-solving skills helps participants learn non-food-related ways of managing day-to-day

conflicts and difficulties, as well as increasing social support to help individuals cope with challenging environments.

Physical Activity

Exercise offers powerful health benefits and is an important influence on longevity (Schoenborn & Stommel, 2011). Regular moderate exercise enhances immunity, lowering the risk of, and speeding recovery to, illnesses (Horn et al., 2015). Exercise reduces risks for heart disease, cancer, diabetes, and at least 20 other illnesses and reduces overall mortality at all times in the lifespan (Rhodes, Janssen, Bredin, Warburton, & Bauman, 2017). Mental health benefits of regular physical activity include improved mood, energy, and ability to cope, as well as lower levels of stress, anxiety, and depression (Hogan, Mata, & Carstensen,

Exercise offers powerful health benefits and is an important influence on longevity.
iStock/verve231

2013; Rebar et al., 2015). In addition, fitness is linked to cognitive performance throughout adulthood. Young adults who demonstrate high levels of cardiovascular fitness tend to perform better on measures of basic cognitive abilities, such as attention, reaction time, working memory, and processing speed, than low-fitness young adults (Newson & Kemps, 2008). Remaining active helps young adults maintain motor skill competencies, such as throwing speed and jumping distance, which predict overall fitness, percentage of body fat, and strength.

How much exercise is enough to reap health benefits? To obtain health benefits such as reduced cholesterol levels, decreased body fat, and reduced risk of developing diabetes or heart disease, national guidelines recommend engaging in at least 150 minutes of moderate activity each week (e.g., brisk walking, raking the lawn, or pushing a lawn mower), or 75 minutes of vigorous activity, plus muscle-strengthening exercises on at least 2 days each week (U.S. Department of Health and Human Services, 2008). About 300 minutes of moderate or 150 minutes of vigorous exercise may be required each week to lose weight. The activity does not have to be performed in a single block of time but may be accumulated in 10-minute increments throughout the day. Unfortunately, physical activity tends to decline from adolescence into emerging adulthood and young adulthood, increasing the risk for poor health outcomes throughout adulthood (Corder et al., 2018).

Sexual Activity

We have seen that today's adolescents initiate sex at older ages than recent generations. At the same time, over the past four decades, adults have become more accepting of consensual premarital sex. In addition, the average number of sexual partners reported by adults rose from 7 in 1988 to 11 in 2012 (18 in males and 6 in females) (Twenge, Sherman, & Wells, 2015).

Most emerging adults are unmarried and, as we will see in Chapter 14, are tasked with exploring their sense of self, including their sexuality. The social script of emerging adulthood as a "time to experiment" is conducive to casual sex, sexual activity outside of romantic relationships (Kuperberg & Padgett, 2016). Causal sex has always existed (Claxton & Van Dulmen, 2016) but has recently received media attention as young people, particularly college students, have increasingly referred to it as hooking up (J. R. Garcia, Reiber, Massey, & Merriwether, 2012). Hooking up is not consistently defined by emerging adults but generally refers to a brief sexual encounter that can range from kissing to intercourse, without the expectation of forming a long-term relationship or attachment (Olmstead, Conrad, & Anders, 2018). An estimated 60% to 80% of college students report at least one hookup (Garcia et al., 2012). For example,

The social script of emerging adulthood as a "time to experiment" is conducive to hookups, alcohol consumption, and casual sex.
Bill Varie / Alamy Stock Photo

in one study of 24,000 students at 22 colleges in the United States surveyed between 2005 and 2011, about 68% of both men and women reported having engaged in hookups (Kuperberg & Padgett, 2016). Of the roughly 12,000 hookup encounters reported by students, 69% included sexual intercourse. The majority of research on casual sex examines heterosexual partners; there is little work examining LGBT adults (R. J. Watson, Snapp, & Wang, 2017).

Hookups often occur within the context of college parties and most frequently involve alcohol use (Bersamin, Paschall, Saltz, & Zamboanga, 2012; Patrick, Maggs, & Lefkowitz, 2015). Some students report enthusiasm about their experiences, but others report distress, particularly when it occurs in the context of drinking (Owen & Fincham, 2011). In one study of over 800 college students, about one third of those who have hooked up while drinking reported that they would not have done so if they had been sober, with women most likely to regret the encounter (Labrie, Hummer, Ghaidarov, Lac, & Kenney, 2014). In research with nearly 4,000 students at 30 colleges across the United States, both men and women who reported casual sex within the previous month scored lower than their peers on measures of psychological well-being (self-esteem, life satisfaction, psychological well-being, and happiness) and higher on measures of distress (anxiety, depression) (Bersamin et al., 2014). Negative emotional consequences are generally more common and more pronounced for women than men (Napper, Montes, Kenney, & LaBrie, 2016).

A double standard exists regarding the social acceptability of sex outside of romantic relationships, in which women receive negative social sanctions while men receive social rewards—and may even experience psychological distress if they do not engage in hookups (Claxton & Van Dulmen, 2016). This double standard regarding sexuality for men and women makes hooking up potentially more damaging for women (Armstrong,

Hamilton, & England, 2010). Despite possible negative consequences, many emerging adults perceive benefits to hooking up, including the belief that such encounters are easier and less time-consuming than traditional romantic relationships and that they have less potential to be "emotionally damaging" than a bad romantic relationship (Napper et al., 2016; Snapp, Ryu, & Kerr, 2015).

In early adulthood, the frequency of sexual activity is closely related to marital status. Married adults are more sexually active than single adults. The average American married couple has coitus two to three times per week when they are in their 20s, with the frequency gradually declining to about weekly in their 30s (Hyde & DeLamater, 2017). Generally speaking, sexual activity is highest among people in young adulthood, from their mid-20s to mid-30s, and declines gradually for people in their 40s and again in their 50s, but the amount of decline is modest (B. M. King, 2019). It is estimated that young adults engage in sexual activity only about one to two times a month more than do their middle-aged counterparts (Herbenick et al., 2010). Not surprisingly, sex predicts positive affect the next day (Debrot, Meuwly, Muise, Impett, & Schoebi, 2017), but there are also long-term associations. Research suggests that the frequency of sexual intercourse is associated with emotional, sexual, and relationship satisfaction, as well as overall happiness, in adults (McNulty, Wenner, & Fisher, 2016).

Sexual Coercion

It is estimated that about one in three women experience nonconsensual sexual activity; that is, they experience sexual assault or rape over their lifetime (S. G. Smith et al., 2017). Nonconsensual is the key to identifying sexual assault: It includes instances in which the victim is coerced by fear tactics, such as threats or use of physical harm, or is incapable of giving consent due to the influence

of drugs or alcohol or because of age. Emerging adulthood is a particularly vulnerable time. It is estimated that between 20% and 30% of emerging adult women experience nonconsensual sexual activity; that is, they experience sexual assault or rape (Fedina, Holmes, & Backes, 2018; Mellins et al., 2017). Nearly 80% of victims experience sexual assault prior to age 25 (Breiding et al., 2014).

Perpetrators of sexual assault are most often acquaintances of their victims. For example, among college students, over three quarters of rapes are committed by someone the victim knows (Sinozich & Langton, 2014). The commonly used term *date rape* for nonconsensual sexual activity with an acquaintance downplays the severity of sexual assault. When alcohol is involved, victims may blame themselves for drinking (Hock, 2015). Many victims wrongly assume that they sent "mixed signals" or that things "got out of hand."

Underreporting of rape is high. The actual number of incidents is hard to determine, but one study found that only about 20% of rapes reported by women had been reported to the police (Sinozich & Langton, 2014). Sometimes victims believe that their attacker will deny the rape; may want to avoid being judged negatively by friends, peers, or future potential dating partners; or may fear being victimized again (Hock, 2015). One meta-analysis of 28 studies (with almost 6,000 participants) found that two thirds of women rape survivors, particularly those who experienced acquaintance rape, did not acknowledge that they had been raped (Wilson & Miller, 2016). Instead, they used more benign labels such as "bad sex" or "miscommunication."

Survivors of sexual assault have a higher than average risk of developing posttraumatic stress disorder (PTSD), anxiety, and depression and of abusing alcohol and other substances (Carey, Norris, Durney, Shepardson, & Carey, 2018; Kirkner, Relyea, & Ullman, 2018). Women who blame themselves for the assault tend to experience more adjustment difficulties, including a higher risk for depression, whereas support from family and friends influences positive adjustment (Orchowski, Untied, & Gidycz, 2013; Sigurvinsdottir & Ullman, 2015; Vickerman & Margolin, 2009).

Male rape is increasingly recognized, and most states have revised their rape laws to be sex neutral (Hock, 2015). Men may feel a greater sense of shame and stigma than women and are even less likely than women to report being sexually assaulted. National surveys have suggested that about 2% of adult men in the United States (i.e., about 2 million) have experienced sexual assault, with the majority committed by acquaintances (Breiding et al., 2014). A recent survey of college students suggested a much higher prevalence of about 12% (Mellins et al., 2017).

Contextual influences, such as the prevalence of rape myths, can affect the prevalence of sexual

The #MeToo movement has drawn attention to the international problem of sexual assault and harrassment.
Gabriel Olsen/WireImage

assault. College men are more accepting of rape myths than are women and are more likely to cling to them following date rape education classes (Maxwell & Scott, 2014; Stewart, 2014). Gender-role stereotyping may contribute to the prevalence of sexual assault, as cultural stereotypes of men's and women's roles, encouraging dominance, aggression, and competition in males and passivity in females, may support attitudes that are accepting of sexual violence. Research with college students has shown that students who are highly gender stereotyped and believe in strict gender roles are more likely than their peers to blame sexual assault survivors, express attitudes condoning nonconsensual sex, and be aroused by depictions of rape (Lambert & Raichle, 2000; Malamuth, Addison, & Koss, 2000). Men who engage in sexual assault tend to interpret women's behavior inaccurately, often perceiving warmth and friendliness as indicating sexual interest (Perilloux, Easton, & Buss, 2012). They buy into rape myths, such as the belief that a victim "asked for it" by dressing attractively or behaving flirtatiously; that nonconsensual sex with a romantic partner, friend, or acquaintance cannot be considered rape; or that men are driven to commit rape by uncontrollable sexual impulses (Malamuth et al., 2000). Effective sexual assault prevention educates men and women about gender socialization and the nature and impact of sexual violence, debunks rape myths, and offers suggestions on how to intervene as a bystander (Stewart, 2014). In women, effective sexual assault prevention includes helping women assess assault risk from acquaintances, overcome emotional barriers in acknowledging danger, and engage in effective verbal and physical self-defense (Senn et al., 2015).

Substance Abuse

Substance use tends to rise during emerging adulthood as young people live away from their parents for the first time in their lives. Emerging adults experience the drive to explore the world at the same time as they feel pressure to complete their education, begin a career, and find a mate. These circumstances, coupled with easy access to drugs and alcohol, increase the risk of alcohol and substance abuse in emerging adulthood.

In North America, substance use, such as drug, alcohol, and tobacco, tends to begin during adolescence, peak in the early 20s, and decline into the 30s (Chen & Jacobson, 2012; Schulenberg & Miech, 2014; Staff et al., 2010). Generally speaking, similar patterns of use during emerging adulthood occur in Australia, New Zealand, and Northern European countries (Andrews & Westling, 2016). Substance use tends to decline as young adults become parents and transition into new family roles; however, substance use remains prevalent in adulthood, with about 15% of adults over age 26 reporting illicit drug use within the past year (National Institute on Drug Abuse, 2017). The following sections examine several commonly used substances: alcohol, marijuana, and tobacco.

Alcohol Use and Abuse

Alcohol is legal for young adults at age 21 in all U.S. states and is the drug of choice for most people throughout adulthood. Of particular concern to professionals are rates of **binge drinking**, defined as consuming five or more drinks in one sitting in men and four drinks in one sitting in women. Heavy drinking is defined as two or more instances of binge drinking within the past 30 days. As shown in Figure 13.5, binge drinking and heavy drinking are highest in emerging and young adulthood, with about one third of adults aged 18 to 24 and 25 to 34 as well as one in five adults aged 35 to 44 reporting binge drinking within the past 30 days (Substance Abuse and Mental Health Services Administration, 2014). Binge drinking is associated with negative short- and long-term consequences for physical and psychological well-being, including academic problems, fatal and nonfatal injuries, violence and crime, sexually transmitted diseases, and sexual assault (Kuntsche, Kuntsche, Thrul, & Gmel, 2017). For example, as shown in Figure 13.6, in 2013, about 20% of 21- to 25-year-olds and 26- to 29-year-olds and about 18% of 30- to 34-year-olds reported driving under the influence of alcohol within the past year (U.S. Department of Health and Human Services, 2014b). Each year, alcohol is implicated in one third of traffic fatalities and in 40% of all crimes (National Council on Alcoholism and Drug Dependence, 2015; National Highway Traffic Safety Administration, 2016).

Research with college students has suggested that binge and heavy drinking may be part of a "stage of life phenomenon" for which the transition out of high school increases the risk (Reckdenwald, Ford, & Murray, 2016). As they enter college, young people experience greater exposure to drinking and encounter higher levels of peer drinking and positive peer attitudes toward alcohol, and alcohol use tends to increase (Simons-Morton et al., 2016). Most emerging adults report experiencing more positive consequences of drinking (such as feeling social) than negative consequences (such as cognitive impairment), which contributes to high rates of binge and heavy drinking in this age group (Lau-Barraco, Linden-Carmichael, Hequembourg, & Pribesh, 2017; C. M. Lee, Maggs, Neighbors, & Patrick, 2011). Although emerging adults who attend college tend to drink more than their non-college-attending peers (Reckdenwald et al., 2016; Simons-Morton et al., 2016), heavy drinking and alcohol-related problems are

FIGURE 13.5

Current, Binge, and Heavy Alcohol Use Among Persons Ages 12 and Older, by Age, 2014

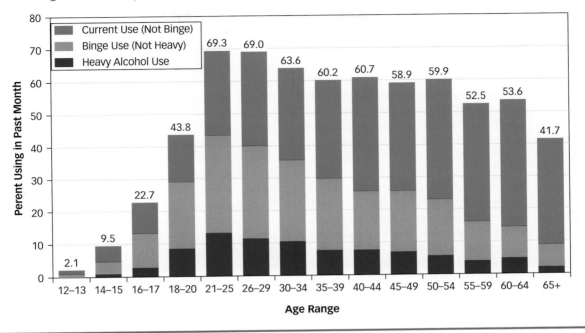

Source: Substance Abuse and Mental Health Services Administration (2014).

FIGURE 13.6

Driving Under the Influence of Alcohol in the Past Year Among People Age 16 or Older, by Age, 2014

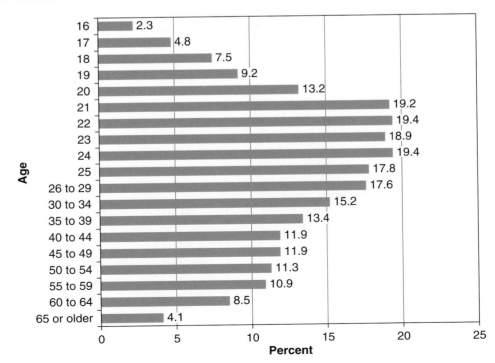

Source: Lipari, Hughes, & Bose, 2016.

more common among emerging adults regardless of college enrollment (Merrill & Carey, 2016).

Often referred to as "maturing out," alcohol use tends to decline as young people enter early adulthood. Generally, young adults in their 20s continue to drink frequently but consume less alcohol on each occasion (Arria et al., 2016). The transition to adult responsibilities such as career, marriage, and parenthood typically predicts declines in heavy drinking and alcohol-related problems (M. R. Lee, Chassin, & Villalta, 2013). Yet heavy drinking and binge drinking remain prevalent in adulthood, with 14% of middle-aged adults reporting binge drinking within the past month (Kanny, Liu, Brewer, & Lu, 2013).

Binge and heavy drinking are concerns because they both involve intermittent but high levels of alcohol consumption, which increases the risk of developing **alcohol dependence** and abuse (Simons, Wills, & Neal, 2014). Alcohol dependence, also known as alcohol use disorder, is a maladaptive pattern of alcohol use that leads to clinically significant impairment or distress. Alcohol dependence is signaled by tolerance, cravings and withdrawal, inability to reduce drinking, drinking more or for longer than intended, neglect of activities and obligations, and continued use of alcohol despite alcohol-related psychological or physical problems (American Psychiatric Association, 2013).

Although there are genetic risk factors for alcohol dependence and alcoholism, environmental factors, personal choices, and circumstances also influence whether an individual turns to alcohol as a coping mechanism (Enoch, 2013). Alcohol dependence and chronic excessive alcohol consumption increase the risk for chronic diseases such as cardiovascular disease, intestinal problems, neurologic impairment, liver disease, and several types of cancer (Rehm, 2011). Brain damage from chronic alcohol abuse can eventually lead to memory and concentration problems, confusion, and apathy (Stavro, Pelletier, & Potvin, 2013). Successful treatments for alcohol dependence include individual and family counseling, group support, coping skills, and possibly aversion therapy (the use of medication that produces negative reactions to alcohol such as vomiting) to spur a distaste for alcohol (McCrady, 2017).

Marijuana

By far the most commonly used substance, after alcohol, is marijuana, with 20% of 18- to 25-year-old emerging adults and 13% of 26- to 34-year-old young adults reporting use in the past month (Azofeifa et al., 2016; Miech et al., 2017). Young people consume marijuana for different reasons; those who cite experimentation as their primary reason tend to report fewer marijuana-related problems than do those who list coping, relaxation, and enjoyment (Patrick, Bray, & Berglund, 2016). Emerging adults are more likely to report recreational use rather than medical reasons for marijuana use; medical use becomes more common with age, especially into middle adulthood (Compton, Han, Hughes, Jones, & Blanco, 2017). For most young people, marijuana use is sporadic and limited in duration, but regular sustained use is associated with current and future dependence and adverse health and social outcomes, including the use of other substances (Griffin, Bang, & Botvin, 2010; Palamar, Griffin-Tomas, & Kamboukos, 2015).

Sustained marijuana use is associated with self-reported cognitive difficulties and personal problems during the middle to late 20s, including lower levels of academic attainment, lower income, greater levels of unemployment, conflict with partners, and poor life satisfaction (Conroy, Kurth, Brower, Strong, & Stein, 2015; Hall, 2014; Silins et al., 2014; C. Zhang, Brook, Leukefeld, & Brook, 2016). Heavy use of marijuana interferes with thinking, impairing a person's ability to shift attention from one item to another and to learn, form memories, and recall material (Bartholomew, Holroyd, & Heffernan, 2010; Crean, Crane, & Mason, 2011). Heavy marijuana use also interferes with executive functioning—problem solving, abstract reasoning, and judgment—and the earlier the age of onset, the greater the negative effects (Crean et al., 2011; Gruber, Sagar, Dahlgren, Racine, & Lukas, 2011). Regular marijuana use can interfere with completing developmental tasks of young adulthood, such as reaching education and career goals, forming intimate relationships and marriage, and taking on adult roles. Marijuana users tend to be less responsive to negative consequences in making decisions (Wesley, Hanlon, & Porrino, 2011). Finally, marijuana smokers experience many of the same respiratory problems common to tobacco smokers, such as cough, more frequent chest illnesses, and cancers. Marijuana smoke contains irritants and carcinogens and appears to have up to about 80% more carcinogens than tobacco smoke (Tashkin, 2013).

Although U.S. federal laws prohibit the sale and possession of marijuana, a growing number of U.S. states have joined many countries, such as Germany, the Netherlands, Australia, Spain, India, and Canada, in authorizing its sale for medical and, increasingly, recreational purposes (Kalvapallé, 2017; Rodriguez, 2017). The issue of marijuana legalization in the United States is examined in the Applying Developmental Science feature.

APPLYING DEVELOPMENTAL SCIENCE

 # Marijuana Legalization

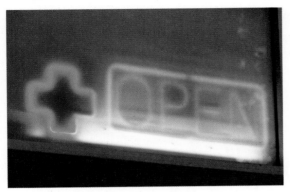

Although many states have legalized marijuana for medical purposes, it remains illegal under federal law.
iStock/400tmax

In response to anecdotal reports and some research suggesting that marijuana may be useful for easing symptoms of serious illnesses, such as cancer and AIDS, California passed Proposition 215 in 1996, legalizing marijuana sale and use for medical purposes. Yet despite Proposition 215, marijuana sale and possession remain federal offenses. The U.S. federal government does not distinguish medical marijuana from illicit marijuana. Although federal statues have not changed, as of this writing, 29 states have legalized medical marijuana (National Conference of State Legislatures, 2018).

Medical scientists argue that medical marijuana has not been subjected to the careful scientific study and medical trials that other drugs are subjected to, and there are no reliable guidelines on use or implications of prolonged use (S. C. Martin, 2016; Monte, Zane, & Heard, 2015). Although there is some evidence to support pain- and nausea-relieving effects, currently there is little evidence for other uses (Hill, 2015; Wilkinson, Radhakrishnan, & D'Souza, 2016). Additional research is needed to substantiate its purported benefits. In addition, since a common mode of ingesting marijuana remains smoking, users may be exposed to a variety of health threats common to cigarette smoke.

In 2012, Colorado and Washington became the first U.S. states to legalize the sale and possession of marijuana for recreational use. Currently, nine states permit recreational marijuana (M. Robinson, Berke, & Gould, 2018). Each regulates marijuana in a way similar to alcohol, allowing possession of a small quantity to adults ages 21 and older, with provisions against operating motor vehicles under the influence,

similar to alcohol laws (Steinmetz, 2016). The laws allow for commercial cultivation and sale subject to state regulation and taxation. Despite state legislation, marijuana remains illegal under federal statute. In 2009, the Justice Department announced that the federal government would not prosecute medical marijuana providers and consumers who were in compliance with state laws, suggesting support for state laws. However, in 2018, the federal government rescinded this position (Savage & Healy, 2018).

Currently, about 60% of U.S. adults support marijuana legalization, and support has increased substantially over the past 50 years. As Figure 13.7 illustrates, the Millennial and Gen X cohorts are most supportive; however, all generations have become more approving. Supporters of legalized marijuana contend that taxes on the sale of marijuana can produce significant tax revenue. For example, Colorado's legal marijuana sales generated more than $135 million in revenue from taxes and fees that the state put toward public projects such as school construction and renovation (Huddleston, 2016). At the same time, marijuana-related emergency room visits and hospitalizations as well as poison center calls increased about 1% per month over the first year since legalization (Davis et al., 2016). The number of children evaluated in the emergency department for unintentional marijuana ingestion has also increased substantially (Monte et al., 2015; Wang et al., 2016). Some experts expect heavy use to increase after recreational legalization (Hall & Lynskey, 2016).

One concern of marijuana legalization is the effect on children and adolescents. Although this area of research is somewhat new, some studies have suggested that medical marijuana laws are not associated with increases in recreational use by adolescents in states where medical marijuana is legal (Ammerman et al., 2015; Hasin et al., 2015; Pacula, Powell, Heaton, & Sevigny, 2015). Comparisons of 10th-grade students in Washington from 2000 to 2014 found that the prevalence of adolescent use remained stable before and after the legalization of recreational marijuana (Fleming, Guttmannova, Cambron, Rhew, & Oesterle, 2016). However, across time, young people showed more risks for marijuana use and abuse, including more favorable attitudes about use, less perceived harm of use, and perceived community attitudes favorable to use. Likewise, Washington State parents of adolescents reported increased parental use of marijuana and approval of adult use, as well as

(Continued)

(Continued)

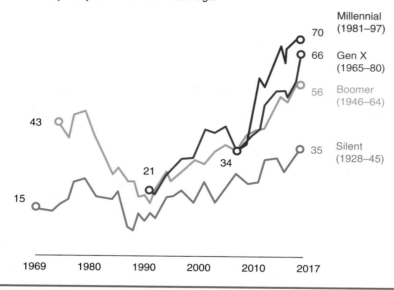

FIGURE 13.7

U.S. Public Opinion on Legalizing Marijuana, 1969–2017

% who say marijuana should be made legal

Millennial (1981–97) — 70
Gen X (1965–80) — 66
Boomer (1946–64) — 56
Silent (1928–45) — 35

43
21
34
15

1969   1980   1990   2000   2010   2017

Source: Reprinted with permission from "About six in ten Americans support marijuana legalization," Pew Research Center, Washington, DC (January, 2018). http://www.pewresearch.org/fact-tank/2018/01/05/americans-support-marijuana-legalization/

reductions in perceived harm after legalization of recreational use (Kosterman et al., 2016). Yet parents also showed wide opposition to marijuana use by adolescents and were opposed to allowing its use in the presence of children. Overall, high school students and their parents generally believe that their marijuana-related attitudes and behaviors changed little as a result of the law (Mason, Hanson, Fleming, Ringle, & Haggerty, 2015). The long-term effects of marijuana legislation, particularly for recreational use, have yet to be determined.

What Do You Think?

Suppose you wanted to study effects of legalizing marijuana on children, adolescents, and adults.

1. What variables would you examine (e.g., health, injuries, attitudes, and substance use)?

2. What design would you choose (review Chapter 1)?

3. What would you expect to find? Why? ●

Tobacco

Smoking is the leading cause of disease in the United States, responsible for one in five deaths each year (Office of the Surgeon General, 2016). Nearly 90% of smokers have their first cigarette before age 18, but regular or daily smoking often does not begin until about age 20 or later, and the overall risk of initiating smoking plateaus at about age 22 and is rare after 24 (Edwards, Carter, Peace, & Blakely, 2013; U.S. Department of Health and Human Services, 2014a). About 13% of emerging adults ages 18 to 24 are current smokers, compared with 18% of adults ages 25 to 44 years (Jamal et al., 2016). Many smokers do not consider themselves smokers because they only engage in occasional social smoking, "bumming" cigarettes rather than buying them and smoking in social groups rather than as a daily habit. In one study, 62% of young adults who indicated they had recently smoked identified themselves as social smokers (Song & Ling, 2011). Most social smokers report no immediate desire to quit, and although they acknowledge smoking-related health risks, they minimize them as being personally irrelevant (Brown, Carpenter, & Sutfin, 2011).

The life transitions that come with young adulthood, such as dramatic changes in social networks, living arrangements, and school and work settings, influence susceptibility to smoking and patterns of smoking behavior. During transitions

Smoking is highly addictive, leading many smokers to ignore health warnings.
iStock/DanBrandenburg

to marriage, parenthood, and occupational roles, young adults may either reject tobacco use or begin smoking regularly so that it becomes an established addiction. Education acts as a protective factor: Non-college-educated adults aged 18 to 34 are more than twice as likely to smoke as their college-educated peers (Centers for Disease Control and Prevention, 2011; Green et al., 2007; Lawrence, Fagan, Backinger, Gibson, & Hartman, 2007).

Why is smoking such a tenacious habit? With each cigarette, a smoker consumes one to two milligrams of nicotine, which enters the blood and reaches the brain quickly and stimulates reward pathways. Withdrawal symptoms of nicotine begin quickly, within a few hours after the last cigarette; these include irritability, craving, anxiety, and attention deficits, which often send the smoker in search of another cigarette. Other withdrawal symptoms include depression, sleep problems, and increased appetite. When a smoker quits, withdrawal symptoms often peak within the first few days of smoking cessation and usually subside within a few weeks, but some people continue to experience symptoms for months. Nearly 35 million people in the United States wish to quit smoking each year, but more than 85% of those who try to quit relapse, often within a week (National Institute on Drug Abuse, 2009).

Some smokers turn to e-cigarettes as an alternative to tobacco cigarettes, viewing e-cigarettes as safer than conventional cigarettes (Goniewicz, Lingas, & Hajek, 2013; Huerta, Walker, Mullen, Johnson, & Ford, 2017). E-cigarettes aerosolize nicotine and produce a vapor that emulates that of conventional cigarettes (Yamin, Bitton, & Bates, 2010). E-cigarettes are the most commonly used tobacco product among young adults, with about 40% of emerging adults ages 18 to 25 reporting use in the past month (Ramo, Young-Wolff, & Prochaska, 2015). Although many people believe that e-cigarettes are a healthy alternative to smoking (Farsalinos &

Polosa, 2014), research instead suggests that nicotine and the aerosol created by e-cigarettes can include chemicals, heavy metals, and ultrafine particles that reach the lungs and are linked to lung disease (Ghosh et al., 2018; Murthy, 2017). Moreover, e-cigarette users show increased risk for transitioning to tobacco smoking (Andrews, Hampson, Severson, Westling, & Peterson, 2016; Soneji et al., 2017).

THINKING IN CONTEXT 13.3

1. What aspects of young adulthood increase young people's risk for obesity and poor health behaviors, such as engaging in little physical activity or smoking?

2. Explain some of the reasons why substance use is highest in young adulthood. What contributes to its decline?

3. Apply the bioecological framework to explain the myriad of factors that influence eating and exercise habits over early adulthood. Identify factors at the microsystem, mesosystem, exosystem, and macrosystem levels that can act as risk and protective factors to health. How do these shift from adolescence into emerging adulthood and from emerging adulthood into early adulthood?

COGNITIVE DEVELOPMENT IN EMERGING AND EARLY ADULTHOOD

» LO 13.4 Compare postformal reasoning, pragmatic thought, and cognitive-affective complexity.

For Alexander, a college junior majoring in biology, weighing hypotheses on evolutionary theory is easy. As he sees it, there is one account that is clearly more rational and supported by data than the others. However, like most emerging adults, Alexander finds personal decisions much more difficult because many are vague and have multiple options with both costs and benefits.

As individuals progress toward adulthood, their thinking becomes increasingly flexible and practical. Adults come to expect uncertainty and ambiguity, as well as recognize that everyday problems are influenced by emotion and experience rather than pure reasoning. Researchers who study adult cognition often focus on **epistemic cognition**—the ways in which individuals understand the nature of knowledge and how they arrive at ideas, beliefs, and conclusions.

Postformal Reasoning

According to Piaget's cognitive-developmental theory, adolescents demonstrate formal operational reasoning, including the ability to think abstractly and to solve hypothetical problems. Although formal operational reasoning is the end point of Piaget's scheme, representing what he believed to be the most advanced form of reasoning, many researchers believe that there is much more to adult thinking than logical abstract reasoning. Specifically, Piaget's final stage of cognitive development may not adequately describe adult cognition. Instead, adults develop a more advanced form of thinking known as **postformal reasoning,** which integrates abstract reasoning with practical considerations (Sinnott, 1998). Young adults who demonstrate postformal reasoning recognize that most problems have multiple causes and solutions, that some solutions are better choices than others, and that all problems involve uncertainty. People's understanding of the nature of knowledge advances along a predictable path in emerging and early adulthood, especially among college students.

When they enter college, individuals tend to view knowledge as a set of facts that hold true across people and contexts (P. M. King & Kitchener, 2016; Perry, 1970). Beginning college students tend to display **dualistic thinking,** in which knowledge and accounts of phenomena are viewed as either right or wrong with no in between. Learning is viewed as a matter of acquiring and assessing facts. At the dualistic stage of reasoning, individuals tend to have difficulty grasping that several contradictory arguments can each have supporting evidence. The entering college student may sit through class lectures, wondering, "Which theory is right?" and become frustrated when the professor explains that multiple theories each have various strengths and weaknesses.

With experience and exposure to multiple viewpoints, multiple arguments, and their inherent contradictions, individuals become aware of the diversity of viewpoints that exist in every area of study. Their thinking becomes more flexible, and they relinquish the belief in absolute knowledge that characterizes dualistic, black-and-white thinking. Next, young adults move toward **relativistic thinking,** in which most knowledge is viewed as relative, dependent on the situation and thinker (P. M. King & Kitchener, 2016; Perry, 1970). Relativistic thinkers recognize that beliefs are subjective, that there are multiple perspectives on a given issue, and that all perspectives are defensible, at least to a certain extent. At first, relativistic thinkers may become overwhelmed by relativism—the great many opinions and options—and conclude that most topics are simply a matter of opinion and all views are correct. For example, they may conclude that all solutions to a problem are correct as it all depends on a person's perspective. The more mature thinker who displays **reflective judgment,** however, acknowledges the multiple options and carefully evaluates them to choose the most adequate solution. He or she recognizes that options and opinions can be evaluated—and generates criteria to do so (Sinnott, 2003). As shown in Table 13.1, reflective judgment is the most mature type of reasoning as it synthesizes contradictions among perspectives. Although reasoning tends to advance throughout the college years, ultimately few adults demonstrate reflective judgment (Hamer & van Rossum, 2017).

Postformal cognitive development depends on experience and metacognition, the ability to reflect on one's thought process. When individuals are exposed to situations and reasoning that challenges their knowledge and belief systems, they may be motivated to consider the adequacy of their own reasoning processes and modify them as needed (Sandoval, Greene, & Bråten, 2016). Social interaction is critical to postformal development. Discussing and considering multiple perspectives and solutions to a problem can spur individuals to evaluate their own reasoning. With maturation, young people become more likely to compare their reasoning process and justifications with others. When their justifications fall short, adults seek a more adequate explanation and adjust their thinking accordingly. Advancement to postformal reasoning is associated with contextual factors—specifically, exposure to realistic but ambiguous problems with diverging information, as well as supportive guidance, such as that which is often a part of college education within Western cultures (Stahl, Ferguson, & Kienhues, 2016; Zeidler, Sadler, Applebaum, & Callahan, 2009).

Given that postformal reasoning is influenced by experience, not all emerging and young adults display it. For example, Chinese college students generally do not display the typical advancement from dualism to relativism to reflective judgment (L. Zhang, 2004). When compared with their U.S. counterparts, Chinese students tend to lack opportunities for making their own choices and decisions in many areas such as curricula, career choices, academic majors, and residential arrangements (L. Zhang, 1999). Experience in decision making matters. Some theorists argue that even in Western cultures, the most advanced level of postformal reasoning (commitment within relativism) may come only with graduate study and wrestling with challenging philosophical and practical problems (Hamer & van Rossum, 2017; P. M. King & Kitchener, 2016). People's

TABLE 13.1

Postformal Reasoning

	UNDERSTANDING OF KNOWLEDGE	EXAMPLES FROM INTERVIEWS WITH YOUNG ADULTS
Dualistic thinking	Knowledge is a collection of facts, and a given idea is either right or wrong.	"… theory might be convenient … but … the facts are what's there … and … should be the main thing" (Perry, 1970/1998).
Relativistic thinking	Knowledge is relative, dependent on the situation and thinker, and a matter of opinion and perspective.	"I really can't [choose a point of view] on this issue. It depends on your beliefs since there is no way of proving either one … I believe they're both the same as far as accuracy" (King & Kitchener, 2004, p. 6). "People think differently and so they attack the problem differently. Other theories could be as true as my own but based on different evidence" (King & Kitchener, 2004, p. 7).
Reflective judgment	Knowledge is a synthesis of contradictory information and perspectives whose evidence can be evaluated according to certain criteria.	"[When approaching a problem] there are probably several ways to do it. What are they? Which one's most efficient? Which one will give us the most accurate results?" (Marra & Palmer, 2004, p. 117) . "One can judge an argument by how well thought-out the positions are, what kinds of reasoning and evidence are used to support it, and how consistent the way one argues on this topic is as compared with how one argues on other topics" (King & Kitchener, 2004, p. 7). "It is very difficult in this life to be sure. There are degrees of sureness. You come to a point at which you are sure enough for a personal stance on the issue" (King & Kitchener, 2004, p. 7).

reasoning advances throughout adulthood; however, reasoning and decision making are not simply cognitive endeavors but are influenced by emotion.

Pragmatic Thought and Cognitive-Affective Complexity

Cognitive advances permit adults to reason about hypothetical and academic problems in more sophisticated ways, but they also influence young adults' everyday functioning. Adults apply their postformal reasoning abilities, specifically reflective judgment, to solve everyday problems. This ability to accept inconsistencies and use reasoning to determine the best alternatives, to apply reflective judgment in real-world contexts, is known as to **pragmatic thought** (Labouvie-Vief, 2015). Managing various roles and tackling the problems of everyday life requires thinking that is adaptive and accepting of contradiction. For example, adults must come to terms with their relative power across various contexts: At home they have autonomy and are able to carve out their own niche, whereas at work they must follow the directions of their employer. Coordinating dynamic roles as spouse, parent, friend, employee, and manager requires flexibility.

However, reasoning in everyday situations is not simply a matter of logic—it is fused with emotion. Our evaluations of potential solutions to problems are influenced by our emotions—positive and negative feelings about each option. Sometimes our cognitive and emotional evaluations conflict. Over the course of adulthood, individuals become better at understanding and regulating their emotions and become less swayed by emotions, which influences their reasoning in everyday situations (Mather, 2012; T. L. Watson & Blanchard-Fields, 1998). Successfully coordinating emotion and cognition improves people's capacity to adapt to the complexities of adult life and the inherent balancing of many roles and obligations (Labouvie-Vief, 2006). This capacity to be aware of emotions, integrate positive and negative feelings about an issue, and regulate intense emotions to make logical decisions about complicated issues is known as **cognitive-affective complexity** (Labouvie-Vief, 2015; Mikels et al., 2010).

Cognitive-affective complexity increases from early adulthood through late middle adulthood. With gains in cognitive-affective complexity, adults better understand others, including their perspectives, feelings, and motivations. This, in turn, helps them to interact with others in more sensitive and complex ways, potentially enhancing their relationships.

Evaluating Cognitive-Developmental Approaches to Adult Development

Similar to research on the development of formal operations, advances in postformal reasoning and cognitive-affective complexity vary among individuals. Adults are more likely than adolescents to demonstrate postformal reasoning, but not all adults reach the most advanced levels of reasoning

(Hamer & van Rossum, 2017). In fact, most do not. People seem to show more mature reasoning when considering material and problems with which they have the greatest experience.

As with findings with younger ages, the ways in which researchers ask questions influence individuals' responses and, ultimately, what is concluded about cognition (Ojalehto & Medin, 2015). For example, researchers have learned that more complex responses are yielded when they ask participants to consider systems of causation using prompts such as, "How are x and y related to each other and to the larger system?" as compared with prompts that encourage reasoning about individual causal links ("Does x cause y?"). This work has shown that there is cultural variation in reasoning about causal events (Ojalehto & Medin, 2015). Westerners who tend to explain events use a single or few direct causes. In contrast, people from East Asian cultures tend to explain events as caused by multiple factors that interact, creating a ripple effect whereby one event holds many complex consequences that may not be easily anticipated (Maddux & Yuki, 2006). This reasoning is conceptually similar to the interacting systems posited by Bronfenbrenner (see Chapter 1). Other research has shown that a multifactor interactive view of causality is present among people of many non-Western cultural communities. For example, indigenous Itza' Maya and Native American Menominee people tend to emphasize complex interactions across many entities, such as animal and spiritual entities; contexts, such as habitats; and time frames (Atran & Medin, 2008; Unsworth et al., 2012).

Likewise, cognitive-affective complexity relies on advances in emotional awareness and regulation. The ability to coordinate sophisticated emotions and cognitions varies with situations, tasks, contexts, and motivations (Labouvie-Vief, 2015). Furthermore, advanced forms of pragmatic reasoning likely do not suddenly appear but rather emerge with gains in knowledge, experience, and information processing capacity (Kuhn, 2013; Moshman & Moshman, 2011).

EDUCATION AND DEVELOPMENT IN EMERGING AND EARLY ADULTHOOD

» LO 13.5 Explain how attending college influences young adults' development, and identify challenges faced by first-generation and nontraditional students.

Unlike childhood and adolescence, when education is mandated and virtually all students progress with their peers on the same schedule, emerging and early adulthood offers a wide range of educational and vocational opportunities and challenges. College represents an increasingly common transition from secondary school to the workplace.

Developmental Impact of Attending College

Attending college, at least for a time, has become a normative experience for emerging adults. In 2015, 69% of high school graduates in the United States enrolled in 2- or 4-year colleges (National Center for Education Statistics, 2017b). Students enroll in college to learn about a specific field of study (i.e., a major) and to prepare for careers, but attending college is also associated with many positive developmental outcomes. Adults of all ages often view their college years as highly influential in shaping their thoughts, values, and worldview (Patton, Renn, Guido-DiBrito, & Quaye, 2016). In addition to academic learning, college presents young people with new perspectives and encourages experimentation with alternative behavior, beliefs, and values. College courses

There are intellectual, psychological, and social benefits of attending college.
iStock/Rawpixel

THINKING IN CONTEXT 13.4

1. Can you identify examples of postformal reasoning in your own thinking? What are some challenges of evaluating one's own thinking?

2. 2. What kinds of experiences foster the development of postformal reasoning? In your view, is higher education necessary to develop the capacity for postformal reasoning? Why or why not?

often require students to construct arguments and solve complex problems, fostering the development of postformal reasoning (P. M. King & Kitchener, 2016). Attending college is associated with advances in moral reasoning, identity development, and social development (Lapsley & Hardy, 2017; Patton et al., 2016).

The positive impact of attending college is not simply a matter of the type of college one attends; research indicates that all institutions, public and private, selective and open enrollment, advance cognitive and psychological development (Mayhew et al., 2016). In addition, students at 2-year community colleges show similar cognitive and academic gains to those of their peers at 4-year institutions (Monaghan & Attewell, 2015). Rather than the type of institution attended, developmental outcomes are most influenced by student involvement in campus life and peer interaction in academic and social contexts. Students who are active in campus life and feel a sense of belonging tend to show greater educational attainment (Mayhew et al., 2016). Students who live in residence halls have more opportunities to interact with peers and become involved in the academic and social aspects of campus life—and show the greatest cognitive gains in the college years (Bronkema & Bowman, 2017).

Despite these benefits, however, many students do not complete college. Only about two thirds of students who enroll in 4-year institutions graduate within 6 years and one third of students enrolled at 2-year institutions graduate within 3 years (National Center for Education Statistics, 2017d). Generally, student attrition is highest in colleges with open enrollment and those with relatively low admission requirements.

First-Generation College Students

Students whose parents do not have 4-year degrees are known as first-generation college students. About one third of students are first-generation students (Skomsvold, 2014). First-generation college students experience a higher risk of dropout than students with parents who have earned 4-year degrees. Students of color and those of low socioeconomic status are disproportionately likely to be first-generation college students. In 2016, about 14% of all college students enrolled in the United States were African American and 18% were Hispanic (as compared with 57% White) (National Center for Education Statistics, 2017c).

First-generation students tend to be less active in campus and extracurricular activities and less academically prepared than their peers, two factors that often aid students in adjusting to college and are risk factors for college dropout (Feldman, 2017).

In addition, first-generation college students often face economic circumstances that interfere with their ability to participate on campus. For example, first-generation students are more likely than their peers to be enrolled part-time, hold a job, and have mixed feelings about college (Ward, Siegel, & Davenport, 2012). With few family and peer models of how to succeed in college, first-generation and minority students may feel isolated and find it difficult to understand and adjust to the college student role and expectations. First-generation students report having fewer opportunities to talk about their negative experiences and are more likely to feel guilty about their educational achievement (Jury et al., 2017).

Many students experience a cultural mismatch between their college environment and their sense of self and the communities in which they identify (Phillips, Stephens, & Townsend, 2016). Many first-generation college students live in families and communities characterized by norms of interdependence, where community members "look out" for one another, which often contrasts with the norms of independence that are prevalent in college environments (Stephens, Fryberg, Markus, Johnson, & Covarrubias, 2012). For example, in one study, Latino first-generation students revealed that many experienced conflicts between their home and school values and responsibilities that interfered with their academic achievement and sense of well-being. Conflicts included providing assistance to family versus doing academic work and allocating funds to the family or for travel to see family versus allocating money for educational expenses (Vasquez-Salgado, Greenfield, & Burgos-Cienfuegos, 2015). Likewise, some Latino students report feeling guilty for attending college and not offering their families daily assistance (Covarrubias & Fryberg, 2015).

Students' transition to and success in college are also influenced by the college environment. Institutions that are responsive to the academic, social, and cultural needs of students help them adjust to college and, ultimately, succeed (Mayhew et al., 2016). Reaching out to at-risk students during the first weeks of college can help them to feel connected to the institution. Colleges and universities can provide opportunities for faculty and students to interact and form connections, help students to develop study skills, and assist students in getting involved on campus. Students who live on campus, see faculty as concerned with their development, establish relationships with faculty and other students, and become involved in campus life are more likely to succeed and graduate from college (Mayhew et al., 2016). When students feel that they are part of a campus community, they are more likely to persist and graduate.

Nontraditional College Students

Virtually all research on the effects of college tends to focus on what most people think of as the typical college student, ages 18 through 22. However, 23% of students enrolled in public 2-year colleges and 11% enrolled in public 4-year colleges are so-called nontraditional college students, adult learners over age 25 (National Center for Education Statistics, 2017a).

Why do students return to college or attend for the first time in their mid-20s or beyond? Adult learners tend to have some or all of the following characteristics: are older than the typical-age student, are independent for financial aid purposes, have one or more dependents, attend college part-time, and may work full-time (Radford, Cominole, & Skomsvold, 2015). Each of these factors poses significant challenges to nontraditional students' success in college (MacDonald, 2018). They are more likely than other college students to juggle multiple life roles, such as worker, spouse, parent, and caregiver. Sometimes the demands of school, family, and work conflict. For example, work-related travel is often disruptive to child care as well as academic demands, resulting in class absences and missed assignments. Over one third of nontraditional students are people of color, and the majority are women ("Time & Money," 2016). Adult learners often seek a college degree to be eligible for higher paying and more satisfying careers. Others enroll in college to change career paths. Employers sometimes encourage students to enroll in college to learn new skills.

However, nontraditional students bring several strengths. They tend to show a readiness to learn and a problem-centered orientation toward learning that emphasizes acquiring the knowledge and skills needed for career advancement (Ross-Gordon, 2011). Adult learners tend to have a more complex knowledge base from which to draw and emphasize seeking meaning and applying what they learn to their lives. Their experience and multiple roles can help nontraditional learners make meaning of theoretical concepts that may be purely abstract to younger learners (Osam, Bergman, & Cumberland, 2017).

Many adult learners may find the practical details of college difficult to navigate, as most colleges are oriented toward emerging adults (Osam et al., 2017). For example, classes that meet 2 or 3 days each week often conflict with work schedules. Evening classes often meet once per week, providing convenience at the expense of continuity and frequent contact with professors. Some students may find that required courses are offered only during the day. They may have difficulty accessing advisors and student support services. Many colleges and universities increasingly support the needs of nontraditional students by extending student services beyond business hours, providing adequate and close parking for those students who rush from work to school, and offering affordable on-campus child care for full- and part-time students, including evening students (Hope, 2017). Some also offer orientation programs for adult learners to provide information about support resources as well as help nontraditional students connect with one another and begin to build a social support network of peers.

The Forgotten Third

It can be said that attending college is part of the American dream and has become expected of many young people. Yet, each year, about one third of high school graduates in the United States transition from high school to work without enrolling in college. In 2016, only 36% of adults held college degrees by age 29 (National Center for Education Statistics, 2016). While some academically well-prepared students report forgoing college because of a desire to work or a lack of interest in academics, many cite economic barriers, such as the high cost of college or the need to support their family, as reasons for nonattendance (Bozick & DeLuca, 2011). The population of non-college-bound youth has been referred to in the literature as "forgotten" by educators, scholars, and policy makers, because relatively few resources are directed toward learning about or assisting them, as compared with college-bound young adults.

Young adults who enter the workforce immediately after high school have fewer work opportunities than those of prior generations. The rate of unemployment for high school graduates is about twice that of bachelor's degree holders (Dennis Vilorio, 2016; U.S. Bureau of Labor Statistics, 2015a). In addition, many young people with high school degrees spend their first working years in jobs that are similar to those they

Adults return to college for many reasons, including to change career paths, obtain higher paying and more satisfying careers, learn new skills, and fulfill personal goals.
iStock/Rawpixel

FIGURE 13.8

Unemployment Rates and Earnings by Educational Attainment in 2017

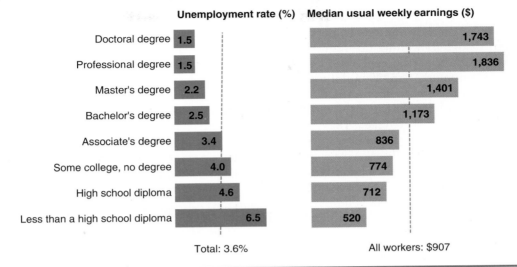

Total: 3.6%   All workers: $907

Source: U.S. Bureau of Labor Statistics, 2018.

held in high school: unskilled, with low pay and little security (Rosenbaum & Person, 2003). As illustrated in Figure 13.8, at all ages, high school graduates earn less and are more likely to be unemployed than peers with college degrees.

The curricula of most secondary schools tend to be oriented toward college-bound students, and counseling tends to focus on helping students gain admission to college (Krei & Rosenbaum, 2000). Some argue that over the past three decades, secondary education has shifted toward emphasizing academics and reducing vocational training, leaving young adults who do not attend college ill prepared for the job market (Symonds, Schwartz, & Ferguson, 2011). A solution proposed in the Pathways to Prosperity report from Harvard Graduate School of Education is for the U.S. educational system to support multiple pathways

in the transition to adulthood (Ferguson & Lamback, 2014; Symonds, Schwartz, & Ferguson, 2011b). Opportunities for vocational training and to obtaining relevant work experience will help young people try out careers and get relevant training for specific jobs. In addition, training programs should relay specific expectations for youth with regard to their responsibility in career training and decision making as well as the educational and vocational support they can expect in return (Symonds et al., 2011).

CAREER DEVELOPMENT IN EMERGING AND EARLY ADULTHOOD

» LO 13.6 **Discuss vocational choice and the transition to work.**

Selecting an occupation is one of the most important decisions that young people make. Children often fantasize about careers as astronauts, actors, and rock stars—careers that bear little resemblance to the choices they ultimately make when they grow up. How do people select occupations in real life?

Occupational Stages

Developmental theorist Donald Super proposed that the development of occupational goals progresses through five stages (Super, 1990). According to Super's model, vocational maturity reflects the degree to which an individual's occupational

THINKING IN CONTEXT 13.5

1. What are some of the reasons why a young adult might not attend college or might drop out? What can schools, colleges, parents, or policy makers do to help young adults attend college?

2. First-generation and nontraditional students have unique circumstances that influence their likelihood of success in college. Identify personal and contextual strengths and resources that may help them to be resilient and may support their success in college.

behaviors and status match the age-appropriate occupational stage. The first stage of occupational development, known as *crystallization,* begins in adolescence. Adolescents from ages 14 through 18 begin to think about careers in increasingly complex ways, considering their own interests, personality, abilities, and values as well as the requirements of each career. Similar to the exploration entailed in identity development, career exploration is at first tentative. Adolescents seek information about careers by talking with family, friends, and teachers, as well as through Internet searches. They compare what they learn with their own interests.

The next stage is the *specification* stage (at about ages 18–21), in which individuals identify specific occupational goals and pursue the education needed to achieve them. As a first-year college student, Imani knew that she wanted to do something related to business but had not yet selected among several possible majors. Imani considered several business-related majors, including accounting, management, and entrepreneurship, and completed an internship at an investment firm before deciding to major in finance.

The third stage, *implementation,* typically from ages 21 to 24, is when emerging adults complete training, enter the job market, and make the transition to become employees. The developmental task of the implementation stage is to reconcile expectations about employment and career goals with available jobs. Young people may take temporary jobs or change jobs as they learn about work roles and attempt to match their goals with available positions. For example, Yolanda majored in education but found no teaching positions available at schools near her home. She accepted a temporary position running an after-school program while she applied for jobs in other cities and states. Even young adults who attain their "dream jobs" often find that they must tailor and adapt their expectations and goals in light of their career setting.

In the *stabilization* stage, young adults from ages 25 to 35 become established in a career; they settle into specific jobs, gain experience, and adapt to changes in their workplace and in their field of work. Toward the end of early adulthood, from age 35 and up, individuals progress through the final stage, consolidation. They accumulate experience and advance up the career ladder, moving into supervisory positions and becoming responsible for the next generation of workers.

Although a stage-oriented approach to understanding career development remains useful, it is important to recognize that career development does not follow a universal pattern. Not everyone progresses through the stages in the prescribed order and at the same pace. For many adults, career development does not progress in a linear fashion; in fact, most adults do not hold the same occupation throughout adulthood. For example, adults in their 50s today have had an average of nine occupations between the ages of 18 and 40 (U.S. Bureau of Labor Statistics, 2015b). Likewise, today's young adults in their 20s are likely to have held six different jobs between ages 18 and 26 (U.S. Bureau of Labor Statistics, 2014). Young adults can expect to change career paths one or more times throughout their lives. Nevertheless, in considering an adult's perspective on careers, it is useful to conceptualize career development as entailing the five stages outlined by Super: crystallization, specification, implementation, stabilization, and consolidation.

Influences on Vocational Choice

Many factors influence how emerging adults perceive and evaluate occupational choices, but perhaps the most important factor in selecting a career is the match between their personality traits and abilities and their occupational interests. We are most satisfied when we select occupations that match our personalities and other individual traits, such as intelligence and skills. John Holland (1997) proposed that occupational choices can be categorized by six personality types, as shown in Table 13.2. Holland explained that each personality type is best suited to a particular type of vocation.

It is useful to consider careers in terms of Holland's six personality types, but most people have traits that correspond to more than one personality type and are able to successfully pursue several career paths (Holland, 1997; Spokane & Cruza-Guet, 2005). Furthermore, many careers entail a variety of skills and talents that cross the boundaries of the six-factor typology.

While personality is an important influence on vocational choice, contextual influences such as family and educational opportunities also determine our choice of career. Parents influence their children's career development in a variety of ways. Parents tend to share personality characteristics and abilities with their children and influence educational attainment, which in turn influences career choice (Ellis & Bonin, 2003; Schoon & Parsons, 2002). Parents act as role models. Socioeconomic status and parents' occupational fields influence career choice (Schoon & Polek, 2011).

Young people in high-SES households are more likely to receive career information from parents. In one study, African American mothers with at least some exposure to college were more likely than other mothers to use a variety of strategies to aid their daughters' progress on academic and career goals, such as gathering information about career

TABLE 13.2

Personality and Vocational Choice

PERSONALITY TYPE	VOCATIONAL CHOICES
Investigative	Enjoys working with ideas; likely to select a scientific career (e.g., biologist, physicist).
Social	Enjoys interacting with people; likely to select a human services career (e.g., teaching, nursing, counseling).
Realistic	Enjoys working with objects and real-world problems; likely to select a mechanical career (carpenter, mechanic, plumber).
Artistic	Enjoys individual expression; likely to select a career in the arts, including writing and performing arts.
Conventional	Prefers well-structured tasks; values social status; likely to select a career in business (e.g., accounting, banking).
Enterprising	Enjoys leading and persuading others; values adventure; likely to select a career in sales or politics.

options, colleges, and professionals from whom to seek advice (Kerpelman, Shoffner, & Ross-Griffin, 2002). Regardless of socioeconomic status, parents can provide support and motivation. Among low-SES first-generation college students, a sense of ethnic identity and maternal support predicted career expectations and, in turn, school engagement—the behavior needed to achieve vocational goals (Kantamneni, McCain, Shada, Hellwege, & Tate, 2016). Research with college students in the Philippines showed that parent and teacher support predicted career optimism (P. R. J. M. Garcia, Restubog, Bordia, Bordia, & Roxas, 2015). Parental expectations and encouragement for academic success and pursuit of high-status occupations also predict vocational choice and success (Maier, 2005).

Considering that most adults spend nearly one third of their waking hours at work, it is not surprising that the career setting is an important context for psychosocial development in early adulthood. Career development does not end with selecting a vocation. Young adults must obtain a job, learn about their role and tasks, develop proficiency, work well with others, respond to direction, and develop a good working relationship with supervisors. Work life influences young people's sense of competence, independence, and financial security and often is a source of new friendships (Brooks & Everett, 2008).

Transition to Work

Many young people find themselves employed in careers that are not their first choice, often explaining that they simply "fell into it," without exerting much effort or a choice. Young people's jobs frequently do not match their interests and education. These mismatches are common during the early years of employment as young adults are learning about their competencies and preferences and comparing them with the reality they encounter in the workplace. For example, one study of 1,200 Australian young adults found that 7 years after completing their schooling, only 20% were working in a field that represented their greatest interest (Athanasou, 2002). The day-to-day tasks entailed by a given occupation often differ from young people's expectations, as young people are typically faced with more clerical and other paperwork, longer work hours, less supportive and instructive supervisors, and lower pay than expected (Hatcher & Crook, 1988). The reality that vocational expectations are not always achieved can be a shock and can influence self-concept and occupational development as young adults revise their expectations.

Managing expectations in light of reality often leads young adults to resign and seek alternative jobs and careers. It is not uncommon for an individual to undergo as many as seven job changes by age 28 (U.S. Bureau of Labor Statistics, 2014). By another estimate, young adults hold, on average, four jobs between the ages of 18 and 21, three between 22 and 24, and three between 25 and 28 (U.S. Bureau of Labor Statistics, 2016a). The median length of job tenure (i.e., time spent in a particular position) is about 4 years, on average, but varies with age. The median tenure of older workers ages 55 to 64 is 10 years, as compared with 3 years for young adults ages 25 to 34 (U.S. Bureau of Labor Statistics, 2016c).

Career development follows a myriad of paths. In Western industrialized societies, men most often are employed continuously after completing their formal education and until retirement, whereas women display more varied and discontinuous career trajectories, often interrupting or deferring their career in favor of childrearing and family caretaking (Hite & McDonald, 2003). In this sense, women may experience multiple transitions to and from work, with potential implications for their adjustment and satisfaction.

Women and people of color often face the glass ceiling, an invisible barrier preventing them from advancing to the highest levels of the career ladder.
iStock/track5

Diversity in the Workplace

In recent decades, the workplace in Western industrialized countries has become increasingly diverse as women and ethnic minorities have entered nearly all careers. Throughout Europe and North America, about half of the labor force is female (Eurostat, 2016; The World Bank, 2016). Fifty-seven percent of women in the United States work as compared with 47% of women in Canada (Statistics Canada, 2017; U.S. Bureau of Labor Statistics, 2015c). Likewise, ethnic diversity is increasing in every occupation and every nation. Despite this, women and ethnic minorities face many obstacles to career success, often collectively known as the **glass ceiling,** the invisible barrier that prevents women and ethnic minorities from advancing to the highest levels of the career ladder. (For more on women and the glass ceiling, see the accompanying feature, Lives in Context: Gender and STEM Careers.)

Unfortunately, women and ethnic minorities tend to fill lower-level positions, and their numbers decline with each higher rung on the career ladder. Women in the United States hold about three quarters of office and administrative support positions but only 39% of management positions (U.S. Department of Labor, 2017). The effect is even more striking for ethnic minorities. As shown by Figure 13.9, half of Asian Americans and 40% of White Americans hold managerial and professional

FIGURE 13.9

Employed People by Occupation, Race, and Ethnicity

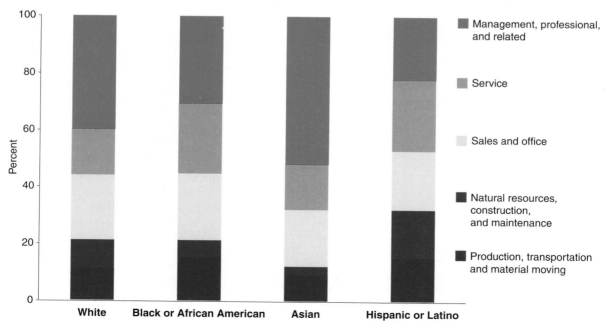

Legend:
- Management, professional, and related
- Service
- Sales and office
- Natural resources, construction, and maintenance
- Production, transportation and material moving

Source: U.S. Bureau of Labor Statistics, 2016.

positions, as compared with less than one third of African Americans and less than one quarter of Hispanic or Latino Americans (U.S. Bureau of Labor Statistics, 2016b).

As shown in Figure 13.10, women, especially ethnic minority women, are less likely than White men to hold senior executive jobs, the top level of management, in public- and private-sector organizations.

Although laws guarantee equal opportunity, racial bias remains an influence, even prior to a job interview. In one study, White male participants were asked to examine résumés that varied in quality (some indicated high qualifications and others low) and by the writer's race (African American, Hispanic, Asian, and White). The participants rated résumés from hypothetical Asian job seekers as highly qualified for high-status jobs, regardless of the actual résumé quality. When they were shown résumés indicating high qualifications, they rated them higher for White and Hispanic job seekers than for African Americans. In fact, they gave African American job seekers negative evaluations regardless of résumé quality. This result indicates how racial discrimination may make it difficult for even highly qualified African American candidates to obtain jobs (E. B. King, Madera, Hebl, Knight, & Mendoza, 2006). In another study, college students judged recommendation letters for hypothetical

---

FIGURE 13.10

U.S. Private Sector Executives, by Gender, Race/Ethnicity, 2014

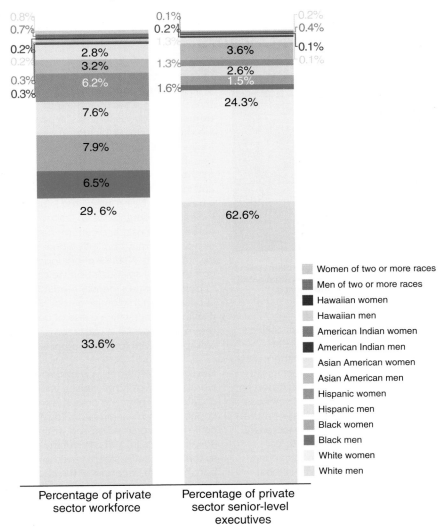

Source: Reproduced with the permission of the American Association of University Women.

job candidates of various ethnicities; the results were similarly biased against African Americans (Morgan, Elder, & King, 2013).

In the workplace, discrimination is often subtle, such as an employer complimenting an African American employee's eloquence (and not her similarly articulate White colleague) or suggesting that an older worker (but not his young adult colleagues) leave work early to rest after a big meeting. Frequently, subtle discrimination is unintentional; however, it is just as damaging as overt discrimination (Jones, Peddie, Gilrane, King, & Gray, 2016). Workers' perceptions of being discriminated against are related to poor physical health, including measures of stress, chronic illness, and acute illness, and mental health, such as depressive and anxiety symptoms (Mouzon, Taylor, Woodward, & Chatters, 2017; Triana, Jayasinghe, & Pieper, 2015).

Minority women are faced with multiple obstacles to their career success, often experiencing both gender and racial discrimination. Minority women who reach career success tend to display high *self-efficacy*, or feelings of personal control, and engage in active problem solving, confronting problems rather than avoiding them (Byars & Hackett, 1998). African American women who become leaders in their professions tend to report close supportive relationships with successful women, such as mentors, colleagues, and similarly successful friends, who help them set high expectations and provide support in achieving them. Mentoring is important for career development of all young adults (Combs & Milosevic, 2016). Women of color report strong desires to be mentored by women of their own ethnicity. However, the ethnic and gender obstacles to career success mean that women of color may find it difficult to establish a

---

Gender and STEM Careers

Gender roles have broadened, but women have been slow to reach equal representation in traditionally male-dominated careers in fields such as medicine, law, and science.
ANNE-CHRISTINE POUJOULAT/AFP/Getty Images

Women are increasingly breaking the glass ceiling, but they have made few overall gains in STEM (science, technology, engineering, and mathematics) fields. However, women have had more success in some STEM fields than others (Figure 13.11) (Cheryan, Ziegler, Montoya, & Jiang, 2017). Biological sciences, chemistry, and mathematics and statistics are more gender balanced and have shown greater increases in the proportion of women over the past three decades, whereas computer science, engineering, and physics tend to be male dominated (National Science Foundation, 2012). What causes the gender disparities in STEM fields?

One explanation lies in gender stereotypes (W. Wood & Eagly, 2012). Some STEM fields, typically those that are more mathematics, are stereotyped as masculine fields (physics), whereas others are viewed as feminine (biology) (Leslie, Cimpian, Meyer, & Freeland, 2015). In U.S. culture, women are negatively stereotyped as having lower abilities in mathematics and science than men. Knowledge and internalization of these stereotypes may deter women from being interested in pursuing STEM (J. L. Smith, Sansone, & White, 2007). STEM fields with a particularly masculine culture, such as engineering and physics, may implicitly signal to women that they do not belong. A sense of belonging to a scientific community of scientists and viewing science as important to one's identity predicts pursuing and succeeding in a scientific career. Women may find it difficult to cultivate a sense of belonging when they are immersed in classrooms, laboratories, and workplaces with few or no other women.

Negative stereotypes may also affect girls' and women's views of their ability. We have seen in prior chapters that girls and boys show similar cognitive capacities and that girls tend to show higher levels of achievement on reading and writing tasks. Yet with advancing grade, and particularly entrance to high school, girls' self-esteem tends to decline, and they become more uncertain of their academic abilities (Jacobs, Lanza, Osgood, Eccles, & Wigfield, 2002). Gender differences in participation in computer

FIGURE 13.11

Percentage of Bachelor's Degrees Awarded to Women in STEM Fields, 1985–2010

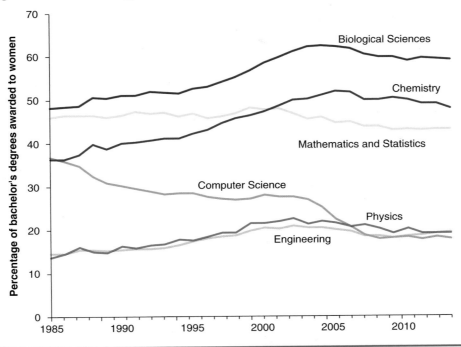

Source: Cheryan et al., 2017.

science, engineering, and physics are evident in high school and continue in college. Interestingly, prior achievement in math and science is not related to gender gaps in science fields, suggesting that women who choose nonscience majors are not less skilled in these areas (Riegle-Crumb, King, Grodsky, & Muller, 2012).

Young women's ambivalence may be exacerbated by debates raised in recent years regarding whether women's professional success is incompatible with career success. As female undergraduate and graduate students advance in their programs, they become more pessimistic about the compatibility of STEM careers and having a family (Beyer, 2014). Some studies suggest that parenthood had a negative effect on women's career success, especially when women give birth to their first child around the same time they enter their careers, whereas men's career success tends to be independent of parenthood (Abele & Spurk, 2011). While male and female students in top mathematics and science graduate programs rate having a flexible schedule and limited work hours as equally important at age 25, the importance of these factors increases for women—but not men—

over time (Ferriman, Lubinski, & Benbow, 2009). As women progress in their education, the work/family conflict may become a bigger deterrent to STEM careers.

Helping young women choose STEM careers entails early encouragement to take math and science courses and aid in accurately evaluating their abilities. Contact and mentoring from women who are successful in STEM careers can help young women advance; however, female models are few, perpetuating gender disparities.

What Do You Think?

1. How did you decide on your major? To what degree have you considered your future roles, a spouse and parent? How might these roles affect your career choices?

2. From your perspective, is there a gender divide in employment opportunities and barriers to careers in science? Why or why not? If so, what can be done to reduce gender differences?

3. Are there gender differences in other, nonscience careers? ●

mentoring relationship with a mentor of their choice (Gonzáles-Figueroa & Young, 2005).

Work and Family

Work–life balance, the challenge of finding time and energy for both a career and personal pursuits such as family, is a concern to most families today, especially to mothers. As shown in Figure 13.12, the proportion of working mothers has increased dramatically over the past four decades. In 2016, the majority of U.S. mothers of children under the age of 18, both married and unmarried, were working (68% vs. 76% for married mothers and unmarried mothers, respectively). Mothers with very young children are only slightly less likely to work than those with older children: Over 66% of mothers with a child under 6 years of age and 57% of mothers with an infant under a year old are in the labor force (U.S. Bureau of Labor Statistics, 2017).

Nearly all married fathers work, and most share child care and household responsibilities with their wives, making work–life balance a task for both spouses. Most parents find it difficult to meet the competing demands of family and career, especially

as the boundaries between today's workplace and home are often blurred because many adults are expected to bring work home or be available during nonwork hours via mobile devices.

Both men and women report feeling conflict between work and family obligations (Ammons & Kelly, 2008; Winslow, 2005). Control over work time predicts satisfaction with work–life balance and lower levels of work–life conflict (Carlson et al., 2011). A perceived loss of control accompanies a sense of role overload. More common among women, **role overload** refers to high levels of stress that result from attempting to balance the demands of multiple roles: employee, mother, and spouse (Higgins, Duxbury, & Lyons, 2010). Role overload is associated with poor health, depressive symptoms, ineffective parenting, and marital conflict (Carnes, 2017; Duxbury, Stevenson, & Higgins, 2018). Successfully managing multiple roles entails setting priorities, such as de-emphasizing household chores and expectations of an immaculate home in favor of spending more time with children (Hewitt, Baxter, & Western, 2006). In addition, research suggests that women who best manage role overload are those who seek physical and emotional support from others (Higgins et al., 2010).

Work–life balance is a concern to adults in most Western countries. For example, research comparing employees across several European countries found that poor work–life balance was associated with perceived health, health complaints, and poor well-being in both men and women (Lunau, Bambra, Eikemo, van der Wel, & Dragano, 2014). Variations in the reported experience of work–life balance differed by country alongside differences in national regulations regarding work hours, suggesting that workplace policies (often regulated by government) influence

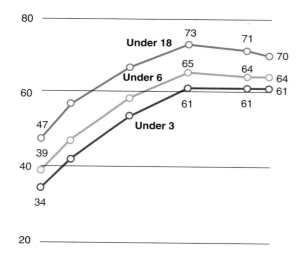

FIGURE 13.12

Labor Force Participation Rates Among Mothers in the United States, 1975–2014

% of mothers who are in the labor force with children

Source: Reprinted with permission from "7 facts about U.S. moms," Pew Research Center, Washington, DC (May, 2018). http://www.pe-wresearch.org/fact-tank/2017/05/11/6-facts-about-u-s-mothers/

THINKING IN CONTEXT 13.6

1. How does career choice illustrate the interplay between an individual's characteristics, development, and capacities and contextual factors, such as opportunities, choices, and socioeconomic status? Provide examples.

2. How might we aid young adults as they transition into the work environment? What factors might improve their competence and satisfaction in their new role?

3. Diversity comes in many forms: ethnic, gender, and parental status, to name a few. What can employers do to help all employees feel included, respected, and treated fairly? How can employers address diversity issues in the workplace and increase morale and productivity?

employees' sense of work–life balance and overall well-being. Workplace policies influence employee morale and productivity. Flexible policies that permit employees to balance home and work responsibilities (e.g., flexible starting and stopping times, opportunities to work from home, and time off to care for sick children) are positively associated with attendance, commitment to the organization, and work performance and negatively associated with distress symptoms (Halpern, 2005). Workplaces with onsite child care show lower rates of employee absenteeism and higher productivity as compared with those without child care (Brandon & Temple, 2007). When adults are able to balance work and family, they are more productive and happy workers, more satisfied spouses, and better parents, and they experience greater well-being at home and work (Herrenkohl, Hong, Klika, Herrenkohl, & Russo, 2013; Lunau et al., 2014; Russo, Shteigman, & Carmeli, 2016).

 APPLY YOUR KNOWLEDGE

Brenda dropped her bags on the floor of her dorm room and introduced herself to her new roommate, Denise. They got along easily, and after talking for some time, Denise left to go to the library. Brenda marveled at their very different lives. Whereas Denise's parents are doctors, Brenda's mother works two jobs to pay the bills. Brenda considers herself very lucky to have won a scholarship to college. She worries about leaving her mother alone with her younger siblings—there's so much work to do, and the little ones need a lot of supervision if they are to stay out of trouble in the neighborhood. Brenda worries that her little brothers will grow up too quickly and make dangerous decisions like joining one of the many neighborhood gangs. She realizes that she is very fortunate to be able to leave her poor community but worries that her absence will harm her family. At the same time, Brenda is delighted to have the opportunity to learn new things, to study with bright students and professors, and to prepare for a career as a doctor. As a premed major, Brenda has a very busy semester ahead, and she hopes that she won't disappoint those who have given her such grand opportunities.

1. Brenda comes from an impoverished neighborhood. In the coming years as she enters early adulthood, how does the context in which she was raised and in which she lives influence her physical development and health?

2. In what ways can Brenda expect to grow cognitively over the years of early adulthood? What contributes to this change? How might cognitive advances influence her functioning and behavior on a practical day-to-day level?

3. How likely is Brenda to earn a college degree? What role does attending college play in career outcomes, employment, and salary in early adulthood?

4. What challenges do first-generation students, like Brenda, face in transitioning to and succeeding in college? What contextual factors influence these risks, and what might serve as protective factors and aid development?

$SAGE edge™

Visit **edge.sagepub.com/kuther2e** to help you accomplish your coursework goals in an easy-to-use learning environment.

LEARNING OBJECTIVES	SUMMARY	KEY TERMS	IN REVIEW
13.1 Describe the features and characteristics of emerging adulthood.	Emerging adulthood is an extended transitional period between adolescence and early adulthood characterized by diversity in lifestyles, identity development, and the subjective sense of being in between. Although emerging adulthood is observed in industrialized cultures around the world, it is not universal as it is influenced by socioeconomic status and contextual changes that have prolonged the transition into adulthood.		What are markers of emerging adulthood? How does context influence emerging adulthood?

LEARNING OBJECTIVES	SUMMARY	KEY TERMS	IN REVIEW
13.2 Summarize the physical developments of emerging and early adulthood.	Physical development continues into the 20s when all of the organs and body systems reach optimum functioning. Age-related physical changes are so gradual that most go unnoticed by young adults. Physical strength peaks at about age 30, then gradually declines, but young adults vary in the rate of change in their performance. Men are capable of reproducing throughout life, but sperm production is impaired by factors that harm the body's functioning. In women, ovulation becomes less regular with age and is impaired by a variety of behavioral and environmental factors.	Senescence	What is senescence? What are typical age-related changes in physical development? Discuss fertility and reproductive capacity in early adulthood.
13.3 Analyze physical and sexual health issues in emerging and early adulthood.	Obesity is influenced by hereditary and contextual factors and is a serious health risk, associated with a range of illnesses and problems. Regular exercise increases longevity, enhances immunity, and promotes stress reduction. Sexual activity, especially casual sexual activity, tends to be highest in early adulthood. Alcohol and substance use tend to peak in emerging adulthood and decline in early adulthood.	Binge drinking Alcohol dependence	Identify causes and consequences of overweight and obesity in adults. What is the nature of sexual activity in emerging and early adulthood? What is sexual coercion, and what are its effects? How does alcohol and substance use and abuse shift over emerging and early adulthood?
13.4 Compare postformal reasoning, pragmatic thought, and cognitive-affective complexity.	People's understanding of the nature of knowledge advances along a predictable path in young adulthood from dualistic thinking, to relativistic thinking, to reflective judgment. Development beyond formal operations is dependent on metacognition and experience. Pragmatic thought refers to the ability to apply reflective judgment to real-world contexts. Cognitive-affective complexity is an advanced form of thought that includes the ability to be aware of emotions, integrate positive and negative feelings about an issue, and regulate intense emotions to make logical decisions about complicated issues.	Epistemic cognition Postformal reasoning Dualistic thinking Relativistic thinking Reflective judgment Pragmatic thought Cognitive-affective complexity	What is postformal reasoning? What key changes underlie the development of postformal reasoning? How do pragmatic thought and cognitive-affective complexity contribute to advances in thinking and reasoning?
13.5 Explain how attending college influences young adults' development, and identify challenges faced by first-generation and nontraditional students.	Attending college is associated with advances in moral reasoning, identity development, and social development. First-generation and nontraditional college students experience a high risk of dropout. Students of color and those of low socioeconomic status are disproportionately likely to be first-generation and nontraditional college students and may perceive a cultural mismatch between their home and neighborhood context and the college environment.		What are some benefits of attending college? What are challenges faced by first-generation and nontraditional college students? What challenges are faced by emerging and young adults who do not attend college?
13.6 Discuss vocational choice and the transition to work.	Vocational development entails choosing and becoming established in a career. Contextual influences such as family, socioeconomic status, and educational opportunities also influence our choice of career. Many adults find the transition to work challenging as it may not match their expectations. Women and people of color are more likely to encounter the glass ceiling and discrimination that can harm their career.	Glass ceiling Work–life balance Role overload	Describe five stages of occupational development. Identify influences on vocational choice. How does experience in the working world influence young people's occupational expectations? What are common career challenges experienced by women and people of color?

PRACTICE AND APPLY WHAT YOU'VE LEARNED

▶ edge.sagepub.com/kuther2e

CHECK YOUR COMPREHENSION ON THE STUDY SITE WITH:

- **Diagnostic Quizzes** to identify opportunities for improvement.

- **Multimedia Resources** that explore chapter content using media and current events.

- **Journal Articles** that support and expand on chapter concepts.

14 Socioemotional Development in Emerging and Early Adulthood

"I guess real life begins now," Sandra remarked to her college roommate, Christiana. "Is my cap straight?" asked Christiana. Sandra adjusted Christiana's cap and stepped back to look at her friend in her graduation cap and gown, "Yep. Here we go!" Later, as she sat through her college commencement, Sandra wondered about her future. Will she like her new job? What will it be like to work full-time? What about her boyfriend, Jamal? They've dated for over a year. Will he propose? Sandra

wasn't sure that she wanted him to propose. There are many things she'd like to do before settling down. "After all, I'm just starting to figure myself out," she thought to herself. "Will I ever be ready to merge my life with someone else's? Will parenthood be right for me? Will I be able to juggle all the demands of work and family life? Do I want to?"

Sandra's ponderings about her future illustrate the developmental task of emerging adulthood: making

Learning Objectives

14.1 Summarize psychosocial development in early adulthood.

14.2 Discuss influences on friendship and mate selection and interactions in early adulthood.

14.3 Analyze the diverse romantic situations that may characterize early adulthood, including singlehood, cohabitation, marriage, and divorce.

14.4 Compare the experiences of young adults as stepparents, never-married parents, and same-sex parents.

Digital Resources

Explore: Young Adulthood: The Crucible of Personality Development

Connect: Hook-Up Culture

▶ **Lives in Context Video 14.1:** Romantic Relationships in Early Adulthood

Connect: Why Marry? Gays and Lesbians Have Different Answers

Listen: Paternity Leave

▶ **Lives in Context Video 14.2:** Planning for Parenthood and Work-Life Balance

---

decisions about relationships, family, career, and lifestyles and then transitioning and committing to these roles. Some young people transition to adult roles very quickly, while others take a more lengthy, winding path to adopting the roles that comprise early adulthood. In this chapter, we take a closer look at the relationships and roles that mark early adulthood. Similar to Chapter 13, the term *emerging adult* will refer to individuals age 25 and under (unless otherwise specified), and *young adult* will refer to all individuals under age 40, including emerging adults (unless otherwise specified).

PSYCHOSOCIAL DEVELOPMENT IN EMERGING ADULTHOOD AND EARLY ADULTHOOD

» LO 14.1   Summarize psychosocial development in early adulthood.

Development is influenced by interactions between the individual and the social world. In his lifespan theory of psychosocial development, Erik Erikson (1950)

posed that at every phase in life, individuals encounter psychological crises that offer both opportunities and risks for psychological development.

Identity Versus Role Confusion

Identity development, posed by Erikson (1950) as the psychosocial task of adolescence, is one of the defining markers of emerging adulthood today. When Erikson published his theory in the mid-20th century, most North Americans entered the workforce after high school, marrying and starting

Emerging adulthood is an exciting time of exploration, independence, and firsts.
iStock/swissmediavision

families soon after. Over the past half-century, college enrollment has increased and an extended transition to adult roles—emerging adulthood—has become more common (Arnett, 2016).

Individuals begin the identity search process in adolescence, but most people do not establish a firm sense of self until emerging adulthood (Arnett, 2014). We adopt a sense of identity in several domains, such as political preference, religious orientation, gender and sexuality, and ethnicity (Schwartz, Zamboanga, Luyckx, Meca, & Ritchie, 2015).

Political identity is illustrated by civic participation, such as voting, beliefs about civic responsibilities, and staying informed about national and local issues (Rekker, Keijsers, Branje, & Meeus, 2017; Sherrod, 2015). Beliefs about civic responsibility predict volunteerism and helping, but civic responsibility is also fostered by engaging in organized community-based activities, suggesting a reciprocal influence/process (Hasford, Abbott, Alisat, Pancer, & Pratt, 2017; Walker & Iverson, 2016). Higher education is associated with civic participation, and participation in civic activities tends to deepen individuals' affiliation (Hart & Life, 2017).

Developing a religious identity entails determining the degree to which religion is integral to the sense of self. Many emerging adults identify themselves as religious, participating in organized religious activities. A substantial number of emerging adults report engaging in prayer, community service, and meditation rather than attending church services (Schwartz et al., 2015). Arnett and Jensen (2002) use the term *congregation of one* to refer to the individualized belief systems many emerging adults develop.

Developing a sense of gender and sexual identity embodies feeling comfortable with one's gender and sense of sexuality (Dillon, Worthington, & Moradi, 2011). Through a variety of sexual experiences, emerging adults explore and consider who they are attracted to and what kinds of sexual behaviors they enjoy. Individuals must also determine the ways in which they are most comfortable expressing affection and love.

Constructing a sense of ethnic identity involves exploring one's ethnic group, including the attitudes, values, and culture associated with that group (Umaña-Taylor, 2016; Umaña-Taylor et al., 2014). Individuals determine what elements to internalize and adopt, develop a sense of belonging, and commit to an identity.

The identity search process is multidimensional. Individuals develop a sense of self across many domains, and each domain is independent. That is, a young adult may have formed a sense of political identity but may continue to experiment and consider religious or gender identities. Identity achievement

is associated with positive outcomes, including a sense of well-being, happiness, and life satisfaction (Lapsley & Hardy 2017; Sumner, Burrow, & Hill, 2015).

Intimacy Versus Isolation

In Erikson's view, the crisis of early adulthood, from ages 18 to 40, is the major psychosocial task of **intimacy versus isolation:** developing the capacity for intimacy and making a permanent commitment to a romantic partner. The formation of intimate relationships is associated with well-being in young adults (Busch & Hofer, 2012). The flip side—not attaining a sense of intimacy and not making personal commitments to others—is the negative psychosocial outcome of isolation, entailing a sense of loneliness and self-absorption.

Establishing an intimate relationship is a challenge for young adults, especially emerging adults, who often continue to struggle with identity issues and who are just gaining social and financial independence. Because developing a sense of intimacy relies on identity development, many emerging adults who are just forming their identities are ill prepared for this task. Young people immersed in Erikson's psychosocial moratorium of identity development are exploring opportunities and are less likely to form successful intimate relationships than those whose identities have been achieved (Markstrom & Kalmanir, 2001). Moreover, emerging adults generally report feeling that they are not ready for a committed, enduring relationship (Collins & van Dulmen, 2006). Adults learn about themselves and relationships through dating. Increasingly, adults meet through online dating sites and mobile apps, as discussed in the Lives in Context feature.

Identity achievement, including a sense of self, values, and goals, predicts readiness for intimate and committed romantic relationships and the capacity to actively seek and establish them (Barry, Madsen, Nelson, Carroll, & Badger, 2009; Beyers &

A primary task of early adulthood is to establish intimate relationships with significant others.
Yasin Ozturk/Anadolu Agency/Getty Images

Internet Dating

With every generation come advances in technology that influence daily life, including romantic relationships. For example, in the mid-1990s, the first online dating sites were launched. Sites like these have flourished over the past two decades, enabling individuals to meet and interact with many potential dates quickly without having to leave their homes. Over one quarter of emerging adults reported using an online dating site or mobile app in 2015 (A. Smith & Anderson, 2016). Online dating is similarly popular among young adults 25 and older.

Why do people choose to date online? Two thirds of online daters report that it is a good way to meet people, and nearly three quarters agree that it helps people find a better romantic match because it gives them access to a wide range of potential partners (A. Smith & Anderson, 2016). Online profiles enable daters to put their best foot forward, managing the impression they send to others (Fullwood & Attrill-Smith, 2018). In addition, in one recent study, Dutch 18- to 30-year-old adults reported using a mobile dating app because it was exciting and easier to communicate, and attention from others enhanced their feelings of self-worth (Sumter, Vandenbosch, & Ligtenberg, 2017).

An online dating relationship usually begins with texts, email messages, or private messages on an app. If the two decide they are interested enough to pursue the contact further, they may meet face-to-face. Thus, in online dating, a great deal of interaction—most of it electronic—occurs before daters meet. The tone, or degree of emotionality, of the messages they exchange influences the daters' impressions of one another. Strong positive emotional words, such as *excited* and *wonderful,* are more likely to elicit a response from a prospective dating partner than less strong emotional words, such as *good* and *fine* (Rosen, Cheever, Cummings, & Felt, 2008). In addition, daters tend to prefer low levels of self-disclosure, a preference that also exists in traditional dating. Indeed, in many ways, people using online dating and the resulting romances are very much like those that originate though friends, school, or work (Hall, Park, Hayeon, & Michael, 2010).

Online dating differs from traditional dating in that it allows daters to exert greater control over their first impressions to potential partners. Typical dating profiles include a self-description and a picture. The accuracy of photos varies. In one study, online daters, independent judges, and trained coders evaluated the accuracy of daters' photos (Hancock & Toma, 2009). While online daters rated their own photos as relatively accurate, independent judges rated approximately one third of the photographs as not accurate. In addition, over half of online daters have felt that others misrepresented themselves in their profiles (A. Smith & Duggan, 2013). Yet one study of online messages suggested that less than 10% were deceptive (Markowitz & Hancock, 2018). Women are more likely to fib about their weight and men about their assets, relationship goals, and personal interests (Hall et al., 2010). (Here, as elsewhere, however, differences between individuals tend to be far greater than those between the sexes.)

Online daters face an ironic challenge. The increased options that dating websites provide may not aid them in finding a suitable partner (Finkel, Eastwick, Karney, Reis, & Sprecher, 2012). As daters face more options, they are less likely to feel satisfied with their selected partners (D'Angelo & Toma, 2017). With seemingly endless opportunities, online daters may find it difficult to make decisions about romantic partners, perhaps undermining their dating efforts as they search for an ideal "Ms./Mr. Right." Indeed, about one third of online daters agree that online dating "keeps people from settling down because they always have options for people to date" (A. Smith & Duggan, 2013).

What Do You Think?

1. In your view, what are the advantages and disadvantages of online dating?

2. Consider friendships and the mate selection process in early adulthood. In what ways is the pursuit of romantic relationships online similar to and different from what we know about friendship formation and mate selection in early adulthood? ●

FIGURE 14.1

Use of Online Dating Sites or Mobile Apps by Young Adults, 2013–2015

% in each age group who have ever used an online dating site and/or mobile dating app

 ■ 2013   ■ 2015

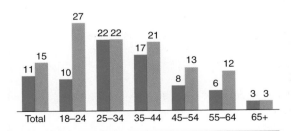

Source: Reprinted with permission from "5 facts about online dating," Pew Research Center, Washington, DC (February, 2016). http://www.pewresearch.org/fact-tank/2016/02/29/5-facts-about-online-dating/

Seiffge-Krenke, 2010). Although Erikson did not draw distinctions between emerging adulthood and early adulthood, today it is clear that many young people do not enter into truly intimate relationships until they have traversed the transition from emerging adulthood to early adulthood. Furthermore, as adults form intimate relationships, they must reshape their identities to include their role as partner and the goals, plans, and interests shared with their partner. Thus, they must resolve identity and intimacy demands that may conflict. For example, as they engage in continued identity development, they must do the work of establishing an intimate relationship—making sacrifices and compromises that may involve a temporary loss of self—before expanding the sense of self to include a partner.

The Social Clock

"There is a time for everything," explained 14-year-old Carissa to her older sister, Erika. "At 18 you graduate high school, 22 you graduate college, 22 or 23 you get engaged, and 24 or 25 you get married." "Silly, those ages fit for some people but not everyone. It depends on your experience, career plans, and personal goals," admonished 20-year-old Erika. Yet Erika wondered to herself whether Carissa was right. Is there a "time for everything"? Developmental theorist Bernice Neugarten (1979; Neugarten & Neugarten, 1996) suggested that there is.

Throughout life, we experience a number of normative age-graded events, life events that most people encounter at specific ages, such as graduating from high school at age 18. Neugarten proposed that the expected timing of normative age-graded events can be expressed as a **social clock**, age-related expectations for major life events such as occupational entry, marriage, parenthood, and retirement. Every society has a timetable for such events, and young people compare their progress on these events with that of their peers. The degree

The social clock marks normative age-graded events, such as graduations, marriage, and parenthood.
iStock/EMPPhotography

to which individuals match their culture's social clock influences their self-esteem and psychological functioning. Most people are aware of their own timing and can describe themselves as early, late, or on time with regard to milestones such as getting married, having children, or retiring.

Since the mid-20th century, Western culture's expectations for the timing of developmental milestones of adulthood have become less age conscious and rigid in that the acceptable age range for norms has widened (C. C. Peterson, 1996). Delayed parenthood is one example; today, few people blink at a 40-year-old first-time parent, whereas a generation ago, late parenthood was unusual. The advent of emerging adulthood offers additional evidence of social changes that may be disrupting the social clock. That said, many adults experience distress and poor self-esteem when they are off-time relative to their peers. Even within a culture, the social clock may vary from one group to the next. For example, ethnic and socioeconomic differences in individuals' educational, career, and family paths can yield differing expectations for the social clock.

THINKING IN CONTEXT 14.1

1. In what ways are the search for identity and a sense of intimacy complementary? How might the typical contexts in which emerging and early adults live contribute to these developmental tasks?

2. Identify elements of the social clock. What are events that most adolescents, emerging adults, and young adults experience? What typical ages accompany these events? Compare yourself to the social clock you have identified. How well does it match your experience?

RELATIONSHIPS IN PSYCHOSOCIAL DEVELOPMENT IN EMERGING AND EARLY ADULTHOOD

» LO 14.2   Discuss influences on friendship and mate selection and interactions in early adulthood.

Young adults satisfy some of their intimacy needs through close friendships. Yet the developmental task of establishing the capacity for intimate relationships is best fulfilled by establishing a romantic relationship with a mate.

Friendship

In adulthood, close friendships are based on reciprocity. This emotional give-and-take entails intimacy, companionship, and support, as well as behaviors such as sharing, exchanging favors, and giving advice (Hartup & Stevens, 1999; Wrzus, Zimmermann, Mund, & Neyer, 2017). At all times in life, friends are likely to be demographically similar to one another, for example, in age, sex, and socioeconomic status (Hall, 2016). However, adults' beliefs influence their friendships, and their flexible thinking enables them to form relationships with peers who are demographically different. Adults who value diversity are more likely to have friends of different ethnicities, religion, and sexual orientation (Bahns, 2018). Shared interests, attitudes, and values are most important to forming and maintaining adult friendships (Wrzus et al., 2017). Friendships may become more ethnically diverse in college, especially on campuses high in racial and ethnic diversity (Fischer, 2008; Stearns, Buchmann, & Bonneau, 2009). Here individuals' values and attitudes interact with their context to influence friendship formation. In one study of students attending 10 colleges, valuing racial diversity increased the likelihood of having racially diverse friendships more on campuses high in racial diversity than less diverse campuses (Bahns, 2018).

Emerging adults' peer relationships share some similarities with those of adolescents. For example, although crowds are generally thought to decline in late adolescence as young people complete secondary school, research suggests that crowd affiliations continue in college. One study of students attending a small U.S. liberal arts college discovered peer crowd groupings similar to those in high school: social, athletic, scholastic, and counterculture (Hopmeyer & Medovoy, 2017). In addition, the crowds included male and female students from every year in college. Emerging adults' affiliation with scholastic and athletic crowds predicts positive social and emotional adjustment and low-risk-related behaviors, whereas affiliation with counterculture crowds was associated with loneliness and low sense of belonging. Both social and counterculture identification predicted risk-related behaviors (Hopmeyer, Troop-Gordon, Medovoy, & Fischer, 2017). Similar to high school, the college environment, especially residential campuses, is conducive to the formation of crowds because emerging adult same-age peers are immersed in a social setting that generally does not include adults of other ages. Although research has not examined crowd formation in emerging adults who do not attend college, it is unlikely that they form crowds, since they are not immersed in a similar peer setting.

The sex differences that characterize friendships in childhood and adolescence continue in adulthood. Women tend to have more intimate and long-lasting friendships and rely more on friends to meet social and emotional needs than do men (Hall, 2016). Men's friendships tend to center on sharing information and activities, such as playing sports, rather than intimate disclosure (David-Barrett et al., 2015). As male friendships endure to become long-lasting ties, self-disclosure increases, and the friends become closer.

Many adults have opposite-sex friendships. These relationships can be important sources of social support but tend not to last as long as same-sex friendships. Among men, friendships with women tend to decline after marriage, but women, especially highly educated women, tend to have more friendships with men throughout adulthood, especially in the workplace (Weger, 2016). Other-sex friendships are a source of companionship and support and offer opportunities to learn about gender differences in the expression of intimacy (R. L. Grover, Nangle, Serwik, & Zeff, 2007). It seems that both men and women gain from other-sex relationships. Men learn about emotional expression and intimacy, and women often report that male friends offer a different, objective point of view on problems. Women most commonly describe their male–female friendships as sibling relationships, and men most frequently label their relationship "just friends" (in contrast with romantic partners). Both of these ways of constructing platonic relationships are related to a high level of friendship satisfaction (Reeder, 2017).

Friendships offer powerful protection against stress for both men and women. Stressors—whether daily hassles or major crises—can tax individuals' coping resources and contribute to illness, aging-related physical changes, and even early death (Aldwin, 2007). Friendship quality is associated with psychological adjustment and well-being, including social competence, life satisfaction, and lower levels of depression and loneliness (Gillespie, Lever, Frederick, & Royce, 2015; Holt, Mattanah, & Long, 2018).

In early adulthood, as in all times of life, close friendships are based on reciprocity, intimacy, companionship, and support.
iStock/DGLimages

Friendship changes over the course of early adulthood. As adults progress through the 20s and take on adult roles, they tend to see their friends less (Nicolaisen & Thorsen, 2017). Young adults who are single tend to rely more heavily on friendships to fulfill needs for social support and acceptance than do married young adults (Wrzus et al., 2017). The more that friendships are characterized by social support and self-disclosure, the more satisfaction single young adults report, and the longer the relationships last (Sanderson, Rahm, & Beigbeder, 2005). As adults establish careers, they often have less time to spend with friends, yet friendship remains an important source of social support and is associated with well-being, positive affect, and self-esteem throughout life (Gillespie et al., 2015; Huxhold, Miche, & Schüz, 2014).

Romantic Relationships

As we have seen, the developmental task of early adulthood is to form long-term intimate relationships that will endure throughout adulthood (Seiffge-Krenke, 2003). Generally speaking, there is continuity in relationship quality such that the quality of romantic relationships in adolescence predicts relationship quality in emerging adulthood and beyond (Shulman & Connolly, 2013). The nature of romantic relationships often does change over time, however. For example, emerging adults tend to fluctuate between relationships or to be involved in short sexual and romantic encounters (Cohen, Kasen, Chen, Hartmark, & Gordon, 2003). Today, emerging adults often experience years of singlehood and dating before partnering.

Mate Selection

What do men and women look for in a mate? Upon first meeting a potential mate, men and women judge attractiveness as the most important influence on romantic interest and desire to pursue further contact (Fletcher, Kerr, Li, & Valentine, 2014). Men and women from many cultures show similar patterns in mate preferences. Men tend to prefer a younger mate and assign greater value to physical attractiveness and domestic skills; from an evolutionary perspective, these are thought to be attributes that signal fertility and the capacity to care for offspring (Li et al., 2013). Women tend to be more cautious and choosy than men (Fletcher et al., 2014). Generally, women assign greater importance to earning potential, intelligence, height, and moral character and seek mates who are the same age or slightly older—characteristics that may increase the likelihood that a woman's offspring will survive and thrive.

Although opposites might attract, it is similarity that breeds relationship satisfaction. Most intimate partners share similarities in demographics, attitudes, and values. Perceived similarity (the degree to which individuals believe they are similar to their partner) predicts attraction to potential and current mates (L. S. Taylor, Fiore, Mendelsohn, & Cheshire, 2011) and is more important in mate selection than actual, measurable similarities (Tidwell, Eastwick, & Finkel, 2013). What similarities do couples typically share? Common similarities include personality style, intelligence, educational aspirations, and attractiveness (Markey & Markey, 2007). Romantic partners often also share similarities in health behaviors (such as smoking), patterns of alcohol use (including binge drinking), and tendencies toward risk taking (Bartel et al., 2017; Smithson & Baker, 2008; Wiersma et al., 2010). Not only do adults tend to choose partners who share similarities with them, but they also often become more similar to each other as their relationships develop. The more similar partners are, in values such as political beliefs, the more likely they are to report being satisfied with their relationship and to remain in the relationship (Leikas, Ilmarinen, Verkasalo, Vartiainen, & Lönnqvist, 2018; Lutz-Zois, Bradley, Mihalik, & Moorman-Eavers, 2006).

Context plays a role in mate selection. For example, the similarities shared by romantic partners may be a function of shared contexts; that is, they may share overlapping contexts, such as workplace, college, clubs or activities, peer group, and community. Partner similarity thus may be due less to active selection than simply the availability of partners (Eastwick, Harden, Shukusky, Morgan, & Joel, 2017).

Context may also play a role in cross-group romantic relationships in which partners identify with different ethnicities and races. For example, a study of Black male and female college students attending historically Black colleges and predominately White colleges found that all students reported insufficient dating options, but females at predominantly White institutions were more likely to report few dating options than were males and students attending historically Black colleges (Stackman, Reviere, & Medley, 2016). Nearly three quarters of all students were favorable to cross-group dating, but students attending historically Black colleges were less supportive. These students' attitudes may be influenced by their context and the perceived availability of same-group partners. Alternatively, it may be that students with a stronger racial identity chose to attend a historically Black college and are more likely to value partners with similar racial identities. Regardless, research suggests that dating relationships among emerging adult cross-group partners generally do not differ in quality, conflict, or satisfaction from those of emerging adults who date within their ethnic or racial group (de Guzman & Nishina, 2017). Most research in this area examines college students. We know less about emerging and young adults who are not enrolled in college. In addition, although the multiracial population of the United States is rapidly increasing, we know even less about relationships among multiracial adults (Buggs, 2017).

Components of Love

Mario and Davida dated for 4 years before marrying. After 15 years of marriage and three children, Davida feels a warm sense of comfort and stability with her husband, who has become her best friend, but she sometimes misses the sparks of their dating years. Corey is planning to propose to his girlfriend of 6 months. "Sure, it's very soon after meeting," he thought to himself, "but I'm crazy about her, can't stop thinking about her, and can't imagine a day without seeing her." Both Davida and Corey are experiencing love, but in different ways.

Interpersonal relationships can be categorized on the basis of different combinations of three components of love: passion, intimacy, and commitment (Sternberg, 2004). New romantic relationships tend to be characterized by passion—the excitement that accompanies physical attraction and physiological arousal (Anderson, 2016). Passion is not always accompanied by intimacy—emotional engagement, warm communication, closeness, and caring for the other person's well-being. Commitment, the decision that partners make to stay with one another, grows as people spend more time together, create shared goals, and solve problems together. According to theorist Robert Sternberg (2004), different combinations of these three components comprise seven different types of love, as shown in Figure 14.2 and Table 14.1.

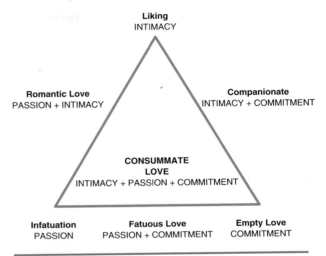

Source: By Lnesa at English Wikipedia, via Wikimedia Commons.

Western ideals of love, such as those depicted in movies and television programs, include all three components. The relative proportions of these components vary over the course of a relationship and with age, however. Young adults tend to experience higher levels of passion in their relationships than older adults, and midlife and older adults tend to experience greater levels of commitment (Sumter, Valkenburg, & Peter, 2013). Novelty plays a role in the euphoria of passion. Intimacy grows with familiarity as partners get to know one another. Commitment emerges over time. Intimacy and commitment, not passion, determine the relationship's fate and the likelihood that a family will form (Clyde Hendrick & Hendrick, 2004). For example, a study of the Hadza people of Tanzania, a hunter-gatherer tribe, revealed that although all of the men and women experienced all three types of love, only commitment predicted the number of children for both men and women, suggesting a reproductive purpose for commitment (Sorokowski et al., 2017).

It has generally been thought that as intimacy and commitment increase, passion subsides for all couples, heterosexual and same-sex, married and unmarried (Anderson, 2016; Kurdek, 2006). However, love is dynamic. Recent studies suggest that intimacy and passion are closely related and can fluctuate from day to day (Graham, 2011; Rubin & Campbell, 2012). Increases in intimacy predict increase in passion and vice versa (Aykutoğlu & Uysal, 2017; Ratelle, Carbonneau, Vallerand, & Mageau, 2013). Many couples show a long-term romantic love characterized by passion and intimacy, which in turn increases marital happiness and enhances their feelings of commitment (Acevedo &

The ratio of passion, intimacy, and commitment changes over the course of a relationship. Love persists, but its nature may shift.
Jessica Hill/For The Washington Post via Getty Images

Aron, 2009). Successful couples acknowledge and appreciate the "ups" in intimacy and passion despite overall declines.

Eastern cultures such as those of China and Japan offer a different perspective on romantic love. Traditional collectivist views common in Eastern cultures value interdependence. The young person is defined through relationships and roles—such as the roles of daughter, son, sibling, husband, and wife—rather than as an individual. Because all relationships are important components of the young person's sense of self, affection is dispersed throughout all relationships, and romantic relationships are less intense than those experienced by Western young people. Chinese and Japanese young adults consider mate selection within the context of their other relationships and responsibilities to others. They are more likely than North American and European young adults to rate companionship, similarity in backgrounds, and career potential as important in choosing a partner and are less likely to rate physical attraction and passion as important factors (Dion & Dion, 1993). Similarly, dating couples in China report feeling less passion than do those in the United States but report similar levels of intimacy and commitment, which in turn predict relationship satisfaction (Gao, 2001). Finally, in a sample of Chinese adults from Hong Kong who were involved in heterosexual romantic relationships, relationship satisfaction was associated with intimacy and commitment, but not passion, suggesting that conceptualizations of romantic love and relationship satisfaction may vary with culture (Ng & Cheng, 2010). Some research suggests that there are neurological correlates of being in love, as discussed in the Brain and Biological Influences on Development feature.

BRAIN AND BIOLOGICAL INFLUENCES ON DEVELOPMENT

 ## Your Brain on Love

People often describe romantic love in terms of physical sensations, such as a throbbing pulse and a rush of feel-good hormones. Is romantic love related to physical functioning? Neurological research suggests that the answer is yes. For example, functional MRI (fMRI) studies of people looking at photographs of someone whom they love suggest that romantic love is accompanied by increased activity in several parts of the brain associated with reward (Bartels & Zeki, 2000).

One recent study examined the relationship between romantic love and the functional architecture of the brain (Song et al., 2015). Individuals who were in love, who had recently ended a love relationship, or who had never been in love were compared as they rested in the fMRI machine while awake, instructed to think about nothing. The adults who were in love showed increased functional connectivity in several areas of the brain thought to be important in processing sensory and emotional information, reward, and motivational processes: the caudate nucleus, nucleus accumbens (NAC), and part of the anterior cingulate cortex (ACC). The caudate nucleus is associated with reward detection, expectation, and representation of goals, and the NAC is rich in receptors for dopamine and oxytocin, neurotransmitters that are associated with rewards, suggesting that the participants who were in love experienced greater neurological rewards even while resting, thinking about nothing. In addition, the increased connectivity in the ACC, associated with cognitive control and the sense of self and other, suggests greater ability to monitor conflict and attend to one's own and others' emotions, activities central to successful social interactions. Finally, being in love was associated with greater connectivity among these regions and the amygdala, a part of the brain involved in emotion, suggesting an enhanced ability to understand and control emotion (Song et al., 2015).

Researchers also found that the functional connectivity just described was positively correlated with the length of time an individual reported being in love, suggesting that romantic love might change the interactions among the parts of the brain responsible for reward, motivation, and emotion regulation. Perhaps these changes are influenced by adults' efforts to monitor their own emotional state and that of their lover, negotiate conflicts, and adjust emotional experience to maintain the romantic relationship.

What Do You Think?

1. What interpersonal skills are needed for a successful romantic relationship?

2. How might socioemotional development influence success at romantic relationships?

3. To what extent do you think that neurological development influences our ability to have romantic relationships? In what ways might having romantic relationships influence our neurological development? ●

TABLE 14.1

Forms of Love

	INTIMACY	PASSION	COMMITMENT	DESCRIPTION
Liking/friendship	X			Close friendship characterized by feelings of warmth but without commitment or a long-term commitment.
Infatuated love		X		Love characterized by passion. Many romantic relationships begin as infatuated love and later become intimate and committed. Relationships characterized by infatuated love may dissolve suddenly.
Empty love			X	Relationship characterized by commitment without love or intimacy. A more complex kind of love may dissolve into empty love. In cultures in which there are arranged marriages—in which partners are selected by their families on the basis of cultural values—relationships of empty love sometimes grow to include intimacy and/or passion.
Romantic love	X	X		Characterized by physical passion and emotional closeness. Many romantic relationships represent romantic love and later develop commitment.
Companionate love	X		X	Similar to friendship, this love is intimate and not passionate; however, it has the element of long-term commitment. It is shared by close friends who have a platonic but strong friendship. It is also characteristic of some marriages in which the passion wanes but strong feelings of emotional connection and commitment remain.
Fatuous love		X	X	Relationship in which commitment is motivated by passion. It might occur in a whirlwind, quick marriage in which the couple does not have the time to form intimacy.
Consummate love	X	X	X	Ideal relationship—passion, intimacy, commitment. The couple displaying consummate love feels close and connected passion and a long-term commitment to each other. Consummate love may be difficult to maintain over time. As passion wanes, it may transform into companionate love.

Source: Based on Sternberg (2004).

Intimate Partner Violence

Violence between intimate partners is a widespread health issue that is not limited by culture, ethnicity, socioeconomic status, sexual orientation, marital status, or gender (Ahmadabadi, Najman, Williams, Clavarino, & d'Abbs, 2018; S. G. Smith et al., 2017). **Intimate partner violence** includes physical, sexual, and emotional abuse directed at a romantic partner. Victims frequently experience several forms of violence. For example, physical violence, such as throwing and breaking possessions, punching holes in walls, and hitting, tends to be accompanied by emotional abuse, including threats and coercive behaviors such as humiliation, control, and isolation from friends and family (Krebs, Breiding, Browne, & Warner, 2011). Intimate partner violence is often situational, occurring during arguments, escalating the emotional intensity of arguments and eliciting retaliatory violence from the victimized partner. Violence that is severe and chronic, characterized by coercive control and repeated battering of a partner, is known as *intimate terrorism,* the most damaging form of intimate partner violence.

Intimate partner violence occurs in couples of all sexual orientations but is most often reported when a male harms a female partner (Barrett, 2015; S. G. Smith et al., 2017). About one third of men and a little more than one third of women report having experienced physical intimate partner violence, such as rape, physical violence, or stalking, at some point in their lifetime and about 5% within the past year (S. G. Smith et al., 2017). Many acts of violence are unreported. Rates of intimate partner violence vary by ethnicity, as shown in Figure 14.3. Although men and women are about equally likely to instigate episodes of intimate violence, women are more likely to miss work, report depression, and be injured or killed by their partners as a result of the violence (Ahmadabadi et al., 2018; Jasinski, Blumenstein, & Morgan, 2014). Men are more likely to report partner aggression as the precipitant to their own aggression,

FIGURE 14.3

Lifetime Rates of Intimate Partner Violence by Sex and Ethnicity

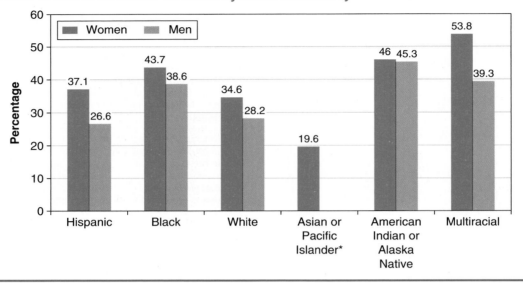

Source: Breiding et al. (2014).

Note: *No data available for Asian or Pacific Islander Males.

whereas women are more likely to report verbal aggression as the trigger to their own aggression (Fincham & Beach, 2010). Note that there is overlap between perpetrator and victim roles; many victims also engage in abusive behavior (Richards, Tillyer, & Wright, 2017; Tillyer & Wright, 2013).

Research is mixed regarding the prevalence of intimate partner violence in the LGBT community, with some proposing rates similar to those in heterosexual populations (Barrett, 2015) and others suggesting higher rates (Edwards, Sylaska, & Neal, 2015; Langenderfer-Magruder, Whitfield, Walls, Kattari, & Ramos, 2016). One review of lesbian couples found that, as with heterosexual couples, all forms of violence occur, but emotional violence was most common (Badenes-Ribera, Bonilla-Campos, Frias-Navarro, & Gemma Pons-Salvador, 2016). Bisexual adults are more likely to experience violence than any other sexual orientation; perceived or real infidelity is most closely linked with perpetration and victimization in bisexual couples (Turell, Brown, & Herrmann, 2018).

A variety of factors contribute to intimate violence. Risk factors regardless of sexual orientation include prior experiences, family history, and substance use (Badenes-Ribera et al., 2016; Buller, Devries, Howard, & Bacchus, 2014; Low, Tiberio, Shortt, Capaldi, & Eddy, 2017). Children who grow up to become abusive spouses are more likely to have observed domestic violence in their homes, to have received physical punishment and coercive discipline, and to have had poor-quality relationships with their parents (Kaufman-Parks, DeMaris,

Giordano, Manning, & Longmore, 2018; Shortt, Low, Capaldi, Eddy, & Tiberio, 2016).

In addition, spouses who abuse often show higher rates of depression, anxiety, and low self-esteem, and they often display possessive, jealous, and controlling behavior toward their partners (Spencer et al., 2018). Attempts to control a partner's behavior predict perpetration and victimization (Giordano, Copp, Longmore, & Manning, 2016). Violence may be more common in cohabiting relationships as well as those low in commitment and poor in quality (Manning, Longmore, & Giordano, 2018).

Contextual factors that contribute to intimate partner violence include economic stressors, such as unemployment and poverty, and lack of community resources, such as poor access to services (Beyer, Wallis, & Hamberger, 2015; Copp, Giordano, Manning, & Longmore, 2016). For example, the experience of poverty and other contextual stressors may underlie the higher rates of domestic violence reported by African American women (Cho, 2012). Minority stress and the experience of discrimination are unique contextual contributors to violence in LGBT couples (Lewis, Mason, Winstead, & Kelley, 2017).

Cultural norms and values also influence rates of partner violence. Worldwide, about one third of women experience intimate partner violence in their lifetimes, but rates vary widely, from 16% in East Asia (including China, Japan, North Korea, and South Korea) and 19% in Western Europe to 41% and 42% in South Asia (including Bangladesh, India, and Pakistan) and parts of Latin America, respectively

Intimate partner violence includes physical, sexual, and emotional abuse directed at a romantic partner. Most victims experience several forms of violence.
AP Photo/K.M. Chaudary

(Breiding, Chen, & Black, 2014; Devries et al., 2013), to 66% in central sub-Saharan Africa (including Chad, Congo, and Rwanda). Cultural norms valuing male dominance and female submissiveness, as well as differences in women's social mobility through education and career, underlie differences in prevalence rates (and gender differences in prevalence rates) throughout the world (Bendall, 2010; Boyle, Georgiades, Cullen, & Racine, 2009; Eng, Li, Mulsow, & Fischer, 2010; World Health Organization, 2005). In Cambodia, for example, the more contact and discussions couples have, the more likely are husbands to assert control and engage in intimate violence because women's more frequent discussion may be viewed as a violation of the cultural belief that wives are to be quiet and submissive (Eng et al., 2010).

Why do victims of intimate violence remain in these relationships? Regardless of sexual orientation, victims often remain in abusive relationships out of fear, financial necessity, love, the embarrassment of alerting authorities, and the hope that their partners will change (Barrett, 2015; Leone, Lape, & Xu, 2013). Many communities provide services to aid victims of intimate violence, including crisis telephone lines, shelters, and clinics that provide counseling, support, and treatment. Yet victims of partner violence often return to the relationship several times before terminating

it. Community services addressing intimate partner violence attempt to empower victims by easing their transition from dangerous homes and fostering self-help skills (Barner & Carney, 2011). Community services often include treatment for abusers, emphasizing communication, anger management, and problem solving, but many perpetrators repeat the pattern of violence despite treatment (Harway & Hansen, 2004; Levesque, Velicer, & Castle, 2008).

 THINKING IN CONTEXT 14.2

1. How might developmental and contextual factors such as neighborhood, age, and life experience influence the formation and course of friendships? In what ways are romantic relationships similar to and different from friendships?

2. How might culture and context influence young adults' perspectives of what characteristics to look for in seeking a romantic partner and mate? How might young people increase their odds of forming a happy and long-lasting relationship?

3. Consider the problem of intimate violence from a bioecological perspective. What microsystem, mesosystem, exosystem, and macrosystem factors may increase the likelihood of violence? What factors might decrease it?

LIFESTYLES AND ROMANTIC PARTNERSHIPS

» LO 14.3 **Analyze the diverse romantic situations that may characterize early adulthood, including singlehood, cohabitation, marriage, and divorce.**

Most young people marry in early adulthood, and others experience alternative living styles, whether by choice or circumstance; they may remain single or cohabit with a partner. Trends such as late marriage, divorce, and an increasing number of adults who choose not to marry mean that most adults in the United States will spend a large part of their adult lives as single; indeed, about 8% will remain single throughout life. Couples who marry are very likely to live together before marriage. Others live together in long-term **cohabitation** that does not lead to marriage.

Singlehood

Singlehood, not living with a romantic partner, is common among U.S. young adults. About one third of 25- to 39-year-olds have never married, including

FIGURE 14.4

Living Arrangements of Emerging Adults

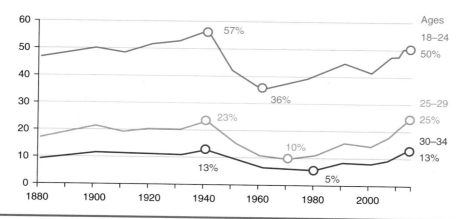

Share of U.S. young adults (ages 18–34) living in their parent(s)' home, by age

Source: Reprinted with permission from "Increase in living with parents driven by those ages 25-34, non-college grads," Pew Research Center, Washington, DC (June, 2016). http://www.pewresearch.org/fact-tank/2016/06/08/increase-in-living-with-parents-driven-by-those-ages-25-34-non-college-grads/ft_16-06-02_livingathome_age-2/

18% of 35- to 39-year-olds (U.S. Bureau of the Census, 2015). About half of single adults say they would like to get married in the future (Wang & Parker, 2014). Younger adults, under the age of 30, are more likely to say they would like to get married (66% compared with 33% of adults 30 and older). About one third of adults ages 18 to 34 live with their parents (Fry, 2016). As shown in Figure 14.4, living with parents remains common in the late 20s.

Women and men differ in rates of singlehood. In contrast with men, women tend to select mates who are the same age or older, are equally or better educated, and are professionally successful. Because of these tendencies, highly educated professional women who are financially independent, and therefore lack an economic incentive to marry, may find few potential mates whom they consider suitable (Sharp & Ganong, 2007). Some women attribute singlehood to focusing more on career goals than marriage, and others point to disappointing romantic relationships or to never having met the right person (Baumbusch, 2004). Overall, women are more likely than men to remain single for many years or for their entire lives.

Adults who are likely to describe themselves as single by choice are those who are self-supporting, feel a sense of control over their romantic lives, and have not encountered anyone they wish to marry (Sharp & Ganong, 2007). Such adults tend to report enjoying singlehood and the freedom to take risks and experiment with lifestyle changes. They also tend to associate singlehood with independence, self-fulfillment, and autonomy throughout their life course, including in old age (Timonen & Doyle, 2013). In contrast, adults who

are involuntarily single, who wish to be married, may feel a sense of romantic loneliness and loss and may be concerned with singlehood's impact on childbearing (Adamczyk, 2017; Jackson, 2018).

Single adults tend to maintain more social connections of both women and men. Compared to their married peers, single adults are more likely to stay in frequent touch with parents, friends, and neighbors and to give and receive help from them, suggesting some important social benefits of singlehood (Sarkisian & Gerstel, 2016).

Cohabitation

The trend for increasing education and delayed career entry that is characteristic of emerging adulthood has led to a rise in cohabitation, the practice of unmarried couples sharing a home. Today, more than half of adults in their 20s have lived with a romantic partner and about 70% of U.S. couples live together before marriage (Manning, 2013). In one recent national poll, emerging adults ages 18 to 24 were about as likely to cohabit as marry (7% and 9%, respectively), but the young adults surveyed (ages 25–34) were much less likely to cohabit (14%) than marry (41%) (Stepler, 2017). Cohabitation is very common in some European countries as well: Over 75% of couples in Northern and Central Europe and the United Kingdom cohabit, as well as about 90% of couples in Sweden and Denmark (Hsueh, Morrison, & Doss, 2009; Manning, 2013; Popenoe, 2009).

Some adults move in with their partners early in the relationships because of changes in employment or housing situations, for the sake of convenience, or in response to pregnancy (Sassler

Most young adults in North America and Europe cohabitate, or live together, in committed relationships.
Sacramento Bee/Tribune/Getty

& Miller, 2011). Adults commonly cite assessing romantic compatibility, convenience, and potential improvement in finances as reasons for cohabiting (Copen, Daniels, & Mosher, 2013). In the United States, young adults of low socioeconomic status, as well as of African American and Puerto Rican heritage, are more likely to cohabit as an alternative to marriage, whereas European American young adults are more likely to marry after a period of cohabitation (Lesthaeghe, López-Colás, & Neidert, 2016).

Cultures differ in the acceptability of cohabitation and have different laws and policies pertaining to it. In many European countries, cohabitation is viewed not as a precursor but rather as an alternative to marriage. Cohabiting couples in those countries often hold legal rights similar to those of married couples and show similar levels of devotion as married couples (Hiekel, Liefbroer, & Poortman, 2014; Perelli-Harris & Gassen, 2012). For example, France, Norway, and the Netherlands offer similar financial protections to married and cohabiting couples, such as insurance, social security, and, in the case of a partner's death, the right to his or her pension (Sánchez Gassen & Perelli-Harris, 2015). In

contrast, cohabitation is nearly unheard of in some countries, such as Ireland, Italy, Japan, and the Philippines, where fewer than 10% of adults have ever lived with an unmarried partner (Batalova & Cohen, 2002; Williams, Kabamalan, & Ogena, 2007).

The stability of cohabiting unions also varies from one country to another. Overall, cohabiting couples in the United States, particularly those without plans to marry, tend to show poor relationship quality, be less satisfied, and have less stable relationships than married couples (Brown, Manning, & Payne, 2017; Jose, Daniel O'Leary, & Moyer, 2010). Most cohabiting couples do not eventually marry (Guzzo, 2014), and research suggests that those who do have unhappier marriages with a greater likelihood of divorce (Copen et al., 2013; Jose et al., 2010; Kulik & Havusha-Morgenstern, 2011). In contrast, in Europe, the rates of dissolution for cohabiting couples are similar to those of married couples (Hiekel et al., 2014; Perelli-Harris & Gassen, 2012). For example, one study included 15,000 British couples who had dissolved their union. Among these unions, cohabiting unions were much shorter in duration—about 4 years, on average, compared with 14 years for married couples (Gravningen et al., 2017). Cohabiting and married couples list similar reasons for breakups: most commonly, growing apart, followed by arguments.

According to some research, as cohabitation becomes more common, its association with marital instability may be weakening (Manning & Cohen, 2012; Reinhold, 2010). Clearly, more research is needed as the association of cohabitation and marital stability is complicated and is influenced by other relationship factors. For example, couples who enter cohabitation with marriage plans, such as while engaged, tend to experience marriages with levels of marital quality, stability, and distress similar to those of married respondents who had not cohabited (Rhoades, Stanley, & Markman, 2009; Stanley, Rhoades, Amato, Markman, & Johnson, 2010). In addition, the correlates of cohabitation vary with the couple's age—older adults show more positive outcomes from cohabitation. Relationship stability is influenced by many factors, not simply whether an unmarried couple lives together.

Marriage

Over the past half-century, marriage rates have declined to record lows—yet nearly all adults in the United States will marry. By age 45, over 80% of adults have married at least once, 90% have married by age 60, and over 95% by age 80 (U.S. Bureau of the Census, 2015). In 2017, the median age of first marriage in the United States was 27.4 for women and 29.5 for men, with dramatic increases over the past

FIGURE 14.5

U.S. Median Age at First Marriage, 1890 to 2017

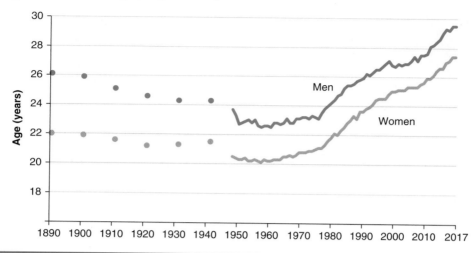

Source: U.S. Bureau of the Census, 2017.

40 years, as shown in Figure 14.5 (U.S. Bureau of the Census, 2017). Similar age increases have occurred in Canada, with the average age at first marriage being 31 for males and 30 for females—up more than 6 years since 1975. Some European countries have experienced increases as well; for example, in 2011 in Sweden, the median age was as high as 36 for men and 33 for women, up 7 years since 1980 (United Nations Economic Commission for Europe, 2015).

Despite this trend, the age of first marriage remains variable. Young people of low socioeconomic status tend to marry at younger ages than do those of higher socioeconomic status (Meier & Allen, 2008). In the United States, African Americans are the least likely to marry, and when they marry, they do so later and spend less time married than European Americans (Dixon, 2009). Factors that contribute to marriage rates of African American adults include the prevalence of more females than males, greater employment instability among African American males, and higher rates of cohabitation compared with other ethnic groups (Lundberg & Pollak, 2016; Raley, Sweeney, & Wondra, 2015).

Generally speaking, marriage offers economic, physical, and psychological benefits. Married people around the world tend to live longer and are happier, physically healthier, wealthier, and in better mental health than nonmarried people (S. Grover & Helliwell, 2014; Koball, Moiduddin, Henderson, Goesling, & Besculides, 2010; Vanassche, Swicegood, & Matthijs, 2012). Nevertheless, the transition to marriage is often challenging, as newlyweds experience multiple changes during their first years of marriage, such as coordinating and making

decisions about living arrangements, housework, eating habits, and sexual activity. Many newlyweds struggle with rising debt, which is associated with higher levels of conflict (Neff & Karney, 2017). Most couples report a decline in relationship satisfaction over the first year of marriage (Lavner & Bradbury, 2014). However, couples who are successful at managing the transition to married life express warmth, empathy, and respect in their relationship (Gadassi et al., 2016). They are able to address differences and resolve conflicts constructively by expressing feelings calmly, listening, accepting responsibility, and compromising (Hanzal & Segrin, 2009). Partners in successful marriages are able to maintain positive emotions for their spouse even in the midst of conflict (Gottman & Gottman, 2017). In contrast, during arguments, unhappy couples easily

The transition to marriage poses many challenges as newlyweds must negotiate household tasks, financial obligations, and new roles.
Bubbles/Alamy

Perceived equity, the sense that work and household responsibilities are distributed fairly, predicts relationship satisfaction in married couples.
AP/Donna McWilliam

sink into negative emotions that are overwhelming and, like quicksand, difficult to escape.

One of the best predictors of marital satisfaction and a long-lasting marriage is the partners' chronological maturity, or age. Generally speaking, the younger the bride and groom, the less likely they are to have a lifelong marriage (Cherlin, 2010). Forging an intimate relationship relies on a secure sense of identity, which many emerging adults are still developing. Marital success is also predicted by the degree of similarity between the members of the couple. Similarities in socioeconomic status, education, religion, and age all contribute to predicting a happy marriage (Gonzaga, Campos, & Bradbury, 2007). In addition, spouses reciprocally influence each other and tend, over a lifetime of marriage, to become more similar to each other in terms of personality (Caspi, Herbener, & Ozer, 1992) and markers of aging (Ko, Berg, Butner, Uchino, & Smith, 2007). They also become more similar in their general well-being, as measured by rates of depression, physical activity, and health, including chronic diseases such as high blood pressure (Bookwala & Jacobs, 2004; Pettee et al., 2006).

The quality of the marital relationship predicts mental health and well-being in both men and women (Robles, 2014). Men generally report being happier with their marriages than women, although the difference is small (Jackson, Miller, Oka, & Henry, 2014). Satisfaction, particularly in women, tends to be highest in egalitarian relationships in which home and family duties are shared and couples view themselves as equal contributors (Helms, Walls, Crouter, & McHale, 2010; Ogolsky, Dennison, & Monk, 2014). This is particularly true in Western nations, where egalitarian marriage roles are increasingly expected (Greenstein, 2009).

In dual-earner marriages today, most men take on many more child care tasks than in prior generations, although they still spend less time than women on housework. Dual-earner couples who view themselves as equal contributors to household duties tend to divide work most equitably and report highest levels of satisfaction (Helms et al., 2010). Although many couples strive for it, true equality in marriage is rare. In determining marital satisfaction, it seems that what matters more than actual equity (how household responsibilities are distributed between partners) is the perception of equity (whether partners feel that responsibilities are distributed fairly); this holds true for both members of the couple but especially for women (Amato & Irving, 2006; Greenstein, 2009). If the division of household responsibilities feels equal, then the couple is likely to report marital satisfaction.

Same-Sex Marriage

Like all people, gay and lesbian adults seek love, partnership, and close intimate relationships. Intimate relationships and marriage have similar meanings for gay and lesbian couples as for heterosexual couples (Cherlin, 2013). Until recently, it was very difficult to study same-sex unions because same-sex marriage was not legal in all U.S. states. Since the 2015 Supreme Court decision in *Obergefell v. Hodges*, discussed in the Applying Developmental Science feature, gay and lesbian couples have begun forming legal unions through marriage (Riggle, Wickham, Rostosky, Rothblum, & Balsam, 2017). The literature comparing these couples with heterosexual couples has been growing, although it is still sparse.

Studies that have compared gay, lesbian, and heterosexual couples have found no significant differences in love, satisfaction, or the partners' evaluations of the strengths and weaknesses of their relationships (Frost, Meyer, & Hammack, 2015; Lavner, Waterman, & Peplau, 2014). Serious problems

Gay and lesbian couples show similar rates of love and satisfaction in their marriages and experience similar benefits of marriage as compared with heterosexual couples.
Kevork Djansezian/Getty Images

The Legalization of Same-Sex Marriage

Marriage confers health, psychosocial, and financial benefits to all couples: same sex or opposite sex (Biblarz & Savci, 2010). However, until the July 2015 Supreme Court decision in *Obergefell v. Hodges,* same-sex couples could not legally marry in many states. The *Obergefell* case combined four cases challenging the right of states to refuse to recognize or license same-sex marriages, thereby denying couples the legal rights and protections that come with marriage (such as the right to jointly adopt children). In the end, the Court ruled that states could not deny these rights to same-sex couples.

Applied developmental scientists played a role in this decision by providing the Court with research-based information about same-sex couples. Specifically, an interdisciplinary group of scientists submitted an amicus curiae ("friend of the court") brief to inform the Supreme Court justices (see http://www.apa.org/about/offices/ogc/amicus/obergefell.pdf). The brief was jointly authored and submitted by more than a dozen professional organizations in psychology, social work, and medicine, including the American Psychological Association (APA), American Medical Association, American Academy of Pediatrics (AAP), National Association of Social Workers, and Association for Marriage and Family Therapy. The brief referred to many of the scientific findings that we have discussed—that same-sex relationships are equivalent to heterosexual relationships in essential respects and that there is no scientific basis for concluding that same-sex couples are not fit parents or that children of same-sex

couples are any less psychologically healthy and well adjusted than children of heterosexual couples. The brief therefore argued that excluding same-sex couples from the institution of marriage denies them social, psychological, and health benefits and is stigmatizing.

With the *Obergefell* ruling, the United States joined the more than a dozen countries with national laws allowing gays and lesbians to marry, including Canada, Finland, Spain, the Netherlands, Argentina, and New Zealand (Pew Research Center, 2015). Moreover, recent surveys of U.S. adults have shown that over two thirds (62%) say they support same-sex marriage, compared with 32% who opposed it (Pew Research Center, 2017). As shown in Figure 14.6, there are large cohort differences in that younger generations express higher levels of support for same-sex marriage, but in recent decades, older generations also have become more supportive.

What Do You Think?

1. What role should developmental scientists take in advising courts and policy makers? Do you think they should participate in writing amicus curiae briefs? Why or why not?

2. What might be some of the reasons we see cohort differences in attitudes toward same-sex marriage? Identify contextual factors that might contribute to some of the generational differences we see. ●

FIGURE 14.6

U.S. Support of Same-Sex Marriage, 2001–2017

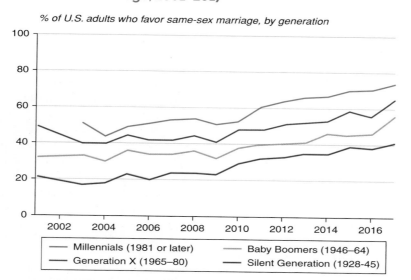

% of U.S. adults who favor same-sex marriage, by generation

Millennials (1981 or later)
Generation X (1965–80)
Baby Boomers (1946–64)
Silent Generation (1928–45)

Source: Reprinted with permission from "Changing Attitudes on Gay Marriage," Pew Research Center, Washington, DC (June, 2017). http://www.pewforum.org/fact-sheet/changing-attitudes-on-gay-marriage/

such as intimate partner violence, for example, exist in both types of relationships (Edwards et al., 2015). Moreover, the breakup rate for same-sex couples is comparable to that for heterosexual couples (Rosenfeld, 2014). The available research suggests that gay and lesbian persons experience the same psychological benefits from legal marriage, civil unions, and registered domestic partnerships as heterosexual couples (Riggle, Rostosky, & Horne, 2010; Rostosky & Riggle, 2017). A study of over 36,000 people in the California Health Interview Survey found that lesbian, gay, and bisexual persons in a legal same-sex marriage were significantly less distressed than their LGB counterparts who were not in a same-sex legal relationship—and the same was true in comparing them with unmarried heterosexual persons. These findings suggest a mental health benefit to legal marriage (Wight, Leblanc, & Lee Badgett, 2013). As with heterosexual couples, marital satisfaction in same-sex unions is influenced by perceived equality and associated with physical and mental health, life satisfaction, and well-being (Cherlin, 2013; Pollitt, Robinson, & Umberson, 2018; Wight et al., 2013).

The stressors that gay men and lesbian women face, such as the experience of stigma and prejudice, might play a role in how same-sex marriage manifests in health and psychological well-being (Cao et al., 2017; Frost et al., 2015; Hatzenbuehler, 2014). Legal marriage may have the potential to offset the mental health impact of these stressors at the individual level and might offset the larger macro-level effects of sanctioned discrimination (Wight et al., 2013). This idea is supported by research conducted prior to the national legalization of marriage, suggesting that same-sex couples living in states with legally sanctioned marriage reported higher levels of self-assessed health, greater self-acceptance, and less isolation than those living in states that barred same-sex marriage (Kail, Acosta, & Wright, 2015; Riggle et al., 2017). Likewise, legally married same-sex older adult couples reported better quality of life and more economic and social resources than unmarried partnered couples (Goldsen et al., 2017). Again, these adults were surveyed prior to the legalization of same-sex marriage in the United States. As you can see from these studies, laws represent an important contextual influence on well-being.

Divorce

In the first few decades following the 1960s, divorce rates tripled in many Western industrialized countries, but since then they have stabilized and even declined (United Nations Statistics Division, 2014). In the United States, for example, the divorce rate increased during the 1970s, peaking at 5.2 divorces per 1,000 people in 1980, and then declined to 2.8 divorces per 1,000 people in 2014 (National Center for Health Statistics, 2015; United Nations Statistics Division, 2017). Despite declines in divorce rates around the world, large international differences remain. The highest divorce rate is in the Russian Federation (4.5 per 1,000 persons) and the lowest in Ireland (.6), suggesting that social contextual factors unique to each culture play an influential role. Most U.S. marriages that end in divorce do so within the first 10 years (Copen, Daniels, Jonathan Vespa, & Mosher, 2012). By 45 years of age, over one third of men and women have been divorced (Kreider & Ellis, 2011).

We have seen that couples who are older and who share similarities in demographics, interests, personality, attitudes, and values are more likely to have successful marriages (Gonzaga et al., 2007). Poor education, economic disadvantage, not attending religious services, and experiencing multiple life stressors and role overload are associated with increased risk of divorce (Härkönen, 2015). Adults who have experienced their parents' divorce may themselves be more prone to divorce. When adult children of divorced families marry, they may have poor coping and conflict resolution skills, experience more conflict in their relationships, and be less able or willing to resolve differences (Amato, 2010). In addition, remarriages experience higher rates of divorce (DeLongis & Zwicker, 2017).

A critical predictor of divorce is the couple's communication and problem-solving style. Negative interaction patterns and difficulty regulating discussions predict later divorce even in newlyweds reporting high marital satisfaction, and these patterns are often evident even before marriage (Gottman & Gottman, 2017; Lavner & Bradbury, 2012). During conflict, troubled couples often experience negative emotions that are overwhelming and interfere with their connection to their partner. Unable to effectively resolve differences, when one member of the couple raises a concern, the other may retreat, reacting with anger, resentment, and defensiveness, creating a negative cycle (Ramos Salazar, 2015). Disagreements over finances are particularly strong predictors of divorce (Dew, Britt, & Huston, 2012).

The process of divorce entails a series of stressful experiences, including conflict, physical separation, moving, distributing property, and, for some, child custody negotiations. Regardless of who initiates a divorce, all family members feel stress and a confusing array of emotions, such as anger, despair, embarrassment, shame, failure—and, sometimes, relief (Härkönen, 2015). Divorce is associated with decreased life satisfaction, heightened risk for a range of illnesses, and even a 20% to 30% increase in early mortality (Björkenstam, Hallqvist, Dalman, & Ljung, 2013; Holt-Lunstad, Smith, & Layton, 2010; Sbarra, Law, & Portley, 2011). Divorce is thought to be more harmful to women's health than to that of men, because it tends to represent a greater economic loss for women, often including a loss of health insurance (Lavelle & Smock, 2012).

Although some adults show poor health outcomes after divorce, most people are resilient and fare well, especially after the initial adjustment (Sbarra & Coan, 2017; Sbarra, Hasselmo, & Bourassa, 2015). For example, in one study of more than 600 German divorcees, nearly three quarters experienced little change in life satisfaction across a 9-year period that included the divorce (Mancini, Bonanno, & Clark, 2011). Women who successfully make the transition through a divorce tend to show positive long-term outcomes. They tend to become more tolerant, self-reliant, and nonconforming—all characteristics that are associated with the increased autonomy and self-reliance demands that come with divorce.

People undergoing divorce often find that their social network shrinks at the same time that their needs for social support increase. Each member of the couple loses supportive in-laws, and in-law relationships may become strained and combative. Friends and neighbors may feel that they are expected to "take sides" and consequently may avoid both members of the divorcing couple. Relocation may cause a spouse to lose contact with friends and neighbors. Recently divorced adults are prone to depression, loneliness, anxiety, an increase in risky behaviors such as drug and alcohol use, promiscuous sexual activity, and poor eating, sleeping, and working habits (Härkönen, 2015; Sbarra et al., 2015). In general, divorced people tend to report lower life satisfaction than married, never-

THINKING IN CONTEXT 14.3

1. Why are singlehood and cohabitation on the rise? What factors within individuals and families might contribute to whether a person remains single or cohabits with a partner? How might neighborhood and societal factors influence the prevalence of singlehood and cohabitation?

2. How might extended singlehood and cohabitation influence young people's attainment of developmental tasks such as intimacy?

3. Provide advice to newlyweds. Given what is known about love, marriage, and divorce, what can they do to ensure a happy marriage and reduce the likelihood of divorce? Alternatively, what can someone who is facing divorce do to aid his or her transition?

TABLE 14.2

Correlates and Influences on Marriage and Divorce

Correlates of Marriage
- Good physical health
- Good mental health
- Positive sense of well-being

Ingredients in Marital Success
- Intimacy and commitment, expressed as warmth, attentiveness, empathy, acceptance, and respect
- Good communication skills, including the ability to express concerns calmly and clarify the other's expressed wishes and needs
- Good conflict management skills, including the ability to compromise, accept responsibility, and avoid defensiveness and criticism
- Effective conflict management and resolution
- Degree of similarity in education, religion, age, and socioeconomic status
- Perception of equity between partners

Risk Factors for Divorce
- Young age
- Multiple life stressors
- Dissimilarities in age, ethnicity, religion, attitudes, and values
- Poor education
- Economic disadvantage
- Poor coping, communication, and conflict resolution skills

Correlates of Divorce
- Loss of income and financial instability
- Risky behaviors such as drug and alcohol use and promiscuous sexual activity
- Poor self-care, including poor eating, sleeping, and working habits
- Negative emotions, such as anger, despair, and shame
- Poor physical and mental health
- Reduced social network and support
- Reduced life satisfaction

married, and widowed people (Næss, Blekesaune, & Jakobsson, 2015). However, spouses in very low-quality relationships may experience divorce as a relief and show increased life satisfaction afterward (Bourassa, Sbarra, & Whisman, 2015). Most find that their happiness and life satisfaction improve when they find a new romantic partner and establish a relationship.

Overall, 40% of new marriages involve remarriage of one or both partners (Livingston, 2014). Women are more likely to not want to marry again (54%) as compared with men (30%). Men tend to remarry more quickly after divorce than do women. As with other life challenges, divorce represents an opportunity for growth and development, and adaptive outcomes following divorce appear to be the norm, not the exception (Perrig-Chiello, Hutchison, & Morselli, 2014). Table 14.2 summarizes correlates and influences on marriage and divorce.

PARENTHOOD IN EARLY ADULTHOOD

» LO 14.4 **Compare the experiences of young adults as stepparents, never-married parents, and same-sex parents.**

Until recent generations, having children was considered an inevitable part of adult life. Since the 1960s, effective methods of birth control and changing cultural views on parenthood and childlessness have made having children a choice (Mills, Rindfuss, McDonald, & te Velde, 2011). Consequently, childbearing rates have declined in most industrialized nations. For example, in the 1950s, the average number of children born to a woman in the United States was 3.8; today it is 1.9 (Central Intelligence Agency, 2017). The average number of children is even lower for many industrialized nations, including Canada (1.6), Germany (1.5), and Japan (1.4). In contrast, rates are significantly higher in developing nations such as Niger (6.5), Somalia, (5.8), and Afghanistan (5.1).

Although families in many countries are growing smaller, most married adults still become parents, but later in life than ever before. The average age at which U.S. women give birth has increased over the past three decades, from 21.4 in 1970 to 26.4 in 2014 (see Figure 14.7) (Matthews & Hamilton, 2002, 2016). However, women who postpone childbearing to their early 30s are at increased risk for experiencing fertility difficulties (Schmidt, Sobotka, Bentzen, & Nyboe Andersen, 2012).

Becoming a Parent

The decision of whether to have a child is influenced by personal and circumstantial factors, such as values, health, and financial status. Although women's employment itself does not predict

FIGURE 14.7

Maternal Age at First Birth, 1970–2014

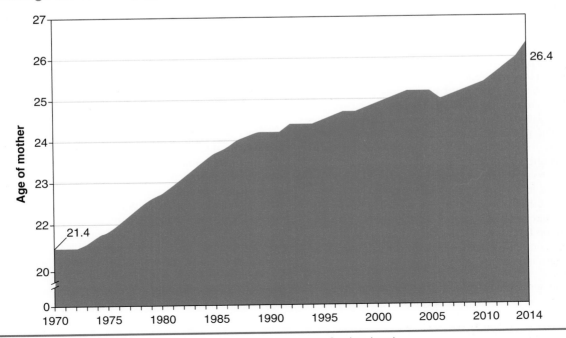

Sources: Matthews and Hamilton (2009); U.S. Department of Health and Human Services (2013).

parenthood, women in high-status and demanding occupations are more likely to delay or decide against childbearing than are women in less demanding occupations (Nilsen et al., 2012). North American adults cite a variety of reasons to have children, including experiencing the parent–child bond; growth, learning, and fun experiences that come with raising a child; and the desire to help someone grow into a productive adult (O'Laughlin & Anderson, 2001). Common disadvantages of parenthood include the loss of freedom and high cost of raising a child. It is estimated that an average middle-income parent (whose income falls within the middle third of the income distribution for two-parent families with children) will spend about $234,000 over the course of raising a child from birth to age 18 (U.S. Department of Agriculture, 2017). Parents with incomes in the lowest third spend about $175,000 and those in the highest third spend about $372,000.

The transition to parenthood is challenging for adults of all ages. New parents experience the exciting yet overwhelming task of getting to know their infant while meeting his or her needs for constant attention, affection, and care. They are greeted with new caregiving responsibilities, added housework, financial demands, loss of sleep, and diminished leisure time. Such pressures are associated with a reduced sense of well-being and self-esteem after the birth of a child (Bleidorn et al., 2016; Nelson, Kushlev, & Lyubomirsky, 2014). Many new parents report not feeling prepared for the roller coaster of emotions ranging from joy to frustration and exhaustion that accompany parenthood (Galatzer-Levy, Mazursky, Mancini, & Bonanno, 2011; Stanca, 2012). Some research suggests that, even years after becoming parents, many people are unable to regain the happiness and life satisfaction that they enjoyed before having a child (Clark, Diener, Georgellis, & Lucas, 2008). Some theorize that parents' perceptions of the joys of parenthood that "it's all worth it" may be a way of balancing the challenges, frustrations, and drops in happiness that accompany parenthood (Eibach & Mock, 2011). For example, new parents, especially men, experience

CULTURAL INFLUENCES ON DEVELOPMENT

Family Leave Policies

Most adults find managing the multiple demands of work and family challenging. There are many times in life when an adult may take on additional caretaking responsibilities, such as after the birth or adoption of a child or when a family member is seriously ill. People in most industrial nations are able to interrupt their employment to care for newborns and young children through various forms of leave.

Maternity leave is granted to mothers and is usually intended to protect the health and welfare of women and their newborns around the time of birth. Beginning in the 1950s, many countries in Europe established maternity leave policies (Moss & Deven, 2006). In 1992, the European Union introduced a policy establishing minimum standards, including at least partial pay, for maternity leave in all of its member states. As shown in Figure 14.8, maternity leave is nearly universal today. New mothers in Finland are entitled to up to 3 years' worth of paid leave. In Norway, mothers can get up to 91 weeks of paid leave. Canada allows 1 year of leave and the United Kingdom up to 39 weeks. The United States is the only industrialized nation that does not offer paid family leave (Ingraham, 2018).

In addition to maternity leave, some countries provide paternity leave. Generally, paternity leave is granted to fathers only around the time of birth and is intended to enable fathers to provide support to their partner and to care for older children. Eighteen of 27 EU countries offer paternity leave. The average length of paternity leave is 12.5 days (Van Belle, 2016).

Parental leave is another type of leave intended to enable parents to care for young children. In 1998, the European Union endorsed a parental leave policy requiring all member states to permit working parents, men and women, up to a minimum of 4 months of leave to care for children up to 8 years of age (Sahadi, 2016). In most of these countries, the leave is partially paid.

While the United States does not mandate maternity, paternity, or parental leave, the Family and Medical Leave Act, signed in 1993, grants workers in companies of 50 or more employees up to 12 weeks of unpaid leave for the birth or adoption of a child and for the care of a sick child, spouse, or parent with a serious health condition. It also guarantees job security, in that an employee is entitled to return to the same or a comparable job. In addition, it requires the employer to maintain health benefits as if the employee had never taken leave. In 2015, the Family and Medical Leave Act was extended to include legally married same-sex spouses (U.S. Department of Labor, 2018). Critics of the Family and Medical Leave Act note that the policy is limited in scope. Only employers with 50 or more employees must provide leave, so it is estimated that the policy covers only about half of U.S. employees (Wisensale, 2006). Furthermore, because it is unpaid, most single parents and low-income couples can't afford to take it even if given the opportunity.

The United States was one of the last industrialized nations to establish a family leave policy (Wisensale, 2006). However, at the time the law was signed, more than 30 states had already adopted some form of leave policy. Indeed, today, state legislation may provide more extensive benefits than does the federal legislation. In 2002, California enacted a paid family leave law and Rhode Island, New Jersey, and New York have since established paid family leave programs as well. Laws in these states require full or partial wage replacement for up to 6 weeks to enable an employee to care for a newborn or newly adopted child or to care for a family member who is suffering from a serious medical condition (National Conference of State Legislatures, 2018). Washington, D.C. will put paid family leave into effect in 2020.

What Do You Think?

1. To what extent do you think national differences in family leave reflect cultural views of parenting?

2. Why do you think family leave policies often spark debate in the United States?

3. Given what you know about children and families, as well as young adults' careers, what family policies, such as the length of leave, would you suggest? ●

FIGURE 14.8

Paid Maternity Leave in the Wealthy World

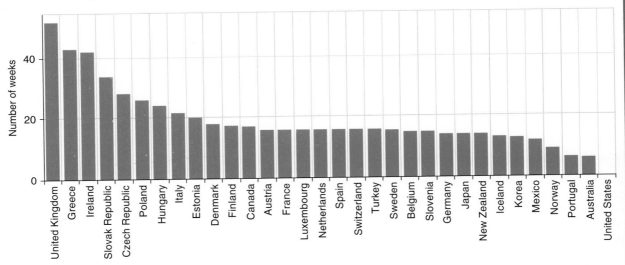

Source: OECD (2013). Length of maternity leave, parental leave and paid father-specific leave. http://www.oecd.org/gender/data/length-of-maternity-leave-parental-leave-and-paid-father-specific-leave.htm

Note: Total duration of paid maternity leave, parental leave, and paid father-specific leave, 2013, most recent data available.

a greater sense of meaning in life, suggesting that, although challenging, parenting contributes to their sense of meaning (Brandel, Melchiorri, & Ruini, 2018).

The parenthood transition places stress on even the best of relationships and marriages. Parenthood is associated with sudden declines in marital satisfaction for both partners in same-sex and opposite-sex relationships (Doss & Rhoades, 2017). Conflict tends to rise in response to increased financial, household, and parental demands and decreased leisure time (Don & Mickelson, 2014; Trillingsgaard, Baucom, & Heyman, 2014). Declines in satisfaction are higher in couples who experienced problems prior to the birth, have temperamentally difficult infants, and have an insecure attachment to their spouse or child (Doss & Rhoades, 2017; Simpson & Rholes, 2019).

During the transition to parenthood, most North American and European opposite-sex couples, even those in relatively egalitarian marriages, shift toward traditional marital roles and division of labor (Dribe & Stanfors, 2009; Katz-Wise, Priess, & Hyde, 2010; Koivunen, Rothaupt, & Wolfgram, 2009). In one study in which mothers and fathers kept a daily diary, mothers reported a greater increase in caregiving load with the birth of a child than did fathers, without reducing their outside workload (Yavorsky, Kamp Dush, & Schoppe-Sullivan, 2015). Furthermore, the gender gap emerged after the birth, with women doing more than 2 hours of additional work per day compared with an additional 40 minutes for men. Other research confirms that mothers tend to report more stress and a higher caregiving workload with the advent of parenthood than do fathers, and this shift influences their relationship satisfaction (Le, McDaniel, Leavitt, & Feinberg, 2016; Widarsson et al., 2013). Mothers' satisfaction with the division of childrearing responsibilities predicts their ratings of relationship quality (Adamsons, 2013). We know less about how same-sex partners share the caregiving workload that comes with new parenthood, but one small study of male same-sex couples found that most perceived an equitable share of work (Tornello, Kruczkowski, & Patterson, 2015). As with opposite-sex couples, perceived equity was associated with high perceived relationship quality. Planning ahead for the changes that accompany a newborn serves a protective role for the spousal relationship (Lawrence, Rothman, Cobb, & Bradbury, 2010). Paid family leave can support parents in adjusting to parenthood by reducing some of the career and financial pressures associated with the transition to parenthood. Not all countries, however, support paid family leave, as discussed in the Cultural Influences on Development feature.

Never-Married Single Parent

Four in 10 infants in the United States are born to never-married mothers each year, and many of these mothers remain single after giving birth (Hamilton, Martin, Osterman, Curtin, & Mathews, 2015). About 44% of all single mothers have never been married (Wang, Parker, & Taylor, 2013). In recent years, more single professional women in their 30s have become single parents by choice. However, these women are

Never-married mothers often experience better mental health than married mothers. However, outcomes vary with contextual factors such as social support and socioeconomic status.
iStock/lewkmiller

dissimilar to the typical never-married single parent, and we know little about the development of children born to single women with high-powered careers. Instead, never-married parents in the United States are less likely to have attended college and are more likely to live at or near the poverty level; this is true in the European Union as well (Bernardi & Mortelmans, 2018; Chzhen & Bradshaw, 2012).

African American women are disproportionately likely to be never-married parents, comprising 40% of never-married mothers (compared with 32% for White non-Hispanic and 24% for Hispanic; Caumont, 2013). In addition, African American women are more likely to postpone marriage after childbirth than are women of other ethnic groups. Higher rates of job loss, mortality, and persistent unemployment among many African American men influence young African American women's decisions. About one third of never-married African American mothers marry within 9 years after the birth of their first child, often to a man who is not the child's biological father, and the resulting family is much like any other first-marriage family (Dixon 2009; Wu, Bumpass, & Musick, 2001).

Although some research suggests that never-married mothers tend to be similar to married mothers in mental health (Afifi, Cox, & Enns, 2006; Z. E. Taylor & Conger, 2014), other work suggests that never-married single mothers are less happy (Baranowska-Rataj, Matysiak, & Mynarska, 2013) and are more likely to have poor health in middle and older adulthood (Berkman et al., 2015). The experiences of never-married single mothers vary with other contextual influences such as social support. African American and Latino parents are more likely to report receiving family support, which influence maternal and child outcomes (Z. E. Taylor & Conger, 2014). Regardless of ethnicity, children in single-mother homes are disproportionately likely to live in poverty (Damaske, Bratter, & Frech, 2017). Indeed, the primary challenge never-married mothers face is economic. They are less likely to receive child support than divorced mothers, and about one half have more than one child (Wu et al., 2001). A large study of unmarried mothers suggested that nonmarital childbearing is adversely associated with the ability to marry an economically attractive mate and maintain a long-term marital union (Graefe & Lichter, 2007). As we have discussed, poverty and low socioeconomic status hold vast implications for children's development.

Same-Sex Parents

Most gay and lesbian young adults in the United States plan to raise children one day (D'augelli, Rendina, Sinclair, & Grossman, 2006). It is estimated that 35% of female spousal couples and 28% of male spousal couples are raising biological, step, or adopted children. For unmarried partners, the estimates are 21% and 5%, respectively (Gates, 2013). About 23% of lesbian women are parents, compared with about 68% of heterosexual women (Brewster, Tillman, & Jokinen-Gordon, 2013). Lesbian women become parents through a more diverse set of pathways than heterosexual women, including adoption and parenting a spouse or partner's child. The majority of children in same-sex parented homes were conceived through previous heterosexual relationships, but an increasing number of gay men and lesbian women become parents through adoption and reproductive technologies (Henehan, Rothblum, Solomon, & Balsam, 2007).

In the past, many state laws assumed that gay men and lesbian women could not be competent parents. For example, until recently, most states permitted adoption to LGBT single adults, but few permitted same-sex couples to adopt (Raley, Fisher, Halder, & Shanmugan, 2013). In 2017, joint adoption by same-sex couples became legal in all U.S. states (Movement Advancement Project, 2018). However, families created through reproductive technology face unique challenges. For example, in many states, a social (nonbiological) mother does not have an automatic legal connection to her spouse's offspring, as male fathers do in opposite-sex marriages. Instead, U.S. states vary in their definitions of parenthood (Harris, 2017). Parents in same-sex families who seek to protect their legal rights as parents often formally adopt their children (Chang & Simmons-Duffin, 2017). The adoption process is similar to that for parents who wish to adopt for the first time. That is, the adopting parents must complete a physical examination, blood work, fingerprinting, and a home visit by a social worker. Same-sex parents who have raised their children from birth often find this process stigmatizing and biased as heterosexual married couples do not face a similar process to obtain legal rights for their children (Harris, 2017). Such bias and discrimination pose threats to same-sex parents' well-being (Prendergast & MacPhee, 2018). In a very important ruling in 2017, the U.S. Supreme Court ruled that nonbiological parents can be listed on newborns' birth certificates, acknowledging their rights as parents (Wolf, 2017).

As discussed in Chapter 9, children reared by lesbian and gay parents do not differ from those reared by heterosexual parents in social development, psychological adjustment, and gender and sexual orientation (Bos, Kuyper, & Gartrell, 2018; Fedewa, Black, & Ahn, 2014). Similarly, same-sex parents do not differ from heterosexual parents in competence or commitment to their roles as parents (Gartrell & Bos, 2010; Perrin & Siegel, 2013). The parenting role that same-sex partners take varies with the way in which the family formed. Generally speaking, the biological parent tends to assume most of the parenting responsibility when the child is the result of a previous heterosexual relationship. As parents, gay and lesbian couples tend to coparent more equally than heterosexual partners; however, their relationship dynamics often shift in similar ways as those of heterosexual parents (Biblarz & Savci, 2010). For example, lesbian couples with children may move from shared employment, decision making, and household work in exchange for differentiation between partners in child care and paid employment, similar to heterosexual couples (Goldberg & Perry-Jenkins, 2007). Less is known about gay men, but they seem to not show a domestic hierarchy that values paid work over homemaking. Instead, paid work may be seen as a compromise that takes the working partner away from spending time with their children (Kurdek, 2007).

Stepparents

Even under ideal conditions, parenting is challenging. Stepparents face even more difficulties. Stepparents are often placed in the position of providing discipline without the warm attachment bond that characterizes most parent–child relationships. Stepmothers tend to face particularly high levels of conflict, to be more disliked by their stepchildren, and to experience more stress, anxiety, and depression (Doodson, 2014; Gosselin, 2010; Shapiro & Stewart, 2011). Stepmothers may be expected to take on maternal roles and develop relationships quickly. However, stepparent–stepchild bonds take a great deal of time to develop, and stepmothers may feel guilty for not feeling maternal and for preferring life without stepchildren (Church, 2004; Felker, Fromme, Arnaut, & Stoll, 2002).

Stepparents who do not have children of their own may hold unrealistic expectations for family life that sharply contrast with the reality they encounter (Amato & Sobolewski, 2004; Doodson, 2014). Stepparents who have children of their own have an easier time, perhaps because they are more experienced in forming warm attachments with children and may engage children in fun activities; this is particularly the case for stepfathers, as they experience less pressure to take on parenting roles than do stepmothers (Ganong, Coleman, Fine, & Martin, 1999; Hennon, Hildenbrand, & Schedle, 2008).

Stepparenting poses challenges for new marriages. Remarried parents tend to report high levels of tension and conflict about parenting compared with first-married parents (Ganong & Coleman, 2000; Hetherington & Stanley-Hagan, 2002). How well adults adjust to the role of stepparent is influenced by the support of the biological parent as well as the children's perception of their relationship with the stepparent and willingness to accept the adult into the family (Jensen & Howard, 2015). Positive child communication and a high-quality marriage, as well as social support, predict positive coping on the part of stepmothers (Whiting, Smith, Barnett, & Grafsky, 2007). Stepmothers who perceive a lack of control over parenting practices during visitations are more likely to feel powerlessness, anger, and resentment, which may be manifested in depression (Gosselin, 2010; Henry & McCue, 2009). After a challenging transition, many couples adjust to their roles as spouses and parents, and interactions with stepchildren improve (Jensen & Howard, 2015). The difficulties that stepparenting entails are one reason that the divorce rate is higher in couples with stepchildren (Teachman, 2008).

Childlessness

Although most adults have children, some remain childless. In 2014, 15% of all U.S. women ages 40 to 44 had not given birth to any children (Livingston, 2015). It is difficult for researchers to determine the rate of childlessness in men. Frequently, childlessness is involuntary, the result of infertility or of postponing parenthood (te Velde, Habbema, Leridon, & Eijkemans, 2012). About 15% of women ages 30 to 44 experience *impaired fecundity,* the inability to become pregnant or carry a fetus to term (U.S. Department of Health and Human Services, 2013). As shown in Figure 14.9, women who have

never given birth experience impaired fecundity rates up to three times higher than women who have given birth at least once.

Some adults are childless by choice—or *childfree,* the term preferred by some. Common reasons for voluntary childlessness include the desire for flexibility and freedom from child-care responsibilities, pursuit of career aspirations, economic security, environmental reasons (e.g., not wanting to contribute to global overpopulation), and desires to preserve marital satisfaction. It is unclear how many women are childless by choice. One study of Italian women found that one third of those who were childless were so by choice (Koropeckyj-Cox & Pendell, 2007). Others were childless as a result of decisions to delay childbearing or the result of adverse external circumstances such as relationship dissolution.

Consistent predictors of childlessness include education and career status. High levels of education and income predict childlessness in women from Australia, the Netherlands, Finland, Germany, the United Kingdom, and the United States (Frejka, 2017; Waren & Pals, 2013). Women and men who are voluntarily childless tend to be less religious and more assertive, independent, and self-reliant than their peers, attributes that likely influence their adjustment throughout life (Avison & Furnham, 2015). Overall, adults who are childless by choice tend to be just as content with their lives as those who are parents. Positive attitudes toward

FIGURE 14.9

Impaired Fecundity Among Females Aged 15–44 Years, by Age and Parity, 2006–2010

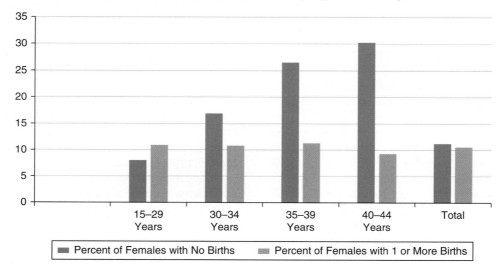

Source: Chandra, Copen, & Stephen, 2013.

childlessness are more common among adults who are college educated, childless, and female, while negative attitudes toward childlessness are more common among adults who are male, are less educated, and have conservative religious beliefs (Koropeckyj-Cox & Pendell, 2007; Koropeckyj-Cox, Romano, & Moras, 2007).

Childlessness appears to interfere with psychosocial development and personal adjustment only when it is involuntary and a result of circumstances beyond an individual's control (Roy, Schumm, & Britt, 2014). In both men and women, involuntary childlessness is associated with life dissatisfaction varying from ambivalence to deep disappointment, especially when it is accompanied by self-blame, rumination, and catastrophizing (Hadley & Hanley, 2011; Nichols & Pace-Nichols, 2000; B. D. Peterson, Gold, & Feingold, 2007). The social context also matters, as the extent to which

childlessness is associated with lower psychological well-being appears to be associated with the degree to which a country and culture's norms are tolerant toward childlessness (Huijts, Kraaykamp, & Subramanian, 2011).

THINKING IN CONTEXT 14.4

1. What personality, developmental, and life experience factors influence whether an adult will become a parent? How might contextual factors play a role in determining whether one becomes a parent and the timing of parenthood?

2. What special challenges do stepparents, single parents, and lesbian and gay parents face? In what ways are the challenges these parents face similar? Different?

APPLY YOUR KNOWLEDGE

In college, Kayla and Meghan were inseparable, sharing friends, majors, and even a dorm room. After college, they obtained entry-level jobs at the same firm and shared an apartment. Feeling that they were more like family than friends, Meghan would often refer to Kayla as her sister, the one who helps her get through her "20s crisis." With each promotion, Kayla and Meghan climbed up the career ladder until one day Meghan came home excitedly talking about her latest promotion, one that would require that she move across the country. Kayla and Meghan vowed to remain best friends forever.

After Meghan moved, their lives began to take different paths. Meghan's extensive business travel took her to faraway places, and her work hours grew longer. Kayla continued on her career path but began to focus more of her energy on her personal life after meeting and falling in love with Joel. Kayla and Joel married within a year, with Meghan as maid of honor. Two years later, Kayla gave birth to a son, naming Meghan as his godmother. Kayla loved her career but hated feeling torn in two directions, between home and career—for example, having to go to work when the baby was sick. After giving birth to her second child, Kayla felt even more out of control and decided to put her career on hold and focus on raising her children.

Unlike Kayla, Meghan never married. She came close, living with someone for over a year, but as time went on, the passion drained from the relationship, leaving two very close friends. Meghan relished her career and

rarely wondered about what could have been. On her 38th birthday, however, Meghan evaluated her life. After visiting Kayla and playing with her godchild, she realized that she wanted a family. Meghan concluded that she may never meet the "right" man and may never marry, but she wanted a family nonetheless. Meghan called her doctor to discuss options for conceiving as a single parent.

1. Meghan and Kayla's lives have taken different paths. Describe the differences. What developmental and contextual factors contribute to them?

2. Is there such a thing as a 20s crisis? If so, what form does it take, and how do contextual factors influence it?

3. How do friendships change over the course of young adulthood?

4. Compare Kayla's and Meghan's experiences with what we know about marriage and cohabitation. What challenges do young adults face with regard to balancing the demands of work and family? How do Kayla and Megan illustrate these themes?

5. Discuss Meghan's decision to pursue parenthood. What challenges might she experience in the coming years? How might she address them?

6. How do you think Kayla and Meghan will fare in the coming years?

$SAGE edge™

Visit **edge.sagepub.com/kuther2e** to help you accomplish your coursework goals in an easy-to-use learning environment.

LEARNING OBJECTIVES	SUMMARY	KEY TERMS	IN REVIEW
14.1 Summarize psychosocial development in early adulthood.	Advances in education have delayed the traditional markers of adulthood. Emerging adulthood is an extended transitional period between adolescence and early adulthood characterized by diversity in lifestyles, identity development, and the subjective sense of being in between. Although emerging adulthood is observed in industrialized cultures around the world, it is not universal as it is influenced by socioeconomic status and contextual changes that have prolonged the transition into adulthood. Erikson proposed that the psychosocial task of early adulthood is establishing an intimate relationship that is mutual and satisfying. Neugarten posed that throughout life, we experience a number of normative events that represent a social clock of age-related expectations for major life events. Every society has a timetable for such events, and the degree that individuals match their culture's social clock influences their adjustment.	Intimacy versus isolation Social clock	According to Erikson, what is the major psychosocial task of early adulthood? What is the social clock, and what role does it play in self-esteem and psychological functioning?
14.2 Discuss influences on friendship and mate selection and interactions in early adulthood.	Like friendships in childhood and adolescence, adult friendships are based on similarity and show gender differences. Men and women from many cultures seek different characteristics in mates. Despite this, most intimate partners share similarities in demographics, attitudes, and values. Violence between intimate partners is not limited by culture, ethnicity, socioeconomic status, sexual orientation, or marital status. A variety of factors contribute to intimate violence, including contextual factors such as poverty, unemployment, drug and alcohol abuse, and cultural norms. Many communities provide services to aid victims as well as perpetrators of intimate violence.	Intimate partner violence	Describe the nature of friendships in emerging and early adulthood. What characteristics do men and women typically look for in mates? What are the components of love, and how do they shift over time? What are influences on intimate partner violence?
14.3 Analyze the diverse romantic situations that may characterize early adulthood, including singlehood, cohabitation, marriage, and divorce.	Most North Americans spend a large part of their adult lives single, and some remain single throughout life. Cohabitation has become increasingly common in the United States and is very common in most European nations. Cohabiting couples in the United States are often less stable than married couples. Most North Americans marry. Marital success is predicted by maturity and similarity in demographic factors. Successful marriages are based on realistic expectations, flexibility, communication, and joint conflict resolution. Risk factors for divorce include being at an economic disadvantage, experiencing multiple life stressors and role overload, and having poor communication and conflict resolution skills. The process of divorce entails a series of stressful experiences. Recently divorced adults are prone to depression, anxiety, and a variety of risky behaviors.	Cohabitation Singlehood	Describe characteristics of adults who remain single or cohabitate. Describe benefits of marriage and challenges associated with the transition to marriage. What factors predict marital success? What are short-term and long-term consequences of divorce?

| 14.4 Compare the experiences of young adults as stepparents, never-married parents, and same-sex parents. | New parents are greeted with a host of new responsibilities and changes. The transition to parenthood is associated with declines in marital satisfaction. In dual-earner couples, the greater the degree of shared parenting responsibilities, the greater the couple's happiness. Most parents report that parenthood has encouraged them to become more empathetic, tolerant, and responsible. Stepparents are often placed in the position of providing discipline without the warm attachment bond that characterizes most parent–child relationships. Remarried parents tend to report high levels of tension and conflict about parenting as compared with first-married parents. After a challenging transition, many couples adjust to their roles as spouses and parents, and interactions with stepchildren improve, but the divorce rate is high for remarried couples with children. The typical never-married parent in the United States is of middle or low socioeconomic status and is most commonly an African American young woman. The primary challenge never-married mothers face is economic. Same-sex parents do not differ from heterosexual parents in competence or commitment to their roles as parents. Children reared by same-sex parents do not differ from those reared by heterosexual parents in mental health, peer relationships, gender identity, and sexual orientation. | | Describe the transition to parenthood.

 What are some challenges faced by stepparents and never-married parents?

 Discuss the parenting experiences of same-sex parents.

 What are characteristics of childless adults? |

PART VII

Middle Adulthood

CHAPTER 15:
Physical and Cognitive Development in Middle Adulthood

CHAPTER 16:
Socioemotional Development in Middle Adulthood

Middle adulthood reflects a changing balance of gains and losses. In addition to sensory changes, many middle-aged adults experience declines in strength and endurance; physical activity, behavior, and experiences influence the rate and extent of change. Women's adjustment to menopause, the end of the reproductive years, is influenced by personal characteristics, circumstances, and internalized societal views about women and aging. Cognitively, middle-aged adults show declines in attention, working memory, and processing speed, but an expanding knowledge base and growing expertise permit them to compensate, showing few changes in functioning within everyday contexts.

The home context takes center stage in middle adulthood. Marital satisfaction increases as childrearing tasks decline and couples have more time to spend with each other. Most parents adjust well to the resulting empty nest as relationships with adult children tend to become closer. The grandparent role often satisfies adults' emerging generative needs. Most middle-aged adults retain the role of adult child and provide increasing assistance to their aging parents. Adults spend much of their days within the work context and job satisfaction increases in middle adulthood, especially with career advancement. Although adults spend less time with friends than with family, friendships improve with age and continue to be important sources of social support. In short, middle-aged adults show positive physical, cognitive, and socioemotional adjustment, as well as a tendency to mellow out, as they interact in the multiple contexts in which they are embedded.

DR. KUTHER'S **CHALK TALKS**

Watch at
edge.sagepub.com/kuther2e

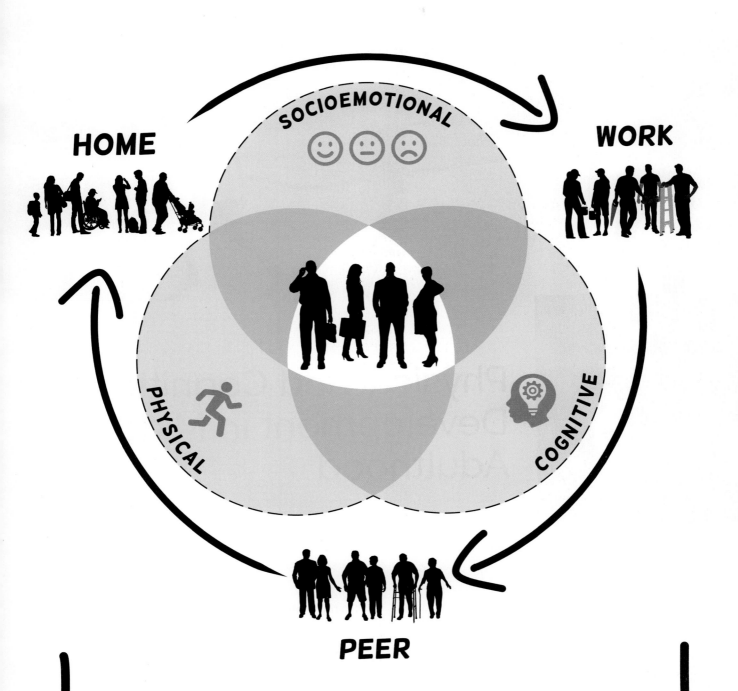

HOME

WORK

SOCIOEMOTIONAL

PHYSICAL

COGNITIVE

PEER

Thomas Barwick/Taxi via Getty Ir

15

Physical and Cognitive Development in Middle Adulthood

As the basketball swooshed through the hoop, Alfonzo called out to his son, Alito, "Yeah! Your dad's still got it!" Alito raced toward his father, beating him for the rebound, "But I'm still faster." "You may be faster, but I'm experienced—and experience makes all the difference," Alfonzo challenged his son.

Who is right, father or son? In many ways, both are. In this chapter, we examine the physical and cognitive changes in middle adulthood. Our discussion will largely mirror this conversation: Middle-aged adults experience mild physical and cognitive declines, but experience and wisdom often permit them to compensate for any decline in capacity.

Learning Objectives

15.1 Summarize age-related physical changes during middle adulthood.

15.2 Discuss common health conditions and illnesses and the roles of stress and hardiness on health during middle adulthood.

15.3 Contrast the findings of cross-sectional and longitudinal studies of crystallized and fluid intelligence over adulthood.

15.4 Analyze changes in cognitive capacities during middle adulthood, including attention, memory, processing speed, and expertise.

Digital Resources

Listen: Menopause in Killer Whales

▶ **Lives in Context Video 15.1:** Career, Health, and Well-Being in Middle Adulthood

Explore: Depression and Anxiety in Diabetes and Arthritis

▶ **Lives in Context Video 15.2:** Resilience and Hardiness in Adulthood

Watch: College in Midlife: Worth the Risk?

▶ **Lives in Context Video 15.3:** Returning to School in Midlife

Connect: The Mind at Midlife

PHYSICAL DEVELOPMENT IN MIDDLE ADULTHOOD

» LO 15.1 Summarize age-related physical changes during middle adulthood.

We define middle adulthood as the years from ages 40 to 65. Unlike the changes that occur in early adolescence, the physical changes that occur in middle adulthood are more gradual. Like Alfonzo, adults often compensate for changes by modifying their behavior. Nevertheless, even active and vibrant middle-aged adults notice some changes in their body shape, strength, speed, and appearance. Most middle-aged adults begin to sense their own mortality, often in response to acute or chronic health conditions and especially after experiencing life-threatening health concerns. Many middle-aged adults begin to think of their lives in terms of years left of life rather than years lived (Neugarten, 1968). Aging itself cannot be controlled, and physical declines are inevitable. However, many middle-aged adults compensate for declines and maximize their physical capacities in order to maintain an active lifestyle.

Theories of Aging: What Causes Aging?

Why do we age? One of the earliest explanations of aging, **wear-and-tear theory,** viewed the body as wearing out from use (Bengston, Gans, Pulney, & Silverstein, 2009). On the contrary, research suggests that we must "use it or lose it." That is, regular exercise is associated with longevity in all people regardless of ethnicity or socioeconomic status (SES) (Muscari et al., 2017; Sanchis-Gomar, Olaso-Gonzalez, Corella, Gomez-Cabrera, & Vina, 2011). Activity is a critical component of a long and healthy life.

Aging is complex and influenced by many factors. Some of aging is likely influenced by genetics. Parents' lifespans predict those of their children, and identical twins share more similar lifespans than do fraternal twins, suggesting a role for heredity in aging (Fedarko, 2018; Montesanto et al., 2011). Yet kin relations for markers of biological age, such as strength, respiratory capacity, blood pressure, and bone density, are relatively small as health is influenced not just by genetics but by context and lifestyle. Lifespans among family members often vary with context and behaviors. Thus, aging reflects the interaction of epigenetic factors, the dynamic interplay between heredity and environment (Mitteldorf, 2016; Moskalev, Aliper, Smit-McBride, Buzdin, & Zhavoronkov, 2014). It may be that it is not lifespan that we inherit but a set of genetic factors that may predict lifespan (Walter et al., 2011).

Ultimately, it is the contextual factors, such as the availability of health care, and lifestyle factors, such as health-related behaviors, that matter in predicting lifespan. Whether genetic predispositions for longevity are realized depends on environmental factors such as diet and exercise, behaviors such as alcohol use or smoking, and exposure to environmental toxins (Govindaraju, Atzmon, & Barzilai, 2015; Tourlouki et al., 2010).

Experiments with animals support the role of caloric restriction in longevity (Speakman & Mitchell, 2011). Animal studies suggest that a nutritious diet that is extremely low in calories, with about 40% fewer than recommended, is associated with a longer lifespan. However, the near-starvation diet is uncomfortable and would be difficult for an adult to sustain (Anton & Leeuwenburgh, 2013; C. Lee & Longo, 2016).

Other research supports the immune system's role in aging by influencing the body's adjustment to external stressors and pathogens encountered throughout life. From this perspective, an aging immune system is less able to differentiate healthy cells from pathology, may direct the body's defenses against healthy cells, and may ignore harmful cells (Montecino-Rodriguez, Berent-Maoz, & Dorshkind, 2013; Salvioli et al., 2013).

Another account of aging relies on cellular mutation, damage to DNA and chromosomes. Research with animals shows that cell mutations increase exponentially with age (Baines, Turnbull, & Greaves, 2014; Milholland, Suh, & Vijg, 2017). Cellular mutations are associated with an increase in age-related diseases and cancers. Some of this damage may be due to **free radicals,** highly reactive and corrosive molecules that form when oxygen corrodes cells and strip off an electron. Free radicals destroy cellular materials in an attempt to replace the missing electrons. Free radicals may increase the likelihood of many age-related diseases such as cancer, cardiovascular disorders, and arthritis (Lagouge & Larsson, 2013; Valko, Jomova, Rhodes, Kuča, & Musílek, 2016) and predict mortality (Schöttker et al., 2015). Environmental factors may work to defend the body from free radicals by producing material that neutralizes free radicals and reduces the harm caused by them. For example, a diet rich in antioxidants, including vitamins C and E and beta-carotene, may protect against damage from free radicals (Harman, 2006). Aging is complex, however, and free radicals may account for only a proportion of change (Ziegler, Wiley, & Velarde, 2015). Recent research suggests that some species tolerate moderately high levels of free radicals, likely because the added stress encourages cells to repair themselves, and other species show longevity despite reduced capacities (Van Houten, Santa-Gonzalez, & Camargo, 2018).

Reductions in the capacity for cell division, specifically the limited capacity for human cells to divide, are the basis for another explanation for aging. Human cells have the capacity to divide about 50 times in their lifespan (Hayflick, 1996). Each time the cell divides, telomeres, tiny caps of DNA located at both ends of the chromosomes, become shorter. Shorter telomeres may protect the cell from common mutations that occur with repeated divisions, but they also reduce the cell's capacity to reproduce itself (Xi, Li, Ren, Zhang, & Zhang, 2013). Telomeres that shorten past a critical length cause the cell to stop dividing altogether, leading to increases in disease, cell death, and body aging (Campisi, 2013; Opresko & Shay, 2017). For example, telomere length is associated with dozens of cancers (Barthel et al., 2017). In this sense, telomere length may serve as a biomarker of aging (Mather, Jorm, Parslow, & Christensen, 2011; Xu, Duc, Holcman, & Teixeira, 2013). Telomere length is thought to be influenced by epigenetic mechanisms—contextual factors that influence how genetic propensities are displayed (Adwan-Shekhidem & Atzmon, 2018). Stress contributes to the shortening of telomeres, as well as oxidative stress, which results from free radicals (Cannon, Einstein, & Tulp, 2017). For people of all ages, regular physical activity contributes to longer telomeres, suggesting that behavioral factors can attenuate telomere shortening and thereby aspects of aging (Arsenis, You, Ogawa, Tinsley, & Zuo, 2017; Blackburn et al., 2015).

Sensory Aging

Suddenly aware that he holds the newspaper at arm's length and still squints to read, 45-year-old Dominic wondered to himself, "When did this happen? I can't see like I used to." Like much of physical development, the changes that take place in our senses represent continuous change. Over the adult years, vision and hearing capacities gradually decline. Like Dominic, most adults notice changes in vision during their 40s and changes in hearing at around age 50. The use of corrective lenses aids vision problems, and hearing aids amplify sounds, permitting better hearing.

Vision

Dominic's need to hold the newspaper at a distance in order to read is not unusual and is related to changes in the eye that occur throughout the adult years. The cornea flattens, the lens loses flexibility, and the muscle that permits the lens to change shape, or accommodate, weakens. The result is that most adults in their 40s develop **presbyopia,** also known as farsightedness—the inability to focus the lens on close objects, such as in reading small print. By age 50, virtually all adults are presbyopic and require reading glasses or other corrective options

(Gil-Cazorla, Shah, & Naroo, 2016; Truscott, 2009). Most also require corrective lenses for distance. Bifocals that combine lenses for nearsightedness and farsightedness are helpful.

In addition to changes in the accommodative ability of the lens, the ability to see in dim light declines because, with age, the lens yellows, the size of the pupil shrinks, and over middle age, most adults have lost about one half of the rods (light receptor cells) in the retina, which reduces the ability to see in dim light and makes adults' night vision decline twice as fast as their day vision (Sörensen, White, & Ramchandran, 2016). As rods are lost, so too are cones (color-receptive cells) because rods secrete substances that permit cones to survive (Barbur & Rodriguez-Carmona, 2015). Color discrimination, thus, becomes limited with gradual declines beginning in the 30s (Paramei & Oakley, 2014). Night vision is further reduced because the vitreous (transparent gel that fills the eyeball) becomes more opaque with age, scattering light that enters the eye (creating glare) and permitting less light to reach the retina (Garcia et al., 2018). In middle adulthood, about one third more light is needed to compensate for these changes that reduce vision (Owsley, McGwin, Jackson, Kallies, & Clark, 2007). All of these changes in vision make driving at night more challenging as headlights from other cars become blinding (Gruber, Mosimann, Müri, & Nef, 2013).

Hearing

In addition to vision, Dominic also noticed that he has difficulty hearing, at least in some situations. When he plays with his 4-year-old nephew, Dominic finds that he has to lean in close to hear the boy's speech. Sometimes he finds himself watching his teenage daughter's lips while she speaks, especially when they are having dinner in a crowded restaurant. Age-related hearing loss, **presbycusis** ("old hearing"), becomes apparent in the 50s and is caused by natural

·A common sign of presbyopia is needing to hold reading materials at a distance.
BSIP/Science Source

cell death that results in the deterioration of the ear structures that convert sound into neural impulses (Quaranta et al., 2015). The loss is first limited to high-pitched sounds, which enable us to distinguish between consonants such as f versus s and p versus t; as a result, the person often can hear most of a message but may misinterpret parts of it, such as names. Middle-aged adults tend to experience more difficulty hearing under conditions of background noise and perform more poorly under that condition than do young adults (Leigh-Paffenroth & Elangovan, 2011). Presbycusis hearing deficits tend to be more apparent in settings with background noise, such as a dinner party (Helfer, Merchant, & Wasiuk, 2017). By late adulthood, hearing loss extends to all sound frequencies. Reduced sensitivity to speech sounds influences processing as older adults show less activation of the auditory cortex in response to speech as compared with younger adults (Wettstein & Wahl, 2016).

Presbycusis is age related and influenced by genetics, but contextual factors play a large role in age-related hearing loss (Wettstein & Wahl, 2016). Generally, men's hearing declines more rapidly than women's, perhaps up to twice as quickly (see Figure 15.1) (Quaranta et al., 2015). Men's rapid hearing decline can be traced to exposure to intense noise (e.g., headphones and concerts), loud work environments (e.g., construction, military, and transportation work), and, in later adulthood, illnesses such as cerebrovascular disease (a disease of the blood vessels that supply the brain, often caused by atherosclerosis), which can lead to a stroke that damages the auditory cortex (Ecob et al., 2008; Helzner et al., 2005). Hearing loss can be lessened and prevented by wearing protective equipment, such as earplugs, and by lowering the volume on MP3 players. Screening to identify risk for hearing loss and early signs of hearing loss can help in delaying loss (Chou, Dana, Bougatsos, Fleming, & Beil, 2011).

Skin, Muscular, and Skeletal Aging

Karen looked at the pictures of her daughter's wedding. "What a beautiful day. Ouch! Look at this picture of me in the sunlight. When did I get so many lines around my eyes?" Like Karen, many adults find that the age-related changes in the skin seemingly appear overnight. Age-related changes in the skin are gradual, predictable, and unavoidable. While most adults in their 30s notice lines developing on their foreheads, by their 40s, these lines are accompanied by crow's feet around the eyes and lines around the mouth—markers of four decades of smiles, frowns, laughter, and other emotions. During middle adulthood, the process continues: Skin becomes less taut as the **epidermis,** the outer protective layer of

FIGURE 15.1

Hearing Loss in Men and Women

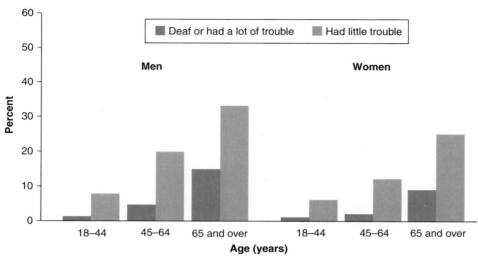

Source: Schoenborn & Heyman, 2008.

the skin that produces new skin cells, loosens its attachment to the thinning **dermis,** the middle layer of skin consisting of connective tissue that gives skin its flexibility (Quan & Fisher, 2015). The resulting loss in elasticity is accompanied by the loss of fat in the **hypodermis,** the innermost layer of skin composed of fat, which leads to wrinkling and loosening of the skin (Robert & Labat-Robert, 2016).

Women tend to experience age-related changes sooner and more quickly than do men. Their dermis is thinner, and as they age, they experience hormonal changes that exacerbate aging, particularly a reduction in the female hormone estrogen (Castelo-Branco & Davila, 2015; Firooz et al., 2017). While age-related changes in the skin are unavoidable, there is great variability in appearance. For people of all skin types and ethnicities, the rate of skin aging is influenced by exposure to the elements—sun, heat, cold, and pollution—and by behavioral factors such as smoking. Exposure to the sun's rays advances skin aging for people of all skin types and ethnicities, as does smoking (Gragnani et al., 2014; Kammeyer & Luiten, 2015; Tobin, 2017; Wiegand, Raschke, & Elsner, 2017).

As we have discussed, although most people reach their peak in muscle strength during their 20s, followed by a small gradual decline through the 30s, changes usually go unnoticed until the mid-to-late 40s. The rate of decline in muscle mass and strength tends to accelerate in the 40s (Keller & Engelhardt, 2013). By age 60, about 10% to 15% of muscle mass and strength are lost. Not all parts of the body age at the same rate (Mitchell et al., 2012). **Isometric**

strength, the subtle contractions used to hold a hand grip, push off against a wall, stretch, or practice yoga, are maintained throughout adulthood (Mitchell et al., 2012). There are also individual differences. Some people experience greater losses and others fewer, depending on their level of physical activity. Loss of endurance tends to occur after age 40, but the decline is generally proportionately less than that of strength (Hayslip, Panek, & Patrick, 2007).

Both men and women tend to experience weight gain in middle adulthood, with an increase in body fat and loss of muscle and bone. Body composition shifts over the course of adulthood as the metabolic rate slows. In men, fat accumulates on the back and upper abdomen, while women experience an increase in fat in the upper arms and around the waist. Over adulthood, muscle mass tends to be replaced by fat; however, good nutrition and an active lifestyle can reduce losses and even increase muscular density. When adults gradually reduce their caloric intake to match their reduced need for calories, age-related weight gain is minimized. For example, a 7-year-long study of about 30,000 women aged 50 to 79 showed that a low-fat diet with lots of vegetables, fruits, and grains predicted weight loss and maintenance, regardless of SES and ethnicity (Howard et al., 2006).

Normal aging brings some loss of bone tissue that begins around age 40. Bone loss increases in the 50s, especially in women, whose bones have less calcium to begin with and who lose the protective influence of estrogen on bones after menopause (Gold, 2016). This bone loss that occurs with reproductive aging increases the risk of

osteoporosis, a disorder entailing severe bone loss that leads to brittle and easily fractured bones (see Chapter 17). Bones become thinner, more porous, and more brittle as calcium is absorbed. As the bones that make up the vertebrae in the spinal column become thin and more brittle, the disks collapse and adults lose height, about an inch or more by age 60 and more thereafter (Hannan et al., 2012). Loss of bone density causes bones to break more easily and heal more slowly, making a broken bone more serious as we age. Losses in bone density can be slowed by behavior, such as avoiding smoking and excess drinking and engaging in weightbearing exercise

Physical activity can offset midlife losses in muscle.
AP/Kathy Kmonicek

(Bleicher et al., 2011). Table 15.1 summarizes some of the physical changes that take place during middle adulthood.

Reproductive Aging

In middle adulthood, the level of sex hormones in the body declines in both men and women. Women experience the end of fertility. Men retain their reproductive capacity but at a diminished level. Despite these changes, sexual activity and enjoyment often continue throughout life.

Reproductive Changes in Women

At about 51 years of age on average, but starting as early as age 42 and as late as 58, women experience **menopause,** the cessation of ovulation and menstruation (Do et al., 2013). The timing of menopause is influenced by heredity but also by lifestyle choices and contextual influences, such as exposure to pollution (Grindler et al., 2015; Hartge, 2009). Menopause occurs earlier in women who smoke, are malnourished, have not given birth, and are of lower SES (Gold et al., 2013; Tawfik et al., 2015). A woman is said to have reached menopause 1 year after her last menstrual period. **Perimenopause** refers to the transition to menopause, extending approximately 3 years before and after menopause. It is during perimenopause that the production of

---

TABLE 15.1

Physical Development During Middle Adulthood

PHYSICAL DEVELOPMENT	AGE-RELATED CHANGE
Vision	Presbyopia affects nearly all adults by age 50. Structural changes of the eye, including the cornea, lens, and retina, cause a decline in night vision.
Hearing	Presbycusis is common by the 50s with the loss first limited to high-pitched sounds and settings in which there is background noise. By late adulthood, it extends to all sound frequencies. Contextual factors, such as exposure to noise, play a role in age-related hearing loss.
Skin	Fine lines are apparent by the 30s, first on the forehead, and by the 40s as crow's feet around the eyes and lines around the mouth. Skin becomes less taut as the epidermis loosens its attachment to the dermis. The resulting loss in elasticity is accompanied by the loss of fat in the hypodermis, which leads to wrinkling and loosening of the skin. Exposure to sun rays is associated with advanced skin aging for people of all skin types and ethnicities.
Muscle	Peak muscle strength is typically reached during the 20s, followed by a gradual decline. Changes usually are not noticeable until about age 45. Loss of endurance tends to occur after age 40. Good nutrition and an active lifestyle can reduce losses and even increase muscular density.
Skeleton	Bone density peaks in the mid to late 30s, after which adults tend to experience gradual bone loss, advancing in the 50s, especially in postmenopausal women. Losses in bone density can be slowed by behaviors such as avoiding smoking and excess drinking and by engaging in weightbearing exercise.

reproductive hormones declines and symptoms associated with menopause first appear (McNamara, Batur, & DeSapri, 2015).

The first indicator of perimenopause is a shorter menstrual cycle, followed by erratic periods (Ketch, Weedin, & Gibson, 2017). Ovulation becomes less predictable, occurring early or late in the cycle; sometimes several ova are released and sometimes none (Nelson, 2008). This unpredictability in ovulation can sometimes lead to a "surprise" late-life pregnancy (Miller, Allen, Kaunitz, & Cwiak, 2018). Other women who waited to have children may find themselves frustrated by the unpredictability of their cycles, the accompanying difficulty getting pregnant, and the closing window of opportunity. The most common and long-lasting symptom of perimenopause is hot flashes, in which the expansion and contraction of blood vessels cause sudden sensations of heat throughout the body accompanied by sweating (McNamara et al., 2015; Sussman et al., 2015). One third to as many as three quarters of U.S. women experience hot flashes, which may persist for 7 or more years (Avis et al., 2015; Santoro, 2016). **Hormone replacement therapy** is designed to address perimenopause symptoms.

Similar to girls' reactions to menarche, how women experience menopause, whether they report severe mood changes and irritability or few psychological and physical consequences, varies with their attitudes and expectations for menopause, which are influenced by personal characteristics, circumstances, and societal views about women and aging (Delanoë et al., 2012; Nosek, Kennedy, & Gudmundsdottir, 2012).

Women who have children may view menopause as providing sexual freedom and enjoyment without worry of contraception or pregnancy. In contrast, women who desire a family, but who have not given birth, may view menopause as the end of fertility and the possibility of childrearing, making menopause a difficult time indeed (Howell & Beth, 2002). High levels of education and high SES are both associated with more positive views of menopause and fewer reports of menopausal symptoms (Lawlor, Ebrahim, & Smith, 2003). Ethnicity is also related to views about menopause. African American and Mexican American women tend to hold more favorable views toward menopause than White non-Hispanic American women, often describing it as a normal part of life, one that many women look forward to (Avis et al., 2001; Sampselle, Harris, Harlow, & Sowers, 2002).

Contextual factors influence how women make sense of menopause (Delanoë et al., 2012; Strauss, 2011). When menopause is viewed as a medical event whose symptoms require treatment, women tend to view it more negatively and report more physical and emotional symptoms (Hvas & Dorte Effersøe, 2008). However, recent generations of women have objected to the notion of menopause as a disease and instead view it as a naturally occurring process. Adults of both sexes, as well as their families, tend to view menopause more positively when it is described as a life transition or symbol of aging, as compared with a medical event whose symptoms are problematic and require treatment (Dillaway, 2008; Hvas & Dorte Effersøe, 2008). In the United States, postmenopausal women tend to view menopause more positively than do younger women (Avis, Brockwell, & Colvin, 2005). They tend to report menopause as causing few difficulties and instead view it as a beginning. In one study of over 2,000 postmenopausal women, about two thirds reported feeling relieved over freedom from birth control (Rossi, 2004). This pattern may also be true cross-culturally. A study of about 1,400 women aged 40 to 55 years from West Bengal, India, revealed that postmenopausal women had more positive attitudes about menopause and aging than did perimenopausal women (Dasgupta & Ray, 2017). Cultural factors also influence how menopause is experienced, as discussed in the Cultural Influences on Development feature.

Reproductive Changes in Men

Do men experience a sudden drop in reproductive ability similar to women? No. Unlike women, men's reproductive ability declines gradually and steadily over the adult years, with declines in testosterone beginning as early as age 30 in some men and continuing at a pace of about a 1% decrease per year to a total decline in testosterone of about 30% by age 70 (Federman & Walford, 2007). Men's bodies produce less testosterone and they become less fertile, but about 75% of men retain testosterone levels in the normal range, with most adult males continuing to produce sperm throughout adulthood; many are able to father children into their 80s and beyond (Ehlert & Fischbacher, 2013). However, the number and quality of sperm produced decline in middle adulthood, beginning at about age 40, and offspring of older men may be at greater risk of congenital abnormalities (Almeida, Rato, Sousa, Alves, & Oliveira, 2017; Johnson, Dunleavy, Gemmell, & Nakagawa, 2015; S. D. Khan, 2017).

Although men experience gradual declines in testosterone over their lifetimes, levels can shift dramatically in response to stress and illness, creating the appearance of a "male menopause" (Shores, 2014). Stress from problems such as unemployment, illness, marital problems, children leaving home, or sexual inactivity can cause reductions in testosterone, which decrease sexual desire and responses. Low levels of testosterone may interfere with a man's ability to

Cultural Perspectives on Menopause

Cultural depictions of menopause influence women's experience of menopause.
Ashley Cooper pics / Alamy Stock Photo

Societal and cultural views influence how menopause is perceived. In societies that value youth, women may fear the bodily changes of menopause and their perceived loss of sex appeal (Howell & Beth, 2002). On the other hand, in cultures where older women are respected and achieve social or religious power with age (e.g., powerful mother-in-law and grandmother roles), women report few complaints about menopausal symptoms (Delanoë et al., 2012).

In Japan, where women gain power and responsibility with age (such as monitoring household finances and caring for dependent parents), women rarely report hot flashes or other menopausal symptoms (Huang, Xu, Nasri, & Jaisamrarn, 2010; Lock & Kaufert, 2001). Middle adulthood is seen as a mature and productive time of life; menopause is not viewed as a marker of decline by Japanese women or their physicians. Research has shown that women in Asian cultures, as well as nonindustrialized cultures, consistently report fewer and less severe menopausal symptoms (Gupta, Sturdee, & Hunter, 2006; Huang et al., 2010). For example, one study of Chinese women found that only one third reported experiencing hot flashes and fewer than one third experienced night sweats (Lu, Liu, & Eden, 2007).

Similarly, Mayan women of the Yucatán achieve increased status with menopause along with freedom from childrearing (Beyene & Martin, 2001). Mayan women marry as teenagers and by their late 30s typically have given birth to many children. Many Mayan women are eager to escape the burden of childrearing and describe menopause in positive terms such as providing freedom, being happy, and feeling like a young girl again. Few report menopausal symptoms such as hot flashes (Beyene & Martin, 2001). In fact, there is no word in the Mayan language to describe hot flashes (Beyene, 1986). Women in rural India also report menopause as a welcomed time that is accompanied by enhanced mobility, freedom from unwanted pregnancy, and increased authority (Gupta et al., 2006).

Women in Western industrialized societies tend to have mixed feelings about menopause. For example, one sample of U.K. women viewed menopause in a variety of ways, as a normal biological process, a distressful transition involving identity loss, and as a liberating transformation involving biological and social change (de Salis, Owen-Smith, Donovan, & Lawlor, 2017). Other women describe the negatives, including a loss of fertility and the physical changes that accompany it, feeling less feminine, and having a clear sign of aging (Chrisler, 2008). However, they also describe it in positive terms, such as the end of dealing with menstrual periods, the end of contraceptive worries, and a sense of liberation. Postmenopausal women tend to have more positive views of menopause than do younger women and are more likely to report feeling a sense of freedom and confidence (Chrisler, 2008).

What Do You Think?

1. From your perspective, how do adults in the United States view menopause? For example, how does television depict menopause or menopausal women? Identify examples in popular media to support your perspective.

2. How might individuals' perception of developments such as menopause influence what they experience (and the reverse)? ●

achieve or maintain an erection, which can influence anxiety about his sexual capacity, which can lead to further declines in testosterone (Seidman & Weiser, 2013). In this way, it might appear as if some men go through a form of menopause, but the sudden declines in testosterone tend to be a correlate of stress and health problems rather than a biological inevitability (Donatelle, 2004). Regardless, media and popular views in the United States and Europe have contributed to the notion of a male menopause and a corresponding medicalization of masculinity in middle and older adulthood through the use of hormone and other treatments (Marshall, 2007; Vainionpää & Topo, 2006). For example, products designed to treat so-called "low T" are commonly advertised on television despite research suggesting that only about

6% to 10% of men experience testosterone deficiency (Araujo et al., 2004; Haring et al., 2010). Similar to the medicalization of menopause, viewing normative hormonal changes experienced by men as a disease contributes to negative views of normal aging.

THINKING IN CONTEXT 15.1

1. Contextual factors, such as socioeconomic status, influence all aspects of physical aging, including the rate and form that aging takes. How might contextual factors influence the sensory changes that occur over the middle adult years? Reproductive changes?

2. The physical changes that accompany middle adulthood can influence how adults view themselves as well as how others view and treat them. What are some of the possible implications of physical aging for adults' sense of self?

3. Compare menopause with menarche. How is the process of menopause similar and different from menarche? What is the role of context in shaping women's experience and perspective on each?

HEALTH IN MIDDLE ADULTHOOD

» **LO 15.2   Discuss common health conditions and illnesses and the roles of stress and hardiness on health during middle adulthood.**

Although the middle adult years are generally characterized by good health, they are a time when many people begin to notice some declines in health and physical abilities. Most adults view themselves as healthy (Centers for Disease Control and Prevention, 2016; Federal Interagency Forum on Aging-Related Statistics, 2016); however, self-reports of health vary by contextual condition. For example, in nearly all countries of the world, self-reports of health and death rates vary by socioeconomic status. In the United States and Europe, high socioeconomic status predicts good health (E. Chen & Miller, 2013; Hu et al., 2016; Mielck et al., 2014). However, socioeconomic status is unrelated to health in developing, low-socioeconomic countries, likely related to an overall lack of resources that affects both high and low-socioeconomic status individuals (Afshar, Roderick, Kowal, Dimitrov, & Hill, 2017). Education is also positively associated with perceived health (Centers for Disease Control and Prevention, 2016).

Common Illnesses

The following sections discuss leading health concerns of middle-aged adults, including cancer, cardiovascular disease, and diabetes. Note that, until recently, nearly all studies of health in adulthood were conducted on men, particularly Caucasian men. Women and people of color are underrepresented in research on prevention and treatment of illness. Researchers have only recently begun to address this deficit in our understanding of illness. The following sections describe what we know about common illnesses in adulthood, discussing sex and ethnic differences when possible.

Cancer

Cancer-related mortality overall has declined 26% since 1991, yet cancer remains the leading cause of death in those ages 45 to 64 (Centers for Disease Control and Prevention, 2018a). It is estimated that nearly 15% of adults will develop cancer between the ages of 50 and 69 (Siegel et al., 2018). Skin cancer is the most common form of cancer. Following skin cancer, across all ages, women are most likely to be diagnosed with breast cancer and men with prostate cancer, as shown in Figure 15.2. Overall, men tend to be diagnosed with cancer at a higher rate than women. Sex differences in cancer that emerge in midlife are influenced by genetics and contextual factors such as workplace exposure to toxins, health-related behaviors such as smoking, and making fewer visits to the doctor.

People of low SES tend to experience cancer at higher rates than do other adults, a difference attributable to a range of causes, including inadequate access to medical care, poor diet, high levels of stress, and occupations that may place them in contact with toxins (Jemal et al., 2008; Kish, Yu, Percy-Laurry, & Altekruse, 2014; Vona-Davis & Rose, 2009). There are large ethnic differences in cancer; the largest difference in incidence and mortality is between middle-age Black men and Asian American men, with the incidence rate of Black men 85% higher than that of Asian American men and 10% higher than that of non-Hispanic White men (Siegel et al., 2018).

What is cancer? Cancerous cells are abnormal cells. Everyone has some of these abnormal cells. Cancer occurs when the genetic program that controls cell growth is disrupted. When this happens, abnormal cells reproduce rapidly and spread to normal tissues and organs (Lin et al., 2007; Vogelstein & Kinzler, 2004). Cancer cells undergo uncontrolled growth for three reasons. Cell mutations may cause cancer genes—known as oncogenes—to undergo abnormal cell division. Other cell mutations may interfere with tumor suppressor genes that keep oncogenes from multiplying (Lin et al., 2007;

FIGURE 15.2

Ten Leading Cancer Types for the Estimated New Cancer Cases and Deaths by Sex, United States, 2018

Estimated New Cases

Male				Female		
Prostate	164,690	19%		Breast	266,120	30%
Lung & bronchus	121,680	14%		Lung & bronchus	112,350	13%
Colon & rectum	75,610	9%		Colon & rectum	64,640	7%
Urinary bladder	62,380	7%		Uterine corpus	63,230	7%
Melanoma of the skin	55,150	6%		Thyroid	40,900	5%
Kidney & renal pelvis	42,680	5%		Melanoma of the skin	36,120	4%
Non-Hodgkin lymphoma	41,730	5%		Non-Hodgkin lymphoma	32,950	4%
Oral cavity & pharynx	37,160	4%		Pancreas	26,240	3%
Leukemia	35,030	4%		Leukemia	25,270	3%
Liver & intrahepatic bile duct	30,610	4%		Kidney & renal pelvis	22,660	3%
All sites	**856,370**	**100%**		**All sites**	**878,980**	**100%**

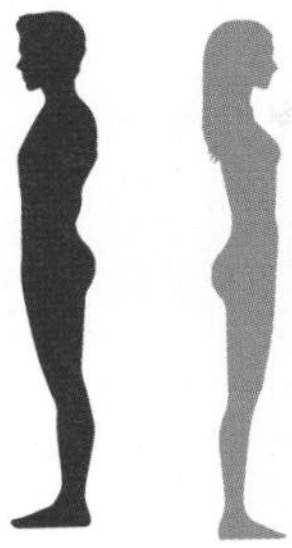

Estimated Deaths

Male				Female		
Lung & bronchus	83,550	26%		Lung & bronchus	70,500	25%
Prostate	29,430	9%		Breast	40,920	14%
Colon & rectum	27,390	8%		Colon & rectum	23,240	8%
Pancreas	23,020	7%		Pancreas	21,310	7%
Liver & intrahepatic bile duct	20,540	6%		Ovary	14,070	5%
Leukemia	14,270	4%		Uterine corpus	11,350	4%
Esophagus	12,850	4%		Leukemia	10,100	4%
Urinary bladder	12,520	4%		Liver & intrahepatic bile duct	9,660	3%
Non-Hodgkin lymphoma	11,510	4%		Non-Hodgkin lymphoma	8,400	3%
Kidney & renal pelvis	10,010	3%		Brain & other nervous system	7,340	3%
All sites	**323,630**	**100%**		**All sites**	**286,010**	**100%**

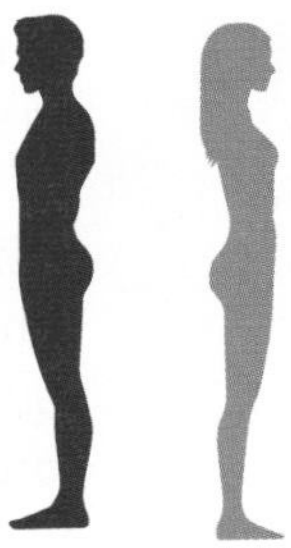

Source: Siegel, Miller, & Jemal, 2018.

Vogelstein & Kinzler, 2004). Finally, cell mutations may prevent cells from repairing the DNA errors that occur as a function of cell division, as well as those that occur from exposure to environmental toxins and free radicals.

Whether an individual develops cancer is affected by a complex web of genetic and environmental influences. U.S. states vary in cancer incidence and are influenced by differences in medical detection practice and the prevalence of risk factors, such as smoking, obesity, and other health behaviors, as well as the national distribution of poverty and access to medical resources (Nguyen, Han, Jemal, & Drope, 2016). For example, the large geographic variation in lung cancer occurrence reflects the historical and continuing differences in smoking prevalence between states (Jemal et al., 2008). Lung cancer incidence rates in Kentucky (where tobacco is grown as part of the local economy), where smoking prevalence continues to be highest, are about 3.5 times higher than those in Utah, where smoking prevalence is lowest (Siegel et al., 2018).

Scientific breakthroughs have increased our knowledge of genetic risk factors for cancer. For example, women now can be tested for mutations in the genes responsible for suppressing the proliferation of breast cancer cells. Genetics, however, is not destiny. Only about 35% to 50% of women who test positive for the genetic mutation actually develop breast cancer. Those who do show more genetic mutations tend to develop breast cancer especially early in life, often before age 30 (Stephens et al., 2012). Whether a genetic risk factor for breast cancer leads to developing breast cancer is influenced by the presence of environmental risk factors, such as heavy alcohol use, being overweight, the use of oral contraceptives, exposure to toxins, and low socioeconomic status (N. Khan, Afaq, & Mukhtar, 2010; Nickels et al., 2013).

Early onset breast cancers are largely inherited, are often invasive, and spread quickly. In contrast, late-onset breast cancers, diagnosed in older adulthood, tend to grow more slowly, are less biologically aggressive, and likely follow extended exposures to environmental stimuli, as well as disruptions in cell division that occur with aging (W. F. Anderson, Rosenberg, Prat, Perou, & Sherman, 2014; Benz, 2008). Although many people persist in the centuries-old belief that a diagnosis of cancer is a death sentence, today's medical advances permit more people to survive cancer, defined as surviving at least 5 years after remission, than ever before.

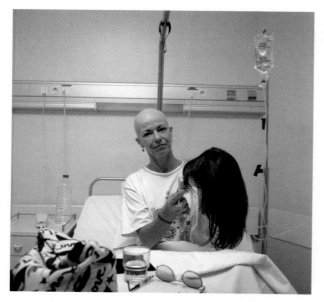

Cancer rates have declined over the last two decades and survival rates have risen to nearly three-quarters of diagnoses, but it remains a leading cause of mortality in middle age.
Manuel Litran/Paris Match/Getty

Cardiovascular Disease

About 40% of men and women ages 40 to 59 have heart disease (Benjamin et al., 2018). **Cardiovascular disease,** commonly referred to as *heart disease*, is responsible for over one quarter of all deaths of middle-aged Americans each year (National Center

for Health Statistics, 2015). It is the second largest killer of adults ages 45 to 64 and the leading cause of death for older adults over age 65 (Centers for Disease Control and Prevention, 2018a). Markers of cardiovascular disease include high blood pressure, high blood cholesterol, plaque buildup in the arteries (atherosclerosis), irregular heartbeat, and, particularly serious, heart attack (blockage of blood flow to the heart caused by a blood clot occurring within a plaque-clogged coronary artery; see Figure 15.3) (Elias & Dore, 2016; Koh, Han, Oh, Shin, & Quon, 2010). Cardiovascular disease can also cause a stroke, a blockage of blood flow to brain cells, which can result in neurological damage, paralysis, and death. A stroke occurs when a blood clot, often originating in the coronary arteries, travels to the brain or when a clot forms in the brain itself.

Awareness of the symptoms of heart attack is critical to surviving it. The most common symptom of heart attack is chest pain, uncomfortable pressure, squeezing, fullness, or pain in the chest that may come and go or last. Other symptoms include discomfort or pain in other areas of the upper body, especially the left arm, but also the back, neck, jaw, or stomach. Shortness of breath, nausea, or lightheadedness can also occur. Cardiovascular disease has been traditionally viewed as an illness affecting

---

FIGURE 15.3

Cardiovascular Disease

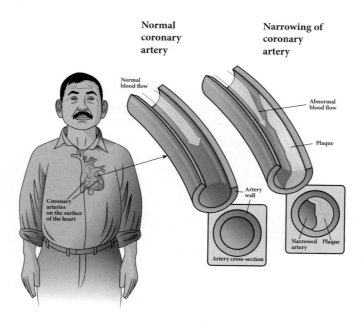

Source: National Heart, Lung, and Blood Institute. (2014).

men, as men are more likely to be diagnosed with cardiovascular disease.

Many people are unaware that women tend to show different symptoms of heart attack (Kirchberger, Heier, Kuch, Wende, & Meisinger, 2011). They are less likely to report chest pain than men. When they do, women are more likely to describe it as pressure or tightness than pain (Mehta & Yeo, 2017). Women are more likely than men to report pain in the left shoulder or arm, pain in the throat or jaw, pain in the upper abdomen, pain between the shoulder blades, nausea, dizziness, and vomiting (Kirchberger, Heier, Kuch, Wende, & Meisinger, 2011). Because of these differences, many women do not recognize their symptoms as severe and life threatening (Madsen & Birkelund, 2016). For these reasons, women are more likely than men to die of cardiovascular disease, especially heart attack (Murphy, Alderman, Voege Harvey, & Harris, 2017).

Risk factors for cardiovascular disease include heredity, age, a diet heavy in saturated and trans fatty acids, and smoking (Go et al., 2013). One important risk factor, hypertension, has increased rapidly in the past two decades to account for over one third of U.S. adults aged 45 to 59 (Nwankwo, Yoon, Burt, & Gu, 2013). Hypertension is a global problem responsible for about 13% of all deaths in the world each year (World Health Organization, 2015). Anxiety, psychological stress, and a poor diet have negative effects on the heart and contribute to hypertension and cardiovascular disease (Backé, Seidler, Latza, Rossnagel, & Schumann, 2012; Holt et al., 2013). As shown in Table 15.2, various behaviors can help to prevent heart disease; however, genetic factors also contribute to cardiovascular disease risk (Kalayinia, Goodarzynejad, Maleki, & Mahdieh, 2018).

Treatment for cardiovascular disease varies depending on the severity. Medication and behavioral changes, such as increasing physical activity, changing diet, and consuming more fish oil, may reduce hypertension and cholesterol levels (Elias & Dore, 2016). Until recently, hormone replacement therapy was prescribed to women to reduce heart disease, among other conditions. For more discussion, see the accompanying Applying Developmental Science feature.

In more severe cases, surgery may be recommended. Angioplasty is a process that involves threading a tube into the arteries and inflating a tiny balloon to flatten plaque deposits against the arterial walls and enabling blood to flow unobstructed. A stent is often placed to prevent the artery from narrowing again after the balloon is removed. In serious cases, a health care provider may recommend coronary bypass surgery, in which damaged coronary blood vessels are replaced with those from the leg.

TABLE 15.2

Preventing Heart Disease

GUIDELINE	DESCRIPTION
Don't smoke or use tobacco.	Smokers have more than twice the risk of heart disease. Chemicals in tobacco and cigarette smoke, including nicotine and carbon monoxide, make your heart work harder by narrowing your blood vessels and increasing blood pressure, leading to atherosclerosis and potentially a heart attack.
Reduce blood cholesterol levels.	Heart disease risk increases along with blood cholesterol levels. Cholesterol contributes to the formation of plaque inside the heart's arteries, leading to atherosclerosis.
Control high blood pressure.	Blood pressure is the force of blood pushing against the walls of the arteries as the heart pumps blood. High blood pressure increases the risk of heart attack and damage to the arteries and heart.
Exercise regularly.	Exercise lowers your risk of heart disease. Regular exercise will also help lower "bad" cholesterol and raise "good" cholesterol. Research has shown that getting at least 30 minutes of moderate physical activity on 5 or more days of the week can help lower blood pressure, lower cholesterol, and keep your weight at a healthy level.
Follow a heart-healthy diet.	Eat a diet low in fat, cholesterol, and salt and rich in fruits, vegetables, whole grains, and low-fat dairy products. Limit red meat, a source of unhealthy fat, and increase consumption of low-fat sources of protein such as beans and fish. Fish is a source of omega-3 fatty acids, a type of healthy fat, which may decrease your risk of heart attack, protect against irregular heartbeats, and lower blood pressure.
Achieve and maintain a healthy weight.	Excess weight strains your heart and is associated with heart disease factors such as diabetes, high blood pressure, and high cholesterol.
Manage stress and anger.	Stress can increase the risk factors for heart disease. For example, people under stress may overeat, start smoking, or smoke more than they otherwise would.

Hormone Replacement Therapy

Hormone replacement therapy is commonly prescribed to manage menopausal symptoms. However, the U.S. Food and Drug Administration recommends that physicians prescribe the smallest dose to reduce menopausal symptoms and for the shortest time.
iStock/MarsBars

From the 1950s until recently, it was common for women to be prescribed hormones to increase the levels of estrogen and/or progesterone in their bodies. Hormone replacement therapy (HRT) was prescribed to reduce severe perimenopause symptoms and manage common symptoms such as hot flashes. HRT was widely prescribed in the belief that it reduced heart disease and improved cognitive function. But in 2002, the Women's Health Initiative Study, a longitudinal study of thousands of perimenopausal women, yielded surprising results. Although HRT reduced the incidence of hot flashes and decreased the risk of osteoporosis, it did not protect the women in this study against heart disease. On the contrary, the results suggested that it may increase the risk of heart disease, stroke, and breast cancer (Nelson et al., 2002). These findings resulted in a dramatic worldwide decline in the use of hormone replacement therapy (Stevenson, Hodis, Pickar, & Lobo, 2009).

However, like most aspects of development, the relation of hormone replacement therapy and health outcomes is much more complex than suggested by the initial findings of the Women's Health Initiative,

which mostly studied women many years after the onset of menopause. More recent analyses indicate a timing effect whereby younger women (ages 50–59 or within 10 years of menopause) can benefit from HRT (Lobo, Pickar, Stevenson, Mack, & Hodis, 2016). In these women, HRT is associated with reduced risk for cardiovascular disease and does not increase the risk of breast cancer or stroke (Benkhadra et al., 2015; Kotsopoulos et al., 2016; Lobo, 2017). The cardiovascular risks associated with HRT increase with age starting only at age 60 (Stevenson et al., 2009). Moreover, research suggests that HRT can help some postmenopausal women with health conditions such as osteoporosis, Type 2 diabetes, atherosclerosis, and some cancers (Arnson et al., 2017; Gambacciani & Levancini, 2014; Panay, Hamoda, Arya, & Savvas, 2013). Although little research has examined ethnic differences in the effectiveness of HRT, some studies have suggested similar effects for White and Black women (Chlebowski et al., 2017; DeBono et al., 2018). Findings such as these suggest that HRT may be a reasonable option to help manage menopausal symptoms over the short term (Hickey, Elliott, & Davison, 2012). The U.S. Food and Drug Administration recommends that physicians prescribe the smallest dose needed to reduce menopausal symptoms and for the shortest time (Hannon, 2010). Ultimately, the decision as to who should use any form of hormone replacement therapy needs to be based on the individual woman's needs, quality of life, and potential risks versus benefits.

What Do You Think?

1. Why have researchers' conclusions regarding the safety of hormone replacement therapy varied so dramatically across studies and over recent decades?
2. What factors do you think are important for women to consider when it comes to hormone replacement therapy? What advice would you give a friend? ●

Diabetes

After each meal we eat, the body digests and breaks down food, releasing glucose into the blood. Insulin, a hormone released by the pancreas, maintains a steady concentration of glucose in the blood, and excess glucose is absorbed by muscle and fat. **Diabetes** is a disease marked by high levels of blood

glucose. Diabetes occurs when the body is unable to regulate the amount of glucose in the bloodstream because there either is not enough insulin produced (Type 1 diabetes) or the body shows insulin resistance and becomes less sensitive to it, failing to respond to it (Type 2 diabetes) (American Diabetes Association, 2014). Symptoms of diabetes include fatigue, great thirst, blurred vision, frequent infections, and slow healing. When glucose levels become too low, hypoglycemia occurs with symptoms of confusion, nervousness, and fainting. Hyperglycemia is characterized by overly high glucose levels, also resulting in serious illness. Managing diabetes entails careful monitoring of the diet and often self-injection of insulin, which permits the body to process glucose, critical to body functioning.

About 17% of adults ages 45 to 64 have diabetes, rising to over one quarter of adults ages 45 to 64 and 25% over the age of 65 (Centers for Disease Control and Prevention, 2018b). Diabetes is the fifth leading cause of death among people ages 55 to 64 and sixth leading cause of death among people ages 45 to 54 and 65 and older (Centers for Disease Control and Prevention, 2018a). Figure 15.4 presents age, sex, and ethnic differences in diabetes diagnoses. African American, Mexican American, and Canadian Aboriginal people are diagnosed with diabetes at higher rates than European Americans because of genetic, as well as contextual, factors, such as the higher rates of obesity, poor health, and a sedentary lifestyle that accompanies poverty (American Diabetes Association, 2014; Best, Hayward, & Hidajat, 2005; Jeffreys et al., 2006). Being overweight at any point during life is associated with an increased risk of diabetes (Djoussé, Driver, Gaziano, Buring, & Lee, 2013). Diabetes has a genetic component (Patel et al., 2016), but behaviors such as diet and exercise are important risk factors that interact with genetic propensities to influence diabetes risk (Jannasch, Kroger, & Schulze, 2017; Leong, Porneala, Dupuis,

Florez, & Meigs, 2016); hence, many researchers emphasize the role of epigenetics in diabetes (Franks & Pare, 2016; Keating, Plutzky, & El-Osta, 2016).

People with diabetes are at risk for a variety of health problems. A high level of glucose in the bloodstream raises the risk of heart attack, stroke, circulation problems in the legs, blindness, and reduced kidney functions (DeFronzo & Abdul-Ghani, 2011). Although women are about as likely as men to be diagnosed with diabetes, for largely unknown reasons, women with diabetes experience a much larger risk for heart attack and stroke than men (Peters, Huxley, & Woodward, 2014). Diabetes has serious cognitive effects, including declines in executive function, processing speed, memory, and motor function (Palta, Schneider, Biessels, Touradji, & Hill-Briggs, 2014). Over time, diabetes is associated with accelerated brain aging, including losses of gray matter, abnormalities in white matter, and a heightened risk of dementia and Alzheimer's disease in older adults (Espeland et al., 2013; Roberts et al., 2014; Vagelatos & Eslick, 2013).

Diabetes also influences psychosocial functioning. Depression is two to three times more common among people with diabetes compared to their peers, and they are more likely to experience chronic depression with up to 80% of those treated for depression experiencing a relapse of depressive symptoms within a 5-year period (M. Park, Katon, & Wolf, 2013; Roy & Lloyd, 2012). Adults with depression are less likely to follow dietary restrictions, comply

FIGURE 15.4

Diabetes Prevalence by Age, Sex, and Ethnicity

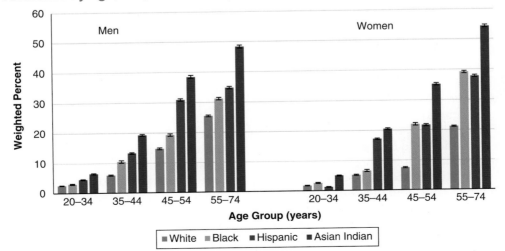

Source: Gujral et al., 2016.

Diabetes poses cognitive and health risks. Managing diabetes entails careful monitoring of the diet and often self-injection of insulin to regulate levels of glucose in the body.
iStock/Drazen_

with medication, and monitor blood glucose—behaviors associated with worse outcomes, including increased risk of mortality (Naicker et al., 2017; van Dooren et al., 2013).

Maintaining a healthy weight through diet and exercise is a powerful way of preventing diabetes. Individuals can successfully manage the disease by adopting a diet that carefully controls the amount of sugar entering the bloodstream as well as engaging in regular exercise (American Diabetes Association, 2014; Jannasch et al., 2017). Frequent blood testing permits the individual to monitor his or her glucose levels and take insulin when needed to lower levels of glucose in the blood. Coping with diabetes requires a great deal of self-monitoring and self-care, but appropriate self-treatment enables adults to manage this chronic illness and live an active life.

Stress

Caught in a traffic jam on the highway, Natasha used her mobile phone to call her husband. "Hi, honey, I'm running late. Can you start cooking dinner?" He replied, "Sorry, I'm not home yet. I've got a late meeting." Natasha sighed, "Okay. Maybe Josh can get a ride home from practice with his friend's mother. I still have to stop at Mom's house to drop off her medicine, and traffic's terrible. I didn't expect Mom's giving up driving to take up so much of my time." Stress is a part of every person's life. Daily hassles such as traffic, child care difficulties, work deadlines, and conflict with family and friends are small stresses that quickly accumulate to influence our mood, ability to cope, and views of our health (Graf, Long, & Patrick, 2017). Often referred to as the "sandwich generation," middle-aged adults are pressed to meet not only the multiple demands of career and family but often the demands of caring for two generations, their children and their own

parents. The resulting stress can influence their mood, ability to cope, and even their health.

Stress is physiologically arousing. When people experience stress, they respond with a "fight-or-flight" stress response in which cortisol is released and the body readies for action, raising blood pressure and heart rate. The fight-or-flight response can motivate behavior, but if experienced daily in response to an excess of daily hassles, the cortisol response can impair health (McEwen, 2018). Individuals who experience chronic stress, such as living in poverty, are more likely to experience negative cardiovascular side effects of stress, such as hypertension (high blood pressure), high cholesterol, and arteriosclerosis (hardening of the arteries, which places more stress on the heart and increases the risk of heart attack and stroke; Harris et al., 2008; Esler, 2017). The stress response and negative consequences of stress tend to be higher in people of low socioeconomic status, perhaps because of the chronic stress associated with living in low-income communities and the lack of resources that accompany low-income communities (Schieman & Koltai, 2017).

Chronic stress is associated with acute illnesses, such as cold and flu, as well as chronic illnesses, such as hypertension, arteriosclerosis, cardiovascular disease, cancer, and autoimmune diseases (e.g., lupus, Graves disease, chronic fatigue syndrome; Connor, 2008; Gouin, Glaser, Malarkey, Beversdorf, & Kiecolt-Glaser, 2012; Marsland, Walsh, Lockwood, & John-Henderson, 2017). Chronic stress is associated with higher rates of anxiety and depression (Leonard & Myint, 2009; Segerstrom & O'Connor, 2012) and can be a trigger for experiencing more serious mental illnesses that have a biological basis, such as bipolar disorder and schizophrenia (Gershon, Johnson, & Miller, 2013; Juster et al., 2011).

Social support can buffer the negative emotional and health consequences that accompany psychological stress. It is associated with lower cortisol levels, suggesting a reduced fight-or-flight response (Ditzen et al., 2008). In addition, when people learn to control their reactions to stress by using relaxation techniques, meditation, and biofeedback, they can reduce the incidence and severity of illness (Sharma & Rush, 2014). Exercise can also reduce stress and promote health and wellness (Gerber & Pühse, 2009). Physically fit individuals show less psychological reactivity (e.g., spikes in blood pressure) to, and improved recovery from, psychological stressors than do unfit individuals (Forcier, Stroud, & Papandonatos, 2006).

Daily stress tends to decline and feelings of well-being increase in the second half of middle adulthood, from age 50 on (Stone, Schneider, & Broderick, 2017). Fortunately, most people tend to show more adaptive responses to stress as they

People often respond to stress with a "fight-or-flight" response that can motivate behavior in times of danger but if experienced in response to daily hassles can impair physical and psychological health.
iStock/DGLimages

progress through middle adulthood. They learn to anticipate stressful events, take steps to avoid them, and approach stressful situations with more realistic attitudes about their ability to change them (Aldwin & Levenson, 2001). Overcoming stressful conditions and personal challenges contributes to a growing sense of self-efficacy over middle adulthood.

Hardiness and Health

Health is influenced not just by behavioral choices, such as coping effectively with stress and maintaining an exercise program, but also by attitudes and personality style. Optimism, conscientiousness, and positive emotions are associated with good health (Dainese et al., 2011; Friedman & Kern, 2014). People who score high on measures of hostility and anger, who tend to view others as having hostile intentions and are easily angered, are at risk for negative health outcomes, such as heart disease and atherosclerosis (Brydon et al., 2010; Friedman & Kern, 2014). Anger is physiologically arousing, and stress hormones course through the body, increasing heart rate and blood pressure. Frequently angry displays and ruminating about events that invoke anger and other negative emotions can lead to high blood pressure that persists and, ultimately, heart disease (Brydon et al., 2010; Ohira et al., 2008).

Some adults are better able than others to adapt to the physical changes of midlife and the stress wrought by the changes in lifestyle that accompany midlife transitions, such as juggling career with caring for children and parents, and tend to display the personal characteristic that researchers refer to as **hardiness** (Maddi, 2016). Individuals who display hardiness tend to have a high sense of self-efficacy, feeling a sense of control over their lives and experiences. They also view challenges as

opportunities for personal growth and feel a sense of commitment to their life choices.

Hardy individuals tend to appraise stressful situations more positively, viewing them as manageable, approach problems with an active problem-focused coping style, and show fewer negative reactions to stressful situations (Bartone, 2006; Vogt, Rizvi, & Shipherd, 2008). The positive appraisals and sense of control that come with hardiness serve a protective function as they are associated with lower emotional reactivity, lower average blood pressure, slower progression of cardiovascular disease, and positive self-ratings of physical and mental health (Maddi, 2013; Sandvik et al., 2013). People who score low in hardiness tend to feel less control, experience more negative reactions to stressful situations, and are more likely to use an emotion-focused style of coping, such as avoidance or denial, which is maladaptive to health and functioning and is associated with higher stress in response to stimuli (Ayala Calvo & García, 2018).

Hardiness can be learned. Training in hardy skills and attitudes, such as coping, social support, relaxation and stress reduction, nutrition, and physical activity, can increase feelings of control, challenge, and commitment that are central to hardiness (Bartone, Jarle Eid, & Hystad, 2016). There is some evidence that hardy leaders can indeed increase hardy cognitions and behaviors in groups, influencing the meaning-making process so that situations are interpreted as interesting, challenging, controllable opportunities to grow (Bartone, Roland, & Picano, 2008; Maddi, 2013).

Sexual Activity

Generally speaking, sexual activity is highest among people in young adulthood, from their mid-20s to mid-30s, and declines gradually for people in their 40s and again in their 50s, but the amount of decline is

Individuals' sense of hardiness can be enhanced by learning stress management and coping techniques, such as meditation.
iStock/FatCamera

modest (King, 2019). It is estimated that heterosexual young adults engage in sexual activity only about one to two times a month more than do their middle-aged counterparts (Herbenick et al., 2010). Research suggests that the frequency of sexual intercourse is associated with emotional, sexual, and relationship satisfaction, as well as overall happiness, in adults in 29 countries (Costa & Brody, 2012; McNulty, Wenner, & Fisher, 2016). For adults in relationships, however, the sexual frequency–happiness link peaks at once a week (Muise, Schimmack, & Impett, 2016). Generally speaking, the research literature examining sexual activity in middle adulthood is sparse, as compared with emerging adulthood, and it is focused nearly exclusively on heterosexual adults.

For midlife adults, the major predictors of sexual activity are health and having a partner (King, 2019; Smith, Gallicchio, & Flaws, 2017). By midlife, there are more women than men in the general population, and women are much more likely to lack a partner. For example, in one study of about 1,300 midlife women, those who were married or cohabiting were eight times more likely than their single peers to be sexually active (Thomas, Hess, & Thurston, 2015).

Physical changes that accompany biological aging can influence sexual activity. For example, declining levels of estrogen slow sexual arousal and reduce vaginal lubrication, sometimes making intercourse uncomfortable or even painful (Simon, 2011; Thomas, Hamm, Hess, & Thurston, 2018), but this is not an indicator of a lack of desire. Vaginal lubricants can relieve this symptom (Herbenick et al., 2011). Many women show no change in sexual interest after menopause, and some show an increased interest as contraception is no longer needed (DeLamater, 2012). Others show a decline in interest (Avis et al., 2017). Complaints about sexual functioning increase with age, with 35% to 40% of women reporting difficulties with sexual functioning, including a reduced sex drive (Torpy, 2007; Walsh & Berman, 2004). For example, one study of women from France, Germany, Italy, the Netherlands, Switzerland, and the United Kingdom found that over one third of the women mentioned experiencing a reduced sex drive, whereas over one half reported a loss of interest in sex (Nappi & Nijland, 2008). Women who report depression following menopause are more likely to report difficulties with sexual functioning (Gallicchio et al., 2007).

With age, men are more likely to experience difficulties establishing or maintaining erections (Walther, Mahler, Debelak, & Ehlert, 2017). The prevalence of erectile dysfunction (ED) ranges from 2% to 9% in men between the ages of 40 and 49 years. It then increases to 20% to 40% in men aged 60 to 69 years (Shamloul & Ghanem, 2013). ED is not inevitable, however, and it has a strong connection with health, with vascular disease as a cause in up to 80% of cases (Moore et al., 2014). Not only is ED frequently due to vasculopathic processes, but it has been well established that ED is a strong predictor of future cardiovascular diagnoses (Fang, Rosen, Vita, Ganz, & Kupelian, 2015). A study of a sample of 651 men (ages 51–60 years) from the Vietnam Era Twin Study of Aging found that men with ED are at a 65% increased relative risk of developing coronary heart disease and a 43% increased risk of stroke within 10 years (Moore et al., 2014). ED has also been associated with poor cognitive performance, particularly on attention–executive–psychomotor speed tasks.

THINKING IN CONTEXT 15.2

1. Genetic tests can reveal whether an individual has a gene for an illness such as cancer. What does a positive test, suggesting the presence of the gene for an illness, mean? Considering the influence of lifestyle and epigenetics (from Chapter 2), what advice would you give to a person who has the gene for an illness such as cancer?

2. Apply the bioecological framework to explain the myriad of factors that influence health and wellness in middle adulthood. Identify factors at the microsystem, mesosystem, exosystem, and macrosystem that can act as risk and protective factors to health during midlife.

3. Provide advice to a friend about what he or she can do to ensure a healthy middle age.

INTELLECTUAL ABILITIES IN MIDDLE ADULTHOOD

» LO 15.3 Contrast the findings of cross-sectional and longitudinal studies of crystallized and fluid intelligence over adulthood.

As we have seen, middle adulthood is a time of change in physical functioning. Are the physical changes of middle adulthood accompanied by cognitive changes? One way of assessing cognitive capacities is with the use of IQ tests. In Chapter 8, we discussed the most commonly used intelligence test, the Wechsler Adult Intelligence Scale (WAIS). The cognitive abilities and skills measured by the WAIS can be classified into two forms of intelligence: fluid and crystallized.

Fluid and Crystallized Intelligence

Intelligent people know a lot. They have a broad knowledge base acquired through experience and education. This accumulation of facts and information comprises **crystallized intelligence** (Horn & Cattell, 1966; Horn & Noll, 1997). Examples of crystallized intelligence include memory of spelling, vocabulary, formulas, and dates in history. People who score high on measures of crystallized intelligence not only know more but also learn more easily and remember more information than do people with lower levels of crystallized intelligence (Brown, 2016).

While crystallized intelligence refers to accumulated knowledge, **fluid intelligence** refers to a person's underlying capacity to make connections among ideas and draw inferences. Fluid intelligence permits flexible, creative, and quick thought, which enables people to solve problems quickly and adapt to complex and rapidly changing situations. Information processing abilities, such as the capacity of working memory, attention, and speed of analyzing information, influence fluid intelligence (Ellingsen & Ackerman, 2016). Fluid and crystallized intelligence are independent components to intelligence, but they interact in the sense that the basic information processing capacities that embody fluid intelligence make it easier for a person to acquire knowledge and develop crystallized intelligence (Nisbett et al., 2013). That said, the relationship is not causal. Longitudinal research with young adults carried out over 6 years, as well as a 16-year study of midlife and older adults, showed no systematic pattern of change between verbal (crystallized) and spatial (fluid) abilities, suggesting that fluid abilities may not drive age changes in crystallized abilities (Christensen, Batterham, & Mackinnon, 2013; Finkel, Reynolds, McArdle, & Pedersen, 2007). Gains in crystallized intelligence help adults compensate and permit adaptive functioning despite fluid losses (Zaval, Li, Johnson, & Weber, 2015).

Intelligence Over the Adult Years

How does intelligence change over the adult years? There is no simple answer to this question. Researchers using different methods have drawn varying conclusions about adult intelligence. Recall from Chapter 1 that researchers learn about how people differ by age and how they change over time with the use of cross-sectional, longitudinal, and cross-sequential research designs. The conclusions that researchers draw regarding intellectual change in adulthood vary with each research design.

Until recently, most researchers believed that intelligence declined with age. Early cross-sectional studies, comparing adults of various ages at once, showed clear age differences in IQ scores whereby intelligence peaked in early adulthood, declined through middle adulthood, and dropped steeply in late adulthood (Salthouse, 2014). Longitudinal studies, however, showed a different picture of intellectual development in adulthood (Ellingsen & Ackerman, 2016). For example, research following people who were evaluated from childhood through middle age (up to age 50) demonstrated that, contrary to prior findings from cross-sectional research, intelligence scores increased into middle adulthood, especially on tests that reflected accumulated knowledge or expertise (Deary, 2014).

Why are the findings of cross-sectional studies very different from those of longitudinal studies? K. Warner Schaie examined this question in his groundbreaking study of intellectual change in adulthood—the Seattle Longitudinal Study. Because cross-sectional and longitudinal studies offer contradictory pictures of intellectual change in adulthood, Schaie employed a cross-sequential design that combined both research methodologies to disentangle the effects of age (change over time) and cohort (change over generations) (Schaie, 2013, 2016). During the first wave of data collection in 1956, adults aged 22 to 70 were tested. These individuals were followed up at regular intervals, and new samples of adults were added. To date, the Seattle Longitudinal Study has examined over 5,000 men and women and has yielded five cross-sectional comparisons and over 60 years of longitudinal data.

The findings of the Seattle Longitudinal Study show a drop in intelligence scores after the mid-30s but also reflect the typical longitudinal finding that there are modest gains through middle age that are sustained into the 60s, followed by gradual declines thereafter (Schaie, 2013, 2016). As shown in Figure 15.5, crystallized and fluid intelligence show different patterns of change over the adult years. The components of crystallized intelligence, such as verbal ability and inductive reasoning, remain stable and even increase into middle adulthood, suggesting that individuals expand and retain their wealth of knowledge over their lifetimes. On the other hand, fluid intelligence, such as perceptual speed and spatial orientation, decreases beginning in the 20s, suggesting that cognitive processing slows, somewhat, with age. Other samples of adults have supported these findings of gains in crystallized intelligence through middle adulthood coupled with gradual declines in fluid intelligence (N. D. Anderson & Craik, 2017; Hartshorne & Germine, 2015). In late adulthood, both types of intelligence decline (Schaie, 2013).

Why does fluid intelligence decline over the adult years? Declines in performance on tasks

FIGURE 15.5

Longitudinal Changes in Crystallized and Fluid Intelligence Over the Adult Years

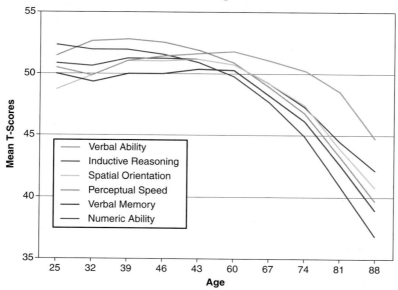

Longitudinal research shows stability over the adult years in most intellectual competencies, especially crystallized abilities, with declines occurring in late adulthood. In contrast, fluid abilities, such as perceptual speed, show steady decline throughout the adult years.

Source: *Developmental Influences on Adult Intelligence: The Seattle Longitudinal Study (p. 127), by K. W. Schaie. © 2005 Oxford University Press. By permission of Oxford University Press, USA.*

measuring fluid intelligence may be due to the biological slowing of the central nervous system, as evident in declines in processing speed (Salthouse & Pink, 2008). Other research points to declines in frontal lobe functioning and reductions in neural interconnectivity in explaining declines in fluid intelligence (Geerligs, Maurits, Renken, & Lorist, 2014). The ability to quickly update one's working memory is closely related to measures of fluid intelligence, and some research suggests that it is the decline in working memory updating rather

than speed that causes age-related changes in fluid intelligence (Unsworth, Fukuda, Awh, & Vogel, 2014). Most notably, training in tasks that tap working memory are associated with improvements in fluid intelligence tasks (Au et al., 2015). An important finding of the Seattle Longitudinal Study is that there are large cohort effects in intelligence. Each cohort of adults has experiences unique to their generation that influence their intellectual development. The Lives in Context feature examines cohort effects in intelligence.

 ## The Flynn Effect: Context and IQ

The cohort differences in intellectual ability documented by the Seattle Longitudinal Study suggest that people are getting "smarter" with each generation. Documented by Flynn (1984) and known as the *Flynn effect*, scores on IQ measures such as the Stanford-Binet and Weschler tests have increased continuously over many years and with each generation (Flynn, 2012). For example, Flynn (1984) discovered a 13.8-point increase in IQ scores

between the years 1932 and 1978, amounting to a rise of about 3 points per decade. More recently, a meta-analysis of 271 samples including nearly 4 million participants from 31 countries confirmed a global increase of about 3 IQ points per decade from 1909 to 2013 (Figure 15.6) (Pietschnig & Voracek, 2015).

From 1889 to 1973, each cohort of adults scored higher in verbal memory and inductive reasoning, and lower in numeric ability, than previous generations (Schaie & Zanjani, 2006). Meta-analyses have shown that patterns of IQ gains are closely associated with historical events. Gains were strong between World Wars I and II but showed a marked decrease during the World War II years and a rise following the 1940s, perhaps reflecting the influences of poor nutrition and marked environmental stress experienced by the general population in regions that were most affected by the world wars (Pietschnig & Voracek, 2015).

The Flynn effect occurs in developed countries, but the gains are especially pronounced in developing countries, such as Kenya, Sudan, China, Brazil, Argentina, and many Caribbean nations (Colom, Flores-Mendoza, & Abad, 2007; Flynn, 2012; Flynn & Rossi-Casé, 2012; Nisbett et al., 2013). The generational increase in IQ is thought to be a function of contextual factors, such as changes in nutrition, health care, education, and environmental stimulation (Flynn & Weiss, 2007; Lynn, 2009; te Nijenhuis, 2013; Trahan, Stuebing, Fletcher, & Hiscock, 2014). With each generation, young people complete more years of education and have more exposure to testing. In addition, advanced levels of education

tend to emphasize logic and self-expression, which are among the skills measured by intelligence tests (Baker et al., 2015; Williams, 2013).

More recent research suggests that the generational gains are leveling off in industrialized countries and already have flattened in Norway, Sweden, and Denmark (Flynn & Weiss, 2007; Pietschnig & Voracek, 2015; Sundet, Barlaug, & Torjussen, 2004; Teasdale & Owen, 2000). If IQ scores are influenced by contextual improvements, such as education and health care, as living conditions optimize in industrialized countries, IQ scores should plateau (Nisbett et al., 2013). Another very large meta-analysis of 285 studies, involving over 14,000 participants since 1951, suggests that the Flynn effect is still at work, yielding an increase of about 2.3 IQ points each decade (Trahan et al., 2014).

What Do You Think?

1. Do you think the generational gains will continue? Why or why not?

2. What factors might contribute to increases, decreases, or plateaus in IQ over generations?. ●

FIGURE 15.6

Change Trajectories

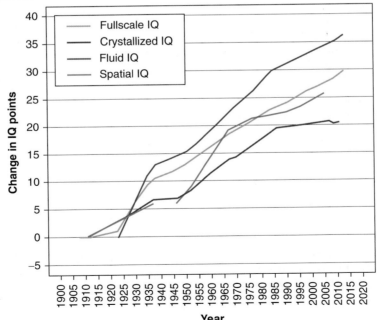

Domain-specific IQ gain trajectories for 1909–2013. Changes are based on weighted average annual IQ changes in all available data.

Overall, intellectual ability is largely maintained over the adult years, especially when individuals are engaged in complex occupational and leisure activities—which are more common among recent cohorts (Schaie, 2013; Schmiedek, 2017). One study examined adult workers over a 17-year period and found that periodically experiencing intellectual challenge in the form of novel work tasks was associated with better processing speed, working memory, and gray matter volume in areas associated with learning and that show age-related decline (Oltmanns et al., 2017). The tendency to engage in mentally simulating activities such as reading is influenced by crystallized intelligence, and engaging in stimulating activities can enhance functional intelligence (Dellenbach & Zimprich, 2008). Moreover, intelligence can influence other domains of functioning. For example, one study of young and middle-aged adults found that fluid intelligence buffered the negative effect of work stress on emotional experience for all adults and crystallized for middle-aged adults (Hyun, Sliwinski, Almeida, Smyth, & Scott, 2018).

> **THINKING IN CONTEXT 15.3**

1. Cross-sectional and longitudinal research designs (see Chapter 1) often result in very different conclusions. Consider this problem using research findings on adult intelligence.

2. Why do we typically find large cohort differences in intellectual abilities? Consider the contextual changes that accompany recent generations. For example, consider your own experiences with those of your parents, grandparents, and even great-grandparents. How were your worlds different, and how might this contribute to differences on intelligence measures?

COGNITIVE DEVELOPMENT IN MIDDLE ADULTHOOD

» LO 15.4 **Analyze changes in cognitive capacities during middle adulthood, including attention, memory, processing speed, and expertise.**

We have seen that middle-age adults experience gradual shifts in intellectual abilities. What do these changes mean for cognition? How do information processing capacities develop over adulthood? Cross-sectional studies suggest that cognitive aging starts in midlife, but longitudinal studies do not document within-individual declines in cognitive performance before the seventh decade (Karlamangla et al., 2014). Most of the research on cognitive development in adulthood tends to compare the tail ends of adulthood, young adults and older adults. Most theorists assume that midlife performance falls somewhere in between that of the young and older adults, but few studies examine this period in life (Lachman, Teshale, & Agrigoroaei, 2015).

Attention

Researchers who study attention examine how much information a person can attend to at once, the ability to divide attention and focus from one task to another in response to situational demands, and the ability to selectively attend and ignore distracters and irrelevant stimuli. From middle adulthood into older adulthood, each of these tasks becomes more difficult (Hartley & Maquestiaux, 2016). For example, research examining the cocktail-party effect, the ability to follow one conversation and switch to another, is studied by presenting an adult with two streams of words to the left and right ear. Adults are instructed to attend to the stream from one ear. With age, adults perform more poorly (Passow et al., 2012). They recall less when asked to report the information from both the target and nontarget streams, suggesting declines in the ability to monitor two sets of stimuli, selectively attend, and switch attention.

With age, adults show more difficulty inhibiting irrelevant information (Hasher, 2016). Response inhibition, the ability to resist interference from irrelevant information, becomes more challenging with age (Zanto & Gazzaley, 2017). Researchers have assessed attention with laboratory tasks in which participants are presented with a series of letter combinations and told to press the space bar only when they see a particular combination (such as T-L); they are to ignore all other combinations. In such tasks, adults' performance declines steadily from the 30s on (Sylvain-Roy, Lungu, & Belleville, 2014).

In everyday life, however, changes in attention are not always evident and vary among adults (Kramer & Madden, 2008). Experience and practice can make a big difference in adults' information processing capacities. People in occupations that require detecting critical stimuli and engaging in multiple complex tasks, such air traffic controllers, develop expertise in focusing and maintaining attention and show smaller declines with age (Kennedy, Taylor, Reade, & Yesavage, 2010; Morrow et al., 2003). Practice also improves performance and reduces age-related decline. For example, training in how to divide attention between two tasks by using selective attention, switching back and forth between

As she paints, this woman must attend carefully to the subject of her painting and her technique. She must ignore distracters and irrelevant stimuli.
iStock/shironosov

mental operations, improves the performance of older adults as much as that of younger adults, although age differences in performance remain (Kramer & Madden, 2008). Although few studies examine middle-aged adults, it is clear that their performance lies between young and older adults (Lachman, 2004).

Memory

The capacity of working memory declines gradually and steadily from the 20s through the 80s, although change is often unnoticed until the 60s (Salthouse, 2016). Changes in attention are related to memory decline (Rowe, Hasher, & Turcotte, 2010; Sylvain-Roy et al., 2014). For example, as we age, it becomes more difficult to tune out irrelevant information, which then leaves less space in working memory for completing a given task. Middle-aged and older adults are less able to recall lists of words and numbers than are young adults; memory for prose shows similar, though less extreme, decline (Davis et al., 2017; Old & Naveh-Benjamin, 2008). Age differences in performance on working memory tasks can be partially explained by a decline in the use of memory strategies, specifically organization and elaboration (Braver & West, 2008; Craik & Rose, 2012). Both of these strategies require the person to link new information with existing knowledge. From middle adulthood into old age, adults begin to have more difficulty retrieving information from long-term memory, which makes them less likely to spontaneously use organization and elaboration as memory strategies.

Many laboratory tests of memory entail tasks that are similar to those encountered in school settings. Middle-aged and older adults may be less motivated by such tasks than younger adults who likely have more recent experience in school

contexts. Laboratory findings, therefore, may not accurately illustrate the everyday memory capacity of middle-aged and older adults (Salthouse, 2012). For example, when the pace of a memory task is slowed, or participants are reminded to use organization or elaboration strategies, middle-aged and older adults show better performance (Braver & West, 2008). In addition, the type of task influences performance. For example, in one study, adults aged 19 to 68 completed memory tests under two conditions: a pressured classroom-like condition and a self-paced condition. When participants were shown a video and tested immediately (classroom-like condition), younger adults showed better recall than did the middle-aged adults. However, when participants were given a packet of information and a video to study on their own (self-paced condition), young and midlife adults did not differ on recall 3 days later (Ackerman & Beier, 2006). The midlife adults performed better when they could apply their own strategies and memorize the material at their own pace.

The declines in memory evident in laboratory research are less apparent in everyday settings (Salthouse, 2012, 2016). Knowledge of facts (e.g., scientific facts), procedures (e.g., how to drive a car), and information related to one's vocation either remains the same or increases over the adult years (Schaie, 2013), and adults' experience and knowledge of their cognitive system (metacognition) enable them to use their memory more effectively. For example, they use external supports and strategies to maximize their memory, such as by organizing their notes or placing their car keys in a designated spot where they can reliably be found (Schwartz & Frazier, 2005). As with attention, memory declines vary with the individual and task. Most adults compensate for declines and show little to no differences in everyday settings; however, chronic stress and negative affect impair working memory (Y. A. Lee & Goto, 2015; Rowell, Green, Teachman, & Salthouse, 2016). Midlife adults who feel overwhelmed in daily life, such as those faced with many conflicting responsibilities and stressors that demand a great deal of multitasking, are more likely to rate their memory competence as poor (Vestergren & Nilsson, 2011). For example, one study of mothers of disabled children found that they reported more stress and showed more declines in episodic memory than mothers of nondisabled children (Song, Mailick, Greenberg, Ryff, & Lachman, 2016).

Processing Speed

The greatest change in information processing capacity with age is a reduction in the speed of processing. Simple reaction time tasks, such as

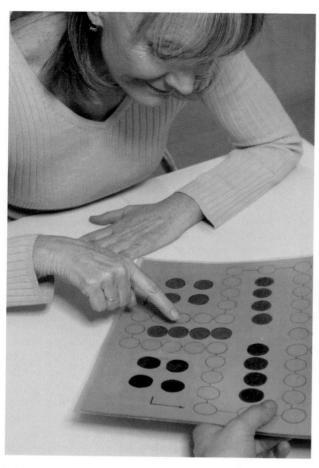

Laboratory tests of memory in middle-aged adults are influenced by factors such as motivation, task, and experience. Laboratory studies may not accurately measure the everyday memory capacity of middle-aged and older adults.
BSIP/Newscom

pushing a button in response to a light, reveal a steady slowing of responses from the 20s into the 90s; see Figure 15.7 (Elgamal, Roy, & Sharratt, 2011; Salthouse, 2016). The more complex the task, the greater the age-related decline in reaction time. However, when reaction time tasks require a vocal response rather than a motor response, age-related declines are less dramatic, suggesting that reaction times may be influenced by motor speed (Low, Crewther, Ong, Perre, & Wijeratne, 2017). Adults' performance on standard tasks measuring processing speed is influenced by their capacities for attention. Adults who are highly distractible show slowed responding on standard tasks measuring processing speed, but their performance improves when tasks are designed to reduce distractions (for example, by listing fewer items on a page) (Lustig, Hasher, & Tonev, 2006; Zanto & Gazzaley, 2017).

Changes in the brain underlie reductions in processing speed. The loss of white matter and myelinated connections reduces processing speed (Bennett & Madden, 2014; Nilsson, Thomas, O'Brien, & Gallagher, 2014). In addition, the loss of neurons forces the remaining neurons to reorganize and form new, often less efficient, connections (Salthouse, 2017). Changes in processing speed influence many of the cognitive declines associated with aging. Declines in processing speed with age predict age-related declines in memory, reasoning, and problem-solving tasks (D. C. Park & Festini, 2017; Salthouse & Madden, 2013). Moreover, the relationship between processing speed and performance on cognitive tasks becomes stronger

FIGURE 15.7

Processing Speed Across the Lifespan

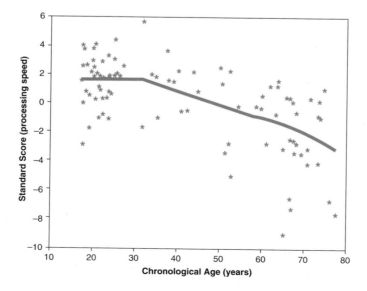

Source: Adapted from Elgamal, Roy, & Sharratt, 2011.

with age (T. Chen & Li, 2007; Salthouse & Pink, 2008). Yet, like attention and memory, the decline in the speed of processing is not as apparent in everyday situations as it is in laboratory tests. Middle-aged and older adults proficiently engage in complex tasks every day, showing performance similar to, or better than, that of younger adults. For example, one classic study tested 19- to 72-year-olds on two tasks: a reaction time task and a typing task. Both tasks measured their speed and accuracy. Although the middle-aged and older adults displayed slower reaction time as compared with young adults, their typing speed and accuracy were no different (Salthouse, 1984). With age, adults compensated for their slower reaction time by looking further ahead in the material to be typed, thereby anticipating keystrokes (Salthouse, 1984). As they age, adults compensate for limitations in processing speed by modifying their activities to emphasize skills that rely on accumulated knowledge and thereby honing their crystallized intelligence (Salthouse, 2016). As discussed in the Brain and Biological Influences on Development feature, sleep may play a role in improving our cognition.

Expertise

Over the course of midlife into old age, many adults gain extensive experience and training in a given area. Many adults develop **expertise,** an elaborate and integrated knowledge base that underlies extraordinary proficiency in a given task (Ericsson, 2017). Experts are not distinguished by extraordinary intellect but by a combination of inherent ability and extensive knowledge and experience (Hambrick, Burgoyne, Macnamara, & Ullén, 2018). Expert knowledge is transformative in that it permits an intuitive approach to approaching problems (Ericsson, 2014). Experts' responses are automatic—well rehearsed, seemingly without thought. This automaticity enables them to process information more quickly and efficiently, and it makes complex tasks routine (Herzmann & Curran, 2011). As expertise grows, experts find that their responses become so automatic that it is hard for them to consciously explain what they do. For example, adults are better than children at tying shoelaces, yet children are far better than adults at explaining how to tie shoelaces (McLeod, Sommerville, & Reed, 2005).

BRAIN AND BIOLOGICAL INFLUENCES ON DEVELOPMENT

 ## Sleep and Neurocognitive Functioning

Although the adult brain weighs only about 3 pounds, it consumes about a quarter of the body's total energy. Brain activity not only uses a great deal of energy but also produces inordinate amounts of biological waste. Recently discovered, the glymphatic system flows cerebrospinal fluid in the spaces between neurons to wash away the cells' daily waste (Jessen, Munk, Lundgaard, & Nedergaard, 2015).

The cognitive benefits of sleep, such as memory consolidation, are well known (Stickgold & Walker, 2013). Sleep also plays a role in forming neural connections and pruning existing connections (Tononi & Cirelli, 2014). Recent research suggests that sleep is even more critical to maintaining neurocognitive functioning because during sleep, the glymphatic system does much of its janitorial work, clearing the brain of biological waste that accumulates as a result of daily thinking (Xie et al., 2013).

In a groundbreaking study, Maiken Nedergaard and colleagues demonstrated that sleep influences the flow of cerebrospinal fluid in mice (Xie et al., 2013). The researchers injected dye into the cerebrospinal fluid of mice and monitored the animals' brains, tracking the movement of dye. When the mice were awake, the dye barely moved, flowing only along the brain's surface. In contrast, when the mice were asleep, the dye indicated

that the cerebrospinal fluid flowed rapidly and reached further into the brain.

Why does the fluid flow more easily during sleep? The team discovered that the increased flow was possible because when mice went to sleep, their brain cells shrank. The space between brain cells increased during sleep, making it easier for fluid to circulate. When an animal woke up, the brain cells enlarged again and the fluid's movement between cells slowed to a trickle. The sleeping mice processed neural wastes, such as excess beta-amyloid, twice as quickly as the awake mice, suggesting that sleep plays a critical role in the brain's waste management. This brain-cleaning process has been observed in rats and baboons but has yet to be studied in humans (DiNuzzo & Nedergaard, 2017; Nedergaard & Goldman, 2016). Yet these findings might explain why we may not think clearly after a sleepless night. More important, the waste management role of cerebrospinal fluid might offer a new way of understanding and perhaps treating brain diseases that involve the buildup of wastes, such as amyloid plaques in Alzheimer's disease (Plog & Nedergaard, 2018).

What Do You Think?

How does sleep affect your thinking and performance? What do these results mean to you? ●

In 2009 Captain Sully Sullenberger successfully executed an emergency water landing of US Airways Flight 1549 in the Hudson River off Manhattan, New York City. He explained to CBS News anchor Katie Couric: "One way of looking at this might be that for 42 years, I've been making small, regular deposits in this bank of experience, education, and training. And on January 15 the balance was sufficient so that I could make a very large withdrawal."

Todd Sumlin/MCT/Newscom

In addition to operating more intuitively and automatically, expert behavior is strategic. Experts have a broader range of strategies, have better strategies than novices, and can better apply them in response to unanticipated problems (Ericsson & Moxley, 2013). Despite showing slower working memory, experts maintain their performance in their areas of expertise, often by relying on external supports, such as notes (Morrow & Schriver, 2007). For example, one study presented airplane pilots with a flight simulation. They were given directions from air traffic controllers and allowed to take notes. The experienced pilots were more likely to take notes than the nonexpert pilots, and their notes tended to be more accurate and complete (Morrow et al., 2003). In actual flights comparing pilots ages 22 to 76, older pilots take more notes than do younger pilots but do not differ in their ability to repeat complex instructions regarding flight plans and conditions. Similarly, expert golfers show fewer declines in performance with age as they compensate for their changing capacities (Ericsson & Pool, 2016; Logan & Baker, 2007). Longitudinal research with expert chess players showed few age effects in chess skill (Moxley & Charness, 2013); players with greater expertise and participation in tournaments showed fewer age-related declines in chess performance but performed similarly in other areas (Roring & Charness, 2007). Intuitive and automatic application of a broad range of strategies permits experts to be more flexible than nonexperts. Experts are more open to deviating from formal procedures when they encounter problems. Experts often approach cases in an individualized way,

varying their approach with contextual factors, and are sensitive to exceptions (Ericsson, 2017; Ormerod, 2005).

Expertise permits selective optimization with compensation, the ability to adapt to changes over time, optimize current functioning, and compensate for losses to preserve performance despite declines in fluid abilities (Baltes & Carstensen, 2003). It is expertise that enables middle-aged and older adults to compensate for declines in processing speed and memory (Ericsson & Moxley, 2013). For example, the typists described earlier compensated for declines in reaction time by looking further ahead in the material to be typed (Salthouse, 1984). A study of food service workers found that gains in expertise compensated for declines in physical performance. In this study, 20- to 60-year-old food service workers were compared in several areas: strength and dexterity, technical knowledge (e.g., of the menu), organizational skills (e.g., setting priorities), and social skills (e.g., providing professional service). Although middle-aged workers showed declines in physical abilities, they performed more efficiently and competently than did young adults, suggesting that expertise in other areas compensated for losses in strength and dexterity (Perlmutter, Kaplan, & Nyquest, 1990).

As people age, they intuitively select and optimize aspects of functioning in which they excel, improving their abilities (Bugg, Zook, DeLosh, Davalos, & Davis, 2006; Salthouse, 1984). In addition to emphasizing their strengths, people naturally devise ways of compensating for declines in physical functioning and fluid ability. Selective optimization with compensation occurs naturally, often without individuals' awareness as their expertise permits them to adapt to developmental changes. Successful aging entails selective optimization with compensation (Freund & Baltes, 2007). The cognitive changes of middle adulthood are summarized in Table 15.3.

THINKING IN CONTEXT 15.4

1. Why are recent generations of adults maintaining their cognitive functioning longer than prior generations? What contextual factors might contribute to this change?

2. Generally speaking, cognitive declines apparent in laboratory settings are less apparent in everyday life. Discuss three examples of this. Why do adults show higher functioning in real-world settings than those in the laboratory?

TABLE 15.3

Cognitive Change During Middle Adulthood

COGNITIVE CAPACITY	AGE-RELATED CHANGE
Crystallized intelligence	Crystallized intelligence increases steadily over the adult years and declines modestly in late adulthood.
Fluid intelligence	Fluid intelligence begins to decline in the 20s and continues throughout adulthood.
Attention	With age, adults show more difficulties with divided attention and inhibition. Declines tend to vary with the individual and task. Most healthy adults compensate for declines and, until old age, show few differences in everyday settings.
Working memory	The capacity of working memory declines from the 20s through the 60s. Changes in working memory are influenced by declines in attention and in the use of memory strategies, such as organization and elaboration, that occur with age. Declines tend to vary with the individual and task. Most healthy adults compensate for declines and, until old age, show few differences in everyday settings.
Processing speed	Processing speed declines steadily from the 20s into the 90s. The more complex the task, the greater the age-related decline in reaction time. Declines in processing speed with age predict age-related declines in memory, reasoning, and problem-solving tasks, and the relationship between processing speed and performance on cognitive tasks becomes stronger with age.
Expertise	With age, most adults develop and expand their expertise. It is expertise that permits middle-aged and older adults to compensate for declines in processing speed.

 APPLY YOUR KNOWLEDGE

Over coffee, Wendy confides in her closest friends:

I sometimes wonder how I got here. I look in the mirror each day and am almost always surprised by the lines in my face and the graying of my hair. My body is changing, and I'm not sure what I think about it. Some is good, some . . . I don't know. Each time I go to aerobics class, I am quickly reminded that I am no longer 20. Yoga classes are a much better experience. I feel healthy, but my doctor still insists on administering a cardiac stress test during my annual checkup.

Her friend Latisha commiserates:

I made the mistake of scheduling my stress test before work. I didn't realize it entailed walking on a treadmill and getting sweaty! Sure, I'm no longer 20, but I'm healthy and I always remind myself that I still have my mind. Every time my son comes home from college, he's surprised that I win nearly every game of Trivial Pursuit we play. I keep reminding him that I have a lot of "useless" knowledge. However, sometimes I feel more forgetful and scattered than ever before. That worries me.

Violet laughs:

Try sitting in my classes. Going back to college has been a real eye-opener. Not only am I the oldest—the "mom" in the room—but it's sometimes embarrassing that I ask the most questions in class. We learned about Piaget last week, and I couldn't help but ask a ton of questions about

what his theory means for my work with preschoolers. Sometimes it seems as though I'm the only one who cares.

1. What physical changes, such as sensory, strength, appearance, and reproductive, can midlife adults expect? How might these physical changes influence their functioning?

2. Do you think that men and women show different patterns of physical changes and corresponding changes in functioning and how they view themselves? Why or why not?

3. Although these friends didn't discuss their health, what heath concerns are typical in midlife? What can men and women do to reduce risks and improve overall health?

4. Why might Latisha feel more scattered and forgetful? What cognitive changes occur during middle adulthood that may influence this? How do situational and contextual factors contribute to adults' feelings of forgetfulness?

5. Do you think Violet's concerns are common to returning students? Why or why not? What might Violet do to improve her experience?

6. What role does socioeconomic status play in physical and cognitive changes and how adults respond to them during middle adulthood? Is this pattern the same for men as for women?

$SAGE edge™

Visit **edge.sagepub.com/kuther2e** to help you accomplish your coursework goals in an easy-to-use learning environment.

LEARNING OBJECTIVES	SUMMARY	KEY TERMS	IN REVIEW
15.1 Summarize age-related physical changes during middle adulthood.	Presbyopia and presbycusis become common over middle adulthood. Declines in strength and endurance become noticeable, but the rate and extent of change are influenced by physical activity. Men and women tend to gain body fat and lose muscle, but these changes can be offset by reducing caloric intake and remaining physically active. Bone density peaks in the mid-to-late 30s, after which adults tend to experience gradual bone loss, advancing in the 50s, especially in postmenopausal women. Menopause is reached at about age 51 and is most commonly accompanied by hot flashes. The timing of menopause is influenced by heredity but also by lifestyle choices, and women experience it in a variety of ways. Men's reproductive ability declines gradually and steadily over the adult years, but most men continue to produce sperm throughout adulthood.	Wear-and-tear theory Free radicals Presbyopia Presbycusis Epidermis Dermis Hypodermis Isometric strength Osteoporosis Menopause Perimenopause Hormone replacement therapy	What are some current explanations for physical aging? What are typical physical changes experienced in middle adulthood? What reproductive changes occur in middle-aged women, and how do contextual factors influence their adjustment? What reproductive changes do men experience?
15.2 Discuss common health conditions and illnesses and the roles of stress and hardiness on health during middle adulthood.	Cancer and chronic health conditions are the result of a complex web of genetic and environmental influences. Advances in medicine have changed the nature of disease. More people survive cancer than ever before. Risk factors for cardiovascular disease include heredity, high blood pressure, poor diet, smoking, and psychological stress. Medication and behavioral changes may reduce hypertension and cholesterol levels. Diabetes is the fifth leading cause of death among people aged 55 to 64. Chronic stress is associated with acute and chronic illnesses. Training in coping, social support, relaxation and stress reduction, nutrition, and physical activity can increase feelings of control, challenge, and commitment that are central to hardiness. Research suggests that the frequency of sexual intercourse is associated with emotional, sexual, and relationship satisfaction, as well as overall happiness. Physical changes that accompany biological aging can influence sexual activity for men and women.	Cardiovascular disease Diabetes Hardiness	Identify risk factors for cancer. Why are women more likely to die of a heart attack than men? What are some of the consequences of diabetes? How can adults manage stress and promote hardiness? What are typical patterns of sexual activity in middle adulthood?
15.3 Contrast the findings of cross-sectional and longitudinal studies of crystallized and fluid intelligence over adulthood.	The cross-sequential Seattle Longitudinal Study shows a cross-sectional drop in fluid intelligence after the mid-30s but also a longitudinal gain in crystallized intelligence in midlife that is sustained into the 60s. In late adulthood, both types of intelligence decline. Declines in performance on tasks measuring fluid intelligence may be due to the biological slowing of the central nervous system; however, intellectual engagement enhances crystallized intelligence as well as functional intelligence over the lifespan.	Crystallized intelligence Fluid intelligence	Provide an example of both crystallized and fluid intelligence. What do cross-sectional studies typically report regarding age changes in intelligence? What are the results of longitudinal studies, such as the Seattle Longitudinal Study?

| 15.4 Analyze changes in cognitive capacities during middle adulthood, including attention, memory, processing speed, and expertise. | With age, it becomes more difficult to divide attention to engage in two complex tasks at once and focus on relevant information as well as to inhibit irrelevant information. The capacity of working memory declines with age because of a decline in the use of memory strategies and changes in attention. Processing speed declines from early adulthood through the middle to late adult years. An expanding knowledge base and growing expertise permit most adults to show few changes in cognitive capacity within everyday contexts and compensate for declines in processing speed. | Expertise | How do attention, memory, and processing speed change with age? What is expertise? What are some of its benefits? How can it be developed? |

Sonja Pacho/

16 Socioemotional Development in Middle Adulthood

"I'm going to be late. I have a parent–teacher conference at John's school," Hal told the babysitter. Another middle-aged adult, Lena, called her assistant while catching the bus to work, "Block out the weekend of the 15th because I'm taking my daughter to college." At a nearby child care center, Danielle said, "Mommy's going to work now. Bye-bye. I love you," as her infant daughter clutched her tightly. Meanwhile, Seymour wondered if he had enough time to straighten the house before his grandchildren arrived. These adults

have very different life experiences and occupy a variety of roles: parent to an infant, parent to an older child, parent to a college student, and grandparent—yet all are middle-aged adults.

We have seen that the middle adult years span a broad period of life, from roughly age 40 to 65. Over these two and one-half decades, we undergo many life changes. Similar to other periods in life, concerns, priorities, and developmental tasks shift over middle adulthood (Hutteman, Hennecke, Orth, Reitz, & Specht,

Learning Objectives

16.1 Summarize the theories and research on psychosocial development during middle adulthood.

16.2 Describe the changes that occur in self-concept, identity, and personality during middle adulthood.

16.3 Analyze relationships in middle adulthood, including friend, spousal, parent–child, and grandparent relationships.

16.4 Discuss influences on job satisfaction and retirement planning during middle adulthood.

Digital Resources

Watch: Generativity and Fathering

Explore: Active Self-Acceptance

Connect: "Your Friend 'Til the End"

▶ **Lives in Context Video 16.1:** Relationships With Adult Children

▶ **Lives in Context Video 16.2:** Family Diversity in Midlife

Listen: A Career Change-Up

▶ **Lives in Context Video 16.3:** Retirement Planning in Midlife

---

2014). For example, parenting demands are highest when adults raise young children but typically decline in the 40s as children age and require less care. Middle-aged adults experience a wide range of concerns to accompany a wide range of life circumstances. A 40-year-old mother of young children faces different developmental and contextual issues than a 55-year-old mother whose child has begun college and left her with an empty nest, a transitional time of parenting when the youngest child leaves home (Wray, 2007). In the past, this time was considered a difficult transition for parents, but it can also be a time for improved relationships and new opportunities, as discussed later in this chapter. Career concerns shift from achieving and maintaining professional status early in midlife to preparing for retirement in the late 50s and 60s. In this chapter, we explore socioemotional development in middle adulthood, changes in developmental tasks, and changes in middle adults' sense of self, personality, relationships, and career.

PSYCHOSOCIAL DEVELOPMENT IN MIDDLE ADULTHOOD

» LO 16.1 Summarize the theories and research on psychosocial development during middle adulthood.

Compared to childhood and old age, middle adulthood has come under study very recently and is perhaps the least understood period of life (Espinola, DeVinney,

& Steinberg, 2017; Lachman, Teshale, & Agrigoroaei, 2015). One challenge of studying middle adulthood is that it comprises several decades during which adults hold multiple roles as spouse, parent, grandparent, caregiver, and worker, for example. Developmental concerns change over the decades, yet we know relatively little about these shifts and adults' adjustment during this period. Popular views associate middle age with psychological awakening and growth, as well as crises. These conflicting views suggest that there are multiple paths through middle adulthood, many factors influence outcomes for better or worse, and well-being and life satisfaction vary among middle-aged adults.

Erikson's Generativity Versus Stagnation

Naomi spent several mornings each week coaching her daughter's softball team. Eduardo hired several high school students to work as interns at his firm and learn about his career path. Francesca volunteered her time at a child advocacy center, helping to write grant proposals to earn the funds needed for the center to remain open. Each of these adults is "giving back" to others. For Erik Erikson (1959), middle-aged adults face the psychosocial stage of **generativity versus stagnation**. The developmental task of this stage entails cultivating a sense of generativity, a concern and sense of responsibility for future generations and society as a whole. In early midlife, generativity is often expressed through childrearing (Syed & McLean, 2017).

Over the middle adult years, generativity expands to include a concern and commitment to the social world beyond oneself and one's immediate family to future generations and even the species itself (McAdams, 2014). Generativity fulfills adults' needs to feel needed and to make contributions that will last beyond their lifetimes, achieving a sense of immortality (Nantais & Stack, 2017). Generativity also serves a societal need for adults to guide the next generation, sharing their wisdom with youth through their roles as parents, teachers, and mentors. Adults fulfill generative needs through teaching and mentoring others in the workplace and community, volunteering, and engaging in creative work. For the active and generative, middle adulthood is the prime of life even as they experience multiple conflicting demands.

A minority of adults, however, experience disappointment in middle adulthood. After not achieving career and family goals or finding them dissatisfying, some middle-aged adults remain self-absorbed. They focus on their own comfort and security rather than seeking challenges, being productive, and making contributions to help others and make the world a better place (Nantais & Stack, 2017). Adults who fail to develop a sense of generativity experience stagnation, self-absorption that interferes with personal growth and prevents them from contributing to the welfare of others.

Generativity is good for others, but it is also good for the middle-aged adult as it promotes personal growth (Villar, 2012). Generativity is associated with life satisfaction, self-acceptance, low rates of anxiety and depression, cognitive function, and overall well-being (An & Cooney, 2006; Cox, Wilt, Olson, & McAdams, 2010; Steinberg et al., 2017). Creativity is associated with generativity, and the most generative adults are proactive problem solvers who approach problems by investigating multiple solutions and exploring several options before committing to any one (Adams-Price, Nadorff, Morse, Davis, & Stearns, 2018; Beaumont & Pratt, 2011).

Generativity increases from the 30s through the 60s in adults of all ethnicities and socioeconomic backgrounds (Ackerman, Zuroff, & Moskowitz, 2000; Nantais & Stack, 2017; Newton & Stewart, 2010). However, it is characterized by an interesting gender difference. Men who have children tend to score higher in measures of generativity than do childless men, although having children is not related to generativity in women (Marks, Bumpass, & Jun, 2004). Likewise, engaging in child care activities is associated with increases in generativity in men but not women (McKeering & Pakenham, 2000). Having children may draw men's attention to the need to care for the next generation while women may already be socialized to nurture young. However, men and women who are involuntarily childless may experience difficulty developing a sense of generativity (R. M. Moore, Allbright-Campos, & Strick, 2017). For both men and women, generativity is influenced by psychosocial issues addressed earlier in life and reflects a lifetime of

psychosocial development, including the ability to trust others and oneself, understand one's self, and sustain meaningful relationships (Syed & McLean, 2017; Wilt, Cox, & McAdams, 2010).

Levinson's Seasons of Life

Similar to Erikson, Daniel Levinson (1978, 1996) viewed development as consisting of qualitative shifts in challenges that result from the interplay of intrapersonal and social forces. Based on interviews with 40 men aged 35 to 45 and, later, 45 women aged 35 to 45—both the men and the women were workers in a wide variety of occupations—Levinson concluded that adults progress through a common set of phases that he called **seasons of life**.

The key element of Levinson's psychosocial theory is the **life structure**, which refers to the overall organization of a person's life: relationships with significant others as well as institutions such as marriage, family, and vocation. In Levinson's model, individuals progress through several seasons over the lifespan in which their life structures are constructed, then tested and modified in response to intrapersonal and social demands.

During the transition to early adulthood (ages 17 to 22), according to Levinson, we construct our life structure by creating a dream, an image of what we are to be in the adult world, which then guides our life choices. Young adults then work to realize their dreams and construct the resulting life structure (ages 22 to 28). Levinson explained that men tend to emphasize the occupational role and construct images of themselves as independent and successful in career settings, whereas women often create dual images that emphasize both marriage and career.

The age *30 transition* (28 to 33) entails a reconsideration of the life structure in which adults may shift priorities from career to family or vice versa. Adults who do not have satisfying experiences at home or work may struggle to revise their life structure and may experience the age 30 transition as a crisis. Men tend to experience the mid-to-late 30s (34 to 40) as a period of settling down, focusing on some goals and relationships and giving up others based on their overall values. Women were thought to remain unsettled through middle adulthood because they generally take on new career or family commitments and balance multiple roles and aspirations.

Levinson observed that as adults transition to middle adulthood (40 to 45), they become aware of the passage of time, that half of life is spent. Middle-aged adults reexamine their dream established in early adulthood and evaluate their progress, coming to terms with the fact that they will not realize many of them. In areas where they have achieved hoped-for success, they must reconcile reality with their dream and perhaps wonder whether the experience was "worth it" or whether they are missing out on some other aspects of life. Some middle-aged adults make substantial changes to their life structure by changing careers, divorcing, or beginning a new project such as writing a book.

Many people find the seasons of life conceptualization intuitively pleasing, but it is vital to note that Levinson based his ideas on a very small sample of adults who were highly educated, White, and of high socioeconomic status (Dare, 2011). The seasons of life are likely influenced by context because the process of evaluating and revising the life structure is influenced by the social opportunities and situations around us.

Contexts of disadvantage—poverty, discrimination, or limited opportunities—deplete individuals of the energy and social resources needed to examine and revise the life structure. The seasons of life model likely does not apply to all men and women across ethnicity, socioeconomic status, and social contexts. That said, adults who construct dreams, revise them in light of opportunity and experience, and are successful in achieving them are likely to be well positioned to focus on the developmental tasks of middle adulthood, such as becoming generative and developing a more comprehensive sense of self. Some adults use mindfulness meditation as a tool to aid in becoming more aware of themselves, as

---

Mindfulness Meditation and the Brain

Mindfulness meditation may influence areas of the brain responsible for emotion regulation.
iStock/Rawpixel

Emotional regulation skills develop throughout life. Recently, researchers have suggested that we can advance our emotional regulation skills through becoming proficient in mindfulness meditation (Kurth, Cherbuin, & Luders, 2017). Mindfulness meditation refers to focusing attention and becoming aware of one's ongoing sensory, cognitive, and emotional experiences with an accepting, nonjudgmental stance (Kong, Wang, Song, & Liu, 2016).

Adults who practice mindfulness meditation learn to become aware of their surroundings and observe their thoughts and emotional states. The resulting increased emotional awareness is coupled with less rumination about feelings (Teper & Inzlicht, 2014).

Mindfulness meditation may affect neural processes. It is associated with greater cortical thickness (Tang, Hölzel, & Posner, 2015; Wheeler, Arnkoff, & Glass, 2017). MRI research has suggested that several brain regions

are involved in mindfulness meditation, most notably the prefrontal cortex, responsible for executive function (Falcone & Jerram, 2018). Activity within the prefrontal cortex may contribute to awareness of oneself and the surroundings. Mindfulness meditation is also associated with activity in the sensory cortex, which is related to body awareness, suggesting that individuals might get better at reading their bodies.

In addition, mindfulness meditation stimulates the anterior cingulate cortex, which is associated with the sense of self, attention, and emotion regulation (Falcone & Jerram, 2018; Tang et al., 2015). Mindfulness meditation might improve prefrontal control of brain regions relevant to emotional processing such as the amygdala (Tang et al., 2015). For example, research suggests that mindfulness meditation is associated with diminished activation of the amygdala in response to emotional stimuli, suggesting a decrease in emotional arousal.

Interventions to teach mindfulness meditation skills help individuals learn emotion regulation and stress management skills. The increased self-awareness and ability to control negative emotions is associated with a variety of positive outcomes, such as improved physical health, reductions in anxiety and depression, and engagement in positive health behaviors, such as exercise and reductions in smoking (Creswell, 2017).

What Do You Think?

Some argue that mindfulness skills should be taught to individuals of all ages, from children through older adults.

1. What might be the benefits of teaching mindfulness meditation to children, adolescents, and adults?

2. Can you identify challenges that a middle-aged adult might face when beginning a mindfulness meditation program? ●

discussed in the Brain and Biological Influences on Development feature.

Midlife Crisis

The 45-year-old who purchases a red convertible sports car; the middle-aged person who suddenly leaves a spouse and moves out of the home, beginning a new life in a new city; the midlifer who is suddenly gripped with anxiety over the future, the fear that half of life is over, and despair that life has not turned out as planned and little time remains to make changes—each of these people embodies aspects of the most popular stereotype about middle age. Depicted in television dramas and self-help magazine articles, the **midlife crisis** is proposed as a stressful time in the early to middle 40s when adults are thought to evaluate their lives. The term arose in the public consciousness in the 1970s after publication of several popular books, including *Seasons of Life*, in which Daniel Levinson (1978) articulated his theory of adult development, discussed in the preceding section.

Although the existence of a midlife crisis is widely accepted among laypersons (Wethington, 2000), research is at odds with this popular view. Surveys of adults over age 40 have revealed that only about 10% to 20% report having experienced a midlife crisis (Wethington et al., 2004). Instead, research suggests that a period of crisis or psychological disturbance is not universal among middle-aged adults but instead exhibits significant individual differences and occurs at various periods of life (Brim, Ryff, & Kessler, 2004; McCrae & Costa, 2006; Rosenberg, Rosenberg, & Farrell, 1999). Adults who believe that they have experienced a midlife crisis have usually experienced upheavals at other times in their lives (Freund & Ritter, 2009). Personal characteristics may determine whether a person experiences middle adulthood, or any other point in life, as a crisis. For example, men who scored higher on measures of psychological problems earlier in adulthood were more likely to report experiencing a midlife crisis 10 years later than did men who scored lower on psychological problems (McCrae & Costa, 2006). Outside events that can occur at any time in adulthood, such as job loss, financial problems, or illness, may trigger responses that adults and their families may interpret as midlife crises (Beutel, Glaesmer, Wiltink, Marian, & Brähler, 2010).

Middle adulthood is unquestionably a transition and is perhaps the most stressful time in life, given changes in adults' bodies, families, careers, and contexts. Most developmental scientists adopt the perspective that midlife represents a transition similar to the transition to adulthood; it entails creating, clarifying, and evaluating values, goals, and priorities (Lachman et al., 2015). A close examination of this kind can lead to insights about oneself, revisions in identity, and decisions to revise life plans (Rathunde & Isabella, 2017). Most adults respond to these changes by making minor

FIGURE 16.1

Views of Midlife, by Age

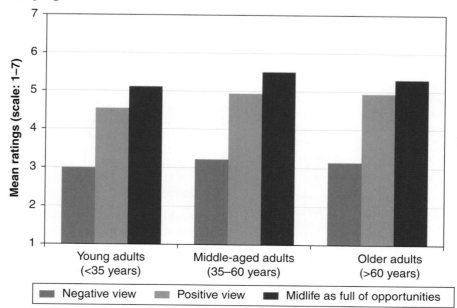

Source: Freund and Ritter (2009). Reprinted with permission.

adjustments, creating turning points in their lives rather than dramatic changes. If they cannot revise their life paths, they try to develop a positive outlook (Vandewater & Stewart, 2006; Wethington, Kessler, & Pixley, 2004). Moreover, goals are not set in stone. Adults assess and adjust goals throughout life, often without awareness (Freund, 2017).

The concept of a midlife crisis remains popular in our culture, perhaps because it describes exciting possibilities for making major life changes, or perhaps because it is a simple explanation for the many changes that occur. Despite this, the research suggests that most adults tend to view middle adulthood as a positive time in life, as shown in Figure 16.1 (Freund & Ritter, 2009). Middle adulthood is a time of increasing life satisfaction, self-esteem, and well-being (Arnett, 2018; Lachman et al., 2015; Orth, Trzesniewski, & Robins, 2010). Moreover, longitudinal studies show that personality remains stable from young adulthood through middle adulthood to older adulthood, suggesting that a period of upheaval and turmoil does not exist in midlife or at least is not evidenced in personality change (McCrae & Costa, 2006).

THINKING IN CONTEXT 16.1

1. According to Erikson's lifespan psychosocial theory, each psychosocial stage builds on the last. How does resolution of the tasks of infancy, childhood, adolescence, and young adulthood contribute to adults' capacities to address the task of middle adulthood, developing a sense of generativity?

2. Identify instances in which a midlife crisis is depicted in popular media. In your view, how accurate are these depictions? Why?

THE SELF IN MIDDLE ADULTHOOD

» LO 16.2 Describe the changes that occur in self-concept, identity, and personality during middle adulthood.

It is in middle age that people often first become aware of biological aging, changes in their skin, bodies, and athletic ability. Youthfulness holds an important place in Western society, especially for women (Clarke, 2018). For example, analyses of women's magazines reveal that the fashion industry focuses its promotional efforts on the young and seldom includes images of women over 40 (Lewis, Medvedev, & Seponski, 2011). Television programs portray middle-aged women with youthful bodies

and shapes and sizes of younger women. Like adolescent and young women, middle-aged women who report viewing these media tend to rate their body shapes more poorly (Hefner et al., 2014). Many adults attempt to stop or reverse the aging process in an effort to maintain an ageless sense of self.

However, changes in body image, while salient, are not always adults' biggest concerns regarding aging. In one study of British African Caribbean, British Muslim, West Indian, and Pakistani women, all tended to perceive physical changes, but most reported that the most important body concern was maintaining physical activity and avoiding dependence on family (Wray, 2007). A recent study of middle-aged U.S. women echoes this theme as the women emphasized maintaining health over physical attractiveness (Hofmeier et al., 2017). Less socioeconomically advantaged adults tend to perceive themselves as older, likely because of their worse health and less favorable predictions of future health as compared with their wealthier peers (Barrett, 2003). Health inequalities can shape the subjective experience of aging, including how old we feel and how we experience aging itself.

Self-Concept in Middle Adulthood

The process of development continues throughout adulthood as self-concept becomes more complex and integrated (Lodi-Smith & Roberts, 2010). In addition to describing themselves in more complex ways, adults are increasingly likely to integrate autobiographical information and experiences into their self-descriptions as they grow older (Pasupathi & Mansour, 2006).

Subjective Age

Throughout life, subjective evaluations of age are important parts of the sense of self (Barrett & Montepare, 2015). Children, adolescents, and

Self-concept becomes more complicated in middle adulthood and includes subjective age, how old we feel.
iStock/RossHelen

emerging adults tend to perceive themselves as older than their chronological age, but as shown in Figure 16.2, adults older than 30 tend to have younger subjective ages, and the discrepancy between subjective and chronological age increases into middle adulthood (Bergland, Nicolaisen, & Thorsen, 2014; Shinan-Altman & Werner, 2018). Adults tend to consistently identify with their younger selves, perhaps as a compensatory strategy to counteract the negative cultural messages associated with aging and to maximize their happiness. Subjective age is multidimensional, and people are more likely to feel younger in areas that tend to be associated with negative age-related stereotypes, such as cognitive aging and health (Kornadt, Hess, Voss, & Rothermund, 2018). Longitudinal samples suggest that older adults feel about 13 years younger, on average, than their chronological age (Kleinspehn-Ammerlahn, Kotter-Gruhn, & Smith, 2008). Cross-cultural research found this difference between subjective and chronological age among adults in 18 countries (Barak, 2009).

As compared with men, women tend to hold more youthful self-concepts, perhaps because Western cultures tend to define aging as a more negative experience for women than men (Izard, 2007). Women with younger age identities tend to be more optimistic than men about their cognitive competencies, their ability to maintain memory, and other aspects of cognitive abilities regardless of their actual age, although this effect is also seen in men to some degree (Schafer & Shippee, 2010). In one recent study, adults reported how old they felt and thought they looked, and observers assessed the participants' age based on photos on two occasions, about 10 years apart (Agrigoroaei, Lee-Attardo, & Lachman, 2017). Adults who reported higher levels of financial stress at Time 1 felt older and were perceived by peers as older than their actual age at both time points (Agrigoroaei, Lee-Attardo, & Lachman, 2017). In addition, stressed adults showed greater increases in self-rated and perceived age than the adults who were less stressed. Adults who perceive themselves as older might be more likely to seek to alter their appearance, as discussed in the Cultural Influences on Development feature.

Adults who view themselves as younger than their chronological age (e.g., those who feel 35 years old when in fact they are 45 years old) tend to score high on measures of well-being, mental health, and life satisfaction (Keyes & Westerhof, 2012; Ryff, 2014). Longitudinal studies have shown that adults who reported feeling younger relative to their peers tended to show better performance and slower declines in episodic memory, executive function, and health over a 10-year period than same-age peers (Hughes & Lachman, 2016; Stephan, Caudroit, Jaconelli, & Terracciano, 2014). Other research, however, suggests that older subjective age predicts poor life satisfaction only when adults have negative attitudes about aging but not when aging attitudes are more favorable (Mock & Eibach, 2011). Ultimately, the adults with the greatest well-being are those who recognize their age but remain active, engage in preventive health habits, and do not become distressed by age-related physical changes (Ryff, 2014; Vandewater & Stewart, 2006).

FIGURE 16.2

Subjective Age Across the Lifespan

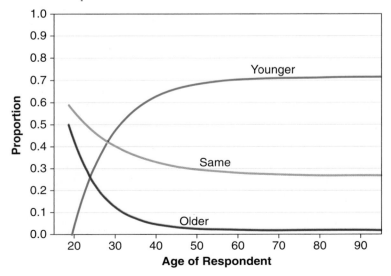

Source: Rubin and Berntsen (2006). With permission from Springer Science+Business Media.

CULTURAL INFLUENCES ON DEVELOPMENT

Use of Cosmetic Procedures in Middle Adulthood

Changes in appearance are hard to deny in middle adulthood. As people age, their concerns about their appearance increasingly focus on the face (Honigman & Castle, 2006). It is not uncommon for middle-aged adults, especially women, to develop concerns and worries about losing their attractiveness, as judged by Western beauty standards that emphasize youth (Barrett & Robbins, 2008).

Many adults seek to improve their appearance through cosmetic procedures, both surgical and nonsurgical. As the name suggests, surgical cosmetic procedures entail surgery. Nearly 1.8 million surgical cosmetic procedures were conducted in 2017, most commonly including procedures such as breast augmentation, liposuction, nose reshaping, eyelid surgery, and tummy tucks (American Society of Plastic Surgeons, 2018). Nonsurgical cosmetic procedures are far more common, with 15.7 million conducted in 2017. The most common noninvasive procedures include Botox injections (which paralyze facial muscles, making them unable to contract and "wrinkle"), so-called injectable fillers (substances injected into wrinkles, temporarily filling them), and chemical peels (which remove the outermost layers of skin, purporting to reveal smooth new skin).

At all ages, about 90% of cosmetic procedures are conducted on women and, as shown in Figure 16.3, middle-aged women are most likely to obtain cosmetic procedures (American Society of Plastic Surgeons, 2017). Most report turning to cosmetic procedures to improve their appearance (Sobanko et al., 2015). Those who fear being negatively judged by others tend to have more positive attitudes about cosmetic procedures (Dunaev, Schulz, & Markey, 2016). Nearly three quarters of women who obtain cosmetic procedures are White.

The ethnic differences in rates of cosmetic procedures suggest that individual and contextual factors influence whether women obtain cosmetic procedures. Western cultural norms equate women's aging with a decline in physical attractiveness. There is little research on ethnic differences in cosmetic procedures, but examinations of body image suggest that at all ages, Black women are more satisfied with their bodies than White women (Grabe & Hyde, 2006). As young adults, African American women report feeling less pressure to conform to Western beauty ideas as portrayed by the media and are less likely to internalize thin ideals for body shape (Warren, Gleaves, & Rakhkovskaya, 2013). African American women may hold a definition of attractiveness that is multifaceted and extends beyond a small body size to include factors such as dress attire and race (D. S. Davis, Sbrocco, Odoms-Young, & Smith, 2010). Likewise, research with adolescent girls has suggested that they identify beauty as defined through attitude, style, personality, and presence (Rubin, Fitts, & Rubin, 2003). Cultural depictions of beauty may protect African American women from negative depictions of aging in mainstream culture.

Cultural views about the wisdom that comes with age may influence adults' beliefs about their own aging and the value of cosmetic procedures. Elders, especially grandmothers, are valued in African American culture as matriarchs and sources of wisdom (Kelch-Oliver, 2011). Aging may afford cultural status.

What Do You Think?

1. In your opinion, why are cosmetic procedures most popular in midlife?

2. What are some of the advantages and disadvantages or risks of such procedures?

3. How might someone make a decision about whether to pursue cosmetic procedures? ●

FIGURE 16.3

Cosmetic Procedures by Age and Ethnicity in the United States, 2016

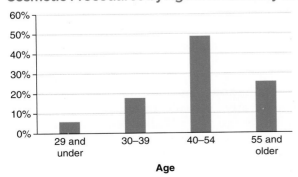

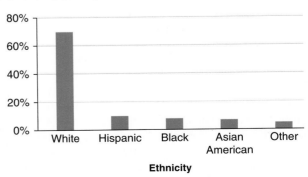

Source: American Society of Plastic Surgeons (2017).

Possible Selves

Possible selves, individuals' conceptions of who they might become in the future, are self-orientations that guide and motivate choices and future-oriented behaviors (Cross & Markus, 1991). The possible self is a motivator of behavior from early adulthood into older adulthood (J. Smith & Freund, 2002; Voss, Kornadt, & Rothermund, 2017). People are motivated to try to become the hoped-for ideal self and avoid becoming the feared self—the self that they hope never to become. As they approach middle adulthood, people compare their real self and the lives they have achieved with their hoped-for ideal self; the degree of match between the two influences life satisfaction. Failure to achieve the hoped-for self, or failure to avoid the feared self, results in negative self-evaluations and affect. However, people often protect themselves from failure by revising their possible selves to be more consistent with their actual experience, thereby avoiding disappointment and frustration.

Possible selves shift throughout adulthood. Many young adults in their 20s describe the aspirations of their possible selves as idealistic and grand—visions of fame, wealth, exceptional health, and athletic prowess. By middle adulthood, most people realize that their time and life opportunities are limited, and they become motivated to balance images of their possible selves with their experiences to find meaning and happiness in their lives. Thus, middle adulthood is an important time of self-growth (Lilgendahl, Helson, & John, 2013). Over their lifetimes, adults revise their possible selves to be more practical and realistic (Lapp & Spaniol, 2016), typically aspiring to competently perform the roles of worker, spouse, and parent and to be wealthy enough to live comfortably and meet the needs of children and aging parents (Bybee & Wells, 2003).

Gender Identity in Middle Adulthood

Adults' views of gender and the roles they adopt tend to shift over the lifespan. Some theorists argue that adult gender roles are shaped by the parental imperative, the need for mothers and fathers to adopt different roles to successfully raise children (Gutmann, 1985). In many cultures, young and middle-aged men emphasize their ability to feed and protect families, characteristics that rely on traditionally masculine traits (often referred to as instrumental traits because they are associated with acting on the world). Young and middle-aged women emphasize their potential to nurture the young and care for families, traditional female traits (expressive traits that are associated with maintaining relationships).

Although today most men and women in developed nations express more flexible views of gender than traditional roles dictate (Brooks & Bolzendahl, 2004; Twenge, 1997), parenthood often signals a shift in couples' behavior and division of labor. Most couples adopt traditional roles after the birth of a child (Schober, 2013; Yavorsky, Dush, & Schoppe-Sullivan, 2015). For example, couples tend to agree that mothers do more of the housework and the fathers do less (Goldberg & Perry-Jenkins, 2004; Katz-Wise, Priess, & Hyde, 2010). In one study that followed 205 first-time and 198 experienced mothers and fathers from 5 months pregnant to 12 months postpartum, parents became more traditional in their gender role attitudes and behavior following the child's birth; for example, mothers did more of the housework than fathers (Katz-Wise et al., 2010). Overall, women showed greater changes in gender role attitudes and behavior than did men, and first-time parents changed more than experienced parents. Gender differences in couples' division of labor continue throughout childhood. For example, the American Time Use Survey found that with most couples, the mother typically spends about twice as much time as the father on both housework and child care, whereas fathers spend more time working outside the home (37 hours as compared with 21 hours for mothers) (Parker & Wang, 2013). However, it should be noted that fathers today spend twice as much time doing household chores than in 1965 (from an average of about 4 hours per week in 1965 to about 10 hours per week today), suggesting a shift in perceived responsibility (Parker & Wang, 2013).

As children grow up and leave the nest, adults' activities shift away from parenting. Some theorists argue that as adults are freed of the parental imperative, they become less tied to traditional gender roles (Gutmann, 1985). Over the middle adult years, individuals' identification with the masculine or feminine gender role tends to become more fluid and integrated. Many middle-aged adults begin to integrate instrumental and expressive aspects of themselves, becoming more similar and more androgynous (James & Lewkowicz, 1995). That is, men begin to adopt more traditionally expressive characteristics, such as being sensitive, considerate, and dependent, and women adopt more traditionally instrumental characteristics, such as confidence, self-reliance, and assertiveness (Lemaster, Delaney, & Strough, 2017). In one study that followed a representative sample of third-grade Finnish children for 30 years (Pulkkinen, Feldt, & Kokko, 2005), boys and girls adopted traditional gender characteristics in adolescence, but by age 40, the men had become less aggressive and more conforming, in contrast to the women, who showed a reverse pattern of becoming more assertive. Longitudinal research following adults from their 30s to 80s mirrors this finding: Although there are individual differences, the average man, initially low in expressive traits, becomes more expressive across the lifespan; the average woman, initially high in expressive traits, becomes less expressive across the lifespan (Jones, Peskin, & Livson, 2011; Jones, Peskin, & Wandeler, 2017). This pattern of gender convergence increases in middle adulthood in Western nations, as well as in non-Western cultures, such as the Mayan people of Guatemala and the Druze of the Middle East (C. L. Fry, 1985).

Androgyny, integrating instrumental and expressive characteristics, provides adults with a greater repertoire of skills for meeting the demands of middle and late adulthood. Middle-aged women who may be newly independent after experiencing divorce, death of a partner, or the end of childrearing may enter the workplace, seek advancement in current careers, or enroll in college. Successfully meeting these new challenges requires self-reliance, assertiveness, and confidence. Men, on the other hand, may become more sensitive and self-reflective as they complete generative tasks of mentoring and caring for the next generation. A great deal of research has shown that androgyny predicts positive adjustment and is associated with high self-

esteem, advanced moral reasoning, psychosocial maturity, and life satisfaction in later years (Bem, 1985; Lefkowitz & Zeldow, 2006; Pilar Matud, Bethencourt, & Ibáñez, 2014). Men and women with androgynous gender roles have a greater repertoire of skills, both instrumental and expressive, which permits them to adapt to a variety of situations with greater ease than do those who adopt either a masculine or feminine gender role.

Self and Well-Being in Middle Adulthood

Throughout the lifespan, the sense of self and identity are important influences on people's overall functioning and their sense of well-being (Sneed, Whitbourne, Schwartz, & Huang, 2012). Middle-aged adults are more likely than young adults to acknowledge and accept both their good and bad qualities and feel positively about themselves (Ryff, 1991, 1995). Revised, more modest, possible selves influence adults' sense of self-esteem and well-being (Orth, Trzesniewski, & Robins, 2010). Self-esteem increases throughout middle adulthood, with longitudinal studies suggesting that self-esteem peaks at about ages 50 to 60 (Orth, Maes, & Schmitt, 2015) and cross-sectional studies suggesting a later peak in early older adulthood, as shown in Figure 16.4 (Robins et al., 2002). Self-esteem is associated with positive emotional, social, and career outcomes throughout life, from adolescence through older adulthood (Orth, Robins, & Widaman, 2012).

Although self-esteem increases in middle adulthood, paradoxically, well-being shows a U-shaped curve, with its lowest point in early middle age, typically the early 40s (López Ulloa, Møller, & Sousa-Poza, 2013; Ryff, 2014). Perhaps the overall decline in well-being in middle adulthood is related to the great many roles most middle-aged adults occupy. In a prior chapter, we discussed the challenge that role overload poses to well-being. When accompanied by a sense of control, multiple role involvement predicts positive well-being, more trusting and positive relations with others, a positive sense of life purpose, and greater overall well-being (Chrouser Ahrens & Ryff, 2006). Perceived control is associated with life satisfaction, and multiple demands that middle-aged adults face often test their sense of control (de Quadros-Wander, McGillivray, & Broadbent, 2013). Positive processing, a tendency to interpret events in a favorable light, is associated with high levels of well-being in middle adulthood (Lilgendahl & McAdams, 2011). Multiple roles must be accompanied by a sense of control or mastery in that area to influence well-being.

Although most people experience midlife shifts in well-being, they typically rate their subjective life

In middle age, adults become less tied to gender stereotypes for their own behavior. Men tend to adopt more expressive characteristics, such as being warm and sensitive, and women adopt more instrumental characteristics, such as becoming more assertive.
iStock/Essentials

FIGURE 16.4

Age Differences in Self-Esteem Across the Lifespan

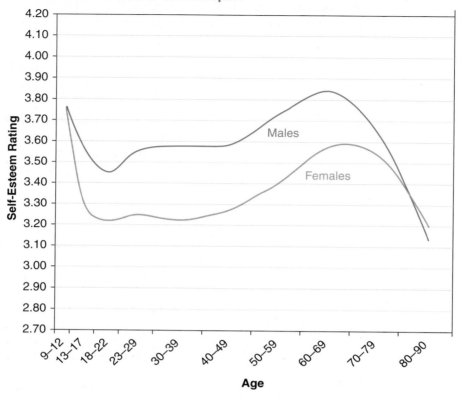

Source: Robins et al. (2002).

FIGURE 16.5

Adults' Mean Ratings of Their Past (10 Years Ago) and Present Life Satisfaction

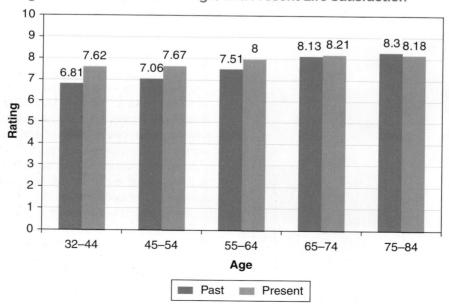

Source: Röcke & Lachman (2008).

Note: The life satisfaction scale can range from 1 (low satisfaction) to 10 (high satisfaction).

satisfaction in the moderate to high range. As shown in Figure 16.5, one national sample of 25- to 75-year-old adults studied over a 9-year span found that on average, all ages reported feeling moderate to high levels of life satisfaction in the present as well as 10 years ago and rated their satisfaction as increasing from past to present (Röcke & Lachman, 2008). One recent study of middle-aged adults found that most believed that this time in their life is stressful but also fun and exciting, a time of freedom, and when anything is possible, suggesting that positive views coexist with stress (Arnett, 2018).

Personality in Middle Adulthood

We have seen that self-concept becomes more defined, but the content remains much the same over adulthood. Does personality show similar stability? One view of personality, evolved through research conducted with multiple samples over several decades, has resulted in an empirically based theory that has collapsed the many characteristics on which people differ into five clusters of personality traits. Collectively known as the **Big 5 personality traits**, they are openness, conscientiousness, extroversion, agreeableness, and neuroticism. These personality factors are shown in Table 16.1 (McCrae & Costa, 2008). The Big 5 personality factors are thought to reflect inherited predispositions that persist throughout life, and a growing body of evidence supports their genetic basis (Power & Pluess, 2015; Vukasović & Bratko, 2015).

Big 5 personality traits predict career, family, and personal choices in adulthood. For example, people who are high in conscientiousness are more likely to complete college, those high in extroversion are more likely to marry, and those

high in neuroticism are more likely to divorce (Hill, Turiano, Mroczek, & Roberts, 2012; Shiota & Levenson, 2007). People who are high in extroversion, agreeableness, and conscientiousness and low in neuroticism report higher levels of well-being (Cox, Wilt, Olson, & McAdams, 2010). High scores on measures of conscientiousness predict better performance on cognitive tasks and slower rates of cognitive decline (Bogg & Roberts, 2013; Curtis, Windsor, & Soubelet, 2015; Luchetti, Terracciano, Stephan, & Sutin, 2015). Big 5 traits, especially low conscientiousness, even predict mortality (Graham et al., 2017). Conscientiousness has an especially close association with health as it influences the behaviors persons engage in—exercise, eating habits, and risky behaviors such as smoking—and these behaviors affect the likelihood of good or poor health outcomes (Friedman & Kern, 2014; Turiano, Chapman, Gruenewald, & Mroczek, 2015). In fact, conscientiousness measured in childhood predicts health in middle adulthood (Hampson et al., 2016).

Individual differences in Big 5 personality traits are large as people show unique patterns of traits, and those patterns and individual differences in personality traits are highly stable over periods of time ranging from 3 to 30 years (McAdams & Olson, 2010; Wängqvist, Lamb, Frisén, & Hwang, 2015). For example, someone who is highly extroverted in young adulthood, perhaps with a very active social life, will also be highly extroverted in middle adulthood, perhaps manifested as being active in a parent–teacher organization, leading a scout troop, or participating in a book group. Continuity in personality traits increases with age, from early adulthood, peaking in the late 30s into middle adulthood and decreasing in older adulthood (Lucas & Donnellan, 2011; McAdams & Olson, 2010).

TABLE 16.1

Big 5 Personality Traits

TRAIT	DESCRIPTION
Openness	The degree to which one is open to experience, ranging from curious, explorative, and creative to disinterested, uncreative, and not open to new experiences.
Conscientiousness	The tendency to be responsible, disciplined, task oriented, and planful. This trait relates to effortful self-regulation. Individuals low in this trait tend to be irresponsible, impulsive, and inattentive.
Extroversion	Includes social outgoingness, high activity, enthusiastic interest, and assertive tendencies. This trait is related to positive emotionality. On the opposite pole, descriptors include social withdrawal and constrictedness.
Agreeableness	This trait includes descriptors such as trusting, cooperative, helpful, caring behaviors and attitudes toward others. Individuals low in agreeableness are seen as difficult, unhelpful, oppositional, and stingy.
Neuroticism	This trait relates to negative emotionality. Descriptors include moodiness, fear, worry, insecurity, and irritability. The opposite pole includes traits such as self-confidence.

Despite findings of within-person stability, research also shows age differences in Big 5 factors, as shown in Figure 16.6 (Soto, John, Gosling, & Potter, 2011). Personality traits shift subtly over adulthood. Cross-sectional studies of adults in 26 countries, including Canada, Germany, Italy, Japan, Russia, South Korea, and the United States, have found that agreeableness and conscientiousness increase and neuroticism, extroversion, and openness decline into middle adulthood, suggesting that adults mellow with age (Löckenhoff et al., 2009; McCrae & Costa, 2006; McCrae, Terracciano, & The Personality Profiles of Cultures Project, 2005; Soto et al., 2011). These patterns continue into older adulthood. Extroversion and openness to experience decline with age from 30 to 90, with the most pronounced drops after the mid-50s (Lucas & Donnellan, 2011; Mroczek, Spiro, & Griffin, 2006; Srivastava, John, Gosling, & Potter, 2003). Conscientiousness increases from emerging adulthood to mid-adulthood, peaks

between 50 and 70, and then declines; agreeableness tends to increase with age (Leszko, Elleman, Bastarache, Graham, & Mroczek, 2016; McCrae, 2002; McCrae & Costa, 2006). Thus, cross-cultural similarities in patterns of change support arguments that personality itself and age-related changes have biological origins; however, cultures often share some contextual similarities.

Although there are predictable age-related shifts in Big 5 traits, there are also individual differences in the pattern and magnitude of change (Graham & Lachman, 2012). Not all individuals follow the normative increase in conscientiousness scores over adulthood, for example. Some people change more than others, and some change in ways that are contrary to general population trends (McAdams & Olson, 2010). How do we make sense of age trends in light of substantial data supporting stability in personality traits over the lifespan? Research with large groups of people indicates general age-related

FIGURE 16.6

Age Differences in Big 5 Personality Traits

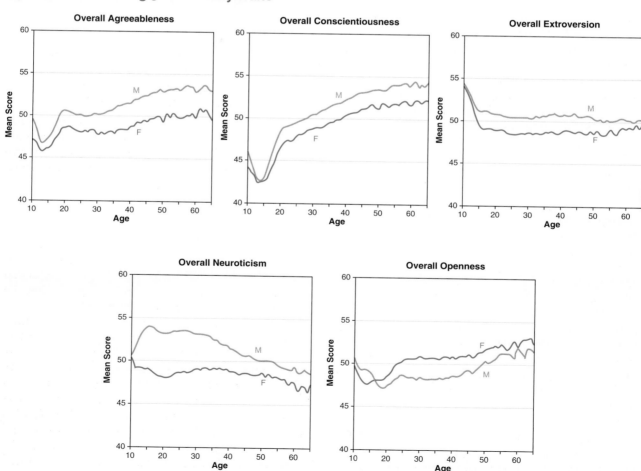

Source: Soto et al. (2011).

patterns of change. At the same time, individuals' relative position with regard to traits does not change (Deary, Pattie, & Starr, 2013; Roberts & Mroczek, 2008). In other words, someone who is high in openness relative to age peers will remain high in openness over time, even though as a group, the adults may show a decline over the adult years.

Why does an individual's personality remain largely the same over a lifetime? Personality influences a person's life choices and experiences, yet folk wisdom usually adheres to the opposite: that a personality in adulthood is influenced by events and experience over a lifetime. The logic goes that after a humiliating experience at a party, a person becomes more introverted and anxious about social gatherings. However, research suggests that experience rarely causes dramatic changes in personality and that instead, it is our personalities that influence our choices and experiences (Bleidorn, Hopwood, & Lucas, 2018; McCrae & Costa, 2006). That is, introverted and socially anxious people may be prone to find parties and social gatherings challenging—and in their distress, they may behave in ways that increase the likelihood of humiliating experiences (e.g., grasping a cup too tightly and inadvertently spilling its contents). People choose behaviors, lifestyles, mates, and contexts based on their personalities, and then the outcomes of these choices and life experiences may strengthen and stabilize personality traits (Soto, 2015; Wrzus, Wagner, & Riediger, 2016). In one study conducted over a 9-year period, social well-being correlated positively with extroversion, agreeableness, conscientiousness, emotional stability, and openness, and changes in social well-being coincided with changes in these traits (Hill et al., 2012). In this sense, stability of personality is influenced by individuals' behaviors and choice of environments as well as by environmental factors themselves (Kandler et al., 2010).

Contextual factors play a role in stabilizing personality throughout adulthood as social, living, and working contexts and social roles, such as spouse or parent, become established and, for most people, are largely stable over adulthood contributing to continuity in personality and individual differences in personality (Kandler, Kornadt, Hagemeyer, & Neyer, 2015; Roberts, Walton, & Viechtbauer, 2006). Dramatic life changes, such as divorce, serious illness, or widowhood, may bring about new behaviors and patterns of traits, but more commonly such events evoke and strengthen existing patterns of traits (Mroczek et al., 2006; Roberts & Caspi, 2003). Personality traits can be expressed in many ways, depending on the situation and on the individual's personality makeup. Most people are motivated to maintain a stable sense of personality as part of developing and maintaining a consistent sense of self (Kandler et al., 2010).

THINKING IN CONTEXT 16.2

1. Consider your self-concept. Identify your possible self and feared self. In what ways do you think these have changed since your adolescent years? Consider the life tasks that you expect to engage in 20 years from now. What might your possible and feared selves look like?

2. Middle-aged adults operate within multiple contexts and roles. What factors might influence middle-aged adults' personality, self-concept, and sense of well-being? Identify factors at the micro-, meso-, and exosystem levels of Bronfenbrenner's bioecological context. How might these factors influence psychosocial functioning? What macrosystem factors might influence psychosocial adjustment in middle adulthood?

3. Adult gender development is linked with roles and contexts. Agree or disagree? Explain your reasoning given the discussion thus far.

RELATIONSHIPS IN MIDDLE ADULTHOOD

» LO 16.3 Analyze relationships in middle adulthood, including friend, spousal, parent–child, and grandparent relationships.

Middle-aged adults' changing sense of self, changing family formations, and changing roles and responsibilities in the workforce and at home influence their social relationships with friends, spouses, children, and parents.

Friendships

Over the course of middle adulthood, most people spend more time with family than friends, but friendships continue to be important sources of social support and are associated with well-being, positive affect, and self-esteem (Blieszner, 2014; Huxhold, Miche, & Schüz, 2014). Like young adults, middle-aged adults tend to share demographic similarities with their friends. Women's friendships continue to be more intimate, and they report having more close friends and experience more pleasure and satisfaction in their friendships than men, whose friendships tend to center on activities (Fiori & Denckla, 2015). Work and family demands tend to reduce the available time and resources adults have for friends, leading adults to prune their social networks (Wrzus, Zimmermann, Mund, & Neyer, 2017). The number of friends and the amount of

Middle-aged adults often have less time for their friends, but friendships continue to be important sources of social support and are associated with well-being, positive affect, and self-esteem.
iStock/andresr

contact with them tend to decrease. Middle-aged adults therefore report having fewer friends and spending less time with friends than young adults, but the friendships that have endured tend to be described as close and few to none are ambivalent or troubled (Fingerman, Hay, & Birditt, 2004).

Friendships offer powerful protection against stress for both men and women (Blieszner, 2014). Adults turn to close friends for support with daily hassles as well as major stressors (Birditt, Antonucci, & Tighe, 2012). Increasingly, friends offer companionship and support from afar, via participation in social media, permitting interactions despite limited time (Dare & Green, 2011; Meng, Martinez, Holmstrom, Chung, & Cox, 2017). For example, one study found that the empty nest is associated with an immediate increase in social media use by midlife adults that persists for up to 2 years (Tanis, van der Louw, & Buijzen, 2017).

Marriage and Divorce

Although marriage rates have declined to record lows over the past half-century, nearly all adults will marry. Over 80% of adults marry by age 45, 90% by age 60, and over 95% by age 80 (U.S. Bureau of the Census, 2015). In comparison, in 1960, only 7% of men and 6% of women had never married by age 45 (M. Wang & Parker, 2014). Similar to early adulthood, marriage is positively associated with physical and mental health for both opposite-sex and same-sex partners (Cherlin, 2013; Goldsen et al., 2017; Grover & Helliwell, 2014; Wight, Leblanc, & Lee Badgett, 2013).

Men generally report being happier with their marriages than women, although the difference is small (Jackson, Miller, Oka, & Henry, 2014). For both opposite-sex and same-sex marriages, satisfaction tends to be highest in egalitarian relationships in which home and family duties are shared and

couples view themselves as equal contributors (Ogolsky, Dennison, & Monk, 2014; Pearson et al., 2014; Pollitt, Robinson, & Umberson, 2018). The most satisfying marriages reflect congruence in which partners' attributes complement one another (Rammstedt, Spinath, Richter, & Schupp, 2013). Successful marriage partners balance similarity and differences, such that partners have enough shared interests, goals, and interaction styles to get along but also some differences that generate and sustain interest in one another. Marital satisfaction tends to wax and wane over the decades. In middle adulthood, marital satisfaction tends to increase as childrearing tasks and stress decline, family incomes rise, and spouses get better at understanding each other and have more time to spend together (Fincham, Beach, & Davila, 2007). The advances in emotion regulation that typically come with age may also improve the quality of marital interactions and predict satisfaction (Bloch, Haase, & Levenson, 2014).

Divorces most often occur within the first 10 years of marriage, but about 10% of marriages break up after 20 years or longer (U.S. Bureau of the Census, 2015). By 45 years of age, over one third of men and women have ever divorced (Kreider, Ellis, & U.S. Bureau of the Census, 2011). Overall, middle-aged adults list similar reasons for divorce as do young adults: communication problems, relationship inequality, adultery, physical and verbal abuse, and desires for autonomy (Rokach, Cohen, & Dreman, 2004; Sakraida, 2005). Women are more likely than men to initiate divorce, and women who are the initiators tend to fare better than those who do not initiate the divorce (Steiner, Suarez, Sells, & Wykes, 2011).

The process of divorce entails a series of stressful experiences, such as conflict, physical separation, moving, distributing property, and, for some, child custody negotiations. Regardless of who initiates a divorce, all family members feel stress and a confusing array of emotions, such as anger, despair, embarrassment, shame, failure, and, sometimes, relief (Clarke-Stewart & Brentano, 2006; Härkönen, 2015). Divorce is associated with decreased life satisfaction, heightened risk for a range of illnesses, and even a 20% to 30% increase in early mortality (Björkenstam, Hallqvist, Dalman, & Ljung, 2013; Holt-Lunstad, Smith, & Layton, 2010; Sbarra, Law, & Portley, 2011). Divorce is thought to be more harmful to women's health than to that of men, because it tends to represent a greater economic loss for women, often including a loss of health insurance (Lavelle & Smock, 2012). However, some research suggests that, in women, illness often precedes divorce, suggesting that illness is simply a correlate of divorce or perhaps a contributor rather than outcome of divorce (Karraker & Latham, 2015). Women tend

In middle adulthood, marital satisfaction tends to increase as childrearing tasks and stress decline.
iStock/mapodile

to report ruminating more about arguments, having more detailed memories of conflicts, and feeling more depressed after arguments than men (Lorenz, Wickrama, Conger, & Elder, 2006; Steiner et al., 2011), all of which predict poor health outcomes (Kross, Gard, Deldin, Clifton, & Ayduk, 2012; Sbarra, Smith, & Mehl, 2012).

Although some adults show poor health outcomes of divorce, most people are resilient and fare well after divorce, especially after the initial adjustment (Sbarra & Coan, 2017; Sbarra, Hasselmo, & Bourassa, 2015). For example, in one study of more than 600 German divorcees, nearly three quarters experienced little change in life satisfaction across a 9-year period that included the divorce (Mancini, Bonanno, & Clark, 2011). Women who successfully make the transition through a divorce tend to show positive long-term outcomes. They tend to become more tolerant, self-reliant, and nonconforming—all characteristics that are associated with the increased autonomy and self-reliance demands that come with divorce.

Divorce is challenging, but middle-aged persons generally show less of a decline in psychological well-being and show overall better adaptation than do young adults (H. Wang & Amato, 2000). It may be that increases in experience, flexibility, and problem-solving and coping skills in middle adulthood aid adaptation. As with other life challenges, divorce represents an opportunity for growth and development (Baum, Rahav, & Sharon, 2005; Schneller & Arditti, 2004), and adaptive outcomes following divorce appear to be the norm, not the exception (Perrig-Chiello, Hutchison, & Morselli, 2014).

Parent–Child Relationships

The dynamic lifelong challenge of parenting taps adults' capacities for adaptation. Just as parents become proficient at meeting children's developmental demands at a given age, children advance, posing new challenges and requiring a transformation of skills. Middle-aged adults are parents to children ranging in age from infancy to adulthood. However, some time in middle adulthood, most parents launch their adult children into the world. Many parents view their children's graduation from high school in a positive light while also experiencing some regrets, especially a sense of lost time with their children that cannot be regained (DeVries, Kerrick, & Oetinger, 2007).

Parents to Adult Children

A son's or daughter's moving out of the family home is an important experience for parents and children as it marks the child's entry to adulthood and independent living. Mothers report the move as more stressful than fathers (Seiffge-Krenke, 2010), but most parents adjust well to their children's transition to independent living and the resulting empty nest (Mitchell & Lovegreen, 2009). However, the extended transition to adulthood common today means that middle-aged adults have more contact with their emerging adult children for a longer period of time and often provide more emotional and financial support than parents of prior generations (Fingerman & Suitor, 2017). How parents view their continued involvement with their adult child influences their well-being. For example, in one study, when parents provided support to grown children several times a week, parents' ratings of the child's neediness were associated with parental well-being. Parents who viewed their grown children as more needy than other young adults reported poorer well-being, but the frequency of support the parents provided was not associated with the parents' well-being (Fingerman, Cheng, Wesselmann, et al., 2012). Nevertheless, most parents report having positive interactions with their grown children on a regular basis. For example, one study followed parents over a week and found that 90% reported having an enjoyable encounter with a grown child, and 89% reported laughing with a grown child (Fingerman, Kim, Birditt, & Zarit, 2016). Negative interactions with adult children, however, are consistently associated with parent reports of negative affect and predict daily patterns of the stress hormone cortisol (Birditt, Manalel, Kim, Zarit, & Fingerman, 2017).

Frequently, the adult child's transition to independent living is gradual and nonlinear, involving intermittent moves back home (Mitchell, 2016). Especially after the economic recession that affected much of the world in 2007 to 2008, it has become increasingly common for adult children to return home at some point in their 20s. Over one third of U.S. young adults ages 18 to 31 live with their parents (R. Fry, 2016). Some research suggests that

FIGURE 16.7

Increase in Living at Home

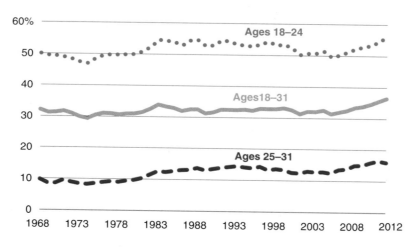

% living at home of parent(s)

Source: Reprinted with permission from "A Rising Share of Young Adults Live in Their Parents' Home," Pew Research Center, Washington, DC (August, 2013). http://www.pewsocialtrends.org/2013/08/01/long-term-changes-in-young-adult-living-arrangements/

having at least one post-college-age child living at home is associated with lower psychological well-being among mothers (Pudrovska, 2009). More recent research suggests that contextual factors—specifically, the increasingly normative nature of so-called boomerang adult children—are associated with parental adjustment. Middle-aged parents surveyed in 2008 reported relatively low parental quality if an adult child was living in the home but not when they were surveyed in 2013—adult children in the home became increasingly common in the intervening years, accounting for the change, as shown in Figure 16.7 (E. M. Davis, Kim, & Fingerman, 2016). Thus, norms for parental involvement with grown children and the economic context may shape the implications of that involvement for parents' marital ties and well-being. Parents are harmed when they believe their grown children should be more autonomous (Pillemer, Suitor, Riffin, & Gilligan, 2017).

Children's success in life influences their midlife parents' sense of well-being. Both mothers and fathers show negative emotional responses to their adult children's unmet career and relationship goals (Cichy, Lefkowitz, Davis, & Fingerman, 2013). Adult children's problems are associated with low parental well-being, including more negative than positive affect, low levels of self-esteem, marital quality, and poor parent–child relationships (Bouchard, 2018; Greenfield, Marks, Hay, Fingerman, & Lefkowitz, 2008). In one study of middle-aged adults, having an adult child with problems predicted poor parental well-being, regardless of the presence of another

successful child, and the more problems in the family, the worse parental well-being (Fingerman, Cheng, Birditt, & Zarit, 2012). Parents who perceive their grown children as needing too much support report lower life satisfaction (Fingerman, Cheng, Wesselmann, et al., 2012).

Around the world, families who live apart continue to provide various forms of emotional and physical support to one another, including advice, babysitting, loans, car repair, and more. How much support family members provide each other depends on many factors, such as attachment, relationship quality, cultural norms, and resources. Familism is a value that mandates that the family comes before all else and that family members have a duty to care for one another, regardless of the problem or situation, whether personal, financial, or legal (Carlo, Koller, Raffaelli, & De Guzman, 2007); it is common in Hispanic cultures, among others. Financial resources also influence the level and types of support that family members provide. Poverty often leads family members to provide financial and physical assistance to each other, including living together. For example, in most nations, low-income families, such as single parents, immigrants, and members of minority groups, are more likely to live together in three-generation households (parents, children, and grandchildren) (Burr & Mutchler, 1999). Generally speaking, early midlife parents continue to give children more assistance than they receive, especially when children are unmarried or facing challenging life transitions such as unemployment

A son's or daughter's moving out of the family home is an important experience for parents and children as it marks the child's entry to adulthood and independent living. Most parents adjust well to the empty nest.
iStock/kali9

and career change or divorce (Fingerman & Suitor, 2017; Zarit & Eggebeen, 2002).

Generally speaking, there is continuity in parent–child relationships throughout the lifespan. In one longitudinal study of New Zealand families, parental warmth and support in childhood and adolescence predicted contact and closeness with children in early adulthood (Belsky, Jaffee, Hsieh, & Silva, 2001). Most parents are happy in their roles, but their satisfaction varies with parental age, health, ethnic background, parent–child relationship quality, and perception of how their children "turn out," which influence their subjective levels of happiness (Mitchell, 2010).

Parents to Infants and Young Children

Most middle-aged parents have adult children; however, a growing minority of adults postpone parenthood into early midlife. Today it is not uncommon for adults in their 40s and early 50s to raise young children. We have discussed the biological changes in reproductive capacity that occur throughout young adulthood and middle adulthood. Whether through assisted reproduction, adoption, or chance, a growing number of new parents in industrialized nations are middle aged.

The transition to parenthood entails many changes for all parents. Middle-aged parents, however, may find the social side of their new role challenging as their daily experiences may not match those of their peers. Middle-aged parents of infants, for example, have different concerns and needs than their friends. A new mother may find that her social clock is discordant with her same-age peers who may be sending their children to college or planning for weddings and grandchildren. At the same time, a middle-aged mother may find herself much older than many of the other parents of infants

she meets at child care, play groups, and parks. For these reasons, older parents may find the social side of parenting a challenge.

When asked, middle-aged parents cite benefits to being an older parent. Many midlife adults have established careers with financial security, enabling flexibility in how they spend their time. Middle-aged parents also feel that they are better prepared for parenthood than they would have been at a younger age. They feel mature, competent, and generative, and they tend to be less stressed than younger parents (MacDougall, Beyene, & Nachtigall, 2012). Middle-aged parents also tend to experience greater increases in life satisfaction with the birth of their children and are less prone to depressive symptoms (Luhmann, Hofmann, Eid, & Lucas, 2012). They tend to take a more youthful perspective, seeing middle age as extending longer and old age as starting later than do those who have children early in life (Toothman & Barrett, 2011). The most common complaints of older parents include having less energy for parenting and feeling stigmatized as older parents (MacDougall et al., 2012).

Children also benefit from being raised by older parents. The cognitive and emotional changes that take place from early to middle adulthood contribute to midlife adults' readiness to parent. In some studies, mothers who were older when their first child was born tended to demonstrate more positive parenting behaviors, such as hugs, kisses, and praise, and fewer negative ones, such as threats or slaps (Barnes, Gardiner, Sutcliffe, & Melhuish, 2013; Camberis, McMahon, Gibson, & Boivin, 2016). Finally, children raised by older mothers tend to be healthier, having fewer visits to the hospital, a greater likelihood of receiving all of their immunizations by 9 months of age, and higher scores on measures of cognitive, language, and social development through age 5 (Sutcliffe, Barnes, Belsky, Gardiner, & Melhuish, 2012; Tearne, 2015).

Grandparenthood

Most U.S. adults are grandparents by the time they reach their late 40s and early 50s (with an average age of 49 for women and 52 for men) (Leopold & Skopek, 2015). In both the United States and Canada, grandparenthood is coming significantly later, yet adults are spending more years as grandparents than ever before (Margolis, 2016). Just as parenthood arrives later with each generation, so does the median age of grandparenthood. Similar to patterns of marriage and childbirth, grandparenthood occurs up to 3 years earlier in Eastern European countries (e.g., Poland, Ukraine, and Bulgaria) and up to 8 years later in Western European countries (e.g., the Netherlands, Switzerland, and Austria) compared

FIGURE 16.8

Distribution of Grandparents by Age and Gender in the United States, 2001 and 2015

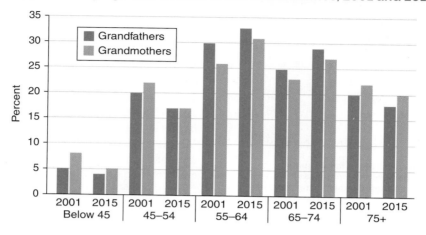

Source: "The Long (Long) Wait to Be a Grandparent" by Anne Tergesen, The Wall Street Journal, March 30, 2014. Reprinted with permission.

with the United States (Leopold & Skopek, 2015). The role of grandparent is an important one for adults because, with increasing lifespans, many will spend one third of their lives as grandparents (see Figure 16.8).

The timing of the transition to grandparenthood influences adults' experience of this role. Adults who become grandparents early or late relative to their peers may experience a more challenging transition (Hank, Cavrini, Di Gessa, & Tomassini, 2018). For example, adults who become grandparents earlier than the norm may find themselves in the position of parenting young children and adolescents while fulfilling the care and support functions of the grandparent role (Fuller-Thomson & Minkler, 2001). The grandparent role is rewarding, and time caring for a new grandchild is associated with positive mental health (Condon, Luszcz, & McKee, 2018). However, for many adults, it may be accompanied by role strain as they may juggle expectations of employers, spouses, children, adult children, and grandchildren.

Grandparent involvement is associated with child well-being and adolescent adjustment (Griggs, Tan, Buchanan, Attar-Schwartz, & Flouri, 2010). For example, close nurturing relationships with grandparents are associated with positive adjustment and relatively few problem behaviors in adolescents in divorced and single-parent homes (Attar-Schwartz, Tan, Buchanan, Flouri, & Griggs, 2009; Henderson, Hayslip, Sanders, & Louden, 2009). In low-income families, grandparents often take on important financial and caregiving roles. Grandparent involvement is high in many ethnic minority households, such as Chinese, Korean, Mexican American, Native American, and

Being a grandparent provides opportunities to enjoy spending time and playing with children without the responsibility of parenthood.
iStock/Milan Marjanovic

Canadian Aboriginal—this is especially the case for grandmothers, who take on caregiver, mentor, and disciplinarian roles (Kamo, 1998; Werner, 1991; N. Williams & Torrez, 1998). Grandparent involvement is predated by regular contact, close relationships with grandchildren, and parental encouragement to visit with grandchildren. Grandparents who are engaged and spend time with their grandchildren tend to report high levels of life satisfaction (S. M. Moore & Rosenthal, 2015). Research with 14 European countries suggests that this is especially true for those who live in countries with high grandparent obligations, such as Italy and Greece (Neuberger & Haberkern, 2013). In some cases, grandparents step in as primary caretakers for their grandchildren, as discussed in the Lives in Context feature.

Relationships between grandparents and grandchildren are influenced by several factors, including grandparent and grandchild gender, geographic proximity, socioeconomic status, and culture. In most cultures, grandparents and grandchildren of the same sex tend to be closer than those of the opposite sex, especially grandmothers and granddaughters. Generally, grandmothers tend to have more contact with their grandchildren than do grandfathers, and they tend to report higher satisfaction with the grandparent role (Silverstein & Marenco, 2001; Soliz, 2015). Grandparents who live closer to their children tend to have closer relationships with their grandchildren than do those who have contact only on special occasions like holidays and birthdays. Yet in Western nations, most grandparents remain involved in their grandchildren's lives despite distance (AARP, 2002). Because parents tend to regulate grandparent–grandchildren contact, grandparents' relationships with their own children influence their contact and relationships with their grandchildren.

The grandparent role provides adults opportunities to satisfy generative needs by nurturing a new generation, enjoy spending time and playing with children without the responsibility of parenthood, and gain a sense of immortality by passing along family and personal history as well as a second generation of progeny (S. M. Moore & Rosenthal, 2015; Soliz, 2015). Some theorists argue that grandparental investment, the tendency for grandparents to be involved in their grandchildren's lives and transfer resources to them, stems from its provision of evolutionary benefits such as a correlation between the presence of the maternal grandmother and child survival (Coall & Hertwig, 2011).

Similar to parent–child relationships, grandparent–grandchild relationships show continuity over time. Close grandparent–grandchild relationships in childhood predict close relations in adulthood (Geurts, Van Tilburg, & Poortman, 2012). Grandparents and adult grandchildren tend to agree that their relationships are close and enduring (Hayslip & Blumenthal, 2016; Villar, Celdrán, & Triadó, 2012). Grandparents offer an important source of emotional support for their grandchildren (Huo, Kim, Zarit, & Fingerman, 2018). Over time, contact with grandchildren tends to decline as young and middle-aged grandchildren take on time-consuming family and work roles, but affection between grandchildren and grandparents remains strong (Silverstein & Marenco, 2001; Thiele & Whelan, 2008).

LIVES IN CONTEXT

 ## Grandparents Raising Grandchildren

Raising a grandchild is challenging, yet custodial grandparents frequently mention a sense of satisfaction in parenting and in seeing grandchildren's accomplishments.
Nikki Kahn/Washington Post/Getty Images

Raising a child is both challenging and rewarding. Although childrearing is generally regarded as a one-time phase in the lifespan, some adults find themselves raising multiple cohorts of children as they take over the parenting of their children's children.

About 2.6 million grandparents are raising grandchildren (U.S. Bureau of the Census, 2017). African American and Hispanic grandparents are more likely to be the primary caregiver for a grandchild than White non-Hispanic grandparents (Ellis & Simmons, 2014). The majority of custody arrangements are informal, with no involvement from child welfare agencies. Grandparents often obtain custody of their grandchildren in response to parental absence or incapacitation from substance abuse, HIV/AIDS, incarceration, abandonment, mental or physical difficulties, or death (Hayslip, Fruhauf, & Dolbin-MacNab, 2017).

The transition to parenting grandchildren is not easy, partly because the reasons for parental absence, such as incarceration or illness, are stressful to both the grandparent and grandchildren. Grandchildren often enter grandparent custodial arrangements

(Continued)

(Continued)

with preexisting problems due to poor parenting and harsh contextual conditions (G. C. Smith & Hancock, 2010; M. N. Williams, 2011). Many children experience internalizing and externalizing difficulties, such as anxiety, depression, aggression, academic difficulties, behavior problems, anger, and guilt (Billing, Ehrle, & Kortenkamp, 2002; Guzell-Roe, Gerard, & Landry-Meyer, 2005). In addition, contextual factors make custodial grandparenting more difficult. Grandparent caregiver arrangements are especially common in low-income communities, as kin offer a safety net for families in crisis. About one quarter of grandparent-headed households live in poverty (U.S. Bureau of the Census, 2017).

As grandparent caregiving is not part of typical midlife development, it can be particularly difficult and stressful for adults (Hayslip & Blumenthal, 2016). Perhaps because of the stress, financial difficulties, feelings of grief and anger toward the parent, and feelings of social isolation, grandparent caregivers tend to suffer more mental and physical health problems than those who do not care for their grandchildren (Edwards & Benson, 2010). Grandparents who care for grandchildren with emotional and behavioral problems tend to experience higher rates of anxiety, stress, and depression, and they tend to report less life satisfaction (Doley, Bell, Watt, & Simpson, 2015). African American and Latino grandparents tend to experience greater risk of health problems because they are more likely to live in poverty and in disadvantaged neighborhoods (Chen, Mair, Bao, & Yang, 2015; Whitley & Fuller-Thomson, 2017); however, social support can buffer some negative outcomes (Doley et al., 2015; Hayslip, Blumenthal, & Garner, 2015).

Despite these challenges, many grandparent caregivers adjust and report positive aspects of caregiving (Hayslip et al., 2017). Many report enjoying the love and companionship of their grandchildren and the opportunity to influence their development. Some grandparents report that raising their grandchildren is easier than parenting their own children because of greater wisdom and experience, feeling more relaxed, and having more time and attention to give to grandchildren (Dolbin-MacNab, 2006). Social support is an important influence on grandparent caregivers' sense of well-being and adjustment. Grandparents who feel that they have a social support network to turn to for emotional and physical assistance tend to show better adjustment, fewer problems, and a greater sense of well-being (Hayslip et al., 2017; Williams, 2011).

What Do You Think?

1. In what ways do you think parenting a grandchild is different from raising one's own child?

2. What challenges might grandparents face in raising their grandchildren?

3. In what ways might raising a grandchild be easier than raising one's own child? ●

Caring for Aging Parents

Despite the popular image of the "sandwich generation"—middle-aged adults scrambling to meet the needs of both dependent children and frail elderly parents and thus sandwiched between the two (Riley & Bowen, 2005)—some experts argue that it is not very accurate (Grundy & Henretta, 2006). In 2012, only 15% of U.S. middle-aged adults reported providing financial support to a parent age 65 or older while raising a minor child or supporting a grown child (Parker & Patten, 2013). Rather than raising young children, most middle-aged parents have adult children. Middle-aged adults with adult children and parents over the age of 65 are more than twice as likely to provide financial support for their children than their parents, but they provide similar levels of emotional support to both generations (Birditt et al., 2017; Parker & Patten, 2013). Although the popular "sandwich" metaphor may exaggerate the number of middle-aged adults who *financially* support two generations, most adults do provide *emotional* support and assistance to multiple generations (Figure 16.9).

Adults report a range of motivations for providing emotional and financial care to their aging parents, including obligation, reciprocity, and the quality of the relationship (Stuifbergen, Dykstra, Lanting, & van Delden, 2010). Young adults tend to adopt an idealistic perspective, perceiving strong obligations and ability to care for their parents, regardless of the level of care needed. In contrast, middle-aged adults adopt a more realistic perspective as they anticipate the need to provide care and appreciate the responsibilities and sacrifices given the specific level and nature of care needed by a parent (Gans & Silverstein, 2006).

The care that adult children provide aging parents is influenced by the parent–child relationship as well as family circumstances and ethnicity.

FIGURE 16.9

Middle-Aged Adults Provide More Emotional Support to Two Generations Than Financial

% of adults ages 40 to 59 who …

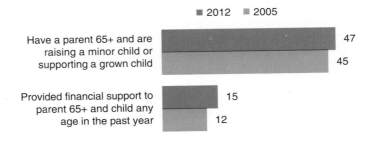

■ 2012 ■ 2005

Have a parent 65+ and are raising a minor child or supporting a grown child	47 / 45
Provided financial support to parent 65+ and child any age in the past year	15 / 12

Source: Reprinted with permission from "The sandwich generation: Rising financial burdens for middle-aged Americans," Pew Research Center, Washington, DC (January, 2013). http://www.pewsocialtrends.org/2013/01/30/the-sandwich-generation/

In one large sample of middle-aged adults in the Netherlands, having few siblings, a widowed parent without a new partner, and a short geographical distance between the parent's and child's homes was positively associated with adult children's provision of care and support to parents (Stuifbergen, Van Delden, & Dykstra, 2008). African American and Hispanic adults at all income levels are more likely than European American non-Hispanic adults to provide aging parents with financial and caregiving assistance; this may reflect the cultural value of familism, mentioned earlier (Shuey & Hardy, 2003). Similarly, Chinese, Japanese, and Korean women tend to provide care for their husband's aging parents, who tend to live with them (Montgomery, Rowe, & Kosloski, 2007; Zhan, 2004). In Thai families, intergenerational relations between older-age parents and their children remain close throughout life, with over 70% of older persons living with or next to a child (Knodel & Chayovan, 2009).

Generally speaking, parents and adult children who have a lifetime of close and positive relations tend to remain close, with adult children providing more assistance than do those whose family relations are less positive (Whitbeck & Hoyt, 1994). In middle age, many people look back and gain more appreciation for their parents' assistance and sacrifices over the years. Relationships between mothers and daughters, usually closer than other parent–child relationships, tend to become more intimate and complex as daughters enter middle age (Fingerman, 2000, 2001; Lefkowitz & Fingerman, 2003). Although parent–child ties influence caregiving, adults with weak parent–child relationships often provide care to parents out of a sense of duty (Silverstein, Conroy, Wang, Giarrusso, & Bengtson, 2002). Daughters, especially those who live in close proximity, are most likely to be parental caregivers (Pillemer & Suitor, 2014).

Middle-aged adults often provide emotional support to their parents.
Alistair Heap / Alamy Stock Photo

As adults' caregiving responsibilities increase, such as when an elderly parent develops dementia, they are more likely to experience conflicts among their many roles. Caregivers can feel overwhelmed by their obligations to parents, children, spouses, employers, and friends, and this role overload is associated with anxiety, exhaustion, and depression

(Killian, Turner, & Cain, 2005; Savia, Almeida, Davey, & Zant, 2008). One study found that relationship quality declined over a 5-year period as older adults' disability increased and their children provided more assistance with self-care tasks (Kim et al., 2016). Adults of ethnic and cultural groups that emphasize familism and the duty to care for elders may experience more anxiety and depression with caregiving than adults from other ethnicities (Dilworth-Anderson, Goodwin, & Williams, 2004).

There are also career and economic costs associated with caregiving. For example, men and women who participated in the Survey of Health, Ageing, and Retirement in Europe showed that giving informal care to one's elderly parents was associated with significant costs in terms of employment opportunities and participation (Bolin, Lindgren, & Lundborg, 2008). Among a U.S. sample of caregivers who reduced their work hours or left the workforce to care for a parent, about half reported losing income (Aumann, Galinsky, Sakai, Brown, & Bond, 2010). As women are more likely than men to be expected to provide care, caregiving can interfere with women's employment, causing losses in hours and earnings. According to one estimate, women who become caregivers to their parents may lose over $300,000, on average, in income and benefits over their lifetime (MetLife Mature Market Institute, National Alliance for Caregiving, & Center for Long Term Care Research and Policy, 2011). Caregiving responsibilities for parents may place female caregivers at risk of living in poverty and requiring public assistance later in life (Lee, Tang, Kim, & Albert, 2015). Caregivers who face multiple career and childrearing demands are at risk for role strain, depressive symptoms, and a reduced sense of personal mastery and self-efficacy, and they engage in fewer outside activities (Mausbach et al., 2012; Y.-N. Wang, Shyu, Chen, & Yang, 2011).

THINKING IN CONTEXT 16.3

1. What are the effects of divorce during the adult years? What contextual factors influence adaptation to divorce, and how might these factors change over the adult years?

2. Imagine that you are studying a family with middle-aged parents and an emerging adult child. What factors might influence family interactions and relationships?

3. What are some of the challenges of becoming a parent in middle adulthood? How might adults address these?

CAREERS IN MIDDLE ADULTHOOD

>> **LO 16.4** **Discuss influences on job satisfaction and retirement planning during middle adulthood.**

Throughout adult life, work is usually the mainstay that structures people's days, contributes to a sense of identity and self-esteem, and provides a number of benefits aside from income. Through work, people have opportunities to interact with others; to display generativity by creating products, items, and ideas by advising and mentoring others; and to contribute to the support of their families and communities. Young adults tend to gravitate toward jobs that emphasize extrinsic rewards such as high salaries and employee benefits, whereas middle-aged employees tend to place greater importance on the intrinsic rewards of work, such as friendships with coworkers, job satisfaction, self-esteem, and feeling that one is making a difference (Sterns & Huyck, 2001). As described in the following section, job satisfaction is more closely associated with the pleasures of surmounting challenges, engaging in creative pursuits, being productive, and other intrinsic rewards of work than with high pay and other extrinsic rewards.

Job Satisfaction

A job is a source of income, but job satisfaction is influenced by more than high pay, as evidenced by research on gender differences in the workplace. Regardless of work experience, women tend to earn less than men (i.e., women earn, on average, $.80 for every dollar men earn) (AAUW, 2017). The gender pay gap also grows with age. In 2015, among full-time workers ages 20 to 24, women were paid 90% of what men were paid on a weekly basis. By the time workers reach 55 to 64 years old, women are paid only 74% of what their male peers are paid. Paradoxically, however, women tend to show higher job satisfaction than men or, in some cases, similar levels of satisfaction to men (Donohue & Heywood, 2013; Zou, 2015). Research with European samples suggests that the gender–job satisfaction paradox is more apparent in countries where the job market is more challenging for women and nonexistent in countries that offer equal opportunities for women (Kaiser, 2007). Some research suggests that the gender difference lies in work orientations and preferences for extrinsic versus intrinsic rewards. Job satisfaction is more closely associated with intrinsic rewards (e.g., the pleasures of surmounting challenges, engaging in creative pursuits, and being productive) than with extrinsic rewards (e.g., high salaries and benefits).

For women, job satisfaction is positively linked to both extrinsic and intrinsic rewards, but for men, job satisfaction tends to be positively linked primarily to extrinsic rewards (Linz & Semykina, 2013).

Samples of adults from the United States, Europe, China, Turkey, and Japan show that age is generally associated with increases in job satisfaction (Barnes-Farrell & Matthews, 2007). Age-related increases in satisfaction are related to shifts in reward preferences. Young adults tend to gravitate toward jobs that emphasize extrinsic rewards, whereas middle-aged employees tend to place greater importance on intrinsic rewards of work, including friendships with coworkers, self-esteem, and feeling that they are making a difference (Kehr, Strasser, & Paulus, 2018). Age-related increases in job satisfaction are greater for professionals than blue-collar workers (Ng & Feldman, 2010). Blue-collar workers tend to have more highly structured jobs with fewer opportunities to control their activities than do white-collar workers, which may contribute to their relatively lower level of job satisfaction (Avolio & Sosik, 1999; Hu, Kaplan, & Dalal, 2010). Males in physically demanding occupations, such as laborers and construction workers, may find that the physical changes that occur over the course of middle adulthood make them less able to perform the tasks their jobs require (Gilbert & Constantine, 2005). In addition, older workers face increased risk of experiencing age discrimination, discussed in the accompanying Applying Developmental Science feature.

Some midlife adults experience job burnout, a sense of mental exhaustion that accompanies long-term job stress, excessive workloads, and reduced feelings of control. Burnout is relatively frequent in professions that are interpersonally demanding and whose demands may exceed workers' coping skills, such as in the helping professions of health care, human services, and teaching (Malinen & Savolainen, 2016; Shanafelt et al., 2015). Employee burnout is a serious problem in the workplace, not simply through its association with poor job satisfaction. Burnout is linked with impairments in attention and concentration abilities, depression, illnesses, poor job performance, workplace injuries, and high levels of employee absenteeism and turnover (Deligkaris, Panagopoulou, Montgomery, & Masoura, 2014; Shirom & Melamed, 2005). When workers receive social support, assistance in managing workloads and reducing stress, and opportunities to participate in creating an attractive workplace environment, they are less likely to experience job burnout (Warr, 2007).

APPLYING DEVELOPMENTAL SCIENCE

Age Discrimination

As workers approach later midlife they are more likely to experience age discrimination in the workplace.
Joe Radle/Getty

With their increased lifespan, better health, and later childbearing relative to prior generations, baby boomers, adults in their early 50s to early 70s, are spending more years in the workforce than their parents and grandparents. In 2017, baby boomers comprised one quarter of the U.S. workforce (R. Fry, 2018). Workers over 50 are often valued for

their experience, knowledge, and ability to keep cool in crisis (Dennis & Thomas, 2007). However, older workers are also at risk to experience age discrimination in the workplace.

Examples of age discrimination include older workers being turned down for a job or promotion in favor of younger workers who are paid less, being disproportionately targeted in company layoffs, or being excluded from important meetings and key assignments. Older workers are also sometimes stereotyped as inflexible, conservative, less engaged, less sharp, unwilling to adapt to technology, and having physical limitations that may cost a company more for health insurance and related benefits (Gee, Pavalko, & Long, 2007). Blatant forms of ageism include jokes or patronizing behavior accompanying assumptions of frailty, mental incompetence, or age-related health ailments (Palmore, Branch, & Harris, 2005). Overall, the risk of experiencing age discrimination shows two peaks: as workers approach age 50 and as they near retirement (Roscigno, Mong, Byron, & Tester, 2007).

(Continued)

(Continued)

One recent study examined the prevalence of age discrimination by sending three resumes that differed only in respondent age (about ages 30, 40, and 65) to 13,000 jobs posted online in 12 U.S. cities (Neumark et al., 2017). Even though the resumes listed identical skills and experience, older candidates were less likely to receive callbacks from employers. Women experienced greater rates of age discrimination than men. Given women's longer life expectancy, age discrimination may be more financially damaging. Women who report age discrimination tend to report greater financial strain and lower levels of life satisfaction (Shippee, Wilkinson, Schafer, & Shippee, 2017). Research with U.K. adults suggests that people of color are more likely to experience age discrimination (Drydakis, MacDonald, Chiotis, & Somers, 2018). Age discrimination is not unique to the United States or United Kingdom. It has been documented in 29 countries (Bratt, Abrams, Swift, Vauclair, & Marques, 2018). Age discrimination in online job applications may include dropdown menus for year that go back only to the 1980s, effectively screening out anyone who graduated or had work experience before those dates (Terrell, 2017). Others list a preference for "digital natives"—people who grew up using computers—deterring middle-aged adults.

In 1967, President Lyndon B. Johnson signed the Age Discrimination in Employment Act (ADEA), a formal acknowledgment of the existence of ageism in the workplace. The purpose of the ADEA is "to promote the employment of older persons based on ability rather than age, to prohibit arbitrary age discrimination in employment and to help employers and workers find ways to address problems arising from the impact of age on employment" (29 USC 621(b)). The original legislation protected employees between the ages of 40 and 65. In 1978, Congress passed an amendment to extend the age of the protected group from 65 to 70, and on January 1, 1987, the age cap was lifted completely (McCann, 2003). There is an exemption, however, for workers who are responsible for public safety, including firefighters, police officers, pilots, and others (Dennis & Thomas, 2007). These workers are required to retire at an earlier age, often by 55 or 60. Although the ADEA has existed for over three decades, age discrimination persists in and out of the workplace.

What Do You Think?

1.   What might be the psychological effects of experiencing age discrimination?

2.   How might employers reduce age discrimination in the workplace?

3.   What advice do you have for an adult experiencing age discrimination? ●

Planning for Retirement

Retirement planning is a process that often begins once the adult becomes aware that it is looming on the horizon; however, it should begin much earlier. Retirement planning is important because retirement represents a major life transition, and adults who plan ahead for the financial and lifestyle changes that accompany retirement tend to show better adjustment and greater life satisfaction (Adams & Rau, 2011).

Although most U.S. adults will spend many years in retirement, most are not financially prepared for it. Less than half of U.S. adults report thinking about financial planning for retirement sometimes or never (U.S. Federal Reserve, 2014). It is estimated that workers should plan for retirement income of at least 70% to 80% of their current preretirement income, yet about one third of middle-class households have no savings, including nearly 20% of adults ages 55 to 61 (Wells Fargo, 2014). The median retirement account savings balance among all households headed by adults ages 56 to 61 was only about $17,000—and only $8,000 for those ages 50 to 55 (Morrissey, 2016). People with a college degree are more likely to have retirement savings (75%) than those with a high school degree (41%) or no high school degree (20%) (U.S. Federal Reserve, 2017). White non-Hispanic adults are about twice as likely to have retirement savings accounts (60%) than Black (34%) or Hispanic (30%) adults. There are also large racial disparities in retirement savings, with White non-Hispanic adults having saved over three times as much as those who are Black or Hispanic (a median of $77,000, $25,000, and $23,000, respectively) (U.S. Federal Reserve, 2017). Income disparities associated with low levels of education and ethnic minority status contribute to differences in retirement savings. Retirement planning is also influenced by psychological factors. For example, adults with more positive beliefs about their ability to control aspects of aging are more likely to financially plan for retirement as compared with those with an intermittent, rather than constant, awareness of the aging process (Heraty & McCarthy, 2015).

Financial resources often are the determining factor with regard to whether and when an older adult retires. Changing economics influence older adults' abilities to retire, as personal retirement investments such as IRAs and 401(k) plans may lose value unexpectedly. The creation of Social Security was designed to aid elders in affording retirement. Yet in 2012, about 4 in 10 of all U.S. adults expressed concern over whether they would have enough income and assets in retirement (Morin & Fry, 2012).

Most adults are aware that retirement planning entails preparing for changes in income, but planning for retirement should also include recognition of impending lifestyle changes and changes in the amount of free time available and how it will be used. Retirement represents a major life transition, and adults who plan ahead for the financial and lifestyle changes that accompany retirement tend to show better adjustment and greater life satisfaction than those who do not plan (Adams & Rau, 2011; M. Wang, Henkens, & van Solinge, 2011). Work activities encompass much of adults' days, beginning in early adulthood. With retirement, most adults find that they need to determine how they will spend their time, often for the first time in their lives. With virtually unlimited possibilities, some adults may feel overwhelmed, at least temporarily; others are glad

to devote themselves to endeavors they have "always wanted" to pursue or to seek out entirely new activities and areas of interest. Some "give back" to the community or to their preretirement careers by volunteering. Others may learn a new language, accomplish home renovations, or spend more time with family members. In contrast, retirees who do not plan how they will spend their time may find themselves adrift. Planning an active life also contributes to postretirement adjustment and happiness (Noone, Stephens, & Alpass, 2009).

THINKING IN CONTEXT 16.4

1. What are some of the contextual factors that might influence job satisfaction? Consider the type of job, location, individual characteristics and skills, as well as demographic characteristics such as sex, ethnicity, and socioeconomic status.

2. Suppose you were to create an intervention or workshop to encourage middle-aged adults to plan for their retirement. What information would you include? Identify considerations in advising middle-aged adults.

APPLY YOUR KNOWLEDGE

"I'm so exhausted," said Marilyn. "I'm working so hard and juggling so much that I can't keep up." At 52, Marilyn held multiple roles but didn't feel a sense of control or competence in any of them. Her job was a source of stress and disappointment. Passed up for managerial work, Marilyn remained at the lower rungs of the corporate ladder despite the many new young hires each year. Sometimes she feels out of touch at meetings as she no longer keeps up with the technology and slang. For example, in a marketing meeting, she was embarrassed to ask the speaker for a definition of *tweet*.

Marilyn's home life is filled with adjustments. After her youngest child moved out, Marilyn and her husband, Gene, began to feel that they no longer knew or cared deeply about each other; their connection was lost. Soon Gene moved out and began divorce proceedings. Many days, Marilyn finds it hard to get out of bed and get dressed for work, feeling that the good years of her life are over and the few remaining decades will simply get worse.

Upon her daughter's arrest for drug use and subsequent stay at a long-term substance abuse treatment facility, Marilyn took on responsibility as guardian for her 7-year-old grandson, Mikey. Marilyn was furious with her daughter's irresponsibility and felt that both she and her daughter had failed as mothers. She loved Mikey dearly but felt ill equipped to care for a child while working

full-time and managing her own sadness over the divorce and her daughter's behavior. Mikey's special needs for attention as he missed his mother often led to trouble at school.

Marilyn began to experience anxiety attacks on her way to work each morning. "I never know what the day will bring, and I didn't expect my life to turn out this way," she said to her best friend, Jalna. She and Jalna had been friends for 30 years and knew everything about each other. Marilyn doesn't get to see her often because the business of life gets in the way, but her friendship with Jalna helps her cope with the many changes of her life.

1. Does Marilyn's experience reflect normative midlife changes? In what ways is Marilyn's experience typical of middle-aged adults? Which of her experiences are unique to her, reflecting development that is not normative?

2. Compare Marilyn's experiences with marriage, divorce, and grandparenting to research findings in this area.

3. Discuss factors that may influence Marilyn's adjustment to life changes. What contextual factors might ease her adjustment?

4. What changes can the typical middle-aged adult expect with regard to the sense of self, personality, career, marriage, family, and friends?

$SAGE edge™

Visit **edge.sagepub.com/kuther2e** to help you accomplish your coursework goals in an easy-to-use learning environment.

LEARNING OBJECTIVES	SUMMARY	KEY TERMS	IN REVIEW
16.1 Summarize the theories and research on psychosocial development during middle adulthood.	For Erik Erikson, the psychosocial task of middle adulthood is cultivating a sense of generativity. Adults fulfill generative needs through volunteering, teaching, and mentoring others in the workplace and community. Generativity is associated with well-being. Daniel Levinson proposed that the life structure refers to the overall organization of a person's life. During the midlife transition, adults reexamine their life dream established in early adulthood, evaluate their success in achieving it, reevaluate their goals and their relations with their social context, and modify their life structures accordingly. The most popular stereotype about middle age is the midlife crisis, a stressful time in the early to middle 40s when adults are thought to evaluate their lives. Successfully traversing the midlife crisis requires that adults modify their life structure, reevaluate their goals and their relations within their social context, and develop a sense of generativity. The midlife crisis is not universal and depends on individual factors and circumstances rather than age.	Empty nest Generativity versus stagnation Seasons of life Life structure Midlife crisis	According to Erikson, what is the major developmental task of middle adulthood? What is the life structure, and how does it change in middle adulthood? What does research reveal about the existence of the midlife crisis?
16.2 Describe the changes that occur in self-concept, identity, and personality during middle adulthood.	Self-concept becomes more complex and integrated into middle adulthood yet shows remarkable consistency. Over the middle adult years, many adults begin to integrate instrumental and expressive aspects of themselves, becoming more androgynous. Androgyny provides adults with a greater repertoire of skills, which permits them to adapt to a variety of situations with greater ease than do those who are not androgynous. People show unique patterns of Big 5 traits and individual differences in personality traits are highly stable, yet cross-sectional research suggests subtle changes, with agreeableness and conscientiousness increasing and neuroticism, extroversion, and openness declining into middle adulthood, suggesting that adults mellow out with age.	Possible selves Androgyny Big 5 personality traits	What are the roles of subjective age and possible selves in self-concept? How does gender identity shift in middle adulthood? How are Big 5 personality traits associated with well-being?
16.3 Analyze relationships in middle adulthood, including friend, spousal, parent–child, and grandparent relationships.	Friendships improve with age. Similar to earlier periods in life, middle-aged friends share demographic similarities, experiences, and values that make them useful sources of advice for dealing with serious problems. Marital satisfaction tends to increase over the middle adult years. Divorce is challenging at all ages, but middle-aged persons show less of a decline in psychological well-being and overall better adaptation than do young adults. Parents and adult children tend to become closer as they mature. Grandparent involvement is associated with child well-being and adolescent adjustment. The level of care that adult children provide aging parents is influenced by the parent–child relationship as well as family circumstances and ethnicity. Adults who care for aging parents may experience role overload.		Describe friendships in middle adulthood. What is the nature of marriage and divorce in middle adulthood? Discuss the diverse parenting roles middle-aged adults may experience. What types of care do middle-aged adults typically provide their parents? Describe the roles grandparents play in the lives of their grandchildren.

| 16.4 Discuss influences on job satisfaction and retirement planning during middle adulthood. | Job satisfaction tends to increase in middle adulthood, especially with career advancement but more so for professionals than blue-collar workers and men than women. The glass ceiling (lower rates of career advancement) that women and minority members face contributes to lower rates of job satisfaction. Some middle-aged adults experience a rise in job burnout, which is associated with cognitive and mental health impairments, reductions in productivity, and increases in injuries, absenteeism, and turnover. Retirement planning entails planning for not only changes in income but also changes in lifestyle and how we spend our time. Retirement planning is associated with better adjustment and satisfaction. | | What is job satisfaction, and what factors influence it?

Summarize recent trends in retirement planning. |

PART VIII

Late Adulthood

CHAPTER 17:
Physical and Cognitive Development in Late Adulthood

CHAPTER 18:
Socioemotional Development in Late Adulthood

In late adulthood, the balance of gains and losses shifts. Physical losses increase; however, older adults' functioning varies widely. They compensate for losses by modifying their behaviors and environment. The benefits of regular exercise in late adulthood include increases in strength, balance, and endurance as well as improved physiological function, better mental health, and higher quality of life. Although older adults show declines in fluid intelligence, they remain adaptive problem solvers throughout adulthood, performing best on everyday problems that are relevant to the contexts they experience in their daily lives. Motivated to engage in reminiscence and life review, older adults work to find continuity, come to terms with choices, and assign meaning to their lives.

Within the home context, marital satisfaction increases in late adulthood. Parent–child relationships shift as adult children provide increasing assistance to their elderly parents. With increases in leisure time, the peer context rises in salience in older adulthood. Friendships become more important, more fulfilling, and more activity based. Most elderly friendships are old relationships, established much earlier in life. Retirement and the loss of the work context is an important transition for many older adults, and success is influenced by a sense of control over the decision. Overall, the developmental changes older adults experience in physical and cognitive domains are offset by gains in socioemotional functioning and are influenced by the multiple interacting contexts in which they are embedded.

DR. KUTHER'S
CHALK TALKS

Watch at
edge.sagepub.com/kuther2e

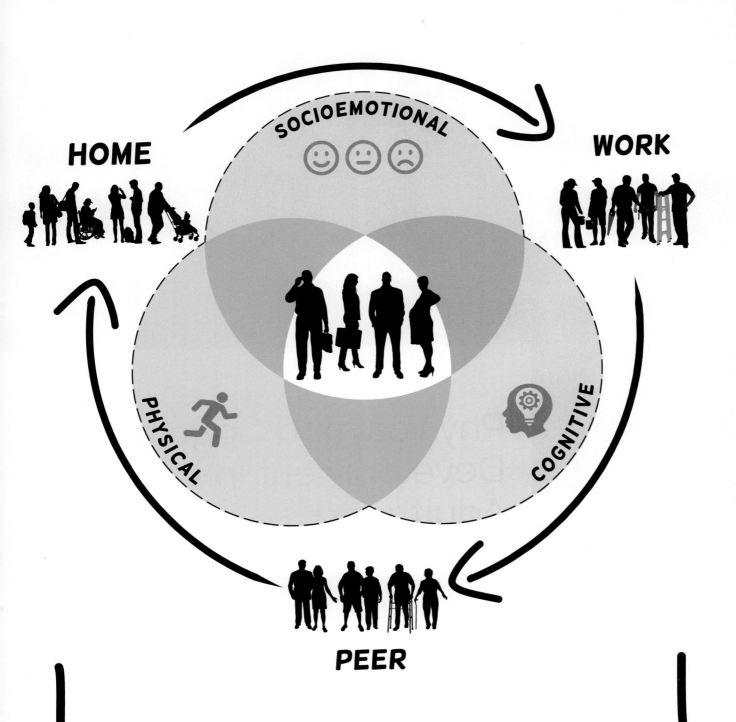

HOME

WORK

SOCIOEMOTIONAL

PHYSICAL

COGNITIVE

PEER

Kirill Kukhmar\TASS via Getty I

17

Physical and Cognitive Development in Late Adulthood

"See you next week, Grandma!" Travis called out to his grandmother, Sylvia, as he headed toward his car. At 75 years of age, Sylvia lives alone in a condo located in a development designed for senior citizens. Thanks to careful monitoring of her finances—and some help from her children—Sylvia is able to afford a housekeeper who does house cleaning and laundry once a week and an aide who stops by a couple of days a week to help

Sylvia with tasks such as grocery shopping. Because of poor vision, Sylvia no longer drives at night—and avoids driving when she can. As Sylvia explained, "Without my hearing aid, I'm no fun at the dinner table. Physically, I'm not as quick as I used to be, but I get along just fine. The days of 5K races are over for me." Sylvia has noticed that she often forgets new information, like people's names, so she works hard to remember names by repeating

Learning Objectives

17.1 Discuss age-related changes in brain and body systems in late adulthood, and identify ways that older adults may compensate for changes.

17.2 Identify risk and protective factors for health in late adulthood.

17.3 Summarize common dementias, including characteristics, risk and protective factors, and treatment.

17.4 Analyze patterns of cognitive change in late adulthood.

Digital Resources

Connect: Life Expectancy

Watch: Exercise: The Fountain of Youth

▶ **Lives in Context Video 17.1:** Health Profiles and Successful Aging: Late Adulthood

Connect: Preventing Dementia With Mental Stimulation

Explore: With Age Comes Wisdom

▶ **Lives in Context Video 17.2:** Caring for Older Adults

---

them. Overall, she feels that she is still good at making decisions. Her grandchildren—even the oldest, who recently graduated from medical school—turn to her for advice and tell her she is wise. In many ways, Sylvia is the picture of successful aging.

As is the case with people in other ages in life, older adults vary in their health and functioning. Many, like Sylvia, remain free of serious physical and cognitive disabilities. All older adults experience declines in physical and cognitive areas, and many experience chronic illnesses that pose demands for adaptation. In this chapter, we examine the physical and cognitive side of aging, including the challenges to physical and mental health that older adults face.

PHYSICAL DEVELOPMENT IN LATE ADULTHOOD

» LO 17.1 Discuss age-related changes in brain and body systems in late adulthood, and identify ways that older adults may compensate for changes.

By late adulthood, biological aging affects all body structures and systems. Although senescence began in early adulthood, the changes are gradual. Most adults show little awareness of the changes until they are faced with clear evidence of aging in their appearance, such as a full head of silver hair; decreased athletic performance, such as difficulty carrying heavy groceries up a flight of stairs; or age-related ailments, such as cataracts or osteoporosis.

Appearance

The skin loses collagen and elasticity throughout adulthood and becomes more dry as oil glands become less active (Quan & Fisher, 2015). Pigmented marks called age spots often appear on the hands and face. The skin also thins and loses the layer of fat underneath it, making blood vessels more visible, and older adults are more sensitive to cold (Tobin, 2017). Exposure to sunlight exacerbates these changes (Flament, Bazin, & Piot, 2013). The nose and ears grow larger and broader in older adulthood (Farage, Miller, & Maibach, 2015). Hair whitens, and both men and women experience hair loss as hair follicles die, while thin downy hair begins to grow from the scalp follicles of men with hereditary baldness.

Body shape changes in older adulthood as fat is redistributed and accumulates in the abdomen. Sarcopenia, the age-related loss of muscle mass and strength, continues with average losses of 10% to 20%

by 60 to 70 years of age and 30% to 50% from age 70 to 80 (Buford et al., 2010). As discussed later in this chapter, physical activity, especially resistance exercise, can strengthen muscles and offset losses into the 90s (Peterson, Rhea, Sen, & Gordon, 2010; Serra-Rexach et al., 2011).

Brain Aging

As we age, the brain changes in predictable ways. Brain volume shrinks as dendrites contract and are lost, accompanied by a decrease in synapses and a loss of glial cells (Raz & Daugherty, 2018). Many neural fibers lose their coating of myelin, and communication among neurons slows accordingly. Declines are especially marked in the prefrontal cortex, responsible for executive functioning and judgment (Lu et al., 2013). However, the reduction in brain volume is, on average, less than half of 1% each year throughout adulthood (Salthouse, 2011). Also, estimates of age-related changes in brain volume vary with measurement and across research studies. For example, some cross-sectional samples that compare adults of different ages at one time show greater age differences in brain volume than do longitudinal samples, which tend to show more continuous and gradual changes in brain volume that are less tied to age (Salthouse, 2011). A program of aerobic exercise has been shown to restore brain volume, especially in the hippocampus, a brain region closely involved with memory, supporting the role individuals have in their own development. For more information about how exercise can improve brain function and cognition, see the Brain and Biological Influences on Development feature on Aerobic Exercise and the Brain.

BRAIN AND BIOLOGICAL INFLUENCES ON DEVELOPMENT

 ## Aerobic Exercise and the Brain

Exercise is associated with neural plasticity, including increases in volume and connectivity.
iStock/Mikolette

One of the most important findings about neurological development in recent years is that the brain retains some plasticity, the capacity to grow and change, throughout life. Physical health is associated with neurological health and plasticity throughout adulthood (U. Braun, Muldoon, & Bassett, 2015). Can improvements in health improve brain function? We know that physical activity has a protective function on health; does it influence neurological and cognitive function? The emerging consensus from a growing body of research is yes, physical activity and cognitive abilities are linked. More physically fit and active older adults tend to show greater brain volume and more efficient activity in areas key to memory and abstract thought (Erickson et al.,

2010; Prakash, Voss, Erickson, & Kramer, 2015). Moreover, exercise training, particularly aerobic exercise, is associated with increases in brain volume and cognitive function, especially executive function in older adults (Kramer & Colcombe, 2018; Stillman, Weinstein, Marsland, Gianaros, & Erickson, 2017).

Cardiovascular exercise and activities that improve coordination are associated with increases in volume and connectivity in the frontal cortex, temporal lobe, and the hippocampus, areas responsible for memory and higher-level cognitive functioning, such as planning and problem solving, and prone to age-related deterioration (Niemann, Godde, & Voelcker-Rehage, 2014; ten Brinke et al., 2015). Aerobic exercise is associated with neurogenesis, the creation of new neurons, in the hippocampus (van Praag, 2008) and prevents age-related atrophy in this area (Firth et al., 2018). Exercise also protects the brain through its positive effect on cardiovascular health, reducing the likelihood of stroke, and increases blood flow to the brain, which protects brain function (Hsu et al., 2018).

Older adults who begin a program of moderate aerobic exercise show improvements in brain function and cognition (Loprinzi, Edwards, Crush, Ikuta, & Del Arco, 2018). In one study (shown in Figure 17.1), greater amounts of physical activity were associated with greater gray matter volume in several areas of the brain, including the prefrontal cortex and hippocampus, over a 9-year period and a reduced risk for cognitive impairment (Erickson et al., 2010). Moreover, even sedentary older adults introduced to a long-term program of moderate physical activity show increases in hippocampal volume over a 2-year period, suggesting that it is never too late to improve physical and neurological function (Rosano et al., 2017). Changes in fitness levels and hippocampal volumes are associated with improvements in recognition and spatial memory (Maass et al., 2015). These exercise experiments demonstrate that the brain remains modifiable throughout adulthood and that aerobic exercise offers important opportunities for neural plasticity (Hötting & Röder, 2013).

Although the phrase "use it or lose it" is often used in reference to cognitive function, recent research suggests that the aging brain can do more than just retain its functions; plasticity means that it can also grow. Perhaps the phrase should be changed to "use it to improve it."

What Do You Think?

1. How do these findings illustrate the lifespan principle that domains of development, such as physical, cognitive, and socioemotional development, interact? (See Chapter 1.)

2. How might you convey these findings to an older adult family member? What advice would you provide? ●

FIGURE 17.1

Changes in Hippocampal Volume With Aerobic Exercise

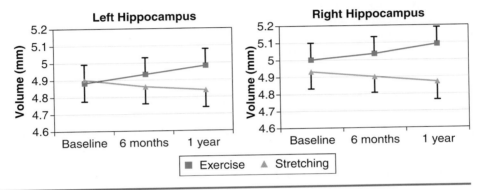

Source: Erickson et al. (2011). Reprinted with permission.

FIGURE 17.2

Age Differences in Neural Activity During a Memory Task

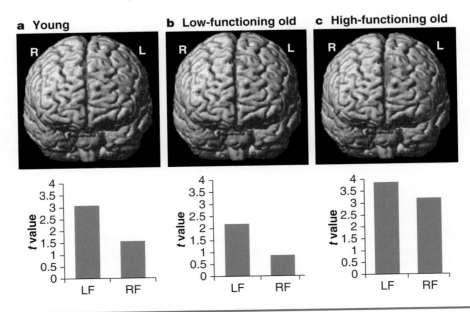

Source: Hedden and Gabrieli (2004). Reprinted with permission.

Myelin losses contribute to cognitive declines with aging (Peters & Kemper, 2012). The last areas of the brain to myelinate are also the first to show reductions in myelin, a pattern some experts call the "last-in first-out" hypothesis of brain aging (Bender, Völkle, & Raz, 2016). The sensory regions of the brain, including the areas responsible for vision and hearing, and the motor cortex are the first brain areas to myelinate in infancy; they are also the last areas to show loss with age (Wu, Kumar, & Yang, 2016). Finally, some myelination continues throughout adulthood, but at a slower rate, permitting some plasticity (S. Wang & Young, 2014).

The brain retains plasticity and compensates for structural changes throughout older adulthood. Older adults' brains compensate for cognitive declines by showing more brain activity and using different brain areas in solving problems than younger adults (Turner & Spreng, 2012). Older adults often show brain activity (indicated in red in Figure 17.2) that is spread out over a larger area, including both hemispheres, compensating for neural losses (Daselaar & Cabeza, 2005; Reuter-Lorenz & Cappell, 2008). Sometimes neural compensation can help older adults perform as well as young adults. For example, in one study, older adults compensated for lower levels of activity in the parietal and occipital lobes with greater activity in the frontal lobes and performed better on a working memory task than did younger adults (Osorio, Fay, Pouthas, & Ballesteros, 2010).

Age-related brain changes are not always apparent in adults' functioning. Adults' brains naturally compensate for losses through **cognitive reserve**, the ability to make flexible and efficient use of available brain resources that permits cognitive efficiency, flexibility, and adaptability (Barulli & Stern, 2013; Nair, Sabbagh, Tucker, & Stern, 2014). Cognitive reserve is a type of plasticity cultivated throughout life from experience and environmental factors. Educational and occupational attainment and engagement in leisure activities allow some adults to cope with age-related changes better than others and show more successful aging (Barulli & Stern, 2013; Chapko, McCormack, Black, Staff, & Murray, 2018). For example, bilingualism is associated with cognitive benefits throughout life. Adults who have daily experiences in using two languages, such as determining when to use one and inhibit another, show enhanced cognitive control abilities, more mental flexibility, and better ability to handle tasks involving switching, inhibition, and conflict monitoring (Grant, Dennis, & Li, 2014; L. Li et al., 2017). In addition, bilingual older adults show preserved white matter integrity, especially in the frontal lobe, as compared with their monolingual peers (Olsen et al., 2015; Pliatsikas, Moschopoulou, & Saddy, 2015).

A particularly exciting finding is that neurogenesis, the creation of new neurons, continues throughout life. New neurons are created in the hippocampus and striatum (a subcortical part of the brain responsible for coordinating motivation with body movement) and the olfactory bulb throughout life but at a much slower rate than prenatally (Ernst et al., 2014; Gonçalves, Schafer, & Gage, 2016; Sailor, Schinder, & Lledo, 2017). Most of these neurons die off, but some survive, especially if exposed to experiences that require learning. Research with mice suggests that intense physical activity, such as running, may promote the survival of new neurons (Trinchero et al., 2017). As with neurogenesis early in life, surviving neurons migrate to the parts of the brain where they will function and create synapses with other neurons (S. M. G. Braun & Jessberger, 2014), permitting lifelong plasticity (Obernier, Tong, & Alvarez-Buylla, 2014). It is estimated that about 2% of neurons are renewed each year (Spalding et al., 2013). The corresponding synaptogenesis is associated with learning and plays a role in cognition and in stress and emotional responses, contributing to plasticity and the maintenance of cognitive abilities and advances in psychosocial maturing in the adult years (Cameron & Glover, 2015; Gonçalves et al., 2016; Nelson & Alkon, 2015; Sailor et al., 2017).

The Senses

As we age, the way in which our senses process information changes. Over the adult years, vision, hearing, and taste and smell gradually decline. These changes can affect older adults' everyday activities, abilities to engage in self-care tasks, and social interactions.

Vision

As in middle adulthood (see Chapter 15), virtually all older adults have difficulty seeing objects up close. In later adulthood, the lens yellows, the vitreous clouds, less light reaches the retina, and it becomes more difficult to see in dim light and to adapt to dramatic changes in light, such as those that accompany night driving (Owsley, 2016). Many adults develop **cataracts**, a clouding of the lens resulting in blurred, foggy vision that makes driving hazardous and can lead to blindness (Kline & Li, 2005). Cataracts are the result of a combination of hereditary and environmental factors associated with oxidative damage, including illnesses such as diabetes and behaviors such as smoking (David, Nancy, & Ying-Bo, 2010; J. S. L. Tan et al., 2008). By age 80, more than half of adults have cataracts (American Academy of Ophthalmology, 2011), which can be corrected through a surgical procedure in which the lens is replaced with an artificial lens.

In addition to the lens, other parts of the eye show structural changes (see Figure 17.3). Cells in the retina and optical nerve are lost with aging (Owsley, 2016). Some older adults experience **macular degeneration**, a substantial loss of cells in the center area of the retina, the macula, causing blurring and eventual loss of central vision (Chakravarthy, Evans, & Rosenfeld, 2010; Owsley, 2016). Hereditary and environmental factors, such as smoking and atherosclerosis, influence the onset of macular degeneration (Myers et al., 2014). A healthy diet, including green leafy vegetables high in Vitamins A, C, and E, as well as vegetables rich in carotenoids, such as carrots, may protect the retina and offset damage caused by free radicals (Mares, Millen, Lawler, & Blomme, 2017; Sin, Liu, & Lam, 2013). Laser surgery, medication, and corrective eyewear can sometimes restore some vision and treat the early stages of macular degeneration. However, macular degeneration is the leading cause of blindness (Chakravarthy et al., 2010; Jager, Mieler, & Miller, 2008).

Most of these changes in vision are so gradual that they may go unnoticed in people who do not visit an ophthalmologist regularly for eye examinations (Owsley, 2016). Substantial vision loss, however, can have a serious effect on older adults' daily lives as it interferes not only with driving but also with reading, watching television, and doing a variety of daily activities from cooking to banking. Not surprisingly,

Presbyopia tends to worsen in older adulthood, making everyday tasks such as reading fine print on a label challenging.
iStock/DaveMcDPhoto

older adults with vision loss participate less than their peers in recreational and sports activities (Alma et al., 2011) and are more likely to be depressed (Tabrett & Latham, 2010), especially when vision loss interferes with their day-to-day functioning and independence (van Nispen, Vreeken, Comijs, Deeg, & van Rens, 2016). In a sample of adults from 10 European countries, vision loss was associated with concentration difficulty; losing interest and enjoyment in activities; feeling fatigued, irritable, and tearful; having less hope for the future; and even wishing for death (Mojon-Azzi, Sousa-Poza, & Mojon, 2008).

Hearing

As described in Chapter 15, age-related hearing loss (known as presbycusis) typically begins in middle adulthood. It increases in older adulthood, with cell losses in the inner ear and cortex (Quaranta et al., 2015). Older adults experience difficulty distinguishing high-frequency sounds, soft sounds of all frequencies, and complex tone patterns and show less activation of the auditory cortex in response to speech as compared with younger adults (Hwang, Li, Wu, Chen, & Liu, 2007; Wettstein & Wahl, 2016). As in middle adulthood, men tend to suffer hearing loss earlier and to a greater extent than do women (Cruickshanks et al., 2010; Helzner et al., 2005). About two thirds of older adults experience hearing loss (F. R. Lin, Thorpe, Gordon-Salant, & Ferrucci, 2011), which can greatly diminish quality of life and poses health risks. The inability to hear car horns and other street sounds or to hear the telephone or doorbell is a risk to safety but also to self-esteem. Turning up the volume to hear a television or radio program and then being asked by others to turn down the volume can be frustrating to older adults and their loved ones. Difficulty hearing others' speech can socially

FIGURE 17.3

Age-Related Changes in the Eye

Older Eye

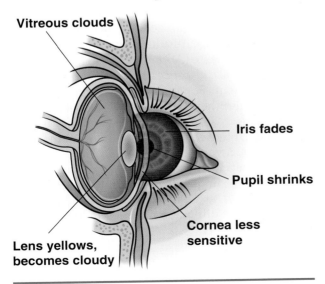

Vitreous clouds

Iris fades

Pupil shrinks

Cornea less sensitive

Lens yellows, becomes cloudy

isolate older adults, reducing their social network, increasing feelings of loneliness and depression, and reducing life satisfaction.

Many older adults compensate for their hearing loss by reducing background noise, when possible, and paying attention to nonverbal cues such as lip movements, facial expressions, and body language to optimize their ability to hear and participate in conversations. Hearing aids are widely available, but research suggests they are underused for several reasons: social attitudes that undervalue the importance of hearing, stigma associated with being seen wearing hearing aids, and their cost, which is typically not covered by health insurance (Laplante-Lévesque, Hickson, & Worrall, 2010). Quality of life for older adults can be improved with successful hearing loss management, which may include education about communication effectiveness, hearing aids, assistive listening devices, and cochlear implants for severe hearing loss (Wettstein & Wahl, 2016). When hearing aids no longer provide benefit, cochlear

Presbycusis and other forms of hearing loss become more common in older adulthood. Hearing loss management, including examinations and communication with physicians, can improve quality of life in older adults who experience losses.
iStock/FangXiaNuo

implantation is the treatment of choice with excellent results even in octogenarians (Quaranta et al., 2015).

Smell and Taste

Sensitivity to smell declines throughout adulthood beginning as early as the 20s (Margran & Boulton, 2005) but is usually not noticeable until late in midlife (Finkelstein & Schiffman, 1999; Hawkes, 2006). By the 60s, olfaction tends to decline markedly (J. Wang, Sun, & Yang, 2016). About one third of adults experience substantial disruptions in their ability to smell by age 80 (Attems, Walker, & Jellinger, 2015). In a classic study, young, middle, and older adults were asked to identify 40 different smells, such as peanut butter and gas (Doty et al., 1984). Young and middle adults performed at similar levels, but performance declined rapidly at age 60, more rapidly for men than women (Morgan, Covington, Geisler, Polich, & Murphy, 1997). However, individuals vary. Some show marked declines and others more gradual change. The odor itself might matter in determining adults' performance on olfactory tasks. Research suggests that older adults are as able as younger adults to identify and remember unpleasant odors, but they show decline in their abilities to identify and remember pleasant odors (Larsson, Oberg-Blåvarg, & Jönsson, 2009).

Recent research with over 1,100 Swedish adults ages 40 to 90 has suggested that poor olfactory performance predicts mortality over a 10-year period (Ekström et al., 2017). Similar findings occurred with a U.S. sample of 2,400 adults ages 53 to 97 followed for 17 years (Schubert et al., 2016), suggesting that olfactory loss might indicate deteriorating health.

Smell and taste are linked such that declines in olfactory abilities hold implications for their abilities to taste. Older adults are generally less sensitive to taste as compared with young and middle-aged adults (Schubert et al., 2012). They also produce less saliva with age, resulting in a dry mouth that interferes with taste (Abrams, 2014). There are also large individual differences, similar to other aspects of development. Some individuals show marked declines while others retain ability. Most older adults report that food seems more bland, and they tend to prefer more intense flavors, especially sweetness (de Graaf, Polet, & van Staveren, 1994). They may lose interest in eating or, alternatively, may overuse salt and spicy seasonings with poor health consequences. A poor sense of taste can even be a health hazard by making it more difficult for an older adult to detect spoiled food.

Developmental changes in both smell and taste are influenced by many factors, such as general health, chronic disease, medications, and smoking (Imoscopi, Inelmen, Sergi, Miotto, &

FIGURE 17.4

Prevalence of Cardiovascular Disease in Adults, by Age and Sex

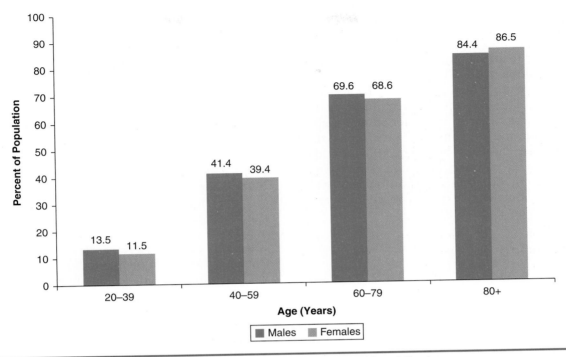

Manzato, 2012; Schiffman, 2009). Most men show greater deficits with age than do women. This is likely the result of different work environments, since men are more likely to work in factories and other environments that expose them to chemicals that can damage sensory abilities. Changes in smell and taste, like other physical capacities, are influenced by our lifelong interactions within our contexts.

Cardiovascular, Respiratory, and Immune Systems

Most adults in their 60s become aware of changes in their cardiovascular and respiratory systems, such as feeling their heart pound and taking longer to catch their breath after running to catch a train. There is a physiological reason for this: With age, the heart experiences cell loss and becomes more rigid. The heart contains pacemaker cells that signal when to initiate a contraction; over time, these cells diminish significantly, by nearly one half, and the heart becomes less responsive to their signals (Mironov, 2009). The arteries stiffen, and the walls accumulate cholesterol and fat plaques, which reduce blood flow; this condition is known

as atherosclerosis and is a cause of heart disease (Paneni, Diaz Cañestro, Libby, Lüscher, & Camici, 2017). As discussed in Chapter 15, cardiovascular disease may be manifested as heart valve problems, arrhythmia, heart attack, and stroke. Heart disease becomes more common with age, as shown in Figure 17.4 (Benjamin et al., 2018).

Just as the heart undergoes changes with age, changes in the respiratory system also reduce the flow of oxygen to the body. Specifically, the lungs gradually lose cells and elasticity over the adult years, substantially reducing the amount of oxygen that enters the system and is absorbed by the blood (B. D. Miller, Wood, & Smith, 2010). Older adults have more trouble breathing, feel more out of breath during physical exertion, and have a harder time catching their breath than younger adults. Experience and lifestyle influence cardiovascular and respiratory system changes. Smoking and exposure to environmental toxins increases damage to the cardiovascular and respiratory systems while physical activity and good nutrition can compensate for decreases in cardiovascular and respiratory function (Paneni et al., 2017).

With age, the immune system becomes less efficient and adaptive (Fenn, Corona, & Godbout, 2013). Declines in immune function place older adults at higher risk of diseases such as flu and pneumonia, cancers, and autoimmune diseases such as rheumatoid arthritis (Gomez, Nomellini, Faunce, & Kovacs, 2008; Lindstrom & Robinson, 2010). Exposure to stress reduces immune function, and the effects increase with age: Older adults often show greater immune impairment in response to stress than younger adults (Vitlic, Lord, & Phillips, 2014). The body's T cells become less effective at protecting the body by attacking foreign substances, and the immune system becomes more likely to malfunction and display an autoimmune response by turning against body tissues. There are, however, large individual differences in immune function. Some people retain strong immune functioning into older adulthood, but most experience at least some declines (Fenn et al., 2013).

Motor Aging

Motor skills change in predictable ways over the lifespan. One study of fine and gross motor performance found that performance showed a pattern of improvement with age up until early adulthood and a decline with age thereafter. Specifically, performance improved from 7- to 9-year-old children through 19- to 25-year-old young adults and then declined from young adulthood into older adulthood, in 66- to 80-year-old adults (Leversen, Haga, Sigmundsson, Rebollo, & Colom, 2012). We have seen that physical activity can compensate for age-related declines in muscle and strength. A lifetime of regular physical activity is associated with greater mobility in older adulthood (Boyer, Andriacchi, & Beaupre, 2012).

Changes in *balance*, the ability to control the body's position in space, is a particularly important influence on older adults' mobility (Payne & Isaacs, 2016). Balance involves integrating sensory information with awareness of the position of one's body in space and in the surrounding environment (Payne & Isaacs, 2016). As we will see later in this chapter, sensory abilities tend to decline in function, and these declines make balance more difficult to achieve and sustain. However, just as muscle strength can be improved, so can balance. Interventions that encourage exercise and promote strength and balance, such as Tai Chi, can increase balance and strength and offset loss (Khanuja, Joki, Bachmann, & Cuccurullo, 2018; Lesinski, Hortobágyi, Muehlbauer, Gollhofer, & Granacher, 2015). With age, balance requires more attention and taps more cognitive resources. In one study, researchers administered four challenging balance tasks to a large sample of healthy 50- to 64-year-old and 65- to 75-year-old participants (Aslan et al., 2008). Balance tasks included a forward

reach that required participants to stand with their feet together and reach forward as far as they could without losing balance; a timed task that recorded how quickly the adults could stand from a chair, walk 10 feet, return, and sit back down; standing from a seated position in a chair five times, fully straightening the legs each time before sitting back down; and a timed task in which participants stepped up on a 4-inch step five times. Balance performance declined with age. Tasks that ask older adults to multitask and perform cognitive tasks (such as counting backwards by threes) show even greater decrements, suggesting that age-related changes are influenced by the ability to allocate attention and that neurological change plays a role in motor performance (Granacher, Muehlbauer, & Gruber, 2012).

Walking is the result of many integrated functions, including neurological, muscular, and sensory systems (Holtzer, Epstein, Mahoney, Izzetoglu, & Blumen, 2014; Sorond et al., 2015). Gait (the speed at which people walk) speed naturally declines with age, with declines in muscle strength, bone density, and flexibility (Payne & Isaacs, 2016). Many adults compensate for a slowed gait by talking longer steps (Jerome et al., 2015). However, rapid or steep decline in gait speed may indicate overall physiological declines that predict mortality because motor function, specifically gait speed, is a marker of overall health and is used in geriatric assessment in addition to measures of blood pressure, respiration, temperature, and pulse (Kuys, Peel, Klein, Slater, & Hubbard, 2014; Studenski, 2011).

THINKING IN CONTEXT 17.1

1. How might the age-related changes that adults experience in vision and hearing influence their day-to-day functioning and interactions with others? Consider adults' roles in the workplace and at home, as employees, parents, spouses, and friends. What are the practical implications of these developmental changes?

2. To what extent does the phrase "use it or lose it" apply to physical functioning in late adulthood? Provide examples considering areas such as the brain and cardiovascular, respiratory, and immune systems.

3. Contextual factors, such as socioeconomic status, influence all aspects of physical aging, including the rate and form that aging takes. Describe and provide examples of contextual factors that might influence physical development in older adulthood. To what extent do these forces operate earlier in life?

HEALTH IN LATE ADULTHOOD

» LO 17.2 Identify risk and protective factors for health in late adulthood.

Adults today live longer than ever before. The increase in life expectancy over the past century can be attributed to the influence of contextual factors such as advances in health care, nutrition, sanitation, and especially the reduction in infant mortality (Dong, Milholland, & Vijg, 2016). Death during childbirth, a common hazard to women in the early 1900s, is rare in industrialized nations. Breakthroughs in medicine and increases in the availability of health care mean that fewer people die of common ailments such as flu, pneumonia, and heart disease. A greater understanding of the role of behavioral factors such as smoking, exercise habits, and diet also contributes to advances in longevity (White, Greene, Kivimaki, & Batty, 2018). Although cancer remains a leading cause of death, the cancer survival rate, defined as living 5 years after diagnosis, is higher than ever. By 2007, over two thirds of adults diagnosed with cancer in the United States and Canada were survivors, as compared with about one half in 1977 (DeSantis et al., 2014; Siegel, Ma, Zou, & Jemal, 2014).

Advances in life expectancy have led gerontologists to categorize older adults into the **young-old, old-old,** and **oldest-old**. The young-old, ages 65 to 74, tend to be active, healthy, and financially and physically independent. Old-old adults (75 to 84) typically live independently but often experience some physical and mental impairment. The oldest-old, adults 85 years and older, are at highest risk for physical and mental health problems and often are unable to live independently, requiring physical and social support to carry out the tasks of daily life. Although these age categories are thought to predict physical health and dependency, some adults in their mid-60s show advanced signs of aging characteristic of the oldest-old, while others in their late 80s function similarly to old-old adults. Because of this, many developmental researchers categorize older adults not by chronological age but by functioning, using terms such as **successful aging** and impaired aging (Kok, Aartsen, Deeg, & Huisman, 2015). The sections that follow examine health in older adults, including behavioral factors such as nutrition and exercise, as well as chronic illnesses and injuries.

Centenarians, individuals who live past 100 years, are becoming more common (see Lives in Context). There were over 72,000 centenarians recorded in the United States in 2014, about 44% more than in 2000 (J. Xu, 2016). The longest recorded human lifespan is 122 years (Whitney, 1997). The number of centenarians is expected to rise rapidly in the coming decades.

LIVES IN CONTEXT

 ## Centenarians

Adults 90 years of age and older are the fastest growing population in Western countries. Centenarians, once an oddity, are increasingly common.
darolyn quayle / Alamy Stock Photo

It was once thought that it was impossible to live past 100 years of age; however, medical and technological advances have led to a rise in the prevalence of centenarians. In fact, adults 90 years of age and older are the fastest growing population in Western countries, such as Denmark, Italy, Japan, the United Kingdom, the United States, and others (Administration on Aging, 2014; Santos-Lozano Alejandro et al., 2015).

Centenarians tend to be healthier than their same-age peers all throughout life, often delaying the onset of mortality-related diseases and disability until well into their 90s (Ailshire, Beltrán-Sánchez, & Crimmins, 2015; Brandão, Ribeiro, Afonso, & Paúl, 2017). Like all older adults, most centenarians experience chronic age-related diseases, but up to one quarter reach age 100 with no chronic disease

(Continued)

(Continued)

(Ash et al., 2015). For example, in one sample of Australian centenarians, one fifth reported reaching age 100 without experiencing any of the following common diseases: osteoporosis, dementia, cardiovascular disease, respiratory illnesses, cancers, anxiety, and depression. An additional one third reported experiencing one or more of these ailments only after age 80 (Richmond, Law, & KayLambkin, 2012). Moreover, centenarians seem to manage chronic illnesses more effectively than other older adults, with many not experiencing disability until well into their 90s (Sebastiani & Perls, 2012).

With regard to cognitive functioning, research suggests that centenarians fall into two distinct groups. About one half to two thirds appear to reach 100 without cognitive impairment (Ailshire et al., 2015; Corrada, Brookmeyer, Paganini-Hill, Berlau, & Kawas, 2010). Other data with Japanese centenarians showed that primary memory was influenced by advanced age; specifically, the ability to store information declines but the ability to process information is maintained (Inagaki et al., 2009). In contrast, about one third to one half of centenarians show a pattern of lower cognitive performance and dementia (Davey et al., 2013).

Longevity is influenced by both genes and lifestyle factors through epigenetics (Armstrong et al., 2017). (Recall from Chapter 2 that epigenetics is the interactive process by which external or environmental factors can "switch" genes on and off.) For example, families tend to show similarities in lifespan. A particular gene known as the *APOE* gene is associated with longevity, and centenarians show different patterns of *APOE* activation that may be linked with their lower likelihood of disease and longer lifespan (Arai, Sasaki, & Hirose, 2017; Ryu, Atzmon, Barzilai, Raghavachari, & Suh, 2016; Shadyab & LaCroix, 2015). Behavioral and environmental factors, such as nutrition, stress, education, and smoking, may show epigenetic effects on longevity by turning particular genes on and off (Govindaraju, Atzmon, & Barzilai, 2015; Ishioka et al., 2016; Rea & Mills, 2018).

Living a long life may sound appealing, but what most people really aspire to is a long, high-quality life. What factors contribute to quality of life for those who live to an advanced age? One thing that people can choose to pursue is an engaged lifestyle, characterized by positive psychosocial functioning, such as having good relationships with children and being involved with family, friends, and community. Optimism, not feeling lonely, perceiving a sense of control over health issues, and adaptability are all associated with high ratings of perceived health among centenarians (Scelzo et al., 2018; Tigani, Artemiadis, Alexopoulos, Chrousos, & Darviri, 2012). Life satisfaction predicts future happiness and longevity and influences how centenarians frame their subjective evaluations of their own health status (Bishop, Martin, MacDonald, & Poon, 2010; Jopp, Boerner, & Rott, 2016; Yorgason et al., 2018). Centenarians tend to attribute their longevity to lifestyle choices, social relationships and support, and their own attitudes about life, including optimism and adaptability (Freeman, Garcia, & Marston, 2013). In addition, personality traits such as emotional stability, extroversion, openness, and conscientiousness are associated with maintaining a high level of cognitive and adaptive functioning among centenarians (Martin, Baenziger, MacDonald, Siegler, & Poon, 2009).

What Do You Think?

1. Identify some of the challenges and opportunities that come with the rapid increase of the number of centenarians in our society.

2. Provide at least two reasons why you would like to live to become a centenarian and two reasons why you would not want to become a centenarian. ●

Nutrition

As adults age, their nutritional needs change. Losses in muscle mass contribute to weight loss and a slowed metabolism. For this reason, older adults require fewer calories than younger adults, and their diets must be more nutrient dense to meet their nutritional needs with fewer calories (Bernstein, 2017). Their changing dietary needs mean that older adults are less likely to get all of their nutritional needs met through their diet and are therefore at risk for a nutritional deficiency. In fact, it is estimated that two thirds of older adults in many developed countries, including Germany, Italy, Japan, the Netherlands, and the United States, are at risk for malnutrition (Kaiser et al., 2010; van Bokhorst-de van der Schueren et al., 2013). Malnutrition is associated with illness, functional disability, and mortality (Charlton et al., 2013).

Age-related declines in taste and smell may influence older adults' eating habits (Ogawa, Annear, Ikebe, & Maeda, 2017). As adults lose their sense of taste, they may eat less food or choose stronger flavors. Nutrition surveys suggest that older adults consume more sweet and salty foods (Sergi, Bano, Pizzato, Veronese, & Manzato, 2017). Older adults who live alone may be reluctant to shop, cook, and eat by themselves. Bereavement, social isolation, depression, and illnesses, such as cancer, are associated with malnutrition (Boulos, Salameh, & Barberger-Gateau, 2017; van den Broeke et al., 2018). Medication can alter older adults' nutritional needs (Reilly & Ilich, 2017). For example, medications that treat hypertension are associated with increased risk for deficiencies in potassium, magnesium, and zinc, contributors to metabolism, muscle function, bone density, as well as the nervous system, organ functioning, and immunity.

A diet of nutritious foods, including fruits, whole grains, low-fat dairy products, leafy green vegetables, and healthy sources of protein, such as fish, nuts, beans, and chicken, can counter nutrition deficits common in older adulthood. However, this is easier said than done given that many older adults have a lifelong pattern of less healthy food preferences. More critically, many older adults lack access to healthy foods, because of difficulty shopping, stores that lack healthy food options, or affordable food choices.

Vitamin and mineral supplements that provide levels of nutrients equivalent to that of a healthy diet can fill in gaps in older adults' diet. Most (80%) older adults report taking at least one dietary supplement (Gahche, Bailey, Potischman, & Dwyer, 2017). However, the evidence for health benefits for additional nutritional supplementation is mixed. Vitamin D and calcium can help reduce the risk of fractures (Saad, Fausto, & Maisch, 2018). The effects of vitamin supplements on cardiovascular disease and cancer are less clear, with some studies suggesting a protective effect and others none (Blumberg, Bailey, Sesso, & Ulrich, 2018; Rautiainen et al., 2017; Woodside, McGrath, Lyner, & McKinley, 2015).

Catechin, a polyphenol found in green tea, has an antioxidative effect and may protect against age-related declines in cognitive functions such as those associated with learning and memory, as well as progressive neurodegenerative disorders such as Parkinson's and Alzheimer's diseases (Assuncao & Andrade, 2015; Song, Xu, Liu, & Feng, 2011). In one 12-week study, older adults who consumed a catechin supplement showed greater improvements in cognition, specifically attention, language skills, and memory, than did those who consumed a placebo (Calapai et al., 2017).

Omega-3, an oil found in fish that is high in polyunsaturated fatty acids, promotes vascular health and is associated with reduced risk of cardiovascular disease (Lorente-Cebrián et al., 2013). Omega-3 is associated with reduced inflammation and degenerative diseases such as arthritis and potentially Alzheimer's disease (Lorente-Cebrián et al., 2015). In one double-blind study, healthy older adults aged 50 to 75 showed increases in executive function and improvements in white matter integrity and gray matter volume, suggesting that omega-3 may have important implications for neurological health and functioning (Witte et al., 2014). Moreover, consumption of omega-3 appears to have an epigenetic effect on longevity through its action on telomeres, the caps covering the tips of DNA. Recall from Chapter 13 that telomeres shorten with every cell division until they reach a critical length, stopping cell division and preceding cell death. The consumption of omega-3 is associated with slowed and even reduced telomere shortening over 5- to 8-year periods (Farzaneh-Far et al., 2010; Paul, 2011), suggesting that cell aging can be slowed and even extended. Improved nutrition holds the promise of protection against age-related cognitive changes, but more research is needed.

Exercise

As in early and middle adulthood, exercise offers powerful health benefits to older adults. Individuals as old as 80 who begin a program of cardiovascular activity, such as walking, cycling, or aerobic dancing, show gains similar to those of much younger adults. Weightbearing exercise begun as late as 90 years of age can improve blood flow to the muscles and increase muscle size (Bechshøft et al., 2017). The physical benefits of regular exercise influence increases in strength, balance, posture, and endurance and permit older adults to carry out everyday activities such as grocery shopping, lifting grandchildren, reaching for objects, and opening jars and bottles (Peterson et al., 2010). Throughout the adult years, moderate physical activity is associated with improved physiological function, a decreased incidence of disease, and reduced incidence of disability (Barengo, Antikainen, Borodulin, Harald, & Jousilahti, 2017; Fielding et al., 2017).

Exercise is good not only for the body but also for the mind. Just as earlier in life, exercise offers older adults stress relief, protects against depression, and is associated with higher quality of life (Windle, Hughes, Linck, Russell, & Woods, 2010). The increased blood flow to the brain that comes with exercise is protective. Older adults who are physically active show less neural and glial cell losses throughout their cortex and less cognitive decline than do those who are sedentary (Muscari et al., 2010; Sampaio-Baptista & Johansen-Berg, 2017). Perhaps more significant is that exercise in older adults is associated with increased hippocampal volume (recall that new neurons are created there) (Dumas, 2017; Ryan & Nolan, 2016). In addition, adults who get regular cardiovascular exercise, such as brisk walks, show increased brain activity in areas

FIGURE 17.5

Current Health Status Among Adults Aged 18 and Older in the United States, 2015

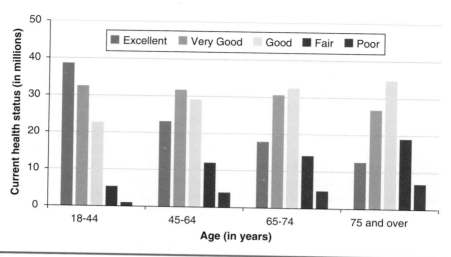

Source: Adapted from CDC/National Center for Health Statistics.

that control attention and perform better on tasks measuring attention than do sedentary adults. They also demonstrate improved performance on tasks examining executive function, processing speed, memory, and other cognitive processes (Erickson et al., 2011; Hindin & Zelinski, 2012). Moreover, patients with dementia who engage in a program of physical exercise, specifically cardiovascular exercise, show improvements in cognitive function, regardless of the intervention frequency or the specific dementia diagnosis (Groot et al., 2016), suggesting that exercise has powerful benefits for cognitive health.

National guidelines recommend that older adults engage in similar levels of physical activity than other adults: at least 150 minutes of moderate activity each week (or 75 minutes of vigorous activity), plus muscle strengthening exercises on at least 2 days each week (U.S. Department of Health and Human Services, 2008). The activity does not have to be performed in a single block of time but may be accumulated in 10-minute increments throughout the day. When older adults cannot perform 150 minutes of moderate-intensity exercise, they should be as physically active as possible. In addition, older adults should do exercises that maintain or improve balance.

Unfortunately, similar to younger adults, most older adults are not active enough. Common barriers to physical activity reported by adults include fears of falling, neighborhood safety, bad weather, and chronic conditions (Belza et al., 2004). Many older adults believe that the best way to manage chronic illnesses such as arthritis

is to rest and that exercise will make symptoms worse. Instead, exercise offers physical and mental benefits that slow the negative effects of aging. Older adults who exercise often report feeling more energetic, experience greater life enhancement, and have a more positive psychological outlook than sedentary elders (Ruppar & Schneider, 2007). In addition, older adults who identify themselves as physical exercisers and physically fit show greater levels of life satisfaction (Strachan, Brawley, Spink, & Glazebrook, 2010).

Chronic Illness

Chronic illnesses become more common with age. Nearly all older adults suffer from one chronic illness or another, and many have multiple diagnoses (Administration on Aging, 2014). Yet, like younger people, older adults tend to view their health as good or better, as shown in Figure 17.5.

Arthritis

One illness that goes hand in hand with aging is arthritis, a degenerative joint disease. There are more than 100 different types of arthritis; the most common is **osteoarthritis**, which affects joints that are injured by overuse, most commonly the hips, knees, lower back, and hands. The cartilage that protects the ends of bones where they meet at joints wears away and joints become less flexible and swell. Those who suffer from osteoarthritis experience a loss of movement and a great deal of pain. Aging is the most prominent risk factor for osteoarthritis; it often first appears in middle adulthood, occurring in about one third of adults ages 45 to 64, but becomes more common and worsens in severity during older adulthood (Aigner, Haag, Martin, & Buckwalter, 2007; Cooper, Javaid, & Arden, 2014). About half of adults aged 65 or older report a diagnosis of arthritis, and it is likely that many more cases remain undiagnosed (National Center for Health Statistics, 2018). Nearly all older adults show at least some signs of osteoarthritis, but there are great individual differences. People whose job or leisure activities rely on repetitive movements are most likely to experience osteoarthritis. Office workers who type every day, for example, might experience osteoarthritis in their hands. Runners might experience it in their knees. Obesity can also be a cause as it places abnormal pressure on joints.

A second common type of arthritis, rheumatoid arthritis, is not age or use related. **Rheumatoid arthritis** is an autoimmune illness in which the connective tissues, the membranes that line the joints, become inflamed and stiff. They thicken and release enzymes that digest bone and cartilage, often causing the affected joint to lose its shape and alignment. Most people are diagnosed with rheumatoid arthritis between ages 20 and 50, and the prevalence increases with age (Lindstrom & Robinson, 2010). Older adults with rheumatoid arthritis often have lived with a painful chronic illness for many years and likely experience multiple physical disabilities.

Arthritis is a chronic disease because it is managed, not cured. When inflammation flares, more rest is needed, as well as pain relief. However, instead of uninterrupted rest, it is best to deal with an arthritis flareup with some activities or exercises to help the muscles maintain flexibility, known as range of motion. People whose osteoarthritis is related to obesity may experience some relief with weight loss. In some cases, a synthetic material can be injected into a joint to provide more cushioning and improve movement, or a severely affected joint, such as the hip or knee, can be surgically replaced. Joint replacement surgery has become increasingly common in recent decades.

Because adults with arthritis live with chronic pain and reduced ability to engage in activities, they are often at risk for depression (E. H. B. Lin, 2008; Margaretten, Katz, Schmajuk, & Yelin, 2013). In one study, over one third of a sample of Latino adults with arthritis experienced depression (Withers, Moran, Nicassio, Weisman, & Karpouzas, 2015). Although arthritis-related stressors are the predominant factors affecting well-being for European American women with arthritis, well-being in African Americans with arthritis is also closely tied to broader life contextual

Osteoarthritis, a degenerative joint disease, often occurs in the hands, knees, and hips.
iStock/Signature

stressors (McIlvane, Baker, & Mingo, 2008). African American patients with rheumatoid arthritis are less likely to receive medication and to seek care from a specialist (Solomon et al., 2012). Low socioeconomic status (SES) is associated with a delay in seeking care, greater arthritis-related symptoms, poorer well-being, and greater use of maladaptive coping strategies among African Americans, yet SES does not predict depressive symptoms and coping among European Americans diagnosed with arthritis (McIlvane, 2007; Molina, del Rincon, Restrepo, Battafarano, & Escalante, 2015).

Osteoporosis

In middle adulthood, women undergo hormonal changes accompanying menopause. These changes are associated with bone loss, increasing women's risk for osteoporosis, a disorder characterized by severe bone loss resulting in brittle and easily fractured bones (Siris et al., 2014; J. Walker, 2008). We tend to think of our bones as static and unchanging— almost like sticks of concrete—but the skeleton is actually a dynamic organ made of living cells that continually dissolve and regenerate. In the first 10 years after menopause, women typically lose about 25% of their bone mass, largely due to menopausal declines in estrogen; this loss increases to about 50% by late adulthood (Avis, Brockwell, & Colvin, 2005; Vondracek, 2010). Men experience a more gradual and less extreme loss of bone, because age-related decreases in testosterone, which their bodies convert to estrogen, occur slowly, and therefore the loss of bone mass that occurs with declines in estrogen occurs gradually over the adult years (Avis & Crawford, 2006; J. Walker, 2008). About 30% of women and 16% of men have osteoporosis, extreme bone loss (Figure 17.6) (Wright, Saag, Dawson-Hughes, Khosla, & Siris, 2017); these conditions can be identified through a routine, noninvasive bone scan. Most people—men and women—are diagnosed with osteoporosis only after experiencing bone fractures, but one out of every two women and one in four men over 50 will have an osteoporosis-related fracture in their lifetime (NIH Osteoporosis and Related Bone Diseases National Resource Center, 2007). Risk factors for osteoporosis in men include low body mass, sedentary lifestyle, and advanced age (Cawthon, Shahnazari, Orwoll, & Lane, 2016). Because women are more widely known to be at risk, however, men often go undiagnosed and untreated (H. Liu et al., 2008).

Heredity and lifestyle contribute to the risk of osteoporosis. For example, at least 15 genes contribute to osteoporosis susceptibility (W. F. Li et al., 2010). Identical twins are more likely to share a diagnosis of osteoporosis than are fraternal twins (S. J. Andersen, 2007). Thin, small-framed women tend to attain a lower peak bone mass than do other women and are at relatively higher risk of osteoporosis. Other risk factors include a sedentary lifestyle, calcium deficiency, cigarette smoking, and heavy alcohol consumption (Bleicher et al., 2011; Nachtigall, Nazem, Nachtigall, & Goldstein, 2013).

The risk of osteoporosis can be reduced by encouraging individuals to maximize their peak bone density by consuming a diet rich in calcium and Vitamin D and engaging in regular exercise from childhood into emerging adulthood when bone reaches its peak density (Nachtigall et al., 2013; Weaver et al., 2016). These same guidelines, specifically having a bone-healthy lifestyle by consuming a diet rich in calcium and Vitamin D, avoiding smoking and heavy drinking, moderating alcohol consumption, and engaging in weightbearing exercise, can offset bone loss in postmenopausal women (Bleicher et al., 2011; Cosman et al., 2014). Medication can increase the absorption of calcium and slow the bone loss associated with osteoporosis in middle and late adulthood (Vondracek, 2010).

Injuries

Deaths from unintentional injuries rise dramatically in later adulthood. They account for 45.01 deaths per 100,000 in 65- to 69-year-old adults and a striking 365.7 in adults age 85 and older (see Figure 17.7) (Centers for Disease Control and Prevention, 2018). Such injuries arise from a variety of causes, including motor vehicle accidents and falls.

FIGURE 17.6

Osteoporosis

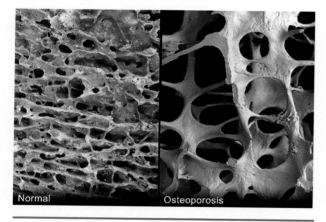

Normal   Osteoporosis

Source: © Scott Camazine/Phototake; Alan Boyde/Visuals Unlimited.

FIGURE 17.7

Fatal Unintentional Injury Rate by Age in the United States

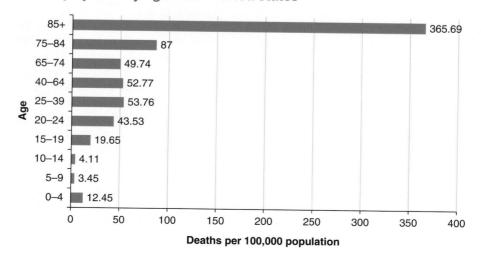

Source: Centers for Disease Control and Prevention, 2018.

Over one quarter of U.S. older adults fall each year. Exercise programs such as Tai Chi and strength and agility training can improve older adults' strength, balance, and confidence. Environmental modifications such as addressing slippery floors, installing handrails on steps, and equipping shower/bath facilities with grip bars, can also help to prevent falls.
iStock/Imagesbybarbara

Motor Vehicle Accidents

Driving a car represents autonomy. Many older adults continue to drive as long as they are able to because driving provides a sense of control and freedom. As the Baby Boom generation ages, older adults are more likely to keep their driver's licenses, make up a larger proportion of the driving population, and drive more miles than ever before. The proportion of the 70-and-older drivers increased by one third between 1997 and 2012, as have the typical miles traveled (Insurance Institute for Highway Safety, 2015). Accidents involving older drivers, both nonfatal and fatal, have declined over the past two decades, but there remain predictable age-related increases in accidents in older adulthood. Per mile traveled, crash rates and fatal crash rates also start increasing when the driver reaches age 70 (see Figure 17.8).

Compared with younger drivers, senior drivers are more likely to be involved in collisions in intersections, when merging into traffic, and switching lanes (Cicchino & McCartt, 2015). Although they drive more slowly and carefully than young adults, older adults are more likely to miss traffic signs, make inappropriate turns, fail to yield the right of way, and show slower reaction time—all risks to safe driving. Declines in vision account for much of the decline in older adults' driving performance (Owsley, McGwin, Jackson, Kallies, & Clark, 2007). They are likely to have difficulty with night vision and reading the dashboard. Changes in working memory and attention also account for some of the problems in older adults' driving competence. Many older adults appear to adapt to these changes, naturally reducing their driving as they notice that their vision and reaction time are less acute (see Figure 17.9). In this way, they may, at least partially, compensate for their higher risk for motor vehicle accidents (Festa, Ott, Manning, Davis, & Heindel, 2013; Sandlin, McGwin, & Owsley, 2014).

FIGURE 17.8

Rate of Vehicle Accidents per Million Miles Traveled in the United States, by Driver Age, 2015

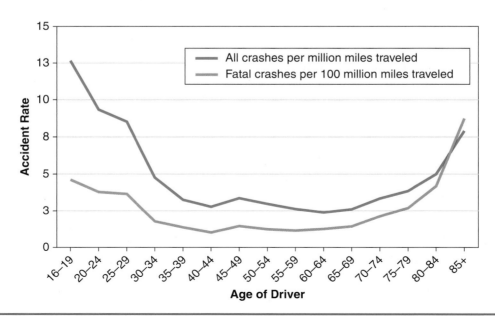

Source: Insurance Institute for Highway Safety (2015), Arlington, Virginia. www.iihs.org. Reprinted with permission.

FIGURE 17.9

Older Adult Drivers Who Tend to Avoid Driving Under Specific Conditions by Gender, 2015

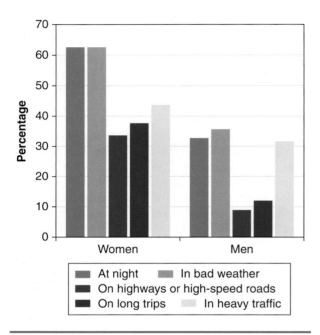

Legend:
- At night
- In bad weather
- On highways or high-speed roads
- On long trips
- In heavy traffic

Source: Centers for Disease Control and Prevention (2015).

Falls

Over one quarter of U.S. adults over the age of 65 fall each year (Crews, Chou, Stevens, & Saaddine, 2016), including about half of those over the age of 80 (Hosseini & Hosseini, 2008). Many aspects of aging increase the risk of falls, including changes in vision, hearing, motor skills and neuromuscular control, and cognition (Dhital, Pey, & Stanford, 2010). Older adults are less able than their younger counterparts to balance and regulate body sway (Johansson, Nordstrom, Gustafson, Westling, & Nordstrom, 2017; H. J. Lee & Chou, 2007), have reduced muscular density (i.e., strength) (Frank-Wilson et al., 2016), and are less adept at navigating and avoiding obstacles (Weerdesteyn, Nienhuis, Geurts, & Duysens, 2007). Declines in cognition, particularly in executive functioning and processing speed, also increase the risk of falls (Mirelman et al., 2012; Welmer, Rizzuto, Laukka, Johnell, & Fratiglioni, 2016).

Falls are a serious hazard for older adults because the natural loss of bone and high prevalence of osteoporosis increase the risk of bone fractures, especially a fractured hip. Hip fractures are particularly dangerous as they immobilize an older adult, are painful, and take a great deal of time to

heal. Following hip fracture, many elderly adults lose the capacity for independent living, and up to 25% die as a result of complications, such as infection within a year after the fall (Panula et al., 2011).

After experiencing a fall, at least half of older adults report fear of falling (Visschedijk, Achterberg, van Balen, & Hertogh, 2010). Adults who fear falling tend to become more cautious, avoiding activities that pose a risk of falling but also limiting opportunities for physical activities that support physical health, retention of mobility, psychological well-being, and social connections (Visschedijk et al., 2010). There are a variety of ways to prevent falls and help older adults become more confident about their mobility. Exercise programs such as Tai Chi and strength and agility training can improve older adults' strength, balance, and confidence (Kaniewski, Stevens, Parker, & Lee, 2015; Tricco et al., 2017). Environmental modifications such as addressing slippery floors, installing handrails on steps, and equipping shower/bath facilities with grip bars can also help to prevent falls.

 THINKING IN CONTEXT 17.2

1. Identify older adults' most important health needs. What resources do they need to maintain their health, prevent chronic illnesses, and treat already existing illnesses?

2. What are potential barriers to older adults' meeting these needs? How might contextual influences support or challenge older adults in meeting their needs? What recommendations do you make given this analysis?

3. Recall from Chapter 1 that domains or types of development interact. Changes in one area of development hold implications for other areas of functioning. How might chronic illnesses in adulthood, such diabetes or arthritis, influence cognitive and socioemotional development? How might these changes influence individuals' interactions within all of the contexts in which they are embedded?

DEMENTIA IN LATE ADULTHOOD

» LO 17.3 Summarize common dementias, including characteristics, risk and protective factors, and treatment.

Some loss of neural connections is part of normal aging and does not prevent older adults from engaging in everyday activities. Some older adults, however, experience high rates of cell death and severe brain deterioration that characterize

FIGURE 17.10

Projected Growth in Dementia Prevalence: Low-Income vs. High-Income Countries, 2013–2050 (Projected)

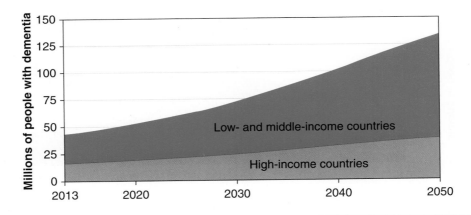

Source: Adapted from Alzheimer's Disease International (2015).

dementia. **Dementia** refers to a progressive deterioration in mental abilities due to changes in the brain that influence higher cortical functions, such as thinking, memory, comprehension, and emotional control, and are reflected in impaired thought and behavior, interfering with the older adult's capacity to engage in everyday activities (Alzheimer's Association, 2018; World Health Organization, 2012). Given that dementia can take many forms, with similar and different neurological features, the most recent version of the *Diagnostic and Statistical Manual of Mental Disorders (DSM-5)* has replaced the term *dementia* with *neurocognitive disorder* (American Psychiatric Association, 2013). Throughout our discussion, we will use the more commonly used term, *dementia*.

There are nearly 47 million people worldwide living with dementia, and this number may reach 135 million in 2050 (Alzheimer's Disease International, 2015; Prince, Comas-Herrera, Knapp, Guerchet, & Karagiannidou, 2016). Much of the increase will be in low-income developing countries, as shown in Figure 17.10. Worldwide, currently 62% of people with dementia live in developing countries; by 2050, this will rise to 71%. The fastest growth in the elderly population is taking place in China, India, and their south Asian and western Pacific neighbors (Alzheimer's Disease International, 2015). Poor access to education, health care, and nutrition contributes to geographic differences in dementia rates.

The most common cause of dementia is Alzheimer's disease, followed by vascular dementia. Dementia, even in its very early stages, is associated with higher rates of mortality (K. Andersen, Lolk, Martinussen, & Kragh-Sørensen, 2010). Dementias

often co-occur and adults may suffer from multiple types of dementia (Corriveau et al., 2016; Iadecola, 2013). The most common forms of dementia are discussed in the following sections.

Alzheimer's Disease

Alzheimer's disease is a neurodegenerative disorder that progresses from general cognitive decline to include personality and behavior changes, motor complications, severe dementia, and death (Agronin, 2014). The risk of Alzheimer's disease grows exponentially with age, doubling approximately every 5 to 6 years in most Western countries (see Figure 17.11). Currently, 5.8 million Americans, including one in nine people over the age of 65, have Alzheimer's disease (Alzheimer's Association, 2018). Of those with Alzheimer's disease, an estimated 4% are under age 65, 16% are 65 to 74, 44% are 75 to 84, and 38% are 85 or older.

Alzheimer's disease is characterized by widespread brain deterioration associated with inflammation and accumulations of *beta-amyloid,* a protein present in the tissue that surrounds neurons in the healthy brain (Graham, Bonito-Oliva, & Sakmar, 2017). Patients with Alzheimer's disease experience inflammation that causes the beta-amyloid to accumulate and join with clumps of dead neurons and glial cells, forming large masses called **amyloid plaques** (see Figure 17.12). It is thought that amyloid plaques disrupt the structure and function of cell membranes and contribute to the formation of **neurofibrillary tangles**, twisted bundles of threads of a protein called *tau* that occur when neurons collapse (Takahashi, Nagao,

FIGURE 17.11

Projected Prevalence of Alzheimer's Disease in the U.S. Population, 2010–2050

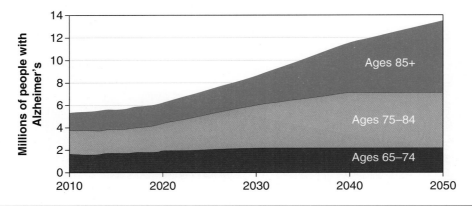

Source: Alzheimer's Association (2015). Reprinted with permission.

& Gouras, 2017). Even healthy brains have some tangles, but in cases of Alzheimer's disease, there is inflammation and a proliferation of plaques and tangles, as well as a progressive loss of neurons that interfere with brain functioning. As neurons die, brain functioning declines. Alzheimer's disease is associated with altered neurogenesis and atrophy in the hippocampus, impairing the generation and development of new neurons (Josephs et al., 2017; Valero et al., 2017).

Diagnosis of Alzheimer's Disease

Because the characteristic beta-amyloid plaques can only be assessed by examining brain tissue, Alzheimer's disease is generally diagnosed in living patients through exclusion: by ruling out all other causes of dementia (Alzheimer's Association, 2018). Symptoms, a medical history, a comprehensive set of neurological and cognitive tests, and conversations with the adult and family members can provide useful information about a person's level of functioning. Brain imaging can help physicians rule out other, potentially treatable, causes of dementia, such as a tumor or stroke (Hort, O'Brien, et al., 2010).

Advances in brain imaging techniques offer opportunities to diagnose Alzheimer's disease by studying changes in brain volume and activity. MRI scans indicating larger spaces surrounding some of the blood vessels in the brain are associated with Alzheimer's disease (Banerjee et al., 2017). Research with animals as well as postmortem humans has suggested that MRI scans can capture images of amyloid plaques and tangles associated with diagnoses of Alzheimer's disease (Raman et al., 2016). The most promising research to date examines biomarkers, genetic or biological traces, of the disease

(Castro-Chavira, Fernandez, Nicolini, Diaz-Cintra, & Prado-Alcala, 2015). For example, cerebrospinal fluid (CSF) concentrations of beta-amyloid appear to serve as biomarkers for Alzheimer's disease (Counts, Ikonomovic, Mercado, Vega, & Mufson, 2017; Kang et al., 2015; Olsson et al., 2016). These biomarkers are used in clinically diagnosing Alzheimer's disease in Europe; however, countries vary in the cutoff values used to diagnose Alzheimer's disease (Hort, Bartos, Pirttilä, & Scheltens, 2010). Searching for biomarkers is not part of a routine diagnosis in North America; researchers have concluded that such markers have promise but have not yet determined specific criteria to diagnose individuals (Blennow, Mattsson, Schöll, Hansson, & Zetterberg, 2015; Frisoni et al., 2017).

Progression of Alzheimer's Disease

Alzheimer's disease progresses through several predictable steps, including specific patterns of cognitive and memory loss. The earliest symptoms of Alzheimer's disease are memory problems, likely because the neurological disruptions that comprise Alzheimer's disease usually begin in the hippocampus, which is influential in memory (Guzmán-Vélez, Warren, Feinstein, Bruss, & Tranel, 2016). First, the older adult experiences impairments in memory that are usually attributed to absentmindedness. The person may forget the names of new people, recent events, appointments, and tasks such as taking a tea kettle off of the stove or turning off the iron. Memory deficits are accompanied by impaired attentional control, which, to an outside observer, may appear as further absentmindedness and inattention, being "lost" in one's own world (Huntley, Hampshire, Bor, Owen, & Howard, 2017). Early Alzheimer's disease can be hard

FIGURE 17.12

Alzheimer's Disease

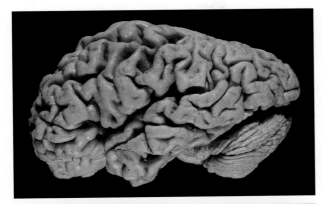

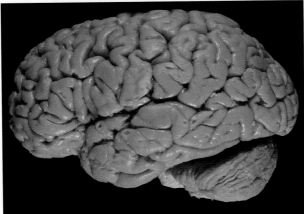

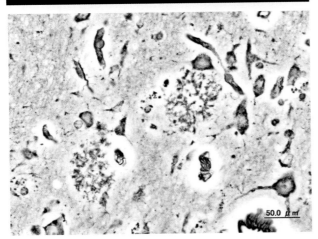

Alzheimer's disease entails a wasting of the brain, as illustrated by the decreased size in the diseased brain (top) as compared with the healthy brain (middle). Alzheimer's disease is characterized by the presence of plaques (bottom) that damage neurons and disrupt functioning.

Source: Wikimedia Commons.

to distinguish from normal aging—or at least popular views and stereotypes of aging.

Over time, the cognitive impairments broaden to include severe problems with concentration coupled with more severe memory problems. Older adults may set the TV remote control down and, a moment later, be unable to find it. The person may ask the same question repeatedly, forgetting that an answer had just been given moments earlier. As memory problems increase, the patient with Alzheimer's disease is frequently confused (Carson, Vanderhorst, & Koenig, 2015). The older adult's vocabulary becomes more limited as he or she is likely to forget or mix up words. Bilingual adults may shift from one language to another (Gollan, Stasenko, Li, & Salmon, 2017). Speech becomes more long-winded and tangential. Communication skills deteriorate, and the person sometimes becomes unpredictably angry or paranoid (Carson et al., 2015). Some adults may show unpredictable aggressive outbursts (Agronin, 2014). Others may become more withdrawn. Personality changes may occur and are associated with CSF biomarkers (Tautvydaitė, Antonietti, Henry, von Gunten, & Popp, 2017).

Up to 50% of patients with Alzheimer's disease experience depression or depressive symptoms (Chi, Yu, Tan, & Tan, 2014; Starkstein, Jorge, Mizrahi, & Robinson, 2005). Some researchers believe that depression may occur prior to and increase the risk for Alzheimer's disease, but the mechanism is not clear (Herbert & Lucassen, 2016). Depression is particularly harmful to patients with Alzheimer's disease as it is associated with greater cognitive and behavioral impairment, disability in activities of daily living, and a faster cognitive decline (Spalletta et al., 2012; Starkstein, Mizrahi, & Power, 2008; Van der Mussele et al., 2013). A predictable routine filled with activities that are enjoyed can provide structure to aid adults who are sometimes confused about their surroundings. Although antidepressants are commonly prescribed to treat depressive symptoms in patients with Alzheimer's disease, little research has examined the effectiveness (Orgeta, Tabet, Nilforooshan, & Howard, 2017). Some patients' depressive symptoms improve with the use of antidementia medication, commonly prescribed drugs that improve memory by increasing the chemical activity in various parts of the brain (Chi et al., 2014).

As the disease progresses, patients become unable to care for themselves. They may forget to eat, to dress themselves properly for the weather, or how to get back inside their home after they step outside—for example, to bring in the mail or daily newspaper. Eventually, the brain will fail to process information and no longer recognize objects, faces, and familiar people (Lavallée et al., 2016). A woman may insist on seeing her daughter and not realize that the woman in front of her is her daughter. In the final stages of the disease, patients with Alzheimer's disease lose the ability to comprehend and produce speech, to control bodily functions, and to respond to stimuli (Carson et al., 2015). They

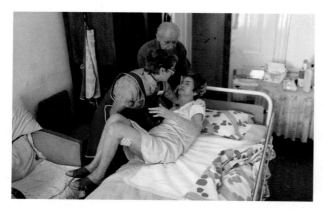

In the final stages of Alzheimer's disease, brain deterioration interferes with the individual's ability to comprehend and produce speech, to control bodily functions, and to respond to stimuli.
Reuters/Nacho Doce

show heightened vulnerability to infections and illnesses that often lead to death. Eventually, brain functions deteriorate to the point where organs fail and life cannot be sustained. The average patient progresses to the final stage of Alzheimer's disease over the course of about 10 years, with a typical range of 7 to 15 years (Rektorova, Rusina, Hort, & Matej, 2009).

Risk Factors for Alzheimer's Disease

A person's risk for developing Alzheimer's disease varies with gender, age, and ethnicity. Women are at greater risk than men, perhaps because of their longer lifespans (Kirbach & Mintzer, 2008). In the United States, African Americans and Hispanic older adults are disproportionately more likely to have Alzheimer's disease and other dementias than their European American counterparts (Alzheimer's Association, 2015). See the accompanying Cultural Influences on Development feature, which discusses Ethnicity and Alzheimer's Disease.

Alzheimer's disease has genetic influences and often runs in families (Bettens, Sleegers, & Van Broeckhoven, 2013; Naj & Schellenberg, 2017). Several chromosomes are implicated, including the 21st chromosome. Individuals with Down syndrome, trisomy 21, are at high risk to develop Alzheimer's disease as many show plaques and tangles in their brains as early as age 40 (Lemere, 2013; Wiseman et al., 2015). Contextual and behavioral factors also matter. Research suggests that the same factors that contribute to cardiovascular risk, such as high blood pressure and obesity, also heighten the risk for Alzheimer's disease (Knopman & Roberts, 2010; J. Li et al., 2016; Tosto et al., 2016). Good nutrition is linked with cardiovascular health and might serve a protective role against Alzheimer's disease, but research is

mixed (Daviglus et al., 2010; Douaud et al., 2013; Schelke et al., 2016).

Education acts as an important protective factor against Alzheimer's disease. The process of learning that accompanies higher education and occupational complexity promotes neural activity and increases connections among neurons, thickening the cortex and boosting cognitive reserve (Boots et al., 2015; Y. Liu et al., 2012; Sattler, Toro, Schönknecht, & Schröder, 2012). Cognitive reserves can protect patients from the handicapping effects of brain atrophy and synaptic loss (W. Xu, Yu, Tan, & Tan, 2015). One recent study showed that patients with higher levels of education showed similar cognitive functioning to those with lower levels of education despite demonstrating more severe neurofibrillary tangles, suggesting that their greater cognitive reserve buffered against losses (Hoenig et al., 2017). Conversely, low socioeconomic status predicts mortality in adults diagnosed with dementia, likely through the limited access to health care and social resources that promote cognitive reserve (van de Vorst, Koek, Stein, Bots, & Vaartjes, 2016).

It is not simply education that buffers against losses. People who remain socially and physically active show a lower risk of Alzheimer's disease as well because such activities stimulate and improve blood flow to the brain and increase synaptic connections (Gallaway et al., 2017; Z. S. Tan et al., 2016). One recent study showed that mice who voluntarily engage in regular running showed reductions in the neurological hallmarks of Alzheimer's disease, as well as reduced neuronal loss, increased hippocampal neurogenesis, and reduced spatial memory loss (Tapia-Rojas, Aranguiz, Varela-Nallar, & Inestrosa, 2016). Regular physical exercise may not only prevent but also reverse neural damage.

Vascular Dementia

Vascular dementia, sometimes known as *multi-infarct dementia,* is the second most common form of dementia and loss of mental ability in older adulthood worldwide (O'Brien & Thomas, 2015). Vascular dementia is caused by strokes, or blockages of blood vessels in the brain (Vinters et al., 2018). Whereas individuals with Alzheimer's disease show slow and steady decrements in mental abilities, those with vascular dementia tend to show sudden, but often mild, losses with each stroke (Kalaria, 2016; Korczyn, Vakhapova, & Grinberg, 2012; Raz, Rodrigue, Kennedy, & Acker, 2007). As time passes, individuals tend to show improvement because the brain's plasticity leads other neurons to take on functions of those that were lost. Additional strokes usually follow, however, and with each stroke, brain matter is lost and it becomes harder

Ethnicity and Alzheimer's Disease

Social and cultural factors, such as socioeconomic status, diet, and health, influence ethnic differences in Alzheimer's and other dementias.
Yoon S. Byun/The Boston Globe via Getty Images

Alzheimer's disease knows no bounds. It is diagnosed in adults around the world, but ethnic differences appear in rates of diagnoses. As shown in Figure 17.13, there are dramatic ethnic differences in cognitive impairment with age. Alzheimer's disease shows a similar pattern. For example, African Americans are twice as likely, and Hispanic populations one and one half times as likely, to be diagnosed with Alzheimer's disease than non-Hispanic Whites (Mayeda, Glymour, Quesenberry, & Whitmer, 2016; Mehta & Yeo, 2017).

There is a genetic component to Alzheimer's disease, but genetics is not thought to influence ethnic differences in rates of diagnoses (Raj et al., 2017). Instead, social and cultural factors are found to play a large role in ethnic differences in Alzheimer's disease and other dementias. High blood pressure, diabetes, and cardiovascular disease, risk factors for many dementias, are more common among African American and Hispanic groups. These chronic diseases have a large lifestyle component and are influenced by diet, which often varies dramatically across cultural groups. Differences in educational attainment may also influence risk for Alzheimer's disease. One study of African American, Latino, and non-Latino White adults found that level of education was strongly associated with rates of dementia and, when age and education were taken into account, ethnic differences in rates of Alzheimer's disease were no longer consistent (Gurland et al., 1999). Differences in education and socioeconomic status, important contextual factors that influence access to opportunities, may account for some of the ethnic differences in susceptibility to Alzheimer's disease (Manly, 2006).

Other contextual factors that contribute to Alzheimer's disease include cultural beliefs about aging, spirituality, and views of the medical profession. African Americans are more likely than White adults to express beliefs that Alzheimer's disease symptoms, such as substantial memory loss, are just a normal part of aging (Connell, Scott Roberts, McLaughlin, & Akinleye, 2009; Jackson et al., 2017; Roberts et al., 2003). Differences in knowledge about normative aging and Alzheimer's disease may partially explain why African Americans often receive delayed care for dementia (Chin, Negash, & Hamilton, 2011). Religious and spiritual beliefs may also influence views of Alzheimer's disease. One study found that a larger proportion of African Americans indicated that they believed "God's will" determined who developed Alzheimer's disease (Connell et al., 2009). Patients may question the efficacy of medicines in treating a disease that stems from a spiritual cause or may resist acting in opposition to a divine plan. In this way, religion and spirituality may play a strong role in the health of African Americans (Chin et al., 2011).

Finally, individuals from minority communities may be distrustful of the medical establishment. Discrimination, including historic events in which minority groups have been denied equal medical treatment, influences individuals' views of the health care system and doctors. Whether or not a patient trusts his or her doctor may determine whether or not he or she will report symptoms of dementia. An understanding of these cultural and contextual influences can help those who work with older adults to be more effective in identifying symptoms of Alzheimer's disease.

What Do You Think?

Apply a bioecological perspective in considering risk and protective factors for Alzheimer's disease in African American older adults.

1. What microsystem and mesosystem factors may increase African American adults' risk for Alzheimer's disease?

2. Identify two exosystem factors and two macrosystem factors that may contribute to the risk for Alzheimer's disease.

3. How can we reduce the risk for Alzheimer's disease in African American older adults? Specifically, what can researchers, physicians and health care practitioners, policy makers, and communities do to help reduce African Americans' risk for Alzheimer's disease? ●

(Continued)

(Continued)

FIGURE 17.13

Proportion of Americans Aged 55 and Older With Cognitive Impairment, by Race/Ethnicity, 2006

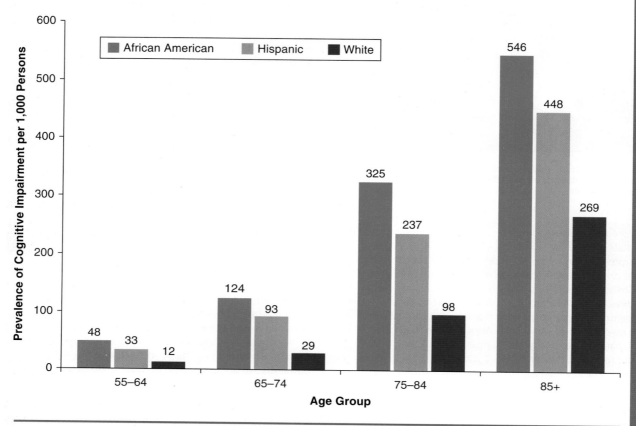

Source: Assistant Secretary for Planning and Evaluation, U.S. Department of Health and Human Services.

for the remaining neurons to compensate for losses (Troncoso et al., 2008).

As vascular dementia worsens, the symptoms are similar to those of Alzheimer's disease (Korczyn et al., 2012; O'Brien & Thomas, 2015). However, vascular dementia is neurologically different from Alzheimer's disease. The damage caused by small strokes is visible on MRI scans and localized to specific areas of the brain (Vinters et al., 2018). Postmortem analyses of the brains of people with vascular dementia show substantial deterioration of areas of the brain and disruptions in white matter but not the widespread abundance of plaques and tangles that accompany Alzheimer's disease (Hase, Horsburgh, Ihara, & Kalaria, 2018; Iadecola, 2013).

Like many disorders, vascular dementia is influenced by both genetic and environmental factors (Schmidt, Freudenberger, Seiler, & Schmidt, 2012; Srinivasan, Braidy, Chan, Xu, & Chan, 2016; Sun et al., 2015). Cardiovascular disease significantly increases the risk of vascular dementia (Sharp, Aarsland, Day, Sønnesyn, & Ballard, 2011; Vinters et al., 2018). As we have discussed, genetics may influence factors that are known to be linked with vascular dementia, such as obesity, diabetes, and cardiovascular disease. Men are more likely to suffer early vascular dementia, in their 60s, than are women because of their heightened vulnerability to cardiovascular disease. Behavioral influences on vascular dementia such as heavy alcohol use, smoking, inactivity, stress, and poor diet are more prevalent in men (Andel et al., 2012; Seshadri & Wolf, 2007).

Factors that prevent cardiovascular disease, such as physical activity, can also prevent or slow the progression of vascular dementia (Aarsland, Sardahaee, Anderssen, & Ballard, 2010; Gallaway et al., 2017; Verdelho et al., 2012). Thus, prevention and management of vascular risks may be the best weapon in a fight against age-related cognitive decline (Chertkow, 2008; Corriveau et al., 2016; Raz et al., 2007). In addition, when symptoms of stroke arise, such as sudden vision loss, weakening or numbness in part of the body, or problems producing or understanding speech, anticlotting drugs can prevent the blood from clotting and forming additional strokes.

Parkinson's Disease

Some dementias first damage the subcortical parts of the brain, areas below the cortex. These dementias are characterized by a progressive loss of motor control. Because the damage occurs first in the subcortical areas of the brain, mental abilities, which are controlled by the cortex, are not initially affected. As the disease progresses and brain deterioration spreads to include the cortex, thought and memory deficits appear (Toulouse & Sullivan, 2008). The most common cause of subcortical dementia is Parkinson's disease.

Parkinson's disease is a brain disorder that occurs when neurons in a part of the brain called the substantia nigra die or become impaired. Neurons in this part of the brain produce the neurotransmitter dopamine, which enables coordinated function of the body's muscles and smooth movement. Parkinson's disease symptoms appear when at least 50% of the nerve cells in the substantia nigra are damaged (National Parkinson Foundation, 2008).

Parkinson's disease is characterized by a specific progression of motor symptoms, including tremors, slowness of movement, difficulty initiating movement, rigidity, difficulty with balance, and a shuffling walk (Postuma et al., 2015). Typically, these symptoms occur in one part of the body and slowly spread to the extremities on the same side of the body before appearing on the opposite side of the body (Truong & Wolters, 2009). Because the stiffness and rigidity are first located in one part of the body, individuals may assume that it is ordinary stiffness, perhaps the result of too much activity or simply because of aging. As the disease progresses, individuals have difficulties with balance and controlling their body movements. As neurons continue to degenerate, cognitive symptoms emerge. Brain functioning declines and cognitive and speech abilities deteriorate. Dementia appears in about three quarters of patients, usually within 10 years after diagnosis (Postuma et al., 2015).

Similar to Alzheimer's disease, among patients with Parkinson's disease, those with larger cognitive reserves and more synaptic connections among neurons have shown a slower progression of neurological changes before dementia appears. The prevalence of Parkinson's disease and its associated dementia increases with age, and Parkinson's disease is found throughout the world, with similar rates occurring in Asia, Africa, South America, Europe, North America, and Australia (Hirsch, Jette, Frolkis, Steeves, & Pringsheim, 2016; Pringsheim, Jette, Frolkis, & Steeves, 2014; Savica, Grossardt, Rocca, & Bower, 2018). People diagnosed with Parkinson's disease at advanced ages tend to develop dementia earlier into their disease than do younger people, likely because of age-related differences in cognitive capacities and neural reserves (Grossman, Bergmann, & Parker, 2006).

Multiple studies support a genetic component to Parkinson's disease (Nalls et al., 2014; Wirdefeldt, Adami, Cole, Trichopoulos, & Mandel, 2011). However, there are few consistent findings regarding environmental and lifestyle influences (Wirdefeldt et al., 2011), suggesting that Parkinson's disease might be influenced by the complex gene–environment interactions characteristic of epigenetics (Cannon & Greenamyre, 2013; Feng, Jankovic, & Wu, 2014). Physical activity may act as a protective factor in developing Parkinson's disease, slowing its progression, and improving motor control (Bellou, Belbasis, Tzoulaki, Evangelou, & Ioannidis, 2016; Paillard et al., 2015).

Diagnosing Parkinson's disease is difficult because, like Alzheimer's disease, no test confirms the presence of the disease. Incorrect diagnoses are common, potentially delaying treatment to patients with Parkinson's disease (Rizzo et al., 2015). It is diagnosed by exclusion, by a thorough examination to rule out other possible causes. Similar to Alzheimer's disease, researchers are searching for biomarkers that may be used to diagnose Parkinson's disease, but the work is still in its early stages (D. B. Miller & O'Callaghan, 2015; Parnetti, Cicognola, Eusebi, & Chiasserini, 2016). Recent research shows that brain scans can detect changes in the substantia nigra associated with Parkinson's disease, suggesting that, in the future, such scans might be used for diagnosis (Atkinson-Clement, Pinto, Eusebio, & Coulon, 2017).

Parkinson's disease symptoms can be treated. Some research has suggested that deep brain stimulation, stimulating specific parts of the brain with electricity, as well as resistance training, can improve some of the motor symptoms, such as poor gait and posture (Lamotte et al., 2015; Roper et al., 2016). Most medications either

Boxer Muhammad Ali (1942–2016) and actor Michael J. Fox, both diagnosed with Parkinson's disease, pretend to spar before giving their testimony before the 2002 U.S. Senate Appropriations Subcommittee on Health and Human Services, advocating that more funding be directed to finding a cure for the disease.
Mark Wilson/Getty

replace or mimic dopamine, which temporarily improves the motor symptoms of the disease; anti-inflammatory medications may also help reduce neurodegeneration; and medication can help alleviate the symptoms of dementia (Aarsland et al., 2017; Brichta, Greengard, & Flajolet, 2013; Emre, Ford, Bilgiç, & Uç, 2014). Medication can temporarily reduce symptoms and perhaps slow its path, but Parkinson's disease is not curable.

Lewy Body Dementia

Lewy body dementia is thought to be about as common as vascular dementia, vying for the second most common form of dementia (Z. Walker, Possin, Boeve, & Aarsland, 2017). The biggest challenge in the diagnosis of dementia with Lewy bodies is differentiating it from Alzheimer's disease. Central features of Lewy body dementia are common to Alzheimer's disease and include progressive dementia that interferes with social or occupational functions and deficits on cognitive tasks, such as attention, visuospatial ability, and executive function (Bonanni, Franciotti, Delli Pizzi, Thomas, & Onofrj, 2018). Lewy body dementia can be distinguished from Alzheimer's disease by the presence of visual hallucinations, cognitive symptoms that fluctuate (improving and worsening), some Parkinson's-like motor symptoms, and, especially, sleep disorders in which individuals sleepwalk and act out their dreams (Hamilton et al., 2012).

The hallmark of Lewy body dementia is the presence of Lewy bodies, spherical protein deposits, accompanied by neural loss (Z. Walker, Possin, Boeve, & Aarsland, 2015). Lewy bodies are also common to Parkinson's dementia. The genetics of dementia with Lewy bodies and Parkinson's

disease overlap, suggesting that the disorders are linked (Meeus et al., 2012). Unfortunately, damage caused by Lewy bodies is usually not apparent on MRI scans until very late in the disease or after death. Like Alzheimer's disease, Lewy body dementia is diagnosed by exclusion, ruling out other causes of dementia (Bonanni et al., 2018). The search is on for biomarkers of Lewy body dementia, but research is in its early stages (Siderowf, Aarsland, Mollenhauer, Goldman, & Ravina, 2018). Like other dementias, Lewy body dementia is managed but not cured. Medication can treat many of the symptoms of Lewy body dementia, such as sleep problems, hallucinations, and cognitive problems, but Lewy body dementia is a progressive neurodegenerative disease that eventually causes death.

Delirium

Not all dementia symptoms represent progressive and irreversible brain damage. Symptoms of dementia sometimes are caused by psychological and behavioral factors that can be reversed. For example, older adults who are socially isolated and lonely can show declines in mental functioning that reverse with the provision of social support (Fisher, Yury, & Buchanan, 2006). Dementia-like symptoms such as problems with attention and reasoning that develop quickly and are temporary are known as **delirium** (DSM). Delirium is treatable and can be cured. However, given common stereotypes of aging, delirium may go unrecognized and untreated in older adults (Oh, Fong, Hshieh, & Inouye, 2017). Reviews of medical records have suggested that 7% to 18% of the dementia cases had treatable causes (Djukic, Wedekind, Franz, Gremke, & Nau, 2015; Muangpaisan, Petcharat, & Srinonprasert, 2012). Another review of over 340 medical records over a 10-year period revealed that of the 193 patients with dementia, 37 (19%) likely were experiencing delirium (Bello & Schultz, 2011).

Other common causes of delirium are poor nutrition and dehydration (Gupta, Chari, & Ali, 2015; Muangpaisan et al., 2012; Panza, Solfrizzi, & Capurso, 2004; Srikanth & Nagaraja, 2005). As we have discussed, older adults require fewer calories than do younger adults, but nutritional demands remain or increase with age. In addition, older adults may eat less than younger adults because of depression or a loss of appetite that occurs with some medications. As a result, older adults are at risk for malnutrition and vitamin deficiencies, which are associated with declines in mental abilities and increases in psychological distress, including depression and anxiety (Baker, 2007). Specifically, Vitamin B12 deficiencies can mirror dementia symptoms, yet correcting for this deficiency restores older adults' functioning (Ringman & Varpetian, 2009).

Prescription and nonprescription drugs and drug interactions can also contribute to symptoms of dementia. Many medications impair nutrition by reducing the body's ability to absorb vitamins. Some painkillers, corticosteroid drugs, and other medications can cause confusion and erratic behavior similar to dementia (Bansal & Parle, 2014; Fisher et al., 2006). Older adults may be more easily overmedicated than younger adults because of their slower metabolism. Physical illnesses themselves can sometimes cause dementia symptoms such as memory loss and agitation that go away as the illness is treated.

Symptoms of depression and anxiety in older adults, such as attention, forgetfulness, disorientation, and other cognitive difficulties, are often mistaken for dementia (de la Torre, 2016; Engmann, 2011). If anxiety or depressive symptoms are misdiagnosed as dementia, the older adult may be prescribed medications that can increase dementia-like symptoms such as fatigue and slowed mental

reactions to stimuli and events. Treating anxiety and depression with combinations of antianxiety and antidepressant medications as well as therapy reduces the cognitive symptoms commonly mistaken for dementia (Davies & Thorn, 2002).

> **THINKING IN CONTEXT 17.3**

1. Identify differences among the various forms of dementia. What behaviors characterize each? How can you tell them apart?

2. What would you suggest to someone who wishes to reduce his or her risk for dementia? What behaviors would you suggest? How might someone take advantage of contextual factors to reduce the risk of dementia or show better adjustment in the face of dementia?

COGNITIVE DEVELOPMENT IN LATE ADULTHOOD

» LO 17.4 Analyze patterns of cognitive change in late adulthood.

Cognition continues to change over late adulthood alongside physical development. Sensory capacities, such as vision and hearing, decline with age and are associated with age-related declines in cognition (Baldwin & Ash, 2011). Sensory impairments may prevent some information from getting into the cognitive system in the first place, so that older adults may never be aware that they have missed it. Cognition changes in several predictable ways over older adulthood.

Attention

In old age, it becomes more difficult to divide attention, to engage in two complex tasks at once and focus on relevant information (Radvansky, Zacks, & Hasher, 2005). As with other capacities, age-related declines in attention are not uniform across adults, and these differences predict variations in cognitive performance. For example, in one study of young, middle-aged, and older adults, those who performed better on cognitive tasks were more attracted to and spent more time viewing novel stimuli than those who performed at average levels (Daffner, Chong, & Riis, 2007). The magnitude of the difference between adults with exceptional versus average performance grew from middle adulthood into old age—and engagement and a preference for novelty were better predictors of cognitive performance with age.

Response inhibition becomes more challenging with age, and adults find it increasingly difficult

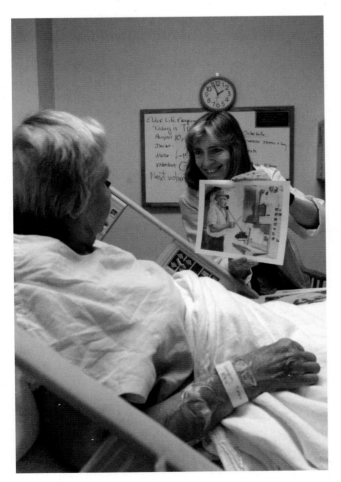

Sometimes physical and psychological health conditions, such as depression or dehydration, or medications can cause delirium, dementia-like cognitive symptoms that are temporary.
Bill Greene/The Boston Globe via Getty Images

to resist interference from irrelevant information to stay focused on the task at hand (Sylvain-Roy, Lungu, & Belleville, 2014). Researchers have assessed attention with laboratory tasks in which participants are presented with a series of letter combinations and told to press the space bar only when they see a particular combination (such as T-L); they are to ignore all other combinations. In such tasks, adults' performance declines steadily from the 30s on. Older adults make more errors of commission—pressing the space bar after incorrect letter combinations—suggesting that they are less able to inhibit responding to extraneous information (Mani, Bedwell, & Miller, 2005). Older adults also make more errors of omission—not pressing the space bar in response to the correct sequence—when the task was accompanied by extraneous noise. Older adults are less likely to inhibit irrelevant items, are slower at inhibiting a response, and are more likely to retrieve irrelevant items, especially in tasks that are complex and include the presence of distracters (Bloemendaal et al., 2016; Gazzaley, Sheridan, Cooney, & D'Esposito, 2007; Rowe, Hasher, & Turcotte, 2010). In everyday life, these changes in attention might make older adults appear more easily distracted, less able to attend, and less able to take in information.

Working Memory

As we have discussed in prior chapters, age-related declines in working memory span from young through older adulthood and influence a range of cognitive tasks, including problem solving, decision making, and learning (Darowski, Helder, Zacks, Hasher, & Hambrick, 2008; Emery, Hale, & Myerson, 2008; McCabe, Roediger, McDaniel, Balota, & Hambrick, 2010). Changes in attention influence declines in working memory (Rowe et al., 2010; Sylvain-Roy et al., 2014). With age, older adults become more susceptible to distraction and are less likely to discard distracting information from working memory, which then leaves less space in working memory for completing a given task (Radvansky et al., 2005; Van Gerven, Van Boxtel, Meijer, Willems, & Jolles, 2007).

However, once material is encoded in working memory, healthy adults of all ages retain the ability to exert control over working memory—they are able to orient their attention within working memory (and stay on task) (Mok, Myers, Wallis, & Nobre, 2016). Problems with working memory vary with the number of tasks and task demands: The greater the number of tasks and demands, the worse the performance (Kessels, Meulenbroek, Fernandez, & Olde Rikkert, 2010; Voelcker-Rehage, Stronge, & Alberts, 2006). Consider an experiment that requires adults to attend and respond to two tasks at once,

such as tapping a computer screen on two alternating targets whose sizes vary systematically at the same time as generating a list of random numbers, spoken at 2-second intervals. With age, most adults find it is more difficult to simultaneously perform a motor and cognitive task such as this than it is to perform either task alone. However, practice in the motor task makes it more automatic, reducing the demands on working memory. In this way, practice can reduce (but not eliminate) age-related deficits in cognitive performance (Voelcker-Rehage & Alberts, 2007).

Age-related decline is less apparent in cognitive tasks that are more passive and less attentionally demanding, such as digit recall and visual pattern recall tasks (Bisiacchi, Borella, Bergamaschi, Carretti, & Mondini, 2008). When working memory maintenance systems are taxed, as in the case of interference, older adults perform more poorly than young and middle-aged adults. **Proactive interference** occurs when information that has previously been remembered interferes with memory for new information (Bowles & Salthouse, 2003). For example, students may experience proactive interference if they have studied a foreign language for a couple of years and then switch to beginner-level classes in another foreign language. The language they have already learned can interfere with ability to learn and use the new language. Older adults are more susceptible to interference effects than are younger adults, even when they have learned the material equally well (Jacoby, Wahlheim, Rhodes, Daniels, & Rogers, 2010). Researchers study this with working memory span tasks, in which participants are presented with repeated trials of material that they are asked to remember, recall, and then forget. Frequently the old, supposedly forgotten material interferes with older adults' ability to store new material.

Context, Task Demands, and Memory Performance

Many laboratory tests of working memory entail tasks that are similar to those encountered in school settings. Middle-aged and older adults may be less motivated by such tasks than younger adults, who likely have more recent experience in school contexts. Laboratory findings, therefore, may not accurately illustrate the everyday memory capacity of middle-aged and older adults (Salthouse, 2012). For example, when the pace of a memory task is slowed, or participants are reminded to use organization or elaboration strategies, middle-aged and older adults show better performance (Braver & West, 2008). In addition, the type of task influences performance. In one study, adults aged 19 to 68 completed memory tests under two conditions: a pressured classroom-like condition and a self-paced condition. When participants were shown a video and tested immediately (classroom-like condition), younger adults showed better recall than did the middle-aged adults. However, when participants were given a packet of information and a video to study on their own (self-paced condition), midlife adults performed just as well as young adults on recall 3 days later (Ackerman & Beier, 2006; Beier & Ackerman, 2005). This suggests that the ways in which we learn and remember change with age and experience.

The declines in memory evident in laboratory research are less apparent in everyday settings (Salthouse, 2012). Knowledge of facts (e.g., scientific facts), procedures (e.g., how to drive a car), and information related to one's vocation either remain the same or increase over the adult years (Schaie, 2013), and adults' experience and knowledge of their cognitive system (metacognition) enable them to use their memory more effectively. For example, they use external supports and strategies to maximize their memory, such as by organizing their notes or placing their car keys in a designated spot where they can be found reliably (Schwartz & Frazier, 2005). As with attention, memory declines vary with the individual and task. Most adults compensate for declines and show little to no differences in everyday settings; however, chronic stress impairs working memory (Y. A. Lee & Goto, 2015). Midlife adults who feel overwhelmed in daily life, such as those faced with many conflicting responsibilities and stressors that demand a great deal of multitasking, are more likely to rate their memory competence as poor (Vestergren & Nilsson, 2011). Multitasking is difficult for all adults, but it becomes more challenging in older adulthood. Managing and coordinating multiple tasks by switching attention among two sets of stimuli is associated with greater disruptions in working memory in older adults as compared with younger adults (Clapp, Rubens, Sabharwal, & Gazzaley, 2011). If, however, older adults have the opportunity to slow down to a pace with which they feel comfortable, they

APPLYING DEVELOPMENTAL SCIENCE

Disclosing a Dementia Diagnosis

Most adults prefer to be informed of a dementia diagnosis.
iStock/AlexRaths

The recognition of patients' autonomy, their right to understand and make decisions about their treatment, is a cornerstone of modern physician–patient relations. There is wide agreement that offering clear, honest information about diagnoses can improve psychological adjustment and reduce distress in patients (Keightley & Mitchell, 2004). For these reasons, most ethical guidelines strongly promote disclosure of a diagnosis of dementia to the affected individual (Briggs, McHale, Fitzhenry, O'Neill, & Kennelly, 2018; Fisk, Beattie, Donnelly, Byszewski, & Molnar, 2007). However, the practice of nondisclosure of dementia diagnoses is common. It is estimated that 50% of patients with Alzheimer's disease are not told about their diagnosis (Alzheimer's Association, 2015). The defense for withholding information is based on the duty of doctors to do no harm because of the lack of certainty about the diagnosis, lack of treatment or cure, cognitive decline leading to poor retention of diagnostic information, and the possibility that receiving such a diagnosis may cause or worsen an existing depression.

However, the majority of people without cognitive impairment as well as those referred to memory clinics say that they wish to know of a diagnosis of dementia (Hort, O'Brien, et al., 2010; van den Dungen et al., 2014). Learning of a diagnosis of dementia may give people with dementia and their families time to adjust and, for people with dementia, to discuss their management and care preferences and engage in advanced decision making regarding care. Disclosure has been found to decrease anxiety and depression in patients and caregivers, perhaps providing a sense of relief in finding a recognizable cause for their symptoms (Hort, O'Brien, et al., 2010; Mitchell, McCollum, & Monaghan, 2013).

The process of disclosure begins when cognitive impairment is first suspected and evolves over time

(Continued)

(Continued)

as information is obtained. Physicians should modify disclosure practices and descriptions to the patients' level of understanding, adopting an individualized patient-centered approach that maintains the individual's personal integrity (Fisk et al., 2007). Whenever possible and appropriate, this process should involve not only the affected individual but also his or her family and/or other current or potential future care providers (Mastwyk, Ames, Ellis, Chiu, & Dow, 2014). Effective disclosure is accompanied by attempts to express empathy, respond to adults' emotions, provide information, and guide decision making (Wynn & Carpenter, 2018). Follow-ups

can provide a progressive disclosure process to address issues, including discussions of diagnostic uncertainty, treatment options, future plans, financial planning, assigning power of attorney, wills and "living wills," and available support services.

What Do You Think?

In your view, should older adults diagnosed with dementia be informed of their diagnosis? Discuss the characteristics and qualities of dementia that influence your decision of whether to inform a patient. ●

---

can show performance on working memory tasks similar to that of younger adults (Verhaeghen, Steitz, Sliwinski, & Cerella, 2003).

The sensitive subject of informing a patient that he or she has a dementia diagnosis is discussed in the Applying Developmental Science feature.

Emotion and Working Memory

Age differences in working memory are usually assessed by tasks that require older and younger adults to complete various tasks in a laboratory setting. Although standard lab tasks often show age-related declines in working memory, there are instances in which older adults show capacities similar to those of younger adults. Older adults score better on measures of complex thinking when the task evokes positive feelings than when the task is designed to evoke neutral or negative feelings (Carpenter, Peters, Västfjäll, & Isen, 2013). For example, one study examined age differences in working memory for emotional versus visual information. Findings demonstrate that, despite an age-related deficit for visual information, working memory for emotion was unimpaired (Mikels, Larkin, Reuter-Lorenz, & Cartensen, 2005). Positive mood enhances working memory capacity so that adults are better able to hold onto information while processing task-irrelevant information when in a positive mood. However, a negative mood is not related to either an increase or decrease in working memory (Storbeck & Maswood, 2016). In another study, although young adults were better able to recall neutral words than were older adults, there were no age differences in recall of emotional words such as *peace, joy, love,* or *smile* (Mammarella, Borella, Carretti, Leonardi, & Fairfield, 2013). A meta-analysis of the positivity effect of 100 studies shows that older adults are

naturally biased toward recalling positive over negative information, while younger adults show the reverse, with more attention on the negative (Reed, Chan, & Mikels, 2014).

What are the reasons for this positivity effect in older adults' memories? It may be due to their greater focus on managing their emotions. That is, older adults may use cognitive control mechanisms that enhance positive and diminish negative information to feel good (Mather & Carstensen, 2005). This finding has appeared in research with Chinese and Korean adults, suggesting that the positivity bias with age may appear cross-culturally (Gutchess & Boduroglu, 2015). Although they are often studied separately, emotion and cognition are intertwined (Reed & Carstensen, 2012). Emotion characterizes most real-life decisions, suggesting that older adults are likely able to focus their attention and cognitive capacities on the task at hand, if it has real-world emotional relevance, such as decisions about health care, financial, and living situations (Samanez-Larkin, Robertson, Mikels, Carstensen, & Gotlib, 2009).

Long-Term Memory

Age-related changes in working memory also contribute to changes in long-term memory. As cognitive processing slows, most adults show difficulties with recall. For example, while watching a television show, an older adult may retain fewer details than a young adult. However, the various types of long-term memory show different patterns of change. Semantic memory, memory for factual material, shows little age-related decline, while episodic memory, memory for experiences, tends to deteriorate with age (St. Laurent, Abdi, Burianová, & Grady, 2011).

FIGURE 17.14

Age and Cohort Differences in Cognitive Aging

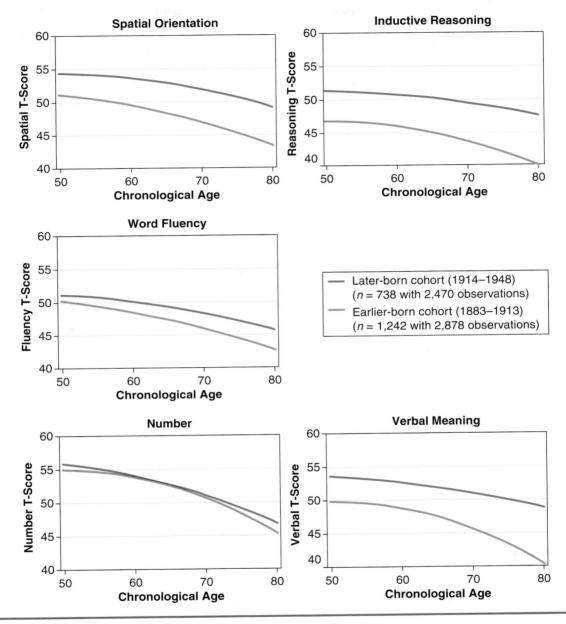

Source: Gerstorf et al. (2011).

Autobiographical memory shows predictable patterns of deterioration. When older adults are asked to discuss a personal memory or experience that comes to mind in response to cue words, such as the words *surprise* or *song*, they commonly recall experiences they had during adolescence and early adulthood. Similarly, when asked to create a timeline of memorable events in their lives, older adults tend to remember events from adolescence through early adulthood; they also remember recent events better than midlife events (Rubin, 2000; Schroots,

van Dijkum, & Assink, 2004). In addition, they are more likely to remember happy events that occurred between ages 10 and 30 than those that occurred any other time in life (Berntsen & Rubin, 2002).

Why does long-term memory follow this pattern? Perhaps we process events differently during our adolescent and early adult years, a time when we are constructing our identities. And perhaps we are less adept at recalling events from middle adulthood because of interference, as new memories interfere with our recall of older memories. Similarities among events may make it difficult to distinguish them. Throughout life, memory is malleable, and we often revise our memories in light of new experiences. However, it also appears that older adults recall fewer details from recent events (within the past 5 years) and different types of details than do younger adults. This suggests that older and younger adults differ in what stimuli they attend to and select for processing (Gaesser, Sacchetti, Addis, & Schacter, 2011; Piolino et al., 2006; Pascale Piolino et al., 2010).

Contextual factors play a role in the rate of cognitive change. As shown in Figure 17.14, similar to findings of cohort differences in intelligence scores, generational differences in overall cognitive performance are maintained throughout life. Specifically, younger cohorts show better performance on a range of cognitive measures and less steep age-related declines (Gerstorf, Ram, Hoppmann, Willis, & Schaie, 2011). Possible factors underlying cohort differences include secular trends in educational systems, disease prevalence, years of education, and quality of education.

Aging and Language

Language comprehension, the ability to understand spoken or written language and retrieve the meaning of words, shows little to no change with age. In fact, older adults maintain or improve their knowledge of words and word meanings, an example of the increases in crystallized intelligence that occur into older adulthood (Shafto & Tyler, 2014).

Changes in sensory and cognitive processing, however, can affect language comprehension and production. Hearing loss can make it more difficult to hear all of the words spoken in a conversation, so that listeners must work hard to make sense of what other people are saying, especially in the presence of background noise (Stine-Morrow, Shake, & Noh, 2010). Older adults might miss critical pieces of information and have difficulty effectively participating in conversations. Yet older adults also have a rich backlog of experiences from which to draw when they listen, enabling them to compensate for impaired hearing. Even if they are unable to hear each word, they are often able to derive the meaning of the collective words used in a straightforward conversation (Stewart & Wingfield, 2009). For example, after watching a particular soap opera for many years, an adult can often anticipate and understand what the characters are saying as well as the content of interactions even without hearing every spoken word (Stine-Morrow, Soederberg Miller, Gagne, & Hertzog, 2008).

Most older adults experience some deficits in the accuracy and speed of word retrieval and naming (Owens, 2015). Picture naming studies show that older adults name objects less accurately and more slowly than do young adults (Feyereisen, Demaeght, & Samson, 1998; Stine-Morrow et al., 2010). In conversations, older adults produce more ambiguous references and more filled pauses (e.g., saying *um* or *er*) and reformulate their words more than young adults do (Horton, Spieler, & Shriberg, 2010), suggesting that older adults have difficulty retrieving the appropriate words when speaking. They use more unclear references and speak more slowly, taking time to retrieve words. The most common language-related deficit that older adults report is difficulty recalling specific words while in conversation (Ossher, Flegal, & Lustig, 2013). For example, older adults are more prone to the *"tip-of-the-tongue" phenomenon,* in which one temporarily cannot recall a specific word but can recall words with similar meaning (Schwartz & Frazier, 2005). Although people of all ages suffer such word-finding failures, older adults experience more tip-of-the-tongue errors than do younger adults (Mortensen, Meyer, & Humphreys, 2006; Shafto, Stamatakis, Tam, & Tyler, 2010). Older adults are therefore more likely than younger adults to use indefinite words, such as *thing,* in place of specific names. This is likely due to deficits in working memory and slower processing speed (Burke & Shafto, 2004; Mortensen et al., 2006; Salthouse & Madden, 2013).

Difficulties in retrieving words and producing language may diminish older adults' success in communicating and weaken their and others' views of their own language competence. Negative self-appraisals promote withdrawal from social interaction. Yet similar to managing other cognitive declines, older adults often compensate for losses. They may take more time in speaking and simplify their sentences and grammar to devote their cognitive resources to retrieving words and producing speech that others can comprehend.

Problem Solving and Wisdom

Cognitive changes in older adulthood are also reflected in problem-solving skills. For example, laboratory studies of problem solving that rely on traditional hypothetical problems show declines with age (Sinnott, 2003). Yet when decisions tap into relevant experience or knowledge, older adults tend to be as effective at making decisions as younger adults (Denney, Pearce, & Palmer, 1982). Moreover, examinations of problem-solving skills in everyday settings show that people remain efficient decision makers throughout adulthood. For example, older adults tend to show adaptive problem solving in response to health-related decisions; they are actually better than younger adults at making decisions about whether they require medical attention and seeking medical care (Artistico, Orom, Cervone, Krauss, & Houston, 2010; Löckenhoff & Carstensen, 2007). In one study, the quality of reasoning behind decisions of 60- to 74-year-olds and 75- to 85-year-olds did not differ from that of college students, but older adults processed the problems more slowly (Ratcliff, Thapar, & McKoon, 2006).

Generally speaking, adults perform better on everyday problems that are relevant to the contexts they experience in their daily lives (Artistico et al., 2010). Specifically, older adults outperformed young and middle-aged adults on problems set in older adult contexts, such as medical care, suggesting that age-related declines observed in laboratory settings may not be observed in everyday life. In addition, older adults are more likely to act efficiently and decisively in solving problems that they feel are under their control (Thornton & Dumke, 2005). Older adults may be better at matching their strategies to their goals than are young adults, perhaps because experience and crystallized knowledge provide an extensive base for making real-life decisions and aligning goals with decisions (Hoppmann & Blanchard-Fields, 2010). In older adults, crystallized intelligence is a better predictor of performance on everyday problem-solving tasks than fluid intelligence, suggesting importance of experience (Chen, Hertzog, & Park, 2017). Finally, older adults are more likely than younger people to report that they turn to spouses, children, and friends for input in making decisions (Strough, Patrick, & Swenson, 2003).

Related to everyday problem solving, it is commonly thought that older adults become wiser with age. **Wisdom** refers to "expertise in the conduct and meanings of life," characterized by emotional maturity and the ability to show insight and apply it to problems (P. B. Baltes & Kunzmann, 2003; Staudinger, Kessler, & Dörner, 2006). It requires knowledge, not in the "book smarts" sense, but the ability to analyze real-world dilemmas in which clean and neat abstractions often give way to messy, disorderly, conflicting concrete interests. Wisdom requires metacognition, being aware of one's thought process, creativity, and insightfulness.

The belief that age brings wisdom is reflected in many societies' respect for older adults as society elders and leaders. Research, on the other hand, shows variability in the extent to which older adults actually display wisdom (Karelitz et al., 2010). In typical studies examining wisdom, researchers rated adults aged 20 to 89 in their response to hypothetical situations reflecting uncertain events, such as what to do if a friend is contemplating suicide (Staudinger, Dörner, & Mickler, 2005). Researchers rated each response for the degree to which it illustrates several components of wisdom: knowledge about fundamental concerns of life such as human nature,

strategies for applying that knowledge to making life decisions, ability to consider multiple contextual demands, and awareness and management of ambiguity in that many problems have no perfect solutions. A small number of adults at all ages scored high in wisdom; they had experience in dealing with human problems, such as that which occurs in human service careers or in leadership roles (Staudinger & Baltes, 1996; Staudinger et al., 2006). When both age and experience were taken into account, older adults were indeed more likely to show wisdom than were younger adults. In other studies, however, college education is an important predictor of wisdom for adults of all ages, suggesting that wisdom does not necessarily come with age but rather with the opportunity and motivation to pursue its development (Ardelt, 2010; Ardelt, Pridgen, & Nutter-Pridgen, 2018).

Wisdom is especially likely to be shown when considering personal problems that are most relevant to individuals. For example, in one study, younger and older adults completed traditional measures of wisdom (hypothetical dilemmas) as well as were asked to discuss personal problems relevant to young adults, specifically, marital conflict. Marital conflict problems were presented in written vignettes and in video clips. There were no age differences in the traditional wisdom task, but in the marital conflict tasks, the young adults gave responses more indicative of wisdom than did the older adults. It appears that relevance matters—we see age differences in wise reasoning about fundamental life issues depend on relevance of problems (Thomas & Kunzmann, 2014).

Life experience, particularly facing and managing adversity, contributes to the development of wisdom. One study of people who came of age during the Great Depression of the 1930s found that, 40 years later, older adults who had experienced and overcome economic adversity demonstrated higher levels of wisdom than their peers (Ardelt, 1998). Experience, particularly expertise in solving the problems of everyday life, is associated with wisdom (P. B. Baltes & Staudinger, 2000). It is not simply experience that matters, however. Those who are wise are reflective; they attempt to find meaning in their experiences (Weststrate & Glück, 2017). They also have advanced cognition and emotional regulation skills, qualities that contribute to the development of wisdom but are also associated with better physical health, higher levels of education, openness to experience, positive social relationships, and overall psychological well-being (Zacher & Staudinger, 2018). What can we conclude about wisdom? Perhaps that it is a rare quality, one that can be found at all ages but that typically improves with age and is associated with well-being. And, older adults are more likely to be among the very wise.

Older adults are more likely to display insight into the meanings of life and to apply it to problems—to be wise.
Liu Guangming/Xinhua Press/Corbis

Influences on Cognitive Change in Adulthood

Cognitive abilities tend to remain stable, relative to peers, over the lifespan. For example, high intelligence early in life (e.g., at age 11) is predictive of intelligence in old age (through age 87) (Gow, Corley, Starr, & Deary, 2012). However, with advancing age comes greater diversity in cognitive ability. Centenarians, people age 100 or older, show greater variations in cognitive performance than do older adults aged 85 to 90 (L. S. Miller et al., 2010; Paúl, Ribeiro, & Santos, 2010). Differences in experience and lifestyle can account for many differences in cognitive change over adulthood.

Cross-sectional research shows that education, measured by years of formal schooling or by literacy levels on reading tests, is a strong and consistent predictor of cognitive performance and problem-solving tasks in old age (Kavé, Eyal, Shorek, & Cohen-Mansfield, 2008). In fact, findings from the Georgia Centenarian Study suggest that education accounted for the largest proportion of cognitive differences among the centenarians studied (Davey

et al., 2010). Recall from Chapter 1 that cross-sectional and longitudinal studies often yield different results. Similar to research on cognitive change in older adulthood, the influence of education on cognitive change varies depending on whether the study is cross-sectional or longitudinal (Van Dijk, Van Gerven, Van Boxtel, Van Der Elst, & Jolles, 2008). Longitudinal research studies with older adults from Germany, Australia, and the United States, spanning 7 to 13 years in length with testing occurring at three to six time points, do not find a relationship between education and cognitive decline at older age (Anstey, Hofer, & Luszcz, 2003; Van Dijk et al., 2008). The effects of education are debated, but it is generally recognized that throughout life, cognitive engagement—through mentally stimulating career, educational, and leisure activities—predicts the maintenance of mental abilities (Bielak, 2010; Schaie, 2013).

Another predictor of cognitive performance and impairment across the lifespan is physical health (Blondell, Hammersley-Mather, & Veerman, 2014; S. Wang, Luo, Barnes, Sano, & Yaffe, 2014). Health conditions such as cardiovascular disease, osteoporosis, and arthritis are associated with cognitive declines (M. M. Baltes & Carstensen, 2003; Okonkwo et al., 2010). Longitudinal studies also suggest that poor mental health, such as depression and anxiety, is associated with declines in processing speed, long-term memory, and problem solving (Lönnqvist, 2010; Margrett et al., 2010). It is difficult to disentangle the directional effects of health and cognitive decline, however, because people who score higher on cognitive measures are more likely to engage in health-promoting behaviors.

Interventions that train older adults and encourage them to use cognitive skills can preserve and even reverse some age-related cognitive declines. One study of participants in the Seattle Longitudinal Study examined the effects of cognitive training on cognitive development in older adulthood (Schaie, 2013). Older adults were administered 51 hours' worth of guided practice completing test items similar to those on a mental ability test and then were tested on two mental ability tests. Two thirds of adults showed gains in performance, and 40% of those who showed cognitive decline prior to the study returned to their level of functioning 14 years earlier. Training improved strategy use and performance on verbal memory, working memory, and short-term memory tasks. Most promising is that 7 years later, older adults who had received training scored higher on mental ability tests than their peers. In other research, training improved measures of processing speed and fluid intelligence, and these improvements were retained over an 8-month period (Borella, Carretti, Riboldi, & De Beni, 2010). Older adults' improvement with intervention is often similar in magnitude to that of younger adults, including gains in working memory, sustained attention, and fewer complaints about memory (Brehmer, Westerberg, & Bäckman, 2012). Other research suggests that gains from working memory interventions generalize to other measures of fluid intelligence (Stepankova et al., 2014). One meta-analysis concluded that working memory and executive functioning training leads to large gains in the trained tasks and large transfer effects to similar tasks measuring the same construct as the trained tasks. There were also clear but smaller transfer effects for different cognitive abilities than those tested. Overall, it seems that generalization takes place in people of all ages who receive cognitive training (Karbach & Verhaeghen, 2014).

However, these findings should be taken with caution. A meta-analysis of 87 studies of working memory training found immediate transfer right after training on measured tasks—but these improvements were short term and specific. They did not transfer to other cognitive skills, nor did they generalize to real-world cognitive skills (Melby-Lervåg, Redick, & Hulme, 2016).

Although older adults experience cognitive declines, there is a great deal of variability in everyday functioning. It is possible to retain and improve cognitive skills in older adulthood. The challenge is to encourage older adults to seek the experiences that will help them retain their mental abilities. Older adults who maintain a high cognitive functioning tend to engage in selective optimization with compensation: They compensate for declines in cognitive reserve or energy by narrowing their goals and selecting activities that will permit them to maximize their strengths and existing capacities. In all, healthy older adults retain the capacity to engage in efficient controlled processing of information.

 THINKING IN CONTEXT 17.4

1. Consider the cognitive changes that occur over the lifespan. In your view, are cognitive development, reasoning, and decision making best described as developing continuously or discontinuously? (Recall these concepts from Chapter 1.) Why?

2. An important theme of lifespan development is that development is characterized by gains and losses. How might the cognitive changes that adults experience illustrate this?

3. What factors might make older adults better decision makers than young adults? Worse?

 APPLY YOUR KNOWLEDGE

"Do you really think she can go back home?" Elliot asked his sister, Judith. "I don't know. The next fall might be much more serious," Judith replied. "I want to go home. I'll be fine," insisted their mother, Ruth. Hospitalized over the past 2 days, 85-year-old Ruth is impatient and ready to go home. Like many other older adults, she no longer drives because her vision is poor. She often finds herself not hungry so sometimes skips meals. Despite her poor eating habits, Ruth has felt that she manages her diabetes well and keeps her blood glucose levels in a healthy range. Osteoarthritis, however, makes Ruth's daily routine more challenging. She has difficulty opening pill bottles, reading newspapers, and sometimes working doorknobs. Ruth has adapted to these challenges by purchasing tools and gadgets, such as nonchildproof pill bottles and nonslip grips for doorknobs. Ruth's children worry about their mother's ability to manage her daily life, and more important, they fear that she will injure herself in a fall or accident.

1. What developmental changes make it more difficult for older adults to live independently?

2. In your view, is Ruth capable of independent living? Why or why not? If not, what supports can help her live as independently as possible?

3. How do her illnesses complicate Ruth's ability to live independently?

4. Ruth's children worry about injuries. Is their worry founded? Discuss factors that influence injuries in older adulthood as well as the possible consequences of injuries.

$SAGE edge™

Visit **edge.sagepub.com/kuther2e** to help you accomplish your coursework goals in an easy-to-use learning environment.

LEARNING OBJECTIVES	SUMMARY	KEY TERMS	IN REVIEW
17.1 Discuss age-related changes in brain and body systems in late adulthood, and identify ways that older adults may compensate for changes.	The loss of neurons contributes to reduced brain volume, especially in the prefrontal cortex. Reductions in myelination contribute to slower communication among neurons. Structural changes in the eye make it difficult to see in dim light and to adapt to dramatic changes in light. Vision may be impaired by the presence of cataracts and macular degeneration. Hearing loss from presbycusis increases from middle into older adulthood. Older adults compensate for sensory losses by modifying their behaviors and environment as well as through surgery and medication. With age, body systems become less efficient.	Cognitive reserve Cataracts Macular degeneration	Describe typical changes in appearance in late adulthood. What age-related brain changes occur and how does the brain compensate for these changes? Describe sensory and physical changes and their impact on older adults. How do motor skills change, and how do these changes influence older adults' day-to-day functioning?
17.2 Identify risk and protective factors for health in late adulthood.	Nutrition is an important influence on immunity and overall health. Moderate physical activity is associated with improved physiological function, less disease and disability, better mental health, and higher quality of life. Nearly all older adults show signs of osteoarthritis. Injury-related fatalities rise dramatically in older adulthood. In older adulthood, brittle bones mean that falls result in fractures, especially hip fractures, which immobilize an older adult, are painful, and take a great deal of time to heal.	Young-old Old-old Oldest-old Successful aging Osteoarthritis Rheumatoid arthritis	Differentiate among three age categories of older adults. How does nutrition and exercise contribute to health and well-being in late adulthood? Describe common chronic illnesses in late adulthood. What types of injuries are most common among older adults? What are some risk and protective factors associated with these types of injuries?
17.3 Summarize common dementias, including characteristics, risk and protective factors, and treatment.	Alzheimer's disease is characterized by widespread brain deterioration and the presence of beta-amyloid plaques and neurofibrillary tangles in the cerebral cortex. Vascular dementia is caused by a series of strokes. Lewy body dementia is caused by a proliferation of Lewy bodies. Parkinson's disease occurs when neurons in the substantia nigra die or become impaired and are unable to produce dopamine. Dementia emerges in the late stages of Parkinson's disease. Each disease has a predictable course. Genetic and environmental factors contribute to dementia. Generally, the symptoms of dementia are treated as most cannot be cured.	Dementia Alzheimer's disease Amyloid plaques Neurofibrillary tangles Vascular dementia Parkinson's disease Lewy body dementia Delirium	For each of the following forms of dementia, identify characteristics, risk and protective factors, and treatments: Alzheimer's disease Vascular disease Parkinson's disease Lewy body dementia What are common causes of delirium?
17.4 Analyze patterns of cognitive change in late adulthood.	Declines in working memory are influenced by reduced sensory capacity and reduced processing speed. The various types of long-term memory show different patterns of change. People remain adaptive problem solvers throughout adulthood. Adults perform best on everyday problems that are relevant to the contexts they experience in their daily lives. Wisdom does not necessarily come with age but rather with the opportunity and motivation to pursue its development. Older adults with higher levels of education, engaging careers, and leisure activities tend to retain their mental abilities. Many physical and mental conditions are associated with cognitive decline. Older adults who maintain a high cognitive functioning tend to compensate for declines in cognitive reserve or energy by modifying their goals and activities.	Proactive interference Wisdom	How do attention and working memory change in late adulthood? How do contextual and emotional factors influence adults' performance on memory tasks? Identify common age-related changes in language abilities. Does wisdom come with age? What factors influence cognitive change in late adulthood?

PRACTICE AND APPLY WHAT YOU'VE LEARNED

▶ edge.sagepub.com/kuther2e

CHECK YOUR COMPREHENSION ON THE STUDY SITE WITH:

- **Diagnostic Quizzes** to identify opportunities for improvement.

- **Multimedia Resources** that explore chapter content using media and current events.

- **Journal Articles** that support and expand on chapter concepts.

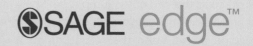

18 Socioemotional Development in Late Adulthood

"Hold the end, and swing it gently in time with your sister," 72-year-old Jennifer instructed her grandson as he grasped the end of the jump rope. She watched as he and his sister swung the rope and a third grandchild hopped in between them, beginning a game of jump rope. "When I was little I could jump double Dutch. Do you know what that is?" Jennifer asks her grandchildren. Jennifer thinks back in time, closes her eyes, and smiles before she begins her explanation.

The "terrible twos" of toddlerhood, adolescent angst, and the midlife crisis are periods of development that are accompanied by stereotypes—beliefs about commonalities shared by members of a given age group. Older adulthood is no different. Ageist attitudes abound in popular culture. Stereotypes of older adults include the belief that they are lonely, lack close friends and family, have a higher rate of mood disorders, and are rigid, unable to cope with age-related declines,

Learning Objectives

18.1 Examine the contributions of self-concept, personality, and religiosity to older adults' well-being.

18.2 Identify social contexts in which older adults live and their influence on development.

18.3 Summarize features of older adults' relationships with friends, spouses, children, and grandchildren, and identify how these relationships affect older adults' functioning.

18.4 Discuss influences on the timing of retirement and adaptation to retirement.

Digital Resources

Explore: The Life Review in Early Dementia

Listen: Overprescribed in Nursing Homes

▶ **Lives in Context Video 18.1:** Multigenerational Family

Connect: Aging Well With a Little Help From One's Friends

Watch: Retirement: The Best Years

▶ **Lives in Context Video 18.2:** Retirement Transition and Adjustment

one-dimensional, sick, dependent, and cognitive and psychologically impaired. Common stereotypes about elders' cognitive functioning and mental health are misguided. As shown in Figure 18.1, older adults experience fewer challenges of aging than young and middle-age adults expect.

In this chapter, we examine the socioemotional transitions of older adulthood, including changes in

how elders view themselves, changes in the contexts in which they live, their evolving relationships, and changes in work habits. Again, it will be apparent that the reality of life in late adulthood does not conform to many of the stereotypes or commonly held views about older adults.

FIGURE 18.1

Challenges of Aging as Expected and Experienced by Older Adults

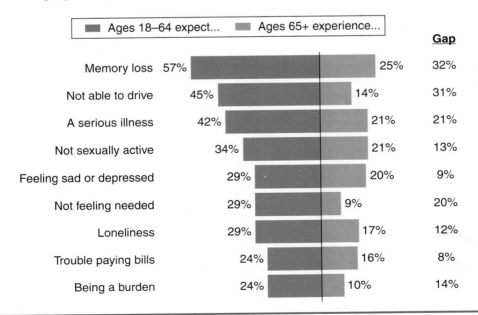

	Ages 18–64 expect...	Ages 65+ experience...	Gap
Memory loss	57%	25%	32%
Not able to drive	45%	14%	31%
A serious illness	42%	21%	21%
Not sexually active	34%	21%	13%
Feeling sad or depressed	29%	20%	9%
Not feeling needed	29%	9%	20%
Loneliness	29%	17%	12%
Trouble paying bills	24%	16%	8%
Being a burden	24%	10%	14%

Source: Reprinted with permission from "Growing Old in America: Expectations vs. Reality," Pew Research Center, Washington, DC (July, 2009). http://www.pewsocialtrends.org/2009/06/29/growing-old-in-america-expectations-vs-reality/.

THE SELF IN LATE ADULTHOOD

» LO 18.1   Examine the contributions of self-concept, personality, and religiosity to older adults' well-being.

Although global self-esteem tends to decline in late life, most adults maintain a positive view of themselves, expressing more positive than negative self-evaluations well into old age (Meier, Orth, Denissen, & Kühnel, 2011; Orth, 2017). For example, both old (70 to 84) and very old (85 to 103) adults rated themselves more positively than negatively with regard to a variety of domains, including hobbies, interests, family, health, and personality, and these positive self-evaluations predicted psychological well-being (Freund & Smith, 1999). Older adults tend to compartmentalize their self-concept more so than younger and middle-aged adults by categorizing the positive and negative aspects of self as separate roles, whereas younger and middle-aged adults tend to integrate them into one (Ready, Carvalho, & Åkerstedt, 2012). Life experience and advances in cognitive affective complexity (see Chapter 15) underlie older adults' multifaceted self-

 ## Cultural Attitudes Toward Old Adults

How are older adults viewed? Are they viewed in a positive or negative light? Why?
iStock/PamelaJoeMcFarlane

Attitudes toward older adults influence how they are treated and hold the potential to influence how older adults view themselves. Some research suggests that people tend to have more negative attitudes toward older adults than younger adults, but these studies have been conducted with North Americans and Europeans (Zhang et al., 2016). Western values emphasizing the individual, self-interest, and freedom may be to blame. Few studies have examined attitudes toward older adults across cultures.

Eastern collectivist cultures emphasize social interdependence, commitment to family, and self-sacrifice. For example, the cultural practice of filial piety refers to children's obligation to care for their aging parents physically, emotionally, and financially, and this may influence attitudes toward older adults. Collectivist values may support more positive attitudes toward older adults than individualist values (S. C. Tan & Barber, 2018).

Research, however, is mixed. Some comparisons of young adults from Eastern and Western cultures have shown more positive attitudes in Eastern than Western cultures, others report the opposite, and still others show no difference (Cuddy et al., 2009; Huang, 2013; Luo, Zhou, Jin, Newman, & Liang, 2013). One explanation for the mixed findings draws a distinction between cultural values and personal values (Zhang et al., 2016).

Frequently, personal values are consistent with cultural values, but sometimes personal values differ (Markus & Kitayama, 2010). People may adopt values at the cultural level, but their self-concept is constructed at a personal level and may differ from cultural values. A cross-cultural data set including over 45,000 people from 35 nations contrasted country-level cultural values with personal values (Zhang et al., 2016). The results showed that individuals' attitude toward older adults was more influenced by personal values than by cultural values. Measures of individualism at the country level were unrelated to attitude toward old adults; however, communal values at the individual level were. This suggests that, across cultures, people tend to hold a more positive attitude toward older adults if they have strong personal values of communalism, but a cultural value toward individualism does not have an adverse effect on attitudes about older adults (Zhang et al., 2016).

What Do You Think?

What factors might contribute to individuals' views of older adults? How might we foster communal views in people? ●

conceptions and evaluations. The developmental task for older adults is to accept their weaknesses and compensate by focusing on their strengths. Over time, adults reframe their sense of self by revising their possible selves in light of experience and emphasizing goals related to the sense of self, relationships, and health (Smith & Freund, 2002). Adults' reports of life satisfaction and well-being typically increase into old age, along with corresponding decreases in negative affect (Darbonne, Uchino, & Ong, 2012; Jeste & Oswald, 2014). Cultural views about aging, as discussed in the Cultural Influences on Development feature, may also influence older adults' perceptions.

Subjective Age

Throughout life, perceived age is an important part of our self-concept. Most older adults tend to feel that they are younger than their years, and this tendency increases with age (Bergland, Nicolaisen, & Thorsen, 2014; Shinan-Altman & Werner, 2018). Research with U.S., German, and Chinese adults suggests that this pattern occurs cross-culturally (O'Brien et al., 2017).

Why do older adults feel younger than their years? One reason may have to do with avoiding the self-categorization of being old (Kornadt & Rothermund, 2012). Categorizing oneself as a member of one's age group influences how individuals think about themselves, their competencies, and their future (D. Weiss & Lang, 2012). Given the negative stereotypes associated with aging, adults may employ strategies to avoid the negative consequences of identification with their age group such as denying or hiding their age by excluding themselves from the "old age" category (Heckhausen & Brim, 1997). Adults with more negative self-views are more likely to feel older than their years over time (Kornadt, Hess, Voss, & Rothermund, 2018). In addition, individuals experiencing challenging contexts and situations, such as those experiencing financial distress, tend to report older subjective ages (Agrigoroaei, Lee-Attardo, & Lachman, 2017).

Subjective age is associated with health and well-being, including the risk for cardiovascular disease, engagement in health behaviors, life satisfaction, and longevity (Kornadt & Rothermund, 2012; Mock & Eibach, 2011). Individuals who feel younger than their years are less likely to internalize negative stereotypes about aging and they remain active, which promotes good heath (Kotter-Grühn, Kornadt, & Stephan, 2016). Younger subjective ages are associated with physical functioning, such as grip strength (Stephan, Chalabaev, Kotter-Grühn, & Jaconelli, 2013). Cognitive performance is also related to subjective age. For example, in one longitudinal study, older adults who reported feeling younger relative to their peers tended to show better performance and slower declines in recall tasks over a 10-year period (Stephan, Caudroit, Jaconelli, & Terracciano, 2014).

Subjective age is malleable in response to contextual conditions. For example, one study found that older adults reported feeling older after taking a working memory test but not after a vocabulary test (Hughes, Geraci, & De Forrest, 2013). Recall from Chapter 15 that age-related declines are seen in tasks tapping fluid intelligence, such as working memory, but not tasks tapping crystallized intelligence, such as vocabulary. More important, simply expecting to take a memory test was associated with feeling subjectively older, suggesting that perception of abilities in various domains can influence perceived age (Hughes et al., 2013). Collectively, these findings suggest that the old adage, "You're only as old as you feel," is partially true as one's perception of one's own age is dynamically associated with health, well-being, and cognitive performance.

Reminiscence and Life Review

Self-concept remains stable over the lifespan. Adults who have lived a relatively long life tend to reminisce and review their past experiences and achievements, reaffirming their sense of self (Prebble, Addis, & Tippett, 2013). They often tell stories and discuss their thoughts about people and events they have experienced. **Reminiscence,** the vocal or silent recall of events in a person's life, happens naturally in everyday conversations and serves a variety of functions (Demiray, Mischler, & Martin, 2018;

Engaging in healthy behaviors, such as exercise and social interaction, positively impacts subjective age.
istockphoto/Django

D. B. King, Cappeliez, Canham, & O'Rourke, 2018). Older adults who engage in knowledge-based reminiscence recall problems that they have encountered and problem-solving strategies they have used. Recalling past experience and acquired knowledge and sharing it with young people is rewarding, life enriching, and positively associated with well-being (O'Rourke, Cappeliez, & Claxton, 2011; Westerhof, Bohlmeijer, & Webster, 2010). A study of Canadian older adults surveyed three times, each about 8 months apart, found that the tendency to reminisce about positive experiences predicted physical and mental health 8 and 16 months later (D. B. King et al., 2018). Reminiscence can also help adults in managing life transitions, such as retirement or widowhood, and provide a sense of personal continuity, preserving a sense of self despite these changes. The tendency to reminisce and the positive or negative content of shared memories tend to remain stable over time. For example, in one study of adults over the age of 50, people who reminisced about positive experiences continued to do so 16 months later (O'Rourke, King, & Cappeliez, 2017). Unfortunately, ruminating over negative events was also stable. When adults focus and ruminate bitterly over difficult events, they sustain and even increase negative emotions, as well as show poor adjustment (Cully, LaVoie, & Gfeller, 2001).

Related to reminiscence, but more comprehensive, is **life review,** reflecting on past experiences and contemplating the meaning of those experiences and their role in shaping one's life (R. N. Butler, 1963). Life review permits self-understanding and helps older adults assign meaning to their lives (R. N. Butler, 1974; Erikson, 1982). Specifically, life review can help elders adapt to and accept the triumphs and disappointments of their lives, become more tolerant and accepting of others, become free of the feeling that time is running out, and enhance emotional integration, life satisfaction, and well-being.

Individual and group interventions can encourage and aid older adults in reminiscence and life review (Davis & Degges-White, 2008). Reminiscence is fostered by encouraging autobiographical storytelling to teach others, remember positive events, and enhance positive feelings. Life review interventions, often conducted by therapists and case workers at community mental health centers and senior centers, tend to focus on helping older adults to evaluate and integrate positive and negative life events into a coherent life story (Webster, Bohlmeijer, & Westerhof, 2010; Westerhof, 2015). Social support may facilitate the life review process in elders, as interaction with others can help to point out blind spots and self-serving biases that arise in the

The ways in which we describe ourselves, self-concept, tends to remain stable over our lives.
iStock/Wicki58

process of autobiographical reconstruction (Korte, Drossaert, Westerhof, & Bohlmeijer, 2014). Close family members and friends can provide feedback and guidance that enhance the life review process (Krause, 2007). Encouraging adults to engage in reminiscence and life review is associated with increases in a sense of mastery, well-being, purpose in life, positive mental health (including the reduction of depressive symptoms), and social integration (Pinquart & Forstmeier, 2012; Westerhof & Bohlmeijer, 2014).

Ego Integrity

Life review, reflecting on the cumulative choices that compose the story of the individual's life, is integral to developing a sense of **ego integrity versus despair,** the last stage in Erikson's (1950, 1982) psychosocial theory, in which older adults find a sense of coherence in life experiences and ultimately conclude that their lives are meaningful and valuable (Whiting & Bradley, 2007). Adults who achieve ego integrity can see their lives within a larger global and historical context and recognize that their own experiences, while important, are only a very small part of the big picture. Viewing one's life within the context of humanity can make death less fearsome, more a part of life, and simply the next step in one's path (Vaillant, 1994, 2004).

According to Erikson, the alternative to developing a sense of integrity is despair, the tragedy experienced if the retrospective looks at one's life are evaluated as meaningless and disappointing, emphasizing faults, mistakes, and what could have been (Whiting & Bradley, 2007). The despairing older adult may ruminate over lost chances and feel overwhelmed with bitterness and defeat, becoming contemptuous toward others in order to mask self-contempt. As might be expected, elders who do not develop a sense of ego integrity are more likely to experience a poor sense of well-being and depression (Dezutter, Toussaint, & Leijssen, 2014).

How does one attain ego integrity? A sense of ego integrity relies on cognitive development, such as complexity and maturity in moral judgment and thinking style, tolerance for ambiguity, and dialectical reasoning (Hearn et al., 2011). The ability to realize that there are multiple solutions to problems and recognize that one's life path may have taken many different courses is integral to developing a sense of ego identity. Ego integrity is also predicted by social factors, including social support, generativity, and good family relationships (James & Zarrett, 2006; Sheldon & Kasser, 2001). Similar to the development of identity and generativity, ego integrity is influenced by interactions with others. When older adults relay their experiences, tell family stories from their lives, and provide advice, they have opportunities to engage in the self-evaluation that can lead to ego integrity.

Personality

As in other life periods, personality traits remain stable into late adulthood such that older adults' scores relative to peers remain stable over their lifetimes. For example, adults who scored high in extroversion relative to their peers at age 30 tend to continue to score high relative to their peers in old age (Graham & Lachman, 2012). Research examining Big 5 personality traits suggests that the stereotype of older adults becoming rigid and set in their ways is untrue. Personality traits shift subtly over the life course in patterns suggesting that most people experience a mellowing of personality characteristics with age. For example, a longitudinal study that examined adults aged 60 through their 80s found that over one third of the sample scored highest on agreeableness in their 80s (A. Weiss et al., 2005). Extroversion and openness to experience decline with age from 30 to 90, with the most pronounced drops after the mid-50s (Lucas & Donnellan, 2011; Wortman, Lucas, & Donnellan, 2012). Conscientiousness increases from emerging to mid-adulthood, peaks between 50 and 70, and then declines. These findings are also supported by cross-cultural research with adults from 50 countries (McCrae, Terracciano, & The Personality Profiles of Cultures Project, 2005).

Individuals' patterns of Big 5 personality traits predict physical and cognitive functioning. For example, conscientiousness is associated with health and longevity, as well as better performance on cognitive tasks (Bogg & Roberts, 2013; Goodwin & Friedman, 2006; Mõttus, Luciano, Starr, Pollard, & Deary, 2013). Neuroticism, on the other hand, is associated with worse average cognitive functioning and a steeper rate of decline (Chapman et al., 2012; Luchetti, Terracciano, Stephan, & Sutin, 2015). Neuroticism also predicts increasing frailty (Stephan, Sutin, Canada, & Terracciano, 2017).

Big 5 personality traits show complex associations with well-being. Specifically, well-being correlates with higher levels of extroversion, agreeableness, and conscientiousness and with lower levels of neuroticism (Cox, Wilt, Olson, & McAdams, 2010). Moreover, this relationship may be bidirectional. A study of 16,000 Australian adults revealed that their personality traits predicted changes in well-being, yet changes in well-being in turn influenced their traits (Soto, 2015). Individuals who were initially extroverted, agreeable, conscientious, and emotionally stable subsequently increased in well-being and in turn became even more agreeable, conscientious, emotionally stable, and extroverted. We have seen that well-being tends to increase over the adult years. Research from the Big 5 trait approach to personality supports this, as people in their later years tend to become happier (more agreeable and less neurotic), more self-contented and self-centered (less extroverted and open), more laid back and satisfied with what they have, and less preoccupied with productivity (less conscientious) (Kandler et al., 2015; Marsh, Nagengast, & Morin, 2012). This mellowing of personality aids older adults in adjusting to change, contributing to well-being (Reitz & Staudinger, 2017).

Religiosity in Late Adulthood

Nearly three quarters of U.S. adults report being "absolutely certain" of the existence of God or a similar spiritual entity (Pew Forum on Religious and Public Life, 2008). Religiosity can take the form of behaviors (attendance at religious services) or attitudes and orientation, such as religious affiliation and private religious practices (such as prayer; George, Ellison, & Larson, 2002). People tend to consider participation in personal religious activity such as prayer more important as they age (see Figure 18.2) (Atchley, 2016; Wink & Dillon, 2002).

Religious views vary around the world, as shown in Figure 18.3. In some countries, such as Pakistan, older and younger adults share strong beliefs about the importance of religion. In other countries, older adults report that religion is more important to them than do younger adults. Comparisons of groups of adults often reveal age differences, but longitudinal research suggests that there is stability in most adults' views of religion. For example, in a 20-year-old study of British older samples, most showed stability in their views of the importance of religion, with nearly all indicating that religion is very important to them (P. G. Coleman, Ivani-Chalian, & Robinson, 2004). Similarly, U.S. adults maintained consistent levels of religiosity and spirituality over a 40-year span, from the 1930s to the 1970s (Wink & Dillon, 2002). Other research suggests that, with age, U.S. adults experience an increase in religious intensity and strength of beliefs, supporting the role of individual differences in religiosity (Atchley, 2016; Bengtson, Silverstein, Putney, & Harris, 2015). Adults are also more likely to attend religious services with age, from middle adulthood into late adulthood. Although religious attendance declines in late adulthood, this is likely due to changes in health, mobility, and transportation (Hayward & Krause, 2013).

In North America, low socioeconomic status (SES) ethnic minority groups, such as African American, Hispanic, Native American, and Canadian Aboriginal elders, show the highest rates of religious participation. For

FIGURE 18.2

Importance of Religion by Age Groups

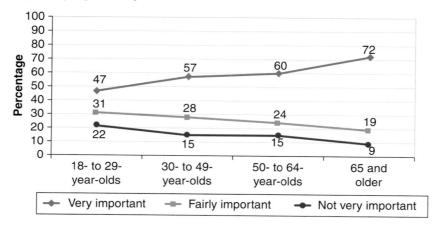

Source: Newport, F. (November 29, 2006). Religion Most Important to Blacks, Women, and Older Americans: Gallup Poll. Reprinted with permission.

FIGURE 18.3

Religiosity Across Countries

Percent responding in the affirmative to specific questions on the World Values Survey, 2010–2014

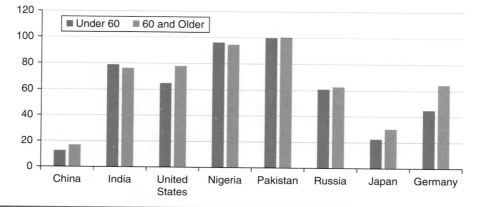

Source: Adapted from Zimmer et al. (2016).

example, African American older adults tend to report higher levels of private religious practice and daily spiritual experiences, as well as perceptions of God as holding a great deal of control over the world, than do their European American counterparts (Krause, 2005; E. K. O. Lee & Sharpe, 2007). Among U.S. residents, 79% report that religion is very important in their lives, as compared with 56% of the U.S. population overall (Pew Research Center, 2009). For many older adults, the church is a place of worship that enables them to find meaning in their lives. For African American older adults, the church often provides tangible support in the form of social connections, health interventions, and activities that improve welfare. In one study, African American respondents identified God as both their primary source of social support and their personal consultant for health-related matters, whereas European American respondents identified a variety of secular sources of help from family, friends, professionals, and clergy (E. K. O. Lee & Sharpe, 2007). Throughout adulthood, women show higher rates of religiosity and religious participation than men (Levin & Taylor, 1994; Pew Research Center, 2016; Simpson, Cloud, Newman, & Fuqua, 2008). This may be because women find religion helpful in buffering the stresses that accompany juggling multiple roles such as parent, employee, and caregiver. Although adults generally show increases in religiosity and spirituality with age, women tend to show greater increases than men (Wink & Dillon, 2002).

Religiosity in adulthood is positively associated with physical health, including more time exercising, reductions in hypertension, and increased longevity (Boswell, Kahana, & Dilworth-Anderson, 2006; Homan & Boyatzis, 2010; E. K. O. Lee, 2007; Wink, Dillon, & Prettyman, 2007; Ysseldyk, Haslam, & Haslam, 2013). Religiosity and spirituality are also associated with well-being throughout adulthood and especially in older adulthood (Abu-Raiya, Pargament, Krause, & Ironson, 2015; Galek, Flannelly, Ellison, Silton, & Jankowski, 2015; Green & Elliott, 2010). A strong sense of religiosity can buffer stress in the face of disadvantages and stressful life events and help older adults to find meaning in life (Zimmer et al., 2016). It is also associated with optimism, a sense of self-worth, life satisfaction, and low rates of depression (Keyes & Reitzes, 2007; Reed & Neville, 2014; Ronneberg, Miller, Dugan, & Porell, 2016; Ysseldyk et al., 2013).

Religious attendance may facilitate mental health through social means by increasing an older adult's connections with other people in the community, both in giving and in receiving

support (Zimmer et al., 2016). Church attendance is positively associated with social network size, frequency of social contact, and perceived support (Keyes & Reitzes, 2007; E. K. O. Lee & Sharpe, 2007). One study of nearly 1,200 older adults who attended church regularly found that most—and especially African Americans—perceived increases in the amount of emotional support they gave

Most older adults report religious or spiritual beliefs. Religiosity in older adulthood is positively associated with physical health, well-being, life satisfaction, and longevity.
iStock/PeopleImages

THINKING IN CONTEXT 18.1

1. In what ways is older adults' sense of self an important resource to help them adapt to physical and cognitive changes of aging?

2. Why might it be adaptive to have a younger subjective age? Are there any disadvantages or potential harms of feeling younger than one's age?

3. How might a family member or friend help an older adult with the process of coming to a sense of ego integrity?

and received over a 7-year period and were more satisfied with the support they received (Hayward & Krause, 2013). Social engagement and feeling part of a community are important benefits of religious service attendance.

LATE ADULTHOOD AND SOCIAL CONTEXTS

>> **LO 18.2 Identify social contexts in which older adults live and their influence on development.**

At all periods in life, we are immersed in a social context that influences our physical functioning, thoughts, and relationships. Older adults' physical and psychological health can benefit from social interaction and a sense of support from significant others.

Social Support in Older Adulthood

Spouses and children are primary sources of support, as are siblings and other relatives. Assistance and support send the message that older adults are valued and help them to feel a sense of belonging and see their place in the wider social order. Social support from family and friends is associated with life satisfaction and protects elders from the negative effects of stress, promotes longevity, and enhances well-being (McLaughlin, Adams, Vagenas, & Dobson, 2011; Nguyen, Chatters, Taylor, & Mouzon, 2016).

Sometimes it is not the actual level of social support that matters but rather the level that the person perceives he or she is receiving. Low levels of perceived social support are associated with higher rates of cardiovascular disease, cancer, infectious diseases, and mortality (Ikeda et al., 2013; Uchino, 2006). People who perceive social support are more likely to engage in health maintenance behaviors such as exercising, eating right, and not smoking, and they are more likely to adhere to medical regimens (S. E. Taylor, 2011). Social support is thought to influence health and longevity by enhancing positive feelings and a sense of control as well as buffering the negative effects of stress.

Family, neighbors, and friends often provide tangible assistance, such as help with shopping or meal preparation. As discussed in Chapters 15 and 17, successful aging entails selective optimization with compensation. An older adult might choose to focus attention and effort on writing a novel or volunteering at a local child care center—asserting control over and optimizing an activity that interests her and is within her scope of capabilities—while accepting assistance in day-

Social support from family and friends protects against the negative effects of stress, promotes longevity and satisfaction, and enhances well-being.
iStock/rjlerich

to-day activities that she finds difficult, such as maintaining a tidy house and yard. Frequently, psychological outcomes and well-being are influenced more by the perception of having others to turn to rather than the actual amount of help provided (S. E. Taylor, 2011).

Aging and the Social World

Social support is important for well-being. However, social interaction tends to decline in older adulthood as social networks become smaller (Antonucci, Akiyama, & Takahashi, 2004; Shaw, Krause, Liang, & Bennett, 2007). Several perspectives account for changes in social interaction and elders' psychological functioning.

Disengagement, Activity, and Continuity Theories

Why do older adults have fewer friends? An early perspective, **disengagement theory**, proposed that older adults disengage from society as they anticipate death. At the same time, society disengages from them (DeLiema & Bengtson, 2017). Older adults withdraw and relinquish valued social roles, reduce their social interaction, and turn inward, spending more time thinking and reflecting. Society pulls away, reducing employment obligations and social responsibilities as they are transferred to younger people. According to disengagement theory, elders' withdrawal and society's simultaneous disengagement serve to allow older adults to advance into very old age and minimize the disruptive nature of their deaths to society. In this way, they benefit both the older person and society.

In the years since disengagement theory was proposed, however, it has become apparent that its central tenet is not true. Rather than disengage, most older individuals prefer to remain active and engaged with others, and they benefit from social engagement (Bengtson & DeLiema, 2016; Johnson & Mutchler, 2014). Any amount of social activity is more beneficial than a lack of involvement (Hinterlong, Morrow-Howell, & Rozario, 2007). Many people continue rewarding aspects of their work after retirement or adopt new roles in their communities. Most older adults retain the same leisure activities from worker to retiree, and many develop new hobbies (Scherger, Nazroo, & Higgs, 2011). Some have argued that disengagement does not reflect healthy development but rather a lack of opportunities for social engagement (Lang, Featherman, & Nesselroade, 1997).

In contrast to disengagement theory, **activity theory** says that declines in social interaction are not a result of elders' desires but are instead a function of social barriers to engagement (DeLiema & Bengtson, 2017). When they lose roles due to retirement or disability, they attempt to replace lost roles in an effort to stay active and busy. Volunteer work, for example, can replace career roles and protect against decline in health and psychological well-being (Hao, 2008). A 13-year longitudinal study following more than 2,700 elders aged 65 and older found that civic engagement in social and productive activities reduced mortality as much as did physical fitness (Glass, Mendes De Leon, Bassuk, & Berkman, 2006). Yet it is not simply the quantity of activity and social relationships that influences health and well-being but the quality, and individuals differ in their needs and desires (Bengtson & DeLiema, 2016; Pushkar et al., 2010). The more active elders are in roles they value—such as spouse, parent, friend, and volunteer—the more likely they are to report high levels of well-being and life satisfaction and to live longer, healthier lives (K. B. Adams, Leibbrandt, & Moon, 2011; Cherry et al., 2013; Litwin, 2003).

From the perspective of **continuity theory**, successful aging entails not simply remaining active but maintaining a sense of consistency in self across their past into the future (DeLiema & Bengtson, 2017). Despite changing roles, people are motivated to maintain their habits, personalities, and lifestyles, adapting as needed to maintain a sense of continuity, that they are the same person they have always been (Breheny & Griffiths, 2017). This entails acknowledging and minimizing losses, integrating them with their sense of self, and optimizing their strengths to construct a life path that maintains their sense of remaining the same person over time despite physical, cognitive, emotional, and social changes (Bengtson & DeLiema, 2016). Older adults tend to seek routine: familiar people, familiar activities, and familiar settings. Most of older adults' friends are old friends. Engaging in familiar activities with familiar people preserves a sense of self and offers comfort, social support, self-esteem, mastery, and identity (Pushkar et al., 2010).

Successful aging entails remaining active and maintaining a sense of continuity in self, in habits, personalities, and lifestyles.
kali9/E+/Getty Images

Socioemotional Selectivity Theory

Older adults' narrowing social circles may rest on the uniquely human ability to monitor time. With advancing age, people become increasingly aware of their shrinking time horizon—that they have little time left to live (Zacher & Kirby, 2015). This awareness causes them to shift their goals and priorities and accounts for continuity and change in social relationships. According to **socioemotional selectivity theory**, older adults become increasingly motivated to derive emotional meaning from life and thereby cultivate emotionally close relationships and disengage from more peripheral social ties (Carstensen et al., 2011; English & Carstensen, 2016).

As perceived time left diminishes, people tend to discard peripheral relationships and focus on important ones, such as those with close family members and friends (English & Carstensen, 2014). In support of this, aging is related to steep declines in social relationships. A recent meta-analysis confirmed that during young adulthood, people continue to accumulate friends; hence, their friendship networks increase (Wrzus, Hänel, Wagner, & Neyer, 2013). Older adults have fewer relationships in comparison with young adults, but their relationships are particularly close, supportive, and reciprocal (Huxhold, Fiori, & Windsor, 2013; Li, Fok, & Fung, 2011). Older adults place more emphasis on the emotional quality of their social relationships and interactions. As compared with young adults, older adults tend to perceive their social network as eliciting less negative emotion and more positive emotion (English & Carstensen, 2014). Despite an overall decline in the number of relationships, this process of strengthening and pruning relationships is associated with positive well-being; it allows older adults to focus their limited time and energy on relationships that are most beneficial while avoiding those that are inconsequential or detrimental, thereby maximizing their emotional well-being. In this sense, social selectivity is an emotional regulation strategy (Sims, Hogan, & Carstensen, 2015).

According to socioemotional selectivity theory, the functions of social interactions change with age and psychological and cognitive development (English & Carstensen, 2016). Specifically, the information-sharing function of friendship becomes less salient. For example, young adults often turn to friends for information, but older adults often have accumulated decades of knowledge. Therefore, it is the emotion-regulating function of social relationships that becomes more important during older adulthood (Carstensen & Mikels, 2005).

Generally, at all ages, we look to friends to affirm our sense of identity and uniqueness, choose friends who make us feel good, and avoid those who evoke negative feelings. According to socioemotional selectivity theory, the emotional correlates of friendship—feeling good and avoiding feeling bad—become more important over the lifespan. As we age, older adults tend to narrow their circle of friends. They are less likely to approach new people for friendship, and thus they reduce the likelihood of rejection and negative feelings. As physical frailty and psychological changes pose more challenges for adaptation, older adults tend to place emphasis on having positive interactions with others, reducing negative interactions, and avoiding stress. Interacting with a handful of carefully chosen relatives and close friends increases the chances that older adults will have positive interactions. Therefore, smaller social networks are associated with greater life satisfaction in older adults than younger adults (Lang & Fingerman, 2004).

Social contexts are important influences on development, such as changes in physical, cognitive, and social functioning, as well as adaptive functioning. The immediate contexts that influence older adults are neighborhoods and the elder's living environment, whether that is the home, a residential community, or a nursing home.

Neighborhoods

The neighborhoods and communities in which older adults reside influence their adaptation through the provision of physical and social resources. City, suburb, and rural communities offer different opportunities and challenges.

Older adults who live in the suburbs tend to be healthier and wealthier and show higher rates of life satisfaction than those who live in cities (Dandy & Bollman, 2008; DeNavas-Walt & Proctor, 2014). Yet as their neighborhoods are less compact, suburban older adults tend to walk less and show greater declines in walking with age; both influence health and ability to

live independently (A. C. King et al., 2017). Generally, urban elders have better access to transportation and health and social services than do suburban and rural elders, enhancing their opportunities for social participation (Andonian & MacRae, 2011). Older adults in more accessible and safe neighborhood contexts, including walking-friendly sidewalks and the availability of public transportation, are more likely to retain a higher degree of mobility and social activity than those in less accessible contexts (Clarke & Gallagher, 2013; Joshi et al., 2017).

Yet urban older adults' access to resources is influenced by neighborhood factors. Older adults who live in poor neighborhoods experience more physical and mental health problems. For example, Canadian older adults who live in poor neighborhoods are more likely than those in affluent neighborhoods to experience arthritis, diabetes, hypertension, heart disease, depression, and stroke (Menec, Shooshtari, Nowicki, & Fournier, 2010). The degree to which older adults walk in their communities may depend on their perceptions of safety. Australian older adults who reported a sense of trust in their neighborhood and social cohesion

Neighborhood factors, such as walkability and access to transportation, health services, and social opportunities influence health and the ability to live independently.
iStock/Signature

were more likely to report recreational walking in nearby parks than were those who perceived the neighborhood as less safe (Van Cauwenberg et al., 2017). Other research suggests that disordered neighborhoods are associated with poor physical functioning, such as frailty, poor mental health, and increased depressive symptoms (Caldwell, Lee, & Cagney, 2018; Joshi et al., 2017; Y. T. Wu et al., 2015). One study found that Mexican American older adults who viewed their neighborhoods positively and as safe were less likely to report poor self-rated health, controlling for both socioeconomic status and health status (Stroope et al., 2017). Moreover, the effects of neighborhood poverty and disadvantage accumulate over a lifetime, with significant implications for functional decline and mortality (Clarke et al., 2014).

One fourth of U.S. and one third of Canadian older adults live in rural areas where they tend to be more disadvantaged in terms of health, wealth, and availability of services, and they are less likely to live near their children (DeNavas-Walt & Proctor, 2014). Older adults who live in rural areas tend to interact with their neighbors more than their urban and suburban counterparts (Shaw, 2005). Close relationships with friends and neighbors, composed of frequent interaction and high levels of social support, are important emotional and material resources for older adults.

Life satisfaction in all older adults, urban and rural, is associated with living in neighborhoods with many seniors who interact with each other. The family is no longer the sole source of support when older adults have close relationships with friends who can aid their adjustment over older adulthood (Bowling & Gabriel, 2004).

Aging in Place

The majority of older adults prefer to age in their homes, referred to as aging in place, as shown in Figure 18.4 (Fields & Dabelko-Schoeny, 2016). Most older adults live in or near the home they have lived in most of their lives. When elders are healthy and not physically impaired, living in their own home permits them the greatest degree of control over their lives, such as choosing what and when to eat. Because of divorce, widowing, or never marrying, about one third of North American older adults live alone, and over one third of women over 65 live alone (Figure 18.5) (Stepler, 2016). Older adults who live alone are more likely to worry about finances and to live in poverty. (For a discussion about poverty and the older woman, see the accompanying feature on Applying Developmental Science.) Elderly women are about 50% more likely to be poor than elderly men, and the risk of poverty increases as women age.

As health declines, living alone poses physical and psychological risks, including social isolation and loneliness. Declines in health and widowhood often prompt older adults to relocate, but most North Americans remain in their old neighborhoods (Chappell, Gee, McDonald, & Stones, 2003). Despite the challenges, remaining in a lifelong home strengthens elders' feelings of continuity with the past, aids their sense of identity, and maintains connections with the community, an important source of support. When older adults choose to

---

FIGURE 18.4

Living Preferences Among Older Adults

% of adults ages 65 and older who say they would ____ if they could no longer live on their own

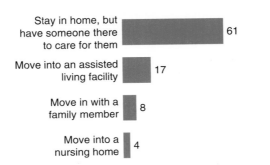

Most older adults want to age in place.

FIGURE 18.5

Living Arrangements of Older Adults, by Sex

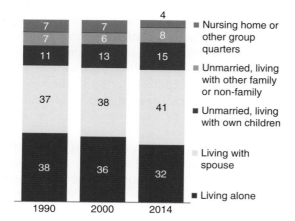

*% among **women** ages 65 and older*

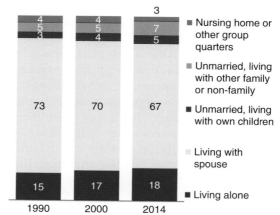

*% among **men** ages 65 and older*

Older women are more likely to live with spouse or children than in 1990; older men are less likely to live with a spouse, but more likely to live with children.

Source: Reprinted with permission from "Smaller share of women ages 65 and older are living alone," Pew Research Center, Washington, DC (February, 2016). http://www.pewsocialtrends.org/2016/02/18/2-living-arrangements-of-older-americans-by-gender/

Note: Older adults who are living with a spouse may also be living with children or other relatives or non-relatives. Unmarried adults include those who are separated, divorced, widowed, have never been married, or married but the spouse is absent from the household. Older adults living alone reside in a household. The share living alone is based on the total population aged 65 and older.

Most adults prefer to age in place and retain their independence. As health declines, living alone poses physical and psychological risks, such as social isolation and loneliness. Despite the challenges, remaining in a lifelong home strengthens elders' feelings of continuity with the past, aids their sense of identity, as well as maintains connections with the community, an important source of support.
iStock/Willowpix

move to new communities, it is often to be closer to children or to relocate to a warm climate.

African American older adults are especially likely to remain in their lifelong neighborhoods and to live in poverty, but they also tend to rely on informal support systems for care, a helper network that includes spouses, children, siblings, friends, neighbors, and church members (Rasheed & Rasheed, 2003). This helper network is the basis for informal caregiving for those older persons who

find themselves unable to maintain complete self-care due to illness or physical infirmities. It provides older adults with instrumental assistance, such as help in grocery shopping, transportation, and meal preparation, and expressive assistance, including emotional support, giving advice, encouragement, companionship, and prayer. Frequently, health care and transportation services are provided informally by friends and relatives to allow the older individual to live out his or her life within the context of home and community.

Many older adults live with kin, in intergenerational families. Older adults often provide child care and share housing and financial assistance with younger family members, adult children, and grandchildren (see Figure 18.6). Grandparents, particularly African American grandmothers, are important agents of socialization, maintaining the role of matriarch and kinkeeper (Barer, 2001). Obligations to care for family members are not unique to African and African American cultures. Adult children of a wide variety of races and ethnicities often feel a strong responsibility to care for aging parents and grandparents (Gans & Silverstein, 2006; Gonzales, 2007). For example, most middle-aged men and women in North America perceive an obligation to assist parents, especially when the parents have serious economic and housing needs (Postigo & Honrubia, 2010). However, when it comes to beginning a coresidence (an older family member giving up his or her own home and moving in with younger family members), an adjustment in attitude is often at issue. The older person may have concerns about not wanting to be a burden, losing autonomy, or losing privacy; younger family members may have similar concerns about an older family member disrupting the household. The new extended family consisting of grandparents, parents, and grandchildren must find a new balance (Hagestad, 2018). Attitudes about coresidence are based on family obligation norms, beliefs about repaying older adults for past help, perceived relationship quality, other demands on the younger adult's resources, the older person's resources, and family members' sense of moral responsibilities to assist (M. Coleman & Ganong, 2008).

FIGURE 18.6

Older Adults Residing in Multigenerational Households in the United States, 1940–2014

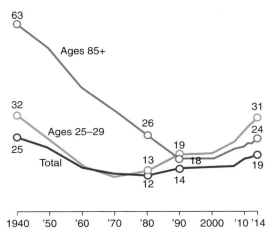

% of population living in multigenerational households

Young adults replace older ones as age group most likely to live in a multigenerational household.

Source: Reprinted with permission from "Record 64 million Americans live in multigenerational households," Pew Research Center, Washington, DC (August, 2016) http://www.pewresearch.org/fact-tank/2018/04/05/a-record-64-million-americans-live-in-multigeneration-al-households/ft_16-08-05_multigeneration_young_old/

APPLYING DEVELOPMENTAL SCIENCE

 Poverty and the Older Woman

Elderly women are more likely to live in poverty than men, and the rate of poverty increases with age.
PhotoFusion/Universal/Getty

Over the past 35 years, the poverty rate among adults aged 65 and older has dropped more than one half, from about 25% in 1970 to about 9% in 2016 (U.S. Bureau of the Census, 2017a). However, the picture is less rosy for older women, particularly older women of color, than it is for older men. Elderly women are about 50% more likely to be poor than elderly men, and the risk of poverty increases as women age (U.S. Bureau of the Census, 2017a). There are large ethnic disparities in poverty, as shown in Figure 18.7.

Older women have fewer sources of retirement income and receive less than two thirds that of men (a median of about $18,000 and $32,000, respectively; U.S. Bureau of the Census, 2017b).

(Continued)

(Continued)

The U.S. Bureau of the Census's poverty threshold for one person in 2018 was about $12,000 (U.S. Department of Health and Human Services, 2018). In other words, the median annual income for older women is just about $6,000 above the U.S. definition of poverty.

The factors that most influence whether older women will become or stay poor during the retirement years are marital status (divorced, widowed, or never married are negatives), prior employment, and health (Willson & Etherington, 2016). Because of longer life expectancy for women, they are more likely to experience the loss of their spouse, live alone in old age, and become financially vulnerable. Women who reach age 65 today are likely to live another 22 years, about 2 years longer than men the same age (Social

FIGURE 18.7

Poverty by Age, Sex, Ethnicity, and Marital Status 2012

Women over 65 are more likely to be poor than men, regardless of race, educational background, and marital status.

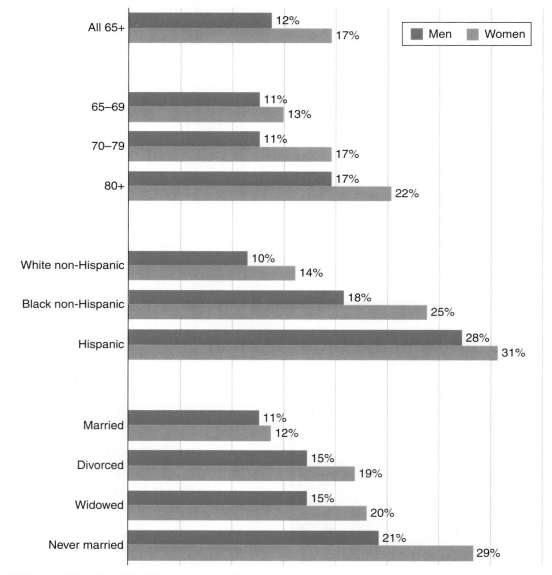

Source: © Economic Policy Institute.

Security Administration, 2018). Most women over 65 will spend some years alone. For women of all racial and ethnic groups, marital disruption, including widowhood, results in a substantial decline in household income and assets; however, the relative loss is greatest for African American and Hispanic women (Addo & Lichter, 2013; Willson & Etherington, 2016).

Women have different work history patterns from men. Interrupting their careers to take care of children often reduces women's opportunities to accumulate Social Security and other retirement benefits and reduces economic well-being (Madero-Cabib & Fasang, 2016; McBride & Parry, 2016). For example, average Social Security benefits for women are about $14,000 per year as compared with about $18,000 for men (U.S. Bureau of the Census, 2017b). Education, especially postsecondary education, has important effects on women's social and economic status during their preretirement years. After controlling for demographic characteristics and employment-related variables, both European American and African American women with

postsecondary education tend to be better off economically and rely less on public assistance income during their retirement (Zhan & Pandey, 2002). Policies that support women's education and aid them in balancing careers, if desired, with family and caregiving can help women develop the educational and career capital to support occupational achievement and economic stability throughout adulthood. Perhaps, then, women may be less likely to experience poverty during their "golden years."

What Do You Think?

1. What solutions would you propose to reduce the age, gender, and ethnic gaps in poverty? For example, do you advocate changes in social policy, stronger incentives for employer retirement programs, or strategies motivating individual women to better plan for their old age?

2. What advice might you give to a young or middle-aged woman who expresses concern about economic stability in her later years? ●

Residential Communities

There are a variety of different types of residential communities for older adults, ranging from single houses, to small collections of condominiums, to large apartment complexes. Homes in residential communities are designed to meet older adults' physical and social needs and may include such features as grab bars in bathrooms, single-level homes, and intercoms for emergency assistance. Some homes are designed for low-income elderly and are subsidized by the government. Most communities, however, are private. Older adults rent or purchase a home in a community complete with recreational facilities for socializing with other elders and obtaining assistance. Other elders live in congregate housing, which permits them to live independently but provides more comprehensive support, including common areas such as a dining room, recreational facilities, meals, and additional supervision and assistance with disabilities. Some older adults opt for "continuing care" communities that are designed to meet their changing needs wherein they begin with independent housing and, when needed, transfer to congregate housing and finally nursing home care.

Residential communities hold many benefits for older adults. Environments that meet elders' changing physical abilities can help offset declines in mobility and aid elders' attempts to remain active (Fonda, Clipp, & Maddox, 2002; Jenkins, Pienta,

There are many types of residential communities and many offer several options for care. Living in a community of older adults provides opportunities for social activities, forming friendships, and offering help to peers.
iStock/CasarsaGuru

& Horgas, 2002). Living in a community of older adults supports social activities, the formation of friendships, and provision of assistance to others, which increase a sense of competence and leadership (Ball et al., 2000; Lawrence & Schigelone, 2002).

How well elders adjust to the move from independent living to life in a residential community varies. Older adults show better adaptation to living in residential communities when they share similar backgrounds and values, have frequent contact and communication with like-minded elders, and feel socially integrated into the community. Conversely, those who perceive a lack of social support and feel disconnected from the community are at risk for depression (K. B. Adams, Sanders, & Auth, 2004). Overall, older adults who reside in residential communities tend to show higher levels of perceived autonomy, sense of security, and quality of life as compared with elders living independently in the neighborhood (van Bilsen, Hamers, Groot, & Spreeuwenberg, 2008). Although elders in residential settings do not differ from those in regular homes with regard to their sense of well-being or feelings of loneliness, those in residential communities participate more frequently in social activities.

Nursing Homes

Contrary to popular belief, only a small number of older adults reside in nursing homes. A nursing home is a facility that provides care to older adults who require assistance with daily care and health issues (Sanford et al., 2015). Nursing homes offer the greatest amount of care, 24 hours a day and 7 days a week, but also are most restrictive of elders' autonomy. Nursing homes tend to be hospital-like settings in which elders often have limited opportunities to control their schedule or interact with others, and their contact with peers generally is determined by staff. Most older people prefer to avoid living in nursing homes, if possible. Family members often experience guilt and anguish when they see no other choice but nursing home placement for their loved one (Seiger Cronfalk, Ternestedt, & Norberg, 2017).

Constraints on autonomy can lead to loneliness, feelings of helplessness, and depression (Anderberg & Berglund, 2010). Among older adults who are not mentally impaired, those in nursing homes tend to show higher rates of depression and anxiety than their peers in the community (Salguero, Martínez-García, Molinero, & Márquez, 2011).

Nursing homes offer round-the-clock care but also restrict adults' autonomy.
iStock/SolStock

Similar to other periods of life, a sense of control and social interaction with others is important to the well-being of elders who reside in nursing homes. Several factors are thought to be most influential in determining the quality of life of older adults: freedom of choice and involvement in decision making, recognition of individuality, right to privacy, continuation of normal social roles, a stimulating environment with age-appropriate opportunities and activities, and a sense of connectedness between home, neighborhood, and community. Well-being is enhanced in nursing homes that are designed to foster a sense of control over day-to-day experiences and social life. Encouraging social interaction in communal spaces, allowing residents to furnish and deinstitutionalize their spaces with some belongings, and modifying their environments to meet their changing needs while retaining as much autonomy as possible can help residents adapt to nursing home living.

THINKING IN CONTEXT 18.2

1. Elders' sense of self and overall well-being is influenced by a variety of factors within the individual as well as by contextual factors. How might the social contexts in which elders reside influence their psychosocial development?

2. In what ways might contexts such as neighborhood, community, and residence influence older adults' developmental status?

RELATIONSHIPS IN LATE ADULTHOOD

» LO 18.3 **Summarize features of older adults' relationships with friends, spouses, children, and grandchildren, and identify how these relationships affect older adults' functioning.**

Social and emotional connections with family and friends are essential for well-being and are important influences on adaptation and happiness. Aging places new constraints on social relationships, but most elders find that social relationships continue to be a source of support, social interaction, and fun.

Friendships

Friendships tend to improve over adulthood. In older adulthood, friendships become more important and more fulfilling, partly due to the declines in family and work responsibilities (R. G. Adams, 2017). With more time to devote to leisure activities, friendships

Older adults have more time to spend with friends than middle-aged adults and their friendships become more fulfilling.
iStock/Horsche

become more centered on activities, such as playing golf or card games, and older adults report having more fun with their friends than do younger adults (Blieszner & Ogletree, 2018). Although friends become fewer in number, older adults form new friendships throughout their lives (Robles, Menkin, Robles, & Menkin, 2015), and they tend to report more meaningful relationships than younger adults (Fingerman & Charles, 2010).

Older adults describe close friendships as entailing mutual interests, a sense of belonging, and opportunities to share feelings (R. G. Adams, Blieszner, & De Vries, 2000). Similar to earlier in life, older adults tend to choose friends who share similarities in age, race, ethnicity, and values. With increasing age and the death of friends, they are more likely to report having friends of different generations (Gillespie, Lever, Frederick, & Royce, 2015). Giving and receiving support from friends is an important influence on older adults' well-being and is protective against depression (Bishop, 2008; Thomas, 2010). Conversely, lack of social contact and friendship is adversely related to physical health (R. G. Adams, 2017). For example, among older adults who suffered a hip fracture, those who had no social contact with friends within 2 weeks prior to the injury were five times more likely to die over the 2 subsequent years than did those who had daily contact with friends during the 2 weeks prior to the fracture (Mortimore et al., 2008). Friendships help adults manage age-related losses in health, are associated with improved well-being and happiness, and can help older adults cope with major life events, such as bereavement at the death of a loved one (R. G. Adams & Taylor, 2015).

Sibling Relationships

Most older adults have a sibling with whom they communicate regularly. Unlike friends, siblings are not chosen, and usually siblings are the only living people who have known the older adult over his or her entire life. The history of personal and family experiences that adult siblings share contributes to a powerful bond. Most older adults feel close to their siblings and consider them to be close friends, even if they do not live near each other and do not visit regularly (Bedford & Avioli, 2016). Siblings grow closer with the experience of family events, hardships, and age-related issues (Myers & Kennedy-Lightsey, 2014). The closeness that siblings share includes sharing experiences, trust, concern for the other, and enjoyment of the sibling relationship.

In addition to emotional support, siblings provide tangible support and are considered important sources of help in times of crisis. Older adults who have never married or who have no children rely more on siblings for support than do those who have been married or have children (Spitze & Trent, 2018). Widowed adults show increased reliance on siblings. Close relationships with siblings influence well-being through pleasurable and self-affirming activities such as reminiscing about shared experiences (Bedford & Avioli, 2016).

Marriage, Divorce, and Cohabitation

Intimate partnerships are important in late adulthood, whether in the form of a decades-long marriage, a second marriage after divorce or widowhood, or a cohabiting relationship.

Marriage

As parenting and employment roles are retired, older adults have more time to spend with their spouse. Marital satisfaction tends to increase from middle adulthood through late adulthood (Ko, Berg, Butner, Uchino, & Smith, 2007). Marriages in older adulthood are characterized by greater satisfaction, less negativity, and more positive interactions than in other developmental periods (Story et al., 2007). Older adults describe their relationships as having less conflict and higher levels of pleasure and report greater positive affect in marital interaction than do younger adults (Carstensen, Fung, & Charles, 2003; Waldinger & Schulz, 2010). Older couples show fewer disagreements and tend to discuss disagreements with more respect and humor and resolve arguments more quickly and constructively with less resulting anger and resentment than younger couples do (Hatch & Bulcroft, 2004).

Compared with middle-aged adults, older adults perceive more positive characteristics and fewer negative characteristics in their partners (Henry, Berg, Smith, & Florsheim, 2007). They also show greater positive sentiment override than middle-aged adults; that is, they appraise their spouse's behavior as more positive than do outside observers (Story et al., 2007). In other words, older married adults tend to view their spouses through rose-colored glasses—and viewing one's spouse positively predicts marital satisfaction (McCoy, Rauer, & Sabey, 2017). To date, research on marital satisfaction in older adulthood nearly exclusively focuses on heterosexual couples. The limited research discussed in prior chapters suggests that romantic partners share similar relationship and family processes regardless of sexual orientation; therefore, it is reasonable to assume that these patterns of increasing marital satisfaction likely apply to same-sex couples as well. For example, one recent study of gay and lesbian older adult couples found that legally married adults reported better quality of life and more economic and social resources than unmarried couples (Goldsen et al., 2017).

A variety of factors contribute to the rise in marital satisfaction over the adult years. The goals emphasized by couples change over the life course. In young adulthood, personal growth is a primary concern; this changes in middle adulthood

Most older adults are very satisfied in their marriages. A lifetime of shared experiences, such as raising families, navigating crises, and building memories together, brings couples closer.
iStock/PeopleImages

to instrumental goals, such as raising children, and in late adulthood to companionship goals (J. E. Lee, Zarit, Rovine, Birditt, & Fingerman, 2011). With grown children and the onset of retirement, adults are no longer faced with the challenges of balancing childrearing and career. Many women perceive greater fairness in their relationships and greater equity in household tasks, as retired men often take on a greater role in completing household tasks than at earlier periods (Kulik, 2002). Retirement provides the opportunity for couples to spend more time together. A lifetime of shared experiences, such as raising families, navigating crises, and building memories together, brings couples closer.

Divorce and Remarriage

Just as marital satisfaction generally tends to increase with age, couples over the age of 65 are less likely to divorce than are younger couples. Similar to younger people, older adults report divorcing because of poor communication, emotional detachment, and few shared interests (Z. Wu & Schimmele, 2007). Adults in long-term marriages may find it more difficult to adjust to divorce than do younger adults. Many find it difficult to separate and feel a sense of failure after spending their lives in a relationship. Divorce poses financial challenges for couples because accumulated assets must be divided and financial security in retirement is at risk. Women face greater financial and emotional difficulties than men as they are more likely to remain single throughout the remainder of their lives (McDonald & Robb, 2004).

Social support is important for well-being throughout adulthood but is especially important in adjusting to divorce. Yet divorce changes relationships with family and friends and can reduce support and pose great challenges to adjustment. Research with U.K. adults 70 years or older, however, found that divorce itself was not related to a decline in support from adult children over a 12-year period (Glaser, Stuchbury, Tomassini, & Askham, 2008). Similarly, samples of U.S. adults show that adult children of divorced parents are just as likely as adult children of widowed parents to give care and money to their mothers but are less likely to care for their fathers after divorce (Lin, 2008). The findings suggest that divorced fathers are likely the population most in need of formal support in old age.

Rates of remarriage decline in older adulthood. Still, a substantial number of adults, particularly older men, remarry after divorce (Huyck & Gutmann, 2006). Single women, whether by divorce or widowhood, are less likely to marry than men. When elders remarry, their unions tend to be more stable than those of younger people. The gains in maturity and perspective may contribute to a more realistic concept of marriage and support the longevity of late-life marriages (Kemp & Kemp, 2002). Many older adults choose cohabitation over remarriage.

Cohabitation

Cohabitation is increasingly common among all adults. Older adults view cohabitation positively, and adults over the age of 50 represent about a quarter of all cohabiting adults (Brown & Wright, 2016). Although the prevalence of cohabitation among adults over age 65 is uncertain, cohabitation has nearly quadrupled for all adults over age 50, from 1.2 million in 2000 to 4 million adults in 2016 (Brown, Bulanda, & Lee, 2012; Stepler, 2017).

Cohabitation is more consistently associated with positive outcomes in older adulthood as compared with younger adulthood. Older adult cohabitors tend to report higher-quality relationships, perceiving more fairness, more time spent alone with their partner, fewer disagreements, and a lower likelihood of heated arguments than their younger peers (Brown & Kawamura, 2010; V. King & Scott, 2005). Compared with younger couples, older adults who cohabit tend to be in relationships of longer duration, are more likely to have experienced the dissolution of a marriage, and tend to report fewer marriage plans, viewing the relationship as an alternative to marriage (Brown et al., 2012). Older adults may be less interested in marriage because they are past the age of childbearing. They also may be more interested in protecting the wealth they have accrued over their lifetime than they are in pooling economic resources.

In older adulthood, cohabiting unions are similar to marriages in terms of adults' reports of emotional satisfaction, pleasure, openness, time spent together, perceived criticism and demands, and overall well-being (Brown & Kawamura, 2010; Wright & Brown, 2017). Among older adults, cohabitation shows similar health benefits to marriage, and this finding holds true in a variety of cultures. For example, one study of Italian men showed that, similar to marriage, cohabitation was associated with reduced mortality as compared with single men who lived alone (Scafato et al., 2008). A longitudinal study of over 2,500 Danish older men showed that cohabitation and marriage were both associated with reduced rates of disability over a nearly 5-year period, whereas, similar to findings on marriage, women did not experience similar benefits of cohabitation as compared with men (Nilsson, Lund, & Avlund, 2008).

Sexuality in Late Adulthood

Media images of sexuality have traditionally portrayed only attractive young people, shaping and reinforcing societal misconceptions that sexuality disappears in older people (Bauer, McAuliffe, & Nay, 2007). Many assume that sexuality is irrelevant to older people, reflecting the stereotype that aging is a feared negative event marked by rapid physical and cognitive decline. Even researchers who study sexuality often overlook the views and experiences of elders by focusing on those under the age of 60. As the population of older adults increases and healthy aging becomes more common, widespread advertising of medications for sexual performance (e.g., to treat erectile dysfunction) may shift assumptions toward the view that older adults desire but are physically unable to have sex. In fact, however, adults remain interested and capable of sexual activity well into older adulthood.

Just as in middle age, good sex in the past predicts good sex in the future (Bell, Reissing, Henry, & VanZuylen, 2017). For example, five decades of research has consistently shown that older people generally maintain sexual interest and remain sexually capable and active well into their 80s and often 90s (DeLamater & Koepsel, 2015; D. M. Lee, Nazroo, O'Connor, Blake, & Pendleton, 2016). Research conducted in Europe, the United States, Australia, and Asia confirms that many older people continue to view sexual interest and activity as important (Bauer, Haesler, & Fetherstonhaugh, 2016; Hyde et al., 2010; Palacios-Ceña et al., 2012).

The frequency of sexual activity declines with age, but sexual satisfaction often remains unchanged (D. M. Lee et al., 2016; Thompson et al., 2011). In one study, 54% of men and 21% of women ages 70 to 80 reported having sexual intercourse within the past year, and nearly one quarter of those men and women had intercourse more than once a week (Nicolosi et al., 2006). One third of a sample of 75- to 85-year-old men reported having at least one sexual encounter within the past year (Hyde, et al., 2010). Likewise, in a 30-year longitudinal study of nearly 2,800 Australian men, 40% of those aged 75 to 79, but only 11% of those aged 90 to 95, reported having had sex in the past year (Doskoch, 2011). Reasons for lack of sexual activity include physical problems, lack of interest, partner's lack of interest, partner's physical problems, and the loss of a partner (Palacios-Ceña et al., 2012).

The nature of sexual expression shifts with age, encompassing an array of behaviors (e.g., self-stimulation, noncoital activity with partners), as well as sexual activity in both long-term and new relationships (McAuliffe, Bauer, & Nay, 2007). Because of the hormonal changes that accompany menopause, women may experience lack of vaginal lubrication and therefore find intercourse uncomfortable (DeLamater & Koepsel, 2015). With increasing age, males' erections tend to take longer to achieve, are less frequent, and are more difficult to sustain than was the case when they were younger; however, these

The nature of sexual expression often changes in older adulthood, but most older adults remain interested in, and satisfied by, sexual activity.
Reuters/Lucy Nicholson

normative changes should not be mistaken for erectile dysfunction (R. S. Tan, 2011). Many factors may diminish sexual response and satisfaction: cigarette smoking, heavy drinking, obesity, poor health, and attitudes toward sexuality and aging, among others (DeLamater, 2012). Many illnesses encountered in advancing age (e.g., arthritis, heart disease, diabetes, Parkinson's disease, stroke, cancer, and depression) can have a negative impact on an individual's interest or participation in sexual activity (Syme, Klonoff, Macera, & Brodine, 2013; A. Taylor & Gosney, 2011). Likewise, prescription drugs, over-the-counter medications, and herbal supplements may have side effects that can alter or impair sexual function.

Sexual activity is a correlate of health, as those who report good health are more likely to be sexually active (DeLamater & Koepsel, 2015; Holden, Collins, Handelsman, Jolley, & Pitts, 2014). However, just as during other phases of life, there is a bidirectional relationship: Sexual activity is likely to enhance health by reducing stress and improving positive affect and well-being (Debrot, Meuwly, Muise, Impett, & Schoebi, 2017; Freak-Poli et al., 2017).

Relationships With Adult Children and Grandchildren

Most North American older adults are parents, usually of middle-aged adults. The nature of the relationship and exchange of help changes over time, from predominantly parent-to-child assistance in childhood through early adulthood to increasing assistance provided by adult children to their elderly parents. Adult child-to-parent assistance most often takes the form of emotional support and companionship, which helps elders cope with and compensate for losses such as disabilities and widowhood. Most older adults and their adult children keep in touch even when they are separated by great distance. Overall, adult daughters tend to be closer and more involved with parents than sons, speaking with and visiting more often than sons. In contrast with emotional support, fewer older adults receive instrumental assistance from adult children. Instead, many older adults, especially those of high socioeconomic status, continue to assist their adult children, primarily with financial assistance (Grundy & Henretta, 2006).

Family relations may take many forms. Some parents and adult children live nearby, engage in frequent contact, and endorse family obligation norms. Support is provided either primarily from parent to adult child or adult to parent. Some older adults are part of multigenerational families that include their children and grandchildren (Gilligan, Karraker, & Jasper, 2018). Other families provide support at a distance where they do not live nearby, engage in frequent contact, endorse fewer family obligation norms, and provide mainly financial support—often from parents to children. Other family relationships are autonomous: not living nearby, engaging in little contact, little endorsement of family obligation norms, and few support exchanges. Each of these types of family relations is found in most European nations and likely the United States (Dykstra & Fokkema, 2010).

Most older adults have grandchildren, and most will see them grow into adults (AARP, 2002). Grandchildren and great-grandchildren increase older adults' opportunities for emotional support. The quality of the grandparent relationship is influenced by the degree of involvement in the grandchild's life. A history of close and frequent contact, positive experiences, and affectionate ties predicts good adult child–grandparent relationships (Geurts, Van Tilburg, & Poortman, 2012; Sheehan & Petrovic, 2008). Adults who share close emotional ties with their grandchildren spend more time listening and providing emotional support and companionship with them as adults (Huo, Kim, Zarit, & Fingerman, 2017). Over time, contact with grandchildren tends to decline as young and middle-aged grandchildren take on time-consuming family and work roles, but affection between grandchildren and grandparents tends to remain strong (Thiele & Whelan, 2008).

Elder Maltreatment

Most older adults maintain positive and healthy relationships with the people around them, including friends, relatives, and caregivers. About 1 in 10 adults, however, experience elder maltreatment—acts or omissions of care that cause harm to the older person and occur within the context of a trusting relationship (Johannesen & LoGiudice, 2013; Roberto, 2016). Elder maltreatment appears in several forms. Many elders fall victim to more than one form of maltreatment (Jackson & Hafemeister, 2016), which may include the following:

- Physical abuse: Intentionally inflicting physical harm or discomfort through cutting, burning, and other acts of physical force

- Sexual abuse: Inflicting unwanted sexual contact

- Psychological abuse: Intentionally inflicting emotional harm through verbal assaults, humiliation, intimidation, or withdrawal of affection

- Financial abuse: Exploiting the elder's financial resources by theft or unauthorized use (e.g., withdrawing funds from savings, selling an elder's jewelry or other possessions, charging purchases to the elder's credit card)

- Physical neglect: Providing inadequate care and failing to meet an elder's basic needs for food, medication, physical comfort, and health care; leaving an elder with special needs unattended

Elder abuse appears in all cultures. Overall, about 6% to 10% of elders in industrialized countries, including Australia, Canada, China, Germany, India, Ireland, Israel, the Netherlands, Taiwan, the United Kingdom, the United States, and others, report experiencing abuse within the past month (Acierno et al., 2010; Cooper, Selwood, & Livingston, 2008; Lowenstein & Doron, 2008; Melchiorre, Penhale, & Lamura, 2014; Podnieks, Anetzberger, Wilson, Teaster, & Wangmo, 2010). Financial abuse is particularly common, as discussed in the Brain and Biological Influences on Development feature.

Similar to child abuse, elder maltreatment is underreported, and prevalence rates are likely

---

BRAIN AND BIOLOGICAL INFLUENCES ON DEVELOPMENT

Neurological Risk for Financial Abuse

Cognitive and neurological changes may place older adults at increased risk of financial abuse.
iStock/GrashAlex

It is estimated that about 5% of older adults experience financial exploitation, or financial abuse (Lachs & Han, 2015). Financial exploitation is likely underestimated (Schafer & Koltai, 2015). Individuals with mild cognitive impairment, Alzheimer's disease, and other dementias experience increased risk of financial exploitation (Spreng, Karlawish, & Marson, 2016). Does normative brain aging increase the risk of financial abuse?

We have seen that neurological aging influences both cognitive and social abilities. Changes in cognitive reasoning skills can influence financial abilities and

increase the risk of financial mismanagement. Most research to date has examined cognitive influences on financial exploitation, but social factors are also important. For example, changes in social cognition can increase adults' vulnerability to social influence, coercion, or deception (Spreng et al., 2016).

A recent functional MRI (fMRI) study compared older adults who had and had not experienced financial exploitation (Spreng et al., 2017). Financial exploitation was defined as theft, misappropriation, and coercion that led to financial loss due to deception, receipt of false information, or withholding of information.

Examination of the fMRI data revealed that the financially exploited older adults had reduced cortical thickness in the anterior insula cortex and parts of the temporal cortex, regions that are related to emotionally based decision making and social cognition (Samanez-Larkin & Knutson, 2015). They also showed reduced connectivity in the anterior insula, which is associated with salience detection, affect-based decision making, and reward anticipation (Uddin, 2015). Differences in the insula may impair older adults' ability to detect threats or disrupt the integration of threat-related information into decision-making processes during social interactions. Reduced threat detection may leave older adults at greater risk for exploitation, particularly in complex or emotionally volatile contexts, as would be the case within families, the most common context for elder exploitation.

(Continued)

(Continued)

In addition, the financially exploited older adults showed reduced connectivity between the medial prefrontal cortex and the posterior cingulate, which play a role in social reasoning and processing of complex social cues to infer the intentions of others (Andrews-Hanna, Smallwood, & Spreng, 2014). Reductions in connectivity might interfere with the processing of social cues, leading to impaired social interactions, and rendering older adults susceptible to deception or undue social influence and vulnerable to exploitation. Perhaps as older adults emphasize rewards, they might be at risk to rely on emotionally salient and possibly misleading information in making social decisions (Spreng et al., 2017).

These results suggest that neurological changes may place older adults at social risk; however, the applied value of these findings is less clear. All of the older adults in this study completed measures of cognition, personality, social interaction, and financial abilities.

The financially exploited and nonexploited groups differed only on two emotions: anger and hostility. The fMRI scans captured structural differences in their brains, but the differences were not visible on behavioral measures. Do changes in the social area of the brain place older adults at risk of financial exploitation? They may influence how information is weighed, but the lack of behavioral differences suggests that social effects might be subtle.

What Do You Think?

1. Why do you think the fMRI findings showed significant differences between the financially exploited and nonexploited groups when the two groups did not differ in other measures?

2. What are the challenges of interpreting findings of fMRI studies? ●

higher than reported (Barboza, 2016). Victims of maltreatment are more likely to be advanced in age and suffer from physical and mental illness, frailty, and impairments with activities of daily living (Chen & Dong, 2017; Laumann, Leitsch, & Waite, 2008). Disadvantaged older adults, including women and adults of color, are more likely to be victimized, as are those who experience a lack of social support or social isolation (Barboza, 2016; Johannesen & LoGiudice, 2013; Sooryanarayana, Choo, & Hairi, 2013). Most cases of elder maltreatment are perpetrated by caregivers, most often spouses or children, who lack social support, experience psychological problems, and feel overwhelmed with the task of caregiving (DeLiema, Yonashiro-Cho, Gassoumis, Yon, & Conrad, 2018; Dong & Simon, 2008). Within nursing homes, institutional factors such as overcrowding and understaffing contribute to caregiver stress and can increase the likelihood of elder maltreatment (Pickering, Nurenberg, & Schiamberg, 2017). Reducing the stressful working conditions for nursing home employees and increasing oversight can reduce the risk of maltreatment in institutional settings. To the extent that elder abuse is an outgrowth of caregiver stress and burnout, aiding caregivers can lessen the likelihood of abuse. Social workers and family counselors can aid caregivers in learning how to cope with anger and manage strong emotions. Respite services such as in-home assistance or elder day care can provide physical assistance, which can reduce the stress of caregiving. The rates of elder abuse can also be reduced through education that helps vulnerable elders understand and identify maltreatment and know where to get help (Ayalon, Lev, Green, & Nevo, 2016; Roberto, 2016).

THINKING IN CONTEXT 18.3

1. What aspects of social relationships (e.g., friendships as well as relationships with siblings and children) are continuous over the lifespan? In what ways do these relationships change?

2. Relationships with spouses are particularly enduring and influential on adjustment and functioning. How do marital relationships form and change over the adult years? What can spouses expect in older adulthood?

3. Many older adults are single, living alone after divorce or widowhood. What challenges to adjustment do each raise? How are males and females' experience of divorce similar and different?

RETIREMENT

» LO 18.4 Discuss influences on the timing of retirement and adaptation to retirement.

In most Western countries, older adults can work longer than ever before because of improved health and the revocation of mandatory retirement ages for most occupations (with exceptions for jobs that entail responsibility for the safety of others, such as air

FIGURE 18.8

Labor Force Participation by Age and Sex, 1996–2026 (Projected)

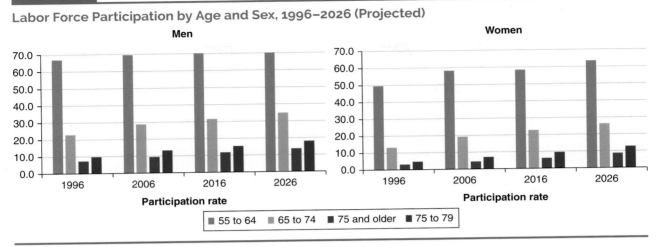

Source: U.S. Bureau of Labor Statistics.

traffic controllers, pilots, and police officers). Despite these changes, increases in life expectancy and declines in the age of retirement mean that over the past century, the period of retirement has lengthened in all Western nations. However, as indicated in Figure 18.8, not all adults retire, and it is projected that adults will increasingly postpone retirement.

Deciding to Retire

Retirement is a process that begins long before the last day of employment. Typically, it begins with imagining the possibility of retirement and what it might be like. Adults then assess their abilities and their resources, determine when is the best time to let go of the work role, and put plans into action (Feldman & Beehr, 2011).

The decision of when to retire is typically influenced by job conditions, health, finances, and personal preferences. Adults with poor health and visual and hearing impairments tend to retire earlier than their unimpaired peers (Gopinath, Liew, Burlutsky, McMahon, & Mitchell, 2017). Among U.S. retirees, 40% of Black retirees and 50% of Hispanic retirees indicate that poor health was at least somewhat important to their decision, as compared with 26% of White retirees (U.S. Federal Reserve, 2018). Workers tend to retire early from jobs that are stressful or hazardous and tend to delay retirement from jobs that are highly stimulating, take place in pleasant environments, and are a source of identity and self-esteem (AARP, 2008). Workers in professional occupations and those who are self-employed tend to stay in their jobs longer as compared with those in blue-collar or clerical positions. A sense of control and perceived working conditions, such as feeling respected by coworkers and leaders, is associated with delaying retirement in German and Finnish older adults (Böckerman, Ilmakunnas, Böckerman, & Ilmakunnas, 2017; Wöhrmann,

Fasbender, & Deller, 2017). Women often retire earlier than men, often to care for an aging relative or spouse (Kim & Moen, 2001). Women in poverty, however, especially African American women, tend to work well into old age because they often lack the financial resources to make retirement possible (S. Lee & Shaw, 2008; Verma, 2003).

Financial resources often are the determining factor with regard to whether and when an older adult retires. Changing economics influence older adults' abilities to retire, as personal retirement investments such as IRAs and 401(k) plans may lose value unexpectedly. The creation of Social Security was designed to aid elders in affording retirement (see the Lives in Context feature). About 4 in 10 of all U.S. adults, including nearly one third of adults over age 65, expressed concern over whether they would have enough income and assets in retirement (Morin & Fry, 2012). Furthermore, 20% of 45- to 59-year-old adults and 19% of adults age 60 and older report that they have no retirement savings (U.S. Federal Reserve, 2018).

Transition to Retirement and Adjustment

The transition to retirement begins years before leaving the workforce and continues well into retirement. Theorists pose that the transition to retirement is a process that follows a predictable set of steps. Adults generally seek to preserve continuity in their sense of self, and this tendency influences their transition to retirement (Atchley, 1989). Adults who are more satisfied at work may see work as central to their sense of self, may experience retirement as a disruption to their sense of self, and may thereby delay retirement. As workers approach retirement, they may adjust their attitudes toward work, revising their views on its importance.

Gains in one domain, such as increased family time, might compensate for losses in another, job-related status. Attitudes toward retirement may be based on their evaluation of the expected balance between the gains and losses associated with leaving working and being retired, and that is shaped in part by the expected disruption to their lifestyle (Davies, Van der Heijden, & Flynn, 2017). The net balance of perceived gains and losses will vary between individuals, with some older adults expecting greater gains or losses than others (Pinquart & Schindler, 2007). Given the scale and scope of potential changes across multiple life domains, attitude toward retirement is likely to be characterized by attitudinal ambivalence in which individuals will hold both favorable and unfavorable attitudes toward the object of retirement (Muratore & Earl, 2015; Newman, Jeon, & Hulin, 2012). Prior to retirement, feelings of well-being and life satisfaction may decline as people worry and anticipate the loss of the work role.

After the retirement event, retirees may experience a short honeymoon phase marked by vacations and new interests or a rest-and-relaxation phase of brief respite from the obligations of work. As retirees become accustomed to the reality of everyday life in retirement, these positive feelings may change to disenchantment. Over time, the adult develops a realistic view of the social and economic opportunities and constraints of retirement, and a period of reorientation occurs in which the person attempts to replace the lost work role with new activities or becomes stressed if he or she cannot (Richardson & Kilty, 1991). Finally, stability occurs once the retirees accommodate and adjust to retirement.

Research on retirement adjustment suggests that the majority of adults show an increase in life satisfaction and adjust well to their postretirement life, but some show poor adjustment (Howe, Matthews, & Heard, 2010; Pinquart & Schindler, 2007). One study of Australian retirees found several patterns of adjustment. Some retirees maintained high life satisfaction across the retirement transition (40%), others experienced declining levels of life satisfaction from a high level prior to retirement (28%), some experienced low levels of life satisfaction that declined further (18%), and some reported increasing life satisfaction from a low level prior to retirement (14%). Overall, retirees who experienced significant declines in life satisfaction tended to have worse health and lower access to a range of social and economic resources prior to retirement, suggesting that preretirement experiences influence adjustment (Heybroek, Haynes, & Baxter, 2015).

Declines in well-being and life satisfaction may occur when the retirement transition causes an important role loss of worker that must be replaced by other social roles over time (Pinquart & Schindler, 2007; Richardson & Kilty, 1991). Work-related roles often become an important part of one's identity and source of self-esteem. The loss of a role central to an adult's identity may be especially stressful, contributing to increases in anxiety, depression, and poor well-being during the retirement transition (Kim & Moen, 2002).

On the other hand, retirees with other role involvements, or those who are retiring from an unpleasant job, may be less troubled by, and even pleased with, the loss of those work roles (G. A. Adams, Prescher, Beehr, & Lepisto, 2002). For individuals who find their job stressful or burdensome, retiring could be a very positive experience, a relief from ongoing strains and conflicts, energizing and fulfilling (Fehr, 2012). Also, for individuals who would like to participate more heavily in the roles of family member and community member, retirement is an opportunity for them to enjoy the rewards and responsibilities tied to those roles. Continuity in other social roles and the ability to adapt to role changes lead to few changes in life satisfaction after retirement (Reitzes & Mutran, 2004). In addition, retirement satisfaction tends to increase for most older adults over the first half dozen years after retirement (Wang, 2007).

Influences on Retirement Adjustment

Adjustment to retirement is influenced by a complex web of influences, including characteristics of the individual, his or her social relationships, and the job (Wang, Henkens, & van Solinge, 2011). Some positive predictors of successful adjustment include physical health, finances, leisure, voluntary retirement, social integration, psychological health, and personality-related attributes (Barbosa, Monteiro, & Murta, 2016). Positive adjustment to retirement is also associated with engagement in satisfying relationships and leisure activities—and planning ahead for the financial and social changes that come with retirement (Grotz et al., 2017; Siguaw, Sheng, & Simpson, 2018; Yeung & Zhou, 2017). Workers in high-stress, demanding jobs, or those that provide little satisfaction, tend to show positive adaptation to retirement (G. A. Adams et al., 2002; Fehr, 2012). For them, retirement often comes as a relief. Those who are in highly satisfying, low-stress, pleasant jobs tend to experience more challenges in adaptation. Generally speaking, the greater the intrinsic value of the older worker's job, the lower the levels of retirement satisfaction (van Solinge & Henkens, 2008).

The characteristics of the retirement transition also matter. Increasingly, adults are taking the route of a gradual retirement, slowly decreasing their involvement and working part-time, rather than an abrupt retirement (Calvo, Haverstick, & Sass, 2009). Workers often view the idea of gradual retirement as a more attractive alternative than a "cold turkey" or

Social Security

President Franklin D. Roosevelt signing the Social Security Act in 1935.
Underwood Archives/Getty

The Great Depression of the 1930s triggered a crisis in the economic life of the United States. It was against this backdrop that the Social Security Act emerged, signed by President Franklin D. Roosevelt in 1935. The act created a social insurance program designed to pay retired workers age 65 or older a continuing income. The original act provided only retirement benefits and only to the worker. In 1939, amendments were enacted to add two new categories of benefits: payments to the spouse and minor children of a retired worker (dependent benefits) and payments to the family in the event of the premature death of a worker (survivor benefits) (Social Security Administration, 2007). Amendments in the 1950s and 1960s allowed disabled workers and their dependents to qualify for benefits. Because of these additional categories of benefits, about one in three Social Security beneficiaries is not a retiree (Shelton, 2007; Social Security Administration, 2008).

Social Security, also known as Old Age and Survivors Insurance and Disability Insurance (OASIDI), is funded by taxes paid by workers; the funds are invested in interest-bearing U.S. securities. Social Security provides older Americans with a dependable monthly income, with automatic increases tied to increases in the cost of living. Social Security has reduced poverty rates for older Americans by more than two thirds, from 35% in 1959 to about 9% in 2016 (U.S. Bureau of the Census, 2017a; Shelton, 2013). More than 90% of U.S. retirees receive monthly Social Security benefit payments (Social Security Administration, 2018).

Social Security was never intended as a sole form of income; instead, it was conceived as a supplement to income from a retirement plan, pension, and savings. However, today most employers do not offer a pension plan, and many workers cannot afford to contribute to a retirement plan (e.g., a 401k or a SEP-IRA) or to set aside savings on a regular basis. In 2017, one half of married couples and nearly three quarters of single adults were getting at least half of their income from Social Security, and for about one quarter and nearly one half, respectively, Social Security was virtually their only income (Social Security Administration, 2018). Moreover, Social Security provides critical income to older women and minorities, who are more likely than married and nonminority elders to rely on Social Security for 90% or more of their income (Social Security Administration, 2016).

Social Security is a pay-as-you-go retirement system. The Social Security taxes paid by today's workers and their employers are used to pay the benefits for today's retirees and other beneficiaries. There is considerable debate over whether Social Security trust funds can remain solvent over the long term because people are living longer than ever before. In addition, more than 80 million Baby Boomers started retiring in 2008. By 2050, when the surviving Baby Boomers will be over the age of 85, the population of older adults aged 65 and over is projected to be 83.7 million, about double that in the early 2010s (Ortman, Velkoff, & Hogan, 2014). At the same time, the number of workers paying into Social Security per beneficiary will drop from 2.8 for each 2.1 collecting benefits in 2016 to about 2.1 paying workers for each person collecting benefits in 2034 (Social Security Administration, 2018). These demographic changes will strain Social Security financing.

Proposed strategies to make Social Security solvent over the long term include increasing payroll taxes, decreasing benefits, and privatizing Social Security. The age to receive full benefits is rising to age 67 in 2022, but more drastic measures may be needed. Some propose raising Social Security taxes. Others advocate raising the income cap above which high-income earners are exempt from Social Security payroll contributions. Yet critics argue that payroll taxes are already very high, having been raised 20 times since the program began, and that eventually Social Security taxes would have to be raised by about 50% to pay for all benefits owed.

(Continued)

(Continued)

What Do You Think?

1. Do you agree or disagree with the phasing in of higher eligibility ages for receiving Social Security retirement benefits? Give reasons for your answer.

2. What information should researchers and policy makers gather to determine a fair and sustainable plan to make Social Security solvent? Consider each bioecological level. For example, what factors at the macrosystem level might be useful to policy makers? Exosystem factors? What microsystem or mesosystem factors might help policy makers in planning Social Security changes? ●

abrupt retirement. One study of Australian retirees found that those who had retired abruptly were more likely to rate their health as having deteriorated, whereas those who had retired gradually tended to report better adjustment to retirement life (De Vaus, Wells, Kendig, & Quine, 2007). However, the length of the transition, whether abrupt or gradual, matters less in determining happiness after retirement than the worker's sense of control over the transition—whether the retirement is chosen or forced (Calvo et al., 2009; De Vaus et al., 2007; Quine, Wells, de Vaus, & Kendig, 2007). Having a sense of control over the decision to retire, as well as the timing and manner of leaving work, has an important positive impact on psychological and social well-being that lasts throughout the retirement transition (Siguaw et al., 2018).

Social support also influences adjustment. Among married retirees, relationship satisfaction aids the transition to retirement, and in turn, the increased time together that retirement brings can serve to enhance marital satisfaction. In contrast, adults who are lonely or recently divorced are more likely to experience difficulty (Damman, Henkens, & Kalmijn, 2015; Segel-Karpas, Ayalon, & Lachman, 2018). Maintaining multiple roles after retirement promotes well-being (S. S. Butler & Eckart, 2007). For example, volunteer work offers older adults opportunities to share their experience, mentor others, and develop and sustain social relationships, all of which may enhance their well-being (Tang, 2008; Windsor, Anstey, & Rodgers, 2008).

THINKING IN CONTEXT 18.4

1. Identify individual and contextual influences on the decision to retire and adjustment to retirement.

2. In what ways might the characteristics of jobs, individuals' education and experience, and other microsystem, macrosystem, and exosystem factors influence retirement decisions and subsequent adjustment?

 APPLY YOUR KNOWLEDGE

On their 50th wedding anniversary, Mike and Carol celebrated with a big party, with family and friends. Their 4 children and 13 grandchildren attended. Nearly all of the grandchildren were married, with children of their own—some teenagers. In addition, a few very close friends attended, some from the neighborhood and a few lifelong friends they met when they were very young. "How fortunate we are," Mike remarked in a toast. His friend called out, "We hear that another congratulations is in order—you've just retired!" Carol replied, "Yes. It will be so nice to have him home with me." "Mom, don't you think he'll get underfoot?" "We'll see."

1. In what ways is Mike and Carol's social world similar to and different from those of most older adults?

2. What can the couple expect with Mike's retirement? How might it affect their marriage? What can Carol expect with regard to Mike's adjustment to retirement? How can the couple aid this adjustment?

3. What can the couple expect in the coming years? What developmental challenges will they face in their twilight?

Visit **edge.sagepub.com/kuther2e** to help you accomplish your coursework goals in an easy-to-use learning environment.

LEARNING OBJECTIVES	SUMMARY	KEY TERMS	IN REVIEW
18.1 Examine the contributions of self-concept, personality, and religiosity to older adults' well-being.	Self-conceptions are more multifaceted, complex, and stable in old age than at other periods of life. Most older adults maintain a positive view of themselves by accepting their weaknesses and compensating by focusing on their strengths. Reminiscence and life review help adults find continuity in their lives, come to term with choices, and develop ego integrity. As in other life periods, the Big 5 personality traits largely remain stable into late adulthood, but most adults experience subtle shifts. Most adults become more religious as they age, often providing support and a buffer against stress.	Reminiscence Life review Ego integrity versus despair	What is the major psychosocial task of late adulthood? What is the role of life review and reminiscence on the sense of self? How do Big 5 personality traits change during old age, and how do they predict well-being? What forms do religiosity take in late adulthood? What are the benefits of religious involvement?
18.2 Identify social contexts in which older adults live and their influence on development.	Most older adults prefer to age in place. There are a variety of different types of residential communities for older adults, ranging from single houses, to small collections of condominiums, to large apartment complexes. Only a small number of older adults reside in nursing homes, which offer the greatest amount of care but also the greatest restriction of elders' autonomy. Factors that influence the quality of living environments for older adults include freedom of choice, involvement in decision making, right to privacy, stimulating environment, age-appropriate opportunities and activities, and sense of connectedness.	Disengagement theory Activity theory Continuity theory Socioemotional selectivity theory	Compare disengagement, continuity, and activity theories. What is socioemotional selectivity theory? What does it mean to age in place? What are the challenges? Compare and contrast the influence of the following social contexts on older adults' development and well-being. • Neighborhoods • Residential communities • Nursing homes
18.3 Summarize features of older adults' relationships with friends, spouses, children, and grandchildren, and identify how these relationships affect older adults' functioning.	In older adulthood, friendships become more important and more fulfilling. Marital satisfaction increases in older adulthood. Older adult cohabiters do not differ from marrieds in their reports of emotional satisfaction, pleasure, openness, time spent together, criticism, and demands. The nature of the relationship and the exchange of help between elderly parents and their adult children change from predominantly parent-to-child assistance in childhood through early adulthood to increasing assistance provided by adult children to their elderly parents. Child-to-parent assistance most often takes the form of emotional support. Regardless of distance and contact, affection between grandchildren and grandparents tends to remain strong. Elder maltreatment appears in several forms, and many elders fall victim to more than one form of maltreatment: physical abuse, sexual abuse, psychological abuse, financial abuse, or physical neglect.		What roles do friends, siblings, and marital partners play in older adults' functioning and overall well-being? What are some recent trends in cohabitation among older adults? What is the nature of sexuality in late adulthood? How do relationships with adult children and grandchildren influence older adults' well-being?
18.4 Discuss influences on the timing of retirement and adaptation to retirement.	The period of retirement has lengthened in all Western nations. The decision of when to retire is influenced by job conditions, health, finances, and personal preferences. Financial resources often are the determining factor with regard to whether and when an older adult retires. Workers in high-stress, demanding jobs or those that provide little satisfaction tend to show positive adaptation to retirement. Research suggests the worker's sense of control influences the transition to retirement. Continuity in other social roles and the ability to adapt to role changes lead to few changes in life satisfaction after retirement. Engagement in leisure activities and volunteer work increases retirement satisfaction.		What factors influence the decision of when to retire? When does the transition to retirement actually begin, and what factors influence adjustment to retirement?

PART IX

Endings

CHAPTER 19:
Death and Dying

Death is a complex concept, and our understanding of it shifts over our lifespan. Children's views of death change with cognitive development, from viewing it as a temporary and reversible state to a final biological inevitability. Conceptions of death continue to change in subtle ways over the course of the lifespan.

Reactions to death change with development. Children may fear abandonment, whereas adolescents' need for autonomy often drives them to participate in decision making. Older adults tend to show less anxiety about death compared with people of other ages. Losing a loved one poses challenges to adjustment at all times in life. The nature of grief varies with the relationship of the bereaved to the deceased as well as with the individuals' understanding of death and capacities for emotional regulation.

Cultural beliefs about the nature of death vary. For example, some cultures view life and death as phases of a cycle, and others view death as a continuation of life. In some cultures, parents shield children from death, and in others, they encourage children to participate in mourning rituals. Cultures also mourn the dead in different ways, such as by ceasing all activity or, alternatively, engaging in jovial celebrations of life.

There are many ways of understanding death and many ways of grieving—all of which are influenced by our context.

DR. KUTHER'S
CHALK TALKS

Watch at
edge.sagepub.com/kuther2e

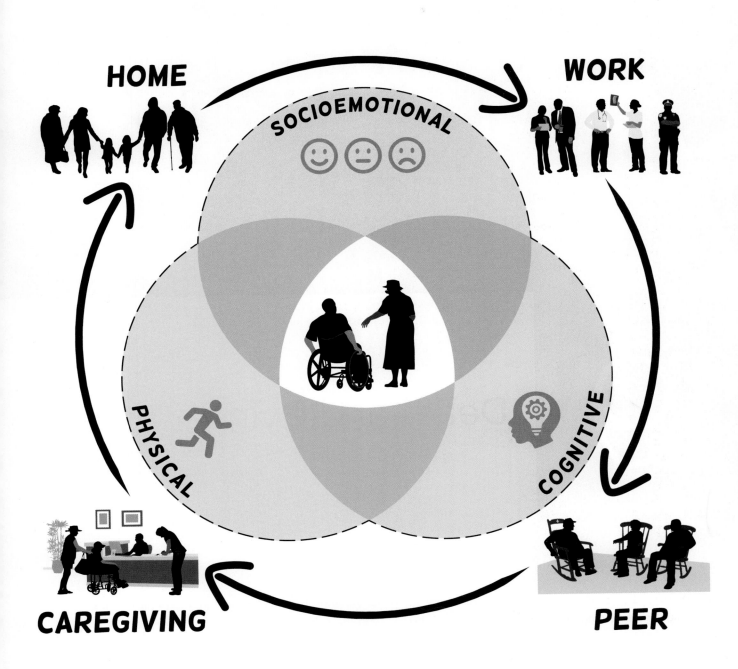

HOME

WORK

SOCIOEMOTIONAL

PHYSICAL

COGNITIVE

CAREGIVING

PEER

Images: ©iStock.com

Mario Tama/Getty Images News via Getty In

19 Death and Dying

At its simplest, death is the absence of life. It is unavoidable, comes hand-in-hand with life, and is the final state of the lifespan. In this chapter, we examine death and death-related issues across the lifespan, including evolving definitions of death, how people of varying ages understand and experience death, and the bereavement processes. The circumstances that surround death and its timing in the lifespan have changed radically over the past century, alongside advances in life expectancy.

Learning Objectives

19.1 Identify ways in which death has been defined and end-of-life issues that may arise.

19.2 Contrast children's, adolescents', and adults' understanding of death.

19.3 Discuss the physical and emotional process of dying as it is experienced over the lifespan.

19.4 Summarize typical grief reactions to the loss of loved ones and the influence of development on bereavement.

Digital Resources

Watch: Hospice Misconceptions

Explore: Children's Understanding of Death

▶ **Lives in Context Video 19.1:** Developmental Tasks of Dying

Connect: Lessons From Kubler-Ross

Connect: Helping Children Understand a Pet's Death

▶ **Lives in Context Video 19.2:** Dealing With a Parent's Death

PATTERNS OF MORTALITY AND DEFINING DEATH

» LO 19.1 Identify ways in which death has been defined and end-of-life issues that may arise.

Most babies born in 1900 did not live past age 50, but infants born in the United States today can expect to live to about age 80—and even longer in some countries, such as Japan (85 years) (Central Intelligence Agency, 2018). The rapid decline in mortality rates over the past 100 years can be attributed to advances in medicine and sanitation. Many once-fatal conditions and diseases are now treatable. In 1900, the leading causes of death were infectious diseases, specifically pneumonia and flu, tuberculosis, and gastrointestinal infections (National Institute of Aging, 2011). Today, each of these illnesses can be prevented and treated.

Mortality

In the United States, mortality across all ages declined 60% between 1935 and 2010 and about an additional 2% through 2014 (Hoyert, 2012; Kochanek, Murphy, Xu, & Arias, 2017) (see Figure 19.1). People of all ages demonstrate a reduced mortality rate, but as you can see in Figure 19.2, the risk of dying has especially plummeted for infants and young children, with a 94% reduction in death rates among children ages 1 to 4, compared with a 38% decline for adults age 85 or more from 1960 through 2010 (Hoyert, 2012). Similar changes have also occurred in the United Kingdom and other Western countries (Mathers, Stevens, Boerma, White, & Tobias, 2014; Office for National Statistics, 2014). Today women are less likely to die in childbirth, infants are more likely to survive their first year, children and adolescents are more likely to grow to adulthood, and adults are likely to overcome conditions that were once fatal.

As shown in Figure 19.3, the leading causes of death vary by age. Infants under a year of age are most likely to die from genetic, prenatal, and birth complications, with sudden infant death syndrome the third most common cause of death. Childhood deaths are most often due to accidents, illnesses, and, alarmingly, homicide (which is most often the result of child maltreatment).

Adolescents and adults through age 44 are most likely to die from unintentional injuries, such as falls and traffic accidents, but most often from drug overdose. In early adolescence, suicide is the second leading cause of death and remains so in early adulthood and into the mid-30s. Illnesses are a leading source of mortality throughout life, but homicide is a more common source of injury death from ages 15 to 34.

Over middle adulthood, cancer, heart disease, and injury become the top three causes, respectively. Suicide, the number four killer of adults ages 45 to 54, becomes less common in the later middle adulthood years, dropping to eighth place. Chronic illnesses

FIGURE 19.1

Infant, Neonatal, and Postneonatal Mortality Rates, United States, 1940–2014

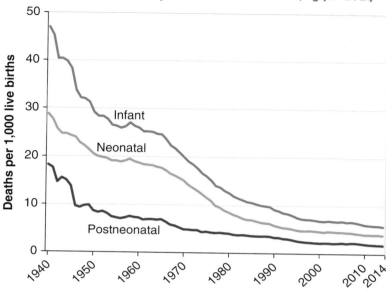

Source: Kochanek et al., 2016.

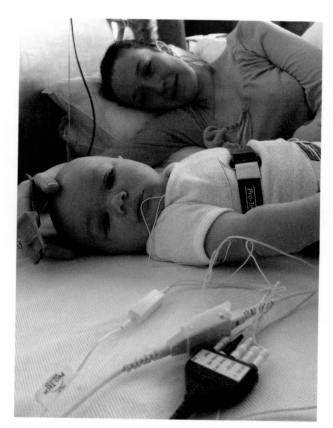

This baby boy is participating in a sleep study that examines the sleep patterns of mothers and babies when bed sharing, which researchers hope will help combat SIDS.
Owen Humphreys - PA Images/PA Images/Getty Images

such as diabetes and diseases of the liver and respiratory system emerge as sources of mortality in midlife, particularly late midlife. Older adults over the age of 65 are most likely to die of chronic illnesses, with heart disease as the number one killer, followed by cancer. Alzheimer's disease emerges as the fifth most common cause of death in adults age 65 and older.

Although unintentional injuries are the leading causes of death through age 44, the most common sources of injuries vary with age. For example, accidental suffocation is common in infancy and childhood, and drowning is a top source of unintentional death from childhood through early adulthood, becoming less so in middle adulthood. Unintentional poisoning, most often through drug overdose, is the second leading cause of injury death from ages 15 to 25 and the leading cause of injury deaths throughout early and middle adulthood, from ages 25 to 64. The opioid crisis is responsible for most overdose deaths, as discussed in the Lives in Context feature.

Defining Death

The actual moment of death is not easy to determine. In prior centuries, death was defined as the cessation of cardiopulmonary function. A person was dead once the heart stopped beating,

FIGURE 19.2

Death Rates by Age and Sex in the United States, 1955–2014

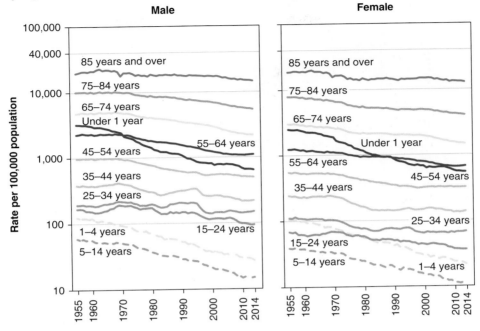

Source: Sherry et al., 2017.

FIGURE 19.3

Leading Causes of Death, by Age, 2016

Rank	<1	1–4	5–9	10–14	15–24	25–34	35–44	45–54	55–64	65+	Total
1	Congenital Anomalies 4,825	Unintentional Injury 1,235	Unintentional Injury 755	Unintentional Injury 763	Unintentional Injury 12,514	Unintentional Injury 19,795	Unintentional Injury 17,818	Malignant Neoplasms 43,054	Malignant Neoplasms 116,122	Heart Disease 507,138	Heart Disease 633,842
2	Short Gestation 4,084	Congenital Anomalies 435	Malignant Neoplasms 437	Malignant Neoplasms 428	Suicide 5,491	Suicide 6,947	Malignant Neoplasms 10,909	Heart Disease 34,248	Heart Disease 76,872	Malignant Neoplasms 419,389	Malignant Neoplasms 595,930
3	SIDS 1,568	Homicide 369	Congenital Anomalies 181	Suicide 409	Homicide 4,733	Homicide 4,863	Heart Disease 10,387	Unintentional Injury 21,499	Unintentional Injury 19,488	Chronic Low Respiratory Disease 131,804	Chronic Low Respiratory Disease 155,041
4	Maternal Pregnancy Comp. 1,522	Malignant Neoplasms 354	Homicide 140	Homicide 158	Malignant Neoplasms 1,469	Malignant Neoplasms 3,704	Suicide 6,936	Liver Disease 8,874	Chronic Low. Respiratory Disease 17,457	Cerebro-vascular 120,156	Unintentional Injury 146,571
5	Unintentional Injury 1,291	Heart Disease 147	Heart Disease 85	Congenital Anomalies 156	Heart Disease 997	Heart Disease 3,522	Homicide 2,895	Suicide 8,751	Diabetes Mellitus 14,166	Alzheimer's Disease 109,495	Cerebro-vascular 140,323
6	Placenta Cord. Membranes 910	Influenza & Pneumonia 88	Chronic Low Respiratory Disease 80	Heart Disease 125	Congenital Anomalies 386	Liver Disease 844	Liver Disease 2,861	Diabetes Mellitus 6,212	Liver Disease 13,278	Diabetes Mellitus 56,142	Alzheimer's Disease 110,561
7	Bacterial Sepsis 599	Septicemia 54	Influenza & Pneumonia 44	Chronic Low Respiratory Disease 93	Chronic Low Respiratory Disease 202	Diabetes Mellitus 798	Diabetes Mellitus 1,986	Cerebro-vascular 5,307	Cerebro-vascular 12,116	Unintentional Injury 51,395	Diabetes Mellitus 79,535
8	Respiratory Distress 462	Perinatal Period 50	Cerebro-vascular 42	Cerebro-vascular 42	Diabetes Mellitus 196	Cerebro-vascular 567	Cerebro-vascular 1,788	Chronic Low Respiratory Disease 4,345	Suicide 7,739	Influenza & Pneumonia 48,774	Influenza & Pneumonia 57,062
9	Circulatory System Disease 428	Cerebro-vascular 42	Benign Neoplasms 39	Influenza & Pneumonia 39	Influenza & Pneumonia 184	HIV 529	HIV 1,055	Septicemia 2,542	Septicemia 5,774	Nephritis 41,258	Nephritis 49,959
10	Neonatal Hemorrhage 406	Chronic Low Respiratory Disease 40	Septicemia 31	Two Tied: Benign Neo./Septicemia 33	Cerebro-vascular 166	Congenital Anomalies 443	Septicemia 829	Nephritis 2,124	Nephritis 5,452	Septicemia 30,817	Suicide 44,193

Source: National Center for Injury Prevention and Control, CDC.

The Opioid Epidemic

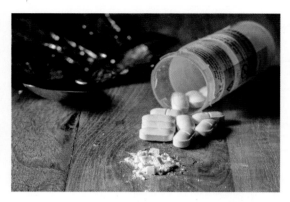

Deemed an epidemic by the U.S. Department of Health and Human Services, opioid overdoses are responsible for the decline in life expectancy since 2015.
iStock/BackyardProduction

Over the past two decades, the use of prescription and nonprescription opioid drugs has skyrocketed in the United States and Canada. Opioids are a class of strong painkillers, including prescription drugs such as oxycodone and illegal drugs such as heroin. Commonly prescribed to treat severe pain, opioids are highly addictive, leading many adults to continue their use to ease withdrawal symptoms or for recreational purposes. Individuals unable to obtain or afford prescriptions often transition to nonprescription opioids, most often heroin. The transition from prescription pills to heroin use may be influenced by the desire to get a more potent high and by heroin being easier to use, cheaper (given the low cost of heroin in the United States), and more easily available compared to prescription opioids (Martins, Santaella-Tenorio, Marshall, Maldonado, & Cerdá, 2015).

In addition to being highly addictive, opioids carry a high risk of overdose. Opioids have a sedative effect and, in high doses, can impair the part of the brain that regulates breathing, slowing and ceasing breathing, leading to death. Drug overdose deaths have increased rapidly since the late 1990s and are now the leading cause of death from young adulthood into middle adulthood, more than traffic accidents and gun-related deaths. It is estimated that two thirds of overdose deaths are from opioids and one half are from prescription drugs (Centers for Disease Control and Prevention, 2017; Katz, 2017). The greater social acceptance of prescribed opioids, as compared with illegal opioids, contributes to the problem. Moreover, overdoses continue to rise, increasing up to 30% in some areas of the United

States from July 2016 through September 2017 (Centers for Disease Control and Prevention, 2018). Canada has experienced similar increases, with a 2017 report noting that emergency department visits as a result of opiate overdose rose 1,000% in the 5 years prior (Ubelacker, 2017).

As we have discussed, the trend over the past century is toward longer lives, but in 2015, for the first time in recorded history, life expectancy fell—and in 2016, it fell again, from 78.7 to 78.6 (Kochanek, Murphy, Xu, & Arias, 2017). The decline in life expectancy is influenced by the increase in overdose deaths in adults under age 50.

In the United States, opioid addiction and overdose are exponentially more prevalent and have increased more rapidly in White non-Hispanics compared with African Americans and Hispanics (Martins et al., 2015; Seth, Scholl, Rudd, & Bacon, 2018). African Americans and Hispanics have been less likely to receive prescriptions for opioid medication (Singhal, Tien, & Hsia, 2016). One recent study suggested that medical students who held false beliefs about biological differences between Blacks and Whites, such as in pain tolerance or likelihood of addiction, were less likely to advocate prescribing strong painkillers to Black patients as compared with White patients (Hoffman, Trawalter, Axt, & Oliver, 2016). In this way, it is argued that racial bias may have protected people of color from the opiate epidemic (Ballesteros, 2017).

Deemed an epidemic by the U.S. Department of Health and Human Services, federal attempts to curb the opioid crisis focus on improving access to prevention, treatment, and recovery services; increasing the availability of overdose-treating drugs to prevent overdose deaths; and regulating and reducing the prescription of opioid drugs for pain (U.S. Department of Health and Human Services, 2018).

It is recommended that physicians and medical staff be trained to consider alternative medications and to recognize the symptoms of addiction. Physicians and pharmacists are encouraged to contribute to prescription drug monitoring databases to track prescriptions and patient use of opioid medications. In practice, the effects of prescription monitoring programs are mixed, as they are implemented inconstantly (Finley et al., 2017; Matusow, Rosenblum, & Parrino, 2018).

The highly addictive nature of opioids makes treatment very difficult. A combination of medical and behavioral treatment is most effective. Medical treatment includes prescription and monitoring of drugs to ease withdrawal symptoms. Behavioral treatment teaches patients strategies for avoiding opiates and managing physical and emotional symptoms of withdrawal and desires for use. Given the strong addictive effects of opiates, behavioral treatments are less likely to be successful in the absence of medical treatments to aid symptoms of physical withdrawal (Kolodny et al., 2015).

What Do You Think?

1. What might draw individuals to use opioid drugs? Do adolescents, adults, and older adults have similar reasons?

2. How might treatment be tailored to the diverse needs of adolescents, adults, and older adults? ●

---

now referred to as **clinical death**. When the heart stops beating, blood, and thereby oxygen, no longer circulates throughout the body and permanent brain damage can occur after 3 minutes of oxygen deprivation (Dennis, 2008). However, today's medical practices, including the widespread dissemination of cardiopulmonary resuscitation (CPR) techniques, have permitted many people to regain a heartbeat and be "revived" from clinical death. A heartbeat is no longer a clear marker of life or, in its absence, death.

Advances in technology have led to new ways of defining death. As mechanical ventilators became commonplace in operating rooms and intensive care settings, it became possible to artificially maintain patients who had irreversible injuries, to keep patients alive on ventilators. It is possible for the heart to continue to beat even though the person cannot eat, think, or breathe on his or her own. Therefore, more precise definitions of death are needed. A 1968 physician-led committee at Harvard Medical School concluded that patients who meet criteria for specific severe neurological injuries may be pronounced dead before cardiopulmonary cessation occurs (Harvard Medical School Ad Hoc Committee, 1968). **Whole brain death** refers to the irreversible loss of functioning in the entire brain, including the higher and lower brain regions, the cortex and brainstem, without the possibility of resuscitation (McMahan, 2001). Whole brain death may occur prior to clinical death (Burkle, Sharp, & Wijdicks, 2014). Death is declared if all criteria are met and other conditions that may mimic death, such as a drug overdose or deep coma, are ruled out. Patients who are brain dead may be temporarily sustained artificially for the purpose of organ donation.

The President's Commission for the Ethical Study of Problems in Medicine, Biomedical, and Behavioral Research (1981) established the criteria used to diagnose whole brain death:

1. No spontaneous movement in response to stimuli

2. No spontaneous respiration for at least 1 hour

3. Total lack of responsiveness to even the most painful stimuli

4. No eye movements, blinking, or pupil responses

5. No postural activity, swallowing, yawning, or vocalizing

6. No motor reflexes

7. A flat electroencephalogram (EEG) for at least 10 minutes

8. No change in any of these criteria when they are tested again 24 hours later

The 2008 report of the President's Council on Bioethics reaffirmed the whole brain definition of death. Under the Uniform Determination of Death Act, all 50 U.S. states and the District of Columbia apply the whole brain standard in defining death, thereby permitting a person to be declared legally dead and removed from life support.

The most controversial definition of death looks beyond the whole brain standard. In the late 19th century, several researchers and physicians noted instances in which brain damage caused a cease in cortical functioning while the heart continued to beat. The cortex is the part of the brain most vulnerable to conditions of *anoxia*, the loss of oxygen. Inadequate blood supply to the brain after heart attack, stroke, drowning, or traumatic brain injury can irreparably damage the cortex while leaving the brainstem intact and functional. The neurons of the brainstem often survive stressors that kill cortex neurons (Brisson, Hsieh, Kim, Jin, & Andrew, 2014), resulting in cortical death, or a **persistent vegetative state (PVS)**, in which the person appears awake but is not aware, due to the permanent loss of all activity in the cortex (Laureys et al., 2010). Despite cortical death, PVS patients retain an intact brainstem, which permits heart rate, respiration, and gastrointestinal activity to continue.

The PVS patient is neither clinically dead nor meets the criteria for whole brain death. He or she remains biologically alive despite lacking the capacity to regain awareness and cognitive capacities. The patient may open his or her eyelids and show sleep-wake cycles but does not show cognitive function, as indicated by measures of brain activity, such as MRI, EEG, and positron emission tomography scans (Bender, Jox, Grill, Straube, & Lulé, 2015). Loved ones may be misled by spontaneous reflexive movements of the arms and legs and random facial expressions to believe that the patient is capable of cognitive functions and experiences emotions (Cranford, 2004). However, reflexes are controlled by the spinal cord and lower regions of the brain that are not involved in conscious awareness. When the condition first appears, it is referred to as a vegetative state, but after 4 weeks, the patient is diagnosed with persistent vegetative state (The Multi-Society Task Force on PVS, 1994). Approximately 30,000 U.S. patients are held captive in this condition (Brisson et al., 2014).

Although the medical community typically defines a PVS patient as dead given the irrevocable lack of awareness and loss of cortical function, PVS is does not meet the criteria for whole brain death (and, thereby, death) and is not recognized as death by U.S. legal statute (McMahan, 2001). Canada and several other countries, however, acknowledge cortical death (Teitelbaum & Shemie, 2016). Supporters of the cortical definition of death argue that the cortex is responsible for what makes us human—thought, emotion, and personality. From this view, when higher cortical functions have ceased, these capacities are lost. Courts require authoritative medical opinion that recovery is not possible before terminating life-prolonging activities (Cranford, 2004). Several lengthy and dramatic court cases have caused many people to consider and communicate their own wishes regarding how they want to die.

End-of-Life Issues

People of all ages desire a sense of control in what happens to them, whether it is as simple as an infant's choice of play toy or as complex as an older adult's

Nieves Melendez tends to her son, former professional boxer Prichard Colon, while he lies in a vegetative state after suffering a traumatic brain injury during his bout against Terrel Williams.
The Washington Post/The Washington Post/Getty Images

choice of living situation. This is especially true when it comes to the many decisions that surround death. **Dying with dignity** refers to ending life in a way that is true to one's preferences, controlling one's end-of-life care (Guo & Jacelon, 2014; Kastenbaum, 2012).

Advance Directives

Planning and communication are key to helping people die with dignity. The individuals' wishes must be known ahead of time because dying patients are usually unable to express their wishes. Without prior communication, dying patients often cannot participate in decisions about their own end-of-life care, such as pain management, life-prolonging treatment, and memorial services. These decisions will likely be made by the persons who surround them—spouse, children, family members, friends, or health care workers—and these persons may well have views that differ from those of the patients. The Patient Self-Determination Act (PSA) of 1990 guaranteed the right of all competent adults to have a say in decisions about their health care by putting their wishes regarding end-of-life and life-sustaining treatment in writing.

Advance directives, including a living will and a durable power of attorney, are an important way of ensuring that people's preferences regarding end-of-life care are known and respected.

A **living will** is a legal document that permits people to make known their wishes regarding medical care if they are incapacitated by an illness or accident and are unable to speak for themselves. The individuals can identify what, if any, medical intervention should be used to prolong their lives if they are unable to express a preference. For example, should artificial respiration or a feeding tube be used? They can also explicitly designate the medical treatment they do not want. A **durable**

power of attorney for health care is a document in which individuals legally authorize a trusted relative or friend (called a *health care proxy*) to make health care decisions on their behalf if they are unable to do so. It is important to have both a living will and a durable power of attorney, as they each fulfill different functions.

Determining final wishes and communicating them in advance directives can ease the process of dying, both for dying persons and for their families. **Advance directives** permit patients to take control over their health care, their deaths, and what happens to their bodies and possessions after death. They facilitate communication about health care needs and preferences and can reduce anxiety on the part of patients (Nelson & Nelson, 2014). Advance directives foster patients' autonomy and help them to retain a sense of dignity as they die. Caregivers benefit from advance directives because an understanding of the patients' wishes can help in decision making and in reducing stress, emotional strain, and, potentially, guilt (Radwany et al., 2009).

Despite the many benefits of advance directives, they are underused. Overall, about one quarter of U.S. adults have written some form of advance directive (Rao, Anderson, Lin, & Laux, 2014). Older adults are most likely to have completed advance directives (about 50%), and they are typically the ones to initiate conversations with family members about end-of-life issues (Pew Research Center, 2009). About one third of 50- to 64-year-old adults and only about one fifth of 30- to 49-year-old adults report having written down their wishes for end-of-life treatment. Yet advance directives are not just for the old or the ill. Many argue that it is the healthy—especially the young and healthy—who benefit most from living wills and health care proxies (Khan, 2014). Young people and their families are often unprepared for the decisions that may accompany the sudden loss of decision-making capacities and consciousness, such as from an accident or serious illness. Advance directives can spare spouses and families the anguish, guilt, and potential conflict among family members of making decisions for a loved one without knowing his or her wishes.

Euthanasia

Through a living will, one might articulate when life-prolonging care may be withdrawn and under what conditions euthanasia is acceptable. **Euthanasia** ("easy death") refers to the practice of assisting terminally ill people in dying more quickly (Jecker, 2006; van der Maas, 1991). It is controversial, but the courts have permitted euthanasia in many hopeless cases, such as that of a patient named Nancy Cruzan. On January 11, 1983, then 25-year-old Nancy Cruzan lost control of her car, was thrown from the vehicle, and landed face down in a water-filled ditch. She was resuscitated by paramedics after about 15 minutes without breathing. After 3 weeks in a coma, Nancy was diagnosed as being in a persistent vegetative state. She remained alive as a PVS patient until 1987, when Nancy's parents asked that her feeding tube be removed. Although a county judge authorized the request, the state of Missouri contested it. The resulting Supreme Court decision in *Cruzan v. Director, Missouri Department of Health,* held that treatment can be refused in extraordinary circumstances, but clear and convincing evidence of Nancy's own wishes would be needed. The court accepted testimony from friends and family that Nancy had told them she would not want to live in a disabled condition. Nancy Cruzan died 2 weeks after her feeding tube was removed, in December 1990. The Cruzan case was pivotal in supporting the right-to-die movement.

Distinctions are commonly made between passive and active euthanasia (Jecker, 2006). **Passive euthanasia** occurs when life-sustaining treatment, such a ventilator, is withheld or withdrawn, allowing a person to die naturally, as happened in the case of Nancy Cruzan. In **active euthanasia**, death is deliberately induced, such as by administering a fatal dose of pain medication. More than two thirds of U.S. adults and 95% of physicians support passive euthanasia (Curlin, Nwodim, Vance, Chin, & Lantos, 2008; Pew Research Center, 2013). Most adults say there are at least some situations in which they, personally, would want to halt medical treatment and be allowed to die. For example, 57% say they would tell their doctors to stop treatment if they had a disease with no hope of improvement and were suffering a great deal of pain. And about half (52%) say they would ask their doctors to stop treatment if they had an incurable disease and were totally dependent on someone else for their care. Yet, about a third of adults (35%) say they would tell their doctors to do everything possible to keep them alive—even in dire circumstances, such as having a disease with no hope of improvement and experiencing a great deal of pain (Pew Research Center, 2013). These are difficult questions, and there is no clear consensus on solutions.

Physician-Assisted Suicide

Physician-assisted suicide is a type of voluntary active euthanasia in which terminally ill patients make the conscious decision that they want their life to end before dying becomes a protracted

Dr. Jack Kevorkian (1928–2011) helped over 100 terminally ill patients end their lives, prompting a continuing debate over physician-assisted suicide.
Detroit News/PSG/Newscom

process. Patients receive from physicians the medical tools needed to end their lives. The patient self-administers the medication. Physician-assisted suicide is legal in the Netherlands, Luxembourg, and Switzerland (Grosse & Grosse, 2015) and is often tacitly accepted in other countries. Until recently, assisting a suicide was illegal throughout North America; however, Canada adopted physician-assisted suicide starting in 2016, and physician-assisted suicide is legal in several U.S. states (Fine, 2015; Ollove, 2015).

The most widely publicized cases of physician-assisted suicide involved Dr. Jack Kevorkian, a Michigan physician who helped over 100 terminally ill patients end their lives. In 1989, Kevorkian created a "suicide machine" that allowed a patient to press a button to self-administer anesthesia and medication that stops the heart. In 1998, Kevorkian was arrested after a segment televised on the program *60 Minutes* aired in which he assisted in the death of a 52-year-old man who suffered from a terminal neurological disease. Although it was flagrantly displayed on television, the procedure was illegal and led to Kevorkian's arrest, trial, and conviction on second-degree murder charges. He was released from prison in 2007 after serving 8 years of a 10 to 25-year sentence. He died in 2011 after being diagnosed with liver cancer.

As of 2018, the practice of physician-assisted suicide is legal in the U.S. states of California, Colorado, Hawaii, Montana, Oregon, Vermont, and Washington and the District of Columbia (Ollove, 2018). Oregon was the first U.S. state to legalize assisted suicide. Under Oregon's Death With Dignity Act, enacted in 1997, terminally ill Oregonians may end their lives through the voluntary self-administration of lethal medications, expressly prescribed by a physician for that purpose.

Under the Oregon law, an adult Oregon resident who has been diagnosed by a physician with a terminal illness that will kill the patient within 6 months may request in writing a prescription for a lethal dose of medication for ending the patient's life. The patient must initiate the request and must be free of any mental condition that might impair judgment. The request must be confirmed by two witnesses, and at least one of them (1) must not be related to the patient, (2) must not be entitled to any portion of the patient's estate, (3) must not be the patient's physician, and (4) must not be employed by a health care facility caring for the patient. After the request is made, a second physician must examine the patient's medical records and confirm the diagnosis. If the request is authorized, the patient must wait an additional 15 days to make a second oral request before the prescription can be written.

Since the Oregon law was enacted in 1997, a total of 1,749 people have had prescriptions written, and 1,127 patients have died from ingesting medication prescribed under the act (Oregon Public Health Division, 2017). Eighty percent of the 1,126 patients who died were over the age of 65, and the median age at time of death was 73. Over three quarters had been diagnosed with cancer. The top three concerns reported by patients as influences on their decisions were being less able to engage in activities to enjoy life, loss of autonomy, and loss of dignity (Oregon Public Health Division, 2017).

The Oregon Death With Dignity Act has permitted many suffering adults to end their lives on their own timetable; however, physician-assisted suicide remains controversial in the United States. As shown in Figure 19.4, most U.S. adults in 2016 (69%) agreed that euthanasia should be legal and that doctors should be allowed to end a patient's life by painless means. Moreover, 51% said they would consider ending their lives if faced with terminal illness (Swift, 2016). Yet debates regarding physician-assisted suicide are unlikely to be resolved at any time soon.

Hospice

The desire to die with dignity, minimal pain, and on one's own terms has advanced the hospice movement. **Hospice** is an approach to end-of-life care that emphasizes dying patients' needs for pain management; psychological, spiritual, and social support; and death with dignity (Connor, 2018). The philosophy of the hospice approach does not emphasize prolonging life but rather prolonging quality of life. Although death occurs most often in hospitals, most dying people express the desire to die at home with family and friends (Weitzen, Teno,

FIGURE 19.4

Physician-Assisted Suicide

When a person has a disease that cannot be cured and is living in severe pain, do you think doctors should or should not be allowed by law to assist the patient to commit suicide if the patient requests it?

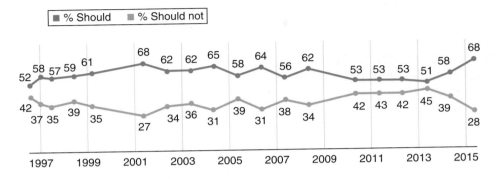

Source: Dugan, 2015.

Fennell, & Mor, 2003). Dying persons have needs that set them apart from other hospital patients, and hospital settings are often not equipped to meet these needs. Rather than medical treatment, dying patients require **palliative care**, focusing on controlling pain and related symptoms. Hospice services are enlisted after the physician and patient believe that the illness is terminal, and no treatment or cure is possible.

Hospice services may be provided on an inpatient basis, at a formal hospice site that provides all care to patients, but they are frequently provided on an outpatient basis in a patient's home (Connor, 2018). Outpatient hospice service is becoming more common because it is cost-effective and enables the patient to remain in the familiar surroundings of his or her home. Home hospice care is associated with increased satisfaction by patients and families (Candy, Holman, Leurent, Davis, & Jones, 2011). Whether hospice care is given on an inpatient or outpatient basis, the patient care team typically includes physicians, nurses, social workers,

Hospice services permit dying patients to remain in their home, comfortable, and feel a sense of control in the death process. Counseling services help families assist the dying person, cope with their own needs, and strengthen connections with the dying person. Hospice services permit death with dignity that honors a loved one's wishes.
John Moore/Gettyritualistic

THINKING IN CONTEXT 19.1

1. Evaluate the right-to-die concept. In your view, what is the value of this concept? How well is it embodied in advance directives, euthanasia, physician-assisted suicide, and hospice? Which of these approaches do you endorse, if any?

2. What advantages and disadvantages do you see to choosing hospice instead of standard medical care? Should some patients be required to transition to hospice? Why or why not?

3. From a bioecological perspective, discuss contextual factors that contribute to the declining mortality rate. Provide examples of influences at each bioecological level with particular attention to exosystem and macrosystem influences.

and counselors who act as spiritual and bereavement counselors who support the patient in facing his or her impending death and help the patient's loved ones cope with the loss.

CONCEPTIONS OF DEATH ACROSS THE LIFESPAN

» LO 19.2   Contrast children's, adolescents', and adults' understanding of death.

There are many ways of conceptualizing death, and cultural beliefs about the nature of death vary. For example, many cultures within the South Pacific do not differentiate death as a separate category of functioning. Melanesians use the term *mate* to refer to the very old, the very sick, and the dead; all other living people are referred to as *toa* (Counts & Counts, 1985). Other South Pacific cultures explain that the life force leaves the body during sleep and illness; therefore, people experience forms of death over the course of their lifetime before experiencing a final death (Counts & Counts, 1985). The Kwanga of Papua New Guinea believe that most deaths are the result of magic and witchcraft (Brison, 1995). The Hopi Indians of North America view life and death as phases of a cycle, with death representing an altered state.

Many children and adults in various cultures express beliefs in **noncorporeal continuation**, the view that some form of life and personal continuity exists after the physical body has died (Kenyon, 2001). For example, a spirit may endure, life may persist in heaven, or a soul may be reincarnated into another body. These beliefs are consistent with the doctrine of many religions and can coexist with mature understandings of death as the irreversible and inevitable ceasing of biological functioning (Corr & Corr, 2013). Researchers generally agree that, in Western cultures, a person has a mature understanding of death when the following four components are understood (Barrett & Behne, 2005; Kenyon, 2001; Panagiotaki, Nobes, Ashraf, & Aubby, 2015; Slaughter & Griffiths, 2007).

1. *Nonfunctionality,* the understanding that death entails the complete and final end of all life-defining abilities or functional capacities, internal and external, that are typically attributed to a living body.

2. *Irreversibility,* the understanding that the processes involved in the transition from being alive to being dead and the resulting state of being dead cannot be undone. Once a thing dies, its physical body cannot be made alive again.

3. *Inevitability,* the understanding that death is universal, that all living things will someday die.

4. *Biological causality,* the understanding that death is caused by events or conditions that trigger natural processes within the organism and that it is not caused by bad behavior or wishes.

Children's Understanding of Death

Children do not understand loss and death in the same way as adults, but they often have a more mature understanding of these events than many adults expect (Gaab, Owens, & Macleod, 2013). Even infants can sense that something unusual is happening when the adults around them grieve. They notice changes in the emotional tone of their families, changes in caregivers, and the degree to which their emotional needs are met or interrupted (Leming & Dickinson, 2016). Young children, similarly, perceive events around them before they have developed the ability to understand or explain them.

Children encounter death in many ways. Grandparents, parents, other important adults, siblings, and friends may die. Pets are often children's first experience with unconditional love, and most children will experience the death of a pet as a significant experience (Leming & Dickinson, 2016). Children have more exposure to death and death themes than many adults realize. They overhear adults talking about the deaths of elderly relatives or public figures. Television reports describe car

Children visit a relative's grave during the *día de los muertos* celebration.
ALFREDO ESTRELLA/AFP/Getty Images

crashes, homicides, disasters, and war. Death is a common topic in television programs. Considering such exposure to the subject of death, it is not surprising that children's play is riddled with death-related themes (Bettelheim, 1977; Opie & Opie, 1969). We have seen that play is the work of childhood, and as such, it is a way that children make sense of the world, including death (Corr, 2010b). Children often act out crashes with their cars or killing with toy soldiers. Death themes appear in children's rhymes, songs, and fairytales (Lamers, 1995). The song "Rock-a-Bye, Baby" culminates with a falling cradle (Achté, Fagerström, Pentikäinen, & Farberow, 1989), and the child's prayer "Now I lay me down to sleep" asks for safekeeping against danger and death. The wicked stepmother demands Snow White's heart as proof of her death, and the big bad wolf in the "Three Little Pigs" falls down the chimney of the third pig's house into a pot of boiling water. Death themes in rhymes and play may help children work through fears related to loss in safe ways.

Young children between the ages of 3 and 5 tend to view death as temporary and reversible. They believe dead things can become alive spontaneously and as the result of medical intervention, after eating or drinking, and by magic, wishful thinking, or prayer (Corr, 2010b; Slaughter, 2005). They may imagine that the person who has died is actually still living but under alternative circumstances (Barrett & Behne, 2005; Slaughter & Griffiths, 2007). They may describe death as sleep, with the corresponding ability to wake up, or a trip from which a person can return. They may personify death as a figure, a spirit that comes and "gets" you (Leming & Dickinson, 2016). They may believe that only people who want to die or who are bad die. Before they understand nonfunctionality, children view dead things as possessing reduced or diminished capacities but retaining some functions such as the ability to feel hunger pangs, wishes, beliefs, and love (Bering & Bjorklund, 2004). Before they understand the inevitability of death, young children think that there are actions they could take to avoid death, such as being clever enough to outsmart it or being lucky (Speece & Brent, 1984). A mature understanding of biological death gradually emerges alongside cognitive development.

The understanding that death is final, irreversible, and inevitable typically emerges between 5 and 7 years of age, corresponding to the transition from preoperational reasoning to concrete operational reasoning in Piaget's theory. Biological causality is the most complex element of the death concept and the final element to be acquired, emerging as early as 6 or 7, but more typically in late childhood (Bonoti, Leondari, & Mastora, 2013; Slaughter & Griffiths, 2007). Advances in executive function are closely related with the emergence of a biological theory of death as these cognitive capacities permit the abstract thinking needed for mature conceptions of death (Zaitchik, Iqbal, & Carey, 2014). Typically, an understanding of the biological nature of death is mastered by about age 10 (Bonoti et al., 2013; Renaud, Engarhos, Schleifer, & Talwar, 2015). Research comparing White British, Muslim British, and Muslim Pakistani children suggests that this pattern of change in biological explanations for death occurs cross-culturally (Panagiotaki et al., 2015). Such findings are consistent with those from children in Australia (Slaughter & Griffiths, 2007), the United States (Lazar & Torney-Purta, 1991), and Israel (Schonfeld & Smilansky, 1989).

Despite cross-cultural similarities in biological conceptions of death, there are contextual differences in children's exposure to death, and these differences influence children's conceptions of death. Some children receive more exposure to death through media depictions of war, accidents, and devastating living conditions. Others experience death firsthand. Many children in all parts of the world, including North America, are exposed directly to violence within their families and communities and may witness or be aware of traumatic events and deaths at home and in their neighborhoods. Children who reside in war-torn and poverty-stricken nations often experience multiple losses (Masten, Narayan, Silverman, & Osofsky, 2015). How children make sense of these events and how they understand death changes with age and experience. Children who have direct, personal experience of death tend to show a more advanced and realistic understanding of death than their peers (Bonoti et al., 2013; Hunter & Smith, 2008).

How parents talk to children about death, and whether they talk about death, influences children's understanding. Parents of young children, ages 3 to 6, tend to believe that their children hold misconceptions about death. They avoid talking about death, believing that children are not capable of grasping or coping with it (Miller & Rosengren, 2014; Nguyen & Rosengren, 2004). U.S. parents often shield their young children from death by not taking them to funerals or memorial services, controlling their access to death in television and movies, and talking with them about death minimally, indirectly, or not at all (Miller & Rosengren, 2014). Parents are most likely to report having discussed death when the child has experienced a death of some kind, regardless of age; more conversations took place as the child's age increased (Renaud et al., 2015).

Culture is a powerful influence on conceptions of death. European American parents, for instance, tend to shield their children from death. In contrast, Mexican and Mexican American parents are likely to believe that children should become familiar with death and are likely to include them as active participants in rituals related to death, such as wakes and funerals (Gutiérrez, Rosengren, & Miller, 2014). These attitudes are supported by traditional Mexican practices, such as the *día de los muertos* (Day of the Dead), a national holiday held each year from October 31 to November 2. At this time, dead relatives are said to return to their homes to eat, drink, and visit with the living. The celebration includes images such as skeletons in festive outfits engaging in everyday activities: dancing, playing instruments, getting married, and so forth. Children participate with other community members in celebrations and vigils held in cemeteries (Gutierrez, 2009). The *día de los muertos* holiday is intended to welcome the dead and to celebrate death as the continuation of life. It is not surprising that young Mexican American children are more likely than their European American peers to attribute biological and psychological properties to the dead (Gutiérrez et al., 2014).

Culture also influences individuals' views of spirituality, which in turn affect their views of death. Children often develop spiritual or religious explanations in addition to biological explanations for death (Legare, Evans, Rosengren, & Harris, 2012). Still, the extent to which children use religious or biological terms may vary by culture (Harris & Gimenez, 2005; Nguyen & Rosengren, 2004).

Harris and Gimenez (2005) found that belief in the afterlife among Spanish children increased between the ages of 7 and 11, along with religious explanations for death. However, children were more likely to offer religious explanations for death in response to vignettes highlighting religious themes than in response to vignettes highlighting medical themes indicating that children hold multiple conceptions of death, depending on context. Children who grow up in cultures that endorse both religious and biological views of death may hold explanations about death that appear incompatible, such as biological irreversibility and religious or spiritual continuity (Gutiérrez et al., 2014; Panagiotaki, Hopkins, Nobes, Ward, & Griffiths, 2018; Panagiotaki et al., 2015). It is not until later in development, particularly adolescence, that children gain the cognitive competence to integrate these ideas. For more on the cultural beliefs about the nature of death, see the accompanying Cultural Influences on Development feature.

Adolescents' Understanding of Death

Adolescents often describe death as an enduring abstract state of nothingness that accompanies the inevitable and irreversible end of biological processes (S. B. Brent, Lin, Speece, Dong, & Yang, 1996). Adolescents' understanding of death reflects the intersection of biological, cognitive, and socioemotional development. As adolescents experience the rapid biological changes of puberty, this process may heighten their awareness of the inevitability of the biological changes of life. Although adolescents are cognitively aware that death is universal and can happen to anyone, at any time, this awareness often is not reflected in their risk-taking behavior. Instead, adolescents are prone to the personal fable (see Chapter 11), viewing themselves as unique and invulnerable to the negative consequences of risky behaviors, including death (Alberts, Elkind, & Ginsberg, 2007). The risk-taking behavior characteristic of adolescence is a form of cheating death, an event that is perceived as a distant, but unlikely, possibility.

Adolescents' advances in abstract reasoning are reflected in their interest in considering the meaning of death, as well as whether some psychological functions, such as knowing and feeling, persist in a dying person after biological processes have ceased (Noppe & Noppe, 2004). Adolescents and adults across cultures often share a belief in an afterlife, whether religious or supernatural in origin (Bering & Bjorklund, 2004). This belief often arises in childhood, but it is in adolescence that we are first able to simultaneously hold a mature biological understanding of death as the end of all body functions alongside cultural and religious beliefs about an afterlife (Panagiotaki et al., 2018). The two conceptions coexist and can be called upon as needed depending on the situation and what adolescents are trying to explain (Legare et al., 2012). For example, the Vezo people in rural Madagascar believe that dead ancestors are present among the living, watching and guiding (Astuti & Harris, 2008). Vezo children tend to emphasize biological explanations for death, but adolescents and adults hold both biological and spiritual explanations, reflecting their cognitive abilities to hold two differing perspectives at once.

Adults' Understanding of Death

Conceptions of death change in subtle ways over the course of adulthood. Young adults begin to

Cultural Rituals Surrounding Death

The Cremation Ceremony held in Bali, Indonesia, is a ritual performed to send the deceased to the next life. The body is placed in a wood coffin inside a temple-like structure made of paper and wood. The structure and body are burned to release the deceased's spirit and enable reincarnation.
© istock.com/laughingmango

There is great variability in cultural views of the meaning of death and the rituals or other behaviors that express grief (Rosenblatt, 2008). Perhaps the most well-known death rituals were practiced by the ancient Egyptians. They believed that the body must be preserved through mummification to permanently house the spirit of the deceased in his or her new eternal life. The mummies were surrounded by valued objects and possessions and buried in elaborate tombs. Family members would regularly visit, bringing food and necessities to sustain them in the afterlife. Egyptian mummies are the most well known, but mummies have been found in other parts of the world such as the Andes mountains of Peru (Whitbourne, 2007).

The Bornu of Nigeria require family members to wash the deceased, wrap the body in a white cloth, and carry it to the burial ground (Cohen, 1967). In the French West Indies, the deceased's neighbors wash the body with rum, pour a liter or more of rum down the throat, and place the body on a bed (Horowitz, 1967).

In South Korea today, a small minority of people still choose to employ the services of a *mudang* (Korean "shaman") to conduct a lengthy ritual known as *Ogu Kut,* in which the *mudang* summons the deceased's spirit into the ritual space; expresses the latter's feelings of unhappiness through song, dance, and the spoken word; and encourages the bereaved to express his or her own grievances within symbolic psychodrama. Once the emotional ties between the bereaved and the deceased have been loosened, prayers for protection are offered to various deities, and the *mudang* guides the spirit toward the Buddhist paradise. Finally, the deceased's earthly possessions are cremated and the bereaved are left better able to move on in their lives (Mills, 2012).

Death rituals vary among religions. Among Hindus, a good death is a holy death, one that is welcomed by the dying person, who rests on the ground and is surrounded by family and friends chanting prayers (Dennis, 2008). Buddhists believe that the dying person's task is to gain insight. Death is not an end, as the individual will be reincarnated in the hopes of reaching nirvana, an ultimate, perfect state of enlightenment. Among Jews, the dying person remains part of the community and is never left alone before or immediately after death. Christians generally believe that death is the entry to an eternity in heaven or hell and thereby is an event to be welcomed (generally) or feared (rarely). In Islam, death is united with life, because it is believed that the achievements and concerns of this life are fleeting, and everyone should be mindful and ready for death. Muslim death rituals, such as saying prayers and washing the body, aid in the dying person's transition to the afterlife.

What Do You Think?

1. In your view, what purpose do death rituals fulfill?

2. Given the ethnic and religious diversity in the United States, many people have opportunities to learn about different cultural and religious approaches to coping with death. What customs, if any, have you observed? ●

apply their mature understanding of death to themselves. The personal fable declines, and as they take on adult roles, young adults begin to acknowledge their vulnerability. Risky activity declines and young adults' behavior begins to better align with their understanding of the inevitability of death.

An awareness of death increases as individuals progress through middle adulthood, when they are likely to gain experience through the deaths of parents, friends, siblings, and colleagues. As midlife adults watch their children take on adult roles and as they become aware of their own aging bodies and minds, they develop a more personalized sense of their own mortality and the inevitability of the life cycle (Doka, 2015). The awareness of death can cause midlife adults to reevaluate their priorities, often leading them to pursue a sense of generativity, the need to give back and leave a lasting legacy (McAdams, 2014). Midlife adults who look beyond their own losses to consider the profound meaning of their absence to significant others, such as spouses and children, may be deeply saddened by the thought of their own death.

Older adults are likely to have exposure to death many times over. With the deaths of many friends and family members, older adults may become socialized to the nature and inevitability of death (Cicirelli, 2002). They often talk about aging and death, perhaps helping them to prepare for the inevitability of their own death (Hallberg, 2013). They also spend more time thinking about the process and circumstances of dying than the state of death, as compared with midlife adults (Corr, 2019).

Cross-sectional and longitudinal studies suggest that death anxiety declines over the lifespan; older adults tend to report lower levels of death anxiety than young and middle-aged adults (Chopik, 2017; Russac, Gatliff, Reece, & Spottswood, 2007). Advances in psychosocial development, such an increasing ability to manage negative emotions, influence how older adults approach death, and may account for their reduced anxiety compared to younger adults. In addition, religion, specifically a religious sense of hope (e.g., the conviction that their religious beliefs will bring opportunities or make things turn out well), reduces death anxiety among older adults (Krause, Pargament, & Ironson, 2016). The psychosocial task of older adulthood is to consider the meaning of life and death. Engaging in life review and establishing a sense of ego integrity help older adults reduce regrets and construct a sense that their lives have been well lived (Erikson, 1982).

DYING AND THE EXPERIENCE OF DEATH

» LO 19.3 Discuss the physical and emotional process of dying as it is experienced over the lifespan.

When does dying begin? How does it occur? How is it experienced? These are questions that are challenging to answer. In the following sections, we consider the biological changes that occur with death, as well as the cognitive and socioemotional experience of death, and finally we consider how people experience their own deaths.

The Dying Process

There is great variability in the **dying trajectory**, or the rate of decline that people show prior to death (Cohen-Mansfield, Skornick-Bouchbinder, & Brill, 2017; Lunney, Lynn, Foley, Lipson, & Guralnik, 2003). Dying trajectories vary by duration and descent and can be categorized into four patterns. The first trajectory is the *abrupt-surprise death,* which is sudden, unexpected, and instantaneous, such as an accident, a shooting, or a heart attack, or, in the case of infants, sudden infant death syndrome (see the Applying Developmental Science feature). As shown in Figure 19.5, the person shows normal functioning until a steep, catastrophic decline occurs, bringing a sudden death without warning. The dying person and his or her family have no time to prepare or adjust beforehand. A second trajectory, the *short-term expected death* is a steady predictable decline due to a terminal illness such as cancer. A third dying trajectory is referred to as an *expected lingering death* because it is anticipated but prolonged, such as in the case of frailty and old age. The fourth trajectory is referred to as *entry-reentry*

THINKING IN CONTEXT 19.2

1. How do children's and adolescents' understanding of death reflect their cognitive development? Explain how cognitive advances from Piagetian and information processing perspectives may underlie children's and adolescents' conceptions of death.

2. Recall Erikson's psychosocial stages of development (Chapter 1). How are the developmental tasks of adolescence and adulthood reflected in how people understand death? Provide specific examples of how tasks, such as identity development and the search for intimacy and generativity, might influence people's views of death.

FIGURE 19.5

Theoretical Trajectories of Dying

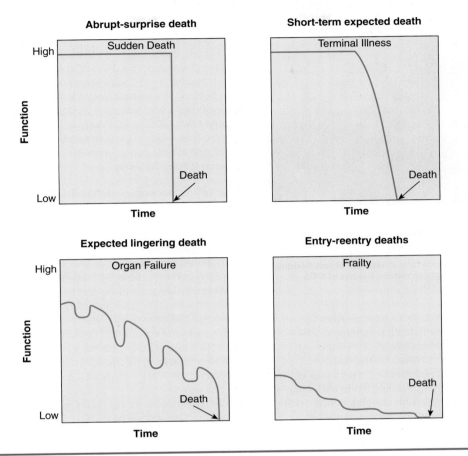

Source: Lunney et al., 2002.

deaths, because slow declines are punctuated by a series of crises and partial recoveries; the dying person may have repeated hospital stays, returning home between stays. The dying trajectory influences adaptation on the part of the dying person and his or her family. Typically, the short-term expected death is most predictable and most likely to be experienced in hospice care as the lifespan is clearly identified as limited. Lingering and entry-reentry deaths are prolonged. They can tax caregivers' coping skills as such deaths are often not afforded hospice care until death is imminent.

Predictable changes and symptoms occur in the dying person hours and days before death; however, people vary in the number and severity of symptoms (Gavrin & Chapman, 1995). Toward the end of life, many people lose their appetite, which is often distressing to family as the patient may show dramatic weight loss. People suffering from lengthy illnesses, such as cancer, AIDS, and

neurodegenerative disorders, often show extreme weight loss and the loss of muscle mass, known as *cachexia* (W. J. Evans et al., 2008). As death is imminent, the person sleeps most of the time, may be disoriented and less able to see, and may experience visual and auditory hallucinations. Many terminally ill patients experience declines in cognitive function in the weeks prior to death.

The dying person may experience pain, shortness of breath, irregular breathing, nausea, disrupted bladder and bowel function, and lethargy (Gavrin & Chapman, 1995). As the person is closer to death, he or she will lose interest in and the ability to eat, drink, and talk, as well as show reduced mobility and drowsiness (Lichter & Hunt, 1990). Breathing will be difficult and the person may experience dry mouth and difficulty swallowing. Breathing becomes noisy, a gurgling or crackling sound with each breath that is referred to as the *death rattle.* The average time from the onset of the death rattle to death is

Sudden Infant Death Syndrome

Sudden infant death syndrome (SIDS) is the leading cause of death of infants under the age of 1. It is not well understood, but placing infants on their backs to sleep and providing a safe sleep environment (such as the use of a firm sleep surface, avoidance of soft bedding and infant overheating) can reduce the risk of SIDS.
Clare Coe / Alamy Stock Photo

The leading cause of death of infants under the age of 1 is sudden infant death syndrome (SIDS) (Bajanowski & Vennemann, 2017). *SIDS* is the diagnostic term used to describe the sudden unexpected death of an infant less than 1 year of age that occurs seemingly during sleep and remains unexplained after a thorough investigation, including an autopsy and review of the circumstances of death and the infant's clinical history (Task Force on Sudden Infant Death Syndrome, 2016).

What causes SIDS? It is believed to be the result of an interaction of factors, including an infant's biological vulnerability to SIDS coupled with exposure to a trigger or stressor that occurs during a critical period of development (R. Y. Moon & Task Force on Sudden Infant Death Syndrome, 2016; Spinelli, Collins-Praino, Van Den Heuvel, & Byard, 2017). The first factor is unknown biological vulnerabilities, such as genetic abnormalities and mutations and prematurity, that may place infants at risk for SIDS. For example, a recent 10-year review of hundreds of SIDS cases in Australia confirmed that, although the underlying cause of SIDS remains unknown, mutations and genetic variants likely play a role (A. Evans, Bagnall, Duflou, & Semsarian, 2013). Second, environmental stressors or events that might trigger SIDS include risks such as having the infant sleep on his or her stomach or side, use of soft bedding or other inappropriate sleep surfaces (including sofas), bed sharing, and exposure to tobacco smoke (Carlin & Moon, 2017). One review of several hundred cases in the United Kingdom found that over a third of SIDS deaths infants were

co-sleeping with adults at the time of death (Blair, Sidebotham, Berry, Evans, & Fleming, 2006). Finally, there are developmental periods in which infants are most vulnerable to SIDS. Most cases of SIDS occur between the second and fifth months of life (Bajanowski & Vennemann, 2017). Therefore, it is thought that SIDS is most likely to occur when the triple risks—biological vulnerability, triggering events, and critical period of development—converge (Filiano & Kinney, 1994; Spinelli et al., 2017).

Ethnic differences appear in the prevalence of SIDS, with Native Americans and Blacks showing the highest rates of SIDS in the United States, followed by non-Hispanic Whites. Asian American and Hispanic infants show lower rates of SIDS than White infants (Parks, Erck Lambert, & Shapiro-Mendoza, 2017). Ethnic differences in SIDS are likely due to differences in socioeconomic and lifestyle factors associated with SIDS, such as lack of prenatal care, low rates of breastfeeding, maternal smoking, and low maternal age. Cultural practices, such as adult–infant bed sharing, providing infants with soft bedding, and placing the sleeping baby in a separate room from caregivers, increase SIDS risk (Colson et al., 2013; Parks et al., 2017; Shapiro-Mendoza et al., 2014). However, ethnic differences in SIDS are complex and influenced by context. For example, in one study of infants, Mexican American U.S.-born mothers had a 50% greater rate of SIDS than infants of Mexican foreign-born mothers after controlling for factors associated with SIDS, including birthweight, maternal age, education, marital status, prenatal care, and socioeconomic status (Collins, Papacek, Schulte, & Drolet, 2001). Differences in acculturation and associated child care practices likely play a role in influencing SIDS risk, but they are not well understood (Parks et al., 2017).

As shown in Figure 19.6, SIDS declined dramatically in the 1990s after the American Academy of Pediatrics, based on data from Europe, Australia, and the United States, recommended that infants be placed for sleep in a nonprone position (i.e., a supine position: on their backs) as a strategy to reduce the risk of SIDS (see Figure 19.6) (American Academy of Pediatrics AAP Task Force on Infant Positioning and SIDS: Positioning and SIDS, 1992). Initiated in 1992, the "Back to Sleep" campaign publicized the importance of nonprone sleeping. Between 1992 and 2001, the SIDS rate declined dramatically in the United States and other countries that implemented nonprone/supine sleeping campaigns (Bajanowski & Vennemann, 2017; Bergman, 2015; R. Y. Moon &

Task Force on Sudden Infant Death Syndrome, 2016), consistent with the steady increase in the prevalence of supine sleeping. In addition to placing infants on their backs to sleep, other recommendations for a safe sleep environment include the use of a firm sleep surface, avoidance of soft bedding and infant overheating, and sharing a room with the infant without sharing a bed. Avoid placing infants in sitting devices, such as car seats, strollers, and infant carriers, for routine sleep. Couches and armchairs are extremely dangerous places for infants. Additional recommendations for SIDS risk reduction include breastfeeding, routine immunizations, use of a pacifier, and avoidance of smoking.

What Do You Think?

Write a letter to a new parent explaining SIDS, risk factors for it, and what parents can do to help protect their infants. ●

FIGURE 19.6

Trends in Sudden Unexpected Infant Death (SUID) by Cause, 1990–2015

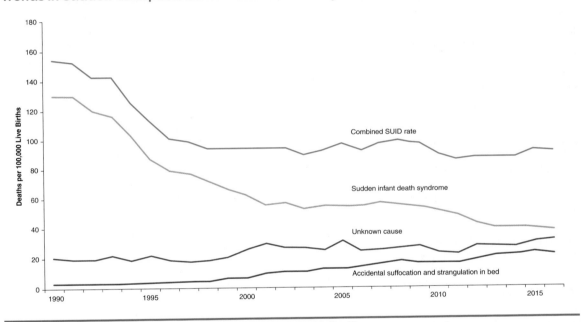

Source: CDC/NCHS, National Vital Statistics System, Compressed Mortality File.

about 16 hours (Peskin, 2017). Fluids may accumulate in the abdomen and extremities, leading to bloating. Psychological symptoms such as anxiety, depression, confusion, the inability to recognize family members, and delirium are common (Enck, 2003).

Emotional Reactions to Dying

People tend to show a range of emotional reactions to the knowledge that they are dying. After conducting more than 200 interviews with terminally ill people, psychiatrist Elisabeth Kübler-Ross categorized people's reactions into five types or ways in which people deal with death: denial, anger, bargaining, depression, and acceptance (Kübler-Ross, 1969). Although Kübler-Ross described these reactions as a series of stages, not everyone experiences all of them or proceeds through them at the same pace or in the same order (Corr, Nabe, & Corr, 2009; Kübler-Ross, 1974).

Upon learning that one has a terminal illness, the first reaction is likely shock. For most people, denial ("It's not possible!") is the first stage of processing death, reflecting the initial reaction to the news. The person may not believe the diagnosis, deny that it is true, and might seek a second or third opinion. Once the dying person realizes that he or she is terminally ill, anger may set in. Dying people might ask themselves, "Why me?" Feeling cheated and robbed out of life, the person may harbor resentment and envy toward family, friends, and caregivers, as it may seem unfair that others live while they must die. Anger is a very difficult stage, but with time and effort, most dying people manage and resolve their hostilities. The bargaining stage, like the other stages of dying, is common but not universal. The dying person bargains to find a way out. Perhaps a deal can be struck with God or fate. The dying person might promise to be a better person and help others if only he or she can survive. A parent might attempt to bargain a timetable, such as, "Just let me live to see my daughter give birth." Eventually, when the person realizes that death cannot be escaped, prolonged, or bargained with, depression is common—especially as the illness becomes more evident because of pain, surgery, or a loss of functioning. Knowing it is the end brings profound sadness. During this stage, the dying person feels great loss and sorrow with the knowledge that, for example, he or she will never return to work or home, that all relationships will end, and that the future is lost. The person may feel guilt over the illness and its consequences for loved ones. Many dying people will tend to withdraw from emotional attachments to all but the few people with whom they have the most meaningful relationships. Sharing their feelings with others can help dying people come to an acceptance of death, the final stage. In this stage, dying people no longer fight death. They accept that death is inevitable, seem at peace, and begin to detach themselves from the world.

Although it is useful to think of these reactions to impending death as stages, a stage view ignores the relevance of context—including relationships, illness, family, and situation (Kastenbaum, 2012). Dying is an individual experience. The dying person has a myriad of emotions and must be allowed to experience and express them to come to terms with his or her grief, complete unfinished business with loved ones, and, ultimately, accept death (Corr & Corr, 2013). It is difficult to predict the psychological state and needs of a dying person as they vary greatly according to factors like age, experience, and the situation (Gavrin & Chapman, 1995). Many dying people experience a sense of calm toward the end, releasing denial, anger, and fear to die in peace (Renz et al., 2018).

The Experience of One's Death

Children, adolescents, and adults have very different sets of abilities and experiences that lead them to view the world in ways that are unique to their age group. We have seen that conceptions of death grow in complexity over time. How do children, adolescents, and adults experience their own deaths?

The Dying Child

Physicians and parents often find it difficult to talk to children about their prognosis and death (Bates & Kearney, 2015). As a result, children are less likely to develop a clear understanding of their condition and imminent death. Dying children who have been ill for a long time have been observed to show a maturity beyond their years (Leming & Dickinson, 2016). In a hospital setting, it is natural for children to acquire information about their disease during the progression of the illness, although parents and doctors are often unaware that they are doing so (Corr, 2010a). Children's experiences are an important determinant of how they view the concepts of sickness, more so than age or intellectual ability (Corr, 2010b). A 3- or 4-year-old child who is dying might understand more about impending death than an older child who is well. Likewise, it is experience with the disease and its treatment that advances children's awareness of dying (Bluebond-Langner, 1989; Cotton & Range, 2010; Hunter & Smith, 2008).

Children with life-threatening diseases tend to show a greater awareness of death than their healthy or chronically ill peers (Jay, Green, Johnson, Caldwell, & Nitschke, 1987; O'Halloran & Altmaier, 1996). Anthropologist Myra Bluebond-Langner (1989) observed terminally ill 3- to 9-year-old children and noted that all became aware of the fact that they were dying before death was imminent. They also knew that death was a final and irreversible process, suggesting a mature concept of death. The children she studied showed awareness that they were dying by noting that they were never going back to school or that they would not be around for a birthday or holiday; some frankly said, "I am going to die." Other researchers observed that not only did children know that they were dying before death was imminent, but many kept that knowledge a secret (Stevens, Rytmeister, Protor, & Bolster, 2010). Just as parents try to protect children, children may keep their knowledge that they are dying from their parents—perhaps in an attempt to protect them from distress.

Pediatricians, social workers, and parents should arrive at a shared understanding of how to approach a terminally ill child's questions and what type of information is appropriate for the child. Because dying children tend to want to know about their illness and treatment (Bates & Kearney, 2015), experts advise that discussions about death should use concrete terms. Open-ended questions can gauge children's knowledge, and children's questions should be answered honestly and directly, in language suited to the child's developmental level (Slaughter & Griffiths, 2007). Part of the process of discussing the child's illness is simply being present for him or her. Children who are dying tend to express sadness and fears of loneliness, separation, and abandonment (Judd, 2014; Theunissen et al., 2007). Parents and loved ones are advised to stay with a dying child, reading, singing, holding, and sleeping with him or her.

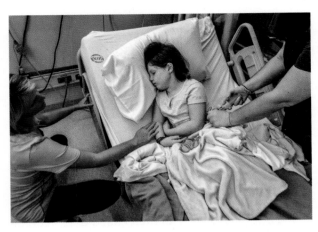

Physicians and parents often find it difficult to talk to children about their prognosis and death but many dying children express desire for the opportunity to seek closure and say goodbye to loved ones.
The Washington Post/The Washington Post/Getty Images

The Dying Adolescent

Adolescents' abilities for abstract reasoning translate into more mature conceptions of death, its finality and permanence (Greydanus & Pratt, 2016). However, adolescents' responses to a terminal illness influence and are influenced by the normative developmental tasks they face. Adolescents tend to feel they have a right to know about their illness and prognosis, consistent with their emerging sense of autonomy (Pousset et al., 2009). The sense of invulnerability that is typical of adolescents can lead some to deny their illness or the need for treatment (Balk, 2009). The side effects of treatment, such as hair loss and weight loss or weight gain, can have devastating consequences for adolescents' body image, often causing much distress (Bates & Kearney, 2015) or even leading them to shun treatment.

Like patients in other age groups, adolescents who are terminally ill often spend a great deal of time in hospitals or other treatment facilities. Given that peer relationships are critical influences on adolescents' development and well-being, these lengthy absences from home and the normal social milieu can distance adolescents from their friends and make them feel increasingly different from their peers. Adolescents tend to focus on the social implications of their illness, such as their ability to attract a boyfriend or girlfriend, be rejected by peers, or lack independence from parents (Stevens & Dunsmore, 1996). Because of their illness, they may have few opportunities to exercise autonomy or experience independence, leading them to feel anger over what they are missing and their need to be dependent on parents and doctors.

As they begin to become aware of the future and develop a future orientation, dying adolescents may mourn the loss of the future. Many adolescents feel angry and cheated, that life is unjust (Corr &

Corr, 2013). Given adolescents' drive for autonomy, it is important that they are informed and involved in planning treatment and decision making (Decker, Phillips, & Haase, 2004; Dunsmore & Quine, 1996; Jacobs et al., 2015). Dying adolescents especially need to live in the present, have the freedom to try out different ways of coping with illness-related challenges, and find meaning and purpose in both their lives and their deaths (Greydanus & Pratt, 2016; Stevens & Dunsmore, 1996).

The Dying Adult

Dying young adults often feel angry and that the world is unfair; they have many developmental tasks that will be unfulfilled. The primary psychosocial task of young adulthood consists of developing relationships, specifically, a sense of intimacy (Erikson, 1959). A terminal illness can pose challenges to satisfying intimacy needs as it is difficult to form close and secure relationships when one is ill and has limited time left to live. Isolation and abandonment are often principal fears of young adults who are dying (Corr & Corr, 2013). Young adults also lose the sense of an unlimited future. Goals, plans, and aspirations are threatened.

Whereas young adults miss out on the future, midlife adults mourn losing the present. They often worry about abandoning family and not having completed their journey. The normative process of taking stock in midlife transitions from planning for the future to putting affairs in order. Midlife adults who are dying have a need to find ways to continue to meet their responsibilities to others, such as children, after they die.

Older adults have a life to look back on. Their developmental task is to come to a sense of integrity after a successful life review (Erikson, 1982). Terminal illness may speed the process, adding stress, so that the elder may find it difficult to do the work involved in life review. Older adults are more likely than their younger counterparts to accept death, feel that it is appropriate, and be free of any sense of unfinished business. Older adults who are dying have a desire to close ties, to make peace with family, and to engage in legacy work, leaving something behind (Leming & Dickinson, 2016).

THINKING IN CONTEXT 16.3

1. Do you think emotional responses to dying follow a stage pattern? Why or why not?

2. Provide examples of how children's, adolescents', and adults' developmental competencies and tasks influence how they experience death.

BEREAVEMENT AND GRIEF

» LO 19.4 Summarize typical grief reactions to the loss of loved ones and the influence of development on bereavement.

The death of a loved one brings on **bereavement**, a state of loss. It triggers an emotional response known as **grief,** which includes an array of emotions such as hurt, anger, guilt, and confusion. **Mourning** refers to culturally patterned ritualistic ways of displaying and expressing bereavement, including special clothing, food, prayers, and gatherings.

One of the first steps in mourning is to organize a funeral or other ritual to mark the occasion of the loved one's death; such customs are different in various cultures around the world. Mourning rituals such as the Jewish custom of sitting *shiva,* ceasing usual activity and instead mourning and receiving visitors at home for a week, provides a sense of structure to help the bereaved manage the first days and weeks of bereavement. The process of coping with the loss of a loved one, however, is personal, complicated, and lengthy.

The Grief Process

There are no rules to grieving. People vary in the intensity of their reactions to loss and in the timing of their reactions. People grieve differently, and the same person may react differently to different losses. Some might feel intense but short-lived grief. Other people may find that grief lingers for many months. Sometimes grief may seem to resolve only to resurface periodically and unexpectedly. Grief is experienced and expressed in many ways, in emotions, physical sensations, and behaviors (Kowalski & Bondmass, 2008; Mallon, 2008). Physical responses such as tightness in the chest, feeling out of breath, stomach pains, and weakness are common manifestations of grief. A range of emotions, from anger, anxiety, loneliness, guilt, helplessness, and even relief, occurs. Behaviors such as looking for the person in crowds and familiar places, absentmindedness, sleep problems, avoiding reminders of the deceased, and loss of interest are common.

Grief is an active coping process in which the grieving person must confront the loss and come to terms with its effects on his or her physical world, interpersonal interactions, and sense of self (Buglass, 2010; Trevino et al., 2018). The person in grief must acknowledge his or her emotions, make sense of them, and learn to manage them. Most important, and most difficult, the grieving person must adjust to life without the deceased (Stroebe,

Schut, & Boerner, 2010). He or she must adapt to the loss by establishing new patterns of behavior and redefining relationships with family and friends in light of the loss (Leming & Dickinson, 2016). The grieving person must construct a new sense of self that takes into account the loss of the deceased and how that loss has changed everyday life.

It was once believed that effective grieving required loosening emotional ties to the deceased, permitting the grieving person to "work through" the death (Buglass, 2010; Wright & Hogan, 2008). During a period of mourning, the survivor would sever attachments to the deceased and become ready for new relationships and attachments. Instead, in recent decades, theorists have come to view the bereaved person's continued attachment to the deceased as normative and adaptive in providing a sense of continuity despite loss (Stroebe et al., 2010). Attachment is illustrated in several behaviors common among the bereaved, such as feeling that the deceased is watching over them, keeping the deceased's possessions, and talking about the deceased to keep their memory alive. Successful adaptation entails moving toward abstract manifestations of attachment, such as thoughts and memories, and away from concrete manifestations, such as possessions (Field, Gal-Oz, & Bonanno, 2003). The deceased remains in mind, however. Grieving appears to involve learning to live with loss, rather than getting over loss.

Models of Grieving

Although people vary in how they experience loss, some theorists suggest phases or stages in grieving that are similar to the stages of emotional adjustment to death posited by Kübler-Ross (1969). People may traverse through several phases of mourning from shock, to intense grieving, to establishing a sense of balance, accommodating the loss into one's sense of being (Buglass, 2010; Wright & Hogan, 2008). For example, the initial reaction to loss is most often shock, a feeling of being dazed, detached, or stunned by the loss. As the person realizes the magnitude of loss, intense feelings of despair arise. The bereaved person may question his or her sense of self in light of the loss. With persistence, the person begins to find a way of living without the loved one. Life will never be the same, but a "new normal" is created. Phases of mourning are useful in describing common reactions to loss; however, they represent a generalization and perhaps oversimplification of the process (Stroebe, Schut, & Boerner, 2017). The progression through grief is not linear; steps do not always occur in sequence, and there is no universal timeframe for processing grief (Maciejewski, Zhang, Block, & Prigerson, 2007).

Other theorists view mourning as a set of tasks to accomplish. The bereaved person must accept the reality of the loss, experience the pain of grief, adjust to a life without the deceased, and develop a new life while maintaining an enduring connection to the deceased (Howarth, 2011; Stroebe et al., 2010). Completing the first task, overcoming the initial sense of denial of the reality of the loss, may be especially difficult if the death was sudden or if the deceased lived far away. As the individual accepts the reality, the pain of grief can become overwhelming. Successfully managing this task requires finding ways of experiencing the pain that are not paralyzing and realizing that grief is to be expected. Adjusting to life without the deceased means that the individual must manage the practical details of life, identify the roles that the deceased filled in the relationship and household, and come to terms with the fact that he or she will no longer fill those roles. For example, children require care even after a parent has died; the surviving spouse must adjust to this reality and determine how to fulfill the roles of the deceased partner. Fulfilling these roles can help many bereaved adapt productively by developing new skills and growing (Jozefowski, 1999).

The final task of mourning is to establish a new life that recognizes the enduring connection to the deceased, who will not be forgotten. This is often experienced as particularly challenging because the bereaved may not want to "move on" and may even feel it is disloyal to do so, but successful grieving entails learning how to live life without the physical presence of the deceased (Leming & Dickinson, 2016).

An alternative view of adaptation to loss emphasizes the stresses that accompany grief. According to the **dual-process model of grief**, bereavement is accompanied by two types of stressors (Stroebe & Schut, 2016). The first is loss oriented and comprises the emotional aspects of grief that accompany the loss of an attachment figure, such as managing emotions and breaking ties to the deceased. Restoration-oriented stressors represent secondary losses; these are the life changes that accompany the death, such as moving to a different residence, social isolation, establishing new roles, and managing practical details, such as paperwork. At any given time, the grieving person may focus on the loss-oriented stressors or the life changes that comprise the restoration-oriented stressors. Healthy adjustment is promoted by alternating focus between the two types. When the person is able, he or she confronts the losses, yet at other times the person may set that task aside to instead consider restoration (Stroebe & Schut, 2010). In this way, the grieving person adaptively copes as he or she is able, gradually moving forward. However, some bereaved individuals experience *overload*, the feeling that he or she has too much to deal with—whether too many losses, too many stimuli, too many stressors—and this can interfere with the grieving process (Stroebe & Schut, 2016).

Contextual Influences on the Grief Process

No two deaths are experienced in the same way. Deaths are interpreted and grieved differently based on a variety of factors, such as the age of the deceased, the nature of the death, and age of the bereaved. The death of a child or young adult is grieved more intensely and is viewed as more catastrophic than that of an older adult (Jecker, 2011). Younger and older adults judge a 19-year-old victim of a fatal car accident as a more tragic and unjust death than that of a 79-year-old victim (Chasteen & Madey, 2003). The young are grieved more intensely as they are viewed as robbed of the chance to experience significant life events such as falling in love or becoming a parent. They are not able to set and fulfill dreams. Generally, off-time deaths, especially those that occur much before our expectations, are particularly difficult (Moos, 1994).

The nature of the death influences how it is experienced and the grief process. Sudden, unexpected deaths are particularly challenging. Mourners are unprepared, with no support group in place. Many feel intense guilt and the need to assign blame and responsibility for accidental deaths. There often is no chance to say goodbye or mend relationships. Anger is a common reaction, especially if the deceased contributed to his or her demise through poor decisions. Traumatic deaths, such as from natural or manmade disasters, can leave losses that are difficult to make sense of. Feeling that a death is traumatic is associated with increased grief, depression, and loneliness (Tang & Chow, 2017).

When death is the result of a prolonged illness, it is no surprise, yet it is still a source of grief. Some theorists have posited the existence of anticipatory grief, feelings of loss that begin before a death occurs but are not fully realized (Coelho, de Brito, & Barbosa, 2018; Siegel & Weinstein, 2008). People grieve losses as they happen. For example, a spouse of a terminally ill patient might grieve the parenting help or physical intimacy that he or she has already lost and anticipate losing the relationship itself. Each loss generates its own grief reaction and mourning process. Knowing that death is to come permits the dying to make decisions, tie loose ends, and strengthen relationships. Although many people believe that

Students embrace at a makeshift memorial for two peers killed in a car accident. Grieving the loss of a young person involves grieving for their lost future.
Jessica Rinaldi/The Boston Globe via Getty Images

having the time and opportunity to prepare for loss will be less distressing, research suggests that this is not true (Coelho et al., 2018; Siegel & Weinstein, 2008; Sweeting & Gilhooly, 1990). All deaths are stressful, just in different ways.

Adjusting to the Death of a Loved One

Grieving is influenced by the relationship between the person and the deceased. Much of the literature on bereavement comes from studying those who have lost a spouse.

Losing a Spouse

The term **widowhood** refers to the status of a person who has lost a spouse through death and has not remarried. About one third of U.S. older adults over the age of 65 are widowed. Women who have lost a spouse (*widows*) live longer than men (*widowers*) and are less likely to remarry. Thirty-five percent of women over the age of 65 are widowed, as compared with 11% of men (Administration on Aging, 2014).

Losing a spouse begins one of the most stressful transitions in life. Widows have lost the person closest to them, a source of companionship, support, status, and income. Widowhood poses a challenge of renegotiating a sense of identity in light of the loss of the role of spouse, often the most long-lasting intimate role held in life. The identity development task posed by the loss of a spouse is to construct a sense of self that is separate from the spouse (Cheek, 2010; Naef, Ward, Mahrer-Imhof, & Grande, 2013). As in earlier periods of life, women who have a myriad of roles apart from spouse tend to fare better in adjusting to the death of a spouse than do women who have few roles, predominantly centered around their husbands. After becoming a widow, most older

adults live alone, often in the same home. Those who relocate often do so for financial reasons, and they tend to move closer to children and grandchildren.

Perhaps the greatest challenge to adjustment that widows and widowers face is loneliness (Kowalski & Bondmass, 2008). Although widowhood marks the loss of a confidant, older adults often maintain and even increase their social participation following spousal loss (Donnelly & Hinterlong, 2010; Isherwood, King, & Luszcz, 2012). In one study in the Netherlands, older adults experienced increased contact and support, especially from their children and siblings, over the first 2 years of widowhood, but the amount of contact and support began to decrease about 2.5 years after widowhood (Guiaux, van Tilburg, & van Groenou, 2007). Other research showed stability in the level of social support received over the 2 years after the loss of a spouse (Powers, Bisconti, & Bergeman, 2014). A prospective study followed widowed adults over an 18-month period and found that close social relationships tended to remain stable, but widowhood brought both losses and gains in social support, which influenced adaptation (Ha, 2010). Specifically, the quality and continuity of support provided by children influences adaptation to spousal loss. Adults who perceived positive support (such as feeling loved, cared for, and heard) from their children 6 months after the death of their spouse showed few depressive symptoms 18 months later. In contrast, negative support (e.g., feeling that children are too demanding or critical) that remains steady, increases, or is accompanied by declines in positive support over time is associated with anger and symptoms of depression and anxiety (Ha, 2010). Maintaining close relationships with family and friends gives widows a sense of continuity, which aids in adjusting to their loss.

Compared with their functioning prior to the loss of a spouse, bereaved adults show increased levels of depression, anxiety, stress, and more poor performance on cognitive tests measuring attention, processing speed, and memory (Rosnick, Small, & Burton, 2010; Ward, Mathias, & Hitchings, 2007). Grief has physical effects, including effects on the brain (see the Brain and Biological Influences on Development feature). The prevalence of anxiety and depression is especially elevated in the first year after the loss of a spouse, with about 22% of newly widowed individuals meeting the diagnostic criteria for major depression (Onrust & Cuijpers, 2006). Social interaction, and especially helping others, aids in reducing depressive symptoms. Specifically, widowed adults who help others by providing instrumental support show an associated decline in depressive symptoms for 6 to 18 months following spousal loss (Brown, Brown, House,

& Smith, 2008). Depression declines with time (Powers et al., 2014), and men and women typically return to prewidowhood levels of depression within 24 months of being widowed (Sasson & Umberson, 2014).

Widowhood also poses risks to physical health. The increased likelihood for a recently widowed person to die, often called the **widowhood effect**, is one of the best documented examples of the relationship between social relations and health (Elwert & Christakis, 2008). The widowhood effect has been found among men and women of all ages throughout the world. Widowhood increases survivors' risk of dying from almost all causes but is especially linked with cardiovascular problems

Losing a spouse begins one of the most stressful transitions in life.
iStock/patat

BRAIN AND BIOLOGICAL INFLUENCES ON DEVELOPMENT

 ## Grief and the Brain

The experience of grief is often described as stifling, a metaphorical weight dulling one's senses and thought. Grief is associated with a variety of cognitive changes, such as reductions in attention, memory, processing speed, and verbal fluency (Rosnick, Small, & Burton, 2010). In one study, individuals experiencing symptoms of grief showed attentional biases toward words associated with the deceased as compared with other words (Freed, Yanagihara, Hirsch, & Mann, 2009). They also were less able to regulate their attention in response to reminders of the deceased. In addition, the strength of the attentional bias was associated with increased amygdala activity and reduced connectivity between regions of the brain that regulate attention and the amygdala, suggesting less control over their cognitive responses to emotional stimuli.

More serious and persisting grief is known as *complicated grief,* which includes a set of symptoms such as persistent intense yearning and longing for and disruptive preoccupation with thoughts of the deceased (Shear, Frank, Houck, & Reynolds, 2005). These symptoms are prominent and elevated at 6 months and beyond after the loss. In one study, compared with either normal-grief or no-grief groups, participants with complicated grief performed worse in domains of executive function and information processing speed, and they had a lower total brain volume as measured by structural brain imaging (Saavedra Pérez et al., 2015).

Neurological research suggests that complicated grief is experienced as pain. Bereaved individuals show increased activity in the anterior cingulate and the insula in response to reminders of the deceased. These regions tend to be activated in response to physical and social pain (such as rejection) (O'Connor, 2012). Other research

showed that when individuals experiencing complicated grief viewed photos of the deceased, they showed more activity in the nucleus accumbens, an area related to rewards, than did bereaved individuals. For individuals with complicated grief, reminders activate reward circuitry, perhaps making it more likely that the individual will perseverate over the lost loved one, which may interfere with adapting to the loss (O'Connor et al., 2008).

In addition, the stress that accompanies grief may influence cognitive and brain function. Adult neurogenesis has been shown to occur primarily in the hippocampus, an area responsible for learning and memory (Mirescu & Gould, 2006; Schoenfeld & Gould, 2013). The hippocampus is richly endowed with receptors sensitive to glucocorticoids, hormones that are released in response to stress, and glucocorticoids play a role in regulating neurogenesis in adults (Egeland, Zunszain, & Pariante, 2015). In addition to its effects on the hippocampus, stress is thought to influence many neural processes, such as the maintenance of dendrites, neurotransmission, and overall plasticity (Mirescu & Gould, 2006; Schoenfeld & Gould, 2013). The stress that accompanies bereavement influences the emotional experience of grief and has neurological consequences with the potential to impair cognition.

What Do You Think?

1. How might the experience of grief illustrate the lifespan principle that domains of development interact?

2. What might be some implications of this principle for helping bereaved individuals? ●

(Fagundes et al., 2018; Subramanian, Elwert, & Christakis, 2008). One study of Norwegian adults found that the rate of mortality was highest for adults in late midlife (55–64); generally, the risk for death declined over time after the spousal loss, but it remained high 7 years later (Brenn & Ytterstad, 2016).

One analysis put the excess mortality of widowhood (compared with marriage) among the elderly between 40% and 50% in the first 6 months (J. R. Moon, Kondo, Glymour, & Subramanian, 2011). However, the cause of spousal death matters. The mortality rate for widowed adults following spouses' death from Alzheimer's disease or Parkinson's disease is lower, suggesting that anticipatory grief may provide a buffer from the widowhood effect (Elwert & Christakis, 2008). This suggests that it may be the predictability of the death rather than the duration of the spouse's terminal illness that shields the survivor from some of the adverse consequences of bereavement.

Losing a spouse poses risks to mental and physical health for both men and women, but men tend to show more health problems, including an increased risk for dementia, and higher rates of mortality (Bennett, Hughes, & Smith, 2005; Gerritsen et al., 2017). Men tend to sustain a high level of depression 6 to 10 years after losing a spouse (Jadhav & Weir, 2017). In addition, widowers of all ages are at higher risk of suicide than their married counterparts (Erlangsen, Jeune, Bille-Brahe, & Vaupel, 2004). Men often rely on their spouses for maintaining relationships with friends and family, managing household tasks, and assistance in coping with stress and managing emotions—and when the wife is no longer present to fulfill these roles, men tend to have difficulty asking for assistance (Lund & Caserta, 2001). Widowers are more likely to remarry than are widows, partly because there are far more single elderly women than men, but also because men have fewer social outlets and sources of support than women (Carr, 2004).

The degree to which a spouse adapts to widowhood is influenced by a variety of factors, such as the circumstances surrounding the spouse's death and his or her age (McNamara & Rosenwax, 2010). Death of a spouse following a long illness such as cancer or Alzheimer's disease can evoke complex emotional responses because such illnesses involve drastic physical and mental deterioration and intense demands for caregiving (Rossi Ferrario, Cardillo, Vicario, Balzarini, & Zotti, 2004). In such cases, in addition to loss, the spouse may feel relief from watching a partner slip away and from the pressures of caregiving (Bonanno, Wortman, & Nesse, 2004). The complex intermingling of sorrow and relief may be confusing, and the widowed spouse may feel guilty. Losing a spouse in young or middle

adulthood is likely experienced very differently than in old age; however, there is little research on off-time widowhood. Unfulfilled roles, unfinished business, and an unlived life can make adjusting to an early widowhood especially difficult. Younger widowed adults likely have been married fewer years than older widowed adults, and they probably have greater responsibilities for dependent children and jobs. These responsibilities can be stressful, but on the positive side, children and coworkers may provide comfort and emotional support to young widowed adults.

Adults vary in the degree to which they show resilience in the face of a partner's death. Personal characteristics influence how people manage the transition to widowhood. Those who are outgoing, have high self-esteem, and have a high sense of perceived self-efficacy in managing tasks of daily living tend to fare best (Corr, 2019; Leming & Dickinson, 2016). One study of Australian adults who experienced spousal loss found that although about two thirds showed increased life satisfaction over time, only 19% and 26% of individuals showed resilience with regard to negative affect (e.g., feeling down, worn out, tired, or unable to be cheered) and positive affect (feeling full of life, energetic, peaceful, or happy), respectively (Infurna & Luthar, 2017b). About one third appeared to be resilient in terms of self-reported health and physical functioning. Very few adults showed resilience across all domains, and about 20% were not resilient in any domain, suggesting that losing a spouse may pose lifelong challenges to physical and emotional health (Infurna & Luthar, 2017b).

Losing a Child

The most difficult of deaths to grieve is the loss of a child. It violates the perceived order of natural life and compromises the continuity of the family life cycle. Parenthood is a developmental achievement that provides a sense of purpose and engenders a sense of identity in people (Cao, Mills-Koonce, Wood, & Fine, 2016). For parents, the loss of a child entails the loss of self and the loss of hopes and dreams for the child and the future (Wijngaards-de Meij et al., 2008). Parents grieve what could have been and what did not occur, the life their child did not have. In this way, they lack a sense of closure (Woodgate, 2006).

Research suggests that the age of the child has little effect on the severity of the grief. Parents, especially mothers, often experience severe grief after miscarriages, stillbirths, or the loss of a young infant (Adolfsson, 2011; Avelin, Rådestad, Säflund, Wredling, & Erlandsson, 2013; Robinson, 2014). Parents of neonates and young infants grieve for the infant and the lost attachment but also the lack of memories and being robbed of the opportunity to become a parent (Avelin et al., 2013; Cacciatore, 2010). Parents of children of all ages mourn unfulfilled dreams, unfinished tasks, and the resulting void in the family.

Guilt is a common response to losing a child (Leming & Dickinson, 2016). Parents may question their adequacy in providing care. This is especially true if the death resulted from a preventable accident or when the causes of death are not understood, as in cases of SIDS. Loss of a child is associated with short- and long-term problems in physical health, mental health, and even mortality (Rogers, Floyd, Seltzer, Greenberg, & Hong, 2008; Song, Floyd, Seltzer, Greenberg, & Hong, 2010).

Bereaved parents tend to experience grief over a longer period than other bereaved people, with grief symptoms often lasting throughout the remainder of the parent's life (Keesee, Currier, & Neimeyer, 2008; Rogers et al., 2008). Parents often have difficulty finding meaning in their loss as the loss of a child is often perceived as "senseless" (Keesee et al., 2008; Wheeler, 2001). Transforming their identity as parent represents a crisis as adults must reshape their sense of purpose, identity, and legacy (De Vries, Lana, & Falck, 1994). Parents typically struggle with this task for years, if not a lifetime. One study of 156 bereaved parents (on average about 6 years after the child's death) found that only about half found a sense of meaning in the death (Lichtenthal, Currier, Neimeyer, & Keesee, 2010). While about half of bereaved parents might show a reduction in negative affect over time, less than half report high levels of life satisfaction, about one third report good health, and a fifth or less report positive affect and physical functioning (Infurna & Luthar, 2017a). Mourning a child appears to be a lifelong event for most parents (Keesee et al., 2008). Older adults who have lost a child many years ago report the loss as their most negative life experience (Bratt, Stenström, & Rennemark, 2018).

Losing a Parent

Most adults expect their parents to precede them in death, yet even the expected death of a parent is difficult (Marks, Jun, & Song, 2007). It is the loss of a lifelong relationship, attachment, and shared experiences. Adult children who acted as caregivers for their parents have devoted much time and energy to care for their parent, often reorganizing their lives to provide care (Weitzner, Haley, & Chen, 2000). The loss of a parent may cause further household upheaval, and the adult child may be unprepared to redirect his or her attention, efforts, and time (Hebert, Dang, & Schulz, 2006). Feelings of guilt and fear that one has not provided adequate care may be combined and heightened if the adult child felt overburdened by the level of care. Adult children may mourn lost opportunities to improve relationships and make amends for unfinished business.

The loss of a parent influences adults' sense of self. It often enhances adults' feelings of mortality as the loss of parents marks adult children as the oldest generation. The parents are no longer the buffer or generational protection against old age and death. The death of a parent often sparks a shift in development, causing adult children to alter their sense of selves and realize their responsibilities to others. In this way, it can impart a sense of generativity to the next generation (Umberson, 2003). Some adults experience tension between grieving their parents' death and facing one's own death and their own grief over perceived lost opportunities.

The death of a parent influences sibling relationships. They must reevaluate the meaning of family and their roles without the grounding role of their parents. The pattern of sibling relationships over the lifespan tends to intensify, such that good relationships often get better and, without the parent, poor relationships may worsen or disrupt. A parent's death changes the fabric of family relations.

Bereavement in Childhood and Adolescence

Losing a loved one in childhood or adolescence brings special challenges to the process of mourning. Cognitive and socioemotional development influence how children and adolescents understand, make sense of, and adjust to loss.

Adolescents tend to have mature conceptions about death, but their experience of grief is often influenced by their ability to understand and manage their own emotions.
glenda/Shutterstock.com

Bereavement in Childhood

Like adults, children's experience of grief is influenced by the deceased's role in their life. Children's grief is uniquely affected by their developmental level, including cognitive and socioemotional development, as well as their understanding of the nature of death (Corr, 2010b). Children's first experience with death is often that of a grandparent. How this affects the child depends on his or her proximity to and contact with the grandparent. Children with close relationships to grandparents, who experience their grandparents as caregivers and sources of unconditional love, are more likely to find death traumatic than are children whose grandparents live far away and with whom they have less contact. Many children find seeing parents and other adults upset distressing, perhaps increasing their sense of loss. However, there are no rules for children's grief (Leming & Dickinson, 2016).

Bereaved children often experience guilt. Many wonder if they caused the death to happen or if the loved one "went away" because of them. The degree to which children feel and express the fear that the death is somehow their fault varies with development (Wolfelt, 2013). This fear is most commonly and openly expressed by young children who are least able to understand the nature of death, but even older children worry. This is especially true in the case of sudden and accidental deaths. Children also worry about who will take care of them. If they conceptualize death as magic, they may fear that they are in danger. In cases of natural disasters and terror attacks, children may feel worry about threats to themselves and their family. The replay of such disasters on television and in the media may intensify children's anxiety.

Bereaved children may experience grief for their parent for a longer period of time than do adults as they must grow up with the loss; their developmental milestones are affected, and the death robs them of emotional support from caregivers (Wolfelt, 2013). Many children strive to maintain a connection to the deceased parent by talking to him or her, feeling that the parent is watching them, dreaming of the parent, and holding on to symbolic objects—particular dolls, pictures, or the parent's possessions.

Bereaved children need support, nurturance, and continuity in their lives. They need accurate information about the death and to have their fears addressed. Children want to know that they will be cared for. Adults should reassure children that they are not to blame, as well as provide support and listen (Corr & Corr, 2013). Children, especially younger children, will often require help in understanding and managing their conflicting emotions. Engaging in routine activities can help children gain a sense of normalcy despite all of the changes (Stokes, 2009). Adults should attempt to model healthy mourning by sharing their own grief and providing an example of how to experience grief in constructive ways (Saldinger, Porterfield, & Cain, 2014).

Bereavement in Adolescence

Adolescents' advancing cognitive abilities and their emerging sense of self influence how they grieve (Christ, Siegel, & Christ, 2002). Adolescents who lose a parent tend to feel intense loss, isolation, and the sense that the parent is irreplaceable and that loss cannot be overcome (Tyson-Rawson, 1996). Adolescents may be plagued by a strong sense that life is unfair. They are at risk to suffer social and interpersonal difficulties in adjustment, including internalizing symptoms such as anxiety and depression (Stikkelbroek, Bodden, Reitz, Vollebergh, & van Baar, 2016), yet often show a strong desire for others to include them and take interest in them (Meshot & Leitner, 1992). Many feel a strong presence of the deceased in dreams and in daily life, which can offer a sense of comfort and support (Meshot & Leitner, 1992).

Adolescents tend to have mature conceptions about death, but their experience of grief is often influenced by their ability to understand and manage their emotions as well as their experience of egocentric thought. The existence of the personal fable may lead them to view their grief as unique and incomprehensible—that others could not understand and certainly do not feel the way they do. Mourning adolescents commonly display intense emotional outbursts that are brief but cyclical, punctuated by periods during which they resume normal activity (Christ et al., 2002; Noppe & Noppe, 2004). Alternatively, some adolescents may suppress their emotions altogether, out of fear of a loss of control (Robin & Omar, 2014). Adolescents may retreat into themselves, reading and listening to music, or they may act out, engaging in risky behaviors. With each developmental shift, adolescents must reinterpret the death in light of their new cognitive and emotional understanding (D. A. Brent, Melhem, Masten, Porta, & Payne, 2012).

The tasks of grieving intertwine and potentially interfere with the normative developmental tasks of adolescence, such as developing a sense of emotional autonomy as well as intimate relationships with friends (Robin & Omar, 2014). Adolescents who were concerned with establishing a sense of emotional autonomy prior to the parent's death may feel intense guilt. The grieving adolescent may find it challenging to develop a sense of autonomy while maintaining connection to the deceased parent, resulting in distress and often guilt. Grieving adolescents may feel that they are different from peers, and this "different" perception may impair their feelings of peer acceptance. They may also worry about how to act while grieving. Young adolescents who are concerned with peer acceptance may be reluctant to share their grief with friends, whereas middle and older adolescents who have formed intimate relationships with peers may find that support from friends can help them work through their pain (Dopp & Cain, 2012). However, if their friends do not understand their pain or are rejecting, the adolescent may be devastated and grieve not only the loss of the parent but of his or her friends too (Gray, 1989).

Bereaved adolescents need adults who are open to discussing whatever they would like to explore and who are careful listeners. Grieving adolescents commonly worry that they will forget the person they have lost (Robin & Omar, 2014). Adults should attend to the feelings that underlie what the adolescent is saying and help the adolescent to understand that their feelings are important, real, and normal. Adults can help them to find ways to remember the deceased and make meaningful connections that retain their attachment with the deceased loved one.

Death and loss are not easy topics to consider. We have seen that, regardless of age, both dying and grieving people have some common needs. All need to move past denial and accept the death, whether upcoming or having passed. Both the dying and grieving require help managing their emotional reactions to loss, including common physical reactions, such as stomachaches, headaches, and lethargy. People of all ages have a need to express their reactions to the loss and may need help identifying and articulating their reactions that may feel very strange and unfamiliar to them. Finally, the dying and the bereaved need to make some sense of the loss. The dying must connect to their loved ones and accept the loss. The bereaved, in turn, must find a way to maintain the connection to the deceased while moving on in their life, recognizing that in some ways, they will never be the same.

THINKING IN CONTEXT 19.4

1. Identify factors within the person and context that may influence the degree and duration of grief. Explain these influences.

2. From your perspective, is the process of adjusting to the death of a loved one continuous or discontinuous? (Review these terms in Chapter 1.)

3. Much of what we know about bereavement comes from studying people who have lost a spouse. From your perspective, what are some of the challenges in extending conclusions regarding widowhood to other forms of loss?

APPLY YOUR KNOWLEDGE

Lying in bed, 88-year-old Margaret wakes and takes in her surroundings. Her daughter and granddaughter are in the room, one reading a magazine and the other reading her phone. Margaret is fortunate to have a private room in her nursing home, where she has been living since she suffered a stroke. Life here is better than she expected. The nurses are responsive, especially the kind night nurse who tells Margaret's daughter that she will check in often and does. The only thing Margaret doesn't like is that the nurses pressure her to socialize in the lounge each day. She'd rather sleep than be pushed out in her wheelchair to play games and watch television with the other elders. Her daughter urges her to eat, but she finds that she isn't very hungry anymore. Margaret feels lucky to have family who live nearby and visit very often. Margaret's children notice a change in their mother. She seems less sharp and each day seems a little bit more confused. She's often too tired to talk and drifts in and out of sleep.

With time, Margaret sleeps nearly all of the time. In addition to her stroke-related impairments, she has congestive heart failure, which is not responding to treatment. A few days before her 89th birthday, the doctors tell Margaret's daughter that the time is near. Margaret's children and grandchildren gather in her room, waiting. They talk about old times and everyday life. Margaret is largely unconscious but now and then she calls out, moans, or talks to herself, reaching her arms out in front of her. As time goes on, her breathing becomes more labored and heavy with occasional gasps. Margaret's children watch carefully and wait, attempting to talk with one another and retain a sense of normalcy. Finally, the room is quiet. Margaret's children know that she is gone. After 88 years and surrounded by family, Margaret has died.

1. What type of death trajectory does Margaret show? Explain your reasoning.

2. How might Margaret's 6-year-old grandchild understand her death? What might a child's grieving look like?

3. What would you expect from a 16-year-old grandchild?

4. How might children and adolescents' responses differ when considering a parent's death?

5. How might the adult child grieve for a parent?

$SAGE edge™

Visit **edge.sagepub.com/kuther2e** to help you accomplish your coursework goals in an easy-to-use learning environment.

LEARNING OBJECTIVES	SUMMARY	KEY TERMS	IN REVIEW
19.1 Identify ways in which death has been defined and end-of-life issues that may arise.	Clinical death occurs when the heart stops beating. Advances in medicine have led to a definition of death as entailing whole brain death. Cortical death, but survival of the brainstem, is known as a persistent vegetative state. Advance directives, including a living will and durable power of attorney, permit individuals to make their wishes regarding end-of-life care known. Euthanasia refers to the practice of assisting terminally ill people in dying naturally. Physician-assisted suicide occurs when terminally ill patients make the conscious decision that they want their life to end and seek assistance from a physician.	Clinical death Whole brain death Persistent vegetative state (PVS) Dying with dignity Living will Durable power of attorney Advance directive Euthanasia Passive euthanasia Active euthanasia Physician-assisted suicide Hospice Palliative care	What are three ways of defining death? What is a persistent vegetative state? What is dying with dignity? What are ways of controlling one's end-of-life care?
19.2 Contrast children's, adolescents', and adults' understanding of death.	Young children tend to view death as temporary and reversible. Children's understanding of death gradually emerges alongside cognitive development. Most adolescents evidence a mature conception of death, as the inevitable and irreversible end of biological processes, yet they often have difficulty appreciating it as an inevitability for themselves. Adolescents and adults across cultures often share a belief in an afterlife, whether religious or supernatural in origin. Conceptions of death change in subtle ways over the course of adulthood. Young adults begin to apply their mature understanding of death to themselves, acknowledging their own vulnerability. The awareness of death can cause midlife adults to reevaluate their priorities, often leading them to pursue a sense of generativity. Older adults experience less anxiety about death than younger adults.	Noncorporeal continuation	What are four components of a mature understanding of death? How do children and adolescents' understanding of death reflect their cognitive development? How does the conception of death change over adulthood?
19.3 Discuss the physical and emotional process of dying as it is experienced over the lifespan.	People tend to show a range of emotional reactions to the knowledge that they are dying, including denial, anger, bargaining, depression, and acceptance. Although described as stages, not everyone experiences all of them or proceeds through them at the same pace or in the same order. Children who are dying tend to express fears of loneliness, separation, and abandonment. Adolescents' sense of invulnerability can lead some to deny their illness or the need for treatment. Dying adolescents mourn the future and have a need to live in the present and to be involved in planning treatment and decision making. Young adults often feel angry and that the world is unfair. Midlife adults tend to mourn losing the present, abandoning family. Dying midlife adults have a need to find ways to continue to meet their responsibilities to others after death. Older adults talk more about death, think about it more, have more experience with it, and are more likely to accept death and feel that it is appropriate.	Dying trajectory	What is the dying trajectory? What are physiological and emotional processes associated with dying? How do the concerns and needs of dying individuals differ with development?

| 19.4 Summarize typical grief reactions to the loss of loved ones and the influence of development on bereavement. | Some theorists suggest phases or stages in grieving that are similar to the stages of emotional adjustment to death. Other theorists view mourning as a set of tasks to accomplish. According to the dual-process model, bereavement is accompanied by loss-oriented stressors and restoration-oriented stressors. Healthy adjustment is promoted by alternating focus between the two types of stressors. Bereavement is associated with increased levels of depression, anxiety, stress, and poor performance on cognitive tests and poor health. Bereaved parents often experience grief symptoms throughout their lives and often have difficulty finding meaning in their loss. Children's grief is uniquely affected by their cognitive and socioemotional development, as well as their understanding of the nature of death. Adolescents tend to have mature conceptions about death, but their experience of grief is often influenced by their ability to understand and manage their emotions, their experience of egocentric thought, and their emerging sense of self. | Bereavement

Grief

Mourning

Dual-process model of grief

Widowhood

Widowhood effect | Define bereavement, grief, and mourning.

What is the dual-process model of grief?

What are contextual influences on the grief process?

How does the relationship of the person to the deceased influence the grief process?

What developmental factors influence children's and adolescents' grief process? |

GLOSSARY

academically centered preschool programs: An approach to early childhood education that emphasizes providing children with structured learning environments in which teachers deliver direct instruction on letters, numbers, shapes, and academic skills.

accommodation: In Piaget's theory, the process by which schemas are modified or new schemas created in light of experience.

achievement motivation: The willingness to persist at challenging tasks and meet high standards of accomplishment.

active euthanasia: The practice of assisting terminally ill people in dying more quickly by deliberate means, such as by administering a fatal dose of pain medication.

activity theory: The view that older adults want to remain active and that declines in social interaction are not a result of elders' desires but are a function of social barriers to engagement.

adolescent egocentrism: A characteristic of adolescents' thinking in which they have difficulty separating others' perspectives from their own; composed of the imaginary audience and personal fable.

adolescent growth spurt: The first outward sign of puberty, refers to a rapid gain in height and weight that generally begins in girls at about age 10 and in boys about age 12.

adoption: A legal process in which a person assumes the parenting rights and responsibilities of a child.

advance directive: A document or order that allows patients to make decisions about their health care, death, and what happens to their bodies and possessions after death.

affordances: Refers to the actional properties of objects—their nature, opportunities, and limits.

age of viability: The age at which the fetus may survive if born prematurely; begins about 22 weeks after conception.

aggressive behavior: Behavior that harms or violates the rights of others; can be physical or relational.

alcohol dependence: A maladaptive pattern of alcohol use that leads to clinically significant impairment or distress, as indicated by tolerance, withdrawal, and inability to reduce drinking; also known as alcohol use disorder.

allele: A variation of a gene that influences an individual's characteristics.

Alzheimer's disease: A neurodegenerative disorder characterized by dementia and the deterioration of memory and personality, as well as marked by the presence of amyloid plaques and neurofibrillary tangles in the cerebral cortex.

amniocentesis: A prenatal diagnostic procedure in which a small sample of the amniotic fluid is extracted from the mother's uterus and subject to genetic analysis.

amyloid plaque: Found in the brains of patients with Alzheimer's disease, deposits of beta-amyloid accumulate along with clumps of dead neurons and glial cells.

androgyny: The gender identity of those who score high on both instrumental and expressive traits.

anencephaly: A neural tube defect that results in the failure of all or part of the brain to develop, resulting in death prior or shortly after birth.

animism: The belief that inanimate objects are alive and have feelings and intentions; a characteristic of preoperational reasoning.

anorexia nervosa: An eating disorder characterized by compulsive starvation and extreme weight loss and accompanied by a distorted body image.

Apgar scale: A quick overall assessment of a baby's immediate health at birth, including appearance, pulse, grimace, activity, and respiration.

appearance–reality distinction: The ability to distinguish between what something appears to be from what it really is.

applied developmental science: A field that studies lifespan interactions between individuals and the contexts in which they live and applies research findings to real-world settings, such as to influence social policy and create interventions.

artificial insemination: A means of conception in which sperm are injected into the vagina by a means other than sexual intercourse.

assimilation: In Piaget's theory, the process by which new experiences are interpreted and integrated into preexisting schemas.

attachment: A lasting emotional tie between two individuals who strive to maintain closeness and act to ensure that the relationship continues.

attention: The ability to direct one's awareness.

attention-deficit/hyperactivity disorder: A condition characterized by persistent difficulties with attention and/or impulsivity that interfere with performance and behavior in school and daily life.

authoritarian parenting style: An approach to childrearing that emphasizes high behavioral control and low levels of warmth and autonomy granting.

authoritative parenting style: An approach to childrearing in which parents are warm and sensitive to children's needs, grant appropriate autonomy, and exert firm control.

autistic spectrum disorder: Refers to a family of disorders that range in severity and are marked by social and communication deficits, often accompanied by restrictive and repetitive behaviors.

autobiographical memory: The recollection of a personally meaningful event that took place at a specific time and place in one's past.

autonomous morality: Piaget's second stage of morality in which children have a more flexible view of rules as they begin to value fairness and equality and account for factors like act, intent, and situation.

autonomy: The ability to make and carry out decisions independently.

autonomy versus shame and doubt: In Erikson's theory, the psychosocial crisis of toddlerhood in which individuals must establish the sense that they can make choices and guide their actions and bodies.

babbling: An infant's repetition of syllables such as "ba-ba-ba-ba" and "ma-ma-ma,"which begins at about 6 months of age.

basic emotions: Emotions that are universal in humans, appear early in life, and are thought to have a long evolutionary history, includes happiness, interest, surprise, fear, anger, sadness, and disgust.

behavioral genetics: The field of study that examines how genes and environment combine to influence the diversity of human traits, abilities, and behaviors.

behaviorism: A theoretical approach that studies how observable behavior is controlled by the physical and social environment through conditioning.

bereavement: The process of coping with the sense of loss that follows a loved one's death.

Big 5 personality traits: Five clusters of personality traits that reflect an inherited predisposition that is stable throughout life. The five traits are openness, conscientiousness, extroversion, agreeableness, and neuroticism.

binge drinking: Heavy episodic drinking; consuming five or more alcoholic beverages in one sitting for men and four drinks in one sitting for women.

bioecological systems theory: A theory introduced by Bronfenbrenner that emphasizes the role of context in development, positing that contexts are organized into a series of systems in which individuals are embedded and that interact with one another and the person to influence development.

blastocyst: A thin-walled, fluid-filled sphere containing an inner mass of cells from which the embryo will develop; is implanted into the uterine wall during the germinal period.

blended family: A family composed of a biological parent and a nonrelated adult, most commonly a mother and stepfather.

body image dissatisfaction: Dissatisfaction with one's physical appearance as shown by a discrepancy between one's ideal body figure and actual body figure.

body mass index (BMI): A measure of body fat based on weight in kilograms divided by height in meters squared (kg/m2).

Brazelton Neonatal Behavioral Assessment Scale (NBAS): The most common neurobehavioral assessment administered to newborns that is administered a few days after birth to assess neurological functioning, including the strength of 20 inborn reflexes, responsiveness to the physical and social environment, and changes in state.

breech position: A feet-first birth position that poses risks to the neonate's health; often results in a cesarean section.

Broca's area: The region in the brain that controls the ability to use language for expression; damage to the area inhibits fluent speech.

bulimia nervosa: An eating disorder characterized by recurrent episodes of binge eating and subsequent purging usually by induced vomiting and the use of laxatives.

bully-victim: An individual who attacks or inflicts harm on others and who is also attacked or harmed by others; the child is both bully and victim.

canalization: The tendency for a trait that is biologically programmed to be restricted to only a few outcomes.

canonical babbling: A type of babbling with well-formed syllables that sounds like language.

cardiovascular disease: A disease marked by high blood pressure, high blood cholesterol, plaque buildup in the arteries, irregular heartbeat, and risk factor for heart attack and stroke.

care orientation: Gilligan's feminine mode of moral reasoning, characterized by a desire to maintain relationships and a responsibility to avoid hurting others.

carrier: An individual who is heterozygous for a particular trait, in which a recessive gene is not expressed in the phenotype yet may be passed on to the carrier's offspring.

cataract: A clouding of the lens of the eye, resulting in blurred, foggy vision and can lead to blindness.

categorical self: A classification of the self based on broad ways in which people differ, such as sex, age, and physical characteristics, which children use to guide their behavior.

categorization: An adaptive mental process in which objects are grouped into conceptual categories, allowing for organized storage of information in memory, efficient retrieval of that information, and the capacity to respond with familiarity to new stimuli from a common class.

cell differentiation: The process by which cells become specialized to form different parts of the body; begins roughly 72 hours after fertilization when the organism consists of about 16 to 32 cells.

central executive: In information processing, the part of our mental system that directs the flow of information and regulates cognitive activities such as attention, action, and problem solving.

centration: The tendency to focus on one part of a stimulus, situation, or idea and exclude all others; a characteristic of preoperational reasoning.

cephalocaudal development: The principle that growth proceeds from the head downward; the head and upper regions of the body develop before the lower regions.

cesarean section: Also known as a C-section; a surgical procedure that removes the fetus from the uterus through the abdomen.

child abuse: Any intentional harm to a minor (under the age of 18), including actions that harm the child physically, emotionally, sexually, or through neglect; also known as child maltreatment.

child-centered preschool programs: A constructivist approach to early childhood education that encourages children to actively build their own understanding of the world through observing, interacting with objects and people, and engaging in a variety of activities that allow them to manipulate materials and interact with teachers and peers.

Child maltreatment: Also known as child abuse, any intentional harm to a minor, including actions that harm the child physically, emotionally, sexually, or through neglect.

chorionic villus sampling (CVS): Prenatal diagnostic test that is conducted on cells sampled from the chorion to detects chromosomal abnormalities.

chromosome: One of 46 rod-like molecules that contain 23 pairs of DNA found in every body cell and collectively contain all of the genes.

chronosystem: In bioecological systems theory, refers to how the people and contexts change over time.

circular reaction: In Piaget's cognitive-developmental theory, the repetition of an action and its response in which infants repeat a newly discovered event caused by their own motor activity.

circumcision: surgery that involves the removal of the foreskin of the penis.

classical conditioning: A form of learning in which an environmental stimulus becomes associated with stimuli that elicit reflex responses.

classification: The ability to organize things into groups based on similar characteristics.

class inclusion: Involves understanding hierarchical relationships among items.

clinical death: Defines death as the moment the heart stops beating.

clique: A tightly knit peer group of about three to eight close friends who share similarities such as demographics and attitudes.

cognitive development: Maturation of mental processes and tools individuals use to obtain knowledge, think, and solve problems.

cognitive reserve: The ability to make flexible and efficient use of available brain resources that permits cognitive efficiency, flexibility, and adaptability; it is cultivated throughout life from experience and environmental factors.

cognitive-affective complexity: A form of mature thinking that involves emotional awareness, the ability to integrate and regulate intense emotions, and the recognition and appreciation of individual experience.

cognitive-developmental theory: A perspective posited by Piaget that views individuals as active explorers of their world, learning by interacting with the world around them, and describes cognitive development as progressing through stages.

cognitive schema: A mental representation, such as concepts, ideas, and ways of interacting with the world.

cohabitation: An arrangement in which a committed, unmarried couple lives together in the same home.

cohort: A generation of people born at the same time, influenced by the same historical and cultural conditions.

concrete operational stage of reasoning: Piaget's third stage of reasoning, from about 6 to 11, in which thought becomes logical and is applied to direct tangible experiences but not to abstract problems.

conservation: The principle that a physical quantity, such as number, mass, or volume, remains the same even when its appearance changes.

context: Unique conditions in which a person develops, including aspects of the physical and social environment such as family, neighborhood, culture, and historical time period.

continuity theory: The perspective that older adults strive to maintain continuity and consistency in self across the past and into the future; successful elders retain a sense that they are the same person they have always been despite physical, cognitive, emotional, and social changes.

continuous development: The view that development consists of gradual cumulative changes in existing skills and capacities.

conventional moral reasoning: The second level of Kohlberg's theory in which moral decisions are based on conforming to social rules.

cooing: An infant's repetition of sounds, such as "ahhhh," "ohhh," and "eeee," that begins between 2 and 3 months of age.

corpus callosum: A thick band of nerve fibers that connects the left and right hemispheres of the brain, allowing communication.

correlational research: A research design that measures relationships among participants' measured characteristics, behaviors, and development.

cortex: The outermost part of the brain containing the greatest numbers of neurons and accounting for thought and consciousness.

cross-sectional research study: A developmental research design that compares people of different ages at a single point in time to infer age differences.

crowd: A large groups of adolescents grouped based on perceived shared characteristics, interests, and reputation.

crystallized intelligence: Intellectual ability that reflects accumulated knowledge acquired through experience and learning.

cyberbullying: Bullying, or repeated acts intended to hurt a victim, carried via electronic means such as text messaging, posting in chat rooms and discussion boards, and creating websites and blogs.

dating violence: The actual or threatened physical or sexual violence or psychological abuse directed toward a current or former boyfriend girlfriend or dating partner.

deferred imitation: Imitating the behavior of an absent model; illustrates infants' capacity for mental representation.

delayed phase preference: Change in pubertal hormone levels causes adolescents' sleep patterns to shift such that they tend to remain awake late at night and are groggy early in the morning.

delirium: Dementia-like symptoms caused by psychological and behavioral factors that can be treated.

dementia: A progressive deterioration in mental abilities due to changes in the brain that influence higher cortical functions such as thinking, memory, comprehension, and emotional control and are reflected in impaired thought and behavior, interfering with the older adult's ability to engage in everyday activities.

deoxyribonucleic acid (DNA): The chemical structure, shaped like a twisted ladder, that contains all of the genes.

dependent variable: The behavior under study in an experiment; it is expected to be affected by changes in the independent variable.

dermis: Middle layer of skin consisting of connective tissue that gives skin its flexibility.

developmental delays: The condition in which a child is less physically or cognitively developed than the norm for his or her age.

developmental dyslexia: The most commonly diagnosed learning disability characterized by unusual difficulty in matching letters to sounds and difficulty with word recognition and spelling despite adequate instruction and intelligence and intact sensory abilities.

diabetes: A disease marked by high levels of blood glucose that occurs when the body is unable to regulate the amount of glucose in the bloodstream because there is not enough insulin produced (Type 1 diabetes) or the body shows insulin resistance and becomes less sensitive to it, failing to respond to it (Type 2 diabetes). Symptoms include fatigue, great thirst, blurred vision, frequent infections, and slow healing.

difficult temperament: A temperament characterized by irregularity in biological rhythms, slow adaptation to change, and a tendency for intense negative reactions.

discontinuous development: The view that growth entails abrupt transformations in abilities and capacities in which new ways of interacting with the world emerge.

disengagement theory: The view that declines in social interaction in older age are due to mutual withdrawal between older adults and society as they anticipate death.

dizygotic (DZ) twin: Also known as a fraternal twin; occurs when two ova are released and each is fertilized by a different sperm; the resulting offspring share 50% of the genetic material.

dominant–recessive inheritance: A form of genetic inheritance in which the phenotype reflects only the dominant allele of a heterozygous pair.

doula: A caregiver who provides support to an expectant mother and her partner throughout the birth process.

Down syndrome: Also known as trisomy 21; a condition in which a third, extra chromosome appears at the 21st site. Down syndrome is associated with distinctive physical characteristics accompanied by developmental disability.

dualistic thinking: Polar reasoning in which knowledge and accounts of phenomena are viewed as absolute facts, either right or wrong with no in-between.

dual-language learning: Also known as two-way immersion; an approach in which children are taught and develop skills in two languages.

dual-process model of grief: Poses that bereavement is accompanied by loss-oriented stressors (emotional attachment) and restoration-oriented stressors (life changes); healthy adjustment is promoted by alternating focus between the two types.

dual-systems model: A model of the brain consisting of two systems, one emotional and the other rational, that develop on different timeframes, accounting for typical adolescent behavior.

durable power of attorney: A document in which individuals legally authorize a trusted relative or friend to make legal, financial, or health care decisions on their behalf if they are unable to do so.

dying trajectory: Refers to the variability in the rate of decline that people show prior to death.

dying with dignity: Ending one's life in a way that is true to one's preferences and controlling end-of-life care.

dynamic systems theory: A framework describing motor skills as resulting from ongoing interactions among physical, cognitive, and socioemotional influences and environmental supports in which previously mastered skills are combined to provide more complex and effective ways of exploring and controlling the environment.

dyscalculia: Mathematics disability; difficulty learning and understanding mathematical concepts such as counting, addition, and subtraction.

easy temperament: A temperament characterized by regularity in biological rhythms, the tendency to adapt easily to new experiences, and a general cheerfulness.

ectoderm: The outer layer of the embryonic disk, which will develop into the skin, nails, hair, teeth, sensory organs, and the nervous system.

egocentrism: Piaget's term for children's inability to take another person's point of view or perspective and to assume that others share the same feelings, knowledge, and physical view of the world.

ego integrity versus despair: The final stage in Erikson's psychosocial theory, in which older adults find a sense of coherence in life experiences and conclude that their lives are meaningful and valuable.

elaboration: A memory strategy in which one imagines a scene or story to link the material to be remembered.

embryo: Prenatal organism between about 2 and 8 weeks after conception; a period of major structural development.

embryonic disk: A mass of cells that differentiates into three layers that will develop into the embryo.

embryonic period: Occurs from about 2 to 8 weeks after pregnancy, in which rapid structural development takes place.

emerging adulthood: An extended transition to adulthood that takes place from ages 18 to 25, in which a young person is no longer an adolescent yet has not assumed the roles that comprise adulthood.

emotional display rule: Unstated cultural guidelines for acceptable emotions and emotional expression that are communicated to children via parents' emotional behavior, expressions, and socialization.

emotion regulation: The ability to adjust and control our emotional state to influence how and when emotions are expressed.

empathy: The capacity to understand another person's emotions and concerns.

empty nest: A transitional time of parenting when the youngest child leaves home.

endoderm: The inner layer of an embryonic disk, which will develop into the digestive system, liver, lungs, pancreas, salivary glands, and respiratory system.

epidermis: The outer protective layer of the skin that produces new skin cells.

epidural: A method of pain management often used during labor in which a regional anesthetic drug is administered to a small space between the vertebrae of the lower spine to numb the woman's lower body.

epigenetics: A perspective that development results from dynamic interactions between genetics and the environment such that the expression of genetic inheritance is influenced by environmental forces.

episodic memory: Memory for everyday experiences.

epistemic cognition: The ways in which an individual understands how he or she arrived at ideas, beliefs, and conclusions.

estrogen: The primary female sex hormone responsible for development and regulation of the female reproductive system and secondary sex characteristics.

ethnic identity: A sense of membership to an ethnic group and viewing the attitudes and practices associated with that group as an enduring part of the self.

ethology: Emphasizes the evolutionary basis of behavior and its adaptive value in ensuring survival of a species.

euthanasia: Refers to the practice of assisting terminally ill people in dying more quickly.

evolutionary developmental theory: A perspective that applies principles of evolution and scientific knowledge about the interactive influence of genetic and environmental mechanisms to understand the adaptive value of developmental changes that are experienced with age.

executive function: The set of cognitive operations that support planning, decision making, and goal-setting abilities, such as the ability to control attention, coordinate information in working memory, and inhibit impulses.

exosystem: In bioecological systems theory, social settings in which an individual does not participate but has an indirect influence on development.

expansion: Adult responses to children's speech that elaborate and enrich its complexity.

experience-dependent brain development: Brain growth and development in response-specific learning experiences.

experience-expectant brain development: Brain growth and development that are dependent on basic environmental experiences, such as visual and auditory stimulation, in order to develop normally.

experimental research: A research design that permits inferences about cause and effect by exerting control, systematically manipulating a variable, and studying the effects on measured variables.

expertise: An elaborate and integrated knowledge base that underlies extraordinary proficiency in given area.

extremely low birthweight: Refers to a birthweight of less than 750 grams (1 lb., 10 oz.); poses serious risks for survival, developmental challenges, and handicaps.

failure to thrive: A term indicating insufficient weight gain or inappropriate weight loss such that the child's weight is below the fifth percentile for their age.

false-belief task: A task that requires children to understand that someone does not share their knowledge.

fast mapping: A process by which children learn new words after only a brief encounter, connecting it with their own mental categories.

fetal alcohol spectrum disorders: The continuum of physical, mental, and behavioral outcomes caused by prenatal exposure to alcohol.

fetal alcohol syndrome (FAS): The most severe form of fetal alcohol spectrum disorder accompanying heavy prenatal exposure to alcohol, including a distinct pattern of facial characteristics, growth deficiencies, and deficits in intellectual development.

fetal MRI: Applies MRI technology to image the fetus's body and diagnose malformations.

fetal period: Occurs during the ninth week of prenatal development to birth, in which the fetus grows rapidly, and its organs become more complex and begin to function.

fetoscopy: A technique that uses a small camera, inserted through a small incision on the mother's abdomen or cervix and placed into the amniotic sac to examine and perform procedures on the fetus during pregnancy.

fetus: The prenatal organism from about the ninth week of pregnancy to delivery; a period of rapid growth and maturation of body structures.

fine motor development: The ability to control small movements of the fingers such as reaching and grasping.

fluid intelligence: Intellectual ability that reflects basic information processing skills, including working memory, processing speed, and the ability to detect relations among stimuli and draw inferences. Underlies learning, is not influenced by culture, and reflects brain functioning.

Flynn effect: The rise in IQ scores over generations in many nations.

formal operational reasoning: Piaget's fourth stage of cognitive development, characterized by abstract, logical, and systematic thinking.

fragile X syndrome: An example of a dominant–recessive disorder carried on the X chromosome characterized by intellectual disability, cardiac defects, and behavioral mannerisms common in individuals with autistic spectrum disorders; occurs in both males and females but is more severe in males.

free radical: A highly reactive, corrosive substance that forms when a cell is exposed to oxygen. Through chemical reactions, free radicals destroy DNA, proteins, and other cellular materials.

gamete: A reproductive cell; sperm in males and ovum in females.

gender: The adoption of male or female characteristics.

gender constancy: A child's understanding of the biological permanence of gender and that it does not change regardless of appearance, activities, or attitudes.

gender identity: Awareness of oneself as a male or female.

gender role norms: The activities, attitudes, skills, and characteristics that are considered appropriate for males or females.

gender schema: A concept or a mental structure that organizes gender-related information and embodies a person's understanding of what it means to be a male or female and is used as a guide to attitudes and behaviors.

gender stereotypes: Refer to broad generalized judgments of the activities, attitudes, skills, and characteristics deemed appropriate for males or females in a given culture.

gender typing: The process in which young children acquire the characteristics and attitudes that are considered appropriate for males or females.

gene: The basic unit of heredity; a small section of a chromosome that contains the string of chemicals (DNA) that provide instructions for the cell to manufacture proteins.

gene–environment interactions: Refer to the dynamic interplay between our genes and our environment in determining out characteristics, behavior, physical, cognitive, and social development as well as health.

generativity versus stagnation: The seventh stage in Erikson's theory in which adults seek to move beyond a concern for their own personal goals and welfare in order to guide future generations and give back to society.

genetic counseling: A medical specialty that helps prospective parents determine the probability that their children will inherit genetic defects and chromosomal abnormalities.

genomic imprinting: The instance when the expression of a gene is determined by whether it is inherited from the mother or father.

genotype: An individual's collection of genes that contain instructions for all physical and psychological characteristics, including hair, eye color, personality, health, and behavior.

germinal period: Also referred to as the period of the zygote; refers to the first 2 weeks after conception.

glass ceiling: Metaphor for the invisible barrier that prevents women and people of color from advancing to the highest levels of the career ladder.

glial cell: A type of brain cell that nourishes neurons and provides structure to the brain.

global self-esteem: An overall evaluation of self-worth.

goodness of fit: The compatibility between a child's temperament and his or her environment, especially the parent's temperament and childrearing methods; the greater the degree of match, the more favorable the child's adjustment.

grammar: The rules of language.

grief: The affective response to bereavement that includes distress and an intense array of emotions such as hurt, anger, and guilt.

gross motor development: The ability to control large movements of the body, such as walking and jumping.

growth norm: The expectation for typical gains and variations in height and weight for children based on their chronological age and ethnic background.

guided participation: Also known as apprenticeship in thinking; the process by which people learn from others who guide them, providing a scaffold to help them accomplish more than the child could do alone.

habituation: The gradual decline in the intensity, frequency, or duration of a response when repeatedly exposed to a stimulus; indicates learning.

hardiness: Personal qualities, including a sense of control, orientation toward personal growth, and commitment to life choices, that influence adults'ability to adapt to changes and life circumstances.

hemispheric dominance: A process in which one hemisphere becomes stronger and more adept than the other.

hemophilia: An X-linked chromosomal disorder involving abnormal blood clotting.

heritability: The statistic that indicates the extent to which variation of a certain trait can be traced to genes.

heteronomous morality: Piaget's first stage of morality when children become aware of rules and view them as absolute and unalterable.

heterozygous: Refers to a chromosomal pair consisting of two different alleles.

holophrase: A one-word expression used to convey a complete thought.

homozygous: Refers to a chromosomal pair consisting of two identical alleles.

hormone: A chemical that is produced and secreted into the bloodstream to affect and influence physiological functions.

hormone replacement therapy: Compensating for reductions in hormones, such as in menopause, by taking hormones.

hospice: An approach to end-of-life care that emphasizes a dying patient's need for pain management; psychological, spiritual, and social support; and death with dignity.

human immunodeficiency virus (HIV): Infection most commonly passed through sexual activity and intravenous drug use, which causes acquired immune deficiency syndrome (AIDS).

hypodermis: Innermost layer of skin composed of fat.

hypothesis: A proposed explanation for a phenomenon that can be tested.

hypothetical–deductive reasoning: The ability to consider propositions and probabilities, generate and systematically test hypotheses, and draw conclusions.

identity: A coherent organized sense of self that includes values, attitudes, and goals to which one is committed.

identity achievement: The identity state in which, after undergoing a period of exploration, a person commits to self-chosen values and goals.

identity achievement status: The identity state that requires that individuals construct a sense of self through reflection, critical examination, and exploring or trying out new ideas and belief systems.

identity diffusion: The identity state in which an individual has not undergone exploration or committed to self-chosen values and goals.

identity foreclosed: The identity state in which an individual has not undergone exploration but has committed to values and goals chosen by an authority figure.

identity status: The degree to which individuals have explored possible selves and whether they have committed to specific beliefs and goals, assessed by administering interview and survey measures, and categorized into four identity statuses.

imaginary audience: A manifestation of adolescent egocentrism in which they assume that they are the focus of others'attention.

immersion: A strategy in which all instruction occurs in the majority language; children learn a second language, such as English, and course content simultaneously.

implantation: The process by which the blastocyst becomes attached to the uterine wall, completed by about 10 days after fertilization.

in vitro fertilization: Fertilization, the creation of zygotes, that takes place outside of a woman's body by mixing sperm with ova that have been surgically removed from the woman's body.

incomplete dominance: A genetic inheritance pattern in which both genes are expressed in the phenotype.

independent variable: The factor proposed to change the behavior under study in an experiment; it is systematically manipulated during an experiment.

inductive discipline: Strategy to control children's behavior that relies on reasoning and discussion.

industry versus inferiority: Erikson's fourth stage in which children attempt new skills, developing feelings of competence in their success or feeling inferior or incompetent.

information processing theory: A perspective that uses a computer analogy to describe how the mind receives information and manipulates, stores, recalls, and uses it to solve problems.

informed consent: A participant's informed (knowledge of the scope of the research and potential harm and benefits of participating), rational, and voluntary agreement to participate in a study.

initiative versus guilt: Erikson's third psychosocial stage in which young children develop a sense of purposefulness, trying new skills and activities, and take pride in their accomplishments, as well as feel guilt if they are unsuccessful.

insecure–avoidant attachment: An attachment pattern in which an infant avoids connecting with the caregiver, showing no distress when separated from a caregiver, such as during the Strange Situation, and does not seem to care about the caregiver's return.

insecure–disorganized attachment: An attachment in which an infant shows inconsistent, contradictory behavior in the Strange Situation, suggesting a conflict between approaching and fleeing the caregiver and perhaps fear.

insecure–resistant attachment: An attachment pattern in which an infant shows anxiety and uncertainty, showing great distress at separation from the caregiver during the Strange Situation and simultaneously seeks and avoids contact upon the caregiver's return.

instrumental aggression: Behavior that hurts someone else in order to achieve a goal such as gaining a possession.

intellectual disability: Characterized by deficits in cognitive functioning and age-appropriate adaptive behavior, such as social, communication, and self-care skills that begin before 18 years of age; formerly known as mental retardation.

intelligence: An individual's ability to adapt to the environment.

intelligence test (IQ test): A test designed to measure the aptitude to learn at school, intellectual aptitude.

intermodal perception: The process of combining information from more than one sensory system such as visual and auditory senses.

internal working model: A set of expectations about one's worthiness of love and the availability of attachment figures during times of distress.

intimacy versus isolation: Erikson's sixth psychosocial stage in which individuals demonstrate the capacity to feel closeness and bond with another individual to make a permanent commitment to a romantic partner.

intimate partner violence: Physical, sexual, and psychological abuse within a romantic relationship.

irreversibility: A characteristic of preoperational reasoning in which a child does not understand that an action can be reversed and a thing restored to its original state.

isometric strength: Subtle contractions in which the length of the muscle does not change, is maintained through adulthood.

Jacob's syndrome: A sex chromosome abnormality experienced by men in which they produce high levels of testosterone; also known as XYY syndrome.

justice orientation: A male mode of moral reasoning proposed by Gilligan that emphasizes the abstract principles of fairness and individualism.

kangaroo care: An intervention for low-birthweight babies in which the infant is placed vertically against the parent's chest, under the shirt, providing skin-to-skin contact.

Klinefelter syndrome: Sex chromosome abnormality in which a male has an extra X chromosome (XXY).

kwashiorkor: A malnutritive disease in children caused by deprivation of protein and calories and characterized by lethargy and the bloating and swelling of the stomach.

labor: Also known as childbirth, occurs at about 40 weeks of pregnancy, or 38 weeks after conception.

language acquisition device (LAD): In Chomsky's theory, an innate facilitator of language that allows infants to quickly and efficiently analyze everyday speech and determine its rules, regardless of their native language.

lanugo: A fine, down-like hair that covers the fetus's body.

lateralization: The process by which the two hemispheres of the brain become specialized to carry out different functions.

learned helplessness orientation: An orientation characterized by a fixed mind-set and the attribution of poor performance to internal factors.

Lewy body dementia: Common form of dementia characterized by the formation of spherical protein deposits known as Lewy bodies.

life review: The reflection on past experiences and one's life, permitting greater self-understanding and the assignment of meaning to their lives.

lifespan human development: An approach to studying human development that examines ways in which individuals grow, change, and stay the same throughout their lives, from conception to death.

life structure: In Levenson's theory, a person's overall organization of his or her life, particularly dreams, goals, and relationships with significant others as well as institutions, such as marriage, family, and vocation.

limbic system: A collection of brain structures responsible for emotion.

living will: A legal document that permits a person to make his or her wishes known regarding medical care in the event that the person is incapacitated by an illness or accident and is unable to speak for himself or herself.

logical extension: A strategy children use to increase their vocabulary in which they extend a new word to other objects in the same category.

longitudinal research study: A developmental study in which one group of participants is studied repeatedly to infer age changes.

long-term memory: The component of the information processing system that is an unlimited store that holds information indefinitely, until it is retrieved to manipulate working memory.

low birthweight: Classifies infants who weigh less than 2,500 grams (5.5 pounds) at birth.

macrosystem: In bioecological systems theory, the sociohistorical context—cultural values, laws, and cultural values—in which the microsystem, mesosystem, and exosystem are embedded, posing indirect influences on individuals.

macular degeneration: A substantial loss of cells in the center area of the retina (the macula), causing blurring and eventual loss of central vision; its onset is influenced by heredity and environmental factors.

mandated reporter: A professional who is legally obligated to report suspected child maltreatment to law enforcement.

marasmus: A wasting disease in which the body's fat and muscle are depleted; growth stops and the body wastes away, taking on a hollow appearance.

mastery orientation: A belief that success stems from trying hard and that failures are influenced by factors that can be controlled, like effort.

meiosis: The process by which a gamete is formed, containing one half of the cell's chromosomes, producing ova and sperm with 23 single, unpaired chromosomes.

memory strategy: Deliberate cognitive activities that make an individual more likely to remember information.

menarche: A girl's first menstrual period.

menopause: The end of menstruation and a woman's reproductive capacity.

mental representation: An internal depiction of an object; thinking of an object using mental pictures.

mesoderm: The middle layer of the embryonic disk; develops into the muscles, skeleton, circulatory system, and internal organs.

mesosystem: In bioecological systems theory, the relations and interactions among microsystems.

metacognition: The ability to think about thinking; knowledge of how the mind works.

metamemory: An aspect of metacognition that refers to the understanding of memory and how to use strategies to enhance memory.

microsystem: In bioecological systems theory, the innermost level of context, which includes an individual's immediate physical and social environment.

midlife crisis: A period of self-doubt and stress attributed to entering midlife once thought to contribute to a major reorganization of personality in midlife. Now thought to occur in a small minority of adults and to be related to history more than age.

midwife: A health care professional, usually a nurse, who specializes in childbirth. Midwives provide health care throughout pregnancy and supervise home births.

mindset: The degree to which an individual believes his or her abilities and characteristics are modifiable (growth mindset) or enduring (fixed mindset).

mitosis: The process of cell duplication in which DNA is replicated and the resulting cell is genetically identical to the original.

monozygotic (MZ) twin: Also known as an identical twin; occurs when the zygote splits apart early in development. The resulting offspring share 100% of their genetic material.

mourning: The ceremonies and rituals a culture prescribes for expressing bereavement.

multiple intelligence theory: Gardner's proposition that human intelligence is composed of a varied set of abilities.

mutation: A sudden permanent change in the structure of genes.

mutual exclusivity assumption: When learning new words, young children assume that objects have only one label or name.

myelination: The process in which neurons are coated in a fatty substance, myelin, which contributes to faster neural communication.

naming explosion: Also known as a vocabulary spurt; a period of rapid vocabulary learning that occurs from about 16 to 24 months of age.

naturalistic observation: A research method in which a researcher views and records an individual's behavior in natural, real-world settings.

nature–nurture issue: A debate within the field of human development regarding whether development is caused by nature (genetics or heredity) or nurture (the physical and social environment).

neurofibrillary tangle: A twisted bundle of threads of a protein called tau that occur in the brain when neurons collapse; found in individuals with Alzheimer's disease.

neurogenesis: The production of new neurons.

neuron: A nerve cell that stores and transmits information; billions of neurons comprise the brain.

niche-picking: An active gene–environment correlation in which individuals seek out experiences and environments that complement their genetic tendencies.

noncorporeal continuation: The view that some form of life and personal continuity exists after the physical body has died.

noninvasive prenatal testing (NIPT): A prenatal diagnostic that samples cell-free fetal DNA from the mother's blood for chromosomal abnormalities.

obesity: In children, defined as having a body mass index at or above the 95th percentile for height and age.

object permanence: The understanding that objects continue to exist outside of sight.

observational learning: Learning that occurs by watching and imitating models, as posited by social learning theory.

oldest-old: Adults aged 85 and older, who are most likely to depend on others for physical and social support to complete daily tasks.

old-old: Adults aged 75 to 84, who typically live independently but often experience some physical and mental impairment.

one-child policy: Policy instituted by the People's Republic of China from 1979 to 2015; restricted the number of children married couples could have to one in an effort to curb population growth.

open-ended interview: A research method in which a researcher asks a participant questions using a flexible, conversational style and may vary the order of questions, probe, and ask follow-up questions based on the participant's responses.

operant conditioning: A form of learning in which behavior increases or decreases based on environmental consequences.

organization: Memory strategy in which items to remember are categorized or grouped by theme or type.

osteoarthritis: The most common type of arthritis; it affects joints that are injured by overuse, most commonly the hips, knees, lower back, and hands, in which the cartilage protecting the ends of the bones where they meet at the joints wears away, and joints become less flexible and swell.

osteoporosis: A condition characterized by severe loss of bone mass, leading to increased risk of fractures.

overextension: A vocabulary error in which the infant applies a word too broadly to a wider class of objects than appropriate.

overregularization errors: Grammatical mistakes that children make because they apply grammatical rules too stringently to words that are exceptions.

ovum: The female reproductive cell or egg cell.

palliative care: An alternative to medical treatment in which dying patients receive medications to control pain and related symptoms.

parental monitoring: Parents' awareness of their children's activities, whereabouts, and companions.

parenting style: Enduring sets of childrearing behaviors a parent uses across situations to form a childrearing climate.

Parkinson's disease: A chronic progressive brain disorder caused by deterioration of neurons in the substantia nigra; characterized by muscle rigidity, tremors, and sometimes dementia.

passive euthanasia: Occurs when life-sustaining treatment, such as a ventilator, is withheld or withdrawn, allowing a person to die naturally.

peer acceptance: Likeability or the degree to which a child is viewed as a worthy social partner by his or her peers.

peer rejection: An ongoing interaction in which a child is deliberately excluded by peers.

peer victimization: Also known as bullying; an ongoing interaction in which a child becomes a frequent target of physical, verbal, or social harm by another child or children.

perception: The mental processing of sensory information, which is interpreted as sight, sound, and smell, for example.

perimenopause: Transition to menopause in which the production of reproductive hormones declines and symptoms associated with menopause first appear, such as hot flashes.

permissive parenting style: A childrearing approach characterized by high levels of warmth and low levels of control or discipline.

persistent vegetative state (PVS): Cortical death when the person appears awake but is not aware, due to permanent loss of all activity in the cortex.

personal fable: A manifestation of adolescent egocentrism in which adolescents believe their thoughts, feelings, and experiences are more special and unique than anyone else's, as well as the sense that they are invulnerable.

phenotype: The observable physical or behavioral characteristics of a person's eye color, hair color, or height.

phenylketonuria (PKU): A recessive disorder that prevents the body from producing an enzyme that breaks down phenylalanine (an amino acid) from proteins that, without treatment, leads to buildup that damages the central nervous system.

phonics instruction: An approach to reading instruction that emphasizes teaching children to sound out words and connect sounds to written symbols.

physical development: Body maturation, including body size, proportion, appearance, health, and perceptual abilities.

physician-assisted suicide: A type of voluntary active euthanasia in which terminally ill patients make the conscious decision that they want their life to end before dying becomes a protracted process.

placenta: The principal organ of exchange between the mother and the developing organism, enabling the exchange of nutrients, oxygen, and wastes via the umbilical cord.

plasticity: A characteristic of development refers to malleability or openness to change in response to experience.

polygenic inheritance: Occurs when a trait is a function of the interaction of many genes, such as with height, intelligence, and temperament.

popular children: Children who receive many positive ratings from peers indicating that they are accepted and valued by peers.

possible selves: Future-oriented representations of self-concept into the future; who an individual might become, both hoped for and feared, that guides and motivates choices and behaviors.

postconventional moral reasoning: Kohlberg's third level of moral reasoning emphasizing autonomous decision making based on principles such as valuing human dignity.

postformal reasoning: A stage of cognitive development proposed to follow Piaget's formal operational stage. Thinking and problem solving are restructured in adulthood to integrate abstract reasoning with practical considerations..

posttraumatic stress disorder (PTSD): An anxiety disorder that occurs as a delayed reaction to experiencing a traumatic event and includes flashbacks, nightmares, and feelings of helplessness.

pragmatics: The practical application of language for everyday communication.

pragmatic thought: In Labouvie-Vief's theory, a type of thinking where logic is used as a tool to address everyday problems and contradictions are viewed as part of life.

preconventional reasoning: Kohlberg's first level of reasoning in which young children's behavior is governed by punishment and gaining rewards.

prenatal care: A set of services provided to improve pregnancy outcomes and engage the expectant mother, family members, and friends in pregnancy-related health care decisions.

preoperational reasoning: Piaget's second stage of cognitive development, between about ages 2 and 6, characterized by advances in symbolic thought, but thought is not yet logical.

presbycusis: Age-related hearing loss, first to the high-frequency sounds, gradually spreading.

presbyopia: An age-related condition in which the lens becomes less able to adjust its focus on objects at a close range.

preterm: A birth that occurs 35 or fewer weeks after conception.

primary circular reaction: In Piaget's theory, repeating an action that produced a chance event involving the infant's body.

primary sex characteristic: The reproductive organs; in females, this includes the ovaries, fallopian tubes, uterus, and vagina, and in males, this includes the penis, testes, scrotum, seminal vesicles, and prostate gland.

private speech: Self-directed speech that children use to guide their behavior.

proactive interference: A phenomenon that occurs when information that has previously been remembered interferes with memory for new information.

Project Head Start: Early childhood intervention program funded by the U.S. federal government that provides low-income children with nutritional, health, and educational services, as well as helps parents become involved in their children's development.

prosocial behavior: Actions that are oriented toward others for the pure sake of helping, without a reward.

protective factor: Variable that is thought to reduce the poor outcomes associated with adverse circumstances.

proximodistal development: The principle that growth and development proceed from the center of the body outward.

psychoanalytic theory: A perspective introduced by Freud that development and behavior are stage-like and influenced by inner drives, memories, and conflicts of which an individual is unaware and cannot control.

psychosocial moratorium: In Erikson's theory, a period in which the individual is free to explore identity possibilities before committing to an identity.

puberty: The biological transition to adulthood, in which hormones cause the body to physically mature and permit sexual reproduction.

punishment: In operant conditioning, the process in which a behavior is followed by an aversive or unpleasant outcome that decreases the likelihood of a response.

questionnaire: A research method in which researchers use a survey or set of questions to collect data from large samples of people.

random assignment: A method of assigning participants that ensures each participant has an equal chance of being assigned to the experimental group or control group.

range of reaction: The concept that a genetic trait may be expressed in a wide range of phenotypes dependent on environmental opportunities and constraints.

recall memory: The ability to generate a memory of a stimulus encountered before without seeing it again.

recast: When an adult repeats a child's sentence back to him or her in a new grammatical form, helping the child to acquire grammatical rules more quickly.

reciprocal determinism: A perspective positing that individuals and the environment interact and influence each other.

recognition memory: The ability to identify a previously encountered stimulus.

reflective judgment: Mature type of reasoning that synthesizes contradictions among perspectives.

rehearsal: A mnemonic strategy that involves systematically repeating information to retain it in working memory.

reinforcement: In operant conditioning, the process by which a behavior is followed by a desirable outcome increases the likelihood of a response.

relational aggression: Harming someone through nonphysical acts aimed at harming a person's connections with others, such as by exclusion and rumor spreading.

relativistic thinking: Type of reasoning in which knowledge is viewed as subjective and dependent on the situation.

reminiscence: The process of telling stories from one's past, to oneself or others.

resilience: The ability to adapt to serious adversity.

rheumatoid arthritis: An autoimmune illness in which the connective tissues, the membranes that line the joints, become inflamed and stiff.

risk factors: Individual or contextual challenges that tax an individual's coping capacities and can evoke psychological stress.

role overload: High levels of stress resulting from balancing the demands of multiple conflicting roles.

rough-and-tumble play: Social interaction involving chasing and play fighting with no intent to harm.

scaffolding: Temporary support that permits a child to bridge the gap between his or her current competence level and the task at hand.

scientific method: The process of forming and answering questions using systematic observations and gathering information.

script: Description of what occurs in a certain situation and used as guide to understand and organize daily experiences.

seasons of life: A set of life phases that Levinson concluded adults progress through in which life structures are constructed, tested, and modified, based on experiences and opportunities.

secondary circular reaction: In Piaget's theory, repeating an action that produced a chance event that triggers a response in the external environment.

secondary sex characteristic: Physical traits that indicate sexual maturity but are not directly related to fertility, such as breast development and the growth of body hair.

secular trend: The change from one generation to the next in an aspect of development, such as body size or in the timing of puberty.

secure attachment: The attachment pattern in which an infant uses the caregiver as a secure base from which to explore, seeks contact during reunions, and is easily comforted by the caregiver.

secure base: The use of a caregiver as a foundation from which to explore and return to for emotional support.

security of attachment: The extent to which an individual feels that an attachment object, such as a caregiver, can reliably meet his or her needs; measured by the Strange Situation.

selective attention: The ability to focus on relevant stimuli and ignore others.

self-concept: The set of attributes, abilities, and characteristics that a person uses to describe and define himself or herself.

self-conscious emotion: Emotion that requires cognitive development and an awareness of self, such as empathy, embarrassment, shame, and guilt.

self-esteem: The emotional evaluation of one's own worth.

self-harm: Deliberate and voluntary physical personal injury that is not life-threatening and is without any conscious suicidal intent.

self-recognition: The ability to identify the self, typically measured as mirror recognition.

senescence: A pattern of gradual age-related declines in physical functioning.

sensation: The physical response of sensory receptors when a stimulus is detected (e.g., activity of the sensory receptors in the eye in response to light); awareness of stimuli in the senses.

sensory memory: The first step in the information processing system in which stimuli are stored for a brief moment in its original form to enable it to be processed.

separation anxiety: Also known as separation protest; occurs when infants respond to the departure of an attachment figure with distress and crying.

sequential research design: A developmental design in which multiple groups of participants of different ages are followed over time, combining cross-sectional and longitudinal research.

seriation: A type of classification that involves ordering objects in a series according to a physical dimension such as height, weight, or color.

sexual identity: An individual's sense of self regarding sexuality, including the awareness and comfort regarding personal sexual attitudes, interests, and behaviors, which develops through a period of exploration and commitment.

sexual orientation: A term that refers to whether someone is sexually attracted to others of the same sex, opposite sex, or both.

sickle cell trait: A recessive trait, most often affecting African Americans, that causes red blood cells to become crescent or sickle shaped, resulting in difficulty distributing oxygen throughout the circulatory system.

singlehood: Refers to not living with a romantic partner.

sleeper effects: Teratogenic outcomes or effects that are not visible until many years later.

slow-to-warm-up temperament: A temperament characterized by mild irregularity in biological rhythms, slow adaptation to change, and mildly negative mood.

small for date: Describes an infant who is full term but who has significantly lower weight than expected for the gestational age.

social clock: A timetable based on social norms for age-related life events such as occupational entry, marriage, parenthood, and retirement.

social comparison: The tendency to compare and judge one's abilities, achievements, and behaviors in relation to others.

social learning theory: An approach that emphasizes the role of modeling and observational learning over people's behavior in addition to reinforcement and punishment.

social referencing: Seeking information from caregivers about how to interpret unfamiliar or ambiguous events by observing their emotional expressions and reactions.

social smile: A smile that emerges between 6 and 10 weeks in response to seeing familiar people.

sociocultural theory: Vygotsky's theory that individuals acquire culturally relevant ways of thinking through social interactions with members of their culture.

sociodramatic play: Make-believe play in which children act out roles and themes.

socioemotional development: Maturation of social and emotional functioning, which includes changes in personality, emotions, personal perceptions, social skills, and interpersonal relationships.

socioemotional selectivity theory: The perspective that as the emotional regulation function of social interaction becomes increasingly important to older adults, they prefer to interact with familiar social partners, accounting for the narrowing of the social network with age.

spermarche: A boy's first ejaculation of sperm.

spina bifida: A neural tube that results in spinal nerves growing outside of the vertebrae, often resulting in paralysis and developmental disability.

states of arousal: Degrees of wakefulness; newborns shift among six states of arousal ranging from regular sleep to waking activity.

Strange Situation: A structured laboratory procedure that measures the security of attachment by observing infants'reactions to being separated from the caregiver in an unfamiliar environment.

stranger wariness: Also known as stranger anxiety; an infant's expression of fear of unfamiliar people.

structured interview: A research method in which each participant is asked the same set of questions in the same way.

structured observation: An observational measure in which an individual's behavior is viewed and recorded in a controlled environment; a situation created by the experimenter.

successful aging: Demonstrating high levels of physical, social, and psychological well-being in advanced age.

surrogacy: An alternative form of reproduction known in which a woman (the surrogate) is impregnated and carries a fetus to term and agrees to turn the baby over to a woman, man, or couple who will raise it.

sustained attention: The ability to remain focused on a stimulus for an extended period of time.

synapse: The intersection or gap between the axon of one neuron and the dendrites of other neurons; the gap that neurotransmitters must cross.

synaptic pruning: The process by which synapses, neural connections that are seldom used, disappear.

synaptogenesis: The process in which neurons form synapses and increase connections between neurons.

telegraphic speech: Two-word utterances produced by toddlers that communicate only the essential words.

temperament: Characteristic differences among individuals in emotional reactivity, self-regulation, and activity that influence reactions to the environment and are stable and appear early in life.

teratogen: An environmental factor that causes damage to prenatal development.

teratology: The study of abnormalities in prenatal development.

tertiary circular reaction: In Piaget's theory, repeating an action to explore and experiment in order to see the results and learn about the world.

testosterone: The primary male sex hormone responsible for development and regulation of the male reproductive system and secondary sex characteristics.

theory: An organized set of observations to describe, explain, and predict a phenomenon.

theory of mind: Children's awareness of their own and other people's mental processes and realization that other people do not share their thoughts.

three-mountains task: A classic Piagetian task used to illustrate preoperational children's egocentrism.

transgender: Denotes when a person's sense of identity and gender do not correspond to that person's biological sex.

transitive inference: A classification skill in which a child can infer the relationship between two objects by understanding each object's relationship to a third object.

triarchic theory of intelligence: Sternberg's theory positing three independent forms of intelligence: analytical, creative, and applied.

trust versus mistrust: The first psychosocial crisis in Erikson's theory in which infants must develop a basic sense of trust of the world as a safe place where their basic needs will be met.

Turner syndrome: Sex chromosome abnormality in which a female is born with only one X chromosome; girls with Turner syndrome show abnormal growth patterns, abnormalities in primary and secondary sex characteristics, and other disorders.

ultrasound: Prenatal diagnostic procedure in which high-frequency sound waves are directed at the mother's abdomen to provide clear images of the womb projected onto a video monitor.

underextension: A vocabulary error in which the infant applies a word too narrowly to a single object rather than the more appropriate, wider class of objects.

uninvolved parenting style: A childrearing style characterized by low levels of warmth and acceptance coupled with little control or discipline.

universal grammar: In Chomsky's theory, rules that apply to all human languages.

vascular dementia: Neurocognitive disorder in which sporadic and progressive losses occur, caused by small blockages of blood vessels in the brain.

vernix caseosa: Greasy material that protects the fetal skin from abrasions, chapping, and hardening that can occur from exposure to amniotic fluid.

very low birthweight: Refers to a birthweight less than 1,500 grams (3.5 lbs.); poses risks for developmental disabilities and handicaps.

video deficit effect: A finding that infants and toddlers perform more poorly on tasks demonstrated on video than those demonstrated live.

violation-of-expectation task: A task in which a stimulus appears to violate physical laws.

wear-and-tear theory: An early theory of aging stating that aging is the result of the body wearing out from use.

Wernicke's area: The region of the brain that is responsible for language comprehension; damage to this area impairs the ability to understand others'speech and sometimes the ability to speak coherently.

whole brain death: Refers to the irreversible loss of functioning in the entire brain that may occur prior to clinical death.

widowhood: Refers to the status of a person who has lost a spouse through death and has not remarried.

widowhood effect: Refers to the increased likelihood for a widowed person to die, illustrating the relationship between social relations and health.

wisdom: Expertise in the conduct and meanings of life, characterized by emotional maturity and the ability to show insight and apply it to problems.

working memory: The component of the information processing system that holds and processes information that is being manipulated, encoded, or retrieved and is responsible for maintaining and processing information used in cognitive tasks.

work–life balance: The challenge of finding time and energy for both a career and personal pursuits such as family.

young-old: Older adults aged 65 to 74, who tend to be active, healthy, and financially and physically independent.

zone of proximal development: Gap between the child's competence level—what he or she can accomplish independently—and what he or she can do with assistance of a skilled partner.

zygote: A fertilized ovum.

REFERENCES

Chapter 1

Abdallah, B., Badr, L. K., & Hawwari, M. (2013). The efficacy of massage on short and long term outcomes in preterm infants. *Infant Behavior and Development, 36,* 662–669. doi:10.1016/j.infbeh.2013.06.009

Adolph, K. E., & Franchak, J. M. (2017). The development of motor behavior. *Wiley Interdisciplinary Reviews: Cognitive Science, 8,* e1430. doi:10.1002/wcs.1430

Aizer, A. (2017). The role of children's health in the intergenerational transmission of economic status. *Child Development Perspectives, 11,* 167–172. doi:10.1111/cdep.12231

Alisic, E., Krishna, R. N., Robbins, M. L., & Mehl, M. R. (2016). A comparison of parent and child narratives of children's recovery from trauma. *Journal of Language and Social Psychology, 35,* 224–235. doi:10.1177/0261927X15599557

American Psychological Association. (2010). *Ethical principles of psychologists and code of conduct.* Retrieved from http://www.apa.org/ethics/code/principles.pdf

Anjos, T., Altmäe, S., Emmett, P., Tiemeier, H., Closa-Monasterolo, R., Luque, V., . . . Campoy, C. (2013). Nutrition and neurodevelopment in children: Focus on NUTRIMENTHE project. *European Journal of Nutrition, 52,* 1825–1842. doi:10.1007/s00394-013-0560-4

Baltes, P. B. (1987). Theoretical propositions of life-span developmental psychology: On the dynamics between growth and decline. *Developmental Psychology, 23,* 611–626.

Baltes, P. B., Lindenberger, U., & Staudinger, U. M. (2006). Life span theory in developmental psychology. In R. M. Lerner (Ed.), *Handbook of child psychology: Vol. 1. Theoretical models of human development* (6th ed., pp. 569–664). Hoboken, NJ: John Wiley.

Bandettini, P. A. (2012). Twenty years of functional MRI: The science and the stories. *NeuroImage, 62,* 575–588. doi:10.1016/j.neuroimage.2012.04.026

Bandura, A. (2010). Vicarious learning. In D. Matsumoto (Ed.), *Cambridge dictionary of psychology* (p. 344). New York, NY: Cambridge University Press.

Bandura, A. (2011). But what about that gigantic elephant in the room? In A. Robert (Ed.), *Most underappreciated: 50 prominent social psychologists describe their most unloved work: Arkin* (pp. 51–59). New York, NY: Oxford University Press.

Bandura, A. (2012). Social cognitive theory. In P. A. M. Van Lange, A. W. Kruglanski, & E. T. Higgins (Eds.), *Handbook of theories of social psychology: Vol. 1. Van Lange* (pp. 349–373). Thousand Oaks, CA: Sage.

Bargh, J. A. (2013). Our unconscious mind. *Scientific American, 310,* 30–37. doi:10.1038/scientificamerican0114-30

Bass, R. W., Brown, D. D., Laurson, K. R., & Coleman, M. M. (2013). Physical fitness and academic performance in middle school students. *Acta Paediatrica, 102,* 832–837. doi:10.1111/apa.12278

Bateson, P. (2015). Human evolution and development: An ethological perspective. In W. F. Overton & P. C. M. Molenaar (Eds.), *Handbook of child psychology and developmental science: Vol. 1. Theory and method* (7th ed., pp. 208–243). Hoboken, NJ: John Wiley.

Beran, T. N., Ramirez-Serrano, A., Kuzyk, R., Fior, M., & Nugent, S. (2011). Understanding how children understand robots: Perceived animism in child–robot interaction. *International Journal of Human-Computer Studies, 69,* 539–550.

Birney, D. P., & Sternberg, R. J. (2011). The development of cognitive abilities. In M. H. Bornstein & M. E. Lamb (Eds.), *Developmental science: An advanced textbook* (6th ed., pp. 353–388). New York, NY: Psychology Press.

Bjorklund, D. F. (2018). A metatheory for cognitive development (or "Piaget is dead" revisited). *Child Development.* Advance online publication. doi:10.1111/cdev.13019

Boker, S. M. (2013). Selection, optimization, compensation, and equilibrium dynamics. *GeroPsych: The Journal of Gerontopsychology and Geriatric Psychiatry, 26,* 61–73. doi:10.1024/1662-9647/a000081

Bowlby, J. (1969). *Attachment and loss: Vol. 1. Attachment.* New York, NY: Basic Books.

Bowlby, J. (1973). *Attachment and loss: Vol. 2. Separation: Anxiety and anger.* New York, NY: Basic Books.

Braams, B. R., & Crone, E. A. (2017). Longitudinal changes in social brain development: Processing outcomes for friend and self. *Child Development, 88,* 1952–1965. doi:10.1111/cdev.12665

Brehmer, Y., Westerberg, H., & Bäckman, L. (2012). Working-memory training in younger and older adults: Training gains, transfer, and maintenance. *Frontiers in Human Neuroscience, 6,* 63. doi:10.3389/fnhum.2012.00063

Bronfenbrenner, U., & Morris, P. A. (2006). The bioecological model of human development. In R. M. Lerner & W. Damon (Eds.), *Handbook of child psychology* (Vol. 21, pp. 793–828). Hoboken, NJ: John Wiley.

Brown, H. R., Harvey, E. A., Griffith, S. F., Arnold, D. H., & Halgin, R. P. (2017). Assent and dissent: Ethical considerations in research with toddlers. *Ethics & Behavior, 27,* 651–664. doi:10.1080/10508422.2016.1277356

Callaghan, T., & Corbit, J. (2015). The development of symbolic representation. In L. S. Liben & U. Muller (Eds.), *Handbook of child psychology and developmental science* (pp. 1–46). Hoboken, NJ: John Wiley. doi:10.1002/9781118963418.childpsy207

Cierniak, R. (2011). *X-ray computed tomography in biomedical engineering.* London, England: Springer London. doi:10.1007/978-0-85729-027-4_2

Cole, M., & Packer, M. (2015). A bio-cultural-historical approach to the study of development. In M. J. Gelfand, C. Chiu, & Y. Hong (Eds.), *Handbook of advances in culture and psychology.* New York, NY: Oxford University Press.

Collura, T. F. (1993). History and evolution of electroencephalographic instruments and techniques. *Journal of Clinical Neurophysiology, 10,* 476–504. Retrieved from http://www.ncbi.nlm.nih.gov/pubmed/8308144

Coplan, R. J., Ooi, L. L., & Nocita, G. (2015). When one is company and two is a crowd: Why some children prefer solitude. *Child Development Perspectives, 9,* 133–137. doi:10.1111/cdep.12131

Crain, W. C. (2016). *Theories of development: concepts and applications* (4th ed.). New York, NY: Routledge.

DelGiudice, M. (2018). Middle childhood: An evolutionary-developmental synthesis. In N. Halfon, C. B. Forrest, R. M. Lerner, & E. M. Faustman (Eds.), *Handbook of life course health development* (pp. 95–107). Cham, Switzerland: Springer International. doi:10.1007/978-3-319-47143-3_5

Elder, G. H., & George, L. K. (2016). Age, cohorts, and the life course. In M. Shanahan, J. Mortimer, & M. Kirkpatrick Johnson (Eds.), *Handbook of the lifecourse* (pp. 59–85). Cham, Switzerland: Springer. doi:10.1007/978-3-319-20880-0_3

Elder, G. H., Jr., Shanahan, M. J., & Jennings, J. A. (2016). Human development in time and place. In M. H. Bornstein & T. Leventhal (Eds.), *Handbook of child psychology: Vol. 4. Ecological settings and processes* (7th ed., pp. 6–54). Hoboken, NJ: John Wiley.

English, T., & Carstensen, L. L. (2016). Socioemotional selectivity theory. In N. A. Pachana (Ed.), *Encyclopedia of geropsychology* (pp. 1–6). Singapore: Springer. https://doi.org/10.1007/978-981-287-080-3_110-1

Erikson, E. H. (1950). *Childhood and society* (2nd ed.). New York, NY: Norton.

Evans, D. W., Milanak, M. E., Medeiros, B., & Ross, J. L. (2002). Magical beliefs and rituals in young children. *Child Psychiatry and Human Development, 33,* 43–58.

Fisher, C. B., Busch-Rossnagel, N. A., Jopp, D. S., & Brown, J. (2013). Applied developmental science: Contributions and challenges for the 21st century. In I. B. Weiner (Ed.), *Handbook of psychology* (Vol. 6, pp. 517–546). Hoboken, NJ.

Flavell, J. H. (1992). Cognitive development: Past, present, and future. *Developmental Psychology, 28,* 998–1005.

Frankenhuis, W. E., & Tiokhin, L. (2018). Bridging evolutionary biology and developmental psychology: Toward an enduring theoretical infrastructure. *Child Development.* Advance online publication. doi:10.1111/cdev.13021

Garrison, E. G., & Kobor, P. C. (2002). Weathering a political storm: A contextual perspective on a psychological research controversy. *American Psychologist, 57,* 165–175.

Gauvain, M. (2018). From developmental psychologist to water scientist and back again: The role of interdisciplinary research in developmental science. *Child Development Perspectives, 12*, 45–50. doi:10.1111/cdep.12255

Golinkoff, R. M., Hirsh-Pasek, K., Grob, R., & Schlesinger, M. (2017). "Oh, the places you'll go" by bringing developmental science into the world! *Child Development, 88*, 1403–1408. doi:10.1111/cdev.12929

Halford, G. S., & Andrews, G. (2011). Information-processing models of cognitive development. In U. Goswami (Ed.). *The Wiley-Blackwell handbook of childhood cognitive development* (2nd ed., pp. 697–721). Hoboken, NJ: Wiley-Blackwell.

Herman, G. T. (2009). *Fundamentals of computerized tomography: Image reconstruction from projections.* New York, NY: Springer.

Hess, T. M., Leclerc, C. M., Swaim, E., & Weatherbee, S. R. (2009). Aging and everyday judgments: The impact of motivational and processing resource factors. *Psychology and Aging, 24*, 735–740. doi:10.1037/a0016340

Hiriscau, I. E., Stingelin-Giles, N., Stadler, C., Schmeck, K., & Reiter-Theil, S. (2014). A right to confidentiality or a duty to disclose? Ethical guidance for conducting prevention research with children and adolescents. *European Child & Adolescent Psychiatry, 23*, 409–416. doi:10.1007/s00787-014-0526-y

Hoff, E. (2014). *Language development* (M. H. Bornstein & M. E. Lamb, Eds.). In *Developmental science: An advanced textbook* (5th ed.). New York, NY: Psychology Press.

Holmes, C. J., Kim-Spoon, J., & Deater-Deckard, K. (2016). Linking executive function and peer problems from early childhood through middle adolescence. *Journal of Abnormal Child Psychology, 44*, 31–42. doi:10.1007/s10802-015-0044-5

Huston, A. C. (2018). A life at the intersection of science and social issues. *Child Development Perspectives, 12*, 75–79. doi:10.1111/cdep.12265

Jaeger, E. L. (2016). Negotiating complexity: A bioecological systems perspective on literacy development. *Human Development, 59*, 163–187. doi:10.1159/000448743

Kamper-DeMarco, K. E., & Ostrov, J. M. (2017). Prospective associations between peer victimization and social-psychological adjustment problems in early childhood. *Aggressive Behavior, 43*, 471–482. doi:10.1002/ab.21705

Keller, K., & Engelhardt, M. (2013). Strength and muscle mass loss with aging process: Age and strength loss. *Muscles, Ligaments and Tendons Journal, 3*, 346–350. Retrieved from http://europepmc.org/articles/PMC3940510/? report=abstract

Kuther, T. L. (2003). Medical decision-making and minors: Issues of consent and assent. *Adolescence, 38*, 343–359.

Lampl, M., Johnson, M. L., Frongillo Jr., E., & Frongillo, E. A. (2001). Mixed distribution analysis identifies saltation and stasis growth. *Annals of Human Biology, 28*, 403–411.

Legare, C. H., Clegg, J. M., & Wen, N. J. (2018). Evolutionary developmental psychology: 2017 redux. *Child Development.* Advance online publication. doi:10.1111/cdev.13018

Lerner, R. M. (2012). Developmental science: Past, present, and future. *International Journal of Developmental Science, 6*, 29–36. doi:10.3233/DEV-2012-12102

Lerner, R. M., Agans, J. P., DeSouza, L. M., & Hershberg, R. M. (2014). Developmental science in 2025: A predictive review. *Research in Human Development, 11*, 255–272. doi:10.1080/15427609.2014.967046

Lerner, R. M., Johnson, S. K., & Buckingham, M. H. (2015). Relational developmental systems-based theories and the study of children and families: Lerner and Spanier (1978) revisited. *Journal of Family Theory & Review, 7*, 83–104. doi:10.1111/jftr.12067

Lickliter, R., & Witherington, D. C. (2017). Towards a truly developmental epigenetics. *Human Development, 60*, 124–138. doi:10.1159/000477996

Lorenz, K. (1952). *King Solomon's ring.* New York, NY: Crowell.

Luna, B., Marek, S., Larsen, B., Tervo-Clemmens, B., & Chahal, R. (2015). An integrative model of the maturation of cognitive control. *Annual Review of Neuroscience, 38*, 151–170. doi:10.1146/annurev-neuro-071714-034054

Luthar, S. S., Crossman, E. J., Small, P. J., Luthar, S. S., Crossman, E. J., & Small, P. J. (2015). Resilience and Adversity. In M. E. Lamb (Ed.), *Handbook of child psychology and developmental science* (pp. 1–40). Hoboken, NJ: Wiley. doi:10.1002/9781118963418.childpsy307

Macapagal, K., Coventry, R., Arbeit, M. R., Fisher, C. B., & Mustanski, B. (2017). I won't out myself just to do a survey: Sexual and gender minority adolescents' perspectives on the risks and benefits of sex research. *Archives of Sexual Behavior, 46*, 1393–1409. doi:10.1007/s10508-016-0784-5

Margrett, J. A., Allaire, J. C., Johnson, T. L., Daugherty, K. E., & Weatherbee, S. R. (2010). Everyday problem solving. In J. C. Cavanaugh, C. K. Cavanaugh, J. Berry, & R. West (Eds.), *Aging in America: Vol. 1. Psychological aspects* (pp. 80–101). Santa Barbara, CA: Praeger/ABC-CLIO.

Markus, H. R., & Kitayama, S. (1991). Culture and the self: Implications for cognition, emotion, and motivation. *Psychological Review, 98*, 224–253. doi:10.1037/0033-295X.98.2.224

Markus, H. R., & Kitayama, S. (2010). Cultures and selves: A cycle of mutual constitution. *Perspectives on Psychological Science, 5*, 420–430. doi:10.1177/1745691610375557

Masten, A. S. (2016). Resilience in developing systems: The promise of integrated approaches. *European Journal of Developmental Psychology, 13*, 297–312. doi:10.1080/17405629.2016.1147344

McAuley, E., Wójcicki, T. R., Gothe, N. P., Mailey, E. L., Szabo, A. N., Fanning, J., . . . Mullen, S. P. (2013). Effects of a DVD-delivered exercise intervention on physical function in older adults. *Journals of Gerontology Series A: Biological Sciences & Medical Sciences, 68*, 1076–1082.

Meaney, M. J. (2017). Epigenetics and the biology of gene × environment interactions. In P. H. Tolan & B. L. Leventhal (Eds.), *Gene-environment transactions in developmental psychopathology* (pp. 59–94). Cham, Switzerland: Springer International. doi:10.1007/978-3-319-49227-8_4

Mehl, M. R. (2017). The electronically activated recorder (EAR). *Current Directions in Psychological Science, 26*, 184–190. doi:10.1177/0963721416680611

Miech, R. A., Johnston, L. D., O'Malley, P. M., Bachman, J. G., Schulenberg, J. E., & Patrick, M. E. (2017). *Monitoring the Future national survey results on drug use, 1975–2016: Vol. 1. Secondary school students.* Retrieved from http://www.monitoringthefuture.org/pubs/monographs/mtf-vol1_2016.pdf

Miller, P. H. (2016). *Theories of developmental psychology* (6th ed.). New York, NY: Worth.

Mistry, J. (2013). Integration of culture and biology in human development. *Advances in Child Development and Behavior, 45*, 287–314. Retrieved from http://www.ncbi.nlm.nih.gov/pubmed/23865120

Mistry, J., & Dutta, R. (2015). Human development and culture. *Handbook of Child Psychology and Developmental Science, 1*, 1–38. doi:10.1002/9781118963418.childpsy110

Mistry, J., Li, J., Yoshikawa, H., Tseng, V., Tirrell, J., Kiang, L., . . . Wang, Y. (2016). An integrated conceptual framework for the development of Asian American children and youth. *Child Development, 87*, 1014–1032. doi:10.1111/cdev.12577

Moran, R. J., Symmonds, M., Dolan, R. J., & Friston, K. J. (2014). The brain ages optimally to model its environment: Evidence from sensory learning over the adult lifespan. *PLoS Computational Biology, 10*, 1–8. doi:10.1371/journal.pcbi.1003422

Müller, U., Kerns, K., Müller, U., & Kerns, K. (2015). The development of executive function. In R. M. Lerner (Ed.), *Handbook of child psychology and developmental science* (7th ed., pp. 1–53). New York, NY: John Wiley. doi:10.1002/9781118963418.childpsy214

Newell, B. R., & Shanks, D. R. (2014). Unconscious influences on decision making: A critical review. *Behavioral and Brain Sciences, 38*, 1–19. doi:10.1017/S0140525X12003214

Oulton, K., Gibson, F., Sell, D., Williams, A., Pratt, L., & Wray, J. (2016). Assent for children's participation in research: Why it matters and making it meaningful. *Child: Care, Health and Development, 42*, 588–597. doi:10.1111/cch.12344

Overton, W. F., & Molenaar, P. C. M. (2015). Concepts, theory, and method in developmental science: A view of the issues. In W. F. Overton & P. C. M. Molenaar (Eds.), *Handbook of child psychology and developmental science: Vol. 1. Theory and method* (pp. 1–8). Hoboken, NJ: John Wiley.

Oyserman, D. (2016). What does a priming persepctive reveal about culture: Culture-as-situated cognition. *Current Opinion in Psychology, 12*, 94–99. doi:10.1016/j.copsyc.2016.10.002

Oyserman, D. (2017). Culture three ways: Cultures and subcultures within countries. *Annual Review of Psychology, 68*, 1–29.

Payne, V. G., & Isaacs, L. D. (2016). *Human motor development: A lifespan approach.* New York, NY: McGraw-Hill.

Pezaro, N., Doody, J. S., & Thompson, M. B. (2017). The ecology and evolution of temperature-dependent reaction norms for sex determination in reptiles: A mechanistic conceptual model. *Biological Reviews, 92*, 1348–1364. doi:10.1111/brv.12285

Piaget, J. (1929). *The child's conception of the world.* London, England: Routledge & Kegan Paul.

Portnow, L. H., Vaillancourt, D. E., & Okun, M. S. (2013). The history of cerebral PET scanning: From physiology to cutting-edge technology. *Neurology, 80,* 952–956. doi:10.1212/WNL.0b013e318285c135

Prusaczyk, B., Cherney, S. M., Carpenter, C. R., & DuBois, J. M. (2017). Informed consent to research with cognitively impaired adults: Transdisciplinary challenges and opportunities. *Clinical Gerontologist, 40,* 63–73. doi:10.1080/07317115.2016.1201714

Rind, B., Tromovitch, P., & Bauserman, R. (1998). A meta-analytic examination of assumed properties of child sexual abuse using college samples. *Psychological Bulletin, 124,* 22–53.

Ristic, J., & Enns, J. T. (2015). Attentional development. In L. S. Liben & U. Muller (Eds.), *Handbook of child psychology and developmental science* (pp. 1–45). Hoboken, NJ: John Wiley. doi:10.1002/9781118963418. childpsy205

Rogler, L. H. (2002). Historical generations and psychology: The case of the Great Depression and World War II. *American Psychologist, 57,* 1013–1023.

Rogoff, B. (2016). Culture and participation: A paradigm shift. *Current Opinion in Psychology, 8,* 182–189. doi:10.1016/j.copsyc.2015.12.002

Rogoff, B., Moore, L. C., Correa-Chavez, M., & Dexter, A. L. (2014). Children develop cultural repertoires through engaging in everyday routines and practices. In J. Grusec & P. Hastings (Eds.), *Handbook of socialization: Theory and research* (pp. 472–498). New York, NY: Guilford.

Roth-Cline, M., & Nelson, R. M. (2013). Parental permission and child assent in research on children. *The Yale Journal of Biology and Medicine, 86,* 291–301. Retrieved from http://www.ncbi.nlm.nih.gov/pubmed/24058304

Rutter, M. (2014). Nature–nurture integration. In M. Lewis & K. D. Rudolph (Eds.), *Handbook of developmental psychopathology* (pp. 45–65). Boston, MA: Springer US. doi:10.1007/978-1-4614-9608-3_3

Schwaba, T., & Bleidorn, W. (2017). Individual differences in personality change across the adult life span. *Journal of Personality, 86*(3), 450–484. https://doi.org/10.1111/jopy.12327

Sharkey, J. D., Reed, L. A., & Felix, E. D. (2017). Dating and sexual violence research in the schools: Balancing protection of confidentiality with supporting the welfare of survivors. *American Journal of Community Psychology, 60*(3–4), 361–367. https://doi.org/10.1002/ajcp.12186

Siegler, R. S. (2016). How does change occur? In R. Sternberg, S. Fiske, & D. Foss (Eds.), *Scientists making a difference: One hundred eminent behavioral and brain scientists talk about their most important contributions* (pp. 223–227). New York, NY: Cambridge University Press.

Siekerman, K., Barbu-Roth, M., Anderson, D. I., Donnelly, A., Goffinet, F., & Teulier, C. (2015). Treadmill stimulation improves newborn stepping. *Developmental Psychobiology, 57,* 247–254. doi:10.1002/dev.21270

Simons, S. S. H., Cillessen, A. H. N., & de Weerth, C. (2017). Cortisol stress responses and children's behavioral functioning at school. *Developmental Psychobiology, 59,* 217–224. doi:10.1002/dev.21484

Soares, J. M., Marques, P., Alves, V., & Sousa, N. (2013). A hitchhiker's guide to diffusion tensor imaging. *Frontiers in Neuroscience, 7,* 31. doi:10.3389/fnins.2013.00031

Society for Research in Child Development. (2007). *Ethical standards in research.* Retrieved from http://www.srcd.org/about-us/ethical-standards-research

Tait, A. R., & Geisser, M. E. (2017). Development of a consensus operational definition of child assent for research. *BMC Medical Ethics, 18,* 41. doi:10.1186/s12910-017-0199-4

Triebel, K., Martin, R., Novack, T., Dreer, L., Turner, C., Kennedy, R., & Marson, D. (2014). Recovery over 6 months of medical decision-making capacity after traumatic brain injury. *Archives of Physical Medicine and Rehabilitation, 95,* 2296–2303. doi:10.1016/J.APMR.2014.07.413

Troutman, B. (2015). Viewing parent–child interactions through the lens of behaviorism. In B. Troutman (Ed.), *Integrating behaviorism and attachment theory in parent coaching* (pp. 3–20). Cham, Switzerland: Springer. doi:10.1007/978-3-319-15239-4_1

Tudge, J. R. H., Payir, A., Merçon-Vargas, E., Cao, H., Liang, Y., Li, J., & O'Brien, L. (2016). Still misused after all these years? A reevaluation of the uses of Bronfenbrenner's bioecological theory of human development. *Journal of Family Theory & Review, 8,* 427–445. doi:10.1111/jftr.12165

United Nations General Assembly. (2015). *Transforming our world: The 2030 agenda for sustainable development.* Retrieved from undocs.org/A/RES/70/1.

Vélez-Agosto, N. M., Soto-Crespo, J. G., Vizcarrondo-Oppenheimer, M., Vega-Molina, S., & Garcia Coll, C. (2017). Bronfenbrenner's bioecological theory revision: Moving culture from the macro into the micro. *Perspectives on Psychological Science, 12,* 900–910. doi:10.1177/1745691617704397

Vraga, E., Bode, L., & Troller-Renfree, S. (2016). Beyond self-reports: Using eye tracking to measure topic and style differences in attention to social media content. *Communication Methods and Measures, 10,* 149–164. doi:10.1080/19312458.2016.1150443

Vygotsky, L. S. (1978). *Mind in society: The development of higher psychological processes.* Cambridge, MA: Harvard University Press.

Watson, J. (1925). *Behaviorism.* New York, NY: Norton.

Westen, D. (1998). The scientific legacy of Sigmund Freud: Toward a psychodynamically informed psychological science. *Psychological Bulletin, 124,* 333–371.

Wetzel, N., Buttelmann, D., Schieler, A., & Widmann, A. (2016). Infant and adult pupil dilation in response to unexpected sounds. *Developmental Psychobiology, 58,* 382–392. doi:10.1002/dev.21377

Willis, S. L., & Belleville, S. (2016). Cognitive training in later adulthood. In K. W. Schaie & S. L. Willis (Eds.), *Handbook of the psychology of aging* (8th ed., pp. 219–243). Waltham, MA: Elsevier.

Witherington, D. C., & Lickliter, R. (2016). Integrating development and evolution in psychological science: Evolutionary developmental psychology, developmental systems, and explanatory pluralism. *Human Development, 59,* 200–234. doi:10.1159/000450715

Wolf, R. M., & Long, D. (2016). Pubertal development. *Pediatrics in Review, 37,* 292–300. doi:10.1542/pir.2015-0065

Worobey, J. (2014). Physical activity in infancy: Developmental aspects, measurement, and importance. *American Journal of Clinical Nutrition, 99,* 729S–733S. doi:10.3945/ajcn.113.072397

Wortman, J., Lucas, R. E., & Donnellan, M. B. (2012). Stability and change in the Big Five personality domains: Evidence from a longitudinal study of Australians. *Psychology and Aging, 27,* 867–874. doi:10.1037/a002932210.1037/a0029322.supp

Yoshikawa, H., Mistry, R., & Wang, Y. (2016). Advancing methods in research on Asian American children and youth. *Child Development, 87,* 1033–1050. doi:10.1111/cdev.12576

Zaitchik, D., Iqbal, Y., & Carey, S. (2014). The effect of executive function on biological reasoning in young children: An individual differences study. *Child Development, 85,* 160–175. doi:10.1111/cdev.12145

Chapter 2

Adolph, K. E., & Franchak, J. M. (2017). The development of motor behavior. *Wiley Interdisciplinary Reviews: Cognitive Science, 8,* e1430. doi:10.1002/wcs.1430

Akolekar, R., Beta, J., Picciarelli, G., Ogilvie, C., & D'Antonio, F. (2015). Procedure-related risk of miscarriage following amniocentesis and chorionic villus sampling: A systematic review and meta-analysis. *Ultrasound in Obstetrics & Gynecology, 45,* 16–26. doi:10.1002/uog.14636

American College of Obstetricians and Gynecologists & Society for Maternal-Fetal Medicine. (2014). Practice bulletin No 144. *Obstetrics & Gynecology, 123,* 1118–1132. doi:10.1097/01.AOG.0000446856.51061.3e

Aston, K. I., Peterson, C. M., & Carrell, D. T. (2008). Monozygotic twinning associated with assisted reproductive technologies: A review. *Reproduction, 136,* 377–386. Retrieved from http://www.reproduction-online.org/content/136/4/377.full?sid=0d0ae256-57c7-4146-99fee3866623b5d7

Bakermans-Kranenburg, M. J., & van IJzendoorn, M. H. (2015). The hidden efficacy of interventions: Gene × environment experiments from a differential susceptibility perspective. *Annual Review of Psychology, 66,* 381–409. doi:10.1146/annurev-psych-010814-015407

Bale, T. L. (2015). Epigenetic and transgenerational reprogramming of brain development. *Nature Reviews Neuroscience, 16,* 332–344. doi:10.1038/nrn3818

Balenzano, C., Coppola, G., Cassibba, R., & Moro, G. (2018). Pre-adoption adversities and adoptees' outcomes: The protective role of post-adoption variables in an Italian experience of domestic open adoption. *Children and Youth Services Review, 85,* 307–318. doi:10.1016/J.CHILDYOUTH.2018.01.012

Bardsley, M. Z., Kowal, K., Levy, C., Gosek, A., Ayari, N., Tartaglia, N., . . . Ross, J. L. (2013). 47,XYY syndrome: Clinical phenotype and timing of ascertainment. *Journal of Pediatrics, 163,* 1085–1094. doi:10.1016/j.jpeds.2013.05.037

Barlow-Stewart, K., & Saleh, M. (2012). Prenatal testing overview. Retrieved from http://www.genetics.edu.au/Information/Genetics-Fact-Sheets/PrenatalTesting-Overview-FS17

Barone, L., Lionetti, F., & Green, J. (2017). A matter of attachment? How adoptive parents foster post institutionalized children's social and emotional adjustment. *Attachment & Human Development, 19,* 323–339. doi:10.1080/14616734.2017.1306714

Beach, S. R. H., Brody, G. H., Gunter, T. D., Packer, H., Wernett, P., & Philibert, R. A. (2010). Child maltreatment moderates the association of MAOA with symptoms of depression and antisocial personality disorder. *Journal of Family Psychology, 24,* 12–20. doi:10.1037/a0018074

Beitsch, R. (2017). As surrogacy surges, new parents seek legal protections. Retrieved from http://www.pewtrusts.org/en/research-and-analysis/blogs/stateline/2017/06/29/as-surrogacy-surges-new-parents-seek-legal-protections

Belsky, J., & Hartman, S. (2014). Gene-environment interaction in evolutionary perspective: Differential susceptibility to environmental influences. *World Psychiatry, 13,* 87–89. doi:10.1002/wps.20092

Bhatia, R. (2010). Constructing gender from the inside out: Sex-selection practices in the United States. *Feminist Studies, 36,* 260–291.

Bird, R. J., & Hurren, B. J. (2016). Anatomical and clinical aspects of Klinefelter's syndrome. *Clinical Anatomy, 29,* 606–619. doi:10.1002/ca.22695

Blau, N. (2016). Genetics of phenylketonuria: Then and now. *Human Mutation, 37,* 508–515. doi:10.1002/humu.22980

Blau, N., Shen, N., & Carducci, C. (2014). Molecular genetics and diagnosis of phenylketonuria: State of the art. *Expert Review of Molecular Diagnostics, 14,* 655–671. doi:10.1586/14737159.2014.923760

Boivin, M., Brendgen, M., Vitaro, F., Forget-Dubois, N., Feng, B., Tremblay, R. E., & Dionne, G. (2013). Evidence of gene-environment correlation for peer difficulties: Disruptive behaviors predict early peer relation difficulties in school through genetic effects. *Development and Psychopathology, 25,* 79–92. doi:10.1017/S0954579412000910

Bonomi, M., Rochira, V., Pasquali, D., Balercia, G., Jannini, E. A., & Ferlin, A. (2017). Klinefelter syndrome (KS): Genetics, clinical phenotype and hypogonadism. *Journal of Endocrinological Investigation, 40,* 123–134. doi:10.1007/s40618-016-0541-6

Bouchard, T. J. (2014). Genes, evolution and intelligence. *Behavior Genetics, 44,* 549–577. doi:10.1007/s10519-014-9646-x

Brown, A., Waters, C. S., & Shelton, K. H. (2017). A systematic review of the school performance and behavioural and

emotional adjustments of children adopted from care. *Adoption & Fostering, 41,* 346–368. doi:10.1177/0308575917731064

Buiting, K., Williams, C., & Horsthemke, B. (2016). Angelman syndrome—insights into a rare neurogenetic disorder. *Nature Reviews Neurology, 12,* 584–593. doi:10.1038/nrneurol.2016.133

Burt, A. (2009). A mechanistic explanation of popularity: Genes, rule breaking, and evocative gene environment correlations. *Journal of Personality and Social Psychology, 96,* 783–794. doi:10.1037/a0013702

Butler, M. G., Manzardo, A. M., Heinemann, J., Loker, C., & Loker, J. (2016). Causes of death in Prader Willi syndrome: Prader-Willi Syndrome Association (USA) 40-year mortality survey. *Genetics in Medicine, 19,* 635. doi:10.1038/gim.2016.178

Byrd, A. L., & Manuck, S. B. (2014). MAOA, childhood maltreatment, and antisocial behavior: Meta analysis of a gene-environment interaction. *Biological Psychiatry, 75,* 9–17. doi:10.1016/j.biopsych.2013.05.004

Caspi, A., McClay, J., Moffitt, T. E., Mill, J., Martin, J., Craig, I. W., . . . Poulton, R. (2002). Role of genotype in the cycle of violence in maltreated children. *Science, 297,* 851–854. doi:10.1126/science.1072290

Centers for Disease Control and Prevention. (2017). Infertility. Retrieved from https://www.cdc.gov/reproductivehealth/infertility/index.htm

Chabris, C. F., Lee, J. J., Cesarini, D., Benjamin, D. J., & Laibson, D. I. (2015). The fourth law of behavior genetics. *Current Directions in Psychological Science, 24,* 304–312. doi:10.1177/0963721415580430

Chaibal, S., Bennett, S., Rattanathanthong, K., & Siritaratiwat, W. (2016). Early developmental milestones and age of independent walking in orphans compared with typical home-raised infants. *Early Human Development, 101,* 23–26. doi:10.1016/J.EARLHUMDEV.2016.06.008

Chakravorty, S., & Williams, T. N. (2015). Sickle cell disease: A neglected chronic disease of increasing global health importance. *Archives of Disease in Childhood, 100,* 48–53. doi:10.1136/archdischild-2013-303773

Chan, W., Kwok, Y., Choy, K., Leung, T., & Wang, C. (2013). Single fetal cells for non-invasive prenatal genetic diagnosis: Old myths new prospective. *Medical Journal of Obstetrics and Gynecology, 1,* 1004.

Chhangur, R. R., Weeland, J., Overbeek, G., Matthys, W., Orobio de Castro, B., van der Giessen, D., & Belsky, J. (2017). Genetic moderation of intervention efficacy: Dopaminergic genes, The Incredible Years, and externalizing behavior in children. *Child Development, 88,* 796–811. doi:10.1111/cdev.12612

Christopoulos, P., Deligeoroglou, E., Laggari, V., Christogiorgos, S., & Creatsas, G. (2008). Psychological and behavioural aspects of patients with Turner syndrome from childhood to adulthood: A review of the clinical literature. *Journal of Psychosomatic Obstetrics & Gynaecology, 29,* 45–51. doi:10.1080/01674820701577078

Cicchetti, D., Rogosch, F. A., & Sturge-Apple, M. L. (2007). Interactions of child maltreatment and serotonin transporter and monoamine

oxidase A polymorphisms: Depressive symptomatology among adolescents from low socioeconomic status backgrounds. *Development and Psychopathology, 19,* 1161–1180. doi:10.1017/S0954579407000600

Colls, P., Silver, L., Olivera, G., Weier, J., Escudero, T., Goodall, N., . . . Munné, S. (2009). Preimplantation genetic diagnosis for gender selection in the USA. *Reproductive BioMedicine Online, 19,* 16–22.

Corrigall, K. A., & Schellenberg, E. G. (2015). Predicting who takes music lessons: Parent and child characteristics. *Frontiers in Psychology, 6,* 282. doi:10.3389/fpsyg.2015.00282

Council of Europe. (1997). *Convention for the protection of human rights and dignity of the human being with regard to the application of biology and medicine: Convention on human rights and biomedicine.* Oviedo, Spain. Retrieved from http://conventions.coe.int/Treaty/en/Treaties/Html/164.htm

Coutelle, C., & Waddington, S. N. (2012). The concept of prenatal gene therapy. *Methods in Molecular Biology, 891,* 1–7. doi:10.1007/978-1-61779-873-3_1

Covelli, V., Raggi, A., Meucci, P., Paganelli, C., & Leonardi, M. (2016). Ageing of people with Down's syndrome. *International Journal of Rehabilitation Research, 39,* 20–28. doi:10.1097/MRR.0000000000000147

Croke, K., Ishengoma, D. S., Francis, F., Makani, J., Kamugisha, M. L., Lusingu, J., . . . Mbando, B. P. (2017). Relationships between sickle cell trait, malaria, and educational outcomes in Tanzania. *BMC Infectious Diseases, 17,* 568. doi:10.1186/s12879-017-2644-x

Culen, C., Ertl, D.-A., Schubert, K., Bartha-Doering, L., & Haeusler, G. (2017). Care of girls and women with Turner syndrome: Beyond growth and hormones. *Endocrine Connections, 6,* R39–R51. doi:10.1530/EC-17-0036

Darnovsky, M. (2009). Countries with laws or policies on sex selection. Memo for the April 13 New York City Sex Selection Meeting. Berkeley, CA. Retrieved from http://geneticsandsociety.org/downloads/200904_sex_selection_memo.pdf

Davis, A. S., & Escobar, L. F. (2013). Early childhood cognitive disorders: Down syndrome. In A. S. Davis (Ed.), *Psychopathology of childhood and adolescence: A neuropsychological approach* (pp. 569–580). New York, NY: Springer.

Deater-Deckard, K. (2001). Nonshared environmental processes in social emotional development: An observational study of identical twin differences in the preschool period. *Developmental Science, 4,* 1–7.

Deater-Deckard, K., & O'Connor, T. (2000). Parent-child mutuality in early childhood: Two behavioral genetic studies. *Developmental Psychology, 36,* 561–571.

Deeney, M. (2013). Bioethical considerations of preimplantation genetic diagnosis for sex selection. *Washington University Jurisprudence Review.* Retrieved from http://digitalcommons.law.wustl.edu/jurisprudence/vol5/iss2/5

de Graaf, G., Buckley, F., Dever, J., & Skotko, B. G. (2017). Estimation of live birth and population prevalence of Down syndrome in nine U.S. states. *American Journal of Medical*

Genetics Part A, 173, 2710–2719. doi:10.1002/ajmg.a.38402

Deprest, J. A., Devlieger, R., Srisupundit, K., Beck, V., Sandaite, I., Rusconi, S., . . . Lewi, L. (2010). Fetal surgery is a clinical reality. *Seminars in Fetal & Neonatal Medicine, 15*, 58–67. doi:10.1016/j.siny.2009.10.002

Dodge, K. A., & Rutter, M. (2011). *Gene-environment interactions in developmental psychopathology*. New York, NY: Guilford.

Doherty, B. R., & Scerif, G. (2017). Genetic syndromes and developmental risk for autism spectrum and attention deficit hyperactivity disorders: Insights from fragile X syndrome. *Child Development Perspectives, 11*, 161–166. doi:10.1111/cdep.12227

Dolinoy, D. C. (2008). The agouti mouse model: An epigenetic biosensor for nutritional and environmental alterations on the fetal epigenome. *Nutrition Reviews, 66*, 7–11. doi:10.1111/j.1753-4887.2008.00056.x

Dondorp, W., De Wert, G., Pennings, G., Shenfield, F., Devroey, P., Tarlatzis, B., . . . Diedrich, K. (2013). ESHRE task force on ethics and law 20: Sex selection for non-medical reasons. *Human Reproduction, 28*, 1448–1454. doi:10.1093/humrep/det109

Dubois, L., Ohm Kyvik, K., Girard, M., Tatone-Tokuda, F., Pérusse, D., Hjelmborg, J., . . . Martin, N. G. (2012). Genetic and environmental contributions to weight, height, and BMI from birth to 19 years of age: An international study of over 12,000 twin pairs. *PLoS ONE, 7*(2). doi:10.1371/journal.pone.0030153

Eigsti, I.-M., Weitzman, C., Schuh, J., de Marchena, A., & Casey, B. J. (2011). Language and cognitive outcomes in internationally adopted children. *Development and Psychopathology, 23*, 629 646. doi:10.1017/S0954579411000204

Esposito, G., Truzzi, A., Setoh, P., Putnick, D. L., Shinohara, K., & Bornstein, M. H. (2017). Genetic predispositions and parental bonding interact to shape adults' physiological responses to social distress. *Behavioural Brain Research, 325*, 156–162. doi:10.1016/J.BBR.2016.06.042

Ethics Committee of the American Society for Reproductive Medicine. (2001). Preconception gender selection for nonmedical reasons. *Fertility and Sterility, 75*, 861–864.

Fauser, B. C. J. M., Devroey, P., Diedrich, K., Balaban, B., Bonduelle, M., Delemarre-van de Waal, H. A., . . . Wells, D. (2014). Health outcomes of children born after IVF/ICSI: A review of current expert opinion and literature. *Reproductive BioMedicine Online, 28*, 162–182. doi:10.1016/J.RBMO.2013.10.013

Fergusson, D. M., Boden, J. M., Horwood, L. J., Miller, A. L., & Kennedy, M. A. (2011). MAOA, abuse exposure and antisocial behaviour: 30-year longitudinal study. *British Journal of Psychiatry: Journal of Mental Science, 198*, 457–463. doi:10.1192/bjp.bp.110.086991

Finegold, D. N. (2017). Overview of genetics. *Merck Manual*. Retrieved from http://www.merckmanuals.com/professional/special-subjects/general-principles-of-medicalgenetics/overview-of-genetics

Flatt, T. (2005). The evolutionary genetics of canalization. *Quarterly Review of Biology, 80*, 287–316.

Fox, K. A., & Saade, G. (2012). Fetal blood sampling and intrauterine transfusion.

NeoReviews, 13, e661–e669. doi:10.1542/neo.13-11-e661

Garber, K. J., & Grotevant, H. D. (2015). "YOU were adopted?!" *The Counseling Psychologist, 43*, 435–462. doi:10.1177/0011000014566471

Ghezzo, A., Salvioli, S., Solimando, M. C., Palmieri, A., Chiostergi, C., Scurti, M., . . . Franceschi, C. (2014). Age-related changes of adaptive and neuropsychological features in persons with Down syndrome. *PLoS ONE, 9*, e113111. doi:10.1371/journal.pone.0113111

Glasson, E. J., Dye, D. E., & Bittles, A. H. (2014). The triple challenges associated with age-related comorbidities in Down syndrome. *Journal of Intellectual Disability Research, 58*, 393–398. doi:10.1111/jir.12026

Glennen, S. (2014). A longitudinal study of language and speech in children who were internationally adopted at different ages. *Language, Speech, and Hearing Services in Schools, 45*, 185–203. doi:10.1044/2014_LSHSS-13-0035

Goldberg, A. E., Downing, J. B., & Moyer, A. M. (2012). Why parenthood, and why now? Gay men's motivations for pursuing parenthood. *Family Relations, 61*, 157–174. Retrieved from http://www.ncbi.nlm.nih.gov/pubmed/22563135

Golombok, S. (2013). Families created by reproductive donation: Issues and research. *Child Development Perspectives, 7*, 61–65. doi:10.1111/cdep.12015

Golombok, S., Ilioi, E., Blake, L., Roman, G., & Jadva, V. (2017). A longitudinal study of families formed through reproductive donation: Parent–adolescent relationships and adolescent adjustment at age 14. *Developmental Psychology, 53*, 1966–1977. doi:10.1037/dev0000372

Gong, L., Parikh, S., Rosenthal, P. J., & Greenhouse, B. (2013). Biochemical and immunological mechanisms by which sickle cell trait protects against malaria. *Malaria Journal. 12*, 317. doi:10.1186/1475-2875-12-317

Gottlieb, G. (2000). Environmental and behavioral influences on gene activity. *Current Directions in Psychological Science, 9*, 93–97. doi: 10.1111/1467-8721.00068

Gottlieb, G. (2007). Probabilistic epigenesis. *Developmental Science, 10*, 1–11. doi:10.1111/j.1467-7687.2007.00556.x

Gregg, A. R., Gross, S. J., Best, R. G., Monaghan, K. G., Bajaj, K., Skotko, B. G., . . . Watson, M. S. (2013). ACMG statement on noninvasive prenatal screening for fetal aneuploidy. *Genetics in Medicine, 15*, 395–398. doi:10.1038/gim.2013.29

Grieco, J., Pulsifer, M., Seligsohn, K., Skotko, B., & Schwartz, A. (2015). Down syndrome: Cognitive and behavioral functioning across the lifespan. *American Journal of Medical Genetics Part C: Seminars in Medical Genetics, 169*, 135–149. doi:10.1002/ajmg.c.31439

Griffiths, P. D., Bradburn, M., Campbell, M. J., Cooper, C. L., Graham, R., Jarvis, D., . . . Wailoo, A. (2017). Use of MRI in the diagnosis of fetal brain abnormalities in utero (MERIDIAN): A multicentre, prospective cohort study. *The Lancet, 389*, 538–546. doi:10.1016/S01406736(16)31723-8

Grotevant, H. D., Lo, A. Y. H., Fiorenzo, L., & Dunbar, N. D. (2017). Adoptive identity and adjustment from adolescence to emerging

adulthood: A person-centered approach. *Developmental Psychology, 53*, 2195–2204. doi:10.1037/dev0000352

Grotevant, H. D., & McDermott, J. M. (2014). Adoption: Biological and social processes linked to adaptation. *Annual Review of Psychology, 65*, 235–265. doi:10.1146/annurevpsych-010213-115020

Hagerman, R. J., Berry-Kravis, E., Hazlett, H. C., Bailey, D. B., Moine, H., Kooy, R. F., . . . Hagerman, P. J. (2017). Fragile X syndrome. *Nature Reviews Disease Primers, 3*, 17065. doi:10.1038/nrdp.2017.65

Harwood, R., Feng, X., & Yu, S. (2013). Preadoption adversities and postadoption mediators of mental health and school outcomes among international, foster, and private adoptees in the United States. *Journal of Family Psychology, 27*, 409–420. doi:10.1037/a0032908

Hawks, Z. W., Strube, M. J., Johnson, N. X., Grange, D. K., & White, D. A. (2018). Developmental trajectories of executive and verbal processes in children with phenylketonuria. *Developmental Neuropsychology, 43*, 207–218. doi:10.1080/87565641.2018.1438439

Herlihy, A. S., & McLachlan, R. I. (2015). Screening for Klinefelter syndrome. *Current Opinion in Endocrinology & Diabetes and Obesity, 22*, 224–229. doi:10.1097/MED.0000000000000154

Hithersay, R., Hamburg, S., Knight, B., & Strydom, A. (2017). Cognitive decline and dementia in Down syndrome. *Current Opinion in Psychiatry, 30*, 102–107. doi:10.1097/YCO.0000000000000307

Improda, N., Rezzuto, M., Alfano, S., Parenti, G., Vajro, P., Pignata, C., & Salerno, M. (2012). Precocious puberty in Turner syndrome: Report of a case and review of the literature. *Italian Journal of Pediatrics, 38*, 54. doi:10.1186/1824-7288-38-54

Ioannides, A. S. (2017). Preconception and prenatal genetic counselling. *Best Practice & Research Clinical Obstetrics & Gynaecology, 42*, 2–10. doi:10.1016/j.bpobgyn.2017.04.003

Jacobs, E., Miller, L. C., & Tirella, L. G. (2010). Developmental and behavioral performance of internationally adopted preschoolers: A pilot study. *Child Psychiatry & Human Development, 41*, 15–29. doi:10.1007/s10578-009-0149-6

Jadva, V., Imrie, S., & Golombok, S. (2015). Surrogate mothers 10 years on: A longitudinal study of psychological well-being and relationships with the parents and child. *Human Reproduction, 30*, 373–379. doi:10.1093/humrep/deu339

Jahja, R., Huijbregts, S. C. J., de Sonneville, L. M. J., van der Meere, J. J., Legemaat, A. M., Bosch, A. M., . . . van Spronsen, F. J. (2017). Cognitive profile and mental health in adult Phenylketonuria: A PKU COBESO study. *Neuropsychology, 31*, 437–447. doi:10.1037/neu0000358

Jelenkovic, A., Sund, R., Hur, Y.-M., Yokoyama, Y., Hjelmborg, J. v. B., Möller, S., . . . Silventoinen, K. (2016). Genetic and environmental influences on height from infancy to early adulthood: An individual-based pooled analysis of 45 twin cohorts. *Scientific Reports, 6*, 28496. doi:10.1038/srep28496

Jennings, S., Mellish, L., Tasker, F., Lamb, M., & Golombok, S. (2014). Why adoption? Gay, lesbian, and heterosexual adoptive parents' reproductive experiences and reasons for adoption. *Adoption Quarterly, 17*, 205–226. doi: 10.1080/10926755.2014.891549

Juffer, F., & van IJzendoorn, M. H. (2007). Adoptees do not lack self-esteem: A meta-analysis of studies on self-esteem of transracial, international, and domestic adoptees. *Psychological Bulletin, 133*, 1067–1083. doi:10.1037/0033-2909.133.6.1067

Juul, A., Aksglaede, L., Bay, K., Grigor, K. M., & Skakkebæk, N. E. (2011). Klinefelter syndrome: The forgotten syndrome. *Acta Paediatrica, 100*, 791–792. doi:10.1111/j.16512227.2011.02283.x

Kahn, J., Koh, A., Luckcuck, R., McNeice, J., Walter, E., Yao, W., . . . Link, T. (2016). A Phenylalanine fiasco: The structure of phenylalanine hydroxylase and its impact on phenylketonuria. *The FASEB Journal, 30*(Suppl 1), 665.8–665.8.

Kalsner, L., & Chamberlain, S. J. (2015). Prader-Willi, Angelman, and 15q11-q13 duplication syndromes. *Pediatric Clinics of North America, 62*, 587–606. doi:10.1016/j.pcl.2015.03.004

Kaufmann, W. E., Kidd, S. A., Andrews, H. F., Budimirovic, D. B., Esler, A., Haas-Givler, B., . . . Berry-Kravis, E. (2017). Autism spectrum disorder in fragile X syndrome: Cooccurring conditions and current treatment. *Pediatrics, 139*(Suppl 3), S194–S206. doi:10.1542/peds.2016-1159F

Kelly, S. T., & Spencer, H. G. (2017). Population-genetic models of sex-limited genomic imprinting. *Theoretical Population Biology, 115*, 35–44. doi:10.1016/j.tpb.2017.03.004

Klahr, A. M., Thomas, K. M., Hopwood, C. J., Klump, K. L., & Burt, S. A. (2013). Evocative gene environment correlation in the mother–child relationship: A twin study of interpersonal processes. *Development and Psychopathology, 25*, 105–118. doi:10.1017/S0954579412000934

Knafo, A., & Jaffee, S. R. (2013). Gene–environment correlation in developmental psychopathology. *Development and Psychopathology, 25*, 1–6. doi:10.1017/S0954579412000855

Knopik, V. S., Neiderhiser, J. M., DeFries, J. C., & Plomin, R. (2017). *Behavioral genetics*. New York, NY: Macmillan Higher Education.

Knopman, J. M., Krey, L. C., Oh, C., Lee, J., McCaffrey, C., & Noyes, N. (2014). What makes them split? Identifying risk factors that lead to monozygotic twins after in vitro fertilization. *Fertility and Sterility, 102*, 82–89. doi:10.1016/j.fertnstert.2014.03.039

Koenen, K. C., Amstadter, A. B., & Nugent, N. (2012). Genetic methods in psychology. In H. Cooper, P. M. Camic, D. L. Long, A. T. Panter, D. Rindskopf, & K. J. Sher (Eds.), *APA handbook of research methods in psychology: Vol. 2. Research designs: Quantitative, qualitative, neuropsychological, and biological* (pp. 663–680). Washington, DC: American Psychological Association. doi:10.1037/13620-000

Kohn, T. P., Kohn, J. R., Darilek, S., Ramasamy, R., & Lipshultz, L. (2016). Genetic counseling for men with recurrent pregnancy loss or recurrent implantation failure due to abnormal sperm chromosomal aneuploidy. *Journal of Assisted Reproduction and Genetics, 33*, 571–576. doi:10.1007/s10815-016-0702-8

Kremen, W. S., Panizzon, M. S., & Cannon, T. D. (2016). Genetics and neuropsychology: A merger whose time has come. *Neuropsychology. 30*, 1–5. doi:10.1037/neu0000254

Krüger, O., Korsten, P., & Hoffman, J. I. (2017). The rise of behavioral genetics and the transition to behavioral genomics and beyond. In J. Call, G. M. Burghardt, I. M. Pepperberg, C. T. Snowdon, & T. Zentall (Eds.), *APA handbook of comparative psychology: Basic concepts, methods, neural substrate, and behavior* (pp. 365–379). Washington, DC: American Psychological Association. doi:10.1037/0000011-018

Kruszka, P., Porras, A. R., Sobering, A. K., Ikolo, F. A., La Qua, S., Shotelersuk, V., . . . Muenke, M. (2017). Down syndrome in diverse populations. *American Journal of Medical Genetics Part A, 173*, 42–53. doi:10.1002/ajmg.a.38043

Larion, S., Warsof, S., Maher, K., Peleg, D., & Abuhamad, A. (2016). Success of universal carrier screening for fetal diagnosis of genetic disease. *Obstetrics & Gynecology, 127*, 128S. doi:10.1097/01.AOG.0000483518.67531.79

Lee, N. C., Chien, Y. H., & Hwu, W. L. (2017). A review of biomarkers for Alzheimer's disease in Down syndrome. *Neurology and Therapy, 6*, 69–81. doi:10.1007/s40120-017-0071-y

The Leiden Conference on the Development and Care of Children Without Permanent Parents. (2012). The development and care of institutionally reared children. *Child Development Perspectives, 6*, 174–180. doi:10.1111/j.1750-8606.2011.00231.x

Lerner, R. M., & Overton, W. F. (2017). Reduction to absurdity: Why epigenetics invalidates all models involving genetic reduction. *Human Development, 60*, 107–123. doi:10.1159/000477995

Lester, B. M., Conradt, E., & Marsit, C. (2016). Introduction to the special section on epigenetics. *Child Development, 87*, 29–37. doi:10.1111/cdev.12489

Lewis, R. (2017). *Human genetics*. New York, NY: McGraw-Hill Education.

Lickliter, R., & Witherington, D. C. (2017). Towards a truly developmental epigenetics. *Human Development, 60*, 124–138. doi:10.1159/000477996

Lindenburg, I. T. M., van Kamp, I. L., & Oepkes, D. (2014). Intrauterine blood transfusion: Current indications and associated risks. *Fetal Diagnosis and Therapy, 36*, 263–271. doi:10.1159/000362812

Lynch, K. (2016). Gene-environment correlation. In V. Zeigler-Hill & T. K. Shackelford (Eds.), *Encyclopedia of personality and individual differences* (pp. 1–4). Cham, Switzerland: Springer International. doi:10.1007/978-3319-28099-8_1470-1

Maakaron, J. E. & Taher, A. (2012). Sickle cell anemia. Retrieved from http://emedicine.medscape.com/article/205926-overview#a0156

Malm, K., & Welti, K. (2010). Exploring motivations to adopt. *Adoption Quarterly, 13*, 185–208. doi: 10.1080/10926755.2010.524872

Manuck, S. B., & McCaffery, J. M. (2014). Gene–environment interaction. *Annual Review of Psychology, 65*, 41–70. doi:10.1146/annurev-Psych-010213-115100.

Martin, J. A., Hamilton, B. E., Osterman, M. J., Driscoll, A. K., & Drake, P. (2018). Births: Final data for 2016. *National Vital Statistics Reports, 67*. Retrieved from https://stacks.cdc.gov/view/cdc/51199

Mason, P., & Narad, C. (2005). International adoption: A health and developmental perspective. *Seminars in Speech and Language, 26*, 1–9.

McGue, M., & Christensen, K. (2013). Growing old but not growing apart: Twin similarity in the latter half of the lifespan. *Behavior Genetics, 43*. 1–12. doi:10.1007/s10519-012-9559-5

McKusick, V. A. (1998). *Mendelian inheritance in man: A catalog of human genes and genetic disorders* (12th ed.). Baltimore, MD: Johns Hopkins University Press.

McKusick, V. A. (2007). Mendelian inheritance in man and its online version, OMIM. *American Journal of Human Genetics, 80*, 588–604. doi:10.1086/514346

McKusick-Nathans Institute of Genetic Medicine. (2017). OMIM—online mendelian inheritance in man. Retrieved from http://www.omim.org/about

McRae, K., Rhee, S. H., Gatt, J. M., Godinez, D., Williams, L. M., & Gross, J. J. (2017). Genetic and environmental influences on emotion regulation: A twin study of cognitive reappraisal and expressive suppression. *Emotion, 17*, 772–777. doi:10.1037/emo0000300

Meaney, M. J. (2017). Epigenetics and the biology of gene × environment interactions. In P. H. Tolan & B. L. Leventhal (Eds.), *Gene-environment transactions in developmental psychopathology* (pp. 59–94). Cham, Switzerland: Springer International. doi:10.1007/978-3-319-49227-8_4

Medford, E., Hare, D. J., & Wittkowski, A. (2017). *Demographic and psychosocial influences on treatment adherence for children and adolescents with PKU: A systematic review*. Berlin, Germany: Springer. doi:10.1007/8904_2017_52

Merz, E. C., Harlé, K. M., Noble, K. G., & McCall, R. B. (2016). Executive function in previously institutionalized children. *Child Development Perspectives, 10*, 105–110. doi:10.1111/cdep.12170

Milani, H. J., Araujo Júnior, E., Cavalheiro, S., Oliveira, P. S., Hisaba, W. J., Barreto, E. Q. S., . . . Moron, A. F. (2015). Fetal brain tumors: Prenatal diagnosis by ultrasound and magnetic resonance imaging. *World Journal of Radiology, 7*, 17–21. doi:10.4329/wjr.v7.i1.17

Miller, L., Tseng, B., Tirella, L., Chan, W., & Feig, E. (2008). Health of children adopted from Ethiopia. *Maternal & Child Health Journal, 12*, 599–605. doi:10.1007/s10995-0070274-4

Minkoff, H., & Berkowitz, R. (2014). The case for universal prenatal genetic counseling. *Obstetrics & Gynecology, 123*, 1335–1338. doi:10.1097/AOG.0000000000000267

Misca, G. (2014). The "quiet migration": Is intercountry adoption a successful intervention in the lives of vulnerable children? *Family Court Review, 52*, 60–68. doi:10.1111/fcre.12070

Mohanty, J. (2015). Ethnic identity and psychological well-being of international transracial adoptees: A curvilinear relationship. *New Directions for Child and Adolescent Development, 2015*, 33–45. doi:10.1002/cad.20117

Moore, D. S. (2017). Behavioral epigenetics. *Wiley Interdisciplinary Reviews: Systems Biology and Medicine, 9*, e1333. doi:10.1002/wsbm.1333

Morrison, M. L., & McMahon, C. J. (2018). Congenital heart disease in Down syndrome. In S. Dey (Ed.), *Advances in research on Down syndrome* (pp. 128–144). London, UK: InTech Open. doi:10.5772/intechopen.71060

Næss, K. A. B., Nygaard, E., Ostad, J., Dolva, A. S., & Lyster, S. A. H. (2017). The profile of social functioning in children with Down syndrome. *Disability and Rehabilitation, 39*, 1320–1331. doi:10.1080/09638288.2016.1194901

Nance, M. A. (2017). Genetic counseling and testing for Huntington's disease: A historical review. *American Journal of Medical Genetics Part B: Neuropsychiatric Genetics, 174*, 75–92. doi:10.1002/ajmg.b.32453

National Association for Down Syndrome. (2017). Facts about Down syndrome. Retrieved from http://www.nads.org/resources/facts-about-down-syndrome/

National Library of Medicine. (2013). Home reference handbook—help me understand genetics. Retrieved from http://ghr.nlm.nih.gov/handbook

National Library of Medicine. (2017). Home reference handbook—help me understand genetics. Retrieved from http://ghr.nlm.nih.gov/handbook

Nikulina, V., Widom, C. S., & Brzustowicz, L. M. (2012). Child abuse and neglect, MAOA, and mental health outcomes: A prospective examination. *Biological Psychiatry, 71*, 350–357. doi:10.1016/j.biopsych.2011.09.008

Odibo, A. O. (2015). Amniocentesis, chorionic villus sampling, and fetal blood sampling. In A. Milunsky & J. M. Milunsky (Eds.), *Genetic disorders and the fetus* (pp. 68–97). Mahwah, NJ: John Wiley. doi:10.1002/9781118981559.ch2

Ojodu, J., Hulihan, M. M., Pope, S. N., & Grant, A. M. (2014). Incidence of sickle cell trait—United States, 2010. *Morbidity and Mortality Weekly Report, 63*, 1155–1158. Retrieved from https://www.cdc.gov/mmwr/preview/mmwrhtml/mm6349a3.htm

Palacios, J., & Brodzinsky, D. (2010). Review: Adoption research: Trends, topics, outcomes. *International Journal of Behavioral Development, 34*, 270–284. doi:10.1177/0165025410362837

Palacios, J., Román, M., Moreno, C., León, E., & Peñarrubia, M.-G. (2014). Differential plasticity in the recovery of adopted children after early adversity. *Child Development Perspectives, 8*, 169–174. doi:10.1111/cdep.12083

Papp, Z., & Fekete, T. (2003). The evolving role of ultrasound in obstetrics/gynecology practice. *International Journal of Gynecology & Obstetrics, 82*, 339–347.

Pappas, K. B., Migeon, C. J., Pappas, K. B., & Migeon, C. J. (2017). Sex chromosome abnormalities. In D. N. Cooper (Ed.), *eLS* (pp. 1–9). Chichester, England: John Wiley. doi:10.1002/9780470015902.a0005943.pub2

Patenaude, Y., Pugash, D., Lim, K., Morin, L., Lim, K., Bly, S., . . . Salem, S. (2014). The use of magnetic resonance imaging in the obstetric patient. *Journal of Obstetrics and Gynaecology Canada, 36*, 349–355. doi:10.1016/S1701-2163(15)30612-5

Pecker, L. H., & Little, J. (2018). Clinical manifestations of sickle cell disease across the lifespan. In E. R. Meier, A. Abraham, & R. M. Fasano (Eds.), *Sickle cell disease and hematopoietic stem cell transplantation* (pp. 3–39). Cham, Switzerland: Springer International. doi:10.1007/978-3-319-62328-3_1

Penke, L., & Jokela, M. (2016). The evolutionary genetics of personality revisited. *Current Opinion in Psychology, 7*, 104–109. doi:10.1016/J.COPSYC.2015.08.021

Pinderhughes, E. E., Zhang, X., & Agerbak, S. (2015). "American" or "multiethnic"? Family ethnic identity among transracial adoptive families, ethnic-racial socialization, and children's self-perception. *New Directions for Child and Adolescent Development, 2015*, 5–18. doi:10.1002/cad.20118

Pinsker, J. E. (2012). Turner syndrome: Updating the paradigm of clinical care. *Journal of Clinical Endocrinology & Metabolism, 97*, E994–E1003. doi:10.1210/jc.2012-1245

Pison, G., Monden, C., & Smits, J. (2015). Twinning rates in developed countries: Trends and explanations. *Population and Development Review, 41*, 629–649. doi:10.1111/j.1728-4457.2015.00088.x

Plomin, R., & Deary, I. J. (2015). Genetics and intelligence differences: Five special findings. *Molecular Psychiatry, 20*, 98–108. doi:10.1038/mp.2014.105

Plomin, R., DeFries, J. C., Knopik, V. S., & Neiderhiser, J. M. (2013). *Behavioral genetics* (6th ed.). New York, NY: Worth.

Plomin, R., DeFries, J. C., Knopik, V. S., & Neiderhiser, J. M. (2016). Top 10 replicated findings from behavioral genetics. *Perspectives on Psychological Science, 11*, 3–23. doi:10.1177/1745691615617439

Plomin, R., & Spinath, F. M. (2004). Intelligence: Genetics, genes, and genomics. *Journal of Personality & Social Psychology, 86*, 112–129. doi:10.1037/0022-3514.86.1.112

Posadas, D. M., & Carthew, R. W. (2014). MicroRNAs and their roles in developmental canalization. *Current Opinion in Genetics & Development, 27*, 1–6. doi:10.1016/j.gde.2014.03.005

Rakhlin, N., Hein, S., Doyle, N., Hart, L., Macomber, L., Ruchkin, V., . . . Grigorenko, E. L. (2015). Language development of internationally adopted children: Adverse early experiences outweigh the age of acquisition effect. *Journal of Communication Disorders, 57*, 66–80.

Ram, G., & Chinen, J. (2011). Infections and immunodeficiency in Down syndrome. *Clinical and Experimental Immunology, 164*, 9–16. doi:10.1111/j.1365-2249.2011.04335.x

Raspa, M., Wheeler, A. C., & Riley, C. (2017). Public health literature review of fragile X syndrome. *Pediatrics, 139*(Suppl 3), S153–S171. doi:10.1542/peds.2016-1159C

Ritz, B. R., Chatterjee, N., Garcia-Closas, M., Gauderman, W. J., Pierce, B. L., Kraft, P., . . . McAllister, K. (2017). Lessons learned from past gene-environment interaction successes. *American Journal of Epidemiology, 186*, 778–786. doi:10.1093/aje/kwx230

Robertson, J. A., & Hickman, T. (2013). Should PGD be used for elective gender selection? American Society for Reproductive Medicine. Retrieved from http://contemporaryobgyn.modernmedicine.com/contemporary-obgyn/news/should-pgd-beused-elective-gender-selection

Romani, C., Palermo, L., MacDonald, A., Limback, E., Hall, S. K., & Geberhiwot, T. (2017). The impact of phenylalanine levels on cognitive outcomes in adults with phenylketonuria: Effects across tasks and developmental stages. *Neuropsychology, 31*, 242–254. doi:10.1037/neu0000336

Rosnati, R., Pinderhughes, E. E., Baden, A. L., Grotevant, H. D., Lee, R. M., & Mohanty, J. (2015). New trends and directions in ethnic identity among internationally transracially adopted persons: Summary of special issue. *New Directions for Child and Adolescent Development, 2015*, 91–95. doi:10.1002/cad.20121

Rushton, J. P., & Bons, T. A. (2005). Mate choice and friendship in twins: Evidence for genetic similarity. *Psychological Science, 16*, 555–559. doi:10.1111/j.0956-7976.2005.01574.x

Rutter, M. (2012). Gene–environment interdependence. *European Journal of Developmental Psychology, 9*, 391–412.

Sadler, T. L. (2015). *Langman's medical embryology* (13th ed.). New York, NY: Lippincott Williams & Wilkins.

Sala, P., Prefumo, F., Pastorino, D., Buffi, D., Gaggero, C. R., Foppiano, M., & De Biasio, P. (2014). Fetal surgery. *Obstetrical & Gynecological Survey, 69*, 218–228. doi:10.1097/OGX.0000000000000061

Saleem, S. N. (2014). Fetal MRI: An approach to practice: A review. *Journal of Advanced Research, 5*, 507–523. doi:10.1016/J.JARE.2013.06.001

Saswati, S., Kissin, D. M., Crawford, S. B., Folger, S. G., Jamieson, D. J., Warner, L., & Barfield, W. D. (2017). Assisted reproductive technology surveillance—United States, 2014. *Morbidity and Mortality Weekly Report, 66*, 1–24.

Scarr, S. (1992). Developmental theories for the 1990s: Development and individual differences. *Child Development, 63*, 1–19. doi:10.1111/1467-8624.ep9203091721

Scarr, S., & McCartney, K. (1983). How people make their own environments: A theory of genotype environment effects. *Child Development, 54*, 424. doi:10.1111/14678624.ep8877295

Seggers, J., Pontesilli, M., Ravelli, A. C. J., Painter, R. C., Hadders-Algra, M., Heineman, M. J., . . . Ensing, S. (2016). Effects of in vitro fertilization and maternal characteristics on perinatal outcomes: A population-based study using siblings. *Fertility and Sterility, 105*, 590–598.e2. doi:10.1016/J.FERTNSTERT.2015.11.015

Shah, K., DeRemigis, A., Hageman, J. R., Sriram, S., & Waggoner, D. (2017). Unique characteristics of the X chromosome and related disorders. *NeoReviews, 18*, e209–e216. doi:10.1542/neo.18-4-e209

Shahbazian, N., Barati, M., Arian, P., & Saadati, N. (2012). Comparison of complications of chorionic villus sampling and amniocentesis.

International Journal of Fertility & Sterility, 5, 241–244.

Shim, S. S., Malone, F., Canick, J., Ball, R., Nyberg, D., Comstock, C., . . . Abuhamad, A. (2014). Chorionic villus sampling. *Journal of Genetic Medicine, 11,* 43–48. doi:10.5734/JGM.2014.11.2.43

Söderström-Anttila, V., Wennerholm, U.-B., Loft, A., Pinborg, A., Aittomäki, K., Romundstad, L. B., & Bergh, C. (2015). Surrogacy: Outcomes for surrogate mothers, children and the resulting families—a systematic review. *Human Reproduction Update, 22,* dmv046. doi:10.1093/humupd/dmv046

Soubry, A., Hoyo, C., Jirtle, R. L., & Murphy, S. K. (2014). A paternal environmental legacy: Evidence for epigenetic inheritance through the male germ line. *BioEssays: News and Reviews in Molecular, Cellular and Developmental Biology, 36,* 359–371. doi:10.1002/bies.201300113

Spruyt, K., Braam, W., & Curfs, L. M. (2018). Sleep in Angelman syndrome: A review of evidence. *Sleep Medicine Reviews, 37,* 69–84. doi:10.1016/J.SMRV.2017.01.002

Stephenson, J. (2005). Fetal ultrasound safety. *JAMA: Journal of the American Medical Association, 293,* 286.

Sullivan-Pyke, C. S., Senapati, S., Mainigi, M. A., & Barnhart, K. T. (2017). In vitro fertilization and adverse obstetric and perinatal outcomes. *Seminars in Perinatology, 41,* 345–353. doi:10.1053/J.SEMPERI.2017.07.001

Szyf, M. (2015). Nongenetic inheritance and transgenerational epigenetics. *Trends in Molecular Medicine, 21,* 134–144. doi:10.1016/j.molmed.2014.12.004

Tabor, H. K., Murray, J. C., Gammill, H. S., Kitzman, J. O., Snyder, M. W., Ventura, M., . . . Shendure, J. (2012). Non-invasive fetal genome sequencing: Opportunities and challenges. *American Journal of Medical Genetics Part A, 158A,* 2382–2384. doi:10.1002/ajmg.a.35545

Theodora, M., Antsaklis, A., Antsaklis, P., Blanas, K., Daskalakis, G., Sindos, M., . . . Papantoniou, N. (2016). Fetal loss following second trimester amniocentesis. Who is at greater risk? How to counsel pregnant women? *Journal of Maternal-Fetal & Neonatal Medicine, 29,* 590–595. doi:10.3109/14767058.2015.1012061

Thoma, M. E., McLain, A. C., Louis, J. F., King, R. B., Trumble, A. C., Sundaram, R., & Buck Louis, G. M. (2013). Prevalence of infertility in the United States as estimated by the current duration approach and a traditional constructed approach. *Fertility and Sterility, 99,* 1324–1331.e1. doi:10.1016/j.fertnstert.2012.11.037

Uhlmann, W. R., Schuette, J. L., & Yashar, B. (2009). *A guide to genetic counseling* (2nd ed.). Hoboken, NJ: Wiley-Blackwell.

Ulrich, D. A., Lloyd, M. C., Tiernan, C. W., Looper, J. E., & Angulo-Barroso, R. M. (2008). Effects of intensity of treadmill training on developmental outcomes and stepping in infants with Down syndrome: A randomized trial. *Physical Therapy, 88,* 114–122.

U.S. Department of State. (2014). *FY 2013 annual report on intercountry adoption.* Retrieved from http://adoption.state.gov/content/pdf/fy2013_annual_report.pdf

Vanhees, K., Vonhögen, I. G. C., van Schooten, F. J., & Godschalk, R. W. L. (2014). You are what you eat, and so are your children: The impact of micronutrients on the epigenetic programming of offspring. *Cellular and Molecular Life Sciences, 71,* 271–285. doi:10.1007/s00018-013-1427-9

Vink, J., & Quinn, M. (2018a). Amniocentesis. In J. Copel, M. E. D'Alton, H. Feltovich, E. Gratacos, A. O. Odibo, L. Platt, & B. Tutschek (Eds.), *Obstetric imaging: Fetal diagnosis and care* (pp. 473–475). Philadelphia, PA: Elsevier. doi:10.1016/B978-0-323-44548-1.00111-X

Vink, J., & Quinn, M. (2018b). Chorionic villus sampling. In J. Copel, M. E. D'Alton, H. Feltovich, E. Gratacos, A. O. Odibo, L. Platt, & B. Tutschek (Eds.), *Obstetric imaging: Fetal diagnosis and care* (pp. 479–481). Philadelphia, PA: Elsevier. doi:10.1016/B978-0-323-44548-1.00113-3

Vissers, L. E. L. M., Gilissen, C., & Veltman, J. A. (2016). Genetic studies in intellectual disability and related disorders. *Nature Reviews Genetics, 17,* 9–18. doi:10.1038/nrg3999

Waddington, C. H. (1971). Concepts of development. In E. Tobach, L. R. Aronson, & E. Shaw (Eds.), *The biopsychology of development* (pp. 17–23). San Diego, CA: Academic Press.

Ware, R. E., de Montalembert, M., Tshilolo, L., & Abboud, M. R. (2017). Sickle cell disease. *The Lancet, 390,* 311–323. doi:10.1016/S0140-6736(17)30193-9

Warsof, S. L., Larion, S., & Abuhamad, A. Z. (2015). Overview of the impact of noninvasive prenatal testing on diagnostic procedures. *Prenatal Diagnosis, 35,* 972–979. doi:10.1002/pd.4601

Waterland, R. A., & Jirtle, R. L. (2003). Transposable elements: Targets for early nutritional effects on epigenetic gene regulation. *Molecular and Cellular Biology, 23,* 5293–5300. doi:10.1128/MCB.23.15.5293-5300.2003

Wentz, E. E. (2017). Importance of initiating a "tummy time" intervention early in infants with Down syndrome. *Pediatric Physical Therapy, 29,* 68–75. doi:10.1097/PEP.0000000000000335

Wigby, K., D'Epagnier, C., Howell, S., Reicks, A., Wilson, R., Cordeiro, L., & Tartaglia, N. (2016). Expanding the phenotype of triple X syndrome: A comparison of prenatal versus postnatal diagnosis. *American Journal of Medical Genetics Part A, 170,* 2870–2881. doi:10.1002/ajmg.a.37688

Wiik, K. L., Loman, M. M., Van Ryzin, M. J., Armstrong, J. M., Essex, M. J., Pollak, S. D., & Gunnar, M. R. (2011). Behavioral and emotional symptoms of post-institutionalized children in middle childhood. *Journal of Child Psychology & Psychiatry, 52,* 56–63. doi:10.1111/j.1469-7610.2010.02294.x

Wilkinson, P. O., Trzaskowski, M., Haworth, C. M. A., & Eley, T. C. (2013). The role of gene–environment correlations and interactions in middle childhood depressive symptoms. *Development and Psychopathology, 25,* 93–104. doi:10.1017/S0954579412000922

Wilson, S. L., & Weaver, T. L. (2009). Follow-up of developmental attainment and behavioral adjustment for toddlers adopted internationally into the USA.

International Social Work, 52, 679–684. doi:10.1177/0020872809337684

Wiseman, F. K., Al-Janabi, T., Hardy, J., Karmiloff-Smith, A., Nizetic, D., Tybulewicz, V. L. J., . . . Strydom, A. (2015). A genetic cause of Alzheimer disease: Mechanistic insights from Down syndrome. *Nature Reviews. Neuroscience, 16,* 564–574. doi:10.1038/nrn3983

Wistuba, J., Brand, C., Zitzmann, M., & Damm, O. S. (2017). Genetics of Klinefelter syndrome: Experimental exploration. *Genetics of Human Infertility, 21,* 40–56. doi:10.1159/000477277

Zampieri, B. L., Biselli-Périco, J. M., de Souza, J. E. S., Bürger, M. C., Silva Júnior, W. A., Goloni-Bertollo, E. M., . . . Flavell, R. (2014). Altered expression of immune-related genes in children with Down syndrome. *PLoS ONE, 9,* e107218. doi:10.1371/journal.pone.0107218

Zill, N. (2015). The paradox of adoption. Retrieved from https://ifstudies.org/blog/the-paradox-ofadoption/

Chapter 3

Adams-Chapman, I., Hansen, N. I., Shankaran, S., Bell, E. F., Boghossian, N. S., Murray, J. C., . . . (2013). Ten-year review of major birth defects in VLBW infants. *Pediatrics, 132,* 49–61. doi:10.1542/peds.2012-3111

Adzick, N. S. (2013). Fetal surgery for spina bifida: Past, present, future. *Seminars in Pediatric Surgery, 22,* 10–17. doi:10.1053/j.sempedsurg.2012.10.003

Alati, R., Davey Smith, G., Lewis, S. J., Sayal, K., Draper, E. S., Golding, J., . . . Gray, R. (2013). Effect of prenatal alcohol exposure on childhood academic outcomes: Contrasting maternal and paternal associations in the ALSPAC study. *PLoS ONE, 8,* e74844. doi:10.1371/journal.pone.0074844

Alcohol Policy Information System. (2018). *Reporting requirements: Data on a specific state—2017—| APIS—Alcohol Policy Information System.* Retrieved May 8, 2018, from https://alcoholpolicy.niaaa.nih.gov/apis-policy-topics/reporting-requirements/23?sd=2017-01-01

Alshaarawy, O., Breslau, N., & Anthony, J. C. (2016). Monthly estimates of alcohol drinking during pregnancy: United States, 2002–2011. *Journal of Studies on Alcohol and Drugs, 77,* 272–276. doi:10.15288/JSAD.2016.77.272

American College of Obstetricians and Gynecologists. (2011). *Substance abuse reporting and pregnancy: The role of the obstetrician–gynecologist.* Retrieved from http://www.acog.org/~;/media/Committee Opinions/Committee on Health Care for Underserved Women/co473.pdf?dmc=1&ts=20140604T1051541013

American Medical Association. (2014). *Pregnant women's rights.* Retrieved April 6, 2014, from http://www.ama-assn.org//ama/pub/physician-resources/legal-topics/litigation-center/casesummaries-topic/pregnant-womens-rights.page

Andescavage, N. N., du Plessis, A., McCarter, R., Serag, A., Evangelou, I., Vezina, G., . . . Limperopoulos, C. (2016). Complex trajectories of brain development in the healthy human fetus. *Cerebral Cortex, 27,* 5274–5283. doi:10.1093/cercor/bhw306

Apgar, V. (1953). A proposal for a new method of evaluation in the newborn infant. *Current Research in Anesthesia and Analgesia, 32,* 260–267.

Arditi-Babchuk, H., Feldman, R., & Eidelman, A. I. (2009). Rapid eye movement (REM) in premature neonates and developmental outcome at 6 months. *Infant Behavior & Development, 32,* 27–32. doi:10.1016/j .infbeh.2008.09.001

Bada, H. S., Bann, C. M., Whitaker, T. M., Bauer, C. R., Shankaran, S., Lagasse, L., . . . Higgins, R. (2012). Protective factors can mitigate behavior problems after prenatal cocaine and other drug exposures. *Pediatrics, 130,* e1479–e1488. doi:10.1542/ peds.2011-3306

Bartram, S. C., Barlow, J., & Wolke, D. (2015). The Neonatal Behavioral Assessment Scale (NBAS) and Newborn Behavioral Observations system (NBO) for supporting caregivers and improving outcomes in caregivers and their infants. In S. C. Bartram (Ed.), *Cochrane database of systematic reviews.* Chichester, England: John Wiley. doi:10.1002/14651858.CD011754

Bazinet, A. D., Squeglia, L., Riley, E., & Tapert, S. F. (2016). *Effects of drug exposure on development* (K. J. Sher, Ed., Vol. 1). Oxford, UK: Oxford University Press. doi:10.1093/ oxfordhb/9780199381708.013.21

Bazzano, A. N., Kirkwood, B., Tawiah-Agyemang, C., Owusu-Agyei, S., & Adongo, P. (2008). Social costs of skilled attendance at birth in rural Ghana. *International Journal of Gynecology & Obstetrics, 102,* 91–94. doi:10.1016/j.ijgo.2008.02.004

Behnke, M., & Smith, V. C. (2013). Prenatal substance abuse: Short- and long-term effects on the exposed fetus. *Pediatrics, 131,* e1009–e1024. doi:10.1542/peds.2012-3931

Benasich, A. A., & Brooks-Gunn, J. (1996). Maternal attitudes and knowledge of child-rearing: Associations with family and child outcomes. *Child Development, 67,* 1186–1205.

Benzies, K. M., Magill-Evans, J. E., Hayden, K., Ballantyne, M., Raju, T., Higgins, R., . . . Dahl, L. (2013). Key components of early intervention programs for preterm infants and their parents: A systematic review and meta-analysis. *BMC Pregnancy and Childbirth, 13*(Suppl. 1), S10. doi:10.1186/14712393-13-S1-S10

Berlin, I., Golmard, J. L., Jacob, N., Tanguy, M. L., & Heishman, S. J. (2017). Cigarette smoking during pregnancy: Do complete abstinence and low level cigarette smoking have similar impact on birth weight? *Nicotine & Tobacco Research, 19,* 518–524. doi:10.1093/ntr/ ntx033

Bianchi, E., & Wright, G. J. (2016). Sperm meets egg: The genetics of mammalian fertilization. *Annual Review of Genetics, 50,* 93–111. doi:10.1146/annurev-genet-121415-121834

Bienstock, J. L., Fox, H. E., & Wallach, E. E. (2015). *The Johns Hopkins manual of gynecology and obstetrics.* Retrieved from http://www. lww.co.uk/johns-hopkins-manual-of-gynecology-and-obstetrics

Blanchette, N., Smith, M., Fernandes-Penney, A., King, S., & Read, S. (2001). Cognitive and motor development in children with vertically transmitted HIV infection. *Brain and Cognition, 46,* 50–53.

Boundy, E. O., Dastjerdi, R., Spiegelman, D., Fawzi, W. W., Missmer, S. A., Lieberman, E., . . . Guedes, Z. (2015). Kangaroo mother care and neonatal outcomes: A meta-analysis. *Pediatrics, 365,* 891–900. doi:10.1542/ peds.2015-2238

Bouthry, E., Picone, O., Hamdi, G., Grangeot-Keros, L., Ayoubi, J. M., & Vauloup-Fellous, C. (2014). Rubella and pregnancy: Diagnosis, management and outcomes. *Prenatal Diagnosis, 34,* 1246–1253. doi:10.1002/ pd.4467

Brazelton, T. B. (1977). Implications of infant development among the Mayan Indians of Mexico. In P. H. Liederman, S. R. Tulikn, & A. Rosenfeld (Eds.), *Culture and infancy* (pp. 336–352). New York, NY: Academic Press.

Brocklehurst, P., Hardy, P., Hollowell, J., Linsell, L., Macfarlane, A., McCourt, C., . . . Stewart, M. (2011). Perinatal and maternal outcomes by planned place of birth for healthy women with low risk pregnancies: The Birthplace in England national prospective cohort study. *BMJ (Clinical Research Ed.), 343,* d7400. doi:10.1136/BMJ.D7400

Calhoun, S., Conner, E., Miller, M., & Messina, N. (2015). Improving the outcomes of children affected by parental substance abuse: A review of randomized controlled trials. *Substance Abuse and Rehabilitation, 6,* 15–24. doi:10.2147/SAR.S46439

Camerota, M., Willoughby, M. T., Cox, M., Greenberg, M. T., & the Family Life Project Investigators. (2015). Executive function in low birth weight preschoolers: The moderating effect of parenting. *Journal of Abnormal Child Psychology, 43,* 1551–1562. doi:10.1007/s10802-015-0032-9

Centers for Disease Control and Prevention. (2017a). *Birth defects: Data and statistics.* Retrieved from https://www.cdc.gov/ ncbddd/birthdefects/data.html

Centers for Disease Control and Prevention. (2017b). *Preterm birth.* Retrieved December 8, 2017, from https://www.cdc.gov/ reproductivehealth/maternalinfanthealth/ pretermbirth.htm

Centers for Disease Control and Prevention. (2017c). *Microcephaly & other birth defects.* Retrieved from https://www.cdc.gov/zika/ healtheffects/birth_defects .html

Centers for Disease Control and Prevention. (2018). *Table 5. low birthweight live births, by detailed race and Hispanic origin of mother: United States, selected years 1970–2015.* Retrieved May 8, 2018, from https://www. cdc.gov/nchs/data/hus/2016/005.pdf

Chang, D. S., Lasley, F. D., Das, I. J., Mendonca, M. S., & Dynlacht, J. R. (2014). Radiation effects in the embryo and fetus. In *Basic radiotherapy physics and biology* (pp. 313–316). Cham, Switzerland: Springer International. doi:10.1007/978-3-319-06841-1_32

Chang, S. M., Grantham-McGregor, S. M., Powell, C. A., Vera-Hernández, M., Lopez-Boo, F., Baker Henningham, H., . . . Aboud, F. (2015). Integrating a parenting intervention with routine primary health care: A cluster randomized trial. *Pediatrics, 136,* 272–280. doi:10.1542/peds.2015-0119

Charness, M. E., Riley, E. P., & Sowell, E. R. (2016). Drinking during pregnancy and the developing brain: Is any amount safe? *Trends in Cognitive Sciences, 20,* 80–82. doi:10.1016/j.tics.2015.09.011

Charpak, N., Gabriel Ruiz, J., Zupan, J., Cattaneo, A., Figueroa, Z., Tessier, R., . . . Worku, B. (2005). Kangaroo mother care: 25 years after. *Acta Paediatrica, 94,* 514–522. doi:10.1111/j.16512227.2005.tb01930.x

Chasnoff, I. J. (2017). Medical marijuana laws and pregnancy: Implications for public health policy. *American Journal of Obstetrics and Gynecology, 216,* 27–30. doi:10.1016/J. AJOG.2016.07.010

Chen, L. W., Wu, Y., Neelakantan, N., Chong, M. F. F., Pan, A., & van Dam, R. M. (2014). Maternal caffeine intake during pregnancy is associated with risk of low birth weight: A systematic review and dose response meta-analysis. *BMC Medicine, 12,* 174. doi:10.1186/ s12916-014-0174-6

Chen, L. W., Wu, Y., Neelakantan, N., Chong, M. F. F., Pan, A., & van Dam, R. M. (2016). Maternal caffeine intake during pregnancy and risk of pregnancy loss: A categorical and dose–response meta-analysis of prospective studies. *Public Health Nutrition, 19,* 1233–1244. doi:10.1017/S1368980015002463

Chmurzynska, A. (2010). Fetal programming: Link between early nutrition, DNA methylation, and complex diseases. *Nutrition Reviews, 68,* 87–98. doi:10.1111/j.1753-4887.2009.00265.x

Cicchetti, D., & Toth, S. L. (2015). Child maltreatment. In M. E. Lamb (Ed.), *Handbook of child psychology and developmental science* (pp. 1–51). Hoboken, NJ: John Wiley. doi:10.1002/9781118963418.childpsy313

Conlon, J. L. (2017). Diethylstilbestrol. *Journal of the American Academy of Physician Assistants, 30,* 49–52. doi:10.1097/01. JAA.0000511800.91372.34

Crnic, K., & Ross, E. (2017). Parenting stress and parental efficacy. In K. Deater-Deckard & R. Panneton (Eds.), *Parental stress and early child development* (pp. 263–284). Cham, Switzerland: Springer International. doi:10.1007/978-3-319-55376-4_11

Daniels, P., Noe, G. F., & Mayberry, R. (2006). Barriers to prenatal care among Black women of low socioeconomic status. *American Journal of Health Behavior, 30,* 188–198.

Davis, E. P., Glynn, L. M., Waffarn, F., & Sandman, C. A. (2011). Prenatal maternal stress programs infant stress regulation. *Journal of Child Psychology and Psychiatry, and Allied Disciplines, 52,* 119–129. doi:10.1111/j.1469-7610.2010.02314.x

Declercq, E. R., Sakala, C., Corry, M. P., Applebaum, S., & Herrlich, A. (2014). Major survey findings of listening to Mothers(SM) III: Pregnancy and birth: Report of the Third National U.S. Survey of Women's Childbearing Experiences. *Journal of Perinatal Education, 23,* 9–16. doi:10.1891/1058-1243.23.1.9

de Jonge, A., Geerts, C., van der Goes, B., Mol, B., Buitendijk, S., & Nijhuis, J. (2015). Perinatal mortality and morbidity up to 28 days after birth among 743 070 low-risk planned home and hospital births: A cohort study based on three merged national perinatal databases. *BJOG: An International Journal of Obstetrics & Gynaecology, 122,* 720–728. doi:10.1111/1471-0528.13084

Diener, M. (2000). Gift from the gods: A Balinese guide to early child rearing. In J. DeLoache & A. Gotlieb (Eds.), *A world of babies: Imagined childcare guiles for seven societies.* Cambridge, England: Cambridge University Press.

Donnan, J., Walsh, S., Sikora, L., Morrissey, A., Collins, K., & MacDonald, D. (2017). A systematic review of the risks factors associated with the onset and natural progression of spina bifida. *NeuroToxicology, 61,* 20–31. doi:10.1016/J.NEURO.2016.03.008

Durik, A., Hyde, J., & Clark, R. (2000). Sequelae of cesarean and vaginal deliveries: Psychosocial outcomes for mothers and infants. *Developmental Psychology, 36,* 251–260.

Durkin, M. S., Benedict, R. E., Christensen, D., Dubois, L. A., Fitzgerald, R. T., Kirby, R. S., . . . Yeargin-Allsopp, M. (2016). Prevalence of cerebral palsy among 8-year-old children in 2010 and preliminary evidence of trends in its relationship to low birthweight. *Paediatric and Perinatal Epidemiology, 30,* 496–510. doi:10.1111/ppe.12299

Eckerman, C. O., Hsu, H. C., Molitor, A., Leung, E. H. L., & Goldstein, R. F. (1999). Infant arousal as an en-face exchange with a new partner: Effects of prematurity and perinatal biological risk. *Developmental Psychology, 35,* 282–293.

El Marroun, H., Tiemeier, H., Franken, I. H. A., Jaddoe, V. W. V., van der Lugt, A., Verhulst, F. C., . . . White, T. (2016). Prenatal cannabis and tobacco exposure in relation to brain morphology: A prospective neuroimaging study in young children. *Biological Psychiatry, 79,* 971–979. doi:10.1016/J.BIOPSYCH.2015.08.024

Elkarmi, A., Abu-Samak, M., & Al-Qaisi, K. (2007). Modeling the effects of prenatal exposure to aspirin on the postnatal development of rat brain. *Growth, Development, and Aging, 70,* 13–24. Retrieved from http://www.ncbi.nlm.nih.gov/pubmed/18038927

Eryigit Madzwamuse, S., Baumann, N., Jaekel, J., Bartmann, P., & Wolke, D. (2015). Neuro-cognitive performance of very preterm or very low birth weight adults at 26 years. *Journal of Child Psychology and Psychiatry, 56,* 857–864. doi:10.1111/jcpp.12358

Fallone, M. D., LaGasse, L. L., Lester, B. M., Shankaran, S., Bada, H. S., & Bauer, C. R. (2014). Reactivity and regulation of motor responses in cocaine-exposed infants. *Neurotoxicology and Teratology, 43,* 25–32. doi:10.1016/j.ntt.2014.02.005

Feldman, P. J., Dunkel-Schetter, C., Sandman, C. A., & Wadhwa, P. D. (2000). Maternal social support predicts birth weight and fetal growth in human pregnancy. *Psychosomatic Medicine, 62,* 715–725.

Field, T. (2011). Prenatal depression effects on early development: A review. *Infant Behavior & Development, 34,* 1–14. doi:10.1016/j.infbeh.2010.09.008

Flak, A. L., Su, S., Bertrand, J., Denny, C. H., Kesmodel, U. S., & Cogswell, M. E. (2014). The association of mild, moderate, and binge prenatal alcohol exposure and child neuropsychological outcomes: A meta analysis. *Alcoholism: Clinical and Experimental Research, 38,* 214–226. doi:10.1111/acer.12214

Fogel, A. (2007). *Infancy: Infant, family, and society* (7th ed.). Cornwall-on-Hudson, NY: Sloan Educational Publishing.

Fracasso, M. P., & Busch-Rossnagel, N. A. (1992). Children and parents of Hispanic origin. In M. E. Procidno & C. B. Fisher (Eds.), *Families: A handbook for school professionals* (pp. 83–98). New York, NY: Teachers College Press.

Fraga, L. R., Diamond, A. J., Vargesson, N., Fraga, L. R., Diamond, A. J., & Vargesson, N. (2016). Thalidomide and birth defects. In *eLS* (pp. 1–11). Chichester, England: John Wiley. doi:10.1002/9780470015902.a0026052

Gabbe, S. G., Niebyl, J., Simpson, J., Landon, M., Galan, H., Jauniaux, E., . . . Grobman, W. (2016). *Obstetrics: Normal and problem pregnancies.* Philadelphia, PA: Elsevier.

Gardiner, H. W., & Kosmitzki, C. (2018). *Lives across cultures: Cross-cultural human development* (6th ed.). Boston, MA: Pearson.

Georgsdottir, I., Haraldsson, A., & Dagbjartsson, A. (2013). Behavior and well-being of extremely low birth weight teenagers in Iceland. *Early Human Development, 89,* 999–1003. doi:10.1016/j.earlhumdev.2013.08.018

Ghosh, J. K. C., Wilhelm, M. H., Dunkel-Schetter, C., Lombardi, C. A., & Ritz, B. R. (2010). Paternal support and preterm birth, and the moderation of effects of chronic stress: A study in Los Angeles County mothers. *Archives of Women's Mental Health, 13,* 327–338. doi:10.1007/s00737-009-0135-9

Glover, V. (2011). Annual research review: Prenatal stress and the origins of psychopathology: An evolutionary perspective. *Journal of Child Psychology and Psychiatry, 52,* 356–367. doi:10.1111/j.1469-7610.2011.02371.x

Granier-Deferre, C., Ribeiro, A., Jacquet, A.-Y., & Bassereau, S. (2011). Near-term fetuses process temporal features of speech. *Developmental Science, 14,* 336–352. doi:10.1111/j.1467 7687.2010.00978.x

Grant, K. S., Petroff, R., Isoherranen, N., Stella, N., & Burbacher, T. M. (2018). Cannabis use during pregnancy: Pharmacokinetics and effects on child development. *Pharmacology & Therapeutics, 182,* 133–151. doi:10.1016/J.PHARMTHERA.2017.08.014

Grewen, K., Burchinal, M., Vachet, C., Gouttard, S., Gilmore, J. H., Lin, W., . . . Gerig, G. (2014). Prenatal cocaine effects on brain structure in early infancy. *NeuroImage, 101,* 114–123. doi:10.1016/J.NEUROIMAGE.2014.06.070

Grigg-Damberger, M. M., & Wolfe, K. M. (2017). Infants sleep for brain. *Journal of Clinical Sleep Medicine, 13,* 1233–1234. doi:10.5664/jcsm.6786

Grotegut, C. A., Chisholm, C. A., Johnson, L. N. C., Brown, H. L., Heine, R. P., & James, A. H. (2014). Medical and obstetric complications among pregnant women aged 45 and older. *PLoS ONE, 9,* e96237. doi:10.1371/journal.pone.0096237

Gunn, J. K. L., Rosales, C. B., Center, K. E., Nuñez, A., Gibson, S. J., Christ, C., & Ehiri, J. E. (2016). Prenatal exposure to cannabis and maternal and child health outcomes: A systematic review and meta-analysis. *BMJ Open, 6,* e009986. doi:10.1136/bmjopen-2015-009986

Gupta, K. K., Gupta, V. K., & Shirasaka, T. (2016). An update on fetal alcohol syndrome-pathogenesis, risks, and treatment. *Alcoholism: Clinical and Experimental Research, 40,* 1594–1602. doi:10.1111/acer.13135

Gupta, R. C. (2017). *Reproductive and developmental toxicology.* Cambridge, MA: Elsevier Science.

Guttmacher Institute. (2018). *Substance use during pregnancy—May 1, 2018.* Retrieved May 8, 2018, from https://www.guttmacher.org/state-policy/explore/substance-use-during-pregnancy

Hacker, N. F., Gambone, J. C., & Hobel, C. J. (2016). *Hacker & Moore's essentials of obstetrics and gynecology.* Philadelphia, PA: Elsevier.

Hamilton, B. E., Martin, J. A., Osterman, M. J. K. S., Driscoll, A. K., & Rossen, L. M. (2017). *Vital statistics rapid release births: Provisional data for 2016.* Retrieved May 8, 2018, from https://www.cdc.gov/nchs/data/vsrr/report002.pdf

Hatzis, D., Dawe, S., Harnett, P., & Barlow, J. (2017). Quality of caregiving in mothers with illicit substance use: A systematic review and meta-analysis. *Substance Abuse: Research and Treatment.* Advance online publication. doi:10.1177/1178221817694038

Hazlett, H. C., Hammer, J., Hooper, S. R., & Kamphaus, R. W. (2011). Down syndrome. In S. Goldstein & C. R. Reynolds (Eds.), *Handbook of neurodevelopmental and genetic disorders in children* (2nd ed., pp. 362–381). New York, NY: Guilford.

He, Y., Chen, J., Zhu, L. H., Hua, L. L., & Ke, F. F. (2017). Maternal smoking during pregnancy and ADHD. *Journal of Attention Disorders.* Advance online publication. doi:10.1177/1087054717696766

Heaman, M. I., Sword, W., Elliott, L., Moffatt, M., Helewa, M. E., Morris, H., . . . Brown, J. (2015). Barriers and facilitators related to use of prenatal care by inner-city women: Perceptions of health care providers. *BMC Pregnancy and Childbirth, 15,* 2. doi:10.1186/s12884-015-0431-5

Henry, D., Dormuth, C., Winquist, B., Carney, G., Bugden, S., Teare, G., . . . CNODES (Canadian Network for Observational Drug Effect Studies) Investigators. (2016). Occurrence of pregnancy and pregnancy outcomes during isotretinoin therapy. *CMAJ: Canadian Medical Association Journal, 188,* 723–730. doi:10.1503/cmaj.151243

Hepper, P. (2015). Behavior during the prenatal period: Adaptive for development and survival. *Child Development Perspectives, 9,* 38–43. doi:10.1111/cdep.12104

Herrera-Gómez, A., Luna-Bertos, E. De, Ramos-Torrecillas, J., Ocaña-Peinado, F. M., García-Martinez, O., & Ruiz, C. (2017). The effect of epidural analgesia alone and in association with other variables on the risk of cesarean section. *Biological Research for Nursing, 19,* 393–398. doi:10.1177/1099800417706023

Hillerer, K. M., Jacobs, V. R., Fischer, T., & Aigner, L. (2014). The maternal brain: An organ with peripartal plasticity. *Neural Plasticity, 2014,* 574159. doi:10.1155/2014/574159

Hoekzema, E., Barba-Müller, E., Pozzobon, C., Picado, M., Lucco, F., García-Garcia, D., . . . Vilarroya, O. (2017). Pregnancy leads to long-lasting changes in human brain structure. *Nature Neuroscience, 20,* 287–296. doi:10.1038/nn.4458

Hoggatt, K. J., Flores, M., Solorio, R., Wilhelm, M., & Ritz, B. (2012). The "Latina epidemiologic paradox" revisited: The role of birthplace and acculturation in predicting infant low birth weight for Latinas in Los Angeles, CA.

Journal of Immigrant and Minority Health, 14, 875–884. doi:10.1007/s10903-011-9556-4

Howe, T.-H., Sheu, C.-F., Wang, T.-N., & Hsu, Y.-W. (2014). Parenting stress in families with very low birth weight preterm infants in early infancy. *Research in Developmental Disabilities, 35,* 1748–1756. doi:10.1016/j.ridd.2014.02.015

Hoyme, H. E., Kalberg, W. O., Elliott, A. J., Blankenship, J., Buckley, D., Marais, A.-S., . . . May, P. A. (2016). Updated clinical guidelines for diagnosing fetal alcohol spectrum disorders. *Pediatrics, 138,* e20154256. doi:10.1542/peds.2015-4256

Hui, K., Angelotta, C., & Fisher, C. E. (2017). Criminalizing substance use in pregnancy: Misplaced priorities. *Addiction, 112,* 1123–1125. doi:10.1111/add.13776

Hussain, F. N., & Ashmead, G. G. (2017). The safety of over-the-counter medications in pregnancy. *Topics in Obstetrics, 37,* 8. doi:10.1097/01.pgo.0000524652.07036.fb

Hutchinson, E. A., De Luca, C. R., Doyle, L. W., Roberts, G., Anderson, P. J., & Victorian Infant Collaborative Study Group. (2013). School-age outcomes of extremely preterm or extremely low birth weight children. *Pediatrics, 131,* e1053–e1061. doi:10.1542/peds.2012-2311

Jaekel, J., Pluess, M., Belsky, J., & Wolke, D. (2015). Effects of maternal sensitivity on low birth weight children's academic achievement: A test of differential susceptibility versus diathesis stress. *Journal of Child Psychology and Psychiatry, 56,* 693–701. doi:10.1111/jcpp.12331

Jansen, I. (2006). Decision making in childbirth: The influence of traditional structures in a Ghanaian village. *International Nursing Review, 53,* 41–46.

Jean, A. D. L., & Stack, D. M. (2012). Full-term and very-low-birth-weight preterm infants' self-regulating behaviors during a Still-Face interaction: Influences of maternal touch. *Infant Behavior and Development, 35,* 779–791. doi:10.1016/j.infbeh.2012.07.023

Jefferies, A. L. (2012). Kangaroo care for the preterm infant and family. *Paediatrics & Child Health, 17,* 141–146.

Jha, A. K., Baliga, S., Kumar, H. H., Rangnekar, A., & Baliga, B. S. (2015). Is there a preventive role for vernix caseosa? An intuitive study. *Journal of Clinical and Diagnostic Research, 9,* SC13–SC16. doi:10.7860/JCDR/2015/14740.6784

Jones, L., Rowe, J., & Becker, T. (2009). Appraisal, coping, and social support as predictors of psychological distress and parenting efficacy in parents of premature infants. *Children's Health Care, 38,* 245–262. doi:10.1080/02739610903235976

Joubert, B. R., Felix, J. F., Yousefi, P., Bakulski, K. M., Just, A. C., Breton, C., . . . London, S. J. (2016). DNA methylation in newborns and maternal smoking in pregnancy: Genome-wide consortium meta analysis. *American Journal of Human Genetics, 98,* 680–696. doi:10.1016/J.AJHG.2016.02.019

Jouhki, M.-R., Suominen, T., & Åstedt-Kurki, P. (2017). Giving birth on our own terms: Women's experience of childbirth at home. *Midwifery, 53,* 35–41. doi:10.1016/j.midw.2017.07.008

Juárez, S. P., & Merlo, J. (2013). Revisiting the effect of maternal smoking during pregnancy on offspring birthweight: A quasi-experimental sibling analysis in Sweden. *PLoS ONE, 8,* e61734. doi:10.1371/journal.pone.0061734

Kaiser, L., Allen, L., & American Dietetic Association. (2008). Position of the American Dietetic Association: Nutrition and lifestyle for a healthy pregnancy outcome. *Journal of the American Dietetic Association, 108,* 553–561. doi:10.1016/j.jada.2008.01.030

Kang, H.-K. (2014). Influence of culture and community perceptions on birth and perinatal care of immigrant women: Doulas' perspective. *Journal of Perinatal Education, 23,* 25–32. doi:10.1891/1058-1243.23.1.25

Kapoor, A., Lubach, G. R., Ziegler, T. E., & Coe, C. L. (2016). Hormone levels in neonatal hair reflect prior maternal stress exposure during pregnancy. *Psychoneuroendocrinology, 66,* 111–117. doi:10.1016/j.psyneuen.2016.01.010

Kenny, L. C., Lavender, T., McNamee, R., O'Neill, S. M., Mills, T., & Khashan, A. S. (2013). Advanced maternal age and adverse pregnancy outcome: Evidence from a large contemporary cohort. *PLoS ONE, 8,* e56583. doi:10.1371/journal.pone.0056583

Khalil, A., Syngelaki, A., Maiz, N., Zinevich, Y., & Nicolaides, K. H. (2013). Maternal age and adverse pregnancy outcome: A cohort study. *Ultrasound in Obstetrics & Gynecology, 42,* 634–643. doi:10.1002/uog.12494

Kingston, D., Tough, S., & Whitfield, H. (2012). Prenatal and postpartum maternal psychological distress and infant development: A systematic review. *Child Psychiatry and Human Development, 43,* 683–714. doi:10.1007/s10578-012-0291-4

Kinsley, C. H., & Amory-Meyer, E. (2011). Why the maternal brain? *Journal of Neuroendocrinology, 23,* 974–983. doi:10.1111/j.1365-2826.2011.02194.x

Kisilevsky, B. S., & Hains, S. M. (2011). Onset and maturation of fetal heart rate response to the mother's voice over late gestation. *Developmental Science, 14,* 214–223. doi:10.1111/j.14677687.2010.00970.x

Kobayashi, T., Good, C., Mamiya, K., Skinner, R., & Garcia-Rill, E. (2004). Development of REM sleep drive and clinical implications. *Journal of Applied Physiology, 96,* 735–746.

Korotchikova, I., Stevenson, N. J., Livingstone, V., Ryan, C. A., & Boylan, G. B. (2016). Sleep-wake cycle of the healthy term newborn infant in the immediate postnatal period. *Clinical Neurophysiology, 127,* 2095–2101. doi:10.1016/j.clinph.2015.12.015

Kozhimannil, K. B., Hardeman, R. R., Alarid-Escudero, F., Vogelsang, C. A., Blauer-Peterson, C., & Howell, E. A. (2016). Modeling the cost-effectiveness of doula care associated with reductions in preterm birth and cesarean delivery. *Birth, 43,* 20–27. doi:10.1111/birt.12218

Lamaze, F. (1956). *Painless childbirth: Psychoprophylactic method.* New York, NY: Contemporary Books.

Lambert, B. L., & Bauer, C. R. (2012). Developmental and behavioral consequences of prenatal cocaine exposure: A review. *Journal of Perinatology, 32,* 819–828. doi:10.1038/jp.2012.90

Lau, R., & Morse, C. A. (2003). Stress experiences of parents with premature infants in a special care nursery. *Stress and Health, 19,* 69–78.

Laughton, B., Cornell, M., Boivin, M., & Van Rie, A. (2013). Neurodevelopment in perinatally HIV-infected children: A concern for adolescence. *Journal of the International AIDS Society, 16,* 18603. doi:10.7448/IAS.16.1.18603

Lee, L. J., & Lupo, P. J. (2013). Maternal smoking during pregnancy and the risk of congenital heart defects in offspring: A systematic review and metaanalysis. *Pediatric Cardiology, 34,* 398–407. doi:10.1007/s00246-012-0470-x

Levine, T. A., & Woodward, L. J. (2018). Early inhibitory control and working memory abilities of children prenatally exposed to methadone. *Early Human Development, 116,* 68–75. doi:10.1016/j.earlhumdev.2017.11.010

Li, D., Liu, L., & Odouli, R. (2003). Exposure to non-steroidal anti-inflammatory drugs during pregnancy and risk of miscarriage: Population based cohort study. *British Medical Journal, 327,* 368–371.

Lottero-Leconte, R., Isidro Alonso, C. A., Castellano, L., & Perez Martinez, S. (2017). Mechanisms of the sperm guidance, an essential aid for meeting the oocyte. *Translational Cancer Research, 6,* S427–S430. doi:10.21037/12829

Lundsberg, L. S., Illuzzi, J. L., Belanger, K., Triche, E. W., & Bracken, M. B. (2015). Low-to-moderate prenatal alcohol consumption and the risk of selected birth outcomes: A prospective cohort study. *Annals of Epidemiology, 25,* 46–54.e3. doi:10.1016/j.annepidem.2014.10.011

MacDorman, M. F., & Declercq, E. (2016). Trends and characteristics of United States out-of-hospital births 2004–2014: New information on risk status and access to care. *Birth, 43,* 116–124. doi:10.1111/birt.12228

MacKay, D. F., Smith, G. C. S., Dobbie, R., & Pell, J. P. (2010). Gestational age at delivery and special educational need: Retrospective cohort study of 407,503 schoolchildren. *PLoS Medicine, 7,* e1000289. doi:10.1371/journal.pmed.1000289

Mamluk, L., Edwards, H. B., Savović, J., Leach, V., Jones, T., Moore, T. H. M., . . . Zuccolo, L. (2016). Prenatal alcohol exposure and pregnancy and childhood outcomes: A systematic review of alternative analytical approaches. *The Lancet, 388,* S73. doi:10.1016/S0140-6736(16)32309-1

Mamluk, L., Edwards, H. B., Savović, J., Leach, V., Jones, T., Moore, T. H. M., . . . Zuccolo, L. (2017). Low alcohol consumption and pregnancy and childhood outcomes: Time to change guidelines indicating apparently "safe" levels of alcohol during pregnancy? A systematic review and meta-analyses. *BMJ Open, 7,* e015410. doi:10.1136/bmjopen-2016-015410

March of Dimes. (2015). *Caffeine in pregnancy.* White Plains, NY: Author. Retrieved from https://www.marchofdimes.org/pregnancy/caffeine-in-pregnancy.aspx

Martin, J. A., Hamilton, B. E., Osterman, M. J. K., Curtin, S. C., & Mathews, T. J. (2013). Births: Final data for 2012. *National Vital Statistics Reports, 62.* Retrieved from http://www.cdc.gov/nchs/data/nvsr/nvsr62/nvsr62_09.pdf#table21

Martin, J. A., Hamilton, B. E., Osterman, M. J., Driscoll, A. K., & Drake, P. (2018). Births: Final data for 2016. *National Vital Statistics Reports, 67*. Retrieved from https://stacks.cdc.gov/view/cdc/51199

Mathews, T. J., & MacDorman, M. F. (2013). Infant mortality statistics from the 2010 period linked birth/infant death data set. *National Vital Statistics Reports, 62*. Retrieved from http://www.cdc.gov/nchs/data/nvsr/nvsr62/nvsr62_08.pdf

Maupin, R., Lyman, R., Fatsis, J., Prystowiski, E., Nguyen, A., Wright, C., . . . Miller, J. (2004). Characteristics of women who deliver with no prenatal care. *Journal of Maternal-Fetal and Neonatal Medicine, 16*, 45–50.

May, P. A., Baete, A., Russo, J., Elliott, A. J., Blankenship, J., Kalberg, W. O., . . . Hoyme, H. E. (2014). Prevalence and characteristics of fetal alcohol spectrum disorders. *Pediatrics, 134*, 855–866. doi:10.1542/peds.2013-3319

Mazul, M. C., Salm-Ward, T. C., & Ngui, E. M. (2016). Anatomy of good prenatal care: Perspectives of low income African-American women on barriers and facilitators to prenatal care. *Journal of Racial and Ethnic Health Disparities, 4*, 79–86. doi:10.1007/s40615-015-0204-x

McGlade, M. S., Saha, S., & Dahlstrom, M. E. (2004). The Latina paradox: An opportunity for restructuring prenatal care delivery. *American Journal of Public Health, 94*, 2062–2065.

Mehta, P. K. (2016). Pregnancy with chicken pox. In A. Gandhi, N. Malhotra, J. Malhotra, N. Gupta, & N. M. (Eds.), *Principles of critical care in obstetrics* (pp. 21–30). New Delhi: Springer India. doi:10.1007/978-81-322-2686-4_4

Meins, E., Fernyhough, C., Fradley, E., & Tuckey, M. (2001). Rethinking maternal sensitivity: Mothers' comments on infants' mental processes predict security of attachment at 12 months. *Journal of Child Psychology and Psychiatry, 42*, 637–648. doi:10.1017/S0021963001007302

Miller, J. E., Hammond, G. C., Strunk, T., Moore, H. C., Leonard, H., Carter, K. W., . . . Burgner, D. P. (2016). Association of gestational age and growth measures at birth with infection-related admissions to hospital throughout childhood: A population-based, data-linkage study from Western Australia. *The Lancet Infectious Diseases, 16*, 952–961. doi:10.1016/S1473-3099(16)00150-X

Min, M. O., Minnes, S., Yoon, S., Short, E. J., & Singer, L. T. (2014). Self-reported adolescent behavioral adjustment: Effects of prenatal cocaine exposure. *Journal of Adolescent Health, 55*, 167–174. doi:10.1016/j.jadohealth.2013.12.032

Moon, C., Cooper, R. P., & Fifer, W. P. (1993). Two-day-old infants prefer their native language. *Infant Behavior and Development, 16*, 495–500.

Moore, D. S. (2017). Behavioral epigenetics. *Wiley Interdisciplinary Reviews: Systems Biology and Medicine, 9*, e1333. doi:10.1002/wsbm.1333

Moore, K. L., & Persaud, T. V. N. (2016). *Before we are born: Essentials of embryology and birth defects* (9th ed.). Philadelphia, PA: Saunders.

Muggli, E., Matthews, H., Penington, A., Claes, P., O'Leary, C., Forster, D., . . . Halliday, J. (2017). Association between prenatal alcohol exposure and craniofacial shape of children at 12 months of age. *JAMA Pediatrics, 171*, 771. doi:10.1001/jamapediatrics.2017.0778

Nagy, G. R., Győrffy, B., Nagy, B., & Rigó, J. (2013). Lower risk for Down syndrome associated with longer oral contraceptive use: A case-control study of women of advanced maternal age presenting for prenatal diagnosis. *Contraception, 87*, 455–458. doi:10.1016/j.contraception.2012.08.040

National Institute of Allergy and infectious Diseases. (2014). *NIH trial tests very early anti-HIV therapy in HIV infected newborns.* Retrieved from http://www.niaid.nih.gov/news/newsreleases/2014/Pages/IMPAACTP1115.aspx

Neshat, H., Jebreili, M., Seyyedrasouli, A., Ghojazade, M., Hosseini, M. B., & Hamishehkar, H. (2016). Effects of breast milk and vanilla odors on premature neonate's heart rate and blood oxygen saturation during and after venipuncture. *Pediatrics & Neonatology, 57*, 225–231. doi:10.1016/J.PEDNEO.2015.09.004

Nugent, J. K. (2013). The competent newborn and the Neonatal Behavioral Assessment Scale: T. Berry Brazelton's legacy. *Journal of Child and Adolescent Psychiatric Nursing, 26*, 173–179. doi:10.1111/jcap.12043

Paltrow, L. M., & Flavin, J. (2013). Arrests of and forced interventions on pregnant women in the United States, 1973–2005: Implications for women's legal status and public health. *Journal of Health Politics, Policy and Law, 38*, 299–343. doi:10.1215/03616878-1966324

Panczakiewicz, A. L., Glass, L., Coles, C. D., Kable, J. A., Sowell, E. R., Wozniak, J. R., . . . CIFASD. (2016). Neurobehavioral deficits consistent across age and sex in youth with prenatal alcohol exposure. *Alcoholism, Clinical and Experimental Research, 40*, 1971–1981. doi:10.1111/acer.13153

Partridge, S., Balayla, J., Holcroft, C., & Abenhaim, H. (2012). Inadequate prenatal care utilization and risks of infant mortality and poor birth outcome: A retrospective analysis of 28,729,765 U.S. deliveries over 8 years. *American Journal of Perinatology, 29*, 787–794. doi:10.1055/s-0032-1316439

Pearson, R. M., Lightman, S. L., & Evans, J. (2009). Emotional sensitivity for motherhood: Late pregnancy is associated with enhanced accuracy to encode emotional faces. *Hormones and Behavior, 56*, 557–563. doi:10.1016/j.yhbeh.2009.09.013

Pierrehumbert, B., Nicole, A., Muller-Nix, C., Forcada-Guex, M., & Ansermet, F. (2003). Parental post-traumatic reactions after premature birth: Implications for sleeping and eating problems in the infant. *Archives of Disease in Childhood—Fetal and Neonatal Edition, 88*, 400F–404F. doi:10.1136/fn.88.5.F400

Pollack, A., & McNeil, D. G., Jr. (2013). In medical first, a baby with H.I.V. is deemed cured. *New York Times.* Retrieved from http://www.nytimes.com/2013/03/04/health/for-first-time-baby-cured-of-hivdoctors-say.html?pagewanted=all&_r=0

Popova, S., Lange, S., Probst, C., Parunashvili, N., & Rehm, J. (2017). Prevalence of alcohol consumption during pregnancy and fetal alcohol spectrum disorders among the general and Aboriginal populations in Canada and the United States. *European Journal of Medical Genetics, 60*, 32–48. doi:10.1016/J.EJMG.2016.09.010

Prakalapakorn, S. G., Meaney-Delman, D., Honein, M. A., & Rasmussen, S. A. (2017). The eyes as a window to improved understanding of the prenatal effects of Zika virus infection. *Journal of AAPOS, 21*, 259–261. doi:10.1016/j.jaapos.2017.07.001

Prechtl, H. F. R. (1974). The behavioural states of the newborn infant (a review). *Brain Research, 76*, 185–212. doi:10.1016/0006-8993(74)90454-5

Procianoy, R. S., Mendes, E. W., & Silveira, R. C. (2010). Massage therapy improves neurodevelopment outcome at two years corrected age for very low birth weight infants. *Early Human Development, 86*, 7–11. doi:10.1016/j.earlhumdev.2009.12.001

Raffaeli, G., Cavallaro, G., Allegaert, K., Wildschut, E. D., Fumagalli, M., Agosti, M., . . . Mosca, F. (2017). Neonatal abstinence syndrome: Update on diagnostic and therapeutic strategies. *Pharmacotherapy, 37*, 814–823. doi:10.1002/phar.1954

Rainwater-Lovett, K., Luzuriaga, K., & Persaud, D. (2015). Very early combination antiretroviral therapy in infants: Prospects for cure. *Current Opinion in HIV and AIDS, 10*, 4–11. doi:10.1097/COH.0000000000000127

Rangmar, J., Hjern, A., Vinnerljung, B., Strömland, K., Aronson, M., & Fahlke, C. (2015). Psychosocial outcomes of fetal alcohol syndrome in adulthood. *Pediatrics, 135*, e52–e58. doi:10.1542/peds.20141915

Renfrew, M. J., McFadden, A., Bastos, M. H., Campbell, J., Channon, A. A., Cheung, N. F., . . . Declercq, E. (2014). Midwifery and quality care: Findings from a new evidence-informed framework for maternal and newborn care. *The Lancet, 384*, 1129–1145. doi:10.1016/S0140-6736(14)60789-3

Richardson, G. A., Goldschmidt, L., Larkby, C., & Day, N. L. (2015). Effects of prenatal cocaine exposure on adolescent development. *Neurotoxicology and Teratology, 49*, 41–48. doi:10.1016/J.NTT.2015.03.002

Ritchie, K., Bora, S., & Woodward, L. J. (2015). Social development of children born very preterm: A systematic review. *Developmental Medicine & Child Neurology, 57*, 899–918. doi:10.1111/dmcn.12783

Roberge, S., Bujold, E., & Nicolaides, K. H. (2017). Aspirin for the prevention of preterm and term preeclampsia: Systematic review and meta-analysis. *American Journal of Obstetrics and Gynecology, 218*, 287–293. doi:10.1016/J.AJOG.2017.11.561

Roberts, S. C. M., & Nuru-Jeter, A. (2012). Universal screening for alcohol and drug use and racial disparities in child protective services reporting. *Journal of Behavioral Health Services & Research, 39*, 3–16. doi:10.1007/s11414-011-9247-x

Rotstein, M., Stolar, O., Uliel, S., Mandel, D., Mani, A., Dollberg, S., . . . Leitner, Y. (2015). Facial expression in response to smell and taste stimuli in small and appropriate for gestational age newborns. *Journal of Child Neurology, 30*, 1466–1471. doi:10.1177/0883073815570153

Ruiz, J. M., Hamann, H. A., Mehl, M. R., & OConnor, M.-F. (2016). The Hispanic health paradox: From epidemiological phenomenon to contribution opportunities for psychological science. *Group Processes & Intergroup Relations, 19*, 462–476. doi:10.1177/1368430216638540

Sadler, T. L. (2015). *Langman's medical embryology* (13th ed.). New York, NY: Lippincott Williams & Wilkins.

Sanchez-Vaznaugh, E. V., Braveman, P. A., Egerter, S., Marchi, K. S., Heck, K., & Curtis, M. (2016). Latina birth outcomes in California: Not so paradoxical. *Maternal and Child Health Journal, 20*, 1849–1860. doi:10.1007/s10995-016-1988-y

Schetter, C. D., & Tanner, L. (2012). Anxiety, depression and stress in pregnancy: Implications for mothers, children, research, and practice. *Current Opinion in Psychiatry, 25*, 141–148. doi:10.1097/YCO.0b013e3283503680

Schreiber, J. (1977). Birth, the family and the community: A southern Italian example. *Birth and the Family Journal, 4*, 153–157.

Schurz, M., Radua, J., Aichhorn, M., Richlan, F., & Perner, J. (2014). Fractionating theory of mind: A meta analysis of functional brain imaging studies. *Neuroscience & Biobehavioral Reviews, 42*, 9–34. doi:10.1016/j.neubiorev.2014.01.009

Seiler, N. K. (2016). Alcohol and pregnancy: CDC's health advice and the legal rights of pregnant women. *Public Health Reports, 131*, 623–627. doi:10.1177/0033354916662222

Servey, J., & Chang, J. (2014). Over-the-counter medications in pregnancy. *American Family Physician, 90*, 548–555. Retrieved from http://www.ncbi.nlm.nih.gov/pubmed/25369643

Sherr, L., Mueller, J., & Varrall, R. (2009). A systematic review of cognitive development and child human immunodeficiency virus infection. *Psychology, Health & Medicine, 14*, 387–404. doi:10.1080/13548500903012897

Sinclair, K. D., & Watkins, A. J. (2013). Parental diet, pregnancy outcomes and offspring health: Metabolic determinants in developing oocytes and embryos. *Reproduction, Fertility, and Development, 26*, 99–114. doi:10.1071/RD13290

Singer, L. T., Minnes, S., Min, M. O., Lewis, B. A., & Short, E. J. (2015). Prenatal cocaine exposure and child outcomes: A conference report based on a prospective study from Cleveland. *Human Psychopharmacology: Clinical and Experimental, 30*, 285–289. doi:10.1002/hup.2454

Smith, A. M., Mioduszewski, O., Hatchard, T., Byron-Alhassan, A., Fall, C., & Fried, P. A. (2016). Prenatal marijuana exposure impacts executive functioning into young adulthood: An fMRI study. *Neurotoxicology and Teratology, 58*, 53–59. doi:10.1016/J.NTT.2016.05.010

Stoll, B. J., Hansen, N. I., Bell, E. F., Walsh, M. C., Carlo, W. A., Shankaran, S., . . . Higgins, R. D. (2015). Trends in care practices, morbidity, and mortality of extremely preterm neonates, 1993–2012. *JAMA, 314*, 1039. doi:10.1001/jama.2015.10244

Suarez, S. S. (2016). Mammalian sperm interactions with the female reproductive tract. *Cell and Tissue Research, 363*, 185–194. doi:10.1007/s00441-015-2244-2

Sullivan, J. L. (2003). Prevention of mother-to-child transmission of HIV: What next?

Journal of Acquired Immune Deficiency Syndromes, 34(Suppl. 1), S67–S72.

Sutin, A. R., Flynn, H. A., & Terracciano, A. (2017). Maternal cigarette smoking during pregnancy and the trajectory of externalizing and internalizing symptoms across childhood: Similarities and differences across parent, teacher, and self reports. *Journal of Psychiatric Research, 91*, 145–148. doi:10.1016/J.JPSYCHIRES.2017.03.003

Taylor, H. G., Klein, N., Minich, N. M., & Hack, M. (2001). Long-term family outcomes for children with very low birth weights. *Archives of Pediatrics & Adolescent Medicine, 155*, 155–161.

Tehranifar, P., Wu, H.-C., McDonald, J. A., Jasmine, F., Santella, R. M., Gurvich, I., . . . Terry, M. B. (2018). Maternal cigarette smoking during pregnancy and offspring DNA methylation in midlife. *Epigenetics, 13*, 129–134. doi:10.1080/15592294.2017.1325065

Tinker, S. C., Cogswell, M. E., Devine, O., & Berry, R. J. (2010). Folic acid intake among U.S. women aged 15–44 years, National Health and Nutrition Examination Survey, 2003–2006. *American Journal of Preventive Medicine, 38*, 534–542. doi:10.1016/j.amepre.2010.01.025

Tong, V. T., England, L. J., Rockhill, K. M., & D'Angelo, D. V. (2017). Risks of preterm delivery and small for gestational age infants: Effects of nondaily and low-intensity daily smoking during pregnancy. *Paediatric and Perinatal Epidemiology, 31*, 144–148. doi:10.1111/ppe.12343

Torpey, K., Kabaso, M., Kasonde, P., Dirks, R., Bweupe, M., Thompson, C., & Mukadi, Y. D. (2010). Increasing the uptake of prevention of mother-to-child transmission of HIV services in a resource-limited setting. *BMC Health Services Research, 10*, 29–36. doi:10.1186/1472-6963-10-29

Torpey, K., Kasonde, P., Kabaso, M., Weaver, M. A., Bryan, G., Mukonka, V., . . . Colebunders, R. (2010). Reducing pediatric HIV infection: Estimating mother-to-child transmission rates in a program setting in Zambia. *Journal of Acquired Immune Deficiency Syndromes (1999), 54*, 415–422.

Tsimis, M. E., & Sheffield, J. S. (2017). Update on syphilis and pregnancy. *Birth Defects Research, 109*, 347–352. doi:10.1002/bdra.23562

United Nations Children's Fund. (2013). *Towards an AIDS-free generation: Children and AIDS sixth stocktaking report.* Retrieved from http://www.childinfo.org/files/str6_full_report_29-11-2013.pdf

U.S. Department of Agriculture. (2017). *Food security status of U.S. households in 2016.* Retrieved from https://www.ers.usda.gov/topics/food-nutrition-assistance/food-security-in-the-us/key-statisticsgraphics.aspx

U.S. Department of Health and Human Services. (2014). *Child Health USA 2014.* Retrieved from http://www.mchb.hrsa.gov/chusa14/index.html

U.S. Food and Drug Administration. (2010). iPLEDGE information. Retrieved from https://www.fda.gov/Drugs/DrugSafety/PostmarketDrugSafetyInformationforPatientsandProviders/cm094307.htm

Van den Bergh, B. R. H., van den Heuvel, M. I., Lahti, M., Braeken, M., de Rooij, S. R., Entringer, S., . . . Schwab, M. (2017). Prenatal developmental origins of behavior and mental health: The influence of maternal stress in pregnancy. *Neuroscience & Biobehavioral Reviews.* Advance online publication. doi:10.1016/J.NEUBIOREV.2017.07.003

Ventura, A. K., & Worobey, J. (2013). Early influences on the development of food preferences. *Current Biology, 23*, R401–R408. doi:10.1016/J.CUB.2013.02.037

Vigeh, M., Yokoyama, K., Matsukawa, T., Shinohara, A., & Ohtani, K. (2014). Low level prenatal blood lead adversely affects early childhood mental development. *Journal of Child Neurology, 29*, 1305–1311. doi:10.1177/0883073813516999

Visscher, M., & Narendran, V. (2014). Vernix caseosa: Formation and functions. *Newborn and Infant Nursing Reviews, 14*, 142–146. doi:10.1053/j.nainr.2014.10.005

Viswanathan, M., Treiman, K. A., Kish-Doto, J., Middleton, J. C., Coker-Schwimmer, E. J. L., & Nicholson, W. K. (2017). Folic acid supplementation for the prevention of neural tube defects. *JAMA, 317*, 190. doi:10.1001/jama.2016.19193

Viteri, O., Soto, E., Bahado-Singh, R., Christensen, C., Chauhan, S., & Sibai, B. (2015). Fetal anomalies and long term effects associated with substance abuse in pregnancy: A literature review. *American Journal of Perinatology, 32*, 405–416. doi:10.1055/s-0034-1393932

Vouloumanos, A., Hauser, M. D., Werker, J. F., & Martin, A. (2010). The tuning of human neonates' preference for speech. *Child Development, 81*, 517–527. doi:10.1111/j.14678624.2009.01412.x

Warton, F. L., Meintjes, E. M., Warton, C. M. R., Molteno, C. D., Lindinger, N. M., Carter, R. C., . . . Jacobson, S. W. (2018). Prenatal methamphetamine exposure is associated with reduced subcortical volumes in neonates. *Neurotoxicology and Teratology, 65*, 51–59. doi:10.1016/J.NTT.2017.10.005

Webster, S., Morris, G., & Kevelighan, E. (2018). *Essential human development.* Hoboken, NJ: John Wiley.

Weinhold, B. (2009). Environmental factors in birth defects. *Environmental Health Perspectives, 117*, A440–A447.

Wilbur, M. B., Little, S., & Szymanski, L. M. (2015). Is home birth safe? *New England Journal of Medicine, 373*, 2683–2685. doi:10.1056/NEJMclde1513623

Wilhoit, L. F., Scott, D. A., & Simecka, B. A. (2017). Fetal alcohol spectrum disorders: Characteristics, complications, and treatment. *Community Mental Health Journal, 53*, 711–718. doi:10.1007/s10597-017-0104-0

Williams, J., Mai, C. T., Mulinare, J., Isenburg, J., Flood, T. J., Ethen, M., . . . Centers for Disease Control and Prevention. (2015). Updated estimates of neural tube defects prevented by mandatory folic acid fortification—United States, 1995–2011. *MMWR. Morbidity and Mortality Weekly Report, 64*, 1–5.

Wilson, R. D. (2016). A preventable teratology: Isotretinoin. *CMAJ: Canadian Medical Association Journal, 188*, 901. doi:10.1503/cmaj.1150114

Wolff, P. H. (1966). The causes, controls and organization of behavior in the neonate. *Psychological Issues Monograph Series, 5,* 1–105.

Wolke, D., Eryigit-Madzwamuse, S., & Gutbrod, T. (2014). Very preterm/very low birthweight infants' attachment: Infant and maternal characteristics. *Archives of Disease in Childhood. Fetal and Neonatal Edition, 99,* F70–F75. doi:10.1136/archdischild-2013-303788

World Health Organization. (2010). Guidelines on HIV and infant feeding 2010: Principles and recommendations for feeding in the context of HIV and a summary of evidence. Geneva, Switzerland: World Health Organization.

World Health Organization. (2011). *WHO | Progress report 2011: Global HIV/AIDS response.* Retrieved from http://www .who.int/hiv/pub/progress_report 2011/en/

World Hunger Education Service. (2017). *2016 World hunger and poverty facts and statistics.* Retrieved from https://www.worldhunger .org/2015-world-hunger-and-poverty-facts -and-statistics/

Xie, X., Ding, G., Cui, C., Chen, L., Gao, Y., Zhou, Y., . . . Tian, Y. (2013). The effects of low-level prenatal lead exposure on birth outcomes. *Environmental Pollution, 175,* 30–34. doi:10.1016/j.envpol.2012.12.013

Yaniv, S. S., Levy, A., Wiznitzer, A., Holcberg, G., Mazor, M., & Sheiner, E. (2011). A significant linear association exists between advanced maternal age and adverse perinatal outcome. *Archives of Gynecology and Obstetrics, 283,* 755–759. doi:10.1007/s00404-010-1459-4

Yau, G., Schluchter, M., Taylor, H. G., Margevicius, S., Forrest, C. B., Andreias, L., . . . Hack, M. (2013). Bullying of extremely low birth weight children: Associated risk factors during adolescence. *Early Human Development, 89,* 333–338. doi:10.1016/j.earlhumdev.2012.11.004

Zielinski, R., Ackerson, K., & Kane Low, L. (2015). Planned home birth: Benefits, risks, and opportunities. *International Journal of Women's Health, 7,* 361–377. doi:10.2147/IJWH.S55561

Chapter 4

AAP Task Force on Circumcision. (2012). Circumcision policy statement. *Pediatrics, 130,* 585–586. doi:10.1542/peds.2012-1989

Abdelhadi, R. A., Bouma, S., Bairdain, S., Wolff, J., Legro, A., Plogsted, S., . . . ASPEN Malnutrition Committee. (2016). Characteristics of hospitalized children with a diagnosis of malnutrition: United States, 2010. *Journal of Parenteral and Enteral Nutrition, 40,* 623–635. doi:10.1177/0148607116633800

Adolph, K. E., Cole, W. G., Komati, M., Garciaguirre, J. S., Badaly, D., Lingeman, J. M., . . . Sotsky, R. B. (2012). How do you learn to walk? Thousands of steps and dozens of falls per day. *Psychological Science, 23,* 1387–1394. doi:10.1177/0956797612446346

Adolph, K. E., & Franchak, J. M. (2017). The development of motor behavior. *Wiley Interdisciplinary Reviews: Cognitive Science, 8,* e1430. doi:10.1002/wcs.1430

Adolph, K. E., & Kretch, K. S. (2015). Gibson's theory of perceptual learning. In H. Keller (Ed.), *International encyclopedia of social and behavioral sciences.* Retrieved from https://nyuscholars.nyu.edu/en/publications/gibsons-theory-of-perceptual-learning

Adolph, K. E., Kretch, K. S., & LoBue, V. (2014). Fear of heights in infants? *Current Directions in Psychological Science, 23,* 60–66. doi:10.1177/0963721413498895

Adolph, K. E., & Robinson, S. R. (2015). Motor development. In L. S. Liben & U. Muller (Eds.), *Handbook of child psychology and developmental science* (pp. 1–45). Hoboken, NJ: John Wiley. doi:10.1002/9781118963418.childpsy204

Adolph, K. E., & Tamis-LeMonda, C. S. (2014). The costs and benefits of development: The transition from crawling to walking. *Child Development Perspectives, 8,* 187–192. doi:10.1111/cdep.12085

Agyei, S. B., van der Weel, F. R. R., & van der Meer, A. L. H. (2016). Development of visual motion perception for prospective control: Brain and behavioral studies in infants. *Frontiers in Psychology, 7,* 100. doi:10.3389/fpsyg.2016.00100

Alaimo, K., Olson, C. M., & Frongillo Jr., E. A. (2001). Food insufficiency and American school-aged children's cognitive, academic, and psychosocial development. *Pediatrics, 108,* 44–53.

Alanis, M. C., & Lucidi, R. S. (2004). Neonatal circumcision: A review of the world's oldest and most controversial operation. *Obstetrical and Gynecological Survey, 59,* 379–395.

American Academy of Pediatrics (AAP) Task Force on Circumcision Policy. (1999). Circumcision policy statement. *Pediatrics, 103,* 686–693.

American Medical Association. (1999). *Neonatal circumcision.* Chicago, IL: Author.

Amitay, E. L., Dubnov Raz, G., & Keinan-Boker, L. (2016). Breastfeeding, other early life exposures and childhood leukemia and lymphoma. *Nutrition and Cancer, 68,* 968–977. doi:10.1080/01635581.2016.1190020

Ampaabeng, S. K., & Tan, C. M. (2013). The long-term cognitive consequences of early childhood malnutrition: The case of famine in Ghana. *Journal of Health Economics, 32,* 1013–1027. doi:10.1016/j.jhealeco.2013.08.001

Annett, M. (2002). *Handedness and brain asymmetry: The right shift theory.* London, UK: Psychology Press.

Ari-Even Roth, D., Hildesheimer, M., Roziner, I., & Henkin, Y. (2016). Evidence for a right-ear advantage in newborn hearing screening results. *Trends in Hearing, 20,* 233121651668116. doi:10.1177/2331216516681168

Aslin, R. N. (2014). Infant learning: Historical, conceptual, and methodological challenges. *Infancy, 19,* 2–27. doi:10.1111/infa.12036

Ball, H. L., Hooker, E., & Kelly, P. J. (1999). Where will the baby sleep? Attitudes and practices of new and experienced parents regarding co-sleeping with their new-born infants. *American Anthropologist, 101,* 1–9.

Ball, H. L., Hooker, E., & Kelly, P. J. (2000). Parent-infant co-sleeping: Fathers' roles and perspectives. *Infant and Child Development, 9,* 67–74.

Banich, M. T. (1998). Integration of information between the cerebral hemispheres. *Current Directions in Psychological Science, 7,* 32–37.

Banich, M. T., & Heller, W. (1998). Evolving perspectives on lateralization of function. *Current Directions in Psychological Science, 7,* 1–2.

Barros, M. C. M., Mitsuhiro, S., Chalem, E., Laranjeira, R. R., & Guinsburg, R. (2011). Neurobehavior of late preterm infants of adolescent mothers. *Neonatology, 99,* 133–139. doi:10.1159/000313590

Beal, J. A. (2017). Neonatal male circumcision. *American Journal of Maternal/Child Nursing, 42,* 233. doi:10.1097/NMC.0000000000000352

Beauchamp, G. K., & Mennella, J. A. (2011). Flavor perception in human infants: Development and functional significance. *Digestion, 83*(Suppl. 1), 1–6. doi:10.1159/000323397

Benatar, M., & Benatar, D. (2003). Between prophylaxis and child abuse: The ethics of neonatal male circumcision. *American Journal of Bioethics, 3,* 35–48.

Berardi, N., Sale, A., & Maffei, L. (2015). Brain structural and functional development: Genetics and experience. *Developmental Medicine & Child Neurology, 57,* 4–9. doi:10.1111/dmcn.12691

Berger, S. E., Theuring, C., & Adolph, K. E. (2007). How and when infants learn to climb stairs. *Infant Behavior & Development, 30,* 36–49. doi:10.1016/j.infbeh.2006.11.002

Bernier, A., Calkins, S. D., & Bell, M. A. (2016). Longitudinal associations between the quality of mother-infant interactions and brain development across infancy. *Child Development, 87,* 1159–1174. doi:10.1111/cdev.12518

Bertenthal, B. I., Campos, J. J., & Barrett, K. (1984). Self-produced locomotion: An organizer of emotional, cognitive, and social development in infancy. In R. Emde & R. Harmon (Eds.), *Continuities and discontinuities in development* (pp. 174–210). New York, NY: Plenum.

Bick, J., & Nelson, C. A. (2017). Early experience and brain development. *Wiley Interdisciplinary Reviews: Cognitive Science, 8,* e1387. doi:10.1002/wcs.1387

Binder, E., Dovern, A., Hesse, M. D., Ebke, M., Karbe, H., Saliger, J., . . . Weiss, P. H. (2017). Lesion evidence for a human mirror neuron system. *Cortex, 90,* 125–137. doi:10.1016/J.CORTEX.2017.02.008

Binner, S. L., Mastrobattista, J. M., Day, M.-C., Swaim, L. S., & Monga, M. (2002). Effect of parental education on decision-making about neonatal circumcision. *Southern Medical Journal, 95,* 457–461.

Blass, E. M., Ganchrow, J. R., & Steiner, J. E. (1984). Classical conditioning in newborn humans 2-48 hours of age. *Infant Behavior and Development, 7,* 223–235.

Bloomfield, F. H., Alexander, T., Muelbert, M., & Beker, F. (2017). Smell and taste in the preterm infant. *Early Human Development, 114,* 31–34. doi:10.1016/J.EARLHUMDEV.2017.09.012

Blumberg, M. S., Gall, A. J., & Todd, W. D. (2014). The development of sleep-wake rhythms and the search for elemental circuits in the infant brain. *Behavioral Neuroscience, 128,* 250–263. doi:10.1037/a0035891

Bo, X., & Goldman, H. (2008). Newborn circumcision in Victoria, Australia: Reasons and parental attitudes. *ANZ Journal of Surgery, 78,* 1019–1022. doi:10.1111/j.1445-2197.2008.04723.x

Bornstein, M. H., & Lamb, M. E. (1992). *Development in infancy* (3rd ed.). New York, NY: McGraw-Hill.

Bower, T. G. R., Broughton, J. M., & Moore, M. K. (1970). The coordination of vision and tactile input in infancy. *Perception and Psychophysics, 8,* 51–53.

Brown, T. T., & Jernigan, T. L. (2012). Brain development during the preschool years. *Neuropsychology Review, 22,* 313–333. doi:10.1007/s11065-012-9214-1

Bruner, J. S. (1973). *Beyond the information given: Studies in the psychology of knowing.* Oxford, England: W. W. Norton.

Cabinian, A., Sinsimer, D., Tang, M., Zumba, O., Mehta, H., Toma, A., . . . Richardson, B. (2016). Transfer of maternal immune cells by breastfeeding: Maternal cytotoxic T lymphocytes present in breast milk localize in the Peyer's patches of the nursed infant. *PLoS ONE, 11,* e0156762. doi:10.1371/journal.pone.0156762

Centers for Disease Control and Prevention. (2013). Progress in increasing breastfeeding and reducing racial/ethnic differences—United States, 2000–2008 births. *MMWR. Morbidity and Mortality Weekly Report, 62,* 77–80. Retrieved from http://www.ncbi.nlm.nih.gov/pubmed/23388550

Centers for Disease Control and Prevention. (2017). *Breastfeeding among U.S. children born 2002–2014, CDC National Immunization Survey.* Retrieved December 22, 2017, from https://www.cdc.gov/breastfeeding/data/nis_data/results.html

Chaibal, S., Bennett, S., Rattanathanthong, K., & Siritaratiwat, W. (2016). Early developmental milestones and age of independent walking in orphans compared with typical home-raised infants. *Early Human Development, 101,* 23–26. doi:10.1016/j.earlhumdev.2016.06.008

Chambers, A. M. (2017). The role of sleep in cognitive processing: Focusing on memory consolidation. *Wiley Interdisciplinary Reviews: Cognitive Science, 8,* e1433. doi:10.1002/wcs.1433

Chen, X., Striano, T., & Rakoczy, H. (2004). Auditory–oral matching behavior in newborns. *Developmental Science, 7,* 42–47.

Cheng, D. T., Meintjes, E. M., Stanton, M. E., Dodge, N. C., Pienaar, M., Warton, C. M. R., . . . Jacobson, S. W. (2016). Functional MRI of human eyeblink classical conditioning in children with fetal alcohol spectrum disorders. *Cerebral Cortex, 27,* 3752–3767. doi:10.1093/cercor/bhw273

Chevalier, N., Kurth, S., Doucette, M. R., Wiseheart, M., Deoni, S. C. L. S., Dean, D. C. D., . . . Greenstein, D. (2015). Myelination is associated with processing speed in early childhood: Preliminary insights. *PLoS ONE, 10,* e0139897. doi:10.1371/journal.pone.0139897

Child Trends Databank. (2015). *Immunization. Child trends databank.* Retrieved from https://www.childtrends.org/?indicators=immunization

Clifford, A., Franklin, A., Davies, I. R. L., & Holmes, A. (2009). Electrophysiological markers of categorical perception of color in 7-month old infants. *Brain & Cognition, 71,* 165–172. doi:10.1016/j.bandc.2009.05.002

Clifton, R. K., Rochat, P., Robin, D. J., & Berthier, N. E. (1994). Multimodal perception in the control of infant reaching. *Journal of Experimental Psychology: Human Perception and Performance, 20,* 876–886.

Cochet, H. (2012). Development of hand preference for object-directed actions and pointing gestures: A longitudinal study between 15 and 25 months of age. *Developmental Psychobiology, 54,* 105–111. doi:10.1002/dev.20576

Cole, S. Z., & Lanham, J. S. (2011). Failure to thrive: An update. *American Family Physician, 83,* 829–834.

Cole, W. G., Lingeman, J. M., & Adolph, K. E. (2012). Go naked: Diapers affect infant walking. *Developmental Science, 15,* 783–790. doi:10.1111/j.1467-7687.2012.01169.x

Cole, W. G., Robinson, S. R., & Adolph, K. E. (2016). Bouts of steps: The organization of infant exploration. *Developmental Psychobiology, 58,* 341–354. doi:10.1002/dev.21374

Coleman-Jensen, A., Rabbitt, M., Gregory, C., & Singh, A. (2016). *Household food security in the United States in 2015.* Retrieved from https://www.ers.usda.gov/publications/pub-details/?pubid=79760

Colombo, J., Brez, C. C., & Curtindale, L. M. (2015). Infant perception and cognition. In I. B. Weiner, R. M. Lerner, M. A. Easterbrooks, & J. Mistry (Eds.), *Handbook of psychology: Developmental psychology* (pp. 61–90). Hoboken, NJ: John Wiley.

Cook, R., Bird, G., Catmur, C., Press, C., & Heyes, C. (2014). Mirror neurons: From origin to function. *The Behavioral and Brain Sciences, 37,* 177–192. doi:10.1017/S0140525X13000903

Corbetta, D., & Snapp-Childs, W. (2009). Seeing and touching: The role of sensory-motor experience on the development of infant reaching. *Infant Behavior & Development, 32,* 44–58. doi:10.1016/j.infbeh.2008.10.004

D'Souza, H., Cowie, D., Karmiloff-Smith, A., & Bremner, A. J. (2017). Specialization of the motor system in infancy: From broad tuning to selectively specialized purposeful actions. *Developmental Science, 20,* e12409. doi:10.1111/desc.12409

Dahl, A., Campos, J. J., Anderson, D. I., Uchiyama, I., Witherington, D. C., Ueno, M., & Barburoth, M. (2013). The epigenesis of wariness of heights. *Psychological Science, 24,* 1361–1367. doi:10.1177/0956797613476047

de Onis, M., & Branca, F. (2016). Childhood stunting: A global perspective. *Maternal & Child Nutrition, 12,* 12–26. doi:10.1111/mcn.12231

de Sousa Freire, N. B., Santos Garcia, J. B., & Carvalho Lamy, Z. (2008). Evaluation of analgesic effect of skin-to-skin contact compared to oral glucose in preterm neonates. *Pain, 139,* 28–33. doi:10.1016/j.pain.2008.02.031

Dehaene-Lambertz, G. (2017). The human infant brain: A neural architecture able to learn language. *Psychonomic Bulletin & Review, 24,* 48–55. doi:10.3758/s13423-016-1156-9

Deming, D. M., Reidy, K. C., Fox, M. K., Briefel, R. R., Jacquier, E., & Eldridge, A. L. (2017). Cross-sectional analysis of eating patterns and snacking in the US Feeding Infants and Toddlers Study 2008. *Public Health Nutrition, 20,* 1584–1592. doi:10.1017/S136898001700043X

Dennis, W. (1960). Causes of retardation among institutional children: Iran. *Journal of Genetic Psychology, 96,* 47–59.

Dennis, W., & Dennis, M. G. (1991). The effect of cradling practices upon the onset of walking in Hopi children. *Journal of Genetic Psychology, 152,* 563–572.

Der, G., Batty, G. D., & Deary, I. J. (2006). Effect of breast feeding on intelligence in children: Prospective study, sibling pairs analysis, and meta-analysis. *BMJ: British Medical Journal (International Edition), 333,* 945–948.

Diamond, A. (2013). Executive functions. *Annual Review of Psychology, 64,* 135–168. doi:10.1146/annurev-psych-113011-143750

Diego, M. A., Field, T., Hernandez-Reif, M., Deeds, O., Ascencio, A., & Begert, G. (2007). Preterm infant massage elicits consistent increases in vagal activity and gastric motility that are associated with greater weight gain. *Acta Paediatrica, 96,* 1588–1591. doi:10.1111/j.1651-2227.2007.00476.x

DiPietro, J. A. (2000). Baby and the brain: Advances in child development. *Annual Review of Public Health, 21,* 455–471.

Domsch, H., Thomas, H., & Lohaus, A. (2010). Infant attention, heart rate, and looking time during habituation/dishabituation. *Infant Behavior and Development, 33,* 321–329. doi:10.1016/j.infbeh.2010.03.008

Doyon, J., Gabitov, E., Vahdat, S., Lungu, O., & Boutin, A. (2018). Current issues related to motor sequence learning in humans. *Current Opinion in Behavioral Sciences, 20,* 89–97. doi:10.1016/j.cobeha.2017.11.012

Duboc, V., Dufourcq, P., Blader, P., & Roussigné, M. (2015). Asymmetry of the brain: Development and implications. *Annual Review of Genetics, 49,* 647–672. doi:10.1146/annurev-genet-112414-055322

Dziewolska, H., & Cautilli, J. (2006). The effects of a motor training package on minimally assisted standing behavior in a three-month-old infant. *The Behavior Analyst Today, 7,* 111–120.

Efron, R. (1990). *The decline and fall of hemispheric specialization.* Hillsdale, NJ: Lawrence Erlbaum.

Ennouri, K., & Bloch, H. (1996). Visual control of hand approach movements in newborns. *British Journal of Developmental Psychology, 14,* 327–338. doi:10.1111/j.2044-835X.1996.tb00709.x

Fagard, J., Spelke, E., & von Hofsten, C. (2009). Reaching and grasping a moving object in 6-, 8-, and 10-month-old infants: Laterality and performance. *Infant Behavior & Development, 32,* 137–146. doi:10.1016/j.infbeh.2008.12.002

Fantz, R. L. (1961). The origin of form perception. *Scientific American, 204,* 66–72.

Feigelman, S., & Keane, V. (2017). Failure to thrive. In R. Kliegman, P. S. Lye, B. J. Bordini, H. Toth, & D. Basel (Eds.), *Nelson pediatric symptom-based diagnosis* (p. 896). Philadelphia, PA: Elsevier.

Ferber, S. G., & Makhoul, I. R. (2008). Neurobehavioural assessment of skin-to-skin effects on reaction to pain in preterm infants: A randomized, controlled within-subject trial. *Acta Paediatrica, 97,* 171–176. doi:10.1111/j.1651-2227.2007.00607.x

Fetters, L., & Hsiang-han, H. (2007). Motor development and sleep, play, and feeding positions in very-low-birthweight infants with and without white matter disease. *Developmental Medicine & Child Neurology, 49,* 807–813. doi:10.1111/j.1469-8749.2007.00807.x

Figueiredo, B., Dias, C. C., Pinto, T. M., & Field, T. (2016). Infant sleep-wake behaviors at two weeks, three and six months. *Infant Behavior and Development, 44,* 169–178. doi:10.1016/J.INFBEH.2016.06.011

Floccia, C., Christophe, A., & Bertoncini, J. (1997). High-amplitude sucking and newborns: The quest for underlying mechanisms. *Journal of Experimental Child Psychology, 64,* 175–198.

Fogel, A. (2007). *Infancy: Infant, family, and society* (7th ed.). Cornwall-on-Hudson, NY: Sloan Educational Publishing.

Forestell, C. A. (2016). The development of flavor perception and acceptance: The roles of nature and nurture. *Nestle Nutrition Institute Workshop Series, 85,* 135–143. doi:10.1159/000439504

Frank, M. C., Vul, E., & Johnson, S. P. (2009). Development of infants' attention to faces during the first year. *Cognition, 110,* 160–170. doi:10.1016/j.cognition.2008.11.010

Freedman, A. L. (2016). The circumcision debate: Beyond benefits and risks. *Pediatrics, 137,* e20160594. doi:10.1542/peds.2016-0594

Friedrich, M., Wilhelm, I., Mölle, M., Born, J., & Friederici, A. D. (2017). The sleeping infant brain anticipates development. *Current Biology, 27,* 2374–2380.e3. doi:10.1016/J.CUB.2017.06.070

Frisch, M., Aigrain, Y., Barauskas, V., Bjarnason, R., Boddy, S.-A., Czauderna, P., . . . Wijnen, R. (2013). Cultural bias in the AAP's 2012 technical report and policy statement on male circumcision. *Pediatrics, 131.* Retrieved from http://pediatrics.aappublications.org/content/131/4/796.short

Gabriel, M. A. M., Alonso, C. R. P., Bértolo, J. D. L. C., Carbonero, S. C., Maestro, M. L., Pumarega, M. M., . . . Pablos, D. L. (2009). Age of sitting unsupported and independent walking in very low birth weight preterm infants with normal motor development at 2 years. *Acta Paediatrica, 98,* 1815–1821. doi:10.1111/j.1651-2227.2009.01475.x

Galland, B. C., Taylor, B. J., Elder, D. E., & Herbison, P. (2012). Normal sleep patterns in infants and children: A systematic review of observational studies. *Sleep Medicine Reviews, 16,* 213–222. doi:10.1016/J.SMRV.2011.06.001

Galler, J. R., Bryce, C. P., Zichlin, M. L., Fitzmaurice, G., Eaglesfield, G. D., & Waber, D. P. (2012). Infant malnutrition is associated with persisting attention deficits in middle adulthood. *Journal of Nutrition, 142,* 788–794. doi:10.3945/jn.111.145441

Galloway, J. C., & Thelen, E. (2004). Feet first: Object exploration in young infants. *Infant Behavior Development, 27,* 107–112.

Gaultney, J. F., & Gingras, J. L. (2005). Fetal rate of behavioral inhibition and preference for novelty during infancy. *Early Human Development, 81,* 379–386.

Gervain, J., Macagno, F., Cogoi, S., Peña, M., & Mehler, J. (2008). The neonate brain detects speech structure. *Proceedings of the National Academy of Sciences of the United States of America, 105,* 14222–14227. doi:10.1073/pnas.0806530105

Gervain, J., & Mehler, J. (2010). Speech perception and language acquisition in the first year of life. *Annual Review of Psychology, 61,* 191–218. doi:10.1146/annurev.psych.093008.100408

Gettler, L. T., & McKenna, J. J. (2011). Evolutionary perspectives on mother-infant sleep proximity and breastfeeding in a laboratory setting. *American Journal of Physical Anthropology, 144,* 454–462. doi:10.1002/ajpa.21426

Geva, R., Yaron, H., & Kuint, J. (2016). Neonatal sleep predicts attention orienting and distractibility. *Journal of Attention Disorders, 20,* 138–150. doi:10.1177/1087054713491493

Ghassabian, A., Sundaram, R., Bell, E., Bello, S. C., Kus, C., & Yeung, E. (2016). Gross motor milestones and subsequent development. *Pediatrics, 138,* e20154372. doi:10.1542/peds.2015-4372

Gibb, R., & Kovalchuk, A. (2018). Brain development. In R. Gibb & B. Kolb (Eds.), *The neurobiology of brain and behavioral development* (pp. 3–27). Cambridge, MA: Academic Press. doi:10.1016/B978-0-12-804036-2.00001-7

Gibson, E. J., & Pick, A. D. (2000). *An ecological approach to perceptual learning and development.* New York, NY: Oxford University Press.

Gibson, E. J., & Walk, R. D. (1960). The visual cliff. *Scientific American, 202,* 64–71.

Gibson, J. (1979). *The ecological approach to visual perception.* Boston, MA: Houghton, Mifflin.

Gliga, T., Elsabbagh, M., Andravizou, A., & Johnson, M. (2009). Faces attract infants' attention in complex displays. *Infancy, 14,* 550–562. doi:10.1080/15250000903144199

Godfrey, J. R., & Lawrence, R. A. (2010). Toward optimal health: The maternal benefits of breastfeeding. *Journal of Women's Health, 19,* 1597–1602. doi:10.1089/jwh.2010.2290

Goubet, N., Strasbaugh, K., & Chesney, J. (2007). Familiarity breeds content? Soothing effect of a familiar odor on full-term newborns. *Journal of Developmental & Behavioral Pediatrics, 28,* 189–194. doi:10.1097/dbp.0b013e31802d0b8d

Gradin, M., Eriksson, M., Schollin, J., Holmqvist, G., & Holstein, A. (2002). Pain reduction at venipuncture in newborns: Oral glucose compared with local anesthetic cream. *Pediatrics, 110,* 1053–1057.

Griffiths, L. J., Tate, A. R., & Lucy, J. G. (2007). Do early infant feeding practices vary by maternal ethnic group? *Public Health Nutrition, 10,* 957–964.

Haith, M. M. (1993). Preparing for the 21st century: Some goals and challenges for studies of infant sensory and perceptual development. *Developmental Review, 13,* 354–371.

Hampton, T. (2007). Food insecurity harms health, well-being of millions in the United States. *JAMA: Journal of the American Medical Association, 298,* 1851–1853.

Harker, A. (2018). Social dysfunction. In R. Gibb & B. Kolb (Eds.), *The neurobiology of brain and behavioral development* (pp. 439–467). Philadelphia, PA: Elsevier. doi:10.1016/B978-0-12-804036-2.00016-9

Harriman, A. E., & Lukosius, P. A. (1982). On why Wayne Dennis found Hopi infants retarded in age at onset of walking. *Perceptual & Motor Skills, 55,* 79–86.

Hauck, Y. L., Fenwick, J., Dhaliwal, S. S., & Butt, J. (2011). A Western Australian survey of breastfeeding initiation, prevalence and early cessation patterns. *Maternal & Child Health Journal, 15,* 260–268. doi:10.1007/s10995-009-0554-2

He, M., Walle, E. A., & Campos, J. J. (2015). A cross-national investigation of the relationship between infant walking and language development. *Infancy, 20,* 283–305. doi:10.1111/infa.12071

Hensch, T. K. (2018). Critical periods in cortical development. In R. Gibb & B. Kolb (Eds.), *The neurobiology of brain and behavioral development* (pp. 133–151). Philadelphia, PA: Elsevier. doi:10.1016/B978-0-12-804036-2.00006-6

Henry, O., Brzostek, J., Czajka, H., Leviniene, G., Reshetko, O., Gasparini, R., . . . Innis, B. (2018). One or two doses of live varicella virus-containing vaccines: Efficacy, persistence of immune responses, and safety six years after administration in healthy children during their second year of life. *Vaccine, 36,* 381–387. doi:10.1016/J.VACCINE.2017.11.081

Hepper, P. G. (2013). The developmental origins of laterality: Fetal handedness. *Developmental Psychobiology, 55,* 588–595. doi:10.1002/dev.21119

Hepper, P. G. (2015). Behavior during the prenatal period: Adaptive for development and survival. *Child Development Perspectives, 9,* 38–43. doi:10.1111/cdep.12104

Herbert, J., Eckerman, C. O., Goldstein, R. F., & Stanton, M. E. (2004). Contrasts in classical eyeblink conditioning as a function of premature birth. *Infancy, 5,* 367–383.

Hernandez-Pavon, J. C., Sosa, M., Lutter, W. J., Maier, M., & Wakai, R. T. (2008). Auditory evoked responses in neonates by MEG. *AIP Conference Proceedings, 1032,* 114–117. doi:10.1063/1.2979244

Hernandez-Reif, M., Diego, M., & Field, T. (2007). Preterm infants show reduced stress behaviors and activity after 5 days of massage therapy. *Infant Behavior Development, 30,* 557–561. doi:10.1016/j.infbeh.2007.04.002

Hodel, A. S., Hunt, R. H., Cowell, R. A., Van Den Heuvel, S. E., Gunnar, M. R., & Thomas, K. M. (2015). Duration of early adversity and structural brain development in post-institutionalized adolescents. *NeuroImage, 105,* 112–119. doi:10.1016/J.NEUROIMAGE.2014.10.020

Homan, G. J. (2016). Failure to thrive: A practical guide. *American Family Physician, 94,* 295–299.

Hopkins, B. (1991). Facilitating early motor development: An intercultural study of West Indian mothers and their infants living in Britain. In J. K. Nugent, B. M.

Lester, & T. B. Brazelton (Eds.), *The cultural context of infancy: Vol. 2. Multicultural and interdisciplinary approaches to parent-infant relations.* Norwood, NJ: Ablex.

Hopkins, B., & Westra, T. (1989). Maternal expectations of their infants' development: Some cultural differences. *Developmental Medicine Child Neurology, 31,* 384–390.

Hopkins, B., & Westra, T. (1990). Motor development, maternal expectations, and the role of handling. *Infant Behavior & Development, 13,* 117–122.

Hunnius, S., & Geuze, R. H. (2004). Developmental changes in visual scanning of dynamic faces and abstract stimuli in infants: A longitudinal study. *Infancy, 6,* 231–255.

Imdad, A., Yakoob, M. Y., & Bhutta, Z. A. (2011). Effect of breastfeeding promotion interventions on breastfeeding rates, with special focus on developing countries. *BMC Public Health, 11*(Suppl. 3), 1–8. doi:10.1186/1471-2458-11-s3-s24

Isaacs, E. B., Fischl, B. R., Quinn, B. T., Chong, W. K., Gadian, D. G., & Lucas, A. (2010). Impact of breast milk on intelligence quotient, brain size, and white matter development. *Pediatric Research, 67,* 357–362.

Islami, F., Liu, Y., Jemal, A., Zhou, J., Weiderpass, E., Colditz, G., . . . Weiss, M. (2015). Breastfeeding and breast cancer risk by receptor status—a systematic review and meta-analysis. *Annals of Oncology, 26,* mdv379. doi:10.1093/annonc/mdv379

James, D. K. (2010). Fetal learning: A critical review. *Infant & Child Development, 19,* 45–54. doi:10.1002/icd.653

Jenkins, J. M., & Foster, E. M. (2014). The effects of breastfeeding exclusivity on early childhood outcomes. *American Journal of Public Health, 104*(Suppl.), S128–S135. doi:10.2105/AJPH.2013.301713

Johnson, S. P., & Hannon, E. E. (2015). Perceptual development. In L. S. Liben & U. Muller *Handbook of child psychology and developmental science* (pp. 1–50). Hoboken, NJ: John Wiley. doi:10.1002/9781118963418.childpsy203

Kail, R. V. (2003). Information processing and memory. In M. H. Bornstein & L. Davidson (Eds.), *Well-being: Positive development across the life course* (pp. 269–279). Mahwah, NJ: Lawrence Erlbaum.

Kaplan, H., & Dove, H. (1987). Infant development among the Ache of eastern Paraguay. *Developmental Psychology, 23,* 190–198.

Karasik, L. B., Tamis-LeMonda, C. S., Adolph, K. E., & Bornstein, M. H. (2015). Places and postures: A cross-cultural comparison of sitting in 5-month-olds. *Journal of Cross-Cultural Psychology, 46,* 1023–1038. doi:10.1177/0022022115593803

Kavšek, M. (2004). Predicting later IQ from infant visual habituation and dishabituation: A meta-analysis. *Journal of Applied Developmental Psychology, 25,* 369–393. doi:10.1016/j.appdev.2004.04.006

Kavšek, M., & Bornstein, M. H. (2010). Visual habituation and dishabituation in preterm infants: A review and meta-analysis. *Research in Developmental Disabilities, 31,* 951–975. doi:10.1016/j.ridd.2010.04.016

Kawai, N. (2010). Towards a new study on associative learning in human fetuses: Fetal associative learning in primates. *Infant &*

Child Development, 19, 55–59. doi:10.1002/icd.654

Kayed, N. S., Farstad, H., & van der Meer, A. L. H. (2008). Preterm infants' timing strategies to optical collisions. *Early Human Development, 84,* 381–388. doi:10.1016/j.earlhumdev.2007.10.006

Keller, H. (2003). Socialization for competence: Cultural models of infancy. *Human Development, 46,* 288–311.

Keven, N., & Akins, K. A. (2017). Neonatal imitation in context: Sensorimotor development in the perinatal period. *Behavioral and Brain Sciences, 40,* e381. doi:10.1017/S0140525X16000911

Kim, S., Fleisher, B., & Sun, J. Y. (2017). The long-term health effects of fetal malnutrition: Evidence from the 1959–1961 China great leap forward famine. *Health Economics, 26,* 1264–1277. doi:10.1002/hec.3397

Kisilevsky, B. S. (2016). Fetal auditory processing: Implications for language development? In N. Reissland & B. S. Kisilevsky (Eds.), *Fetal development* (pp. 133–152). Cham, Switzerland: Springer International. doi:10.1007/978-3-319-22023-9_8

Kit, B. K., Akinbami, L. J., Isfahani, N. S., & Ulrich, D. A. (2017). Gross motor development in children aged 3–5 years, United States 2012. *Maternal and Child Health Journal, 21,* 1–8. doi:10.1007/s10995-017-2289-9

Kliegman, R., Stanton, B., St. Geme, J. W., Schor, N. F., Behrman, R. E., & Nelson, W. E. (2016). *Nelson textbook of pediatrics.* Philadelphia, PA: Elsevier.

Kolb, B. (2018). Overview of factors influencing brain development. In R. Gibb & B. Kolb (Eds.), *The neurobiology of brain and behavioral development* (pp. 51–79). Philadelphia, PA: Elsevier. doi:10.1016/B978-0-12-804036-2.00003-0

Kolb, B., Mychasiuk, R., & Gibb, R. (2014). Brain development, experience, and behavior. *Pediatric Blood & Cancer, 61,* 1720–1723. doi:10.1002/pbc.24908

Kolb, B., Whishaw, I., & Teskey, G. C. (2016). *An introduction to brain and behavior.* New York, NY: Worth.

Kotwica, K. A., Ferre, C. L., & Michel, G. F. (2008). Relation of stable hand-use preferences to the development of skill for managing multiple objects from 7 to 13 months of age. *Developmental Psychobiology, 50,* 519–529. doi:10.1002/dev.20311

Krafchuk, E. E., Tronick, E. Z., & Clifton, R. K. (1983). Behavioral and cardiac responses to sound in preterm infants varying in risk status: A hypothesis of their paradoxical reactivity. In T. Field & A. Sostek (Eds.), *Infants born at risk: Physiological, perceptual, and cognitive processes* (pp. 99–128). New York, NY: Grune & Stratton.

Kramer, M. S., Fombonne, E., Igumnov, S., Vanilovich, I., Matush, L., Mironova, E., . . . Platt, R. W. (2008). Effects of prolonged and exclusive breastfeeding on child behavior and maternal adjustment: Evidence from a large, randomized trial. *Pediatrics, 121,* e435–e440.

Kretch, K. S., & Adolph, K. E. (2017). The organization of exploratory behaviors in infant locomotor planning. *Developmental Science, 20,* e12421. doi:10.1111/desc.12421

Kretch, K. S., Franchak, J. M., & Adolph, K. E. (2014). Crawling and walking infants see the world differently. *Child Development, 85,* 1503–1518. doi:10.1111/cdev.12206

Krueger, J. M., Frank, M. G., Wisor, J. P., & Roy, S. (2016). Sleep function: Toward elucidating an enigma. *Sleep Medicine Reviews, 28,* 46–54. doi:10.1016/J.SMRV.2015.08.005

Kuo, Y.-L., Liao, H.-F., Chen, P.-C., Hsieh, W.-S., & Hwang, A.-W. (2008). The influence of wakeful prone positioning on motor development during the early life. *Journal of Developmental and Behavioral Pediatrics, 29,* 367–376. doi:10.1097/DBP.0b013e3181856d54

Kurosky, S. K., Davis, K. L., & Krishnarajah, G. (2017). Effect of combination vaccines on completion and compliance of childhood vaccinations in the United States. *Human Vaccines & Immunotherapeutics, 13,* 2494–2502. doi:10.1080/21645515.2017.1362515

Lampl, M., & Johnson, M. L. (2011). Infant growth in length follows prolonged sleep and increased naps. *Sleep, 34,* 641–650. doi:10.1093/sleep/34.5.641

Lampl, M., Johnson, M. L., & Frongillo, E. A., Jr. (2001). Mixed distribution analysis identifies saltation and stasis growth. *Annals of Human Biology, 28,* 403–411.

Larson-Nath, C., & Biank, V. F. (2016). Clinical review of failure to thrive in pediatric patients. *Pediatric Annals, 45,* e46–e49. doi:10.3928/00904481-20160114-01

Lee, B. K., & McGrath, J. J. (2015). Advancing parental age and autism: Multifactorial pathways. *Trends in Molecular Medicine, 21,* 118–125. doi:10.1016/J.MOLMED.2014.11.005

Lee, H., & Galloway, J. C. (2012). Control in very young infants. *Physical Therapy, 92,* 935–947.

Lewis, S. (2017). Sleep: Dream a little dream. *Nature Reviews Neuroscience, 18,* 324–324. doi:10.1038/nrn.2017.66

Lewkowicz, D. J., Leo, I., & Simion, F. (2010). Intersensory perception at birth: Newborns match nonhuman primate faces and voices. *Infancy, 15,* 46–60. doi:10.1111/j.1532-7078.2009.00005.x

Libertus, K., Gibson, J., Hidayatallah, N. Z., Hirtle, J., Adcock, R. A., & Needham, A. (2013). Size matters: How age and reaching experiences shape infants' preferences for different sized objects. *Infant Behavior & Development, 36,* 189–198. doi:10.1016/j.infbeh.2013.01.006

Libertus, K., Joh, A. S., & Needham, A. W. (2016). Motor training at 3 months affects object exploration 12 months later. *Developmental Science, 19,* 1058–1066. doi:10.1111/desc.12370

Libertus, K., & Needham, A. (2010). Teach to reach: The effects of active vs. passive reaching experiences on action and perception. *Vision Research, 50,* 2750–2757. doi:10.1016/j.visres.2010.09.001

Lipsitt, L. P., & Kaye, H. (1964). Conditioned sucking in the human newborn. *Psychonomic Science, 1,* 29–30.

Litovsky, R. Y., & Ashmead, D. H. (1997). Development of binaural and spatial hearing in infants and children. In R. H. Gilkey & T. R. Anderson (Eds.), *Binaural and special hearing in real and virtual environments* (pp. 571–592). Mahwah, NJ: Lawrence Erlbaum.

Little, A. H., Lipsitt, L. P., & Rovee-Collier, C. K. (1984). Classical conditioning and retention of the infant's eyelid response: Effects of age and interstimulus interval. *Journal of Experimental Child Psychology, 37*, 512–524.

Lobo, M. A., & Galloway, J. C. (2012). Enhanced handling and positioning in early infancy advances development throughout the first year. *Child Development, 83*, 1290–1302. doi:10.1111/j.1467-8624.2012.01772.x

Lohaus, A., Keller, H., Lamm, B., Teubert, M., Fassbender, I., Freitag, C., . . . Schwarzer, G. (2011). Infant development in two cultural contexts: Cameroonian Nso farmer and German middleclass infants. *Journal of Reproductive and Infant Psychology, 29*, 148–161. doi:10.1080/02646838.2011.558074

Lozoff, B., Wolf, A. W., & Davis, N. S. (1984). Cosleeping in urban families with young children in the United States. *Pediatrics, 74*, 171–182.

Lyall, A. E., Shi, F., Geng, X., Woolson, S., Li, G., Wang, L., . . . Gilmore, J. H. (2015). Dynamic development of regional cortical thickness and surface area in early childhood. *Cerebral Cortex, 25*, 2204–2212. doi:10.1093/cercor/bhu027

Lynch, A., Lee, H. M., Bhat, A., & Galloway, J. C. (2008). No stable arm preference during the pre-reaching period: A comparison of right and left hand kinematics with and without a toy present. *Developmental Psychobiology, 50*, 390–398. doi:10.1002/dev.20297

Macfarlane, A. J. (1975). Olfaction in the development of social preferences in the human neonate. *Ciba Foundation Symposia, 33*, 103–117.

Markant, J. C., & Thomas, K. M. (2013). *Postnatal brain development* (P. D. Zelazo, Ed.). Oxford, UK: Oxford University Press. doi:10.1093/oxfordhb/9780199958450.013.0006

Marlier, L., & Schaal, B. (2005). Human newborns prefer human milk: Conspecific milk odor is attractive without postnatal exposure. *Child Development, 76*, 155–168.

Martin, L. R., & Petrie, K. J. (2017). Understanding the dimensions of anti-vaccination attitudes: The Vaccination Attitudes Examination (VAX) scale. *Annals of Behavioral Medicine, 51*, 652–660. doi:10.1007/s12160-017-9888-y

Matlin, M. W., & Foley, H. J. (1997). *Sensation and perception* (4th ed.). Boston, MA: Allyn & Bacon.

Matsuda, E. (2017). Sucrose for analgesia in newborn infants undergoing painful procedures. *Nursing Standard, 31*, 61–63. doi:10.7748/ns.2017.e10827

Maurer, D. (2017). Critical periods re-examined: Evidence from children treated for dense cataracts. *Cognitive Development, 42*, 27–36. doi:10.1016/j.cogdev.2017.02.006

Maurer, D., & Lewis, T. L. (2013). *Sensitive periods in visual development* (P. D. Zelazo, Ed.). Oxford, UK: Oxford University Press. doi:10.1093/oxfordhb/9780199958450.013.0008

May, L., Gervain, J., Carreiras, M., & Werker, J. F. (2018). The specificity of the neural response to speech at birth. *Developmental Science, 21*, e12564. doi:10.1111/desc.12564

McCall, R. B. (1994). What process mediates predictions of childhood IQ from infant habituation and recognition memory? Speculations on the roles of inhibition and rate of information processing. *Intelligence, 18*, 107–125.

McCorry, N. K., & Hepper, P. G. (2007). Fetal habituation performance: Gestational age and sex effects. *British Journal of Developmental Psychology, 25*, 277–292.

McKenna, J. J. (2001). Why we never ask "Is it safe for infants to sleep alone?" *Academy of Breast Feeding Medicine News and Views, 7*, 32, 38.

McKenna, J. J., & Volpe, L. E. (2007). Sleeping with baby: An Internet-based sampling of parental experiences, choices, perceptions, and interpretations in a Western industrialized context. *Infant and Child Development, 16*, 359–385. doi:10.1002/icd.525

McLaughlin, K. A., Sheridan, M. A., & Nelson, C. A. (2017). Neglect as a violation of species-expectant experience: Neurodevelopmental consequences. *Biological Psychiatry, 82*, 462–471. doi:10.1016/J.BIOPSYCH.2017.02.1096

Meltzoff, A. N., & Borton, R. W. (1979). Intermodal matching by human neonates. *Nature, 282*, 403–404.

Meltzoff, A. N., & Kuhl, P. K. (1994). Faces and speech: Intermodal processing of biologically relevant signals in infants and adults. In D. J. Lewkowicz & R. Lickliter (Eds.), *The development of intersensory perception* (pp. 335–369). Hillsdale, NJ: Lawrence Erlbaum.

Meltzoff, A. N., & Moore, M. K. (1977). Imitation of facial and manual gestures by human neonates. *Science, 198*, 75–78.

Mennella, J. A., & Beauchamp, G. K. (2002). Flavor experiences during formula feeding are related to preferences during childhood. *Early Human Development, 68*, 71–82.

Mercuri, E., Baranello, G., Romeo, D. M. M., Cesarini, L., & Ricci, D. (2007). The development of vision. *Early Human Development, 83*, 795–800. doi:10.1016/j.earlhumdev.2007.09.014

Michel, G. F., Campbell, J. M., Marcinowski, E. C., Nelson, E. L., & Babik, I. (2016). Infant hand preference and the development of cognitive abilities. *Frontiers in Psychology, 7*, 410. doi:10.3389/fpsyg.2016.00410

Miles, G., & Siega-Riz, A. M. (2017). Trends in food and beverage consumption among infants and toddlers: 2005–2012. *Pediatrics, 139*, e20163290. doi:10.1542/peds.2016-3290

Mindell, J. A., Sadeh, A., Wiegand, B., How, T. H., & Goh, D. Y. T. (2010). Cross-cultural differences in infant and toddler sleep. *Sleep Medicine, 11*, 274–280. doi:10.1016/J.SLEEP.2009.04.012

Mitchell, E. A. (2009). Risk factors for SIDS. *BMJ: British Medical Journal, 339*, 873–874. doi:10.1136/bmj.b3466

Modabbernia, A., Velthorst, E., & Reichenberg, A. (2017). Environmental risk factors for autism: An evidence-based review of systematic reviews and meta-analyses. *Molecular Autism, 8*, 13. doi:10.1186/s13229-017-0121-4

Monk, C. S., Webb, S. J., & Nelson, C. A. (2001). Prenatal neurobiological development: Molecular mechanisms and anatomical change. *Developmental Neuropsychology, 19*, 211–236.

Moon, C., Cooper, R. P., & Fifer, W. P. (1993). Two-day-old infants prefer their native language. *Infant Behavior and Development, 16*, 495–500.

Morelli, G., Rogoff, B., Oppenheim, D., & Goldsmith, D. (1992). Cultural variation in infants' sleeping arrangements: Questions of independence. *Developmental Psychology, 28*, 604–613.

Morley, J. E. (2016). Protein-energy undernutrition (PEU). *Merck Manual*. Retrieved from http://www.merckmanuals.com/professional/nutritional-disorders/undernutrition/protein-energy-undernutrition-peu

Morokuma, S., Fukushima, K., Kawai, N., Tomonaga, M., Satoh, S., & Nakano, H. (2004). Fetal habituation correlates with functional brain development. *Behavioural Brain Research, 153*, 459–463.

Morris, B. J., Kennedy, S. E., Wodak, A. D., Mindel, A., Golovsky, D., Schrieber, L., . . . Ziegler, J. B. (2017). Early infant male circumcision: Systematic review, risk-benefit analysis, and progress in policy. *World Journal of Clinical Pediatrics, 6*, 89–102. doi:10.5409/wjcp.v6.i1.89

Morris, B. J., Wamai, R. G., Henebeng, E. B., Tobian, A. A., Klausner, J. D., Banerjee, J., & Hankins, C. A. (2016). Estimation of country-specific and global prevalence of male circumcision. *Population Health Metrics, 14*, 4. doi:10.1186/s12963-016-0073-5

Mowery, T. M., Kotak, V. C., & Sanes, D. H. (2016). The onset of visual experience gates auditory cortex critical periods. *Nature Communications, 7*, 10416. doi:10.1038/ncomms10416

Muenssinger, J., Matuz, T., Schleger, F., Kiefer-Schmidt, I., Goelz, R., Wacker-Gussmann, A., . . . Preissl, H. (2013). Auditory habituation in the fetus and neonate: An fMEG study. *Developmental Science, 16*, 287–295. doi:10.1111/desc.12025

Mummert, A., Schoen, M., & Lampl, M. (2018). Growth and life course health development. In N. Halfon, C. B. Forrest, R. M. Lerner, & E. M. Faustman (Eds.), *Handbook of life course health development* (pp. 405–429). Cham, Switzerland: Springer International. doi:10.1007/978-3-319-47143-3_17

Nadel, J., & Butterworth, G. (1999). *Imitation in infancy*. Cambridge, England: Cambridge University Press.

Nagy, E., Pilling, K., Orvos, H., & Molnar, P. (2013). Imitation of tongue protrusion in human neonates: Specificity of the response in a large sample. *Developmental Psychology, 49*, 1628–1638. doi:10.1037/a0031127

Nakano, T., Watanabe, H., Homae, F., & Taga, G. (2009). Prefrontal cortical involvement in young infants' analysis of novelty. *Cerebral Cortex, 19*, 455–463. doi:10.1093/cercor/bhn096

Náñez Sr., J. E., & Yonas, A. (1994). Effects of luminance and texture motion on infant defensive reactions to optical collision. *Infant Behavior & Development, 17*, 165–174.

NCD Risk Factor Collaboration (NCD-RisC). (2016). A century of trends in adult human height. *eLife, 5*, e13410. doi:10.7554/eLife.13410

Nelson, C. A., Fox, N. A., Zeanah, C. H., Nelson, C. A., Fox, N. A., & Zeanah, C. H. (2016). The effects of early psychosocial deprivation on brain and behavioral development: Findings from the Bucharest Early Intervention Project. In D. Cicchetti (Ed.), *Developmental psychopathology* (pp. 1–37). Hoboken, NJ: John Wiley. doi:10.1002/9781119125556.devpsy418

Nelson, E. L., Campbell, J. M., & Michel, G. F. (2013). Unimanual to bimanual: Tracking the development of handedness from 6 to 24 months. *Infant Behavior & Development, 36,* 181–188. doi:10.1016/j.infbeh.2013.01.009

Nelson, E. L., Campbell, J. M., & Michel, G. F. (2015). Early handedness in infancy predicts language stability in toddlers. *Developmental Psychology, 50,* 809–814. doi:10.1037/a0033803.Early

Neville, H. J., & Bavelier, D. (2001). Variability of developmental plasticity: Carnegie Mellon symposia on cognition. In J. L. McClelland & R. S. Siegler (Eds.), *Mechanisms of cognitive development: Behavioral and neural perspectives* (pp. 271–301). Mahwah, NJ: Lawrence Erlbaum.

Newell, F. N. (2004). Cross-modal object recognition. In G. A. Calvert, C. Spence, & B. E. Stein (Eds.), *The handbook of multisensory processes.* (pp. 123–139). Cambridge, MA: MIT Press.

Nishitani, S., Miyamura, T., Tagawa, M., Sumi, M., Takase, R., Doi, H., . . . Shinohara, K. (2009). The calming effect of a maternal breast milk odor on the human newborn infant. *Neuroscience Research, 63,* 66–71. doi:10.1016/j.neures.2008.10.007

Nishiyori, R., Bisconti, S., Meehan, S. K., & Ulrich, B. D. (2016). Developmental changes in motor cortex activity as infants develop functional motor skills. *Developmental Psychobiology, 58,* 773–783. doi:10.1002/dev.21418

Northern, J. L., Downs, M. P., & Hayes, D. (2014). *Hearing in children.* San Diego, CA: Plural.

Olsen, E. M. (2006). Failure to thrive: Still a problem of definition. *Clinical Pediatrics, 45,* 1–6.

Oostenbroek, J., Suddendorf, T., Nielsen, M., Redshaw, J., Kennedy-Costantini, S., Davis, J., . . . Slaughter, V. (2016). Comprehensive longitudinal study challenges the existence of neonatal imitation in humans. *Current Biology, 26,* 1334–1338. doi:10.1016/j.cub.2016.03.047

Owings, M., Uddin, S., & Williams, S. (2013). Trends in circumcision among male newborns born in U.S. hospitals: 1979–2010. *NCHS Health E-Stat.* Retrieved from http://www.cdc.gov/nchs/data/hestat/circumcision_2013/circumcision_2013.htm

Paix, B. R., Peterson, S. E. (2012). Circumcision of neonates and children without appropriate anaesthesia is unacceptable practice. *Anaesthesia & Intensive Care, 40,* 511.

Papousek, H. (1967). Conditioning during early postnatal development. In Y. Brackbill & G. G. Thompson (Eds.), *Behavior in infancy and early childhood* (pp. 268–284). New York, NY: Free Press.

Pascalis, O., Dechonen, S., Morton, J., Duruelle, C., & Grenet, F. (1995). Mother's face recognition in neonates: A replication and an extension. *Infant Behavior and Development, 18,* 79–85.

Payne, V. G., & Isaacs, L. D. (2016). *Human motor development: A lifespan approach.* New York,

NY: McGraw-Hill. Retrieved from http://dl.acm.org/citation.cfm?id=1214267

Peter, C. J., Fischer, L. K., Kundakovic, M., Garg, P., Jakovcevski, M., Dincer, A., . . . Akbarian, S. (2016). DNA methylation signatures of early childhood malnutrition associated with impairments in attention and cognition. *Biological Psychiatry, 80,* 765–774. doi:10.1016/J.BIOPSYCH.2016.03.2100

Piaget, J. (1952). *The origins of intelligence in children.* New York, NY: International Universities Press. (Original work published 1936)

Porter, R., Varendi, H., Christensson, K., Porter, R. H., & Winberg, J. (1998). Soothing effect of amniotic fluid smell in newborn infants. *Early Human Development, 51,* 47–55.

Previc, F. H. (1991). A general theory concerning the prenatal origins of cerebral lateralization in humans. *Psychological Review, 98,* 299–334. doi:10.1037/0033-295X.98.3.299

Qiu, A., Mori, S., & Miller, M. I. (2015). Diffusion tensor imaging for understanding brain development in early life. *Annual Review of Psychology, 66,* 853–876. doi:10.1146/annurev-psych-010814-015340

Racine, E. F., Frick, K., Guthrie, J. F., & Strobino, D. (2009). Individual net-benefit maximization: A model for understanding breastfeeding cessation among low-income women. *Maternal & Child Health Journal, 13,* 241–249. doi:10.1007/s10995-008-0337-1

Ratnarajah, N., Rifkin-Graboi, A., Fortier, M. V, Chong, Y. S., Kwek, K., Saw, S.-M., . . . Qiu, A. (2013). Structural connectivity asymmetry in the neonatal brain. *NeuroImage, 75,* 187–194. doi:10.1016/j.neuroimage.2013.02.052

Rattaz, C., Goubet, N., & Bullinger, A. (2005). The calming effect of a familiar odor on full-term newborns. *Journal of Developmental and Behavioral Pediatrics, 26,* 86–92.

Remer, J., Croteau-Chonka, E., Dean, D. C., D'Arpino, S., Dirks, H., Whiley, D., & Deoni, S. C. L. (2017). Quantifying cortical development in typically developing toddlers and young children, 1–6 years of age. *NeuroImage, 153,* 246–261. doi:10.1016/J.NEUROIMAGE.2017.04.010

Richards, J. E. (1997). Effects of attention on infant's preference for briefly exposed visual stimuli in the paired-comparison recognition-memory paradigm. *Developmental Psychology, 32,* 22–31.

Richards, J. E., & Holley, F. B. (1999). Infant attention and the development of smooth pursuit tracking. *Developmental Psychology, 35,* 856–867.

Richmond, S., Johnson, K. A., Seal, M. L., Allen, N. B., & Whittle, S. (2016). Development of brain networks and relevance of environmental and genetic factors: A systematic review. *Neuroscience & Biobehavioral Reviews, 71,* 215–239. doi:10.1016/j.neubiorev.2016.08.024

Rizzolatti, G., Sinigaglia, C., & Anderson, F. (2008). *Mirrors in the brain: How our minds share actions and emotions.* New York, NY: Oxford University Press.

Roelants, M., Hauspie, R., & Hoppenbrouwers, K. (2010). Breastfeeding, growth and growth standards: Performance of the WHO growth standards for monitoring growth of Belgian children. *Annals of Human Biology, 37,* 2–9. doi:10.3109/03014460903089500

Ross, E. S. (2017). Flavor and taste development in the first years of life. *Nestle Nutrition Institute Workshop Series, 87,* 49–58. doi:10.1159/000448937

Rovee-Collier, C. K. (1987). Learning and memory. In J. D. Osofsky (Ed.), *Handbook of infant development* (2nd ed., pp. 98–148). New York, NY: John Wiley.

Sadeh, A., De Marcas, G., Guri, Y., Berger, A., Tikotzky, L., & Bar-Haim, Y. (2015). Infant sleep predicts attention regulation and behavior problems at 3–4 years of age. *Developmental Neuropsychology, 40,* 122–137. doi:10.1080/87565641.2014.973498

Sai, F. Z. (2005). The role of the mother's voice in developing mother's face preference: Evidence for intermodal perception at birth. *Infant & Child Development, 14,* 29–50.

Salmon, D. A., Dudley, M. Z., Glanz, J. M., & Omer, S. B. (2015). Vaccine hesitancy: Causes, consequences, and a call to action. *Vaccine, 33,* D66–D71. doi:10.1016/J.VACCINE.2015.09.035

Sann, C., & Streri, A. (2007). Perception of object shape and texture in human newborns: Evidence from cross-modal transfer tasks. *Developmental Science, 10,* 399–410. doi:10.1111/j.1467-7687.2007.00593.x

Savelsbergh, G., van der Kamp, J., & van Wermeskerken, M. (2013). The development of reaching actions. In P. D. Zelazo (Ed.), *The Oxford handbook of developmental psychology* (Vol. 1). Oxford, UK: Oxford University Press. doi:10.1093/oxfordhb/9780199958450.013.0014

Schaal, B. (2017). Infants and children making sense of scents. In *Springer handbook of odor* (pp. 107–108). Cham, Switzerland: Springer International. doi:10.1007/978-3-319-26932-0_43

Schaal, B., Montagner, H., Hertling, E., Bolzoni, D., Moyse, R., & Quichon, R. (1980). Olfactory stimulations in mother-infant relationships. *Reproduction, Nutrition, Development, 20,* 843–858.

Schoenmaker, C., Juffer, F., van IJzendoorn, M. H., van den Dries, L., Linting, M., van der Voort, A., & Bakermans-Kranenburg, M. J. (2015). Cognitive and health-related outcomes after exposure to early malnutrition: The Leiden longitudinal study of international adoptees. *Children and Youth Services Review, 48,* 80–86. doi:10.1016/j.childyouth.2014.12.010

Schuldiner, O., & Yaron, A. (2015). Mechanisms of developmental neurite pruning. *Cellular and Molecular Life Sciences, 72,* 101–19. doi:10.1007/s00018-014-1729-6

Schulze, P. A., & Carlisle, S. A. (2010). What research does and doesn't say about breastfeeding: A critical review. *Early Child Development & Care, 180,* 703–718. doi:10.1080/03004430802263870

Shaw, D. J., & Czekóová, K. (2013). Exploring the development of the mirror neuron system: Finding the right paradigm. *Developmental Neuropsychology, 38,* 256–271. doi:10.1080/87565641.2013.783832

Sheridan, M. A., & McLaughlin, K. A. (2014). Dimensions of early experience and neural development: Deprivation and threat. *Trends in Cognitive Sciences, 18,* 580–585. doi:10.1016/J.TICS.2014.09.001

Siekerman, K., Barbu-Roth, M., Anderson, D. I., Donnelly, A., Goffinet, F., & Teulier, C. (2015).

Treadmill stimulation improves newborn stepping. *Developmental Psychobiology, 57,* 247–254. doi:10.1002/dev.21270

Simmons, K. (2015). *Sub-Saharan Africa makes progress against poverty but has long way to go.* Retrieved December 20, 2017, from http://www.pewresearch.org/fact-tank/2015/09/24/sub-saharan-africa-makes-progress-against-poverty-but-has-long-way-to-go/

Slater, A., Rose, D., & Morison, V. (1984). Newborn infants' perception of similarities and differences between two- and three-dimensional stimuli. *British Journal of Developmental Psychology, 3,* 211–220.

Sloan, S., Stewart, M., & Dunne, L. (2010). The effect of breastfeeding and stimulation in the home on cognitive development in one-year-old Infants. *Child Care in Practice, 16,* 101–110. doi:10.1080/13575270903529136

Smith-Gagen, J., Hollen, R., Walker, M., Cook, D. M., & Yang, W. (2014). Breastfeeding laws and breastfeeding practices by race and ethnicity. *Women's Health Issues, 24,* e11–e19. doi:10.1016/J.WHI.2013.11.001

Spencer, J. P., Vereijken, B., Diedrich, F. J., & Thelen, E. (2000). Posture and the emergence of manual skills. *Developmental Science, 3,* 216–217.

Spencer, R. M. C., Walker, M. P., & Stickgold, R. (2017). Sleep and memory consolidation. In S. Chokroverty (Ed.), *Sleep disorders medicine* (pp. 205–223). New York, NY: Springer. doi:10.1007/978-1-4939-6578-6_13

Springer, S. P., & Deutsch, G. (1998). *Left brain, right brain: Perspectives from cognitive neuroscience* (5th ed.). New York, NY: Freeman.

Steiner, J. E. (1979). Human facial expressions in response to taste and smell stimulations. In L. P. Lipsitt & H. W. Reese (Eds.), *Advances in child development* (Vol. 13, pp. 257–295). New York, NY: Academic Press.

Stiles, J., Brown, T. T., Haist, F., Jernigan, T. L., Stiles, J., Brown, T. T., . . . Jernigan, T. L. (2015). Brain and cognitive development. In L. S. Liben & U. Muller (Eds.), *Handbook of child psychology and developmental science* (pp. 1–54). Hoboken, NJ: John Wiley. doi:10.1002/9781118963418.childpsy202

Stiles, J., & Jernigan, T. L. (2010). The basics of brain development. *Neuropsychology Review, 20,* 327–348. doi:10.1007/s11065-010-9148-4

Su, J. R., Leroy, Z., Lewis, P. W., Haber, P., Marin, M., Leung, J., . . . Shimabukuro, T. T. (2017). Safety of second-dose single-antigen varicella vaccine. *Pediatrics, 139,* e20162536. doi:10.1542/peds.2016-2536

Suddendorf, T., Oostenbroek, J., Nielsen, M., & Slaughter, V. (2013). Is newborn imitation developmentally homologous to later social-cognitive skills? *Developmental Psychobiology, 55,* 52–58. doi:10.1002/dev.21005

Sugita, Y. (2004). Experience in early infancy is indispensable for color perception. *American Journal of Ophthalmology, 138,* 902.

Super, C. M., & Harkness, S. (1982). The infant's niche in rural Kenya and metropolitan America. In L. L. Adler (Ed.), *Cross-cultural research at issue* (pp. 247–255). New York, NY: Academic Press.

Super, C. M., & Harkness, S. (2015). Charting infant development. In L. A. Jensen (Ed.), *The Oxford handbook of human development and culture.* Oxford, UK: Oxford University Press. doi:10.1093/oxfordhb/9780199948550.013.6

Tamis-LeMonda, C. S., Song, L., & Bornstein, M. H. (1989). Habituation and maternal encouragement of attention in infancy as predictors of toddler language, play, and representational competence. *Child Development, 60,* 738–751.

Tamnes, C. K., Herting, M. M., Goddings, A.-L., Meuwese, R., Blakemore, S.-J., Dahl, R. E., . . . Mills, K. L. (2017). Development of the cerebral cortex across adolescence: A multisample study of inter-related longitudinal changes in cortical volume, surface area, and thickness. *Journal of Neuroscience, 37,* 3402–3412. doi:10.1523/JNEUROSCI.3302-16.2017

Tanaka, K., Kon, N., Ohkawa, N., Yoshikawa, N., & Shimizu, T. (2009). Does breastfeeding in the neonatal period influence the cognitive function of very-low-birth-weight infants at 5 years of age? *Brain Development, 31,* 288–293. doi:10.1016/j.braindev.2008.05.011

Tarullo, A. R., Isler, J. R., Condon, C., Violaris, K., Balsam, P. D., & Fifer, W. P. (2016). Neonatal eyelid conditioning during sleep. *Developmental Psychobiology, 58,* 875–882. doi:10.1002/dev.21424

Task Force on Sudden Infant Death Syndrome. (2016). SIDS and other sleep-related infant deaths: Updated 2016 recommendations for a safe infant sleeping environment. *Pediatrics, 138,* e20162938. doi:10.1542/peds.2016-2938

Taylor, L. E., Swerdfeger, A. L., & Eslick, G. D. (2014). Vaccines are not associated with autism: An evidence-based meta-analysis of case-control and cohort studies. *Vaccine, 32,* 3623–3629. doi:10.1016/j.vaccine.2014.04.085

Taylor, N., Donovan, W., & Leavitt, L. (2008). Consistency in infant sleeping arrangements and mother-infant interaction. *Infant Mental Health Journal, 29,* 77–94. doi:10.1002/imhj.20170

Teller, D. Y. (1997). First glances: The vision of infants. *Investigative Ophthalmology & Visual Science, 38,* 2183–2203.

Teller, D. Y. (1998). Spatial and temporal aspects of infant color vision. *Vision Research, 38,* 3275–3282.

Tham, E. K., Schneider, N., & Broekman, B. F. (2017). Infant sleep and its relation with cognition and growth: A narrative review. *Nature and Science of Sleep, 9,* 135–149. doi:10.2147/NSS.S125992

Thelen, E. (1995). Motor development: A new synthesis. *American Psychologist, 50,* 79–95. doi:10.1037/0003-066X.50.2.79

Thelen, E. (2000). Motor development as foundation and future of developmental psychology. *International Journal of Behavioral Development, 24,* 385–397.

Thoman, E. B., & Ingersoll, E. W. (1993). Learning in premature infants. *Developmental Psychology, 28,* 692–700.

Tiemeier, H., Lenroot, R. K., Greenstein, D. K., Tran, L., Pierson, R., & Giedd, J. N. (2010). Cerebellum development during childhood and adolescence: A longitudinal morphometric MRI study. *NeuroImage, 49,* 63–70. doi:10.1016/j.neuroimage.2009.08.016

Tononi, G., & Cirelli, C. (2014). Sleep and the price of plasticity: From synaptic and cellular homeostasis to memory consolidation and integration. *Neuron, 81,* 12–34. doi:10.1016/j.neuron.2013.12.025

Tramacere, A., Pievani, T., & Ferrari, P. F. (2017). Mirror neurons in the tree of life: Mosaic evolution, plasticity and exaptation of sensorimotor matching responses. *Biological Reviews, 92,* 1819–1841. doi:10.1111/brv.12310

Trettien, A. W. (1990). Creeping and walking. *American Journal of Psychology, 12,* 1–57.

Turfkruyer, M., & Verhasselt, V. (2015). Breast milk and its impact on maturation of the neonatal immune system. *Current Opinion in Infectious Diseases, 28,* 199–206. doi:10.1097/QCO.0000000000000165

Turner, B. O., Marinsek, N., Ryhal, E., & Miller, M. B. (2015). Hemispheric lateralization in reasoning. *Annals of the New York Academy of Sciences, 1359,* 47–64. doi:10.1111/nyas.12940

U.K. Department of Health. (2005). *Reduce the risk of cot death: An easy guide.* London: UK Department of Health.

U.S. Department of Health and Human Services. (2011). *The Surgeon General's call to action to support breastfeeding.* Washington, DC: Author.

van Heteren, C. F., Boekkooi, P. F., Jongsma, H. W., & Nijhuis, J. G. (2000). Fetal learning and memory. *The Lancet, 356,* 1169–1170.

Vannasing, P., Florea, O., González-Frankenberger, B., Tremblay, J., Paquette, N., Safi, D., . . . Gallagher, A. (2016). Distinct hemispheric specializations for native and non-native languages in one-day-old newborns identified by fNIRS. *Neuropsychologia, 84,* 63–69. doi:10.1016/j.neuropsychologia.2016.01.038

Vereijken, B., & Thelen, E. (1997). Training infant treadmill stepping: The role of individual pattern stability. *Developmental Psychobiology, 30,* 89–102.

Victora, C. G., Bahl, R., Barros, A. J. D., França, G. V. A., Horton, S., Krasevec, J., . . . Rollins, N. C. (2016). Breastfeeding in the 21st century: Epidemiology, mechanisms, and lifelong effect. *The Lancet, 387,* 475–490. doi:10.1016/S0140-6736(15)01024-7

Vilasboas, T., Herbet, G., & Duffau, H. (2017). Challenging the myth of right nondominant hemisphere: Lessons from corticosubcortical stimulation mapping in awake surgery and surgical implications. *World Neurosurgery, 103,* 449–456. doi:10.1016/j.wneu.2017.04.021

Vincini, S., Jhang, Y., Buder, E. H., & Gallagher, S. (2017). Neonatal imitation: Theory, experimental design, and significance for the field of social cognition. *Frontiers in Psychology, 8,* 1323. doi:10.3389/fpsyg.2017.01323

von Hofsten, C., & Rönnqvist, L. (1993). The structuring of neonatal arm movements. *Child Development, 64,* 1046–1057. Retrieved from http://www.ncbi.nlm.nih.gov/pubmed/8404256

Waber, D. P., Bryce, C. P., Fitzmaurice, G. M., Zichlin, M. L., McGaughy, J., Girard, J. M., & Galler, J. R. (2014). Neuropsychological outcomes at midlife following moderate to severe malnutrition in infancy.

Neuropsychology, 28, 530–540. doi:10.1037/neu0000058

Walk, R. D. (1968). Monocular compared to binocular depth perception in human infants. *Science, 162*, 473–475.

Waltes, R., Duketis, E., Knapp, M., Anney, R. J. L., Huguet, G., Schlitt, S., . . . Chiocchetti, A. G. (2014). Common variants in genes of the postsynaptic FMRP signalling pathway are risk factors for autism spectrum disorders. *Human Genetics, 133*, 781–792. doi:10.1007/s00439-013-1416-y

Wang, G., Johnson, S., Gong, Y., Polk, S., Divall, S., Radovick, S., . . . Wang, X. (2016). Weight gain in infancy and overweight or obesity in childhood across the gestational spectrum: A prospective birth cohort study. *Scientific Reports, 6*, 29867. doi:10.1038/srep29867

Watson, J. B., & Raynor, R. (1920). Conditioned emotional reactions. *Journal of Experimental Psychology, 3*, 1–14.

Weaver, J., Crespi, S., Tosetti, M., & Morrone, M. (2015). Map of visual activity in the infant brain sheds light on neural development. *PLoS Biology, 13*, e1002261. doi:10.1371/journal.pbio.1002261

Wessel, L. (2017). Vaccine myths. *Science, 356*, 368–372. doi:10.1126/science.356.6336.368

Whitehouse, A. J. O., Robinson, M., Li, J., & Oddy, W. H. (2011). Duration of breast feeding and language ability in middle childhood. *Paediatric & Perinatal Epidemiology, 25*, 44–52. doi:10.1111/j.1365-3016.2010.01161.x

Wilson, R. S., & Harpring, E. B. (1972). Mental and motor development in infant twins. *Developmental Psychology, 7*, 277–287.

Witherington, D. C., Campos, J. J., Anderson, D. I., Lejeune, L., & Seah, E. (2005). Avoidance of heights on the visual cliff in newly walking infants. *Infancy, 7*, 285–298. doi:10.1207/s15327078in0703_4

Wojcicki, J. M., Heyman, M. B., Elwan, D., Lin, J., Blackburn, E., & Epel, E. (2016). Early exclusive breastfeeding is associated with longer telomeres in Latino preschool children. *American Journal of Clinical Nutrition, 104*, 397–405. doi:10.3945/ajcn.115.115428

World Health Organization. (2009). *WHO child growth standards and the identification of severe acute malnutrition in infants and children: A joint statement.* Retrieved from http://www.who.int/nutrition/publications/severemalnutrition/9789241598163/en/

Xiao-na, H., Hui-shan, W., Li-jin, Z., & Xi-cheng, L. (2010). Co-sleeping and children's sleep in China. *Biological Rhythm Research, 41*, 169–181. doi:10.1080/09291011003687940

Young, G. (2016). Lateralization and specialization of the brain. In G. Young (Ed.), *Unifying causality and psychology* (pp. 177–200). Cham, Switzerland: Springer International. doi:10.1007/978-3-319-24094-7_8

Zelazo, N. A., Zelazo, P. R. D. R., Cohen, K. M., & Zelazo, P. R. D. R. (1993). Specificity of practice effects on elementary neuromotor patterns. *Developmental Psychology, 29*, 686–691. doi:10.1037/0012-1649.29.4.686

Zelazo, P. R. (1983). The development of walking: New findings on old assumptions. *Journal of Motor Behavior, 2*, 99–137.

Chapter 5

Abraham, L. M., Crais, E., & Vernon-Feagans, L. (2013). Early maternal language use during book sharing in families from low-income environments. *American Journal of Speech Language Pathology/American Speech-Language-Hearing Association, 22*, 71–83. doi:10.1044/1058-0360(2012/11-0153)

Acredolo, L. P., & Goodwyn, S. (1985). Symbolic gesturing in language development. *Human Development, 28*, 40–49. doi:10.1159/10.1159/000272934

Acredolo, L. P., & Goodwyn, S. (1988). Symbolic gesturing in normal infants. *Child Development, 59*, 450–466.

Acredolo, L. P., Goodwyn, S., & Abrams, D. (2009). *Baby signs: How to talk with your baby before your baby can talk* (3rd ed.). New York, NY: McGraw-Hill.

Ahmed, A., & Ruffman, T. (1998). Why do infants make A not B errors in a search task, yet show memory for location of hidden objects in a non-search task? *Developmental Psychology, 34*, 441–453.

Aiello, L. C., & Dunbar, R. I. M. (1993). Neocortex size, group size, and the evolution of language. *Current Anthropology, 34*, 184–193. doi:10.1086/204160

Akhtar, N., Jipson, J., & Callanan, M. A. (2001). Learning words through overhearing. *Child Development, 72*, 416–430.

American Academy of Pediatrics. (2017). *AAP agenda for children.* Retrieved September 17, 2017, from https://www.aap.org/en-us/about-the-aap/aap-facts/AAP-Agenda-for-Children-Strategic-Plan/Pages/AAP-Agenda-for-Children-Strategic-Plan.aspx

American Academy of Pediatrics Council on Communications and Media. (2016). Media and young minds. *Pediatrics, 138*. Retrieved from http://pediatrics.aappublications.org/content/138/5/e20162591

Anderson, D. R., & Pempek, T. A. (2005). Television and very young children. *American Behavioral Scientist, 48*, 505–522. doi:10.1177/0002764204271506

Andruski, J. E., Casielles, E., & Nathan, G. (2013). Is bilingual babbling language-specific? Some evidence from a case study of Spanish–English dual acquisition. *Bilingualism: Language and Cognition, 17*, 660–672. doi:10.1017/S1366728913000655

Baddeley, A. (2012). Working memory: Theories, models, and controversies. *Annual Review of Psychology, 63*, 1–29.

Baddeley, A. (2016). Working memory. In R. J. Sternberg, S. T. Fiske, & D. J. Foss (Eds.), *Scientists making a difference: One hundred eminent behavioral and brain scientist talk about their most important contributions.* New York, NY: Cambridge University Press.

Baillargeon, R. (1987). Object permanence in 3 1/2- and 4 1/2-month-old-infants. *Developmental Psychology, 23*, 655–664.

Baillargeon, R., Scott, R. M., & Bian, L. (2016). Psychological reasoning in infancy. *Annual Review of Psychology, 67*, 159–186. doi:10.1146/annurev-psych-010213-115033

Barr, R. (2010). Transfer of learning between 2D and 3D sources during infancy: Informing theory and practice. *Developmental Review, 30*, 128–154. doi:10.1016/j.dr.2010.03.001

Barr, R. (2013). Memory constraints on infant learning from picture books, television, and touchscreens. *Child Development Perspectives, 7*, 205–210. doi:10.1111/cdep.12041

Barr, R., Marrott, H., & Rovee-Collier, C. (2003). The role of sensory preconditioning in memory retrieval by preverbal infants. *Learning & Behavior, 31*, 111–123.

Bassano, D. (2000). Early development of nouns and verbs in French: Exploring the interface between lexicon and grammar. *Journal of Child Language, 27*, 521–559.

Bates, E., Bretherton, I., & Snyder, L. (1988). *From first words to grammar.* Cambridge, England: Cambridge University Press.

Bayley, N. (1949). Consistency and variability in the growth of intelligence from birth to eighteen years. *The Pedagogical Seminary and Journal of Genetic Psychology, 75*, 165–196. doi:10.1080/08856559.1949.10533516

Bayley, N. (1969). *Manual for the Bayley scales of infant development.* San Antonio, TX: Psychological Corporation.

Bayley, N. (2005). *Bayley scales of infant and toddler development* (3rd ed.). San Antonio, TX: Psychological Corporation.

Bergelson, E., & Swingley, D. (2012). At 6–9 months, human infants know the meanings of many common nouns. *Proceedings of the National Academy of Sciences of the United States of America, 109*, 3253–3258. doi:10.1073/pnas.1113380109

Berry, D., Blair, C., Willoughby, M., Garrett-Peters, P., Vernon-Feagans, L., & Mills-Koonce, W. R. (2016). Household chaos and children's cognitive and socio-emotional development in early childhood: Does childcare play a buffering role? *Early Childhood Research Quarterly, 34*, 115–127. doi:10.1016/J.ECRESQ.2015.09.003

Berwick, R. C., & Chomsky, N. (2016). *Why only us: Language and evolution.* Cambridge: MIT Press.

Berwick, R. C., Chomsky, N., & Piattelli Palmarini, M. (2013). Poverty of the stimulus stands: Why recent challenges fail. In M. Piattelli-Palmarini & R. C. Berwick (Eds.), *Rich languages from poor inputs* (pp. 18–42). Oxford, UK: Oxford University Press. doi:10.1093/acprof:oso/9780199590339.003.0002

Betancourt, L. M., Avants, B., Farah, M. J., Brodsky, N. L., Wu, J., Ashtari, M., & Hurt, H. (2016). Effect of socioeconomic status (SES) disparity on neural development in female African-American infants at age 1 month. *Developmental Science, 19*, 947–956. doi:10.1111/desc.12344

Bjorklund, D. F. (2018). A metatheory for cognitive development (or "Piaget is dead" revisited). *Child Development.* Advance online publication. doi:10.1111/cdev.13019

Bjorklund, D. F., & Myers, A. (2015). The development of cognitive abilities. In M. H. Bornstein & M. E. Lamb (Eds.), *Developmental science: An advanced textbook* (pp. 391–441). New York, NY: Psychology Press.

Bogartz, R. S., Shinskey, J. L., & Schilling, T. H. (2000). Object permanence in five-and-a-half month-old infants? *Infancy, 1*, 403–428. doi:10.1207/S15327078IN0104_3

Bohannon. J. N., Padgett, R. J., Nelson, K. E., & Mark, M. (1996). Useful evidence on negative evidence. *Developmental Psychology, 32,* 551–555.

Bohannon, J. N., & Stanowicz, L. (1988). The issue of negative evidence: Adult responses to children's language errors. *Developmental Psychology, 24,* 684–689.

Bornstein, M. H., & Arterberry, M. E. (2010). The development of object categorization in young children: Hierarchical inclusiveness, age, perceptual attribute, and group versus individual analyses. *Developmental Psychology, 46,* 350–365. doi:10.1037/a0018411

Bornstein, M. H., Arterberry, M. E., & Mash, C. (2004). Long-term memory for an emotional interpersonal interaction occurring at 5 months of age. *Infancy, 6,* 407–416.

Bornstein, M. H., Cote, L. R., Maital, S., Painter, K., Park, S. Y., Pascual, L., . . . Vyt, A. (2004). Cross-linguistic analysis of vocabulary in young children: Spanish, Dutch, French, Hebrew, Italian, Korean, and American English. *Child Development, 75,* 1115–1139.

Bornstein, M. H., Slater, A., Brown, E., Roberts, E., & Barrett, J. (1997). Stability of mental development from infancy to later childhood: Three "waves" of research. In G. Bremner, A. Slater, & G. Butterworth (Eds.), *Infant development: Recent advances* (pp. 191–215). Philadelphia, PA: Psychology Press.

Boysson-Bardies, B. De, Sagart, L., Durand, C., Eimas, P. D., Siqueland, E. R., Jusczyk, P., . . . Oller, D. K. (1984). Discernible differences in the babbling of infants according to target language. *Journal of Child Language, 11,* 1–15. doi:10.1017/S0305000900005559

Bremner, J. G., Slater, A. M., & Johnson, S. P. (2015). Perception of object persistence: The origins of object permanence in infancy. *Child Development Perspectives, 9,* 7–13. doi:10.1111/cdep.12098

Broesch, T. L., & Bryant, G. A. (2015). Prosody in infant-directed speech is similar across western and traditional cultures. *Journal of Cognition and Development, 16,* 31–43. doi:10.1080/15248372.2013.833923

Brooks, P. J., & Kempe, V. (2014). *Encyclopedia of language development.* Thousand Oaks, CA: Sage.

Bryant, G. A., Liénard, P., & Barrett, H. C. (2012). Recognizing infant-directed speech across distant cultures: Evidence from Africa. *Journal of Evolutionary Psychology, 10,* 47–59. doi:10.1556/jep.10.2012.2.1

Carey, S., Zaitchik, D., & Bascandziev, I. (2015). Theories of development: In dialog with Jean Piaget. *Developmental Review, 38,* 36–54. doi:10.1016/J.DR.2015.07.003

Chen, L. M., & Kent, R. D. (2010). Segmental production in Mandarin-learning infants. *Journal of Child Language, 37,* 341–371. doi:10.1017/s0305000909009581

Cheour, M., Ceponiene, R., Leppanen, P., Alho, K., Kujala, T., Renlund, M., . . . Naatanen, R (2002). The auditory sensory memory trace decays rapidly in newborns. *Scandinavian Journal of Psychology, 43,* 33–39. doi:10.1111/1467-9450.00266

Chomsky, N. (1959). Review of B. F. Skinner's verbal behavior. *Language, 35,* 26–58.

Chomsky, N. (2017). Language architecture and its import for evolution. *Neuroscience & Biobehavioral Reviews, 81,* 295–300. doi:10.1016/J.NEUBIOREV.2017.01.053

Christodoulou, J., Lac, A., & Moore, D. S. (2017). Babies and math: A meta-analysis of infants' simple arithmetic competence. *Developmental Psychology, 53,* 1405–1417. doi:10.1037/dev0000330

Cohen, L. B., & Cashon, C. H. (2006). Infant cognition. In D. Kuhn, R. S. Siegler, W. Damon, & R. M. Lerner (Eds.), *Handbook of child psychology: Vol. 2. Cognition, perception, and language* (6th ed., pp. 214–251). Hoboken, NJ: Wiley.

Coubart, A., Izard, V., Spelke, E. S., Marie, J., & Streri, A. (2014). Dissociation between small and large numerosities in newborn infants. *Developmental Science, 17,* 11–22. doi:10.1111/desc.12108

Courage, M. L. (2017). Screen media and the youngest viewers: Implications for attention and learning. In F. C. Blumberg & P. J. Brooks (Eds.), *Cognitive development in digital contexts* (pp. 3–28). Cambridge, MA: Elsevier. doi:10.1016/B978-0-12-809481-5.00001-8

Courage, M. L., & Cowan, N. (2009). *The development of memory in infancy and childhood* (2nd ed.). New York, NY: Psychology Press.

Courage, M. L., & Howe, M. L. (2010). To watch or not to watch: Infants and toddlers in a brave new electronic world. *Developmental Review, 30,* 101–115. doi:10.1016/j.dr.2010.03.002

Courage, M. L., Reynolds, G. D., & Richards, J. E. (2006). Infants' attention to patterned stimuli: Developmental change from 3 to 12 months of age. *Child Development, 77,* 680–695. doi:10.1111/j.1467-8624.2006.00897.x

Cuevas, K., & Bell, M. A. (2010). Developmental progression of looking and reaching performance on the A-not-B task. *Developmental Psychology, 46,* 1363–1371. doi:10.1037/a0020185

Dąbrowska, E. (2015). What exactly is universal grammar, and has anyone seen it? *Frontiers in Psychology, 6,* 852. doi:10.3389/fpsyg.2015.00852

de Houwer, A., & Gillis, S. (1998). *The acquisition of Dutch.* Amsterdam, the Netherlands: Benjamins.

Dediu, D., & Christiansen, M. H. (2016). Language evolution: Constraints and opportunities from modern genetics. *Topics in Cognitive Science, 8,* 361–370. doi:10.1111/tops.12195

Dehaene-Lambertz, G. (2017). The human infant brain: A neural architecture able to learn language. *Psychonomic Bulletin & Review, 24,* 48–55. doi:10.3758/s13423-016-1156-9

Dehaene-Lambertz, G., & Spelke, E. S. (2015). The infancy of the human brain. *Neuron, 88,* 93–109. doi:10.1016/j.neuron.2015.09.026

DeLoache, J. S., Chiong, C., Sherman, K., Islam, N., Vanderborght, M., Troseth, G. L., . . . O'Doherty, K. (2010). Do babies learn from baby media? *Psychological Science, 21,* 1570–1574. doi:10.1177/0956797610384145

Diamond, A. (1991). Neuropsychological insights into the meaning of object concept development. In S. Carey & R. Gelman (Eds.), *The epigenesis of mind: Essays on biology and cognition* (pp. 67–110). Hillsdale, NJ: Lawrence Erlbaum.

Dickerson, A., & Popli, G. K. (2016). Persistent poverty and children's cognitive development: Evidence from the UK Millennium Cohort study. *Journal of the Royal Statistical Society: Series A (Statistics in Society), 179,* 535–558. doi:10.1111/rssa.12128

Dirix, C. E. H., Nijhuis, J. G., Jongsma, H. W., & Hornstra, G. (2009). Aspects of fetal learning and memory. *Child Development, 80,* 1251–1258. doi:10.1111/j.1467-8624.2009.01329.x

Doherty-Sneddon, G. (2008). *The great baby signing debate: Academia meets public interest.* Leicester: British Psychological Society. Retrieved from https://dspace.stir.ac.uk/handle/1893/385

Elsabbagh, M., Hohenberger, A., Campos, R., Van Herwegen, J., Serres, J., de Schonen, S., . . . Karmiloff-Smith, A. (2013). Narrowing perceptual sensitivity to the native language in infancy: Exogenous influences on developmental timing. *Behavioral Sciences, 3,* 120–132. doi:10.3390/bs3010120

Englund, K., & Behne, D. (2006). Changes in infant directed speech in the first six months. *Infant & Child Development, 15,* 139–160.

Estes, K. G., & Hurley, K. (2012). Infant-directed prosody helps infants map sounds to meanings. *Infancy, 18,* 797–824. doi:10.1111/infa.12006

Esteve-Gilbert, N., Prieto, P., Balog, H. L., Brentari, D., Davis, B. L., MacNeilage, P. F., . . . Liszkowski, U. (2013). Prosody signals the emergence of intentional communication in the first year of life: Evidence from Catalan-babbling infants. *Journal of Child Language, 40,* 919–944. doi:10.1017/S0305000912000359

Evans, G. W., & Kim, P. (2013). Childhood poverty, chronic stress, self-regulation, and coping. *Child Development Perspectives, 7,* 43–48. doi:10.1111/cdep.12013

Fagan, J. F. (2011). Intelligence in infancy. In R. J. Sternberg & S. B. Kaufman (Eds.), *The Cambridge handbook of intelligence* (pp. 130–142). Cambridge, UK: Cambridge University Press.

Fenstermacher, S. K., Barr, R., Salerno, K., Garcia, A., Shwery, C. E., Calvert, S. L., & Linebarger, D. L. (2010). Infant-directed media: An analysis of product information and claims. *Infant & Child Development, 19,* 556–557. doi:10.1002/icd.718

Ferguson, C. J., & Donnellan, M. B. (2014). Is the association between children's baby video viewing and poor language development robust? A reanalysis of Zimmerman, Christakis, and Meltzoff (2007). *Developmental Psychology, 50,* 129–137. doi:10.1037/a0033628

Fernald, A., Marchman, V. A., & Weisleder, A. (2013). SES differences in language processing skill and vocabulary are evident at 18 months. *Developmental Science, 16,* 234–248. doi:10.1111/desc.12019

Fernald, A., & Morikawa, H. (1993). Common themes and cultural variations in Japanese and American mothers' speech to infants. *Child Development, 64,* 657–674.

Fisher, S. E. (2017). Evolution of language: Lessons from the genome. *Psychonomic Bulletin & Review, 24,* 34–40. doi:10.3758/s13423-016-1112-8

Fitneva, S. A., & Matsui, T. (2015). The emergence and development of language across cultures. In L. A. Jensen (Ed.), *The Oxford handbook of human development and culture.* Oxford, UK: Oxford University Press. doi:10.1093/oxfordhb/9780199948550.013.8

Friederici, A. D. (2017). Evolution of the neural language network. *Psychonomic Bulletin & Review, 24,* 41–47. doi:10.3758/s13423-016-1090-x

Gershkoff-Stowe, L. (2002). Object naming, vocabulary growth, and the development of word retrieval abilities. *Journal of Memory & Language, 46,* 665.

Giofrè, D., Mammarella, I. C., & Cornoldi, C. (2013). The structure of working memory and how it relates to intelligence in children. *Intelligence, 41,* 396–406. doi:10.1016/j.intell.2013.06.006

Goldstein, M. H., & Schwade, J. A. (2008). Social feedback to infants' babbling facilitates rapid phonological learning. *Psychological Science, 19,* 515–523. doi:10.1111/j.1467-9280.2008.02117.x

Goodwyn, S. W., & Acredolo, L. P. (1998). Encouraging symbolic gestures: A new perspective on the relationship between gesture and speech. *New Directions for Child and Adolescent Development, 1998,* 61–73. doi:10.1002/cd.23219987905

Gopnik, A., & Choi, S. (1995). *Beyond names for things: Children's acquisition of verbs.* Hillsdale, NJ: Lawrence Erlbaum.

Hackman, D. A., Gallop, R., Evans, G. W., & Farah, M. J. (2015). Socioeconomic status and executive function: Developmental trajectories and mediation. *Developmental Science, 18,* 686–702. doi:10.1111/desc.12246

Hadley, P. A., Rispoli, M., Fitzgerald, C., & Bahnsen, A. (2011). Predictors of morphosyntactic growth in typically developing toddlers: Contributions of parent input and child sex. *Journal of Speech Language and Hearing Research, 54,* 549. doi:10.1044/1092-4388(2010/09-0216)

Hair, N. L., Hanson, J. L., Wolfe, B. L., Pollak, S. D., & Knight, R. T. (2015). Association of child poverty, brain development, and academic achievement. *JAMA Pediatrics, 169,* 822. doi:10.1001/jamapediatrics.2015.1475

Hanson, J. J. L., Hair, N., Shen, D. G., Shi, F., Gilmore, J. H. J., Wolfe, B. B. L., . . . Hickie, I. (2013). Family poverty affects the rate of human infant brain growth. *PLoS ONE, 8,* e80954. doi:10.1371/journal.pone.0080954

Hauser, M. D., Yang, C., Berwick, R. C., Tattersall, I., Ryan, M. J., Watumull, J., . . . Lewontin, R. C. (2014). The mystery of language evolution. *Frontiers in Psychology, 5,* 401. doi:10.3389/fpsyg.2014.00401

Hayne, H., Boniface, J., & Barr, R. (2000). The development of declarative memory in human infants: Age-related changes in deferred imitation. *Behavioral Neuroscience, 114,* 77–83. doi:10.1037/0735-7044.114.1.77

Heimann, M., & Meltzoff, A. N. (1996). Deferred imitation in 9- and 14-month-old infants: A longitudinal study of a Swedish sample. *British Journal of Developmental Psychology, 14,* 55–64. doi:10.1111/j.2044-835X.1996.tb00693.x

Hespos, S. J., & Baillargeon, R. (2008). Young infants' actions reveal their developing knowledge of support variables: Converging evidence for violation-of-expectation findings. *Cognition, 107,* 304–316. doi:10.1016/J.COGNITION.2007.07.009

Hespos, S. J., Ferry, A. L., Anderson, E. M., Hollenbeck, E. N., & Rips, L. J. (2016). Five-month-old infants have general knowledge of how nonsolid substances behave and interact. *Psychological Science, 27,* 244–256. doi:10.1177/0956797615617897

Heyes, C. (2014). False belief in infancy: A fresh look. *Developmental Science, 17,* 647–659. doi:10.1111/desc.12148

Hoff, E. (2015). Language development. *Developmental science: An advanced textbook* (5th ed.). New York, NY: Cengage Learning.

Hoff, E., Naigles, L., & Nigales, L. (2002). How children use input to acquire a lexicon. *Child Development, 73,* 418–433.

Howe, M. L. (2015). Memory development. In L. S. Liben & U. Muller (Eds.), *Handbook of child psychology and developmental science* (pp. 1–47). Hoboken, NJ: John Wiley. doi:10.1002/9781118963418.childpsy206

Hurtado, N., Marchman, V. A., & Fernald, A. (2008). Does input influence uptake? Links between maternal talk, processing speed and vocabulary size in Spanish-learning children. *Developmental Science, 11,* F31–F39. doi:10.1111/j.1467-7687.2008.00768.x

Huttenlocher, J., Waterfall, H., Vasilyeva, M., Vevea, J., & Hedges, L. V. (2010). Sources of variability in children's language growth. *Cognitive Psychology, 61,* 343–365. doi:10.1016/j.cogpsych.2010.08.002

Ibbotson, P., & Tomasello, M. (2016). Evidence rebuts Chomsky's theory of language learning. *Scientific American, 315,* 70–75. doi:10.1038/scientificamerican1116-70

Iverson, J. M., & Goldin-Meadow, S. (2005). Gesture paves the way for language development. *Psychological Science, 16,* 367–371. doi:10.1111/j.0956-7976.2005.01542.x

Johnson, S. B., Riis, J. L., & Noble, K. G. (2016). State of the art review: Poverty and the developing brain. *Pediatrics.* Retrieved from http://pediatrics.aappublications.org/content/early/2016/03/03/peds.2015-3075

Johnston, J. C. (2005). Teaching gestural signs to infants to advance child development: A review of the evidence. *First Language, 25,* 235–251. doi:10.1177/0142723705050340

Jones, E. J. H., & Herbert, J. S. (2006). Exploring memory in infancy: Deferred imitation and the development of declarative memory. *Infant & Child Development, 15,* 195–205.

Just, M. A., & Carpenter, P. A. (1992). A capacity theory of comprehension: Individual differences in working memory. *Psychological Review, 99,* 122–149.

Kan, P. F., & Kohnert, K. (2008). Fast mapping by bilingual preschool children. *Journal of Child Language, 35,* 495–514. doi:10.1017/S0305000907008604

Kavšek, M. (2013). The comparator model of infant visual habituation and dishabituation: Recent insights. *Developmental Psychobiology, 55,* 793–808. doi:10.1002/dev.21081

Kirk, E., Howlett, N., Pine, K. J., & Fletcher, B. C. (2013). To sign or not to sign? The impact of encouraging infants to gesture on infant language and maternal mind-mindedness. *Child Development, 84,* 574–590. doi:10.1111/j.1467-8624.2012.01874.x

Kitamura, C., & Burnham, D. (2003). Pitch and communicative intent in mother's speech: Adjustments for age and sex in the first year. *Infancy, 4,* 85–110.

Koball, H., & Jiang, Y. (2018). *Basic facts about low income children.* Retrieved May 18, 2018, from http://www.nccp.org/publications/pub_1194.html

Kolling, T., Goertz, C., Stefanie, F., & Knopf, M. (2010). Memory development throughout the second year: Overall developmental pattern, individual differences, and developmental trajectories. *Infant Behavior & Development, 33,* 159–167. doi:10.1016/j.infbeh.2009.12.007

Kressley-Mba, R. A., Lurg, S., & Knopf, M. (2005). Testing for deferred imitation of 2- and 3-step action sequences with 6-month-olds. *Infant Behavior & Development, 28,* 82–86.

Kuhl, P. K. (2015). Baby talk. *Scientific American, 313,* 64–69. doi:10.1038/scientificamerican1115-64

Kuhl, P. K. (2016). Language and the social brain: The power of surprise in science. In R. J. Sternberg, S. T. Fiske, & D. J. Foss (Eds.), *Scientists making a difference: One hundred eminent behavioral and brain scientists talk about their most important contributions.* New York, NY: Cambridge University Press.

Kuhl, P. K., Andruski, J. E., Christovich, I. A., Christovich, L. A., Kozhevnikova, E. V, & Ryskina, V. L. (1997). Cross-language analysis of phonetic units in language addressed to infants. *Science, 277,* 684–686.

Kuhl, P. K., Stevens, E., Hayashi, A., Deguchi, T., Kiritani, S., & Iverson, P. (2006). Infants show a facilitation effect for native language phonetic perception between 6 and 12 months. *Developmental Science, 9,* F13–F21. doi:10.1111/j.1467-7687.2006.00468.x

Kuhl, P. K., Tsao, F. M., & Liu, H. M. (2003). Foreign-language experience in infancy: Effects of short-term exposure and social interaction on phonetic learning. *Proceedings of the National Academy of Sciences of the United States of America, 100,* 9096–9101. doi:10.1073/pnas.1532872100

Lany, J., Shoaib, A., Thompson, A., & Estes, K. G. (2018). Infant statistical-learning ability is related to real-time language processing. *Journal of Child Language, 45,* 368–391. doi:10.1017/S0305000917000253

Learmonth, A. E., Lamberth, R., & Rovee-Collier, C. (2004). Generalizations of deferred imitation during the first year of life. *Journal of Experimental Child Psychology, 88,* 297–318.

Levitt, A. G., Aydelott Utman, J. G., Jakobson, R., Menn, L., Oller, D. K., & Stark, R. E. (1992). From babbling towards the sound systems of English and French: A longitudinal two-case study. *Journal of Child Language, 19,* 19. doi:10.1017/S0305000900013611

Libertus, K., Joh, A. S., & Needham, A. W. (2016). Motor training at 3 months affects object exploration 12 months later. *Developmental Science, 19,* 1058–1066. doi:10.1111/desc.12370

Libertus, M. E., Starr, A., & Brannon, E. M. (2014). Number trumps area for 7-month-old infants. *Developmental Psychology, 50,* 108–112. doi:10.1037/a0032986

Lieven, E., & Stoll, S. (2010). Language. In M. H. Bornstein (Ed.), *Handbook of cultural developmental science* (pp. 143–160). New York, NY: Psychology Press.

Linebarger, D. L., & Vaala, S. E. (2010). Screen media and language development in infants and toddlers: An ecological perspective. *Developmental Review, 30,* 176–202. doi:10.1016/j.dr.2010.03.006

Luttikhuizen dos Santos, E. S., de Kieviet, J. F., Königs, M., van Elburg, R. M., & Oosterlaan, J. (2013). Predictive value of the Bayley scales of infant development on development of very preterm/very low birth weight children: A meta-analysis. *Early Human Development, 89,* 487–496. doi:10.1016/j.earlhumdev.2013.03.008

MacWhinney, B., MacWhinney, & Brian. (2015). Language development. In L. S. Liben & U.Muller (Eds.), *Handbook of child psychology and developmental science* (pp. 1–43). Hoboken, NJ: John Wiley.

Maital, S. L., Dromi, E., Sagi, A., & Bornstein, M. H. (2000). The Hebrew communicative development inventory: Language specific properties and cross-linguistic generalizations. *Journal of Child Language, 27,* 43–67.

Mandel, D. R., Jusczyk, P. W., & Pisoni, D. B. (1995). Infants' recognition of the sound patterns of their own names. *Psychological Science, 6,* 314–317.

Mandler, J. M. (2004). *The foundations of mind: Origins of conceptual thought.* New York, NY: Oxford University Press.

Mandler, J. M., & McDonough, L. (1998). On developing a knowledge base in infancy. *Developmental Psychology, 34,* 1274–1288.

Marcovitch, S., Clearfield, M. W., Swingler, M., Calkins, S. D., & Bell, M. A. (2016). Attentional predictors of 5-month-olds' performance on a looking A-not-B task. *Infant and Child Development, 25,* 233–246. doi:10.1002/icd.1931

Marinellie, S. A., & Kneile, L. A. (2012). Acquiring knowledge of derived nominals and derived adjectives in context. *Language Speech and Hearing Services in Schools, 43,* 53. doi:10.1044/0161-1461(2011/10-0053)

May, L., Gervain, J., Carreiras, M., & Werker, J. F. (2018). The specificity of the neural response to speech at birth. *Developmental Science, 21,* e12564. doi:10.1111/desc.12564

McClure, E. R., Chentsova-Dutton, Y. E., Holochwost, S. J., Parrott, W. G., & Barr, R. (2018). Look at That! Video chat and joint visual attention development among babies and toddlers. *Child Development, 89,* 27–36. doi:10.1111/cdev.12833

McMurray, B. (2007). Defusing the childhood vocabulary explosion. *Science, 317,* 631. doi:10.1126/science.1144073

Meltzoff, A. N., & Moore, M. K. (1994). Imitation, memory, and the representation of persons. *Infant Behavior & Development, 17,* 83–99. doi:10.1016/0163-6383(94)90024-8

Miller, P. H. (2016). *Theories of developmental psychology* (6th ed.). New York, NY: Worth.

Mix, K. S., Huttenlocher, J., & Levine, S. C. (2002). Multiple cues for quantification in infancy: Is number one of them? *Psychological Bulletin, 128,* 278–294.

Moore, C., Angelopoulos, M., & Bennett, P. (1999). Word learning in the context of referential and salience cues. *Developmental Psychology, 35,* 60–68.

Mueller, V., & Sepulveda, A. (2014). Parental perception of a baby sign workshop on stress and parent–child interaction. *Early Child Development and Care, 184,* 450–468. doi:10.1080/03004430.2013.797899

Muenssinger, J., Matuz, T., Schleger, F., Kiefer-Schmidt, I., Goelz, R., Wacker-Gussmann, A., . . . Preissl, H. (2013). Auditory habituation in the fetus and neonate: An fMEG study. *Developmental Science, 16,* 287–295. doi:10.1111/desc.12025

Myers, L. J., LeWitt, R. B., Gallo, R. E., & Maselli, N. M. (2017). Baby FaceTime: Can toddlers learn from online video chat? *Developmental Science, 20,* e12430. doi:10.1111/desc.12430

Nelson, L. H., White, K. R., & Grewe, J. (2012). Evidence for website claims about the benefits of teaching sign language to infants and toddlers with normal hearing. *Infant and Child Development, 21,* 474–502. doi:10.1002/icd.1748

Neuman, S. B., Kaefer, T., Pinkham, A., & Strouse, G. (2014). Can babies learn to read? A randomized trial of baby media. *Journal of Educational Psychology, 106,* 815–830. doi:10.1037/a0035937

Noble, K. G., Houston, S. M., Brito, N. H., Bartsch, H., Kan, E., Kuperman, J. M., . . . Sowell, E. R. (2015). Family income, parental education and brain structure in children and adolescents. *Nature Neuroscience, 18,* 773–778. doi:10.1038/nn.3983

Oakes, L. M. (2010). Using habituation of looking time to assess mental processes in infancy. *Journal of Cognition & Development, 11,* 255–268. doi:10.1080/15248371003699977

Oberauer, K., Farrell, S., Jarrold, C., & Lewandowsky S. (2016). What limits working memory capacity? *Psychological Bulletin, 142,* 758–799. doi:10.1037/bul0000046

Ochs, E., & Schieffein, B. (1984). Language acquisition and socialization: Three developmental stories and their implications. In R. A. Shweder & R. A. Levine (Eds.), *Culture theory: Essays on mind, self, and emotion* (pp. 276–320). Cambridge, UK: Cambridge University Press.

Oller, D. K., Eilers, R. E., & Basinger, D. (2001). Intuitive identification of infant vocal sounds by parents. *Developmental Science, 4,* 49–60.

Owens, R. E. (2016). *Language development: An introduction.* New York, NY: Pearson.

Paquette, N., Lassonde, M., Vannasing, P., Tremblay, J., González-Frankenberger, B., Florea, O., . . . Gallagher, A. (2015). Developmental patterns of expressive language hemispheric lateralization in children, adolescents and adults using functional near-infrared spectroscopy. *Neuropsychologia, 68,* 117–125. doi:10.1016/J.NEUROPSYCHOLOGIA.2015.01.007

Pascoe, J. M., Wood, D. L., Duffee, J. H., & Kuo, A. (2016). Mediators and adverse effects of child poverty in the United States. *Pediatrics, 137,* e20160340. doi:10.1542/peds.2016-0340

Patel, S., Gaylord, S., & Fagen, J. (2013). Generalization of deferred imitation in 6-, 9-, and 12 month-old infants using visual and auditory contexts. *Infant Behavior and Development, 36,* 25–31. doi:10.1016/J.INFBEH.2012.09.006

Pelaez, M., Virues-Ortega, J., & Gewirtz, J. L. (2011). Reinforcement of vocalizations through contingent vocal imitation. *Journal of Applied Behavior Analysis, 44,* 33–40. doi:10.1901/jaba.2011.44-33

Perry, L. K. (2015). To have and to hold: Looking vs. touching in the study of categorization. *Frontiers in Psychology, 6,* 178. doi:10.3389/fpsyg.2015.00178

Perszyk, D. R., & Waxman, S. R. (2018). Linking language and cognition in infancy. *Annual Review of Psychology, 69,* 231–250. doi:10.1146/annurev-psych-122216-011701

Peter, V., Kalashnikova, M., Santos, A., & Burnham, D. (2016). Mature neural responses to infant-directed speech but not adult-directed speech in pre-verbal infants. *Scientific Reports, 6,* 34273. doi:10.1038/srep34273

Petursdottir, A. I., & Mellor, J. R. (2017). Reinforcement contingencies in language acquisition. *Policy Insights from the Behavioral and Brain Sciences, 4,* 25–32. doi:10.1177/2372732216686083

Piaget, J. (1952). *The origins of intelligence in children.* New York, NY: International Universities Press. (Original work published 1936)

Piaget, J. (1962). *Play, dreams, and imitation in childhood.* New York, NY: Norton.

Piantadosi, S. T., & Cantlon, J. F. (2017). True numerical cognition in the wild. *Psychological Science, 28,* 462–469. doi:10.1177/0956797616686862

Posner, M. I. (2001). The developing human brain. *Developmental Science, 4,* 253–387.

Qiu, A., Mori, S., & Miller, M. I. (2015). Diffusion tensor imaging for understanding brain development in early life. *Annual Review of Psychology, 66,* 853–876. doi:10.1146/annurev-psych-010814-015340

Quinn, P. C. (2016). Establishing cognitive organization in infancy. In L. Balter & C. S. Tamis LeMonda (Eds.), *Child psychology: A handbook of contemporary issues.* Philadelphia, PA: Psychology Press.

Quinn, P. C., Doran, M. M., Reiss, J. E., & Hoffman, J. E. (2010). Neural markers of subordinate level categorization in 6- to 7-month-old infants. *Developmental Science, 13,* 499–507. doi:10.1111/j.1467-7687.2009.00903.x

Quinn, P. C., Eimas, P. D., & Rosenkrantz, S. L. (1993). Evidence for representations of perceptual similar natural categories by 3 and 4 month old infants. *Perception, 22,* 463–475.

Ramsdell, H. L., Oller, D. K., Buder, E. H., Ethington, C. A., & Chorna, L. (2012). Identification of prelinguistic phonological categories. *Journal of Speech, Language, and Hearing Research, 55,* 1626–1639. doi:10.1044/1092-4388(2012/11-0250)

Redick, T. S., Unsworth, N., Kelly, A. J., & Engle, R. W. (2012). Faster, smarter? Working memory capacity and perceptual speed in relation to fluid intelligence. *Journal of Cognitive Psychology, 24,* 844–854. doi:10.1080/20445911.2012.704359

Reynolds, G. D. (2015). Infant visual attention and object recognition. *Behavioural Brain Research, 285,* 34–43. doi:10.1016/j.bbr.2015.01.015

Reynolds, G. D., Zhang, D., & Guy, M. W. (2013). Infant attention to dynamic audiovisual stimuli: Look duration from 3 to 9 months of age. *Infancy, 18*, 554–577. doi:10.1111/j.1532-7078.2012.00134.x

Richards, J. E. (2010). The development of attention to simple and complex visual stimuli in infants: Behavioral and psychophysiological measures. *Developmental Review, 30*, 203–219. doi:10.1016/j.dr.2010.03.005

Rigney, J., & Wang, S. (2015). Delineating the boundaries of infants' spatial categories: The case of containment. *Journal of Cognition and Development, 16*, 420–441. doi:10.1080/15248372.2013.848868

Ristic, J., & Enns, J. T. (2015). Attentional development. In L. S. Liben & U. Muller (Eds.), *Handbook of child psychology and developmental science* (pp. 1–45). Hoboken, NJ: John Wiley. doi:10.1002/9781118963418.childpsy205

Rivera, S. M., Wakely, A., & Langer, J. (1999). The drawbridge phenomenon: Representational reasoning or perceptual preference? *Developmental Psychology, 35*, 427–435.

Rodriguez, E. T., & Tamis-LeMonda, C. S. (2011). Trajectories of the home learning environment across the first 5 years: Associations with children's vocabulary and literacy skills at prekindergarten. *Child Development, 82*, 1058–1075. doi:10.1111/j.1467-8624.2011.01614.x

Rose, S. A., & Feldman, J. F. (1995). Prediction of IQ and specific cognitive abilities from infancy measures. *Developmental Psychology, 31*, 685–696.

Rose, S. A., Feldman, J. F., & Jankowski, J. J. (2009). Information processing in toddlers: Continuity from infancy and persistence of preterm deficits. *Intelligence, 37*, 311–320. doi:10.1016/j.intell.2009.02.002

Rose, S. A., Feldman, J. F., & Jankowski, J. J. (2012). Implications of infant cognition for executive functions at age 11. *Psychological Science, 23*, 1345–1355. doi:10.1177/0956797612444902

Rose, S. A., Feldman, J. F., Jankowski, J. J., & Van Rossem, R. (2011). The structure of memory in infants and toddlers: An SEM study with fullterms and preterms. *Developmental Science, 14*, 83–91. doi:10.1111/j.1467-7687.2010.00959.x

Rose, S. A., Feldman, J. F., Jankowski, J. J., & Van Rossem, R. (2012). Information processing from infancy to 11 years: Continuities and prediction of IQ. *Intelligence, 40*, 445–457. doi:10.1016/j.intell.2012.05.007

Rosenberg, R. D., & Feigenson, L. (2013). Infants hierarchically organize memory representations. *Developmental Science, 16*, 610–621. doi:10.1111/desc.12055

Rovee-Collier, C. K., & Bhatt, R. S. (1993). Evidence of long-term memory in infancy. *Annals of Child Development, 9*, 1–45.

Rowe, M. L. (2012). A longitudinal investigation of the role of quantity and quality of child directed speech in vocabulary development. *Child Development, 83*, 1762–1774. doi:10.1111/j.1467-8624.2012.01805.x

Saffran, J. R., & Kirkham, N. Z. (2018). Infant statistical learning. *Annual Review of Psychology, 69*, 181–203. doi:10.1146/annurev-psych-122216-011805

Samuelson, L. K., & McMurray, B. (2017). What does it take to learn a word? *Wiley Interdisciplinary Reviews: Cognitive Science, 8*, e1421. doi:10.1002/wcs.1421

Sansavini, A., Bertoncini, J., & Giovanelli, G. (1997). Newborns discriminate the rhythm of multisyllabic stressed words. *Developmental Psychology, 33*, 3–11.

Saxton, M. (1997). The contrast theory of negative input. *Journal of Child Language, 24*, 139–161.

Schachner, A., & Hannon, E. E. (2011). Infant-directed speech drives social preferences in 5 month-old infants. *Developmental Psychology, 47*, 19–25. doi:10.1037/a0020740

Segal, J., & Newman, R. S. (2015). Infant preferences for structural and prosodic properties of infant-directed speech in the second year of life. *Infancy, 20*, 339–351. doi:10.1111/infa.12077

Shapiro, B., Fagen, J., Prigot, J., Carroll, M., & Shalan, J. (1998). Infants' emotional and regulatory behaviors in response to violations of expectancies. *Infant Behavior and Development, 27*, 299–313.

Sheppard, L. D. (2008). Intelligence and speed of information-processing: A review of 50 years of research. *Personality & Individual Differences, 44*, 533–549.

Sheridan, M. A., Sarsour, K., Jutte, D., D'Esposito, M., & Boyce, W. T. (2012). The impact of social disparity on prefrontal function in childhood. *PLoS ONE, 7*, e35744. doi:10.1371/journal.pone.0035744

Shinskey, J. L. (2012). Disappearing décalage: Object search in light and dark at 6 Months. *Infancy, 17*, 272–294. doi:10.1111/j.1532-7078.2011.00078.x

Singh, L., Nestor, S., Parikh, C., & Yull, A. (2009). Influences of infant-directed speech on early word recognition. *Infancy, 14*, 654–666. doi:10.1080/15250000903263973

Skinner, B. F. (1957). *Verbal behavior*. New York, NY: Appleton-Century-Crofts.

Spelke, E. S. (2016). Core knowledge and conceptual change. In D. Barner & A. S. Baron (Eds.), *Core knowledge and conceptual change* (pp. 279–300). New York, NY: Oxford University Press.

Spelke, E. S. (2017). Core knowledge, language, and number. *Language Learning and Development, 13*, 147–170. doi:10.1080/15475441.2016.1263572

Streri, A., Hevia, M., Izard, V., & Coubart, A. (2013). What do we know about neonatal cognition? *Behavioral Sciences, 3*, 154–169. doi:10.3390/bs3010154

Sundberg, U. (1998). *Mother tongue-phonetic aspects of infant-directed speech* (Unpublished doctoral dissertation). PERILUS, Stockholm.

Tamariz, M., & Kirby, S. (2016). The cultural evolution of language. *Current Opinion in Psychology, 8*, 37–43. doi:10.1016/J.COPSYC.2015.09.003

Tamis-Lemonda, C., & Bornstein, M. (2015). Infant word learning in biopsychosocial perspective. In S. Calkins (Ed.), *Handbook of infant development: A biopsychosocial perspective*. Retrieved from https://nyuscholars.nyu.edu/en/publications/infant-word-learning-in-biopsychosocial-perspective

Tamis-LeMonda, C. S., Bornstein, M. H., & Baumwell, L. (2001). Maternal responsiveness and children's achievement of language milestones. *Child Development, 72*, 748–767.

Tamis-Lemonda, C., Bornstein, MH., Cyphers, L., Toda, S., & Ogino, M. (1992). Language and play at one year: A comparison of toddlers and mothers in the United States and Japan. *International Journal of Behavioral Development, 15*, 19–42.

Tamis-LeMonda, C. S., Kuchirko, Y., & Song, L. (2014). Why is infant language learning facilitated by parental responsiveness? *Current Directions in Psychological Science, 23*, 121–126. doi:10.1177/0963721414522813

Tamis-LeMonda, C. S., Shannon, J. D., Cabrera, N. J., & Lamb, M. E. (2004). Fathers and mothers at play with their 2- and 3-year-olds: Contributions to language and cognitive development. *Child Development, 75*, 1806–1820. doi:10.1111/j.1467-8624.2004.00818.x

Tardif, T., Fletcher, P., Liang, W., Zhang, Z., Kaciroti, N., & Marchman, V. A. (2008). Baby's first 10 words. *Developmental Psychology, 44*, 929–938. doi:10.1037/0012-1649.44.4.929

Tardif, T., Shatz, M., & Naigles, L. (1997). Caregiver speech and children's use of nouns versus verbs: A comparison of English, Italian, and Mandarin. *Journal of Child Language, 24*, 535–565.

Thiessen, E. D., Hill, E. A., & Saffran, J. R. (2005). Infant-directed speech facilitates word segmentation. *Infancy, 7*, 53–71.

Tomalski, P., Marczuk, K., Pisula, E., Malinowska, A., Kawa, R., & Niedźwiecka, A. (2017). Chaotic home environment is associated with reduced infant processing speed under high task demands. *Infant Behavior and Development, 48*, 124–133. doi:10.1016/J.INFBEH.2017.04.007

Tomasello, M. (2012). A usage-based approach to child language acquisition. *Proceedings of the Annual Meeting of the Berkeley Linguistics Society, 26*, 305–319.

Tronick, E. Z., Als, H., Adamson, L., Wise, S., & Brazelton, B. (1978). The infants' response to entrapment between contradictory messages in face-to-face interaction. *American Academy of Child Psychiatry, 1*, 1–13.

Turnbull, K., & Justice, L. M. (2016). *Language development from theory to practice*. New York, NY: Pearson.

Ursache, A., & Noble, K. G. (2016). Neurocognitive development in socioeconomic context: Multiple mechanisms and implications for measuring socioeconomic status. *Psychophysiology, 53*, 71–82. doi:10.1111/psyp.12547

Vaala, S. E., & LaPierre, M. A. (2014). Marketing genius: The impact of educational claims and cues on parents' reactions to infant/toddler DVDs. *Journal of Consumer Affairs, 48*, 323–350. doi:10.1111/joca.12023

Vallotton, C. D., Decker, K. B., Kwon, A., Wang, W., & Chang, T. (2017). Quantity and quality of gestural input: Caregivers' sensitivity predicts caregiver-infant bidirectional communication through gestures. *Infancy, 22*, 56–77. doi:10.1111/infa.12155

Vannasing, P., Florea, O., González-Frankenberger, B., Tremblay, J., Paquette, N., Safi, D., . . . Gallagher, A. (2016). Distinct hemispheric specializations for native and non-native languages in one-day-old newborns identified by fNIRS. *Neuropsychologia, 84*, 63–69. doi:10.1016/j.neuropsychologia.2016.01.038

von Hofsten, C., Kochukhova, O., & Rosander, K. (2007). Predictive tracking over occlusions by 4-month-old infants. *Developmental Science, 10*, 625–640. doi:10.1111/j.1467-7687.2006.00604.x

Waxman, S., Fu, X., Arunachalam, S., Leddon, E., Geraghty, K., & Song, H. (2013). Are nouns learned before verbs? Infants provide insight into a long-standing debate. *Child Development Perspectives, 7*, 155–159. doi:10.1111/cdep.12032

Weinberg, M. K., & Tronick, E. Z. (1994). Beyond the face: An empirical study of infant affective configurations of facial, vocal, gestural, and regulatory behaviors. *Child Development, 65*, 1503–1515.

Weisleder, A., & Fernald, A. (2013). Talking to children matters: Early language experience strengthens processing and builds vocabulary. *Psychological Science, 24*, 2143–2152. doi:10.1177/0956797613488145

Werker, J. F., Yeung, H. H., & Yoshida, K. A. (2012). How do infants become experts at native speech perception? *Current Directions in Psychological Science, 21*, 221–226. doi:10.1177/0963721412449459

Westermann, G. (2016). Experience-dependent brain development as a key to understanding the language system. *Topics in Cognitive Science, 8*, 446–458. doi:10.1111/tops.12194

Woodward, A. L., Markman, E. M., & Fitzsimmons, C. M. (1994). Rapid word learning in 13- and 18-month-olds. *Developmental Psychology, 30*, 553–556.

Xu, F., & Kushnir, T. (2013). Infants are rational constructivist learners. *Current Directions in Psychological Science, 22*, 28–32.

Yang, C., Crain, S., Berwick, R. C., Chomsky, N., & Bolhuis, J. J. (2017). The growth of language: Universal grammar, experience, and principles of computation. *Neuroscience & Biobehavioral Reviews, 81*, 103–119. doi:10.1016/J.NEUBIOREV.2016.12.023

Yoshikawa, H., Aber, J. L., & Beardslee, W. R. (2012). The effects of poverty on the mental, emotional, and behavioral health of children and youth: Implications for prevention. *American Psychologist, 67*, 272–284. doi:10.1037/a0028015

Zammit, M., & Atkinson, S. (2017). The relations between "babysigning," child vocabulary and maternal mind-mindedness. *Early Child Development and Care, 187*, 1887–1895. doi:10.1080/03004430.2016.1193502

Zelazo, P. D., Reznick, J. S., & Spinazzola, J. (1998). Representational flexibility and response control in a multistep, multilocation search task. *Developmental Psychology, 34*, 203–214.

Chapter 6

Addabbo, M., Longhi, E., Marchis, I. C., Tagliabue, P., & Turati, C. (2018). Dynamic facial expressions of emotions are discriminated at birth. *PLoS ONE, 13*, e0193868. doi:10.1371/journal.pone.0193868

Ainsworth, M. D. S., Blehar, M. C., Waters, E., & Wall, S. (1978). *Patterns of attachment.* Hillsdale, NJ: Lawrence Erlbaum.

Andersson, B. E. (1989). Effects of public day-care: A longitudinal study. *Child Development, 60*, 857. doi:10.1111/1467-8624.ep9676141

Axe, J. B. (2007). Child care and child development: Results from the NICHD study of early child care and youth development. *Education & Treatment of Children, 30*, 129–136.

Axia, V. D., & Weisner, T. S. (2002). Infant stress reactivity and home cultural ecology of Italian infants and families. *Infant Behavior & Development, 25*, 255.

Bard, K. A., Todd, B. K., Bernier, C., Love, J., & Leavens, D. A. (2006). Self-awareness in human and chimpanzee infants: What is measured and what is meant by the Mark and Mirror test? *Infancy, 9*, 191–219. doi:10.1207/s15327078in0902_6

Barr, R. G., Konner, M., Bakeman, R., & Adamson, L. (1991). Crying in !Kung San infants: A test of the cultural specificity hypothesis. *Developmental Medicine & Child Neurology, 33*, 601–610.

Bates, E. (1990). Language about me and you: Pronominal reference and the emerging concept of self. In D. Cicchetti & M. Beeghly (Eds.), *The self in transition: Infancy to childhood* (pp. 165–182). Chicago, IL: University of Chicago Press.

Bates, J., Pettit, G., Dodge, K., & Ridge, B. (1998). Interaction of temperamental resistance to control and restrictive parenting in the development of externalizing behavior. *Developmental Psychology, 34*, 982–995.

Beebe, B., Jaffe, J., Markese, S., Buck, K., Chen, H., Cohen, P., . . . Feldstein, S. (2010). The origins of 12-month attachment: A microanalysis of 4-month mother-infant interaction. *Attachment & Human Development, 12*, 3–141. doi:10.1080/14616730903338985

Beebe, B., Messinger, D., Bahrick, L. E., Margolis, A., Buck, K. A., & Chen, H. (2016). A systems view of mother–infant face-to-face communication. *Developmental Psychology, 52*, 556–571. doi:10.1037/a0040085

Behrens, K. Y., Parker, A. C., & Haltigan, J. D. (2011). Maternal sensitivity assessed during the Strange Situation procedure predicts child's attachment quality and reunion behaviors. *Infant Behavior & Development, 34*, 378–381. doi:10.1016/j.infbeh.2011.02.007

Belsky, J. (2005). Attachment theory and research in ecological perspective: Insights from the Pennsylvania infant and family development project and the NICHD study of early child care. In K. E. Grossmann, K. Grossmann, & E. Waters (Eds.), *Attachment from infancy to adulthood: The major longitudinal studies* (pp. 71–97). New York, NY: Guilford.

Bennett, D. S., Bendersky, M., & Lewis, M. (2005). Does the organization of emotional expression change over time? Facial expressivity from 4 to 12 months. *Infancy, 8*, 167–187. doi:10.1207/s15327078in0802_4

Berry, D., Blair, C., Willoughby, M., Garrett-Peters, P., Vernon-Feagans, L., & Mills-Koonce, W. R. (2016). Household chaos and children's cognitive and socio-emotional development

in early childhood: Does childcare play a buffering role? *Early Childhood Research Quarterly, 34*, 115–127. doi:10.1016/J.ECRESQ.2015.09.003

Best, D. L., House, A. S., Barnard, A. E., & Spicker, B. S. (1994). Parent-child interactions in France, Germany, and Italy: The effects of gender and culture. *Journal of Cross-Cultural Psychology, 25*, 181–193. doi:10.1177/0022022194252002

Białecka-Pikul, M., Byczewska-Konieczny, K., Kosno, M., Białek, A., & Stępień-Nycz, M. (2018). Waiting for a treat. Studying behaviors related to self-regulation in 18- and 24-month-olds. *Infant Behavior and Development, 50*, 12–21. doi:10.1016/J.INFBEH.2017.10.004

Biro, S., Alink, L. R. A., van IJzendoorn, M. H., & Bakermans-Kranenburg, M. J. (2014). Infants' monitoring of social interactions: The effect of emotional cues. *Emotion, 14*, 263–271.

Blair, C. (2010). Stress and the development of self-regulation in context. *Child Development Perspectives, 4*, 181–188. doi:10.1111/j.1750-8606.2010.00145.x

Bleah, D. A., & Ellett, M. L. (2010). Infant crying among recent African immigrants. *Health Care for Women International, 31*, 652–663. doi:10.1080/07399331003628446

Boldt, L. J., Kochanska, G., Yoon, J. E., & Koenig Nordling, J. (2014). Children's attachment to both parents from toddler age to middle childhood: Links to adaptive and maladaptive outcomes. *Attachment & Human Development, 16*, 211–229. doi:10.1080/14616734.2014.889181

Booth-LaForce, C., Groh, A. M., Burchinal, M. R., Roisman, G. I., Owen, M. T., & Cox, M. J. (2014). Caregiving and contextual sources of continuity and change in attachment security from infancy to late adolescence. *Monographs of the Society for Research in Child Development, 79*, 67–84. doi:10.1111/mono.12114

Bornstein, M. H., Arterberry, M. E., & Lamb, M. E. (2013). *Development in infancy: A contemporary introduction.* Philadelphia, PA: Psychology Press.

Bornstein, M. H., & Lamb, M. E. (2011). *Developmental science: An advanced textbook* (6th ed.). Philadelphia, PA: Psychology Press.

Bornstein, M. H., Putnick, D. L., Gartstein, M. A., Hahn, C.-S., Auestad, N., & O'Connor, D. L. (2015). Infant temperament: Stability by age, gender, birth order, term status, and socioeconomic status. *Child Development, 86*, 844–863. doi:10.1111/cdev.12367

Bornstein, M. H., Putnick, D. L., Rigo, P., Esposito, G., Swain, J. E., Suwalsky, J. T. D., . . . Venuti, P. (2017). Neurobiology of culturally common maternal responses to infant cry. *Proceedings of the National Academy of Sciences of the United States of America, 114*, E9465–E9473. doi:10.1073/pnas.1712022114

Bornstein, M. H., Suwalsky, J. T. D., & Breakstone, D. A. (2012). Emotional relationships between mothers and infants: Knowns, unknowns, and unknown unknowns. *Development and Psychopathology, 24*, 113–23. doi:10.1017/S0954579411000708

Bosquet Enlow, M., King, L., Schreier, H. M., Howard, J. M., Rosenfield, D., Ritz, T., & Wright, R. J. (2014). Maternal sensitivity and infant autonomic and endocrine stress responses. *Early Human Development, 90,* 377–385. doi:10.1016/J.EARLHUMDEV.2014.04.007

Bowlby, J. (1969). Attachment and loss. In *Attachment* (Vol. 1). New York, NY: Basic Books.

Brandl, J. L. (2018). The puzzle of mirror self-recognition. *Phenomenology and the Cognitive Sciences.* Advance online publication. doi:10.1007/s11097-016-9486-7

Braungart-Rieker, J. M., Hill-Soderlund, A. L., & Karrass, J. (2010). Fear and anger reactivity trajectories from 4 to 16 months: The roles of temperament, regulation, and maternal sensitivity. *Developmental Psychology, 46,* 791–804. doi:10.1037/a0019673

Bretherton, I., Fritz, J., Zahn-Waxler, C., & Ridgeway, D. (1986). Learning to talk about emotions: A functionalist perspective. *Child Development, 57,* 529–548.

Bretherton, I., & Munholland, K. (2016). The internal working model construct in light of contemporary neuroimaging research. In J. Shaver & P. R. Cassidy (Eds.), *Handbook of attachment: Theory, research, and clinical applications* (pp. 63–68). New York, NY: Guilford.

Bridgett, D. J., Gartstein, M. A., Putnam, S. P., McKay, T., Iddins, E., Robertson, C., . . . Rittmueller, A. (2009). Maternal and contextual influences and the effect of temperament development during infancy on parenting in toddlerhood. *Infant Behavior & Development, 32,* 103–116. doi:10.1016/j.infbeh.2008.10.007

Broberg, A. G., Wessels, H., Lamb, M. E., & Hwang, C. P. (1997). Effects of day care on the development of cognitive abilities in 8-year-olds: A longitudinal study. *Developmental Psychology, 33,* 62–69. doi:10.1037/0012-1649.33.1.62

Broekhuizen, M. L., van Aken, M. A. G., Dubas, J. S., & Leseman, P. P. M. (2018). Child care quality and Dutch 2- and 3-year-olds' socio-emotional outcomes: Does the amount of care matter? *Infant and Child Development, 27,* e2043. doi:10.1002/icd.2043

Broesch, T., Rochat, P., Olah, K., Broesch, J., & Henrich, J. (2016). Similarities and differences in maternal responsiveness in three societies: Evidence from Fiji, Kenya, and the United States. *Child Development, 87,* 700–711. doi:10.1111/cdev.12501

Brooker, R. J., Buss, K. A., Lemery-Chalfant, K., Aksan, N., Davidson, R. J., & Goldsmith, H. H. (2013). The development of stranger fear in infancy and toddlerhood: Normative development, individual differences, antecedents, and outcomes. *Developmental Science, 16,* 864–878. doi:10.1111/desc.12058

Brooks, R., & Meltzoff, A. N. (2008). Infant gaze following and pointing predict accelerated vocabulary growth through two years of age: A longitudinal, growth curve modeling study. *Journal of Child Language, 35,* 207–220. doi:10.1017/s030500090700829x

Brown, G. L., Mangelsdorf, S. C., & Neff, C. (2012). Father involvement, paternal sensitivity, and father-child attachment security in the first 3 years. *Journal of Family Psychology, 26,* 421–430. doi:10.1037/a0027836

Bullock, M., & Lutkenhaus, P. (1990). Who am I? Self-understanding in toddlers. *Merrill-Palmer Quarterly, 36,* 217–238.

Butterworth, G. (1992). Origins of self-perception in infancy. *Psychological Inquiry, 3,* 103–111. doi:10.1207/s15327965pli0302_1

Carlson, V. J., & Harwood, R. L. (2003). Attachment, culture, and the caregiving system: The cultural patterning of everyday experiences among Anglo and Puerto Rican mother-infant pairs. *Infant Mental Health Journal, 24,* 53–73.

Cassibba, R., Sette, G., Bakermans-Kranenburg, M. J., & Ijzendoorn, M. H. (2013). Attachment the Italian way: In search of specific patterns of infant and adult attachments in Italian typical and atypical samples. *European Psychologist, 18,* 47–58. doi:10.1027/1016-9040/a000128

Celeghin, A., Diano, M., Bagnis, A., Viola, M., & Tamietto, M. (2017). Basic emotions in human neuroscience: Neuroimaging and beyond. *Frontiers in Psychology, 8,* 1432. doi:10.3389/fpsyg.2017.01432

Chen, X., & Schmidt, L. A. (2015). Temperament and personality. In R. Lerner (Ed.), *Handbook of child psychology and developmental science* (pp. 1–49). Hoboken, NJ: John Wiley. doi:10.1002/9781118963418.childpsy305

Cheng, N., Lu, S., Archer, M., & Wang, Z. (2018). Quality of maternal parenting of 9-month-old infants predicts executive function performance at 2 and 3 years of age. *Frontiers in Psychology, 8,* 2293. doi:10.3389/fpsyg.2017.02293

Chess, S., & Thomas, A. (1984). *Origins and evolution of behavior disorders.* New York, NY: Brunner/Mazel.

Chess, S., & Thomas, A. (1991). Temperament and the concept of goodness of fit. In J. Strelau & A. Angleitner (Eds.), *Explorations in temperament: International perspectives on theory and measurement* (pp. 15–28). New York, NY: Plenum.

Cicchetti, D., Rogosch, F. A., Toth, S. L., & Spagnola, M. (1997). Affect, cognition, and the emergence of self-knowledge in the toddler offspring. *Journal of Experimental Child Psychology, 67,* 338.

Clearfield, M. W. (2011). Learning to walk changes infants' social interactions. *Infant Behavior & Development, 34,* 15–25. doi:10.1016/j.infbeh.2010.04.008

Combs-Orme, T., & Renkert, L. E. (2009). Fathers and their infants: Caregiving and affection in the modern family. *Journal of Human Behavior in the Social Environment, 19,* 394–418. doi:10.1080/10911350902790753

Conradt, E. (2017). Using principles of behavioral epigenetics to advance research on early-life stress. *Child Development Perspectives, 11,* 107–112. doi:10.1111/cdep.12219

Cordaro, D. T., Sun, R., Keltner, D., Kamble, S., Huddar, N., & McNeil, G. (2018). Universals and cultural variations in 22 emotional expressions across five cultures. *Emotion, 18,* 75–93. doi:10.1037/emo0000302

Courage, M. L., Edison, S. C., & Howe, M. L. (2004). Variability in the early development of visual self-recognition. *Infant Behavior & Development, 27,* 509–532. doi:10.1016/j.infbeh.2004.06.001

Dagan, O., & Sagi-Schwartz, A. (2018). Early attachment network with mother and father: An unsettled issue. *Child Development Perspectives, 12,* 115–121. doi:10.1111/cdep.12272

Dehaan, L. (2006). Child care and development: Results from the NICHD study of early child care and youth development. The NICHD early child care research network. *Journal of Marriage & Family, 68,* 252–253. doi:10.1111/j.1741-3737.2006.00245.x

Dempsey, J., McQuillin, S., Butler, A. M., & Axelrad, M. E. (2016). Maternal depression and parent management training outcomes. *Journal of Clinical Psychology in Medical Settings, 23,* 240–246. doi:10.1007/s10880-016-9461-z

Dondi, M., Simion, F., & Caltran, G. (1999). Can newborns discriminate between their own cry and the cry of another newborn infant? *Developmental Psychology, 35,* 418–426.

Duschinsky, R. (2015). The emergence of the disorganized/disoriented (D) attachment classification, 1979–1982. *History of Psychology, 18,* 32–46. doi:10.1037/a0038524

Dyson, M. W., Olino, T. M., Durbin, C. E., Goldsmith, H. H., Bufferd, S. J., Miller, A. R., & Klein, D. N. (2015). The structural and rank-order stability of temperament in young children based on a laboratory-observational measure. *Psychological Assessment, 27,* 1388–1401. doi:10.1037/pas0000104

Easterbrooks, M. A., Bartlett, J. D., Beeghly, M., & Thompson, R. A. (2012). Social and emotional development in infancy. In I. B. Weiner, R. M. Lerner, M. A. Easterbrooks, & J. Mistry (Eds.), *Handbook of psychology, developmental psychology* (p. 752). Hoboken, NJ: John Wiley.

Erikson, E. H. (1950). *Childhood and society* (2nd ed.). New York, NY: Norton.

Farroni, T., Menon, E., Rigato, S., & Johnson, M. H. (2007). The perception of facial expressions in newborns. *European Journal of Developmental Psychology, 4,* 2–13. doi:10.1080/17405620601046832

Federal Interagency Forum on Child and Family Statistics. (2014). *America's children: Key national indicators of well-being, 2013.* Retrieved from http://www.childstats.gov/americaschildren

Feeney, B. C., & Monin, J. K. (2016). Divorce through the lens of attachment theory. In J. Shaver & P. R. Cassidy (Eds.), *Handbook of attachment: Theory, research, and clinical applications* (pp. 941–965). New York, NY: Guilford.

Feldman, R. (2003). Infant–mother and infant–father synchrony: The coregulation of positive arousal. *Infant Mental Health Journal, 24,* 1–23. doi:10.1002/imhj.10041

Feldman, R., Dollberg, D., & Nadam, R. (2011). The expression and regulation of anger in toddlers: Relations to maternal behavior and mental representations. *Infant Behavior & Development, 34,* 310–320. doi:10.1016/j.infbeh.2011.02.001

Flanders, J. L., Leo, V., Paquette, D., Pihl, R. O., & Séguin, J. R. (2009). Rough-and-tumble play and the regulation of aggression: An observational study of father–child play dyads. *Aggressive Behavior, 35,* 285–295. doi:10.1002/ab.20309

Friedlmeier, W., Çorapçi, F., & Benga, O. (2015). Early emotional development in cultural perspective. In L. A. Jensen (Ed.), *The*

Oxford handbook of human development and culture (pp. 127–148). Oxford, UK: Oxford University Press. doi:10.1093/oxfordhb/9780199948550.013.9

Frodi, A. M., Lamb, M. E., Hwang, C. P., & Frodi, M. (1983). Father–mother infant interaction in traditional and nontraditional Swedish families: A longitudinal study. *Alternative Lifestyles, 5*, 142–163. doi:10.1007/bf01091325

Gardiner, H. W., & Kosmitzki, C. (2018). *Lives across cultures: Cross-cultural human development* (6th ed.). Boston, MA: Pearson.

Gartstein, M. A., & Iverson, S. (2014). Attachment security: The role of infant, maternal, and contextual factors. *International Journal of Psychology & Psychological Therapy, 14*, 261–276.

Gartstein, M. A., Putnam, S. P., Aron, E. N., & Rothbart, M. K. (2016). *Temperament and personality* (S. Maltzman, Ed.) (Vol. 1). Oxford, UK: Oxford University Press. doi:10.1093/oxfordhb/9780199739134.013.2

Gialamas, A., Mittinty, M. N., Sawyer, M. G., Zubrick, S. R., & Lynch, J. (2014). Child care quality and children's cognitive and socio-emotional development: An Australian longitudinal study. *Early Child Development and Care, 184*, 977–997. doi:10.1080/03004430.2013.847835

Goodman, S. H., & Garber, J. (2017). Evidence-based interventions for depressed mothers and their young children. *Child Development, 88*, 368–377. doi:10.1111/cdev.12732

Goodvin, R., Thompson, R. A., & Winer, A. C. (2015). The individual child: Temperament, emotion, self, and personality. In M. Bornstein & M. Lamb (Eds.), *Developmental psychology: An advanced textbook* (pp. 491–533). Philadelphia, PA: Psychology Press.

Gothe-Snape, J. (2017). *How other countries address affordable childcare*. Retrieved from https://www.sbs.com.au/news/how-other-countries-address-affordable-childcare

Grady, J. S., & Karraker, K. (2017). Mother and child temperament as interacting correlates of parenting sense of competence in toddlerhood. *Infant and Child Development, 26*, e1997. doi:10.1002/icd.1997

Granat, A., Gadassi, R., Gilboa-Schechtman, E., & Feldman, R. (2017). Maternal depression and anxiety, social synchrony, and infant regulation of negative and positive emotions. *Emotion, 17*, 11–27. doi:10.1037/emo0000204

Granqvist, P., Sroufe, L. A., Dozier, M., Hesse, E., Steele, M., van IJzendoorn, M., . . . Duschinsky, R. (2017). Disorganized attachment in infancy: A review of the phenomenon and its implications for clinicians and policy-makers. *Attachment & Human Development, 19*, 534–558. doi:10.1080/14616734.2017.1354040

Groh, A. M., Fearon, R. M. P., van IJzendoorn, M. H., Bakermans-Kranenburg, M. J., & Roisman, G. I. (2017). Attachment in the early life course: Meta-analytic evidence for its role in socioemotional development. *Child Development Perspectives, 11*, 70–76. doi:10.1111/cdep.12213

Grossmann, K. E., Spangler, G., Suess, G., & Unzner, L. (1985). Maternal sensitivity and newborns' orientation responses as related to quality of attachment in northern Germany. *Monographs of the Society for Research in Child Development, 50*(1–2, Serial No. 209), 233–256.

Grossmann, K., Grossman, K. E., Fremmer-Bombik, E., Kindler, H., Scheuerer-Englisch, H., & Zimmermann, P. (2002). The uniqueness of the child–father attachment relationship: Fathers' sensitive and challenging play as a pivotal variable in a 16-year longitudinal study. *Social Development, 11*, 301–337.

Guo, Y., Leu, S. Y., Barnard, K. E., Thompson, E. A., & Spieker, S. J. (2015). An examination of changes in emotion co-regulation among mother and child dyads during the Strange Situation. *Infant and Child Development, 24*, 256–273. doi:10.1002/icd.1917

Halberstadt, A. G., & Lozada, F. T. (2011). Emotion development in infancy through the lens of culture. *Emotion Review, 3*, 158–168. doi:10.1177/1754073910387946

Harlow, H. F., & Zimmerman, R. (1959). Affectional responses in the infant monkey. *Science, 130*, 421–432.

Harrison, L. J., & Ungerer, J. A. (2002). Maternal employment and infant–mother attachment security at 12 months postpartum. *Developmental Psychology, 38*, 758–773.

Harwood, R. L., Scholmerich, A., Schulze, P. A., & Gonzalez, Z. (1999). Cultural differences in maternal beliefs and behaviors: A study of middle class Anglo and Puerto Rican mother–infant pairs in four everyday situations. *Child Development, 70*, 1005–1016.

Hewlett, B. S. (2008). Fathers and infants among Aka pygmies. In R. A. LeVine & R. S. New (Eds.), *Anthropology and child development: A cross-cultural reader* (pp. 84–99). Malden, MA: Blackwell.

Hewlett, B. S., Lamb, M. E., Shannon, D., Leyendecker, B., & Scholmerich, A. (1998). Culture and early infancy among central African foragers and farmers. *Developmental Psychology, 34*, 653–661.

Hewlett, B. S., & MacFarlan, S. J. (2010). Fathers, roles in hunter-gatherer and other small-scale cultures. In M. E. Lamb (Ed.), *The roles of the father in child development* (5th ed., pp. 41–44). Hoboken, NJ: John Wiley.

Hock, A., Oberst, L., Jubran, R., White, H., Heck, A., & Bhatt, R. S. (2017). Integrated emotion processing in infancy: Matching of faces and bodies. *Infancy, 22*, 608–625. doi:10.1111/infa.12177

Hollon, S. D., DeRubeis, R. J., Fawcett, J., Amsterdam, J. D., Shelton, R. C., Zajecka, J., . . . Gallop, R. (2016). Notice of retraction and replacement. Hollon et al. Effect of cognitive therapy with antidepressant medications vs antidepressants alone on the rate of recovery in major depressive disorder: A randomized clinical trial. JAMA Psychiatry. 2014;71(10):1157–1164. *JAMA Psychiatry, 73*, 639. doi:10.1001/jamapsychiatry.2016.0756

Hossain, Z., Field, T., Pickens, J., Malphurs, J., & Del Valle, C. (1997). Fathers' caregiving in low income African-American and Hispanic-American families. *Early Development & Parenting, 6*, 73–82. doi:10.1002/(sici)1099-0917(199706)6:2<73::aid-edp145>3.0.co;2-o

Hossain, Z., Roopnarine, J. L., Ismail, R., Hashmi, S. I., & Sombuling, A. (2007). Fathers' and mothers' reports of involvement in caring for infants in Kadazan families in Sabah, Malaysia. *Fathering: A Journal of Theory, Research, & Practice about Men as Fathers, 5*, 58–72. doi:10.3149/fth.0501.58

Howell, B. R., McMurray, M. S., Guzman, D. B., Nair, G., Shi, Y., McCormack, K. M., . . . Sanchez, M. M. (2017). Maternal buffering beyond glucocorticoids: Impact of early life stress on corticolimbic circuits that control infant responses to novelty. *Social Neuroscience, 12*, 50–64. doi:10.1080/17470919.2016.1200481

Huang, Z. J., Lewin, A., Mitchell, S. J., & Zhang, J. (2012). Variations in the relationship between maternal depression, maternal sensitivity, and child attachment by race/ethnicity: Findings from a nationally representative cohort study. *Maternal and Child Health Journal, 16*, 40–50. doi:10.1007/s10995-010-0716-2

Huston, A. C., Bobbitt, K. C., & Bentley, A. (2015). Time spent in child care: How and why does it affect social development? *Developmental Psychology, 51*, 621–634. doi:10.1037/a0038951

Izard, C. E., Woodburn, E. M., & Finlon, K. J. (2010). Extending emotion science to the study of discrete emotions in infants. *Emotion Review, 2*, 134–136. doi:10.1177/1754073909355003

Jacob, J. I. (2009). The socio-emotional effects of non-maternal childcare on children in the USA: A critical review of recent studies. *Early Child Development & Care, 179*, 559–570. doi:10.1080/03004430701292988

Jin, M. K., Jacobvitz, D., Hazen, N., & Jung, S. H. (2012). Maternal sensitivity and infant attachment security in Korea: Cross-cultural validation of the Strange Situation. *Attachment & Human Development, 14*, 33–44. doi:10.1080/14616734.2012.636656

Jonas, W., Atkinson, L., Steiner, M., Meaney, M. J., Wazana, A., & Fleming, A. S. (2015). Breastfeeding and maternal sensitivity predict early infant temperament. *Acta Paediatrica, 104*, 678–686. doi:10.1111/apa.12987

Kagan, J. (2013). Temperamental contributions to inhibited and uninhibited profiles. In P. D. Zelazo (Ed.), *The Oxford handbook of developmental psychology: Vol. 2. Self and other* (pp. 142–165). Oxford, UK: Oxford University Press. doi:10.1093/oxfordhb/9780199958474.013.0007

Kagan, J., Arcus, D., Snidman, N., Feng, W., Handler, J., & Greene, S. (1994). Reactivity in infants: A cross national comparison. *Developmental Psychology, 30*, 342–345.

Kawakami, K., Takai-Kawakami, K., Kawakami, F., Tomonaga, M., Suzuki, M., & Shimizu, Y. (2008). Roots of smile: A preterm neonates' study. *Infant Behavior & Development, 31*, 518–522. doi:10.1016/j.infbeh.2008.03.002

Kim, B. R., & Teti, D. M. (2014). Maternal emotional availability during infant bedtime: An ecological framework. *Journal of Family Psychology, 28*, 1–11. doi:10.1037/a0035157

Kochanska, G. (2000). Mother-child mutually responsive orientation and conscience development: From toddler to early school age. *Child Development, 71*, 417.

Kochanska, G., & Kim, S. (2013). Early attachment organization with both parents and future behavior problems: From infancy to middle childhood. *Child Development, 84*, 283–296. doi:10.1111/j.1467-8624.2012.01852.x

Kojima, H. (1986). Becoming nurturant in Japan: Past and present. In A. Fogel & G. F. Melson (Eds.), *Origins of nurturance: Developmental, biological, and cultural perspectives on caregiving* (pp. 359–376). Hillsdale, NJ: Lawrence Erlbaum.

Kragel, P. A., & LaBar, K. S. (2016). Decoding the nature of emotion in the brain. *Trends in Cognitive Sciences, 20*, 444–455. doi:10.1016/J.TICS.2016.03.011

Krassner, A. M., Gartstein, M. A., Park, C., Dragan, W. Ł., Lecannelier, F., & Putnam, S. P. (2016). East–west, collectivist-individualist: A cross-cultural examination of temperament in toddlers from Chile, Poland, South Korea, and the U.S. *European Journal of Developmental Psychology, 14*, 449–464. doi:1 0.1080/17405629.2016.1236722

Kringelbach, M. L., Stark, E. A., Alexander, C., Bornstein, M. H., & Stein, A. (2016). On cuteness: Unlocking the parental brain and beyond. *Trends in Cognitive Sciences, 20*, 545–558. doi:10.1016/J.TICS.2016.05.003

Lamb, M. E., & Lewis, C. (2015). The role of parent–child relationships in child development. In M. H. Bornstein & M. E. Lamb (Eds.), *Developmental science: An advanced textbook* (7th ed., pp. 469–517). New York, NY: Psychology Press.

Lamb, M. E., & Lewis, C. (2016). The role of parent–child relationships in development. In M. H. Bornstein & M. E. Lamb (Eds.), *Developmental science: An advanced textbook* (7th ed., pp. 535–585). New York, NY: Psychology Press.

Langfur, S. (2013). The you-I event: On the genesis of self-awareness. *Phenomenology and the Cognitive Sciences, 12*, 769–790. doi:10.1007/s11097-012-9282-y

Laurent, H. K., & Ablow, J. C. (2013). A face a mother could love: Depression-related maternal neural responses to infant emotion faces. *Social Neuroscience, 8*, 228–239. doi:10.1080/17470919.2012.762039

Laurent, H. K., Harold, G. T., Leve, L., Shelton, K. H., & Van Goozen, S. H. M. (2016). Understanding the unfolding of stress regulation in infants. *Development and Psychopathology, 28*(4, Pt. 2), 1431–1440. doi:10.1017/S0954579416000171

Laurin, J. C., & Joussemet, M. (2017). Parental autonomy-supportive practices and toddlers' rule internalization: A prospective observational study. *Motivation and Emotion, 41*, 562–575. doi:10.1007/s11031-017-9627-5

Lemerise, E. A., & Dodge, K. A. (2008). The development of anger and hostile interactions. In M. Lewis, J. M. Haviland-Jones, & L. F. Barrett (Eds.), *Handbook of emotions* (3rd ed., pp. 730–741). New York, NY: Guilford.

Lemery-Chalfant, K., Kao, K., Swann, G., & Goldsmith, H. H. (2013). Childhood temperament: Passive gene–environment correlation, gene–environment interaction, and the hidden importance of the family environment. *Development and Psychopathology, 25*, 51–63. doi:10.1017/S0954579412000892

Lench, H. C., Baldwin, C. L., An, D., & Garrison, K. E. (2018). The emotional toolkit: Lessons from the science of emotion. In L. C. Lench (Ed.), *The function of emotions* (pp. 253–261).

Cham, Switzerland: Springer International. doi:10.1007/978-3-319-77619-4_13

Leppanen, J. M. (2011). Neural and developmental bases of the ability to recognize social signals of emotions. *Emotion Review, 3*, 179–188. doi:10.1177/1754073910387942

Leventon, J. S., & Bauer, P. J. (2013). The sustained effect of emotional signals on neural processing in 12-month-olds. *Developmental Science, 16*, 485–498. doi:10.1111/desc.12041

Levine, L. E. (1983). Mine: Self-definition in 2-year-old boys. *Developmental Psychology, 19*, 544–549.

Levine, R. A., Levine, S., Dixon, S., Richman, A., Keefer, C. H., Leiderman, P. H., & Brazelton, T. B. (1994). *Child care and culture: Lessons from Africa.* New York, NY: Cambridge University Press.

Lewis, M. (2011). Inside and outside: The relation between emotional states and expressions. *Emotion Review, 3*, 189–196. doi:10.1177/1754073910387947

Lewis, M. (2016). Self-conscious emotions: Embarrassment, pride, shame, guilt, and hubris. In L. F. Barrett, M. Lewis, & J. M. Haviland-Jones (Eds.), *Handbook of emotions* (p. 928). New York, NY: Guilford.

Lewis, M., & Brooks-Gunn, J. (1979). *Social cognition and the acquisition of self.* New York, NY: Plenum.

Lewis, M., & Carmody, D. P. (2008). Self-representation and brain development. *Developmental Psychology, 44*, 1329–1334.

Lewis, M., Hitchcock, D. F. A., & Sullivan, M. W. (2004). Physiological and emotional reactivity to learning and frustration. *Infancy, 6*, 121–143.

Lewis, M., Ramsay, D. S., & Kawakami, K. (1993). Differences between Japanese infants and Caucasian American infants in behavioral and cortisol response to inoculation. *Child Development, 64*, 1722–1731. doi:10.1111/j.1467-8624.1993.tb04209.x

Lickenbrock, D. M., & Braungart-Rieker, J. M. (2015). Examining antecedents of infant attachment security with mothers and fathers: An ecological systems perspective. *Infant Behavior and Development, 39*, 173–187. doi:10.1016/J.INFBEH.2015.03.003

Liu, Y., Kaaya, S., Chai, J., McCoy, D. C., Surkan, P. J., Black, M. M., . . . Smith-Fawzi, M. C. (2017). Maternal depressive symptoms and early childhood cognitive development: A meta-analysis. *Psychological Medicine, 47*, 680–689. doi:10.1017/S003329171600283X

Lucassen, N., Tharner, A., Van IJzendoorn, M. H., Bakermans-Kranenburg, M. J., Volling, B. L., Verhulst, F. C., . . . Tiemeier, H. (2011). The association between paternal sensitivity and infant-father attachment security: A meta-analysis of three decades of research. *Journal of Family Psychology, 25*, 986–992. doi:10.1037/a0025855

Lyons-Ruth, K., & Jacobvitz, D. (2016). Attachment disorganization from infancy to adulthood: Neurobiological correlates, parenting contexts, and pathways to disorder. In J. Cassidy & P. R. Shaver (Eds.), *Handbook of attachment: Theory, research, and clinical applications* (pp. 667–695). New York, NY: Guilford.

Main, M., & Solomon, J. (1986). Discovery of an insecure, disorganized/disoriented attachment pattern: Procedures, findings, and implications for the classification of behavior. In M. Yogman & T. B. Brazelton (Eds.), *Affective development in infancy* (pp. 95–124). Norwood, NJ: Ablex.

Malatesta, C. Z., & Haviland, J. M. (1982). Learning display rules: The socialization of emotion expression in infancy. *Child Development, 53*, 991–1003.

Mangelsdorf, S. C. (1992). Developmental changes in infant-stranger interaction. *Infant Behavior & Development, 15*, 191–208. doi:10.1016/0163-6383(92)80023-n

Mangelsdorf, S. C., Shapiro, J. R., & Marzolf, D. (1995). Developmental and temperamental differences in emotion regulation in infancy. *Child Development, 66*, 1817–1828.

Marvin, R. S., Britner, P. A., & Russell, B. S. (2016). Normative development: The ontogeny of attachment in childhood. In J. Cassidy & P. R. Shaver (Eds.), *Handbook of attachment, third edition: Theory, research, and clinical applications* (pp. 273–289). New York, NY: Guilford.

McMahan True, M., Pisani, L., & Oumar, F. (2001). Infant–mother attachment among the Dogon of Mali. *Child Development, 72*, 1451.

Meehan, C. L., & Hawks, S. (2013). Cooperative breeding and attachment among the Aka Foragers. In N. Quinn & J. Marie Mageo (Eds.), *Attachment reconsidered* (pp. 85–113). New York, NY: Palgrave Macmillan US. doi:10.1057/9781137386724_4

Meléndez, L. (2005). Parental beliefs and practices around early self-regulation: The impact of culture and immigration. *Infants & Young Children, 18*, 136–146.

Meltzoff, A. N. (1990). Towards a developmental cognitive science. *Annals of the New York Academy of Sciences, 608*, 1–37.

Meltzoff, A. N. (2007). "Like me": A foundation for social cognition. *Developmental Science, 10*, 126–134. doi:10.1111/j.1467-7687.2007.00574.x

Mesman, J., van IJzendoorn, M. H., & Sagi-Schwartz, A. (2016). Cross-cultural patterns of attachment: Universal and contextual dimensions. In J. Cassidy & P. R. Shaver (Eds.), *Handbook of attachment, third edition: Theory, research, and clinical applications* (pp. 852–876) New York, NY: Guilford.

Messer, E. P., Ammerman, R. T., Teeters, A. R., Bodley, A. L., Howard, J., Van Ginkel, J. B., & Putnam, F. W. (2018). Treatment of maternal depression with in-home cognitive behavioral therapy augmented by a parenting enhancement: A case report. *Cognitive and Behavioral Practice, 25*, 402–415. doi:10.1016/J.CBPRA.2017.10.002

Messinger, D., & Fogel, A. (2007). The interactive development of social smiling. In R. V. Kail (Ed.), *Advances in child development and behavior* (Vol. 35, pp. 327–366). San Diego, CA: Elsevier Academic Press.

Morelli, G. (2015). The evolution of attachment theory and cultures of human attachment in infancy and early childhood. In L. A. Jensen (Ed.), *The Oxford handbook of human development and culture* (pp. 149–164). Oxford, UK: Oxford University Press. doi:10.1093/oxfordhb/9780199948550.013.10

Mortensen, J. A., & Barnett, M. A. (2015). Teacher–child interactions in infant/toddler child care and socioemotional development. *Early Education and Development, 26*, 209–229. doi:10.1080/10409289.2015.985878

Neisser, U. (1993). *The perceived self: Ecological and interpersonal sources of self-knowledge.* New York, NY: Cambridge University Press.

Newland, R. P., Parade, S. H., Dickstein, S., & Seifer, R. (2016). The association between maternal depression and sensitivity: Child-directed effects on parenting during infancy. *Infant Behavior and Development, 45*, 47–50. doi:10.1016/J.INFBEH.2016.09.001

NICHD Early Child Care Research Network. (2005). Early child care and children's development in the primary grades: Follow-up results from the NICHD study of early child care. *American Educational Research Journal, 42*, 537–570. doi:10.3102/00028312042003537

Oddi, K. B., Murdock, K. W., Vadnais, S., Bridgett, D. J., & Gartstein, M. A. (2013). Maternal and infant temperament characteristics as contributors to parenting stress in the first year postpartum. *Infant and Child Development, 22*, 553–579. doi:10.1002/icd.1813

Pallini, S., Chirumbolo, A., Morelli, M., Baiocco, R., Laghi, F., & Eisenberg, N. (2018). The relation of attachment security status to effortful self-regulation: A meta-analysis. *Psychological Bulletin, 144*, 501–531. doi:10.1037/bul0000134

Papageorgiou, K., Smith, T. J., Wu, R., Johnson, M. H., Kirkham, N. Z., & Ronald, A. (2014). Individual differences in infant fixation duration relate to attention and behavioral control in childhood. *Psychological Science, 25*, 1371–1379. doi:10.1177/0956797614531295

Papoušek, M., & Papoušek, H. (1990). Excessive infant crying and intuitive parental care: Buffering support and its failures in parent–infant interaction. *Early Child Development and Care, 65*, 117–126. doi:10.1080/0300443900650114

Paulussen-Hoogeboom, M. C., Stams, G. J. J. M., Hermanns, J. M. A., & Peetsma, T. T. D. (2007). Child negative emotionality and parenting from infancy to preschool: A meta-analytic review. *Developmental Psychology, 43*, 438–453. doi:10.1037/0012-1649.43.2.438

Pemberton Roben, C. K., Bass, A. J., Moore, G. A., Murray-Kolb, L., Tan, P. Z., Gilmore, R. O., Teti, L. O. (2012). Let me go: The influences of crawling experience and temperament on the development of anger expression. *Infancy, 17*, 558–577. doi:10.1111/j.1532-7078.2011.00092.x

Pinquart, M., Feußner, C., & Ahnert, L. (2013). Meta-analytic evidence for stability in attachments from infancy to early adulthood. *Attachment & Human Development, 15*, 189–218. doi:10.1080/14616734.2013.746257

Planalp, E. M., Van Hulle, C., Lemery-Chalfant, K., & Goldsmith, H. H. (2017). Genetic and environmental contributions to the development of positive affect in infancy. *Emotion, 17*, 412–420. doi:10.1037/emo0000238

Pluess, M., Birkbeck, J. B., & Belsky, J. (2010). Differential susceptibility to parenting and quality child care. *Developmental Psychology, 46*, 379–390. doi:10.1037/a0015203

Poehlmann, J., Schwichtenberg, A. J. M., Shlafer, R. J., Hahn, E., Bianchi, J.-P., & Warner, R. (2011). Emerging self-regulation in toddlers born preterm or low birth weight: Differential susceptibility to parenting? *Development & Psychopathology, 23*, 177–193. doi:10.1017/s0954579410000726

Posner, M. I., & Rothbart, M. K. (2018). Temperament and brain networks of attention. *Philosophical Transactions of the Royal Society of London Series B, Biological Sciences, 373*, 20170254. doi:10.1098/rstb.2017.0254

Potegal, M., Robison, S., Anderson, F., Jordan, C., & Shapiro, E. (2007). Sequence and priming in 15 month-olds' reactions to brief arm restraint: Evidence for a hierarchy of anger responses. *Aggressive Behavior, 33*, 508–518. doi:10.1002/ab.20207

Prady, S. L., Kiernan, K., Fairley, L., Wilson, S., & Wright, J. (2014). Self-reported maternal parenting style and confidence and infant temperament in a multi-ethnic community: Results from the Born in Bradford cohort. *Journal of Child Health Care, 18*, 31–46. doi:10.1177/1367493512473855

Prenoveau, J. M., Craske, M. G., West, V., Giannakakis, A., Zioga, M., Lehtonen, A., . . . Stein, A. (2017). Maternal postnatal depression and anxiety and their association with child emotional negativity and behavior problems at two years. *Developmental Psychology, 53*, 50–62. doi:10.1037/dev0000221

Priel, B., & deSchonen, S. (1986). Self-recognition: A study of a population without mirrors. *Journal of Experimental Child Psychology, 41*, 237–250.

Raby, K. L., Steele, R. D., Carlson, E. A., & Sroufe, L. A. (2015). Continuities and changes in infant attachment patterns across two generations. *Attachment & Human Development, 17*, 414–428. doi:10.1080/14616734.2015.1067824

Roben, C. K. P., Cole, P. M., & Armstrong, L. M. (2013). Longitudinal relations among language skills, anger expression, and regulatory strategies in early childhood. *Child Development, 84*, 891–905. doi:10.1111/cdev.12027

Roben, C. K. P., Moore, G. A., Cole, P. M., Molenaar, P., Leve, L. D., Shaw, D. S., . . . Neiderhiser, J. M. (2015). Transactional patterns of maternal depressive symptoms and mother-child mutual negativity in an adoption sample. *Infant and Child Development, 24*, 322–342. doi:10.1002/icd.1906

Rochat, P. (1998). Self-perception and action in infancy. *Experimental Brain Research, 123*, 102–109. doi:10.1007/s002210050550

Rochat, P. (2010). Emerging self-concept. In J. G. Bremner & T. D. Wachs (Eds.), *The Wiley-Blackwell handbook of infant development* (pp. 320–344). Oxford, England: Wiley-Blackwell. doi:10.1002/9781444327564.ch10

Rochat, P. (2013). Self-conceptualizing in development. In P. D. Zelazo (Ed.), *The Oxford handbook of developmental psychology: Vol. 2. Self and other* (pp. 378–396). Oxford, UK: Oxford University Press. doi:10.1093/oxfordhb/9780199958474.013.0015

Rolls, E. T. (2017). Evolution of the emotional brain. In S. Watanabe, M. A. Hofman, & T. Shimizu (Eds.), *Evolution of the brain, cognition, and emotion in vertebrates* (pp. 251–272). Tokyo: Springer Japan. doi:10.1007/978-4-431-56559-8_12

Roopnarine, J. L., Talukder, E., Jain, D., Joshi, P., & Srivastav, P. (1992). Personal well-being, kinship tie, and mother–infant and father–infant interactions in single-wage and dual-wage families in New Delhi, India. *Journal of Marriage & Family, 54*, 293–301.

Rothbart, M. K. (2011). *Becoming who we are: Temperament and personality in development.* New York, NY: Guilford.

Rothbart, M. K., & Bates, J. E. (1998). Temperament. In N. Eisenberg (Ed.), *Handbook of child psychology: Vol. 3. Social, emotional, and personality development* (5th ed., pp. 105–176). New York, NY: John Wiley.

Rothbart, M. K., & Bates, J. E. (2007). Temperament. In *Handbook of child psychology* (pp. 207–212). Hoboken, NJ: John Wiley. doi:10.1002/9780470147658.chpsy0303

Rothbaum, F., Weisz, J., Pott, M., Miyake, K., & Morelli, G. (2000). Attachment and culture: Security in the United States and Japan. *American Psychologist, 55*, 1093–1104.

Rubin, K. H., Hastings, P., Chen, X., Stewart, S., & McNichol, K. (1998). Interpersonal and maternal correlates of aggression, conflict, and externalizing problems in toddlers. *Child Development, 69*, 1614–1629.

Saarni, C., Mumme, D. L., & Campos, J. J. (1998). Emotional development: Action, communication, and understanding. In N. Eisenberg & W. Damon (Eds.), *Handbook of child psychology: Social, emotional, and personality development* (5th ed., Vol. 3, pp. 237–309). Hoboken, NJ: John Wiley.

Safdar, S., Friedlmeier, W., Matsumoto, D., Yoo, S. H., Kwantes, C. T., Kakai, H., & Shigemasu, E. (2009). Variations of emotional display rules within and across cultures: A comparison between Canada, USA, and Japan. *Canadian Journal of Behavioural Science/Revue Canadienne Des Sciences Du Comportement, 41*, 1–10. doi:10.1037/a0014387

Sagi, A., Lamb, M. E., Lewkowicz, K. S., Shoham, R., Dvir, R., & Estes, D. (1985). Security of infant-mother, -father, and -metapelet attachments among kibbutz-reared Israeli children. *Monographs of the Society for Research in Child Development, 50*, 257–275. doi:10.1111/1540-5834.ep11890146

Sagi, A., Van IJzendoorn, M. H., & Koren-Karie, N. (1991). Primary appraisal of the Strange Situation: A cross-cultural analysis of preseparation episodes. *Developmental Psychology, 27*, 587–596.

Salter, M. D. (1940). *An evaluation of adjustment based upon the concept of security.* Toronto: University of Toronto Press.

Sarkadi, A., Kristiansson, R., Oberklaid, F., & Bremberg, S. (2008). Fathers' involvement and children's developmental outcomes: A systematic review of longitudinal studies. *Acta Paediatrica, 97*, 153–158. doi:10.1111/j.1651-2227.2007.00572.x

Saudino, K. J., & Micalizzi, L. (2015). Emerging trends in behavioral genetic studies of child temperament. *Child Development*

Perspectives, 9, 144–148. doi:10.1111/cdep.12123

Schulte, B., & Durana, A. (2016). *The new America care report.* Retrieved January 2, 2018, from https://www.newamerica.org/better-life-lab/policy-papers/new-america-care-report/

Seifer, R., Dickstein, S., Parade, S., Hayden, L. C., Magee, K. D., & Schiller, M. (2014). Mothers' appraisal of goodness of fit and children's social development. *International Journal of Behavioral Development, 38,* 86–97. doi:10.1177/0165025413507172

Sethna, V. F., Perry, E., Domoney, J., Iles, J., Psychogiou, L., Rowbotham, N. E. L., . . . Ramchandani, P. G. (2016). Father–child interactions at 3-months and 2 years: Contributions to children's cognitive development at 2 years. *Infant Mental Health Journal, 38,* 378–390. doi:10.1002/imhj.21642

Sockol, L. E. (2015). A systematic review of the efficacy of cognitive behavioral therapy for treating and preventing perinatal depression. *Journal of Affective Disorders, 177,* 7–21. doi:10.1016/J.JAD.2015.01.052

Spinelli, M., & Mesman, J. (2018). The regulation of infant negative emotions: The role of maternal sensitivity and infant-directed speech prosody. *Infancy, 23,* 502–518. doi:10.1111/infa.12237

Sroufe, L. A. (2016). The place of attachment in development. In J. Cassidy & P. R. Shaver (Eds.), *Handbook of attachment: Theory, research, and clinical applications* (pp. 997–1010). New York, NY: Guilford.

Sroufe, L. A. (1977). Wariness of strangers and the study of infant development. *Child Development, 48,* 731–746.

Sroufe, L. A. (1997). Psychopathology as an outcome of development. *Development and Psychopathology, 7,* 323–336.

Sroufe, L. A., & Waters, E. (1976). The ontogenesis of smiling and laughter: A perspective on the organization of development in infancy. *Psychological Review, 83,* 173–189. doi:10.1037/0033-295x.83.3.173

Stapel, J. C., van Wijk, I., Bekkering, H., & Hunnius, S. (2017). Eighteen-month-old infants show distinct electrophysiological responses to their own faces. *Developmental Science, 20,* e12437. doi:10.1111/desc.12437

Stenberg, G. (2017). Does contingency in adults' responding influence 12-month-old infants' social referencing? *Infant Behavior and Development, 46,* 67–79. doi:10.1016/j.infbeh.2016.11.013

Stern, J. A., & Cassidy, J. (2018). Empathy from infancy to adolescence: An attachment perspective on the development of individual differences. *Developmental Review, 47,* 1–22. doi:10.1016/J.DR.2017.09.002

Stipek, D. (1995). *The development of pride and shame in toddlers* (J. P. Tangney & K. W. Fischer, Eds.). New York, NY: Guilford.

Stipek, D., Gralinski, J. H., & Kopp, C. B. (1990). Self-concept development in the toddler years. *Developmental Psychology, 26,* 972–977. doi:10.1037/0012-1649.26.6.972

Strathearn, L., Jian, L., Fonagy, P., & Montague, P. R. (2008). What's in a smile? Maternal brain responses to infant facial cues. *Pediatrics, 122,* 40–51. doi:10.1542/peds.2007-1566

Sullivan, M. W., & Lewis, M. (2003). Contextual determinants of anger and other negative expressions in young infants. *Developmental Psychology, 39,* 693–705. doi:10.1037/0012-1649.39.4.693

Super, C. M., & Harkness, S. (2010). Culture and infancy. In J. G. Bremner & T. D. Wachs (Eds.), *The Wiley-Blackwell handbook of infant development* (pp. 623–649). Oxford, England: Wiley-Blackwell. doi:10.1002/9781444327564.ch21

Suurland, J., van der Heijden, K. B., Smaling, H. J. A., Huijbregts, S. C. J., van Goozen, S. H. M., & Swaab, H. (2017). Infant autonomic nervous system response and recovery: Associations with maternal risk status and infant emotion regulation. *Development and Psychopathology, 29,* 759–773. doi:10.1017/S0954579416000456

Swartz, H. A., Cyranowski, J. M., Cheng, Y., Zuckoff, A., Brent, D. A., Markowitz, J. C., . . . Frank, E. (2016). Brief psychotherapy for maternal depression: Impact on mothers and children. *Journal of the American Academy of Child & Adolescent Psychiatry, 55,* 495–503.e2. doi:10.1016/J.JAAC.2016.04.003

Takahashi, K. (1990). Are the key assumptions of the "Strange Situation" procedure universal? A view from Japanese research. *Human Development, 33,* 23–30.

Tamis-LeMonda, C. S., Kahana-Kalman, R., & Yoshikawa, H. (2009). Father involvement in immigrant and ethnically diverse families from the prenatal period to the second year: Prediction and mediating mechanisms. *Sex Roles, 60,* 496–509. doi:10.1007/s11199-009-9593-9

Tan, E. S., McIntosh, J. E., Kothe, E. J., Opie, J. E., & Olsson, C. A. (2018). Couple relationship quality and offspring attachment security: A systematic review with meta-analysis. *Attachment & Human Development, 20,* 349–377. doi:10.1080/14616734.2017.1401651

Thomas, A., & Chess, S. (1977). *Temperament and development.* New York, NY: Brunner/Mazel.

Thomas, A., Chess, S., & Birch, H. G. (1970). The origin of personality. *Scientific American, 223,* 102–109.

Thompson, R. A. (2013). Attachment theory and research: Précis and prospect. In P. D. Zelazo (Ed.), *The Oxford handbook of developmental psychology: Vol. 2. Self and other* (2nd ed., pp. 191–216). New York, NY: Oxford University Press. doi:10.1093/oxfordhb/9780199958474.013.0009

Thompson, R. A. (2016). Early attachment and later development: Reframing the questions. In J. Cassidy & P. R. Shaver (Eds.), *Handbook of attachment, third edition: Theory, research, and clinical applications* (pp. 330–347). New York, NY: Guilford.

Thurman, S. L., & Corbetta, D. (2017). Spatial exploration and changes in infant–mother dyads around transitions in infant locomotion. *Developmental Psychology, 53,* 1207–1221. doi:10.1037/dev0000328

Tronick, E. Z., Morelli, G. A., & Ivey, P. K. (1992). The Efe forager infant and toddler's pattern of social relationships: Multiple and simultaneous. *Developmental Psychology, 28,* 568–577.

Turecki, G., & Meaney, M. J. (2016). Effects of the social environment and stress on glucocorticoid receptor gene methylation: A systematic review. *Biological Psychiatry, 79,* 87–96. doi:10.1016/j.biopsych.2014.11.022

Turner, J. H. (2014). *The evolution of human emotions.* Dordrecht, The Netherlands: Springer. doi:10.1007/978-94-017-9130-4_2

U.S. Bureau of Labor Statistics. (2016). *Employment characteristics of families—2015.* Retrieved from https://www.bls.gov/news.release/pdf/famee.pdf

Ursache, A., Blair, C., Stifter, C., Voegtline, K., & The Family Life Project Investigators. (2013). Emotional reactivity and regulation in infancy interact to predict executive functioning in early childhood. *Developmental Psychology, 40,* 760.

Vaish, A., Grossmann, T., & Woodward, A. (2008). Not all emotions are created equal: The negativity bias in social-emotional development. *Psychological Bulletin, 134,* 383–403. doi:10.1037/0033-2909.134.3.383

Vallotton, C., & Ayoub, C. (2011). Use your words: The role of language in the development of toddlers' self-regulation. *Early Childhood Research Quarterly, 26,* 169–181.

Van IJzendoorn, M. H., & Kroonenberg, P. M. (1988). Cross-cultural patterns of attachment: A meta-analysis of the strange situation. *Child Development, 59,* 147–156.

Van Ryzin, M. J., Carlson, E. A., & Sroufe, L. A. (2011). Attachment discontinuity in a high-risk sample. *Attachment & Human Development, 13,* 381–401. doi:10.1080/14616734.2011.584403

Vandell, D. L., Belsky, J., Burchinal, M., Steinberg, L., & Vandergrift, N. (2010). Do effects of early child care extend to age 15 years? Results from the NICHD study of early child care and youth development. *Child Development, 81,* 737–756. doi:10.1111/j.1467-8624.2010.01431.x

Vandell, D. L., Burchinal, M., & Pierce, K. M. (2016). Early child care and adolescent functioning at the end of high school: Results from the NICHD study of early child care and youth development. *Developmental Psychology, 52,* 1634–1645. doi:10.1037/dev0000169

Verhage, M. L., Oosterman, M., & Schuengel, C. (2013). Parenting self-efficacy predicts perceptions of infant negative temperament characteristics, not vice versa. *Journal of Family Psychology, 27,* 844–849. doi:10.1037/a0034263

Verissimo, M., Santos, A. J., Fernandes, C., Shin, N., & Vaughn, B. E. (2014). Associations between attachment security and social competence in preschool children. *Merrill-Palmer Quarterly, 60,* 80. doi:10.13110/merrpalmquar1982.60.1.0080

Walle, E. A., Reschke, P. J., & Knothe, J. M. (2017). Social referencing: Defining and delineating a basic process of emotion. *Emotion Review, 9,* 245–252. doi:10.1177/1754073916669594

Watamura, S. E., Phillips, D. A., Morrissey, T. W., McCartney, K., & Bub, K. (2011). Double jeopardy: Poorer social-emotional outcomes for children in the NICHD SECCYD experiencing home and child-care environments that confer risk. *Child Development, 82,* 48–65. doi:10.1111/j.1467-8624.2010.01540.x

Waters, S. F., West, T. V., Karnilowicz, H. R., & Mendes, W. B. (2017). Affect contagion between mothers and infants: Examining valence and touch. *Journal of Experimental*

Psychology: General, 146, 1043–1051. doi:10.1037/xge0000322

Waters, S. F., West, T. V., & Mendes, W. B. (2014). Stress contagion: Physiological covariation between mothers and infants. *Psychological Science, 25,* 934–942. doi:10.1177/0956797613518352

Webb, R., & Ayers, S. (2015). Cognitive biases in processing infant emotion by women with depression, anxiety and post-traumatic stress disorder in pregnancy or after birth: A systematic review. *Cognition and Emotion, 29,* 1278–1294. doi:10.1080/02699931.2014.977849

Weinfield, N. S., Sroufe, L. A., Egeland, B., & Carlson, E. (2008). Individual differences in infant caregiver attachment: Conceptual and empirical aspects of security. In J. Cassidy & P. R. Shaver (Eds.), *Handbook of attachment: Theory, research, and clinical applications* (pp. 78–101). New York, NY: Guilford.

Wolke, D., Eryigit-Madzwamuse, S., & Gutbrod, T. (2014). Very preterm/very low birthweight infants' attachment: Infant and maternal characteristics. *Archives of Disease in Childhood, Fetal and Neonatal Edition, 99,* F70–F75. doi:10.1136/archdischild-2013-303788

Zimmer-Gembeck, M. J., Webb, H. J., Pepping, C. A., Swan, K., Merlo, O., Skinner, E. A., . . . Dunbar, M. (2017). Is parent–child attachment a correlate of children's emotion regulation and coping? *International Journal of Behavioral Development, 41,* 74–93. doi:10.1177/0165025415618276

Chapter 7

Al-Namlah, A. S., Meins, E., & Fernyhough, C. (2012). Self-regulatory private speech relates to children's recall and organization of autobiographical memories. *Early Childhood Research Quarterly, 27,* 441–446. doi:10.1016/j.ecresq.2012.02.005

Alarcón-Rubio, D., Sánchez-Medina, J. A., & Prieto-Garcia, J. R. (2014). Executive function and verbal self-regulation in childhood: Developmental linkages between partially internalized private speech and cognitive flexibility. *Early Childhood Research Quarterly, 29,* 95–105. doi:10.1016/j.ecresq.2013.11.002

Alferink, L. A., & Farmer-Dougan, V. (2010). Brain-(not) based education: Dangers of misunderstanding and misapplication of neuroscience research. *Exceptionality, 18,* 42–52. doi:10.1080/09362830903462573

Anderson, S., & Phillips, D. (2017). Is pre-K classroom quality associated with kindergarten and middle-school academic skills? *Developmental Psychology, 53,* 1063–1078. doi:10.1037/dev0000312

Anderson, V. A., Spencer-Smith, M. M., Coleman, L., Anderson, P. J., Greenham, M., Jacobs, R., . . . Leventer, R. J. (2014). Predicting neurocognitive and behavioural outcome after early brain insult. *Developmental Medicine and Child Neurology, 56,* 329–336. doi:10.1111/dmcn.12387

Aslan, A., & Bäuml, K.-H. T. (2010). Retrieval-induced forgetting in young children. *Psychonomic Bulletin & Review, 17,* 704–709. doi:10.3758/pbr.17.5.704

Astington, J. W. (1993). *The child's discovery of the mind.* Cambridge, MA: Harvard University Press.

Backscheider, A. G., Shatz, M., & Gelman, S. A. (1993). Preschoolers' ability to distinguish living kinds as a function of regrowth. *Child Development, 64,* 1242–1257.

Baddeley, A. (2016). Working memory. In R. J. Sternberg, S. T. Fiske, & D. J. Foss (Eds.), *Scientists making a difference: One hundred eminent behavioral and brain scientist talk about their most important contributions* (pp. 119–122). New York: Cambridge University Press.

Baker-Ward, L., Gordon, B. N., Ornstein, P. A., Larus, D. M., & Clubb, P. A. (1993). Young children's long-term retention of a pediatric examination. *Child Development, 64,* 1519–1533.

Bandura, A. (1977). *Social learning theory.* Englewood Cliffs, NJ: Prentice Hall.

Bandura, A. (1986). *Social foundations of thought and action: A social cognitive theory.* Englewood Cliffs, NJ: Prentice Hall.

Bandura, A., & McDonald, F. J. (1963). The influence of social reinforcement and the behavior of models in shaping children's moral judgments. *Journal of Abnormal and Social Psychology, 67,* 274–281.

Barnett, W. S., Carolan, M. E., Squires, J. H., & Clarke Brown, K., & Horowitz, M. (2015). *The state of preschool 2014: State preschool yearbook.* New Brunswick, NJ: National Institute for Early Education Research.

Bauer, P. J. (1996). Development of memory in early childhood. In N. Cowan (Ed.), *The development of memory in childhood* (pp. 83–112). Hove, England: Psychology Press.

Bauer, P. J. (2015). Development of episodic and autobiographical memory: The importance of remembering forgetting. *Developmental Review, 38,* 146–166. doi:10.1016/J.DR.2015.07.011

Behrend, D. A., Scofield, J., & Kleinknecht, E. E. (2001). Beyond fast mapping: Young children's extensions of novel words and novel facts. *Developmental Psychology, 37,* 698–705.

Benigno, J. P., Byrd, D. L., McNamara, J. P., Berg, W. K., & Farrar, M. J. (2011). Talking through transitions: Microgenetic changes in preschoolers' private speech and executive functioning. *Child Language Teaching and Therapy, 27,* 269–285. doi:10.1177/0265659010394385

Benjamin Neelon, S. E., Vaughn, A., Ball, S. C., McWilliams, C., & Ward, D. S. (2012). Nutrition practices and mealtime environments of North Carolina Child Care Centers. *Childhood Obesity, 8,* 216–223. doi:10.1089/chi.2011.0065

Benson, J. E., Sabbagh, M. A., Carlson, S. M., & Zelazo, P. D. (2013). Individual differences in executive functioning predict preschoolers' improvement from theory-of-mind training. *Developmental Psychology, 49,* 1615–1627. doi:10.1037/a0031056

Berger, P. K., Hohman, E. E., Marini, M. E., Savage, J. S., & Birch, L. L. (2016). Girls' picky eating in childhood is associated with normal weight status from ages 5 to 15 y. *American Journal of Clinical Nutrition, 104,* 1577–1582. doi:10.3945/ajcn.116.142430

Berk, L. E. (1986). Development of private speech among preschool children. *Early Child Development and Care, 24,* 113–136.

Berk, L. E. (1992). The extracurriculum. In P. W. Jackson (Ed.), *Handbook of research on curriculum* (pp. 1003–1043). New York, NY: Macmillan.

Berk, L. E., & Garvin, R. A. (1984). Development of private speech among low-income Appalachian children. *Developmental Psychology, 20,* 271–286.

Bernard, S., & Deleau, M. (2007). Conversational perspective-taking and false belief attribution: A longitudinal study. *British Journal of Developmental Psychology, 25,* 443–460. doi:10.1348/026151006X171451

Birch, S. A. J. (2005). When knowledge is a curse: Biases in mental state attribution. *Current Directions in Psychological Science, 14,* 25–29.

Bjorklund, D. F., & Myers, A. (2015). The development of cognitive abilities. In M. H. Bornstein & M. E. Lamb (Eds.), *Developmental science: An advanced textbook* (pp. 391–441). New York, NY: Psychology Press.

Bloom, L. (2000). Commentary: Breaking the language barrier: An emergentist coalition model for the origins of word learning. *Monographs of the Society for Research in Child Development, 65*(3, Serial No. 262), 124–135.

Bodrova, E., & Leong, D. J. (2018). Tools of the mind: A Vygotskian early childhood curriculum. In M. Fleer & B. I. Oers (Eds.), *International handbook of early childhood education* (pp. 1095–1111). Dordrecht, The Netherlands: Springer. doi:10.1007/978-94-024-0927-7_56

Bower, B. (1993). A child's theory of mind. *Science News, 144,* 40–42.

Brinums, M., Imuta, K., & Suddendorf, T. (2018). Practicing for the future: Deliberate practice in early childhood. *Child Development.* Advance online publication. doi:10.1111/cdev.12938

Bronfenbrenner, U. (1979). *The ecology of human development: Experiments by nature and design.* Cambridge, MA: Harvard University Press.

Brown, D. A., & Lamb, M. E. (2015). Can children be useful witnesses? It depends how they are questioned. *Child Development Perspectives, 9,* 250–255. doi:10.1111/cdep.12142

Brubacher, S. P., Glisic, U. N. A., Roberts, K. P., & Powell, M. (2011). Children's ability to recall unique aspects of one occurrence of a repeated event. *Applied Cognitive Psychology, 25,* 351–358. doi:10.1002/acp.1696

Bruer, J. T. (2008). In search of . . . brain-based education. In M. H. Immordino-Yang (Ed.), *The Jossey-Bass reader on the brain and learning* (pp. 51–69). San Francisco, CA: Jossey-Bass.

Bryck, R. L., & Fisher, P. A. (2012). Training the brain: Practical applications of neural plasticity from the intersection of cognitive neuroscience, developmental psychology, and prevention science. *American Psychologist, 67,* 87–100.

Bussey, K. (1992). Lying and truthfulness: Children's definitions, standards, and evaluative reactions. *Child Development, 63,* 129–137.

Busso, D. S., & Pollack, C. (2014). No brain left behind: Consequences of neuroscience discourse for education. *Learning, Media and Technology, 40*, 168–186. doi:10.1080/17439884.2014.908908

Callaghan, T., Rochat, P., Lillard, A., Claux, M. L., Odden, H., Itakura, S., . . . Singh, S. (2005). Synchrony in the onset of mental-state reasoning. *Psychological Science, 16*, 378–384.

Campbell, F. A., Pungello, E. P., Burchinal, M., Kainz, K., Pan, Y., Wasik, B. H., . . . Ramey, C. T. (2012). Adult outcomes as a function of an early childhood educational program: An Abecedarian Project follow-up. *Developmental Psychology, 48*, 1033–1043. doi:10.1037/a0026644

Campbell, F. A., & Ramey, C. T. (1994). Effects of early intervention on intellectual and academic achievement: A follow-up study of children from low-income families. *Child Development, 65*, 684–698. doi:10.1111/j.1467-8624.1994.tb00777.x

Campbell, F. A., Ramey, C. T., Pungello, E., Sparling, J., & Miller-Johnson, S. (2002). Early childhood education: Young adult outcomes from the Abecedarian Project. *Applied Developmental Science, 6*, 42–57.

Cardona Cano, S., Hoek, H. W., van Hoeken, D., de Barse, L. M., Jaddoe, V. W. V., Verhulst, F. C., & Tiemeier, H. (2016). Behavioral outcomes of picky eating in childhood: A prospective study in the general population. *Journal of Child Psychology and Psychiatry, 57*, 1239–1246. doi:10.1111/jcpp.12530

Carlson, S. M., Zelazo, P. D., & Faja, S. (2013). *Executive function* (P. D. Zelazo, Ed.). Oxford, UK: Oxford University Press. doi:10.1093/oxfordhb/9780199958450.013.0025

Cauffman, E., Shulman, E., Bechtold, J., & Steinberg, L. (2015). Children and the law. In M. H. Bornstein, & T. Leventhal (Eds.), *Handbook of child psychology and developmental science* (pp. 1–49). Hoboken, NJ: John Wiley. https://doi.org/10.1002/9781118963418.childpsy312

Ceci, S. J., & Bruck, M. (1998). The ontogeny and durability of true and false memories: A fuzzy trace account. *Journal of Experimental Child Psychology, 71*, 165–169.

Ceci, S. J., Huffman, M. L., Smith, E., & Loftus, E. F. (1994). Repeatedly thinking about a non-event: Source misattributions among preschoolers. *Consciousness and Cognition, 3*, 388–407.

Chandler, M. J., & Carpendale, J. I. (1998). Inching toward a mature theory of mind. In M. Ferrari & R. J. Sternberg (Eds.), *Self-awareness: Its nature and development* (pp. 148–190). New York, NY: Guilford.

Chao, R. K. (1995). Chinese and European American cultural models of the self related in mothers' child rearing beliefs. *Ethos. 23*, 328–354.

Chevalier, N., Kurth, S., Doucette, M. R., Wiseheart, M., Deoni, S. C. L. S., Dean, D. C. D., . . . Greenstein, D. (2015). Myelination is associated with processing speed in early childhood: Preliminary insights. *PLoS ONE, 10*, e0139897. doi:10.1371/journal.pone.0139897

Corballis, M. C., Lalueza-Fox, C., Orlando, L., Enard, W., & Green, R. (2014). Left brain, right brain: Facts and fantasies. *PLoS Biology, 12*, e1001767. doi:10.1371/journal.pbio.1001767

Cox, M. V. (1993). *Children's drawings of the human figure.* Hillsdale, NJ: Lawrence Erlbaum.

Deák, G. O. (2006). Do children really confuse appearance and reality? *Trends in Cognitive Sciences, 10*, 546–550.

Dean, D. C., O'Muircheartaigh, J., Dirks, H., Waskiewicz, N., Walker, L., Doernberg, E., . . . Deoni, S. C. L. (2014). Characterizing longitudinal white matter development during early childhood. *Brain Structure & Function, 220*, 1921–1933. doi:10.1007/s00429-014-0763-3

de Onis, M., & Branca, F. (2016). Childhood stunting: A global perspective. *Maternal & Child Nutrition, 12*, 12–26. doi:10.1111/mcn.12231

de Villiers, J. G., & de Villiers, P. A. (2014). The role of language in theory of mind development. *Topics in Language Disorders, 34*, 313–328. doi:10.1097/TLD.0000000000000037

Devine, R. T., & Hughes, C. H. (2018). Let's talk: Parents' mental talk (not mind-mindedness or mindreading capacity) predicts children's false belief understanding. *Child Development.* Advance online publication. doi:10.1111/cdev.12990

DeVries, R. (1969). Constancy of generic identity in the years three to six. *Monographs of the Society for Research in Child Development, 34*(Serial No. 127).

DeVries, R., & Zan, B. (2003). When children make rules. *Educational Leadership, 61*, 64–67.

Dixson, H. G. W., Komugabe-Dixson, A. F., Dixson, B. J., & Low, J. (2018). Scaling theory of mind in a small-scale society: A case study from Vanuatu. *Child Development.* Advance online publication. doi:10.1111/cdev.12919

Doenyas, C., Yavuz, H. M., & Selcuk, B. (2018). Not just a sum of its parts: How tasks of the theory of mind scale relate to executive function across time. *Journal of Experimental Child Psychology, 166*, 485–501. doi:10.1016/J.JECP.2017.09.014

Duboc, V., Dufourcq, P., Blader, P., & Roussigné, M. (2015). Asymmetry of the brain: Development and implications. *Annual Review of Genetics, 49*, 647–672. doi:10.1146/annurev-genet-112414-055322

Dubois, J., Dehaene-Lambertz, G., Kulikova, S., Poupon, C., Hüppi, P. S., & Hertz-Pannier, L. (2013). The early development of brain white matter: A review of imaging studies in fetuses, newborns and infants. *Neuroscience, 276*, 48–71. doi:10.1016/j.neuroscience.2013.12.044

Duncan, G. J., Ludwig, J., & Magnuson, K. A. (2007). Reducing poverty through preschool interventions. *The Future of Children, 17*, 143–160.

Duncan, G. J., & Magnuson, K. (2013). Investing in preschool programs. *The Journal of Economic Perspectives, 27*, 109–132. doi:10.1257/jep.27.2.109

Education Commission of the States. (2014). *Child must attend kindergarten.* Retrieved from http://ecs.force.com/mbdata/mbquestRT?rep=Kq1403

Eisbach, A. O. (2004). Children's developing awareness of diversity in people's trains of thoughts. *Child Development, 75*, 1694–1707.

Eisenberg, S. L., Guo, L. Y., & Germezia, M. (2012). How grammatical are 3-year-olds? *Language, Speech, and Hearing Services in Schools, 43*, 36–52. doi:10.1044/0161-1461(2011/10-0093)

Fildes, A., Llewellyn, C., Van Jaarsveld, C. H. M., Fisher, A., Cooke, L., & Wardle, J. (2014). Common genetic architecture underlying food fussiness in children, and preference for fruits and vegetables. *Appetite, 76*, 200. doi:10.1016/j.appet.2014.01.023

Fischer, U., Suggate, S. P., Schmirl, J., & Stoeger, H. (2018). Counting on fine motor skills: Links between preschool finger dexterity and numerical skills. *Developmental Science, 21*, e12623. doi:10.1111/desc.12623

Fivush, R. (2011). The development of autobiographical memory. *Annual Review of Psychology, 62*, 559–582. doi:10.1146/annurev.psych.121208.131702

Fivush, R., Hudson, J., & Nelson, K. (1983). Children's long-term memory for a novel event: An exploratory study. *Merrill-Palmer Quarterly, 30*, 303–316.

Flavell, J. H. (1993). The development of children's understanding of false belief and the appearance-reality distinction. *International Journal of Psychology, 28*, 595–604.

Flavell, J. H. (1999). Cognitive development: Children's knowledge about the mind. *Annual Review of Psychology, 50*, 21–45.

Flavell, J. H., Everett, B. H., Croft, K., & Flavell, E. R. (1981). Young children's knowledge about visual perception: Further evidence for the level 1–level 2 distinction. *Developmental Psychology, 17*, 99–103.

Flavell, J. H., Green, F. L., & Flavell, E. R. (1986). Development of knowledge about the appearance-reality distinction. *Monographs of the Society for Research in Child Development, 51*(1, Serial No. 212).

Flavell, J. H., Green, F. L., & Flavell, E. R. (1995). Young children's knowledge about thinking. *Monographs of the Society for Research in Child Development, 60*(1, Serial No. 243).

Gabbard, C. P. (2012). *Lifelong motor development* (6th ed.). Boston, MA: Pearson.

Gallagher, A. (2008). *Developing thinking with four and five year old pupils: The impact of a cognitive acceleration programme through early science skill development.* Dublin, Ireland: Education Department and School of Chemical Sciences, Dublin City University.

Gibbs, J. C. (1991). Sociomoral developmental delay and cognitive distortion: Implications for the treatment of antisocial youth. In W. M. Kurtines & J. L. Gewirtz (Eds.), *Handbook of moral behavior and development: Vol. 3. Application* (pp. 95–110). Hillsdale, NJ: Lawrence Erlbaum.

Gibbs, J. C. (2003). *Moral development and reality: Beyond the theories of Kohlberg and Hoffman.* Thousand Oaks, CA: Sage.

Gilliard, J. L., & Moore, R. A. (2007). An investigation of how culture shapes curriculum in early care and education programs on a Native American Indian reservation. *Early Childhood Education Journal, 34*, 251–258. doi:10.1007/s10643-006-0136-5

Gilmore, J. H., Knickmeyer, R. C., & Gao, W. (2018). Imaging structural and functional brain development in early childhood. *Nature Reviews Neuroscience, 19*, 123–137. doi:10.1038/nrn.2018.1

Gjersoe, N. L., Hall, E. L., & Hood, B. (2015). Children attribute mental lives to toys when they are emotionally attached to them. *Cognitive Development, 34*, 28–38. doi:10.1016/j.cogdev.2014.12.002

Göncü, A., & Gauvain, M. (2012). Sociocultural approaches to educational psychology: Theory, research, and application. In J. Harris, K. R. Graham, S. Urdan, T. McCormick, C. B. Sinatra, & G. M. Sweller (Ed.), *APA educational psychology handbook: Vol. 1. Theories, constructs, and critical issues* (pp. 125–154). Washington, DC: American Psychological Association. doi:10.1037/13273-006

Goodman, G. S., & Aman, C. J. (1990). Children's use of anatomically detailed dolls to recount an event. *Child Development, 61*, 1859–1871.

Goodman, G. S., Rudy, L., Bottoms, B. L., & Aman, C. (1990). Children's concerns and memory: Issues of ecological validity in the study of children's eyewitness testimony. In R. Fivush & J. A. Hudson (Eds.), *Knowing and remembering in young children* (pp. 249–284). New York, NY: Cambridge University Press.

Gordon, A. M., & Browne, K. W. (2016). *Beginning essentials in early childhood education.* Belmont, CA: Cengage Learning.

Gormley, W. T., Jr., Phillips, D., Adelstein, S., & Shaw, C. (2010). Head Start's comparative advantage: Myth or reality? *Policy Studies Journal, 38*, 397–418. doi:10.1111/j.1541-0072.2010.00367.x

Grosse Wiesmann, C., Friederici, A. D., Singer, T., & Steinbeis, N. (2017). Implicit and explicit false belief development in preschool children. *Developmental Science, 20*, e12445. doi:10.1111/desc.12445

Grusec, J. E. (1992). Social learning theory and developmental psychology: The legacies of Robert Sears and Albert Bandura. *Developmental Psychology, 28*, 776–786.

Grusec, J. E., & Goodnow, J. J. (1994). Impact of parental discipline methods on the child's internalization of values: A reconceptualization of current points of view. *Developmental Psychology, 30*, 4–19.

Haden, C. A., & Fivush, F. (1996). Contextual variation in maternal conversational styles. *Merrill-Palmer Quarterly, 42*, 200–227.

Hafstad, G. S., Abebe, D. S., Torgersen, L., & von Soest, T. (2013). Picky eating in preschool children: The predictive role of the child's temperament and mother's negative affectivity. *Eating Behaviors, 14*, 274–277. doi:10.1016/j.eatbeh.2013.04.001

Hanania, R., & Smith, L. B. (2010). Selective attention and attention switching: Towards a unified developmental approach. *Developmental Science, 13*, 622–635. doi:10.1111/j.1467-7687.2009.00921.x

Hansen, M. B., & Markman, E. M. (2009). Children's use of mutual exclusivity to learn labels for parts of objects. *Developmental Psychology, 45*, 592–596. doi:10.1037/a0014838

Harris, J., Golinkoff, R. M., & Hirsh-Pasek, K. (2011). Lessons from the crib for the classroom: How children really learn vocabulary. In S. B. Neuman & D. K. Dickinson (Eds.), *Handbook of early literacy research* (Vol. 3, pp. 49–65). New York, NY: Guilford.

Helming, K. A., Strickland, B., & Jacob, P. (2014). Making sense of early false-belief understanding. *Trends in Cognitive Sciences, 18*, 167–170. doi:10.1016/j.tics.2014.01.005

Hess, J., & Slavin, J. (2014). Snacking for a cause: Nutritional insufficiencies and excesses of U.S. children, a critical review of food consumption patterns and macronutrient and micronutrient intake of U.S. children. *Nutrients, 6*, 4750–4759. doi:10.3390/nu6114750

Heyes, C. (2014). False belief in infancy: A fresh look. *Developmental Science, 17*, 647–659. doi:10.1111/desc.12148

Holloway, S. D. (1999). Divergent cultural models of child rearing and pedagogy in Japanese preschools. *New Directions for Child and Adolescent Development, 83*, 61–75.

Honomichl, R. D., & Zhe, C. (2011). Relations as rules: The role of attention in the dimensional change card sort task. *Developmental Psychology, 47*, 50–60. doi:10.1037/a0021025

Howard-Jones, P. A. (2014). Neuroscience and education: Myths and messages. *Nature Reviews Neuroscience, 15*, 817–824. doi:10.1038/nrn3817

Hudson, J. A., Fivush, R., & Kuebli, J. (1992). Scripts and episodes: The development of event memory. *Applied Cognitive Psychology, 6*, 483–505.

Hughes, C. H., & Devine, R. T. (2015). A social perspective on theory of mind. In M. E. Lamb (Ed.), *Handbook of child psychology and developmental science* (pp. 1–46). Hoboken, NJ: John Wiley. doi:10.1002/9781118963418.childpsy314

Hughes, C. H., & Ensor, R. (2007). Executive function and theory of mind: Predictive relations from ages 2 to 4. *Developmental Psychology, 43*, 1447–1459. doi:10.1037/0012-I 649.43.6.1447

Huston, A. C. (2008). From research to policy and back. *Child Development, 79*, 1–12. doi:10.1111/j.1467-8624.2007.01107.x

Huttenlocher, J., Vasilyeva, M., Cymerman, E., & Levine, S. (2002). Language input and child syntax. *Cognitive Psychology, 45*, 337.

Hyde. K. L., Lerch, J., Norton, A., Forgeard, M., Winner, E., Evans, A. C., & Schlaug, G. (2009). Musical training shapes structural brain development. *Journal of Neuroscience, 29*, 3019–3025. doi:10.1523/JNEUROSCI.5118-08.2009

Jansen, P. W., de Barse, L. M., Jaddoe, V. W. V., Verhulst, F. C., Franco, O. H., & Tiemeier, H. (2017). Bi-directional associations between child fussy eating and parents' pressure to eat: Who influences whom? *Physiology & Behavior, 176*, 101–106. doi:10.1016/j.physbeh.2017.02.015

Janssens, J. M. A. M., & Dekovic, M. (1997). Child rearing, prosocial moral reasoning, and prosocial behaviour. *International Journal of Behavioral Development, 20*, 509–527.

Jaswal, V. K. (2010). Believing what you're told: Young children's trust in unexpected testimony about the physical world. *Cognitive Psychology, 61*, 248–272. doi:10.1016/j.cogpsych.2010.06.002

Jernigan, T. L., & Stiles, J. (2017). Construction of the human forebrain. *Wiley Interdisciplinary Reviews: Cognitive Science, 8*, e1409. doi:10.1002/wcs.1409

Jipson, J. L., Gülgöz, S., & Gelman, S. A. (2016). Parent–child conversations regarding the ontological status of a robotic dog. *Cognitive Development, 39*, 21–35. doi:10.1016/j.cogdev.2016.03.001

Joo, M. (2010). Long-term effects of Head Start on academic and school outcomes of children in persistent poverty: Girls vs. boys. *Children & Youth Services Review, 32*, 807–814. doi:10.1016/j.childyouth.2010.01.018

Kenward, B., & Dahl, M. (2011). Preschoolers distribute scarce resources according to the moral valence of recipients' previous actions. *Developmental Psychology, 47*, 1054–1064. doi:10.1037/a0023869.10.1037/a0023869.supp

Killen, M., McGlothlin, H., & Lee-Kim, J. (2002). Between individuals and culture: Individuals' evaluations of exclusion from social groups. In H. Keller, Y. Poortinga, & A. Schoelmerich (Eds.), *Between biology and culture: Perspectives on Ontogenetic Development B2—Between Biology and Culture: Perspectives on Ontogenetic Development* (pp. 159–190). Cambridge, England: Cambridge University Press.

Killen, M., & Nucci, L. P. (1995). Morality, autonomy, and social conflict. In M. Killen & D. Hart (Eds.), *Morality in everyday life: Developmental perspectives* (pp. 52–86). Cambridge, England: Cambridge University Press.

Király, I., Takács, S., Kaldy, Z., & Blaser, E. (2017). Preschoolers have better long-term memory for rhyming text than adults. *Developmental Science, 20*, e12398. doi:10.1111/desc.12398

Kliegman, R., Stanton, B., St. Geme, J. W., Schor, N. F., Behrman, R. E., & Nelson, W. E. (2016). *Nelson textbook of pediatrics.* Philadelphia, PA: Elsevier.

Kochanska, G., Casey, R. J., & Fukumoto, A. (1995). Toddlers' sensitivity to standard violations. *Child Development, 66*, 643–656.

Kohlberg, L. (1969). Stage and sequence: The cognitive-developmental approach to socialization. In D. A. Goslin (Ed.), *Handbook of socialization* (pp. 347–480). Chicago, IL: Rand McNally.

Kohlberg, L. (1976). Moral stages and moralization: The cognitive developmental approach. In T. Lickona (Ed.), *Moral development and moral behavior: Theory, research, and social issues* (pp. 31–53). New York, NY: Holt, Rinehart & Winston.

Kostelnik, M. J., Soderman, A. K., Whiren, A. P., & Rupiper, M. Q. (2015). *Developmentally appropriate curriculum: Best practices in early childhood education.* Boston, MA: Pearson.

Kucker, S. C., McMurray, B., & Samuelson, L. K. (2015). Slowing down fast mapping: Redefining the dynamics of word learning. *Child Development Perspectives, 9*, 74–78. doi:10.1111/cdep.12110

La Rooy, D., Lamb, M. E., & Pipe, M. (2011). Repeated interviewing: A critical evaluation of the risks and potential benefits. In K. Kuehnle & M. Connell (Eds.), *The evaluation of child sexual abuse allegations:*

A comprehensive guide to assessment and testimony (pp. 327–361). Chichester, England: Wiley-Blackwell.

Lam, J. (2015). Picky eating in children. *Frontiers in Pediatrics, 3,* 41. doi:10.3389/fped.2015.00041

Lecce, S., Demicheli, P., Zocchi, S., & Palladino, P. (2015). The origins of children's metamemory: The role of theory of mind. *Journal of Experimental Child Psychology, 131,* 56–72. doi:10.1016/j.jecp.2014.11.005

Leow, C., & Wen, X. (2017). Is full day better than half day? A propensity score analysis of the association between Head Start program intensity and children's school performance in kindergarten. *Early Education and Development, 28,* 224–239. doi:10.1080/1040 9289.2016.1208600

Lerkkanen, M. K., Kiuru, N., Pakarinen, E., Poikkeus, A. M., Rasku-Puttonen, H., Siekkinen, M., & Nurmi, J. E. (2016). Child-centered versus teacher-directed teaching practices: Associations with the development of academic skills in the first grade at school. *Early Childhood Research Quarterly, 36,* 145–156. doi:10.1016/j. ecresq.2015.12.023

Lewis, M., Stanger, C., & Sullivan, M. W. (1989). Deception in 3-year-olds. *Developmental Psychology, 25,* 439–443. http://dx.doi. org/10.1037/0012-1649.25

Liu, D., Wellman, H. M., Tardif, T., & Sabbagh, M. A. (2008). Theory of mind development in Chinese children: A meta-analysis of false-belief understanding across cultures and languages. *Developmental Psychology, 44,* 523–531. doi:10.1037/0012-1649.44.2.523

Lockl, K., & Schneider, W. (2007). Knowledge about the mind: Links between theory of mind and later metamemory. *Child Development, 78,* 148–167. doi:10.1111/j.1467-8624.2007.00990.x

Lohmann, H., & Tomasello, M. (2003). The role of language in the development of false belief understanding: A training study. *Child Development, 74,* 1130–1144. doi:10.1111/1467-8624.00597

Ma, L., & Ganea, P. A. (2010). Dealing with conflicting information: Young children's reliance on what they see versus what they are told. *Developmental Science, 13,* 151–160. doi:10.1111/j.1467-7687.2009.00878.x

MacConnell, A., & Daehler, M. W. (2004). The development of representational insight: Beyond the model/room paradigm. *Cognitive Development, 19,* 345–362.

MacWhinney, B.. (2015). Language development. In L. S. Liben & U. Muller (Eds.), *Handbook of child psychology and developmental science* (pp. 1–43). Hoboken, NJ: John Wiley. doi:10.1002/9781118963418.childpsy208

Manfra, L., & Winsler, A. (2006). Preschool children's awareness of private speech. *International Journal of Behavioral Development, 30,* 537–549.

Marcon, R. A. (1999). Positive relationships between parent-school involvement and public school inner-city preschoolers' development and academic performance. *School Psychology Review, 28,* 395–412.

Marcus, G. (2000). Children's overregularization and its implications for cognition. In P. Broeder & J. Murre (Eds.), *Models of language acquisition* (pp. 154–176). Oxford, UK: Oxford University Press. Retrieved

from https://nyuscholars.nyu.edu/en/publications/childrens-overregularization-and-its-implications-for-cognition

Markman, E. M., & Wachtel, G. F. (1988). Children's use of mutual exclusivity to constrain the meaning of words. *Cognitive Psychology, 20,* 121–157. doi:10.1016/0010-0285(88)90017-5

Markman, E. M., Wasow, J. L., & Hansen, M. B. (2003). Use of the mutual exclusivity assumption by young word learners. *Cognitive Psychology, 47,* 241–275. doi:10.1016/S0010-0285(03)00034-3

Markowitz, A. J., Bassok, D., & Hamre, B. (2018). Leveraging developmental insights to improve early childhood education. *Child Development Perspectives, 12,* 87–92. doi:10.1111/cdep.12266

Mayer, A., & Träuble, B. (2015). The weird world of cross-cultural false-belief research: A true- and false-belief study among Samoan children based on commands. *Journal of Cognition and Development, 16,* 650–665. doi:10.1080/15248372.2014.926273

McAlister, A. R., & Peterson, C. C. (2013). Siblings, theory of mind, and executive functioning in children aged 3–6 years: New longitudinal evidence. *Child Development, 84,* 1442–1458. doi:10.1111/cdev.12043

McGonigle-Chalmers, M., Slater, H., & Smith, A. (2014). Rethinking private speech in preschoolers: The effects of social presence. *Developmental Psychology, 50,* 829–836. doi:10.1037/a0033909

Mermelshtine, R. (2017). Parent–child learning interactions: A review of the literature on scaffolding. *British Journal of Educational Psychology, 87,* 241–254. doi:10.1111/bjep.12147

Milligan, K., Astington, J. W., & Dack, L. A. (2007). Language and theory of mind: Meta-analysis of the relation between language ability and false-belief understanding. *Child Development, 78,* 622–646.

Miyake, A., & Friedman, N. P. (2012). The nature and organization of individual differences in executive functions. *Current Directions in Psychological Science, 21,* 8–14. doi:10.1177/0963721411429458

Mori, A., & Cigala, A. (2016). Perspective taking: Training procedures in developmentally typical preschoolers. Different intervention methods and their effectiveness. *Educational Psychology Review, 28,* 267–294. doi:10.1007/s10648-015-9306-6

Moriguchi, Y. (2014). The early development of executive function and its relation to social interaction: A brief review. *Frontiers in Psychology, 5,* 388. doi:10.3389/fpsyg.2014.00388

Moriguchi, Y., Kanda, T., Ishiguro, H., Shimada, Y., & Itakura, S. (2011). Can young children learn words from a robot? *Interaction Studies: Social Behaviour and Communication in Biological and Artificial Systems, 12,* 107–118.

Moses, L. J., Coon, J. A., & Wusinich, N. (2000). Young children's understanding of desire information. *Developmental Psychology, 36,* 77–90.

Muennig, P., Robertson, D., Johnson, G., Campbell, F., Pungello, E. P., & Neidell, M. (2011). The effect of an early education program on adult health: The Carolina Abecedarian Project randomized

controlled trial. *American Journal of Public Health, 101,* 512–516. doi:10.2105/AJPH.2010.200063

Murachver, T., Pipe, M., Gordon, R., Owens, J. L., & Fivush, R. (1996). Do, show, and tell: Children's event memories acquired through direct experience, observation, and stories. *Child Development, 67,* 3029–3044.

Mussen, P., & Eisenberg-Berg, N. (1977). *Roots of caring, sharing, and helping.* San Francisco, CA: Freeman.

Myers, N. A., & Perlmutter, M. (2014). Memory in the years from two to five. In P. A. Ornstein (Ed.), *Memory development in children* (pp. 191–218). New York, NY: Psychology Press.

Nagayama, M., & Gilliard, J. L. (2005). An investigation of Japanese and American early care and education. *Early Childhood Education Journal, 33,* 137–143.

Natale, V., & Rajagopalan, A. (2014). Worldwide variation in human growth and the World Health Organization growth standards: A systematic review. *BMJ Open, 4,* e003735. doi:10.1136/bmjopen-2013-003735

Nederkoorn, C., Jansen, A., & Havermans, R. C. (2015). Feel your food. The influence of tactile sensitivity on picky eating in children. *Appetite, 84,* 7–10. doi:10.1016/J.APPET.2014.09.014

Newcombe, N., & Huttenlocher, J. (1992). Children's early ability to solve perspective-taking problems. *Developmental Psychology, 28,* 635–643.

Nieto, M., Ros, L., Ricarte, J. J., & Latorre, J. M. (2018). The role of executive functions in accessing specific autobiographical memories in 3- to 6-year-olds. *Early Childhood Research Quarterly, 43,* 23–32. doi:10.1016/j.ecresq.2017.11.004

Nobes, G., & Pawson, C. (2003). Children's understanding of social rules and social status. *Merrill-Palmer Quarterly, 49,* 77–99.

Nuttall, A. K., Valentino, K., Comas, M., McNeill, A. T., & Stey, P. C. (2014). Autobiographical memory specificity among preschool-aged children. *Developmental Psychology, 50,* 1963–1972.

Otgaar, H., Howe, M. L., Merckelbach, H., & Muris, P. (2018). Who is the better eyewitness? Adults and children—city research online. *Current Directions in Psychological Science.* Retrieved from http://openaccess.city. ac.uk/19272/

Owens, R. E. (2015). *Language development: An introduction.* Boston, MA: Pearson.

Pantell, R. H., & Committee on Psychosocial Aspects of Child and Family Health. (2017). The child witness in the courtroom. *Pediatrics, 139,* e20164008. doi:10.1542/peds.2016-4008

Park, C. J., Yelland, G. W., Taffe, J. R., & Gray, K. M. (2012). Brief report: The relationship between language skills, adaptive behavior, and emotional and behavior problems in pre-schoolers with autism. *Journal of Autism and Developmental Disorders, 42,* 2761–2766.

Pavarini, G., Hollanda Souza, D., & Hawk, C. K. (2012). Parental practices and theory of mind development. *Journal of Child and Family Studies, 22,* 844–853. doi:10.1007/s10826-012-9643-8

Payne, V. G., Isaacs, L. D., & Larry, D. (2016). *Human motor development: A lifespan approach.* New York, NY: McGraw-Hill.

Phillips, D., Gormley, W., & Anderson, S. (2016). The effects of Tulsa's CAP Head Start program on middle-school academic outcomes and progress. *Developmental Psychology, 52,* 1247–1261. doi:10.1037/dev0000151

Piaget, J. (1932). *The moral judgment of the child.* New York, NY: Harcourt Brace.

Piaget, J., & Inhelder, B. (1967). *The child's conception of space.* New York, NY: Norton.

Pillow, B. H. (2008). Development of children's understanding of cognitive activities. *Journal of Genetic Psychology, 169,* 297–321.

Polak, A., & Harris, P. L. (1999). Deception by young children following noncompliance. *Developmental Psychology, 35,* 561–568.

Poole, D. A., & White, L. T. (1991). Effects of question repetition on the eyewitness testimony of children and adults. *Developmental Psychology, 27,* 975–986.

Poole, D. A., & White, L. T. (1993). Two years later: Effects of question repetition and retention interval on the eyewitness testimony of children and adults. *Developmental Psychology, 29,* 844–853.

Qiu, A., Mori, S., & Miller, M. I. (2015). Diffusion tensor imaging for understanding brain development in early life. *Annual Review of Psychology, 66,* 853–876. doi:10.1146/annurev-psych-010814-015340

Rakoczy, H., Warneken, F., & Tomasello, M. (2007). "This way!" "No! That way!": 3-year olds know that two people can have mutually incompatible desires. *Cognitive Development, 22,* 47–68.

Ristic, J., & Enns, J. T. (2015). Attentional development. In L. S. Liben & U. Muller (Eds.), *Handbook of child psychology and developmental science* (pp. 1–45). Hoboken, NJ: John Wiley.

Robbins, J. (2005). Contexts, collaboration, and cultural tools: A sociocultural perspective on researching children's thinking. *Contemporary Issues in Early Childhood, 6,* 140. doi:10.2304/ciec.2005.6.2.4

Robinson, J. B., Burns, B. M., & Davis, D. W. (2009). Maternal scaffolding and attention regulation in children living in poverty. *Journal of Applied Developmental Psychology, 30,* 82–91. doi:10.1016/j.appdev.2008.10.013

Roediger, H. L., & Marsh, E. J. (2003). Episodic and autobiographical memory. In I. B. Weiner (Ed.), *Handbook of psychology: Part Six. Complex learning and memory processes.* Hoboken, NJ: John Wiley.

Rogoff, B. (2014). Learning by observing and pitching in to family and community endeavors: An orientation. *Human Development, 57,* 69–81. doi:10.1159/000356757

Rogoff, B. (2015). Human teaching and learning involve cultural communities, not just individuals. *Behavioral and Brain Sciences, 38,* e60. doi:10.1017/S0140525X14000818

Rogoff, B., Callanan, M., Gutiérrez, K. D., & Erickson, F. (2016). The organization of informal learning. *Review of Research in Education, 40,* 356–401. doi:10.3102/0091732X16680994

Roseberry, S., Hirsh-Pasek, K., & Golinkoff, R. M. (2014). Skype me! Socially contingent interactions help toddlers learn language. *Child Development, 85,* 956–970. doi:10.1111/cdev.12166

Rosenkoetter, L. I. (1973). Resistance to temptation: Inhibitory and disinhibitory effects of models. *Developmental Psychology, 8,* 80–84.

Rueda, M. R. (2013). Development of attention. In K. Ochsner & S. M. Kosslyn (Eds.), *The Oxford handbook of cognitive neuroscience: Vol. 1. Core topics* (p. 656). Oxford, UK: Oxford University Press.

Ryalls, B. O. (2000). Dimensional adjectives: Factors affecting children's ability to compare objects using novel words. *Journal of Experimental Child Psychology, 76,* 26–49.

Saarni, C. (1984). An observational study of children's attempt to monitor their expressive behavior. *Child Development, 55,* 1504–1513. doi: 10.2307/1130020

Sabbagh, M. A., Xu, F., Carlson, S. M., Moses, L. J., & Lee, K. (2006). The development of executive functioning and theory of mind. *Psychological Science, 17,* 74–81.

Sapp, F., Lee, K., & Muir, D. (2000). Three-year-olds' difficulty with the appearance-reality distinction: Is it real or is it apparent? *Developmental Psychology, 36,* 547–560.

Schnur, E., & Belanger, S. (2000). What works in Head Start. In M. P. Kluger, G. Alexander, & P. A. Curtis (Eds.), *What works in child welfare* (pp. 277–284). Washington, DC: Child Welfare League of America.

Schwebel, D. C., Rosen, C. S., & Singer, J. L. (1999). Preschoolers' pretend play and theory of mind: The role of jointly constructed pretence. *British Journal of Developmental Psychology, 17,* 333–348. doi:10.1348/026151099165320

Schweinhart, L. J., Montie, J., Iang, Z., Barnett, W. S., Belfield, C. R., & Nores, M. (2005). *Lifetime effects: The High/Scope Perry Preschool Study through age 40.* Ypsilanti, MI: High/Scope Press.

Scott, R. M., & Baillargeon, R. (2017). Early false-belief understanding. *Trends in Cognitive Sciences, 21,* 237–249. doi:10.1016/J.TICS.2017.01.012

Shahaeian, A., Peterson, C. C., Slaughter, V., & Wellman, H. M. (2011). Culture and the sequence of steps in theory of mind development. *Developmental Psychology, 47,* 1239–1247. doi:10.1037/a0023899

Sills, J., Rowse, G., & Emerson, L.-M. (2016). The role of collaboration in the cognitive development of young children: A systematic review. *Child: Care, Health and Development, 42,* 313–324. doi:10.1111/cch.12330

Silva, M., Strasser, K., & Cain, K. (2014). Early narrative skills in Chilean preschool: Questions scaffold the production of coherent narratives. *Early Childhood Research Quarterly, 29,* 205–213. doi:10.1016/j.ecresq.2014.02.002

Skitka, L. J., Bauman, C. W., & Mullen, E. (2016). Morality and justice. In C. Sabbagh & M. Schmitt (Eds.), *Handbook of social justice theory and research* (pp. 407–423). New York, NY: Springer. doi:10.1007/978-1-4939-3216-0_22

Slaughter, V., & Perez-Zapata, D. (2014). Cultural variations in the development of mind reading. *Child Development Perspectives, 8,* 237–241. doi:10.1111/cdep.12091

Slaughter, V., Peterson, C. C., & Mackintosh, E. (2007). Mind what mother says: Narrative input and theory of mind in typical children and those on the autism spectrum. *Child Development, 78,* 839–858. doi:10.1111/j.1467-8624.2007.01036.x

Smetana, J. G. (1995). Morality in context: Abstractions, ambiguities, and applications. In R. Vasta (Ed.), *Annals of child development* (Vol. 10, pp. 83–130). London, England: Jessica Kingsley.

Smetana, J. G., & Braeges, J. L. (1990). The development of toddler's moral and conventional judgments. *Merrill-Palmer Quarterly, 36,* 329–346.

Sousa, D. A. (2001). *How the brain learns: A classroom teacher's guide.* Thousand Oaks, CA: Corwin Press.

Stagi, S., Scalini, P., Farello, G., & Verrotti, A. (2017). Possible effects of an early diagnosis and treatment in patients with growth hormone deficiency: The state of art. *Italian Journal of Pediatrics, 43,* 81. doi:10.1186/s13052-017-0402-8

Steinsbekk, S., Bonneville-Roussy, A., Fildes, A., Llewellyn, C. H., & Wichstrøm, L. (2017). Child and parent predictors of picky eating from preschool to school age. *International Journal of Behavioral Nutrition and Physical Activity, 14,* 87. doi:10.1186/s12966-017-0542-7

Stiles, J. (2017). Principles of brain development. *Wiley Interdisciplinary Reviews: Cognitive Science, 8,* e1402. doi:10.1002/wcs.1402

Stipek, D., Feiler, R., Daniels, D., & Milburn, S. (1995). Effects of different instructional approaches on young children's achievement and motivation. *Child Development, 66,* 209–223.

Stone, M. M., Blumberg, F. C., Blair, C., & Cancelli, A. A. (2016). The "EF" in deficiency: Examining the linkages between executive function and the utilization deficiency observed in preschoolers. *Journal of Experimental Child Psychology, 152,* 367–375. doi:10.1016/j.jecp.2016.07.003

Stulp, G., & Barrett, L. (2016). Evolutionary perspectives on human height variation. *Biological Reviews, 91,* 206–234. doi:10.1111/brv.12165

Taumoepeau, M. (2015). From talk to thought. *Journal of Cross-Cultural Psychology, 46,* 1169–1190. doi:10.1177/0022022115604393

Taylor, C. M., Wernimont, S. M., Northstone, K., & Emmett, P. M. (2015). Picky/fussy eating in children: Review of definitions, assessment, prevalence and dietary intakes. *Appetite, 95,* 349–359. doi:10.1016/J.APPET.2015.07.026

Taylor, K. (2017, April 24). New York City will offer free preschool for all 3-year-olds. *New York Times.* Retrieved from https://www.nytimes.com/2017/04/24/nyregion/de-blasio-pre-k-expansion.html?_r=0

Titz, C., & Karbach, J. (2014). Working memory and executive functions: Effects of training on academic achievement. *Psychological Research, 78,* 852–868. doi:10.1007/s00426-013-0537-1

Trawick-Smith, J., & Dziurgot, T. (2011). "Good-fit" teacher–child play interactions and the subsequent autonomous play of preschool children. *Early Childhood Research Quarterly, 26,* 110–123. doi:10.1016/j.ecresq.2010.04.005

Tulving, E. (2002). Episodic memory: From mind to brain. *Annual Review of Psychology, 53,* 1–25.

Turiel, E. (1998). The development of morality. In N. Eisenberg (Ed.), *Handbook of child psychology: Vol. 3. Social, emotional, and personality development* (5th ed., pp. 863–932). New York, NY: John Wiley.

Turiel, E., & Nucci, L. (2017). Moral development in context. In A. Dick & U. Muller (Eds.), *Advancing developmental science: Philosophy, theory, and method* (pp. 107–121). New York: Routledge.

Turnbull, K., & Justice, L. M. (2016). *Language development from theory to practice.* New York: Pearson.

Uhl, E. R., Camilletti, C. R., Scullin, M. H., & Wood, J. M. (2016). Under pressure: Individual differences in children's suggestibility in response to intense social influence. *Social Development, 25,* 422–434. doi:10.1111/sode.12156

U.S. Department of Health and Human Services & Administration for Children and Families. (2010). *Head Start impact study: Final report.* Washington, DC: U.S. Department of Health and Human Services.

Vandermaas-Peeler, M., Massey, K., & Kendall, A. (2016). Parent guidance of young children's scientific and mathematical reasoning in a science museum. *Early Childhood Education Journal, 44,* 217–224. doi:10.1007/s10643-015-0714-5

Veer, I. M., Luyten, H., Mulder, H., van Tuijl, C., & Sleegers, P. J. C. (2017). Selective attention relates to the development of executive functions in 2.5- to 3-year-olds: A longitudinal study. *Early Childhood Research Quarterly, 41,* 84–94. doi:10.1016/J.ECRESQ.2017.06.005

Vinden, P. (1996). Junin Quechua children's understanding of mind. *Child Development, 67,* 1707–1716.

Vygotsky, L. S. (1978). *Mind in society: The development of higher psychological processes.* Cambridge, MA: Harvard University Press.

Vygotsky, L. S., & Minick, N. (1987). *Thinking and speech.* (T. N. Minick, Ed.). New York, NY: Plenum.

Walker, L. J., & Taylor, J. H. (1991). Family interactions and the development of moral reasoning. *Child Development, 62,* 264–283.

Walton, K., Kuczynski, L., Haycraft, E., Breen, A., & Haines, J. (2017). Time to re-think picky eating? A relational approach to understanding picky eating. *International Journal of Behavioral Nutrition and Physical Activity, 14,* 62. doi:10.1186/s12966-017-0520-0

Walton, M., Dewey, D., & Lebel, C. (2018). Brain white matter structure and language ability in preschool-aged children. *Brain and Language, 176,* 19–25. doi:10.1016/J.BANDL.2017.10.008

Wang, X., Bernas, R., & Eberhard, P. (2008). Responding to children's everyday transgressions in Chinese working-class families. *Journal of Moral Education, 37,* 55–79. doi:10.1080/03057240701803684

Wass, R., & Golding, C. (2014). Sharpening a tool for teaching: The zone of proximal development. *Teaching in Higher Education, 19,* 671–684. doi:10.1080/13562517.2014.901958

Wellman, H. M. (2017). The development of theory of mind: Historical reflections. *Child Development Perspectives, 11,* 207–214. doi:10.1111/cdep.12236

Wellman, H. M., & Banerjee, M. (1991). Mind and emotion: Children's understanding of the emotional consequences of beliefs and desires. *British Journal of Developmental Psychology, 9,* 191–214.

Wellman, H. M., Cross, D., & Watson, J. (2001). Meta-analysis of theory-of-mind development: The truth about false belief. *Child Development, 72,* 655. doi:10.1111/1467-8624.00304

Wellman, H. M., Fang, F., & Peterson, C. C. (2011). Sequential progressions in a theory-of-mind scale: Longitudinal perspectives. *Child Development, 82,* 780–792. doi:10.1111/j.1467-8624.2011.01583.x

Wellman, H. M., Somerville, S. C., & Haake, R. J. (1979). Development of search procedures in real-life spatial environments. *Developmental Psychology, 15,* 530–542.

Welshman, J. (2010). From Head Start to sure start: Reflections on policy transfer. *Children & Society, 24,* 89–99. doi:10.1111/j.1099-0860.2008.00201.x

Wertsch, J. V. (1998). *Mind as action.* New York, NY: Oxford University Press.

Williams, E. (2015). *Pre-kindergarten across states.* Retrieved from http://www.edcentral.org/prekstatefunding/

Willis, J. (2007). Which brain research can educators trust? *Phi Delta Kappan, 88,* 697–699.

Winsler, A., Fernyhough, C., & Montero, I. (2009). *Private speech, executive functioning, and the development of verbal self-regulation.* Cambridge, England: Cambridge University Press.

Woolley, J. D., & E Ghossainy, M. (2013). Revisiting the fantasy-reality distinction: Children as naïve skeptics. *Child Development, 84,* 1496–1510. doi:10.1111/cdev.12081

Wysman, L., Scoboria, A., Gawrylowicz, J., & Memon, A. (2014). The cognitive interview buffers the effects of subsequent repeated questioning in the absence of negative feedback. *Behavioral Sciences & the Law, 32,* 207–219. doi:10.1002/bsl.2115

Yamagata, K. (2007). Differential emergence of representational systems: Drawings, letters, and numerals. *Cognitive Development, 22,* 244–257.

Yarrow, M. R., Scott, P. M., & Waxler, C. Z. (1973). Learning concern for others. *Developmental Psychology, 8,* 240–260.

Yau, J., & Smetana, J. G. (2003). Conceptions of moral, social-conventional, and personal events among Chinese preschoolers in Hong Kong. *Child Development, 74,* 647–658.

Yuill, N., & Perner, J. (1988). Intentionality and knowledge in children's judgments of actor's responsibility and recipient's emotional reaction. *Developmental Psychology, 24,* 358–365.

Zaitchik, D., Iqbal, Y., & Carey, S. (2014). The effect of executive function on biological reasoning in young children: An individual differences study. *Child Development, 85,* 160–175. doi:10.1111/cdev.12145

Zhai, F., Brooks-Gunn, J., & Waldfogel, J. (2011). Head Start and urban children's school readiness: A birth cohort study in 18 cities. *Developmental Psychology, 47,* 134–152. doi:10.1037/a0020784

Zigler, E., & Styfco, S. J. (2004). Moving Head Start to the states: One experiment too many. *Applied Developmental Science, 8,* 51–55.

Zosh, J. M., Brinster, M., & Halberda, J. (2013). Optimal contrast: Competition between two referents improves word learning. *Applied Developmental Science, 17,* 20–28. doi:10.1080/10888691.2013.748420

Zuckerman, G. (2007). Child-adult interaction that creates a zone of proximal development. *Journal of Russian & East European Psychology, 45,* 43–69. doi:10.2753/RPO1061-0405450302

Chapter 8

AAP Committee on Psychosocial Aspects of Child and Family Health. (1998). Guidance for effective discipline. *Pediatrics, 101,* 723–728.

Arthur, A. E., Bigler, R. S., & Ruble, D. N. (2009). An experimental test of the effects of gender constancy on sex typing. *Journal of Experimental Child Psychology, 104,* 427–446. doi:10.1016/j.jecp.2009.08.002

Baker, E. R., Tisak, M. S., & Tisak, J. (2016). What can boys and girls do? Preschoolers' perspectives regarding gender roles across domains of behavior. *Social Psychology of Education, 19,* 23–39. doi:10.1007/s11218-015-9320-z

Balan, R., Dobrean, A., Roman, G. D., & Balazsi, R. (2017). Indirect effects of parenting practices on internalizing problems among adolescents: The role of expressive suppression. *Journal of Child and Family Studies, 26,* 40–47. doi:10.1007/s10826-016-0532-4

Ball, C. L., Smetana, J. G., & Sturge-Apple, M. L. (2017). Following my head and my heart: Integrating preschoolers' empathy, theory of mind, and moral judgments. *Child Development, 88,* 597–611. doi:10.1111/cdev.12605

Bandura, A., & Bussey, K. (2004). On broadening the cognitive, motivational, and sociostructural scope of theorizing about gender development and functioning: Comment on Martin, Ruble, and Szkrybalo (2002). *Psychological Bulletin, 130,* 691–701.

Barth, R. P., Scarborough, A., Lloyd, E. C., Losby, J., Casanueva, C., & Mann, T. (2007). *Developmental status and early intervention service needs of maltreated children.* Washington, DC: U.S. Department of Health and Human Services, Office of the Assistant Secretary for Planning and Evaluation.

Basow, S. (2008). Gender socialization, or how long a way has baby come? In J. C. Chrisler, C. Golden, & P. D. Rozee (Eds.), *Lectures on the psychology of women* (4th ed., pp. 81–95). New York, NY: McGraw-Hill.

Baumrind, D. (1971). Current patterns of parental authority. *Developmental Psychology, 4*(Monograph 1), 1–103.

Baumrind, D. (2012). Differentiating between confrontive and coercive kinds of parental power-assertive disciplinary practices. *Human Development, 55*, 35–51. doi:10.1159/000337962

Baumrind, D. (2013). Authoritative parenting revisited: History and current status. In R. E. Larzelere, A. S. Morris, & A. W. Harrist (Eds.), *Authoritative parenting: Synthesizing nurturance and discipline for optimal child development* (pp. 11–34). Washington, DC: APA.

Baumrind, D., Larzelere, R. E., & Owens, E. B. (2010). Effects of preschool parents' power assertive patterns and practices on adolescent development. *Parenting: Science & Practice, 10*, 157–201. doi:10.1080/15295190903290790

Beal, C. R. (1994). *Boys and girls: The development of gender roles.* New York, NY: McGraw-Hill.

Bem, S. L. (1974). The measurement of psychological androgyny. *Journal of Consulting and Clinical Psychology, 42*, 155–162.

Berenbaum, S. A. (2018). Beyond pink and blue: The complexity of early androgen effects on gender development. *Child Development Perspectives, 12*, 58–64. doi:10.1111/cdep.12261

Berger, R. H., Miller, A. L., Seifer, R., Cares, S. R., & Lebourgeois, M. K. (2012). Acute sleep restriction effects on emotion responses in 30- to 36-month-old children. *Journal of Sleep Research, 21*, 235–246. doi:10.1111/j.1365-2869.2011.00962.x

Best, D. L., & Bush, C. D. (2016). Gender roles in childhood and adolescence. In U. P. Gielen & J. L. Roopnarine (Eds.), *Childhood and adolescence: Cross-cultural perspectives and applications* (pp. 209–240). Santa Barbara, CA: Praeger.

Bian, L., Leslie, S. J., & Cimpian, A. (2017). Gender stereotypes about intellectual ability emerge early and influence children's interests. *Science, 355*, 389–391. doi:10.1126/science.aah6524

Black, K., Marola, J., Littman, A., Chrisler, J., & Neace, W. (2009). Gender and form of cereal box characters: Different medium, same disparity. *Sex Roles, 60*, 882–889. doi:10.1007/s11199-008-9579-z

Blakemore, J. E. O., Berenbaum, S. A., & Liben, L. S. (2009). *Gender development.* New York, NY: Psychology Press.

Boseovski, J. J. (2010). Evidence for "rose colored glasses": An examination of the positivity bias in young children's personality judgments. *Child Development Perspectives, 4*, 212–218. doi:10.1111/j.1750-8606.2010.00149.x

Bouldin, P. (2006). An investigation of the fantasy predisposition and fantasy style of children with imaginary companions. *Journal of Genetic Psychology, 167*, 17–29.

Brownell, C. A. (2016). Prosocial behavior in infancy: The role of socialization. *Child Development Perspectives, 10*, 222–227. doi:10.1111/cdep.12189

Burgdorf, J., Kroes, R. A., & Moskal, J. R. (2017). Rough-and-tumble play induces resilience to stress in rats. *NeuroReport, 28*, 1122–1126. doi:10.1097/WNR.0000000000000864

Bussey, K. (2013). Gender development. In M. K. Ryan & N. R. Branscombe (Eds.), *The Sage handbook of gender and psychology* (pp. 81–100). Thousand Oaks, CA: Sage.

Camras, L. A., & Halberstadt, A. G. (2017). Emotional development through the lens of affective social competence. *Current Opinion in Psychology, 17*, 113–117. doi:10.1016/J.COPSYC.2017.07.003

Canevello, A. (2016). Gender schema theory. In V. Zeigler-Hill & T. K. Shackelford (Eds.), *Encyclopedia of personality and individual differences* (pp. 1–3). Cham, Switzerland: Springer International. doi:10.1007/978-3-319-28099-8_978-1

Carlson, M., Oshri, A., & Kwon, J. (2015). Child maltreatment and risk behaviors: The roles of callous/unemotional traits and conscientiousness. *Child Abuse & Neglect, 50*, 234–243. doi:10.1016/j.chiabu.2015.07.003

Carson, A. S., & Banuazizi, A. (2008). "That's not fair": Similarities and differences in distributive justice reasoning between American and Filipino children. *Journal of Cross-Cultural Psychology, 39*, 493–514.

Carter, C. S. (2014). Oxytocin pathways and the evolution of human behavior. *Annual Review of Psychology, 65*, 17–39. doi:10.1146/annurev-psych-010213-115110

Casanueva, C., Goldman-Fraser, J., Ringeisen, H., Lederman, C., Katz, L., & Osofsky, J. (2010). Maternal perceptions of temperament among infants and toddlers investigated for maltreatment: Implications for services need and referral. *Journal of Family Violence, 25*, 557–574. doi:10.1007/s10896-010-9316-6

Cauce, A. M. (2008). Parenting, culture, and context: Reflections on excavating culture. *Applied Developmental Science, 12*, 227–229. doi:10.1080/10888690802388177

Cecil, C. A. M., Viding, E., Fearon, P., Glaser, D., & McCrory, E. J. (2017). Disentangling the mental health impact of childhood abuse and neglect. *Child Abuse & Neglect, 63*, 106–119. doi:10.1016/j.chiabu.2016.11.024

Chao, R. K. (2001). Extending research on the consequences of parenting style for Chinese Americans and European Americans. *Child Development, 72*, 1832–1843.

Chaplin, T. M., & Aldao, A. (2013). Gender differences in emotion expression in children: A meta-analytic review. *Psychological Bulletin, 139*, 735–765. doi:10.1037/a0030737

Cheah, C. S. L., Leung, C. Y. Y., Tahseen, M., & Schultz, D. (2009). Authoritative parenting among immigrant Chinese mothers of preschoolers. *Journal of Family Psychology, 23*, 311–320. doi:10.1037/a0015076

Child Welfare Information Gateway. (2013). *What is child abuse and neglect? Recognizing the signs and symptoms.* Retrieved from https://www.childwelfare.gov/pubpdfs/whatiscan.pdf

Choe, D. E., Olson, S. L., & Sameroff, A. J. (2013). The interplay of externalizing problems and physical and inductive discipline during childhood. *Developmental Psychology, 49*, 2029–2039. doi:10.1037/a0032054

Cicchetti, D. (2016). Socioemotional, personality, and biological development: Illustrations from a multilevel developmental psychopathology perspective on child maltreatment. *Annual Review of Psychology, 67*, 187–211. doi:10.1146/annurev-psych-122414-033259

Cicchetti, D., & Banny, A. (2014). A developmental psychopathology perspective on child maltreatment. In M. Lewis & K. D. Rudolph (Eds.), *Handbook of developmental psychopathology* (pp. 723–741). Boston, MA: Springer US. doi:10.1007/978-1-4614-9608-3

Cicchetti, D., & Toth, S. L. (2015). Child maltreatment. In M. Lamb (Ed.), *Handbook of child psychology and developmental science* (pp. 1–51). Hoboken, NJ: John Wiley. doi:10.1002/9781118963418.childpsy313

Cimpian, A., Hammond, M. D., Mazza, G., & Corry, G. (2017). Young children's self-concepts include representations of abstract traits and the global self. *Child Development, 88*, 1786–1798. doi:10.1111/cdev.12925

Coley, R. L., Kull, M. A., & Carrano, J. (2014). Parental endorsement of spanking and children's internalizing and externalizing problems in African American and Hispanic families. *Journal of Family Psychology, 28*, 22–31. doi:10.1037/a0035272

Conron, K. J., Scott, G., Stowell, G. S., & Landers, S. J. (2012). Transgender health in Massachusetts: Results from a household probability sample of adults. *American Journal of Public Health, 102*, 118–122. doi:10.2105/AJPH.2011.300315

Coplan, R. J., & Arbeau, K. A. (2009). Peer interactions and play in early childhood. In K. H. Rubin, W. M. Bukowski, & B. Laursen (Eds.), *Handbook of peer interactions, relationships, and groups* (pp. 143–161). New York, NY: Guilford.

Côté, S. M. (2009). A developmental perspective on sex differences in aggressive behaviours. In R. E. Tremblay, M. A. G. van Aken, & W. Koops (Eds.), *Development and prevention of behaviour problems: From genes to social policy* (pp. 143–163). New York, NY: Psychology Press.

Coyne, S. M., Linder, J. R., Rasmussen, E. E., Nelson, D. A., & Birkbeck, V. (2016). Pretty as a princess: Longitudinal effects of engagement with Disney princesses on gender stereotypes, body esteem, and prosocial behavior in children. *Child Development, 87*, 1909–1925. doi:10.1111/cdev.12569

Crespo, L. M., Trentacosta, C. J., Aikins, D., & Wargo-Aikins, J. (2017). Maternal emotion regulation and children's behavior problems: The mediating role of child emotion regulation. *Journal of Child and Family Studies, 26*, 2797–2809. doi:10.1007/s10826-017-0791-8

Cuartas, J. (2018). Neighborhood crime undermines parenting: Violence in the vicinity of households as a predictor of aggressive discipline. *Child Abuse & Neglect, 76*, 388–399. doi:10.1016/J.CHIABU.2017.12.006

Cuellar, J., Jones, D. J., & Sterrett, E. (2013). Examining parenting in the neighborhood context: A review. *Journal of Child and Family Studies, 24*, 195–219. doi:10.1007/s10826-013-9826-y

de Waal, F. B. M. (1993). Sex differences in chimpanzee (and human) behavior: A matter of social values? In M. Hechter, L. Nadel,

& R. E. Michod (Eds.), *The origin of values* (pp. 285–303). New York, NY: Aldine de Gruyter.

Dahl, A. (2015). The developing social context of infant helping in two U.S. samples. *Child Development, 86*, 1080–1093. doi:10.1111/cdev.12361

Damon, W. (1977). *The social world of the child.* San Francisco, CA: Jossey-Bass.

Davis, P. E., Meins, E., & Fernyhough, C. (2014). Children with imaginary companions focus on mental characteristics when describing their real-life friends. *Infant and Child Development, 23*, 622–633. doi:10.1002/icd.1869

Deneault, J., & Ricard, M. (2013). Are emotion and mind understanding differently linked to young children's social adjustment? Relationships between behavioral consequences of emotions, false belief, and SCBE. *Journal of Genetic Psychology, 174*, 88–116. doi:10.1080/00221325.2011.642028

Dennis, T. A., Cole, P. M., Zahn-Waxler, C., & Mizuta, I. (2002). Self in context: Autonomy and relatedness in Japanese and U.S. mother-preschooler dyads. *Child Development, 73*, 1803–1817.

D'Souza, A. J., Russell, M., Wood, B., Signal, L., & Elder, D. (2016). Attitudes to physical punishment of children are changing. *Archives of Disease in Childhood, 101*, 690–693. doi:10.1136/archdischild-2015-310119

Durwood, L., McLaughlin, K. A., & Olson, K. R. (2017). Mental health and self-worth in socially transitioned transgender youth. *Journal of the American Academy of Child and Adolescent Psychiatry, 56*, 116–123.e2. doi:10.1016/j.jaac.2016.10.016

Dyer, S., & Moneta, G. B. (2006). Frequency of parallel, associative, and cooperative play in British children of different socioeconomic status. *Social Behavior & Personality: An International Journal, 34*, 587–592.

Eisenberg, N., Spinrad, T. L., & Knafo-Noam, A. (2015). Prosocial development. In M. Lamb (Ed.), *Handbook of child psychology and developmental science* (pp. 1–47). Hoboken, NJ: John Wiley. doi:10.1002/9781118963418.childpsy315

Eisenberg, N., Spinrad, T. L., & Morris, A. S. (2013). Prosocial development. In P. D. Zelazo (Ed.), *The Oxford handbook of developmental psychology: Vol. 2. Self and other* (Vol. 1, pp. 300–324). Oxford, UK: Oxford University Press. doi:10.1093/oxfordhb/9780199958474.013.0013

Eisner, M. P., & Malti, T. (2015). Aggressive and violent behavior. In M. Lamb (Ed.), *Handbook of child psychology and developmental science* (pp. 1–48). Hoboken, NJ: John Wiley. doi:10.1002/9781118963418.childpsy319

Else-Quest, N. M., Higgins, A., Allison, C., & Morton, L. C. (2012). Gender differences in self-conscious emotional experience: A meta-analysis. *Psychological Bulletin, 138*, 947–981. doi:10.1037/a0027930

Else-Quest, N. M., Hyde, J. S., Goldsmith, H. H., & Van Hulle, C. A. (2006). Gender differences in temperament: A meta-analysis. *Psychological Bulletin, 132*, 33–72. doi:10.1037/0033-2909.132.1.33

Endendijk, J. J., Groeneveld, M. G., van der Pol, L. D., van Berkel, S. R., Hallers-Haalboom, E. T., Bakermans-Kranenburg, M. J., &

Mesman, J. (2017). Gender differences in child aggression: Relations with gender-differentiated parenting and parents' gender-role stereotypes. *Child Development, 88*, 299–316. doi:10.1111/cdev.12589

England, D. E., Descartes, L., & Collier-Meek, M. A. (2011). Gender role portrayal and the Disney princesses. *Sex Roles, 64*, 555–567. doi:10.1007/s11199-011-9930-7

Enright, R. D., Bjerstedt, Å., Enright, W. F., Levy Jr., V. M., Lapsley, D. K., Buss, R. R., . . . Zindler, M. (1984). Distributive justice development: Cross-cultural, contextual, and longitudinal evaluations. *Child Development, 55*, 1737. Retrieved from 10.1111/1467-8624.ep7304494

Erikson, E. H. (1950). *Childhood and society* (2nd ed.). New York, NY: Norton.

Evans, J. (1998). Princesses are not into war "n things, they always scream and run off": Exploring gender stereotypes in picture books. *Reading, 32*, 5–11.

Fast, A. A., & Olson, K. R. (2018). Gender development in transgender preschool children. *Child Development, 89*, 620–637. doi:10.1111/cdev.12758

Fay-Stammbach, T., Hawes, D. J., & Meredith, P. (2014). Parenting influences on executive function in early childhood: A review. *Child Development Perspectives, 8*, 258–264. doi:10.1111/cdep.12095

Fitzpatrick, M., & McPherson, B. (2010). Coloring within the lines: Gender stereotypes in contemporary coloring books. *Sex Roles, 62*, 127–137. doi:10.1007/s11199-009-9703-8

Font, S. A., & Berger, L. M. (2014). Child maltreatment and children's developmental trajectories in early to middle childhood. *Child Development, 86*, 536–556. doi:10.1111/cdev.12322

Frahsek, S., Mack, W., Mack, C., Pfalz-Blezinger, C., & Knopf, M. (2010). Assessing different aspects of pretend play within a play setting: Towards a standardized assessment of pretend play in young children. *British Journal of Developmental Psychology, 28*, 331–345. doi:10.1348/026151009x413666

Frawley, T. J. (2008). Gender schema and prejudicial recall: How children misremember, fabricate, and distort gendered picture book information. *Journal of Research in Childhood Education, 22*, 291–303.

Freeman, N. (2007). Preschoolers' perceptions of gender appropriate toys and their parents' beliefs about genderized behaviors: Miscommunication, mixed messages, or hidden truths? *Early Childhood Education Journal, 34*, 357–366. doi:10.1007/s10643-006-0123-x

Fuss, J., Auer, M. K., & Briken, P. (2015). Gender dysphoria in children and adolescents. *Current Opinion in Psychiatry, 28*, 430–434. doi:10.1097/YCO.0000000000000203

Gagnon, S. G., Huelsman, T. J., Reichard, A. E., Kidder-Ashley, P., Griggs, M. S., Struby, J., & Bollinger, J. (2013). Help me play! Parental behaviors, child temperament, and preschool peer play. *Journal of Child and Family Studies, 23*, 872–884. doi:10.1007/s10826-013-9743-0

Gaskins, S. (2014). Children's play as cultural activity. In E. Brooker, M. Blaise, & S. Edwards (Eds.), *Sage handbook of play and learning in early childhood* (pp. 31–42). Thousand Oaks, CA: Sage.

Gates, G. J. (2011). *How many people are lesbian, gay, bisexual and transgender?* Retrieved from https://escholarship.org/uc/item/09h684x2

Gershoff, E. T. (2013). Spanking and child development: We know enough now to stop hitting our children. *Child Development Perspectives, 7*, 133–137. doi:10.1111/cdep.12038

Gershoff, E. T., & Grogan-Kaylor, A. (2016). Spanking and child outcomes: Old controversies and new meta-analyses. *Journal of Family Psychology, 30*, 453–469. doi:10.1037/fam0000191

Ginsburg, K. R. (2007). The importance of play in promoting healthy child development and maintaining strong parent-child bonds. *Pediatrics, 119*, 182–191.

Gioia, K. A., & Tobin, R. M. (2010). Role of sociodramatic play in promoting self-regulation. In C. E. Schaefer (Ed.), *Play therapy for preschool children* (pp. 181–198). Washington, DC: American Psychological Association. doi:10.1037/12060-009

Gleason, T. R., & Kalpidou, M. (2014). Imaginary companions and young children's coping and competence. *Social Development, 24*, 820–839. doi:10.1111/sode.12078

Gleason, T. R., Sebanc, A. M., & Hartup, W. W. (2000). Imaginary companions of preschool children. *Developmental Psychology, 36*, 419–428.

Goldstein, T. R., & Lerner, M. D. (2018). Dramatic pretend play games uniquely improve emotional control in young children. *Developmental Science, 21*, e12603. doi:10.1111/desc.12603

Gómez, R. L., & Edgin, J. O. (2015). Sleep as a window into early neural development: Shifts in sleep-dependent learning effects across early childhood. *Child Development Perspectives, 9*, 183–189. doi:10.1111/cdep.12130

Goodvin, R., Meyer, S., Thompson, R. A., & Hayes, R. (2008). Self-understanding in early childhood: Associations with child attachment security and maternal negative affect. *Attachment & Human Development, 10*, 433–450. doi:10.1080/14616730802461466

Goodvin, R., Thompson, R. A., & Winer, A. C. (2015). The individual child: Temperament, emotion, self, and personality. In M. Bornstein & M. Lamb (Eds.), *Developmental psychology: An advanced textbook* (pp. 377–409). New York, NY: Psychology Press.

Gower, A. L., Lingras, K. A., Mathieson, L. C., Kawabata, Y., & Crick, N. R. (2014). The role of preschool relational and physical aggression in the transition to kindergarten: Links with social-psychological adjustment. *Early Education and Development, 25*, 619–640. doi:10.1080/10409289.2014.844058

Grogan-Kaylor, A., Ma, J., & Graham-Bermann, S. A. (2018). The case against physical punishment. *Current Opinion in Psychology, 19*, 22–27. doi:10.1016/J.COPSYC.2017.03.022

Guimond, S., Chatard, A., & Lorenzi-Cioldi, F. (2013). The social psychology of gender across cultures. In M. K. Ryan (Ed.), *The SAGE handbook of gender and psychology* (pp. 216–233). Thousand Oaks, CA: Sage. doi:10.4135/9781446269930.n14

Guzman, M. R. de, Do, K. A., & Kok, C. (2014). *The cultural contexts of children's prosocial behaviors.* Faculty Publications, Department of Child, Youth, and Family Studies. Retrieved from http://digitalcommons.unl.edu/famconfacpub/103

Halim, M. L. (2016). Princesses and superheroes: Social-cognitive influences on early gender rigidity. *Child Development Perspectives, 10,* 155–160. doi:10.1111/cdep.12176

Halim, M. L., Ruble, D. N., Tamis-LeMonda, C. S., Shrout, P. E., & Amodio, D. M. (2017). Gender attitudes in early childhood: Behavioral consequences and cognitive antecedents. *Child Development, 88,* 882–889. doi:10.1111/cdev.12642

Halim, M. L., Ruble, D. N., Tamis-LeMonda, C. S., Zosuls, K. M., Lurye, L. E., & Greulich, F. K. (2014). Pink frilly dresses and the avoidance of all things "girly": Children's appearance rigidity and cognitive theories of gender development. *Developmental Psychology, 50,* 1091–1101. doi:10.1037/a0034906

Halim, M. L., Ruble, D., Tamis-LeMonda, C., & Shrout, P. E. (2013). Rigidity in gender-typed behaviors in early childhood: A longitudinal study of ethnic minority children. *Child Development, 84,* 1269–1284. doi:10.1111/cdev.12057

Halpern, H. P., & Perry-Jenkins, M. (2016). Parents' gender ideology and gendered behavior as predictors of children's gender-role attitudes: A longitudinal exploration. *Sex Roles, 74,* 527–542. doi:10.1007/s11199-015-0539-0

Hammond, S. I., & Carpendale, J. I. M. (2015). Helping children help: The relation between maternal scaffolding and children's early help. *Social Development, 24,* 367–383. doi:10.1111/sode.12104

Hanish, L. D., Fabes, R. A., Leaper, C., Bigler, R., Hayes, A. R., Hamilton, V., & Beltz, A. M. (2013). Gender: Early socialization. In D. A. C. Elizabeth, T. Gershoff, & R. S. Mistry (Eds.), *Societal contexts of child development: Pathways of influence and implications for practice and policy.* Oxford, UK: Oxford University Press.

Harter, S. (2012). Emerging self-processes during childhood and adolescence. In M. R. Leary & J. P. Tangney (Eds.), *Handbook of self and identity* (pp. 680–715). New York, NY: Guilford.

Hay, D. F., Hurst, S. L., Waters, C. S., & Chadwick, A. (2011). Infants' use of force to defend toys: The origins of instrumental aggression. *Infancy, 16,* 471–489. doi:10.1111/j.1532-7078.2011.00069.x

Hein, T. C., & Monk, C. S. (2017). Research review: Neural response to threat in children, adolescents, and adults after child maltreatment: A quantitative meta-analysis. *Journal of Child Psychology and Psychiatry, 58,* 222–230. doi:10.1111/jcpp.12651

Hepach, R., Vaish, A., & Tomasello, M. (2012). Young children are intrinsically motivated to see others helped. *Psychological Science, 23,* 967–972. doi:10.1177/0956797612440571

Hicks-Pass, S. (2009). Corporal punishment in America today: Spare the rod, spoil the child? A systematic review of the literature. *Best Practice in Mental Health: An International Journal, 5,* 71–88.

Hines, M. (2015). Gendered development. In M. Lamb (Ed.), *Handbook of child psychology and developmental science* (pp. 1–46). Hoboken, NJ: John Wiley. doi:10.1002/9781118963418.childpsy320

Hines, M., Pasterski, V., Spencer, D., Neufeld, S., Patalay, P., Hindmarsh, P. C., . . . Acerini, C. L. (2016). Prenatal androgen exposure alters girls' responses to information indicating gender-appropriate behaviour. *Philosophical Transactions of the Royal Society of London B: Biological Sciences, 371.* Retrieved from http://rstb.royalsocietypublishing.org/content/371/1688/20150125

Hinkelman, L., & Bruno, M. (2008). Identification and reporting of child sexual abuse: The role of elementary school professionals. *Elementary School Journal, 108,* 376–391.

Hoeve, M., Dubas, J. S., Gerris, J. R. M., van der Laan, P. H., & Smeenk, W. (2011). Maternal and paternal parenting styles: Unique and combined links to adolescent and early adult delinquency. *Journal of Adolescence, 34,* 813–827. doi:10.1016/j.adolescence.2011.02.004

Hoffmann, J., & Russ, S. (2012). Pretend play, creativity, and emotion regulation in children. *Psychology of Aesthetics, Creativity, and the Arts, 6,* 175–184.

Honaker, S. M., & Meltzer, L. J. (2014). Bedtime problems and night wakings in young children: An update of the evidence. *Pediatric Respiratory Reviews, 15,* 333–339. doi:10.1016/j.prrv.2014.04.011

Huntsinger, C. S., Jose, P. E., & Larson, S. L. (1998). Do parent practices to encourage academic competence influence the social adjustment of young European American and Chinese American children? *Developmental Psychology, 34,* 747–756.

Hyde, J. S. (2014). Gender similarities and differences. *Annual Review of Psychology, 65,* 373–398. doi:10.1146/annurev-psych-010213-115057

Hyde, J. S. (2016). Sex and cognition: Gender and cognitive functions. *Current Opinion in Neurobiology, 38,* 53–56. doi:10.1016/j.conb.2016.02.007

Jewell, J. D., Krohn, E. J., Scott, V. G., Carlton, M., & Meinz, E. (2008). The differential impact of mothers' and fathers' discipline on preschool children's home and classroom behavior. *North American Journal of Psychology, 10,* 173–188.

Jones, D. J., Lewis, T., Litrownik, A., Thompson, R., Proctor, L. J., Isbell, P., . . . Runyan, D. (2013). Linking childhood sexual abuse and early adolescent risk behavior: The intervening role of internalizing and externalizing problems. *Journal of Abnormal Child Psychology, 41,* 139–150. doi:10.1007/s10802-012-9656-1

Kahlenberg, S. G., & Hein, M. M. (2010). Progression on Nickelodeon? Gender-role stereotypes in toy commercials. *Sex Roles, 62,* 830–847. doi:10.1007/s11199-009-9653-1

Keefe-Cooperman, K., & Brady-Amoon, P. (2014). Preschooler sleep patterns related to cognitive and adaptive functioning. *Early Education and Development, 25,* 859–874. doi:10.1080/10409289.2014.876701

Kim, H., Wildeman, C., Jonson-Reid, M., & Drake, B. (2017). Lifetime prevalence of investigating child maltreatment among US children. *American Journal of Public Health, 107,* 274–280. doi:10.2105/AJPH.2016.303545

Kimball, M. M. (1986). Television and sex-role attitudes. In T. M. Williams (Ed.), *The impact of television: A natural experiment in three communities* (pp. 265–301). Orlando, FL: Academic Press.

Knafo-Noam, A., Uzefovsky, F., Israel, S., Davidov, M., & Zahn-Waxler, C. (2015). The prosocial personality and its facets: Genetic and environmental architecture of mother-reported behavior of 7-year-old twins. *Frontiers in Psychology, 6,* 112. doi:10.3389/fpsyg.2015.00112

Kohlberg, L. (1966). A cognitive-developmental analysis of children's sex-role concepts and attitudes. In E. E. Maccoby (Ed.), *The development of sex differences* (pp. 82–173). Stanford, CA: Stanford University Press.

Kramer, L. (2014). Learning emotional understanding and emotion regulation through sibling interaction. *Early Education and Development, 25,* 160–184. doi:10.1080/10409289.2014.838824

Kuhlmeier, V., Dunfield, K., & O'Neill, A. (2014). Selectivity in early prosocial behavior. *Frontiers in Psychology, 5.* doi:10.3389/fpsyg.2014.00836

Lambert, M. C., & Kelley, H. M. (2011). Initiative versus guilt. In S. Goldstein & J. A. Naglieri (Eds.), *Encyclopedia of child behavior and development* (pp. 816–817). Boston, MA: Springer US. doi:10.1007/978-0-387-79061-9_1499

Lancy, D. (2008). *The anthropology of childhood: Cherubs, chattel, changelings.* Utah State University Faculty Monographs. Retrieved from http://digitalcommons.usu.edu/usufaculty_monographs/15

Lansford, J. E., Deater-Deckard, K., Dodge, K. A., Bates, J. E., & Pettit, G. S. (2004). Ethnic differences in the link between physical discipline and later adolescent externalizing behaviors. *Journal of Child Psychology & Psychiatry, 45,* 801–812. doi:10.1111/j.1469-7610.2004.00273.x

Leaper, C. (2013). Gender development during childhood. In P. D. Zelaz (Ed.), (*The Oxford handbook of developmental psychology: Vol. 2. Self and other* (pp. 326–376). Oxford, UK: Oxford University Press.

Lee, Y. E., Brophy-Herb, H. E., Vallotton, C. D., Griffore, R. J., Carlson, J. S., & Robinson, J. L. (2016). Do young children's representations of discipline and empathy moderate the effects of punishment on emotion regulation? *Social Development, 25,* 120–138. doi:10.1111/sode.12141

Levy, G. D., & Haaf, R. A. (1994). Detection of gender-related categories by 10-month-old infants. *Infant Behavior & Development, 17,* 457–459. doi:10.1016/0163-6383(94)90037-x

Lewis, M., Takai-Kawakami, K., Kawakami, K., & Sullivan, M. W. (2010). Cultural differences in emotional responses to success and failure. *International Journal of Behavioral Development, 34,* 53–61. doi:10.1177/0165025409348559

Liben, L. S., Bigler, R. S., & Hilliard, L. J. (2013). Gender development. In D. A. C. Elizabeth, T. Gershoff, & R. S. Mistry (Ed.), *Societal* contexts of child development: Pathways of influence and implications for practice and policy (pp. 3–18). Oxford, UK: Oxford University Press.

Lillard, A. S. (2015). The development of play. In M. Lamb (Ed.), *Handbook of child psychology and developmental science* (pp. 1–44). Hoboken, NJ: John Wiley. doi:10.1002/9781118963418.childpsy211

Lindsey, E. W., & Colwell, M. J. (2013). Pretend and physical play: Links to preschoolers' affective social competence. *Merrill-Palmer Quarterly, 59*, 330–360. doi:10.1353/mpq.2013.0015

LoBue, V., Nishida, T., Chiong, C., DeLoache, J. S., & Haidt, J. (2011). When getting something good is bad: Even three-year-olds react to inequality. *Social Development, 20*, 154–170. doi:10.1111/j.1467-9507.2009.00560.x

Lockenhoff, C. E., Chan, W., McCrae, R. R., De Fruyt, F., Jussim, L., De Bolle, M., . . . Terracciano, A. (2014). Gender stereotypes of personality: Universal and accurate? *Journal of Cross-Cultural Psychology, 45*, 675–694. doi:10.1177/0022022113520075

Magee, C. A., Gordon, R., & Caputi, P. (2014). Distinct developmental trends in sleep duration during early childhood. *Pediatrics, 133*, e1561–e1567. doi:10.1542/peds.2013-3806

Malti, T., & Dys, S. P. (2018). From being nice to being kind: Development of prosocial behaviors. *Current Opinion in Psychology, 20*, 45–49. doi:10.1016/J.COPSYC.2017.07.036

Maniglio, R. (2013). Child sexual abuse in the etiology of anxiety disorders: A systematic review of reviews. *Trauma, Violence & Abuse, 14*, 96–112. doi:10.1177/1524838012470032

Martin, C., Fabes, R., Hanish, L., Leonard, S., & Dinella, L. (2011). Experienced and expected similarity to same-gender peers: Moving toward a comprehensive model of gender segregation. *Sex Roles, 65*, 421–434. doi:10.1007/s11199-011-0029-y

Martin, C., Kornienko, O., Schaefer, D. R., Hanish, L. D., Fabes, R. A., & Goble, P. (2013). The role of sex of peers and gender-typed activities in young children's peer affiliative networks: A longitudinal analysis of selection and influence. *Child Development, 84*, 921–37. doi:10.1111/cdev.12032

Martin, C., & Ruble, D. N. (2010). Patterns of gender development. *Annual Review of Psychology, 61*, 353–381. doi:10.1146/annurev.psych.093008.100511

McClelland, M. M., & Cameron, C. E. (2011). Self-regulation and academic achievement in elementary school children. *New Directions for Child and Adolescent Development, 2011*, 29–44. doi:10.1002/cd.302

McKinney, C., & Renk, K. (2011). A multivariate model of parent-adolescent relationship variables in early adolescence. *Child Psychiatry and Human Development, 42*, 442–462. doi:10.1007/s10578-011-0228-3

McLoyd, V. C., & Smith, J. (2002). Physical discipline and behavior problems in African American, European American, and Hispanic children: Emotional support as a moderator. *Journal of Marriage and Family, 64*, 40–53.

Miller, A. L., Seifer, R., Crossin, R., & Lebourgeois, M. K. (2015). Toddler's self-regulation strategies in a challenge context are nap-dependent. *Journal of Sleep Research, 24*, 279–287. doi:10.1111/jsr.12260

Miller, C. F., Trautner, H. M., & Ruble, D. N. (2006). The role of gender stereotypes in children's preferences and behavior. In L. Balter & C. S. Tamis-LeMonda (Eds.), *Child psychology: A handbook of contemporary issues* (2nd ed., pp. 293–323). New York, NY: Psychology Press.

Miller, D. I., & Halpern, D. F. (2014). The new science of cognitive sex differences. *Trends in Cognitive Sciences, 18*, 37–45. doi:10.1016/j.tics.2013.10.011

Miller, J. G. (2018). Physiological mechanisms of prosociality. *Current Opinion in Psychology, 20*, 50–54. doi:10.1016/J.COPSYC.2017.08.018

Mindell, J. A., Meltzer, L. J., Carskadon, M. A., & Chervin, R. D. (2009). Developmental aspects of sleep hygiene: Findings from the 2004 National Sleep Foundation Sleep in America poll. *Sleep Medicine, 10*, 771–779. doi:10.1016/j.sleep.2008.07.016

Molnar, B. E., Goerge, R. M., Gilsanz, P., Hill, A., Subramanian, S. V, Holton, J. K., . . . Beardslee, W. R. (2016). Neighborhood-level social processes and substantiated cases of child maltreatment. *Child Abuse & Neglect, 51*, 41–53. doi:10.1016/j.chiabu.2015.11.007

Morawska, A., & Sanders, M. (2011). Parental use of time out revisited: A useful or harmful parenting strategy? *Journal of Child & Family Studies, 20*, 1–8. doi:10.1007/s10826-010-9371-x

Muris, P., & Meesters, C. (2014). Small or big in the eyes of the other: On the developmental psychopathology of self-conscious emotions as shame, guilt, and pride. *Clinical Child and Family Psychology Review, 17*, 19–40. doi:10.1007/s10567-013-0137-z

Murry, V. M., Brody, G. H., Simons, R. L., Cutrona, C. E., & Gibbons, F. X. (2008). Disentangling ethnicity and context as predictors of parenting within rural African American families. *Applied Developmental Science, 12*, 202–210. doi:10.1080/10888690802388144

Newton, E., & Jenvey, V. (2011). Play and theory of mind: Associations with social competence in young children. *Early Child Development & Care, 181*, 761–773. doi:10.1080/03004430.2010.486898

Newton, E., Laible, D., Carlo, G., Steele, J. S., & McGinley, M. (2014). Do sensitive parents foster kind children, or vice versa? Bidirectional influences between children's prosocial behavior and parental sensitivity. *Developmental Psychology, 50*, 1808–1816. doi:10.1037/a0036495

Nugent, B. M., & McCarthy, M. M. (2011). Epigenetic underpinnings of developmental sex differences in the brain. *Neuroendocrinology, 93*, 150–158. doi:10.1159/000325264

Ochs, E., & Izquierdo, C. (2009). Responsibility in childhood: Three developmental trajectories. *Ethos, 37*, 391–413. doi:10.1111/j.1548-1352.2009.01066.x

Olson, K. R., Durwood, L., DeMeules, M., & McLaughlin, K. A. (2016). Mental health of transgender children who are supported in their identities. *Pediatrics, 137*, e20153223. doi:10.1542/peds.2015-3223

Olson, K. R., Key, A. C., & Eaton, N. R. (2015). Gender cognition in transgender children. *Psychological Science, 26*, 467–474. doi:10.1177/0956797614568156

Ostrov, J. M., & Godleski, S. A. (2010). Toward an integrated gender-linked model of aggression subtypes in early and middle childhood. *Psychological Review, 117*, 233–242. doi:10.1037/a0018070

Oveisi, S., Eftekhare Ardabili, H., Majdzadeh, R., Mohammadkhani, P., Alaqband Rad, J., & Loo, J. (2010). Mothers' attitudes toward corporal punishment of children in Qazvin-Iran. *Journal of Family Violence, 25*, 159–164. doi:10.1007/s10896-009-9279-7

Paradise, R., & Rogoff, B. (2009). Side by side: Learning by observing and pitching in. *Ethos, 37*, 102–138. doi:10.1111/j.1548-1352.2009.01033.x

Parten, M. (1932). Social participation among preschool children. *Journal of Abnormal and Social Psychology, 27*, 243–269.

Paulus, M., & Moore, C. (2014). The development of recipient-dependent sharing behavior and sharing expectations in preschool children. *Developmental Psychology, 50*, 914–921. doi:10.1037/a0034169

Pellegrini, A. D., & Roseth, C. J. (2006). Relational aggression and relationships in preschoolers: A discussion of methods, gender differences, and function. *Journal of Applied Developmental Psychology, 27*, 269–276.

Piaget, J. (1962). *Play, dreams, and imitation in childhood.* New York, NY: Norton.

Pinquart, M. (2017). Associations of parenting dimensions and styles with externalizing problems of children and adolescents: An updated meta-analysis. *Developmental Psychology, 53*, 873–932. doi:10.1037/dev0000295

Piotrowski, J. T., Lapierre, M. A., & Linebarger, D. L. (2013). Investigating correlates of self-regulation in early childhood with a representative sample of English-speaking American families. *Journal of Child and Family Studies, 22*, 423–436. doi:10.1007/s10826-012-9595-z

Quinn, M., & Hennessy, E. (2010). Peer relationships across the preschool to school transition. *Early Education & Development, 21*, 825–842. doi:10.1080/10409280903329013

Quinn, P. C., & Liben, L. S. (2014). A sex difference in mental rotation in infants: Convergent evidence. *Infancy, 19*, 103–116. doi:10.1111/infa.12033

Quinn, P. C., Yahr, J., Kuhn, A., Slater, A. M., & Pascalis, O. (2002). Representation of the gender of human faces by infants: A preference for female. *Perception, 31*, 1109–1121. doi:10.1068/p3331

Reed, T., & Brown, M. (2001). The expression of care in the rough and tumble play of boys. *Journal of Research in Childhood Education, 15*, 104–116.

Roby, A. C., & Kidd, E. (2008). The referential communication skills of children with imaginary companions. *Developmental Science, 11*, 531–540. doi:10.1111/j.1467-7687.2008.00699.x

Rochat, P. (2013). Self-conceptualizing in development. In P. D. Zelazo (Ed.), *The Oxford handbook of developmental psychology: Vol. 2. Self and other* (pp. 378–396). Oxford, UK: Oxford University Press. doi:10.1093/oxfordhb/9780199958474.013.0015

Roopnarine, J. L., Hossain, Z., Gill, P., & Brophy, H. (1994). Play in the East Indian context. In J. L. Roopnarine, J. E. Johnson, & F. H. Hooper (Eds.), *Children's play in diverse cultures* (pp. 9–30). Albany: State University of New York Press.

Roopnarine, J. L., Lasker, J., Sacks, M., & Stores, M. (1998). The cultural contexts of children's play. In O. N. Saracho & B. Spodek (Eds.), *Multiple perspectives on play in early childhood education* (pp. 194–219). Albany: State University of New York Press.

Rose, J., Roman, N., Mwaba, K., & Ismail, K. (2018). The relationship between parenting and internalizing behaviours of children: A systematic review. *Early Child Development and Care, 199*, 1468–1486. doi:10.1080/03004430.2016.1269762

Ross, J. (2017). You and me: Investigating the role of self-evaluative emotion in preschool prosociality. *Journal of Experimental Child Psychology, 155*, 67–83. doi:10.1016/J.JECP.2016.11.001

Rothbaum, F., Pott, M., Azuma, H., Miyake, K., & Weisz, J. (2000). The development of close relationships in Japan and the United States: Paths of symbiotic harmony and generative tension. *Child Development, 71*, 1121–1142.

Rubin, K. H., Bukowski, W. M., & Bowker, J. C. (2015). Children in peer groups. In M. H. Borntein & T. Leventhal (Eds.), *Handbook of child psychology and developmental science* (pp. 1–48). Hoboken, NJ: John Wiley. doi:10.1002/9781118963418.childpsy405

Ryan, C., Russell, S. T., Huebner, D., Diaz, R., & Sanchez, J. (2010). Family acceptance in adolescence and the health of LGBT young adults. *Journal of Child and Adolescent Psychiatric Nursing, 23*, 205–213. doi:10.1111/j.1744-6171.2010.00246.x

Sadler, T. L. (2015). *Langman's medical embryology* (13th ed.). New York, NY: Lippincott Williams & Wilkins.

Sala, M. N., Pons, F., & Molina, P. (2014). Emotion regulation strategies in preschool children. *British Journal of Developmental Psychology, 32*, 440–453. doi:10.1111/bjdp.12055

Schumacher, A. M., Miller, A. L., Watamura, S. E., Kurth, S., Lassonde, J. M., & LeBourgeois, M. K. (2017). Sleep moderates the association between response inhibition and self-regulation in early childhood. *Journal of Clinical Child and Adolescent Psychology, 46*, 222–235. doi:10.1080/15374416.2016.1204921

Sebanc, A. M., Kearns, K. T., Hernandez, M. D., & Galvin, K. B. (2007). Predicting having a best friend in young children: Individual characteristics and friendship features. *Journal of Genetic Psychology, 168*, 81–96. doi:10.3200/GNTP.168.1.81-96

Signorella, M., & Liben, L. S. (1984). Recall and reconstruction of gender-related pictures: Effects of attitude, task difficulty, and age. *Child Development, 55*, 393–405.

Silkenbeumer, J. R., Schiller, E. M., & Kärtner, J. (2018). Co- and self-regulation of emotions in the preschool setting. *Early Childhood Research Quarterly, 44*, 72–81. doi:10.1016/J.ECRESQ.2018.02.014

Simons, L., Schrager, S. M., Clark, L. F., Belzer, M., & Olson, J. (2013). Parental support and mental health among transgender adolescents. *Journal of Adolescent Health, 53*, 791–793. doi:10.1016/j.jadohealth.2013.07.019

Smith, C. E., Blake, P. R., & Harris, P. L. (2013). I should but I won't: Why young children endorse norms of fair sharing but do not follow them. *PLoS ONE, 8*, e59510. doi:10.1371/journal.pone.0059510

Sorkhabi, N. (2005). Applicability of Baumrind's parent typology to collective cultures: Analysis of cultural explanations of parent socialization effects. *International Journal of Behavioral Development, 29*, 552–563.

Sosic-Vasic, Z., Kröner, J., Schneider, S., Vasic, N., Spitzer, M., & Streb, J. (2017). The association between parenting behavior and executive functioning in children and young adolescents. *Frontiers in Psychology, 8*, 472. doi:10.3389/fpsyg.2017.00472

Spinrad, T. L., & Gal, D. E. (2018). Fostering prosocial behavior and empathy in young children, *Current Opinion in Psychology, 20*, 40–44. doi:10.1016/J.COPSYC.2017.08.004

Stacks, A. M., Oshio, T., Gerard, J., & Roe, J. (2009). The moderating effect of parental warmth on the association between spanking and child aggression: A longitudinal approach. *Infant & Child Development, 18*, 178–194. doi:10.1002/icd.596

Steensma, T. D., & Cohen-Kettenis, P. T. (2011). Gender transitioning before puberty? *Archives of Sexual Behavior, 40*, 649–650. doi:10.1007/s10508-011-9752-2

Ștefan, C. A., & Avram, J. (2018). The multifaceted role of attachment during preschool: Moderator of its indirect effect on empathy through emotion regulation. *Early Child Development and Care, 188*, 62–76. doi:10.1080/03004430.2016.1246447

Stern, J. A., & Cassidy, J. (2018). Empathy from infancy to adolescence: An attachment perspective on the development of individual differences. *Developmental Review, 47*, 1–22. doi:10.1016/J.DR.2017.09.002

Sullivan, M. W., Carmody, D. P., & Lewis, M. (2010). How neglect and punitiveness influence emotion knowledge. *Child Psychiatry and Human Development, 41*, 285–298. doi:10.1007/s10578-009-0168-3

Svetlova, M., Nichols, S. R., & Brownell, C. A. (2010). Toddlers prosocial behavior: From instrumental to empathic to altruistic helping. *Child Development, 81*, 1814–1827. doi:10.1111/j.1467-8624.2010.01512.x

Tamis-LeMonda, C. S., Briggs, R. D., McClowry, S. G., & Snow, D. L. (2009). Maternal control and sensitivity, child gender, and maternal education in relation to children's behavioral outcomes in African American families. *Journal of Applied Developmental Psychology, 30*, 321–331. doi:10.1016/j.appdev.2008.12.018

Tannock, M. (2011). Observing young children's rough-and-tumble play. *Australasian Journal of Early Childhood, 36*, 13–20.

Taylor, M. (1999). *Imaginary companions and the children who create them*. New York, NY: Oxford University Press.

Taylor, M., Shawber, A. B., & Mannering, A. M. (2009). Children's imaginary companions: What is it like to have an invisible friend? In K. D. Markman, W. M. P. Klein, & J. A. Suhr (Eds.), *Handbook of imagination and mental simulation* (pp. 211–224). New York, NY: Psychology Press.

Taylor, Z. E., Eisenberg, N., Spinrad, T. L., Eggum, N. D., & Sulik, M. J. (2013). The relations of ego-resiliency and emotion socialization to the development of empathy and prosocial behavior across early childhood. *Emotion, 13*, 822–831.

Thompson, A. E., & Voyer, D. (2014). Sex differences in the ability to recognise non-verbal displays of emotion: A meta-analysis. *Cognition and Emotion, 28*, 1164–1195. doi:10.1080/02699931.2013.875889

Thompson, R., Kaczor, K., Lorenz, D. J., Bennett, B. L., Meyers, G., & Pierce, M. C. (2017). Is the use of physical discipline associated with aggressive behaviors in young children? *Academic Pediatrics, 17*, 34–44. doi:10.1016/J.ACAP.2016.02.014

Thompson, R. A., & Goodvin, R. (2007). Taming the tempest in the teapot: Emotion regulation in toddlers. In C. A. Brownell & C. B. Kopp (Eds.), *Transitions in early socioemotional development: The toddler years* (pp. 320–341). New York, NY: Guilford.

Thompson, R. A., & Newton, E. K. (2013). Baby altruists? Examining the complexity of prosocial motivation in young children. *Infancy, 18*, 120–133. doi:10.1111/j.1532-7078.2012.00139.x

Thompson, R. A., & Virmani, E. A. (2010). Self and personality. In M. H. Bornstein (Ed.), *Handbook of cultural developmental science* (pp. 195–207). New York, NY: Psychology Press.

Tremblay, R. E. (2014). Early development of physical aggression and early risk factors for chronic physical aggression in humans. *Current Topics in Behavioral Neurosciences, 17*, 315–327. doi:10.1007/7854_2013_262

Tremblay, R. E., Nagin, D. S., Séguin, J. R., Zoccolillo, M., Zelazo, P. D., Boivin, M., . . . Japel, C. (2004). Physical aggression during early childhood: Trajectories and predictors. *Pediatrics, 114*, e43–e50.

Trionfi, G., & Reese, E. (2009). A good story: Children with imaginary companions create richer narratives. *Child Development, 80*, 1301–1313. doi:10.1111/j.1467-8624.2009.01333.x

Tucker, B., & Young, A. (2005). Growing up Mikea: Children's time allocation and tuber foraging in southwestern Madagascar. In B. S. Hewlett & M. E. Lamb (Eds.), *Huntergatherer childhoods: Evolutionary, developmental and cultural perspectives* (pp. 147–174). New Brunswick, NJ: Transaction.

Turner, P. J., & Gervai, J. (1995). A multidimensional study of gender typing in preschool children and their parents: Personality, attitudes, preferences, behavior, and cultural differences. *British Journal of Developmental Psychology, 11*, 323–342.

Tzeng, O., Jackson, J., & Karlson, H. (1991). *Theories of child abuse and neglect: Differential perspectives, summaries, and evaluations*. New York, NY: Praeger.

U.S. Department of Health and Human Services. (2013). *Child maltreatment 2012*. Retrieved from http://www.acf.hhs.gov/programs/cb/resource/child-maltreatment-2012

U.S. Department of Health and Human Services. (2016). *Child maltreatment, 2014*. Retrieved from http://www.acf.hhs.gov/sites/default/files/cb/cm2014.pdf

Vaish, A. (2018). The prosocial functions of early social emotions: The case of guilt. *Current Opinion in Psychology, 20*, 25–29. doi:10.1016/J.COPSYC.2017.08.008

Van de Vondervoort, J. W., & Hamlin, J. K. (2016). Evidence for intuitive morality: Preverbal infants make sociomoral evaluations. *Child Development Perspectives, 10*, 143–148. doi:10.1111/cdep.12175

van Dijken, M. W., Stams, G. J. J. M., & de Winter, M. (2016). Can community-based interventions prevent child maltreatment? *Children and Youth Services Review, 61*, 149–158. doi:10.1016/j.childyouth.2015.12.007

van Hoogdalem, A.-G., Singer, E., Eek, A., & Heesbeen, D. (2013). Friendship in young children: Construction of a behavioural sociometric method. *Journal of Early Childhood Research, 11*, 236–247. doi:10.1177/1476718X13488337

Vaughn, B. E., Elmore-Staton, L., Shin, N., & El-Sheikh, M. (2015). Sleep as a support for social competence, peer relations, and cognitive functioning in preschool children. *Behavioral Sleep Medicine, 13*, 92–106. doi:10.1080/15402002.2013.845778

Vygotsky, L. S. (1978). *Mind in society: The development of higher psychological processes*. Cambridge, MA: Harvard University Press.

Wagner, M. F., Milner, J. S., McCarthy, R. J., Crouch, J. L., McCanne, T. R., & Skowronski, J. J. (2015). Facial emotion recognition accuracy and child physical abuse: An experiment and a meta-analysis. *Psychology of Violence, 5*, 154–162. doi:10.1037/a0036014

Waldman, I. D., Tackett, J. L., Van Hulle, C. A., Applegate, B., Pardini, D., Frick, P. J., & Lahey, B. B. (2011). Child and adolescent conduct disorder substantially shares genetic influences with three socioemotional dispositions. *Journal of Abnormal Psychology, 120*, 57–70. doi:10.1037/a0021351

Wang, F., Christ, S. L., Mills-Koonce, W. R., Garrett-Peters, P., & Cox, M. J. (2013). Association between maternal sensitivity and externalizing behavior from preschool to preadolescence. *Journal of Applied Developmental Psychology, 34*, 89–100. doi:10.1016/j.appdev.2012.11.003

Wang, Q. (2004). The emergence of cultural self-constructs: Autobiographical memory and self-description in European American and Chinese children. Developmental Psychology, 40, 3–15.

Warneken, F., Lohse, K., Melis, A. P., & Tomasello, M. (2011). Young children share the spoils after collaboration. *Psychological Science, 22*, 267–273. doi:10.1177/0956797610395392

Weinberg, M. K., Tronick, E. Z., Cohn, J. F., & Olson, K. L. (1999). Gender differences in emotional expressivity and self-regulation during early infancy. *Developmental Psychology, 35*, 175–188. doi:10.1037/0012-1649.35.1.175

Weis, R., & Toolis, E. E. (2010). Parenting across cultural contexts in the USA: Assessing parenting behaviour in an ethnically and socioeconomically diverse sample. *Early Child Development and Care, 180*, 849–867. doi:10.1080/03004430802472083

Weisgram, E. S. (2016). The cognitive construction of gender stereotypes: Evidence for the dual pathways model of gender differentiation. *Sex Roles, 75*, 301–313. doi:10.1007/s11199-016-0624-z

Wellman, H. M. (2017). The development of theory of mind: Historical reflections. *Child Development Perspectives, 11*, 207–214. doi:10.1111/cdep.12236

Whiting, B. B., & Whiting, J. W. (1975). *Children of six cultures: A psycho-cultural analysis.* Cambridge, MA: Harvard University Press.

Widom, C. S. (2014). Handbook of child maltreatment. In J. E. Korbin & R. D. Krugman (Eds.), *Handbook of child maltreatment* (Vol. 2, pp. 225–247). Dordrecht, The Netherlands: Springer Netherlands. doi:10.1007/978-94-007-7208-3

Williams, J. E., & Best, D. L. (1982). *Measuring sex stereotypes: A thirty-nation study.* Beverly Hills, CA: Sage.

Xu, Y., Farver, J. A. M., Zhang, Z., Zeng, Q., Yu, L., & Cai., B. (2005). Mainland Chinese parenting styles and parent-child interaction. *International Journal of Behavioral Development, 29*, 524–531.

Yaoying, X., & Xu, Y. (2010). Children's social play sequence: Parten's classic theory revisited. *Early Child Development and Care, 180*, 489–498. doi:10.1080/03004430802090430

Zahn-Waxler, C., Friedman, R. J., Cole, P. M., Mizuta, I., & Hiruma, N. (1996). Japanese and United States preschool children's responses to conflict and distress. *Child Development, 67*, 2462–2477.

Zeman, J., Cassano, M., & Adrian, M. C. (2013). Socialization influences on children's and adolescents' emotional self-regulation processes. In K. Caplovitz Barrett, N. A. Fox, G. A. Morgan, & D. J. Fidler (Eds.), *Handbook of self-regulatory processes in development* (pp. 79–107). New York, NY: Psychology Press.

Zosuls, K. M., Andrews, N. C. Z., Martin, C. L., England, D. E., & Field, R. D. (2016). Developmental changes in the link between gender typicality and peer victimization and exclusion. *Sex Roles, 75*, 243–256. doi:10.1007/s11199-016-0608-z

Zosuls, K. M., Ruble, D. N., Tamis-LeMonda, C. S., Shrout, P. E., Bornstein, M. H., & Greulich, F. K. (2009). The acquisition of gender labels in infancy: Implications for gender-typed play. *Developmental Psychology, 45*, 688–701. doi:10.1037/a0014053

Zucker, K. J., Wood, H., Singh, D., & Bradley, S. J. (2012). A developmental, biopsychosocial model for the treatment of children with gender identity disorder. *Journal of Homosexuality, 59*, 369–397. doi:10.1080/00918369.2012.653309

Chapter 9

Ablewhite, J., Peel, I., McDaid, L., Hawkins, A., Goodenough, T., Deave, T., . . . Kessel, A. (2015). Parental perceptions of barriers and facilitators to preventing child unintentional injuries within the home: A qualitative study. *BMC Public Health, 15*, 280. doi:10.1186/s12889-015-1547-2

Acar, E., Dursun, O. B., Esin, İ. S., Öğütlü, H., Özcan, H., & Mutlu, M. (2015). Unintentional injuries in preschool age children: Is there a correlation with parenting style and parental attention deficit and hyperactivity symptoms. *Medicine, 94*, e1378. doi:10.1097/MD.0000000000001378

Afshin, A., Reitsma, M. B., & Murray, C. J. L. (2017). Health effects of overweight and obesity in 195 countries. *The New England Journal of Medicine, 377*, 1496–1497. doi:10.1056/NEJMc1710026

Aguiar, A., Eubig, P. A., & Schantz, S. L. (2010). Attention deficit/hyperactivity disorder: A focused overview for children's environmental health researchers. *Environmental Health Perspectives, 118*, 1646–1653. doi:10.1289/ehp.1002326

Ainscow, M., & Messiou, K. (2018). Engaging with the views of students to promote inclusion in education. *Journal of Educational Change, 19*, 1–17. doi:10.1007/s10833-017-9312-1

Albuquerque, D., Nóbrega, C., Manco, L., & Padez, C. (2017). The contribution of genetics and environment to obesity. *British Medical Bulletin, 123*, 159–173. doi:10.1093/bmb/ldx022

Allen, S. E. M., & Crago, M. B. (1996). Early passive acquisition in Inukitut. *Journal of Child Language, 23*, 129–156.

Allen, T. (2007). Witchcraft, sexuality and HIV/AIDS among the Azande of Sudan. *Journal of Eastern African Studies, 1*, 359–396. doi:10.1080/17531050701625789

Alviola, P. A., Nayga, R. M., Thomsen, M. R., Danforth, D., & Smartt, J. (2014). The effect of fast-food restaurants on childhood obesity: A school level analysis. *Economics & Human Biology, 12*, 110–119. doi:10.1016/j.ehb.2013.05.001

American Association on Intellectual and Developmental Disabilities. (2010). *Intellectual disability: Definition, classification, and systems of supports.* Washington, DC: Author.

American Psychiatric Association. (2013). *Diagnostic and statistical manual of mental disorders* (5th ed.). Washington, DC: Author.

Annie E. Casey Foundation. (2017). *Children who speak a language other than English at home.* Retrieved from https://datacenter.kidscount.org/data#USA/1/0/char/0

Ardila, A. (2013). Development of metacognitive and emotional executive functions in children. *Applied Neuropsychology. Child, 2*, 82–87. doi:10.1080/21622965.2013.748388

Armon-Lotem, S., Haman, E., Jensen de López, K., Smoczynska, M., Yatsushiro, K., Szczerbinski, M., . . . van der Lely, H. (2016). A large-scale cross-linguistic investigation of the acquisition of passive. *Language Acquisition, 23*, 27–56. doi:10.1080/10489223.2015.1047095

Artman, L., & Cahan, S. (1993). Schooling and the development of transitive inference. *Developmental Psychology, 29*, 753–759.

Baker, M., Currie, J., & Schwandt, H. (2017). *Mortality inequality in Canada and the U.S.: Divergent or convergent trends?* Cambridge, MA: National Bureau of Economic Research doi:10.3386/w23514

Barac, R., & Bialystok, E. (2012). Bilingual effects on cognitive and linguistic development: Role of language, cultural background, and education. *Child Development, 83*, 413–422. doi:10.1111/j.1467-8624.2011.01707.x

Barac, R., Bialystok, E., Castro, D. C., & Sanchez, M. (2014). The cognitive development of young dual language learners: A critical review. *Early Childhood Research Quarterly, 29*, 699–714. doi:10.1016/j.ecresq.2014.02.003

Barnett, S. M., Ceci, S. J., & Williams, W. M. (2006). Is the ability to make a bacon sandwich a mark of intelligence? and other issues: Some reflections on Gardner's theory of multiple intelligences. In J. A. Schaler (Ed.), *Howard Gardner under fire: The rebel psychologist faces his critics* (pp. 95–114). Chicago, IL: Open Court.

Baus, C., Costa, A., & Carreiras, M. (2013). On the effects of second language immersion on first language production. *Acta Psychologica, 142*, 402–409. doi:10.1016/j.actpsy.2013.01.010

Becker, A. E., Keel, P., Anderson-Fye, E. P., & Thomas, J. J. (2004). Genes and/or jeans? Genetic and socio-cultural contributions to risk for eating disorders. *Journal of Addictive Diseases, 23*, 81–103. doi:10.1300/J069v23n03_07

Benner, G. J., Nelson, J. R., & Epstein, M. H. (2002). The language skills of students with emotional and behavioral disorders: A literature review. *Journal of Emotional and Behavioral Disorders, 10*, 43–59.

Berge, J. M., Wall, M., Hsueh, T.-F., Fulkerson, J. A., Larson, N., & Neumark-Sztainer, D. (2015). The protective role of family meals for youth obesity: 10-year longitudinal associations. *Journal of Pediatrics, 166*, 296–301. doi:10.1016/j.jpeds.2014.08.030

Berninger, V., Abbott, R., Cook, C. R., & Nagy, W. (2017). Relationships of attention and executive functions to oral language, reading, and writing skills and systems in middle childhood and early adolescence. *Journal of Learning Disabilities, 50*, 434–449. doi:10.1177/0022219415617167

Best, R. M., Dockrell, J. E., & Braisby, N. R. (2006). Real-world word learning: Exploring children's developing semantic representations of a science term. *British Journal of Developmental Psychology, 24*, 265–282. Retrieved from r.best@lancaster.ac.uk

Bialystok, E. (2015). Bilingualism and the development of executive function: The role of attention. *Child Development Perspectives, 9*, 117–121. doi:10.1111/cdep.12116

Bialystok, E., Peets, K. F., & Moreno, S. (2014). Producing bilinguals through immersion education: Development of metalinguistic awareness. *Applied Psycholinguistics, 35*, 177–191. doi:10.1017/S0142716412000288

Black, I. E., Menzel, N. N., & Bungum, T. J. (2015). The relationship among playground areas and physical activity levels in children. *Journal of Pediatric Health Care, 29*, 156–168. doi:10.1016/j.pedhc.2014.10.001

Borst, G., Poirel, N., Pineau, A., Cassotti, M., & Houdé, O. (2013). Inhibitory control efficiency in a Piaget-like class-inclusion task in school-age children and adults: A developmental negative priming study. *Developmental Psychology, 49*, 1366–1374. doi:10.1037/a0029622

Bosch, L., & Ramon-Casas, M. (2014). First translation equivalents in bilingual toddlers' expressive vocabulary: Does form similarity matter? *International Journal of Behavioral Development, 38*, 317–322. doi:10.1177/0165025414532559

Brady, S. A. (2011). Efficacy of phonics teaching for reading outcomes: Indications from post-NRP research. In S. A. Brady, D. Braze, & C. A. Fowler (Eds.), *Explaining individual differences in reading: Theory and evidence.* New York, NY: Psychology Press.

Bryant, B. R., Bryant, D. P., Porterfield, J., Dennis, M. S., Falcomata, T., Valentine, C., . . . Bell, K. (2016). The effects of a tier 3 intervention on the mathematics performance of second grade students with severe mathematics difficulties. *Journal of Learning Disabilities, 49*, 176–188. doi:10.1177/0022219414538516

Bush, N. R., Allison, A. L., Miller, A. L., Deardorff, J., Adler, N. E., & Boyce, W. T. (2017). Socioeconomic disparities in childhood obesity risk: Association with an oxytocin receptor polymorphism. *JAMA Pediatrics, 171*, 61. doi:10.1001/jamapediatrics.2016.2332

Cadima, J., Doumen, S., Verschueren, K., & Buyse, E. (2015). Child engagement in the transition to school: Contributions of self-regulation, teacher–child relationships and classroom climate. *Early Childhood Research Quarterly, 32*, 1–12. doi:10.1016/J.ECRESQ.2015.01.008

Carbonneau, K. J., Marley, S. C., & Selig, J. P. (2013). A meta-analysis of the efficacy of teaching mathematics with concrete manipulatives. *Journal of Educational Psychology, 105*, 380–400. doi:10.1037/a0031084

Carlo, G., Mestre, M. V., Samper, P., Tur, A., & Armenta, B. E. (2011). The longitudinal relations among dimensions of parenting styles, sympathy, prosocial moral reasoning, and prosocial behaviors. *International Journal of Behavioral Development, 35*, 116–124. doi:10.1177/0165025410375921

Carrion-Castillo, A., Franke, B., & Fisher, S. E. (2013). Molecular genetics of dyslexia: An overview. *Dyslexia (Chichester, England), 19*, 214–240. doi:10.1002/dys.1464

Carson, A. S., & Banuazizi, A. (2008). "That's not fair": Similarities and differences in distributive justice reasoning between American and Filipino children. *Journal of Cross-Cultural Psychology, 39*, 493–514. Retrieved from carsona@mville.edu

Case, R. (1999). Cognitive development. In M. Bennett (Ed.), *Developmental psychology: Achievements and prospects* (pp. 36–54). Philadelphia, PA: Taylor & Francis.

Castro, D. C., Páez, M. M., Dickinson, D. K., & Frede, E. (2011). Promoting language and literacy in young dual language learners: Research, practice, and policy. *Child Development Perspectives, 5*, 15–21. doi:10.1111/j.1750-8606.2010.00142.x

Chen, Y.-C., Sudre, G., Sharp, W., Donovan, F., Chandrasekharappa, S. C., Hansen, N., . . . Shaw, P. (2018). Neuroanatomic, epigenetic and genetic differences in monozygotic twins discordant for attention deficit hyperactivity disorder. *Molecular Psychiatry, 23*, 683–690. doi:10.1038/mp.2017.45

Child Trends Databank. (2014). *Unintentional injuries.* Retrieved from http://www.childtrends.org/?indicators=unintentional-injuries

Child Trends Databank. (2016). *Infant, child, and teen mortality—Child trends.* Retrieved January 20, 2018, from https://www.childtrends.org/indicators/infant-child-and-teen-mortality/

Chung, A., Backholer, K., Wong, E., Palermo, C., Keating, C., & Peeters, A. (2016). Trends in child and adolescent obesity prevalence in economically advanced countries according to socioeconomic position: A systematic review. *Obesity Reviews, 17*, 276–295. doi:10.1111/obr.12360

Clark, K. A., Helland, T., Specht, K., Narr, K. L., Manis, F. R., Toga, A. W., & Hugdahl, K. (2014). Neuroanatomical precursors of dyslexia identified from pre-reading through to age 11. *Brain: A Journal of Neurology, 137*, 3136–3141. doi:10.1093/brain/awu229

Clark, L., & Tiggemann, M. (2008). Sociocultural and individual psychological predictors of body image in young girls: A prospective study. *Developmental Psychology, 44*, 1124–1134. Retrieved from 10.1037/0012-1649.44.4.1124

Clark, E. V. (2017). *Language in children: A brief introduction.* Retrieved from https://www.routledge.com/Language-in-Children/Clark/p/book/9781138906075

Cliffordson, C., & Gustafsson, J. E. (2008). Effects of age and schooling on intellectual performance: Estimates obtained from analysis of continuous variation in age and length of schooling. *Intelligence, 36*, 143–152. doi:10.1016/j.intell.2007.03.006

Collette, F., & Van der Linden, M. (2002). Brain imaging of the central executive component of working memory. *Neuroscience & Biobehavioral Reviews, 26*, 105–125.

Cormier, D. C., McGrew, K. S., Bulut, O., & Funamoto, A. (2017). Revisiting the relations between the WJ-IV measures of Cattell-Horn-Carroll (CHC) cognitive abilities and reading achievement during the school-age years. *Journal of Psychoeducational Assessment, 35*, 731–754. doi:10.1177/0734282916659208

Costa, L. D., Silva, D. A., Alvarenga, M. D., & de Assis Guedes de Vasconcelos, F. (2016). Association between body image dissatisfaction and obesity among schoolchildren aged 7–10 years. *Physiology & Behavior, 160*, 6–11. doi:10.1016/J.PHYSBEH.2016.03.022

Cottini, M., Basso, D., & Palladino, P. (2018). The role of declarative and procedural metamemory in event-based prospective memory in school-aged children. *Journal of Experimental Child Psychology, 166*, 17–33. doi:10.1016/J.JECP.2017.08.002

Coughlin, C., Leckey, S., & Ghetti, S. (2018). Development of episodic memory: Processes and implications. In S. Ghetti (Ed.), *Stevens' handbook of experimental psychology and cognitive neuroscience* (pp. 1–25). Hoboken, NJ: John Wiley. doi:10.1002/9781119170174.epcn404

Cowan, N., Hismjatullina, A., AuBuchon, A. M., Saults, J. S., Horton, N., Leadbitter, K., & Towse, J. (2010). With development, list recall includes more chunks, not just larger ones. *Developmental Psychology, 46*, 1119–1131. doi:10.1037/a0020618

Crone, E. A., & Steinbeis, N. (2017). Neural perspectives on cognitive control development during childhood and adolescence. *Trends in Cognitive Sciences, 21,* 205–215. doi:10.1016/J.TICS.2017.01.003

Cunningham, P. M. (2013). *Phonics they use: Words for reading and writing.* Boston, MA: Pearson.

Daley, C. E., & Onwuegbuzie, A. J. (2011). Race and intelligence. In R. J. Sternberg & S. B. Kaufman (Eds.), *The Cambridge handbook of intelligence* (pp. 293–308). Cambridge, UK: Cambridge University Press.

Damon, W. (1977). *The social world of the child.* San Francisco, CA: Jossey-Bass.

Damon, W. (1980). Patterns of change in children's social reasoning: A two-year longitudinal study. *Child Development, 51,* 1010–1017.

Damon, W. (1988). *The moral child.* New York, NY: Free Press.

Danovitch, J., & Bloom, P. (2009). Children's extension of disgust to physical and moral events. *Emotion (Washington, D.C.), 9,* 107–112. doi:10.1037/a0014113

Dasen, P. R. (1994). Culture and cognitive development from a Piagetian perspective. In W. J. Lonner & R. Malpass (Eds.), *Psychology and culture* (pp. 145–149). Boston, MA: Allyn & Bacon.

Decety, J., Michalska, K. J., & Kinzler, K. D. (2012). The contribution of emotion and cognition to moral sensitivity: A neurodevelopmental study. *Cerebral Cortex, 22,* 209–220. doi:10.1093/cercor/bhr111

de Onis, M., Blössner, M., & Borghi, E. (2010). WHO | Global prevalence and trends of overweight and obesity among preschool children. *American Journal of Clinical Nutrition, 92,* 1257–1264. doi:10.3945/ajcn.2010.29786

De Neys, W., & Glumicic, T. (2008). Conflict monitoring in dual process theories of thinking. *Cognition, 106,* 1248–1299. doi:10.1016/j.cognition.2007.06.002

de Wilde, A., Koot, H. M., & van Lier, P. A. C. (2016). Developmental links between children's working memory and their social relations with teachers and peers in the early school years. *Journal of Abnormal Child Psychology, 44,* 19–30. doi:10.1007/s10802-015-0053-4

Dellinger, A., & Gilchrist, J. (2018). Leading causes of fatal and nonfatal unintentional injury for children and teens and the role of lifestyle clinicians. *American Journal of Lifestyle Medicine.* Advance online publication. doi:10.1177/1559827617696297

Deneault, J., & Ricard, M. (2006). The assessment of children's understanding of inclusion relations: Transitivity, asymmetry, and quantification. *Journal of Cognition & Development, 7,* 551–570.

Diamond, A. (2013). Executive functions. *Annual Review of Psychology, 64,* 135–168. doi:10.1146/annurev-psych-113011-143750

Dion, J., Hains, J., Vachon, P., Plouffe, J., Laberge, L., Perron, M., . . . Leone, M. (2016). Correlates of body dissatisfaction in children. *Journal of Pediatrics, 171,* 202–207. doi:10.1016/J.JPEDS.2015.12.045

Dohnt, H. K., & Tiggemann, M. (2005). Peer influences on body dissatisfaction and dieting awareness in young girls. *British Journal of Developmental Psychology, 23,* 103–116.

Dubois, L., Ohm Kyvik, K., Girard, M., Tatone-Tokuda, F., Pérusse, D., Hjelmborg, J., . . . Martin, N. G. (2012). Genetic and environmental contributions to weight, height, and BMI from birth to 19 years of age: An international study of over 12,000 twin pairs. *PLoS ONE, 7,* e30153. doi:10.1371/journal.pone.0030153

Duchin, O., Marin, C., Mora-Plazas, M., Mendes de Leon, C., Lee, J. M., Baylin, A., & Villamor, E. (2015). A prospective study of body image dissatisfaction and BMI change in school-age children. *Public Health Nutrition, 18,* 322–328. doi:10.1017/S1368980014000366

Duyme, M., Dumaret, A. C., & Tomkiewicz, S. (1999). How can we boost IQs of "dull children"? A late adoption study. *Proceedings of the National Academy of Sciences of the United States of America, 96,* 8790–8794. doi:10.1073/PNAS.96.15.8790

Ehmke, T., Drechsel, B., & Carstensen, C. H. (2010). Effects of grade retention on achievement and self-concept in science and mathematics. *Studies in Educational Evaluation, 36,* 27–35. doi:10.1016/j.stueduc.2010.10.003

Ellis, K. J., Abrams, S. A., & Wong, W. W. (1997). Body composition of a young, multiethnic female population. *American Journal of Clinical Nutrition, 65,* 724–731.

Entwisle, D. R., Alexander, K. L., & Steffel Olson, L. (2005). First grade and educational attainment by age 22: A new story. *American Journal of Sociology, 110,* 1458–1502.

Ericsson, K. A., & Moxley, J. H. (2013). Experts' superior memory: From accumulation of chunks to building memory skills that mediate improved performance and learning. In D. S. L. Timothy J Perfect (Ed.), *The SAGE handbook of applied memory* (pp. 404–420). Thousand Oaks, CA: Sage.

Eshraghi, A. A., Liu, G., Kay, S. I. S., Eshraghi, R. S., Mittal, J., Moshiree, B., & Mittal, R. (2018). Epigenetics and autism spectrum disorder: Is there a correlation? *Frontiers in Cellular Neuroscience, 12,* 78. doi:10.3389/fncel.2018.00078

Evans, S. W., Owens, J. S., Wymbs, B. T., & Ray, A. R. (2018). Evidence-based psychosocial treatments for children and adolescents with attention deficit/hyperactivity disorder. *Journal of Clinical Child & Adolescent Psychology, 47,* 157–198. doi:10.1080/15374416.2017.1390757

Evans, E. H., Tovée, M. J., Boothroyd, L. G., & Drewett, R. F. (2013). Body dissatisfaction and disordered eating attitudes in 7- to 11-year-old girls: Testing a sociocultural model. *Body Image, 10,* 8–15. doi:10.1016/j.bodyim.2012.10.001

Everitt, B. J., Cardinal, R. N., Parkinson, J. A., & Robbins, T. W. (2003). Appetitive behavior. *Annals of the New York Academy of Sciences, 985,* 233–250.

Fan, M., & Jin, Y. (2014). Do neighborhood parks and playgrounds reduce childhood obesity? *American Journal of Agricultural Economics, 96,* 26–42. doi:10.1093/ajae/aat047

Fandakova, Y., Selmeczy, D., Leckey, S., Grimm, K. J., Wendelken, C., Bunge, S. A., & Ghetti, S. (2017). Changes in ventromedial prefrontal and insular cortex support the development of metamemory from childhood into adolescence. *Proceedings of the National Academy of Sciences of the United States of America, 114,* 7582–7587. doi:10.1073/pnas.1703079114

Farber, D. A., & Beteleva, T. G. (2011). Development of the brain's organization of working memory in young schoolchildren. *Human Physiology, 37,* 1–13. doi:10.1134/s0362119710061015

Farooq, M. A., Parkinson, K. N., Adamson, A. J., Pearce, M. S., Reilly, J. K., Hughes, A. R., . . . Reilly, J. J. (2018). Timing of the decline in physical activity in childhood and adolescence: Gateshead Millennium Cohort Study. *British Journal of Sports Medicine, 52,* 1002–1006. doi:10.1136/bjsports-2016-096933

Federal Interagency Forum on Child and Family Statistics. (2017). *America's children: Key national indicators of well-being, 2017.* Washington, DC: U.S. Department of Health and Human Services.

Filippova, E., & Astington, J. W. (2008). Further development in social reasoning revealed in discourse irony understanding. *Child Development, 79,* 126–138. Retrieved from e.filippova@utoronto.ca

Fink, S. K., Racine, E. F., Mueffelmann, R. E., Dean, M. N., & Herman-Smith, R. (2014). Family meals and diet quality among children and adolescents in North Carolina. *Journal of Nutrition Education and Behavior, 46,* 418–422. doi:10.1016/J.JNEB.2014.05.004

Flanagan, D. P., & Alfonso, V. C. (2017). *Essentials of WISC-V assessment.* Hoboken, NJ: John Wiley.

Flynn, J. R. (1987). Massive IQ gains in 14 nations: What IQ tests really measure. *Psychological Bulletin of the World Health Organization, 101,* 171–191.

Flynn, J. R. (1998). IQ gains over time: Toward finding the causes. In I. U. Neisser (Ed.), *The rising curve: Long-term gains in IQ and related measures* (pp. 25–66). Washington, DC: American Psychological Association.

Flynn, J. R., & Weiss, L. G. (2007). American IQ gains from 1932 to 2002: The WISC subtests and educational progress. *International Journal of Testing, 7,* 209–224. doi:10.1080/15305050701193587

Franić, S., Dolan, C. V., Broxholme, J., Hu, H., Zemojtel, T., Davies, G. E., . . . Boomsma, D. I. (2015). Mendelian and polygenic inheritance of intelligence: A common set of causal genes? Using next-generation sequencing to examine the effects of 168 intellectual disability genes on normal-range intelligence. *Intelligence, 49,* 10–22. doi:10.1016/j.intell.2014.12.001

Frederickson, N. L., & Simmonds, E. A. (2008). Special needs, relationship type and distributive justice norms in early and later years of middle childhood. *Social Development, 17,* 1056–1073. Retrieved from 10.1111/j.1467-9507.2008.00477.x

Fry, A. F., & Hale, S. (1996). Processing speed, working memory, and fluid intelligence: Evidence for a developmental cascade. *Psychological Science, 7,* 237–241.

Fuchs, L. S., Malone, A. S., Schumacher, R. F., Namkung, J., & Wang, A. (2017). Fraction intervention for students with mathematics difficulties: Lessons learned from five randomized controlled trials. *Journal of Learning Disabilities, 50,* 631–639. doi:10.1177/0022219416677249

Gabbard, C. (2018). *Lifelong motor development.* Philadelphia, PA: Wolters-Kluwer.

Gardner, H. (2013). *The unschooled mind: How children think and how schools should teach* (Vol. 25). New York, NY: Basic Books.

Gardner, H. (2016). Multiple intelligences: Prelude, theory, and aftermath. In R. J. Sternberg, S. T. Fiske, & D. J. Foss (Eds.), *Scientists making a difference: One hundred eminent behavioral and brain scientists talk about their most important contributions* (pp. 167–170). New York, NY: Cambridge University Press.

Gardner, H. (2017). Taking a multiple intelligences (MI) perspective. *Behavioral and Brain Sciences, 40,* e203. doi:10.1017/S0140525X16001631

Gathercole, S. E., Pickering, S. J., Ambridge, B., & Wearing, H. (2004). A structural analysis of working memory from 4 to 15 years of age. *Developmental Psychology, 40,* 177–190.

Gattario, K. H., Frisén, A., & Anderson-Fye, E. (2014). Body image and child well-being. In B. Asher, F. Casas, I. Frønes, & J. E. Korbin (Eds.), *Handbook of child well-being* (pp. 2409–2436). Dordrecht, The Netherlands: Springer.

Gauvain, M., Perez, S., Gauvain, M., & Perez, S. (2015). Cognitive development and culture. In L. S. Liben & U. Muller (Eds.), *Handbook of child psychology and developmental science* (pp. 1–43). Hoboken, NJ: John Wiley. doi:10.1002/9781118963418.childpsy220

Genesee, F. (2006). Bilingual first language acquisition in perspective. In P. McCardle & E. Hoff (Eds.), *Childhood bilingualism: Research on infancy through school age* (pp. 45–67). Clevedon, England: Multilingual Matters.

Georgas, J., Weiss, L. G., van de Vijver, F. J. R., & Saklofske, D. H. (2003). Cross-cultural psychology, intelligence, and cognitive processes. In J. Georgas, L. G. Weiss, F. J. R. Van de Vijver, & D. H. Saklofske (Eds.), *Culture and children's intelligence: Cross-cultural analysis of the WISC-III* (pp. 23–37). San Diego, CA: Academic Press.

Gilmore, C. K., McCarthy, S. E., & Spelke, E. S. (2010). Non-symbolic arithmetic abilities and mathematics achievement in the first year of formal schooling. *Cognition, 115,* 394–406. doi:10.1016/j.cognition.2010.02.002

Glenwright, M., & Pexman, P. M. (2010). Development of children's ability to distinguish sarcasm and verbal irony. *Journal of Child Language, 37,* 429. doi:10.1017/S0305000909009520

Goodarzi, M. O. (2018). Genetics of obesity: What genetic association studies have taught us about the biology of obesity and its complications. *The Lancet Diabetes & Endocrinology, 6,* 223–236. doi:10.1016/S2213-8587(17)30200-0

Goodnow, J. J., Lawrence, J. A., Goodnow, J. J., & Lawrence, J. A. (2015). Children and cultural context. In M. H Bornstein & T. Leventhal (Eds.), *Handbook of child psychology and developmental science* (pp. 1–41). Hoboken, NJ: John Wiley. doi:10.1002/9781118963418.childpsy419

Goodwin, G. P., & Johnson-Laird, P. N. (2008). Transitive and pseudo-transitive inferences. *Cognition, 108,* 320–352. Retrieved from 10.1016/j.cognition.2008.02.010

Greene, J., & Haidt, J. (2002). How (and where) does moral judgment work? *Trends in Cognitive Sciences, 6,* 517–523. doi:10.1016/S1364-6613(02)02011-9

Grosjean, F. (2010). *Bilingual: Life and reality.* Cambridge, MA: Harvard University Press.

Guo, Y., Sun, S., Breit-Smith, A., Morrison, F. J., & Connor, C. M. (2015). Behavioral engagement and reading achievement in elementary-school-age children: A longitudinal cross-lagged analysis. *Journal of Educational Psychology, 107,* 332–347. doi:10.1037/a0037638

Haidt, J. (2008). Morality. *Perspectives on Psychological Science, 3,* 65–72. doi:10.1111/j.1745-6916.2008.00063.x

Hall, L. J. (2018). *Autism spectrum disorders: From theory to practice.* Retrieved from https://www.vitalsource.com/educators/products/autism-spectrum-disorders-laura-j-hall-v9780134461168

Hanley, J. R., Cortis, C., Budd, M. J., & Nozari, N. (2016). Did I say dog or cat? A study of semantic error detection and correction in children. *Journal of Experimental Child Psychology, 142,* 36–47. doi:10.1016/j.jecp.2015.09.008

Harrist, A. W., Swindle, T. M., Hubbs-Tait, L., Topham, G. L., Shriver, L. H., & Page, M. C. (2016). The social and emotional lives of overweight, obese, and severely obese children. *Child Development, 87,* 1564–1580. doi:10.1111/cdev.12548

Hawk, L. W., Fosco, W. D., Colder, C. R., Waxmonsky, J. G., Pelham, W. E., & Rosch, K. S. (2018). How do stimulant treatments for ADHD work? Evidence for mediation by improved cognition. *Journal of Child Psychology and Psychiatry.* Advance online publication. doi:10.1111/jcpp.12917

Heath, S. B. (1989). Oral and literate tradition among black Americans living in poverty. *American Psychologist, 44,* 367–373.

Heikura, U., Taanila, A., Hartikainen, A. L., Olsen, P., Linna, S. L., von Wendt, L., & Järvelin, M. R. (2008). Variations in prenatal sociodemographic factors associated with intellectual disability: A study of the 20-year interval between two birth cohorts in northern Finland. *American Journal of Epidemiology, 167,* 169–177. doi:10.1093/aje/kwm291

Helms, J. E. (1992). Why is there no study of cultural equivalence in standardized cognitive ability testing? *American Psychologist, 47,* 1083–1101.

Helwig, C. C., & Prencipe, A. (1999). Children's judgments of flags and flag-burning. *Child Development, 70,* 132–143.

Hindman, A. H., & Wasik, B. A. (2015). Building vocabulary in two languages: An examination of Spanish-speaking dual language learners in Head Start. *Early Childhood Research Quarterly, 31,* 19–33. doi:10.1016/j.ecresq.2014.12.006

Hinshaw, S. P. (2018). Attention deficit hyperactivity disorder (ADHD): Controversy, developmental mechanisms, and multiple levels of analysis. *Annual Review of Clinical Psychology, 14,* 291–316. doi:10.1146/annurev-clinpsy-050817-084917

Hitch, G. J., Towse, J. N., & Hutton, U. (2001). What limits children's working memory span? Theoretical accounts and applications for scholastic development. *Journal of Experimental Psychology: General, 130,* 184–198.

Hoddinott, J., Alderman, H., Behrman, J. R., Haddad, L., & Horton, S. (2013). The economic rationale for investing in stunting reduction. *Maternal & Child Nutrition, 9*(Suppl. 2), 69–82. doi:10.1111/mcn.12080

Hoff, E. (2015). *Language development. Developmental science: An advanced textbook* (5th ed.). New York, NY: Cengage Learning.

Hoff, E., & Core, C. (2015). What clinicians need to know about bilingual development. *Seminars in Speech and Language, 36,* 89–99. doi:10.1055/s-0035-1549104

Hoff, E., Rumiche, R., Burridge, A., Ribot, K. M., & Welsh, S. N. (2014). Expressive vocabulary development in children from bilingual and monolingual homes: A longitudinal study from two to four years. *Early Childhood Research Quarterly, 29,* 433–444. doi:10.1016/j.ecresq.2014.04.012

Hong, G., & Yu, B. (2007). Early-grade retention and children's reading and math learning in elementary years. *Educational Evaluation and Policy Analysis, 29,* 239–261.

Horning, M. L., Schow, R., Friend, S. E., Loth, K., Neumark-Sztainer, D., & Fulkerson, J. A. (2017). Family dinner frequency interacts with dinnertime context in associations with child and parent BMI outcomes. *Journal of Family Psychology, 31,* 945–951. doi:10.1037/fam0000330

Houdé, O., Pineau, A., Leroux, G., Poirel, N., Perchey, G., Lanoë, C., . . . Mazoyer, B. (2011). Functional magnetic resonance imaging study of Piaget's conservation-of-number task in preschool and school-age children: A neo-Piagetian approach. *Journal of Experimental Child Psychology, 110,* 332–346. doi:10.1016/j.jecp.2011.04.008

Hughes, J. N., Cao, Q., West, S. G., Allee Smith, P., & Cerda, C. (2017). Effect of retention in elementary grades on dropping out of school early. *Journal of School Psychology, 65,* 11–27. doi:10.1016/J.JSP.2017.06.003

Huttenlocher, J., Levine, S., & Vevea, J. (1998). Environmental input and cognitive growth: A study using time-period comparisons. *Child Development, 69,* 1012–1029.

Huynh, H. T., Demeter, N. E., Burke, R. V., & Upperman, J. S. (2017). The role of adult perceptions and supervision behavior in preventing child injury. *Journal of Community Health, 42,* 649–655. doi:10.1007/s10900-016-0300-9

Inhelder, B., & Piaget, J. (1964). *The early growth of logic in the child: Classification and seriation.* New York, NY: Harper & Row.

Jacob, B. A. (2016). *The wisdom of mandatory grade retention.* Retrieved from https://www.brookings.edu/research/the-wisdom-of-mandatory-grade-retention/

Jambon, M., & Smetana, J. G. (2014). Moral complexity in middle childhood: Children's evaluations of necessary harm. *Developmental Psychology, 50,* 22–33. doi:10.1037/a0032992

Janssen, I., Katzmarzyk, P. T., Boyce, W. F., Vereecken, C., Mulvihill, C., Roberts, C., . . . Health Behaviour in School-Aged Children Obesity Working Group. (2005). Comparison of overweight and obesity prevalence in school-aged youth from 34 countries and their relationships with physical activity and dietary patterns. *Obesity Reviews, 6*, 123–132.

Jia, G., & Aaronson, D. (2003). A longitudinal study of Chinese children and adolescents learning English in the United States. *Applied Psycholinguistics, 24*, 131–161. doi:10.1017/S0142716403000079

Jimerson, S. R., & Renshaw, T. L. (2012). Retention and social promotion: Principal leadership. *Retention and Social Promotion. Principal Leadership, 13*, 12–16.

Jonsson, B., Wiklund-Hörnqvist, C., Nyroos, M., & Börjesson, A. (2014). Self-reported memory strategies and their relationship to immediate and delayed text recall and working memory capacity. *Education Inquiry, 5*, 22850. doi:10.3402/edui.v5.22850

Junaid, K. A., & Fellowes, S. (2006). Gender differences in the attainment of motor skills on the movement assessment battery for children. *Physical & Occupational Therapy in Pediatrics, 26*, 5–11.

Jung, W. H., Prehn, K., Fang, Z., Korczykowski, M., Kable, J. W., Rao, H., & Robertson, D. C. (2016). Moral competence and brain connectivity: A resting-state fMRI study. *NeuroImage, 141*, 408–415. doi:10.1016/j.neuroimage.2016.07.045

Kann, L., Kinchen, S., Shanklin, S. L., Flint, K. H., Kawkins, J., Harris, W. A., . . . Centers for Disease Control and Prevention (CDC). (2014). Youth risk behavior surveillance—United States, 2013. *Morbidity and Mortality Weekly Report, 63*(Suppl. 4), 1–168. Retrieved from http://www.ncbi.nlm.nih.gov/pubmed/24918634

Kantomaa, M. T., Stamatakis, E., Kankaanpää, A., Kaakinen, M., Rodriguez, A., Taanila, A., . . . Tammelin, T. (2013). Physical activity and obesity mediate the association between childhood motor function and adolescents' academic achievement. *Proceedings of the National Academy of Sciences of the United States of America, 110*, 1917–1922. doi:10.1073/pnas.1214574110

Katz, A. M. (2017). Psycholinguistic approaches to metaphor acquisition and use. In E. Semino & Z. Demjén (Eds.), *The Routledge handbook of metaphor and language*. New York, NY: Routledge.

Kaufman, J. C., Kaufman, S. B., & Plucker., J. A. (2013). Contemporary theories of intelligence. In D. Reisberg (Ed.), *Oxford handbook of cognitive psychology* (pp. 811–822). Oxford, UK: Oxford University Press.

Kaufmann, L., Mazzocco, M. M., Dowker, A., von Aster, M., Göbel, S. M., Grabner, R. H., . . . Nuerk, H.-C. (2013). Dyscalculia from a developmental and differential perspective. *Frontiers in Psychology, 4*, 516. doi:10.3389/fpsyg.2013.00516

Kendrick, D., Barlow, J., Hampshire, A., Stewart-Brown, S., & Polnay, L. (2008). Parenting interventions and the prevention of unintentional injuries in childhood: Systematic review and meta-analysis. *Child: Care, Health and Development, 34*, 682–695. doi:10.1111/j.1365-2214.2008.00849.x

Kharitonova, M., Winter, W., & Sheridan, M. A. (2015). As working memory grows: A developmental account of neural bases of working memory capacity in 5- to 8-year old children and adults. *Journal of Cognitive Neuroscience, 27*, 1775–1788. doi:10.1162/jocn_a_00824

Killen, M., & Smetana, J. G. (2015). Origins and development of morality. In M. Lamb (Ed.), *Handbook of child psychology and developmental science* (pp. 701–749). Hoboken, NJ: John Wiley. doi:10.1002/9781118963418.childpsy317

Kitsao-Wekulo, P. K., Holding, P., Taylor, H. G., Abubakar, A., Kvalsvig, J., & Connolly, K. (2013). Nutrition as an important mediator of the impact of background variables on outcome in middle childhood. *Frontiers in Human Neuroscience, 7*, 713. doi:10.3389/fnhum.2013.00713

Kohlberg, L. (1976). Moral stages and moralization: The cognitive developmental approach. In T. Lickona (Ed.), *Moral development and moral behavior: Theory, research, and social issues* (pp. 31–53). New York, NY: Holt, Rinehart & Winston.

Kohnert, K. J., and Bates, E. (2002). Balancing bilinguals II. *Journal of Speech Language and Hearing Research, 45*, 347. doi:10.1044/1092-4388(2002/027)

Kucian, K., & von Aster, M. (2015). Developmental dyscalculia. *European Journal of Pediatrics, 174*, 1–13. doi:10.1007/s00431-014-2455-7

Kumar, S., & Kelly, A. S. (2017). Review of childhood obesity: From epidemiology, etiology, and comorbidities to clinical assessment and treatment. *Mayo Clinic Proceedings, 92*, 251–265. doi:10.1016/j.mayocp.2016.09.017

Lange, H., Buse, J., Bender, S., Siegert, J., Knopf, H., & Roessner, V. (2016). Accident proneness in children and adolescents affected by ADHD and the impact of medication. *Journal of Attention Disorders, 20*, 501–509. doi:10.1177/1087054713518237

Laukkanen, A., Pesola, A., Havu, M., Sääkslahti, A., & Finni, T. (2014). Relationship between habitual physical activity and gross motor skills is multifaceted in 5- to 8-year-old children. *Scandinavian Journal of Medicine & Science in Sports, 24*, e102–e110. doi:10.1111/sms.12116

Leather, C. V., & Henry, L. A. (1994). Working memory span and phonological awareness tasks as predictors of early reading ability. *Journal of Experimental Child Psychology, 58*, 88–111.

Legare, C. H., Evans, E. M., Rosengren, K. S., & Harris, P. L. (2012). The coexistence of natural and supernatural explanations across cultures and development. *Child Development, 83*, 779–793. doi:10.1111/j.1467-8624.2012.01743.x

Legare, C. H., & Gelman, S. A. (2008). Bewitchment, biology, or both: The co-existence of natural and supernatural explanatory frameworks across development. *Cognitive Science, 32*, 607–642. Retrieved from 10.1080/03640210802066766

Lerkkanen, M. K., Kiuru, N., Pakarinen, E., Poikkeus, A. M., Rasku-Puttonen, H., Siekkinen, M., & Nurmi, J. E. (2016). Child-centered versus teacher-directed teaching practices: Associations with the development of academic skills in the first grade at school. *Early Childhood Research Quarterly, 36*, 145–156. doi:10.1016/j.ecresq.2015.12.023

Lewis, R. B., Wheeler, J. J., & Carter, S. L. (2017). *Teaching students with special needs in general education classrooms*. Boston, MA: Pearson.

Lobstein, T., Jackson-Leach, R., Moodie, M. L., Hall, K. D., Gortmaker, S. L., Swinburn, B. A., . . . McPherson, K. (2015). Child and adolescent obesity: Part of a bigger picture. *Lancet, 385*, 2510–2520. doi:10.1016/S0140-6736(14)61746-3

Lonigan, C. J. (2015). Literacy development. In L. S. Liben & U. Muller (Eds.), *Handbook of child psychology and developmental science* (pp. 763–804). Hoboken, NJ: John Wiley. doi:10.1002/9781118963418.childpsy218

Luo, Q., Nakic, M., Wheatley, T., Richell, R., Martin, A., & Blair, R. J. R. (2006). The neural basis of implicit moral attitude-An IAT study using event-related fMRI. *NeuroImage, 30*, 1449–1457. doi:10.1016/j.neuroimage.2005.11.005

Lynn, R. (2013). Who discovered the Flynn effect? A review of early studies of the secular increase of intelligence. *Intelligence, 41*, 765–769. doi:10.1016/j.intell.2013.03.008

Mackintosh, N. J. (2011). *IQ and human intelligence.* (2nd ed.). Oxford, UK: Oxford University Press.

MacWhinney, B. (2015). Language development. In L. S. Liben & U. Muller (Eds.), *Handbook of child psychology and developmental science* (pp. 296–338). Hoboken, NJ: John Wiley. doi:10.1002/9781118963418.childpsy208

Maldonado-Carreño, C., & Votruba-Drzal, E. (2011). Teacher-child relationships and the development of academic and behavioral skills during elementary school: A within- and between-child analysis. *Child Development, 82*, 601–616. doi:10.1111/j.1467-8624.2010.01533.x

Malti, T., & Latzko, B. (2010). Children's moral emotions and moral cognition: Towards an integrative perspective. *New Directions for Child & Adolescent Development, 2010*, 1–10. doi:10.1002/cd.272

Manoach, D. S., Schlaug, G., Siewert, B., Darby, D. G., Bly, B. M., Benfield, A., Edelman, R. R., & Warach, S. (1997). Prefrontal cortex fMRI signal changes are correlated with working memory load. *NeuroReport, 8*, 545–549.

Masi, A., DeMayo, M. M., Glozier, N., & Guastella, A. J. (2017). An overview of autism spectrum disorder, heterogeneity and treatment options. *Neuroscience Bulletin, 33*, 183–193. doi:10.1007/s12264-017-0100-y

Mastropieri, M. A., & Scruggs, T. E. (2017). *The inclusive classroom: Strategies for effective differentiated instruction*. Boston, MA: Pearson.

McCabe, M. P., Connaughton, C., Tatangelo, G., Mellor, D., & Busija, L. (2017). Healthy me: A gender-specific program to address body image concerns and risk factors among preadolescents. *Body Image, 20*, 20–30. doi:10.1016/J.BODYIM.2016.10.007

McClure, R., Kegler, S., Davey, T., & Clay, F. (2015). Contextual determinants of childhood injury: A systematic review of studies with multilevel analytic methods. *American Journal of Public Health, 105,* e37–e43. doi:10.2105/AJPH.2015.302883

McDonell, J. R. (2014). Neighborhood characteristics and children's safety. In A. C. Michalos (Ed.), *Encyclopedia of quality of life and well-being research* (pp. 4314–4318). Dordrecht, The Netherlands: Springer Netherlands. doi:10.1007/978-94-007-0753-5_3773

McKenzie, K., Milton, M., Smith, G., & Ouellette-Kuntz, H. (2016). Systematic review of the prevalence and incidence of intellectual disabilities: Current trends and issues. *Current Developmental Disorders Reports, 3,* 104–115. doi:10.1007/s40474-016-0085-7

McVey, G. L., Levine, M., Piran, N., & Ferguson, H. B. (2013). *Preventing eating-related and weight-related disorders: Collaborative research, advocacy, and policy change.* Ontario, Canada: Wilfrid Laurier University Press.

Menon, V. (2016). Working memory in children's math learning and its disruption in dyscalculia. *Current Opinion in Behavioral Sciences, 10,* 125–132. doi:10.1016/j.cobeha.2016.05.014

Michael, S. L., Wentzel, K., Elliott, M. N., Dittus, P. J., Kanouse, D. E., Wallander, J. L., . . . Schuster, M. A. (2014). Parental and peer factors associated with body image discrepancy among fifth-grade boys and girls. *Journal of Youth and Adolescence, 43,* 15–29. doi:10.1007/s10964-012-9899-8

Miller, S., McCulloch, S., & Jarrold, C. (2015). The development of memory maintenance strategies: Training cumulative rehearsal and interactive imagery in children aged between 5 and 9. *Frontiers in Psychology, 6,* 524. doi:10.3389/fpsyg.2015.00524

Mitchell, J. A., Rodriguez, D., Schmitz, K. H., & Audrain-McGovern, J. (2013). Greater screen time is associated with adolescent obesity: A longitudinal study of the BMI distribution from ages 14 to 18. *Obesity (Silver Spring, Md.), 21,* 572–575. doi:10.1002/oby.20157

Modabbernia, A., Velthorst, E., & Reichenberg, A. (2017). Environmental risk factors for autism: An evidence-based review of systematic reviews and meta-analyses. *Molecular Autism, 8,* 13. doi:10.1186/s13229-017-0121-4

Morey, C. C., Mareva, S., Lelonkiewicz, J. R., & Chevalier, N. (2018). Gaze-based rehearsal in children under 7: A developmental investigation of eye movements during a serial spatial memory task. *Developmental Science, 21,* e12559. doi:10.1111/desc.12559

Mouratidi, P. S., Bonoti, F., & Leondari, A. (2016). Children's perceptions of illness and health: An analysis of drawings. *Health Education Journal, 75,* 434–447. doi:10.1177/0017896915599416

Mpofu, E., & Vijver, F. J. R. van de. (2000). Taxonomic structure in early to middle childhood: A longitudinal study with Zimbabwean schoolchildren. *International Journal of Behavioral Development, 24,* 204–212.

Murdock, G. P. (1980). *Theories of illness: A world survey.* Retrieved from https://repository.library.georgetown.edu/handle/10822/785785

Myant, K. A., & Williams, J. M. (2005). Children's concepts of health and illness: Understanding of contagious illnesses, non-contagious illnesses and injuries. *Journal of Health Psychology, 10,* 805–819.

National Association of School Psychologists. (2003). *Position statement on student grade retention and social promotion.* Retrieved from http://www.nasponline.org/about_nasp/pospaper_graderetent.aspx

National Center for Education Statistics. (2017a). *2015 mathematics and reading assessments.* Retrieved from https://www.nationsreportcard.gov/reading_math_2015/

National Center for Education Statistics. (2017b). *Status and trends in the education of racial and ethnic groups.* Retrieved February 12, 2018, from https://nces.ed.gov/programs/raceindicators/index.asp

Neisser, U., Boodoo, G., Bouchard Jr., T. J., Boykin, A. W., Brody, N., Ceci, S. J., . . . Sternberg, R. J. (1996). Intelligence: Knowns and unknowns. *American Psychologist, 51,* 77–101.

Ninio, A. (2014). Pragmatic development. In P. J. Brooks & V. Kempe (Eds.), *Encyclopedia of language development.* Thousand Oaks, CA: Sage. doi:10.4135/9781483346441.n153

Nisbett, R. E., Aronson, J., Blair, C., Dickens, W., Flynn, J., Halpern, D. F., & Turkheimer, E. (2013). Intelligence: New findings and theoretical developments. *American Psychologist, 67,* 130–159. doi:10.1037/a0026699

O'Dea, J. A., & Yager, Z. (2011). School-based psychoeducational approaches to prevention. In I. T. F. Cash & L. Smolak (Eds.), *Body image: A handbook of science, practice, and prevention* (pp. 434–441). New York, NY: Guilford.

Ogden, C. L., Carroll, M. D., Fryar, C. D., & Flegal, K. M. (2015). *Prevalence of obesity among adults and youth: United States, 2011–2014. NCHS Data Brief* (Vol. 219). Retrieved from https://www.cdc.gov/nchs/data/databriefs/db219.pdf

Okagaki, L., & Sternberg, R. J. (1993). Parental beliefs and children's school performance. *Child Development, 64,* 36–56.

Owens, R. E. (2016). *Language development: An introduction.* Boston, MA: Pearson.

Peng, P., Barnes, M., Wang, C., Wang, W., Li, S., Swanson, H. L., . . . Tao, S. (2018). A meta-analysis on the relation between reading and working memory. *Psychological Bulletin, 144,* 48–76. doi:10.1037/bul0000124

Perlman, S. B., Huppert, T. J., & Luna, B. (2016). Functional near-infrared spectroscopy evidence for development of prefrontal engagement in working memory in early through middle childhood. *Cerebral Cortex, 26,* 2790–2799. doi:10.1093/cercor/bhv139

Perone, S., Almy, B., & Zelazo, P. D. (2018). Toward an understanding of the neural basis of executive function development. In R. Gibb & B. Kolb (Eds.), *The neurobiology of brain and behavioral development* (pp. 291–314). New York, NY: Elsevier. doi:10.1016/B978-0-12-804036-2.00011-X

Peterson, R. L., & Pennington, B. F. (2012). Developmental dyslexia. *Lancet, 379,* 1997–2007. doi:10.1016/S0140-6736(12)60198-6

Pexman, P. M. (2014). Nonliteral language use. In P. J. Brooks & V. Kempe (Eds.), *Encyclopedia of language development.* Thousand Oaks, CA: Sage. doi:10.4135/9781483346441.n132

Piaget, J. (1932). *The moral judgment of the child.* New York, NY: Harcourt Brace.

Piek, J. P., Dawson, L., Smith, L. M., & Gasson, N. (2008). The role of early fine and gross motor development on later motor and cognitive ability. *Human Movement Science, 27,* 668–681.

Plomin, R., & Deary, I. J. (2015). Genetics and intelligence differences: Five special findings. *Molecular Psychiatry, 20,* 98–108. doi:10.1038/mp.2014.105

Plomin, R., DeFries, J. C., Knopik, V. S., & Neiderhiser, J. M. (2016). Top 10 replicated findings from behavioral genetics. *Perspectives on Psychological Science, 11,* 3–23. doi:10.1177/1745691615617439

Poirel, N., Borst, G. G., Simon, G., Rossi, S., Cassotti, M., Pineau, A., . . . Jouvent, R. (2012). Number conservation is related to children's prefrontal inhibitory control: An fMRI study of a Piagetian task. *PLoS ONE, 7,* e40802. doi:10.1371/journal.pone.0040802

Prehn, K., Wartenburger, I., Mériau, K., Scheibe, C., Goodenough, O. R., Villringer, A., . . . Heekeren, H. R. (2008). Individual differences in moral judgment competence influence neural correlates of socio-normative judgments. *Social Cognitive and Affective Neuroscience, 3,* 33–46. doi:10.1093/scan/nsm037

Pulgarón, E. R. (2013). Childhood obesity: A review of increased risk for physical and psychological comorbidities. *Clinical Therapeutics, 35,* A18–A32. doi:10.1016/j.clinthera.2012.12.014

Quek, Y. H., Tam, W. W. S., Zhang, M. W. B., & Ho, R. C. M. (2017). Exploring the association between childhood and adolescent obesity and depression: A meta-analysis. *Obesity Reviews, 18,* 742–754. doi:10.1111/obr.12535

Ramus, F. (2014). Neuroimaging sheds new light on the phonological deficit in dyslexia. *Trends in Cognitive Sciences, 18,* 274–275. doi:10.1016/j.tics.2014.01.009

Rapin, I. (2016). Dyscalculia and the calculating brain. *Pediatric Neurology, 61,* 11–20. doi:10.1016/j.pediatrneurol.2016.02.007

Reilly, J. J. (2007). Childhood obesity: An overview. *Children & Society, 21,* 390–396.

Relji, G., Ferring, D., & Martin, R. (2015). A meta-analysis on the effectiveness of bilingual programs in Europe. *Review of Educational Research, 85,* 92–128. doi:10.3102/0034654314548514

Richardson, S. M., Paxton, S. J., & Thomson, J. S. (2009). Is BodyThink an efficacious body image and self-esteem program? A controlled evaluation with adolescents. *Body Image, 6,* 75–82. doi:10.1016/j.bodyim.2008.11.001

Rideout, V. J. (2013). *Zero to eight: Children's media use in America 2013.* Retrieved from https://www.commonsensemedia.org/research/zero-to-eight-childrens-media-use-in-america-2013

Rindermann, H., & Thompson, J. (2013). Ability rise in NAEP and narrowing ethnic gaps? *Intelligence, 41,* 821–831. doi:10.1016/j.intell.2013.06.016

Ristic, J., & Enns, J. T. (2015). The changing face of attentional development. *Current Directions in Psychological Science, 24,* 24–31. doi:10.1177/0963721414551165

Robbins, E., Starr, S., & Rochat, P. (2016). Fairness and distributive justice by 3- to 5-year-old Tibetan children. *Journal of Cross-Cultural Psychology, 47,* 333–340. doi:10.1177/0022022115620487

Roberts, G., Quach, J., Mensah, F., Gathercole, S., Gold, L., Anderson, P., . . . Wake, M. (2015). Schooling duration rather than chronological age predicts working memory between 6 and 7 years. *Journal of Developmental & Behavioral Pediatrics, 36,* 68–74. doi:10.1097/DBP.0000000000000121

Rochat, P., Dias, M. D. G., Guo Liping, G., Broesch, T., Passos-Ferreira, C., Winning, A., & Berg, B. (2009). Fairness in distributive justice by 3- and 5-year-olds across seven cultures. *Journal of Cross-Cultural Psychology, 40,* 416–442. doi:10.1177/0022022109332844

Rogoff, B., & Chavajay, P. (1995). What's become of research on the cultural basis of cognitive development? *American Psychologist, 50,* 859–877.

Rogoff, B., & Waddell, K. J. (1982). Memory for information organized in a scene by children from two cultures. *Child Development, 53,* 1224–1228.

Runions, K. C., Vitaro, F., Cross, D., Shaw, T., Hall, M., & Boivin, M. (2014). Teacher–child relationship, parenting, and growth in likelihood and severity of physical aggression in the early school years. *Merrill-Palmer Quarterly, 60,* 274–301.

Ruzgis, P., & Grigorenko, E. L. (1994). Cultural meaning systems, intelligence, and personality. In R. J. Sternberg & P. Ruzgis (Eds.), *Personality and intelligence* (pp. 248–270). New York, NY: Cambridge University Press.

Safe Kids Worldwide. (2015). *Overview of childhood injury morbidity and mortality in the U.S.* Retrieved from https://www.safekids.org/sites/default/files/documents/skw_overview_fact_sheet_november_2014.pdf

Salend, S. J. (2015). *Creating inclusive classrooms: Enhanced effective, differentiated and reflective practices.* Boston, MA: Pearson.

Sandin, S., Lichtenstein, P., Kuja-Halkola, R., Hultman, C., Larsson, H., & Reichenberg, A. (2017). The heritability of autism spectrum disorder. *JAMA, 318,* 1182–1184. doi:10.1001/jama.2017.12141

Sattler, J. M. (2014). *Foundations of behavioral, social and clinical assessment of children.* La Mesa, CA: Jerome M. Sattler.

Schachar, R. (2014). Genetics of attention deficit hyperactivity disorder (ADHD): Recent updates and future prospects. *Current Developmental Disorders Reports, 1,* 41–49. doi:10.1007/s40474-013-0004-0

Schalock, R. L. (2015). Intellectual disability. In R. L. Cautin & S. O. Lilienfeld (Eds.), *The encyclopedia of clinical psychology* (pp. 1–7). Hoboken, NJ: John Wiley. doi:10.1002/9781118625392.wbecp062

Schneider, W., & Bjorklund, D. F. (1992). Expertise, aptitude, and strategic remembering. *Child Development, 63,* 461–473. doi:10.1111/j.1467-8624.1992.tb01640.x

Schneider, W., & Ornstein, P. A. (2015). The development of children's memory. *Child Development Perspectives, 9,* 190–195. doi:10.1111/cdep.12129

Schneider, W., & Pressley, M. (2013). *Memory development between two and twenty* (3rd ed.). Mahwah, NJ: Erlbaum.

Schurz, M., Wimmer, H., Richlan, F., Ludersdorfer, P., Klackl, J., & Kronbichler, M. (2015). Resting-state and task-based functional brain connectivity in developmental dyslexia. *Cerebral Cortex, 25,* 3502–3514. doi:10.1093/cercor/bhu184

Schwerdt, G., West, M. R., & Winters, M. A. (2017). The effects of test-based retention on student outcomes over time: Regression discontinuity evidence from Florida. *Journal of Public Economics, 152,* 154–169. doi:10.1016/J.JPUBECO.2017.06.004

Senbanjo, I. O., Oshikoya, K. A., Odusanya, O. O., & Njokanma, O. F. (2011). Prevalence of and risk factors for stunting among school children and adolescents in Abeokuta, southwest Nigeria. *Journal of Health, Population, and Nutrition, 29,* 364–370.

Serpell, R. (1974). Aspects of intelligence in a developing country. *African Social Research, 17,* 578–596.

Serpell, R., & Jere-Folotiya, J. (2008). Developmental assessment, cultural context, gender, and schooling in Zambia. *International Journal of Psychology, 43,* 88–96.

Shea, S. E. (2012). Intellectual disability (mental retardation). *Pediatrics in Review, 33,* 110–121. doi:10.1542/pir.33-3-110

Shearer, C. B., & Karanian, J. M. (2017). The neuroscience of intelligence: Empirical support for the theory of multiple intelligences? *Trends in Neuroscience and Education, 6,* 211–223. doi:10.1016/J.TINE.2017.02.002

Siegel, L. S. (1994). Working memory and reading: A life-span perspective. *International Journal of Behavioural Development, 17,* 109–124.

Simard, D., & Gutiérrez, X. (2018). The study of metalinguistic constructs in second language acquisition research. In P. Garrett & J. M. Cots (Eds.), *The Routledge handbook of language awareness.* Retrieved from https://www.routledge.com/The-Routledge-Handbook-of-Language-Awareness/Garrett-Cots/p/book/9781138937048

Simmonds, M., Llewellyn, A., Owen, C. G., & Woolacott, N. (2016). Predicting adult obesity from childhood obesity: a systematic review and meta-analysis. *Obesity Reviews, 17,* 95–107. https://doi.org/10.1111/obr.12334

Slater, A., & Tiggemann, M. (2016). Little girls in a grown up world: Exposure to sexualized media, internalization of sexualization messages, and body image in 6–9 year-old girls. *Body Image, 18,* 19–22.

Smetana, J. G., Jambon, M., & Ball, C. (2014). The social domain approach to children's moral and social judgments. In M. Killen & J. G. Smetana (Eds.), *Handbook of moral development* (pp. 23–45). New York, NY: Psychology Press. doi:10.4324/9780203581957

Smith, C. E., & Warneken, F. (2016). Children's reasoning about distributive and retributive justice across development. *Developmental Psychology, 52,* 613–628. doi:10.1037/a0040069

Smolak, L. (2011). Body image development in childhood. In T. F. Cash & L. Smolak (Eds.), *Body image: A handbook of science, practice, and prevention* (pp. 67–75). New York, NY: Guilford.

Snowling, M. J. (2013). Early identification and interventions for dyslexia: A contemporary view. *Journal of Research in Special Educational Needs, 13,* 7–14. doi:10.1111/j.1471-3802.2012.01262.x

Spilt, J. L., Hughes, J. N., Wu, J. Y., & Kwok, O. M. (2012). Dynamics of teacher–student relationships: Stability and change across elementary school and the influence on children's academic success. *Child Development, 83,* 1180–1195. doi:10.1111/j.1467-8624.2012.01761.x

Srour, M., & Shevell, M. (2014). Genetics and the investigation of developmental delay/intellectual disability. *Archives of Disease in Childhood, 99,* 386–389. doi:10.1136/archdischild-2013-304063

Sternberg, R. J. (1985). *Beyond IQ: A triarchic theory of human intelligence.* Cambridge, England: Cambridge University Press.

Sternberg, R. J. (2011). The theory of successful intelligence. In R. J. Sternberg & S. B. Kaufman (Eds.), *The Cambridge handbook of intelligence* (pp. 504–527). Cambridge, UK: Cambridge University Press.

Sternberg, R. J. (2014). The development of adaptive competence: Why cultural psychology is necessary and not just nice. *Developmental Review, 34,* 208–224. doi:10.1016/j.dr.2014.05.004

Sternberg, R. J., & Grigorenko, E. L. (2008). Ability testing across cultures. In L. A. Suzuki & J. G. Ponterotto (Eds.), *Handbook of multicultural assessment: Clinical, psychological, and educational applications* (pp. 449–470). San Francisco, CA: Jossey-Bass.

Sternberg, R. J., Grigorenko, E. L., & Bundy, D. A. (2001). The predictive value of IQ. *Merrill-Palmer Quarterly, 47,* 1–41.

Stone, M. M., Blumberg, F. C., Blair, C., & Cancelli, A. A. (2016). The "EF" in deficiency: Examining the linkages between executive function and the utilization deficiency observed in preschoolers. *Journal of Experimental Child Psychology, 152,* 367–375. doi:10.1016/j.jecp.2016.07.003

Subrahmanyam, K., & Greenfield, P. M. (1996). Effect of video game practice on spatial skills in girls and boys. In P. M. Greenfield & R. R. Cocking (Eds.), *Interacting with video* (pp. 95–114). Norwood, NJ: Ablex.

Super, C. M., & Harkness, S. (1982). The infant's niche in rural Kenya and metropolitan America. In L. L. Adler (Ed.), *Cross-cultural research at issue* (pp. 247–255). New York, NY: Academic Press.

Tarver, J., Daley, D., & Sayal, K. (2014). Attention-deficit hyperactivity disorder (ADHD): An updated review of the essential facts. *Child: Care, Health and Development, 40,* 762–774. doi:10.1111/cch.12139

te Nijenhuis, J. (2013). The Flynn effect, group differences, and g loadings. *Personality and Individual Differences, 55,* 224–228. doi:10.1016/j.paid.2011.12.023

Thapar, A., Cooper, M., Eyre, O., & Langley, K. (2013). What have we learnt about the causes of ADHD? *Journal of Child Psychology and Psychiatry, and Allied Disciplines, 54,* 3–16. doi:10.1111/j.1469-7610.2012.02611.x

Thornberg, R., Thornberg, U. B., Alamaa, R., & Daud, N. (2016). Children's conceptions of bullying and repeated conventional transgressions: Moral, conventional, structuring and personal-choice reasoning. *Educational Psychology, 36,* 95–111. doi:10.1080/01443410.2014.915929

Tiemeier, H., Lenroot, R. K., Greenstein, D. K., Tran, L., Pierson, R., & Giedd, J. N. (2010). Cerebellum development during childhood and adolescence: A longitudinal morphometric MRI study. *NeuroImage, 49,* 63–70. doi:10.1016/j.neuroimage.2009.08.016

Tsujimoto, S., Kuwajima, M., & Sawaguchi, T. (2007). Developmental fractionation of working memory and response inhibition during childhood. *Experimental Psychology, 54,* 30–37.

Turiel, E., & Nucci, L. (2017). Moral development in context. In A. Dick & U. Muller (Eds.), *Advancing developmental science: Philosophy, theory, and method* (pp. 107–121). New York, NY: Routledge.

Turnbull, K., & Justice, L. M. (2016). *Language development from theory to practice.* Boston, MA: Pearson.

U.S. Bureau of the Census. (2015). *Census bureau reports at least 350 languages spoken in U.S. homes.* Retrieved from https://www.census.gov/newsroom/press-releases/2015/cb15-185.html

Van Craeyevelt, S., Verschueren, K., Vancraeyveldt, C., Wouters, S., & Colpin, H. (2017). The role of preschool teacher-child interactions in academic adjustment: An intervention study with Playing-2-gether. *British Journal of Educational Psychology, 87,* 345–364. doi:10.1111/bjep.12153

Vaughn, S., & Klingner, J. K. (1998). Students' perceptions of inclusion and resource room settings. *Journal of Special Education, 32,* 79–88.

Visser, S. N., Danielson, M. L., Bitsko, R. H., Holbrook, J. R., Kogan, M. D., Ghandour, R. M., . . . Blumberg, S. J. (2014). Trends in the parent-report of health care provider-diagnosed and medicated attention-deficit/hyperactivity disorder: United States, 2003-2011. *Journal of the American Academy of Child and Adolescent Psychiatry, 53,* 34–46. e2. doi:10.1016/j.jaac.2013.09.001

Wang, Y., & Lim, H. (2012). The global childhood obesity epidemic and the association between socio-economic status and childhood obesity. *International Review of Psychiatry (Abingdon, England), 24,* 176–188. doi:10.3109/09540261.2012.688195

Wang, Y., Zhang, Y., Liu, L., Cui, J., Wang, J., Shum, D. H. K., . . . Chan, R. C. K. (2017). A meta-analysis of working memory impairments in autism spectrum disorders. *Neuropsychology Review, 27,* 46–61. doi:10.1007/s11065-016-9336-y

Warren, J. R., & Saliba, J. (2012). First through eighth grade retention rates for all 50 states: A new method and initial results.

Educational Researcher, 41, 320–329. doi:10.3102/0013189X12457813

Watson-Jones, R. E., Busch, J. T. A., & Legare, C. H. (2015). Interdisciplinary and cross-cultural perspectives on explanatory coexistence. *Topics in Cognitive Science, 7,* 611–623. doi:10.1111/tops.12162

Watson, S. M. R., & Gable, R. A. (2013). Unraveling the complex nature of mathematics learning disability: Implications for research and practice. *Learning Disability Quarterly, 36,* 178–187. doi:10.1177/0731948712461489

Wechsler, D. (1944). *The measurement of adult intelligence* (3rd ed.). Baltimore, MD: Williams & Wilkins.

Wechsler, D. (2014). *Wechsler intelligence scale for children* (5th ed.). San Antonio, TX: NCS Pearson.

White, K. M. (2013). Associations between teacher–child relationships and children's writing in kindergarten and first grade. *Early Childhood Research Quarterly, 28,* 166–176. doi:10.1016/j.ecresq.2012.05.004

Wigfield, A., Gladstone, J. R., & Turci, L. (2016). Beyond cognition: Reading motivation and reading comprehension. *Child Development Perspectives, 10,* 190–195. doi:10.1111/cdep.12184

Williams, N. A., Fournier, J., Coday, M., Richey, P. A., Tylavsky, F. A., & Hare, M. E. (2013). Body esteem, peer difficulties and perceptions of physical health in overweight and obese urban children aged 5 to 7 years. *Child: Care, Health and Development, 39,* 825–834. doi:10.1111/j.1365-2214.2012.01401.x

World Health Organization. (2009). *BMI classification.* Retrieved from http://apps.who.int/bmi/index.jsp? introPage=intro_3.html

Wright, B. C., & Smailes, J. (2015). Factors and processes in children's transitive deductions. *Journal of Cognitive Psychology, 27,* 967–978. doi:10.1080/20445911.2015.1063641

Wu, W., West, S. G., & Hughes, J. N. (2010). Effect of grade retention in first grade on psychosocial outcomes. *Journal of Educational Psychology, 102,* 135–152. doi:10.1037/a0016664

Xu, J., Murphy, S. L., Kochanek, K. D., & Bastian, B. A. (2016). Deaths: Final data for 2013. *National Vital and Statistics Reports, 1, 64.* Retrieved from http://www.cdc.gov/nchs/data/nvsr/nvsr64/nvsr64_02.pdf

Yang, S., & Sternberg, R. J. (1997). Conceptions of intelligence in ancient Chinese philosophy. *Journal of Theoretical and Philosophical Psychology, 17,* 101–119.

Young, L., & Koenigs, M. (2008). Investigating emotion in moral cognition: A review of evidence from functional neuroimaging and neuropsychology. *British Medical Bulletin, 84,* 69–79. doi:10.1093/bmb/ldm031

Zafiropoulou, M., Sotiriou, A., & Mitsiouli, V. (2007). Relation of self-concept in kindergarten and first grade to school adjustment. *Perceptual & Motor Skills, 104,* 1313–1327. Retrieved from 10.2466/PMS.104.4.1313-1327

Zhu, L., Liu, G., & Tardif, T. (2009). Chinese children's explanations for illness. *International Journal of Behavioral Development, 33,* 516–519. doi:10.1177/016502540934374

Chapter 10

Afifi, T. O., & MacMillan, H. L. (2011). Resilience following child maltreatment: A review of protective factors. *La Résilience Après La Maltraitance Clans L'enfance: Une Revue Des Facteurs Protecteurs, 56,* 266–272.

Alaggia, R., Collin-Vézina, D., & Lateef, R. (2018). Facilitators and barriers to child sexual abuse (CSA) disclosures. *Trauma, Violence, & Abuse.* Advance online publication. doi:10.1177/1524838017697312

Amato, P. R. (2010). Research on divorce: Continuing trends and new developments. *Journal of Marriage & Family, 72,* 650–666. doi:10.1111/j.1741-3737.2010.00723.x

Amato, P. R., & Anthony, C. J. (2014). Estimating the effects of parental divorce and death with fixed effects models. *Journal of Marriage and Family, 76,* 370–386. doi:10.1111/jomf.12100

Archer, L., DeWitt, J., Osborne, J., Dillon, J., Willis, B., & Wong, B. (2012). Science aspirations, capital, and family habitus: How families shape children's engagement and identification with science. *American Educational Research Journal, 49,* 881–908. doi:10.3102/0002831211433290

Arseneault, L. (2018). Annual research review: The persistent and pervasive impact of being bullied in childhood and adolescence: Implications for policy and practice. *Journal of Child Psychology and Psychiatry, 59,* 405–421. doi:10.1111/jcpp.12841

Bastaits, K., & Mortelmans, D. (2016). Parenting as mediator between post-divorce family structure and children's well-being. *Journal of Child and Family Studies, 25,* 2178–2188. doi:10.1007/s10826-016-0395-8

Bennett, K. M. (2006). Does marital status and marital status change predict physical health in older adults? *Psychological Medicine, 36,* 1313–1320.

Berger, L. M., Font, S. A., Slack, K. S., & Waldfogel, J. (2017). Income and child maltreatment in unmarried families: Evidence from the earned income tax credit. *Review of Economics of the Household, 15,* 1345–1372. doi:10.1007/s11150-016-9346-9

Bierman, K. L., Kalvin, C. B., & Heinrichs, B. S. (2014). Early childhood precursors and adolescent sequelae of grade school peer rejection and victimization. *Journal of Clinical Child and Adolescent Psychology, 44,* 367–379. doi:10.1080/15374416.2013.873983

Bing, N. M., Nelson, W. M., & Wesolowski, K. L. (2009). Comparing the effects of amount of conflict on children's adjustment following parental divorce. *Journal of Divorce & Remarriage, 50,* 159–171. doi:10.1080/10502550902717699

Blakemore, S. J. (2012). Imaging brain development: The adolescent brain. *NeuroImage, 61,* 397–406. doi:10.1016/j.neuroimage.2011.11.080

Blandon, A. Y., Calkins, S. D., Grimm, K. J., Keane, S. P., & O'Brien, M. (2010). Testing a developmental cascade model of emotional and social competence and early peer acceptance. *Development and Psychopathology, 22,* 737–748. doi:10.1017/S0954579410000428

Bos, H. M. W., Knox, J. R., van Rijn-van Gelderen, L., & Gartrell, N. K. (2016). Same-sex and different-sex parent households and child health outcomes. *Journal of Developmental & Behavioral Pediatrics, 37*, 179–187. doi:10.1097/DBP.0000000000000288

Boseovski, J. J. (2010). Evidence for "rose colored glasses": An examination of the positivity bias in young children's personality judgments. *Child Development Perspectives, 4*, 212–218. doi:10.1111/j.1750-8606.2010.00149.x

Boutwell, B. B., Meldrum, R. C., & Petkovsek, M. A. (2017). General intelligence in friendship selection: A study of preadolescent best friend dyads. *Intelligence, 64*, 30–35. doi:10.1016/J.INTELL.2017.07.002

Bowker, J. C., Fredstrom, B. K., Rubin, K. H., Rose-Krasnor, L., Booth-LaForce, C., & Laursen, B. (2010). Distinguishing children who form new best-friendships from those who do not. *Journal of Social and Personal Relationships, 27*, 707–725. doi:10.1177/0265407510373259

Bradley, R. H., & Corwyn, R. F. (2008). Infant temperament, parenting, and externalizing behavior in first grade: A test of the differential susceptibility hypothesis. *Journal of Child Psychology & Psychiatry, 49*, 124–131. doi:10.1111/j.1469-7610.2007.01829.x

Bradley, R. H., Iida, M., Pennar, A., Owen, M. T., & Vandell, D. L. (2017). The dialectics of parenting: Changes in the interplay of maternal behaviors during early and middle childhood. *Journal of Child and Family Studies, 26*, 3214–3225. doi:10.1007/s10826-017-0805-6

Brassard, M. R., & Fiorvanti, C. M. (2015). School-based child abuse prevention programs. *Psychology in the Schools, 52*, 40–60. doi:10.1002/pits.21811

Bratberg, E., & Tjøtta, S. (2008). Income effects of divorce in families with dependent children. *Journal of Population Economics, 21*, 439–461. doi:10.1007/s00148-005-0029-8

Brown, S. L., Manning, W. D., & Stykes, J. B. (2015). Family structure and child well-being: Integrating family complexity. *Journal of Marriage and the Family, 77*, 177–190. doi:10.1111/jomf.12145

Brumariu, L. E. (2015). Parent-child attachment and emotion regulation. *New Directions for Child and Adolescent Development, 2015*, 31–45. doi:10.1002/cad.20098

Brummelman, E. (2018). The emergence of narcissism and self-esteem: A social-cognitive approach. *European Journal of Developmental Psychology.* Advance online publication. doi:10.1080/17405629.2017.1419953

Buckley, C. (2015). China ends one-child policy, allowing families two children. *New York Times.* Retrieved February 25, 2018, from https://www.nytimes.com/2015/10/30/world/asia/china-end-one-child-policy.html

Buist, K. L., & Vermande, M. (2014). Sibling relationship patterns and their associations with child competence and problem behavior. *Journal of Family Psychology, 28*, 529–537. doi:10.1037/a0036990

Burnham, J. J. (2009). Contemporary fears of children and adolescents: Coping and resiliency in the 21st century. *Journal of Counseling & Development, 87*, 28–35.

Burnham, J. J., Lomax, R. G., & Hooper, L. M. (2012). Gender, age, and racial differences in self-reported fears among school-aged youth. *Journal of Child and Family Studies, 22*, 268–278. doi:10.1007/s10826-012-9576-2

Cabeza, R., & Nyberg, L. (2000). Neural bases of learning and memory: Functional neuroimaging evidence. *Current Opinion in Neurology, 13*, 415–421.

Chen, X., Rubin, K. H., & Li, B. (1994). Only children and sibling children in urban China: A re-examination. *International Journal of Behavioral Development, 17*, 413–421.

Child Trends. (2013). *Measures of flourishing.* Retrieved from http://www.childtrends.org/? indicators=measures-of-flourishing#sthash.ODuubJhm.dpuf

Child Trends Databank. (2015). *Family structure.* Retrieved from https://www.childtrends.org/? indicators=family-structure

Cicchetti, D. (2016). Socioemotional, personality, and biological development: Illustrations from a multilevel developmental psychopathology perspective on child maltreatment. *Annual Review of Psychology, 67*, 187–211. doi:10.1146/annurev-psych-122414-033259

Cooley, J. L., & Fite, P. J. (2016). Peer victimization and forms of aggression during middle childhood: The role of emotion regulation. *Journal of Abnormal Child Psychology. 44*, 535–546. doi:10.1007/s10802-015-0051-6

Copen, C. E., Daniels, K., & Mosher, W. D. (2013). First premarital cohabitation in the United States: 2006–2010 National Survey of Family Growth. *National Health Statistics Reports, 64*, 1–15.

Copen, C. E., Daniels, K., Vespa, J., Mosher, W. D. (2012). First marriages in the United States: Data from the 2006–2010 National Survey of Family Growth. *National Health Statistics Reports, 49*, 1–21. Retrieved from http://www.ncbi.nlm.nih.gov/pubmed/22803221

Coplan, R. J., Ooi, L. L., & Nocita, G. (2015). When one is company and two is a crowd: Why some children prefer solitude. *Child Development Perspectives, 9*, 133–137. doi:10.1111/cdep.12131

Coplan, R. J., Rose-Krasnor, L., Weeks, M., Kingsbury, A., Kingsbury, M., & Bullock, A. (2013). Alone is a crowd: Social motivations, social withdrawal, and socioemotional functioning in later childhood. *Developmental Psychology, 49*, 861–875.

Cornell, D., & Limber, S. P. (2015). Law and policy on the concept of bullying at school. *The American Psychologist, 70*, 333–343. doi:10.1037/a0038558

Cummings, E. M., Goeke-Morey, M. C., Merrilees, C. E., Taylor, L. K., & Shirlow, P. (2014). A social-ecological, process-oriented perspective on political violence and child development. *Child Development Perspectives, 8*, 82–89. doi:10.1111/cdep.12067

Cutuli, J. J., Ahumada, S. M., Herbers, J. E., Lafavor, T. L., Masten, A. S., & Oberg, C. N. (2017). Adversity and children experiencing family homelessness: Implications for health. *Journal of Children and Poverty, 23*, 41–55. doi:10.1080/10796126.2016.1198753

Damaske, S., Bratter, J. L., & Frech, A. (2017). Single mother families and employment, race, and poverty in changing economic times. *Social Science Research, 62*, 120–133. doi:10.1016/j.ssresearch.2016.08.008

Davidson, R. D., O'Hara, K. L., & Beck, C. J. A. (2014). Psychological and biological processes in children associated with high conflict parental divorce. *Juvenile and Family Court Journal, 65*, 29–44. doi:10.1111/jfcj.12015

Davies, P., & Martin, M. (2014). Children's coping and adjustment in high-conflict homes: The reformulation of emotional security theory. *Child Development Perspectives, 8*, 242–249. doi:10.1111/cdep.12094

Davis-Kean, P. E., Jager, J., & Andrew Collins, W. (2009). The self in action: An emerging link between self-beliefs and behaviors in middle childhood. *Child Development Perspectives, 3*, 184–188. doi:10.1111/j.1750-8606.2009.00104.x

DeNavas-Walt, C., & Proctor, B. D. (2014). *Income and poverty in the United States: 2013.* Retrieved from http://www.census.gov/hhes/www/poverty/data/incpovhlth/2013/

Denissen, J. J. A., Zarrett, N. R., & Eccles, J. S. (2007). I like to do it, I'm able, and I know I am: Longitudinal couplings between domain-specific achievement, self-concept, and interest. *Child Development, 78*, 430–447.

Domhardt, M., Münzer, A., Fegert, J. M., & Goldbeck, L. (2015). Resilience in survivors of child sexual abuse: A systematic review of the literature. *Trauma, Violence & Abuse, 16*, 476–493. doi:10.1177/1524838014557288

Doodson, L., & Morley, D. (2006). Understanding the roles of non-residential stepmothers. *Journal of Divorce & Remarriage, 45*, 109–130. doi:10.1300/J087v45n03-06

Drapeau, S., Gagne, M. H., Saint-Jacques, M. C., Lepine, R., & Ivers, H. (2009). Post-separation conflict trajectories: A longitudinal study. *Marriage & Family Review, 45*, 353–373. doi:10.1080/01494920902821529

Dunn, J. (2002). Sibling relationships. In P. K. Smith & C. H. Hart (Eds.), *Blackwell handbook of childhood social development* (pp. 223–237). Oxford, England: Blackwell.

Dweck, C. S. (2017). The journey to children's mindsets-and beyond. *Child Development Perspectives, 11*, 139–144. doi:10.1111/cdep.12225

Eisenberg, N., Haugen, R., Spinrad, T. L., Hofer, C., Chassin, L., Qing, Z., . . . Liew, J. (2010). Relations of temperament to maladjustment and ego resiliency in at-risk children. *Social Development, 19*, 577–600. doi:10.1111/j.1467-9507.2009.00550.x

Elliott, J. G., & Place, M. (2018). Practitioner review: School refusal: Developments in conceptualisation and treatment since 2000. *Journal of Child Psychology and Psychiatry.* Advance online publication. doi:10.1111/jcpp.12848

Ellis, B. J., Bianchi, J., Griskevicius, V., & Frankenhuis, W. E. (2017). Beyond risk and protective factors: An adaptation-based approach to resilience. *Perspectives on Psychological Science, 12*, 561–587. doi:10.1177/1745691617693054

Erdley, C. A., & Day, H. J. (2017). Friendship in childhood and adolescence. In M. Hojjat &

A. Moyer (Eds.), *The psychology of friendship* (pp. 3–19). Oxford, UK: Oxford University Press.

Erikson, E. H. (1950). *Childhood and society* (2nd ed.). New York, NY: Norton.

Espelage, D. L., Low, S. K., & Jimerson, S. R. (2014). Understanding school climate, aggression, peer victimization, and bully perpetration: Contemporary science, practice, and policy. *School Psychology Quarterly, 29*, 233–237.

Ettekal, I., & Ladd, G. W. (2015). Developmental pathways from childhood aggression-disruptiveness, chronic peer rejection, and deviant friendships to early-adolescent rule breaking. *Child Development, 86*, 614–631. doi:10.1111/cdev.12321

Evans-Lacko, S., Takizawa, R., Brimblecombe, N., King, D., Knapp, M., Maughan, B., & Arseneault, L. (2017). Childhood bullying victimization is associated with use of mental health services over five decades: A longitudinal nationally representative cohort study. *Psychological Medicine, 47*, 127–135. doi:10.1017/S0033291716001719

Evans, G. W., Li, D., & Whipple, S. S. (2013). Cumulative risk and child development. *Psychological Bulletin, 139*, 1342–1396. doi:10.1037/a0031808

Falbo, T., Poston, D. L., Jr., Triscari, R. S., & Zhang, X. (1997). Self-enhancing illusions among Chinese schoolchildren. *Journal of Cross-Cultural Psychology, 28*, 172–191.

Farr, R. H. (2017). Does parental sexual orientation matter? A longitudinal follow-up of adoptive families with school-age children. *Developmental Psychology, 53*, 252–264. doi:10.1037/dev0000228

Fedewa, A. L., Black, W. W., & Ahn, S. (2014). Children and adolescents with same-gender parents: A meta-analytic approach in assessing outcomes. *Journal of GLBT Family Studies, 11*, 1–34. doi:10.1080/1550428X.2013.869486

Feinberg, M. E., Solmeyer, A. R., & McHale, S. M. (2012). The third rail of family systems: Sibling relationships, mental and behavioral health, and preventive intervention in childhood and adolescence. *Clinical Child and Family Psychology Review, 15*, 43–57. doi:10.1007/s10567-011-0104-5

Fergusson, D. M., McLeod, G. F. H., & Horwood, L. J. (2013). Childhood sexual abuse and adult developmental outcomes: Findings from a 30-year longitudinal study in New Zealand. *Child Abuse & Neglect, 37*, 664–674. doi:10.1016/j.chiabu.2013.03.013

Fink, E., Begeer, S., Peterson, C. C., Slaughter, V., & de Rosnay, M. (2015). Friendlessness and theory of mind: A prospective longitudinal study. *British Journal of Developmental Psychology, 33*, 1–17. doi:10.1111/bjdp.12060

Fink, E., Patalay, P., Sharpe, H., & Wolpert, M. (2018). Child- and school-level predictors of children's bullying behavior: A multilevel analysis in 648 primary schools. *Journal of Educational Psychology, 110*, 17–26. doi:10.1037/edu0000204

Finkelhor, D., Ormrod, R. K., & Turner, H. A. (2009). The developmental epidemiology of childhood victimization. *Journal of Interpersonal Violence, 24*, 711–731.

Finkelhor, D., Shattuck, A., Turner, H. A., & Hamby, S. L. (2014). The lifetime prevalence of child sexual abuse and sexual assault assessed in late adolescence. *Journal of Adolescent Health, 55*, 329–333. doi:10.1016/j.jadohealth.2013.12.026

Fite, P. J., Hendrickson, M., Rubens, S. L., Gabrielli, J., & Evans, S. (2013). The role of peer rejection in the link between reactive aggression and academic performance. *Child & Youth Care Forum, 42*, 193–205. doi:10.1007/s10566-013-9199-9

Fryda, C. M., & Hulme, P. A. (2015). School-based childhood sexual abuse prevention programs: An integrative review. *Journal of School Nursing, 31*, 167–182. doi:10.1177/1059840514544125

Gagnier, C., & Collin-Vézina, D. (2016). The disclosure experiences of male child sexual abuse survivors. *Journal of Child Sexual Abuse, 25*, 221–241. doi:10.1080/10538712.2016.1124308

Ganong, L., & Coleman, M. (2017). Siblings, half-siblings, and stepsiblings. In L. Ganong & M. Coleman (Eds.), *Stepfamily relationships* (pp. 191–204). Boston, MA: Springer US. doi:10.1007/978-1-4899-7702-1_10

Ganong, L., Coleman, M., & Russell, L. T. (2015). Children in diverse families. In M. H. Bornstein & T. Leventhal (Eds.), *Handbook of child psychology and developmental science* (pp. 1–42). Hoboken, NJ: Wiley. doi:10.1002/9781118963418.childpsy404

Gao, G. (2015). *Americans' ideal family size is smaller than it used to be.* Retrieved from http://www.pewresearch.org/fact-tank/2015/05/08/ideal-size-of-the-american-family/

Gass, K., Jenkins, J., & Dunn, J. (2007). Are sibling relationships protective? A longitudinal study. *Journal of Child Psychology & Psychiatry, 48*, 167–175.

Gates, G. J. (2013). *LGBT parenting in the United States.* Retrieved from http://williamsinstitute.law.ucla.edu/wp-content/uploads/LGBT-Parenting.pdf

Golombok, S., Blake, L., Slutsky, J., Raffanello, E., Roman, G. D., & Ehrhardt, A. (2018). Parenting and the adjustment of children born to gay fathers through surrogacy. *Child Development, 89*, 1223–1233. doi:10.1111/cdev.12728

Golombok, S., Mellish, L., Jennings, S., Casey, P., Tasker, F., & Lamb, M. E. (2014). Adoptive gay father families: Parent-child relationships and children's psychological adjustment. *Child Development, 85*, 456–468. doi:10.1111/cdev.12155

Golombok, S., & Tasker, F. (2015). Socioemotional development in changing families. In M. E. Lamb (Ed.), *Handbook of child psychology and developmental science* (pp. 1–45). Hoboken, NJ: John Wiley. doi:10.1002/9781118963418.childpsy311

Gómez-Ortiz, O., Romera, E. M., & Ortega-Ruiz, R. (2016). Parenting styles and bullying: The mediating role of parental psychological aggression and physical punishment. *Child Abuse & Neglect, 51*, 132–143. doi:10.1016/j.chiabu.2015.10.025

Goodvin, R., Thompson, R. A., & Winer, A. C. (2015). The individual child: Temperament, emotion, self, and personality. In M. Bornstein & M. Lamb (Eds.), *Developmental psychology: An advanced textbook* (pp. 377–409). New York, NY: Psychology Press.

Goodwin, P., Mosher, W., & Chandra, A. (2010). Marriage and cohabitation In the United States: A statistical portrait based on cycle 6 (2002) of the National Survey of Family Growth. *Vital and Health Statistics, 23*, 1–45.

Graham, S., Munniksma, A., & Juvonen, J. (2014). Psychosocial benefits of cross-ethnic friendships in urban middle schools. *Child Development, 85*, 469–483. doi:10.1111/cdev.12159

Grassetti, S. N., Hubbard, J. A., Smith, M. A., Bookhout, M. K., Swift, L. E., & Gawrysiak, M. J. (2018). Caregivers' advice and children's bystander behaviors during bullying incidents. *Journal of Clinical Child & Adolescent Psychology.* Advance online publication. doi:10.1080/15374416.2017.1295381

Guo, L., Yang, L., Liu, Z., & Song, T. (2005). An experimental research on the formation of primary school pupils' self-confidence. *Psychological Science (China), 28*, 1068–1071.

Haimovitz, K., & Dweck, C. S. (2017). The origins of children's growth and fixed mindsets: New research and a new proposal. *Child Development, 88*, 1849–1859. doi:10.1111/cdev.12955

Hakvoort, E. M., Bos, H. M. W., van Balen, F., & Hermanns, J. M. A. (2010). Family relationships and the psychosocial adjustment of school-aged children in intact families. *Journal of Genetic Psychology, 171*, 182–201.

Halevi, G., Djalovski, A., Vengrober, A., & Feldman, R. (2016). Risk and resilience trajectories in war-exposed children across the first decade of life. *Journal of Child Psychology and Psychiatry, 57*, 1183–1193. doi:10.1111/jcpp.12622

Hamm, M. P., Newton, A. S., Chisholm, A., Shulhan, J., Milne, A., Sundar, P., . . . Hartling, L. (2015). Prevalence and effect of cyberbullying on children and young people. *JAMA Pediatrics, 169*, 770. doi:10.1001/jamapediatrics.2015.0944

Harper, S., & Ruicheva, I. (2010). Grandmothers as replacement parents and partners: The role of grandmotherhood in single parent families. *Journal of Intergenerational Relationships, 8*, 219–233. doi:10.1080/15350770.2010.498779

Hart, D., Atkins, R., & Tursi, N. (2006). Origins and developmental influences on self-esteem. In M. H. Kernis (Ed.), *Self-esteem issues and answers: A sourcebook of current perspectives* (pp. 157–162). New York, NY: Psychology Press.

Harter, S. (2012a). Emerging self-processes during childhood and adolescence. In M. R. Leary & J. P. Tangney (Eds.), Handbook of self and identity (pp. 680–715). New York, NY: Guilford.

Harter, S. (2012b). The construction of the self: Developmental and sociocultural foundations (2nd ed.). New York, NY: Guilford.

Hartup, W. W. (2006). Relationships in early and middle childhood. In A. L. Vangelisti & D. Perlman (Eds.), *The Cambridge handbook of personal relationships* (pp. 177–190). New York: Cambridge University Press.

Havik, T., Bru, E., & Ertesvåg, S. K. (2013). Parental perspectives of the role of school factors in school refusal. *Emotional and Behavioural*

Difficulties, 19, 131–153. doi:10.1080/1363275
2.2013.816199

Havik, T., Bru, E., & Ertesvåg, S. K. (2015). School factors associated with school refusal- and truancy-related reasons for school non-attendance. *Social Psychology of Education, 18*, 221–240. doi:10.1007/s11218-015-9293-y

Herrenkohl, T. I., Hong, S., Klika, J. B., Herrenkohl, R. C., & Russo, M. J. (2013). Developmental impacts of child abuse and neglect related to adult mental health, substance use, and physical health. *Journal of Family Violence, 28*, 191–199. doi:10.1007/s10896-012-9474-9

Hill, N. E., Bush, K. R., & Roosa, M. W. (2003). Parenting and socialization strategies and children's mental health: Low-income Mexican-American and Euro-American mothers and children. *Child Development, 74*, 189–204.

Hillis, S., Mercy, J., Amobi, A., & Kress, H. (2016). Global prevalence of past-year violence against children: A systematic review and minimum estimates. *Pediatrics, 137*, e20154079. doi:10.1542/peds.2015-4079

Hinduja, S., & Patchin, J. (2015). *State cyberbullying laws: A brief review of state cyberbullying laws and policies*. Retrieved from http://www.cyberbullying.us/Bullying-and-Cyberbullying-Laws.pdf

Holliday, K. (2014, October 21). *China to ease 1-child rule further, but do people care?* CNBC News. Retrieved from http://www.cnbc.com/id/102104640#

Homma, Y., Wang, N., Saewyc, E., & Kishor, N. (2012). The relationship between sexual abuse and risky sexual behavior among adolescent boys: A meta-analysis. *Journal of Adolescent Health, 51*, 18–24. doi:10.1016/j.jadohealth.2011.12.032

Hopkins, K. D., Taylor, C. L., D'Antoine, H., & Zubrick, S. R. (2012). Predictors of resilient psychosocial functioning in Western Australian aboriginal young people exposed to high family-level risk. In M. Ungar (Ed.), *The social ecology of resilience* (pp. 425–440). New York, NY: Springer. doi:10.1007/978-1-4614-0586-3_33

Huesmann, L. R., Dubow, E. F., Boxer, P., Landau, S. F., Gvirsman, S. D., Shikaki, K., . . . Sapolsky, R. M. (2016). Children's exposure to violent political conflict stimulates aggression at peers by increasing emotional distress, aggressive script rehearsal, and normative beliefs favoring aggression. *Development and Psychopathology, 36*, 1–12. doi:10.1017/S0954579416001115

Hutson, E., Kelly, S., & Militello, L. K. (2018). Systematic review of cyberbullying interventions for youth and parents with implications for evidence-based practice. *Worldviews on Evidence-Based Nursing, 15*, 72–79. doi:10.1111/wvn.12257

Hymel, S., & Swearer, S. M. (2015). Four decades of research on school bullying: An introduction. *American Psychologist, 70*, 293–299. doi:10.1037/a0038928

Ilmarinen, V. J., Vainikainen, M. P., Verkasalo, M. J., & Lönnqvist, J. E. (2017). Homophilous friendship assortment based on personality traits and cognitive ability in middle childhood: The moderating effect of peer network size. *European Journal of Personality, 31*, 208–219. doi:10.1002/per.2095

Inglés, C. J., Gonzálvez-Maciá, C., García-Fernández, J. M., Vicent, M., & Martínez-Monteagudo, M. C. (2015). Current status of research on school refusal. *European Journal of Education and Psychology, 8*, 37–52. doi:10.1016/J.EJEPS.2015.10.005

Iqbal, H., Neal, S., & Vincent, C. (2017). Children's friendships in super-diverse localities: Encounters with social and ethnic difference. *Childhood, 24*, 128–142. doi:10.1177/0907568216633741

Jaeger, M. M. (2012). The extended family and children's educational success. *American Sociological Review, 77*, 903–922. doi:10.1177/0003122412464040

Jayakody, R., & Kalil, A. (2002). Social fathering in low-income, African American families with preschool children. *Journal of Marriage and Family, 64*, 504–516.

Ji-Yeon, K., McHale, S. M., Crouter, A. C., & Osgood, D. W. (2007). Longitudinal linkages between sibling relationships and adjustment from middle childhood through adolescence. *Developmental Psychology, 43*, 960–973.

Jones, D. J., Lewis, T., Litrownik, A., Thompson, R., Proctor, L. J., Isbell, P., . . . Runyan, D. (2013). Linking childhood sexual abuse and early adolescent risk behavior: The intervening role of internalizing and externalizing problems. *Journal of Abnormal Child Psychology, 41*, 139–150. doi:10.1007/s10802-012-9656-1

Juvonen, J., & Graham, S. (2014). Bullying in schools: The power of bullies and the plight of victims. *Annual Review of Psychology, 65*, 159–185. doi:10.1146/annurev-psych-010213-115030

Kärnä, A., Voeten, M., Poskiparta, E., & Salmivalli, C. (2010). Vulnerable children in varying classroom contexts: Bystanders' behaviors moderate the effects of risk factors on victimization. *Merrill-Palmer Quarterly: Journal of Developmental Psychology, 56*, 261–282.

Kawabata, Y., & Crick, N. R. (2011). The significance of cross-racial/ethnic friendships: Associations with peer victimization, peer support, sociometric status, and classroom diversity. *Developmental Psychology, 47*, 1763–1775. doi:10.1037/a0025399

Kawabata, Y., Crick, N. R., & Hamaguchi, Y. (2010). The role of culture in relational aggression: Associations with social-psychological adjustment problems in Japanese and US school-aged children. *International Journal of Behavioral Development, 34*, 354–362. doi:10.1177/0165025409339151

Kearney, C. A., Diliberto, R., Kearney, C. A., & Diliberto, R. (2013). School refusal behavior. In S. Hoffman (Ed.), *The Wiley handbook of cognitive behavioral therapy* (pp. 875–892). Chichester, England: John Wiley. doi:10.1002/9781118528563.wbcbt37

Keijsers, L., Loeber, R., Branje, S., & Meeus, W. H. J. (2011). Bidirectional links and concurrent development of parent-child relationships and boys' offending behavior. *Journal of Abnormal Psychology, 210*, 878–889. doi:10.1037/a0024588

Kennedy, S., & Bumpass, L. (2008). Cohabitation and children's living arrangements: New estimates from the United State. *Demographic Research, 19*, 1663–1692.

Kennedy, S., & Fitch, C. A. (2012). Measuring cohabitation and family structure in the United States: Assessing the impact of new data from the Current Population Survey. *Demography, 49*, 1479–1498. doi:10.1007/s13524-012-0126-8

Kenny, D. (2018). *Children, sexuality and child sexual abuse*. New York, NY: Routledge.

Kenny, M. C., & McEachern, A. (2009). Children's self-concept: A multicultural comparison. *Professional School Counseling, 12*, 207–212.

Killen, M., Kelly, M., Richardson, C., Crystal, D., & Ruck, M. (2010). European-American children's and adolescents' evaluations of interracial exclusion. *Group Processes & Intergroup Relations, 13*, 283–300. doi:10.1177/1368430209346700

Kim, H., Drake, B., & Jonson-Reid, M. (2018). An examination of class-based visibility bias in national child maltreatment reporting. *Children and Youth Services Review, 85*, 165–173. doi:10.1016/J.CHILDYOUTH.2017.12.019

Klima, T., & Repetti, R. L. (2008). Children's peer relations and their psychological adjustment: Differences between close friendships and the larger peer group. *Merrill-Palmer Quarterly, 54*, 151–178.

Koehn, A. J., & Kerns, K. A. (2018). Parent–child attachment: Meta-analysis of associations with parenting behaviors in middle childhood and adolescence. *Attachment & Human Development, 20*, 378–405. doi:10.108 0/14616734.2017.1408131

Kornbluh, M., & Neal, J. W. (2016). Examining the many dimensions of children's popularity. *Journal of Social and Personal Relationships, 33*, 62–80. doi:10.1177/0265407514562562

Kowalski, R. M., Giumetti, G. W., Schroeder, A. N., & Lattanner, M. R. (2014). Bullying in the digital age: A critical review and meta-analysis of cyberbullying research among youth. *Psychological Bulletin, 140*, 1073–1137. doi:10.1037/a0035618

Kramer, L. (2010). The essential ingredients of successful sibling relationships: An emerging framework for advancing theory and practice. *Child Development Perspectives, 4*, 80–86. doi:10.1111/j.1750-8606.2010.00122.x

Labella, M. H., Narayan, A. J., McCormick, C. M., Desjardins, C. D., & Masten, A. S. (2018). Risk and adversity, parenting quality, and children's social-emotional adjustment in families experiencing homelessness. *Child Development*. Advance online publication. doi:10.1111/cdev.12894

Ladd, G. W., & Kochenderfer-Ladd, B. (2016). Research in educational psychology: Social exclusion in school. In P. Riva & J. Eck (Eds.), *Social exclusion* (pp. 109–132). Cham, Switzerland: Springer International. doi:10.1007/978-3-319-33033-4_6

LaFontana, K. M., & Cillessen, A. H. N. (2010). Developmental changes in the priority of perceived status in childhood and adolescence. *Social Development, 19*, 130–147. doi:10.1111/j.1467-9507.2008.00522.x

Laible, D., McGinley, M., Carlo, G., Augustine, M., & Murphy, T. (2014). Does engaging in prosocial behavior make children see the world through rose-colored glasses? *Developmental Psychology, 50*, 872–880.

Lamb, M. E. (2012). Mothers, fathers, families, and circumstances: Factors affecting children's adjustment. *Applied Developmental Science, 16*, 98–111. doi:10.1080/10888691.2012.667344

Lamb, M. E., & Lewis, C. (2015). The role of parent-child relationships in child development. In M. H. Bornstein & M. E. Lamb (Eds.), *Developmental science: An advanced textbook* (7th ed., pp. 469–517). New York, NY: Psychology Press.

Lansford, J. E. (2014). Parenting across cultures. In H. Selin (Ed.), *Parenting across cultures* (Vol. 7, pp. 445–458). Dordrecht: Springer Netherlands. doi:10.1007/978-94-007-7503-9

Lansford, J. E., Staples, A. D., Bates, J. E., Pettit, G. S., & Dodge, K. A. (2013). Trajectories of mothers' discipline strategies and interparental conflict: Interrelated change during middle childhood. *Journal of Family Communication, 13*, 178–195. doi:10.1080/15267431.2013.796947

Laursen, B. (2017). Making and keeping friends: The importance of being similar. *Child Development Perspectives, 11*, 282–289. doi:10.1111/cdep.12246

Layne, C. M., Saltzman, W. R., Poppleton, L., Burlingame, G. M., Pašalić, A., Duraković, E., . . . Pynoos, R. S. (2008). Effectiveness of a school-based group psychotherapy program for war-exposed adolescents: A randomized controlled trial. *Journal of the American Academy of Child & Adolescent Psychiatry, 47*, 1048–1062. doi:10.1097/CHI.0b013e31817eecae

Leclerc, B., & Wortley, R. (2015). Predictors of victim disclosure in child sexual abuse: Additional evidence from a sample of incarcerated adult sex offenders. *Child Abuse & Neglect, 43*, 104–111. doi:10.1016/J.CHIABU.2015.03.003

Lee, L., Howes, C., & Chamberlain, B. (2007). Ethnic heterogeneity of social networks and cross-ethnic friendships of elementary school boys and girls. *Merrill-Palmer Quarterly, 53*, 325–346.

Levenson, E. (2017). *China's two-child policy sparks immediate increase in babies.* CNN. Retrieved February 25, 2018, from https://www.cnn.com/2017/01/23/world/china-two-child/index.html

Limber, S. P., & Small, M. A. (2003). State laws and policies to address bullying in schools. *School Psychology Review, 32*, 445–455.

Livingston, G. (2013). *The rise of single fathers.* Retrieved from http://www.pewsocialtrends.org/2013/07/02/the-rise-of-single-fathers/

Luthar, S. S., Crossman, E. J., Small, P. J., Luthar, S. S., Crossman, E. J., & Small, P. J. (2015). Resilience and adversity. In M. E. Lamb (Ed.), *Handbook of child psychology and developmental science* (pp. 1–40). Hoboken, NJ: John Wiley. doi:10.1002/9781118963418.childpsy307

Maikovich-Fong, A. K., & Jaffee, S. R. (2010). Sex differences in childhood sexual abuse characteristics and victims' emotional and behavioral problems: Findings from a national sample of youth. *Child Abuse & Neglect, 34*. 429–437. doi:10.1016/j.chiabu.2009.10.006

Maniglio, R. (2011). The role of child sexual abuse in the etiology of substance-related disorders. *Journal of Addictive Diseases, 30*, 216–228. doi:10.1080/10550887.2011.581987

Maniglio, R. (2013). Child sexual abuse in the etiology of anxiety disorders: A systematic review of reviews. *Trauma, Violence & Abuse, 14*, 96–112. doi:10.1177/1524838012470032

Manning, W. D. (2015). Cohabitation and child wellbeing. *The Future of Children, 25*, 51–66.

Manning, W. D., & Brown, S. (2006). Children's economic well-being in married and cohabiting parent families. *Journal of Marriage & Family, 68*, 345–362.

Maric, M., Heyne, D. A., MacKinnon, D. P., van Widenfelt, B. M., & Westenberg, P. M. (2013). Cognitive mediation of cognitive-behavioural therapy outcomes for anxiety-based school refusal. *Behavioural and Cognitive Psychotherapy, 41*, 549–564. doi:10.1017/S1352465812000756

Marks, A. K., Szalacha, L. A., Lamarre, M., Boyd, M. J., & Coll, C. G. (2007). Emerging ethnic identity and interethnic group social preferences in middle childhood: Findings from the Children of Immigrants Development in Context (CIDC) study. *International Journal of Behavioral Development, 31*, 501–513.

Marks, P. E. L. (2017). Introduction to the special issue: 20th-century origins and 21st-century developments of peer nomination methodology. *New Directions for Child and Adolescent Development, 2017*, 7–19. doi:10.1002/cad.20205

Markus, H. R., & Kitayama, S. (1991). Culture and the self: Implications for cognition, emotion, and motivation. *Psychological Review, 98*, 224–253. doi:10.1037/0033-295X.98.2.224

Marriott, C., Hamilton-Giachritsis, C., & Harrop, C. (2014). Factors promoting resilience following childhood sexual abuse: A structured, narrative review of the literature. *Child Abuse Review, 23*, 17–34. doi:10.1002/car.2258

Masten, A. S. (2016). Resilience in developing systems: The promise of integrated approaches. *European Journal of Developmental Psychology, 13*, 297–312. doi:10.1080/17405629.2016.1147344

Masten, A. S., Cicchetti, D., Masten, A. S., & Cicchetti, D. (2016). Resilience in development: Progress and transformation. In D. Cicchetti (Ed.), *Developmental psychopathology* (pp. 1–63). Hoboken, NJ: John Wiley. doi:10.1002/9781119125556.devpsy406

Masten, A. S., & Monn, A. R. (2015). Child and family resilience: A call for integrated science, practice, and professional training. *Family Relations, 64*, 5–21. doi:10.1111/fare.12103

Masten, A. S., Narayan, A. J., Silverman, W. K., & Osofsky, J. D. (2015). Children in war and disaster. In M. H. Bornstein & T. Leventhal (Eds.), *Handbook of child psychology and developmental science* (pp. 1–42). Hoboken, NJ: John Wiley. doi:10.1002/9781118963418.childpsy418

Maynard, B. R., Brendel, K. E., Bulanda, J. J., Heyne, D., Thompson, A. M., & Pigott, T. D. (2015). Campbell systematic reviews psychosocial interventions for school refusal with primary and secondary school students: A systematic review. Unpublished manuscript.

Maynard, B. R., Heyne, D., Brendel, K. E., Bulanda, J. J., Thompson, A. M., & Pigott, T. D. (2018). Treatment for school refusal among children and adolescents. *Research on Social Work Practice, 28*, 56–67. doi:10.1177/1049731515598619

McClure, J., Meyer, L. H., Garisch, J., Fischer, R., Weir, K. F., & Walkey, F. H. (2011). Students' attributions for their best and worst marks: Do they relate to achievement? *Contemporary Educational Psychology, 36*, 71–81. doi:10.1016/j.cedpsych.2010.11.001

McDonald, K. L., Dashiell-Aje, E., Menzer, M. M., Rubin, K. H., Oh, W., & Bowker, J. C. (2013). Contributions of racial and sociobehavioral homophily to friendship stability and quality among same-race and cross-race friends. *Journal of Early Adolescence, 33*, 897–919. doi:10.1177/0272431612472259

McDougall, P., & Vaillancourt, T. (2015). Long-term adult outcomes of peer victimization in childhood and adolescence: Pathways to adjustment and maladjustment. *The American Psychologist, 70*, 300–310. doi:10.1037/a0039174

McGlothlin, H., & Killen, M. (2006). Intergroup attitudes of European American children attending ethnically homogeneous schools. *Child Development, 77*, 1375–1386.

McHale, S. M., Updegraff, K. A., & Whiteman, S. D. (2012). Sibling relationships and influences in childhood and adolescence. *Journal of Marriage and the Family, 74*, 913–930.

McLoughlin, C. S. (2005). The coming-of-age of China's single-child policy. *Psychology in the Schools, 42*, 305–313. doi:10.1002/pits.20081

Meece, J. L., Anderman, E. M., & Anderman, L. H. (2006). Classroom goal structure, student motivation, and academic achievement. *Annual Review of Psychology, 57*, 487–503. doi:10.1146/annurev.psych.56.091103.070258

Melvin, G. A., & Tonge, B. J. (2012). School refusal. In P. Sturmey & M. Hersen (Eds.), *Handbook of evidence-based practice in clinical psychology.* Hoboken, NJ: John Wiley.

Menesini, E., & Salmivalli, C. (2017). Bullying in schools: The state of knowledge and effective interventions. *Psychology, Health & Medicine, 22*, 240–253. doi:10.1080/13548506.2017.1279740

Menting, B., Koot, H., & van Lier, P. (2014). Peer acceptance and the development of emotional and behavioural problems: Results from a preventive intervention study. *International Journal of Behavioral Development, 39*, 530–540. doi:10.1177/0165025414558853

Menting, B., van Lier, P. A. C., & Koot, H. M. (2011). Language skills, peer rejection, and the development of externalizing behavior from kindergarten to fourth grade. *Journal of Child Psychology & Psychiatry, 52*, 72–79. doi:10.1111/j.1469-7610.2010.02279.x

Miller, B. G., Kors, S., & Macfie, J. (2017). No differences? Meta-analytic comparisons of psychological adjustment in children of gay fathers and heterosexual parents. *Psychology of Sexual Orientation and Gender Diversity, 4*, 14–22. doi:10.1037/sgd0000203

Mills, K. L., Goddings, A. L., Clasen, L. S., Giedd, J. N., & Blakemore, S. J. (2014). The developmental mismatch in structural brain maturation during adolescence.

Developmental Neuroscience, 36, 147–160. doi:10.1159/000362328

Mills, K. L., Lalonde, F., Clasen, L. S., Giedd, J. N., & Blakemore, S. J. (2014). Developmental changes in the structure of the social brain in late childhood and adolescence. *Social Cognitive and Affective Neuroscience, 9*, 123–131. doi:10.1093/scan/nss113

Mishna, F., Cook, C., Gadalla, T., Daciuk, J., & Solomon, S. (2010). Cyber bullying behaviors among middle and high school students. *American Journal of Orthopsychiatry, 80*, 362–374. doi:10.1111/j.1939-0025.2010.01040.x

Moore, J. S. B., & Smith, M. (2018). Children's levels of contingent self-esteem and social and emotional outcomes. *Educational Psychology in Practice, 334*, 113–130. doi:10.1080/02667363.2017.1411786

Moore, S. E., Norman, R. E., Suetani, S., Thomas, H. J., Sly, P. D., & Scott, J. G. (2017). Consequences of bullying victimization in childhood and adolescence: A systematic review and meta-analysis. *World Journal of Psychiatry, 7*, 60–76. doi:10.5498/wjp.v7.i1.60

Morcillo, C., Ramos-Olazagasti, M. A., Blanco, C., Sala, R., Canino, G., Bird, H., & Duarte, C. S. (2015). Socio-cultural context and bulling others in childhood. *Journal of Child and Family Studies, 24*, 2241–2249. doi:10.1007/s10826-014-0026-1

Mosher, S. W. (2006). China's one-child policy: Twenty-five years later. *Human Life Review, 32*, 76–101.

Muenks, K., Wigfield, A., & Eccles, J. S. (2018). I can do this! The development and calibration of children's expectations for success and competence beliefs. *Developmental Review, 48*, 24–39. doi:10.1016/J.DR.2018.04.001

Munniksma, A., & Juvonen, J. (2012). Cross-ethnic friendships and sense of social-emotional safety in a multiethnic middle school: An exploratory study. *Merrill-Palmer Quarterly, 58*, 489–506. doi:10.1353/mpq.2012.0023

Murray-Close, D., Nelson, D. A., Ostrov, J. M., Casas, J. F., & Crick, N. R., (2016). Relational aggression: A developmental psychopathology perspective. In D. Cicchetti (Ed.), *Developmental psychopathology* (pp. 1–63). Hoboken, NJ: John Wiley. doi:10.1002/9781119125556.devpsy413

National Center for Health Statistics. (2015). *National marriage and divorce rate trends.* Washington, DC: Author.

Nemeroff, C. B. (2016). Paradise lost: The neurobiological and clinical consequences of child abuse and neglect. *Neuron, 89*, 892–909. doi:10.1016/J.NEURON.2016.01.019

Nese, R. N. T., Horner, R. H., Dickey, C. R., Stiller, B., & Tomlanovich, A. (2014). Decreasing bullying behaviors in middle school: Expect respect. *School Psychology Quarterly, 29*, 272–286.

Ng, F. F. Y., Pomerantz, E. M., & Lam, S. (2007). European American and Chinese parents' responses to children's success and failure: Implications for children's responses. *Developmental Psychology, 43*, 1239–1255. doi:10.1037/0012-1649.43.5.1239

Nikolaou, D. (2017). Do anti-bullying policies deter in-school bullying victimization? *International Review of Law and Economics, 50*, 1–6. doi:10.1016/J.IRLE.2017.03.001

Nixon, E., Hadfield, K., Nixon, E., & Hadfield, K. (2016). Blended families. In C. L. Sheehan (Ed.), *Encyclopedia of family studies* (pp. 1–5). Hoboken, NJ: John Wiley. doi:10.1002/9781119085621.wbefs207

Northoff, G., & Hayes, D. J. (2011). Is our self nothing but reward? *Biological Psychiatry, 69*, 1019–1025. doi:10.1016/j.biopsych.2010.12.014

Olweus, D. (2013). School bullying: Development and some important challenges. *Annual Review of Clinical Psychology, 9*, 751–780. doi:10.1146/annurev-clinpsy-050212-185516

Olweus, D., & Limber, S. P. (2010). Bullying in school: Evaluation and dissemination of the Olweus Bullying Prevention Program. *American Journal of Orthopsychiatry, 80*, 124–134. doi:10.1111/j.1939-0025.2010.01015.x

Orkin, M., May, S., & Wolf, M. (2017). How parental support during homework contributes to helpless behaviors among struggling readers. *Reading Psychology, 38*, 506–541. doi:10.1080/02702711.2017.1299822

Orth, U. (2017). The family environment in early childhood has a long-term effect on self-esteem: A longitudinal study from birth to age 27 years. *Journal of Personality and Social Psychology, 114*, 637–655. doi:10.1037/pspp0000143

Osborne, C., Manning, W. D., & Smock, P. J. (2007). Married and cohabiting parents' relationship stability: A focus on race and ethnicity. *Journal of Marriage & Family, 69*, 1345–1366.

Parkinson, M., & Creswell, C. (2011). Worry and problem-solving skills and beliefs in primary school children. *British Journal of Clinical Psychology, 50*, 106–112. doi:10.1348/014466510x523887

Parra-Cardona, J. R., Cordova, D., Holtrop, K., Villarruel, F. A., & Wieling, E. (2008). Shared ancestry, evolving stories: Similar and contrasting life experiences described by foreign born and U.S. born Latino parents. *Family Process, 47*, 157–172. doi:10.1111/j.1545-5300.2008.00246.x

Patterson, C. J. (2017). Parents' sexual orientation and children's development. *Child Development Perspectives, 11*, 45–49. doi:10.1111/cdep.12207

Pérez-Fuentes, G., Olfson, M., Villegas, L., Morcillo, C., Wang, S., & Blanco, C. (2013). Prevalence and correlates of child sexual abuse: A national study. *Comprehensive Psychiatry, 54*, 16–27. doi:10.1016/j.comppsych.2012.05.010

Pérez-González, A., Guilera, G., Pereda, N., & Jarne, A. (2017). Protective factors promoting resilience in the relation between child sexual victimization and internalizing and externalizing symptoms. *Child Abuse & Neglect, 72*, 393–403. doi:10.1016/J.CHIABU.2017.09.006

Perren, S., Ettekal, I., & Ladd, G. (2013). The impact of peer victimization on later maladjustment: Mediating and moderating effects of hostile and self-blaming attributions. *Journal of Child Psychology and Psychiatry, and Allied Disciplines, 54*, 46–55. doi:10.1111/j.1469-7610.2012.02618.x

Perrin, E. C., & Siegel, B. S. (2013). Promoting the well-being of children whose parents are gay or lesbian. *Pediatrics, 131*, e1374–e1383. doi:10.1542/peds.2013-0377

Pesu, L., Viljaranta, J., & Aunola, K. (2016). The role of parents' and teachers' beliefs in children's self-concept development. *Journal of Applied Developmental Psychology, 44*, 63–71. doi:10.1016/j.appdev.2016.03.001

Pew Research Center. (2015). *Parenting in America: The American family today.* Retrieved from http://www.pewsocialtrends.org/2015/12/17/1-the-american-family-today/

Pfeifer, J. H., Kahn, L. E., Merchant, J. S., Peake, S. J., Veroude, K., Masten, C. L., . . . Dapretto, M. (2013). Longitudinal change in the neural bases of adolescent social self-evaluations: Effects of age and pubertal development. *Journal of Neuroscience, 33*, 7415–7419. doi:10.1523/JNEUROSCI.4074-12.2013

Pfeifer, J. H., Lieberman, M. D., & Dapretto, M. (2007). "I know you are but what am I?!": Neural bases of self- and social knowledge retrieval in children and adults. *Journal of Cognitive Neuroscience, 19*, 1323–1337. doi:10.1162/jocn.2007.19.8.1323

Pfeifer, J. H., & Peake, S. J. (2012). Self-development: Integrating cognitive, socioemotional, and neuroimaging perspectives. *Developmental Cognitive Neuroscience, 2*, 55–69. doi:10.1016/j.dcn.2011.07.012

Pomerantz, E. M., & Dong, W. (2006). Effects of mothers' perceptions of children's competence: The moderating role of mothers' theories of competence. *Developmental Psychology, 42*, 950–961. doi:10.1037/0012-1649.42.5.950

Pomerantz, E. M., Ng, F. F. Y., Cheung, C. S. S., & Qu, Y. (2014). Raising happy children who succeed in school: Lessons from China and the United States. *Child Development Perspectives, 8*, 71–76. doi:10.1111/cdep.12063

Pomerantz, E. M., & Saxon, J. L. (2001). Conceptions of ability as stable and self-evaluative processes: A longitudinal examination. *Child Development, 72*, 152–173. doi:10.1111/1467-8624.00271

Potter, D. (2010). Psychosocial well-being and the relationship between divorce and children's academic achievement. *Journal of Marriage & Family, 72*, 933–946. doi:10.1111/j.1741-3737.2010.00740.x

Poulin, F., & Chan, A. (2010). Friendship stability and change in childhood and adolescence. *Developmental Review, 30*, 257–272. doi:10.1016/j.dr.2009.01.001

Pozzoli, T., Gini, G., & Vieno, A. (2012). The role of individual correlates and class norms in defending and passive bystanding behavior in bullying: A multilevel analysis. *Child Development, 83*, 1917–1931. doi:10.1111/j.1467-8624.2012.01831.x

Punamäki, R. L., Palosaari, E., Diab, M., Peltonen, K., & Qouta, S. R. (2014). Trajectories of posttraumatic stress symptoms (PTSS) after major war among Palestinian children: Trauma, family- and child-related predictors. *Journal of Affective Disorders, 172C*, 133–140. doi:10.1016/j.jad.2014.09.021

Raftery, J. N., Grolnick, W. S., & Flamm, E. S. (2012). Families as facilitators of student engagement: Toward a home-school partnership model. In S. L. Christenson, A. L. Reschly, & C. Wylie (Eds.), *Handbook of research on student engagement* (pp. 343–364). Boston, MA: Springer US. doi:10.1007/978-1-4614-2018-7_16

Rajendran, K., Kruszewski, E., & Halperin, J. M. (2016). Parenting style influences bullying: A longitudinal study comparing children with and without behavioral problems. *Journal of Child Psychology and Psychiatry, 57*, 188–195. doi:10.1111/jcpp.12433

Reavis, R. D., Keane, S. P., & Calkins, S. D. (2010). Trajectories of peer victimization: The role of multiple relationships. *Merrill-Palmer Quarterly: Journal of Developmental Psychology, 56*, 303–332.

Reising, M. M., Watson, K. H., Hardcastle, E. J., Merchant, M. J., Roberts, L., Forehand, R., & Compas, B. E. (2013). Parental depression and economic disadvantage: The role of parenting in associations with internalizing and externalizing symptoms in children and adolescents. *Journal of Child and Family Studies, 22*, 335–343. doi:10.1007/s10826-012-9582-4

Reyna, C. (2008). Ian is intelligent but Leshaun is lazy: Antecedents and consequences of attributional stereotypes in the classroom. *European Journal of Psychology of Education, 23*, 439–458. doi:10.1007/BF03172752

Rose-Greenland, F., & Smock, P. J. (2013). Living together unmarried: What do we know about cohabiting families? In G. W. Peterson & K. R. Bush (Eds.), *Handbook of marriage and the family* (pp. 255–273). New York, NY: Springer.

Rubin, K. H., Bukowski, W. M., & Bowker, J. C. (2015). Children in peer groups. In M. H. Bornstein & T. Leventhal (Eds.), *Handbook of child psychology and developmental science* (pp. 1–48). Hoboken, NJ: John Wiley. doi:10.1002/9781118963418.childpsy405

Rubin, K. H., Coplan, R. J., & Bowker, J. C. (2009). Social withdrawal in childhood. *Annual Review of Psychology, 60*, 141–171. doi:10.1146/annurev.psych.60110707.163642

Rubin, K. H., Coplan, R. J., Chen, X., Bowker, J. C., McDonald, K. L., & Heverly-Fitt, S. (2015). Peer relationships. In M. H. Bornstein & M. Lamb (Eds.), *Developmental science: An advanced textbook* (pp. 587–644). New York, NY: Psychology Press.

Rubin, K. H., Wojslawowicz, J. C., Rose-Krasnor, L., Booth-LaForce, C., & Burgess, K. B. (2006). The best friendships of shy/withdrawn children: Prevalence, stability, and relationship quality. *Journal of Abnormal Child Psychology, 34*, 143–157. doi:10.1007/s10802-005-9017-4

Ryan, R. M., Claessens, A., & Markowitz, A. J. (2015). Associations between family structure change and child behavior problems: The moderating effect of family income. *Child Development, 86*, 112–127. doi:10.1111/cdev.12283

Sabia, J. J., & Bass, B. (2017). Do anti-bullying laws work? New evidence on school safety and youth violence. *Journal of Population Economics, 30*, 473–502. doi:10.1007/s00148-016-0622-z

Salmivalli, C. (2014). Participant roles in bullying: How can peer bystanders be utilized in interventions? *Theory Into Practice, 53*, 286–292. doi:10.1080/00405841.2014.947222

Saraiya, A., Garakani, A., & Billick, S. B. (2013). Mental health approaches to child victims of acts of terrorism. *The Psychiatric Quarterly, 84*, 115–124. doi:10.1007/s11126-012-9232-4

Schneider, B. H. (2016). *Childhood friendships and peer relations: Friends and enemies.* New York, NY: Routledge.

Schwartz, D., Lansford, J. E., Dodge, K. A., Pettit, G. S., & Bates, J. E. (2015). Peer victimization during middle childhood as a lead indicator of internalizing problems and diagnostic outcomes in late adolescence. *Journal of Clinical Child and Adolescent Psychology, 44*, 393–404. doi:10.1080/15374416.2014.881293

Shetgiri, R., Lin, H., & Flores, G. (2013). Trends in risk and protective factors for child bullying perpetration in the United States. *Child Psychiatry and Human Development, 44*, 89–104. doi:10.1007/s10578-012-0312-3

Shi, B., & Xie, H. (2012). Popular and nonpopular subtypes of physically aggressive preadolescents: Continuity of aggression and peer mechanisms during the transition to middle school. *Merrill-Palmer Quarterly, 58*, 530–553. doi:10.1353/mpq.2012.0025

Sim, A., Fazel, M., Bowes, L., & Gardner, F. (2018). Pathways linking war and displacement to parenting and child adjustment: A qualitative study with Syrian refugees in Lebanon. *Social Science & Medicine, 200*, 19–26. doi:10.1016/J.SOCSCIMED.2018.01.009

Simpkins, S. D., Delgado, M. Y., Price, C. D., Quach, A., & Starbuck, E. (2013). Socioeconomic status, ethnicity, culture, and immigration: Examining the potential mechanisms underlying Mexican-origin adolescents' organized activity participation. *Developmental Psychology, 49*, 706–721. doi:10.1037/a0028399

Slaughter, V., Imuta, K., Peterson, C. C., & Henry, J. D. (2015). Meta-analysis of theory of mind and peer popularity in the preschool and early school years. *Child Development, 86*, 1159–1174. doi:10.1111/cdev.12372

Slone, M., & Mann, S. (2016). Effects of war, terrorism and armed conflict on young children: A systematic review. *Child Psychiatry & Human Development, 47*, 950–965. doi:10.1007/s10578-016-0626-7

Smith, S. L., & Moyer-Gusé, E. (2006). Children and the war on Iraq: Developmental differences in fear responses to television news coverage. *Media Psychology, 8*, 213–237. doi:10.1207/s1532785xmep0803_2

Srabstein, J., Joshi, P. T., Due, P., Wright, J., Leventhal, B., Merrick, J., . . . Riibner, K. (2008). Antibullying legislation: A public health perspective. *Journal of Adolescent Health, 42*, 11–20. doi:10.1016/j.jadohealth.2007.10.007

Sroufe L.A. (2016). The place of attachment in development. In J. Cassidy & P. R. Shaver (Eds.), *Handbook of attachment: Theory, research, and clinical applications.* Retrieved from https://www.guilford.com/books/Handbook-of-Attachment/Cassidy-Shaver/9781462525294/contents

Stevenson, H. W., Lee, S., & Mu, X. (2000). Successful achievement in mathematics: China and the United States. In C. F. M. van Lieshout & P. G. Heymans (Eds.), *Developing talent across the life span* (pp. 167–183). New York, NY: Psychology Press.

Strohschein, L. (2005). Parental divorce and child mental health trajectories. *Journal of Marriage and Family, 67*, 1286–1300.

Swearer, S. M., & Hymel, S. (2015). Understanding the psychology of bullying: Moving toward a social-ecological diathesis-stress model. *The American Psychologist, 70*, 344–353. doi:10.1037/a0038929

Tasker, F., & Patterson, C. J. (2007). Research on gay and lesbian parenting: Retrospect and prospect. *Journal of GLBT Family Studies, 3*, 9–34.

Taylor, Z. E., & Conger, R. D. (2017). Promoting strengths and resilience in single-mother families. *Child Development, 88*, 350–358. doi:10.1111/cdev.12741

Thomaes, S., Reijntjes, A., Orobio de Castro, B., Bushman, B. J., Poorthuis, A., & Telch, M. J. (2010). I like me if you like me: On the interpersonal modulation and regulation of preadolescents' state self-esteem. *Child Development, 81*, 811–825. doi:10.1111/j.1467-8624.2010.01435.x

Thomas, H. J., Connor, J. P., & Scott, J. G. (2017). Why do children and adolescents bully their peers? A critical review of key theoretical frameworks. *Social Psychiatry and Psychiatric Epidemiology, 53*, 437–451. doi:10.1007/s00127-017-1462-1

Toyama, M. (2001). Developmental changes in social comparison in pre-school and elementary school children: Perceptions, feelings, and behavior. *Japanese Journal of Educational Psychology, 49*, 500–507.

Traub, F., & Boynton-Jarrett, R. (2017). Modifiable resilience factors to childhood adversity for clinical pediatric practice. *Pediatrics, 139*, e20162569. doi:10.1542/peds.2016-2569

Troutman, D. R., & Fletcher, A. C. (2010). Context and companionship in children's short-term versus long-term friendships. *Journal of Social & Personal Relationships, 27*, 1060–1074. doi:10.1177/0265407510381253

Turcotte Benedict, F., Vivier, P. M., & Gjelsvik, A. (2015). Mental health and bullying in the United States among children aged 6 to 17 years. *Journal of Interpersonal Violence, 30*, 782–795. doi:10.1177/0886260514536279

Ungar, M. (2015). Practitioner review: Diagnosing childhood resilience—a systemic approach to the diagnosis of adaptation in adverse social and physical ecologies. *Journal of Child Psychology and Psychiatry, 56*, 4–17. doi:10.1111/jcpp.12306

U.S. Department of Health and Human Services. (2017). *Laws & Policies | StopBullying.gov.* Retrieved February 25, 2018, from https://www.stopbullying.gov/laws/index.html

U.S. Department of Health and Human Services. (2018). *Child maltreatment, 2016.* Retrieved from https://www.acf.hhs.gov/cb/resource/child-maltreatment-2016

van den Berg, Y. H. M., Deutz, M. H. F., Smeekens, S., & Cillessen, A. H. N. (2017). Developmental pathways to preference and popularity in middle childhood. *Child Development, 88*, 1629–1641. doi:10.1111/cdev.12706

van Dijk, A., Poorthuis, A. M. G., & Malti, T. (2017). Psychological processes in young bullies versus bully-victims. *Aggressive Behavior, 43*, 430–439. doi:10.1002/ab.21701

Vaillancourt, T., Faris, R., & Mishna, F. (2017). Cyberbullying in children and youth: Implications for health and clinical practice. *Canadian Journal of Psychiatry, 62*, 368–373. doi:10.1177/0706743716684791

Waasdorp, T. E., & Bradshaw, C. P. (2011). Examining student responses to frequent bullying: A latent class approach. *Journal of Educational Psychology, 103*, 336–352. doi:10.1037/a0022747

Waasdorp, T. E., & Bradshaw, C. P. (2015). The overlap between cyberbullying and traditional bullying. *Journal of Adolescent Health, 56*, 483–488. doi:10.1016/j.jadohealth.2014.12.002

Waldfogel, J., Craigie, T. A., & Brooks-Gunn, J. (2010). Fragile families and child wellbeing. *The Future of Children, 20*, 87–112.

Wang, D., Kato, N., Inaba, Y., Tango, T., Yoshida, Y., Kusaka, Y., . . . Zhang, Q. (2000). Physical and personality traits of preschool children in Fuzhou, China: Only child vs sibling. *Child: Care, Health & Development, 26*, 49–60.

Weaver, J. M., & Schofield, T. J. (2015). Mediation and moderation of divorce effects on children's behavior problems. *Journal of Family Psychology, 29*, 39–48. doi:10.1037/fam0000043

Wentzel, K. R. (2002). Are effective teachers like good parents? Teaching styles and student adjustment in early adolescence. *Child Development, 73*, 287–301.

Werner, E. E. (2012). Children and war: Risk, resilience, and recovery. *Development and Psychopathology, 24*, 553–558.

Whiteside, M. F., & Becker, B. J. (2000). Parental factors and the young child's postdivorce adjustment: A meta-analysis with implications for parenting arrangements. *Journal of Family Psychology, 14*, 5–26.

Wigfield, A., Eccles, J. S., Fredricks, J. A., Simpkins, S., Roeser, R. W., Schiefele, U. (2015). Development of achievement motivation and engagement. In M. Lamb (Ed.), *Handbook of child psychology and developmental science* (pp. 1–44). Hoboken, NJ: John Wiley. doi:10.1002/9781118963418.childpsy316

Will, G. J., van Lier, P. A. C., Crone, E. A., & Güroğlu, B. (2016). Chronic childhood peer rejection is associated with heightened neural responses to social exclusion during adolescence. *Journal of Abnormal Child Psychology, 44*, 43–55. doi:10.1007/s10802-015-9983-0

Wojslawowicz Bowker, J. C., Rubin, K. H., Burgess, K. B., Booth-Laforce, C., & Rose-Krasnor, L. (2006). Behavioral characteristics associated with stable and fluid best friendship patterns in middle childhood. *Merrill-Palmer Quarterly, 52*, 671–693.

Yang, J. (2007). The one-child policy and school attendance in China. *Comparative Education Review, 51*, 471–495.

Yeager, D. S., & Dweck, C. S. (2012). Mindsets that promote resilience: When students believe that personal characteristics can be developed. *Educational Psychologist, 47*, 302–314. doi:10.1080/00461520.2012.722805

Zhu, W. X., Lu, L., & Hesketh, T. (2009). China's excess males, sex selective abortion, and one child policy: Analysis of data from 2005 National Intercensus survey. *BMJ: British Medical Journal, 338*, 920–923.

Zych, I., Farrington, D. P., Llorent, V. J., & Ttofi, M. M. (2017). *Protecting children against bullying and its consequences.* Cham, Switzerland: Springer International. doi:10.1007/978-3-319-53028-4

Chapter 11

Aïte, A., Cassotti, M., Linzarini, A., Osmont, A., Houdé, O., & Borst, G. (2018). Adolescents' inhibitory control: Keep it cool or lose control. *Developmental Science, 21*, e12491. doi:10.1111/desc.12491

Akos, P., Rose, R. A., & Orthner, D. (2014). Sociodemographic moderators of middle school transition effects on academic achievement. *Journal of Early Adolescence, 35*, 170–198. doi:10.1177/0272431614529367

Albert, D., Chein, J., & Steinberg, L. (2013). The teenage brain: Peer influences on adolescent decision making. *Current Directions in Psychological Science, 22*, 114–120. doi:10.1177/0963721412471347

Alberts, A., Elkind, D., & Ginsberg, S. (2007). The personal fable and risk-taking in early adolescence. *Journal of Youth & Adolescence, 36*, 71–76.

Alivernini, F., & Lucidi, F. (2011). Relationship between social context, self-efficacy, motivation, academic achievement, and intention to drop out of high school: A longitudinal study. *Journal of Educational Research, 104*, 241–252. doi:10.1080/00220671003728062

Allen, J. P., & Antonishak, J. (2008). Adolescent peer influences: Beyond the dark side. In M. J. Prinstein & K. A. Dodge (Eds.), *Understanding peer influence in children and adolescents* (pp. 141–160). New York, NY: Guilford.

Alviola, P. A., Nayga, R. M., Thomsen, M. R., Danforth, D., & Smartt, J. (2014). The effect of fast-food restaurants on childhood obesity: A school level analysis. *Economics & Human Biology, 12*, 110–119. doi:10.1016/j.ehb.2013.05.001

American Academy of Pediatrics & American Academy of Pediatrics Council on Communications and Media. (2013). Children, adolescents, and the media. *Pediatrics, 132*, 958–961. doi:10.1542/peds.2013-2656

Ardila, A. (2013). Development of metacognitive and emotional executive functions in children. *Applied Neuropsychology, Child, 2*, 82–87. doi:10.1080/21622965.2013.748388

Arnett, J. J. (2015). *The Oxford handbook of emerging adulthood.* Oxford, UK: Oxford University Press. doi:10.1093/oxfordhb/9780199795574.001.0001

Assadi, S. M., Zokaei, N., Kaviani, H., Mohammadi, M. R., Ghaeli, P., Gohari, M. R., & van de Vijver, F. J. R. (2007). Effect of sociocultural context and parenting style on scholastic achievement among Iranian adolescents. *Social Development, 16*, 169–180.

Aunola, K., & Stattin, H. (2000). Parenting styles and adolescents' achievement strategies. *Journal of Adolescence, 23*, 205–223.

Baams, L., Dubas, J. S., Overbeek, G., & van Aken, M. A. G. (2015). Transitions in body and behavior: A meta-analytic study on the relationship between pubertal development and adolescent sexual behavior. *Journal of Adolescent Health, 56*, 586–598. doi:10.1016/j.jadohealth.2014.11.019

Balzer, B. W. R., Duke, S.-A., Hawke, C. I., & Steinbeck, K. S. (2015). The effects of estradiol on mood and behavior in human female adolescents: A systematic review. *European Journal of Pediatrics, 174*, 289–298. doi:10.1007/s00431-014-2475-3

Banfield, E. C., Liu, Y., Davis, J. S., Chang, S., & Frazier-Wood, A. C. (2016). Poor adherence to US dietary guidelines for children and adolescents in the National Health and Nutrition Examination survey population. *Journal of the Academy of Nutrition and Dietetics, 116*, 21–27. doi:10.1016/j.jand.2015.08.010

Barrouillet, P., Gavens, N., Vergauwe, E., Gaillard, V., & Camos, V. (2009). Working memory span development: A time-based resource-sharing model account. *Developmental Psychology, 45*, 477–490. doi:10.1037/a0014615

Bartel, K. A., Gradisar, M., & Williamson, P. (2015). Protective and risk factors for adolescent sleep: A meta-analytic review. *Sleep Medicine Reviews, 21*, 72–85. doi:10.1016/j.smrv.2014.08.002

Bava, S., & Tapert, S. F. (2010). Adolescent brain development and the risk for alcohol and other drug problems. *Neuropsychology Review, 20*, 398–413. doi:10.1007/s11065-010-9146-6

Benner, A. D. (2011). The transition to high school: Current knowledge, future directions. *Educational Psychology Review, 23*, 299–328. doi:10.1007/s10648-011-9152-0

Benner, A. D., Boyle, A. E., & Bakhtiari, F. (2017). Understanding students' transition to high school: Demographic variation and the role of supportive relationships. *Journal of Youth and Adolescence, 46*, 2129–2142. doi:10.1007/s10964-017-0716-2

Benner, A. D., & Graham, S. (2009). The transition to high school as a developmental process among multiethnic urban youth. *Child Development, 80*, 356–376. doi:10.1111/j.1467-8624.2009.01265.x

Benoit, A., Lacourse, E., & Claes, M. (2013). Pubertal timing and depressive symptoms in late adolescence: The moderating role of individual, peer, and parental factors. *Development and Psychopathology, 25*, 455–471. doi:10.1017/S0954579412001174

Berenbaum, S. A., Beltz, A. M., & Corley, R. (2015). The importance of puberty for adolescent development: Conceptualization and measurement. *Advances in Child Development and Behavior, 48*, 53–92. doi:10.1016/BS.ACDB.2014.11.002

Berge, J. M., Jin, S. W., Hannan, P., & Neumark-Sztainer, D. (2013). Structural and interpersonal characteristics of family meals: Associations with adolescent body mass index and dietary patterns. *Journal of the Academy of Nutrition and Dietetics, 113*, 816–822. doi:10.1016/j.jand.2013.02.004

Berge, J. M., Wall, M., Hsueh, T. F., Fulkerson, J. A., Larson, N., & Neumark-Sztainer, D. (2015). The protective role of family meals for youth obesity: 10-year longitudinal associations. *Journal of Pediatrics, 166*, 296–301. doi:10.1016/j.jpeds.2014.08.030

Berkowitz, M. W., & Begun, A. L. (1994). Assessing how adolescents think about the morality of substance use. *Drugs & Society, 8*, 111.

Best, C., & Fortenberry, J. D. (2013). Adolescent sexuality and sexual behavior. In W. T. O'Donohue, L. T. Benuto, & L. Woodward Tolle (Eds.), *Handbook of adolescent health psychology* (pp. 271–291). New York, NY: Springer. doi:10.1007/978-1-4614-6633-8_19

Biehl, M., Natsuaki, M., & Ge, X. (2007). The influence of pubertal timing on alcohol use and heavy drinking trajectories. *Journal of Youth & Adolescence, 36,* 153–167.

Birney, D. P., & Sternberg, R. J. (2011). The development of cognitive abilities. In M. H. Bornstein & M. E. Lamb (Eds.), *Developmental science: An advanced textbook* (6th ed., pp. 353–388). New York, NY: Psychology Press.

Biro, F. M., Greenspan, L. C., & Galvez, M. P. (2012). Puberty in girls of the 21st century. *Journal of Pediatric and Adolescent Gynecology, 25,* 289–294. doi:10.1016/j.jpag.2012.05.009

Blakemore, S. J., & Mills, K. L. (2014). Is adolescence a sensitive period for sociocultural processing? *Annual Review of Psychology, 65,* 187–207. doi:10.1146/annurev-psych-010213-115202

Boom, J. J., Wouters, H., & Keller, M. (2007). A cross-cultural validation of stage development: A Rasch re-analysis of longitudinal socio-moral reasoning data. *Cognitive Development, 22,* 213–229.

Booth, M. Z., & Gerard, J. M. (2014). Adolescents' stage-environment fit in middle and high school: The relationship between students' perceptions of their schools and themselves. *Youth & Society, 46,* 735–755. doi:10.1177/0044118X12451276

Bosch, A. M., Hutter, I., & van Ginneken, J. K. (2008). Perceptions of adolescents and their mothers on reproductive and sexual development in Matlab, Bangladesh. *International Journal of Adolescent Medicine and Health, 20,* 329–342.

Bowers, A. J., & Sprott, R. (2012). Examining the multiple trajectories associated with dropping out of high school: A growth mixture model analysis. *Journal of Educational Research, 105,* 176–195. doi:10.1080/00220671.2011.552075

Boyer, T. W., & Byrnes, J. P. (2016). Risk-taking. In J. R. Levesque (Ed.), *Encyclopedia of adolescence* (pp. 1–5). Cham, Switzerland: Springer International. doi:10.1007/978-3-319-32132-5_15-2

Breiner, K., Li, A., Cohen, A. O., Steinberg, L., Bonnie, R. J., Scott, E. S., . . . Galván, A. (2018). Combined effects of peer presence, social cues, and rewards on cognitive control in adolescents. *Developmental Psychobiology, 60,* 292–302. doi:10.1002/dev.21599

Brooks-Gunn, J., & Ruble, D. N. (2013). Developmental processes in the experience of menarche. In J. E. S. A. Baum, J. E. Sin, & A. Baum (Eds.), *Issues in child health and adolescent health: Handbook of psychology and health* (pp. 117–148). New York, NY: Psychology Press.

Brugman, D. (2010). Moral reasoning competence and the moral judgment-action discrepancy in young adolescents. In A. F. S. Willem Koops, D. Brugman, & T. J. Ferguson (Eds.), *The development and structure of conscience* (pp. 119–133). New York, NY: Psychology Press.

Buchanan, C. M., & Bruton, J. H. (2016). Storm and stress. In J. R. Levesque (Ed.), *Encyclopedia of adolescence* (pp. 1–12). Cham, Switzerland: Springer International. doi:10.1007/978-3-319-32132-5_111-2

Bundak, R., Darendeliler, F., Gunoz, H., Bas, F., Saka, N., & Neyzi, O. (2007). Analysis of puberty and pubertal growth in healthy boys. *European Journal of Pediatrics, 166,* 595–600.

Burchinal, M., Roberts, J. E., Zeisel, S. A., Hennon, E. A., & Hooper, S. (2006). Social risk and protective child, parenting, and child care factors in early elementary school years. *Parenting: Science & Practice, 6,* 79–113.

Burgess-Champoux, T. L., Larson, N., Neumark-Sztainer, D., Hannan, P. J., & Story, M. (2009). Are family meal patterns associated with overall diet quality during the transition from early to middle adolescence? *Journal of Nutrition Education & Behavior, 41,* 79–86.

Caprara, G. V., Schwartz, S., Capanna, C., Vecchione, M., & Barbaranelli, C. (2006). Personality and politics: Values, traits, and political choice. *Political Psychology, 27,* 1–28. doi:10.1111/j.1467-9221.2006.00447.x

Carlo, G., Mestre, M. V., Samper, P., Tur, A., & Armenta, B. E. (2011). The longitudinal relations among dimensions of parenting styles, sympathy, prosocial moral reasoning, and prosocial behaviors. *International Journal of Behavioral Development, 35,* 116–124. doi:10.1177/0165025410375921

Carlson, S. M., Zelazo, P. D., & Faja, S. (2013). *Executive function* (P. D. Zelazo, Ed.). Oxford, UK: Oxford University Press. doi:10.1093/oxfordhb/9780199958450.013.0025

Carskadon, M. A. (2009). Adolescents and sleep: Why teens can't get enough of a good thing. *Brown University Child & Adolescent Behavior Letter, 25,* 1–6.

Carskadon, M. A., Acebo, C., & Jenni, O. G. (2004). Regulation of adolescent sleep: Implications for behavior. *Annals of the New York Academy of Sciences, 1021,* 276–291. doi:10.1196/annals.1308.032

Carskadon, M. A., & Tarokh, L. (2014). Developmental changes in sleep biology and potential effects on adolescent behavior and caffeine use. *Nutrition Reviews, 72*(Suppl 1), 60–64. doi:10.1111/nure.12147

Carter, R., Mustafaa, F. N., & Leath, S. (2018). Teachers' expectations of girls' classroom performance and behavior. *Journal of Early Adolescence, 38,* 885–907. doi:10.1177/0272431617699947

Cauffman, E., & Steinberg, L. (2012). Emerging findings from research on adolescent justice. *Victims and Offenders, 7,* 428–449. doi:10.1080/15564886.2012.713901

Centifanti, L. C. M., Modecki, K. L., MacLellan, S., & Gowling, H. (2016). Driving under the influence of risky peers: An experimental study of adolescent risk taking. *Journal of Research on Adolescence, 26,* 207–222. doi:10.1111/jora.12187

Chandra-Mouli, V., & Patel, S. V. (2017). Mapping the knowledge and understanding of menarche, menstrual hygiene and menstrual health among adolescent girls in low- and middle-income countries. *Reproductive Health, 14,* 30. doi:10.1186/s12978-017-0293-6

Chen, F. R., Rothman, E. F., & Jaffee, S. R. (2017). Early puberty, friendship group characteristics, and dating abuse in US girls. *Pediatrics, 139,* e20162847. doi:10.1542/peds.2016-2847

Chen, P., & Vazsonyi, A. T. (2013). Future orientation, school contexts, and problem behaviors: A multilevel study. *Journal of Youth and Adolescence, 42,* 67–81. doi:10.1007/s10964-012-9785-4

Coelho, V. A., Marchante, M., & Jimerson, S. R. (2017). Promoting a positive middle school transition: A randomized-controlled treatment study examining self-concept and self-esteem. *Journal of Youth and Adolescence, 46,* 558–569. doi:10.1007/s10964-016-0510-6

Cohen, A. O., & Casey, B. J. (2017). The neurobiology of adolescent self-control. In T. Egner (Ed.), *The Wiley handbook of cognitive control* (pp. 455–475). Chichester, England: John Wiley. doi:10.1002/9781118920497.ch26

Cohen Kadosh, K., Johnson, M. H., Dick, F., Cohen Kadosh, R., & Blakemore, S.-J. (2013). Effects of age, task performance, and structural brain development on face processing. *Cerebral Cortex, 23,* 1630–1642. doi:10.1093/cercor/bhs150

Colby, A., & Damon, W. (1992). *Some do care: Contemporary lives of moral commitment.* New York, NY: Free Press.

Colrain, I. M., & Baker, F. C. (2011). Changes in sleep as a function of adolescent development. *Neuropsychology Review, 21,* 5–21. doi:10.1007/s11065-010-9155-5

Comunian, A. L., & Gielen, U. P. (2000). Sociomoral reflection and prosocial and antisocial behavior: Two Italian studies. *Psychological Reports, 87,* 161–176.

Conway, J. M., Amel, E. L., & Gerwien, D. P. (2009). Teaching and learning in the social context: A meta-analysis of service learning's effects on academic, personal, social, and citizenship outcomes. *Teaching of Psychology, 36,* 233–245. doi:10.1080/00986280903172969

Cooper, S. M., Kurtz-Costes, B., & Rowley, S. J. (2010). The schooling of African American children. In J. L. Meece & J. S. Eccles (Eds.), *Handbook of research on schools, schooling and human development* (pp. 275–292). New York, NY: Routledge.

Costos, D., Ackerman, R., & Paradis, L. (2002). Recollections of menarche: Communication between mothers and daughters regarding menstruation. *Sex Roles, 46,* 49–59. doi:10.1023/A:1016037618567

Crone, E. A., Peters, S., & Steinbeis, N. (2018). Executive function: Development in adolescence. In S. A. Wiebe & J. Karbach (Eds.), *Executive function: Development across the life span* (pp. 58–72). New York, NY: Routledge.

Crosnoe, R., Benner, A. D., Crosnoe, R., & Benner, A. D. (2015). Children at school. In M. H. Bornstein & T. Leventhal (Eds.), *Handbook of child psychology and developmental science* (pp. 1–37). Hoboken, NJ: John Wiley. doi:10.1002/9781118963418.childpsy407

Crowley, S. J., Acebo, C., & Carskadon, M. A. (2007). Sleep, circadian rhythms, and delayed phase in adolescence. *Sleep Medicine, 8,* 602–612. doi:10.1016/j.sleep.2006.12.002

Cservenka, A., & Brumback, T. (2017). The burden of binge and heavy drinking on the brain: Effects on adolescent and young adult neural structure and function. *Frontiers in Psychology, 8,* 1111. doi:10.3389/fpsyg.2017.01111

Currie, C., Ahluwalia, N., Godeau, E., Nic Gabhainn, S., Due, P., & Currie, D. B. (2012). Is obesity at individual and national level associated with lower age at menarche? Evidence from 34 countries in the Health Behaviour in School-aged Children study. *Journal of Adolescent Health, 50*, 621–626. doi:10.1016/j.jadohealth.2011.10.254

Darchia, N., & Cervena, K. (2014). The journey through the world of adolescent sleep. *Reviews in the Neurosciences, 25*, 585–604. doi:10.1515/revneuro-2013-0065

Dawson, T. L. (2002). New tools, new insights: Kohlberg's moral judgement stages revisited. *International Journal of Behavioral Development, 26*, 154–166.

Deardorff, J., Abrams, B., Ekwaru, J. P., & Rehkopf, D. H. (2014). Socioeconomic status and age at menarche: An examination of multiple indicators in an ethnically diverse cohort. *Annals of Epidemiology, 24*, 727–733. doi:10.1016/j.annepidem.2014.07.002

Deardorff, J., Ekwaru, J. P., Kushi, L. H., Ellis, B. J., Greenspan, L. C., Mirabedi, A., . . . Hiatt, R. A. (2011). Father absence, body mass index, and pubertal timing in girls: Differential effects by family income and ethnicity. *Journal of Adolescent Health, 48*, 441–447. doi:10.1016/j.jadohealth.2010.07.032

Denbow, J. R., James, R., & Thebe, P. C. (2006). *Culture and customs of Botswana.* Westport, CT: Greenwood.

Dorn, L. D., & Biro, F. M. (2011). Puberty and its measurement: A decade in review. *Journal of Research on Adolescence, 21*, 180–195. doi:10.1111/j.1532-7795.2010.00722.x

Dornbusch, S. M., Ritter, P. L., Mont-Reynaud, R., & Chen, Z. (1990). Family decision making and academic performance in a diverse high school population. *Journal of Adolescent Research, 5*, 143–160.

Dotterer, A. M., Lowe, K., & McHale, S. M. (2014). Academic growth trajectories and family relationships among African American youth. *Journal of Research on Adolescence, 24*, 734–747. doi:10.1111/jora.12080

Douglass, S., Yip, T., & Shelton, J. N. (2014). Intragroup contact and anxiety among ethnic minority adolescents: Considering ethnic identity and school diversity transitions. *Journal of Youth and Adolescence, 43*, 1628–1641. doi:10.1007/s10964-014-0144-5

Downs, A. C., & Fuller, M. J. (1991). Recollections of spermarche: An exploratory investigation. *Current Psychology, 10*, 93.

Dreyfuss, M., Caudle, K., Drysdale, A. T., Johnston, N. E., Cohen, A. O., Somerville, L. H., . . . Casey, B. J. (2014). Teens impulsively react rather than retreat from threat. *Developmental Neuroscience, 36*, 220–227. doi:10.1159/000357755

Duell, N., Steinberg, L., Icenogle, G., Chein, J., Chaudhary, N., Di Giunta, L., . . . Chang, L. (2018). Age patterns in risk taking across the world. *Journal of Youth and Adolescence, 47*, 1052–1072. doi:10.1007/s10964-017-0752-y

Duke, S. A., Balzer, B. W. R., & Steinbeck, K. S. (2014). Testosterone and its effects on human male adolescent mood and behavior: A systematic review. *Journal of Adolescent Health, 55*, 315–322. doi:10.1016/j.jadohealth.2014.05.007

Dumith, S. C., Gigante, D. P., Domingues, M. R., & Kohl, H. W. (2011). Physical activity change during adolescence: A systematic review and a pooled analysis. *International Journal of Epidemiology, 40*, 685–698. doi:10.1093/ije/dyq272

Dumontheil, I. (2016). Adolescent brain development. *Current Opinion in Behavioral Sciences, 10*, 39–44. doi:10.1016/j.cobeha.2016.04.012

Dupéré, V., Dion, E., Leventhal, T., Archambault, I., Crosnoe, R., & Janosz, M. (2018). High school dropout in proximal context: The triggering role of stressful life events. *Child Development, 89*, e107–e122. doi:10.1111/cdev.12792

Dupere, V., Leventhal, T., Dion, E., Crosnoe, R., Archambault, I., & Janosz, M. (2015). Stressors and turning points in high school and dropout: A stress process, life course framework. *Review of Educational Research, 85*, 591–629. doi:10.3102/0034654314559845

Eccles, J. S., & Roeser, R. W. (2011). Schools as developmental contexts during adolescence. *Journal of Research on Adolescence, 21*, 225–241. doi:10.1111/j.1532-7795.2010.00725.x

Eccles, J. S., & Roeser, R. W. (2015). School and community influences on human development. In M. H. Bornstein & M. E. Lamb (Eds.), *Developmental science: An advanced textbook* (7th ed., pp. 645–727). New York, NY: Psychology Press

Eisenberg, N., Cumberland, A., Guthrie, I. K., Murphy, B. C., & Shepard, S. A. (2005). Age changes in prosocial responding and moral reasoning in adolescence and early adulthood. *Journal of Research on Adolescence, 15*, 235–260. doi:10.1111/j.1532-7795.2005.00095.x

Elias, C. F. (2012). Leptin action in pubertal development: Recent advances and unanswered questions. *Trends in Endocrinology and Metabolism, 23*, 9–15. doi:10.1016/j.tem.2011.09.002

Elkind, D., & Bowen, R. (1979). Imaginary audience behavior in children and adolescents. *Developmental Psychology, 15*, 38–44.

Emmanuel, M., & Bokor, B. R. (2017). Tanner stages. *StatPearls.* Retrieved from http://www.ncbi.nlm.nih.gov/pubmed/29262142

Espinoza, G., & Juvonen, J. (2011). Perceptions of the school social context across the transition to middle school: Heightened sensitivity among Latino students? *Journal of Educational Psychology, 103*, 749–758. doi:10.1037/a0023811

Farooq, M. A., Parkinson, K. N., Adamson, A. J., Pearce, M. S., Reilly, J. K., Hughes, A. R., . . . Reilly, J. J. (2018). Timing of the decline in physical activity in childhood and adolescence: Gateshead Millennium Cohort Study. *British Journal of Sports Medicine, 52*, 1002–1006. doi:10.1136/bjsports-2016-096933

Felmlee, D., McMillan, C., Inara Rodis, P., & Osgood, D. W. (2018). Falling behind: Lingering costs of the high school transition for youth friendships and grades. *Sociology of Education, 91*, 159–182. doi:10.1177/0038040718762136

Figner, B., Mackinlay, R. J., Wilkening, F., & Weber, E. U. (2009). Affective and deliberative processes in risky choice: Age differences in risk taking in the Columbia Card Task. *Journal of Experimental Psychology: Learning, Memory, and Cognition, 35*, 709–730. doi:10.1037/a0014983

Flanagan, C. A., Kim, T., Collura, J., & Kopish, M. A. (2015). Community service and adolescents' social capital. *Journal of Research on Adolescence, 25*, 295–309. doi:10.1111/jora.12137

Fradkin, C., Wallander, J. L., Elliott, M. N., Cuccaro, P., & Schuster, M. A. (2014). Regular physical activity has differential association with reduced obesity among diverse youth in the United States. *Journal of Health Psychology, 21*, 1607–1619. doi:10.1177/1359105314559622

Fradkin, C., Wallander, J. L., Elliott, M. N., Tortolero, S., Cuccaro, P., & Schuster, M. A. (2015). Associations between socioeconomic status and obesity in diverse, young adolescents: Variation across race/ethnicity and gender. *Health Psychology, 34*, 1–9. doi:10.1037/hea0000099

Frankel, L. L. (2002). "I've never thought about it": Contradictions and taboos surrounding American males' experiences of first ejaculation (semenarche). *Journal of Men's Studies, 11*, 37–54.

Frazier-Wood, A. C., Banfield, E. C., Liu, Y., Davis, J. S., & Chang, S. (2015). Abstract 27: Poor adherence to US dietary guidelines for children and adolescents in the National Health and Nutrition Examination survey (NHANES) 2005-2010 population. *Circulation, 131*(Suppl. 1). Retrieved from http://circ.ahajournals.org/content/131/Suppl_1/A27.short

Frederick, C. B., Snellman, K., & Putnam, R. D. (2014). Increasing socioeconomic disparities in adolescent obesity. *Proceedings of the National Academy of Sciences of the United States of America, 111*, 1338–1342. doi:10.1073/pnas.1321355110

Freeman, J., & Simonsen, B. (2015). Examining the impact of policy and practice interventions on high school dropout and school completion rates: A systematic review of the literature. *Review of Educational Research, 82*, 205–248. doi:10.3102/0034654314554431

Frostad, P., Pijl, S. J., & Mjaavatn, P. E. (2014). Losing all interest in school: Social participation as a predictor of the intention to leave upper secondary school early. *Scandinavian Journal of Educational Research, 59*, 110–122. doi:10.1080/00313831.2014.904420

Fuhrmann, D., Knoll, L. J., & Blakemore, S.-J. (2015). Adolescence as a sensitive period of brain development. *Trends in Cognitive Sciences, 19*, 558–566. doi:10.1016/j.tics.2015.07.008

Fuligni, A. J., Arruda, E. H., Krull, J. L., & Gonzales, N. A. (2018). Adolescent sleep duration, variability, and peak levels of achievement and mental health. *Child Development, 89*, e18–e28. doi:10.1111/cdev.12729

Furby, L., & Beyth-Marom, R. (1992). Risk taking in adolescence: A decision-making perspective. *Developmental Review, 12*, 1–44.

Garg, R., Levin, E., Urajnik, D., & Kauppi, C. (2005). Parenting style and academic achievement for East Indian and Canadian adolescents. *Journal of Comparative Family Studies, 36*, 653–661.

Geier, C. F. (2013). Adolescent cognitive control and reward processing: Implications for risk taking and substance use. *Hormones and Behavior, 64*, 333–342. doi:10.1016/j.yhbeh.2013.02.008

Gentle-Genitty, C. (2009). Best practice program for low-income African American students transitioning from middle to high school. *Children & Schools, 31*, 109–117.

Gibbs, J. C., Basinger, K. S., Grime, R. L., & Snarey, J. R. (2007). Moral judgment development across cultures: Revisiting Kohlberg's universality claims. *Developmental Review, 27*, 443–500. doi:10.1016/j.dr.2007.04.001

Giedd, J. N. (2018). A ripe time for adolescent research. *Journal of Research on Adolescence, 28*, 157–159. doi:10.1111/jora.12378

Giedd, J. N., Lalonde, F. M., Celano, M. J., White, S. L., Wallace, G. L., Lee, N. R., & Lenroot, R. K. (2009). Anatomical brain magnetic resonance imaging of typically developing children and adolescents. *Journal of the American Academy of Child & Adolescent Psychiatry, 48*, 465–470. doi:10.1097/CHI.0b013e31819f215

Gilligan, C. (1982). *In a different voice: Psychological theory and women's development.* Cambridge, MA: Harvard University Press.

Gilligan, C., & Attanucci, J. (1988). Two moral orientations: Gender differences and similarities. *Merrill-Palmer Quarterly, 34*, 223–237.

Goldstein, S. E., Boxer, P., & Rudolph, E. (2015). Middle school transition stress: Links with academic performance, motivation, and school experiences. *Contemporary School Psychology, 19*, 21–29. doi:10.1007/s40688-014-0044-4

Gonzalez, A. L., & Wolters, C. A. (2006). The relation between perceived parenting practices and achievement motivation in mathematics. *Journal of Research in Childhood Education, 21*, 203–217.

Graber, J. A., Nichols, T. R., & Brooks-Gunn, J. (2010). Putting pubertal timing in developmental context: Implications for prevention. *Developmental Psychobiology, 52*, 254–262. doi:10.1002/dev.20438

Hanson, K. L., Thayer, R. E., & Tapert, S. F. (2014). Adolescent marijuana users have elevated risk-taking on the balloon analog risk task. *Journal of Psychopharmacology, 28*, 1080–1087. doi:10.1177/0269881114550352

Hanson, K. L., Winward, J. L., Schweinsburg, A. D., Medina, K. L., Brown, S. A., & Tapert, S. F. (2010). Longitudinal study of cognition among adolescent marijuana users over three weeks of abstinence. *Addictive Behaviors, 35*, 970–976. doi:10.1016/j.addbeh.2010.06.012

Hardy, L. L., Mihrshahi, S., Gale, J., Drayton, B. A., Bauman, A., & Mitchell, J. (2017). 30-Year trends in overweight, obesity and waist-to-height ratio by socioeconomic status in Australian children, 1985 to 2015. *International Journal of Obesity, 41*, 76–82. doi:10.1038/ijo.2016.204

Hart, D., Donnelly, T. M., Youniss, J., & Atkins, R. (2007). High school community service as a predictor of adult voting and volunteering. *American Educational Research Journal, 44*, 197–219. doi:10.3102/0002831206298173

Heaven, P. C. L., & Ciarrochi, J. (2008). Parental styles, conscientiousness, and academic performance in high school: A three-wave longitudinal study. *Personality and Social Psychology Bulletin, 34*, 451–461. doi:10.1177/0146167207311909

Helwig, C. C., Arnold, M. L., Tan, D., & Boyd, D. (2007). Mainland Chinese and Canadian adolescents' judgments and reasoning about the fairness of democratic and other forms of government. *Cognitive Development, 22*, 96–109.

Henry, K. L., Knight, K. E., & Thornberry, T. P. (2012). School disengagement as a predictor of dropout, delinquency, and problem substance use during adolescence and early adulthood. *Journal of Youth and Adolescence, 41*, 156–166. doi:10.1007/s10964-011-9665-3

Herman, K. M., Hopman, W. M., & Sabiston, C. M. (2015). Physical activity, screen time and self-rated health and mental health in Canadian adolescents. *Preventive Medicine, 73*, 112–116. doi:10.1016/J.YPMED.2015.01.030

Herman-Giddens, M. E. (2006). Recent data on pubertal milestones in United States children: The secular trend toward earlier development. *International Journal of Andrology, 29*, 241–246.

Herman-Giddens, M. E., Steffes, J., Harris, D., Slora, E., Hussey, M., Dowshen, S. A., . . . Reiter, E. O. (2012). Secondary sexual characteristics in boys: Data from the Pediatric Research in Office Settings Network. *Pediatrics, 130*, e1058–e1068. doi:10.1542/peds.2011-3291

Hines, A. R., & Paulson, S. E. (2006). Parents' and teachers' perceptions of adolescent storm and stress: Relations with parenting and teaching styles. *Adolescence, 41*, 597–614. Retrieved from http://www.ncbi.nlm.nih.gov/pubmed/17240769

Hodges-Simeon, C. R., Gurven, M., Cárdenas, R. A., & Gaulin, S. J. C. (2013). Voice change as a new measure of male pubertal timing: a study among Bolivian adolescents. *Annals of Human Biology, 40*, 209–219. doi:10.3109/03014460.2012.759622

Hollenstein, T., & Lougheed, J. P. (2013). Beyond storm and stress: Typicality, transactions, timing, and temperament to account for adolescent change. *The American Psychologist, 68*, 444–454. doi:10.1037/a0033586

Inhelder, B., & Piaget, J. (1958). *The growth of logical thinking: From childhood to adolescence.* New York, NY: Basic Books.

Jaffee, S., & Hyde, J. S. (2000). Gender differences in moral orientation: A meta-analysis. *Psychological Bulletin, 126*, 703.

Janssen, H. G., Davies, I. G., Richardson, L. D., & Stevenson, L. (2018). Determinants of takeaway and fast food consumption: A narrative review. *Nutrition Research Reviews, 31*, 16–34. doi:10.1017/S0954422417000178N

Javadi, A. H., Schmidt, D. H. K., & Smolka, M. N. (2014). Differential representation of feedback and decision in adolescents and adults. *Neuropsychologia, 56*, 280–288. doi:10.1016/j.neuropsychologia.2014.01.021

Jia, Y., Konold, T. R., & Cornell, D. (2016). Authoritative school climate and high school dropout rates. *School Psychology Quarterly, 31*, 289–303. doi:10.1037/spq0000139

Juvonen, J., Kogachi, K., & Graham, S. (2018). When and how do students benefit from ethnic diversity in middle school? *Child Development, 89*, 1268–1282. doi:10.1111/cdev.12834

Karafantis, D. M., & Levy, S. R. (2004). The role of children's lay theories about the malleability of human attributes in beliefs about and volunteering for disadvantaged groups. *Child Development, 75*, 236–250. doi:10.1111/j.1467-8624.2004.00666.x

Karbach, J., Gottschling, J., Spengler, M., Hegewald, K., & Spinath, F. M. (2013). Parental involvement and general cognitive ability as predictors of domain-specific academic achievement in early adolescence. *Learning and Instruction, 23*, 43–51. doi:10.1016/j.learninstruc.2012.09.004

Keating, D. P. (2012). Cognitive and brain development in adolescence. *Enfance, 2012*, 267–279. doi:10.4074/S0013754512003035

Keith, T. Z., Keith, P. B., Quirk, K. J., Sperduto, J., Santillo, S., & Killings, S. (1998). Longitudinal effects of parent involvement on high school grades: Similarities and differences. *Journal of School Psychology, 35*, 335–364.

Kelly, Y., Zilanawala, A., Sacker, A., Hiatt, R., & Viner, R. (2017). Early puberty in 11-year-old girls: Millennium Cohort study findings. *Archives of Disease in Childhood, 102*, 232–237. doi:10.1136/archdischild-2016-310475

Kidger, J., Araya, R., Donovan, J., & Gunnell, D. (2012). The effect of the school environment on the emotional health of adolescents: A systematic review. *Pediatrics, 129*, 925–949. doi:10.1542/peds.2011-2248

Kingery, J. N., Erdley, C. A., & Marshall, K. C. (2011). Peer acceptance and friendship as predictors of early adolescents' adjustment across the middle school transition. *Merrill-Palmer Quarterly, 57*, 215–243. doi:10.1353/mpq.2011.0012

Kleanthous, K., Dermitzaki, E., Papadimitriou, D. T., Papaevangelou, V., & Papadimitriou, A. (2017). Secular changes in the final height of Greek girls are levelling off. *Acta Paediatrica, 106*, 341–343. doi:10.1111/apa.13677

Knox, P. L., Fagley, N. S., & Miller, P. M. (2004). Care and justice moral orientation among African American college students. *Journal of Adult Development, 11*, 41–45.

Kohlberg, L. (1969). Stage and sequence: The cognitive-developmental approach to socialization. In D. A. Goslin (Ed.), *Handbook of socialization* (pp. 347–480). Chicago, IL: Rand McNally.

Kohlberg, L., Levine, C., & Hewer, A. (1983). Moral stages: A current formulation and a response to critics. *Contributions to Human Development, 10*, 174.

Kohlberg, L., & Ryncarz, R. A. (1990). Beyond justice reasoning: Moral development and consideration of a seventh stage. In C. N. Alexander & E. J. Langer (Eds.), *Higher stages of human development: Perspectives on adult growth* (pp. 191–207). New York, NY: Oxford University Press.

Kretsch, N., Mendle, J., Cance, J. D., & Harden, K. P. (2016). Peer group similarity in perceptions of pubertal timing. *Journal of Youth and Adolescence, 45*, 1696–1710. doi:10.1007/s10964-015-0275-3

Kretsch, N., Mendle, J., & Harden, K. P. (2016). A twin study of objective and subjective pubertal timing and peer influence on risk-taking. *Journal of Research on Adolescence, 26*, 45–59. doi:10.1111/jora.12160

Kuhn, D. (2012). The development of causal reasoning. *Wiley Interdisciplinary Reviews: Cognitive Science, 3*, 327–335. doi:10.1002/wcs.1160

Kuhn, D. (2013). Reasoning. In P. D. Zelazo (Ed.), *The Oxford handbook of developmental psychology: Vol. 21. Body and mind* (pp. 744–764). Oxford, UK: Oxford University Press. doi:10.1093/oxfordhb/9780199958450.013.0026

Kuhn, D., Pease, M., & Wirkala, C. (2009). Coordinating the effects of multiple variables: A skill fundamental to scientific thinking. *Journal of Experimental Child Psychology, 103*, 268–284. doi:10.1016/j.jecp.2009.01.009

Kuther, T. L., & Higgins-D'Alessandro, A. (2000). Bridging the gap between moral reasoning and adolescent engagement in risky behavior. *Journal of Adolescence, 23*, 409–423.

Labouvie-Vief, G. (2015). *Integrating emotions and cognition throughout the lifespan.* New York, NY: Springer. doi:10.1007/978-3-319-09822-7

Lacroix, A. E., & Whitten, R. A. (2017). Menarche. *StatPearls.* Retrieved from http://www.ncbi.nlm.nih.gov/pubmed/29261991

Lamb, C. S., & Crano, W. D. (2014). Parents' beliefs and children's marijuana use: Evidence for a self-fulfilling prophecy effect. *Addictive Behaviors, 39*, 127–132. doi:10.1016/J.ADDBEH.2013.09.009

Larson, R., & Csikszentmihalyi, M. (2014). The experience sampling method. In M. Csikszentmihalyi (Ed.), *Flow and the foundations of positive psychology* (pp. 21–34). Retrieved from http://link.springer.com/chapter/10.1007/978-94-017-9088-8_3

Larson, R., Csikszentmihalyi, M., & Graef, R. (2014). Mood variability and the psycho-social adjustment of adolescents. In M. Csikszentmihalyi (Ed.), *Applications of flow in human development and education* (pp. 285–304). Retrieved from http://link.springer.com/chapter/10.1007/978-94-017-9094-9_15

Lawson, G. M., Hook, C. J., & Farah, M. J. (2018). A meta-analysis of the relationship between socioeconomic status and executive function performance among children. *Developmental Science, 21*, e12529. doi:10.1111/desc.12529

Lebel, C., & Deoni, S. (2018). The development of brain white matter microstructure. *NeuroImage.* Advance online publication. doi:10.1016/J.NEUROIMAGE.2017.12.097

Leenders, I., & Brugman, D. D. (2005). Moral/non-moral domain shift in young adolescents in relation to delinquent behaviour. *British Journal of Developmental Psychology, 23*, 65–79.

Lehman, D. R., & Nisbett, R. E. (1990). A longitudinal study of the effects of undergraduate training on reasoning. *Developmental Psychology, 26*, 952–960.

Lerner, R. M., Buckingham, M. H., Champine, R. B., Greenman, K. N., Warren, D. J. A., Weiner, M. B., . . . Weiner, M. B. (2015). Positive

development among diverse youth. In R. A. Scott, S. M. Kosslyn, & M. Buchmann (Eds.), *Emerging trends in the social and behavioral sciences* (pp. 1–14). Hoboken, NJ: John Wiley. doi:10.1002/9781118900772.etrds0260

Lisdahl, K. M., Gilbart, E. R., Wright, N. E., & Shollenbarger, S. (2013). Dare to delay? The impacts of adolescent alcohol and marijuana use onset on cognition, brain structure, and function. *Frontiers in Psychiatry, 4*, 53. doi:10.3389/fpsyt.2013.00053

Loeb, E., Hessel, E. T., & Allen, J. (2016). The self-fulfilling prophecy of adolescent social expectations. *International Journal of Behavioral Development, 40*, 555–564. doi:10.1177/0165025415618274

Loessl, B., Valerius, G., Kopasz, M., Hornyak, M., Riemann, D., & Voderholzer, U. (2008). Are adolescents chronically sleep-deprived? An investigation of sleep habits of adolescents in the southwest of Germany. *Child: Care, Health & Development, 34*, 549–556. doi:10.1111/j.1365-2214.2008.00845.x

Lopez-Larson, M. P., Rogowska, J., Bogorodzki, P., Bueler, C. E., McGlade, E. C., & Yurgelun-Todd, D. A. (2012). Cortico-cerebellar abnormalities in adolescents with heavy marijuana use. *Psychiatry Research: Neuroimaging, 202*, 224–232. doi:10.1016/j.pscychresns.2011.11.005

Lubman, D. I., Cheetham, A., & Yücel, M. (2015). Cannabis and adolescent brain development. *Pharmacology & Therapeutics, 148*, 1–16. doi:10.1016/j.pharmthera.2014.11.009

Luna, B., Garver, K. E., Urban, T. A., Lazar, N. A., & Sweeney, J. A. (2004). Maturation of cognitive processes from late childhood to adulthood. *Child Development, 75*, 1357–1372. doi:10.1111/j.1467-8624.2004.00745.x

Luna, B., Marek, S., Larsen, B., Tervo-Clemmens, B., & Chahal, R. (2015). An integrative model of the maturation of cognitive control. *Annual Review of Neuroscience, 38*, 151–170. doi:10.1146/annurev-neuro-071714-034054

Luna, B., Paulsen, D. J., Padmanabhan, A., & Geier, C. (2013). The teenage brain: Cognitive control and motivation. *Current Directions in Psychological Science, 22*, 94–100. doi:10.1177/0963721413478416

Malti, T., Keller, M., & Buchmann, M. (2013). Do moral choices make us feel good? The development of adolescents' emotions following moral decision making. *Journal of Research on Adolescence, 23*, 389–397. doi:10.1111/jora.12005

Malti, T., & Latzko, B. (2010). Children's moral emotions and moral cognition: Towards an integrative perspective. *New Directions for Child & Adolescent Development, 2010*, 1–10. doi:10.1002/cd.272

Marshall, L. (1999). *Nyae Nyae!Kung beliefs and rites.* Cambridge, MA: Peabody Museum of Archaeology and Ethnology, Harvard University.

Marti, E., & Rodriguez, C. (2012). *After Piaget.* New Brunswick, NJ: Transaction Publishers.

McFarland, D. A., & Thomas, R. J. (2006). Bowling young: How youth voluntary associations influence adult political participation. *American Sociological Review, 71*, 401–425. doi:10.1177/000312240607100303

McGinley, M., Lipperman-Kreda, S., Byrnes, H. F., & Carlo, G. (2010). Parental, social and dispositional pathways to Israeli adolescents' volunteering. *Journal of Applied Developmental Psychology, 31*, 386–394. doi:10.1016/j.appdev.2010.06.001

Mendle, J. (2014). Beyond pubertal timing: New directions for studying individual differences in development. *Current Directions in Psychological Science, 23*, 215–219. doi:10.1177/0963721414530144

Mendle, J., Turkheimer, E., D'Onofrio, B. M., Lynch, S. K., Emery, R. E., Slutske, W. S., & Martin, N. G. (2006). Family structure and age at menarche: A children-of-twins approach. *Developmental Psychology, 42*, 533–542.

Meruelo, A. D., Castro, N., Cota, C. I., & Tapert, S. F. (2017). Cannabis and alcohol use, and the developing brain. *Behavioural Brain Research, 325*(Pt. A), 44–50. doi:10.1016/j.bbr.2017.02.025

Miller, J. G. (2018). Physiological mechanisms of prosociality. *Current Opinion in Psychology, 20*, 50–54. doi:10.1016/J.COPSYC.2017.08.018

Miller, M. B., Janssen, T., & Jackson, K. M. (2017). The prospective association between sleep and initiation of substance use in young adolescents. *Journal of Adolescent Health, 60*, 154–160. doi:10.1016/j.jadohealth.2016.08.019

Mills, K. L., Goddings, A. L., Clasen, L. S., Giedd, J. N., & Blakemore, S. J. (2014). The developmental mismatch in structural brain maturation during adolescence. *Developmental Neuroscience, 36*, 147–160. doi:10.1159/000362328

Minges, K. E., & Redeker, N. S. (2016). Delayed school start times and adolescent sleep: A systematic review of the experimental evidence. *Sleep Medicine Reviews, 28*, 86–95. doi:10.1016/j.smrv.2015.06.002

Mitchell, J. A., Rodriguez, D., Schmitz, K. H., & Audrain-McGovern, J. (2013a). Greater screen time is associated with adolescent obesity: A longitudinal study of the BMI distribution from ages 14 to 18. *Obesity 21*, 572–575. doi:10.1002/oby.20157

Mitchell, J. A., Rodriguez, D., Schmitz, K. H., & Audrain-McGovern, J. (2013b). Sleep duration and adolescent obesity. *Pediatrics, 131*, e1428–e1434. doi:10.1542/peds.2012-2368

Modecki, K. L. (2014). Maturity of judgment. In J. Levesque (Ed.), *Encyclopedia of adolescence* (pp. 1660–1665). New York, NY: Springer. Retrieved from http://link.springer.com/referenceworkentry/10.1007%2F978-1-4419-1695-2_213

Moilanen, K. L., Rasmussen, K. E., & Padilla-Walker, L. M. (2015). Bidirectional associations between self-regulation and parenting styles in early adolescence. *Journal of Research on Adolescence, 25*, 246–262. doi:10.1111/jora.12125

Moore, S. R., Harden, K. P., & Mendle, J. (2014). Pubertal timing and adolescent sexual behavior in girls. *Developmental Psychology, 50*, 1734–1745. doi:10.1037/a0036027

Morris, A. S., Criss, M. M., Silk, J. S., & Houltberg, B. J. (2017). The impact of parenting on emotion regulation during childhood and adolescence. *Child Development Perspectives, 11*, 233–238. doi:10.1111/cdep.12238

Morris, A. S., Squeglia, L. M., Jacobus, J., & Silk, J. S. (2018). Adolescent brain development: Implications for understanding risk and resilience processes through neuroimaging research. *Journal of Research on Adolescence, 28*, 4–9. doi:10.1111/jora.12379

Moshman, D., & Moshman, D. (2011). *Adolescent rationality and development: Cognition, morality, and identity.* New York, NY: Psychology Press.

Motta-Mena, N. V., & Scherf, K. S. (2017). Pubertal development shapes perception of complex facial expressions. *Developmental Science, 20*, e12451. doi:10.1111/desc.12451

Mrug, S., Elliott, M. N., Davies, S., Tortolero, S. R., Cuccaro, P., & Schuster, M. A. (2014). Early puberty, negative peer influence, and problem behaviors in adolescent girls. *Pediatrics, 133*, 7–14. doi:10.1542/peds.2013-0628

Mueller, C. E., & Anderman, E. M. (2010). Middle school transitions and adolescent development. In J. L. Meece & J. S. Eccles (Eds.), *Handbook of research on schools, schooling and human development* (pp. 216–233). New York, NY: Routledge. doi:10.4324/9780203874844-24

Müller, U., & Kerns, K. (2015). The development of executive function. In L. Liben & U. Muller (Eds.), *Handbook of child psychology and developmental science* (pp. 1–53). Hoboken, NJ: John Wiley. doi:10.1002/9781118963418.childpsy214

Müller-Oehring, E. M., Kwon, D., Nagel, B. J., Sullivan, E. V, Chu, W., Rohlfing, T., . . . Pohl, K. M. (2018). Influences of age, sex, and moderate alcohol drinking on the intrinsic functional architecture of adolescent brains. *Cerebral Cortex, 28*, 1049–1063. doi:10.1093/cercor/bhx014

Munthali, A. C., & Zulu, E. M. (2007). The timing and role of initiation rites in preparing young people for adolescence and responsible sexual and reproductive behaviour in Malawi. *African Journal of Reproductive Health, 11*, 150–167. Retrieved from https://journals.co.za/content/ajrh/11/3/EJC134431

National Center for Educational Statistics. (2017). *Dropout rates.* Retrieved from https://nces.ed.gov/programs/coe/indicator_coj.asp

Natsuaki, M. N., Samuels, D., & Leve, L. D. (2015). Puberty, identity, and context. In K. C. McLean & M. Syed (Eds.), *The Oxford handbook of identity development* (pp. 389–405). Oxford, UK: Oxford University Press. doi:10.1093/oxfordhb/9780199936564.013.005

Neberich, W., Penke, L., Lehnart, J., & Asendorpf, J. B. (2010). Family of origin, age at menarche, and reproductive strategies: A test of four evolutionary-developmental models. *European Journal of Developmental Psychology, 7*, 153–177. doi:10.1080/17405620801928029

Nguyen-Louie, T. T., Brumback, T., Worley, M. J., Colrain, I. M., Matt, G. E., Squeglia, L. M., & Tapert, S. F. (2018). Effects of sleep on substance use in adolescents: A longitudinal perspective. *Addiction Biology, 23*, 750–760. doi:10.1111/adb.12519

Nhlekisana, R. O. (2017). From childhood to womanhood: puberty rites of !Xoo girls of Zutshwa. *Marang: Journal of Language and Literature, 29*, 31–41.

Noë, B., Turner, L. D., Linden, D. E. J., Allen, S. M., Maio, G. R., & Whitaker, R. M. (2017). Timing rather than user traits mediates mood sampling on smartphones. *BMC Research Notes, 10*, 481. doi:10.1186/s13104-017-2808-1

Noll, J. G., Trickett, P. K., Long, J. D., Negriff, S., Susman, E. J., Shalev, I., . . . Putnam, F. W. (2017). Childhood sexual abuse and early timing of puberty. *Journal of Adolescent Health, 60*, 65–71. doi:10.1016/j.jadohealth.2016.09.008

Obeidallah, D., Brennan, R. T., Brooks-Gunn, J., & Earls, F. (2004). Links between pubertal timing and neighborhood contexts: Implications for girls' violent behavior. *Journal of the American Academy of Child & Adolescent Psychiatry, 43*, 1460–1468.

Obeidallah, D., Brennan, R. T., Brooks-Gunn, J., Kindlon, D., & Earls, F. (2000). Socioeconomic status, race, and girls' pubertal maturation: Results from the project on human development in Chicago neighborhoods. *Journal of Research on Adolescence, 10*, 443–464.

Offer, D., Ostrov, E., Howard, K. I., & Atkinson, R. (1988). *The teenage world: Adolescents' self-image in ten countries* (Vol. 11). New York, NY: Springer.

Omar, H., McElderry, D., & Zakharia, R. (2003). Educating adolescents about puberty: What are we missing? *International Journal of Adolescent Medicine and Health, 15*, 79–83.

Ottoni-Wilhelm, M., Estell, D. B., & Perdue, N. H. (2014). Role-modeling and conversations about giving in the socialization of adolescent charitable giving and volunteering. *Journal of Adolescence, 37*, 53–66. doi:10.1016/j.adolescence.2013.10.010

Owens, J. A., Belon, K., & Moss, P. (2010). Impact of delaying school start time on adolescent sleep, mood, and behavior. *Archives of Pediatrics & Adolescent Medicine, 164*, 608–614. doi:10.1001/archpediatrics.2010.96

Owens, J. A., Dearth-Wesley, T., Herman, A. N., Oakes, J. M., & Whitaker, R. C. (2017). A quasi-experimental study of the impact of school start time changes on adolescent sleep. *Sleep Health, 3*, 437–443. doi:10.1016/j.sleh.2017.09.001

Paksarian, D., Rudolph, K. E., He, J.-P., & Merikangas, K. R. (2015). School start time and adolescent sleep patterns: Results from the U.S. National Comorbidity survey—Adolescent supplement. *American Journal of Public Health, 105*, 1351–1357. doi:10.2105/AJPH.2015.302619

Papadimitriou, A. (2016a). The evolution of the age at menarche from prehistorical to modern times. *Journal of Pediatric and Adolescent Gynecology, 29*, 527–530. doi:10.1016/j.jpag.2015.12.002

Papadimitriou, A. (2016b). Timing of puberty and secular trend in human maturation. In P. Kumanov & A. Agarwal (Eds.), *Puberty* (pp. 121–136). Cham, Switzerland: Springer International. doi:10.1007/978-3-319-32122-6_9

Paulsen, D. J., Hallquist, M. N., Geier, C. F., & Luna, B. (2014). Effects of incentives, age, and behavior on brain activation during inhibitory control: A longitudinal fMRI study. *Developmental Cognitive Neuroscience, 11*, 105–115. doi:10.1016/j.dcn.2014.09.003

Payne, V. G., & Isaacs, L. D. (2016). *Human motor development: A lifespan approach.* New York, NY: McGraw-Hill.

Pearson, N., Griffiths, P., Biddle, S. J., Johnston, J. P., McGeorge, S., & Haycraft, E. (2017). Clustering and correlates of screen-time and eating behaviours among young adolescents. *BMC Public Health, 17*, 533. doi:10.1186/s12889-017-4441-2

Peeters, M., Janssen, T., Monshouwer, K., Boendermaker, W., Pronk, T., Wiers, R., & Vollebergh, W. (2015). Weaknesses in executive functioning predict the initiating of adolescents' alcohol use. *Developmental Cognitive Neuroscience, 16*, 139–146. doi:10.1016/j.dcn.2015.04.003

Piaget, J. (1972). Intellectual evolution from adolescence to adulthood. *Human Development, 51*, 40–47. doi:10.1159/000112531

Pieters, S., Burk, W. J., Van der Vorst, H., Dahl, R. E., Wiers, R. W., & Engels, R. C. M. E. (2015). Prospective relationships between sleep problems and substance use, internalizing and externalizing problems. *Journal of Youth and Adolescence, 44*, 379–388. doi:10.1007/s10964-014-0213-9

Poppen, P. (1974). Sex differences in moral judgment. *Personality and Social Psychology Bulletin, 1*, 313–315. doi:10.1177/014616727400100106

Power, F. C., Higgins, A., & Kohlberg, L. (1989). *Lawrence Kohlberg's approach to moral education.* New York, NY: Columbia University Press.

Pratt, M. W., Hunsberger, B., Pancer, S. M., & Alisat, S. (2003). A longitudinal analysis of personal values socialization: Correlates of a moral self-ideal in late adolescence. *Social Development, 12*, 563–585. doi:10.1111/1467-9507.00249

Qu, Y., Pomerantz, E. M., Wang, M., Cheung, C., & Cimpian, A. (2016). Conceptions of adolescence: Implications for differences in engagement in school over early adolescence in the United States and China. *Journal of Youth and Adolescence, 45*, 1512–1526. doi:10.1007/s10964-016-0492-4

Rai, R., Mitchell, P., Kadar, T., & Mackenzie, L. (2016). Adolescent egocentrism and the illusion of transparency: Are adolescents as egocentric as we might think? *Current Psychology, 35*, 285–294. doi:10.1007/s12144-014-9293-7

Rembeck, G., Möller, M., & Gunnarsson, R. (2006). Attitudes and feelings towards menstruation and womanhood in girls at menarche. *Acta Paediatrica, 95*, 707–714.

Reyna, V. F., & Rivers, S. E. (2008). Current theories of risk and rational decision making. *Developmental Review, 28*, 1–11. doi:10.1016/j.dr.2008.01.002

Reynolds, B. M., & Repetti, R. L. (2008). Contextual variations in negative mood and state self-esteem: What role do peers play? *Journal of Early Adolescence, 28*, 405–427.

Richmond, S., Johnson, K. A., Seal, M. L., Allen, N. B., & Whittle, S. (2016). Development of brain networks and relevance of environmental and genetic factors: A systematic review. *Neuroscience & Biobehavioral Reviews, 71*, 215–239. doi:10.1016/j.neubiorev.2016.08.024

Rickard, I. J., Frankenhuis, W. E., & Nettle, D. (2014). Why are childhood family factors associated with timing of maturation? A role for internal prediction. *Perspectives on Psychological Science, 9,* 3–15. doi:10.1177/1745691613513467

Rideout, V. J. (2010). *Generation M2: Media in the lives of 8- to 18-year-olds.* Menlo Park, CA. Retrieved from http://kff.org/other/event/generation-m2-media-in-the-lives-of/

Rudolph, K. D., Troop-Gordon, W., Lambert, S. F., & Natsuaki, M. N. (2014). Long-term consequences of pubertal timing for youth depression: Identifying personal and contextual pathways of risk. *Development and Psychopathology, 26*(4, Pt. 2), 1423–1444.

Rueger, S. Y., Chen, P., Jenkins, L. N., & Choe, H. J. (2014). Effects of perceived support from mothers, fathers, and teachers on depressive symptoms during the transition to middle school. *Journal of Youth and Adolescence, 43,* 655–670. doi:10.1007/s10964-013-0039-x

Sadler, K. (2017). Pubertal development. In M. A. Goldstein (Ed.), *The mass general hospital for children adolescent medicine handbook* (pp. 19–26). Cham, Switzerland: Springer International. doi:10.1007/978-3-319-45778-9_3

Sanchez-Garrido, M. A., & Tena-Sempere, M. (2013). Metabolic control of puberty: Roles of leptin and kisspeptins. *Hormones and Behavior, 64,* 187–194. doi:10.1016/j.yhbeh.2013.01.014

Sanders, J. O., Qiu, X., Lu, X., Duren, D. L., Liu, R. W., Dang, D., . . . Cooperman, D. R. (2017). The uniform pattern of growth and skeletal maturation during the human adolescent growth spurt. *Scientific Reports, 7,* 16705. doi:10.1038/s41598-017-16996-w

Schelleman-Offermans, K., Knibbe, R. A., & Kuntsche, E. (2013). Are the effects of early pubertal timing on the initiation of weekly alcohol use mediated by peers and/or parents? A longitudinal study. *Developmental Psychology, 49,* 1277–1285.

Schlegel, A. (2008). A cross-cultural approach to adolescence. In D. L. Browning (Ed.), *Adolescent identities: A collection of readings* (pp. 31–44). New York, NY: The Analytic Press/Taylor & Francis.

Schonert-Reichl, K. A. (1999). Relations of peer acceptance, friendship adjustment, and social behavior to moral reasoning during early adolescence. *Journal of Early Adolescence, 19,* 31.

Schreier, H. M. C., & Chen, E. (2013). Socioeconomic status and the health of youth: A multilevel, multidomain approach to conceptualizing pathways. *Psychological Bulletin, 139,* 606–654. doi:10.1037/a0029416

Schwartz, P. D., Maynard, A. M., & Uzelac, S. M. (2008). Adolescent egocentrism: A contemporary view. *Adolescence, 43,* 441–448.

Scott, E. S., Duell, N., & Steinberg, L. (2018). *Brain development, social context and justice policy.* Retrieved from https://papers.ssrn.com/sol3/papers.cfm?abstract_id=3118366

Seaton, E. K., & Carter, R. (2018). Pubertal timing, racial identity, neighborhood, and school context among Black adolescent females. *Cultural Diversity and Ethnic Minority Psychology, 24,* 40–50. doi:10.1037/cdp0000162

Seidman, E., Aber, J. L., & French, S. E. (2004). The organization of schooling and adolescent development. In K. I. Maton, C. J. Schellenbach, B. J. Leadbeater, & A. L. Solarz (Eds.), *Investing in children, youth, families, and communities: Strengths-based research and policy* (pp. 233–250). Washington, DC: American Psychological Association.

Sheppard, P., & Sear, R. (2012). Father absence predicts age at sexual maturity and reproductive timing in British men. *Biology Letters, 8,* 237–240. doi:10.1098/rsbl.2011.0747

Shulman, E. P., & Cauffman, E. (2013). Reward-biased risk appraisal and its relation to juvenile versus adult crime. *Law and Human Behavior, 37,* 412–423. doi:10.1037/lhb0000033

Shulman, E. P., Smith, A. R., Silva, K., Icenogle, G., Duell, N., Chein, J., & Steinberg, L. (2016). The dual systems model: Review, reappraisal, and reaffirmation. *Developmental Cognitive Neuroscience, 17,* 103–117. doi:10.1016/j.dcn.2015.12.010

Sigmund, E., Badura, P., Sigmundová, D., Voráčová, J., Zacpal, J., Kalman, M., . . . Hamrik, Z. (2018). Trends and correlates of overweight/obesity in Czech adolescents in relation to family socioeconomic status over a 12-year study period (2002–2014). *BMC Public Health, 18,* 122. doi:10.1186/s12889-017-5013-1

Silveri, M. M., Dager, A. D., Cohen-Gilbert, J. E., & Sneider, J. T. (2016). Neurobiological signatures associated with alcohol and drug use in the human adolescent brain. *Neuroscience & Biobehavioral Reviews, 70,* 244–259. doi:10.1016/J.NEUBIOREV.2016.06.042

Sisk, C. L. (2017). Development: Pubertal hormones meet the adolescent brain. *Current Biology, 27,* R706–R708. doi:10.1016/J.CUB.2017.05.092

Skoog, T., & Bayram Özdemir, S. (2016). Explaining why early-maturing girls are more exposed to sexual harassment in early adolescence. *Journal of Early Adolescence, 36,* 490–509. doi:10.1177/0272431614568198

Skoog, T., & Stattin, H. (2014). Why and under what contextual conditions do early-maturing girls develop problem behaviors? *Child Development Perspectives, 8,* 158–162. doi:10.1111/cdep.12076

Smetana, J. G., Jambon, M., & Ball, C. (2013). The social domain approach to children's moral and social judgments. In M. Killen & J. G. Smetana (Eds.), *Handbook of moral development* (pp. 23–44). New York, NY: Psychology Press.

Smetana, J. G., Tasopoulos-Chan, M., Gettman, D. C., Villalobos, M., Campione-Barr, N., & Metzger, A. (2009). Adolescents' and parents' evaluations of helping versus fulfilling personal desires in family situations. *Child Development, 80,* 280–294. doi:10.1111/j.1467-8624.2008.01259.x

Smith, A. R., Chein, J., & Steinberg, L. (2013). Impact of socio-emotional context, brain development, and pubertal maturation on adolescent risk-taking. *Hormones and Behavior, 64,* 323–232. doi:10.1016/j.yhbeh.2013.03.006

Smith, A. R., Rosenbaum, G. M., Botdorf, M. A., Steinberg, L., & Chein, J. M. (2018). Peers influence adolescent reward processing, but not response inhibition. *Cognitive, Affective, & Behavioral Neuroscience, 18,* 284–295. doi:10.3758/s13415-018-0569-5

Smith, A. R., Steinberg, L., Strang, N., & Chein, J. (2015). Age differences in the impact of peers on adolescents' and adults' neural response to reward. *Developmental Cognitive Neuroscience, 11,* 75–82. doi:10.1016/j.dcn.2014.08.010

Spear, L. P. (2018). Effects of adolescent alcohol consumption on the brain and behaviour. *Nature Reviews Neuroscience, 19,* 197–214. doi:10.1038/nrn.2018.10

Spera, C. (2005). A review of the relationship among parenting practices, parenting styles, and adolescent school achievement. *Educational Psychology Review, 17,* 125–146.

Spielberg, J. M., Olino, T. M., Forbes, E. E., & Dahl, R. E. (2014). Exciting fear in adolescence: Does pubertal development alter threat processing? *Developmental Cognitive Neuroscience, 8,* 86–95. doi:10.1016/j.dcn.2014.01.004

Stang, J. S., & Stotmeister, B. (2017). Nutrition in adolescence. In N. J. Temple, T. Wilson, & G. A. Bray (Eds.), *Nutrition guide for physicians and related healthcare professionals* (pp. 29–39). Cham, Switzerland: Springer International. doi:10.1007/978-3-319-49929-1_4

Stein, J. H., & Reiser, L. W. (1994). A study of white middle-class adolescent boys' responses to "semenarche" (the first ejaculation). *Journal of Youth and Adolescence, 23,* 373–384. doi:10.1007/BF01536725

Steinberg, L. (2013). Does recent research on adolescent brain development inform the mature minor doctrine? *Journal of Medicine and Philosophy, 38,* 256–267. doi:10.1093/jmp/jht017

Steinberg, L. (2017). Adolescent brain science and juvenile justice policymaking. *Psychology, Public Policy, and Law, 23,* 410–420. doi:10.1037/law0000128

Steinberg, L., Icenogle, G., Shulman, E. P., Breiner, K., Chein, J., Bacchini, D., . . . Takash, H. M. S. (2018). Around the world, adolescence is a time of heightened sensation seeking and immature self-regulation. *Developmental Science, 21,* e12532. doi:10.1111/desc.12532

Steinberg, L., & Lerner, R. M. (2004). The scientific study of adolescence: A brief history. *Journal of Early Adolescence, 24,* 45–54. doi:10.1177/0272431603260879

Steinberg, L., & Scott, E. S. (2003). Less guilty by reason of adolescence: Developmental immaturity, diminished responsibility, and the juvenile death penalty. *American Psychologist, 58,* 1009–1018.

Stidham-Hall, K., Moreau, C., & Trussell, J. (2012). Patterns and correlates of parental and formal sexual and reproductive health communication for adolescent women in the United States, 2002–2008. *Journal of Adolescent Health, 50,* 410–413. doi:10.1016/j.jadohealth.2011.06.007

Stojković, I. (2013). Pubertal timing and self-esteem in adolescents: The mediating role of body-image and social relations. *European Journal of Developmental Psychology, 10,* 359–377. doi:10.1080/17405629.2012.682145

Stroud, C. B., & Davila, J. (2016). Pubertal timing. In J. Levesque (Ed.), *Encyclopedia of adolescence* (pp. 1–9). Cham, Switzerland: Springer International. doi:10.1007/978-3-319-32132-5_14-2

Sun, Y., Mensah, F. K., Azzopardi, P., Patton, G. C., & Wake, M. (2017). Childhood social disadvantage and pubertal timing: A National Birth Cohort from Australia. *Pediatrics, 139,* e20164099. doi:10.1542/peds.2016-4099

Takagi, M., Youssef, G., & Lorenzetti, V. (2016). Neuroimaging of the human brain in adolescent substance users. In D. De Micheli, A. L. M. Andrade, E. A. da Silva, & M. L. O. de Souza Formigoni (Eds.), *Drug abuse in adolescence* (pp. 69–99). Cham, Switzerland: Springer International. doi:10.1007/978-3-319-17795-3_6

Tapia-Rojas, C., Carvajal, F. J., Mira, R. G., Arce, C., Lerma-Cabrera, J. M., Orellana, J. A., . . . Quintanilla, R. A. (2017). Adolescent binge alcohol exposure affects the brain function through mitochondrial impairment. *Molecular Neurobiology, 55,* 4473–4491. doi:10.1007/s12035-017-0613-4

Tanner, J. M. (1990). *Foetus into man: Physical growth from conception to maturity.* Cambridge, MA: Harvard University Press.

Tarry, H., & Emler, N. (2007). Attitude, values and moral reasoning as predictors of delinquency. *British Journal of Developmental Psychology, 25,* 169–183. doi:10.1348/026151006x113671

Telzer, E. H., Fuligni, A. J., Lieberman, M. D., & Galván, A. (2013). The effects of poor quality sleep on brain function and risk taking in adolescence. *NeuroImage, 71,* 275–283. doi:10.1016/j.neuroimage.2013.01.025

Tinggaard, J., Mieritz, M. G., Sørensen, K., Mouritsen, A., Hagen, C. P., Aksglaede, L., . . . Juul, A. (2012). The physiology and timing of male puberty. *Current Opinion in Endocrinology, Diabetes, and Obesity, 19,* 197–203. doi:10.1097/MED.0b013e3283535614

Tomova, A. (2016). Body weight and puberty. In P. Kumanov & A. Agarwal (Eds.), *Puberty* (pp. 95–108). Cham, Switzerland: Springer International. doi:10.1007/978-3-319-32122-6_7

Tomova, A., Lalabonova, C., Robeva, R. N., & Kumanov, P. T. (2011). Timing of pubertal maturation according to the age at first conscious ejaculation. *Andrologia, 43,* 163–166. doi:10.1111/j.1439-0272.2009.01037.x

Tomova, A., Robeva, R., & Kumanov, P. (2015). Influence of the body weight on the onset and progression of puberty in boys. *Journal of Pediatric Endocrinology and Metabolism, 28,* 859–865. doi:10.1515/jpem-2014-0363

Tønnessen, E., Svendsen, I. S., Olsen, I. C., Guttormsen, A., & Haugen, T. (2015). Performance development in adolescent track and field athletes according to age, sex and sport discipline. *PLoS ONE, 10,* e0129014. doi:10.1371/journal.pone.0129014

Tottenham, N., & Galván, A. (2016). Stress and the adolescent brain: Amygdala-prefrontal cortex circuitry and ventral striatum as developmental targets. *Neuroscience & Biobehavioral Reviews, 70,* 217–227. doi:10.1016/J.NEUBIOREV.2016.07.030

Toufexis, D., Rivarola, M. A., Lara, H., & Viau, V. (2014). Stress and the reproductive axis. *Journal of Neuroendocrinology, 26,* 573–586. doi:10.1111/jne.12179

Tu, W., Wagner, E. K., Eckert, G. J., Yu, Z., Hannon, T., Pratt, J. H., & He, C. (2015). Associations between menarche-related genetic variants and pubertal growth in male and female adolescents. *Journal of Adolescent Health, 56,* 66–72. doi:10.1016/j.jadohealth.2014.07.020

Tunau, K., Adamu, A., Hassan, M., Ahmed, Y., & Ekele, B. (2012). Age at menarche among school girls in Sokoto, Northern Nigeria. *Annals of African Medicine.* Retrieved from http://www.ajol.info/index.php/aam/article/view/75230

Tyler, J. H., & Lofstrom, M. (2009). Finishing high school: Alternative pathways and dropout recovery. *The Future of Children/Center for the Future of Children, the David and Lucile Packard Foundation, 19,* 77–103. Retrieved from http://europepmc.org/abstract/med/21141706

Ullsperger, J. M., & Nikolas, M. A. (2017). A meta-analytic review of the association between pubertal timing and psychopathology in adolescence: Are there sex differences in risk? *Psychological Bulletin, 143,* 903–938. doi:10.1037/bul0000106

van der Stel, M., & Veenman, M. V. J. (2013). Metacognitive skills and intellectual ability of young adolescents: A longitudinal study from a developmental perspective. *European Journal of Psychology of Education, 29,* 117–137. doi:10.1007/s10212-013-0190-5

van Duijvenvoorde, A. C. K., Huizenga, H. M., Somerville, L. H., Delgado, M. R., Powers, A., Weeda, W. D., . . . Figner, B. (2015). Neural correlates of expected risks and returns in risky choice across development. *Journal of Neuroscience, 35,* 1549–1560. doi:10.1523/JNEUROSCI.1924-14.2015

van Duijvenvoorde, A. C. K., Peters, S., Braams, B. R., & Crone, E. A. (2016). What motivates adolescents? Neural responses to rewards and their influence on adolescents' risk taking, learning, and cognitive control. *Neuroscience & Biobehavioral Reviews, 70,* 135–147. doi:10.1016/J.NEUBIOREV.2016.06.037

van Goethem, A. A. J., van Hoof, A., van Aken, M. A. G., Orobio de Castro, B., & Raaijmakers, Q. A. W. (2014). Socialising adolescent volunteering: How important are parents and friends? Age dependent effects of parents and friends on adolescents' volunteering behaviours. *Journal of Applied Developmental Psychology, 35,* 94–101. doi:10.1016/j.appdev.2013.12.003

Vernon, L., Modecki, K. L., & Barber, B. L. (2018). Mobile phones in the bedroom: Trajectories of sleep habits and subsequent adolescent psychosocial development. *Child Development, 89,* 66–77. doi:10.1111/cdev.12836

Vikraman, S., Fryar, C. D., & Ogden, C. L. (2015). Caloric intake from fast food among children and adolescents in the United States, 2011–2012. *NCHS Data Brief.* Retrieved from http://www.ncbi.nlm.nih.gov/pubmed/26375457

Virtanen, M., Kivimäki, H., Ervasti, J., Oksanen, T., Pentti, J., Kouvonen, A., . . . Vahtera, J. (2015). Fast-food outlets and grocery stores near school and adolescents' eating habits and overweight in Finland. *European Journal of Public Health, 25,* 650–655. doi:10.1093/eurpub/ckv045

Walker, L. J. (2004). Progress and prospects in the psychology of moral development. *Merrill-Palmer Quarterly, 50,* 546–557.

Wang, J. L., Jackson, L. A., Zhang, D. J., & Su, Z. Q. (2012). The relationships among the Big Five personality factors, self-esteem, narcissism, and sensation-seeking to Chinese University students' uses of social networking sites (SNSs). *Computers in Human Behavior, 28,* 2313–2319. doi:10.1016/j.chb.2012.07.001

Wang, M. T., & Dishion, T. J. (2012). The trajectories of adolescents' perceptions of school climate, deviant peer affiliation, and behavioral problems during the middle school years. *Journal of Research on Adolescence, 22,* 40–53. doi:10.1111/j.1532-7795.2011.00763.x

Wang, M. T., & Fredricks, J. A. (2014). The reciprocal links between school engagement, youth problem behaviors, and school dropout during adolescence. *Child Development, 85,* 722–737. doi:10.1111/cdev.12138

Wang, M. T., Hill, N. E., & Hofkens, T. (2014). Parental involvement and African American and European American adolescents' academic, behavioral, and emotional development in secondary school. *Child Development, 85,* 2151–2168. doi:10.1111/cdev.12284

Wang, Y., & Lim, H. (2012). The global childhood obesity epidemic and the association between socio-economic status and childhood obesity. *International Review of Psychiatry, 24,* 176–188. doi:10.3109/09540261.2012.688195

Waters, S. K., Lester, L., & Cross, D. (2014). Transition to secondary school: Expectation versus experience. *Australian Journal of Education, 58,* 153–166. doi:10.1177/0004944114523371

Watson, N. F., Martin, J. L., Wise, M. S., Carden, K. A., Kirsch, D. B., Kristo, D. A., . . . American Academy of Sleep Medicine Board of Directors. (2017). Delaying middle school and high school start times promotes student health and performance: An American Academy of Sleep medicine position statement. *Journal of Clinical Sleep Medicine, 13,* 623–625. doi:10.5664/jcsm.6558

Watts, A. W., Loth, K., Berge, J. M., Larson, N., & Neumark-Sztainer, D. (2017). No time for family meals? Parenting practices associated with adolescent fruit and vegetable intake when family meals are not an option. *Journal of the Academy of Nutrition and Dietetics, 117,* 707–714. doi:10.1016/j.jand.2016.10.026

Way, N., Reddy, R., & Rhodes, J. (2007). Students' perceptions of school climate during the middle school years: Associations with trajectories of psychological and behavioral adjustment. *American Journal of Community Psychology, 40,* 194–213. doi:10.1007/s10464-007-9143-y

Webster, G. D., Graber, J. A., Gesselman, A. N., Crosier, B. S., & Schember, T. O. (2014). A life history theory of father absence and menarche: A meta-analysis. *Evolutionary Psychology, 12,* 147470491401200. doi:10.1177/147470491401200202

Weil, L. G., Fleming, S. M., Dumontheil, I., Kilford, E. J., Weil, R. S., Rees, G., . . . Blakemore, S.-J. (2013). The development of metacognitive ability in adolescence. *Consciousness and Cognition, 22*, 264–271.

Weinstein, S. M., & Mermelstein, R. (2007). Relations between daily activities and adolescent mood: The role of autonomy. *Journal of Clinical Child & Adolescent Psychology, 36*, 182–194. doi:10.1080/15374410701274967

Weisz, A. N., & Black, B. M. (2002). Gender and moral reasoning: African American youth respond to dating dilemmas. *Journal of Human Behavior in the Social Environment, 5*, 35–52.

White, E. S., & Mistry, R. S. (2016). Parent civic beliefs, civic participation, socialization practices, and child civic engagement. *Applied Developmental Science, 20*, 44–60. doi:10.1080/10888691.2015.1049346

Whittle, S., Vijayakumar, N., Simmons, J. G., Dennison, M., Schwartz, O., Pantelis, C., . . . Allen, N. B. (2017). Role of positive parenting in the association between neighborhood social disadvantage and brain development across adolescence. *JAMA Psychiatry, 74*, 824. doi:10.1001/jamapsychiatry.2017.1558

Winward, J. L., Hanson, K. L., Tapert, S. F., & Brown, S. A. (2014). Heavy alcohol use, marijuana use, and concomitant use by adolescents are associated with unique and shared cognitive decrements. *Journal of the International Neuropsychological Society, 20*, 784–795. doi:10.1017/S1355617714000666

Wolfson, A. R., Spaulding, N. L., Dandrow, C., & Baroni, E. M. (2007). Middle school start times: The importance of a good night's sleep for young adolescents. *Behavioral Sleep Medicine, 5*, 194–209. doi:10.1080/15402000701263809

Wong, M. M., & Brower, K. J. (2012). The prospective relationship between sleep problems and suicidal behavior in the National Longitudinal Study of Adolescent Health. *Journal of Psychiatric Research, 46*, 953–959. doi:10.1016/j.jpsychires.2012.04.008

Wong, M. M., Robertson, G. C., & Dyson, R. B. (2015). Prospective relationship between poor sleep and substance-related problems in a national sample of adolescents. *Alcoholism, Clinical and Experimental Research, 39*, 355–362. doi:10.1111/acer.12618

Wray-Lake, L., & Syvertsen, A. K. (2011). The developmental roots of social responsibility in childhood and adolescence. *New Directions for Child and Adolescent Development, 2011*, 11–25. doi:10.1002/cd.308

Wray-Lake, L., Syvertsen, A. K., & Flanagan, C. A. (2016). Developmental change in social responsibility during adolescence: An ecological perspective. *Developmental Psychology, 52*, 130–142. doi:10.1037/dev0000067

Wu, T., Mendola, P., & Buck, G. M. (2002). Ethnic differences in the presence of secondary sex characteristics and menarche among US girls: The third National Health and Nutrition Examination survey, 1988–1994. *Pediatrics, 110*, 752.

Yates, M., & Youniss, J. (1996). Community service and political-moral identity in adolescents. *Journal of Research on Adolescence, 6*, 271–284.

Yau, J. C., & Reich, S. M. (2018). "It's just a lot of work": Adolescents' self-presentation norms and practices on Facebook and Instagram. *Journal of Research on Adolescence.* Advance online publication. doi:10.1111/jora.12376

Yousefi, M., Karmaus, W., Zhang, H., Roberts, G., Matthews, S., Clayton, B., & Arshad, S. H. (2013). Relationships between age of puberty onset and height at age 18 years in girls and boys. *World Journal of Pediatrics, 9*, 230–238. doi:10.1007/s12519-013-0399-z

Yurgelun-Todd, D. (2007). Emotional and cognitive changes during adolescence. *Current Opinion in Neurobiology, 17*, 251–257.

Yurgelun-Todd, D., & Killgore, W. D. S. (2006). Fear-related activity in the prefrontal cortex increases with age during adolescence: A preliminary fMRI study. *Neuroscience Letters, 406*, 194–199. doi:10.1016/J.NEULET.2006.07.046

Zhai, Z. W., Pajtek, S., Luna, B., Geier, C. F., Ridenour, T. A., & Clark, D. B. (2015). Reward-modulated response inhibition, cognitive shifting, and the orbital frontal cortex in early adolescence. *Journal of Research on Adolescence, 25*, 753–764. doi:10.1111/jora.12168

Zhou, D., Lebel, C., Treit, S., Evans, A., & Beaulieu, C. (2015). Accelerated longitudinal cortical thinning in adolescence. *NeuroImage, 104*, 138–145. doi:10.1016/j.neuroimage.2014.10.005

Chapter 12

Ackard, D. M., Fulkerson, J. A., & Neumark-Sztainer, D. (2011). Stability of eating disorder diagnostic classifications in adolescents: Five-year longitudinal findings from a population-based study. *Eating Disorders, 19*, 308–322. doi:10.1080/10640266.2011.584804

Adams, R. E., & Laursen, B. (2007). The correlates of conflict: Disagreement is not necessarily detrimental. *Journal of Family Psychology, 21*, 445–458.

Al-Owidha, A., Green, K. E., & Kroger, J. (2009). On the question of an identity status category order: Rasch model step and scale statistics used to identify category order. *International Journal of Behavioral Development, 33*, 88–96. doi:10.1177/0165025408100110

Almy, B., Long, K., Lobato, D., Plante, W., Kao, B., & Houck, C. (2016). Perceptions of siblings' sexual activity predict sexual attitudes among at-risk adolescents. *Journal of Developmental and Behavioral Pediatrics, 36*, 258–266.

American Academy of Child and Adolescent Psychiatry. (2008). *Teen suicide. Facts for families.* Retrieved from http://www.aacap.org/galleries/FactsForFamilies/10_teen_suicide.pdf

American Psychiatric Association. (2013). *Diagnostic and statistical manual of mental disorders* (5th ed.). Washington, DC: Author.

Andersen, T. S. (2015). Race, ethnicity, and structural variations in youth risk of arrest: Evidence from a national longitudinal sample. *Criminal Justice and Behavior, 42*, 900–916. doi:10.1177/0093854815570963

Angley, M., Divney, A., Magriples, U., & Kershaw, T. (2015). Social support, family functioning and parenting competence in adolescent parents. *Maternal and Child Health Journal, 19*, 67–73. doi:10.1007/s10995-014-1496-x

Arnett, J. J. (2015). Identity development from adolescence to emerging adulthood. In K. C. McLean & M. Syed (Eds.), *The Oxford handbook of identity development* (pp. 53–64). Oxford, UK: Oxford University Press. doi:10.1093/oxfordhb/9780199936564.013.009

Årseth, A. K., Kroger, J., Martinussen, M., & Marcia, J. E. (2009). Meta-analytic studies of identity status and the relational issues of attachment and intimacy. *Identity, 9*, 1–32. doi:10.1080/15283480802579532

Australian Institute of Health and Welfare. (2016). *Leading causes of death.* Retrieved from http://www.aihw.gov.au/deaths/leading-causes-of-death/

Bachman, J. G., O'Malley, P. M., Freedman-Doan, P., Trzesniewski, K. H., & Donnellan, M. B. (2011). Adolescent self-esteem: Differences by race/ethnicity, gender, and age. *Self and Identity, 10*, 445–473. doi:10.1080/15298861003794538

Bagci, S. C., Rutland, A., Kumashiro, M., Smith, P. K., & Blumberg, H. (2014). Are minority status children's cross-ethnic friendships beneficial in a multiethnic context? *British Journal of Developmental Psychology, 32*, 107–115. doi:10.1111/bjdp.12028

Baglivio, M. T., Jackowski, K., Greenwald, M. A., & Howell, J. C. (2014). Serious, violent, and chronic juvenile offenders. *Criminology & Public Policy, 13*, 83–116. doi:10.1111/1745-9133.12064

Bailey, J. M., Vasey, P. L., Diamond, L. M., Breedlove, S. M., Vilain, E., & Epprecht, M. (2016). Sexual orientation, controversy, and science. *Psychological Science in the Public Interest, 17*, 45–101. doi:10.1177/1529100616637616

Bauman, S., Toomey, R. B., & Walker, J. L. (2013). Associations among bullying, cyberbullying, and suicide in high school students. *Journal of Adolescence, 36*, 341–350. doi:10.1016/j.adolescence.2012.12.001

Becht, A. I., Nelemans, S. A., Branje, S. J. T., Vollebergh, W. A. M., Koot, H. M., Denissen, J. J. A., & Meeus, W. H. J. (2016). The quest for identity in adolescence: Heterogeneity in daily identity formation and psychosocial adjustment across 5 years. *Developmental Psychology, 52*, 2010–2021. doi:10.1037/dev0000245

Benowitz-Fredericks, C. A., Garcia, K., Massey, M., Vasagar, B., & Borzekowski, D. L. G. (2012). Body image, eating disorders, and the relationship to adolescent media use. *Pediatric Clinics of North America, 59*, 693–704, ix. doi:10.1016/j.pcl.2012.03.017

Bentley, K. H., Nock, M. K., & Barlow, D. H. (2014). The four-function model of nonsuicidal self-injury: Key directions for future research. *Clinical Psychological Science, 2*, 638–656. doi:10.1177/2167702613514563

Berndt, T. J., & Murphy, L. M. (2002). Influences of friends and friendships: Myths, truths, and research recommendations. In R. V Kail (Ed.), *Advances in child development and behavior* (Vol. 30, pp. 275–310). San Diego, CA: Academic Press.

Bersamin, M., Todd, M., Fisher, D. A., Hill, D. L., Grube, J. W., & Walker, S. (2008). Parenting practices and adolescent sexual behavior: A longitudinal study. *Journal of Marriage & Family, 70,* 97–112. doi:10.1111/j.1741-3737.2007.00464.x

Berzonsky, M. D., & Kuk, L. S. (2000). Identity status, identity processing style, and the transition to university. *Journal of Adolescent Research, 15,* 81–99.

Birkeland, M. S., Breivik, K., & Wold, B. (2014). Peer acceptance protects global self-esteem from negative effects of low closeness to parents during adolescence and early adulthood. *Journal of Youth and Adolescence, 43,* 70–80. doi:10.1007/s10964-013-9929-1

Birkett, M., Newcomb, M. E., & Mustanski, B. (2015). Does it get better? A longitudinal analysis of psychological distress and victimization in lesbian, gay, bisexual, transgender, and questioning youth. *Journal of Adolescent Health, 56,* 280–285. doi:10.1016/j.jadohealth.2014.10.275

Bjärehed, J., Wångby-Lundh, M., & Lundh, L.-G. (2012). Nonsuicidal self-injury in a community sample of adolescents: Subgroups, stability, and associations with psychological difficulties. *Journal of Research on Adolescence, 22,* 678–693. doi:10.1111/j.1532-7795.2012.00817.x

Bleidorn, W., Arslan, R. C., Denissen, J. J. A., Rentfrow, P. J., Gebauer, J. E., Potter, J., & Gosling, S. D. (2016). Age and gender differences in self-esteem—A cross-cultural window. *Journal of Personality and Social Psychology, 111,* 396–410. doi:10.1037/pspp0000078

Bornstein, M. H., & Putnick, D. L. (2018). Parent–adolescent relationships in global perspective. In J. E. Lansford & P. Banati (Eds.), *Handbook of adolescent development research and its impact on global policy.* Oxford, UK: Oxford University Press.

Bosse, J. D., & Chiodo, L. (2016). It is complicated: Gender and sexual orientation identity in LGBTQ youth. *Journal of Clinical Nursing, 25,* 3665–3675. https://doi.org/10.1111/jocn.13419

Bowker, A., & Ramsay, K. (2016). Friendship characteristics. In R. J. R. Levesque (Ed.), *Encyclopedia of adolescence* (pp. 1–8). Cham, Switzerland: Springer. doi:10.1007/978-3-319-32132-5_49-2

Bowman, M. A., Prelow, H. M., & Weaver, S. R. (2007). Parenting behaviors, association with deviant peers, and delinquency in African American adolescents: A mediated-moderation model. *Journal of Youth & Adolescence, 36,* 517–527.

Boyes, M. C., & Chandler, M. (1992). Cognitive development, epistemic doubt, and identity formation in adolescence. *Journal of Youth and Adolescence, 21,* 277–304.

Braams, B. R., van Duijvenvoorde, A. C. K., Peper, J. S., & Crone, E. A. (2015). Longitudinal changes in adolescent risk-taking: A comprehensive study of neural responses to rewards, pubertal development, and risk-taking behavior. *Journal of Neuroscience, 35,* 7226–7238.

Branje, S. (2018). Development of parent-adolescent relationships: Conflict interactions as a mechanism of change.

Child Development Perspectives, 12, 171–176. doi:10.1111/cdep.12278

Branje, S., Laursen, B., & Collins, W. A. (2013). Parent-child communication during adolescence. In A. L. Vangelisti (Ed.), *Routledge handbook of family communication* (p. 601). New York, NY. Routledge.

Brechwald, W. A., & Prinstein, M. J. (2011). Beyond homophily: A decade of advances in understanding peer influence processes. *Journal of Research on Adolescence, 21,* 166–179. doi:10.1111/j.1532-7795.2010.00721.x

Brooks-Russell, A., Simons-Morton, B., Haynie, D., Farhat, T., & Wang, J. (2014). Longitudinal relationship between drinking with peers, descriptive norms, and adolescent alcohol use. *Prevention Science, 15,* 497–505. doi:10.1007/s11121-013-0391-9

Brown, B., Bank, H., & Steinberg, L. (2008). Smoke in the looking glass: Effects of discordance between self- and peer rated crowd affiliation on adolescent anxiety, depression and self-feelings. *Journal of Youth & Adolescence, 37,* 1163–1177. doi:10.1007/s10964-007-9198-y

Brown, B., Lohr, M. J., & McClenahan, E. L. (1986). Early adolescents' perceptions of peer pressure. *Journal of Early Adolescence, 6,* 139–154.

Brumback, T., Worley, M., Nguyen-Louie, T. T., Squeglia, L. M., Jacobus, J., & Tapert, S. F. (2016). Neural predictors of alcohol use and psychopathology symptoms in adolescents. *Development and Psychopathology, 28*(4, Pt. 1), 1209–1216. doi:10.1017/S0954579416000766

Bruni, V., & Dei, M. (2018). Eating disorders in adolescence. In A. M. Fulghesu (Ed.), *Good practice in pediatric and adolescent gynecology* (pp. 131–141). Cham, Switzerland: Springer International. doi:10.1007/978-3-319-57162-1_8

Burrus, B. B. (2018). Decline in adolescent pregnancy in the United States: A success not shared by all. *American Journal of Public Health, 108,* S5–S6. doi:10.2105/AJPH.2017.304273

Calzo, J. P., Antonucci, T. C., Mays, V. M., & Cochran, S. D. (2011). Retrospective recall of sexual orientation identity development among gay, lesbian, and bisexual adults. *Developmental Psychology, 47,* 1658–1673. doi:10.1037/a0025508

Calzo, J. P., Masyn, K. E., Austin, S. B., Jun, H.-J., & Corliss, H. L. (2017). Developmental latent patterns of identification as mostly heterosexual versus lesbian, gay, or bisexual. *Journal of Research on Adolescence, 27,* 246–253. doi:10.1111/jora.12266

Canetto, S. S., & Sakinofsky, I. (1998). The gender paradox in suicide. *Suicide and Life-Threatening Behavior, 28,* 1–23.

Carbia, C., Cadaveira, F., López-Caneda, E., Caamaño-Isorna, F., Rodriguez Holguin, S., & Corral, M. (2017). Working memory over a six-year period in young binge drinkers. *Alcohol, 61,* 17–23. doi:10.1016/j.alcohol.2017.01.013

Carlson, D. L., McNulty, T. L., Bellair, P. E., & Watts, S. (2014). Neighborhoods and racial/ethnic disparities in adolescent sexual risk behavior. *Journal of Youth and Adolescence, 43,* 1536–1549. doi:10.1007/s10964-013-0052-0

Carlsson, J., Wängqvist, M., & Frisén, A. (2016). Life on hold: Staying in identity diffusion in the late twenties. *Journal of Adolescence, 47,* 220–229. doi:10.1016/j.adolescence.2015.10.023

Casares, W. N., Lahiff, M., Eskenazi, B., & Halpern-Felsher, B. L. (2010). Unpredicted trajectories: The relationship between race/ethnicity, pregnancy during adolescence, and young women's outcomes. *Journal of Adolescent Health, 47,* 143–150. doi:10.1016/j.jadohealth.2010.01.013

Casey Copen, E., Chandra, A., & Martinez, G. (2012). Prevalence and timing of oral sex with opposite-sex partners among females and males aged 15–24 years: United States, 2007–2010. *National Health Statistics Reports, 56.* Retrieved from http://web.csulb.edu/~nmatza/powerpoint/HSc411BAssign/Course Docs/HSC 411b Docs/oral.sex.teens2012.pdf

Cauce, A., & Domenech-Rodriguez, M. (2002). Latino families: Myths and realities. In J. Contreras, A. Neal-Barnett, & K. Kerns (Eds.), *Latino children and families in the United States* (pp. 2–25). Westport, CT: Praeger.

Centers for Disease Control and Prevention. (2015). *HIV in the United States: At a glance.* Retrieved from http://stacks.cdc.gov/view/cdc/35661/cdc_35661_DS1.pdf

Centers for Disease Control and Prevention. (2016a). *Sexually transmitted disease surveillance 2015.* Retrieved from https://www.cdc.gov/std/stats15/default.htm

Centers for Disease Control and Prevention. (2016b). *Teen pregnancy in the United States.* Retrieved from https://www.cdc.gov/teenpregnancy/about/

Centers for Disease Control and Prevention. (2017). *10 Leading causes of death, by age group, United States—2015.* Retrieved from https://www.cdc.gov/injury/images/lc-charts/leading_causes_of_death_age_group_2015_1050w740h.gif

Chaplin, T. M., Sinha, R., Simmons, J. A., Healy, S. M., Mayes, L. C., Hommer, R. E., & Crowley, M. J. (2012). Parent–adolescent conflict interactions and adolescent alcohol use. *Addictive Behaviors, 37,* 605–612. doi:10.1016/j.addbeh.2012.01.004

Chein, J., Albert, D., O'Brien, L., Uckert, K., & Steinberg, L. (2011). Peers increase adolescent risk taking by enhancing activity in the brain's reward circuitry. *Developmental Science, 14,* F1–F10. doi:10.1111/J.1467-7687.2010.01035.X

Chen, P., Voisin, D. R., & Jacobson, K. C. (2013). Community violence exposure and adolescent delinquency: Examining a spectrum of promotive factors. *Youth & Society, 48,* 33–57. doi:10.1177/0044118X13475827

Child Trends Databank. (2015). *Oral sex behaviors among teens.* Retrieved May 4, 2015, from https://www.childtrends.org/?indicators=oral-sex-behaviors-among-teens

Child Trends Databank. (2017). *Sexually active teens—Child trends.* Retrieved May 25, 2018, from https://www.childtrends.org/indicators/sexually-active-teens/

Choukas-Bradley, S., Giletta, M., Widman, L., Cohen, G. L., & Prinstein, M. J. (2014).

Experimentally measured susceptibility to peer influence and adolescent sexual behavior trajectories: A preliminary study. *Developmental Psychology, 50*, 2221–2227. doi:10.1037/a0037300

Claes, L., Luyckx, K., Baetens, I., Van de Ven, M., & Witteman, C. (2015). Bullying and victimization, depressive mood, and non-suicidal self-injury in adolescents: The moderating role of parental support. *Journal of Child and Family Studies, 24*, 3363–3371. doi:10.1007/s10826-015-0138-2

Cohen, K. M., & Savin-Williams, R. C. (1996). *Developmental perspectives on coming out to self and others.* Retrieved from http://psycnet.apa.org/psycinfo/1996-97027-005

Coley, R. L., Lombardi, C. M., Lynch, A. D., Mahalik, J. R., & Sims, J. (2013). Sexual partner accumulation from adolescence through early adulthood: The role of family, peer, and school social norms. *Journal of Adolescent Health, 53*, 91-7.e1–91-7.e2. doi:10.1016/j.jadohealth.2013.01.005

Collier, K. L., van Beusekom, G., Bos, H. M. W., & Sandfort, T. G. M. (2013). Sexual orientation and gender identity/expression related peer victimization in adolescence: A systematic review of associated psychosocial and health outcomes. *Journal of Sex Research, 50*, 299–317. doi:10.1080/00224499.2012.750639

Collins, W. A., Welsh, D. P., & Furman, W. (2009). Adolescent romantic relationships. *Annual Review of Psychology, 60*, 631–652. doi:10.1146/annurev.psych.60.110707.163459

Connolly, J., & Craig, W. (1999). Conceptions of cross-sex friendships and romantic relationships in early adolescence. *Journal of Youth & Adolescence, 14*, 481–509.

Connolly, J., Craig, W., Goldberg, A., & Pepler, D. (2004). Mixed-gender groups, dating, and romantic relationships in early adolescence. *Journal of Research on Adolescence, 14*, 185–207.

Connolly, J., & McIsaac, C. (2011). Romantic relationships in adolescence. In M. K. Underwood & L. H. Rosen (Eds.), *Social development: Relationships in infancy, childhood, and adolescence* (p. 18). New York, NY: Guilford.

Connolly, J., Nguyen, H. N. T., Pepler, D., Craig, W., & Jiang, D. (2013). Developmental trajectories of romantic stages and associations with problem behaviours during adolescence. *Journal of Adolescence, 36*, 1013–1024. doi:10.1016/j.adolescence.2013.08.006

Coyle, K. K., Guinosso, S. A., Glassman, J. R., Anderson, P. M., & Wilson, H. W. (2017). Exposure to violence and sexual risk among early adolescents in urban middle schools. *Journal of Early Adolescence, 37*, 889–909. doi:10.1177/0272431616642324

Crocetti, E. (2017). Identity formation in adolescence: The dynamic of forming and consolidating identity commitments. *Child Development Perspectives, 11*, 145–150. doi:10.1111/cdep.12226

Crocetti, E., Branje, S., Rubini, M., Koot, H. M., & Meeus, W. (2017). Identity processes and parent-child and sibling relationships in adolescence: A five-wave multi-informant longitudinal study. *Child Development, 88*, 210–228. doi:10.1111/cdev.12547

Crocetti, E., Klimstra, T. A., Hale, W. W., Koot, H. M., & Meeus, W. H. J. (2013). Impact of early adolescent externalizing problem behaviors on identity development in middle to late adolescence: A prospective 7-year longitudinal study. *Journal of Youth and Adolescence, 42*, 1745–1758. doi:10.1007/s10964-013-9924-6

Crocetti, E., Klimstra, T., Keijsers, L., Hale Iii, W. W., & Meeus, W. H. J. (2009). Anxiety trajectories and identity development in adolescence: A five-wave longitudinal study. *Journal of Youth & Adolescence, 38*, 839–849. doi:10.1007/s10964-008-9302-y

Cross, J. R., & Fletcher, K. L. (2009). The challenge of adolescent crowd research: Defining the crowd. *Journal of Youth & Adolescence, 38*, 747–764. doi:10.1007/s10964-008-9307-6

Davis, B., Royne Stafford, M. B., & Pullig, C. (2014). How gay-straight alliance groups mitigate the relationship between gay-bias victimization and adolescent suicide attempts. *Journal of the American Academy of Child and Adolescent Psychiatry, 53*, 1271–1278.e1. doi:10.1016/j.jaac.2014.09.010

De Genna, N., Larkby, C., & Cornelius, M. (2011). Pubertal timing and early sexual intercourse in the offspring of teenage mothers. *Journal of Youth & Adolescence, 40*, 1315–1328. doi:10.1007/s10964-010-9609-3

De La Rue, L., Polanin, J. R., Espelage, D. L., & Pigott, T. D. (2017). A meta-analysis of school-based interventions aimed to prevent or reduce violence in teen dating relationships. *Review of Educational Research, 87*, 7–34. doi:10.3102/0034654316632061

de Water, E., Burk, W. J., Cillessen, A. H. N., & Scheres, A. (2016). Substance use and decision-making in adolescent best friendship dyads: The role of popularity. *Social Development, 26*, 860–875. doi:10.1111/sode.12227

Delsing, M. J. M. H., ter Bogt, T. F. M., Engels, R. C. M. E., & Meeus, W. H. J. (2007). Adolescents' peer crowd identification in the Netherlands: Structure and associations with problem behaviors. *Journal of Research on Adolescence, 17*, 467–480. doi:10.1111/j.1532-7795.2007.00530.x

Desjardins, T., & Leadbeater, B. J. (2017). Changes in parental emotional support and psychological control in early adulthood. *Emerging Adulthood, 5*, 177–190. doi:10.1177/2167696816666974

Diamond, L. M., & Savin-Williams, R. C. (2009). Adolescent sexuality. In R. M. Lerner & L. Steinberg (Eds.), *Handbook of adolescent psychology* (p. 479). Hoboken, NJ: John Wiley.

Dimler, L. M., Natsuaki, M. N., Hastings, P. D., Zahn-Waxler, C., & Klimes-Dougan, B. (2017). Parenting effects are in the eye of the beholder: Parent–adolescent differences in perceptions affects adolescent problem behaviors. *Journal of Youth and Adolescence, 46*, 1076–1088. doi:10.1007/s10964-016-0612-1

Dishion, T. J., & Patterson, G. R. (2016). The development and ecology of antisocial behavior: Linking etiology, prevention, and treatment. In D. Cicchetti (Ed.), *Developmental psychopathology* (pp. 1–32). Hoboken, NJ: John Wiley. doi:10.1002/9781119125556.devpsy315

Dittus, P. J., Michael, S. L., Becasen, J. S., Gloppen, K. M., McCarthy, K., & Guilamo-Ramos, V. (2015). Parental monitoring and its associations with adolescent sexual risk behavior: A meta-analysis. *Pediatrics, 136*, e1587–e1599.

Dotterer, A. M., McHale, S. M., & Crouter, A. C. (2009). Sociocultural factors and school engagement among African American youth: The roles of racial discrimination, racial socialization, and ethnic identity. *Applied Developmental Science, 13*, 61–73. doi:10.1080/10888690902801442

Douglass, S., & Umaña-Taylor, A. J. (2016). Time-varying effects of family ethnic socialization on ethnic-racial identity development among Latino adolescents. *Developmental Psychology, 52*, 1904–1912. doi:10.1037/dev0000141

Douglass, S., & Umaña-Taylor, A. J. (2017). Examining discrimination, ethnic-racial identity status, and youth public regard among Black, Latino, and White adolescents. *Journal of Research on Adolescence, 27*, 155–172. doi:10.1111/jora.12262

Duan, L., Chou, C. P., Andreeva, V., & Pentz, M. (2009). Trajectories of peer social influences as long-term predictors of drug use from early through late adolescence. *Journal of Youth & Adolescence, 38*, 454–465. doi:10.1007/s10964-008-9310-y

East, P. L., Khoo, S. T., Reyes, B. T., & Coughlin, L. (2006). AAP report on pregnancy in adolescents. *Perspectives on Sexual & Reproductive Health, 10*, 12.

East, P. L., Reyes, B. T., & Horn, E. J. (2007). Association between adolescent pregnancy and a family history of teenage births. *Perspectives on Sexual & Reproductive Health, 39*, 108–115.

Easterbrooks, M. A., Chaudhuri, J. H., Bartlett, J. D., & Copeman, A. (2011). Resilience in parenting among young mothers: Family and ecological risks and opportunities. *Children and Youth Services Review, 33*, 42–50. doi:10.1016/j.childyouth.2010.08.010

Ellis, W. E., & Zarbatany, L. (2017). Understanding processes of peer clique influence in late childhood and early adolescence. *Child Development Perspectives, 11*, 227–232. doi:10.1111/cdep.12248

Englund, M. M., Siebenbruner, J., Oliva, E. M., Egeland, B., Chung, C. T., & Long, J. D. (2013). The developmental significance of late adolescent substance use for early adult functioning. *Developmental Psychology, 49*, 1554–1564. doi:10.1037/a0030229

Erdley, C. A., & Day, H. J. (2017). Friendship in childhood and adolescence. In M. Hojjat & A. Moyer (Eds.), *The psychology of friendship* (pp. 3–19). Oxford, UK: Oxford University Press.

Erikson, E. H. (1950). *Childhood and society* (2nd ed.). New York, NY: Norton.

Ethier, K. A., Harper, C. R., Hoo, E., & Dittus, P. J. (2016). The longitudinal impact of perceptions of parental monitoring on adolescent initiation of sexual activity. *Journal of Adolescent Health, 59*, 570–576. doi:10.1016/j.jadohealth.2016.06.011

Evans, S. Z., Simons, L. G., & Simons, R. L. (2014). Factors that influence trajectories of delinquency throughout adolescence. *Journal of Youth and Adolescence, 45*, 156–171. doi:10.1007/s10964-014-0197-5

Exner-Cortens, D., Eckenrode, J., & Rothman, E. (2013). Longitudinal associations between teen dating violence victimization and adverse health outcomes. *Pediatrics, 131,* 71–78. doi:10.1542/peds.2012-1029

Fareri, D. S., & Delgado, M. R. (2014). Social rewards and social networks in the human brain. *The Neuroscientist, 20,* 387–402. doi:10.1177/1073858414521869

Farrington, D. P., & Loeber, R. (2000). Epidemiology of juvenile violence. *Juvenile Violence, 9,* 733–748.

Federal Bureau of Investigation. (2015). *Crime in the United States.* Washington, DC: Author.

Feldstein Ewing, S. W., Sakhardande, A., & Blakemore, S.-J. (2014). The effect of alcohol consumption on the adolescent brain: A systematic review of MRI and fMRI studies of alcohol-using youth. *NeuroImage: Clinical, 5,* 420–437. doi:10.1016/j.nicl.2014.06.011

Fellmeth, G. L., Heffernan, C., Nurse, J., Habibula, S., & Sethi, D. (2013). Educational and skills-based interventions for preventing relationship and dating violence in adolescents and young adults. *Cochrane Database of Systematic Reviews, 6,* 1465–1858. doi:10.1002/14651858.CD004534.pub3

Ferguson, G. M., Hafen, C. A., & Laursen, B. (2010). Adolescent psychological and academic adjustment as a function of discrepancies between actual and ideal self-perceptions. *Journal of Youth and Adolescence, 39,* 1485–1497. doi:10.1007/s10964-009-9461-5

Fergusson, D. M., & Horwood, L. J. (2002). Male and female offending trajectories. *Development and Psychopathology, 14,* 159–177.

Fergusson, D. M., Woodward, L. J., & Horwood, L. J. (2000). Risk factors and life processes associated with the onset of suicidal behaviour during adolescence and early adulthood. *Psychological Medicine, 30,* 23–39.

Finer, L. B., & Philbin, J. M. (2013). Sexual initiation, contraceptive use, and pregnancy among young adolescents. *Pediatrics, 131,* 886–891. doi:10.1542/peds.2012-3495

Fisher, H. L., Moffitt, T. E., Houts, R. M., Belsky, D. W., Arseneault, L., & Caspi, A. (2012). Bullying victimisation and risk of self harm in early adolescence: Longitudinal cohort study. *BMJ (Clinical Research Ed.), 344*(apr26_2), e2683. doi:10.1136/bmj.e2683

Flannery, D. J., Hussey, D., & Jefferis, E. (2005). Adolescent delinquency and violent behavior. In T. P. Gullotta & G. R. Adams (Eds.), *Handbook of adolescent behavioral problems: Evidence-based approaches to prevention and treatment* (pp. 415–438). New York, NY: Springer.

Floyd, F. J., & Bakeman, R. (2006). Coming-out across the life course: Implications of age and historical context. *Archives of Sexual Behavior, 35,* 287–296. doi:10.1007/s10508-006-9022-x

Fortenberry, J. D. (2013). Puberty and adolescent sexuality. *Hormones and Behavior, 64,* 280–287. doi:10.1016/j.yhbeh.2013.03.007

Foshee, V. A., McNaughton Reyes, H. L., Vivolo-Kantor, A. M., Basile, K. C., Chang, L. Y., Faris, R., & Ennett, S. T. (2014). Bullying as a longitudinal predictor of adolescent dating violence. *Journal of Adolescent Health, 55,* 439–444. doi:10.1016/j.jadohealth.2014.03.004

Foshee, V. A., McNaughton Reyes, L., Tharp, A. T., Chang, L. Y., Ennett, S. T., Simon, T. R., . . . Suchindran, C. (2015). Shared longitudinal predictors of physical peer and dating violence. *Journal of Adolescent Health, 56,* 106–112. doi:10.1016/j.jadohealth.2014.08.003

French, D. C., & Cheung, H. S. (2018). Peer relationships. In J. E. Lansford & P. Banati (Eds.), *Handbook of adolescent development research and its impact on global policy.* Oxford, UK: Oxford University Press.

Fuglset, T. S., Landrø, N. I., Reas, D. L., & Rø, Ø. (2016). Functional brain alterations in anorexia nervosa: A scoping review. *Journal of Eating Disorders, 4,* 32. doi:10.1186/s40337-016-0118-y

Furman, W., & Collibee, C. (2014). A matter of timing: Developmental theories of romantic involvement and psychosocial adjustment. *Development and Psychopathology, 26*(4, Pt. 1), 1149–1160. doi:10.1017/S0954579414000182

Galliher, R. V, Jones, M. D., & Dahl, A. (2011). Concurrent and longitudinal effects of ethnic identity and experiences of discrimination on psychosocial adjustment of Navajo adolescents. *Developmental Psychology, 47,* 509–526. doi:10.1037/a0021061

Galupo, M. P., Davis, K. S., Grynkiewicz, A. L., & Mitchell, R. C. (2014). Conceptualization of sexual orientation identity among sexual minorities: Patterns across sexual and gender identity. *Journal of Bisexuality, 14,* 433–456. https://doi.org/10.1080/15299716.2014.933466

Ge, X., Natsuaki, M. N., Neiderhiser, J. M., & Reiss, D. (2009). The longitudinal effects of stressful life events on adolescent depression are buffered by parent-child closeness. *Development & Psychopathology, 21,* 621–635. doi:10.1017/s0954579409000339

Gest, S. D., Davidson, A. J., Rulison, K. L., Moody, J., & Welsh, J. A. (2007). Features of groups and status hierarchies in girls' and boys' early adolescent peer networks. *New Directions for Child & Adolescent Development, 2007,* 43–60.

Giletta, M., Burk, W. J., Scholte, R. H. J., Engels, R. C. M. E., & Prinstein, M. J. (2013). Direct and indirect peer socialization of adolescent nonsuicidal self-injury. *Journal of Research on Adolescence, 23,* 450–463. doi:10.1111/jora.12036

Giordano, P. C., Phelps, K. D., Manning, W. D., & Longmore, M. A. (2008). Adolescent academic achievement and romantic relationships. *Social Science Research, 37,* 37–54. doi:10.1016/j.ssresearch.2007.06.004

Giordano, P. C., Soto, D. A., Manning, W. D., & Longmore, M. A. (2010). The characteristics of romantic relationships associated with teen dating violence. *Social Science Research, 39,* 863–874. doi:10.1016/j.ssresearch.2010.03.009

Gonzales-Backen, M. A., Bámaca-Colbert, M. Y., & Allen, K. (2016). Ethnic identity trajectories among Mexican-origin girls during early and middle adolescence: Predicting future psychosocial adjustment. *Developmental Psychology, 52,* 790–797. doi:10.1037/a0040193

Graham, S., Munniksma, A., & Juvonen, J. (2014). Psychosocial benefits of cross-ethnic friendships in urban middle schools. *Child Development, 85,* 469–483. doi:10.1111/cdev.12159

Greaves, L. M., Barlow, F. K., Lee, C. H. J., Matika, C. M., Wang, W., Lindsay, C.-J., . . . Sibley, C. G. (2017). The diversity and prevalence of sexual orientation self-labels in a New Zealand national sample. *Archives of Sexual Behavior, 46,* 1325–1336. doi:10.1007/s10508-016-0857-5

Greenberg, J. S. (2017). *Exploring the dimensions of human sexuality.* Burlington, MA: Jones & Bartlett.

Griffith, S. F., & Grolnick, W. S. (2013). Parenting in Caribbean families: A look at parental control, structure, and autonomy support. *Journal of Black Psychology, 40,* 166–190. doi:10.1177/0095798412475085

Grossman, A. H., Park, J. Y., & Russell, S. T. (2016). Transgender youth and suicidal behaviors: Applying the interpersonal psychological theory of suicide. *Journal of Gay & Lesbian Mental Health, 20,* 329–349. doi:10.1080/19359705.2016.1207581

Grotevant, H. D., Thorbecke, W., & Meyer, M. L. (1982). An extension of Marcia's identity status interview into the interpersonal domain. *Journal of Youth and Adolescence, 11,* 33–47. doi:10.1007/BF01537815

Gruenenfelder-Steiger, A. E., Harris, M. A., & Fend, H. A. (2016). Subjective and objective peer approval evaluations and self-esteem development: A test of reciprocal, prospective, and long-term effects. *Developmental Psychology, 52,* 1563–1577. doi:10.1037/dev0000147

Guimond, S., Chatard, A., & Lorenzi-Cioldi, F. (2013). The social psychology of gender across cultures. In M. K. Ryan (Ed.), *The SAGE handbook of gender and psychology* (pp. 216–233). Thousand Oaks, CA: Sage. doi:10.4135/9781446269930.n14

Guttmacher Institute. (2014). *American teens' sexual and reproductive health.* Washington, DC: Author. Retrieved from http://www.guttmacher.org/pubs/fb_ATSRH.html

Haas, A. P., Eliason, M., Mays, V. M., Mathy, R. M., Cochran, S. D., D'Augelli, A. R., . . . Clayton, P. J. (2011). Suicide and suicide risk in lesbian, gay, bisexual, and transgender populations: Review and recommendations. *Journal of Homosexuality, 58,* 10–51. doi:10.1080/00918369.2011.534038

Hadiwijaya, H., Klimstra, T. A., Vermunt, J. K., Branje, S. J. T., & Meeus, W. H. J. (2017). On the development of harmony, turbulence, and independence in parent–adolescent relationships: A Five-Wave Longitudinal Study. *Journal of Youth and Adolescence, 46,* 1772–1788. doi:10.1007/s10964-016-0627-7

Hail, L., & Le Grange, D. (2018). Bulimia nervosa in adolescents: Prevalence and treatment challenges. *Adolescent Health, Medicine and Therapeutics, 9,* 11–16. doi:10.2147/AHMT.S135326

Haleem, D. J. (2012). Serotonin neurotransmission in anorexia nervosa. *Behavioural Pharmacology, 23,* 478–495. doi:10.1097/FBP.0b013e328357440d

Hall, B., & Place, M. (2010). Cutting to cope—A modern adolescent phenomenon. *Child: Care, Health & Development, 36,* 623–629. doi:10.1111/j.1365-2214.2010.01095.x

Hall, S. P., & Brassard, M. R. (2008). Relational support as a predictor of identity status in an ethnically diverse early adolescent sample. *Journal of Early Adolescence, 28*, 92–114. doi:10.1177/0272431607308668

Harper, G. W., Serrano, P. A., Bruce, D., & Bauermeister, J. A. (2015). The Internet's multiple roles in facilitating the sexual orientation identity development of gay and bisexual male adolescents. *American Journal of Men's Health, 10*, 359–376. doi:10.1177/1557988314566227

Harris, A. C. (1996). African American and Anglo-American gender identities: An empirical study. *Journal of Black Psychology, 22*, 182–194. doi:10.1177/00957984960222004

Harris, M. A., Gruenenfelder-Steiger, A. E., Ferrer, E., Donnellan, M. B., Allemand, M., Fend, H., . . . Trzesniewski, K. H. (2015). Do parents foster self-esteem? Testing the prospective impact of parent closeness on adolescent self-esteem. *Child Development, 86*, 995–1013. doi:10.1111/cdev.12356

Harris-McKoy, D., & Cui, M. (2012). Parental control, adolescent delinquency, and young adult criminal behavior. *Journal of Child and Family Studies, 22*, 836–843. doi:10.1007/s10826-012-9641-x

Harter, S. (2012a). Emerging self-processes during childhood and adolescence. In M. R. Leary & J. P. Tangney (Eds.), *Handbook of self and identity* (pp. 680–715). New York, NY: Guilford.

Harter, S. (2012b). The construction of the self: Developmental and sociocultural foundations (2nd ed.). New York, NY: Guilford.

Hartl, A. C., Laursen, B., & Cillessen, A. H. N. (2015). A survival analysis of adolescent friendships. *Psychological Science, 26*, 1304–1315. doi:10.1177/0956797615588751

Hartup, W. W., & Stevens, N. (1997). Friendships and adaptation in the life course. *Psychological Bulletin, 121*, 355–370.

Haw, C., Hawton, K., Niedzwiedz, C., & Platt, S. (2013). Suicide clusters: A review of risk factors and mechanisms. *Suicide & Life-Threatening Behavior, 43*, 97–108. doi:10.1111/j.1943-278X.2012.00130.x

Haydon, A. A., Herring, A. H., Prinstein, M. J., & Halpern, C. T. (2012). Beyond age at first sex: Patterns of emerging sexual behavior in adolescence and young adulthood. *Journal of Adolescent Health, 50*, 456–463. doi:10.1016/j.jadohealth.2011.09.006

Helms, S. W., Choukas-Bradley, S., Widman, L., Giletta, M., Cohen, G. L., & Prinstein, M. J. (2014). Adolescents misperceive and are influenced by high-status peers' health risk, deviant, and adaptive behavior. *Developmental Psychology, 50*, 2697–714. doi:10.1037/a0038178

Hepper, P. G., Dornan, J. C., & Lynch, C. (2012). Sex differences in fetal habituation. *Developmental Science, 15*, 373–383. doi:10.1111/j.1467-7687.2011.01132.x

Herpertz-Dahlmann, B. (2017). Treatment of eating disorders in child and adolescent psychiatry. *Current Opinion in Psychiatry, 30*, 438–445. doi:10.1097/YCO.0000000000000357

Herrman, J. W. (2009). There's a fine line . . . adolescent dating violence and prevention. *Pediatric Nursing, 35*, 164–170.

Hiatt, C., Laursen, B., Mooney, K. S., & Rubin, K. H. (2015). Forms of friendship: A person-centered assessment of the quality, stability, and outcomes of different types of adolescent friends. *Personality and Individual Differences, 77*, 149–155. doi:10.1016/j.paid.2014.12.051

Hiatt, C., Laursen, B., Stattin, H., & Kerr, M. (2017). Best friend influence over adolescent problem behaviors: Socialized by the satisfied. *Journal of Clinical Child & Adolescent Psychology, 46*, 695–708. doi:10.1080/15374416.2015.1050723

Hill, R. M., Castellanos, D., & Pettit, J. W. (2011). Suicide-related behaviors and anxiety in children and adolescents: A review. *Clinical Psychology Review, 31*, 1133–1144. doi:10.1016/j.cpr.2011.07.008

Hoeve, M., Dubas, J. S., Gerris, J. R. M., van der Laan, P. H., & Smeenk, W. (2011). Maternal and paternal parenting styles: Unique and combined links to adolescent and early adult delinquency. *Journal of Adolescence, 34*, 813–827. doi:10.1016/j.adolescence.2011.02.004

Hofer, C., Eisenberg, N., Spinrad, T. L., Morris, A. S., Gershoff, E., Valiente, C., . . . Eggum, N. D. (2013). Mother-adolescent conflict: Stability, change, and relations with externalizing and internalizing behavior problems. *Social Development, 22*, 259–279. doi:10.1111/sode.12012

Holman, D. M., Benard, V., Roland, K. B., Watson, M., Liddon, N., & Stokley, S. (2014). Barriers to Human Papillomavirus Vaccination among US adolescents. *JAMA Pediatrics, 168*, 76. doi:10.1001/jamapediatrics.2013.2752

Hopmeyer, A., & Medovoy, T. (2017). Emerging adults' self-identified peer crowd affiliations, risk behavior, and social–emotional adjustment in college. *Emerging Adulthood, 5*, 143–148. doi:10.1177/2167696816665055

Howell, B. R., McMurray, M. S., Guzman, D. B., Nair, G., Shi, Y., McCormack, K. M., . . . Sanchez, M. M. (2017). Maternal buffering beyond glucocorticoids: Impact of early life stress on corticolimbic circuits that control infant responses to novelty. *Social Neuroscience, 12*, 50–64. doi:10.1080/17470919.2016.1200481

Huang, D. Y. C., Murphy, D. A., & Hser, Y.-I. (2011). Parental monitoring during early adolescence deters adolescent sexual initiation: Discrete-time survival mixture analysis. *Journal of Child and Family Studies, 20*, 511–520. doi:10.1007/s10826-010-9418-z

Huey, M., Hiatt, C., Laursen, B., Burk, W. J., & Rubin, K. (2017). Mother–adolescent conflict types and adolescent adjustment: A person-oriented analysis. *Journal of Family Psychology, 31*, 504–512. doi:10.1037/fam0000294

Hughes, D., Hagelskamp, C., Way, N., & Foust, M. D. (2009). The role of mothers' and adolescents' perceptions of ethnic-racial socialization in shaping ethnic-racial identity among early adolescent boys and girls. *Journal of Youth & Adolescence, 38*, 605–626. doi:10.1007/s10964-009-9399-7

Hughes, D. L., Del Toro, J., & Way, N. (2017). Interrelations among dimensions of ethnic-racial identity during adolescence. *Developmental Psychology, 53*, 2139–2153. doi:10.1037/dev0000401

Isomaa, R., Isomaa, A.-L., Marttunen, M., Kaltiala-Heino, R., & Björkqvist, K. (2009). The prevalence, incidence and development of eating disorders in Finnish adolescents—A two-step 3-year follow-up Study. *European Eating Disorders Review, 17*, 199–207. doi:10.1002/erv.919

Jain, S., & Cohen, A. K. (2013). Behavioral adaptation among youth exposed to community violence: A longitudinal multidisciplinary study of family, peer and neighborhood-level protective factors. *Prevention Science, 14*, 606–617. doi:10.1007/s11121-012-0344-8

Jaramillo, N., Buhi, E. R., Elder, J. P., & Corliss, H. L. (2017). Associations between sex education and contraceptive use among heterosexually active, adolescent males in the United States. *Journal of Adolescent Health, 60*, 534–540. doi:10.1016/j.jadohealth.2016.11.025

Jeha, D., Usta, I., Ghulmiyyah, L., & Nassar, A. (2015). A review of the risks and consequences of adolescent pregnancy. *Journal of Neonatal-Perinatal Medicine, 8*, 1–8. doi:10.3233/NPM-15814038

Jespersen, K., Kroger, J., & Martinussen, M. (2013). Identity status and moral reasoning: A meta analysis. *Identity, 13*, 266–280. doi:10.1080/15283488.2013.799472

Johnson, A. Z., Sieving, R. E., Pettingell, S. L., & McRee, A.-L. (2015). The roles of partner communication and relationship status in adolescent contraceptive use. *Journal of Pediatric Health Care, 29*, 61–69. doi:10.1016/j.pedhc.2014.06.008

Johnston, L. D., Miech, R. A., O'Malley, P. M., Bachman, J. G., Schulenberg, J. E., & Patrick, M. E. (2018). *2017 Overview: Key findings on adolescent drug use.* Retrieved March 15, 2018, from http://www.monitoringthefuture.org/pubs/monographs/mtf-overview2017.pdf

Jordan, J. W., Stalgaitis, C. A., Charles, J., Madden, P. A., Radhakrishnan, A. G., & Saggese, D. (2018). Peer crowd identification and adolescent health behaviors: Results from a statewide representative study. *Health Education & Behavior.* Advance online publication. doi:10.1177/1090198118759148

Kaiser Family Foundation. (2014). *Sexual health of adolescents and young adults in the United States.* Retrieved May 4, 2015, from http://kff.org/womens-health-policy/fact-sheet/sexual-health-of-adolescents-and-young-adults-in-the-united-states/

Kann, L., Kinchen, S., Shanklin, S. L., Flint, K. H., Kawkins, J., Harris, W. A., . . . Centers for Disease Control and Prevention (CDC). (2014). Youth risk behavior surveillance—United States, 2013. *Morbidity and Mortality Weekly Report, Surveillance Summaries, 63*(Suppl. 4), 1–168. Retrieved from http://www.ncbi.nlm.nih.gov/pubmed/24918634

Kansky, J., & Allen, J. P. (2018). Long-term risks and possible benefits associated with late adolescent romantic relationship quality. *Journal of Youth and Adolescence, 47*, 1531–1544. doi:10.1007/s10964-018-0813-x

Kapadia, S., & Gala, J. (2015). Gender across cultures. In L. A. Jensen (Ed.), *The Oxford handbook of human development and culture* (pp. 307–326). Oxford, UK: Oxford University Press. doi:10.1093/oxfordhb/9780199948550.013.19

Kawabata, Y., & Crick, N. R. (2011). The significance of cross-racial/ethnic friendships: Associations with peer victimization, peer support, sociometric status, and classroom diversity. *Developmental Psychology, 47*, 1763–1775. doi:10.1037/a0025399

Kaye, W. H., Wierenga, C. E., Bailer, U. F., Simmons, A. N., & Bischoff-Grethe, A. (2013). Nothing tastes as good as skinny feels: The neurobiology of anorexia nervosa. *Trends in Neurosciences, 36*, 110–120. doi:10.1016/j.tins.2013.01.003

Keski-Rahkonen, A., & Mustelin, L. (2016). Epidemiology of eating disorders in Europe. *Current Opinion in Psychiatry, 29*, 340–345. doi:10.1097/YCO.0000000000000278

Kim, S. Y., Chen, Q., Wang, Y., Shen, Y., & Orozco-Lapray, D. (2013). Longitudinal linkages among parent-child acculturation discrepancy, parenting, parent-child sense of alienation, and adolescent adjustment in Chinese immigrant families. *Developmental Psychology, 49*, 900–912. doi:10.1037/a0029169

Kim, S. Y., Qi, C., Jing, L., Xuan, H., & Ui Jeong, M. (2009). Parent–child acculturation, parenting, and adolescent depressive symptoms in Chinese immigrant families. *Journal of Family Psychology, 23*, 426–437. doi:10.1037/a0016019

Kiselica, M. S., & Kiselica, A. M. (2014). The complicated worlds of adolescent fathers: Implications for clinical practice, public policy, and research. *Psychology of Men & Masculinity, 15*, 260.

Klemera, E., Brooks, F. M., Chester, K. L., Magnusson, J., & Spencer, N. (2017). Self-harm in adolescence: Protective health assets in the family, school and community. *International Journal of Public Health, 62*, 631–638. doi:10.1007/s00038-016-0900-2

Klimstra, T. A., Kuppens, P., Luyckx, K., Branje, S., Hale, W. W., Oosterwegel, A., . . . Meeus, W. H. J. (2016). Daily dynamics of adolescent mood and identity. *Journal of Research on Adolescence, 26*, 459–473. doi:10.1111/jora.12205

Kobak, R., Abbott, C., Zisk, A., & Bounoua, N. (2017). Adapting to the changing needs of adolescents: Parenting practices and challenges to sensitive attunement. *Current Opinion in Psychology, 15*, 137–142. doi:10.1016/j.copsyc.2017.02.018

Kochendorfer, L. B., & Kerns, K. A. (2017). Perceptions of parent–child attachment relationships and friendship qualities: Predictors of romantic relationship involvement and quality in adolescence. *Journal of Youth and Adolescence, 46*, 1009–1021. doi:10.1007/s10964-017-0645-0

Kosciw, J. G., Palmer, N. A., & Kull, R. M. (2015). Reflecting resiliency: Openness about sexual orientation and/or gender identity and its relationship to well-being and educational outcomes for LGBT students. *American Journal of Community Psychology, 55*, 167–178. doi:10.1007/s10464-014-9642-6

Kreager, D. A., Molloy, L. E., Moody, J., & Feinberg, M. E. (2016). Friends first? The peer network origins of adolescent dating. *Journal of Research on Adolescence, 26*, 257–269. doi:10.1111/jora.12189

Kroger, J. (2015). Identity development through adulthood: The move toward "wholeness." In K. C. McLean & M. Syed (Eds.), *The Oxford handbook of identity development* (pp. 65–80). Oxford, UK: Oxford University Press.

Kroger, J., Martinussen, M., & Marcia, J. E. (2010). Identity status change during adolescence and young adulthood: A meta-analysis. *Journal of Adolescence, 33*, 683–698. doi:10.1016/j.adolescence.2009.11.002

Laghi, F., Baiocco, R., Lonigro, A., & Baumgartner, E. (2013). Exploring the relationship between identity status development and alcohol consumption among Italian adolescents. *Journal of Psychology, 147*, 277–292. doi:10.1080/00223980.2012.688075

Lam, C. B., Stanik, C., & McHale, S. M. (2017). The development and correlates of gender role attitudes in African American youth. *British Journal of Developmental Psychology, 35*, 406–419. doi:10.1111/bjdp.12182

Lansford, J. E., Costanzo, P. R., Grimes, C., Putallaz, M., Miller, S., & Malone, P. S. (2009). Social network centrality and leadership status: Links with problem behaviors and tests of gender differences. *Merrill-Palmer Quarterly, 55*, 1–25.

Lansford, J. E., Laird, R. D., Pettit, G. S., Bates, J. E., & Dodge, K. A. (2014). Mothers' and fathers' autonomy-relevant parenting: Longitudinal links with adolescents' externalizing and internalizing behavior. *Journal of Youth and Adolescence, 43*, 1877–1889. doi:10.1007/s10964-013-0079-2

Lansford, J. E., Staples, A. D., Bates, J. E., Pettit, G. S., & Dodge, K. A. (2013). Trajectories of mothers' discipline strategies and interparental conflict: Interrelated change during middle childhood. *Journal of Family Communication, 13*, 178–195. doi:10.1080/15267431.2013.796947

Leadbeater, B., Banister, E., Ellis, W., & Yeung, R. (2008). Victimization and relational aggression in adolescent romantic relationships: The influence of parental and peer behaviors, and individual adjustment. *Journal of Youth & Adolescence, 37*, 359–372. doi:10.1007/s10964-007-9269-0

Leaper, C., & Valin, D. (1996). Predictors of Mexican American mothers' and fathers' attitudes toward gender equality. *Hispanic Journal of Behavioral Sciences, 18*, 343–355. doi:10.1177/07399863960183005

Lefkowitz, E. S., Vasilenko, S. A., & Leavitt, C. E. (2016). Oral vs. vaginal sex experiences and consequences among first-year college students. *Archives of Sexual Behavior, 45*, 329–337. doi:10.1007/s10508-015-0654-6

Lenhart, A., Purcell, K., Smith, A., & Zickuhr, K. (2010). *Social media and young adults.* Retrieved from http://www.pewinternet.org/2010/02/03/social-media-and-young-adults/

Lerner, R. M., & Israeloff, R. (2007). The good teen: Rescuing adolescence from the myths of the storm and stress years. New York, NY: Crown.

Levine, J. A., Emery, C. R., & Pollack, H. (2007). The well-being of children born to teen mothers. *Journal of Marriage and Family, 69*, 105–122. doi:10.1111/j.1741-3737.2006.00348.x

Li, J. J., Berk, M. S., & Lee, S. S. (2013). Differential susceptibility in longitudinal models of gene-environment interaction for adolescent depression. *Development and Psychopathology, 25*(4, Pt. 1), 991–1003. doi:10.1017/S0954579413000321

Lillevoll, K. R., Kroger, J., & Martinussen, M. (2013). Identity status and anxiety: A meta-analysis. *Identity, 13*, 214–227. doi:10.1080/15283488.2013.799432

Lindberg, L., Santelli, J., & Desai, S. (2016). Understanding the decline in adolescent fertility in the United States, 2007–2012. *Journal of Adolescent Health, 59*, 577–583. doi:10.1016/j.jadohealth.2016.06.024

Liu, R. T., & Mustanski, B. (2012). Suicidal ideation and self-harm in lesbian, gay, bisexual, and transgender youth. *American Journal of Preventive Medicine, 42*, 221–228. doi:10.1016/j.amepre.2011.10.023

Lockwood, J., Daley, D., Townsend, E., & Sayal, K. (2017). Impulsivity and self-harm in adolescence: A systematic review. *European Child & Adolescent Psychiatry, 26*, 387–402. doi:10.1007/s00787-016-0915-5

Lopez-Tamayo, R., LaVome Robinson, W., Lambert, S. F., Jason, L. A., & Ialongo, N. S. (2016). Parental monitoring, association with externalized behavior, and academic outcomes in urban African-American youth: A moderated mediation analysis. *American Journal of Community Psychology, 57*, 366–379. doi:10.1002/ajcp.12056

Lucassen, M. F., Clark, T. C., Denny, S. J., Fleming, T. M., Rossen, F. V, Sheridan, J., . . . Robinson, E. M. (2015). What has changed from 2001 to 2012 for sexual minority youth in New Zealand? *Journal of Paediatrics and Child Health, 51*, 410–418. doi:10.1111/jpc.12727

Madge, N., Hewitt, A., Hawton, K., De Wilde, E. J., Corcoran, P., Fekete, S., . . . Ystgaard, M. (2008). Deliberate self-harm within an international community sample of young people: Comparative findings from the Child & Adolescent Self-harm in Europe (CASE) study. *Journal of Child Psychology & Psychiatry, 49*, 667–677. doi:10.1111/j.1469-7610.2008.01879.x

Madsen, S. D., & Collins, W. A. (2011). The salience of adolescent romantic experiences for romantic relationship qualities in young adulthood. *Journal of Research on Adolescence, 21*, 789–801. doi:10.1111/j.1532-7795.2011.00737.x

Mahatmya, D., & Lohman, B. (2011). Predictors of late adolescent delinquency: The protective role of after-school activities in low-income families. *Children and Youth Services Review, 33*, 1309–1317. doi:10.1016/j.childyouth.2011.03.005

Malcolm, S., Huang, S., Cordova, D., Freitas, D., Arzon, M., Jimenez, G. L., . . . Prado, G. (2013). Predicting condom use attitudes, norms, and control beliefs in Hispanic problem behavior youth: The effects of family functioning and parent-adolescent communication about sex on condom use. *Health Education & Behavior, 40*, 384–391. doi:10.1177/1090198112440010

Malczyk, B. R., & Lawson, H. A. (2017). Parental monitoring, the parent–child relationship and children's academic engagement in mother-headed single-parent families. *Children and Youth Services Review, 73*, 274–282. doi:10.1016/j.childyouth.2016.12.019

Marcia, J. E. (1966). Development and validation of ego-identity status. *Journal of Personality and Social Psychology, 3*, 551–558.

Markiewicz, D., & Doyle, A. B. (2016). Best friends. In R. J. R. Levesque (Ed.), *Encyclopedia of adolescence* (pp. 1–8). Cham, Switzerland: Springer. doi:10.1007/978-3-319-32132-5_314-2

Marshall, E. J. (2014). Adolescent alcohol use: Risks and consequences. *Alcohol and Alcoholism, 49*, 160–164. doi:10.1093/alcalc/agt180

Marshall, S. K., Tilton-Weaver, L. C., & Stattin, H. (2013). Non-suicidal self-injury and depressive symptoms during middle adolescence: A longitudinal analysis. *Journal of Youth and Adolescence, 42*, 1234–1242. doi:10.1007/s10964-013-9919-3

Masche, J. G. (2010). Explanation of normative declines in parents' knowledge about their adolescent children. *Journal of Adolescence, 33*, 271–284. doi:10.1016/j.adolescence.2009.08.002

Mason, W. A., & Spoth, R. L. (2011). Longitudinal associations of alcohol involvement with subjective well-being in adolescence and prediction to alcohol problems in early adulthood. *Journal of Youth and Adolescence, 40*, 1215–1224. doi:10.1007/s10964-011-9632-z

Maughan, B., Collishaw, S., & Stringaris, A. (2013). Depression in childhood and adolescence. Journal of the Canadian Academy of Child and Adolescent Psychiatry, 22, 35–40. Retrieved from http://www.pubmedcentral.nih.gov/articlerender.fcgi?artid=3565713&tool=pmcentrez&rendertype=abstract

Maynard, M. J., & Harding, S. (2010). Perceived parenting and psychological well-being in UK ethnic minority adolescents. *Child: Care, Health and Development, 36*, 630–638. doi:10.1111/j.1365-2214.2010.01115.x

McAdams, D. P., & Zapata-Gietl, C. (2015). Three strands of identity development across the human life course. In K. C. McLean & M. Syed (Eds.), *The Oxford handbook of identity development* (pp. 81–96). Oxford, UK: Oxford University Press. doi:10.1093/oxfordhb/9780199936564.013.006

McClelland, S. I., & Tolman, D. L. (2014). Adolescent sexuality. In T. Tio (Ed.), *Encyclopedia of critical psychology* (pp. 40–47). New York, NY: Springer.

McKinney, C., & Renk, K. (2011). A multivariate model of parent–adolescent relationship variables in early adolescence. *Child Psychiatry and Human Development, 42*, 442–462. doi:10.1007/s10578-011-0228-3

McLean, K. C., Syed, M., Way, N., & Rogers, O. (2015). [T]hey say black men won't make it, but I know I'm gonna make it. In K. C. McLean & M. Syed (Eds.), *The Oxford handbook of identity development* (pp. 269–287). Oxford, UK: Oxford University Press. doi:10.1093/oxfordhb/9780199936564.013.032

McLeod, J. D., & Knight, S. (2010). The association of socioemotional problems with early sexual initiation. *Perspectives on Sexual and Reproductive Health, 42*, 93–101. doi:10.1363/4209310

McLoughlin, A. B., Gould, M. S., & Malone, K. M. (2015). Global trends in teenage suicide: 2003–2014. *QJM: Monthly Journal of the Association of Physicians, 108*, 765–780. doi:10.1093/qjmed/hcv026

McQuillan, G., Kruszon-Moran, D., Markowitz, L. E., Unger, E. R., & Paulose-Ram, R. (2017). Prevalence of HPV in adults aged 18–69: United States, 2011–2014. *NCHS Data Briefs, 280*. Retrieved from https://www.cdc.gov/nchs/data/databriefs/db280.pdf

Meeus, W. H. J. (2011). The study of adolescent identity formation 2000–2010: A review of longitudinal research. *Journal of Research on Adolescence, 21*, 75–94. doi:10.1111/j.1532-7795.2010.00716.x

Meshi, D., Morawetz, C., & Heekeren, H. R. (2013). Nucleus accumbens response to gains in reputation for the self relative to gains for others predicts social media use. *Frontiers in Human Neuroscience, 7*, 439. doi:10.3389/fnhum.2013.00439

Miconi, D., Moscardino, U., Ronconi, L., & Altoè, G. (2017). Perceived parenting, self-esteem, and depressive symptoms in immigrant and non-immigrant adolescents in Italy: A multigroup path analysis. *Journal of Child and Family Studies, 26*, 345–356. doi:10.1007/s10826-016-0562-y

Miech, R. A., Johnston, L. D., O'Malley, P. M., Bachman, J. G., Schulenberg, J. E., & Patrick, M. E. (2017). *Monitoring the Future national survey results on drug use, 1975–2016: Vol. I. Secondary school students.* Retrieved from http://www.monitoringthefuture.org/pubs/monographs/mtf-vol1_2016.pdf

Miething, A., Almquist, Y. B., Edling, C., Rydgren, J., & Rostila, M. (2017). Friendship trust and psychological well-being from late adolescence to early adulthood: A structural equation modelling approach. *Scandinavian Journal of R. J. R. Levesque Public Health, 45*, 244–252. doi:10.1177/1403494816680784

Milevsky, A. (2016). Parenting styles. In R. J. R. Levesque (Ed.), *Encyclopedia of adolescence* (pp. 1–8). Cham, Switzerland: Springer. doi:10.1007/978-3-319-32132-5_38-2

Miller-Cotto, D., & Byrnes, J. P. (2016). Ethnic/racial identity and academic achievement: A meta-analytic review. *Developmental Review, 41*, 51–70. doi:10.1016/j.dr.2016.06.003

Miranda-Mendizábal, A., Castellví, P., Parés-Badell, O., Almenara, J., Alonso, I., Blasco, M. J., . . . Alonso, J. (2017). Sexual orientation and suicidal behaviour in adolescents and young adults: Systematic review and meta-analysis. *British Journal of Psychiatry.* Retrieved from http://bjp.rcpsych.org/content/early/2017/02/20/bjp.bp.116.196345

Monahan, K. C., Steinberg, L., Cauffman, E., & Mulvey, E. P. (2013). Psychosocial (im)maturity from adolescence to early adulthood: Distinguishing between adolescence-limited and persisting antisocial behavior. *Development and Psychopathology, 25*(4, Pt. 1), 1093–1105. doi:10.1017/S0954579413000394

Moore, S. R., Harden, K. P., & Mendle, J. (2014). Pubertal timing and adolescent sexual behavior in girls. *Developmental Psychology, 50*, 1734–1745. doi:10.1037/a0036027

Moreno, O., Janssen, T., Cox, M. J., Colby, S., & Jackson, K. M. (2017). Parent–adolescent relationships in Hispanic versus Caucasian families: Associations with alcohol and marijuana use onset. *Addictive Behaviors, 74*, 74–81. doi:10.1016/J.ADDBEH.2017.05.029

Mrick, S. E., & Mrtorell, G. A. (2011). Sticks and stones may break my bones: Protective factors for the effects of perceived discrimination on social competence in adolescence. *Personal Relationships, 18*, 487–501. doi:10.1111/j.1475-6811.2010.01320.x

Muehlenkamp, J. J., Claes, L., Havertape, L., & Plener, P. L. (2012). International prevalence of adolescent non-suicidal self-injury and deliberate self-harm. *Child and Adolescent Psychiatry and Mental Health, 6*, 10. doi:10.1186/1753-2000-6-10

Mustanski, B., & Liu, R. T. (2013). A longitudinal study of predictors of suicide attempts among lesbian, gay, bisexual, and transgender youth. *Archives of Sexual Behavior, 42*, 437–448. doi:10.1007/s10508-012-0013-9

Nair, R. L., Roche, K. M., & White, R. M. B. (2018). Acculturation gap distress among Latino youth: Prospective links to family processes and youth depressive symptoms, alcohol use, and academic performance. *Journal of Youth and Adolescence, 47*, 105–120. doi:10.1007/s10964-017-0753-x

Nanayakkara, S., Misch, D., Chang, L., & Henry, D. (2013). Depression and exposure to suicide predict suicide attempt. *Depression and Anxiety, 30*, 991–996. doi:10.1002/da.22143

Natsuaki, M. N., Shaw, D. S., Neiderhiser, J. M., Ganiban, J. M., Harold, G. T., Reiss, D., & Leve, L. D. (2014). Raised by depressed parents: Is it an environmental risk? *Clinical Child and Family Psychology Review, 17*, 357–367. doi:10.1007/s10567-014-0169-z

Negriff, S., Susman, E. J., & Trickett, P. K. (2011). The developmental pathway from pubertal timing to delinquency and sexual activity from early to late adolescence. *Journal of Youth and Adolescence, 40*, 1343–1356. doi:10.1007/s10964-010-9621-7

Nguyen, D. J., Kim, J. J., Weiss, B., Ngo, V., & Lau, A. S. (2018). Prospective relations between parent–adolescent acculturation conflict and mental health symptoms among Vietnamese American adolescents. *Cultural Diversity and Ethnic Minority Psychology, 24*, 151–161. doi:10.1037/cdp0000157

Niolon, P. H., Vivolo-Kantor, A. M., Latzman, N. E., Valle, L. A., Kuoh, H., Burton, T., . . . Tharp, A. T. (2015). Prevalence of teen dating violence and co-occurring risk factors among middle school youth in high-risk urban communities. *Journal of Adolescent Health, 56*, S5–S13. doi:10.1016/j.jadohealth.2014.07.019

Nishina, A., Ammon, N. Y., Bellmore, A. D., & Graham, S. (2006). Body dissatisfaction and physical development among ethnic minority adolescents. *Journal of Youth and Adolescence, 35*, 189–201. doi:10.1007/s10964-005-9012-7

Nock, M. K. (2009). Why do people hurt themselves? New insights into the nature and functions of self-injury. *Current Directions in Psychological Science, 18*, 78–83. doi:10.1111/j.1467-8721.2009.01613.x

Nock, M. K., Prinstein, M. J., & Sterba, S. K. (2009). Revealing the form and function of self-injurious thoughts and behaviors: A real-time ecological assessment study among adolescents and young adults. *Journal of Abnormal Psychology, 118*, 816–827. doi:10.1037/a0016948

Nordin, S. M., Harris, G., & Cumming, J. (2003). Disturbed eating in young, competitive gymnasts: Differences between three gymnastics disciplines. *European Journal of Sport Science, 3*, 1–14.

O'Sullivan, L. F., Cheng, M. M., Harris, K. M., & Brooks-Gunn, J. (2007). I wanna hold your hand: The progression of social, romantic and sexual events in adolescent relationships. *Perspectives on Sexual & Reproductive Health, 39*, 100–107. doi:10.1363/3910007

Oberlander, S. E., Black, M. M., & Starr, J. R. H. (2007). African American adolescent mothers and grandmothers: A multigenerational approach to parenting. *American Journal of Community Psychology, 39*, 37–46. doi:10.1007/s10464-007-9087-2

Office for National Statistics. (2015). *What are the top causes of death by age and gender?* Retrieved from http://visual.ons.gov.uk/what-are-the-top-causes-of-death-by-age-and-gender/

Office of Juvenile Justice and Delinquency Prevention. (2014). *Statistical briefing book.* Retrieved from http://www.ojjdp.gov/ojstatbb/

Oh, J. S., & Fuligni, A. J. (2010). The role of heritage language development in the ethnic identity and family relationships of adolescents from immigrant backgrounds. *Social Development, 19*, 202–220. doi:10.1111/j.1467-9507.2008.00530.x

Orth, U. (2017). The lifespan development of self-esteem. In J. Specht (Ed.), *Personality development across the lifespan* (pp. 181–195). New York, NY: Elsevier. doi:10.1016/B978-0-12-804674-6.00012-0

Oxford, M. L., Gilchrist, L. D., Lohr, M. J., Gillmore, M. R., Morrison, D. M., & Spieker, S. J. (2005). Life course heterogeneity in the transition from adolescence to adulthood among adolescent mothers. *Journal of Research on Adolescence, 15*, 479–504.

Palmer, R. H. C., Young, S. E., Hopfer, C. J., Corley, R. P., Stallings, M. C., Crowley, T. J., & Hewitt, J. K. (2009). Developmental epidemiology of drug use and abuse in adolescence and young adulthood: Evidence of generalized risk. *Drug & Alcohol Dependence, 102*, 78–87. doi:10.1016/j.drugalcdep.2009.01.012

Pazol, K., Whiteman, M. K., Folger, S. G., Kourtis, A. P., Marchbanks, P. A., & Jamieson, D. J. (2015). Sporadic contraceptive use and nonuse: Age-specific prevalence and associated factors. *American Journal of Obstetrics and Gynecology, 212*, 324.e1–324.e8. doi:10.1016/j.ajog.2014.10.004

Phinney, J. S., & Ong, A. D. (2007). Conceptualization and measurement of ethnic identity: Current status and future directions. *Journal of Counseling Psychology, 54*, 271–281. doi:10.1037/0022-067X.54.3.271

Pike, K. M., Hoek, H. W., & Dunne, P. E. (2014). Cultural trends and eating disorders. *Current Opinion in Psychiatry, 27*, 436–442. doi:10.1097/YCO.0000000000000100

Pinquart, M. (2017). Associations of parenting dimensions and styles with externalizing problems of children and adolescents: An updated meta-analysis. *Developmental Psychology, 53*, 873–932. doi:10.1037/dev0000295

Piquero, A. R., & Moffitt, T. E. (2013). Moffitt's developmental taxonomy of antisocial behavior. In G. Bruinsma & D. Weisburd (Eds.), *Encyclopedia of criminology and criminal justice* (pp. 3121–3127). New York, NY: Springer.

Plöderl, M., Wagenmakers, E.-J., Tremblay, P., Ramsay, R., Kralovec, K., Fartacek, C., & Fartacek, R. (2013). Suicide risk and sexual orientation: A critical review. *Archives of Sexual Behavior, 42*, 715–727. doi:10.1007/s10508-012-0056-y

Pompili, M., Lester, D., Forte, A., Seretti, M. E., Erbuto, D., Lamis, D. A., . . . Girardi, P. (2014). Bisexuality and suicide: A systematic review of the current literature. *Journal of Sexual Medicine, 11*, 1903–1913. doi:10.1111/jsm.12581

Poteat, V. P., Sinclair, K. O., DiGiovanni, C. D., Koenig, B. W., & Russell, S. T. (2013). Gay-straight alliances are associated with student health: A multischool comparison of LGBTQ and heterosexual youth. *Journal of Research on Adolescence, 23*, 319–330. doi:10.1111/j.1532-7795.2012.00832.x

Poteat, V. P., Yoshikawa, H., Calzo, J. P., Gray, M. L., DiGiovanni, C. D., Lipkin, A., . . . Shaw, M. P. (2015). Contextualizing gay-straight alliances: Student, advisor, and structural factors related to positive youth development among members. *Child Development, 86*, 176–193. doi:10.1111/cdev.12289

Poulin, F., & Chan, A. (2010). Friendship stability and change in childhood and adolescence. *Developmental Review, 30*, 257–272. doi:10.1016/j.dr.2009.01.001

Preckel, F., Niepel, C., Schneider, M., & Brunner, M. (2013). Self-concept in adolescence: A longitudinal study on reciprocal effects of self-perceptions in academic and social domains. *Journal of Adolescence, 36*, 1165–1175. doi:10.1016/j.adolescence.2013.09.001

Raevuori, A., Keski-Rahkonen, A., & Hoek, H. W. (2014). A review of eating disorders in males. *Current Opinion in Psychiatry, 27*, 426–430. doi:10.1097/YCO.0000000000000113

Raffaelli, M., & Ontai, L. L. (2004). Gender socialization in Latino/a families: Results from two retrospective studies. *Sex Roles, 50*, 287–299. doi:10.1023/B:SERS.0000018886.58945.06

Rafferty, Y., Griffin, K. W., & Lodise, M. (2011). Adolescent motherhood and developmental outcomes of children in early head start: The influence of maternal parenting behaviors, well-being, and risk factors within the family setting. *American Journal of Orthopsychiatry, 81*, 228–245. doi:10.1111/j.1939-0025.2011.01092.x

Ragelienė, T. (2016). Links of Adolescents identity development and relationship with peers: A systematic literature review. *Journal of the Canadian Academy of Child and Adolescent Psychiatry, 25*, 97–105. Retrieved from http://www.ncbi.nlm.nih.gov/pubmed/27274745

Reagan-Steiner, S., Yankey, D., Jeyarajah, J., Elam-Evans, L. D., Curtis, C. R., MacNeil, J., . . . Singleton, J. A. (2016). National, regional, state, and selected local area vaccination coverage among adolescents aged 13–17 years—United States, 2015. *MMWR. Morbidity and Mortality Weekly Report, 65*, 850–858. doi:10.15585/mmwr.mm6533a4

Renk, K., Liljequist, L., Simpson, J. E., & Phares, V. (2005). Gender and age differences in the topics of parent-adolescent conflict. *Family Journal, 13*, 139–149. doi:10.1177/1066480704271190

Rice, E., Rhoades, H., Winetrobe, H., Sanchez, M., Montoya, J., Plant, A., & Kordic, T. (2012). Sexually explicit cell phone messaging associated with sexual risk among adolescents. *Pediatrics, 130*, 667–673. doi:10.1542/peds.2012-0021

Rivas-Drake, D., Seaton, E. K., Markstrom, C., Quintana, S., Syed, M., Lee, R. M., . . . Yip, T. (2014). Ethnic and racial identity in adolescence: Implications for psychosocial, academic, and health outcomes. *Child Development, 85*, 40–57. doi:10.1111/cdev.12200

Rizzo, C. J., Joppa, M., Barker, D., Collibee, C., Zlotnick, C., & Brown, L. K. (2018). Project date SMART: A dating violence (dv) and sexual risk prevention program for adolescent girls with prior DV exposure. *Prevention Science, 19*, 416–442. doi:10.1007/s11121-018-0871-z

Robinson, J. P., & Espelage, D. L. (2013). Peer victimization and sexual risk differences between lesbian, gay, bisexual, transgender, or questioning and nontransgender heterosexual youths in Grades 7–12. *American Journal of Public Health, 103*, 1810–1819. doi:10.2105/AJPH.2013.301387

Rock, P. F., Cole, D. J., Houshyar, S., Lythcott, M., & Prinstein, M. J. (2011). Peer status in an ethnic context: Associations with African American adolescents' ethnic identity. *Journal of Applied Developmental Psychology, 32*, 163–169. doi:10.1016/j.appdev.2011.03.002

Romero, A. J., Edwards, L. M., Fryberg, S. A., & Orduña, M. (2014). Resilience to discrimination stress across ethnic identity stages of development. *Journal of Applied Social Psychology, 44*, 1–11. doi:10.1111/jasp.12192

Romo, D. L., Garnett, C., Younger, A. P., Stockwell, M. S., Soren, K., Catallozzi, M., & Neu, N. (2017). Social media use and its association with sexual risk and parental monitoring among a primarily Hispanic adolescent population. *Journal of Pediatric and Adolescent Gynecology, 30*, 466–473. doi:10.1016/j.jpag.2017.02.004

Rose, A. J., & Asher, S. R. (2017). The social tasks of friendship: Do boys and girls excel in different tasks? *Child Development Perspectives, 11*, 3–8. doi:10.1111/cdep.12214

Ross, S., Heath, N. L., & Toste, J. R. (2009). Non-suicidal self-injury and eating pathology in high school students. *American Journal of Orthopsychiatry, 79*, 83–92. doi:10.1037/a0014826

Rote, W. M., & Smetana, J. G. (2016). Beliefs about parents' right to know: Domain differences and associations with change in concealment. *Journal of Research on Adolescence, 26*, 334–344. doi:10.1111/jora.12194

Rulison, K., Patrick, M. E., & Maggs, J. (2015). Linking peer relationships to substance use across adolescence. In R. A. Zucker & S. A. Brown (Eds.), *The Oxford handbook of adolescent substance abuse*. Oxford,

UK: Oxford University Press. doi:10.1093/oxfordhb/9780199735662.013.019

Russell, S. T., & Fish, J. N. (2016). Mental health in lesbian, gay, bisexual, and transgender (LGBT) youth. *Annual Review of Clinical Psychology, 12,* 465–487. doi:10.1146/annurev-clinpsy-021815-093153

Rutter, M., Giller, H., & Hagell, A. (1998). *Antisocial behavior by young people.* New York, NY: Cambridge University Press.

Ryan, S., Franzetta, K., & Manlove, J. (2007). Knowledge, perceptions, and motivations for contraception. *Youth & Society, 39,* 182–208.

Saewyc, E. M. (2011). Research on adolescent sexual orientation: Development, health disparities, stigma, and resilience. *Journal of Research on Adolescence, 21,* 256–272. doi:10.1111/j.1532-7795.2010.00727.x

Samarova, V., Shilo, G., & Diamond, G. M. (2014). Changes in youths' perceived parental acceptance of their sexual minority status over time. *Journal of Research on Adolescence, 24,* 681–688. doi:10.1111/jora.12071

Sánchez-Queija, I., Oliva, A., & Parra, Á. (2017). Stability, change, and determinants of self-esteem during adolescence and emerging adulthood. *Journal of Social and Personal Relationships, 34,* 1277–1294. doi:10.1177/0265407516674831

Savin-Williams, R. C. (2016). Sexual orientation: Categories or continuum? Commentary on Bailey et al. (2016). *Psychological Science in the Public Interest, 17,* 37–44. doi:10.1177/1529100616637618

Savin-Williams, R. C., Dubé, E. M., & Dube, E. M. (1998). Parental reactions to their child's disclosure of a gay/lesbian identity. *Family Relations, 47,* 7. doi:10.2307/584845

Savin-Williams, R. C., Joyner, K., & Rieger, G. (2012). Prevalence and stability of self-reported sexual orientation identity during young adulthood. *Archives of Sexual Behavior, 41,* 103–110. doi:10.1007/s10508-012-9913-y

Savin-Williams, R. C., & Ream, G. L. (2003). Sex variations in the disclosure to parents of same-sex attractions. *Journal of Family Psychology, 17,* 429–438. doi:10.1037/0893-3200.17.3.429

Savin-Williams, R. C., & Ream, G. L. (2007). Prevalence and stability of sexual orientation components during adolescence and young adulthood. *Archives of Sexual Behavior, 36,* 385–394. doi:10.1007/s10508-006-9088-5

Scalco, M. D., Trucco, E. M., Coffman, D. L., & Colder, C. R. (2015). Selection and socialization effects in early adolescent alcohol use: A propensity score analysis. *Journal of Abnormal Child Psychology, 43,* 1131–1143. doi:10.1007/s10802-014-9969-3

Schaffhuser, K., Allemand, M., & Schwarz, B. (2017). The development of self-representations during the transition to early adolescence: The role of gender, puberty, and school transition. *Journal of Early Adolescence, 37,* 774–804. doi:10.1177/0272431615624841

Schwartz, S. J., Luyckx, K., & Crocetti, E. (2015). What have we learned since Schwartz (2001)? In K. C. McLean & M. Syed (Eds.), *The Oxford handbook of identity development.* (pp. 539–561). Oxford, UK: Oxford University Press. doi:10.1093/oxfordhb/9780199936564.013.028

Schwartz, S. J., Zamboanga, B. L., Luyckx, K., Meca, A., & Ritchie, R. A. (2013). Identity in emerging adulthood: Reviewing the field and looking forward. *Emerging Adulthood, 1,* 96–113. doi:10.1177/2167696813479781

Scoliers, G., Portzky, G., Madge, N., Hewitt, A., Hawton, K., de Wilde, E. J., . . . Van Heeringen, K. (2009). Reasons for adolescent deliberate self-harm: A cry of pain and/or a cry for help? *Social Psychiatry & Psychiatric Epidemiology, 44,* 601–607. doi:10.1007/s00127-008-0469-z

Sears, H. A., Sandra Byers, E., & Lisa Price, E. (2007). The co-occurrence of adolescent boys' and girls' use of psychologically, physically, and sexually abusive behaviours in their dating relationships. *Journal of Adolescence, 30,* 487–504. doi:10.1016/j.adolescence.2006.05.002

Sedgh, G., Finer, L. B., Bankole, A., Eilers, M. A., & Singh, S. (2015). Adolescent pregnancy, birth, and abortion rates across countries: Levels and recent trends. *Journal of Adolescent Health, 56,* 223–230. doi:10.1016/j.jadohealth.2014.09.007

Selby, E. A., Nock, M. K., & Kranzler, A. (2014). How does self-injury feel? Examining automatic positive reinforcement in adolescent self-injurers with experience sampling. *Psychiatry Research, 215,* 417–423. doi:10.1016/j.psychres.2013.12.005

Ševčiková, A. (2016). Girls' and boys' experience with teen sexting in early and late adolescence. *Journal of Adolescence, 51,* 156–162. doi:10.1016/j.adolescence.2016.06.007

Ševčiková, A., Blinka, L., & Daneback, K. (2018). Sexting as a predictor of sexual behavior in a sample of Czech adolescents. *European Journal of Developmental Psychology, 15,* 426–437. doi:10.1080/17405629.2017.1295842

Sherman, L. E., Greenfield, P. M., Hernandez, L. M., & Dapretto, M. (2018). Peer influence via Instagram: Effects on brain and behavior in adolescence and young adulthood. *Child Development, 89,* 37–47. doi:10.1111/cdev.12838

Sherman, L. E., Payton, A. A., Hernandez, L. M., Greenfield, P. M., & Dapretto, M. (2016). The power of the like in adolescence. *Psychological Science, 27,* 1027–1035. doi:10.1177/0956797616645673

Shin, H., & Ryan, A. M. (2014). Early adolescent friendships and academic adjustment: Examining selection and influence processes with longitudinal social network analysis. *Developmental Psychology, 50,* 2462–2672. doi:10.1037/a0037922

Silveri, M. M., Dager, A. D., Cohen-Gilbert, J. E., & Sneider, J. T. (2016). Neurobiological signatures associated with alcohol and drug use in the human adolescent brain. *Neuroscience & Biobehavioral Reviews, 70,* 244–259. doi:10.1016/j.neubiorev.2016.06.042

Sim, T. N., & Koh, S. F. (2003). A domain conceptualization of adolescent susceptibility to peer pressure. *Journal of Research on Adolescence, 13,* 58–80.

Simons, J. S., Wills, T. A., & Neal, D. J. (2014). The many faces of affect: A multilevel model of drinking frequency/quantity and alcohol dependence symptoms among young adults. *Journal of Abnormal Psychology, 123,* 676–694. doi:10.1037/a0036926

Skinner, O. D., & McHale, S. M. (2016). Parent–adolescent conflict in African American families. *Journal of Youth and Adolescence, 45,* 2080–2093. doi:10.1007/s10964-016-0514-2

Smink, F. R. E., van Hoeken, D., & Hoek, H. W. (2013). Epidemiology, course, and outcome of eating disorders. *Current Opinion in Psychiatry, 26,* 543–548. doi:10.1097/YCO.0b013e328365a24f

Smink, F. R. E., van Hoeken, D., Oldehinkel, A. J., & Hoek, H. W. (2014). Prevalence and severity of DSM-5 eating disorders in a community cohort of adolescents. *International Journal of Eating Disorders, 47,* 610–619. doi:10.1002/eat.22316

Smith, A. R., Chein, J., & Steinberg, L. (2014). Peers increase adolescent risk taking even when the probabilities of negative outcomes are known. *Developmental Psychology, 50,* 1564–1568. doi:10.1037/a0035696

Smith-Darden, J. P., Kernsmith, P. D., Reidy, D. E., & Cortina, K. S. (2017). In search of modifiable risk and protective factors for teen dating violence. *Journal of Research on Adolescence, 27,* 423–435. doi:10.1111/jora.12280

Spear, L. P. (2011). Adolescent neurobehavioral characteristics, alcohol sensitivities, and intake: Setting the stage for alcohol use disorders? *Child Development Perspectives, 5,* 231–238. doi:10.1111/j.1750-8606.2011.00182.x

Spencer, M. B., Swanson, D. P., & Harpalani, V. (2015). Development of the self. In M. Lamb (Ed.), *Handbook of child psychology and developmental science* (pp. 1–44). Hoboken, NJ: John Wiley. doi:10.1002/9781118963418.childpsy318

Squeglia, L. M., & Gray, K. M. (2016). Alcohol and drug use and the developing brain. *Current Psychiatry Reports, 18,* 46. doi:10.1007/s11920-016-0689-y

Squeglia, L. M., Tapert, S. F., Sullivan, E. V., Jacobus, J., Meloy, M. J., Rohlfing, T., & Pfefferbaum, A. (2015). Brain development in heavy-drinking adolescents. *American Journal of Psychiatry, 172,* 531–542. doi:10.1176/appi.ajp.2015.14101249

Stanford, S., Jones, M. P., & Hudson, J. L. (2017). Rethinking pathology in adolescent self-harm: Towards a more complex understanding of risk factors. *Journal of Adolescence, 54,* 32–41. doi:10.1016/j.adolescence.2016.11.004

Statistics Canada. (2015). *The 10 leading causes of death, 2011.* Retrieved from http://www.statcan.gc.ca/pub/82-625-x/2014001/article/11896-eng.htm

Steiger, A. E., Allemand, M., Robins, R. W., & Fend, H. A. (2014). Low and decreasing self-esteem during adolescence predict adult depression two decades later. *Journal of Personality and Social Psychology, 106,* 325–338. doi:10.1037/a0035133

Steinberg, L., & Monahan, K. C. (2007). Age differences in resistance to peer influence. *Developmental Psychology, 43,* 1531–1543. doi:10.1037/0012-1649.43.6.1531

Stevens, E. N., Lovejoy, M. C., & Pittman, L. D. (2014). Understanding the relationship between actual:ideal discrepancies and depressive symptoms: A developmental examination. *Journal of Adolescence, 37,* 612–621. doi:10.1016/j.adolescence.2014.04.013

Striegel-Moore, R. H., & Bulik, C. M. (2007). Risk factors for eating disorders. *American Psychologist, 62,* 181–198.

Strober, M., Freeman, R., Lampert, C., Diamond, J., & Kaye, W. (2014). Controlled family study of anorexia nervosa and bulimia nervosa: Evidence of shared liability and transmission of partial syndromes. *American Journal of Psychiatry.* Retrieved from http://ajp.psychiatryonline.org/doi/10.1176/appi.ajp.157.3.393

Substance Abuse and Mental Health Services Administration. (2013). *Results from the 2012 national survey on drug use and health: Mental health findings.* Rockville, MD: Author.

Sussman, S., Pokhrel, P., Ashmore, R. D., & Brown, B. B. (2007). Adolescent peer group identification and characteristics: A review of the literature. *Addictive Behaviors, 32,* 1602–1627.

Syed, M., Walker, L. H. M., Lee, R. M., Umana-Taylor, A. J., Zamboanga, B. L., Schwartz, S. J., . . . Huynh, Q.-L. (2013). A two-factor model of ethnic identity exploration: Implications for identity coherence and well-being. *Cultural Diversity and Ethnic Minority Psychology, 19,* 143–154. doi:10.1037/a0030564

Tang, S., Davis-Kean, P. E., Chen, M., & Sexton, H. R. (2016). Adolescent pregnancy's intergenerational effects: Does an adolescent mother's education have consequences for her children's achievement? *Journal of Research on Adolescence, 26,* 180–193. doi:10.1111/jora.12182

Taylor, J. L. (2009). Midlife impacts of adolescent parenthood. *Journal of Family Issues, 30,* 484–510.

Thapar, A., Collishaw, S., Pine, D. S., & Thapar, A. K. (2012). Depression in adolescence. *Lancet, 379,* 1056–1067. doi:10.1016/S0140-6736(11)60871-4

Thomas, J. J., Eddy, K. T., Ruscio, J., Ng, K. L., Casale, K. E., Becker, A. E., & Lee, S. (2015). Do recognizable lifetime eating disorder phenotypes naturally occur in a culturally Asian population? A combined latent profile and taxometric approach. *European Eating Disorders Review, 23,* 199–209. doi:10.1002/erv.2357

Titzmann, P. F., Brenick, A., & Silbereisen, R. K. (2015). Friendships fighting prejudice: A longitudinal perspective on adolescents' cross-group friendships with immigrants. *Journal of Youth and Adolescence, 44,* 1318–1431. doi:10.1007/s10964-015-0256-6

Trucco, E. M., Colder, C. R., Wieczorek, W. F., Lengua, L. J., & Hawk, L. W. (2014). Early adolescent alcohol use in context: How neighborhoods, parents, and peers impact youth. *Development and Psychopathology, 26,* 425–436. doi:10.1017/S0954579414000042

Ueno, K. (2005). Sexual orientation and psychological distress in adolescence: Examining interpersonal stressors and social support processes. *Social Psychology Quarterly, 68,* 258–277.

Uji, M., Sakamoto, A., Adachi, K., & Kitamura, T. (2013). The impact of authoritative, authoritarian, and permissive parenting styles on children's later mental health in Japan: Focusing on parent and child gender. *Journal of Child and Family Studies, 23,* 293–302. doi:10.1007/s10826-013-9740-3

Umaña-Taylor, A. J. (2016). Ethnic-racial identity conceptualization, development, and youth adjustment. In L. Balter & C. S. Tamis-LeMonda (Eds.), *Child psychology: A handbook of contemporary issues* (p. 505). New York, NY: Routledge.

Umaña-Taylor, A. J., Guimond, A. B., Updegraff, K. A., & Jahromi, L. (2013). A longitudinal examination of support, self-esteem, and Mexican-origin adolescent mothers' parenting efficacy. *Journal of Marriage and the Family, 75,* 746–759. doi:10.1111/jomf.12019

Umaña-Taylor, A. J., Quintana, S. M., Lee, R. M., Cross, W. E., Rivas-Drake, D., Schwartz, S. J., . . . Seaton, E. (2014). Ethnic and racial identity during adolescence and into young adulthood: An integrated conceptualization. *Child Development, 85,* 21–39. doi:10.1111/cdev.12196

Updegraff, K. A., McHale, S. M., Zeiders, K. H., Umaña-Taylor, A. J., Perez-Brena, N. J., Wheeler, L. A., & Rodriguez De Jesús, S. A. (2014). Mexican-American adolescents' gender role attitude development: The role of adolescents' gender and nativity and parents' gender role attitudes. *Journal of Youth and Adolescence, 43,* 2041–2053. doi:10.1007/s10964-014-0128-5

Vagi, K. J., Rothman, E. F., Latzman, N. E., Tharp, A. T., Hall, D. M., & Breiding, M. J. (2013). Beyond correlates: A review of risk and protective factors for adolescent dating violence perpetration. *Journal of Youth and Adolescence, 42,* 633–649. doi:10.1007/s10964-013-9907-7

van de Bongardt, D., Reitz, E., Sandfort, T., & Deković, M. (2014). A meta-analysis of the relations between three types of peer norms and adolescent sexual behavior. *Personality and Social Psychology Review, 19,* 203–234. doi:10.1177/1088868314544223

van de Bongardt, D., Yu, R., Deković, M., & Meeus, W. H. J. (2015). Romantic relationships and sexuality in adolescence and young adulthood: The role of parents, peers, and partners. *European Journal of Developmental Psychology, 12,* 497–515. doi:10.1080/17405629.2015.1068689

Van Dijk, M. P. A., Branje, S., Keijsers, L., Hawk, S. T., Hale, W. W., & Meeus, W. H. J. (2014). Self-concept clarity across adolescence: Longitudinal associations with open communication with parents and internalizing symptoms. *Journal of Youth and Adolescence, 43,* 1861–1876. doi:10.1007/s10964-013-0055-x

Van Doorn, M. D., Branje, S. J. T., & Meeus, W. H. J. (2011). Developmental changes in conflict resolution styles in parent-adolescent relationships: A four-wave longitudinal study. *Journal of Youth and Adolescence, 40,* 97–107. doi:10.1007/s10964-010-9516-7

van Hoorn, J., Crone, E. A., & van Leijenhorst, L. (2017). Hanging out with the right crowd: Peer influence on risk-taking behavior in adolescence. *Journal of Research on Adolescence, 27,* 189–200. doi:10.1111/jora.12265

van Hoorn, J., van Dijk, E., Meuwese, R., Rieffe, C., & Crone, E. A. (2016). Peer influence on prosocial behavior in adolescence. *Journal of Research on Adolescence, 26,* 90–100. doi:10.1111/jora.12173

Van Houdenhove, E., Gijs, L., T'Sjoen, G., & Enzlin, P. (2015). Asexuality: A multidimensional approach. *The Journal of Sex Research, 52,* 669–678. doi:10.1080/00224499.2014.898015

Van Ouytsel, J., Van Gool, E., Ponnet, K., & Walrave, M. (2014). Brief report: The association between adolescents' characteristics and engagement in sexting. *Journal of Adolescence, 37,* 1387–1391. doi:10.1016/j.adolescence.2014.10.004

Vanhalst, J., Luyckx, K., Scholte, R. H. J., Engels, R. C. M. E., & Goossens, L. (2013). Low self-esteem as a risk factor for loneliness in adolescence: Perceived—but not actual—social acceptance as an underlying mechanism. *Journal of Abnormal Child Psychology, 41,* 1067–1081. doi:10.1007/s10802-013-9751-y

Verkooijen, K. T., de Vries, N. K., & Nielsen, G. A. (2007). Youth crowds and substance use: The impact of perceived group norm and multiple group identification. *Psychology of Addictive Behaviors, 21,* 55–61. doi:10.1037/0893-164x.21.1.55

Voelker, D. K., Gould, D., & Reel, J. J. (2014). Prevalence and correlates of disordered eating in female figure skaters. *Psychology of Sport and Exercise, 15,* 696–704. doi:10.1016/j.psychsport.2013.12.002

von Soest, T., Wichstrøm, L., & Kvalem, I. L. (2016). The development of global and domain-specific self-esteem from age 13 to 31. *Journal of Personality and Social Psychology, 110,* 592–608. doi:10.1037/pspp0000060

Wagnsson, S., Lindwall, M., & Gustafsson, H. (2014). Participation in organized sport and self-esteem across adolescence: The mediating role of perceived sport competence. *Journal of Sport & Exercise Psychology, 36,* 584–594. doi:10.1123/jsep.2013-0137

Wang, C., Xia, Y., Li, W., Wilson, S. M., Bush, K., & Peterson, G. (2016). Parenting behaviors, adolescent depressive symptoms, and problem behavior: The role of self-esteem and school adjustment difficulties among Chinese adolescents. *Journal of Family Issues, 37,* 520–542. doi:10.1177/0192513X14542433

Wang, M. T., Dishion, T. J., Stormshak, E. A., & Willett, J. B. (2011). Trajectories of family management practices and early adolescent behavioral outcomes. *Developmental Psychology, 47,* 1324–1341. doi:10.1037/a0024026

Wang, M. T., & Sheikh-Khalil, S. (2014). Does parental involvement matter for student achievement and mental health in high school? *Child Development, 85,* 610–625. doi:10.1111/cdev.12153

Warner, T. D. (2018). Adolescent sexual risk taking: The distribution of youth behaviors and perceived peer attitudes across neighborhood contexts. *Journal of Adolescent Health, 62,* 226–233. doi:10.1016/J.JADOHEALTH.2017.09.007

Warner, T. D., Giordano, P. C., Manning, W. D., & Longmore, M. A. (2011). Everybody's doin' it (right?): Neighborhood norms and sexual activity in adolescence. *Social Science Research, 40*, 1676–1690. doi:10.1016/j.ssresearch.2011.06.009

Way, N., Santos, C., Niwa, E. Y., & Kim-Gervey, C. (2008). To be or not to be: An exploration of ethnic identity development in context. *New Directions for Child & Adolescent Development, 2008*, 61–79.

Weisz, A. N., & Black, B. M. (2008). Peer intervention in dating violence: Beliefs of African-American middle school adolescents. *Journal of Ethnic & Cultural Diversity in Social Work, 17*, 177–196. doi:10.1080/15313200801947223

Wentzel, K. R. (2014). Prosocial behavior and peer relations in adolescence. In G. C. L. M. Padilla-Walker (Ed.), *Prosocial development: A multidimensional approach* (pp. 178–200). Oxford, UK: Oxford University Press.

Wesche, R., Kreager, D. A., Lefkowitz, E. S., & Siennick, S. E. (2017). Early sexual initiation and mental health: A fleeting association or enduring change? *Journal of Research on Adolescence, 27*, 611–627. doi:10.1111/jora.12303

Weymouth, B. B., Buehler, C., Zhou, N., & Henson, R. A. (2016). A meta-analysis of parent-adolescent conflict: Disagreement, hostility, and youth maladjustment. *Journal of Family Theory & Review, 8*, 95–112. doi:10.1111/jftr.12126

White, C. N., & Warner, L. A. (2015). Influence of family and school-level factors on age of sexual initiation. *Journal of Adolescent Health, 56*, 231–237. doi:10.1016/j.jadohealth.2014.09.017

White, R. M. B., Knight, G. P., Jensen, M., & Gonzales, N. A. (2018). Ethnic socialization in neighborhood contexts: Implications for ethnic attitude and identity development among Mexican-origin adolescents. *Child Development, 89*, 1004–1021. doi:10.1111/cdev.12772

Wight, D., Williamson, L., & Henderson, M. (2006). Parental influences on young people's sexual behaviour: A longitudinal analysis. *Journal of Adolescence, 29*, 473–494.

Williams, J. L., Aiyer, S. M., Durkee, M. I., & Tolan, P. H. (2014). The protective role of ethnic identity for urban adolescent males facing multiple stressors. *Journal of Youth and Adolescence, 43*, 1728–1741. doi:10.1007/s10964-013-0071-x

Williams, T. S., Connolly, J., Pepler, D., Laporte, L., & Craig, W. (2008). Risk models of dating aggression across different adolescent relationships: A developmental psychopathology approach. *Journal of Consulting and Clinical Psychology, 76*, 622–632. doi:10.1037/0022-006x.76.4.622

Wilson, G. T., Grilo, C. M., & Vitousek, K. M. (2007). Psychological treatment of eating disorders. *American Psychologist, 62*, 199–216.

Wincentak, K., Connolly, J., & Card, N. (2017). Teen dating violence: A meta-analytic review of prevalence rates. *Psychology of Violence, 7*, 224–241. doi:10.1037/a0040194

Windle, M., & Zucker, R. A. (2010). Reducing underage and young adult drinking: How to address critical drinking problems during this developmental period. *Alcohol Research & Health, 33*, 29–44.

Wouters, S., Doumen, S., Germeijs, V., Colpin, H., & Verschueren, K. (2013). Contingencies of self-worth in early adolescence: The antecedent role of perceived parenting. *Social Development, 22*, 242–258. doi:10.1111/sode.12010

Xu, J., Kochanek, K. D., Murphy, S. L., & Arias, E. (2014). Mortality in the United States, 2012. *NCHS Data Brief*. Retrieved from http://europepmc.org/abstract/med/25296181

Ybarra, M. L., & Mitchell, K. J. (2014). "Sexting" and its relation to sexual activity and sexual risk behavior in a national survey of adolescents. *Journal of Adolescent Health, 55*, 757–764. doi:10.1016/j.jadohealth.2014.07.012

Yip, T. (2014). Ethnic identity in everyday life: The influence of identity development status. *Child Development, 85*, 205–219. doi:10.1111/cdev.12107

Zapolski, T. C. B., Fisher, S., Banks, D. E., Hensel, D. J., & Barnes-Najor, J. (2017). Examining the protective effect of ethnic identity on drug attitudes and use among a diverse youth population. *Journal of Youth and Adolescence, 46*, 1702–1715. doi:10.1007/s10964-016-0605-0

Chapter 13

Abele, A. E., & Spurk, D. (2011). The dual impact of gender and the influence of timing of parenthood on men's and women's career development: Longitudinal findings. *International Journal of Behavioral Development, 35*, 225–232. doi:10.1177/0165025411398181

American Psychiatric Association. (2013). *Diagnostic and statistical manual of mental disorders* (5th ed.). Washington, DC: Author.

Ammerman, S., Ryan, S., Adelman, W. P., Committee on Substance Abuse, the Committee on Adolescence, Eaton, D., Kann, L., . . . Huestis, M. (2015). The impact of marijuana policies on youth: Clinical, research, and legal update. *Pediatrics, 135*, e769–e785. doi:10.1542/peds.2014-4147

Ammons, S. K., & Kelly, E. L. (2008). Social class and the experience of work-family conflict during the transition to adulthood. *New Directions for Child & Adolescent Development, 2008*, 71–84.

Andrews, J. A., Hampson, S. E., Severson, H. H., Westling, E., & Peterson, M. (2016). Perceptions and use of e-cigarettes across time among emerging adults. *Tobacco Regulatory Science, 2*, 70–81. doi:10.18001/TRS.2.1.8

Andrews, J. A., & Westling, E. (2016). Substance use in emerging adulthood. In J. J. Arnett (Ed.), *The Oxford handbook of emerging adulthood* (pp. 521–542). Oxford, UK: Oxford University Press. doi:10.1093/oxfordhb/9780199795574.013.20

Armstrong, E. A., Hamilton, L., & England, P. (2010). Is hooking up bad for young women? *Contexts, 9*, 22–27. doi:10.1525/ctx.2010.9.3.22

Arnett, J. J. (2003). Conceptions of the transition to adulthood among emerging adults in American ethnic groups. *New Directions for Child & Adolescent Development, 2003*, 63–76.

Arnett, J. J. (Ed.). (2016). *The Oxford handbook of emerging adulthood* (Vol. 1). Oxford, UK: Oxford University Press. doi:10.1093/oxfordhb/9780199795574.001.0001

Arnett, J. J. (2016). College students as emerging adults. *Emerging Adulthood, 4*, 219–222. doi:10.1177/2167696815587s422

Arnett, J. J., & Padilla-Walker, L. M. (2015). Brief report: Danish emerging adults' conceptions of adulthood. *Journal of Adolescence, 38*, 39–44. doi:10.1016/J.ADOLESCENCE.2014.10.011

Arnett, J. J., & Schwab, J. (2012). *The Clark University poll of emerging adults: Thriving, struggling, and hopeful*. Retrieved from http://www2.clarku.edu/clark-poll-emerging-adults/pdfs/clark-university-poll-emerging-adults-findings.pdf

Arnett, J. J., Žukauskienė, R., & Sugimura, K. (2014). The new life stage of emerging adulthood at ages 18–29 years: Implications for mental health. *The Lancet Psychiatry, 1*, 569–576. doi:10.1016/S2215-0366(14)00080-7

Arria, A. M., Caldeira, K. M., Allen, H. K., Vincent, K. B., Bugbee, B. A., & O'Grady, K. E. (2016). Drinking like an adult? Trajectories of alcohol use patterns before and after college graduation. *Alcoholism: Clinical and Experimental Research, 40*, 583–590. doi:10.1111/acer.12973

Athanasou, J. A. (2002). Vocational pathways in the early part of a career: An Australian study. *Career Development Quarterly, 51*, 78–86.

Atran, S., & Medin, D. (2008). *The native mind and the cultural construction of nature*. Cambridge: MIT Press.

Azofeifa, A., Mattson, M. E., Schauer, G., McAfee, T., Grant, A., & Lyerla, R. (2016). National estimates of marijuana use and related indicators? National survey on drug use and health, United States, 2002–2014. *MMWR. Surveillance Summaries, 65*, 1–28. doi:10.15585/mmwr.ss6511a1

Badger, S., Nelson, L. J., & Barry, C. M. (2006). Perceptions of the transition to adulthood among Chinese and American emerging adults. *International Journal of Behavioral Development, 30*, 84–93. doi:10.1177/0165025406062128

Bartholomew, J., Holroyd, S., & Heffernan, T. M. (2010). Does cannabis use affect prospective memory in young adults? *Journal of Psychopharmacology, 24*, 241–246. doi:10.1177/0269881109106909

Belson, K. (2013). *Explaining the N.F.L. settlement*. Retrieved from http://www.nytimes.com/2013/08/30/sports/football/nfl-settlement-leaves-many-questions-for-fans.html

Bentov, Y., Yavorska, T., Esfandiari, N., Jurisicova, A., & Casper, R. (2011). The contribution of mitochondrial function to reproductive aging. *Journal of Assisted Reproduction & Genetics, 28*, 773–783. doi:10.1007/s10815-011-9588-7

Bersamin, M. M., Paschall, M. J., Saltz, R. F., & Zamboanga, B. L. (2012). Young adults and casual sex: The relevance of college drinking settings. *Journal of Sex Research, 49*, 274–281. doi:10.1080/00224499.2010.548012

Bersamin, M. M., Zamboanga, B. L., Schwartz, S. J., Donnellan, M. B., Hudson, M., Weisskirch, R. S., . . . Caraway, S. J. (2014). Risky business: Is there an association between casual sex and mental health among emerging adults? *Journal of Sex Research, 51,* 43–51. doi:10.1080/00224499.2013.772088

Beyer, S. (2014). Why are women underrepresented in computer science? Gender differences in stereotypes, self-efficacy, values, and interests and predictors of future CS course-taking and grades. *Computer Science Education, 24,* 153–192. doi:10.1080/08993408.2014.963363

Bonnie, R. J., Stroud, C., & Breiner, H. (2015). *Investing in the health and well-being of young adults.* Washington, DC: National Academies Press.

Bozick, R., & DeLuca, S. (2011). Not making the transition to college: School, work, and opportunities in the lives of American youth. *Social Science Research, 40,* 1249–1262. doi:10.1016/j.ssresearch.2011.02.003

Brahem, S., Mehdi, M., Elghezal, H., & Saad, A. (2011). The effects of male aging on semen quality, sperm DNA fragmentation and chromosomal abnormalities in an infertile population. *Journal of Assisted Reproduction & Genetics, 28,* 425–432. doi:10.1007/s10815-011-9537-5

Brandon, P. D., & Temple, J. B. (2007). Family provisions at the workplace and their relationship to absenteeism, retention, and productivity of workers: Timely evidence from prior data. *Australian Journal of Social Issues, 42,* 447–460.

Breiding, M. J., Smith, S. G., Basile, K. C., Walters, M. L., Chen, J., & Merrick, M. T. (2014). Prevalence and characteristics of sexual violence, stalking, and intimate partner violence victimization—National Intimate Partner and Sexual Violence survey, United States, 2011. *Morbidity and Mortality Weekly Report, 63,* 1–18. Retrieved from https://www.cdc.gov/mmwr/preview/mmwrhtml/ss6308a1.htm

Bronkema, R., & Bowman, N. A. (2017). A residential paradox? Residence hall attributes and college student outcomes. *Journal of College Student Development, 58,* 624–630. doi:10.1353/csd.2017.0047

Brooks, R., & Everett, G. (2008). The predominance of work-based training in young graduates' learning. *Journal of Education & Work, 21,* 61–73. Retrieved from 10.1080/13639080801956966

Brown, A. E., Carpenter, M. J., & Sutfin, E. L. (2011). Occasional smoking in college: Who, what, when and why? *Addictive Behaviors, 36,* 1199–1204. doi:10.1016/j.addbeh.2011.07.024

Byars, A. M., & Hackett, G. (1998). Applications of social cognitive theory to the career development of women of color. *Applied & Preventive Psychology, 7,* 255–267.

Carey, K. B., Norris, A. L., Durney, S. E., Shepardson, R. L., & Carey, M. P. (2018). Mental health consequences of sexual assault among first-year college women. *Journal of American College Health.* Advance online publication. doi:10.1080/07448481.2018.1431915

Carlson, D. S., Grzywacz, J. G., Ferguson, M., Hunter, E. M., Clinch, C. R., & Arcury, T. A. (2011). Health and turnover of working

mothers after childbirth via the work-family interface: An analysis across time. *Journal of Applied Psychology, 96,* 1045–1054. doi:10.1037/a0023964

Carnes, A. M. (2017). Bringing work stress home: The impact of role conflict and role overload on spousal marital satisfaction. *Journal of Occupational and Organizational Psychology, 90,* 153–176. doi:10.1111/joop.12163

Centers for Disease Control and Prevention. (2011). Current cigarette smoking prevalence among working adults—United States, 2004-2010. *MMWR. Morbidity and Mortality Weekly Report, 60,* 1305–1309. Retrieved from http://www.ncbi.nlm.nih.gov/pubmed/21956406

Centers for Disease Control and Prevention. (2017a). *10 leading causes of injury deaths by age group highlighting unintentional injury deaths, United States—2015.* Retrieved March 23, 2018, from https://www.cdc.gov/injury/images/lc-charts/leading_causes_of_death_age_group_2015_1050w740h.gif

Centers for Disease Control and Prevention. (2017b). *10 leading causes of death- by age group—2015.* Retrieved from ftp://ftp.cdc.gov/pub/ncipc/10LC-2003/JPEG/10lc-2003.jpg

Chen, P., & Jacobson, K. C. (2012). Developmental trajectories of substance use from early adolescence to young adulthood: Gender and racial/ethnic differences. *Journal of Adolescent Health:, 50,* 154–163. doi:10.1016/j.jadohealth.2011.05.013

Cheng, H. L., Medlow, S., & Steinbeck, K. (2016). The health consequences of obesity in young adulthood. *Current Obesity Reports, 5,* 30–37. doi:10.1007/s13679-016-0190-2

Cheryan, S., Ziegler, S. A., Montoya, A. K., & Jiang, L. (2017). Why are some STEM fields more gender balanced than others? *Psychological Bulletin, 143,* 1–35. doi:10.1037/bul0000052

Chung, J. M., Robins, R. W., Trzesniewski, K. H., Noftle, E. E., Roberts, B. W., & Widaman, K. F. (2014). Continuity and change in self-esteem during emerging adulthood. *Journal of Personality and Social Psychology, 106,* 469–483. doi:10.1037/a0035135

Claxton, S., & Van Dulmen, M. (2016). Casual sexual relationships and experiences in emerging adulthood. In J. J. Arnett (Ed.), *The Oxford handbook of emerging adulthood* (pp. 245–261). Oxford, UK: Oxford University Press. doi:10.1093/oxfordhb/9780199795574.013.002

Cohen, P., Kasen, S., Chen, H., Hartmark, C., & Gordon, K. (2003). Variations in patterns of developmental transitions in the emerging adulthood period. *Developmental Psychology, 39,* 657. Retrieved from http://www.ncbi.nlm.nih.gov/pubmed/12859120

Combs, G. M., & Milosevic, I. (2016). Workplace discrimination and the wellbeing of minority women: Overview, prospects, and implications. In M. L. Connerley & J. Wu (Eds.), *Handbook on well-being of working women* (pp. 17–31). Dordrecht: Springer Netherlands. doi:10.1007/978-94-017-9897-6_2

Compton, W. M., Han, B., Hughes, A., Jones, C. M., & Blanco, C. (2017). Use of marijuana for medical purposes among adults in the

United States. *JAMA, 317,* 209. doi:10.1001/jama.2016.18900

Conroy, D. A., Kurth, M. E., Brower, K. J., Strong, D. R., & Stein, M. D. (2015). Impact of marijuana use on self-rated cognition in young adult men and women. *American Journal on Addictions/American Academy of Psychiatrists in Alcoholism and Addictions, 24,* 160–165. doi:10.1111/j.1521-0391.2014.12157.x

Corder, K., Winpenny, E., Love, R., Brown, H. E., White, M., & van Sluijs, E. (2018). Change in physical activity from adolescence to early adulthood: A systematic review and meta-analysis of longitudinal cohort studies. *British Journal of Sports Medicine.* Advance online publication. doi:10.1136/bjsports-2016-097330

Cornman, J. C., Glei, D. A., Goldman, N., Ryff, C. D., & Weinstein, M. (2015). Socioeconomic status and biological markers of health: An examination of adults in the United States and Taiwan. *Journal of Aging and Health, 27,* 75–102. doi:10.1177/0898264314538661

Côté, J. E. (2014). The dangerous myth of emerging adulthood: An evidence-based critique of a flawed developmental theory. *Applied Developmental Science, 18,* 177–188.

Covarrubias, R., & Fryberg, S. A. (2015). Movin' on up (to college): First-generation college students' experiences with family achievement guilt. *Cultural Diversity and Ethnic Minority Psychology, 21,* 420–429. doi:10.1037/a0037844

Crean, R. D., Crane, N. A., & Mason, B. J. (2011). An evidence-based review of acute and long-term effects of cannabis use on executive cognitive functions. *Journal of Addiction Medicine, 5,* 1–8. doi:10.1097/ADM.0b013e31820c23fa

Davis, J. M., Mendelson, B., Berkes, J. J., Suleta, K., Corsi, K. F., Booth, R. E., . . . Moos, R. (2016). Public health effects of medical marijuana legalization in Colorado. *American Journal of Preventive Medicine, 50,* 373–379. doi:10.1016/j.amepre.2015.06.034

De Martinis, M., & Timiras, P. S. (2003). The pulmonary respiration, hemotopoiesis and erythrocytes. In P. S. Timiras (Ed.), *Physiological basis of aging and geriatrics* (3rd ed., pp. 319–336). Boca Raton, FL: CRC Press.

Debrot, A., Meuwly, N., Muise, A., Impett, E. A., & Schoebi, D. (2017). More than just sex. *Personality and Social Psychology Bulletin, 43,* 287–299. doi:10.1177/0146167216684124

du Bois-Reymond, M. (2015). Emerging adulthood theory and social class. In J. J. Arnett (Ed.), *The Oxford handbook of emerging adulthood* (Vol. 1). Oxford, UK: Oxford University Press. doi:10.1093/oxfordhb/9780199795574.013.37

Duxbury, L., Stevenson, M., & Higgins, C. (2018). Too much to do, too little time: Role overload and stress in a multi-role environment. *International Journal of Stress Management, 25,* 250–266. doi:10.1037/str0000062

Edwards, R., Carter, K., Peace, J., & Blakely, T. (2013). An examination of smoking initiation rates by age: Results from a large longitudinal study in New Zealand. *Australian and New Zealand Journal of Public Health, 37,* 516–519.

Eisenberg, M. E., Spry, E., & Patton, G. C. (2015). From emerging to established: Longitudinal patterns in the timing of transition events among Australian emerging adults. *Emerging Adulthood, 3,* 277–281. doi:10.1177/2167696815574639

Ellis, L., & Bonin, S. L. (2003). Genetics and occupation-related preferences. Evidence from adoptive and non-adoptive families. *Personality & Individual Differences, 35,* 929.

Enoch, M. A. (2013). Genetic influences on the development of alcoholism. *Current Psychiatry Reports, 15,* 412. doi:10.1007/s11920-013-0412-1

Eurostat. (2016). *Employment statistics.* Retrieved from http://ec.europa.eu/eurostat/statistics-explained/index.php/Employment_statistics

Facio, A., & Micocci, F. (2003). Emerging adulthood in Argentina. In J. J. Arnett & N. L. Galambos (Eds.), *New directions in child development: Vol. 100. Exploring cultural conceptions of the transition to adulthood* (pp. 21–31). San Francisco, CA: Jossey-Bass.

Farsalinos, K. E., & Polosa, R. (2014). Safety evaluation and risk assessment of electronic cigarettes as tobacco cigarette substitutes: A systematic review. *Therapeutic Advances in Drug Safety, 5,* 67–86. doi:10.1177/2042098614524430

Federal Interagency Forum on Child and Family Statistics. (2014). *America's young adults: Special issue, 2014.* Retrieved from http://www.childstats.gov/pdf/ac2014/YA_14.pdf

Fedina, L., Holmes, J. L., & Backes, B. L. (2018). Campus sexual assault: A systematic review of prevalence research from 2000 to 2015. *Trauma, Violence, & Abuse, 19,* 76–93. doi:10.1177/1524838016631129

Feldman, R. S. (2017). *The first year of college: Research, theory, and practice on improving the student experience and increasing retention.* Cambridge, UK: Cambridge University Press.

Ferguson, R. F., & Lamback, S. (2014). *Creating pathways to prosperity: A blueprint for action. Report issued by the pathways to prosperity project at the Harvard Graduate School of Education and the Achievement Gap Initiative at Harvard University.* Retrieved from http://www.agi.harvard.edu/pathways/CreatingPathwaystoProsperityReport2014.pdf

Ferriman, K., Lubinski, D., & Benbow, C. P. (2009). Work preferences, life values, and personal views of top math/science graduate students and the profoundly gifted: Developmental changes and gender differences during emerging adulthood and parenthood. *Journal of Personality and Social Psychology, 97,* 517–532. doi:10.1037/a0016030

Flament, F., Bazin, R., & Piot, B. (2013). Effect of the sun on visible clinical signs of aging in Caucasian skin. *Clinical, Cosmetic and Investigational Dermatology, 6,* 221. doi:10.2147/CCID.S44686

Fleming, C. B., Guttmannova, K., Cambron, C., Rhew, I. C., Oesterle, S. (2016). Examination of the divergence in trends for adolescent marijuana use and marijuana-specific risk factors in Washington state. *Journal of Adolescent Health, 59,* 269–275. doi:10.1016/j.jadohealth.2016.05.008

Flynn, E. (2016). *What is the NFL's concussion protocol?* Retrieved from https://www.si.com/nfl/nfl-concussion-protocol-policy-history

Ford, N. D., Patel, S. A., & Narayan, K. M. V. (2017). Obesity in low- and middle-income countries: Burden, drivers, and emerging challenges. *Annual Review of Public Health, 38,* 145–164. doi:10.1146/annurev-publhealth-031816-044604

Fryar, C. D., Carroll, M. D., & Ogden, C. L. (2016). Prevalence of overweight, obesity, and extreme obesity among adults aged 20 and over: United States, 1960–1962 through 2013–2014. *Health EStats.* Retrieved from http://www.cdc.gov/nchs/data/hestat/obesity_adult_11_12/obesity_adult_11_12.htm

Galambos, N. L., Barker, E. T., & Krahn, H. J. (2006). Depression, self-esteem, and anger in emerging adulthood: Seven-year trajectories. *Developmental Psychology, 42,* 350–365.

Garcia, J. R., Reiber, C., Massey, S. G., & Merriwether, A. M. (2012). Sexual hookup culture: A review. *Review of General Psychology, 16,* 161–176. doi:10.1037/a0027911

Garcia, P. R. J. M., Restubog, S. L. D., Bordia, P., Bordia, S., & Roxas, R. E. O. (2015). Career optimism: The roles of contextual support and career decision-making self-efficacy. *Journal of Vocational Behavior, 88,* 10–18. doi:10.1016/j.jvb.2015.02.004

Ghosh, A., Coakley, R. C., Mascenik, T., Rowell, T. R., Davis, E. S., Rogers, K., . . . Tarran, R. (2018). Chronic e-cigarette exposure alters the human bronchial epithelial proteome. *American Journal of Respiratory and Critical Care Medicine, 198,* 67–76. doi:10.1164/rccm.201710-2033OC

Giskes, K., van Lenthe, F., Avendano-Pabon, M., & Brug, J. (2011). A systematic review of environmental factors and obesogenic dietary intakes among adults: Are we getting closer to understanding obesogenic environments? *Obesity Reviews, 12,* e95–e106. doi:10.1111/j.1467-789X.2010.00769.x

Goniewicz, M. L., Lingas, E. O., & Hajek, P. (2013). Patterns of electronic cigarette use and user beliefs about their safety and benefits: An Internet survey. *Drug and Alcohol Review, 32,* 133–140. doi:10.1111/j.1465-3362.2012.00512.x

Gonzáles-Figueroa, E., & Young, A. M. (2005). Ethnic identity and mentoring among Latinas in professional roles. *Cultural Diversity and Ethnic Minority Psychology, 11,* 213–226.

Gordon, M. (2017). Individual-level and socio-contextual influences on body mass index and achievement in adolescence to young adulthood. *Journal of Adolescent and Family Health, 8.* Retrieved from https://scholar.utc.edu/jafh/vol8/iss1/1

Green, M. P., McCausland, K. L., Xiao, H., Duke, J. C., Vallone, D. M., & Healton, C. G. (2007). A closer look at smoking among young adults: Where tobacco control should focus its attention. *American Journal of Public Health, 97,* 1427–1433.

Griffin, K. W., Bang, H., & Botvin, G. J. (2010). Age of alcohol and marijuana use onset predicts weekly substance use and related psychosocial problems during young adulthood. *Journal of Substance Use, 15,* 174–183. doi:10.3109/14659890903013109

Gruber, S. A., Sagar, K. A., Dahlgren, M. K., Racine, M., & Lukas, S. E. (2012). Age of onset of marijuana use and executive function. *Psychology of Addictive Behaviors, 26,* 496–506. doi:10.1037/a0026269

Hales, C. M., Carroll, M. D., Fryar, C. D., & Ogden, C. L. (2017). Prevalence of obesity among adults and youth: United States, 2015–2016. *NCHS Data Brief.* Retrieved from https://stacks.cdc.gov/view/cdc/49223

Hall, W. (2014). What has research over the past two decades revealed about the adverse health effects of recreational cannabis use? *Addiction, 110,* 19–35. doi:10.1111/add.12703

Hall, W., & Lynskey, M. (2016). Evaluating the public health impacts of legalizing recreational cannabis use in the United States. *Addiction, 111,* 1764–1773. doi:10.1111/add.13428

Halpern, D. F. (2005). How time-flexible work policies can reduce stress, improve health, and save money. *Stress & Health: Journal of the International Society for the Investigation of Stress, 21,* 157–168. Retrieved from 10.1002/smi.1049

Hamamura, T. (2012). Are cultures becoming individualistic? A cross-temporal comparison of individualism–collectivism in the United States and Japan. *Personality and Social Psychology Review, 16,* 3–24. doi:10.1177/1088868311411587

Hamer, R., & van Rossum, E. J. (2017). Six languages in education—Looking for postformal thinking. *Behavioral Development Bulletin, 22,* 377–393. doi:10.1037/bdb0000030

Hasin, D. S., Wall, M., Keyes, K. M., Cerdá, M., Schulenberg, J., O'Malley, P. M., . . . Hall, W. (2015). Medical marijuana laws and adolescent marijuana use in the USA from 1991 to 2014: Results from annual, repeated cross-sectional surveys. *The Lancet Psychiatry, 2,* 601–608. doi:10.1016/S2215-0366(15)00217-5

Hatcher, L., & Crook, J. C. (1988). First-job surprises for college graduates: An exploratory investigation. *Journal of College Student Development, 29,* 441–448.

Heinonen, I., Helajärvi, H., Pahkala, K., Heinonen, O. J., Hirvensalo, M., Pälve, K., . . . Raitakari, O. T. (2013). Sedentary behaviours and obesity in adults: The cardiovascular risk in young Finns study. *BMJ Open, 3,* e002901. doi:10.1136/bmjopen-2013-002901

Hendry, L. B., & Kloep, M. (2010). How universal is emerging adulthood? An empirical example. *Journal of Youth Studies, 13,* 169–179. doi:10.1080/13676260903295067

Henrich, J., Heine, S. J., & Norenzayan, A. (2010). The weirdest people in the world? *Behavioral and Brain Sciences, 33,* 61–83. doi:10.1017/S0140525X0999152X

Herbenick, D., Reece, M., Schick, V., Sanders, S. A., Dodge, B., & Fortenberry, J. D. (2010). Sexual behavior in the United States: Results from a national probability sample of men and women ages 14–94. *Journal of Sexual Medicine, 7,* 255–265. doi:10.1111/J.1743-6109.2010.02012.X

Herrenkohl, T. I., Hong, S., Klika, J. B., Herrenkohl, R. C., & Russo, M. J. (2013). Developmental impacts of child abuse and neglect related to adult mental health, substance use, and physical health. *Journal of Family Violence, 28*, 191–199. doi:10.1007/s10896-012-9474-9

Hewitt, B., Baxter, J., & Western, M. (2006). Family, work and health: The impact of marriage, parenthood and employment on self-reported health of Australian men and women. *Journal of Sociology, 42*, 61–78.

Higgins, C. A., Duxbury, L. E., & Lyons, S. T. (2010). Coping with overload and stress: Men and women in dual-earner families. *Journal of Marriage and Family, 72*, 847–859. doi:10.1111/j.1741-3737.2010.00734.x

Hill, K. P. (2015). Medical marijuana for treatment of chronic pain and other medical and psychiatric problems. *JAMA, 313*, 2474. doi:10.1001/jama.2015.6199

Hite, L. M., & McDonald, K. S. (2003). Career aspirations of non-managerial women: Adjustment and adaptation. *Journal of Career Development, 29*, 221–235.

Hock, R. (2015). *Human sexuality*. Boston, MA: Pearson.

Hogan, C. L., Mata, J., & Carstensen, L. L. (2013). Exercise holds immediate benefits for affect and cognition in younger and older adults. *Psychology and Aging, 28*, 587–594. doi:10.1037/a0032634

Holland, J. L. (1997). *Making vocational choices: A theory of vocational personalities and work environments* (3rd ed.). Odessa, FL: Psychological Assessment Resources.

Hope, J. (2017). Review policy recommendations to support adult learners. *Recruiting & Retaining Adult Learners, 19*, 8. doi:10.1002/nsr.30238

Horn, P. L., West, N. P., Pyne, D. B., Koerbin, G., Lehtinen, S. J., Fricker, P. A., & Cripps, A. W. (2015). Routine exercise alters measures of immunity and the acute phase reaction. *European Journal of Applied Physiology, 115*, 407–415. doi:10.1007/s00421-014-3028-1

Huddleston, T. (2016, February 1). Colorado's legal marijuana industry is worth $1 billion. *Fortune*. Retrieved from http://fortune.com/2016/02/11/marijuana-billion-dollars-colorado/

Huerta, T. R., Walker, D. M., Mullen, D., Johnson, T. J., & Ford, E. W. (2017). Trends in e-cigarette awareness and perceived harmfulness in the U.S. *American Journal of Preventive Medicine, 52*, 339–346. doi:10.1016/j.amepre.2016.10.017

Hughes, M. C. B., Williams, G. M., Baker, P., & Green, A. C. (2013). Sunscreen and prevention of skin aging: A randomized trial. *Annals of Internal Medicine, 158*, 781–90. doi:10.7326/0003-4819-158-11-201306040-00002

Hyde, J. S., & DeLamater, J. D. (2017). *Understanding human sexuality*. New York, NY: McGraw-Hill.

Jacobs, J. E., Lanza, S., Osgood, D. W., Eccles, J. S., & Wigfield, A. (2002). Changes in children's self-competence and values: Gender and domain differences across grades one through twelve. *Child Development, 73*, 509–527.

Jamal, A., King, B. A., Neff, L. J., Whitmill, J., Babb, S. D., & Graffunder, C. M. (2016). Current cigarette smoking among adults—United States, 2005–2015. *MMWR. Morbidity and Mortality Weekly Report, 65*, 1205–1211. doi:10.15585/mmwr.mm6544a2

Jasienska, G., Bribiescas, R. G., Furberg, A. S., Helle, S., & Núñez-de la Mora, A. (2017). Human reproduction and health: An evolutionary perspective. *The Lancet, 390*, 510–520. doi:10.1016/S0140-6736(17)30573-1

Johnson, S. L., Dunleavy, J., Gemmell, N. J., & Nakagawa, S. (2015). Consistent age-dependent declines in human semen quality: A systematic review and meta-analysis. *Ageing Research Reviews, 19C*, 22–33. doi:10.1016/j.arr.2014.10.007

Jones, K. P., Peddie, C. I., Gilrane, V. L., King, E. B., & Gray, A. L. (2016). Not so subtle: A meta-analytic investigation of the correlates of subtle and overt discrimination. *Journal of Management, 42*, 1588–1613. doi:10.1177/0149206313506466

Jury, M., Smeding, A., Stephens, N. M., Nelson, J. E., Aelenei, C., & Darnon, C. (2017). The experience of low-SES students in higher education: Psychological barriers to success and interventions to reduce social-class inequality. *Journal of Social Issues, 73*, 23–41. doi:10.1111/josi.12202

Kalvapallé, R. (2017). *Weed around the world: What legal marijuana looks like in other countries*. Retrieved from http://globalnews.ca/news/3378603/marijuana-laws-around-the-world/

Kanny, D., Liu, Y., Brewer, R. D., & Lu, H. (2013). Binge drinking—United States, 2011. *Morbidity and Mortality Weekly Report, Surveillance Summaries, 62*(Suppl. 3), 77–80. Retrieved from http://www.ncbi.nlm.nih.gov/pubmed/24264494

Kantamneni, N., McCain, M. R. C., Shada, N., Hellwege, M. A., & Tate, J. (2016). Contextual factors in the career development of prospective first-generation college students. Journal of Career Assessment, *26*, 183–196. doi:10.1177/1069072716680048

Kenney, W. L., Wilmore, J., & Costill, D. L. (2015). *Physiology of sport and exercise* (6th ed.). Champaign, IL: Human Kinetics.

Kerpelman, J. L., Shoffner, M. F., & Ross-Griffin, S. (2002). African American mothers' and daughters' beliefs about possible selves and their strategies for reaching the adolescents' future academic and career goals. *Journal of Youth & Adolescence, 31*, 289.

King, B. M. (2019). *Human sexuality today*. Boston, MA: Pearson.

King, E. B., Madera, J. M., Hebl, M. R., Knight, J. L., & Mendoza, S. A. (2006). What's in a name? A multiracial investigation of the role of occupational stereotypes in selection decisions. *Journal of Applied Social Psychology, 36*, 1145–1159.

King, P. M., & Kitchener, K. S. (2004). Reflective judgment: Theory and research on the development of epistemic assumptions through adulthood. *Educational Psychologist, 39*, 5–15.

King, P. M., & Kitchener, K. S. (2016). Cognitive development in the emerging adult. In J. J. Arnett (Ed.), *The Oxford handbook of emerging adulthood* (pp. 205–125). Oxford, UK: Oxford University Press. doi:10.1093/oxfordhb/9780199795574.013.14

Kirkner, A., Relyea, M., & Ullman, S. E. (2018). PTSD and problem drinking in relation to seeking mental health and substance use treatment among sexual assault survivors. *Traumatology, 24*, 1–7. doi:10.1037/trm0000126

Kosterman, R., Bailey, J. A., Guttmannova, K., Jones, T. M., Eisenberg, N., Hill, K. G., . . . Zeger, S. (2016). Marijuana legalization and parents' attitudes, use, and parenting in Washington state. *Journal of Adolescent Health, 59*, 450–456. doi:10.1016/j.jadohealth.2016.07.004

Krei, M. S., & Rosenbaum, J. E. (2000). Career and college advice to the forgotten half: What do counselors and vocational teachers advise? *Teachers College Record, 103*, 823–842. Retrieved from http://eric.ed.gov/?id=EJ638357

Kuhn, D. (2013). Reasoning. In P. D. Zelazo (Ed.), *The Oxford handbook of developmental psychology: Vol. 1. Body and mind* (pp. 744–764). Oxford, UK: Oxford University Press. doi:10.1093/oxfordhb/9780199958450.013.0026

Kuntsche, E., Kuntsche, S., Thrul, J., & Gmel, G. (2017). Binge drinking: Health impact, prevalence, correlates and interventions. *Psychology & Health, 32*, 976–1017. doi:10.1080/08870446.2017.1325889

Kuperberg, A., & Padgett, J. E. (2016). The role of culture in explaining college students' selection into hookups, dates, and long-term romantic relationships. *Journal of Social and Personal Relationships, 33*, 1070–1096. doi:10.1177/0265407515616876

Labouvie-Vief, G. (2006). Emerging structures of adult thought. In J. J. Arnett & J. L. Tanner (Eds.), *Emerging adults in America: Coming of age in the 21st century* (pp. 59–84). Washington, DC: American Psychological Association.

Labouvie-Vief, G. (2015). *Integrating emotions and cognition throughout the lifespan*. New York, NY: Springer. doi:10.1007/978-3-319-09822-7

Labrie, J. W., Hummer, J. F., Ghaidarov, T. M., Lac, A., & Kenney, S. R. (2014). Hooking up in the college context: The event-level effects of alcohol use and partner familiarity on hookup behaviors and contentment. *Journal of Sex Research, 51*, 62–73. doi:10.1080/00224499.2012.714010

Lakerveld, J., & Mackenbach, J. (2017). The upstream determinants of adult obesity. *Obesity Facts, 10*, 216–222. doi:10.1159/000471489

Lambert, A. J., & Raichle, K. (2000). The role of political ideology in mediating judgments of blame in rape victims and their assailants: A test of the just world, personal responsibility, and legitimization hypotheses. *Personality and Social Psychology Bulletin, 26*, 853–863. doi:10.1177/0146167200269010

Lapsley, D., & Hardy, S. A. (2017). Identity formation and moral development in emerging adulthood. In L. M. Padilla-Walker & L. J. Nelson (Ed.), *Flourishing in emerging adulthood: Positive development during the third decade of life* (Vol. 1). Oxford, UK: Oxford University Press. doi:10.1093/acprof:oso/9780190260637.003.0002

Larson, N. I., Story, M. T., & Nelson, M. C. (2009). Neighborhood environments. *American*

Journal of Preventive Medicine, 36, 74–81.e10. doi:10.1016/j.amepre.2008.09.025

Lau-Barraco, C., Linden-Carmichael, A. N., Hequembourg, A., & Pribesh, S. (2017). Motivations and consequences of alcohol use among heavy drinking nonstudent emerging adults. *Journal of Adolescent Research, 32,* 667–695. doi:10.1177/0743558416630812

Lawrence, D., Fagan, P., Backinger, C. L., Gibson, J. T., & Hartman, A. (2007). Cigarette smoking patterns among young adults aged 18–24 years in the United States. *Nicotine & Tobacco Research, 9,* 687–697. doi:10.1080/14622200701365319

Lee, C. M., Maggs, J. L., Neighbors, C., & Patrick, M. E. (2011). Positive and negative alcohol-related consequences: Associations with past drinking. *Journal of Adolescence, 34,* 87–94. doi:10.1016/j.adolescence.2010.01.009

Lee, M. R., Chassin, L., & Villalta, I. K. (2013). Maturing out of alcohol involvement: Transitions in latent drinking statuses from late adolescence to adulthood. *Development and Psychopathology, 25*(4, Pt. 1), 1137–1153. doi:10.1017/S0954579413000424

Leslie, S. J., Cimpian, A., Meyer, M., & Freeland, E. (2015). Expectations of brilliance underlie gender distributions across academic disciplines. *Science, 347,* 262–265. doi:10.1126/science.1261375

Li, Y., Lin, H., Li, Y., & Cao, J. (2011). Association between socio-psycho-behavioral factors and male semen quality: Systematic review and meta-analyses. *Fertility & Sterility, 95,* 116–123. doi:10.1016/j.fertnstert.2010.06.031

Lipari, R. N., Hughes, A., & Bose, J. (2013). *Driving under the influence of alcohol and illicit drugs. The CBHSQ report.* Substance Abuse and Mental Health Services Administration. Retrieved from http://www.ncbi.nlm.nih.gov/pubmed/28252900

Lunau, T., Bambra, C., Eikemo, T. A., van der Wel, K. A., & Dragano, N. (2014). A balancing act? Work-life balance, health and well-being in European welfare states. *European Journal of Public Health, 24,* 422–427. doi:10.1093/eurpub/cku010

MacDonald, K. (2018). A review of the literature: The needs of nontraditional students in postsecondary education. *Strategic Enrollment Management Quarterly, 5,* 159–164. doi:10.1002/sem3.20115

MacLean, P. S., Wing, R. R., Davidson, T., Epstein, L., Goodpaster, B., Hall, K. D., . . . Ryan, D. (2015). NIH working group report: Innovative research to improve maintenance of weight loss. *Obesity, 23,* 7–15. doi:10.1002/oby.20967

Maddux, W. W., & Yuki, M. (2006). The "ripple effect": Cultural differences in perceptions of the consequences of events. *Personality and Social Psychology Bulletin, 32,* 669–683. doi:10.1177/0146167205283840

Maggs, J. L., Jager, J., Patrick, M. E., & Schulenberg, J. (2012). Social role patterning in early adulthood in the USA: Adolescent predictors and concurrent wellbeing across four distinct configurations. *Longitudinal and Life Course Studies, 3,* 190–210. Retrieved from http://www.pubmedcentral.nih.gov/articlerender.fcgi?artid=3495328&tool=pmcentrez&rendertype=abstract

Maier, K. S. (2005). Transmitting educational values: Parent occupation and adolescent development. In B. Schneider & L. J. Waite (Eds.), *Being together, working apart: Dual-career families and the work-life balance* (pp. 396–418). New York, NY: Cambridge University Press.

Malamuth, N. M., Addison, T., & Koss, M. (2000). Pornography and sexual aggression: Are there reliable effects and can we understand them? *Annual Review of Sex Research.* Retrieved from http://psycnet.apa.org/psycinfo/2001-17368-002

Markus, H. R., & Kitayama, S. (2010). Cultures and selves: A cycle of mutual constitution. *Perspectives on Psychological Science, 5,* 420–430. doi:10.1177/1745691610375557

Martin, J. A., Hamilton, B. E., & Osterman, M. J. K. (2017). Births in the United States, 2016. *NCHS Data Brief, 287,* 1–8.

Martin, S. C. (2016). A brief history of marijuana law in America. *Time.* Retrieved from http://time.com/4298038/marijuana-history-in-america/

Martins, W. P., & Jokubkiene, L. (2017). Assessment of the functional ovarian reserve. In S. Guerriero & J. Alcazar (Eds.), *Managing ultrasonography in human reproduction* (pp. 3–12). Cham, Switzerland: Springer International. doi:10.1007/978-3-319-41037-1_1

Mason, W. A., Hanson, K., Fleming, C. B., Ringle, J. L., & Haggerty, K. P. (2015). Washington state recreational marijuana legalization: Parent and adolescent perceptions, knowledge, and discussions in a sample of low-income families. *Substance Use & Misuse, 50,* 541–545. doi:10.3109/10826084.2014.952447

Mather, M. (2012). The emotion paradox in the aging brain. *Annals of the New York Academy of Sciences, 1251,* 33–49. doi:10.1111/j.1749-6632.2012.06471.x

Matsumoto, D. (2002). *The new Japan: Debunking seven cultural stereotypes.* Yarmouth, ME: Intercultural Press. Retrieved from https://wqv282mhk01.storage.googleapis.com/MTg3Nzg2NDkzNQ==01.pdf

Matthews, T. J., & Hamilton, B. E. (2016). *Mean age of mothers is on the rise: United States, 2000–2014.* Retrieved from https://www.cdc.gov/nchs/products/databriefs/db232.htm

Maxwell, L., & Scott, G. (2014). A review of the role of radical feminist theories in the understanding of rape myth acceptance. *Journal of Sexual Aggression, 20,* 40–54. doi:10.1080/13552600.2013.773384

Mayhew, M. J., Rockenbach, A. N., Bowman, N. A., Seifert, T. A., Wolniak, G. C., Pascarella, E. T., & Terenzini, P. Y. (2016). *How college affects students: Vol. 3. 21st century evidence that higher education works.* Hoboken, NJ: John Wiley.

Mayseless, O., & Scharf, M. (2003). What does it mean to be an adult? The Israeli experience. *New Directions for Child & Adolescent Development, 2003,* 5–20.

McCrady, B. S. (2017). Alcohol use disorders. In D. McKay, J. S. Abramowitz, & E. A. Storch (Eds.), *Treatments for psychological problems and syndromes* (pp. 235–247). Chichester, England: John Wiley. doi:10.1002/9781118877142.ch16

McDonald, R. B. (2014). *Biology of aging.* New York, NY: Garland Science.

McIndoe, S. (2017). *How the NHL concussion lawsuit could threaten the future of the league.* Retrieved from https://www.theguardian.com/sport/2017/apr/05/nhl-concussion-lawsuit-could-threaten-future-of-league

McKee, A. C., Stein, T. D., Nowinski, C. J., Stern, R. A., Daneshvar, D. H., Alvarez, V. E., . . . Cantu, R. C. (2013). The spectrum of disease in chronic traumatic encephalopathy. *Brain, 136,* 43–64. doi:10.1093/brain/aws307

McNulty, J. K., Wenner, C. A., & Fisher, T. D. (2016). Longitudinal associations among relationship satisfaction, sexual satisfaction, and frequency of sex in early marriage. *Archives of Sexual Behavior, 45,* 85–97. doi:10.1007/s10508-014-0444-6

Mellins, C. A., Walsh, K., Sarvet, A. L., Wall, M., Gilbert, L., Santelli, J. S., . . . Hirsch, J. S. (2017). Sexual assault incidents among college undergraduates: Prevalence and factors associated with risk. *PLoS ONE, 12,* e0186471. doi:10.1371/journal.pone.0186471

Merrill, J. E., & Carey, K. B. (2016). Drinking over the lifespan: Focus on college ages. *Alcohol Research: Current Reviews, 38,* 103–14. Retrieved from http://www.ncbi.nlm.nih.gov/pubmed/27159817

Mez, J., Daneshvar, D. H., Kiernan, P. T., Abdolmohammadi, B., Alvarez, V. E., Huber, B. R., & McKee, A. C. (2017). Clinicopathological evaluation of chronic traumatic encephalopathy in players of American football. *JAMA, 318,* 360.

Miech, R. A., Johnston, L. D., O'Malley, P. M., Bachman, J. G., Schulenberg, J. E., & Patrick, M. E. (2017). *Monitoring the Future national survey results on drug use, 1975–2016: Vol. I. Secondary school students.* Retrieved from http://www.monitoringthefuture.org/pubs/monographs/mtf-vol1_2016.pdf

Mikels, J. A., Löckenhoff, C. E., Maglio, S. J., Goldstein, M. K., Garber, A., & Carstensen, L. L. (2010). Following your heart or your head: Focusing on emotions versus information differentially influences the decisions of younger and older adults. *Journal of Experimental Psychology, Applied, 16,* 87–95. doi:10.1037/a0018500

Mitchell, L. L., & Syed, M. (2015). Does college matter for emerging adulthood? Comparing developmental trajectories of educational groups. *Journal of Youth and Adolescence, 44,* 2012–2027. doi:10.1007/s10964-015-0330-0

Monaghan, D. B., & Attewell, P. (2015). The community college route to the bachelor's degree. *Educational Evaluation and Policy Analysis, 37,* 70–91. doi:10.3102/0162373714521865

Monte, A. A., Zane, R. D., & Heard, K. J. (2015). The implications of marijuana legalization in Colorado. *JAMA, 313,* 241–242. doi:10.1001/jama.2014.17057

Morgan, W. B., Elder, K. B., & King, E. B. (2013). The emergence and reduction of bias in letters of recommendation. *Journal of Applied Social Psychology, 43,* 2297–2306. doi:10.1111/jasp.12179

Moshman, D., & Moshman, D. (2011). *Adolescent rationality and development: Cognition, morality, and identity.* New York: Psychology Press.

Mouzon, D. M., Taylor, R. J., Woodward, A. T., & Chatters, L. M. (2017). Everyday racial discrimination, everyday non-racial discrimination, and physical health among African-Americans. *Journal of Ethnic & Cultural Diversity in Social Work, 26,* 68–80. doi:10.1080/15313204.2016.1187103

Murthy, V. H. (2017). E-cigarette use among youth and young adults. *JAMA Pediatrics, 171,* 209. doi:10.1001/jamapediatrics.2016.4662

Napper, L. E., Montes, K. S., Kenney, S. R., & LaBrie, J. W. (2016). Assessing the personal negative impacts of hooking up experienced by college students: Gender differences and mental health. *Journal of Sex Research, 53,* 766–775. doi:10.1080/00224499.2015.1065951

National Center for Education Statistics. (2016). *What are the trends in the educational level of the United States population?* Retrieved from https://nces.ed.gov/fastfacts/display.asp?id=27

National Center for Education Statistics. (2017a). *Characteristics of postsecondary students.* Retrieved March 13, 2018, from https://nces.ed.gov/programs/coe/indicator_csb.asp

National Center for Education Statistics. (2017b). *Immediate college enrollment rate.* Retrieved from https://nces.ed.gov/programs/coe/indicator_cpa.asp

National Center for Education Statistics. (2017c). *Status and trends in the education of racial and ethnic groups.* Retrieved February 12, 2018, from https://nces.ed.gov/programs/raceindicators/index.asp

National Center for Education Statistics. (2017d). *Undergraduate retention and graduation rates—Indicator April (2017).* Retrieved March 13, 2018, from https://nces.ed.gov/programs/coe/indicator_ctr.asp

National Conference of State Legislatures. (2018). *State medical marijuana laws—4/21/2017.* Retrieved from http://www.ncsl.org/research/health/state-medical-marijuana-laws.aspx

National Council on Alcoholism and Drug Dependence. (2015). *Alcohol and crime.* Retrieved from https://ncadd.org/learn-about-alcohol/alcohol-and-crime

National Highway Traffic Safety Administration. (2016). *Alcohol impaired driving: Traffic safety facts—2015.* Retrieved from file:///C:/Users/Tara/Desktop/2015 Alcohol-Impaired Driving Traffic Safety Fact Sheet.pdf

National Institute on Drug Abuse. (2009). *Are there effective treatments for tobacco addiction?* Bethesda, MD: National Institutes of Health. Retrieved from http://www.nida.nih.gov/ResearchReports/Nicotine/treatment.html

National Institute on Drug Abuse. (2017). *National survey on drug use and health: Trends in prevalence of various drugs for ages 12 or older, ages 12 to 17, ages 18 to 25, and ages 26 or older; 2015–2016 (in percent).* Retrieved March 12, 2018, from https://www.drugabuse.gov/national-survey-drug-use-health

National Science Foundation. (2012). *Table 2–12. Freshmen intending S&E major, by field, sex, and race/ethnicity: 1995–2010.* Retrieved from http://www.nsf.gov/statistics/seind12/c2/c2s2.htm

Nelson, L. J. (2009). An examination of emerging adulthood in Romanian college students. *International Journal of Behavioral Development, 33,* 402–411. doi:10.1177/0165025409340093

Nelson, L. J., Badger, S., & Wu, B. (2004). The influence of culture in emerging adulthood: Perspectives of Chinese college students. *International Journal of Behavioral Development, 28,* 26–36.

Nelson, L. J., & Luster, S. S. (2015). "Adulthood" by whose definition? In J. J. Arnett (Ed.), *The Oxford handbook of emerging adulthood* (pp. 421–437). Oxford, UK: Oxford University Press. doi:10.1093/oxfordhb/9780199795574.013.24

Newson, R. S., & Kemps, E. B. (2008). Relationship between fitness and cognitive performance in younger and older adults. *Psychology & Health, 23,* 369–386. doi:10.1080/08870440701421545

NHL Public Relations. (2016). *NHL updates concussion protocol.* Retrieved from https://www.nhl.com/news/nhl-updates-concussion-protocol/c-282571624

Nicklas, J. M., Huskey, K. W., Davis, R. B., & Wee, C. C. (2012). Successful weight loss among obese U.S. adults. *American Journal of Preventive Medicine, 42,* 481–485.

Nurkkala, M., Kaikkonen, K., Vanhala, M. L., Karhunen, L., Keränen, A. M., & Korpelainen, R. (2015). Lifestyle intervention has a beneficial effect on eating behavior and long-term weight loss in obese adults. *Eating Behaviors, 18,* 179–185. doi:10.1016/j.eatbeh.2015.05.009

Nutter, S., Russell-Mayhew, S., Arthur, N., & Ellard, J. H. (2018). Weight bias as a social justice issue: A call for dialogue. *Canadian Psychology/Psychologie Canadienne, 59,* 89–99. doi:10.1037/cap0000125

Office of the Surgeon General. (2016). *A report of the surgeon general—Executive summary.* Atlanta, GA: Author.

Ojalehto, B. L., & Medin, D. L. (2015). Perspectives on culture and concepts. *Annual Review of Psychology, 66,* 249–275. doi:10.1146/annurev-psych-010814-015120

Ojalehto, B., & Medin, D. (2015). Emerging trends in culture and concepts. In R. A. Scott & M. C. Buchmann (Ed.), *Emerging trends in the social and behavioral sciences* (pp. 1–15). Hoboken, NJ: John Wiley. doi:10.1002/9781118900772.etrds0064

Olmstead, S. B., Conrad, K. A., & Anders, K. M. (2018). First semester college students' definitions of and expectations for engaging in hookups. *Journal of Adolescent Research, 33,* 275–305. doi:10.1177/0743558417698571

Orchowski, L. M., Untied, A. S., & Gidycz, C. A. (2013). Social reactions to disclosure of sexual victimization and adjustment among survivors of sexual assault. *Journal of Interpersonal Violence, 28,* 2005–2023. doi:10.1177/0886260512471085

Orzano, A. J., & Scott, J. G. (2004). Diagnosis and treatment of obesity in adults: An applied evidence-based review. *Journal of the American Board of Family Practice, 17,* 359–369.

Osam, E. K., Bergman, M., & Cumberland, D. M. (2017). An integrative literature review on the barriers impacting adult learners' return to college. *Adult Learning, 28,* 54–60. doi:10.1177/1045159516658013

Owen, J., & Fincham, F. D. (2011). Young adults' emotional reactions after hooking up encounters. *Archives of Sexual Behavior, 40,* 321–330. doi:10.1007/s10508-010-9652-x

Pacula, R. L., Powell, D., Heaton, P., & Sevigny, E. L. (2015). Assessing the effects of medical marijuana laws on marijuana use: The devil is in the details. *Journal of Policy Analysis and Management, 34,* 7–31.

Palamar, J. J., Griffin-Tomas, M., & Kamboukos, D. (2015). Reasons for recent marijuana use in relation to use of other illicit drugs among high school seniors in the United States. *American Journal of Drug and Alcohol Abuse, 41,* 323–331. doi:10.3109/00952990.2015.1045977

Patrick, M. E., Bray, B. C., & Berglund, P. A. (2016). Reasons for marijuana use among young adults and long-term associations with marijuana use and problems. *Journal of Studies on Alcohol and Drugs, 77,* 881–888. doi:10.15288/jsad.2016.77.881

Patrick, M. E., Maggs, J. L., & Lefkowitz, E. S. (2015). Daily associations between drinking and sex among college students: A longitudinal measurement burst design. *Journal of Research on Adolescence, 25,* 377–386. doi:10.1111/jora.12135

Patton, L. D., Renn, K. A., Guido-DiBrito, F., & Quaye, S. J. (2016). *Student development in college: Theory, research, and practice.* New York, NY: John Wiley.

Payne, V. G., & Isaacs, L. D. (2016). *Human motor development: A lifespan approach.* New York, NY: McGraw-Hill.

Perilloux, C., Easton, J. A., & Buss, D. M. (2012). The misperception of sexual interest. *Psychological Science, 23,* 146–151. doi:10.1177/0956797611424162

Perry, W. G. (1970). *Forms of intellectual and ethical development in the college years: A scheme.* San Francisco, CA: Jossey-Bass.

Phillips, L. T., Stephens, N. M., & Townsend, S. S. M. (2016). *Access is not enough: Cultural mismatch persists to limit first-generation students' opportunities for achievement throughout college.* Retrieved from https://www.scholars.northwestern.edu/en/publications/access-is-not-enough-cultural-mismatch-persists-to-limit-first-ge

Puhl, R. M., Heuer, C. A., & Brownell, K. D. (2011). Stigma and social consequences of obesity. In P. G. Kopelman, I. D. Caterson, & W. H. Dietz (Eds.), *Clinical obesity in adults and children* (pp. 25–40). Hoboken, NJ: John Wiley. doi:10.1002/9781444307627.CH3

Radford, A. W., Cominole, M., & Skomsvold, P. (2015). *Demographic and enrollment characteristics of nontraditional undergraduates: 2011–12.* Retrieved from http://www.voced.edu.au/content/ngv:70505

Ramo, D. E., Young-Wolff, K. C., & Prochaska, J. J. (2015). Prevalence and correlates of electronic-cigarette use in young adults: Findings from three studies over five years. *Addictive Behaviors, 41,* 142–147. doi:10.1016/j.addbeh.2014.10.019

Rao, M., Afshin, A., Singh, G., & Mozaffarian, D. (2013). Do healthier foods and diet patterns cost more than less healthy options? A systematic review and meta-analysis. *BMJ Open, 3,* e004277. doi:10.1136/bmjopen-2013-004277

Ravert, R. D., Stoddard, N. A., & Donnellan, M. B. (2018). A content analysis of the methods used to study emerging adults in six developmental journals from 2013 to 2015. *Emerging Adulthood, 6,* 151–158. doi:10.1177/2167696817720011

Rebar, A. L., Stanton, R., Geard, D., Short, C., Duncan, M. J., & Vandelanotte, C. (2015). A meta-meta-analysis of the effect of physical activity on depression and anxiety in non-clinical adult populations. *Health Psychology Review, 9,* 366–378. doi:10.1080/17437199.2015.1022901

Reckdenwald, A., Ford, J. A., & Murray, B. N. (2016). Alcohol use in emerging adulthood: Can Moffitt's developmental theory help us understand binge drinking among college students? *Journal of Child & Adolescent Substance Abuse, 25,* 497–503. doi:10.1080/1067828X.2015.1103347

Rehm, J. (2011). The risks associated with alcohol use and alcoholism. *Alcohol Research & Health: The Journal of the National Institute on Alcohol Abuse and Alcoholism, 34,* 135–143. doi:Fea-AR&H-65

Rhodes, R. E., Janssen, I., Bredin, S. S. D., Warburton, D. E. R., & Bauman, A. (2017). Physical activity: Health impact, prevalence, correlates and interventions. *Psychology & Health, 32,* 942–975. doi:10.1080/08870446.2017.1325486

Riegle-Crumb, C., King, B., Grodsky, E., & Muller, C. (2012). The more things change, the more they stay the same? Examining gender equality in prior achievement and entry into STEM college majors over time. *American Educational Research Journal, 49,* 1048–1073. doi:10.3102/0002831211435229

Roberts, S. B., & Rosenberg, I. (2006). Nutrition and aging: Changes in the regulation of energy metabolism with aging. *Physiological Reviews, 86,* 651–667. doi:10.1152/physrev.00019.2005

Robinson, E., Sutin, A., & Daly, M. (2017). Perceived weight discrimination mediates the prospective relation between obesity and depressive symptoms in U.S. and U.K. adults. *Health Psychology, 36,* 112–121. doi:10.1037/hea0000426

Robinson, M., Berke, J., & Gould, S. (2018). States where marijuana is legal. *Business Insider.* Retrieved March 14, 2018, from http://www.businessinsider.com/legal-marijuana-states-2018-1

Rodriguez, C. (2017). Marijuana legalization In Europe: Is France next? *Forbes.* Retrieved from https://www.forbes.com/sites/ceciliarodriguez/2017/01/06/marijuana-legalization-in-europe-is-france-next/#669531f6c96e

Rosenbaum, J. E., & Person, A. E. (2003). Beyond college for all: Policies and practices to improve transitions into college and jobs. *Professional School Counseling, 6,* 252.

Ross-Gordon, J. M. (2011). Research on adult learners: Supporting the needs of a student population that is no longer nontraditional. *Peer Review, 3,* 26–29. Retrieved from http://www.aacu.org/publications-research/periodicals/research-adult-learners-supporting-needs-student-population-no

Russo, M., Shteigman, A., & Carmeli, A. (2016). Workplace and family support and work–life balance: Implications for individual psychological availability and energy at work. *Journal of Positive Psychology, 11,* 173–188. doi:10.1080/17439760.2015.1025424

Sandoval, W. A., Greene, J. A., & Bråten, I. (2016). Understanding and promoting thinking about knowledge. *Review of Research in Education, 40,* 457–496. doi:10.3102/0091732X16669319

Savage, C., & Healy, J. (2018). Trump administration takes step that could threaten marijuana legalization movement. *New York Times.* Retrieved March 14, 2018, from https://www.nytimes.com/2018/01/04/us/politics/marijuana-legalization-justice-department-prosecutions.html

Schoenborn, C. A., & Stommel, M. (2011). Adherence to the 2008 adult physical activity guidelines and mortality risk. *American Journal of Preventive Medicine, 40,* 514–521. doi:10.1016/j.amepre.2010.12.029

Schoon, I., & Parsons, S. (2002). Competence in the face of adversity: The influence of early family environment and long-term consequences. *Children & Society, 16,* 260–272.

Schoon, I., & Polek, E. (2011). Teenage career aspirations and adult career attainment: The role of gender, social background and general cognitive ability. *International Journal of Behavioral Development, 35,* 210–217. doi:10.1177/0165025411398183

Schuh-Huerta, S. M., Johnson, N. A., Rosen, M. P., Sternfeld, B., Cedars, M. I., & Reijo Pera, R. A. (2012). Genetic variants and environmental factors associated with hormonal markers of ovarian reserve in Caucasian and African American women. *Human Reproduction, 27,* 594–608. doi:10.1093/humrep/der391

Schulenberg, J. E., & Miech, R. A. (2014). *Monitoring the Future national survey results on drug use, 1975–2013: Vol. 2. College students and adults ages 19–55.* Retrieved from http://www.monitoringthefuture.org//pubs/monographs/mtf-vol2_2013.pdf

Schwartz, S. J. (2016). Turning point for a turning point. *Emerging Adulthood, 4,* 307–317. doi:10.1177/2167696815624640

Schwartz, S. J., Zamboanga, B. L., Luyckx, K., Meca, A., & Ritchie, R. A. (2013). Identity in emerging adulthood: Reviewing the field and looking forward. *Emerging Adulthood, 1,* 96–113. doi:10.1177/2167696813479781

Seiter, L. N., & Nelson, L. J. (2011). An examination of emerging adulthood in college students and nonstudents in India. *Journal of Adolescent Research, 26,* 506–536. doi:10.1177/0743558410391262

Senn, C. Y., Eliasziw, M., Barata, P. C., Thurston, W. E., Newby-Clark, I. R., Radtke, H. L., & Hobden, K. L. (2015). Efficacy of a sexual assault resistance program for university women. *New England Journal of Medicine, 372,* 2326–2335. doi:10.1056/NEJMsa1411131

Sharon, T. (2016). Constructing adulthood: Markers of adulthood and well-being among emerging adults. *Emerging Adulthood, 4,* 161–167. doi:10.1177/2167696815579826

Sigurvinsdottir, R., & Ullman, S. E. (2015). Social reactions, self-blame, and problem drinking in adult sexual assault survivors. *Psychology of Violence, 5,* 192–198. doi:10.1037/a0036316

Silins, E., Horwood, L. J., Patton, G. C., Fergusson, D. M., Olsson, C. A., Hutchinson, D. M., . . . Mattick, R. P. (2014). Young adult sequelae of adolescent cannabis use: An integrative analysis. *The Lancet Psychiatry, 1,* 286–293. doi:10.1016/S2215-0366(14)70307-4

Simons, J. S., Wills, T. A., & Neal, D. J. (2014). The many faces of affect: A multilevel model of drinking frequency/quantity and alcohol dependence symptoms among young adults. *Journal of Abnormal Psychology, 123,* 676–694. doi:10.1037/a0036926

Simons-Morton, B., Haynie, D., Liu, D., Chaurasia, A., Li, K., & Hingson, R. (2016). The effect of residence, school status, work status, and social influence on the prevalence of alcohol use among emerging adults. *Journal of Studies on Alcohol and Drugs, 77,* 121–132. doi:10.15288/JSAD.2016.77.121

Sinnott, J. D. (1998). *The development of logic in adulthood: Postformal thought and its applications.* New York, NY: Plenum.

Sinnott, J. D. (2003). Postformal thought and adult development: Living in balance. In J. Demick & C. Andreoletti (Eds.), *Handbook of adult development* (pp. 221–238). New York, NY: Kluwer.

Sinozich, S., & Langton, L. (2014). *Rape and sexual assault victimization among college-age females, 1995–2013.* Retrieved from https://assets.documentcloud.org/documents/1378364/rsavcaf9513.pdf

Sirsch, U., Dreher, E., Mayr, E., & Willinger, U. (2009). What does it take to be an adult in Austria? Views of adulthood in Austrian adolescents, emerging adults, and adults. *Journal of Adolescent Research, 24,* 275–292.

Skomsvold, P. (2014). *Profile of undergraduate students: 2011–12 (web tables).* Retrieved from https://nces.ed.gov/pubsearch/pubsinfo.asp?pubid=2015167

Smith, J. L., Sansone, C., & White, P. H. (2007). The stereotyped task engagement process: The role of interest and achievement motivation. *Journal of Educational Psychology, 99,* 99–114. Retrieved from https://insights.ovid.com/educational-psychology/jedup/2007/02/000/stereotyped-task-engagement-process/8/00004760

Smith, S. G., Basile, K. C., Gilbert, L. K., Merrick, M. T., Patel, N., Walling, M., & Jain, A. (2017). *National Intimate Partner and Sexual Violence Survey (NISVS): 2010–2012 state report.* Retrieved from https://stacks.cdc.gov/view/cdc/46305

Snapp, S., Ryu, E., & Kerr, J. (2015). The upside to hooking up: College students' positive hookup experiences. *International Journal of Sexual Health, 27,* 43–56. doi:10.1080/19317611.2014.939247

Soneji, S., Barrington-Trimis, J. L., Wills, T. A., Leventhal, A. M., Unger, J. B., Gibson, L. A., . . . Sargent, J. D. (2017). Association between initial use of e-cigarettes and subsequent cigarette smoking among adolescents and young adults: A systematic review and meta-analysis. *JAMA Pediatrics, 171,* 788–797. doi:10.1001/jamapediatrics.2017.1488

Song, A. V., & Ling, P. M. (2011). Social smoking among young adults: Investigation of intentions and attempts to quit. *American Journal of Public Health, 101,* 1291–1296. doi:10.2105/ajph.2010.300012

Spokane, A. R., & Cruza-Guet, M. C. (2005). Holland's theory of vocational personalities in work environments. In S. D. Brown & R. W. Lent (Eds.), *Career development and counseling: Putting theory and research to work* (pp. 24–41). Hoboken, NJ: John Wiley.

Spini, D., Jopp, D. S., Pin, S., & Stringhini, S. (2016). The multiplicity of aging: Lessons for theory and conceptual development from longitudinal studies. In V. L. Bengtson & R. Settersten (Eds.), *Handbook of theories of aging* (3rd ed., pp. 669–692). New York, NY: Springer.

Staff, J., Schulenberg, J. E., Maslowsky, J., Bachman, J. G., O'Malley, P. M., Maggs, J. L., & Johnston, L. D. (2010). Substance use changes and social role transitions: Proximal developmental effects on ongoing trajectories from late adolescence through early adulthood. *Development and Psychopathology, 22,* 917–932. doi:10.1017/S0954579410000544

Stahl, E., Ferguson, L., & Kienhues, D. (2016). Diverging information and epistemic change. In I. B. Jeffrey, A. Greene, & W. A. Sandoval (Eds.), *Handbook of epistemic cognition* (pp. 330–342). New York, NY: Routledge. doi:10.4324/9781315795225-30

Statistics Canada. (2017). *Labour force characteristics by sex and age group.* Retrieved from http://www.statcan.gc.ca/tables-tableaux/sum-som/l01/cst01/labor05-eng.htm

Stavro, K., Pelletier, J., & Potvin, S. (2013). Widespread and sustained cognitive deficits in alcoholism: A meta-analysis. *Addiction Biology, 18,* 203–213. doi:10.1111/j.1369-1600.2011.00418.x

Steinmetz, K. (2016). These states just legalized marijuana. *Time.* Retrieved from http://time.com/4559278/marijuana-election-results-2016/

Stephens, N. M., Fryberg, S. A., Markus, H. R., Johnson, C. S., & Covarrubias, R. (2012). Unseen disadvantage: How American universities' focus on independence undermines the academic performance of first-generation college students. *Journal of Personality and Social Psychology, 102,* 1178–1197. doi:10.1037/a0027143

Stewart, A. L. (2014). The men's project: A sexual assault prevention program targeting college men. *Psychology of Men & Masculinity, 15,* 481–485. doi:10.1037/a0033947

Substance Abuse and Mental Health Services Administration. (2014). *Results from the 2013 National Survey on Drug Use and Health: Summary of national findings.* Retrieved from http://www.samhsa.gov/data/sites/default/files/NSDUHresultsPDFWHTML2013/Web/NSDUHresults2013.pdf

Sugimura, K., Yamazaki, M., Phinney, J. S., & Takeo, K. (2009). Compliance, negotiation, and self-assertion in Japanese adolescents' disagreements with parents. *International Journal of Behavioral Development, 33,* 77–87. doi:10.1177/0165025408098010

Super, D. E. (1990). A life-span, life-space approach to career development. In D. Brown & L. Brooks (Eds.), *Career choice and development: Applying contemporary theories to practice* (2nd ed., pp. 197–261). San Francisco, CA: Jossey-Bass.

Swanson, J. A. (2016). Trends in literature about emerging adulthood. *Emerging Adulthood, 4,* 391–402. doi:10.1177/2167696816630468

Syed, M. (2016). Emerging adulthood: Developmental stage, theory, or nonsense? In J. J. Arnett (Ed.), *The Oxford handbook of emerging adulthood* (pp. 11–25). Oxford, UK: Oxford University Press. doi:10.1093/oxfordhb/9780199795574.013.9

Syed, M., & Mitchell, L. L. (2014). I How race and ethnicity shape emerging adulthood. In J. J. Arnett (Ed.), *The Oxford handbook of emerging adulthood* (pp. 87–101). Oxford, UK: Oxford University Press. doi:10.1093/oxfordhb/9780199795574.013.005

Symonds, W. C., Schwartz, R., & Ferguson., R. F. (2011). *Pathways to prosperity: Meeting the challenge of preparing young Americans.* Retrieved from http://www.sawdc.com/media/5959/pathways_to_prosperity_feb2011.pdf

Tanner, J. L. (2015). Mental health in emerging adulthood. In J. J. Arnett (Ed.), *The Oxford handbook of emerging adulthood* (pp. 499–520). Oxford, UK: Oxford University Press. doi:10.1093/oxfordhb/9780199795574.013.30

Tashkin, D. P. (2013). Effects of marijuana smoking on the lung. *Annals of the American Thoracic Society, 10,* 239–247. Retrieved from http://www.atsjournals.org/doi/abs/10.1513/annalsats.201212-127fr#.ValGhflojxE

Tchernof, A., & Després, J. P. (2013). Pathophysiology of human visceral obesity: An update. *Physiological Reviews, 93,* 359–404. doi:10.1152/physrev.00033.2011

Time & money. (2016). *U.S. News & World Report.* Retrieved from https://mediakit.usnews.com/downloads/insights/USN_PartnerInsights_Strayer.pdf

Tobin, D. J. (2017). Introduction to skin aging. *Journal of Tissue Viability, 26,* 37–46. doi:10.1016/j.jtv.2016.03.002

Triana, M. del C., Jayasinghe, M., & Pieper, J. R. (2015). Perceived workplace racial discrimination and its correlates: A meta-analysis. *Journal of Organizational Behavior, 36,* 491–513. doi:10.1002/job.1988

Twenge, J. M., Sherman, R. A., & Wells, B. E. (2015). Changes in American adults' sexual behavior and attitudes, 1972–2012. *Archives of Sexual Behavior, 44,* 2273–2285. doi:10.1007/s10508-015-0540-2

Unsworth, S. J., Levin, W., Bang, M., Washinawatok, K., Waxman, S. R., & Medin, D. (2012). Cultural differences in children's ecological reasoning and psychological closeness to nature: Evidence from Menominee and European American children. *Journal of Cognition and Culture, 12,* 17–29. doi:10.1163/156853712X633901

U.S. Bureau of Labor Statistics. (2014). *America's young adults at 27: Labor market activity, education, and household composition: Results from a longitudinal survey summary.* Retrieved from http://www.bls.gov/news.release/nlsyth.nr0.htm

U.S. Bureau of Labor Statistics. (2015a). *Labor force statistics from the current population survey: Employment status of the civilian noninstitutional population by age, sex, and race.* Retrieved from http://www.bls.gov/cps/cpsaat03.htm

U.S. Bureau of Labor Statistics. (2015b). *Number of jobs held, labor market activity, and earnings growth among the youngest baby boomers: Results from a longitudinal survey summary.* Retrieved from http://www.bls.gov/news.release/nlsoy.nr0.htm

U.S. Bureau of Labor Statistics. (2015c). *Women in the laborforce: A databook. BLS Reports.* Retrieved from https://www.bls.gov/opub/reports/womens-databook/archive/women-in-the-labor-force-a-databook-2015.pdf

U.S. Bureau of Labor Statistics. (2016a). *America's young adults at 29: Labor market activity, education and partner status: Results from a longitudinal survey.* Retrieved from https://www.bls.gov/news.release/nlsyth.nr0.htm

U.S. Bureau of Labor Statistics. (2016b). Labor force characteristics by race and ethnicity, 2015. *BLS Reports.* Retrieved from https://www.bls.gov/opub/reports/race-and-ethnicity/2015/home.htm

U.S. Bureau of Labor Statistics. (2016c). *Median years of tenure with current employer for employed wage and salary workers by age and sex, selected years, 2006–16.* Washington, DC: Author.

U.S. Bureau of Labor Statistics. (2017). *Employment characteristics of families summary.* Retrieved from https://www.bls.gov/news.release/famee.nr0.htm

U.S. Department of Health and Human Services. (2008). *2008 physical activity guidelines for Americans.* Retrieved from http://www.health.gov/PAGuidelines.

U.S. Department of Health and Human Services. (2014a). *The health consequences of moking—50 years of progress: A report of the Surgeon General.* Retrieved from http://www.surgeongeneral.gov/library/reports/50-years-of-progress/

U.S. Department of Health and Human Services. (2014b). *National Survey on Drug Use and Health, 2013.* Ann Arbor, MI. doi:10.3886/ICPSR35509.v1

U.S. Department of Labor. (2017). *Household data annual averages 11. Employed persons by detailed occupation, sex, race, and Hispanic or Latino ethnicity.* Washington, DC: Author.

Vasquez-Salgado, Y., Greenfield, P. M., & Burgos-Cienfuegos, R. (2015). Exploring home-school value conflicts. *Journal of Adolescent Research, 30,* 271–305. doi:10.1177/0743558414561297

Vickerman, K. A., & Margolin, G. (2009). Rape treatment outcome research: Empirical findings and state of the literature. *Clinical Psychology Review, 29,* 431–448. doi:10.1016/j.cpr.2009.04.004

Vilorio, D. (2016). *Earnings and unemployment rates by educational attainment, 2015.* Retrieved March 13, 2018, from https://www.bls.gov/careeroutlook/2016/data-on-display/education-matters.htm

Wang, G. S., Le Lait, M. C., Deakyne, S. J., Bronstein, A. C., Bajaj, L., & Roosevelt, G. (2016). Unintentional pediatric exposures to marijuana in Colorado, 2009-2015. *JAMA Pediatrics, 170,* e160971. doi:10.1001/jamapediatrics.2016.0971

Ward, L., Siegel, M. J., & Davenport, Z. (2012). *First generation college students: Understanding and improving the experience from recruitment to commencement.* San Francisco, CA: Jossey-Bass.

Watson, R. J., Snapp, S., & Wang, S. (2017). What we know and where we go from here: A review of lesbian, gay, and bisexual youth hookup literature. *Sex Roles, 77,* 801–811. doi:10.1007/s11199-017-0831-2

Watson, T. L., & Blanchard-Fields, F. (1998). Thinking with your head and your heart: Age differences in everyday problem-solving strategy preferences. *Aging, Neuropsychology, and Cognition, 5,* 225–240.

Wesley, M. J., Hanlon, C. A., & Porrino, L. J. (2011). Poor decision-making by chronic marijuana users is associated with decreased functional responsiveness to negative consequences. *Psychiatry Research: Neuroimaging Section, 191,* 51–59. doi:10.1016/j.pscychresns.2010.10.002

Wilkinson, S. T., Radhakrishnan, R., & D'Souza, D. C. (2016). A systematic review of the evidence for medical marijuana in psychiatric indications. *Journal of Clinical Psychiatry, 77,* 1050–1064. doi:10.4088/JCP.15r10036

Wilson, L. C., & Miller, K. E. (2016). Meta-analysis of the prevalence of unacknowledged rape. *Trauma, Violence, & Abuse, 17,* 149–159. doi:10.1177/1524838015576391

Winslow, S. (2005). Work-family conflict, gender, and parenthood, 1977-1997. *Journal of Family Issues, 26,* 727–755. Retrieved from 10.1177/0192513X05277522

Wood, D., Crapnell, T., Lau, L., Bennett, A., Lotstein, D., Ferris, M., & Kuo, A. (2018). Emerging adulthood as a critical stage in the life course. In N. Halfon, C. B. Forrest, R. M. Lerner, & E. M. Faustman (Eds.), *Handbook of life course health development* (pp. 123–143). Cham, Switzerland: Springer International. doi:10.1007/978-3-319-47143-3_7

Wood, W., & Eagly, A. H. (2012). Biosocial construction of sex differences and similarities in behavior. *Advances in Experimental Social Psychology, 46,* 55–123. doi:10.1016/B978-0-12-394281-4.00002-7

The World Bank. (2016). *Labor force, female (% of total labor force).* Retrieved from http://data.worldbank.org/indicator/SL.TLF.TOTL.FE.ZS

Yamin, C. K., Bitton, A., & Bates, D. W. (2010). E-cigarettes: A rapidly growing Internet phenomenon. *Annals of Internal Medicine, 153,* 607–609. doi:10.7326/0003-4819-153-9-201011020-00011

Zeidler, D. L., Sadler, T. D., Applebaum, S., & Callahan, B. E. (2009). Advancing reflective judgment through socioscientific issues. *Journal of Research in Science Teaching, 46,* 74–101. doi:10.1002/tea.20281

Zhang, C., Brook, J. S., Leukefeld, C. G., & Brook, D. W. (2016). Trajectories of marijuana use from adolescence to adulthood as predictors of unemployment status in the early forties. *American Journal on Addictions, 25,* 203–209. doi:10.1111/ajad.12361

Zhang, L. (1999). A comparison of U.S. and Chinese university students' cognitive development: The cross-cultural applicability of Perry's theory. *Journal of Psychology, 133,* 425–440.

Zhang, L. (2004). The Perry scheme: Across cultures, across approaches to the study of human psychology. *Journal of Adult Development, 11,* 123–138.

Zheng, Y., Manson, J. E., Yuan, C., Liang, M. H., Grodstein, F., Stampfer, M. J., . . . Hu, F. B. (2017). Associations of weight gain from early to middle adulthood with major health outcomes later in life. *JAMA, 318,* 255. doi:10.1001/jama.2017.7092

Zimmermann, P., & Iwanski, A. (2014). Emotion regulation from early adolescence to emerging adulthood and middle adulthood. *International Journal of Behavioral Development, 38,* 182–194. doi:10.1177/0165025413515405

Chapter 14

Acevedo, B. P., & Aron, A. (2009). Does a long-term relationship kill romantic love? *Review of General Psychology, 13,* 59–65. doi:10.1037/a0014226

Adamczyk, K. (2017). Voluntary and involuntary singlehood and young adults' mental health: An investigation of mediating role of romantic loneliness. *Current Psychology, 36,* 888–904. doi:10.1007/s12144-016-9478-3

Adamsons, K. (2013). Predictors of relationship quality during the transition to parenthood. *Journal of Reproductive and Infant Psychology, 31,* 160–171. doi:10.1080/02646838.2013.791919

Afifi, T. O., Cox, B. J., & Enns, M. W. (2006). Mental health profiles among married, never-married, and separated/divorced mothers in a nationally representative sample. *Social Psychiatry & Psychiatric Epidemiology, 41,* 122–129.

Ahmadabadi, Z., Najman, J. M., Williams, G. M., Clavarino, A. M., & d'Abbs, P. (2018). Gender differences in intimate partner violence in current and prior relationships. *Journal of Interpersonal Violence.* Advance online publication. doi:10.1177/0886260517730563

Aldwin, C. M. (2007). *Stress, coping, and development: An integrative perspective* (2nd ed.). New York, NY: Guilford.

Amato, P. R. (2010). Research on divorce: Continuing trends and new developments. *Journal of Marriage & Family, 72,* 650–666. doi:10.1111/j.1741-3737.2010.00723.x

Amato, P. R., & Irving, S. (2006). Historical trends in divorce in the United States. In M. A. Fine & J. H. Harvey (Eds.), *Handbook of divorce and relationship dissolution* (pp. 41–57). Mahwah, NJ: Lawrence Erlbaum.

Amato, P. R., & Sobolewski, J. M. (2004). The effects of divorce on fathers and children: Nonresidential fathers and stepfathers. In M. E. Lamb (Ed.), *The role of the father in child development* (4th ed.). (pp. 341–367). Hoboken, NJ: John Wiley.

Anderson, J. W. (2016). Sternberg's triangular theory of love. In C. L. Shehan (Ed.), *Encyclopedia of family studies* (pp. 1–3). Hoboken, NJ: John Wiley. doi:10.1002/9781119085621.wbefs058

Arnett, J. J. (2014). *Emerging adulthood: The winding road from the late teens through the twenties.* New York, NY: Oxford University Press.

Arnett, J. J. (2016). College students as emerging adults. *Emerging Adulthood, 4,* 219–222. doi:10.1177/2167696815587422

Arnett, J. J., & Jensen, L. A. (2002). A congregation of one: Individualized religious beliefs among emerging adults. *Journal of Adolescent Research, 17,* 451–467.

Arnett, J. J., & Schwab, J. (2012). *The Clark University poll of emerging adults: Thriving, struggling, and hopeful.* Retrieved from http://www2.clarku.edu/clark-poll-emerging-adults/pdfs/clark-university-poll-emerging-adults-findings.pdf

Avison, M., & Furnham, A. (2015). Personality and voluntary childlessness. *Journal of Population Research, 32,* 45–67. doi:10.1007/s12546-014-9140-6

Aykutoğlu, B., & Uysal, A. (2017). The relationship between intimacy change and passion: A dyadic diary study. *Frontiers in Psychology, 8,* 2257. doi:10.3389/fpsyg.2017.02257

Badenes-Ribera, L., Bonilla-Campos, A., Frias-Navarro, D., & Gemma Pons-Salvador, H. M.-B. (2016). Intimate partner violence in self-identified lesbians. *Trauma, Violence, & Abuse, 17,* 284–297. doi:10.1177/1524838015584363

Bahns, A. J. (2018). Preference, opportunity, and choice: A multilevel analysis of diverse friendship formation. *Group Processes & Intergroup Relations.* Advance online publication. doi:10.1177/1368430217725390

Baranowska-Rataj, A., Matysiak, A., & Mynarska, M. (2013). Does lone motherhood decrease women's happiness? Evidence from qualitative and quantitative research. *Journal of Happiness Studies, 15,* 1457–1477. doi:10.1007/s10902-013-9486-z

Barner, J. R., & Carney, M. M. (2011). Interventions for intimate partner violence: A historical review. *Journal of Family Violence, 26,* 235–244. doi:10.1007/s10896-011-9359-3

Barrett, B. J. (2015). *Domestic violence in the LGBT community.* Oxford, UK: NASW Press and Oxford University Press. doi:10.1093/acrefore/9780199975839.013.1133

Barry, C. M., Madsen, S. D., Nelson, L. J., Carroll, J. S., & Badger, S. (2009). Friendship and romantic relationship qualities in emerging adulthood: Differential associations with identity development and achieved adulthood criteria. *Journal of Adult Development, 16,* 209–222. doi:10.1007/s10804-009-9067-x

Bartel, S. J., Sherry, S. B., Molnar, D. S., Mushquash, A. R., Leonard, K. E., Flett, G. L., & Stewart, S. H. (2017). Do romantic partners influence each other's heavy episodic drinking? Support for the partner influence hypothesis in a three-year longitudinal study. *Addictive Behaviors, 69,* 55–58. doi:10.1016/J.ADDBEH.2017.01.020

Batalova, J. A., & Cohen, P. N. (2002). Premarital cohabitation and housework: Couples in cross-national perspective. *Journal of Marriage & Family, 64,* 743–755.

Baumbusch, J. L. (2004). Unclaimed treasures: Older women's reflections on lifelong singlehood. *Journal of Women & Aging, 16,* 105–121.

Bendall, C. (2010). The domestic violence epidemic in South Africa: Legal and practical remedies. *Women's Studies, 39,* 100–118. doi:10.1080/00497870903459275

Berkman, L. F., Zheng, Y., Glymour, M. M., Avendano, M., Börsch-Supan, A., & Sabbath,

E. L. (2015). Mothering alone: Cross-national comparisons of later-life disability and health among women who were single mothers. *Journal of Epidemiology and Community Health, 69,* 865–72. doi:10.1136/jech-2014-205149

Bernardi, L., & Mortelmans, D. (2018). In L. Bernardi & D. Mortelmans (Eds.). *Lone parenthood in the life course* (Vol. 8). Cham, Switzerland: Springer International. doi:10.1007/978-3-319-63295-7

Beyer, K., Wallis, A. B., & Hamberger, L. K. (2015). Neighborhood environment and intimate partner violence. *Trauma, Violence, & Abuse, 16,* 16–47. doi:10.1177/1524838013515758

Beyers, W., & Seiffge-Krenke, I. (2010). Does identity precede intimacy? Testing Erikson's theory on romantic development in emerging adults of the 21st century. *Journal of Adolescent Research, 25,* 387–415. doi:10.1177/0743558410361370

Biblarz, T. J., & Savci, E. (2010). Lesbian, gay, bisexual, and transgender families. *Journal of Marriage and Family, 72,* 480–497. doi:10.1111/j.1741-3737.2010.00714.x

Björkenstam, E., Hallqvist, J., Dalman, C., & Ljung, R. (2013). Risk of new psychiatric episodes in the year following divorce in midlife: Cause or selection? A nationwide register-based study of 703,960 individuals. *International Journal of Social Psychiatry, 59,* 801–804. doi:10.1177/0020764012461213

Bleidorn, W., Buyukcan-Tetik, A., Schwaba, T., van Scheppingen, M. A., Denissen, J. J. A., & Finkenauer, C. (2016). Stability and change in self-esteem during the transition to parenthood. *Social Psychological and Personality Science, 7,* 560–569. doi:10.1177/1948550616646428

Bookwala, J., & Jacobs, J. (2004). Age, marital processes, and depressed affect. *Gerontologist, 44,* 328–338.

Bos, H. M. W., Kuyper, L., & Gartrell, N. K. (2018). A population-based comparison of female and male same-sex parent and different-sex parent households. *Family Process, 57,* 148–164. doi:10.1111/famp.12278

Bourassa, K. J., Sbarra, D. A., & Whisman, M. A. (2015). Women in very low quality marriages gain life satisfaction following divorce. *Journal of Family Psychology, 29,* 490–499. doi:10.1037/fam0000075

Boyle, M. H., Georgiades, K., Cullen, J., & Racine, Y. (2009). Community influences on intimate partner violence in India: Women's education, attitudes towards mistreatment and standards of living. *Social Science & Medicine, 69,* 691–697. doi:10.1016/j.socscimed.2009.06.039

Brandel, M., Melchiorri, E., & Ruini, C. (2018). The dynamics of eudaimonic well-being in the transition to parenthood: Differences between fathers and mothers. *Journal of Family Issues.* Advance online publication. doi:10.1177/0192513X18758344

Breiding, M. J., Chen, J., & Black, M. C. (2014). *Intimate partner violence in the United States—2010.* Retrieved from https://www.ncjrs.gov/App/Publications/abstract.aspx?ID=267363

Brewster, K. L., Tillman, K. H., & Jokinen-Gordon, H. (2013). Demographic characteristics of lesbian parents in the United States. *Population Research and Policy Review, 33,* 503–526. doi:10.1007/s11113-013-9296-3

Brown, S. L., Manning, W. D., & Payne, K. K. (2017). Relationship quality among cohabiting versus married couples. *Journal of Family Issues, 38,* 1730–1753. doi:10.1177/0192513X15622236

Buggs, S. G. (2017). Does (mixed-)race matter? The role of race in interracial sex, dating, and marriage. *Sociology Compass, 11,* e12531. doi:10.1111/soc4.12531

Buller, A. M., Devries, K. M., Howard, L. M., & Bacchus, L. J. (2014). Associations between intimate partner violence and health among men who have sex with men: A systematic review and meta-analysis. *PLoS Medicine, 11,* e1001609. doi:10.1371/journal.pmed.1001609

Busch, H., & Hofer, J. (2012). Self-regulation and milestones of adult development: Intimacy and generativity. *Developmental Psychology, 48,* 282–293. doi:10.1037/a0025521

Cao, H., Zhou, N., Fine, M., Liang, Y., Li, J., & Mills-Koonce, W. R. (2017). Sexual minority stress and same-sex relationship well-being: A meta-analysis of research prior to the U.S. nationwide legalization of same-sex marriage. *Journal of Marriage and Family, 79,* 1258–1277. doi:10.1111/jomf.12415

Caspi, A., Herbener, E. S., & Ozer, D. J. (1992). Shared experiences and the similarity of personalities: A longitudinal study of married couples. *Journal of Personality and Social Psychology, 62,* 281–291. Retrieved from 10.1037/0022-3514.62.2.281

Caumont, A. (2013). *More of today's single mothers have never been married.* Retrieved from http://www.pewresearch.org/fact-tank/2013/08/16/more-of-todays-single-mothers-have-never-been-married/

Central Intelligence Agency. (2017). Country comparison: Total fertility rate. In *The world factbook 2017.* Washington, DC: Central Intelligence Agency. Retrieved from https://www.cia.gov/library/publications/the-world-factbook/rankorder/2127rank.html

Chang, A., & Simmons-Duffin, S. (2017). *Same-sex spouses turn to adoption to protect parental rights: NPR.* Retrieved March 24, 2018, from https://www.npr.org/2017/09/22/551814731/same-sex-spouses-turn-to-adoption-to-protect-parental-rights

Cherlin, A. J. (2010). Demographic trends in the United States: A review of research in the 2000s. *Journal of Marriage & Family, 72,* 403–419. doi:10.1111/j.1741-3737.2010.00710.x

Cherlin, A. J. (2013). Health, marriage, and same-sex partnerships. *Journal of Health and Social Behavior, 54,* 64–66. doi:10.1177/0022146512474430

Cho, H. (2012). Racial differences in the prevalence of intimate partner violence against women and associated factors. *Journal of Interpersonal Violence, 27,* 344–363. doi:10.1177/0886260511416469

Church, E. (2004). *Understanding stepmothers: Women share their struggles, successes, and insights.* Toronto, Canada: HarperCollins.

Chzhen, Y., & Bradshaw, J. (2012). Lone parents, poverty and policy in the European Union. *Journal of European Social Policy, 22,* 487–506. doi:10.1177/0958928712456578

Clark, A. E., Diener, E., Georgellis, Y., & Lucas, R. E. (2008). Lags and leads in life satisfaction: A test of the baseline hypothesis. *The Economic Journal, 118,* F222–F243. doi:10.1111/j.1468-0297.2008.02150.x

Cohen, P., Kasen, S., Chen, H., Hartmark, C., & Gordon, K. (2003). Variations in patterns of developmental transitions in the emerging adulthood period. *Developmental Psychology, 39,* 657.

Collins, A., & van Dulmen, M. (2006). Friendships and romance in emerging adulthood: Assessing distinctiveness in close relationships. In J. J. Arnett & J. L. Tanner (Eds.), *Emerging adults in America: Coming of age in the 21st century* (pp. 219–234). Washington, DC: American Psychological Association.

Copen, C. E., Daniels, K., & Mosher, W. D. (2013). First premarital cohabitation in the United States: 2006–2010 National Survey of Family Growth. *National Health Statistics Reports, 64,* 1–15.

Copen, C. E., Daniels, K., Vespa, J., Mosher, W. D. (2012). First marriages in the United States: Data from the 2006–2010 National Survey of Family Growth. *National Health Statistics Reports, 49,* 1–21.

Copp, J. E., Giordano, P. C., Manning, W. D., & Longmore, M. A. (2016). Couple-level economic and career concerns and intimate partner violence in young adulthood. *Journal of Marriage and the Family, 78,* 744–758. doi:10.1111/jomf.12282

D'augelli, A. R., Rendina, J. H., Sinclair, K. O., & Grossman, A. H. (2006). Lesbian and gay youth's aspirations for marriage and raising children. *Journal of LGBT Issues in Counseling, 1,* 77–98.

Damaske, S., Bratter, J. L., & Frech, A. (2017). Single mother families and employment, race, and poverty in changing economic times. *Social Science Research, 62,* 120–133. doi:10.1016/j.ssresearch.2016.08.008

David-Barrett, T., Rotkirch, A., Carney, J., Behncke Izquierdo, I., Krems, J. A., Townley, D., . . . Dunbar, R. I. M. (2015). Women favour dyadic relationships, but men prefer clubs: Cross-cultural evidence from social networking. *PLoS ONE, 10,* e0118329. doi:10.1371/journal.pone.0118329

de Guzman, N. S., & Nishina, A. (2017). 50 Years of loving: Interracial romantic relationships and recommendations for future research. *Journal of Family Theory & Review, 9,* 557–571. doi:10.1111/jftr.12215

DeLongis, A., & Zwicker, A. (2017). Marital satisfaction and divorce in couples in stepfamilies. *Current Opinion in Psychology, 13,* 158–161. doi:10.1016/j.copsyc.2016.11.003

Devries, K. M., Mak, J. Y. T., Garcia-Moreno, C., Petzold, M., Child, J. C., Falder, G., . . . Watts, C. H. (2013). Global health: The global prevalence of intimate partner violence against women. *Science, 340,* 1527–1528. doi:10.1126/science.1240937

Dew, J., Britt, S., & Huston, S. (2012). Examining the relationship between financial issues and divorce. *Family Relations, 61,* 615–628. doi:10.1111/j.1741-3729.2012.00715.x

Dion, K. L., & Dion, K. K. (1993). Gender and ethnocultural comparisons in styles of love. *Psychology of Women Quarterly, 17,* 463–473.

Dixon, P. (2009). Marriage among African Americans: What does the research reveal? *Journal of African American Studies, 13,* 29–46. doi:10.1007/s12111-008-9062-5

Don, B. P., & Mickelson, K. D. (2014). Relationship satisfaction trajectories across the transition to parenthood among low-risk parents. *Journal of Marriage and Family, 76,* 677–692. doi:10.1111/jomf.12111

Doodson, L. J. (2014). Understanding the factors related to stepmother anxiety: A qualitative approach. *Journal of Divorce & Remarriage, 55,* 645–667. doi:10.1080/10502556.2014.9 59111

Doss, B. D., & Rhoades, G. K. (2017). The transition to parenthood: Impact on couples' romantic relationships. *Current Opinion in Psychology, 13,* 25–28. doi:10.1016/J.COPSYC.2016.04.003

Dribe, M., & Stanfors, M. (2009). Does parenthood strengthen a traditional household division of labor? Evidence from Sweden. *Journal of Marriage & Family, 71,* 33–45. doi:10.1111/j.1741-3737.2008.00578.x

Eastwick, P. W., Harden, K. P., Shukusky, J. A., Morgan, T. A., & Joel, S. (2017). Consistency and inconsistency among romantic partners over time. *Journal of Personality and Social Psychology, 112,* 838–859. doi:10.1037/pspi0000087

Edwards, K. M., Sylaska, K. M., & Neal, A. M. (2015). Intimate partner violence among sexual minority populations: A critical review of the literature and agenda for future research. *Psychology of Violence, 5,* 112–121.

Eibach, R. P., & Mock, S. E. (2011). Idealizing parenthood to rationalize parental investments. *Psychological Science, 22,* 203–208. doi:10.1177/0956797610397057

Eng, S., Li, Y., Mulsow, M., & Fischer, J. (2010). Domestic violence against women in Cambodia: Husband's control, frequency of spousal discussion, and domestic violence reported by Cambodian women. *Journal of Family Violence, 25,* 237–246. doi:10.1007/s10896-009-9287-7

Erikson, E. H. (1950). *Childhood and society* (2nd ed.). New York, NY: Norton.

Fedewa, A. L., Black, W. W., & Ahn, S. (2014). Children and adolescents with same-gender parents: A meta-analytic approach in assessing outcomes. *Journal of GLBT Family Studies, 11,* 1–34. doi:10.1080/155042 8X.2013.869486

Felker, J. A., Fromme, D. K., Arnaut, G. L., & Stoll, B. M. (2002). A qualitative analysis of stepfamilies: The stepparent. *Journal of Divorce & Remarriage, 38,* 125.

Fincham, F. D., & Beach, S. R. H. (2010). Marriage in the new millennium: A decade in review. *Journal of Marriage and Family, 72,* 630–649. doi:10.1111/j.1741-3737.2010.00722.x

Finkel, E. J., Eastwick, P. W., Karney, B. R., Reis, H. T., & Sprecher, S. (2012). Online dating: A critical analysis from the perspective of psychological science. *Psychological Science in the Public Interest, 13,* 3–66. http://doi.org/10.1177/1529100612436522

Fischer, M. J. (2008). Does campus diversity promote friendship diversity? A look at interracial friendships in college. *Social Science Quarterly, 89,* 631–655. doi:10.1111/j.1540-6237.2008.00552.x

Fletcher, G. J. O., Kerr, P. S. G., Li, N. P., & Valentine, K. A. (2014). Predicting romantic interest and decisions in the very early stages of mate selection. *Personality and Social Psychology Bulletin, 40,* 540–550. doi:10.1177/0146167213519481

Frejka, T. (2017). Childlessness in the United States. In M. Kreyenfeld & D. Konietzka (Eds.), *Childlessness in Europe: Contexts, causes, and consequences* (pp. 159–179). Cham, Switzerland: Springer. doi:10.1007/978-3-319-44667-7_8

Frost, D. M., Meyer, I. H., & Hammack, P. L. (2015). Health and well-being in emerging adults' same-sex relationships: Critical questions and directions for research in developmental science. *Emerging Adulthood, 3,* 3–13. doi:10.1177/2167696814535915

Fullwood, C., & Attrill-Smith, A. (2018). Up-dating: Ratings of perceived dating success are better online than offline. *Cyberpsychology, Behavior, and Social Networking, 21,* 11–15. http://doi.org/10.1089/cyber.2016.0631

Gadassi, R., Bar-Nahum, L. E., Newhouse, S., Anderson, R., Heiman, J. R., Rafaeli, E., & Janssen, E. (2016). Perceived partner responsiveness mediates the association between sexual and marital satisfaction: A daily diary study in newlywed couples. *Archives of Sexual Behavior, 45,* 109–120. doi:10.1007/s10508-014-0448-2

Galatzer-Levy, I. R., Mazursky, H., Mancini, A. D., & Bonanno, G. A. (2011). What we don't expect when expecting: Evidence for heterogeneity in subjective well-being in response to parenthood. *Journal of Family Psychology, 25,* 384–392. doi:10.1037/a0023759

Ganong, L., Coleman, M., Fine, M., & Martin, P. (1999). Stepparents' affinity-seeking and affinity-maintaining strategies with stepchildren. *Journal of Family Issues, 20,* 299–327.

Ganong, L. H., & Coleman, M. (2000). Remarried families. In C. Hendrick & S. S. Hendrick (Eds.), *Close relationships* (pp. 155–168). Thousand Oaks, CA: Sage.

Gao, G. (2001). Intimacy, passion and commitment in Chinese and US American romantic relationships. *International Journal of Intercultural Relations, 25,* 329–342.

Gartrell, N., & Bos, H. (2010). US National Longitudinal Lesbian Family study: Psychological adjustment of 17-year-old adolescents. *Pediatrics, 126,* 28–36. doi:10.1542/peds2009-3153

Gates, G. J. (2013). *LGBT parenting in the United States.* Retrieved from http://williamsinstitute.law.ucla.edu/wp-content/uploads/LGBT-Parenting.pdf

Gillespie, B. J., Lever, J., Frederick, D., & Royce, T. (2015). Close adult friendships, gender, and the life cycle. *Journal of Social and Personal Relationships, 32,* 709–736. doi:10.1177/0265407514546977

Giordano, P. C., Copp, J. E., Longmore, M. A., & Manning, W. D. (2016). Anger, control, and intimate partner violence in young adulthood. *Journal of Family Violence, 31,* 1–13. doi:10.1007/s10896-015-9753-3

Goldberg, A. E., & Perry-Jenkins, M. (2007). The division of labor and perceptions of parental roles: Lesbian couples across the transition to parenthood. *Journal of Social & Personal Relationships, 24,* 297–318. doi:10.1177/0265407507075415

Goldsen, J., Bryan, A. E. B., Kim, H. J., Muraco, A., Jen, S., & Fredriksen-Goldsen, K. I. (2017). Who says I do: The changing context of marriage and health and quality of life for LGBT older adults. *The Gerontologist, 57*(Suppl. 1), S50–S62. doi:10.1093/geront/gnw174

Gonzaga, G. C., Campos, B., & Bradbury, T. (2007). Similarity, convergence, and relationship satisfaction in dating and married couples. *Journal of Personality and Social Psychology, 93,* 34–48.

Gosselin, J. (2010). Individual and family factors related to psychosocial adjustment in stepmother families with adolescents. *Journal of Divorce & Remarriage, 51,* 108–123. doi:10.1080/10502550903455174

Gottman, J., & Gottman, J. (2017). The natural principles of love. *Journal of Family Theory & Review, 9,* 7–26. doi:10.1111/jftr.12182

Graefe, D. R., & Lichter, D. T. (2007). When unwed mothers marry. *Journal of Family Issues, 28,* 595–622.

Graham, J. M. (2011). Measuring love in romantic relationships: A meta-analysis. *Journal of Social and Personal Relationships, 28,* 748–771. doi:10.1177/0265407510389126

Gravningen, K., Mitchell, K. R., Wellings, K., Johnson, A. M., Geary, R., Jones, K. G., . . . Mercer, C. H. (2017). Reported reasons for breakdown of marriage and cohabitation in Britain: Findings from the third National Survey of Sexual Attitudes and Lifestyles (Natsal-3). *PLoS ONE, 12,* e0174129. doi:10.1371/journal.pone.0174129

Greenstein, T. N. (2009). National context, family satisfaction, and fairness in the division of household labor. *Journal of Marriage & Family, 71,* 1039–1051. doi:10.1111/j.1741-3737.2009.00651.x

Grover, R. L., Nangle, D. W., Serwik, A., & Zeff, K. R. (2007). Girl friend, boy friend, girlfriend, boyfriend: Broadening our understanding of heterosocial competence. *Journal of Clinical Child & Adolescent Psychology, 36,* 491–502.

Grover, S., & Helliwell, J. F. (2014). *How's life at home? New evidence on marriage and the set point for happiness.* Retrieved from http://www.nber.org/papers/w20794

Guzzo, K. B. (2014). Trends in cohabitation outcomes: Compositional changes and engagement among never-married young adults. *Journal of Marriage and the Family, 76,* 826–842. doi:10.1111/jomf.12123

Hadley, R., & Hanley, T. (2011). Involuntarily childless men and the desire for fatherhood. *Journal of Reproductive and Infant Psychology, 29,* 56–68. doi:10.1080/0264683 8.2010.544294

Hall, J. A. (2016). Same-sex friendships. In C. R. Berger, M. E. Roloff, S. R. Wilson, J. P. Dillard, J. Caughlin, & D. Solomon (Eds.), *The international encyclopedia of interpersonal communication* (pp. 1–8). Hoboken, NJ: John Wiley. doi:10.1002/9781118540190.wbeic138

Hall, J. A., Park, N., Hayeon, S., & Michael, J. C. (2010). Strategic misrepresentation in online dating: The effects of gender, self-monitoring, and personality traits. *Journal of Social & Personal Relationships, 27,* 117–135. http://doi.org/10.1177/0265407509349633

Hamilton, B. E., Martin, J. A., Osterman, M., Curtin, S. C., & Mathews, T. J. (2015). Births: Final data for 2014. *National Vital Statistics Reports Statistics Reports, 64*, 1–64.

Hancock, J. T., & Toma, C. L. (2009). Putting your best face forward: The accuracy of online dating photographs. *Journal of Communication, 59*, 367–386. doi:10.1111/j.1460-2466.2009.01420.x

Hanzal, A., & Segrin, C. (2009). The role of conflict resolution styles in mediating the relationship between enduring vulnerabilities and marital quality. *Journal of Family Communication, 9*, 150–169. doi:10.1080/15267430902945612

Härkönen, J. (2015). Divorce. In J. Treas, J. Scott, & M. Richards (Eds.), *The Wiley Blackwell companion to the sociology of families* (pp. 303–322). New York, NY: John Wiley.

Harris, E. A. (2017). Same-sex parents still face legal complications. *New York Times.* Retrieved March 24, 2018, from https://www.nytimes.com/2017/06/20/us/gay-pride-lgbtq-same-sex-parents.html

Hart, D., & Life, A. V. (2017). The role of civic and political participation in successful early adulthood. In L. M. Padilla-Walker & L. J. Nelson (Eds.), Flourishing in emerging adulthood: Positive development during the third decade of life (pp. 139–166). Oxford, UK: Oxford University Press.

Hartup, W. W., & Stevens, N. (1999). Friendships and adaptation across the life span. *Current Directions in Psychological Science, 8*, 76–79.

Harway, M., & Hansen, M. (2004). *Spouse abuse: Assessing & treating battered women, batterers, & their children* (2nd ed.). Sarasota, FL: Professional Resource Press/Professional Resource Exchange.

Hasford, J., Abbott, K., Alisat, S., Pancer, S. M., & Pratt, M. W. (2017). Community involvement and narrative identity in emerging and young adulthood: A longitudinal analysis. *Identity, 17*, 40–54. http://doi.org/10.1080/15283488.2016.1268962

Hatzenbuehler, M. L. (2014). Structural stigma and the health of lesbian, gay, and bisexual populations. *Current Directions in Psychological Science, 23*, 127–132. doi:10.1177/0963721414523775

Helms, H. M., Walls, J. K., Crouter, A. C., & McHale, S. M. (2010). Provider role attitudes, marital satisfaction, role overload, and housework: A dyadic approach. *Journal of Family Psychology, 24*, 568–577. doi:10.1037/a0020637

Hendrick, C., & Hendrick, S. S. (2004). Sex and romantic love: Connects and disconnects. In J. H. Harvey, A. Wenzel, & S. Sprecher (Eds.), *The handbook of sexuality in close relationships* (pp. 159–182). Mahwah, NJ: Lawrence Erlbaum.

Henehan, D., Rothblum, E. D., Solomon, S. E., & Balsam, K. F. (2007). Social and demographic characteristics of gay, lesbian, and heterosexual adults with and without children. *Journal of GLBT Family Studies, 3*, 35–79.

Hennon, C. B., Hildenbrand, B., & Schedle, A. (2008). Stepfamilies and children. In T. P. Gullotta & G. M. Blau (Eds.), *Family influences on childhood behavior and development: Evidence-based prevention and treatment*

approaches (pp. 161–185). New York, NY: Routledge/Taylor & Francis.

Henry, P. J., & McCue, J. (2009). The experience of nonresidential stepmothers. *Journal of Divorce & Remarriage, 50*, 185–205. doi:10.1080/10502550902717780

Hetherington, E. M., & Stanley-Hagan, M. (2002). Parenting in divorced and remarried families. In M. H. Bornstein (Ed.), *Handbook of parenting* (2nd ed., Vol. 3, pp. 287–315). Mahwah, NJ: Lawrence Erlbaum.

Hiekel, N., Liefbroer, A. C., & Poortman, A.-R. (2014). Understanding diversity in the meaning of cohabitation across Europe. *European Journal of Population, 30*, 391–410. doi:10.1007/s10680-014-9321-1

Holt, L. J., Mattanah, J. F., & Long, M. W. (2018). Change in parental and peer relationship quality during emerging adulthood. *Journal of Social and Personal Relationships, 35*, 743–769. doi:10.1177/0265407517697856

Holt-Lunstad, J., Smith, T. B., & Layton, J. B. (2010). Social relationships and mortality risk: A meta-analytic review. *PLoS Medicine, 7*, e1000316. doi:10.1371/journal.pmed.1000316

Hopmeyer, A., & Medovoy, T. (2017). Emerging adults' self-identified peer crowd affiliations, risk behavior, and social–emotional adjustment in college. *Emerging Adulthood, 5*, 143–148. doi:10.1177/2167696816665055

Hopmeyer, A., Troop-Gordon, W., Medovoy, T., & Fischer, J. (2017). Emerging adults' self-identified peer crowd affiliations and college adjustment. *Social Psychology of Education, 20*, 643–667. doi:10.1007/s11218-017-9390-1

Hsueh, A. C., Morrison, K. R., & Doss, B. D. (2009). Qualitative reports of problems in cohabiting relationships: Comparisons to married and dating relationships. *Journal of Family Psychology, 23*, 236–246. doi:10.1037/a0015364

Huijts, T., Kraaykamp, G., & Subramanian, S. V. (2011). Childlessness and psychological well-being in context: A multilevel study on 24 European countries. *European Sociological Review, 29*, 32–47. doi:10.1093/esr/jcr037

Huxhold, O., Miche, M., & Schüz, B. (2014). Benefits of having friends in older ages: Differential effects of informal social activities on well-being in middle-aged and older adults. *Journal of Gerontology Series B: Psychological Sciences and Social Sciences, 69*, 366–75. doi:10.1093/geronb/gbt029

Ingraham, C. (2018). *The world's richest countries guarantee mothers more than a year of paid maternity leave. The U.S. guarantees them nothing.* Retrieved May 26, 2018, from https://www.washingtonpost.com/news/wonk/wp/2018/02/05/the-worlds-richest-countries-guarantee-mothers-more-than-a-year-of-paid-maternity-leave-the-u-s-guarantees-them-nothing/?noredirect=on&utm_term=.5f0bac431041

Jackson, J. B. (2018). The ambiguous loss of singlehood: Conceptualizing and treating singlehood ambiguous loss among never-married adults. *Contemporary Family Therapy, 40*, 210–222. doi:10.1007/s10591-018-9455-0

Jackson, J. B., Miller, R. B., Oka, M., & Henry, R. G. (2014). Gender differences in marital

satisfaction: A meta-analysis. *Journal of Marriage and Family, 76*, 105–129. doi:10.1111/jomf.12077

Jasinski, J., Blumenstein, L., & Morgan, R. (2014). Testing Johnson's typology: Is there gender symmetry in intimate terrorism? *Violence and Victims, 29*, 73–88. doi:10.1891/0886-6708.VV-D-12-00146

Jensen, T. M., & Howard, M. O. (2015). Perceived stepparent–child relationship quality: A systematic review of stepchildren's perspectives. *Marriage & Family Review, 51*, 99–153. doi:10.1080/01494929.2015.1006717

Jose, A., Daniel O'Leary, K., & Moyer, A. (2010). Does premarital cohabitation predict subsequent marital stability and marital quality? A meta-analysis. *Journal of Marriage & Family, 72*, 105–116. doi:10.1111/j.1741-3737.2009.00686.x

Kail, B. L., Acosta, K. L., & Wright, E. R. (2015). State-level marriage equality and the health of same-sex couples. *American Journal of Public Health, 105*, 1101–1105. doi:10.2105/AJPH.2015.302589

Katz-Wise, S. L., Priess, H. A., & Hyde, J. S. (2010). Gender-role attitudes and behavior across the transition to parenthood. *Developmental Psychology, 46*, 18–28. doi:10.1037/a0017820

Kaufman-Parks, A. M., DeMaris, A., Giordano, P. C., Manning, W. D., & Longmore, M. A. (2018). Familial effects on intimate partner violence perpetration across adolescence and young adulthood. *Journal of Family Issues.* Advance online publication. doi:10.1177/0192513X17734586

Ko, K. J., Berg, C. A., Butner, J., Uchino, B. N., & Smith, T. W. (2007). Profiles of successful aging in middle-aged and older adult married couples. *Psychology and Aging, 22*, 705–718.

Koball, H. L., Moiduddin, E., Henderson, J., Goesling, B., & Besculides, M. (2010). What do we know about the link between marriage and health? *Journal of Family Issues, 31*, 1019–1040. doi:10.1177/0192513X10365834

Koivunen, J. M., Rothaupt, J. W., & Wolfgram, S. M. (2009). Gender dynamics and role adjustment during the transition to parenthood: Current perspectives. *Family Journal, 17*, 323–328. doi:10.1177/1066480709347360

Koropeckyj-Cox, T., & Pendell, G. (2007). Attitudes about childlessness in the United States. *Journal of Family Issues, 28*, 1054–1082.

Koropeckyj-Cox, T., Romano, V. R., & Moras, A. (2007). Through the lenses of gender, race, and class: Students' perceptions of childless/childfree individuals and couples. *Sex Roles, 56*, 415–428.

Krebs, C., Breiding, M. J., Browne, A., & Warner, T. (2011). The association between different types of intimate partner violence experienced by women. *Journal of Family Violence, 26*, 487–500. doi:10.1007/s10896-011-9383-3

Kreider, R. M., & Ellis, R. (2011). Number, timing, and duration of marriages and divorces: 2009. *Current Population Reports.* Retrieved from https://www.census.gov/prod/2011pubs/p70-125.pdf

Kulik, L., & Havusha-Morgenstern, H. (2011). Does cohabitation matter? Differences in initial marital adjustment among women who cohabited and those who did not. *Families in Society: Journal of Contemporary Social Services, 92*, 120–127.

Kurdek, L. A. (2006). Differences between partners from heterosexual, gay, and lesbian cohabiting couples. *Journal of Marriage & Family, 68*, 509–528.

Kurdek, L. A. (2007). The allocation of household labor by partners in gay and lesbian couples. *Journal of Family Issues, 28*, 132–148. doi:10.1177/0192513X06292019

Langenderfer-Magruder, L., Whitfield, D. L., Walls, N. E., Kattari, S. K., & Ramos, D. (2016). Experiences of intimate partner violence and subsequent police reporting among lesbian, gay, bisexual, transgender, and queer adults in Colorado. *Journal of Interpersonal Violence, 31*, 855–871. doi:10.1177/0886260514556767

Lapsley, D., & Hardy, S. A. (2017). Identity formation and moral development in emerging adulthood. In L. M. Padilla-Walker & L. J. Nelson (Eds.), *Flourishing in emerging adulthood: Positive development during the third decade of life* (pp. 14–39). Oxford, UK: Oxford University Press. doi:10.1093/acprof:oso/9780190260637.003.0002

Lavelle, B., & Smock, P. J. (2012). Divorce and women's risk of health insurance loss. *Journal of Health and Social Behavior, 53*, 413–431. doi:10.1177/0022146512465758

Lavner, J. A., & Bradbury, T. N. (2012). Why do even satisfied newlyweds eventually go on to divorce? *Journal of Family Psychology, 26*, 1–10. doi:10.1037/a0025966

Lavner, J. A., & Bradbury, T. N. (2014). Marital satisfaction change over newlywed years. In A. C. Michalos (Ed.), *Encyclopedia of quality of life and well-being research* (pp. 3811–3815). Dordrecht: Springer Netherlands. doi:10.1007/978-94-007-0753-5_3856

Lavner, J. A., Waterman, J., & Peplau, L. A. (2014). Parent adjustment over time in gay, lesbian, and heterosexual parent families adopting from foster care. *American Journal of Orthopsychiatry, 84*, 46–53. doi:10.1037/h0098853

Lawrence, E., Rothman, A. D., Cobb, R. J., & Bradbury, T. N. (2010). Marital satisfaction across the transition to parenthood: Three eras of research. In M. S. Schulz, M. K. Pruett, P. K. Kerig, & R. D. Parke (Eds.), *Strengthening couple relationships for optimal child development: Lessons from research and intervention* (pp. 97–114). Washington, DC: American Psychological Association. doi:10.1037/12058-007

Le, Y., McDaniel, B. T., Leavitt, C. E., & Feinberg, M. E. (2016). Longitudinal associations between relationship quality and coparenting across the transition to parenthood: A dyadic perspective. *Journal of Family Psychology, 30*, 918–926. doi:10.1037/fam0000217

Leikas, S., Ilmarinen, V. J., Verkasalo, M., Vartiainen, H. L., & Lönnqvist, J. E. (2018). Relationship satisfaction and similarity of personality traits, personal values, and attitudes. *Personality and Individual Differences, 123*, 191–198. doi:10.1016/J.PAID.2017.11.024

Leone, J. M., Lape, M. E., & Xu, Y. (2013). Women's decisions to not seek formal help for partner violence: A comparison of intimate terrorism

and situational couple violence. *Journal of Interpersonal Violence, 29*, 1850–1876. doi:10.1177/0886260513511701

Lesthaeghe, R. J., López-Colás, J., & Neidert, L. (2016). The social geography of unmarried cohabitation in the USA, 2007–2011. In A. Esteve & R. J. Lesthaeghe (Eds.), *Cohabitation and marriage in the Americas: Geo-historical legacies and new trends* (pp. 101–131). Cham, Switzerland: Springer International. doi:10.1007/978-3-319-31442-6_4

Levesque, D. A., Velicer, W. F., & Castle, P. H. (2008). Resistance among domestic violence offenders: Measurement development and initial validation. *Violence Against Women, 14*, 158–184.

Lewis, R. J., Mason, T. B., Winstead, B. A., & Kelley, M. L. (2017). Empirical investigation of a model of sexual minority specific and general risk factors for intimate partner violence among lesbian women. *Psychology of Violence, 7*, 110–119. doi:10.1037/vio0000036

Li, N. P., Yong, J. C., Tov, W., Sng, O., Fletcher, G. J. O., Valentine, K. A., . . . Balliet, D. (2013). Mate preferences do predict attraction and choices in the early stages of mate selection. *Journal of Personality and Social Psychology, 105*, 757–776. doi:10.1037/a0033777

Livingston, G. (2014). *Four-in-ten couples are saying "I do," again.* Retrieved from http://www.pewsocialtrends.org/2014/11/14/four-in-ten-couples-are-saying-i-do-again/

Livingston, G. (2015). *Childlessness.* Retrieved from http://www.pewsocialtrends.org/2015/05/07/childlessness/

Low, S., Tiberio, S. S., Shortt, J. W., Capaldi, D. M., & Eddy, J. M. (2017). Associations of couples' intimate partner violence in young adulthood and substance use: A dyadic approach. *Psychology of Violence, 7*, 120–127. doi:10.1037/vio0000038

Lundberg, S. J., & Pollak, R. A. (2016). The evolving role of marriage: 1950–2010. *The Future of Children, 25*, 29–50. Retrieved from http://dspace.uib.no/handle/1956/12486

Lutz-Zois, C. J., Bradley, A. C., Mihalik, J. L., & Moorman-Eavers, E. R. (2006). Perceived similarity and relationship success among dating couples: An idiographic approach. *Journal of Social & Personal Relationships, 23*, 865–880.

Mancini, A. D., Bonanno, G. A., & Clark, A. E. (2011). Stepping off the hedonic treadmill. *Journal of Individual Differences, 32*, 144–152. doi:10.1027/1614-0001/a000047

Manning, W. D. (2013). *Trends in cohabitation: Over twenty years of change, 1987–2010* (FP-13-12). Bowling Green, OH: National Center for Family & Marriage Research. Retrieved from http://ncfmr.bgsu.edu/pdf/family_profiles/file130944.pdf

Manning, W. D., & Cohen, J. A. (2012). Premarital cohabitation and marital dissolution: An examination of recent marriages. *Journal of Marriage and the Family, 74*, 377–387. doi:10.1111/j.1741-3737.2012.00960.x

Manning, W. D., Longmore, M. A., & Giordano, P. C. (2018). Cohabitation and intimate partner violence during emerging adulthood: High constraints and low commitment.

Journal of Family Issues, 39, 1030–1055. doi:10.1177/0192513X16686132

Markey, P. M., & Markey, C. N. (2007). Romantic ideals, romantic obtainment, and relationship experiences: The complementarity of interpersonal traits among romantic partners. *Journal of Social & Personal Relationships, 24*, 517–533.

Markowitz, D. M., & Hancock, J. T. (2018). Deception in mobile dating conversations. *Journal of Communication, 68*, 547–569. http://doi.org/10.1093/joc/jqy019

Markstrom, C. A., & Kalmanir, H. M. (2001). Linkages between the psychosocial stages of identity and intimacy and the ego strengths of fidelity and love. *Identity, 1*, 179–196.

Matthews, T. J., & Hamilton, B. E. (2002). Mean age of mother, 1970–2000. *National Vital and Statistics Reports, 51*. Retrieved from https://www.cdc.gov/nchs/data/nvsr/nvsr51/nvsr51_01.pdf

Matthews, T. J., & Hamilton, B. E. (2016). *Mean age of mothers is on the rise: United States, 2000–2014.* Retrieved from https://www.cdc.gov/nchs/products/databriefs/db232.htm

Meier, A., & Allen, G. (2008). Intimate relationship development during the transition to adulthood: Differences by social class. *New Directions for Child & Adolescent Development, 2008*, 25–39.

Mills, M., Rindfuss, R. R., McDonald, P., & te Velde, E. (2011). Why do people postpone parenthood? Reasons and social policy incentives. *Human Reproduction Update, 17*, 848–860.

Moss, P., & Deven, F. (2006). Leave policies and research: A cross-national overview. *Marriage & Family Review, 39*, 255–285.

Movement Advancement Project. (2018). *Foster and adoption laws.* Retrieved March 24, 2018, from http://www.lgbtmap.org/equality-maps/foster_and_adoption_laws

Næss, S., Blekesaune, M., & Jakobsson, N. (2015). Marital transitions and life satisfaction. *Acta Sociologica, 58*, 63–78. doi:10.1177/0001699314563841

National Center for Health Statistics. (2015). *Provisional number of divorces and annulments and rate: United States, 2000–2011.* Retrieved June 5, 2015, from http://www.cdc.gov/nchs/nvss/marriage_divorce_tables.htm

National Conference of State Legislatures. (2018). *Paid family leave resources.* Retrieved May 26, 2018, from http://www.ncsl.org/research/labor-and-employment/paid-family-leave-resources.aspx

Neff, L. A., & Karney, B. R. (2017). Acknowledging the elephant in the room: How stressful environmental contexts shape relationship dynamics. *Current Opinion in Psychology, 13*, 107–110. doi:10.1016/J.COPSYC.2016.05.013

Nelson, S. K., Kushlev, K., & Lyubomirsky, S. (2014). The pains and pleasures of parenting: When, why, and how is parenthood associated with more or less well-being? *Psychological Bulletin, 140*, 846–895. doi:10.1037/a0035444

Neugarten, B. L. (1979). Time, age, and the life cycle. *American Journal of Psychiatry, 136*, 887–894.

Neugarten, B. L., & Neugarten, D. A. (1996). *The meanings of age: Selected papers of Bernice L. Neugarten.* Chicago, IL: University of Chicago Press.

Ng, T. K., & Cheng, H. K. C. (2010). The effects of intimacy, passion, and commitment on satisfaction in romantic relationships among Hong Kong Chinese people. *Journal of Psychology in Chinese Societies, 11,* 123–146.

Nichols, W. C., & Pace-Nichols, M. A. (2000). Childless married couples. In W. C. Nichols, M. A. Pace-Nichols, D. S. Becvar, & A. Y. Napier (Eds.), *Handbook of family development and intervention* (pp. 171–188). Hoboken, NJ: John Wiley.

Nicolaisen, M., & Thorsen, K. (2017). What are friends for? Friendships and loneliness over the lifespan—From 18 to 79 years. *International Journal of Aging and Human Development, 84,* 126–158. doi:10.1177/0091415016655166

Nilsen, A. B. V., Waldenström, U., Hjelmstedt, A., Hjelmsted, A., Rasmussen, S., & Schytt, E. (2012). Characteristics of women who are pregnant with their first baby at an advanced age. *Acta Obstetricia et Gynecologica Scandinavica, 91,* 353–362x. doi:10.1111/j.1600-0412.2011.01335.x

O'Laughlin, E. M., & Anderson, V. N. (2001). Perceptions of parenthood among young adults: Implications for career and family planning. *American Journal of Family Therapy, 29,* 95–108.

Ogolsky, B. G., Dennison, R. P., & Monk, J. K. (2014). The role of couple discrepancies in cognitive and behavioral egalitarianism in marital quality. *Sex Roles, 70,* 329–342. doi:10.1007/s11199-014-0365-9

Perelli-Harris, B., & Gassen, N. S. (2012). How similar are cohabitation and marriage? Legal approaches to cohabitation across Western Europe. *Population and Development Review, 38,* 435–467. doi:10.1111/j.1728-4457.2012.00511.x

Perrig-Chiello, P., Hutchison, S., & Morselli, D. (2014). Patterns of psychological adaptation to divorce after a long-term marriage. *Journal of Social and Personal Relationships, 32,* 386–405. doi:10.1177/0265407514533769

Perrin, E. C., & Siegel, B. S. (2013). Promoting the well-being of children whose parents are gay or lesbian. *Pediatrics, 131,* e1374–e1383. doi:10.1542/peds.2013-0377

Peterson, B. D., Gold, L., & Feingold, T. (2007). The experience and influence of infertility: Considerations for couple counselors. *Family Journal, 15,* 251–257.

Peterson, C. C. (1996). The ticking of the social clock: Adults' beliefs about the timing of transition events. *International Journal of Aging & Human Development, 42,* 189.

Pettee, K. K., Brach, J. S., Kriska, A. M., Boudreau, R., Richardson, C. R., Colbert, L. H., . . . Newman, A. B. (2006). Influence of marital status on physical activity levels among older adults. *Medicine & Science in Sports & Exercise, 38,* 541–546.

Pew Research Center. (2015). *Gay marriage around the world.* Retrieved from http://www.pewforum.org/2013/12/19/gay-marriage-around-the-world-2013/

Pew Research Center. (2017). *Changing attitudes on gay marriage | Pew Research Center.*

Retrieved March 16, 2018, from http://www.pewforum.org/fact-sheet/changing-attitudes-on-gay-marriage/

Pollitt, A. M., Robinson, B. A., & Umberson, D. (2018). Gender conformity, perceptions of shared power, and marital quality in same- and different-sex marriages. *Gender & Society, 32,* 109–131. doi:10.1177/0891243217742110

Popenoe, D. (2009). Cohabitation, marriage, and child wellbeing: A cross-national perspective. *Society, 46,* 429–436. doi:10.1007/s12115-009-9242-5

Prendergast, S., & MacPhee, D. (2018). Family resilience amid stigma and discrimination: A conceptual model for families headed by same-sex parents. *Family Relations, 67,* 26–40. doi:10.1111/fare.12296

Raley, J. A., Fisher, W. M., Halder, R., & Shanmugan, K. (2013). Child custody and homosexual/bisexual parents: A survey of judges. *Journal of Child Custody, 10,* 54–67. doi:10.1080/15379418.2013.781843

Raley, R. K., Sweeney, M. M., & Wondra, D. (2015). The growing racial and ethnic divide in U.S. marriage patterns. *The Future of Children, 25,* 89–109. Retrieved from http://www.ncbi.nlm.nih.gov/pubmed/27134512

Ramos Salazar, L. (2015). The negative reciprocity process in marital relationships: A literature review. *Aggression and Violent Behavior, 24,* 113–119. doi:10.1016/j.avb.2015.05.008

Ratelle, C. F., Carbonneau, N., Vallerand, R. J., & Mageau, G. (2013). Passion in the romantic sphere: A look at relational outcomes. *Motivation and Emotion, 37,* 106–120. doi:10.1007/s11031-012-9286-5

Reeder, H. (2017). "He's like a brother": The social construction of satisfying cross-sex friendship roles. *Sexuality & Culture, 21,* 142–162. doi:10.1007/s12119-016-9387-5

Reinhold, S. (2010). Reassessing the link between premarital cohabitation and marital instability. *Demography, 47,* 719–733. doi:10.1353/dem.0.0122

Rekker, R., Keijsers, L., Branje, S., & Meeus, W. (2017). The dynamics of political identity and issue attitudes in adolescence and early adulthood. *Electoral Studies, 46,* 101–111. http://doi.org/10.1016/J.ELECTSTUD.2017.02.005

Rhoades, G. K., Stanley, S. M., & Markman, H. J. (2009). The pre-engagement cohabitation effect: A replication and extension of previous findings. *Journal of Family Psychology, 23,* 107–111. doi:10.1037/a0014358

Richards, T. N., Tillyer, M. S., & Wright, E. M. (2017). Intimate partner violence and the overlap of perpetration and victimization: Considering the influence of physical, sexual, and emotional abuse in childhood. *Child Abuse & Neglect, 67,* 240–248. doi:10.1016/J.CHIABU.2017.02.037

Riggle, E. D. B., Rostosky, S. S., & Horne, S. G. (2010). Psychological distress, well-being, and legal recognition in same-sex couple relationships. *Journal of Family Psychology, 24,* 82–86. doi:10.1037/a0017942

Riggle, E. D. B., Wickham, R. E., Rostosky, S. S., Rothblum, E. D., & Balsam, K. F. (2017). Impact of civil marriage recognition for long-term same-sex couples. *Sexuality Research*

and Social Policy, 14, 223–232. doi:10.1007/s13178-016-0243-z

Robles, T. F. (2014). Marital quality and health: Implications for marriage in the 21st century. *Current Directions in Psychological Science, 23,* 427–432. doi:10.1177/0963721414549043

Rosen, L. D., Cheever, N. A., Cummings, C., & Felt, J. (2008). The impact of emotionality and self-disclosure on online dating versus traditional dating. *Computers in Human Behavior, 24,* 2124–2157. http://doi.org/10.1016/j.chb.2007.10.003

Rosenfeld, M. J. (2014). Couple longevity in the era of same-sex marriage in the United States. *Journal of Marriage and Family, 76,* 905–918. doi:10.1111/jomf.12141

Rostosky, S. S., & Riggle, E. D. B. (2017). Same-sex couple relationship strengths: A review and synthesis of the empirical literature (2000–2016). *Psychology of Sexual Orientation and Gender Diversity, 4,* 1–13. doi:10.1037/sgd0000216

Roy, R. N., Schumm, W. R., & Britt., S. L. (2014). Voluntary versus involuntary childlessness. In R. N. Roy, W. R. Schumm & S. L. Britt (Eds.), *Transition to parenthood* (pp. 49–68). New York, NY: Springer.

Rubin, H., & Campbell, L. (2012). Day-to-day changes in intimacy predict heightened relationship passion, sexual occurrence, and sexual satisfaction: A dyadic diary analysis. *Social Psychological and Personality Science, 3,* 224–231. doi:10.1177/1948550611416520

Sahadi, J. (2016). *It's good to be a working parent in Europe.* Retrieved May 26, 2018, from http://money.cnn.com/2016/02/17/pf/working-parents-paid-leave/index.html

Sánchez Gassen, N., & Perelli-Harris, B. (2015). The increase in cohabitation and the role of union status in family policies: A comparison of 12 European countries. *Journal of European Social Policy, 25,* 431–449. doi:10.1177/0958928715594561

Sanderson, C. A., Rahm, K. B., & Beigbeder, S. A. (2005). The link between the pursuit of intimacy goals and satisfaction in close same-sex friendships: An examination of the underlying processes. *Journal of Social & Personal Relationships, 22,* 75–98.

Sarkisian, N., & Gerstel, N. (2016). Does singlehood isolate or integrate? Examining the link between marital status and ties to kin, friends, and neighbors. *Journal of Social and Personal Relationships, 33,* 361–384. doi:10.1177/0265407515597564

Sassler, S., & Miller, A. J. (2011). Class differences in cohabitation processes. *Family Relations, 60,* 163–177. doi:10.1111/j.1741-3729.2010.00640.x

Sbarra, D. A., & Coan, J. A. (2017). Divorce and health: Good data in need of better theory. *Current Opinion in Psychology, 13,* 91–95. doi:10.1016/j.copsyc.2016.05.014

Sbarra, D. A., Hasselmo, K., & Bourassa, K. J. (2015). Divorce and health: Beyond individual differences. *Current Directions in Psychological Science, 24,* 109–113. doi:10.1177/0963721414559125

Sbarra, D. A., Law, R. W., & Portley, R. M. (2011). Divorce and death: A meta-analysis and research agenda for clinical, social, and health psychology. *Perspectives* on Psychological Science, 6, 454–474. doi:10.1177/1745691611414724

Schmidt, L., Sobotka, T., Bentzen, J. G., & Nyboe Andersen, A. (2012). Demographic and medical consequences of the postponement of parenthood. Human Reproduction Update, 18, 29–43. doi:10.1093/humupd/dmr040

Schwartz, S. J., Zamboanga, B. L., Luyckx, K., Meca, A., & Ritchie, R. (2015). Identity in emerging adulthood. In J. J. Arnett (Ed.), The Oxford handbook of emerging adulthood (pp. 401–420). Oxford, UK: Oxford University Press. http://doi.org/10.1093/oxfordhb/9780199795574.013.001

Seiffge-Krenke, I. (2003). Testing theories of romantic development from adolescence to young adulthood: Evidence of a developmental sequence. International Journal of Behavioral Development, 27, 519–531. doi:10.1080/01650250344000145

Shapiro, D. N., & Stewart, A. J. (2011). Parenting stress, perceived child regard, and depressive symptoms among stepmothers and biological mothers. Family Relations, 60, 533–544. doi:10.1111/j.1741-3729.2011.00665.x

Sharp, E. A., & Ganong, L. (2007). Living in the gray: Women's experiences of missing the marital transition. Journal of Marriage and Family, 69, 831–844. doi:10.1111/j.1741-3737.2007.00408.x

Sherrod, L. R. (2015). Recognizing civic engagement as a critical domain of human development. Research in Human Development, 12, 312–318. http://doi.org/10.1080/15427609.2015.1068040

Shortt, J. W., Low, S., Capaldi, D.M., Eddy, J. M., & Tiberio, S. S. (2016). Predicting intimate partner violence for at-risk young adults and their romantic partner—NCJ 250668. Retrieved March 21, 2018, from https://www.ncjrs.gov/App/Publications/abstract.aspx?ID=272836

Shulman, S., & Connolly, J. (2013). The challenge of romantic relationships in emerging adulthood: Reconceptualization of the field. Emerging Adulthood, 1, 27–39. doi:10.1177/2167696812467330

Simpson, J. A., & Rholes, W. S. (2019). Adult attachment orientations and well-being during the transition to parenthood. Current Opinion in Psychology, 25, 47–52. doi:10.1016/J.COPSYC.2018.02.019

Smith, A., & Anderson, M. (2016). 5 Facts about online dating | Pew Research Center. Retrieved May 24, 2018, from http://www.pewresearch.org/fact-tank/2016/02/29/5-facts-about-online-dating/

Smith, A., & Duggan, M. (2013). Online dating & relationships. Retrieved from http://www.pewinternet.org/2013/10/21/online-dating-relationships/

Smith, S. G., Basile, K. C., Gilbert, L. K., Merrick, M. T., Patel, N., Walling, M., & Jain, A. (2017). National intimate partner and sexual violence survey (NISVS): 2010–2012 state report. Retrieved from https://stacks.cdc.gov/view/cdc/46305

Smithson, M., & Baker, C. (2008). Risk orientation, loving, and liking in long-term romantic relationships. Journal of Social & Personal Relationships, 25, 87–103. doi:10.1177/0265407507086807

Song, H., Zou, Z., Kou, J., Liu, Y., Yang, L., Zilverstand, A., . . . Zhang, X. (2015). Love-related changes in the brain: A resting-state functional magnetic resonance imaging study. Frontiers in Human Neuroscience, 9, 71. doi:10.3389/fnhum.2015.00071

Sorokowski, P., Sorokowska, A., Butovskaya, M., Karwowski, M., Groyecka, A., Wojciszke, B., & Pawłowski, B. (2017). Love influences reproductive success in humans. Frontiers in Psychology, 8, 1922. doi:10.3389/fpsyg.2017.01922

Spencer, C., Mallory, A. B., Cafferky, B. M., Kimmes, J. G., Beck, A. R., & Stith, S. M. (2018). Mental health factors and intimate partner violence perpetration and victimization: A meta-analysis. Psychology of Violence. Advance online publication. doi:10.1037/vio0000156

Stackman, V. R., Reviere, R., & Medley, B. C. (2016). Attitudes toward marriage, partner availability, and interracial dating among black college students from historically Black and predominantly White institutions. Journal of Black Studies, 47, 169–192. doi:10.1177/0021934715623520

Stanca, L. (2012). Suffer the little children: Measuring the effects of parenthood on well-being worldwide. Journal of Economic Behavior & Organization, 81, 742–750. doi:10.1016/j.jebo.2010.12.019

Stanley, S. M., Rhoades, G. K., Amato, P. R., Markman, H. J., & Johnson, C. A. (2010). The timing of cohabitation and engagement: Impact on first and second marriages. Journal of Marriage and the Family, 72, 906–918. doi:10.1111/j.1741-3737.2010.00738.x

Stearns, E., Buchmann, C., & Bonneau, K. (2009). Interracial friendships in the transition to college: Do birds of a feather flock together once they leave the nest? Sociology of Education, 82, 173–195.

Stepler, R. (2017). Number of cohabiting Americans rises, especially among those 50+ | Pew Research Center. Retrieved March 16, 2018, from http://www.pewresearch.org/fact-tank/2017/04/06/number-of-u-s-adults-cohabiting-with-a-partner-continues-to-rise-especially-among-those-50-and-older/

Sternberg, R. J. (2004). A triangular theory of love. In H. T. Reis & C. E. Rusbult (Eds.), Close relationships: Key readings (pp. 213–227). Philadelphia, PA: Taylor & Francis.

Sumner, R., Burrow, A. L., & Hill, P. L. (2015). Identity and purpose as predictors of subjective well-being in emerging adulthood. Emerging Adulthood, 3, 46–54. http://doi.org/10.1177/2167696814532796

Sumter, S. R., Valkenburg, P. M., & Peter, J. (2013). Perceptions of love across the lifespan: Differences in passion, intimacy, and commitment. International Journal of Behavioral Development, 37, 417–427. doi:10.1177/0165025413492486

Taylor, L. S., Fiore, A. T., Mendelsohn, G. A., & Cheshire, C. (2011). "Out of my league": A real-world test of the matching hypothesis. Personality & Social Psychology Bulletin, 37, 942–954. doi:10.1177/0146167211409947

Taylor, Z. E., & Conger, R. D. (2014). Risk and resilience processes in single-mother families: An interactionist perspective.

In Z. Sloboda & H. Petras (Eds.), Defining prevention science (pp. 195–217). Boston, MA: Springer. doi:10.1007/978-1-4899-7424-2

te Velde, E., Habbema, D., Leridon, H., & Eijkemans, M. (2012). The effect of postponement of first motherhood on permanent involuntary childlessness and total fertility rate in six European countries since the 1970s. Human Reproduction (Oxford, England), 27, 1179–1183. doi:10.1093/humrep/der455

Teachman, J. (2008). Complex life course patterns and the risk of divorce in second marriages. Journal of Marriage & Family, 70, 294–305.

Tidwell, N. D., Eastwick, P. W., & Finkel, E. J. (2013). Perceived, not actual, similarity predicts initial attraction in a live romantic context: Evidence from the speed-dating paradigm. Personal Relationships, 20, 199–215. doi:10.1111/j.1475-6811.2012.01405.x

Tillyer, M. S., & Wright, E. M. (2013). Intimate partner violence and the victim-offender overlap. Journal of Research in Crime and Delinquency, 51, 29–55. doi:10.1177/0022427813484315

Timonen, V., & Doyle, M. (2013). Life-long singlehood: Intersections of the past and the present. Ageing and Society, 34, 1749–1770. doi:10.1017/S0144686X13000500

Tornello, S. L., Kruczkowski, S. M., & Patterson, C. J. (2015). Division of labor and relationship quality among male same-sex couples who became fathers via surrogacy. Journal of GLBT Family Studies, 11, 375–394. doi:10.1080/1550428X.2015.1018471

Trillingsgaard, T., Baucom, K. J. W., & Heyman, R. E. (2014). Predictors of change in relationship satisfaction during the transition to parenthood. Family Relations, 63, 667–679. doi:10.1111/fare.12089

Turell, S. C., Brown, M., & Herrmann, M. (2018). Disproportionately high: An exploration of intimate partner violence prevalence rates for bisexual people. Sexual and Relationship Therapy, 33, 113–131. doi:10.1080/14681994.2017.1347614

U.S. Bureau of the Census. (2015). Estimated median age at first marriage, by sex: 1890 to the present; Current population survey. Retrieved from http://www.census.gov/hhes/families/data/marital.html

U.S. Bureau of the Census. (2015). Marital status of people 15 years and over, by age, sex, personal earnings, race, and Hispanic origin: 2014; Current population survey. Retrieved from https://www.census.gov/hhes/families/data/cps2014A.html

U.S. Bureau of the Census. (2017). Historical marital status tables—Table MS-2. Estimated median age at first marriage, by sex: 1890 to the present. Retrieved March 16, 2018, from https://www.census.gov/data/tables/time-series/demo/families/marital.html

U.S. Department of Agriculture. (2017). Families projected to spend an average of $233,610 raising a child born in 2015 | USDA. Retrieved March 24, 2018, from https://www.usda.gov/media/press-releases/2017/01/09/families-projected-spend-average-233610-raising-child-born-2015

U.S. Department of Health and Human Services. (2013). Child health USA 2013. Retrieved from http://mchb.hrsa.gov/chusa13/index.html

U.S. Department of Labor. (2018). *Family and medical leave act—Wage and hour division (WHD)—U.S. Department of Labor*. Retrieved May 26, 2018, from https://www.dol.gov/whd/fmla/

Umaña-Taylor, A. J., Quintana, S. M., Lee, R. M., Cross, W. E., Rivas-Drake, D., Schwartz, S. J., . . . Seaton, E. (2014). Ethnic and racial identity during adolescence and into young adulthood: An integrated conceptualization. *Child Development, 85*, 21–39. http://doi.org/10.1111/cdev.12196

United Nations Economic Commission for Europe. (2015). *Statistical database*. Retrieved May 5, 2015, from http://w3.unece.org/pxweb/QuickStatistics/IndicatorsList.asp?1#17

United Nations Statistics Division. (2014). *Demographic yearbook: 2013*. Retrieved from http://unstats.un.org/unsd/demographic/products/dyb/dyb2.htm

United Nations Statistics Division. (2017). *Divorces and crude divorce rates by urban/rural residence: 2011–2015*. Retrieved from https://unstats.un.org/Unsd/demographic/products/dyb/dyb2015/Table25.pdf

Vanassche, S., Swicegood, G., & Matthijs, K. (2012). Marriage and children as a key to happiness? Cross-national differences in the effects of marital status and children on well-being. *Journal of Happiness Studies, 14*, 501–524. doi:10.1007/s10902-012-9340-8

Van Belle, J. (2016). *Paternity and parental leave policies across the European Union*. Retrieved May 26, 2018, from https://www.rand.org/content/dam/rand/pubs/research_reports/RR1600/RR1666/RAND_RR1666.pdf

Walker, M., & Iverson, E. (2016). Identity development and political self-regulation in emerging adult political attitudes and behavior. *Emerging Adulthood, 4*, 153–160. http://doi.org/10.1177/2167696815585052

Wang, W., & Parker, K. (2014). *Record share of Americans have never married*. Retrieved from http://www.pewsocialtrends.org/2014/09/24/record-share-of-americans-have-never-married/

Wang, W., Parker, K., & Taylor, P. (2013). *Chapter 4: Single mothers | Pew Research Center*. Retrieved April 9, 2018, from http://www.pewsocialtrends.org/2013/05/29/chapter-4-single-mothers/

Waren, W., & Pals, H. (2013). Comparing characteristics of voluntarily childless men and women. *Journal of Population Research, 30*, 151–170. doi:10.1007/s12546-012-9103-8

Weger, H. (2016). Cross-sex friendships. In C. R. Berger, M. E. Roloff, S. R. Wilson, J. Price, D. J. Caughlin, & D. Solomon (Eds.), *The international encyclopedia of interpersonal communication* (pp. 1–6). Hoboken, NJ: John Wiley. doi:10.1002/9781118540190.wbeic131

Whiting, J. B., Smith, D. R., Barnett, T., & Grafsky, E. L. (2007). Overcoming the Cinderella myth: A mixed methods study of successful stepmothers. *Journal of Divorce & Remarriage, 47*, 95–109.

Widarsson, M., Engström, G., Rosenblad, A., Kerstis, B., Edlund, B., & Lundberg, P. (2013). Parental stress in early parenthood among mothers and fathers in Sweden. *Scandinavian Journal of Caring Sciences, 27*, 839–847. doi:10.1111/j.1471-6712.2012.01088.x

Wiersma, J. D., Fischer, J. L., Harrington Cleveland, H., Reifman, A., & Harris, K. S. (2010). Selection and socialization of drinking among young adult dating, cohabiting, and married partners. *Journal of Social and Personal Relationships, 28*, 182–200. doi:10.1177/0265407510380083

Wight, R. G., Leblanc, A. J., & Lee Badgett, M. V. (2013). Same-sex legal marriage and psychological well-being: Findings from the California Health Interview survey. *American Journal of Public Health, 103*, 339–346. doi:10.2105/AJPH.2012.301113

Williams, L., Kabamalan, M., & Ogena, N. (2007). Cohabitation in the Philippines: Attitudes and behaviors among young women and men. *Journal of Marriage & Family, 69*, 1244–1256.

Wisensale, S. K. (2006). Commentary: What role for the Family and Medical Leave Act in long-term care policy? *Journal of Aging & Social Policy, 18*, 79–93.

Wolf, R. (2017). *Supreme Court rules for same-sex parents' birth certificate rights in Arkansas case*. Retrieved March 24, 2018, from https://www.usatoday.com/story/news/politics/2017/06/26/supreme-court-hear-challenge-same-sex-parents-birth-certificate/102672194/

World Health Organization. (2005). *World Health Organization multi-country study on women's health and domestic violence against women*. Geneva, Switzerland: World Health Organization. Retrieved from http://www.who.int/gender/violence/who_multicountry_study/en/index.html

Wrzus, C., Zimmermann, J., Mund, M., & Neyer, F. J. (2017). Friendships in young and middle adulthood. In M. Hojjat & A. Moyer (Eds.), *The psychology of friendship* (pp. 21–38). Oxford, UK: Oxford University Press. doi:10.1093/acprof: oso/9780190222024.003.0002

Wu. L. L., Bumpass, L. L., & Musick, K. (2001). Historical and life course trajectories of nonmarital childbearing. In L. L. Wu & B. Wolfe (Eds.), *Out of wedlock: Causes and consequences of nonmarital fertility* (pp. 3–48). New York, NY: Russell Sage Foundation.

Yavorsky, J. E., Kamp Dush, C. M., & Schoppe-Sullivan, S. J. (2015). The production of inequality: The gender division of labor across the transition to parenthood. *Journal of Marriage and Family, 77*, 662–679. doi:10.1111/jomf.12189

Zimmermann, P., & Iwanski, A. (2014). Emotion regulation from early adolescence to emerging adulthood and middle adulthood. *International Journal of Behavioral Development, 38*, 182–194. doi:10.1177/0165025413515405

Chapter 15

Ackerman, P. L., & Beier, M. E. (2006). Determinants of domain knowledge and independent study learning in an adult sample. *Journal of Educational Psychology, 98*, 366–381.

Adwan-Shekhidem, H., & Atzmon, G. (2018). The epigenetic regulation of telomere maintenance in aging. In A. Moskalev & A. M. Vaiserman (Eds.). *Epigenetics of aging and longevity* (pp. 119–136). London, UK: Elsevier. doi:10.1016/B978-0-12-811060-7.00005-X

Afshar, S., Roderick, P. J., Kowal, P., Dimitrov, B. D., & Hill, A. G. (2017). Global patterns of multimorbidity: A comparison of 28 countries using the World Health surveys. In M. N. Hoque, B. Pecotte, & M. A. McGehee (Eds.), *Applied demography and public health in the 21st century* (pp. 381–402). New York: Springer. doi:10.1007/978-3-319-43688-3_21

Aldwin, C. M., & Levenson, M. R. (2001). Stress, coping, and health at midlife: A developmental perspective. In M. E. Lachman (Ed.), *Handbook of midlife development* (pp. 188–214). Hoboken, NJ: John Wiley.

Almeida, S., Rato, L., Sousa, M., Alves, M. G., & Oliveira, P. F. (2017). Fertility and sperm quality in the aging male. *Current Pharmaceutical Design, 23*, 4429–4437. doi:10.2174/1381612823666170503150313

American Diabetes Association. (2014). Standards of medical care in diabetes—2014. *Diabetes Care, 37*(Suppl. 1), S11–S66. doi:10.2337/dc13-S011

Anderson, N. D., & Craik, F. I. M. (2017). 50 years of cognitive aging theory. *Journal of Gerontology Series B: Psychological Sciences and Social Sciences, 72*, 1–6. doi:10.1093/geronb/gbw108

Anderson, W. F., Rosenberg, P. S., Prat, A., Perou, C. M., & Sherman, M. E. (2014). How many etiological subtypes of breast cancer: Two, three, four, or more? *Journal of the National Cancer Institute, 106*, dju165. doi:10.1093/jnci/dju165

Anton, S., & Leeuwenburgh, C. (2013). Fasting or caloric restriction for healthy aging. *Experimental Gerontology, 48*, 1003–1005. doi:10.1016/j.exger.2013.04.011

Araujo, A. B., O'Donnell, A. B., Brambilla, D. J., Simpson, W. B., Longcope, C., Matsumoto, A. M., & McKinlay, J. B. (2004). Prevalence and incidence of androgen deficiency in middle-aged and older men: Estimates from the Massachusetts Male Aging study. *Journal of Clinical Endocrinology and Metabolism, 89*, 5920–5926. doi:10.1210/jc.2003-031719

Arnson, Y., Rozanski, A., Gransar, H., Otaki, Y., Doris, M., Wang, F., . . . Berman, D. (2017). Hormone replacement therapy is associated with less coronary atherosclerosis and lower mortality. *Journal of the American College of Cardiology, 69*, 1408. doi:10.1016/S0735-1097(17)34797-6

Arsenis, N. C., You, T., Ogawa, E. F., Tinsley, G. M., & Zuo, L. (2017). Physical activity and telomere length: Impact of aging and potential mechanisms of action. *Oncotarget, 4*, 45008–45019. doi:10.18632/oncotarget.16726

Au, J., Sheehan, E., Tsai, N., Duncan, G. J., Buschkuehl, M., & Jaeggi, S. M. (2015). Improving fluid intelligence with training on working memory: A meta-analysis. *Psychonomic Bulletin & Review, 22*, 366–377. doi:10.3758/s13423-014-0699-x

Avis, N. E., Brockwell, S., & Colvin, A. (2005). A universal menopausal syndrome? *American Journal of Medicine, 118*, 1406. Retrieved from 10.1016/j.amjmed.2005.10.010

Avis, N. E., Colvin, A., Karlamangla, A. S., Crawford, S., Hess, R., Waetjen, L. E., . . . Greendale, G. A. (2017). Change in sexual functioning over the menopausal transition. *Menopause, 24,* 379–390. doi:10.1097/GME.0000000000000770

Avis, N. E., Crawford, S. L., Greendale, G., Bromberger, J. T., Everson-Rose, S. A., Gold, E. B., . . . Study of Women's Health Across the Nation. (2015). Duration of menopausal vasomotor symptoms over the menopause transition. *JAMA Internal Medicine, 175,* 531–539. doi:10.1001/jamainternmed.2014.8063

Avis, N. E., Stellato, R., Crawford, S., Bromberger, J., Ganz, P., Cain, V., & Kagawa-Singer, M. (2001). Is there a menopausal syndrome? Menopausal status and symptoms across racial/ethnic groups. *Social Science & Medicine, 52,* 345.

Ayala Calvo, J. C., & Garcia, G. M. (2018). Hardiness as moderator of the relationship between structural and psychological empowerment on burnout in middle managers. *Journal of Occupational and Organizational Psychology, 91,* 362–384. doi:10.1111/joop.12194

Backé, E. M., Seidler, A., Latza, U., Rossnagel, K., & Schumann, B. (2012). The role of psychosocial stress at work for the development of cardiovascular diseases: A systematic review. *International Archives of Occupational and Environmental Health, 85,* 67–79. doi:10.1007/s00420-011-0643-6

Baines, H. L., Turnbull, D. M., & Greaves, L. C. (2014). Human stem cell aging: Do mitochondrial DNA mutations have a causal role? *Aging Cell, 13,* 201–205. doi:10.1111/acel.12199

Baker, D. P., Eslinger, P. J., Benavides, M., Peters, E., Dieckmann, N. F., & Leon, J. (2015). The cognitive impact of the education revolution: A possible cause of the Flynn effect on population IQ. *Intelligence, 49,* 144–158. doi:10.1016/j.intell.2015.01.003

Baltes, M. M., & Carstensen, L. L. (2003). The process of successful aging: Selection, optimization and compensation. In U. M. Staudinger & U. Lindenberger (Eds.), *Understanding human development: Dialogues with lifespan psychology* (pp. 81–104). Dordrecht, The Netherlands: Kluwer Academic.

Barbur, J. L., & Rodriguez-Carmona, M. (2015). Color vision changes in normal aging. In A. J. Elliot, M. D. Fairchild, & A. Franklin (Eds.), *Handbook of color psychology* (p. 740). Retrieved from http://openaccess.city.ac.uk/12513/

Barthel, F. P., Wei, W., Tang, M., Martinez-Ledesma, E., Hu, X., Amin, S. B., . . . Verhaak, R. G. W. (2017). Systematic analysis of telomere length and somatic alterations in 31 cancer types. *Nature Genetics, 49,* 349–357. doi:10.1038/ng.3781

Bartone, P. T. (2006). Resilience under military operational stress: Can leaders influence hardiness. *Military Psychology, 18,* S131–S148.

Bartone, P. T., Eid, J., & Hystad, S. W. (2016). Training hardiness for stress resilience. In N. Maheshwari & V. V. Kumar (Eds.), *Military psychology: Concepts, trends and interventions* (pp. 231–248). New Delhi, India: Sage.

Bartone, P. T., Roland, R. R., & Picano, J. J. (2008). Psychological hardiness predicts success in U.S. Army Special Forces candidates. *International Journal of Selection and Assessment, 16,* 78–81.

Bengston, V. L., Gans, D., Pulney, N. M., & Silverstein, M. (2009). *Handbook of theories of aging* (2nd ed.). New York, NY: Springer.

Benjamin, E. J., Virani, S. S., Callaway, C. W., Chamberlain, A. M., Chang, A. R., Cheng, S., . . . American Heart Association Council on Epidemiology and Prevention Statistics Committee and Stroke Statistics Subcommittee. (2018). Heart disease and stroke statistics—2018 update: A report from the American Heart Association. *Circulation, 137,* e67–e492. doi:10.1161/CIR.0000000000000558

Benkhadra, K., Mohammed, K., Al Nofal, A., Carranza Leon, B. G., Alahdab, F., Faubion, S., . . . Murad, M. H. (2015). Menopausal hormone therapy and mortality: A systematic review and meta-analysis. *Journal of Clinical Endocrinology & Metabolism, 100,* 4021–4028. doi:10.1210/jc.2015-2238

Bennett, I. J., & Madden, D. J. (2014). Disconnected aging: Cerebral white matter integrity and age-related differences in cognition. *Neuroscience, 276,* 187–205. doi:10.1016/j.neuroscience.2013.11.026

Benz, C. C. (2008). Impact of aging on the biology of breast cancer. *Critical Reviews in Oncology/Hematology, 66,* 65–74. Retrieved from 10.1016/j.critrevonc.2007.09.001

Best, L. E., Hayward, M. D., & Hidajat, M. M. (2005). Life course pathways to adult-onset diabetes. *Social Biology, 52,* 94–111.

Beyene, Y. (1986). Cultural significance and physiological manifestations of menopause a biocultural analysis. *Culture, Medicine and Psychiatry, 10,* 47–71. doi:10.1007/BF00053262

Beyene, Y., & Martin, M. C. (2001). Menopausal experiences and bone density of Mayan women in Yucatan, Mexico. *American Journal of Human Biology, 13,* 505–511.

Blackburn, E. H., Epel, E. S., Lin, J., Sfeir, A., Lange, T. de, Blackburn, E. H., . . . Blau, H. M. (2015). Human telomere biology: A contributory and interactive factor in aging, disease risks, and protection. *Science, 350,* 1193–1198. doi:10.1126/science.aab3389

Bleicher, K., Cumming, R. G., Naganathan, V., Seibel, M. J., Sambrook, P. N., Blyth, F. M., . . . Waite, L. M. (2011). Lifestyle factors, medications, and disease influence bone mineral density in older men: findings from the CHAMP study. *Osteoporosis International, 22,* 2421–2437. doi:10.1007/s00198-010-1478-9

Braver, T. S., & West, R. (2008). Working memory, executive control, and aging. In F. I. M. Craik & T. A. Salthouse (Eds.), *The handbook of aging and cognition* (3rd ed., pp. 311–372). New York, NY: Psychology Press.

Brown, R. E. (2016). Hebb and Cattell: The genesis of the theory of fluid and crystallized intelligence. *Frontiers in Human Neuroscience, 10,* 606. doi:10.3389/fnhum.2016.00606

Brydon, L., Strike, P. C., Bhattacharyya, M. R., Whitehead, D. L., McEwan, J., Zachary, I., & Steptoe, A. (2010). Hostility and physiological responses to laboratory stress in acute coronary syndrome patients. *Journal of Psychosomatic Research, 68,* 109–116. doi:10.1016/j.jpsychores.2009.06.007

Bugg, J. M., Zook, N. A., DeLosh, E. L., Davalos, D. B., & Davis, H. P. (2006). Age differences in fluid intelligence: Contributions of general slowing and frontal decline. *Brain & Cognition, 62,* 9–16. Retrieved from 10.1016/j.bandc.2006.02.006

Campisi, J. (2013). Aging, cellular senescence, and cancer. *Annual Review of Physiology, 75,* 685–705. doi:10.1146/annurev-physiol-030212-183653

Cannon, S. M., Einstein, G. P., & Tulp, O. L. (2017). Analysis of telomere length in aging and age-related illness. *The FASEB Journal, 31*(1, Suppl.), 935.2–935.2. Retrieved from http://www.fasebj.org/content/31/1_Supplement/935.2.short

Castelo-Branco, C., & Davila, J. (2015). Menopause and aging skin in the elderly. In M. A. Farage, K. W. Miller, N. F. Woods, & H. I. Maibach (Eds.), *Skin, mucosa and menopause* (pp. 345–357). Heidelberg, Germany: Springer. doi:10.1007/978-3-662-44080-3_25

Centers for Disease Control and Prevention. (2016). QuickStats: Percentage distribution of respondent-assessed health status among adults aged ≥25 years, by completed education—National Health Interview survey, United States, 2015. *MMWR. Morbidity & Mortality Weekly Report, 65,* 1383. Retrieved from https://www.cdc.gov/mmwr/volumes/65/wr/mm6548a8.htm

Centers for Disease Control and Prevention. (2018a). *10 leading causes of death by age group—2016.* Retrieved from https://www.cdc.gov/injury/images/lc-charts/leading_causes_of_death_age_group_2016_1056w814h.gif

Centers for Disease Control and Prevention. (2018b). *National diabetes statistics report, 2017.* Retrieved from http://www.diabetes.org/assets/pdfs/basics/cdc-statistics-report-2017.pdf

Chen, E., & Miller, G. E. (2013). Socioeconomic status and health: Mediating and moderating factors. *Annual Review of Clinical Psychology, 9,* 723–749. doi:10.1146/annurev-clinpsy-050212-185634

Chen, T., & Li, D. (2007). The roles of working memory updating and processing speed in mediating age-related differences in fluid intelligence. *Aging, Neuropsychology & Cognition, 14,* 631–646.

Chlebowski, R. T., Barrington, W., Aragaki, A. K., Manson, J. E., Sarto, G., O'Sullivan, M. J., . . . Prentice, R. L. (2017). Estrogen alone and health outcomes in black women by African ancestry. *Menopause, 24,* 133–141. doi:10.1097/GME.0000000000000733

Chou, R., Dana, T., Bougatsos, C., Fleming, C., & Beil, T. (2011). Screening adults aged 50 years or older for hearing loss: A review of the evidence for the U.S. preventive services task force. *Annals of Internal Medicine, 154,* 347–355. doi:10.7326/0003-4819-154-5-201103010-00009

Chrisler, J. C. (2008). The menstrual cycle in a biopsychosocial context. In F. L. Denmark & M. A. Paludi (Eds.), *Psychology of women: A handbook of issues and theories* (2nd ed., pp. 400–439). Westport, CT: Praeger/Greenwood.

Christensen, H., Batterham, P. J., & Mackinnon, A. J. (2013). The getting of wisdom: Fluid intelligence does not drive knowledge acquisition. *Journal of Cognition and Development, 14,* 321–331. doi:10.1080/15248372.2012.664590

Colom, R., Flores-Mendoza, C. E., & Abad, F. J. (2007). Generational changes on the draw-a-man test: A comparison of Brazilian urban and rural children tested in 1930, 2002 and 2004. *Journal of Biosocial Science, 39,* 79. doi:10.1017/S0021932005001173

Connor, T. J. (2008). Don't stress out your immune system—Just relax. *Brain, Behavior, and Immunity, 22,* 1128–1129. doi:10.1016/j.bbi.2008.07.009

Costa, R. M., & Brody, S. (2012). Sexual satisfaction, relationship satisfaction, and health are associated with greater frequency of penile–vaginal intercourse. *Archives of Sexual Behavior, 41,* 9–10. doi:10.1007/s10508-011-9847-9

Craik, F. I. M., & Rose, N. S. (2012). Memory encoding and aging: A neurocognitive perspective. *Neuroscience and Biobehavioral Reviews, 36,* 1729–1739. doi:10.1016/j.neubiorev.2011.11.007

Dainese, S. M., Allemand, M., Ribeiro, N., Bayram, S., Martin, M., & Ehlert, U. (2011). Protective factors in midlife: How do people stay healthy? *GeroPsych: The Journal of Gerontopsychology and Geriatric Psychiatry, 24,* 19–29.

Dasgupta, D., & Ray, S. (2017). Is menopausal status related to women's attitudes toward menopause and aging? *Women & Health, 57,* 311–328 . doi:10.1080/03630242.2016.1160965

Davis, D., Bendayan, R., Muniz Terrera, G., Hardy, R., Richards, M., & Kuh, D. (2017). Decline in search speed and verbal memory over 26 years of midlife in a British birth cohort. *Neuroepidemiology, 49,* 121–128. doi:10.1159/000481136

Deary, I. J. (2014). The stability of intelligence from childhood to old age. *Current Directions in Psychological Science, 23,* 239–245. doi:10.1177/0963721414536905

DeBono, N. L., Robinson, W. R., Lund, J. L., Tse, C. K., Moorman, P. G., Olshan, A. F., & Troester, M. A. (2018). Race, menopausal hormone therapy, and invasive breast cancer in the Carolina Breast Cancer study. *Journal of Women's Health, 27,* 377–386. doi:10.1089/jwh.2016.6063

DeFronzo, R. A., & Abdul-Ghani, M. (2011). Assessment and treatment of cardiovascular risk in prediabetes: Impaired glucose tolerance and impaired fasting glucose. *American Journal of Cardiology, 108,* 3B–24B. doi:10.1016/j.amjcard.2011.03.013

DeLamater, J. (2012). Sexual expression in later life: A review and synthesis. *Journal of Sex Research, 49,* 125–141. doi:10.1080/00224499.2011.603168

Delanoë, D., Hajri, S., Bachelot, A., Mahfoudh Draoui, D., Hassoun, D., Marsicano, E., & Ringa, V. (2012). Class, gender and culture in the experience of menopause. A comparative survey in Tunisia and France. *Social Science & Medicine (1982), 75,* 401–409. doi:10.1016/j.socscimed.2012.02.051

Dellenbach, M., & Zimprich, D. (2008). Typical intellectual engagement and cognition in old age. *Aging, Neuropsychology & Cognition, 15,* 208–231. Retrieved from 10.1080/13825580701338094

Dillaway, H. E. (2008). "Why can't you control this?" How women's interactions with intimate partners define menopause and family. *Journal of Women & Aging, 20,* 47–64.

DiNuzzo, M., & Nedergaard, M. (2017). Brain energetics during the sleep–wake cycle. *Current Opinion in Neurobiology, 47,* 65–72. https://doi.org/10.1016/J.CONB.2017.09.010

Ditzen, B., Schmidt, S., Strauss, B., Nater, U. M., Ehlert, U., & Heinrichs, M. (2008). Adult attachment and social support interact to reduce psychological but not cortisol responses to stress. *Journal of Psychosomatic Research, 64,* 479–486. doi:10.1016/j.jpsychores.2007.11.011

Djoussé, L., Driver, J. A., Gaziano, J. M., Buring, J. E., & Lee, I. M. (2013). Association between modifiable lifestyle factors and residual lifetime risk of diabetes. *Nutrition, Metabolism and Cardiovascular Diseases, 23,* 17–22. doi:10.1016/j.numecd.2011.08.002

Do, K. A., Treloar, S., Pandeya, N., Purdie, D., Green, A., Heath, A., & Martin, N. (2013). Predictive factors of age at menopause in a large Australian twin study. *Human Biology.* Retrieved from http://digitalcommons.wayne.edu/humbiol/vol70/iss6/8

Donatelle, R. (2004). *Health: The basics.* San Francisco, CA: Benjamin Cummings.

Ecob, R., Sutton, G., Rudnicka, A., Smith, P., Power, C., Strachan, D., & Davis, A. (2008). Is the relation of social class to change in hearing threshold levels from childhood to middle age explained by noise, smoking, and drinking behaviour? *International Journal of Audiology, 47,* 100–108. doi:10.1080/14992020701647942

Ehlert, U., & Fischbacher, S. (2013). Reproductive health. In M. D. Gellman & J. R. Turner (Eds.), *Encyclopedia of behavioral medicine* (pp. 1658–1665). New York, NY: Springer. doi:10.1007/978-1-4419-1005-9

Elias, M. F., & Dore, G. A. (2016). Cardiovascular disease. In S. K. Whitbourne (Ed.), *The encyclopedia of adulthood and aging* (pp. 1–4). Hoboken, NJ: John Wiley. doi:10.1002/9781118521373.wbeaa216

Ellingsen, V. J., & Ackerman, P. L. (2016). Fluid-crystallized theory of intelligence. In S. K. Whitbourne (Ed.), *The encyclopedia of adulthood and aging* (pp. 1–5). Hoboken, NJ: John Wiley. doi:10.1002/9781118521373.wbeaa022

Ericsson, A., & Pool, R. (2016). *Peak: Secrets from the new science of expertise.* New York, NY: Houghton Mifflin.

Ericsson, K. A. (2014). Expertise. *Current Biology: CB, 24,* R508–R510. doi:10.1016/j.cub.2014.04.013

Ericsson, K. A. (2017). Expertise and individual differences: The search for the structure and acquisition of experts' superior performance. *Wiley Interdisciplinary Reviews: Cognitive Science, 8,* e1382. doi:10.1002/wcs.1382

Ericsson, K. A., & Moxley, J. H. (2013). Experts' superior memory: From accumulation of chunks to building memory skills that mediate improved performance and learning. In D. S. L. Timothy J. Perfect (Ed.), *The SAGE handbook of applied memory* (pp. 404–420). Thousand Oaks, CA: Sage.

Esler, M. (2017). Mental stress and human cardiovascular disease. *Neuroscience & Biobehavioral Reviews, 74,* 269–276. doi:10.1016/J.NEUBIOREV.2016.10.011

Espeland, M. A., Bryan, R. N., Goveas, J. S., Robinson, J. G., Siddiqui, M. S., Liu, S., . . . Resnick, S. M. (2013). Influence of type 2 diabetes on brain volumes and changes in brain volumes: Results from the Women's Health Initiative Magnetic Resonance Imaging studies. *Diabetes Care, 36,* 90–97. doi:10.2337/dc12-0555

Fang, S. C., Rosen, R. C., Vita, J. A., Ganz, P., & Kupelian, V. (2015). Changes in erectile dysfunction over time in relation to Framingham cardiovascular risk in the Boston Area Community Health (BACH) survey. *Journal of Sexual Medicine, 12,* 100–108. doi:10.1111/jsm.12715

Fedarko, N. S. (2018). Theories and mechanisms of aging. In J. G. Reves, S. R. Barnett, J. R. McSwain, & G. A. Rooke (Eds.), *Geriatric anesthesiology* (pp. 19–25). Cham, Switzerland: Springer International. doi:10.1007/978-3-319-66878-9_2

Federal Interagency Forum on Aging-Related Statistics. (2016). *Older Americans 2016 key indicators of well-being.* Retrieved from https://agingstats.gov/docs/LatestReport/Older-Americans-2016-Key-Indicators-of-WellBeing.pdf

Federman, D. D., & Walford, G. A. (2007). Is male menopause real? (Cover story). *Newsweek, 149,* 58–60.

Finkel, D., Reynolds, C. A., McArdle, J. J., & Pedersen, N. L. (2007). Age changes in processing speed as a leading indicator of cognitive aging. *Psychology and Aging, 22,* 558–568.

Firooz, A., Rajabi-Estarabadi, A., Zartab, H., Pazhohi, N., Fanian, F., & Janani, L. (2017). The influence of gender and age on the thickness and echo-density of skin. *Skin Research and Technology, 23,* 13–20. doi:10.1111/srt.12294

Flynn, J. R. (1984). The mean IQ of Americans: Massive gains 1932 to 1978. *Psychological Bulletin, 95,* 29–51. doi:10.1037/0033-2909.95.1.29

Flynn, J. R. (2012). *Are we getting smarter?* Cambridge, UK: Cambridge University Press. doi:10.1017/CBO9781139235679

Flynn, J. R., & Rossi-Casé, L. (2012). IQ gains in Argentina between 1964 and 1998. *Intelligence, 40,* 145–150. doi:10.1016/j.intell.2012.01.006

Flynn, J. R., & Weiss, L. G. (2007). American IQ gains from 1932 to 2002: The WISC subtests and educational progress. *International Journal of Testing, 7,* 209–224. doi:10.1080/15305050701193587

Forcier, K., Stroud, L. R., & Papandonatos, G. D. (2006). Links between physical fitness and cardiovascular reactivity and recovery to psychological stressors: A meta-analysis. *Health Psychology, 25,* 723–739.

Franks, P. W., & Pare, G. (2016). Putting the genome in context: Gene-environment interactions in type 2 diabetes. *Current Diabetes Reports, 16,* 57. doi:10.1007/s11892-016-0758-y

Freund, A. M., & Baltes, P. B. (2007). Toward a theory of successful aging: Selection, optimization, and compensation. In R. Fernández-Ballesteros (Ed.), *Geropsychology: European perspectives for an aging world* (pp. 239–254). Ashland, OH: Hogrefe & Huber.

Friedman, H. S., & Kern, M. L. (2014). Personality, well-being, and health. *Annual Review of Psychology, 65*, 719–742. doi:10.1146/annurev-psych-010213-115123

Gallicchio, L., Schilling, C., Tomic, D., Miller, S. R., Zacur, H., & Flaws, J. A. (2007). Correlates of sexual functioning among mid-life women. *Climacteric, 10*, 132–142.

Gambacciani, M., & Levancini, M. (2014). Hormone replacement therapy and the prevention of postmenopausal osteoporosis. *Przeglad Menopauzalny, 13*, 213–220. doi:10.5114/pm.2014.44996

Garcia, G. A., Khoshnevis, M., Yee, K. M. P., Nguyen, J. H., Nguyen-Cuu, J., Sadun, A. A., & Sebag, J. (2018). The effects of aging vitreous on contrast sensitivity function. *Graefe's Archive for Clinical and Experimental Ophthalmology, 256*, 919–925. doi:10.1007/s00417-018-3957-1

Geerligs, L., Maurits, N. M., Renken, R. J., & Lorist, M. M. (2014). Reduced specificity of functional connectivity in the aging brain during task performance. *Human Brain Mapping, 35*, 319–330. doi:10.1002/hbm.22175

Gerber, M., & Pühse, U. (2009). Do exercise and fitness protect against stress-induced health complaints? A review of the literature. *Scandinavian Journal of Public Health, 37*, 801–819. doi:10.1177/1403494809350522

Gershon, A., Johnson, S. L., & Miller, I. (2013). Chronic stressors and trauma: Prospective influences on the course of bipolar disorder. *Psychological Medicine, 43*, 2583–2592. doi:10.1017/S0033291713000147

Gil-Cazorla, R., Shah, S., & Naroo, S. A. (2016). A review of the surgical options for the correction of presbyopia. *British Journal of Ophthalmology, 100*, 62–70. doi:10.1136/bjophthalmol-2015-306663

Go, A. S., Mozaffarian, D., Roger, V. L., Benjamin, E. J., Berry, J. D., Borden, W. B., . . . Turner, M. B. (2013). Heart disease and stroke statistics—2013 update: A report from the American Heart Association. *Circulation, 127*, e6–e245. doi:10.1161/CIR.0b013e31828124ad

Gold, D. T. (2016). Bone. In S. K. Whitbourne (Ed.), *The encyclopedia of adulthood and aging* (pp. 1–5). Hoboken, NJ: John Wiley. doi:10.1002/9781118521373.wbeaa300

Gold, E. B., Crawford, S. L., Avis, N. E., Crandall, C. J., Matthews, K. A., Waetjen, L. E., . . . Harlow, S. D. (2013). Factors related to age at natural menopause: Longitudinal analyses from SWAN. *American Journal of Epidemiology, 178*, 70–83. doi:10.1093/aje/kws421

Gouin, J. P., Glaser, R., Malarkey, W. B., Beversdorf, D., & Kiecolt-Glaser, J. (2012). Chronic stress, daily stressors, and circulating inflammatory markers. *Health Psychology, 31*, 264–268. doi:10.1037/a0025536

Govindaraju, D., Atzmon, G., & Barzilai, N. (2015). Genetics, lifestyle and longevity: Lessons from centenarians. *Applied & Translational Genomics, 4*, 23–32. doi:10.1016/j.atg.2015.01.001

Graf, A. S., Long, D. M., & Patrick, J. H. (2017). Successful aging across adulthood: Hassles, uplifts, and self-assessed health in daily context. *Journal of Adult Development, 24*, 216–225. doi:10.1007/s10804-017-9260-2

Gragnani, A., Cornick, S. Mac, Chominski, V., Ribeiro de Noronha, S. M., Alves Corrêa de Noronha, S. A., & Ferreira, L. M. (2014). Review of major theories of skin aging. *Advances in Aging Research, 3*, 265–284. doi:10.4236/aar.2014.34036

Grindler, N. M., Allsworth, J. E., Macones, G. A., Kannan, K., Roehl, K. A., & Cooper, A. R. (2015). Persistent organic pollutants and early menopause in U.S. women. *PLoS ONE, 10*, e0116057. doi:10.1371/journal.pone.0116057

Gruber, N., Mosimann, U. P., Müri, R. M., & Nef, T. (2013). Vision and night driving abilities of elderly drivers. *Traffic Injury Prevention, 14*, 477–485. doi:10.1080/15389588.2012.727510

Gupta, P., Sturdee, D. W., & Hunter, M. S. (2006). Mid-age health in women from the Indian subcontinent (MAHWIS): General health and the experience of menopause in women. *Climacteric, 9*, 13–22.

Hambrick, D. Z., Burgoyne, A. P., Macnamara, B. N., & Ullén, F. (2018). Toward a multifactorial model of expertise: Beyond born versus made. *Annals of the New York Academy of Sciences, 1423*, 284–295. doi:10.1111/nyas.13586

Hannan, M. T., Broe, K. E., Cupples, L. A., Dufour, A. B., Rockwell, M., & Kiel, D. P. (2012). Height loss predicts subsequent hip fracture in men and women of the Framingham study. *Journal of Bone and Mineral Research, 27*, 146–152. doi:10.1002/jbmr.557

Hannon, K. (2010). Dealing with the hormone dilemma. *U.S. News & World Report, 147*, 51–52.

Haring, R., Ittermann, T., Völzke, H., Krebs, A., Zygmunt, M., Felix, S. B., . . . Wallaschofski, H. (2010). Prevalence, incidence and risk factors of testosterone deficiency in a population-based cohort of men: Results from the study of health in Pomerania. *The Aging Male, 13*, 247–257. doi:10.3109/13685538.2010.487553

Harman, D. (2006). Free radical theory of aging: an update: Increasing the functional life span. *Annals of the New York Academy of Sciences, 1067*, 10–21.

Harris, W. S., Miller, M., Tighe, A. P., Davidson, M. H., Schaefer, E. J., & Dimsdale, J. E. (2008). Psychological stress and cardiovascular disease. *Journal of the American College of Cardiology, 51*, 1237–1246. Retrieved from 10.1016/j.jacc.2007.12.024

Hartge, P. (2009). Genetics of reproductive lifespan. *Nature Genetics, 41*, 637–638. doi:10.1038/ng0609-637

Hartley, A. A., & Maquestiaux, F. (2016). Attention. In S. K. Whitbourne (Ed.), *The encyclopedia of adulthood and aging* (pp. 1–5). Hoboken, NJ: John Wiley. doi:10.1002/9781118521373.wbeaa133

Hartshorne, J. K., & Germine, L. T. (2015). When does cognitive functioning peak? The asynchronous rise and fall of different cognitive abilities across the life span. *Psychological Science, 26*, 433–443. doi:10.1177/0956797614567339

Hayflick, L. (1996). *How and why we age.* New York, NY: Ballantine.

Hayslip, B. J., Panek, P. E., & Patrick, J. H. (2007). *Adult development and aging* (4th ed.). Malabar, FL: Krieger.

Helfer, K. S., Merchant, G. R., & Wasiuk, P. A. (2017). Age-related changes in objective and subjective speech perception in complex listening environments. *Journal of Speech Language and Hearing Research, 60*, 3009. doi:10.1044/2017_JSLHR-H-17-0030

Helzner, E. P., Cauley, J. A., Pratt, S. R., Wisniewski, S. R., Zmuda, J. M., Talbott, E. O., . . . Newman, A. B. (2005). Race and sex differences in age-related hearing loss: The health, aging and body composition study. *Journal of the American Geriatrics Society, 53*, 2119–2127.

Herbenick, D., Reece, M., Hensel, D., Sanders, S., Jozkowski, K., & Fortenberry, J. D. (2011). Association of lubricant use with women's sexual pleasure, sexual satisfaction, and genital symptoms: A prospective daily diary study. *Journal of Sexual Medicine, 8*, 202–212. doi:10.1111/j.1743-6109.2010.02067.x

Herbenick, D., Reece, M., Schick, V., Sanders, S. A., Dodge, B., & Fortenberry, J. D. (2010). Sexual behavior in the United States: Results from a national probability sample of men and women ages 14–94. *Journal of Sexual Medicine, 7*, 255–265. doi:10.1111/J.1743-6109.2010.02012.X

Herzmann, G., & Curran, T. (2011). Experts' memory: An ERP study of perceptual expertise effects on encoding and recognition. *Memory & Cognition, 39*, 412–432. doi:10.3758/s13421-010-0036-1

Hickey, M., Elliott, J., & Davison, S. L. (2012). Hormone replacement therapy. *BMJ (Clinical Research Ed.), 344*(feb16_2), e763. doi:10.1136/bmj.e763

Holt, R. I. G., Phillips, D. I. W., Jameson, K. A., Cooper, C., Dennison, E. M., & Peveler, R. C. (2013). The relationship between depression, anxiety and cardiovascular disease: Findings from the Hertfordshire Cohort study. *Journal of Affective Disorders, 150*, 84–90. doi:10.1016/j.jad.2013.02.026

Horn, J. L., & Cattell, R. B. (1966). Refinement and test of the theory of fluid and crystallized general intelligences. *Journal of Educational Psychology, 57*, 253–270.

Horn, J. L., & Noll, J. (1997). Human cognitive capabilities: Gf-Gc theory. In D. P. Flanagan, J. L. Genshaft, & P. L. Harrison (Eds.), *Contemporary intellectual assessment: Theories, tests, and issues* (pp. 53–91). New York, NY: Guilford.

Howard, B. V., Van Horn, L., Hsia, J., Manson, J. E., Stefanick, M. L., Wassertheil-Smoller, S., . . . Robbins, J. (2006). Low-fat diet and weight change in postmenopausal women. *JAMA: Journal of the American Medical Association, 296*, 394–395.

Howell, L. C., & Beth, A. (2002). Midlife myths and realities: Women reflect on their experiences. *Journal of Women & Aging, 14*, 189.

Hu, Y., van Lenthe, F. J., Borsboom, G. J., Looman, C. W. N., Bopp, M., Burström, B., . . . Mackenbach, J. P. (2016). Trends in socioeconomic inequalities in self-assessed health in 17 European countries between 1990 and 2010. *Journal of Epidemiology and Community Health, 70*, 644–652. doi:10.1136/jech-2015-206780

Huang, K. E., Xu, L., Nasri, N. I., & Jaisamrarn, U. (2010). The Asian menopause survey: Knowledge, perceptions, hormone treatment and sexual function. *Maturitas, 65,* 276–283. doi:10.1016/j.maturitas.2009.11.015

Hvas, L., & Dorte Effersøe, G. (2008). Discourses on menopause—Part II: How do women talk about menopause? *Health: An Interdisciplinary Journal for the Social Study of Health, Illness & Medicine, 12,* 177–192. doi:10.1177/1363459307086842

Hyun, J., Sliwinski, M. J., Almeida, D. M., Smyth, J. M., & Scott, S. B. (2018). The moderating effects of aging and cognitive abilities on the association between work stress and negative affect. *Aging & Mental Health, 22,* 611–618. doi:10.1080/13607863.2017.1299688

Jannasch, F., Kroger, J., & Schulze, M. B. (2017). Dietary patterns and type 2 diabetes: A systematic literature review and meta-analysis of prospective studies. *Journal of Nutrition, 147,* 1174–1182. doi:10.3945/jn.116.242552

Jeffreys, M., Lawlor, D. A., Galobardes, B., McCarron, P., Kinra, S., Ebrahim, S., & Smith, G. D. (2006). Lifecourse weight patterns and adult-onset diabetes: The Glasgow Alumni and British Women's Heart and Health studies. *International Journal of Obesity, 30,* 507–512.

Jemal, A., Thun, M. J., Ward, E. E., Henley, S. J., Cokkinides, V. E., & Murray, T. E. (2008). Mortality from leading causes by education and race in the United States, 2001. *American Journal of Preventive Medicine, 34,* 1–8.

Jessen, N. A., Munk, A. S. F., Lundgaard, I., & Nedergaard, M. (2015). The glymphatic system: A beginner's guide. *Neurochemical Research, 40,* 2583–2599. https://doi.org/10.1007/s11064-015-1581-6

Johnson, S. L., Dunleavy, J., Gemmell, N. J., & Nakagawa, S. (2015). Consistent age-dependent declines in human semen quality: A systematic review and meta-analysis. *Ageing Research Reviews, 19C,* 22–33. doi:10.1016/j.arr.2014.10.007

Juster, R. P., Bizik, G., Picard, M., Arsenault-Lapierre, G., Sindi, S., Trepanier, L., . . . Lupien, S. J. (2011). A transdisciplinary perspective of chronic stress in relation to psychopathology throughout life span development. *Development and Psychopathology, 23,* 725–776. doi:10.1017/S0954579411000289

Kalayinia, S., Goodarzynejad, H., Maleki, M., & Mahdieh, N. (2018). Next generation sequencing applications for cardiovascular disease. *Annals of Medicine, 50,* 91–109. doi:10.1080/07853890.2017.1392595

Kammeyer, A., & Luiten, R. M. (2015). Oxidation events and skin aging. *Ageing Research Reviews, 21,* 16–29. doi:10.1016/j.arr.2015.01.001

Karlamangla, A. S., Miller-Martinez, D., Lachman, M. E., Tun, P. A., Koretz, B. K., & Seeman, T. E. (2014). Biological correlates of adult cognition: Midlife in the United States (MIDUS). *Neurobiology of Aging, 35,* 387–394. doi:10.1016/j.neurobiolaging.2013.07.028

Keating, S. T., Plutzky, J., & El-Osta, A. (2016). Epigenetic changes in diabetes and cardiovascular risk. *Circulation Research, 118,* 1706–1722. doi:10.1161/CIRCRESAHA.116.306819

Keller, K., & Engelhardt, M. (2013). Strength and muscle mass loss with aging process. Age and strength loss. *Muscles, Ligaments and Tendons Journal, 3,* 346–350.

Kennedy, Q., Taylor, J. L., Reade, G., & Yesavage, J. A. (2010). Age and expertise effects in aviation decision making and flight control in a flight simulator. *Aviation, Space, and Environmental Medicine, 81,* 489–497.

Ketch, C., Weedin, E., & Gibson, B. A. (2017). Management of the symptoms of perimenopause. In D. Shoupe (Ed.), *Handbook of gynecology* (pp. 487–497). Cham, Switzerland: Springer International. doi:10.1007/978-3-319-17798-4_44

Khan, N., Afaq, F., & Mukhtar, H. (2010). Lifestyle as risk factor for cancer: Evidence from human studies. *Cancer Letters, 293,* 133–143. doi:10.1016/j.canlet.2009.12.013

Khan, S. D. (2017). Aging and male reproduction. In K. Gunasekaran & N. Pandiyan (Eds.), *Male infertility* (pp. 197–206). New Delhi: Springer India. doi:10.1007/978-81-322-3604-7_13

King, B. M., & Regan, P. C. (2014). *Human sexuality today.* Boston, MA: Pearson.

Kish, J. K., Yu, M., Percy-Laurry, A., & Altekruse, S. F. (2014). Racial and ethnic disparities in cancer survival by neighborhood socioeconomic status in Surveillance, Epidemiology, and End Results (SEER) registries. Journal of the National Cancer Institute. *Monographs, 2014,* 236–243. doi:10.1093/jncimonographs/lgu020

Koh, K. K., Han, S. H., Oh, P. C., Shin, E. K., & Quon, M. J. (2010). Combination therapy for treatment or prevention of atherosclerosis: Focus on the lipid-RAAS interaction. *Atherosclerosis, 209,* 307–313. doi:10.1016/j.atherosclerosis.2009.09.007

Kotsopoulos, J., Huzarski, T., Gronwald, J., Moller, P., Lynch, H. T., Neuhausen, S. L., . . . Narod, S. A. (2016). Hormone replacement therapy after menopause and risk of breast cancer in BRCA1 mutation carriers: A case-control study. *Breast Cancer Research and Treatment, 155,* 365–373. doi:10.1007/s10549-016-3685-3

Kramer, A. F., & Madden, D. J. (2008). Attention. In F. I. M. Craik & T. A. Salthouse (Eds.), *The handbook of aging and cognition* (3rd ed., pp. 189–249). New York, NY: Psychology Press.

Lachman, M. E. (2004). Development in midlife. *Annual Review of Psychology, 55,* 305–331.

Lachman, M. E., Teshale, S., & Agrigoroaei, S. (2015). Midlife as a pivotal period in the life course: Balancing growth and decline at the crossroads of youth and old age. *International Journal of Behavioral Development, 39,* 20–31. doi:10.1177/0165025414533223

Lagouge, M., & Larsson, N. G. (2013). The role of mitochondrial DNA mutations and free radicals in disease and ageing. *Journal of Internal Medicine, 273,* 529–543. doi:10.1111/joim.12055

Lawlor, D. A., Ebrahim, S., & Smith, G. D. (2003). The association of socio-economic position across the life course and age at menopause: The British Women's Heart and Health study. *BJOG: An International Journal of Obstetrics & Gynaecology, 110,* 1078.

Lee, C., & Longo, V. (2016). Dietary restriction with and without caloric restriction for healthy aging. *F1000Research, 5,* F1000. doi:10.12688/f1000research.7136.1

Lee, Y. A., & Goto, Y. (2015). Chronic stress effects on working memory: Association with prefrontal cortical tyrosine hydroxylase. *Behavioural Brain Research, 286,* 122–127. doi:10.1016/j.bbr.2015.03.007

Leigh-Paffenroth, E. D., & Elangovan, S. (2011). Temporal processing in low-frequency channels: Effects of age and hearing loss in middle-aged listeners. *Journal of the American Academy of Audiology, 22,* 393–404. doi:10.3766/jaaa.22.7.2

Leonard, B. E., & Myint, A. (2009). The psychoneuroimmunology of depression. *Human Psychopharmacology: Clinical & Experimental, 24,* 165–175. doi:10.1002/hup.1011

Leong, A., Porneala, B., Dupuis, J., Florez, J. C., & Meigs, J. B. (2016). Type 2 diabetes genetic predisposition, obesity, and all-cause mortality risk in the U.S.: A multiethnic analysis. *Diabetes Care, 39.* Retrieved from http://care.diabetesjournals.org/content/39/4/539.short

Lin, J., Gan, C. M., Zhang, X., Jones, S., Sjöblom, T., Wood, L. D., . . . Velculescu, V. E. (2007). A multidimensional analysis of genes mutated in breast and colorectal cancers. *Genome Research, 17,* 7.

Lobo, R. A. (2017). Hormone-replacement therapy: Current thinking. *Nature Reviews Endocrinology, 13,* 220–231. doi:10.1038/nrendo.2016.164

Lobo, R. A., Pickar, J. H., Stevenson, J. C., Mack, W. J., & Hodis, H. N. (2016). Back to the future: Hormone replacement therapy as part of a prevention strategy for women at the onset of menopause. *Atherosclerosis, 254,* 282–290. doi:10.1016/j.atherosclerosis.2016.10.005

Lock, M., & Kaufert, P. (2001). Menopause, local biologies, and cultures of aging. *American Journal of Human Biology, 13,* 494–504.

Logan, A. J., & Baker, J. (2007). Cross-sectional and longitudinal profiles of age related decline in golf performance. *Journal of Sport & Exercise Psychology, 29,* S15–S15.

Low, E., Crewther, S. G., Ong, B., Perre, D., & Wijeratne, T. (2017). Compromised motor dexterity confounds processing speed task outcomes in stroke patients. *Frontiers in Neurology, 8,* 484. doi:10.3389/fneur.2017.00484

Lu, J., Liu, J., & Eden, J. (2007). The experience of menopausal symptoms by Arabic women in Sydney. *Climacteric, 10,* 72.

Lustig, C., Hasher, L., & Tonev, S. T. (2006). Distraction as a determinant of processing speed. *Psychonomic Bulletin & Review, 13,* 619–625.

Lynn, R. (2009). What has caused the Flynn effect? Secular increases in the development quotients of infants. *Intelligence, 37,* 16–24. doi:10.1016/j.intell.2008.07.008

Maddi, S. R. (2013). Personal hardiness as the basis for resilience. In S. R. Maddi (Ed.), *Hardiness: Turning stressful circumstances into resilient growth* (pp. 7–17). Dordrecht: Springer Netherlands. doi:10.1007/978-94-007-5222-1

Maddi, S. R. (2016). Hardiness as a pathway to resilience under stress. In U. Kumar (Ed.), *The Routledge international handbook of psychosocial resilience* (p. 104). New York, NY: Routledge.

Madsen, R., & Birkelund, R. (2016). Women's experiences during myocardial infarction: Systematic review and meta-ethnography. *Journal of Clinical Nursing, 25,* 599–609. doi:10.1111/jocn.13096

Marshall, B. L. (2007). Climacteric redux? *Men & Masculinities, 9,* 509–529.

Marsland, A. L., Walsh, C., Lockwood, K., & John-Henderson, N. A. (2017). The effects of acute psychological stress on circulating and stimulated inflammatory markers: A systematic review and meta-analysis. *Brain, Behavior, and Immunity, 64,* 208–219. doi:10.1016/J.BBI.2017.01.011

Mather, K. A., Jorm, A. F., Parslow, R. A., & Christensen, H. (2011). Is telomere length a biomarker of aging? A review. *Journal of Gerontology Series A: Biological Sciences and Medical Sciences, 66,* 202–213. doi:10.1093/gerona/glq180

McEwen, B. S. (2018). Neurobiological and systemic effects of chronic stress. *Chronic Stress.* Advance online publication. doi:10.1177/2470547017692328

McLeod, P., Sommerville, P., & Reed, N. (2005). Are automated actions beyond conscious access? In J. Duncan, P. McLeod, & L. Phillips (Eds.), *Measuring the mind* (pp. 359–371). New York, NY: Oxford University Press.

McNamara, M., Batur, P., & DeSapri, K. T. (2015). In the clinic: Perimenopause. *Annals of Internal Medicine, 162,* ITC1–ITC15. doi:10.7326/AITC201502030

McNulty, J. K., Wenner, C. A., & Fisher, T. D. (2016). Longitudinal associations among relationship satisfaction, sexual satisfaction, and frequency of sex in early marriage. *Archives of Sexual Behavior, 45,* 85–97. doi:10.1007/s10508-014-0444-6

Mehta, K. M., & Yeo, G. W. (2017). Systematic review of dementia prevalence and incidence in United States race/ethnic populations. *Alzheimer's & Dementia, 13,* 72–83. doi:10.1016/j.jalz.2016.06.2360

Mielck, A., Vogelmann, M., Leidl, R., Mielck, A., Reitmeir, P., Vogelmann, M., . . . Williams, A. (2014). Health-related quality of life and socioeconomic status: Inequalities among adults with a chronic disease. *Health and Quality of Life Outcomes, 12,* 58. doi:10.1186/1477-7525-12-58

Milholland, B., Suh, Y., & Vijg, J. (2017). Mutation and catastrophe in the aging genome. *Experimental Gerontology, 94,* 34–40. doi:10.1016/j.exger.2017.02.073

Miller, T. A., Allen, R. H., Kaunitz, A. M., & Cwiak, C. A. (2018). Contraception for midlife women: A review. *Menopause, 25,* 817–827. doi:10.1097/GME.0000000000001073

Mitchell, W. K., Williams, J., Atherton, P., Larvin, M., Lund, J., & Narici, M. (2012). Sarcopenia, dynapenia, and the impact of advancing age on human skeletal muscle size and strength: A quantitative review. *Frontiers in Physiology, 3,* 260. doi:10.3389/fphys.2012.00260

Mitteldorf, J. (2016). An epigenetic clock controls aging. *Biogerontology, 17,* 257–265. doi:10.1007/s10522-015-9617-5

Montecino-Rodriguez, E., Berent-Maoz, B., & Dorshkind, K. (2013). Causes, consequences, and reversal of immune system aging. *Journal of Clinical Investigation, 123,* 958–965. doi:10.1172/JCI64096

Montesanto, A., Latorre, V., Giordano, M., Martino, C., Domma, F., & Passarino, G. (2011). The genetic component of human longevity: Analysis of the survival advantage of parents and siblings of Italian nonagenarians. *European Journal of Human Genetics, 19,* 882–886. doi:10.1038/ejhg.2011.40

Moore, C. S., Grant, M. D., Zink, T. A., Panizzon, M. S., Franz, C. E., Logue, M. W., . . . Lyons, M. J. (2014). Erectile dysfunction, vascular risk, and cognitive performance in late middle age. *Psychology and Aging, 29,* 163–172. doi:10.1037/a0035463

Morrow, D. G., Menard, W. E., Ridolfo, H. E., Stine-Morrow, E. A. L., Teller, T., & Bryant, D. (2003). Expertise, cognitive ability, and age effects on pilot communication. *International Journal of Aviation Psychology, 13,* 345.

Morrow, D. G., & Schriver, A. (2007). External support for pilot communication: Implications for age-related design. *International Journal of Cognitive Technology, 12,* 21–30.

Moskalev, A. A., Aliper, A. M., Smit-McBride, Z., Buzdin, A., & Zhavoronkov, A. (2014). Genetics and epigenetics of aging and longevity. *Cell Cycle, 13,* 1063–1077. doi:10.4161/cc.28433

Moxley, J. H., & Charness, N. (2013). Meta-analysis of age and skill effects on recalling chess positions and selecting the best move. *Psychonomic Bulletin & Review, 20,* 1017–1022. doi:10.3758/s13423-013-0420-5

Muise, A., Schimmack, U., & Impett, E. A. (2016). Sexual frequency predicts greater well-being, but more is not always better. *Social Psychological and Personality Science, 7,* 295–302. doi:10.1177/1948550615616462

Murphy, N., Alderman, P., Voege Harvey, K., & Harris, N. (2017). Women and heart disease: An evidence-based update. *Journal for Nurse Practitioners, 13,* 610–616. doi:10.1016/j.nurpra.2017.07.011

Muscari, A., Bianchi, G., Forti, P., Giovagnoli, M., Magalotti, D., Pandolfi, P., & Zoli, M. (2017). Physical activity and other determinants of survival in the oldest adults. *Journal of the American Geriatrics Society, 65,* 402–406. doi:10.1111/jgs.14569

Naicker, K., Johnson, J. A., Skogen, J. C., Manuel, D., Øverland, S., Sivertsen, B., & Colman, I. (2017). Type 2 diabetes and comorbid symptoms of depression and anxiety: Longitudinal associations with mortality risk. *Diabetes Care, 40,* 352–358. doi:10.2337/dc16-2018

Nappi, R. E., & Nijland, E. A. (2008). Women's perception of sexuality around the menopause: Outcomes of a European telephone survey. *European Journal of Obstetrics & Gynecology & Reproductive Biology, 137,* 10–16. Retrieved from 10.1016/j.ejogrb.2006.10.036

National Center for Health Statistics. (2015). *Deaths: Final data for 2013.* Retrieved from http://www.cdc.gov/nchs/data/nvsr/nvsr64/nvsr64_02.pdf

Nedergaard, M., & Goldman, S. A. (2016). Brain drain. *Scientific American, 314,* 44–49.

Retrieved from http://www.ncbi.nlm.nih.gov/pubmed/27066643

Nelson, H. D. (2008). Menopause. *Lancet, 371,* 760–770.

Nelson, H. D., Humphrey, L. L., LeBlanc, E., Miller, J., Takano, L., Chan, B. K. S., . . . Teutsch, S. M. (2002). *Postmenopausal hormone replacement therapy for primary prevention of chronic conditions.* Summary of the evidence for the U.S. Preventive Services Task Force. Rockville, MD: Agency for Healthcare Research and Quality. Retrieved from http://www.ahrq.gov/clinic/3rduspstf/hrt/hrtsum1.htm

Neugarten, B. L. (1968). The awareness of middle aging. In B. L. Neugarten (Ed.), *Middle age and aging* (pp. 137–147). Chicago, IL: University of Chicago Press.

Nguyen, B. T., Han, X., Jemal, A., & Drope, J. (2016). Diet quality, risk factors and access to care among low-income uninsured American adults in states expanding Medicaid vs. states not expanding under the affordable care act. *Preventive Medicine, 91,* 169–171. doi:10.1016/J.YPMED.2016.08.015

Nickels, S., Truong, T., Hein, R., Stevens, K., Buck, K., Behrens, S., . . . Chang-Claude, J. (2013). Evidence of gene-environment interactions between common breast cancer susceptibility loci and established environmental risk factors. *PLoS Genetics, 9,* e1003284. doi:10.1371/journal.pgen.1003284

Nilsson, J., Thomas, A. J., O'Brien, J. T., & Gallagher, P. (2014). White matter and cognitive decline in aging: A focus on processing speed and variability. *Journal of the International Neuropsychological Society, 20,* 262–267. doi:10.1017/S1355617713001458

Nisbett, R. E., Aronson, J., Blair, C., Dickens, W., Flynn, J., Halpern, D. F., & Turkheimer, E. (2013). Intelligence: New findings and theoretical developments. *American Psychologist, 67,* 130–159. doi:10.1037/a0026699

Nosek, M., Kennedy, H. P., & Gudmundsdottir, M. (2012). Distress during the menopause transition: A rich contextual analysis of midlife women's narratives. *Sage Open, 2.* doi:10.1177/2158244012455178

Nwankwo, T., Yoon, S. S., Burt, V., & Gu, Q. (2013). Hypertension among adults in the United States: National Health and Nutrition Examination survey, 2011-2012. *NCHS Data Brief.* Retrieved from http://www.ncbi.nlm.nih.gov/pubmed/24171916

Ohira, T., Hozawa, A., Iribarren, C., Daviglus, M. L., Matthews, K. A., Gross, M., & Jacobs, D. R. (2008). Longitudinal association of serum carotenoids and tocopherols with hostility: The CARDIA study. *American Journal of Epidemiology, 167,* 42.

Old, S. R., & Naveh-Benjamin, M. (2008). Differential effects of age on item and associative measures of memory: A meta-analysis. *Psychology and Aging, 23,* 104–118. doi:10.1037/0882-7974.23.1.104

Oltmanns, J., Godde, B., Winneke, A. H., Richter, G., Niemann, C., Voelcker-Rehage, C., . . . Staudinger, U. M. (2017). Don't lose your brain at work: The role of recurrent novelty at work in cognitive and brain aging. *Frontiers in Psychology, 8,* 117. doi:10.3389/fpsyg.2017.00117

Opresko, P. L., & Shay, J. W. (2017). Telomere-associated aging disorders. *Ageing Research Reviews, 33,* 52–66. doi:10.1016/j.arr.2016.05.009

Ormerod, T. C. (2005). Planning and ill-defined problems. In R. Morris & G. Ward (Eds.), *The cognitive psychology of planning.* London, England: Psychology Press.

Owsley, C., McGwin, G., Jackson, G. R., Kallies, K., & Clark, M. (2007). Cone- and rod-mediated dark adaptation impairment in age-related maculopathy. *Ophthalmology, 114,* 1728–1735.

Palta, P., Schneider, A. L. C., Biessels, G. J., Touradji, P., & Hill-Briggs, F. (2014). Magnitude of cognitive dysfunction in adults with type 2 diabetes: A meta-analysis of six cognitive domains and the most frequently reported neuropsychological tests within domains. *Journal of the International Neuropsychological Society, 20,* 278–291. doi:10.1017/S1355617713001483

Panay, N., Hamoda, H., Arya, R., & Savvas, M. (2013). The 2013 British Menopause Society & Women's Health Concern recommendations on hormone replacement therapy. *Menopause International, 19,* 59–68. doi:10.1177/1754045313489645

Paramei, G. V., & Oakley, B. (2014). Variation of color discrimination across the life span. *Journal of the Optical Society of America: A, Optics, Image Science, and Vision, 31,* A375–A384. doi:10.1364/JOSAA.31.00A375

Park, D. C., & Festini, S. B. (2017). Theories of memory and aging: A look at the past and a glimpse of the future. *Journal of Gerontology Series B: Psychological Sciences and Social Sciences, 72,* 82–90. doi:10.1093/geronb/gbw066

Park, M., Katon, W. J., & Wolf, F. M. (2013). Depression and risk of mortality in individuals with diabetes: A meta-analysis and systematic review. *General Hospital Psychiatry, 35,* 217–225. doi:10.1016/j.genhosppsych.2013.01.006

Passow, S., Westerhausen, R., Wartenburger, I., Hugdahl, K., Heekeren, H. R., Lindenberger, U., & Li, S. C. (2012). Human aging compromises attentional control of auditory perception. *Psychology and Aging, 27,* 99–105. doi:10.1037/a0025667

Patel, K. A., Oram, R. A., Flanagan, S. E., De Franco, E., Colclough, K., Shepherd, M., . . . Hattersley, A. T. (2016). Type 1 Diabetes Genetic Risk Score: a novel tool to discriminate monogenic and type 1 diabetes. *Diabetes.* Retrieved from http://diabetes.diabetesjournals.org/content/early/2016/03/28/db15-1690

Perlmutter, M., Kaplan, M., & Nyquest, L. (1990). Development of adaptive competence in adulthood. *Human Development, 33,* 185–197.

Peters, S. A. E., Huxley, R. R., & Woodward, M. (2014). Diabetes as a risk factor for stroke in women compared with men: a systematic review and meta-analysis of 64 cohorts, including 775 385 individuals and 12 539 strokes. *The Lancet, 383,* 1973–1980. doi:10.1016/S0140-6736(14)60040-4

Pietschnig, J., & Voracek, M. (2015). One century of global IQ gains: A formal meta-analysis of the Flynn effect (1909–2013). *Perspectives on Psychological Science, 10,* 282–306. doi:10.1177/1745691615577701

Plog, B. A., & Nedergaard, M. (2018). The glymphatic system in central nervous system health and disease: Past, present, and future. *Annual Review of Pathology: Mechanisms of Disease, 13,* 379–394. https://doi.org/10.1146/annurev-pathol-051217-111018

Quan, T., & Fisher, G. J. (2015). Role of age-associated alterations of the dermal extracellular matrix microenvironment in human skin aging: A mini-review. *Gerontology, 61,* 427–434. doi:10.1159/000371708

Quaranta, N., Coppola, F., Casulli, M., Barulli, M. R., Panza, F., Tortelli, R., . . . Logroscino, G. (2015). Epidemiology of age related hearing loss: A review. *Hearing, Balance and Communication, 13,* 77–81. doi:10.3109/21695717.2014.994869

Robert, L., & Labat-Robert, J. (2016). Skin. In S. K. Whitbourne (Ed.), *The encyclopedia of adulthood and aging* (pp. 1–4). Hoboken, NJ: John Wiley. doi:10.1002/9781118521373.wbeaa165

Roberts, R. O., Knopman, D. S., Przybelski, S. A., Mielke, M. M., Kantarci, K., Preboske, G. M., . . . Jack, C. R. (2014). Association of type 2 diabetes with brain atrophy and cognitive impairment. *Neurology, 82,* 1132–1141. doi:10.1212/WNL.0000000000000269

Roring, R. W., & Charness, N. (2007). A multilevel model analysis of expertise in chess across the life span. *Psychology and Aging, 22,* 291–299.

Rossi, A. S. (2004). The menopausal transition and aging processes. In O. G. Brim, C. D. Ryff, & R. C. Kessler (Eds.), *How healthy are we? A national study of well-being at midlife* (pp. 153–201). Chicago, IL: University of Chicago Press.

Rowe, G., Hasher, L., & Turcotte, J. (2010). Interference, aging, and visuospatial working memory: The role of similarity. *Neuropsychology, 24,* 804–807. doi:10.1037/a0020244

Rowell, S. F., Green, J. S., Teachman, B. A., & Salthouse, T. A. (2016). Age does not matter: Memory complaints are related to negative affect throughout adulthood. *Aging & Mental Health, 20,* 1255–1263. doi:10.1080/13607863.2015.1078284

Roy, T., & Lloyd, C. E. (2012). Epidemiology of depression and diabetes: a systematic review. *Journal of Affective Disorders, 142*(Suppl.), S8–S21. doi:10.1016/S0165-0327(12)70004-6

Salthouse, T. A. (1984). Effects of age and skill in typing. *Journal of Experimental Psychology: General, 113,* 345–371.

Salthouse, T. A. (2012). Consequences of age-related cognitive declines. *Annual Review of Psychology, 63,* 201–226. doi:10.1146/annurev-psych-120710-100328

Salthouse, T. A. (2014). Why are there different age relations in cross-sectional and longitudinal comparisons of cognitive functioning? *Current Directions in Psychological Science, 23,* 252–256. doi:10.1177/0963721414535212

Salthouse, T. A. (2016). Continuity of cognitive change across adulthood. *Psychonomic Bulletin & Review, 23,* 932–939. doi:10.3758/s13423-015-0910-8

Salthouse, T. A. (2017). Neural correlates of age-related slowing. In R. Cabeza, L. Nyberg, & D. C. Park (Eds.), *Cognitive neuroscience of aging: Linking cognitive and cerebral aging.* New York, NY: Oxford University Press.

Salthouse, T. A., & Madden, D. J. (2013). Information processing speed and aging. In J. DeLuca & J. H. Kalmar (Eds.), *Information processing speed in clinical populations* (pp. 221–239). New York, NY: Psychology Press.

Salthouse, T. A., & Pink, J. E. (2008). Why is working memory related to fluid intelligence? *Psychonomic Bulletin & Review, 15,* 364–371.

Salvioli, S., Monti, D., Lanzarini, C., Conte, M., Pirazzini, C., Giulia Bacalini, M., . . . Franceschi, C. (2013). Immune system, cell senescence, aging and longevity—Inflamm-aging reappraised. *Current Pharmaceutical Design, 19,* 1675–1679. Retrieved from http://www.ingentaconnect.com/content/ben/cpd/2013/00000019/00000009/art00015

Sampselle, C. M., Harris, V., Harlow, S. D., & Sowers, M. (2002). Midlife development and menopause in African American and Caucasian women. *Health Care for Women International, 23,* 351–363.

Sanchis-Gomar, F., Olaso-Gonzalez, G., Corella, D., Gomez-Cabrera, M. C., & Vina, J. (2011). Increased average longevity among the "Tour de France" cyclists. *International Journal of Sports Medicine, 32,* 644–647. doi:10.1055/s-0031-1271711

Sandvik, A. M., Bartone, P. T., Hystad, S. W., Phillips, T. M., Thayer, J. F., & Johnsen, B. H. (2013). Psychological hardiness predicts neuroimmunological responses to stress. *Psychology, Health & Medicine, 18,* 705–713. doi:10.1080/13548506.2013.772304

Santoro, N. (2016). Perimenopause: From research to practice. *Journal of Women's Health, 25,* 332–339. doi:10.1089/jwh.2015.5556

Schaie, K. W. (2013). *Developmental influences on adult intelligence: The Seattle Longitudinal Study.* New York, NY: Oxford University Press.

Schaie, K. W. (2016). The longitudinal study of adult cognitive development. In R. J. Sternberg, S. T. Fiske, & D. J. Foss (Eds.), *Scientists making a difference: One hundred eminent behavioral and brain* (pp. 218–222). New York, NY: Cambridge University Press.

Schaie, K. W., & Zanjani, F. A. K. (2006). Intellectual development across adulthood. In C. Hoare (Ed.), *Handbook of adult development and learning* (pp. 99–122). New York, NY: Oxford University Press.

Schieman, S., & Koltai, J. (2017). Discovering pockets of complexity: Socioeconomic status, stress exposure, and the nuances of the health gradient. *Social Science Research, 63,* 1–18. doi:10.1016/J.SSRESEARCH.2016.09.023

Schmiedek, F. (2017). Development of cognition and intelligence. In J. Specht (Ed.), *Personality development across the lifespan* (pp. 309–323). New York, NY: Elsevier. doi:10.1016/B978-0-12-804674-6.00019-3

Schöttker, B., Brenner, H., Jansen, E. E. H., Gardiner, J., Peasey, A., Kubínová, R., . . . Tosukhowong, P. (2015). Evidence for the free radical/oxidative stress theory of ageing from the CHANCES consortium: A meta-analysis of individual participant data. *BMC Medicine, 13*, 300. doi:10.1186/s12916-015-0537-7

Schwartz, B. L., & Frazier, L. D. (2005). Tip-of-the-tongue states and aging: Contrasting psycholinguistic and metacognitive perspectives. *Journal of General Psychology, 132*, 377–391.

Segerstrom, S. C., & O'Connor, D. B. (2012). Stress, health and illness: Four challenges for the future. *Psychology & Health, 27*, 128–140. doi:10.1080/08870446.2012.659516

Seidman, S. N., & Weiser, M. (2013). Testosterone and mood in aging men. *The Psychiatric Clinics of North America, 36*, 177–182. doi:10.1016/j.psc.2013.01.007

Shamloul, R., & Ghanem, H. (2013). Erectile dysfunction. *The Lancet, 381*, 153–165. doi:10.1016/S0140-6736(12)60520-0

Sharma, M., & Rush, S. E. (2014). Mindfulness-based stress reduction as a stress management intervention for healthy individuals. *Journal of Evidence-Based Complementary & Alternative Medicine, 19*, 271–286. doi:10.1177/2156587214543143

Shores, M. M. (2014). The implications of low testosterone on mortality in men. *Current Sexual Health Reports, 6*, 235–243. doi:10.1007/s11930-014-0030-x

Siegel, R. L., Miller, K. D., & Jemal, A. (2018). Cancer statistics, 2018. *CA: A Cancer Journal for Clinicians, 68*, 7–30. doi:10.3322/caac.21442

Simon, J. A. (2011). Identifying and treating sexual dysfunction in postmenopausal women: The role of estrogen. *Journal of Women's Health (2002), 20*, 1453–1465. doi:10.1089/jwh.2010.2151

Smith, R. L., Gallicchio, L., & Flaws, J. A. (2017). Factors affecting sexual activity in midlife women: Results from the Midlife Health study. *Journal of Women's Health, 26*, 103–108. doi:10.1089/jwh.2016.5881

Song, J., Mailick, M. R., Greenberg, J. S., Ryff, C. D., & Lachman, M. E. (2016). Cognitive aging in parents of children with disabilities. *Journal of Gerontology Series B: Psychological Sciences and Social Sciences, 71*, 821–830. doi:10.1093/geronb/gbv015

Sörensen, S., White, K., & Ramchandran, R. S. (2016). Vision in mid and late life. In S. K. Whitbourne (Ed.), *The encyclopedia of adulthood and aging* (pp. 1–5). Hoboken, NJ: John Wiley. doi:10.1002/9781118521373.wbeaa189

Speakman, J. R., & Mitchell, S. E. (2011). Caloric restriction. *Molecular Aspects of Medicine, 32*, 159–221. doi:10.1016/j.mam.2011.07.001

Stephens, P. J., Tarpey, P. S., Davies, H., Van Loo, P., Greenman, C., Wedge, D. C., . . . Stratton, M. R. (2012). The landscape of cancer genes and mutational processes in breast cancer. *Nature, 486*, 400–404. doi:10.1038/nature11017

Stevenson, J. C., Hodis, H. N., Pickar, J. H., & Lobo, R. A. (2009). Coronary heart disease and menopause management: The swinging pendulum of HRT. *Atherosclerosis, 207*, 336–340. doi:10.1016/j.atherosclerosis.2009.05.033

Stickgold, R., & Walker, M. P. (2013). Sleep-dependent memory triage: Evolving

generalization through selective processing. *Nature Neuroscience, 16*, 139–145. doi:10.1038/nn.3303

Stone, A. A., Schneider, S., & Broderick, J. E. (2017). Psychological stress declines rapidly from age 50 in the United States: Yet another well-being paradox. *Journal of Psychosomatic Research, 103*, 22–28. doi:10.1016/j.jpsychores.2017.09.016

Strauss, J. R. (2011). Contextual influences on women's health concerns and attitudes toward menopause. *Health & Social Work, 36*, 121–127. doi:10.1093/hsw/36.2.121

Sundet, J. M., Barlaug, D. G., & Torjussen, T. M. (2004). The end of the Flynn effect? A study of secular trends in mean intelligence test scores of Norwegian conscripts during half a century. *Intelligence, 32*, 349–362.

Sussman, M., Trocio, J., Best, C., Mirkin, S., Bushmakin, A. G., Yood, R., . . . Gallia, C. (2015). Prevalence of menopausal symptoms among mid-life women: Findings from electronic medical records. *BMC Women's Health, 15*, 58. doi:10.1186/s12905-015-0217-y

Sylvain-Roy, S., Lungu, O., & Belleville, S. (2014). Normal aging of the attentional control functions that underlie working memory. *Journal of Gerontology, Series B, Psychological Sciences and Social Sciences, 70*, gbt166. doi:10.1093/geronb/gbt166

Tawfik, H., Kline, J., Jacobson, J., Tehranifar, P., Protacio, A., Flom, J. D., . . . Terry, M. B. (2015). Life course exposure to smoke and early menopause and menopausal transition. *Menopause, 22*, 1076–1083. doi:10.1097/GME.0000000000000444

te Nijenhuis, J. (2013). The Flynn effect, group differences, and g loadings. *Personality and Individual Differences, 55*, 224–228. doi:10.1016/j.paid.2011.12.023

Teasdale, T. W., & Owen, D. R. (2000). Forty-year secular trends in cognitive abilities. *Intelligence, 28*, 115–120.

Thomas, H. N., Hamm, M., Hess, R., & Thurston, R. C. (2018). Changes in sexual function among midlife women. *Menopause, 25*, 286–292. doi:10.1097/GME.0000000000000988

Thomas, H. N., Hess, R., & Thurston, R. C. (2015). Correlates of sexual activity and satisfaction in midlife and older women. *Annals of Family Medicine, 13*, 336–342. doi:10.1370/afm.1820

Tobin, D. J. (2017). Introduction to skin aging. *Journal of Tissue Viability, 26*, 37–46. doi:10.1016/j.jtv.2016.03.002

Tononi, G., & Cirelli, C. (2014). Sleep and the price of plasticity: From synaptic and cellular homeostasis to memory consolidation and integration. *Neuron, 81*, 12–34. doi:10.1016/j.neuron.2013.12.025

Torpy, J. M. (2007). Women's sexual concerns after menopause. *JAMA: Journal of the American Medical Association, 297*, 664.

Tourlouki, E., Polychronopoulos, E., Zeimbekis, A., Tsakountakis, N., Bountziouka, V., Lioliou, E., . . . Panagiotakos, D. B. (2010). The "secrets" of the long livers in Mediterranean islands: The MEDIS study. *European Journal of Public Health, 20*, 659–664.

Trahan, L. H., Stuebing, K. K., Fletcher, J. M., & Hiscock, M. (2014). The Flynn effect: A meta-analysis. *Psychological Bulletin, 140*, 1332–1360. doi:10.1037/a0037173

Truscott, R. J. (2009). Presbyopia. Emerging from a blur towards an understanding of the molecular basis for this most common eye condition. *Experimental Eye Research, 88*, 241–247. doi:10.1016/j.exer.2008.07.003

Unsworth, N., Fukuda, K., Awh, E., & Vogel, E. K. (2014). Working memory and fluid intelligence: Capacity, attention control, and secondary memory retrieval. *Cognitive Psychology, 71*, 1–26. doi:10.1016/j.cogpsych.2014.01.003

Vagelatos, N. T., & Eslick, G. D. (2013). Type 2 diabetes as a risk factor for Alzheimer's disease: The confounders, interactions, and neuropathology associated with this relationship. *Epidemiologic Reviews, 35*, 152–160. doi:10.1093/epirev/mxs012

Vainionpää, K., & Topo, P. (2006). The construction of male menopause in Finnish popular magazines. *Critical Public Health, 16*, 19–34.

Valko, M., Jomova, K., Rhodes, C. J., Kuča, K., & Musilek, K. (2016). Redox- and non-redox-metal-induced formation of free radicals and their role in human disease. *Archives of Toxicology, 90*, 1–37. doi:10.1007/s00204-015-1579-5

van Dooren, F. E. P., Nefs, G., Schram, M. T., Verhey, F. R. J., Denollet, J., & Pouwer, F. (2013). Depression and risk of mortality in people with diabetes mellitus: A systematic review and meta-analysis. *PLoS ONE, 8*, e57058. doi:10.1371/journal.pone.0057058

Van Houten, B., Santa-Gonzalez, G. A., & Camargo, M. (2018). DNA repair after oxidative stress: Current challenges. *Current Opinion in Toxicology, 7*, 9–16. doi:10.1016/J.COTOX.2017.10.009

Vestergren, P., & Nilsson, L.-G. (2011). Perceived causes of everyday memory problems in a population-based sample aged 39–99. *Applied Cognitive Psychology, 25*, 641–646. doi:10.1002/acp.1734

Vogelstein, B., & Kinzler, K. W. (2004). Cancer genes and the pathways they control. *Nature Medicine, 10*, 789–799.

Vogt, D. S., Rizvi, S. L., & Shipherd, J. C. (2008). Longitudinal investigation of reciprocal relationship between stress reactions and hardiness. *Personality and Social Psychology Bulletin, 34*, 61–73.

Vona-Davis, L., & Rose, D. P. (2009). The influence of socioeconomic disparities on breast cancer tumor biology and prognosis: A review. *Journal of Women's Health, 18*, 883–893. doi:10.1089/jwh.2008.1127

Walsh, K. E., & Berman, J. R. (2004). Sexual dysfunction in the older woman. *Drugs & Aging, 21*, 655–675.

Walter, S., Atzmon, G., Demerath, E. W., Garcia, M. E., Kaplan, R. C., Kumari, M., . . . Evans, D. A. (2011). A genome-wide association study of aging. *Neurobiology of Aging, 32*, 2109.e15–2109.e28. doi:10.1016/j.neurobiolaging.2011.05.026

Walther, A., Mahler, F., Debelak, R., & Ehlert, U. (2017). Psychobiological protective factors modifying the association between age and sexual health in men: Findings from the Men's Health 40+ study. *American Journal of Men's Health, 11*, 737–747. doi:10.1177/1557988316689238

Wettstein, M., & Wahl, H.-W. (2016). Hearing. In S. K. Whitbourne (Ed.), *The encyclopedia of adulthood and aging* (pp. 1–5). Hoboken, NJ: John Wiley. doi:10.1002/9781118521373.wbeaa202

Wiegand, C., Raschke, C., & Elsner, P. (2017). Skin aging: A brief summary of characteristic changes. In M. A. Farage, K. W. Miller, & H. I. Maibac (Eds.), *Textbook of aging skin* (pp. 55–65). Berlin, Germany: Springer. doi:10.1007/978-3-662-47398-6_5

Williams, R. L. (2013). Overview of the Flynn effect. *Intelligence, 41,* 753–764. doi:10.1016/j.intell.2013.04.010

World Health Organization. (2015). *World health statistics 2015.* Retrieved from http://www.who.int/gho/publications/world_health_statistics/2015/en/

Xi, H., Li, C., Ren, F., Zhang, H., & Zhang, L. (2013). Telomere, aging and age-related diseases. *Aging Clinical and Experimental Research, 25,* 139–146. doi:10.1007/s40520-013-0021-1

Xie, L., Kang, H., Xu, Q., Chen, M. J., Liao, Y., Thiyagarajan, M., . . . Nedergaard, M. (2013). Sleep drives metabolite clearance from the adult brain. *Science, 342,* 373–377. doi:10.1126/science.1241224

Xu, Z., Duc, K. D., Holcman, D., & Teixeira, M. T. (2013). The length of the shortest telomere as the major determinant of the onset of replicative senescence. *Genetics, 194,* 847–857. doi:10.1534/genetics.113.152322

Zanto, T. P., & Gazzaley, A. (2017). Cognitive control and the ageing brain. In T. Egner (Ed.), *The Wiley handbook of cognitive control* (pp. 476–490). Hoboken, NJ: John Wiley.

Zaval, L., Li, Y., Johnson, E. J., & Weber, E. U. (2015). Complementary contributions of fluid and crystallized intelligence to decision making across the life span. In T. M. Hess, J. Strough, & C. E. Löckenhoff (Eds.), *Aging and decision making* (pp. 149–168). London, UK: Elsevier. doi:10.1016/B978-0-12-417148-0.00008-X

Ziegler, D. V., Wiley, C. D., & Velarde, M. C. (2015). Mitochondrial effectors of cellular senescence: Beyond the free radical theory of aging. *Aging Cell, 14,* 1–7. doi:10.1111/acel.12287

Chapter 16

AARP. (2002). *The grandparent study: 2002 report.* Washington, DC: Author.

AAUW. (2017). *The simple truth about the gender pay gap (Spring 2017).* Retrieved from http://www.aauw.org/research/the-simple-truth-about-the-gender-pay-gap/

Ackerman, S., Zuroff, D. C., & Moskowitz, D. S. (2000). Generativity in midlife and young adults: Links to agency, communion, and subjective well-being. *International Journal of Aging & Human Development, 50,* 17–41. doi:10.2190/9F51-LR6T-JHRJ-2QW6

Adams, G. A., & Rau, B. L. (2011). Putting off tomorrow to do what you want today: Planning for retirement. *The American Psychologist, 66,* 180–92. doi:10.1037/a0022131

Adams-Price, C. E., Nadorff, D. K., Morse, L. W., Davis, K. T., & Stearns, M. A. (2018). The creative benefits scale. *The International Journal of Aging and Human Development, 86,* 242–265. doi:10.1177/0091415017699939

Agrigoroaei, S., Lee-Attardo, A., & Lachman, M. E. (2017). Stress and subjective age: Those with greater financial stress look older. *Research on Aging, 39,* 1075–1099. doi:10.1177/0164027516658502

American Society of Plastic Surgeons. (2017). *2016 plastic surgery statistics report.* Retrieved April 9, 2018, from www.plasticsurgery.org

American Society of Plastic Surgeons. (2018). *2017 plastic surgery statistics report.* Retrieved April 9, 2018, from www.plasticsurgery.org

An, J. S., & Cooney, T. M. (2006). Psychological well-being in mid to late life: The role of generativity development and parent–child relationships across the lifespan. *International Journal of Behavioral Development, 30,* 410–421.

Arnett, J. J. (2018). Happily stressed: The complexity of well-being in midlife. *Journal of Adult Development.* Advance online publication. doi:10.1007/s10804-018-9291-3

Attar-Schwartz, S., Tan, J. P., Buchanan, A., Flouri, E., & Griggs, J. (2009). Grandparenting and adolescent adjustment in two-parent biological, lone-parent, and step-families. *Journal of Family Psychology, 23,* 67–75. doi:10.1037/a0014383

Aumann, K., Galinsky, E., Sakai, K., Brown, M., & Bond, J. T. (2010). *The elder care study: Everyday realities and wishes for change.* New York, NY: Families and Work Institute.

Avolio, B. J., & Sosik, J. J. (1999). A life-span framework for assessing the impact of work on white-collar workers. In S. L. Willis & J. D. Reid (Eds.), *Life in the middle: Psychological and social development in middle age* (pp. 249–274). San Diego, CA: Academic Press.

Barak, B. (2009). Age identity: A cross-cultural global approach. *International Journal of Behavioral Development, 33,* 2–11. doi:10.1177/0165025408099485

Barnes, J., Gardiner, J., Sutcliffe, A., & Melhuish, E. (2013). The parenting of preschool children by older mothers in the United Kingdom. *European Journal of Developmental Psychology, 11,* 397–419. doi:10.1080/17405629.2013.863728

Barnes-Farrell, J. L., & Matthews, R. A. (2007). Age and work attitudes. In K. S. Shultz & G. A. Adams (Eds.), *Aging and work in the 21st century* (pp. 139–162). Mahwah, NJ: Lawrence Erlbaum.

Barrett, A. E. (2003). Socioeconomic status and age identity: The role of dimensions of health in the subjective construction of age. *Journals of Gerontology Series B: Psychological Sciences & Social Sciences, 58B,* S101.

Barrett, A. E., & Montepare, J. M. (2015). "It's about time": Applying life span and life course perspectives to the study of subjective age. *Annual Review of Gerontology and Geriatrics, 35,* 55–77. doi:10.1891/0198-8794.35.55

Barrett, A. E., & Robbins, C. (2008). The multiple sources of women's aging anxiety and their relationship with psychological distress. *Journal of Aging and Health, 20,* 32–65. doi:10.1177/0898264307309932

Baum, N., Rahav, G., & Sharon, D. (2005). Changes in the self-concepts of divorced women. *Journal of Divorce & Remarriage, 43,* 47–67.

Beaumont, S. L., & Pratt, M. M. (2011). Identity processing styles and psychosocial balance during early and middle adulthood: The role of identity in intimacy and generativity. *Journal of Adult Development, 18,* 172–183. doi:10.1007/s10804-011-9125-z

Belsky, J., Jaffee, S., Hsieh, K. H., & Silva, P. A. (2001). Child-rearing antecedents of intergenerational relations in young adulthood: A prospective study. *Developmental Psychology, 37,* 801–813.

Bem, S. L. (1985). Androgyny and gender schema theory: A conceptual and empirical integration. In T. B. Sondregger (Ed.), *Nebraska Symposium on Motivation, 1984: Psychology and gender* (pp. 76–103). Lincoln: University of Nebraska Press.

Bergland, A., Nicolaisen, M., & Thorsen, K. (2014). Predictors of subjective age in people aged 40–79 years: A five-year follow-up study. The impact of mastery, mental and physical health. *Aging & Mental Health, 18,* 653–661. doi:10.1080/13607863.2013.869545

Beutel, M. E., Glaesmer, H., Wiltink, J., Marian, H., & Brähler, E. (2010). Life satisfaction, anxiety, depression and resilience across the life span of men. *The Aging Male, 13,* 32–39.

Billing, A., Ehrle, J., & Kortenkamp, K. (2002). *Children cared for by relatives: What do we know about their well-being?* Washington, DC: The Urban Institute.

Birditt, K. S., Antonucci, T. C., & Tighe, L. (2012). Enacted support during stressful life events in middle and older adulthood: An examination of the interpersonal context. *Psychology and Aging, 27,* 728–741. doi:10.1037/a0026967

Birditt, K. S., Manalel, J. A., Kim, K., Zarit, S. H., & Fingerman, K. L. (2017). Daily interactions with aging parents and adult children: Associations with negative affect and diurnal cortisol. *Journal of Family Psychology, 31,* 699–709. doi:10.1037/fam0000317

Björkenstam, E., Hallqvist, J., Dalman, C., & Ljung, R. (2013). Risk of new psychiatric episodes in the year following divorce in midlife: Cause or selection? A nationwide register-based study of 703,960 individuals. *The International Journal of Social Psychiatry, 59,* 801–804. doi:10.1177/0020764012461213

Bleidorn, W., Hopwood, C. J., & Lucas, R. E. (2018). Life events and personality trait change. *Journal of Personality, 86,* 83–96. doi:10.1111/jopy.12286

Blieszner, R. (2014). The worth of friendship: Can friends keep us happy and healthy? *Generations, 38,* 24–30.

Bloch, L., Haase, C. M., & Levenson, R. W. (2014). Emotion regulation predicts marital satisfaction: More than a wives' tale. *Emotion (Washington, D.C.), 14,* 130–144. doi:10.1037/a0034272

Bogg, T., & Roberts, B. W. (2013). The case for conscientiousness: Evidence and implications for a personality trait marker of health and longevity. *Annals of Behavioral Medicine, 45,* 278–288. doi:10.1007/s12160-012-9454-6

Bolin, K., Lindgren, B., & Lundborg, P. (2008). Your next of kin or your own career? Caring and working among the 50+ of Europe. *Journal of Health Economics, 27*, 718–738.

Bouchard, G. (2018). A dyadic examination of marital quality at the empty-nest phase. *The International Journal of Aging and Human Development, 86*, 34–50. doi:10.1177/0091415017691285

Bratt, C., Abrams, D., Swift, H. J., Vauclair, C.-M., & Marques, S. (2018). Perceived age discrimination across age in Europe: From an ageing society to a society for all ages. *Developmental Psychology, 54*, 167–180. doi:10.1037/dev0000398

Brim, O. G., Ryff, C. D., & Kessler, R. C. (2004). *How healthy are we? A national study of well-being at midlife.* Chicago, IL: University of Chicago Press.

Brooks, C., & Bolzendahl, C. (2004). The transformation of US gender role attitudes: Cohort replacement, social-structural change, and ideological learning. *Social Science Research, 33*, 106–133. doi:10.1016/S0049-089X(03)00041-3

Burr, J. A., & Mutchler, J. E. (1999). Race and ethnic variation in norms of filial responsibility among older persons. *Journal of Marriage & the Family, 61*, 674–687.

Bybee, J. A., & Wells, Y. V. (2003). The development of possible selves during adulthood. In J. Demick & C. Andreoletti (Eds.), *Handbook of adult development* (pp. 257–270). New York, NY: Kluwer Academic/Plenum.

Camberis, A. L., McMahon, C. A., Gibson, F. L., & Boivin, J. (2016). Maternal age, psychological maturity, parenting cognitions, and mother-infant interaction. *Infancy, 21*, 396–422. doi:10.1111/infa.12116

Carlo, G., Koller, S., Raffaelli, M., & De Guzman, M. R. T. (2007). Culture-related strengths among Latin American families: A case study of Brazil. *Marriage & Family Review, 42*, 335–360.

Chen, F., Mair, C. A., Bao, L., & Yang, Y. C. (2015). Race/ethnic differentials in the health consequences of caring for grandchildren for grandparents. *Journals of Gerontology Series B: Psychological Sciences and Social Sciences, 70*, 793–803. doi:10.1093/geronb/gbu160

Cherlin, A. J. (2013). Health, marriage, and same-sex partnerships. *Journal of Health and Social Behavior, 54*, 64–66. doi:10.1177/0022146512474430

Chrouser Ahrens, C. J., & Ryff, C. D. (2006). Multiple roles and well-being: Sociodemographic and psychological moderators. *Sex Roles, 55*, 801–815.

Cichy, K. E., Lefkowitz, E. S., Davis, E. M., & Fingerman, K. L. (2013). "You are such a disappointment!": Negative emotions and parents' perceptions of adult children's lack of success. *Journals of Gerontology Series B: Psychological Sciences and Social Sciences, 68*, 893–901. doi:10.1093/geronb/gbt053

Clarke, L. H. (2018). Women, aging, and beauty culture: Navigating the social perils of looking old. *Generations, 41*, 104–108.

Clarke-Stewart, A., & Brentano, C. (2006). *Divorce: Causes and consequences.* New Haven, CT: Yale University Press. http://www.ingentaconnect.com/contentone/asag/gen/2018/00000041/00000004/art00016

Coall, D. A., & Hertwig, R. (2011). Grandparental investment: A relic of the past or a resource for the future? *Current Directions in Psychological Science, 20*, 93–98. doi:10.1177/0963721411403269

Condon, J., Luszcz, M., & McKee, I. (2018). The transition to grandparenthood: A prospective study of mental health implications. *Aging & Mental Health, 22*, 336–343. doi:10.1080/13607863.2016.1248897

Cox, K. S., Wilt, J., Olson, B., & McAdams, D. P. (2010). Generativity, the Big Five, and psychosocial adaptation in midlife adults. *Journal of Personality, 78*, 1185–1208. doi:10.1111/j.1467-6494.2010.00647.x

Creswell, J. D. (2017). Mindfulness interventions. *Annual Review of Psychology, 68*, 491–516. doi:10.1146/annurev-psych-042716-051139

Cross, S., & Markus, H. (1991). Possible selves across the life span. *Human Development, 34*, 230–255.

Curtis, R. G., Windsor, T. D., & Soubelet, A. (2015). The relationship between Big-5 personality traits and cognitive ability in older adults: A review. *Neuropsychology, Development, and Cognition, Section B: Aging, Neuropsychology and Cognition, 22*, 42–71. doi:10.1080/13825585.2014.888392

Dare, J. (2011). Transitions in midlife women's lives: Contemporary experiences. *Health Care for Women International, 32*, 111–133. doi:10.1080/07399332.2010.500753

Dare, J., & Green, L. (2011). Rethinking social support in women's midlife years: Women's experiences of social support in online environments. *European Journal of Cultural Studies, 14*, 473–490. doi:10.1177/1367549411412203

Davis, E. M., Kim, K., & Fingerman, K. L. (2016). Is an empty nest best? Coresidence with adult children and parental marital quality before and after the Great Recession. *Journals of Gerontology Series B: Psychological Sciences and Social Sciences, 55*, gbw022. doi:10.1093/geronb/gbw022

Davis, D. S., Sbrocco, T., Odoms-Young, A., & Smith, D. M. (2010). Attractiveness in African American and Caucasian women: Is beauty in the eyes of the observer? *Eating Behaviors, 11*, 25–32. doi:10.1016/j.eatbeh.2009.08.004

de Quadros-Wander, S., McGillivray, J., & Broadbent, J. (2013). The influence of perceived control on subjective wellbeing in later life. *Social Indicators Research, 115*, 999–1010. doi:10.1007/s11205-013-0243-9

Deary, I. J., Pattie, A., & Starr, J. M. (2013). The stability of intelligence from age 11 to age 90 years: The Lothian Birth Cohort of 1921 *Psychological Science, 24*, 2361–2368. doi:10.1177/0956797613486487

Deligkaris, P., Panagopoulou, E., Montgomery, A. J., & Masoura, E. (2014). *Job burnout and cognitive functioning: A systematic review.* Retrieved from http://www.tandfonline.com/doi/abs/10.1080/02678373.2014.909545

Dennis, H., & Thomas, K. (2007). Ageism in the workplace. *Generations, 31*, 84–89.

DeVries, H. M., Kerrick, S., & Oetinger, M. (2007). Satisfactions and regrets of midlife parents: A qualitative analysis. *Journal of Adult Development, 14*, 6–15.

Dilworth-Anderson, P., Goodwin, P. Y., & Williams, S. W. (2004). Can culture help explain the physical health effects of caregiving over time among African American caregivers? *Journals of Gerontology Series B: Psychological Sciences & Social Sciences, 59B*, S138–S145.

Doley, R., Bell, R., Watt, B., & Simpson, H. (2015). Grandparents raising grandchildren: Investigating factors associated with distress among custodial grandparent. *Journal of Family Studies, 21*, 1–19. doi:10.1080/13229400.2015.1015215

Donohue, S. M., & Heywood, J. S. (2013). Job satisfaction and gender: An expanded specification from the NLSY. *International Journal of Manpower.* Retrieved from http://www.emeraldinsight.com/doi/abs/10.1108/01437720410536007

Drydakis, N., MacDonald, P., Chiotis, V., & Somers, L. (2018). Age discrimination in the UK labour market: Does race moderate ageism? An experimental investigation. *Applied Economics Letters, 25*, 1–4. doi:10.1080/13504851.2017.1290763

Edwards, O. W., & Benson, N. F. (2010). A four-factor social support model to mediate stressors experienced by children raised by grandparents. *Journal of Applied School Psychology, 26*, 54–69. doi:10.1080/15377900903368862

Ellis, R. R., & Simmons, T. (2014). *Coresident grandparents and their grandchildren: 2012.* Retrieved from https://www.census.gov/content/dam/Census/library/publications/2014/demo/p20-576.pdf

Erikson, E. H. (1959). *Identity and the life cycle* (Vol. 64). New York, NY: Norton.

Espinola, M., DeVinney, H., & Steinberg, A. (2017). Women at midlife. In K. A. Kendall-Tackett & L. M. Ruglass (Eds.), *Women's mental health across the lifespan: Challenges, vulnerabilities, and strengths.* New York, NY: Routledge.

Falcone, G., & Jerram, M. (2018). Brain activity in mindfulness depends on experience: A meta-analysis of fMRI studies. *Mindfulness.* Advance online publication. doi:10.1007/s12671-018-0884-5

Fincham, F. D., Beach, S. R. H., & Davila, J. (2007). Longitudinal relations between forgiveness and conflict resolution in marriage. *Journal of Family Psychology, 21*, 542–545.

Fingerman, K. L. (2000). 'We had a nice little chat': Age and generational differences in mothers' and daughters'. *Journals of Gerontology Series B: Psychological Sciences & Social Sciences, 55B*, P95.

Fingerman, K. L. (2001). A distant closeness: Intimacy between parents and their children in later life. *Generations, 25*, 26.

Fingerman, K. L., Cheng, Y. P., Birditt, K., & Zarit, S. (2012). Only as happy as the least happy child: Multiple grown children's problems and successes and middle-aged parents' well-being. *Journals of Gerontology Series B: Psychological Sciences and Social Sciences, 67*, 184–193. doi:10.1093/geronb/gbr086

Fingerman, K. L., Cheng, Y. P., Wesselmann, E. D., Zarit, S., Furstenberg, F., & Birditt, K. S. (2012). Helicopter parents and landing pad kids: Intense parental support of grown children. *Journal of Marriage and Family, 74*, 880–896. doi:10.1111/j.1741-3737.2012.00987.x

Fingerman, K. L., Hay, E. L., & Birditt, K. S. (2004). The best of ties, the worst of ties: Close, problematic, and ambivalent social relationships. *Journal of Marriage & Family, 66,* 792–808.

Fingerman, K. L., Kim, K., Birditt, K. S., & Zarit, S. H. (2016). The ties that bind: Midlife parents' daily experiences with grown children. *Journal of Marriage and Family, 78,* 431–450. doi:10.1111/jomf.12273

Fingerman, K. L., & Suitor, J. J. (2017). Millennials and their parents: Implications of the new young adulthood for midlife adults. *Innovation in Aging, 1,* igx026. doi:10.1093/geroni/igx026

Fiori, K. L., & Denckla, C. A. (2015). Friendship and happiness among middle-aged adults. In M. Demir (Ed.), *Friendship and happiness* (pp. 137–154). Dordrecht: Springer Netherlands. doi:10.1007/978-94-017-9603-3_8

Freund. A. M. (2017). Motivational changes across adulthood: The role of goal representations for adult development and aging. In R. A. Scott & S. Kosslyn (Eds.), *Emerging trends in the social and behavioral sciences* (pp. 1–15). Hoboken, NJ: John Wiley. doi:10.1002/9781118900772.etrds0424

Freund, A. M., & Ritter, J. O. (2009). Midlife crisis: A debate. *Gerontology, 55,* 582–591. doi:10.1159/000227322

Friedman, H. S., & Kern, M. L. (2014). Personality, well-being, and health. *Annual Review of Psychology, 65,* 719–742. doi:10.1146/annurev-psych-010213-115123

Fry, C. L. (1985). Culture, behavior, and aging in the comparative perspective. In J. E. Birren & K. W. Schaie (Eds.), *Handbook of the psychology of aging* (2nd ed., pp. 216–244). New York, NY: Van Nostrand Reinhold Co.

Fry, R. (2016). *For first time in modern era, living with parents edges out other living arrangements for 18- to 34-year-olds.* Retrieved from http://www.pewsocialtrends.org/2016/05/24/for-first-time-in-modern-era-living-with-parents-edges-out-other-living-arrangements-for-18-to-34-year-olds/

Fry, R. (2018). *Millennials are largest generation in the U.S. labor force | Pew Research Center.* Retrieved April 16, 2018, from http://www.pewresearch.org/fact-tank/2018/04/11/millennials-largest-generation-us-labor-force/

Fuller-Thomson, E., & Minkler, M. (2001). American grandparents providing extensive child care to their grandchildren: Prevalence and profile. *The Gerontologist, 41,* 201–209. doi:10.1093/geront/41.2.201

Gans, D., & Silverstein, M. (2006). Norms of filial responsibility for aging parents across time and generations. *Journal of Marriage & Family, 68,* 961–976.

Gee, G. C., Pavalko, E. K., & Long, J. S. (2007). Age, cohort and perceived age discrimination: Using the life course to assess self-reported age discrimination. *Social Forces, 86,* 265–290.

Geurts, T., Van Tilburg, T. G., & Poortman, A.-R. (2012). The grandparent-grandchild relationship in childhood and adulthood: A matter of continuation? *Personal Relationships, 19,* 267–278. doi:10.1111/j.1475-6811.2011.01354.x

Gilbert, R., & Constantine, K. (2005). When strength can't last a lifetime: Vocational challenges of male workers in early and middle adulthood. *Men and Masculinities, 7,* 424–433. Retrieved from 10.1177/1097184X03257582

Goldberg, A. E., & Perry-Jenkins, M. (2004). Division of labor and working-class women's well-being across the transition to parenthood. *Journal of Family Psychology, 18,* 225–236. doi:10.1037/0893-3200.18.1.225

Goldsen, J., Bryan, A. E. B., Kim, H.-J., Muraco, A., Jen, S., & Fredriksen-Goldsen, K. I. (2017). Who says I do: The changing context of marriage and health and quality of life for LGBT older adults. *The Gerontologist, 57*(Suppl. 1), S50–S62. doi:10.1093/geront/gnw174

Grabe, S., & Hyde, J. S. (2006). Ethnicity and body dissatisfaction among women in the United States: A meta-analysis. *Psychological Bulletin, 132,* 622–640. doi:10.1037/0033-2909.132.4.622

Graham, E. K., & Lachman, M. E. (2012). Personality stability is associated with better cognitive performance in adulthood: Are the stable more able? *Journals of Gerontology Series B: Psychological Sciences and Social Sciences, 67,* 545–554. doi:10.1093/geronb/gbr149

Graham, E. K., Rutsohn, J. P., Turiano, N. A., Bendayan, R., Batterham, P. J., Gerstorf, D., . . . Mroczek, D. K. (2017). Personality predicts mortality risk: An integrative data analysis of 15 international longitudinal studies. *Journal of Research in Personality, 70,* 174–186. doi:10.1016/J.JRP.2017.07.005

Greenfield, E. A., Marks, N. F., Hay, E. L., Fingerman, K. L., & Lefkowitz, E. S. (2008). The worries adult children and their parents experience for one another. *International Journal of Aging & Human Development, 67,* 101–127.

Griggs, J., Tan, J. P., Buchanan, A., Attar-Schwartz, S., & Flouri, E. (2010). "They've always been there for me": Grandparental involvement and child well-being. *Children & Society, 24,* 200–214. doi:10.1111/j.1099-0860.2009.00215.x

Grover, S., & Helliwell, J. F. (2014). *How's life at home? New evidence on marriage and the set point for happiness.* Retrieved from http://www.nber.org/papers/w20794

Grundy, E., & Henretta, J. C. (2006). Between elderly parents and adult children: A new look at the intergenerational care provided by the "sandwich generation." *Ageing & Society, 26,* 707–722.

Gutmann, D. L. (1985). The parental imperative revisited: Towards a developmental psychology of adulthood and later life. In J. A. Meacham (Ed.), *Contributions to human development* (pp. 31–60). Basel, Switzerland: S Karger AG. doi:10.1159/000411472

Guzell-Roe, J. R., Gerard, J. M., & Landry-Meyer, L. (2005). Custodial grandparents' perceived control over caregiving outcomes: Raising children the second time around. *Journal of Intergenerational Relationships, 3,* 43–61. Retrieved from 10.1300/J194v03n02_04

Hampson, S. E., Edmonds, G. W., Barckley, M., Goldberg, L. R., Dubanoski, J. P., & Hillier, T. A. (2016). A Big Five approach to self-regulation: Personality traits and health trajectories in the Hawaii longitudinal study of personality and health. *Psychology, Health & Medicine, 21,* 152–162. doi:10.1080/13548506.2015.1061676

Hank, K., Cavrini, G., Di Gessa, G., & Tomassini, C. (2018). What do we know about grandparents? Insights from current quantitative data and identification of future data needs. *European Journal of Ageing.* Advance online publication. doi:10.1007/s10433-018-0468-1

Härkönen, J. (2015). Divorce. In J. Treas, J. Scott, & M. Richards (Eds.), *The Wiley Blackwell companion to the sociology of families* (pp. 303–322). New York, NY: John Wiley.

Hayslip, B., Blumenthal, H., & Garner, A. (2015). Social support and grandparent caregiver health: One-year longitudinal findings for grandparents raising their grandchildren. *Journals of Gerontology Series B: Psychological Sciences and Social Sciences, 70,* 804–812. doi:10.1093/geronb/gbu165

Hayslip, B., Fruhauf, C. A., & Dolbin-MacNab, M. L. (2017). Grandparents raising grandchildren: What have we learned over the past decade? *The Gerontologist.* Advance online publication. doi:10.1093/geront/gnx106

Hayslip, B., Jr., & Blumenthal, H. (2016). Grandparenthood: A developmental perspective. In M. H. Meyer & E. Daniele (Eds.), *Gerontology: Changes, challenges, and solutions* (pp. 271–298). New York, NY: Praeger.

Hefner, V., Woodward, K., Figge, L., Bevan, J. L., Santora, N., & Baloch, S. (2014). The influence of television and film viewing on midlife women's body image, disordered eating, and food choice. *Media Psychology, 17,* 185–207. doi:10.1080/15213269.2013.838903

Henderson, C. E., Hayslip, J. B., Sanders, L. M., & Louden, L. (2009). Grandmother-grandchild relationship quality predicts psychological adjustment among youth from divorced families. *Journal of Family Issues, 30,* 1245–1264.

Heraty, N., & McCarthy, J. (2015). Unearthing psychological predictors of financial planning for retirement among late career older workers: Do self-perceptions of aging matter? *Work, Aging and Retirement.* Advance online publication. doi:10.1093/workar/wav008

Hill, P. L., Turiano, N. A., Mroczek, D. K., & Roberts, B. W. (2012). Examining concurrent and longitudinal relations between personality traits and social well-being in adulthood. *Social Psychological and Personality Science, 3,* 698–705. doi:10.1177/1948550611433888

Hofmeier, S. M., Runfola, C. D., Sala, M., Gagne, D. A., Brownley, K. A., & Bulik, C. M. (2017). Body image, aging, and identity in women over 50: The gender and body image (GABI) study. *Journal of Women & Aging, 29,* 3–14. doi:10.1080/08952841.2015.1065140

Holt-Lunstad, J., Smith, T. B., & Layton, J. B. (2010). Social relationships and mortality risk: A meta-analytic review. *PLoS Medicine, 7,* e1000316. doi:10.1371/journal.pmed.1000316

Honigman, R., & Castle, D. J. (2006). Aging and cosmetic enhancement. *Clinical Interventions in Aging, 1,* 115–119.

Hu, X., Kaplan, S., & Dalal, R. S. (2010). An examination of blue- versus white-collar workers' conceptualizations of job satisfaction facets. *Journal of Vocational Behavior, 76*, 317–325. doi:10.1016/j.jvb.2009.10.014

Hughes, M. L., & Lachman, M. E. (2016). Social comparisons of health and cognitive functioning contribute to changes in subjective age. *Journals of Gerontology Series B: Psychological Sciences and Social Sciences, 57*, 1196. doi:10.1093/geronb/gbw044

Huo, M., Kim, K., Zarit, S. H., & Fingerman, K. L. (2018). Support grandparents give to their adult grandchildren. *Journals of Gerontology Series B: Psychological Sciences and Social Sciences, 73*, 1006–1015. doi:10.1093/geronb/gbw208

Hutteman, R., Hennecke, M., Orth, U., Reitz, A. K., & Specht, J. (2014). Developmental tasks as a framework to study personality development in adulthood and old age. *European Journal of Personality, 28*, 267–278.

Huxhold, O., Miche, M., & Schüz, B. (2014). Benefits of having friends in older ages: Differential effects of informal social activities on well-being in middle-aged and older adults. *Journals of Gerontology Series B: Psychological Sciences and Social Sciences, 69*, 366–375. doi:10.1093/geronb/gbt029

Izard, C. E. (2007). Basic emotions, natural kinds, emotion schemas, and a new paradigm. *Perspectives on Psychological Science, 2*, 260–280. doi:10.1111/j.1745-6916.2007.00044.x

Jackson, J. B., Miller, R. B., Oka, M., & Henry, R. G. (2014). Gender differences in marital satisfaction: A meta-analysis. *Journal of Marriage and Family, 76*, 105–129. doi:10.1111/jomf.12077

James, J. B., & Lewkowicz, C. (1995). Rethinking the gender identity crossover hypothesis: A test of a new model. *Sex Roles, 32*, 185–207.

Jones, C., Peskin, H., & Livson, N. (2011). Men's and women's change and individual differences in change in femininity from age 33 to 85: Results from the intergenerational studies. *Journal of Adult Development, 18*, 155–163. doi:10.1007/s10804-010-9108-5

Jones, C., Peskin, H., & Wandeler, C. (2017). Femininity and dominance across the lifespan: Longitudinal findings from two cohorts of women. *Journal of Adult Development, 24*, 22–30. doi:10.1007/s10804-016-9243-8

Kaiser, L. C. (2007). Genderjob satisfaction differences across Europe. *International Journal of Manpower, 28*, 75–94. doi:10.1108/01437720710733483

Kamo, Y. (1998). Asian grandparents. In M. E. Szinovacz (Ed.), *Handbook on grandparenthood* (pp. 97–112). Westport, CT: Greenwood.

Kandler, C., Bleidorn, W., Riemann, R., Spinath, F. M., Thiel, W., & Angleitner, A. (2010). Sources of cumulative continuity in personality: A longitudinal multiple-rater twin study. *Journal of Personality and Social Psychology, 98*, 995–1008. doi:10.1037/a0019558

Kandler, C., Kornadt, A. E., Hagemeyer, B., & Neyer, F. J. (2015). Patterns and sources of personality development in old age. *Journal of Personality and Social Psychology, 109*, 175–191. doi:10.1037/pspp0000028

Karraker, A., & Latham, K. (2015). In sickness and in health? Physical illness as a risk factor for marital dissolution in later life. *Journal of Health and Social Behavior, 56*, 59–73. doi:10.1177/0022146514568351

Katz-Wise, S. L., Priess, H. A., & Hyde, J. S. (2010). Gender-role attitudes and behavior across the transition to parenthood. *Developmental Psychology, 46*, 18–28. doi:10.1037/a0017820

Kehr, H. M., Strasser, M., & Paulus, A. (2018). Motivation and volition in the workplace. In J. Heckhausen & H. Heckhausen (Eds.), *Motivation and action* (pp. 819–852). Cham, Switzerland: Springer International. doi:10.1007/978-3-319-65094-4_19

Kelch-Oliver, K. (2011). The experiences of African American grandmothers in grandparent-headed families. *The Family Journal, 19*, 73–82. doi:10.1177/1066480710388730

Keyes, C. L. M., & Westerhof, G. J. (2012). Chronological and subjective age differences in flourishing mental health and major depressive episode. *Aging & Mental Health, 16*, 67–74. doi:10.1080/13607863.2011.596811

Killian, T., Turner, J., & Cain, R. (2005). Depressive symptoms of caregiving women in midlife: The role of physical health. *Journal of Women & Aging, 17*, 115–127. Retrieved from 10.1300/J074v17n01_09

Kim, K., Bangerter, L. R., Liu, Y., Polenick, C. A., Zarit, S. H., & Fingerman, K. L. (2016). Middle-aged offspring's support to aging parents with emerging disability. *The Gerontologist, 20*, gnv686. doi:10.1093/geront/gnv686

Kleinspehn-Ammerlahn, A., Kotter-Gruhn, D., & Smith, J. (2008). Self-perceptions of aging: Do subjective age and satisfaction with aging change during old age? *Journals of Gerontology Series B: Psychological Sciences and Social Sciences, 63*, P377–P385. doi:10.1093/geronb/63.6.P377

Knodel, J., & Chayovan, N. (2009). Intergenerational relationships and family care and support for Thai elderly. *Ageing International, 33*, 15–27. doi:10.1007/s12126-009-9026-7

Kong, F., Wang, X., Song, Y., & Liu, J. (2016). Brain regions involved in dispositional mindfulness during resting state and their relation to well-being. *Social Neuroscience, 11*, 331–343. doi:10.1080/17470919.2015.1092469

Kornadt, A. E., Hess, T. M., Voss, P., & Rothermund, K. (2018). Subjective age across the life span: A differentiated, longitudinal approach. *Journals of Gerontology Series B: Psychological Sciences and Social Sciences, 73*, 767–777. doi:10.1093/geronb/gbw072

Kreider, R. M., Ellis, R., & U.S. Bureau of the Census. (2011). Number, timing, and duration of marriages and divorces: 2009. *Current Population Reports*. Retrieved from https://www.census.gov/prod/2011pubs/p70-125.pdf

Kross, E., Gard, D., Deldin, P., Clifton, J., & Ayduk, O. (2012). "Asking why" from a distance: Its cognitive and emotional consequences for people with major depressive disorder. *Journal of Abnormal Psychology, 121*, 559–569. doi:10.1037/a0028808

Kurth, F., Cherbuin, N., & Luders, E. (2017). Promising links between meditation and reduced (brain) aging: An attempt to bridge some gaps between the alleged fountain of youth and the youth of the field. *Frontiers in Psychology, 8*, 860. doi:10.3389/fpsyg.2017.00860

Lachman, M. E., Teshale, S., & Agrigoroaei, S. (2015). Midlife as a pivotal period in the life course: Balancing growth and decline at the crossroads of youth and old age. *International Journal of Behavioral Development, 39*, 20–31. doi:10.1177/0165025414533223

Lapp, L. K., & Spaniol, J. (2016). Aging and self-discrepancy: Evidence for adaptive change across the life span. *Experimental Aging Research, 42*, 212–219. doi:10.1080/0361073X.2016.1132900

Lavelle, B., & Smock, P. J. (2012). Divorce and women's risk of health insurance loss. *Journal of Health and Social Behavior, 53*, 413–431. doi:10.1177/0022146512465758

Lee, Y., Tang, F., Kim, K. H., & Albert, S. M. (2015). The vicious cycle of parental caregiving and financial well-being: A longitudinal study of women. *The Journals of Gerontology Series B: Psychological Sciences and Social Sciences, 70*, 425–431. doi:10.1093/geronb/gbu001

Lefkowitz, E. S., & Fingerman, K. L. (2003). Positive and negative emotional feelings and behaviors in mother-daughter ties in late life. *Journal of Family Psychology, 17*, 607–617.

Lefkowitz, E. S., & Zeldow, P. B. (2006). Masculinity and femininity predict optimal mental health: A belated test of the androgyny hypothesis. *Journal of Personality Assessment, 87*, 95–101.

Lemaster, P., Delaney, R., & Strough, J. (2017). Crossover, degendering, or . . .? A multidimensional approach to life-span gender development. *Sex Roles, 76*, 669–681. doi:10.1007/s11199-015-0563-0

Leopold, T., & Skopek, J. (2015). The demography of grandparenthood: An international profile. *Social Forces, 94*, 801–832. doi:10.1093/sf/sov066

Leszko, M., Elleman, L. G., Bastarache, E. D., Graham, E. K., & Mroczek, D. K. (2016). Future directions in the study of personality in adulthood and older age. *Gerontology, 62*, 210–215. doi:10.1159/000434720

Levinson, D. J. (1978). *The seasons of a man's life.* New York, NY: Knopf.

Levinson, D. J. (1996). *The seasons of a woman's life.* New York, NY: Knopf.

Lewis, D. C., Medvedev, K., & Seponski, D. M. (2011). Awakening to the desires of older women: Deconstructing ageism within fashion magazines. *Journal of Aging Studies, 25*, 101–109. doi:10.1016/j.jaging.2010.08.016

Lilgendahl, J. P., Helson, R., & John, O. P. (2013). Does ego development increase during midlife? The effects of openness and accommodative processing of difficult events. *Journal of Personality, 81*, 403–416. doi:10.1111/jopy.12009

Lilgendahl, J. P., & McAdams, D. P. (2011). Constructing stories of self-growth: How individual differences in patterns of autobiographical reasoning relate to well-being in midlife. *Journal of Personality, 79*, 391–428. doi:10.1111/j.1467-6494.2010.00688.x

Linz, S., & Semykina, A. (2013). Job satisfaction, expectations, and gender: Beyond the European Union. *International Journal of Manpower, 34*, 584–615. doi:10.1108/IJM-06-2013-0149

Löckenhoff, C. E., De Fruyt, F., Terracciano, A., McCrae, R. R., De Bolle, M., Costa, P. T., . . . Yik, M. (2009). Perceptions of aging across 26 cultures and their culture-level associates. *Psychology and Aging, 24*, 941–954. doi:10.1037/a0016901

Lodi-Smith, J., & Roberts, B. W. (2010). Getting to know me: Social role experiences and age differences in self-concept clarity during adulthood. *Journal of Personality, 78*, 1383–1410. doi:10.1111/j.1467-6494.2010.00655.x

López Ulloa, B. F., Møller, V., & Sousa-Poza, A. (2013). How does subjective well-being evolve with age? A literature review. *Journal of Population Ageing, 6*, 227–246. doi:10.1007/s12062-013-9085-0

Lorenz, F. O., Wickrama, K. A. S., Conger, R. D., & Elder, G. H. J. (2006). The short-term and decade-long effects of divorce on women's midlife health. *Journal of Health and Social Behavior, 47*, 111–125.

Lucas, R. E., & Donnellan, M. B. (2011). Personality development across the life span: Longitudinal analyses with a national sample from Germany. *Journal of Personality & Social Psychology, 101*, 847–861. doi:10.1037/a0024298

Luchetti, M., Terracciano, A., Stephan, Y., & Sutin, A. R. (2015). Personality and cognitive decline in older adults: Data from a longitudinal sample and meta-analysis. *Journals of Gerontology Series B: Psychological Sciences and Social Sciences, 71*, gbu184. doi:10.1093/geronb/gbu184

Luhmann, M., Hofmann, W., Eid, M., & Lucas, R. E. (2012). Subjective well-being and adaptation to life events: A meta-analysis. *Journal of Personality and Social Psychology, 102*, 592–615. doi:10.1037/a0025948

MacDougall, K., Beyene, Y., & Nachtigall, R. D. (2012). "Inconvenient biology:" Advantages and disadvantages of first-time parenting after age 40 using in vitro fertilization. *Human Reproduction, 27*, 1058–1065. doi:10.1093/humrep/des007

Malinen, O. P., & Savolainen, H. (2016). The effect of perceived school climate and teacher efficacy in behavior management on job satisfaction and burnout: A longitudinal study. *Teaching and Teacher Education, 60*, 144–152. doi:10.1016/j.tate.2016.08.012

Mancini, A. D., Bonanno, G. A., & Clark, A. E. (2011). Stepping off the hedonic treadmill. *Journal of Individual Differences, 32*, 144–152. doi:10.1027/1614-0001/a000047

Margolis, R. (2016). The changing demography of grandparenthood. *Journal of Marriage and Family, 78*, 610–622. doi:10.1111/jomf.12286

Marks, N. F., Bumpass, L. L., & Jun, H. (2004). Family roles and well-being during the middle life course. In O. G. Brim, C. D. Ryff, & R. C. Kessler (Eds.), *How healthy are we? A national study of well-being at midlife* (pp. 514–549). Chicago, IL: University of Chicago Press.

Mausbach, B. T., Roepke, S. K., Chattillion, E. A., Harmell, A. L., Moore, R., Romero-Moreno, R., . . . Grant, I. (2012). Multiple mediators of the relations between caregiving stress and depressive symptoms. *Aging & Mental Health, 16*, 27–38. doi:10.1080/13607863.2011.615738

McAdams, D. P. (2014). The life narrative at midlife. *New Directions for Child and Adolescent Development, 2014*, 57–69. doi:10.1002/cad.20067

McAdams, D. P., & Olson, B. D. (2010). Personality development: Continuity and change over the life course. *Annual Review of Psychology, 61*, 517–542. doi:10.1146/annurev.psych.093008.100507

McCann, L. (2003). *Age discrimination in employment legislation in the United States experience.* Washington, DC: AARM Foundation Litigation.

McCrae, R. R. (2002). The maturation of personality psychology: Adult personality development and psychological well-being. *Journal of Research in Personality, 36*, 307–317.

McCrae, R. R., & Costa, P. T. J. (2006). Cross-cultural perspectives on adult personality trait development. In D. K. Mroczek & T. D. Little (Eds.), *Handbook of personality development* (pp. 129–145). Mahwah, NJ: Lawrence Erlbaum.

McCrae, R. R., & Costa, P. T., Jr. (2008). The five-factor theory of personality. In O. P. John, R. W. Robins, & L. A. Pervin (Eds.), *Handbook of personality psychology: Theory and research* (3rd ed., pp. 159–181). New York, NY: Guilford.

McCrae, R. R., Terracciano, A., & The Personality Profiles of Cultures Project. (2005). Universal features of personality traits from the observer's perspective: Data from 50 cultures. *Journal of Personality and Social Psychology, 88*, 547–561.

McKeering, H., & Pakenham, K. I. (2000). Gender and generativity issues in parenting: Do fathers benefit more than mothers from involvement in child care activities? *Sex Roles, 43*, 459–480.

Meng, J., Martinez, L., Holmstrom, A., Chung, M., & Cox, J. (2017). Research on social networking sites and social support from 2004 to 2015: A narrative review and directions for future research. *Cyberpsychology, Behavior, and Social Networking, 20*, 44–51. doi:10.1089/cyber.2016.0325

MetLife Mature Market Institute, National Alliance for Caregiving, & Center for Long Term Care Research and Policy. (2011). *The MetLife study of caregiving costs to working caregivers: Double jeopardy for baby boomers caring for their parents.* Retrieved from https://www.caregiving.org/wp-content/uploads/2011/06/mmi-caregiving-costs-working-caregivers.pdf

Mitchell, B. A. (2010). Happiness in midlife parental roles: A contextual mixed methods analysis. *Family Relations, 59*, 326–339.

Mitchell, B. A. (2016). Empty nest. In C L. Shehan (Ed.), *Encyclopedia of family studies* (pp. 1–4). Hoboken, NJ: John Wiley. doi:10.1002/9781119085621.wbefs008

Mitchell, B. A., & Lovegreen, L. D. (2009). The empty nest syndrome in midlife families: A multimethod exploration of parental gender differences and cultural dynamics. *Journal of Family Issues, 30*, 1651–1670.

Mock, S. E., & Eibach, R. P. (2011). Aging attitudes moderate the effect of subjective age on psychological well-being: Evidence from a 10-year longitudinal study. *Psychology and Aging, 26*, 979–986.

Montgomery, R. J. V., Rowe, J. M., & Kosloski, K. (2007). Family caregiving. In J. A. Blackburn & C. N. Dulmus (Eds.), *Handbook of gerontology: Evidence-based approaches to theory, practice, and policy* (pp. 426–454). Hoboken, NJ: John Wiley.

Moore, R. M., Allbright-Campos, M., & Strick, K. (2017). Childlessness in midlife. *The Family Journal, 25*, 40–47. doi:10.1177/1066480716679647

Moore, S. M., & Rosenthal, D. A. (2015). Personal growth, grandmother engagement and satisfaction among non-custodial grandmothers. *Aging & Mental Health, 19*, 136–143. doi:10.1080/13607863.2014.920302

Morin, R., & Fry, R. (2012). *More Americans worry about financing retirement.* Retrieved from http://www.pewsocialtrends.org/2012/10/22/more-americans-worry-about-financing-retirement/

Morrissey, M. (2016). *The state of American retirement: Retirement inequality chartbook.* Retrieved from http://www.epi.org/publication/retirement-in-america/#charts

Mroczek, D. K., Spiro, A. I. I. I., & Griffin, P. W. (2006). Personality and aging. In J. E. Birren & K. W. Schaire (Eds.), *Handbook of the psychology of aging* (6th ed., pp. 363–377). Amsterdam, The Netherlands: Elsevier.

Nantais, C., & Stack, M. (2017). Generativity versus stagnation. In V. Zeigler-Hill & T. K. Shackelford (Eds.), *Encyclopedia of personality and individual differences* (pp. 1–3). Cham, Switzerland: Springer International. doi:10.1007/978-3-319-28099-8_589-1

Neuberger, F. S., & Haberkern, K. (2013). Structured ambivalence in grandchild care and the quality of life among European grandparents. *European Journal of Ageing, 11*, 171–181. doi:10.1007/s10433-013-0294-4

Neumark, D., Burn, I., Button, P., Neumark, D., Burn, I., & Button, P. (2017). Age discrimination and hiring of older workers. *FRBSF Economic Letter.* Retrieved from https://econpapers.repec.org/article/fipfedfel/00121.htm

Newton, N., & Stewart, A. J. (2010). The middle ages: Change in women's personalities and social roles. *Psychology of Women Quarterly, 34*, 75–84. doi:10.1111/j.1471-6402.2009.01543.x

Ng, T. W. H., & Feldman, D. C. (2010). The relationships of age with job attitudes: A meta-analysis. *Personnel Psychology, 63*, 677–718. doi:10.1111/j.1744-6570.2010.01184.x

Noone, J. H., Stephens, C., & Alpass, F. M. (2009). Preretirement planning and well-being in later life: A prospective study. *Research on Aging, 31*, 295–317.

Ogolsky, B. G., Dennison, R. P., & Monk, J. K. (2014). The role of couple discrepancies in cognitive and behavioral egalitarianism in marital quality. *Sex Roles, 70*, 329–342. doi:10.1007/s11199-014-0365-9

Orth, U., Maes, J., & Schmitt, M. (2015). Self-esteem development across the life span: A longitudinal study with a large sample from Germany. *Developmental Psychology, 51*, 248–259. doi:10.1037/a0038481

Orth, U., Robins, R. W., & Widaman, K. F. (2012). Life-span development of self-esteem and its effects on important life outcomes. *Journal of Personality and Social Psychology, 102*, 1271–1288. doi:10.1037/a0025558

Orth, U., Trzesniewski, K. H., & Robins, R. W. (2010). Self-esteem development from young adulthood to old age: A cohort-sequential longitudinal study. *Journal of Personality and Social Psychology, 98*, 645–658. doi:10.1037/a0018769

Palmore, E. B., Branch, L., & Harris, D. K. (2005). *Encyclopedia of ageism*. Binghamton, NY: Haworth Pastoral Press.

Parker, K., & Patten, E. (2013). *The sandwich generation rising financial burdens for middle-aged Americans*. Retrieved from http://www.pewsocialtrends.org/2013/01/30/the-sandwich-generation/

Parker, K., & Wang, W. (2013). *Modern parenthood roles of moms and dads converge as they balance work and family*. Retrieved from http://www.pewsocialtrends.org/2013/03/14/modern-parenthood-roles-of-moms-and-dads-converge-as-they-balance-work-and-family/

Pasupathi, M., & Mansour, E. (2006). Adult age differences in autobiographical reasoning in narratives. *Developmental Psychology, 42*, 798–808.

Pearson, A. L., Bentham, G., Day, P., Kingham, S., Flegal, K., Carroll, M., . . . Brug, J. (2014). Associations between neighbourhood environmental characteristics and obesity and related behaviours among adult New Zealanders. *BMC Public Health, 14*, 553. doi:10.1186/1471-2458-14-553

Perrig-Chiello, P., Hutchison, S., & Morselli, D. (2014). Patterns of psychological adaptation to divorce after a long-term marriage. *Journal of Social and Personal Relationships, 32*, 386–405. doi:10.1177/0265407514533769

Pilar Matud, M., Bethencourt, J. M., & Ibáñez, I. (2014). Relevance of gender roles in life satisfaction in adult people. *Personality and Individual Differences, 70*, 206–211. doi:10.1016/j.paid.2014.06.046

Pillemer, K., & Suitor, J. J. (2014). Who provides care? A prospective study of caregiving among adult siblings. *The Gerontologist, 54*, 589–598. doi:10.1093/geront/gnt066

Pillemer, K., Suitor, J. J., Riffin, C., & Gilligan, M. (2017). Adult children's problems and mothers' well-being. *Research on Aging, 39*, 375–395. doi:10.1177/0164027515611464

Pollitt, A. M., Robinson, B. A., & Umberson, D. (2018). Gender conformity, perceptions of shared power, and marital quality in same- and different-sex marriages. *Gender & Society, 32*, 109–131. doi:10.1177/0891243217742110

Power, R., & Pluess, M. (2015). Heritability estimates of the Big Five personality traits based on common genetic variants. *Translational Psychiatry, 5*, e604. doi:10.1038/tp.2015.96

Pudrovska, T. (2009). Parenthood, stress, and mental health in late midlife and early old age. *International Journal of Aging & Human Development, 68*, 127–147. doi:10.2190/AG.68.2.b

Pulkkinen, L., Feldt, T., & Kokko, K. (2005). Personality in young adulthood and functioning in middle age. In S. L. Willis & M. Martin (Eds.), *Middle adulthood: A lifespan perspective* (pp. 99–141). Thousand Oaks, CA: Sage.

Rammstedt, B., Spinath, F. M., Richter, D., & Schupp, J. (2013). Partnership longevity and personality congruence in couples. *Personality and Individual Differences, 54*, 832–835. doi:10.1016/j.paid.2012.12.007

Rathunde, K., & Isabella, R. (2017). Play, flow, and tailoring identity in middle adulthood. In J. N. Sinnot (Ed.), *Identity flexibility during adulthood* (pp. 211–232). Cham, Switzerland: Springer International. doi:10.1007/978-3-319-55658-1_14

Riley, L. D., & Bowen, C. (2005). The sandwich generation: Challenges and coping strategies of multigenerational families. *Family Journal, 13*, 52–58. Retrieved from 10.1177/1066480704270099

Roberts, B. W., & Caspi, A. (2003). The cumulative continuity model of personality development: Striking a balance between continuity and change in personality traits across the life course. In M. Ursula & U. Lindenberger (Eds.), *Understanding human development: Dialogues with lifespan psychology* (pp. 183–214). Dordrecht, The Netherlands: Kluwer Academic.

Roberts, B. W., & Mroczek, D. (2008). Personality trait change in adulthood. *Current Directions in Psychological Science, 17*, 31–35. Retrieved from 10.1111/j.1467-8721.2008.00543.x

Roberts, B. W., Walton, K. E., & Viechtbauer, W. (2006). Patterns of mean-level change in personality traits across the life course: A meta-analysis of longitudinal studies. *Psychological Bulletin, 132*, 1–25. doi:10.1037/0033-2909.132.1.1

Robins, R. W., Trzesniewski, K. H., Tracy, J. L., Gosling, S. D., & Potter, J. (2002). Global self-esteem across the life span. *Psychology and Aging, 17*, 423–434. Retrieved from http://www.ncbi.nlm.nih.gov/pubmed/12243384

Röcke, C., & Lachman, M. E. (2008). Perceived trajectories of life satisfaction across past, present, and future: Profiles and correlates of subjective change in young, middle-aged, and older adults. *Psychology and Aging, 23*, 833–847. doi:10.1037/a0013680

Rokach, R., Cohen, O., & Dreman, S. J. (2004). Who pulls the trigger? Who initiates divorce among over 45-year-olds. *Journal of Divorce & Remarriage, 42*, 61–83. Retrieved from 10.1300/J087v42n01_03

Roscigno, V. J., Mong, S., Byron, R., & Tester, G. (2007). Age discrimination, social closure and employment. *Social Forces, 86*, 313–334.

Rosenberg, S. D., Rosenberg, H. J., & Farrell, M. P. (1999). The midlife crisis revisited. In S. L. Willis & J. D. Reid (Eds.), *Life in the middle: Psychological and social development in middle age* (pp. 47–73). San Diego, CA: Academic Press.

Rubin, L. R., Fitts, M. L., & Rubin, L. R. (2003). "Whatever feels good in my soul": Body ethics and aesthetics among African American and Latina women. *Culture, Medicine and Psychiatry, 27*, 49–75. doi:10.1023/A:1023679821086

Ryff, C. D. (1991). Possible selves in adulthood and old age: A tale of shifting horizons. *Psychology and Aging, 6*, 286–295.

Ryff, C. D. (1995). Psychological well-being in adult life. *Current Directions in Psychological Science, 4*, 99–104. Retrieved from 10.1111/1467-8721.ep10772395

Ryff, C. D. (2014). Psychological well-being revisited: Advances in the science and practice of eudaimonia. *Psychotherapy and Psychosomatics, 83*, 10–28. doi:10.1159/000353263

Sakraida, T. J. (2005). Common themes in the divorce transition experience of midlife women. *Journal of Divorce & Remarriage, 43*, 69–88.

Savia, J., Almeida, D. M., Davey, A., & Zant, S. H. (2008). Routine assistance to parents: Effects on daily mood and other stressors. *Journals of Gerontology Series B: Psychological Sciences & Social Sciences, 36B*, S154–S161.

Sbarra, D. A., & Coan, J. A. (2017). Divorce and health: Good data in need of better theory. *Current Opinion in Psychology, 13*, 91–95. doi:10.1016/j.copsyc.2016.05.014

Sbarra, D. A., Hasselmo, K., & Bourassa, K. J. (2015). Divorce and health: Beyond individual differences. *Current Directions in Psychological Science, 24*, 109–113. doi:10.1177/0963721414559125

Sbarra, D. A., Law, R. W., & Portley, R. M. (2011). Divorce and death: A meta-analysis and research agenda for clinical, social, and health psychology. *Perspectives on Psychological Science, 6*, 454–474. doi:10.1177/1745691611414724

Sbarra, D. A., Smith, H. L., & Mehl, M. R. (2012). When leaving your ex, love yourself: Observational ratings of self-compassion predict the course of emotional recovery following marital separation. *Psychological Science, 23*, 261–269. doi:10.1177/0956797611429466

Schafer, M. H., & Shippee, T. P. (2010). Age identity, gender, and perceptions of decline: Does feeling older lead to pessimistic dispositions about cognitive aging? *Journals of Gerontology Series B: Psychological Sciences & Social Sciences, 65B*, 91–96.

Schneller, D. P., & Arditti, J. A. (2004). After the breakup: Interpreting divorce and rethinking intimacy. *Journal of Divorce & Remarriage, 42*, 1–37.

Schober, P. S. (2013). The parenthood effect on gender inequality: Explaining the change in paid and domestic work when British couples become parents. *European Sociological Review, 29*, 74–85. doi:10.1093/esr/jcr041

Seiffge-Krenke, I. (2010). Predicting the timing of leaving home and related developmental tasks: Parents' and children's perspectives. *Journal of Social & Personal Relationships, 27*, 495–518. doi:10.1177/0265407510363426

Shanafelt, T. D., Hasan, O., Dyrbye, L. N., Sinsky, C., Satele, D., Sloan, J., & West, C. P. (2015). Changes in burnout and satisfaction with work-life balance in physicians and the general US working population between 2011 and 2014. *Mayo Clinic Proceedings, 90*, 1600–1613. doi:10.1016/j.mayocp.2015.08.023

Shinan-Altman, S., & Werner, P. (2018). Subjective age and its correlates among middle-aged and older adults. *The International Journal of Aging and Human Development*. Advance online publication. doi:10.1177/0091415017752941

Shiota, M. N., & Levenson, R. W. (2007). Birds of a feather don't always fly farthest: Similarity in Big Five personality predicts more negative marital satisfaction trajectories in long-term marriages. *Psychology and Aging, 22,* 666–675.

Shippee, T. P., Wilkinson, L. R., Schafer, M. H., & Shippee, N. D. (2017). Long-term effects of age discrimination on mental health: The role of perceived financial strain. *Journals of Gerontology Series B: Psychological Sciences & Social Sciences.* Advance online publication. doi:10.1093/geronb/gbx017

Shirom, A., & Melamed, S. (2005). Does burnout affect physical health? A review of the evidence. In A. S. G. Antoniou & C. L. Cooper (Eds.), *Research companion to organizational health psychology* (pp. 599–622). Northampton, MA: Edward Elgar.

Shuey, K., & Hardy, M. A. (2003). Assistance to aging parents and parents-in-law: Does lineage affect family allocation decisions? *Journal of Marriage and Family, 65,* 418–431.

Silverstein, M., Conroy, S. J., Wang, H., Giarrusso, R., & Bengtson, V. L. (2002). Reciprocity in parent-child relations over the adult life course. *Journals of Gerontology Series B: Psychological Sciences & Social Sciences, 57B,* 3.

Silverstein, M., & Marenco, A. (2001). How Americans enact the grandparent role across the family life course. *Journal of Family Issues, 22,* 493–522.

Smith, G. C., & Hancock, G. R. (2010). Custodial grandmother-grandfather dyads: Pathways among marital distress, grandparent dysphoria, parenting practice, and grandchild adjustment. *Family Relations, 59,* 45–59. doi:10.1111/j.1741-3729.2009.00585.x

Smith, J., & Freund, A. M. (2002). The dynamics of possible selves in old age. *Journals of Gerontology Series B: Psychological Sciences & Social Sciences, 57B,* P492.

Sneed, J. R., Whitbourne, S. K., Schwartz, S. J., & Huang, S. (2012). The relationship between identity, intimacy, and midlife well-being: Findings from the Rochester Adult Longitudinal study. *Psychology and Aging, 27,* 318–323. doi:10.1037/a0026378

Sobanko, J. F., Taglienti, A. J., Wilson, A. J., Sarwer, D. B. D., Margolis, D. J., Dai, J., . . . Pusic, A. (2015). Motivations for seeking minimally invasive cosmetic procedures in an academic outpatient setting. *Aesthetic Surgery Journal/American Society for Aesthetic Plastic Surgery, 35,* 1014–1020. doi:10.1093/asj/sjv094

Soliz, J. (2015). Communication and the grandparent-grandchild relationship. In C. R. Berger, M. E. Roloff, S. R. Wilson, J. P. Dillard, J. Coughlin, & D. Solomon (Eds.), *The international encyclopedia of interpersonal communication* (pp. 1–5). Hoboken, NJ: John Wiley. doi:10.1002/9781118540190.wbeic221

Soto, C. J. (2015). Is happiness good for your personality? Concurrent and prospective relations of the Big Five with subjective well-being. *Journal of Personality, 83,* 45–55. doi:10.1111/jopy.12081

Soto, C. J., John, O. P., Gosling, S. D., & Potter, J. (2011). Age differences in personality traits from 10 to 65: Big Five domains and facets in a large cross-sectional sample. *Journal of Personality and Social Psychology, 100,* 330–348. doi:10.1037/a0021717

Srivastava, S., John, O. P., Gosling, S. D., & Potter, J. (2003). Development of personality in early and middle adulthood: Set like plaster or persistent change? *Journal of Personality and Social Psychology, 84,* 1041–1053.

Steinberg, L., Icenogle, G., Shulman, E. P., Breiner, K., Chein, J., Bacchini, D., . . . Takash, H. M. S. (2017). Around the world, adolescence is a time of heightened sensation seeking and immature self-regulation. *Developmental Science, 21,* e12532. doi:10.1111/desc.12532

Steiner, L. M., Suarez, E. C., Sells, J. N., & Wykes, S. D. (2011). Effect of age, initiator status, and infidelity on women's divorce adjustment. *Journal of Divorce & Remarriage, 52,* 33–47. doi:10.1080/10502556.2011.534394

Stephan, Y., Caudroit, J., Jaconelli, A., & Terracciano, A. (2014). Subjective age and cognitive functioning: A 10-year prospective study. *American Journal of Geriatric Psychiatry, 22,* 1180–1187. doi:10.1016/j.jagp.2013.03.007

Sterns, H. L., & Huyck, M. H. (2001). The role of work in midlife. In M. E. Lachman (Ed.), *Handbook of midlife development* (pp. 447–486). Hoboken, NJ: John Wiley.

Stuifbergen, M. C., Dykstra, P. A., Lanting, K. N., & van Delden, J. J. M. (2010). Autonomy in an ascribed relationship: The case of adult children and elderly parents. *Journal of Aging Studies, 24,* 257–265. doi:10.1016/j.jaging.2010.05.006

Stuifbergen, M. C., Van Delden, J. J. M., & Dykstra, P. A. (2008). The implications of today's family structures for support giving to older parents. *Ageing & Society, 28,* 413–434.

Sutcliffe, A. G., Barnes, J., Belsky, J., Gardiner, J., & Melhuish, E. (2012). The health and development of children born to older mothers in the United Kingdom: Observational study using longitudinal cohort data. *BMJ (Clinical Research Ed.), 345*(aug21_1), e5116. doi:10.1136/bmj.e5116

Syed, M., & McLean, K. C. (2018). Erikson's theory of psychosocial development. In E. Braaten & B. Willoughby (Eds.), *The Sage encyclopedia of intellectual and developmental disorders* (pp. 577–581). Thousand Oaks, CA; Sage. doi:10.17605/OSF.IO/ZF35D

Tang, Y. Y., Hölzel, B. K., & Posner, M. I. (2015). The neuroscience of mindfulness meditation. *Nature Reviews Neuroscience, 16,* 213–225. doi:10.1038/nrn3916

Tanis, M., van der Louw, M., & Buijzen, M. (2017). From empty nest to social networking site: What happens in cyberspace when children are launched from the parental home? *Computers in Human Behavior, 68,* 56–63. doi:10.1016/J.CHB.2016.11.005

Tearne, J. E. (2015). Older maternal age and child behavioral and cognitive outcomes: A review of the literature. *Fertility and Sterility, 103,* 1381–1391. doi:10.1016/j.fertnstert.2015.04.027

Teper, R., & Inzlicht, M. (2014). Mindful acceptance dampens neuroaffective reactions to external and rewarding performance feedback. *Emotion, 14,* 105–114. doi:10.1037/a0034296

Tergesen, A. (2014, March 30). The long (long) wait to be a grandparent as more couples delay having children, ties between generations are feeling the strain. *Wall Street Journal.* Retrieved from http://www.wsj.com/articles/SB10001424052702303775504579395501172676002

Terrell, K. (2017). *Studies show age discrimination still persists.* Retrieved April 16, 2018, from https://www.aarp.org/work/working-at-50-plus/info-2017/age-discrimination-online-fd.html?intcmp=AE-WOR-W50-AD-R2-C1

Thiele, D. M., & Whelan, T. A. (2008). The relationship between grandparent satisfaction, meaning, and generativity. *International Journal of Aging & Human Development, 66,* 21–48.

Toothman, E. L., & Barrett, A. E. (2011). Mapping midlife: An examination of social factors shaping conceptions of the timing of middle age. *Advances in Life Course Research, 16,* 99–111. doi:10.1016/j.alcr.2011.08.003

Turiano, N. A., Chapman, B. P., Gruenewald, T. L., & Mroczek, D. K. (2015). Personality and the leading behavioral contributors of mortality. *Health Psychology, 34,* 51–60. doi:10.1037/hea0000038

Twenge, J. M. (1997). Attitudes toward women, 1970–1995. *Psychology of Women Quarterly, 21,* 35–51. doi:10.1111/j.1471-6402.1997.tb00099.x

U.S. Bureau of the Census. (2015). *Table A1. Marital status of people 15 years and over, by age, sex, personal earnings, race, and Hispanic origin: 2014.* Retrieved from http://www.census.gov/hhes/families/data/cps2014A.html

U.S. Bureau of the Census. (2017). *National Grandparents Day 2017: Sept. 10.* Retrieved April 16, 2018, from https://www.census.gov/newsroom/facts-for-features/2017/grandparents-day.html

U.S. Federal Reserve. (2014). *Report on the economic well-being of U.S. households in 2013.* Retrieved from http://www.federalreserve.gov/econresdata/2013-report-economic-well-being-us-households-201407.pdf

U.S. Federal Reserve. (2017). *Survey of consumer finances (SCF) chart book.* Retrieved April 7, 2018, from https://www.federalreserve.gov/econres/scfindex.htm

Vandewater, E., & Stewart, A. (2006). Paths to late midlife well-being for women and men: The importance of identity development and social role quality. *Journal of Adult Development, 13,* 76–83.

Villar, F. (2012). Successful ageing and development: The contribution of generativity in older age. *Ageing and Society, 32,* 1087–1105. doi:10.1017/S0144686X11000973

Villar, F., Celdrán, M., & Triadó, C. (2012). Grandmothers offering regular auxiliary care for their grandchildren: An expression of generativity in later life? *Journal of Women & Aging, 24,* 292–312. doi:10.1080/08952841.2012.708576

Voss, P., Kornadt, A. E., & Rothermund, K. (2017). Getting what you expect? Future self-views predict the valence of life events. *Developmental Psychology, 53,* 567–580. doi:10.1037/dev0000285

Vukasović, T., & Bratko, D. (2015). Heritability of personality: A meta-analysis of behavior genetic studies. *Psychological Bulletin, 141,* 769–785. doi:10.1037/bul0000017

Wang, H., & Amato, P. R. (2000). Predictors of divorce adjustment: Stressors, resources, and definitions. *Journal of Marriage & the Family, 62,* 655–668.

Wang, M., Henkens, K., & van Solinge, H. (2011). Retirement adjustment: A review of theoretical and empirical advancements. *American Psychologist, 66,* 204–213. doi:10.1037/a0022414

Wang, W., & Parker, K. (2014). *Record share of Americans have never married.* Retrieved from http://www.pewsocialtrends.org/2014/09/24/record-share-of-americans-have-never-married/

Wang, Y.-N., Shyu, Y.-I. L., Chen, M.-C., & Yang, P.-S. (2011). Reconciling work and family caregiving among adult-child family caregivers of older people with dementia: Effects on role strain and depressive symptoms. *Journal of Advanced Nursing, 67,* 829–840. doi:10.1111/j.1365-2648.2010.05505.x

Wängqvist, M., Lamb, M. E., Frisén, A., & Hwang, C. P. (2015). Child and adolescent predictors of personality in early adulthood. *Child Development, 86,* 1253–1261. doi:10.1111/cdev.12362

Warr, P. (2007). *Work, happiness, and unhappiness.* Mahwah, NJ: Lawrence Erlbaum.

Warren, C. S., Gleaves, D. H., & Rakhkovskaya, L. M. (2013). Score reliability and factor similarity of the Sociocultural Attitudes Towards Appearance Questionnaire-3 (SATAQ-3) among four ethnic groups. *Journal of Eating Disorders, 1,* 14. doi:10.1186/2050-2974-1-14

Wells Fargo. (2014). *2014 Wells Fargo middle class retirement study.* Retrieved from https://www08.wellsfargomedia.com/downloads/pdf/com/retirement-employee-benefits/insights/2014-retirement-study.pdf

Werner, E. E. (1991). Grandparent–grandchild relationships amongst US ethnic groups. In P. K. Smith (Ed.), *The psychology of grandparenthood: An international perspective* (pp. 68–82). Florence, KY: Taylor & Frances/Routledge.

Wethington, E. (2000). Expecting stress: Americans and the "midlife crisis." *Motivation and Emotion, 24,* 85–103.

Wethington, E., Kessler, R. C., & Pixley, J. E. (2004). Turning points in adulthood. In O. G. Brim, C. D. Ryff, & R. C. Kessler (Eds.), *How healthy are we? A national study of well-being at midlife* (pp. 586–613). Chicago, IL: University of Chicago Press.

Wheeler, M. S., Arnkoff, D. B., & Glass, C. R. (2017). The neuroscience of mindfulness: How mindfulness alters the brain and facilitates emotion regulation. *Mindfulness, 8,* 1471–1487. doi:10.1007/s12671-017-0742-x

Whitbeck, L., & Hoyt, D. R. (1994). Early family relationships, intergenerational solidarity, and support provided to parents by. *Journal of Gerontology, 49,* S85.

Whitley, D. M., & Fuller-Thomson, E. (2017). African-American solo grandparents raising grandchildren: A representative profile of their health status. *Journal of Community Health, 42,* 312–323. doi:10.1007/s10900-016-0257-8

Wight, R. G., Leblanc, A. J., & Lee Badgett, M. V. (2013). Same-sex legal marriage and psychological well-being: Findings from the California Health Interview survey. *American Journal of Public Health, 103,* 339–346. doi:10.2105/AJPH.2012.301113

Williams, M. N. (2011). The changing roles of grandparents raising grandchildren. *Journal of Human Behavior in the Social Environment, 21,* 948–962. doi:10.1080/10911359.2011.588535

Williams, N., & Torrez, D. J. (1998). Grandparenthood among Hispanics. In M. E. Szinovacz (Ed.), *Handbook on grandparenthood* (pp. 87–96). Westport, CT: Greenwood.

Wilt, J., Cox, K., & McAdams, D. P. (2010). The Eriksonian life story: Developmental scripts and psychosocial adaptation. *Journal of Adult Development, 17,* 156–161. doi:10.1007/s10804-010-9093-8

Wray, S. (2007). Women making sense of midlife: Ethnic and cultural diversity. *Journal of Aging Studies, 21,* 31–42. doi:10.1016/j.jaging.2006.03.001

Wrzus, C., Wagner, G. G., & Riediger, M. (2016). Personality-situation transactions from adolescence to old age. *Journal of Personality and Social Psychology, 110,* 782–799. doi:10.1037/pspp0000054

Wrzus, C., Zimmermann, J., Mund, M., & Neyer, F. J. (2017). Friendships in young and middle adulthood. In M. Hojjat & A. Moyer (Eds.), *The psychology of friendship* (pp. 21–38). Oxford, UK: Oxford University Press. doi:10.1093/acprof:oso/9780190222024.003.0002

Yavorsky, J. E., Dush, C. M. K., & Schoppe-Sullivan, S. J. (2015). The production of inequality: The gender division of labor across the transition to parenthood. *Journal of Marriage and the Family, 77,* 662–679. doi:10.1111/jomf.12189

Zarit, S. H., & Eggebeen, D. J. (2002). Parent-child relationships in adulthood and later years. In M. H. Bornstein (Ed.), *Handbook of parenting: Vol. 1. Children and parenting* (2nd ed., pp. 135–161). Mahwah, NJ: Lawrence Erlbaum.

Zhan, H. J. (2004). Willingness and expectations: Intergenerational differences in attitudes toward filial responsibility in China. *Marriage & Family Review, 36,* 175–200. Retrieved from 10.1300/J002v36n01_08

Zou, M. (2015). Gender, work orientations and job satisfaction. *Work, Employment & Society, 29,* 3–22. doi:10.1177/0950017014559267

Chapter 17

Aarsland, D., Creese, B., Politis, M., Chaudhuri, K. R., Ffytche, D. H., Weintraub, D., & Ballard, C. (2017). Cognitive decline in Parkinson disease. *Nature Reviews: Neurology, 13,* 217–231. doi:10.1038/nrneurol.2017.27

Aarsland, D., Sardahaee, F. S., Anderssen, S., & Ballard, C. (2010). Is physical activity a potential preventive factor for vascular dementia? A systematic review. *Aging & Mental Health, 14,* 386–395. doi:10.1080/13607860903586136

Abrams, A. P. (2014). Physiology of aging of older adults: Systemic and oral health considerations. *Dental Clinics of North America, 58,* 729–738. doi:10.1016/j.cden.2014.06.002

Ackerman, P. L., & Beier, M. E. (2006). Determinants of domain knowledge and independent study learning in an adult sample. *Journal of Educational Psychology, 98,* 366–381.

Administration on Aging. (2014). *A profile of older Americans: 2014.* Retrieved from http://www.aoa.acl.gov/Aging_Statistics/Profile/index.aspx

Agronin, M. E. (2014). *Alzheimer's disease and other dementias: A practical guide.* New York, NY: Routledge.

Aigner, T., Haag, J., Martin, J., & Buckwalter, J. (2007). Osteoarthritis: Aging of matrix and cells—Going for a remedy. *Current Drug Targets, 8,* 325–331.

Ailshire, J. A., Beltrán-Sánchez, H., & Crimmins, E. M. (2015). Becoming centenarians: Disease and functioning trajectories of older US Adults as they survive to 100. *Journals of Gerontology Series A: Biological Sciences and Medical Sciences, 70,* 193–201. doi:10.1093/gerona/glu124

Alma, M. A., van der Mei, S. F., Melis-Dankers, B. J. M., van Tilburg, T. G., Groothoff, J. W., & Suurmeijer, T. P. B. M. (2011). Participation of the elderly after vision loss. *Disability and Rehabilitation, 33,* 63–72. doi:10.3109/09638288.2010.488711

Alzheimer's Association. (2015). *2015 Alzheimer's disease facts and figures.* Retrieved from http://www.alz.org/facts/downloads/facts_figures_2015.pdf

Alzheimer's Association. (2018). *2018 Alzheimer's disease facts and figures.* Retrieved from https://alz.org/documents_custom/2018-facts-and-figures.pdf

Alzheimer's Disease International. (2015). *World Alzheimer Report 2014: Dementia and risk reduction.* Retrieved from http://www.alz.co.uk/research/world-report-2014

American Academy of Ophthalmology. (2011). *Eye health statistics at a glance.* Retrieved from http://www.aao.org/newsroom/upload/Eye-Health-Statistics-April-2011.pdf

American Psychiatric Association. (2013). *Diagnostic and statistical manual of mental disorders* (5th ed.). Washington, DC: Author.

Andel, R., Crowe, M., Hahn, E. A., Mortimer, J. A., Pedersen, N. L., Fratiglioni, L., . . . Gatz, M. (2012). Work-related stress may increase the risk of vascular dementia. *Journal of the American Geriatrics Society, 60,* 60–67. doi:10.1111/j.1532-5415.2011.03777.x

Andersen, K., Lolk, A., Martinussen, T., & Kragh-Sørensen, P. (2010). Very mild to severe dementia and mortality: A 14-year follow-up—The Odense study. *Dementia & Geriatric Cognitive Disorders, 29,* 61–67. doi:10.1159/000265553

Andersen, S. J. (2007). Osteoporosis in the older woman. *Clinical Obstetrics & Gynecology, 50,* 752–766.

Anstey, K. J., Hofer, S. M., & Luszcz, M. A. (2003). A latent growth curve analysis of late-life sensory and cognitive function over 8 years: Evidence for specific and common factors underlying change. *Psychology and Aging, 18,* 714–726.

Arai, Y., Sasaki, T., & Hirose, N. (2017). Demographic, phenotypic, and genetic characteristics of centenarians in Okinawa and Honshu, Japan: Part 2 Honshu, Japan.

Mechanisms of Ageing and Development, 165, 80–85. doi:10.1016/J.MAD.2017.02.005

Ardelt, M. (1998). Social crisis and individual growth: The long-term effects of the Great Depression. *Journal of Aging Studies, 12,* 291.

Ardelt, M. (2010). Are older adults wiser than college students? A comparison of two age cohorts. *Journal of Adult Development, 17,* 193–207. doi:10.1007/s10804-009-9088-5

Ardelt, M., Pridgen, S., & Nutter-Pridgen, K. L. (2018). The relation between age and three-dimensional wisdom: Variations by wisdom dimensions and education. *Journals of Gerontology Series B: Psychological Sciences & Social Sciences.* Advance online publication. doi:10.1093/geronb/gbx182

Armstrong, N. J., Mather, K. A., Thalamuthu, A., Wright, M. J., Trollor, J. N., Ames, D., . . . Kwok, J. B. (2017). Aging, exceptional longevity and comparisons of the Hannum and Horvath epigenetic clocks. *Epigenomics, 9,* 689–700. doi:10.2217/epi-2016-0179

Artistico, D., Orom, H., Cervone, D., Krauss, S., & Houston, E. (2010). Everyday challenges in context: The influence of contextual factors on everyday problem solving among young, middle-aged, and older adults. *Experimental Aging Research, 36,* 230–247. doi:10.1080/03610731003613938

Ash, A. S., Kroll-Desrosiers, A. R., Hoaglin, D. C., Christensen, K., Fang, H., & Perls, T. T. (2015). Are members of long-lived families healthier than their equally long-lived peers? Evidence from the Long Life Family study. *The Journals of Gerontology Series A: Biological Sciences and Medical Sciences, 70,* 971–976. doi:10.1093/gerona/glv015

Aslan, U. B., Cavlak, U., Yagci, N., Akdag, B., Stewart, A. L., Miller, C. J., & Bloch, D. A. (2008). Balance performance, aging and falling: A comparative study based on a Turkish sample. *Archives of Gerontology and Geriatrics, 46,* 283–292. doi:10.1016/j.archger.2007.05.003

Assuncao, M., & Andrade, J. P. (2015). Protective action of green tea catechins in neuronal mitochondria during aging. *Frontiers in Bioscience, 20,* 247–262.

Atkinson-Clement, C., Pinto, S., Eusebio, A., & Coulon, O. (2017). Diffusion tensor imaging in Parkinson's disease: Review and meta-analysis. *NeuroImage: Clinical, 16,* 98–110. doi:10.1016/J.NICL.2017.07.011

Attems, J., Walker, L., & Jellinger, K. A. (2015). Olfaction and aging: A mini-review. *Gerontology, 61,* 485–490. doi:10.1159/000381619

Avis, N. E., Brockwell, S., & Colvin, A. (2005). A universal menopausal syndrome? *American Journal of Medicine, 118,* 1406.

Avis, N. E., & Crawford, S. (2006). Menopause: Recent research findings. In S. K. Whitbourne & S. L. Willis (Eds.), *The baby boomers grow up: Contemporary perspectives on midlife* (pp. 75–109). Mahwah, NJ: Lawrence Erlbaum.

Baker, H. (2007). Nutrition in the elderly: An overview (Cover story). *Geriatrics, 62,* 28–31.

Baldwin, C. L., & Ash, I. K. (2011). Impact of sensory acuity on auditory working memory span in young and older adults. *Psychology and Aging, 26,* 85–91. doi:10.1037/a0020360

Baltes, M. M., & Carstensen, L. L. (2003). The process of successful aging: Selection, optimization and compensation. In U. M. Staudinger & U. Lindenberger (Eds.), *Understanding human development: Dialogues with lifespan psychology* (pp. 81–104). Dordrecht, The Netherlands: Kluwer Academic.

Baltes, P. B., & Kunzmann, U. (2003). Wisdom. *The Psychologist, 16,* 131–133.

Baltes, P. B., & Staudinger, U. M. (2000). Wisdom: A metaheuristic (pragmatic) to orchestrate mind and virtue toward excellence. *American Psychologist, 55,* 122–136.

Banerjee, G., Kim, H. J., Fox, Z., Jäger, H. R., Wilson, D., Charidimou, A., . . . Werring, D. J. (2017). MRI-visible perivascular space location is associated with Alzheimer's disease independently of amyloid burden. *Brain, 140,* 1107–1116. doi:10.1093/brain/awx003

Bansal, N., & Parle, M. (2014). Dementia: An overview. *Management, 1,* 281–297.

Barengo, N. C., Antikainen, R., Borodulin, K., Harald, K., & Jousilahti, P. (2017). Leisure-time physical activity reduces total and cardiovascular mortality and cardiovascular disease incidence in older adults. *Journal of the American Geriatrics Society, 65,* 504–510. doi:10.1111/jgs.14694

Barulli, D., & Stern, Y. (2013). Efficiency, capacity, compensation, maintenance, plasticity: Emerging concepts in cognitive reserve. *Trends in Cognitive Sciences, 17,* 502–509. doi:10.1016/j.tics.2013.08.012

Bechshøft, R. L., Malmgaard-Clausen, N. M., Gliese, B., Beyer, N., Mackey, A. L., Andersen, J. L., . . . Holm, L. (2017). Improved skeletal muscle mass and strength after heavy strength training in very old individuals. *Experimental Gerontology, 92,* 96–105. doi:10.1016/J.EXGER.2017.03.014

Beier, M. E., & Ackerman, P. L. (2005). Age, ability, and the role of prior knowledge on the acquisition of new domain knowledge: Promising results in a real-world learning environment. *Psychology and Aging, 20,* 341–355.

Bello, V. M. E., & Schultz, R. R. (2011). Prevalence of treatable and reversible dementias: A study in a dementia outpatient clinic. *Dementia & Neuropsychologia, 5,* 44–47.

Bellou, V., Belbasis, L., Tzoulaki, I., Evangelou, E., & Ioannidis, J. P. A. (2016). Environmental risk factors and Parkinson's disease: An umbrella review of meta-analyses. *Parkinsonism & Related Disorders, 23,* 1–9. doi:10.1016/j.parkreldis.2015.12.008

Belza, B., Walwick, J., Shiu-Thornton, S., Schwartz, S., Taylor, M., & LoGerfo, J. (2004). Older adult perspectives on physical activity and exercise: Voices from multiple cultures. *Preventing Chronic Disease, 1,* A09.

Bender, A. R., Völkle, M. C., & Raz, N. (2016). Differential aging of cerebral white matter in middle-aged and older adults: A seven-year follow-up. *NeuroImage, 125,* 74–83. doi:10.1016/j.neuroimage.2015.10.030

Benjamin, E. J., Virani, S. S., Callaway, C. W., Chamberlain, A. M., Chang, A. R., Cheng, S., . . . American Heart Association Council on Epidemiology and Prevention Statistics Committee and Stroke Statistics Subcommittee. (2018). Heart disease and stroke statistics—2018 update: A report from the American Heart Association.

Circulation, 137, e67–e492. doi:10.1161/CIR.0000000000000558

Bernstein, M. (2017). Nutritional needs of the older adult. *Physical Medicine and Rehabilitation Clinics of North America, 28,* 747–766. doi:10.1016/j.pmr.2017.06.008

Berntsen, D., & Rubin, D. C. (2002). Emotionally charged autobiographical memories across the life span: The recall of happy, sad, traumatic and involuntary memories. *Psychology and Aging, 17,* 636–652.

Bettens, K., Sleegers, K., & Van Broeckhoven, C. (2013). Genetic insights in Alzheimer's disease. *The Lancet Neurology, 12,* 92–104. doi:10.1016/S1474-4422(12)70259-4

Bielak, A. A. M. (2010). How can we not "lose it" if we still don't understand how to "use it"? Unanswered questions about the influence of activity participation on cognitive performance in older age—A mini-review. *Gerontology, 56,* 507–519. doi:10.1159/000264918

Bishop, A. J., Martin, P., MacDonald, M., & Poon, L. (2010). Predicting happiness among centenarians. *Gerontology, 56,* 88–92. doi:10.1159/000272017

Bisiacchi, P. S., Borella, E., Bergamaschi, S., Carretti, B., & Mondini, S. (2008). Interplay between memory and executive functions in normal and pathological aging. *Journal of Clinical & Experimental Neuropsychology, 30,* 723–733. Retrieved from 10.1080/13803390701689587

Blackwell, D., Lucas, J., & Clarke, T. (2012). Summary health statistics for U.S. adults: National Health Interview Survey, 2012. *Vital Health Statistics, 10.* Retrieved from http://www.cdc.gov/nchs/data/series/sr_10/sr10_260.pdf

Bleicher, K., Cumming, R. G., Naganathan, V., Seibel, M. J., Sambrook, P. N., Blyth, F. M., . . . Waite, L. M. (2011). Lifestyle factors, medications, and disease influence bone mineral density in older men: Findings from the CHAMP study. *Osteoporosis International, 22,* 2421–2437. doi:10.1007/s00198-010-1478-9

Blennow, K., Mattsson, N., Schöll, M., Hansson, O., & Zetterberg, H. (2015). Amyloid biomarkers in Alzheimer's disease. *Trends in Pharmacological Sciences, 36,* 297–309. doi:10.1016/j.tips.2015.03.002

Bloemendaal, M., Zandbelt, B., Wegman, J., van de Rest, O., Cools, R., & Aarts, E. (2016). Contrasting neural effects of aging on proactive and reactive response inhibition. *Neurobiology of Aging, 46,* 96–106. doi:10.1016/j.neurobiolaging.2016.06.007

Blondell, S. J., Hammersley-Mather, R., & Veerman, J. L. (2014). Does physical activity prevent cognitive decline and dementia? A systematic review and meta-analysis of longitudinal studies. *BMC Public Health, 14,* 510. doi:10.1186/1471-2458-14-510

Blumberg, J., Bailey, R., Sesso, H., & Ulrich, C. (2018). The evolving role of multivitamin/multimineral supplement use among adults in the age of personalized nutrition. *Nutrients, 10,* 248. doi:10.3390/nu10020248

Bonanni, L., Franciotti, R., Delli Pizzi, S., Thomas, A., & Onofrj, M. (2018). Lewy body dementia. In D. Galimberti & E. Scarpini (Eds.), *Neurodegenerative diseases* (pp. 297–312). Cham, Switzerland: Springer International. doi:10.1007/978-3-319-72938-1_14

Boots, E. A., Schultz, S. A., Almeida, R. P., Oh, J. M., Koscik, R. L., Dowling, M. N., . . . Okonkwo, O. C. (2015). Occupational complexity and cognitive reserve in a middle-aged cohort at risk for Alzheimer's disease. *Archives of Clinical Neuropsychology, 30*, 634–642. doi:10.1093/arclin/acv041

Borella, E., Carretti, B., Riboldi, F., & De Beni, R. (2010). Working memory training in older adults: Evidence of transfer and maintenance effects. *Psychology and Aging, 25*, 767–778. doi:10.1037/a0020683

Boulos, C., Salameh, P., & Barberger-Gateau, P. (2017). Social isolation and risk for malnutrition among older people. *Geriatrics & Gerontology International, 17*, 286–294. doi:10.1111/ggi.12711

Bowles, R. P., & Salthouse, T. A. (2003). Assessing the age-related effects of proactive interference on working memory tasks using the Rasch model. *Psychology and Aging, 18*, 608–615.

Boyer, K. A., Andriacchi, T. P., & Beaupre, G. S. (2012). The role of physical activity in changes in walking mechanics with age. *Gait & Posture, 36*, 149–153. doi:10.1016/j.gaitpost.2012.02.007

Brandão, D., Ribeiro, O., Afonso, R. M., & Paúl, C. (2017). Escaping most common lethal diseases in old age: Morbidity profiles of Portuguese centenarians. *European Geriatric Medicine, 8*, 310–314. doi:10.1016/J.EURGER.2017.04.011

Braun, S. M. G., & Jessberger, S. (2014). Adult neurogenesis: Mechanisms and functional significance. *Development, 141*, 1983–1986. doi:10.1242/dev.104596

Braun, U., Muldoon, S. F., & Bassett, D. S. (2015). On human brain networks in health and disease. In *eLS* (pp. 1–9). Chichester, England: John Wiley. doi:10.1002/9780470015902.a0025783

Braver, T. S., & West, R. (2008). Working memory, executive control, and aging. In F. I. M. Craik & T. A. Salthouse (Eds.), *The handbook of aging and cognition* (3rd ed., pp. 311–372). New York, NY: Psychology Press.

Brehmer, Y., Westerberg, H., & Bäckman, L. (2012). Working-memory training in younger and older adults: training gains, transfer, and maintenance. *Frontiers in Human Neuroscience, 6*, 63. doi:10.3389/fnhum.2012.00063

Brichta, L., Greengard, P., & Flajolet, M. (2013). Advances in the pharmacological treatment of Parkinson's disease: Targeting neurotransmitter systems. *Trends in Neurosciences, 36*, 543–554. doi:10.1016/j.tins.2013.06.003

Briggs, R., McHale, C., Fitzhenry, D., O'Neill, D., & Kennelly, S. P. (2018). Dementia, disclosing the diagnosis. *QJM: An International Journal of Medicine, 111*, 215–216. doi:10.1093/qjmed/hcx181

Buford, T. W., Anton, S. D., Judge, A. R., Marzetti, E., Wohlgemuth, S. E., Carter, C. S., . . . Manini, T. M. (2010). Models of accelerated sarcopenia: Critical pieces for solving the puzzle of age-related muscle atrophy. *Ageing Research Reviews, 9*, 369–383. doi:10.1016/j.arr.2010.04.004

Burke, D. M., & Shafto, M. A. (2004). Aging and language production. *Current Directions in Psychological Science, 13*, 21–24. doi:10.1111/j.0963-7214.2004.01301006.x

Calapai, G., Bonina, F., Bonina, A., Rizza, L., Mannucci, C., Arcoraci, V., . . . Alecci, U. (2017). A randomized, double-blinded, clinical trial on effects of a vitis vinifera extract on cognitive function in healthy older adults. *Frontiers in Pharmacology, 8*, 776. doi:10.3389/fphar.2017.00776

Cameron, H. A., & Glover, L. R. (2015). Adult neurogenesis: Beyond learning and memory. *Annual Review of Psychology, 66*, 53–81. doi:10.1146/annurev-psych-010814-015006

Cannon, J. R., & Greenamyre, J. T. (2013). Gene-environment interactions in Parkinson's disease: Specific evidence in humans and mammalian models. *Neurobiology of Disease, 57*, 38–46. doi:10.1016/j.nbd.2012.06.025

Carpenter, S. M., Peters, E., Västfjäll, D., & Isen, A. M. (2013). Positive feelings facilitate working memory and complex decision making among older adults. *Cognition & Emotion, 27*, 184–192. doi:10.1080/02699931.2012.698251

Carson, V. B., Vanderhorst, K., & Koenig, H. G. (2015). *Care giving for Alzheimer's disease: A compassionate guide for clinicians and loved ones.* New York, NY: Springer.

Castro-Chavira, S. A., Fernandez, T., Nicolini, H., Diaz-Cintra, S., & Prado-Alcala, R. A. (2015). Genetic markers in biological fluids for aging-related major neurocognitive disorder. *Current Alzheimer Research, 12*, 200–209.

Cawthon, P. M., Shahnazari, M., Orwoll, E. S., & Lane, N. E. (2016). Osteoporosis in men: Findings from the Osteoporotic Fractures in Men study (MrOS). *Therapeutic Advances in Musculoskeletal Disease, 8*, 15–27. doi:10.1177/1759720X15621227

Centers for Disease Control and Prevention. (2018). *Fatal injury reports, national, regional and state, 1981–2016.* Retrieved April 8, 2018, from https://webappa.cdc.gov/sasweb/ncipc/mortrate.html

Chakravarthy, U., Evans, J., & Rosenfeld, P. J. (2010). Age related macular degeneration. *BMJ: British Medical Journal, 340*, 526–530. doi:10.1136/bmj.c981

Chapko, D., McCormack, R., Black, C., Staff, R., & Murray, A. (2018). Life-course determinants of cognitive reserve (CR) in cognitive aging and dementia—A systematic literature review. *Aging & Mental Health.* Advance online publication. doi:10.1080/13607863.2017.1348471

Charlton, K. E., Batterham, M. J., Bowden, S., Ghosh, A., Caldwell, K., Barone, L., . . . Milosavljevic, M. (2013). A high prevalence of malnutrition in acute geriatric patients predicts adverse clinical outcomes and mortality within 12 months. *E-SPEN Journal, 8*, e120–e125. doi:10.1016/j.clnme.2013.03.004

Chen, X., Hertzog, C., & Park, D. C. (2017). Cognitive predictors of everyday problem solving across the lifespan. *Gerontology, 63*, 372–384. doi:10.1159/000459622

Chertkow, H. (2008). Diagnosis and treatment of dementia: Introduction. *CMAJ: Canadian Medical Association Journal, 178*, 316–321. Retrieved from 10.1503/cmaj.070795

Chi, S., Yu, J. T., Tan, M. S., & Tan, L. (2014). Depression in Alzheimer's disease: Epidemiology, mechanisms, and management. *Journal of Alzheimer's Disease: JAD, 42*, 739–755. doi:10.3233/JAD-140324

Chin, A. L., Negash, S., & Hamilton, R. (2011). Diversity and disparity in dementia: The impact of ethnoracial differences in Alzheimer disease. *Alzheimer Disease and Associated Disorders, 25*, 187–195. doi:10.1097/WAD.0b013e318211c6c9

Cicchino, J. B., & McCartt, A. T. (2015). *Critical older driver errors in a sample of serious U.S. crashes.* Arlington, VA: Insurance Institute for Highway Safety.

Clapp, W. C., Rubens, M. T., Sabharwal, J., & Gazzaley, A. (2011). Deficit in switching between functional brain networks underlies the impact of multitasking on working memory in older adults. *Proceedings of the National Academy of Sciences of the United States of America, 108*, 7212–7217. doi:10.1073/pnas.1015297108

Connell, C. M., Scott Roberts, J., McLaughlin, S. J., & Akinleye, D. (2009). Racial differences in knowledge and beliefs about Alzheimer disease. *Alzheimer Disease & Associated Disorders, 23*, 110–116. doi:10.1097/WAD.0b013e318192e94d

Cooper, C., Javaid, M. K., & Arden, N. (2014). Epidemiology of osteoarthritis. In N. Arden, F. Blanco, C. Cooper, A. Guermazi, D. Hayashi, D. Hunter, . . . F. W. Reginster (Eds.), *Atlas of osteoarthritis* (pp. 21–36). Tarporley, England: Springer Healthcare Ltd. doi:10.1007/978-1-910315-16-3_2

Corrada. M. M., Brookmeyer, R., Paganini-Hill, A., Berlau, D., & Kawas, C. H. (2010). Dementia incidence continues to increase with age in the oldest old: The 90+ study. *Annals of Neurology, 67*, 114–121. doi:10.1002/ana.21915

Corriveau, R. A., Bosetti, F., Emr, M., Gladman, J. T., Koenig, J. I., Moy, C. S., . . . Koroshetz, W. (2016). The science of vascular contributions to cognitive impairment and dementia (VCID): A framework for advancing research priorities in the cerebrovascular biology of cognitive decline. *Cellular and Molecular Neurobiology, 36*, 281–288. doi:10.1007/s10571-016-0334-7

Cosman, F., de Beur, S. J., LeBoff, M. S., Lewiecki, E. M., Tanner, B., Randall, S., & Lindsay, R. (2014). Clinician's guide to prevention and treatment of osteoporosis. *Osteoporosis International, 25*, 2359–2381. doi:10.1007/s00198-014-2794-2

Counts, S. E., Ikonomovic, M. D., Mercado, N., Vega, I. E., & Mufson, E. J. (2017). Biomarkers for the early detection and progression of Alzheimer's disease. *Neurotherapeutics, 14*, 35–53. doi:10.1007/s13311-016-0481-z

Crews, J. E., Chou, C. F., Stevens, J. A., & Saaddine, J. B. (2016). Falls among persons aged 65 years with and without severe vision impairment? United States, 2014. *MMWR. Morbidity and Mortality Weekly Report, 65*, 433–437. doi:10.15585/mmwr.mm6517a2

Cruickshanks, K. J., Nondahl, D. M., Tweed, T. S., Wiley, T. L., Klein, B. E. K., Klein, R., . . . Nash, S. D. (2010). Education, occupation, noise exposure history and the 10-yr cumulative incidence of hearing impairment in older adults. *Hearing Research, 264*, 3–9. doi:10.1016/j.heares.2009.10.008

Daffner, K. R., Chong, H., & Riis, J. (2007). Cognitive status impacts age-related changes in attention to novel and target events in normal adults. *Neuropsychology, 21*, 291–300.

Darowski, E. S., Helder, E., Zacks, R. T., Hasher, L., & Hambrick, D. Z. (2008). Age-related differences in cognition: The role of distraction control. *Neuropsychology, 22,* 638–644.

Daselaar, S., & Cabeza, R. (2005). Age-related changes in hemispheric organization. In R. Cabeza, L. Nyberg, & D. C. Park (Eds.), *Cognitive neuroscience of aging: Linking cognitive and cerebral aging* (pp. 325–353). New York, NY: Oxford University Press.

Davey, A., Dai, T., Woodard, J. L., Miller, L. S., Gondo, Y., Johnson, M. A., . . . Poon, L. W. (2013). Profiles of cognitive functioning in a population-based sample of centenarians using factor mixture analysis. *Experimental Aging Research, 39,* 125–144. doi:10.1080/036 1073X.2013.761869

Davey, A., Elias, M. F., Siegler, I. C., Lele, U., Martin, P., Johnson, M. A., . . . Poon, L. W. (2010). Cognitive function, physical performance, health, and disease: Norms from the Georgia Centenarian study. *Experimental Aging Research, 36,* 394–425. doi:10.1080/0361073x.2010.509010

David, C. B., Nancy, M. H., & Ying-Bo, S. (2010). Oxidative damage and the prevention of age-related cataracts. *Ophthalmic Research, 44,* 155–165.

Davies, C. G., & Thorn, B. L. (2002). Psychopharmacology with older adults in residential care. In R. D. Hill, B. L. Thorn, J. Bowling, & A. Morrison (Eds.), *Geriatric residential care* (pp. 161–181). Mahwah, NJ: Lawrence Erlbaum.

Daviglus, M. L., Bell, C. C., Berrettini, W., Bowen, P. E., Connolly, E. S., Cox, N. J., . . . Trevisan, M. (2010). National Institutes of Health State-of-the-Science Conference statement: Preventing Alzheimer disease and cognitive decline. *Annals of Internal Medicine, 60,* 136–141. doi:10.1059/0003-4819-153-3-201008030-00260

de Graaf, C., Polet, P., & van Staveren, W. A. (1994). Sensory perception and pleasantness of food flavors in elderly subjects. *Journal of Gerontology, 49,* P93–P99. doi:10.1093/geronj/49.3.P93

de la Torre, J. C. (2016). Masquerading as dementia. In J. C. de la Torre (Ed.), *Alzheimer's turning point* (pp. 25–29). Cham, Switzerland: Springer International. doi:10.1007/978-3-319-34057-9_3

Denney, N. W., Pearce, K. A., & Palmer, A. M. (1982). A developmental study of adults' performance on traditional and practical problem-solving tasks. *Experimental Aging Research, 8,* 115–118. doi:10.1080/03610738208258407

DeSantis, C. E., Lin, C. C., Mariotto, A. B., Siegel, R. L., Stein, K. D., Kramer, J. L., . . . Jemal, A. (2014). Cancer treatment and survivorship statistics, 2014. *CA: A Cancer Journal for Clinicians, 64,* 252–271. doi:10.3322/caac.21235

Dhital, A., Pey, T., & Stanford, M. R. (2010). Visual loss and falls: A review. *Eye, 24,* 1437–1446. doi:10.1038/eye.2010.60

Djukic, M., Wedekind, D., Franz, A., Gremke, M., & Nau, R. (2015). Frequency of dementia syndromes with a potentially treatable cause in geriatric in-patients: Analysis of a 1-year interval. *European Archives of Psychiatry and Clinical Neuroscience, 265,* 429–438. doi:10.1007/s00406-015-0583-3

Dong, X., Milholland, B., & Vijg, J. (2016). Evidence for a limit to human lifespan. *Nature, 538,* 257–259. doi:10.1038/nature19793

Doty, R. L., Shaman, P., Applebaum, S. L., Giberson, R., Siksorski, L., & Rosenberg, L. (1984). Smell identification ability: Changes with age. *Science, 226,* 1441–1443. doi:10.1126/science.6505700

Douaud, G., Refsum, H., de Jager, C. A., Jacoby, R., Nichols, T. E., Smith, S. M., & Smith, A. D. (2013). Preventing Alzheimer's disease-related gray matter atrophy by B-vitamin treatment. *Proceedings of the National Academy of Sciences of the United States of America, 110,* 9523–9528. doi:10.1073/pnas.1301816110

Dumas, J. A. (2017). Physical activity and the hippocampus in older adults. *American Journal of Geriatric Psychiatry, 25,* 218–219. doi:10.1016/j.jagp.2016.12.005

Ekström, I., Sjölund, S., Nordin, S., Nordin Adolfsson, A., Adolfsson, R., Nilsson, L. G., . . . Olofsson, J. K. (2017). Smell loss predicts mortality risk regardless of dementia conversion. *Journal of the American Geriatrics Society, 65,* 1238–1243. doi:10.1111/jgs.14770

Emery, L., Hale, S., & Myerson, J. (2008). Age differences in proactive interference, working memory, and abstract reasoning. *Psychology and Aging, 23,* 634–645.

Emre, M., Ford, P. J., Bilgiç, B., & Uç, E. Y. (2014). Cognitive impairment and dementia in Parkinson's disease: Practical issues and management. *Movement Disorders, 29,* 663–672. doi:10.1002/mds.25870

Engmann, B. (2011). Mild cognitive impairment in the elderly: A review of the influence of depression, possible other core symptoms, and diagnostic findings. *GeroPsych: The Journal of Gerontopsychology and Geriatric Psychiatry, 24,* 71–76.

Erickson, K. I., Raji, C. A., Lopez, O. L., Becker, J. T., Rosano, C., Newman, A. B., . . . Kuller, L. H. (2010). Physical activity predicts gray matter volume in late adulthood: The Cardiovascular Health study. *Neurology, 75,* 1415–1422. doi:10.1212/WNL.0b013e3181f88359

Ernst, A., Alkass, K., Bernard, S., Salehpour, M., Perl, S., Tisdale, J., . . . Frisén, J. (2014). Neurogenesis in the striatum of the adult human brain. *Cell, 156,* 1072–1083. doi:10.1016/j.cell.2014.01.044

Farage, M. A., Miller, K. W., & Maibach, H. I. (2015). Degenerative changes in aging skin. In M. A. Farage, K. W. Miller, & H. I. Maibach (Eds.), *Textbook of aging skin* (pp. 1–18). New York, NY: Springer. doi:10.1007/978-3-642-27814-3_4-2

Farzaneh-Far, R., Lin, J., Epel, E. S., Harris, W. S., Blackburn, E. H., & Whooley, M. A. (2010). Association of marine omega-3 fatty acid levels with telomeric aging in patients with coronary heart disease. *JAMA: Journal of the American Medical Association, 303,* 250–257.

Feng, Y., Jankovic, J., & Wu, Y. C. (2014). Epigenetic mechanisms in Parkinson's disease. *Journal of the Neurological Sciences, 349,* 3–9. doi:10.1016/j.jns.2014.12.017

Fenn, A. M., Corona, A. W., & Godbout, J. P. (2013). Aging and the immune system. In A. W. Kusnecov & H. Anisman (Eds.), *The Wiley-Blackwell handbook of psychoneuroimmunology* (pp. 313–329). Chichester, UK: John Wiley. https://doi.org/10.1002/9781118314814

Festa, E. K., Ott, B. R., Manning, K. J., Davis, J. D., & Heindel, W. C. (2013). Effect of cognitive status on self-regulatory driving behavior in older adults: An assessment of naturalistic driving using in-car video recordings. *Journal of Geriatric Psychiatry and Neurology, 26,* 10–18. doi:10.1177/0891988712473801

Feyereisen, P., Demaeght, N., & Samson, D. (1998). Why do picture naming latencies increase with age: General. *Experimental Aging Research, 24,* 21.

Fielding, R. A., Guralnik, J. M., King, A. C., Pahor, M., McDermott, M. M., Tudor-Locke, C., & Rejeski, W. J. (2017). Dose of physical activity, physical functioning and disability risk in mobility-limited older adults: Results from the LIFE study randomized trial. *PLoS ONE, 12,* e0182155. doi:10.1371/journal.pone.0182155

Finkelstein, J. A., & Schiffman, S. S. (1999). Workshop on taste and smell in the elderly: An overview. *Physiology & Behavior, 66,* 173–176. doi:10.1016/S0031-9384(98)00261-3

Firth, J., Stubbs, B., Vancampfort, D., Schuch, F., Lagopoulos, J., Rosenbaum, S., & Ward, P. B. (2018). Effect of aerobic exercise on hippocampal volume in humans: A systematic review and meta-analysis. *NeuroImage, 166,* 230–238. doi:10.1016/J.NEUROIMAGE.2017.11.007

Fisher, J. E., Yury, C., & Buchanan, J. A. (2006). Dementia. In J. E. Fisher & W. T. O'Donohue (Eds.), *Practitioner's guide to evidence-based psychotherapy* (pp. 214–229). New York, NY: Springer Science + Business Media.

Fisk, J. D., Beattie, B. L., Donnelly, M., Byszewski, A., & Molnar, F. J. (2007). Disclosure of the diagnosis of dementia. *Alzheimer's & Dementia, 3,* 404–410.

Flament, F., Bazin, R., & Piot, B. (2013). Effect of the sun on visible clinical signs of aging in Caucasian skin. *Clinical, Cosmetic and Investigational Dermatology, 6,* 221. doi:10.2147/CCID.S44686

Frank-Wilson, A. W., Farthing, J. P., Chilibeck, P. D., Arnold, C. M., Davison, K. S., Olszynski, W. P., & Kontulainen, S. A. (2016). Lower leg muscle density is independently associated with fall status in community-dwelling older adults. *Osteoporosis International, 27,* 2231–2240. doi:10.1007/s00198-016-3514-x

Freeman, S., Garcia, J., & Marston, H. R. (2013). Centenarian self-perceptions of factors responsible for attainment of extended health and longevity. *Educational Gerontology, 39,* 717–728. doi:10.1080/036012 77.2012.750981

Frisoni, G. B., Boccardi, M., Barkhof, F., Blennow, K., Cappa, S., Chiotis, K., . . . Winblad, B. (2017). Strategic roadmap for an early diagnosis of Alzheimer's disease based on biomarkers. *The Lancet Neurology, 16,* 661–676. doi:10.1016/S1474-4422(17)30159-X

Gaesser, B., Sacchetti, D. C., Addis, D. R., & Schacter, D. L. (2011). Characterizing age-related changes in remembering the past and imagining the future. *Psychology and Aging, 26,* 80–84. doi:10.1037/a0021054

Gahche, J. J., Bailey, R. L., Potischman, N., & Dwyer, J. T. (2017). Dietary supplement use was very high among older adults in the United States in 2011–2014. *Journal of Nutrition, 147*, 1968–1976. doi:10.3945/jn.117.255984

Gallaway, P., Miyake, H., Buchowski, M., Shimada, M., Yoshitake, Y., Kim, A., & Hongu, N. (2017). Physical activity: A viable way to reduce the risks of mild cognitive impairment, Alzheimer's disease, and vascular dementia in older adults. *Brain Sciences, 7*, 22. doi:10.3390/brainsci7020022

Gazzaley, A., Sheridan, M. A., Cooney, J. W., & D'Esposito, M. (2007). Age-related deficits in component processes of working memory. *Neuropsychology, 21*, 532–539.

Gerstorf, D., Ram, N., Hoppmann, C., Willis, S. L., & Schaie, K. W. (2011). Cohort differences in cognitive aging and terminal decline in the Seattle Longitudinal Study. *Developmental Psychology, 47*, 1026–1041. doi:10.1037/a0023426

Gollan, T. H., Stasenko, A., Li, C., & Salmon, D. P. (2017). Bilingual language intrusions and other speech errors in Alzheimer's disease. *Brain and Cognition, 118*, 27–44. doi:10.1016/J.BANDC.2017.07.007

Gomez, C. R., Nomellini, V., Faunce, D. E., & Kovacs, E. J. (2008). Innate immunity and aging. *Experimental Gerontology, 43*, 718–728. Retrieved from 10.1016/j.exger.2008.05.016

Gonçalves, J. T., Schafer, S. T., & Gage, F. H. (2016). Adult neurogenesis in the hippocampus: From stem cells to behavior. *Cell, 167*, 897–914. doi:10.1016/j.cell.2016.10.021

Govindaraju, D., Atzmon, G., & Barzilai, N. (2015). Genetics, lifestyle and longevity: Lessons from centenarians. *Applied & Translational Genomics, 4*, 23–32. doi:10.1016/j.atg.2015.01.001

Gow, A. J., Corley, J., Starr, J. M., & Deary, I. J. (2012). Reverse causation in activity-cognitive ability associations: The Lothian Birth Cohort 1936. *Psychology and Aging, 27*, 250–255. doi:10.1037/a0024144

Graham, W. V., Bonito-Oliva, A., & Sakmar, T. P. (2017). Update on Alzheimer's disease therapy and prevention strategies. *Annual Review of Medicine, 68*, 413–430. doi:10.1146/annurev-med-042915-103753

Granacher, U., Muehlbauer, T., & Gruber, M. (2012). A qualitative review of balance and strength performance in healthy older adults: Impact for testing and training. *Journal of Aging Research, 2012*, 708905. doi:10.1155/2012/708905

Grant, A., Dennis, N. A., & Li, P. (2014). Cognitive control, cognitive reserve, and memory in the aging bilingual brain. *Frontiers in Psychology, 5*, 1401. doi:10.3389/fpsyg.2014.01401

Groot, C., Hooghiemstra, A. M., Raijmakers, P. G. H. M., van Berckel, B. N. M., Scheltens, P., Scherder, E. J. A., . . . Ossenkoppele, R. (2016). The effect of physical activity on cognitive function in patients with dementia: A meta-analysis of randomized control trials. *Ageing Research Reviews, 25*, 13–23. doi:10.1016/j.arr.2015.11.005

Grossman, H., Bergmann, C., & Parker, S. (2006). Dementia: A brief review. *Mount Sinai Journal of Medicine, 73*, 985–992.

Gupta, R., Chari, D., & Ali, R. (2015). Reversible dementia in elderly: Really uncommon? *Journal of Geriatric Mental Health, 2*, 30. doi:10.4103/2348-9995.161378

Gurland, B. J., Wilder, D. E., Lantigua, R., Stern, Y., Chen, J., Killeffer, E. H., & Mayeux, R. (1999). Rates of dementia in three ethnoracial groups. *International Journal of Geriatric Psychiatry, 14*, 481–493.

Gutchess, A. H., & Boduroglu, A. (2015). Cognition in adulthood across cultures. In L. A. Jensen (Ed.), *The Oxford handbook of human development and culture* (pp. 621–636). New York, NY: Oxford University Press. doi:10.1093/oxfordhb/9780199948550.013.38

Guzmán-Vélez, E., Warren, D. E., Feinstein, J. S., Bruss, J., & Tranel, D. (2016). Dissociable contributions of amygdala and hippocampus to emotion and memory in patients with Alzheimer's disease. *Hippocampus, 26*, 727–738. doi:10.1002/hipo.22554

Hamilton, J. M., Landy, K. M., Salmon, D. P., Hansen, L. A., Masliah, E., & Galasko, D. (2012). Early visuospatial deficits predict the occurrence of visual hallucinations in autopsy-confirmed dementia with Lewy bodies. *American Journal of Geriatric Psychiatry, 20*, 773–781. doi:10.1097/JGP.0b013e31823033bc

Hase, Y., Horsburgh, K., Ihara, M., & Kalaria, R. N. (2018). White matter degeneration in vascular and other ageing-related dementias. *Journal of Neurochemistry, 144*, 617–633. doi:10.1111/jnc.14271

Hawkes, C. (2006). Olfaction in neurodegenerative disorder. In T. Hummel & A. Welge-Lüssen (Eds.), *Taste and smell* (Vol. 63, pp. 133–151). Basel, Switzerland: Karger. doi:10.1159/000093759

Hedden, T., & Gabrieli, J. D. E. (2004). Insights into the ageing mind: A view from cognitive neuroscience. *Nature Reviews: Neuroscience, 5*, 87–96. doi:10.1038/nrn1323

Helzner, E. P., Cauley, J. A., Pratt, S. R., Wisniewski, S. R., Zmuda, J. M., Talbott, E. O., . . . Newman, A. B. (2005). Race and sex differences in age-related hearing loss: The health, aging and body composition study. *Journal of the American Geriatrics Society, 53*, 2119–2127.

Herbert, J., & Lucassen, P. J. (2016). Depression as a risk factor for Alzheimer's disease: Genes, steroids, cytokines and neurogenesis—What do we need to know? *Frontiers in Neuroendocrinology, 41*, 153–171. doi:10.1016/j.yfrne.2015.12.001

Hindin, S. B., & Zelinski, E. M. (2012). Extended practice and aerobic exercise interventions benefit untrained cognitive outcomes in older adults: A meta-analysis. *Journal of the American Geriatrics Society, 60*, 136–141. doi:10.1111/j.1532-5415.2011.03761.x

Hirsch, L., Jette, N., Frolkis, A., Steeves, T., & Pringsheim, T. (2016). The incidence of Parkinson's disease: A systematic review and meta-analysis. *Neuroepidemiology, 46*, 292–300. doi:10.1159/000445751

Hoenig, M. C., Bischof, G. N., Hammes, J., Faber, J., Fliessbach, K., van Eimeren, T., & Drzezga, A. (2017). Tau pathology and cognitive reserve in Alzheimer's disease. *Neurobiology of Aging, 57*, 1–7. doi:10.1016/j.neurobiolaging.2017.05.004

Holtzer, R., Epstein, N., Mahoney, J. R., Izzetoglu, M., & Blumen, H. M. (2014). Neuroimaging of mobility in aging: A targeted review. *Journals of Gerontology Series A: Biological Sciences and Medical Sciences, 69*, 1375–1388. doi:10.1093/gerona/glu052

Hoppmann, C. A., & Blanchard-Fields, F. (2010). Goals and everyday problem solving: Manipulating goal preferences in young and older adults. *Developmental Psychology, 46*, 1433–1443. doi:10.1037/a0020676

Hort, J., Bartos, A., Pirttilä, T., & Scheltens, P. (2010). Use of cerebrospinal fluid biomarkers in diagnosis of dementia across Europe. *European Journal of Neurology, 17*, 90–96. doi:10.1111/j.1468-1331.2009.02753.x

Hort, J., O'Brien, J. T., Gainotti, G., Pirttila, T., Popescu, B. O., Rektorova, I., . . . Scheltens, P. (2010). EFNS guidelines for the diagnosis and management of Alzheimer's disease. *European Journal of Neurology, 17*, 1236–1248. doi:10.1111/j.1468-1331.2010.03040.x

Horton, W. S., Spieler, D. H., & Shriberg, E. (2010). A corpus analysis of patterns of age-related change in conversational speech. *Psychology and Aging, 25*, 708–713. doi:10.1037/a0019424

Hosseini, H., & Hosseini, N. (2008). Epidemiology and prevention of fall injuries among the elderly. *Hospital Topics, 86*, 15–20.

Hötting, K., & Röder, B. (2013). Beneficial effects of physical exercise on neuroplasticity and cognition. *Neuroscience & Biobehavioral Reviews, 37*, 2243–2257. doi:10.1016/j.neubiorev.2013.04.005

Hsu, C. L., Best, J. R., Davis, J. C., Nagamatsu, L. S., Wang, S., Boyd, L. A., . . . Liu-Ambrose, T. (2018). Aerobic exercise promotes executive functions and impacts functional neural activity among older adults with vascular cognitive impairment. *British Journal of Sports Medicine, 52*, 184–191. doi:10.1136/bjsports-2016-096846

Huntley, J. D., Hampshire, A., Bor, D., Owen, A. M., & Howard, R. J. (2017). The importance of sustained attention in early Alzheimer's disease. *International Journal of Geriatric Psychiatry, 32*, 860–867. doi:10.1002/gps.4537

Hwang, J. H., Li, C. W., Wu, C. W., Chen, J. H., & Liu, T. C. (2007). Aging effects on the activation of the auditory cortex during binaural speech listening in white noise: An fMRI study. *Audiology & Neuro-Otology, 12*, 285–294.

Iadecola, C. (2013). The pathobiology of vascular dementia. *Neuron, 80*, 844–866. doi:10.1016/j.neuron.2013.10.008

Imoscopi, A., Inelmen, E. M., Sergi, G., Miotto, F., & Manzato, E. (2012). Taste loss in the elderly: Epidemiology, causes and consequences. *Aging Clinical and Experimental Research, 24*, 570–579. doi:10.3275/8520

Inagaki, H., Gondo, Y., Hirose, N., Masui, Y., Kitagawa, K., Arai, Y., . . . Homma, A. (2009). Cognitive function in Japanese centenarians according to the mini-mental state examination. *Dementia & Geriatric Cognitive Disorders, 28*, 6–12. doi:10.1159/000228713

Insurance Institute for Highway Safety. (2015). *Older drivers.* Retrieved from http://www.iihs.org/iihs/topics/t/older-drivers/qanda

Ishioka, Y. L., Gondo, Y., Fuku, N., Inagaki, H., Masui, Y., Takayama, M., . . . Hirose, N. (2016). Effects of the APOE ε4 allele and education on cognitive function in Japanese centenarians. *AGE, 38*, 495–503. doi:10.1007/s11357-016-9944-8

Jackson, J. D., Rentz, D. M., Aghjayan, S. L., Buckley, R. F., Meneide, T. F., Sperling, R. A., & Amariglio, R. E. (2017). Subjective cognitive concerns are associated with objective memory performance in Caucasian but not African-American persons. *Age and Ageing, 46*, 988–993. doi:10.1093/ageing/afx077

Jacoby, L. L., Wahlheim, C. N., Rhodes, M. G., Daniels, K. A., & Rogers, C. S. (2010). Learning to diminish the effects of proactive interference: Reducing false memory for young and older adults. *Memory & Cognition, 38*, 820–829. doi:10.3758/mc.38.6.820

Jager, R. D., Mieler, W. F., & Miller, J. W. (2008). Age-related macular degeneration. *New England Journal of Medicine, 358*, 2606–2617. Retrieved from 10.1056/NEJMra0801537

Jerome, G. J., Ko, S., Kauffman, D., Studenski, S. A., Ferrucci, L., & Simonsick, E. M. (2015). Gait characteristics associated with walking speed decline in older adults: Results from the Baltimore Longitudinal study of Aging. *Archives of Gerontology and Geriatrics, 60*, 239–243. doi:10.1016/j.archger.2015.01.007

Johansson, J., Nordstrom, A., Gustafson, Y., Westling, G., & Nordstrom, P. (2017). Increased postural sway during quiet stance as a risk factor for prospective falls in community-dwelling elderly individuals. *Age and Ageing, 10*(Suppl 4), 1–6. doi:10.1093/ageing/afx083

Jopp, D. S., Boerner, K., & Rott, C. (2016). Health and disease at age 100. *Deutsches Arzteblatt International, 113*, 203–210. doi:10.3238/arztebl.2016.0203

Josephs, K. A., Dickson, D. W., Tosakulwong, N., Weigand, S. D., Murray, M. E., Petrucelli, L., . . . Whitwell, J. L. (2017). Rates of hippocampal atrophy and presence of post-mortem TDP-43 in patients with Alzheimer's disease: A longitudinal retrospective study. *The Lancet Neurology, 16*, 917–924. doi:10.1016/S1474-4422(17)30284-3

Kaiser, M. J., Bauer, J. M., Rämsch, C., Uter, W., Guigoz, Y., Cederholm, T., . . . Sieber, C. C. (2010). Frequency of malnutrition in older adults: A multinational perspective using the mini nutritional assessment. *Journal of the American Geriatrics Society, 58*, 1734–1738. doi:10.1111/j.1532-5415.2010.03016.x

Kalaria, R. N. (2016). Neuropathological diagnosis of vascular cognitive impairment and vascular dementia with implications for Alzheimer's disease. *Acta Neuropathologica, 131*, 659–685. doi:10.1007/s00401-016-1571-z

Kang, J. H., Korecka, M., Figurski, M. J., Toledo, J. B., Blennow, K., Zetterberg, H., . . . Shaw, L. M. (2015). The Alzheimer's disease neuroimaging initiative 2 biomarker core: A review of progress and plans. *Alzheimer's & Dementia, 11*, 772–791. doi:10.1016/j.jalz.2015.05.003

Kaniewski, M., Stevens, J. A., Parker, E. M., & Lee, R. (2015). An introduction to the Centers for Disease Control and Prevention's efforts to prevent older adult falls. *Frontiers in Public Health, 2*, e119. doi:10.3389/fpubh.2014.00119

Karbach, J., & Verhaeghen, P. (2014). Making working memory work: A meta-analysis of executive-control and working memory training in older adults. *Psychological Science, 25*, 2027–2037. doi:10.1177/0956797614548725

Karelitz, T. M., Jarvin, L., Sternberg, R. J., Karelitz, T. M., Jarvin, L., & Sternberg, R. J. (2010). The meaning of wisdom and its development throughout life. In W. F. Overton (Ed.), *The handbook of life-span development* (pp. 837–881). Hoboken, NJ: John Wiley. doi:10.1002/9780470880166.hlsd001023

Kavé, G., Eyal, N., Shorek, A., & Cohen-Mansfield, J. (2008). Multilingualism and cognitive state in the oldest old. *Psychology and Aging, 23*, 70–78.

Keightley, J., & Mitchell, A. (2004). What factors influence mental health professionals when deciding whether or not to share a diagnosis of dementia with the person? *Aging & Mental Health, 8*, 13–20.

Kessels, R. P. C., Meulenbroek, O., Fernandez, G., & Olde Rikkert, M. G. M. (2010). Spatial working memory in aging and mild cognitive impairment: Effects of task load and contextual cueing. *Aging, Neuropsychology & Cognition, 17*, 556–574. doi:10.1080/138255 85.2010.481354

Khanuja, K., Joki, J., Bachmann, G., & Cuccurullo, S. (2018). Gait and balance in the aging population: Fall prevention using innovation and technology. *Maturitas, 110*, 51–56. doi:10.1016/j.maturitas.2018.01.021

Kirbach, S. E., & Mintzer, J. (2008). Alzheimer's disease burdens African-Americans: A review of epidemiological risk factors and implications for prevention and treatment. *Current Psychiatry Reviews, 4*, 58–62.

Kline, D. W., & Li, W. (2005). Cataracts and the aging driver. *Ageing International, 30*, 105–121.

Knopman, D. S., & Roberts, R. (2010). Vascular risk factors: Imaging and neuropathologic correlates. *Journal of Alzheimer's Disease, 20*, 699–709. doi:10.3233/jad-2010-091555

Kok, A. A. L., Aartsen, M. J., Deeg, D. J. H., & Huisman, M. (2015). Capturing the diversity of successful aging: An operational definition based on 16-year trajectories of functioning. *The Gerontologist, 57*, gnv127. doi:10.1093/geront/gnv127

Korczyn, A. D., Vakhapova, V., & Grinberg, L. T. (2012). Vascular dementia. *Journal of the Neurological Sciences, 322*, 2–10. doi:10.1016/j.jns.2012.03.027

Kramer, A. F., & Colcombe, S. (2018). Fitness effects on the cognitive function of older adults: A meta-analytic study—Revisited. *Perspectives on Psychological Science, 13*, 213–217. doi:10.1177/1745691617707316

Kuys, S. S., Peel, N. M., Klein, K., Slater, A., & Hubbard, R. E. (2014). Gait speed in ambulant older people in long term care: A systematic review and meta-analysis. *Journal of the American Medical Directors Association, 15*, 194–200. doi:10.1016/j.jamda.2013.10.015

Lamotte, G., Skender, E., Rafferty, M. R., David, F. J., Sadowsky, S., & Corcos, D. M. (2015). Effects of progressive resistance exercise training on the motor and nonmotor features of Parkinson's disease: A review. *Kinesiology Review, 4*, 11–27. doi:10.1123/kr.2014-0074

Laplante-Lévesque, A., Hickson, L., & Worrall, L. (2010). Rehabilitation of older adults with hearing impairment: A critical review. *Journal of Aging & Health, 22*, 143–153. doi:10.1177/0898264309352731

Larsson, M., Oberg-Blåvarg, C., & Jönsson, F. U. (2009). Bad odors stick better than good ones: Olfactory qualities and odor recognition. *Experimental Psychology, 56*, 375–380. doi:10.1027/1618-3169.56.6.375

Lavallée, M. M., Gandini, D., Rouleau, I., Vallet, G. T., Joannette, M., Kergoat, M.-J., . . . Joubert, S. (2016). A qualitative impairment in face perception in Alzheimer's disease: Evidence from a reduced face inversion effect. *Journal of Alzheimer's Disease, 51*, 1225–1236. doi:10.3233/JAD-151027

Lee, H. J., & Chou, L. S. (2007). Balance control during stair negotiation in older adults. *Journal of Biomechanics, 40*, 2530–2536.

Lee, Y. A., & Goto, Y. (2015). Chronic stress effects on working memory: Association with prefrontal cortical tyrosine hydroxylase. *Behavioural Brain Research, 286*, 122–127. doi:10.1016/j.bbr.2015.03.007

Lemere, C. (2013). Alzheimer's disease and Down syndrome. *Alzheimer's & Dementia, 9*, P513. doi:10.1016/j.jalz.2013.04.223

Lesinski, M., Hortobágyi, T., Muehlbauer, T., Gollhofer, A., & Granacher, U. (2015). Effects of balance training on balance performance in healthy older adults: A systematic review and meta-analysis. *Sports Medicine, 45*, 1721–1738. doi:10.1007/s40279-015-0375-y

Leversen, J. S. R., Haga, M., Sigmundsson, H., Rebollo, I., & Colom, R. (2012). From children to adults: Motor performance across the life-span. *PLoS ONE, 7*, e38830. doi:10.1371/journal.pone.0038830

Li, J. Q., Tan, L., Wang, H. F., Tan, M. S., Tan, L., Xu, W., . . . Yu, J. T. (2016). Risk factors for predicting progression from mild cognitive impairment to Alzheimer's disease: A systematic review and meta-analysis of cohort studies. *Journal of Neurology, Neurosurgery & Psychiatry, 87*, 476–484. doi:10.1136/jnnp-2014-310095

Li, L., Abutalebi, J., Emmorey, K., Gong, G., Yan, X., Feng, X., . . . Ding, G. (2017). How bilingualism protects the brain from aging: Insights from bimodal bilinguals. *Human Brain Mapping, 38*, 4109–4124. doi:10.1002/hbm.23652

Li, W. F., Hou, S. X., Yu, B., Li, M. M., Férec, C., Chen, J. M., . . . Jian-Min, C. (2010). Genetics of osteoporosis: Accelerating pace in gene identification and validation. *Human Genetics, 127*, 249–285. doi:10.1007/s00439-009-0773-z

Lin, E. H. B. (2008). Depression and osteoarthritis. *American Journal of Medicine, 121*, S16–S19. Retrieved from 10.1016/j.amjmed.2008.09.009

Lin, F. R., Thorpe, R., Gordon-Salant, S., & Ferrucci, L. (2011). Hearing loss prevalence and risk factors among older adults in the United States. *The Journals of Gerontology Series A: Biological Sciences and Medical Sciences, 66A*, 582–590. doi:10.1093/gerona/glr002

Lindstrom, T. M., & Robinson, W. H. (2010). Rheumatoid arthritis: A role for immunosenescence? *Journal of the American Geriatrics Society, 58*, 1565–1575. doi:10.1111/j.1532-5415.2010.02965.x

Liu, H., Paige, N. M., Goldzweig, C. L., Wong, E., Zhou, A., Suttorp, M. J., . . . Shekelle, P. (2008). Screening for osteoporosis in men: A systematic review for an American College of Physicians guideline. *Annals of Internal Medicine, 148*, 685–W138.

Liu, Y., Julkunen, V., Paajanen, T., Westman, E., Wahlund, L. O., Aitken, A., . . . Soininen, H. (2012). Education increases reserve against Alzheimer's disease: Evidence from structural MRI analysis. *Neuroradiology, 54,* 929–938. doi:10.1007/s00234-012-1005-0

Löckenhoff, C. E., & Carstensen, L. L. (2007). Aging, emotion, and health-related decision strategies: Motivational manipulations can reduce age differences. *Psychology and Aging, 22,* 134–146.

Lönnqvist, J. (2010). Cognition and mental ill-health. *European Psychiatry, 25,* 297–299. doi:10.1016/j.eurpsy.2010.01.006

Loprinzi, P. D., Edwards, M. K., Crush, E., Ikuta, T., & Del Arco, A. (2018). Dose–response association between physical activity and cognitive function in a national sample of older adults. *American Journal of Health Promotion, 32,* 554–560. doi:10.1177/0890117116689732

Lorente-Cebrián, S., Costa, A. G. V., Navas-Carretero, S., Zabala, M., Laiglesia, L. M., Martinez, J. A., & Moreno-Aliaga, M. J. (2015). An update on the role of omega-3 fatty acids on inflammatory and degenerative diseases. *Journal of Physiology and Biochemistry, 71,* 341–349. doi:10.1007/s13105-015-0395-y

Lorente-Cebrián, S., Costa, A. G. V., Navas-Carretero, S., Zabala, M., Martinez, J. A., & Moreno-Aliaga, M. J. (2013). Role of omega-3 fatty acids in obesity, metabolic syndrome, and cardiovascular diseases: A review of the evidence. *Journal of Physiology and Biochemistry, 69,* 633–651. doi:10.1007/s13105-013-0265-4

Lu, P. H., Lee, G. J., Tishler, T. A., Meghpara, M., Thompson, P. M., & Bartzokis, G. (2013). Myelin breakdown mediates age-related slowing in cognitive processing speed in healthy elderly men. *Brain and Cognition, 81,* 131–138. doi:10.1016/j.bandc.2012.09.006

Maass, A., Düzel, S., Goerke, M., Becke, A., Sobieray, U., Neumann, K., . . . Düzel, E. (2015). Vascular hippocampal plasticity after aerobic exercise in older adults. *Molecular Psychiatry, 20,* 585–593. doi:10.1038/mp.2014.114

Mammarella, N., Borella, E., Carretti, B., Leonardi, G., & Fairfield, B. (2013). Examining an emotion enhancement effect in working memory: Evidence from age-related differences. *Neuropsychological Rehabilitation, 23,* 416–428. doi:10.1080/09602011.2013.775065

Mani, T. M., Bedwell, J. S., & Miller, L. S. (2005). Age-related decrements in performance on a brief continuous performance test. *Archives of Clinical Neuropsychology, 20,* 575–586.

Manly, J. J. (2006). Deconstructing race and ethnicity. *Medical Care, 44*(Suppl 3), S10–S16. doi:10.1097/01.mlr.0000245427.22788.be

Mares, J. A., Millen, A. E., Lawler, T. P., & Blomme, C. K. (2017). Diet and supplements in the prevention and treatment of eye diseases. In A. M. Coulston, C. J. Boushey, & M. Ferruzzi (Eds.), *Nutrition in the prevention and treatment of disease* (pp. 393–434). New York, NY: Elsevier. doi:10.1016/B978-0-12-802928-2.00019-9

Margaretten, M. E., Katz, P., Schmajuk, G., & Yelin, E. (2013). Missed opportunities for depression screening in patients with arthritis in the United States. *Journal of General Internal Medicine, 28,* 1637–1642. doi:10.1007/s11606-013-2541-y

Margran, T. H., & Boulton, M. (2005). Sensory impairment. In M. L. Johnson (Ed.), *The Cambridge handbook of age and aging* (pp. 121–130). New York, NY: Cambridge University Press.

Margrett, J., Martin, P., Woodard, J. L., Miller, L. S., MacDonald, M., Baenziger, J., . . . Poon, L. (2010). Depression among centenarians and the oldest old: Contributions of cognition and personality. *Gerontology, 56,* 93–99. doi:10.1159/000272018

Martin, P., Baenziger, J., MacDonald, M., Siegler, I. C., & Poon, L. W. (2009). Engaged lifestyle, personality, and mental status among centenarians. *Journal of Adult Development, 16,* 199–208. doi:10.1007/s10804-009-9066-y

Mastwyk, M., Ames, D., Ellis, K. A., Chiu, E., & Dow, B. (2014). Disclosing a dementia diagnosis: What do patients and family consider important? *International Psychogeriatrics/IPA, 26,* 1263–1272. doi:10.1017/S1041610214000751

Mather, M., & Carstensen, L. L. (2005). Aging and motivated cognition: The positivity effect in attention and memory. *Trends in Cognitive Sciences, 9,* 496–502. doi:10.1016/j.tics.2005.08.005

Mayeda, E. R., Glymour, M. M., Quesenberry, C. P., & Whitmer, R. A. (2016). Inequalities in dementia incidence between six racial and ethnic groups over 14 years. *Alzheimer's & Dementia, 12,* 216–224. doi:10.1016/j.jalz.2015.12.007

McCabe, D. P., Roediger III, H. L., McDaniel, M. A., Balota, D. A., & Hambrick, D. Z. (2010). The relationship between working memory capacity and executive functioning: Evidence for a common executive attention construct. *Neuropsychology, 24,* 222–243. doi:10.1037/a0017619

McIlvane, J. M. (2007). Disentangling the effects of race and SES on arthritis-related symptoms, coping, and well-being in African American and white women. *Aging & Mental Health, 11,* 556–569. Retrieved from 10.1080/13607860601086520

McIlvane, J. M., Baker, T. A., & Mingo, C. A. (2008). Racial differences in arthritis-related stress, chronic life stress, and depressive symptoms among women with arthritis: A contextual perspective. *Journals of Gerontology Series B: Psychological Sciences & Social Sciences, 63B,* S320–S327.

Meeus, B., Verstraeten, A., Crosiers, D., Engelborghs, S., Van den Broeck, M., Mattheijssens, M., . . . Theuns, J. (2012). DLB and PDD: A role for mutations in dementia and Parkinson disease genes? *Neurobiology of Aging, 33,* 629.e5–629.e18. doi:10.1016/j.neurobiolaging.2011.10.014

Mehta, K. M., & Yeo, G. W. (2017). Systematic review of dementia prevalence and incidence in United States race/ethnic populations. *Alzheimer's & Dementia, 13,* 72–83. doi:10.1016/j.jalz.2016.06.2360

Melby-Lervåg, M., Redick, T. S., & Hulme, C. (2016). Working memory training does not improve performance on measures of intelligence or other measures of "Far Transfer": Evidence from a meta-analytic review. *Perspectives on Psychological Science, 11,* 512–534. doi:10.1177/1745691616635612

Mikels, J. A., Larkin, G. R., Reuter-Lorenz, P. A., & Carstensen, L. L. (2005). Divergent trajectories in the aging mind: Changes in working memory for affective versus visual information with age. *Psychology and Aging, 20,* 542–553. doi:10.1037/0882-7974.20.4.542

Miller, B. D., Wood, B. L., & Smith, B. A. (2010). Respiratory illness. In R. J. Shaw & D. R. DeMaso (Eds.), *Textbook of pediatric psychosomatic medicine* (pp. 303–317). Arlington, VA: American Psychiatric Publishing.

Miller, D. B., & O'Callaghan, J. P. (2015). Biomarkers of Parkinson's disease: Present and future. *Metabolism, 64,* S40–S46. doi:10.1016/j.metabol.2014.10.030

Miller, L. S., Mitchell, M. B., Woodard, J. L., Davey, A., Martin, P., & Poon, L. W. (2010). Cognitive performance in centenarians and the oldest old: Norms from the Georgia Centenarian study. *Aging, Neuropsychology & Cognition, 17,* 575–590. doi:10.1080/13825585.2010.481355

Mirelman, A., Herman, T., Brozgol, M., Dorfman, M., Sprecher, E., Schweiger, A., . . . Giladi, N. (2012). Executive function and falls in older adults: New findings from a five-year prospective study link fall risk to cognition. *PLoS ONE, 7,* e40297. doi:10.1371/journal.pone.0040297

Mironov, S. (2009). Respiratory circuits: Function, mechanisms, topology, and pathology. *Neuroscientist, 15,* 194–208.

Mitchell, G., McCollum, P., & Monaghan, C. (2013). The personal impact of disclosure of a dementia diagnosis: A thematic review of the literature. *British Journal of Neuroscience Nursing, 9,* 223–228. doi:10.12968/bjnn.2013.9.5.223

Mojon-Azzi, S. M., Sousa-Poza, A., & Mojon, D. S. (2008). Impact of low vision on well-being in 10 European countries. *Ophthalmologica, 222,* 205–212. https://doi.org/10.1159/000126085

Mok, R. M., Myers, N. E., Wallis, G., & Nobre, A. C. (2016). Behavioral and neural markers of flexible attention over working memory in aging. *Cerebral Cortex, 26,* 1831–1842. doi:10.1093/cercor/bhw011

Molina, E., del Rincon, I., Restrepo, J. F., Battafarano, D. F., & Escalante, A. (2015). Association of socioeconomic status with treatment delays, disease activity, joint damage, and disability in rheumatoid arthritis. *Arthritis Care & Research, 67,* 940–946. doi:10.1002/acr.22542

Morgan, C. D., Covington, J. W., Geisler, M. W., Polich, J., & Murphy, C. (1997). Olfactory event-related potentials: Older males demonstrate the greatest deficits. *Electroencephalography and Clinical Neurophysiology/Evoked Potentials Section, 104,* 351–358. doi:10.1016/S0168-5597(97)00020-8

Mortensen, L., Meyer, A. S., & Humphreys, G. W. (2006). Age-related effects on speech production: A review. *Language & Cognitive Processes, 21,* 238–290. doi:10.1080/01690960444000278

Muangpaisan, W., Petcharat, C., & Srinonprasert, V. (2012). Prevalence of potentially reversible conditions in dementia and mild cognitive impairment in a geriatric clinic. *Geriatrics & Gerontology International, 12,* 59–64. doi:10.1111/j.1447-0594.2011.00728.x

Muscari, A., Giannoni, C., Pierpaoli, L., Berzigotti, A., Maietta, P., Foschi, E., . . . Zoli, M. (2010). Chronic endurance exercise training prevents aging-related cognitive decline in healthy older adults: A randomized controlled trial. *International Journal of Geriatric Psychiatry, 25,* 1055–1064.

Myers, C. E., Klein, B. E. K., Gangnon, R., Sivakumaran, T. A., Iyengar, S. K., & Klein, R. (2014). Cigarette smoking and the natural history of age-related macular degeneration: The Beaver Dam Eye study. *Ophthalmology, 121,* 1949–1955. doi:10.1016/j.ophtha.2014.04.040

Nachtigall, M. J., Nazem, T. G., Nachtigall, R. H., & Goldstein, S. R. (2013). Osteoporosis risk factors and early life-style modifications to decrease disease burden in women. *Clinical Obstetrics and Gynecology, 56,* 650–653. doi:10.1097/GRF.0b013e3182aa1daf

Nair, A. K., Sabbagh, M. N., Tucker, A. M., & Stern, Y. (2014). Cognitive reserve and the aging brain. In A. K. Nair & M. N. Sabbagh (Eds.), *Geriatric neurology* (pp. 118–125). Chichester, England: John Wiley. doi:10.1002/9781118730676

Naj, A. C., & Schellenberg, G. D. (2017). Genomic variants, genes, and pathways of Alzheimer's disease: An overview. *American Journal of Medical Genetics Part B: Neuropsychiatric Genetics, 174,* 5–26. doi:10.1002/ajmg.b.32499

Nalls, M. A., Pankratz, N., Lill, C. M., Do, C. B., Hernandez, D. G., Saad, M., . . . Singleton, A. B. (2014). Large-scale meta-analysis of genome-wide association data identifies six new risk loci for Parkinson's disease. *Nature Genetics, 46,* 989–993. doi:10.1038/ng.3043

National Center for Health Statistics. (2018). *Selected diseases and conditions among adults aged 18 and over, by selected characteristics: United States, 2016.* Retrieved April 8, 2018, from https://www.cdc.gov/nchs/nhis/shs/tables.htm

National Parkinson Foundation. (2008). *About Parkinson's disease.* Retrieved from http://www.parkinson.org/NETCOMMUNITY/Page.aspx?pid=225&srcid=201

Nelson, T. J., & Alkon, D. L. (2015). Molecular regulation of synaptogenesis during associative learning and memory. *Brain Research, 1621,* 239–251. doi:10.1016/j.brainres.2014.11.054

Niemann, C., Godde, B., & Voelcker-Rehage, C. (2014). Not only cardiovascular, but also coordinative exercise increases hippocampal volume in older adults. *Frontiers in Aging Neuroscience, 6,* 170. doi:10.3389/fnagi.2014.00170

NIH Osteoporosis and Related Bone Diseases National Resource Center. (2007). *Osteoporosis.* Retrieved from http://www.niams.nih.gov/Health_Info/Bone/Osteoporosis/default.asp

Obernier, K., Tong, C. K., & Alvarez-Buylla, A. (2014). Restricted nature of adult neural stem cells: Re-evaluation of their potential for brain repair. *Frontiers in Neuroscience, 8,* 162. doi:10.3389/fnins.2014.00162

O'Brien, J. T., & Thomas, A. (2015). Vascular dementia. *The Lancet, 386,* 1698–1706. doi:10.1016/S0140-6736(15)00463-8

Ogawa, T., Annear, M. J., Ikebe, K., & Maeda, Y. (2017). Taste-related sensations in old age. *Journal of Oral Rehabilitation, 44,* 626–635. doi:10.1111/joor.12502

Oh, E. S., Fong, T. G., Hshieh, T. T., & Inouye, S. K. (2017). Delirium in older persons. *JAMA, 318,* 1161. doi:10.1001/jama.2017.12067

Okonkwo, O. C., Cohen, R. A., Gunstad, J., Tremont, G., Alosco, M. L., & Poppas, A. (2010). Longitudinal trajectories of cognitive decline among older adults with cardiovascular disease. *Cerebrovascular Diseases, 30,* 362–373. doi:10.1159/000319564

Olsen, R. K., Pangelinan, M. M., Bogulski, C., Chakravarty, M. M., Luk, G., Grady, C. L., & Bialystok, E. (2015). The effect of lifelong bilingualism on regional grey and white matter volume. *Brain Research, 1612,* 128–139. doi:10.1016/j.brainres.2015.02.034

Olsson, B., Lautner, R., Andreasson, U., Öhrfelt, A., Portelius, E., Bjerke, M., . . . Zetterberg, H. (2016). CSF and blood biomarkers for the diagnosis of Alzheimer's disease: A systematic review and meta-analysis. *The Lancet Neurology, 15,* 673–684. doi:10.1016/S1474-4422(16)00070-3

Orgeta, V., Tabet, N., Nilforooshan, R., & Howard, R. (2017). Efficacy of antidepressants for depression in Alzheimer's disease: Systematic review and meta-analysis. *Journal of Alzheimer's Disease, 58,* 725–733. doi:10.3233/JAD-161247

Osorio, A., Fay, S., Pouthas, V., & Ballesteros, S. (2010). Ageing affects brain activity in highly educated older adults: An ERP study using a word-stem priming task. *Cortex: A Journal Devoted to the Study of the Nervous System and Behavior, 46,* 522–534. doi:10.1016/j.cortex.2009.09.003

Ossher, L., Flegal, K. E., & Lustig, C. (2013). Everyday memory errors in older adults. *Neuropsychology, Development, and Cognition: Section B. Aging, Neuropsychology and Cognition, 20,* 220–242. doi:10.1080/13825585.2012.690365

Owens, R. E. (2015). *Language development: An introduction.* Boston, MA: Pearson.

Owsley, C. (2016). Vision and aging. *Annual Review of Vision Science, 2,* 255–271. doi:10.1146/annurev-vision-111815-114550

Owsley, C., McGwin, G., Jackson, G. R., Kallies, K., & Clark, M. (2007). Cone- and rod-mediated dark adaptation impairment in age-related maculopathy. *Ophthalmology, 114,* 1728–1735.

Paillard, T., Rolland, Y., de Souto Barreto, P., Kalil-Gaspar, P., Marcuzzo, S., & Achaval, M. (2015). Protective effects of physical exercise in Alzheimer's disease and Parkinson's disease: A narrative review. *Journal of Clinical Neurology, 11,* 212. doi:10.3988/jcn.2015.11.3.212

Paneni, F., Diaz Cañestro, C., Libby, P., Lüscher, T. F., & Camici, G. G. (2017). The aging cardiovascular system: Understanding it at the cellular and clinical levels. *Journal of the American College of Cardiology, 69,* 1952–1967. doi:10.1016/J.JACC.2017.01.064

Panula, J., Pihlajamäki, H., Mattila, V. M., Jaatinen, P., Vahlberg, T., Aarnio, P., & Kivelä, S. L. (2011). Mortality and cause of death in hip fracture patients aged 65 or older-a population-based study. *BMC Musculoskeletal Disorders, 12,* 105.

Panza, F., Solfrizzi, V., & Capurso, A. (2004). *Diet and cognitive decline.* Hauppauge, NY: Nova Science.

Parnetti, L., Cicognola, C., Eusebi, P., & Chiasserini, D. (2016). Value of cerebrospinal fluid α-synuclein species as biomarker in Parkinson's diagnosis and prognosis. *Biomarkers in Medicine, 10,* 35–49. doi:10.2217/bmm.15.107

Paúl, C., Ribeiro, O., & Santos, P. (2010). Cognitive impairment in old people living in the community. *Archives of Gerontology & Geriatrics, 51,* 121–124. doi:10.1016/j.archger.2009.09.037

Paul, L. (2011). Diet, nutrition and telomere length. *The Journal of Nutritional Biochemistry, 22,* 895–901. doi:10.1016/j.jnutbio.2010.12.001

Payne, V. G., & Isaacs, L. D. (Larry D. (2016). *Human motor development: A lifespan approach.* New York, NY: McGraw-Hill. Retrieved from http://dl.acm.org/citation.cfm?id=1214267

Peters, A., & Kemper, T. (2012). A review of the structural alterations in the cerebral hemispheres of the aging rhesus monkey. *Neurobiology of Aging, 33,* 2357–2372. doi:10.1016/j.neurobiolaging.2011.11.015

Peterson, M. D., Rhea, M. R., Sen, A., & Gordon, P. M. (2010). Resistance exercise for muscular strength in older adults: A meta-analysis. *Ageing Research Reviews, 9,* 226–237. doi:10.1016/j.arr.2010.03.004

Piolino, P., Coste, C., Martinelli, P., Macé, A.-L., Quinette, P., Guillery-Girard, B., & Belleville, S. (2010). Reduced specificity of autobiographical memory and aging: Do the executive and feature binding functions of working memory have a role? *Neuropsychologia, 48,* 429–440. doi:10.1016/j.neuropsychologia.2009.09.035

Piolino, P., Desgranges, B., Clarys, D., Guillery-Girard, B., Taconnat, L., Isingrini, M., & Eustache, F. (2006). Autobiographical memory, autonoetic consciousness, and self-perspective in aging. *Psychology and Aging, 21,* 510–525.

Pliatsikas, C., Moschopoulou, E., & Saddy, J. D. (2015). The effects of bilingualism on the white matter structure of the brain. *Proceedings of the National Academy of Sciences of the United States of America, 112,* 1334–1337. doi:10.1073/pnas.1414183112

Postuma, R. B., Berg, D., Stern, M., Poewe, W., Olanow, C. W., Oertel, W., . . . Deuschl, G. (2015). MDS clinical diagnostic criteria for Parkinson's disease. *Movement Disorders, 30,* 1591–1601. doi:10.1002/mds.26424

Prakash, R. S., Voss, M. W., Erickson, K. I., & Kramer, A. F. (2015). Physical activity and cognitive vitality. *Annual Review of Psychology, 66,* 769–797. doi:10.1146/annurev-psych-010814-015249

Prince, M., Comas-Herrera, A., Knapp, M., Guerchet, M., & Karagiannidou, M. (2016). *World Alzheimer report 2016: Improving healthcare for people living with dementia: Coverage, quality and costs now and in the future.* Retrieved from http://eprints.lse.ac.uk/67858/

Pringsheim, T., Jette, N., Frolkis, A., & Steeves, T. D. L. (2014). The prevalence of Parkinson's disease: A systematic review and meta-analysis. *Movement Disorders, 29*, 1583–1590. doi:10.1002/mds.25945

Quan, T., & Fisher, G. J. (2015). Role of age-associated alterations of the dermal extracellular matrix microenvironment in human skin aging: A mini-review. *Gerontology, 61*, 427–434. doi:10.1159/000371708

Quaranta, N., Coppola, F., Casulli, M., Barulli, M. R., Panza, F., Tortelli, R., . . . Logroscino, G. (2015). Epidemiology of age related hearing loss: A review. *Hearing, Balance and Communication, 13*, 77–81. doi:10.3109/21695717.2014.994869

Radvansky, G. A., Zacks, R. T., & Hasher, L. (2005). Age and inhibition: The retrieval of situation models. *Journals of Gerontology Series B: Psychological Sciences & Social Sciences, 60B*, P276–P278.

Raj, T., Chibnik, L. B., McCabe, C., Wong, A., Replogle, J. M., Yu, L., . . . De Jager, P. L. (2017). Genetic architecture of age-related cognitive decline in African Americans. *Neurology Genetics, 3*, e125. doi:10.1212/NXG.0000000000000125

Raman, M. R., Schwarz, C. G., Murray, M. E., Lowe, V. J., Dickson, D. W., Jack, C. R., & Kantarci, K. (2016). An MRI-based atlas for correlation of imaging and pathologic findings in Alzheimer's disease. *Journal of Neuroimaging, 26*, 264–268. doi:10.1111/jon.12341

Ratcliff, R., Thapar, A., & McKoon, G. (2006). Aging and individual differences in rapid two-choice decisions. *Psychonomic Bulletin & Review, 13*, 626–635.

Rautiainen, S., Gaziano, J. M., Christen, W. G., Bubes, V., Kotler, G., Glynn, R. J., . . . Sesso, H. D. (2017). Effect of baseline nutritional status on long-term multivitamin use and cardiovascular disease risk. *JAMA Cardiology, 2*, 617. doi:10.1001/jamacardio.2017.0176

Raz, N., & Daugherty, A. M. (2018). Pathways to brain aging and their modifiers: Free-radical-induced energetic and neural decline in senescence (FRIENDS) model—A mini-review. *Gerontology, 64*, 49–57. doi:10.1159/000479508

Raz, N., Rodrigue, K. M., Kennedy, K. M., & Acker, J. D. (2007). Vascular health and longitudinal changes in brain and cognition in middle-aged and older adults. *Neuropsychology, 21*, 149–157.

Rea, I. M., & Mills, K. I. (2018). Living long and aging well. In A. Moskalev & A. M. Vaiserman (Eds.), *Epigenetics of aging and longevity* (pp. 137–152). New York, NY: Elsevier. doi:10.1016/B978-0-12-811060-7.00006-1

Reed, A. E., & Carstensen, L. L. (2012). The theory behind the age-related positivity effect. *Frontiers in Psychology, 3*, 339. doi:10.3389/fpsyg.2012.00339

Reed, A. E., Chan, L., & Mikels, J. A. (2014). Meta-analysis of the age-related positivity effect: Age differences in preferences for positive over negative information. *Psychology and Aging, 29*, 1–15. doi:10.1037/a0035194

Reilly, W., & Ilich, J. (2017). Prescription drugs and nutrient depletion: How much is known? *Advances in Nutrition, 8*, 23–23. doi:10.1093/advances/8.1.23

Rektorova, I., Rusina, R., Hort, J., & Matej, R. (2009). The degenerative dementias. In R. P. Lisak, D. D. Truong, W. M. Carroll, & R. Bhidayasiri (Eds.), *International neurology: A clinical approach* (pp. 126–137). Hoboken, NJ: John Wiley.

Reuter-Lorenz, P. A., & Cappell, K. A. (2008). Neurocognitive aging and the compensation hypothesis. *Current Directions in Psychological Science, 17*, 177–182. Retrieved from 10.1111/j.1467-8721.2008.00570.x

Richmond, R. L., Law, J., & KayLambkin, F. (2012). Morbidity profiles and lifetime health of Australian centenarians. *Australasian Journal on Ageing, 31*, 227–232. doi:10.1111/j.1741-6612.2011.00570.x

Ringman, J. M., & Varpetian, A. (2009). Other dementias. In R. P. Lisak, D. D. Truong, W. M. Carroll, & R. Bhidayasiri (Eds.), *International neurology: A clinical approach* (pp. 137–143). Hoboken, NJ: John Wiley.

Rizzo, G., Arcuti, S., Martino, D., Copetti, M., Fontana, A., & Logroscino, G. (2015). Accuracy of clinical diagnosis of Parkinson's disease: A systematic review and Bayesian meta-analysis (S36.001). *Neurology, 84*(14, Suppl.), S36.001. Retrieved from http://www.neurology.org/content/84/14_Supplement/S36.001.short

Roberts, J. S., Connell, C. M., Cisewski, D., Hipps, Y. G., Demissie, S., & Green, R. C. (2003). Differences between African Americans and Whites in their perceptions of Alzheimer disease. *Alzheimer Disease and Associated Disorders, 17*, 19–26.

Roper, J. A., Kang, N., Ben, J., Cauraugh, J. H., Okun, M. S., & Hass, C. J. (2016). Deep brain stimulation improves gait velocity in Parkinson's disease: A systematic review and meta-analysis. *Journal of Neurology, 263*, 1195–1203. doi:10.1007/s00415-016-8129-9

Rosano, C., Guralnik, J., Pahor, M., Glynn, N. W., Newman, A. B., Ibrahim, T. S., . . . Aizenstein, H. J. (2017). Hippocampal response to a 24-month physical activity intervention in sedentary older adults. *American Journal of Geriatric Psychiatry, 25*, 209–217. doi:10.1016/j.jagp.2016.11.007

Rowe, G., Hasher, L., & Turcotte, J. (2010). Interference, aging, and visuospatial working memory: The role of similarity. *Neuropsychology, 24*, 804–807. doi:10.1037/a0020244

Rubin, D. C. (2000). Autobiographical memory and aging. In D. C. Park & N. Schwarz (Eds.), *Cognitive aging: A primer* (pp. 131–149). New York, NY: Psychology Press.

Ruppar, T. M., & Schneider, J. K. (2007). Self-reported exercise behavior and interpretations of exercise in older adults. *Western Journal of Nursing Research, 29*, 140–157.

Ryan, S. M., & Nolan, Y. M. (2016). Neuroinflammation negatively affects adult hippocampal neurogenesis and cognition: Can exercise compensate? *Neuroscience & Biobehavioral Reviews, 61*, 121–131. doi:10.1016/j.neubiorev.2015.12.004

Ryu, S., Atzmon, G., Barzilai, N., Raghavachari, N., & Suh, Y. (2016). Genetic landscape of APOE in human longevity revealed by high-throughput sequencing. *Mechanisms of Ageing and Development, 155*, 7–9. doi:10.1016/J.MAD.2016.02.010

Saad, M., Fausto, N., & Maisch, N. (2018). Vitamins and dietary supplements for the older adult. *American Journal of Therapeutics, 25*, e173–e182. doi:10.1097/MJT.0000000000000669

Sailor, K. A., Schinder, A. F., & Lledo, P.-M. (2017). Adult neurogenesis beyond the niche: Its potential for driving brain plasticity. *Current Opinion in Neurobiology, 42*, 111–117. doi:10.1016/j.conb.2016.12.001

Salthouse, T. A. (2011). Neuroanatomical substrates of age-related cognitive decline. *Psychological Bulletin, 137*, 753–784. doi:10.1037/a0023262

Salthouse, T. A. (2012). Consequences of age-related cognitive declines. *Annual Review of Psychology, 63*, 201–226. doi:10.1146/annurev-psych-120710-100328

Salthouse, T. A., & Madden, D. J. (2013). Information processing speed and aging. In J. DeLuca & J. H. Kalmar (Eds.), *Information processing speed in clinical populations* (pp. 221–239). New York, NY: Psychology Press.

Samanez-Larkin, G. R., Robertson, E. R., Mikels, J. A., Carstensen, L. L., & Gotlib, I. H. (2009). Selective attention to emotion in the aging brain. *Psychology and Aging, 24*, 519–529. doi:10.1037/a0016952

Sampaio-Baptista, C., & Johansen-Berg, H. (2017). White matter plasticity in the adult brain. *Neuron, 96*, 1239–1251. doi:10.1016/J.NEURON.2017.11.026

Sandlin, D., McGwin, G., & Owsley, C. (2014). Association between vision impairment and driving exposure in older adults aged 70 years and over: A population-based examination. *Acta Ophthalmologica, 92*, e207–e212. doi:10.1111/aos.12050

Santos-Lozano, A., Sanchis-Gomar, F., Pareja-Galeano, H., Fiuza-Luces, C., Emanuele. E., Lucia, A., & Garatachea, N. (2015). Where are supercentenarians located? A worldwide demographic study. *Rejuvenation Research.* Retrieved from http://online.liebertpub.com/doi/abs/10.1089/rej.2014.1609

Sattler, C., Toro, P., Schönknecht, P., & Schröder, J. (2012). Cognitive activity, education and socioeconomic status as preventive factors for mild cognitive impairment and Alzheimer's disease. *Psychiatry Research, 196*, 90–95. doi:10.1016/j.psychres.2011.11.012

Savica, R., Grossardt, B. R., Rocca, W. A., & Bower, J. H. (2018). Parkinson disease with and without Dementia: A prevalence study and future projections. *Movement Disorders, 33*, 537–543. doi:10.1002/mds.27277

Scelzo, A., Di Somma, S., Antonini, P., Montross, L. P., Schork, N., Brenner, D., & Jeste, D. V. (2018). Mixed-methods quantitative–qualitative study of 29 nonagenarians and centenarians in rural southern Italy: Focus on positive psychological traits. *International Psychogeriatrics, 30*, 31–38. doi:10.1017/S1041610217002721

Schaie, K. W. (2013). *Developmental influences on adult intelligence: The Seattle Longitudinal Study.* New York, NY: Oxford University Press.

Schelke, M. W., Hackett, K., Chen, J. L., Shih, C., Shum, J., Montgomery, M. E., . . . Isaacson, R. S. (2016). Nutritional interventions for Alzheimer's prevention: A clinical precision medicine approach. *Annals of the New York Academy of Sciences, 1367*, 50–56. doi:10.1111/nyas.13070

Schiffman, S. S. (2009). Effects of aging on the human taste system. *Annals of the New York Academy of Sciences, 1170,* 725–729. doi:10.1111/j.1749-6632.2009.03924.x

Schmidt, H., Freudenberger, P., Seiler, S., & Schmidt, R. (2012). Genetics of subcortical vascular dementia. *Experimental Gerontology, 47,* 873–877. doi:10.1016/j.exger.2012.06.003

Schroots, J. J. F., van Dijkum, C., & Assink, M. H. J. (2004). Autobiographical memory from a life span perspective. *International Journal of Aging & Human Development, 58,* 69–85.

Schubert, C. R., Cruickshanks, K. J., Fischer, M. E., Huang, G.-H., Klein, B. E. K., Klein, R., . . . Nondahl, D. M. (2012). Olfactory impairment in an adult population: The Beaver Dam Offspring study. *Chemical Senses, 37,* 325–334. doi:10.1093/chemse/bjr102

Schubert, C. R., Fischer, M. E., Pinto, A. A., Klein, B. E. K., Klein, R., Tweed, T. S., & Cruickshanks, K. J. (2016). Sensory impairments and risk of mortality in older adults. *Journals of Gerontology Series A: Biological Sciences and Medical Sciences, 84,* glw036. doi:10.1093/gerona/glw036

Schwartz, B. L., & Frazier, L. D. (2005). Tip-of-the-tongue states and aging: Contrasting psycholinguistic and metacognitive perspectives. *Journal of General Psychology, 132,* 377–391.

Sebastiani, P., & Perls, T. T. (2012). The genetics of extreme longevity: Lessons from the new England centenarian study. *Frontiers in Genetics, 3,* 277. doi:10.3389/fgene.2012.00277

Sergi, G., Bano, G., Pizzato, S., Veronese, N., & Manzato, E. (2017). Taste loss in the elderly: Possible implications for dietary habits. *Critical Reviews in Food Science and Nutrition, 57,* 3684–3689. doi:10.1080/10408398.2016.1160208

Serra-Rexach, J. A., Bustamante-Ara, N., Hierro Villarán, M., González Gil, P., Sanz Ibáñez, M. J., Blanco Sanz, N., . . . Lucia, A. (2011). Short-term, light- to moderate-intensity exercise training improves leg muscle strength in the oldest old: A randomized controlled trial. *Journal of the American Geriatrics Society, 59,* 594–602. doi:10.1111/j.1532-5415.2011.03356.x

Seshadri, S., & Wolf, P. A. (2007). Lifetime risk of stroke and dementia: Current concepts, and estimates from the Framingham Study. *Lancet Neurology, 6,* 1106–1114.

Shadyab, A. H., & LaCroix, A. Z. (2015). Genetic factors associated with longevity: A review of recent findings. *Ageing Research Reviews, 19,* 1–7. doi:10.1016/j.arr.2014.10.005

Shafto, M. A., Stamatakis, E. A., Tam, P. P., & Tyler, L. K. (2010). Word retrieval failures in old age: The relationship between structure and function. *Journal of Cognitive Neuroscience, 22,* 1530–1540. doi:10.1162/jocn.2009.21321

Shafto, M. A., & Tyler, L. K. (2014). Language in the aging brain: The network dynamics of cognitive decline and preservation. *Science, 346,* 583–587. doi:10.1126/science.1254404

Sharp, S. I., Aarsland, D., Day, S., Sønnesyn, H., & Ballard, C. (2011). Hypertension is a potential risk factor for vascular dementia: Systematic review. *International Journal of Geriatric Psychiatry, 26,* 661–669. doi:10.1002/gps.2572

Siderowf, A., Aarsland, D., Mollenhauer, B., Goldman, J. G., & Ravina, B. (2018). Biomarkers for cognitive impairment in Lewy body disorders: Status and relevance for clinical trials. *Movement Disorders, 33,* 528–536. doi:10.1002/mds.27355

Siegel, R. L., Ma, J., Zou, Z., & Jemal, A. (2014). Cancer statistics, 2014. *CA: A Cancer Journal for Clinicians, 64,* 9–29. doi:10.3322/caac.21208

Sin, H. P. Y., Liu, D. T. L., & Lam, D. S. C. (2013). Lifestyle modification, nutritional and vitamins supplements for age-related macular degeneration. *Acta Ophthalmologica, 91,* 6–11. doi:10.1111/j.1755-3768.2011.02357.x

Sinnott, J. D. (2003). Postformal thought and adult development: Living in balance. In J. Demick & C. Andreoletti (Eds.), *Handbook of adult development* (pp. 221–238). New York, NY: Kluwer.

Siris, E. S., Adler, R., Bilezikian, J., Bolognese, M., Dawson-Hughes, B., Favus, M. J., . . . Watts, N. B. (2014). The clinical diagnosis of osteoporosis: A position statement from the National Bone Health Alliance Working Group. *Osteoporosis International, 25,* 1439–1443. doi:10.1007/s00198-014-2655-z

Solomon, D. H., Ayanian, J. Z., Yelin, E., Shaykevich, T., Brookhart, M. A., & Katz, J. N. (2012). Use of disease-modifying medications for rheumatoid arthritis by race and ethnicity in the National Ambulatory Medical Care Survey. *Arthritis Care & Research, 64,* 184–189. doi:10.1002/acr.20674

Song, J., Xu, H., Liu, F., & Feng, L. (2011). Tea and cognitive health in late life: Current evidence and future directions. *Journal of Nutrition, Health & Aging, 16,* 31–34. doi:10.1007/s12603-011-0139-9

Sorond, F. A., Cruz-Almeida, Y., Clark, D. J., Viswanathan, A., Scherzer, C. R., De Jager, P., . . . Lipsitz, L. A. (2015). Aging, the central nervous system, and mobility in older adults: Neural mechanisms of mobility impairment. *Journals of Gerontology Series A: Biological Sciences and Medical Sciences, 70,* 1526–1532. doi:10.1093/gerona/glv130

Spalding, K. L., Bergmann, O., Alkass, K., Bernard, S., Salehpour, M., Huttner, H. B., . . . Frisén, J. (2013). Dynamics of hippocampal neurogenesis in adult humans. *Cell, 153,* 1219–1227. doi:10.1016/j.cell.2013.05.002

Spalletta, G., Caltagirone, C., Girardi, P., Gianni, W., Casini, A. R., & Palmer, K. (2012). The role of persistent and incident major depression on rate of cognitive deterioration in newly diagnosed Alzheimer's disease patients. *Psychiatry Research, 198,* 263–268. doi:10.1016/j.psychres.2011.11.018

Srikanth, S., & Nagaraja, A. V. (2005). A prospective study of reversible dementias: Frequency, causes, clinical profile and results of treatment. *Neurology India, 53,* 291–294.

Srinivasan, V., Braidy, N., Chan, E. K. W., Xu, Y.-H., & Chan, D. K. Y. (2016). Genetic and environmental factors in vascular dementia: an update of blood brain barrier dysfunction. *Clinical and Experimental Pharmacology and Physiology, 43,* 515–521. doi:10.1111/1440-1681.12558

St-Laurent, M., Abdi, H., Burianová, H., & Grady, C. L. (2011). Influence of aging on the neural correlates of autobiographical, episodic, and semantic memory retrieval. *Journal of Cognitive Neuroscience, 23,* 4150–4163. doi:10.1162/jocn_a_00079

Starkstein, S. E., Jorge, R., Mizrahi, R., & Robinson, R. G. (2005). The construct of minor and major depression in Alzheimer's disease. *American Journal of Psychiatry, 162,* 2086–2093. doi:10.1176/appi.ajp.162.11.2086

Starkstein, S. E., Mizrahi, R., & Power, B. D. (2008). Depression in Alzheimer's disease: Phenomenology, clinical correlates and treatment. *International Review of Psychiatry, 20,* 382–388. Retrieved from 10.1080/09540260802094480

Staudinger, U. M., & Baltes, P. B. (1996). Interactive minds: A facilitative setting of wisdom-related performance? *Journal of Personality & Social Psychology, 71,* 746–762.

Staudinger, U. M., Dörner, J., & Mickler, C. (2005). Wisdom and personality. In R. J. Sternberg & J. Jordan (Eds.), *A handbook of wisdom: Psychological perspectives* (pp. 191–219). New York, NY: Cambridge University Press.

Staudinger, U. M., Kessler, E. M., & Dörner, J. (2006). Wisdom in social context. In K. W. Schaie & L. L. Carstensen (Eds.), *Social structures, aging, and self-regulation in the elderly* (pp. 33–67). New York, NY: Springer.

Stepankova, H., Lukavsky, J., Buschkuehl, M., Kopecek, M., Ripova, D., & Jaeggi, S. M. (2014). The malleability of working memory and visuospatial skills: A randomized controlled study in older adults. *Developmental Psychology, 50,* 1049–1059. doi:10.1037/a0034913

Stewart, R., & Wingfield, A. (2009). Hearing loss and cognitive effort in older adults' report accuracy for verbal materials. *Journal of the American Academy of Audiology, 20,* 147–154. doi:10.3766/jaaa.20.2.7

Stillman, C. M., Weinstein, A. M., Marsland, A. L., Gianaros, P. J., & Erickson, K. I. (2017). Body-brain connections: The effects of obesity and behavioral interventions on neurocognitive aging. *Frontiers in Aging Neuroscience, 9,* 115. doi:10.3389/fnagi.2017.00115

Stine-Morrow, E. A. L., Shake, M. C., & Noh, S. R. (2010). Language and communication. In J. C. Cavanaugh, C. K. Cavanaugh, J. Berry, & R. West (Eds.), *Aging in America: Vol. 1. Psychological aspects* (pp. 56–78). Santa Barbara, CA: Praeger/ABC-CLIO.

Stine-Morrow, E. A. L., Soederberg Miller, L. M., Gagne, D. D., & Hertzog, C. (2008). Self-regulated reading in adulthood. *Psychology and Aging, 23,* 131–153. doi:10.1037/0882-7974.23.1.131

Storbeck, J., & Maswood, R. (2016). Happiness increases verbal and spatial working memory capacity where sadness does not: Emotion, working memory and executive control. *Cognition and Emotion, 30,* 925–938. doi:10.1080/02699931.2015.1034091

Strachan, S. M., Brawley, L. R., Spink, K., & Glazebrook, K. (2010). Older adults' physically-active identity: Relationships between social cognitions, physical activity and satisfaction with life. *Psychology of Sport and Exercise, 11,* 114–121. doi:10.1016/j.psychsport.2009.09.002

Strough, J., Patrick, J. H., & Swenson, L. M. (2003). Strategies for solving everyday problems faced by grandparents: The role of experience. In B. Hayslip Jr. & J. H. Patrick (Eds.), *Working with custodial grandparents* (pp. 257–275). New York, NY: Springer.

Studenski, S. (2011). Gait speed and survival in older adults. *JAMA, 305,* 50. doi:10.1001/jama.2010.1923

Sun, J. H., Tan, L., Wang, H. F., Tan, M. S., Tan, L., Li, J. Q., . . . Yu, J. T. (2015). Genetics of vascular dementia: Systematic review and meta-analysis. *Journal of Alzheimer's Disease, 46,* 611–629. doi:10.3233/JAD-143102

Sylvain-Roy, S., Lungu, O., & Belleville, S. (2014). Normal aging of the attentional control functions that underlie working memory. *Journals of Gerontology Series B: Psychological Sciences and Social Sciences, 70,* gbt166. doi:10.1093/geronb/gbt166

Tabrett, D. R., & Latham, K. (2010). Depression and vision loss. *Optician, 240,* 22–29.

Takahashi, R. H., Nagao, T., & Gouras, G. K. (2017). Plaque formation and the intraneuronal accumulation of β-amyloid in Alzheimer's disease. *Pathology International, 67,* 185–193. doi:10.1111/pin.12520

Tan, J. S. L., Wang, J. J., Younan, C., Cumming, R. G., Rochtchina, E., & Mitchell, P. (2008). Smoking and the long-term incidence of cataract: The Blue Mountains Eye study. *Ophthalmic Epidemiology, 15,* 155–161. Retrieved from 10.1080/09286580701840362

Tan, Z. S., Spartano, N. L., Beiser, A. S., DeCarli, C., Auerbach, S. H., Vasan, R. S., & Seshadri, S. (2016). Physical activity, brain volume, and dementia risk: The Framingham study. *Journals of Gerontology Series A: Biological Sciences and Medical Sciences, 31,* glw130. doi:10.1093/gerona/glw130

Tapia-Rojas, C., Aranguiz, F., Varela-Nallar, L., & Inestrosa, N. C. (2016). Voluntary running attenuates memory loss, decreases neuropathological changes and induces neurogenesis in a mouse model of Alzheimer's disease. *Brain Pathology, 26,* 62–74. doi:10.1111/bpa.12255

Tautvydaitė, D., Antonietti, J. P., Henry, H., von Gunten, A., & Popp, J. (2017). Relations between personality changes and cerebrospinal fluid biomarkers of Alzheimer's disease pathology. *Journal of Psychiatric Research, 90,* 12–20. doi:10.1016/j.jpsychires.2016.12.024

ten Brinke, L. F., Bolandzadeh, N., Nagamatsu, L. S., Hsu, C. L., Davis, J. C., Miran-Khan, K., & Liu-Ambrose, T. (2015). Aerobic exercise increases hippocampal volume in older women with probable mild cognitive impairment: A 6-month randomised controlled trial. *British Journal of Sports Medicine, 49,* 248–254. doi:10.1136/bjsports-2013-093184

Thomas, S., & Kunzmann, U. (2014). Age differences in wisdom-related knowledge: Does the age relevance of the task matter? *Journals of Gerontology Series B: Psychological Sciences and Social Sciences, 69,* 897–905. doi:10.1093/geronb/gbt076

Thornton, W. J. L., & Dumke, H. A. (2005). Age differences in everyday problem-solving and decision-making effectiveness: A meta-analytic review. *Psychology and Aging, 20,* 85–99.

Tigani, X., Artemiadis, A. K., Alexopoulos, E. C., Chrousos, G. P., & Darviri, C. (2012). Self-rated health in centenarians: A nation-wide cross-sectional Greek study. *Archives of Gerontology and Geriatrics, 54,* e342–e348. doi:10.1016/j.archger.2012.01.012

Tobin, D. J. (2017). Introduction to skin aging. *Journal of Tissue Viability, 26,* 37–46. doi:10.1016/j.jtv.2016.03.002

Tosto, G., Bird, T. D., Bennett, D. A., Boeve, B. F., Brickman, A. M., Cruchaga, C., . . . Mayeux, R. (2016). The role of cardiovascular risk factors and stroke in familial Alzheimer disease. *JAMA Neurology, 73,* 1231. doi:10.1001/jamaneurol.2016.2539

Toulouse, A., & Sullivan, A. M. (2008). Progress in Parkinson's disease: Where do we stand? *Progress in Neurobiology, 85,* 376–392. Retrieved from 10.1016/j.pneurobio.2008.05.003

Tricco, A. C., Thomas, S. M., Veroniki, A. A., Hamid, J. S., Cogo, E., Strifler, L., . . . Straus, S. E. (2017). Comparisons of interventions for preventing falls in older adults. *JAMA, 318,* 1687. doi:10.1001/jama.2017.15006

Trinchero, M. F., Buttner, K. A., Sulkes Cuevas, J. N., Temprana, S. G., Fontanet, P. A., Monzón-Salinas, M. C., . . . Schinder, A. F. (2017). High plasticity of new granule cells in the aging hippocampus. *Cell Reports, 21,* 1129–1139. doi:10.1016/J.CELREP.2017.09.064

Troncoso, J. C., Zonderman, A. B., Resnick, S. M., Crain, B., Pletnikova, O., & O'Brien, R. J. (2008). Effect of infarcts on dementia in the Baltimore Longitudinal Study of Aging. *Annals of Neurology, 64,* 168–176.

Truong, D. D., & Wolters, E. C. (2009). Recognition and management of Parkinson's disease during the premotor (prodromal) phase. *Expert Review of Neurotherapeutics, 9,* 847–857. doi:10.1586/ern.09.50

Turner, G. R., & Spreng, R. N. (2012). Executive functions and neurocognitive aging: Dissociable patterns of brain activity. *Neurobiology of Aging, 33,* 826.e1–826.e13. doi:10.1016/j.neurobiolaging.2011.06.005

U.S. Department of Health and Human Services. (2008). *2008 physical activity guidelines for Americans.* Retrieved from http://www.health.gov/PAGuidelines

Valero, J., Bernardino, L., Cardoso, F. L., Silva, A. P., Fontes-Ribeiro, C., Ambrósio, A. F., & Malva, J. O. (2017). Impact of neuroinflammation on hippocampal neurogenesis: Relevance to aging and Alzheimer's disease. *Journal of Alzheimer's Disease, 60,* S161–S168. doi:10.3233/JAD-170239

van Bokhorst-de van der Schueren, M. A. E., Lonterman-Monasch, S., de Vries, O. J., Danner, S. A., Kramer, M. H. H., & Muller, M. (2013). Prevalence and determinants for malnutrition in geriatric outpatients. *Clinical Nutrition, 32,* 1007–1011. doi:10.1016/j.clnu.2013.05.007

van de Vorst, I. E., Koek, H. L., Stein, C. E., Bots, M. L., & Vaartjes, I. (2016). Socioeconomic disparities and mortality after a diagnosis of dementia: Results from a nationwide registry linkage study. *American Journal of Epidemiology, 184,* 219–226. doi:10.1093/aje/kwv319

van den Broeke, C., de Burghgraeve, T., Ummels, M., Gescher, N., Deckx, L., Tjan-Heijnen, V., . . . van den Akker, M. (2018). Occurrence of malnutrition and associated factors in community-dwelling older adults: Those with a recent diagnosis of cancer are at higher risk. *Journal of Nutrition, Health & Aging, 22,* 191–198. doi:10.1007/s12603-017-0882-7

van den Dungen, P., van Kuijk, L., van Marwijk, H., van der Wouden, J., Moll van Charante, E., van der Horst, H., & van Hout, H. (2014). Preferences regarding disclosure of a diagnosis of dementia: A systematic review. *International Psychogeriatrics, 26,* 1603–1618. Retrieved from http://journals.cambridge.org/abstract_S1041610214000969

Van der Mussele, S., Bekelaar, K., Le Bastard, N., Vermeiren, Y., Saerens, J., Somers, N., . . . Engelborghs, S. (2013). Prevalence and associated behavioral symptoms of depression in mild cognitive impairment and dementia due to Alzheimer's disease. *International Journal of Geriatric Psychiatry, 28,* 947–958. doi:10.1002/gps.3909

Van Dijk, K. R. A., Van Gerven, P. W. M., Van Boxtel, M. P. J., Van Der Elst, W., & Jolles, J. (2008). No protective effects of education during normal cognitive aging: Results from the 6-year follow-up of the Maastricht Aging study. *Psychology & Aging, 23,* 119–130.

Van Gerven, P. W. M., Van Boxtel, M. P. J., Meijer, W. A., Willems, D., & Jolles, J. (2007). On the relative role of inhibition in age-related working memory decline. *Aging, Neuropsychology & Cognition, 14,* 95–107.

van Nispen, R. M. A., Vreeken, H. L., Comijs, H. C., Deeg, D. J. H., & van Rens, G. H. M. B. (2016). Role of vision loss, functional limitations and the supporting network in depression in a general population. *Acta Ophthalmologica, 94,* 76–82. doi:10.1111/aos.12896

van Praag, H. (2008). Neurogenesis and exercise: Past and future directions. *NeuroMolecular Medicine, 10,* 128–140. doi:10.1007/s12017-008-8028-z

Verdelho, A., Madureira, S., Ferro, J. M., Baezner, H., Blahak, C., Poggesi, A., . . . Inzitari, D. (2012). Physical activity prevents progression for cognitive impairment and vascular dementia: Results from the LADIS (Leukoaraiosis and Disability) study. *Stroke: A Journal of Cerebral Circulation, 43,* 3331–3335. doi:10.1161/STROKEAHA.112.661793

Verhaeghen, P., Steitz, D. W., Sliwinski, M. J., & Cerella, J. (2003). Aging and dual-task performance: A meta-analysis. *Psychology and Aging, 18,* 443–460.

Vestergren, P., & Nilsson, L.-G. (2011). Perceived causes of everyday memory problems in a population-based sample aged 39-99. *Applied Cognitive Psychology, 25,* 641–646. doi:10.1002/acp.1734

Vinters, H. V., Zarow, C., Borys, E., Whitman, J. D., Tung, S., Ellis, W. G., . . . Chui, H. C. (2018). Review: Vascular dementia: Clinicopathologic and genetic considerations. *Neuropathology and Applied Neurobiology, 44,* 247–266. doi:10.1111/nan.12472

Visschedijk, J., Achterberg, W., van Balen, R., & Hertogh, C. (2010). Fear of falling after hip fracture: A systematic review of measurement instruments, prevalence, interventions, and related factors. *Journal of the American Geriatrics Society, 58,* 1739–1748. doi:10.1111/j.1532-5415.2010.03036.x

Vitlic, A., Lord, J. M., & Phillips, A. C. (2014). Stress, ageing and their influence on functional, cellular and molecular aspects of the immune system. *Age (Dordrecht, Netherlands), 36*, 9631. doi:10.1007/s11357-014-9631-6

Voelcker-Rehage, C., & Alberts, J. L. (2007). Effect of motor practice on dual-task performance in older adult. *Journals of Gerontology Series B: Psychological Sciences and Social Sciences, 62*, P141–P148.

Voelcker-Rehage, C., Stronge, A. J., & Alberts, J. L. (2006). Age-related differences in working memory and force control under dual-task conditions. *Aging, Neuropsychology, and Cognition, 13*, 366–384.

Vondracek, S. F. (2010). Managing osteoporosis in postmenopausal women. *American Journal of Health-System Pharmacy, 67*, S9–S19. doi:10.2146/ajhp100076

Walker, J. (2008). Osteoporosis: Pathogenesis, diagnosis and management. *Nursing Standard, 22*, 48–56.

Walker, Z., Possin, K. L., Boeve, B. F., & Aarsland, D. (2015). Lewy body dementias. *Lancet (London, England), 386*, 1683–1697. doi:10.1016/S0140-6736(15)00462-6

Walker, Z., Possin, K. L., Boeve, B. F., & Aarsland, D. (2017). Lewy body dementias. *Focus, 15*, 85–100. doi:10.1176/appi.focus.15105

Wang, J., Sun, X., & Yang, Q. X. (2016). Early aging effect on the function of the human central olfactory system. *The Journals of Gerontology Series A: Biological Sciences and Medical Sciences, 21*, glw104. doi:10.1093/gerona/glw104

Wang, S., Luo, X., Barnes, D., Sano, M., & Yaffe, K. (2014). Physical activity and risk of cognitive impairment among oldest-old women. *The American Journal of Geriatric Psychiatry:, 22*, 1149–1157. doi:10.1016/j.jagp.2013.03.002

Wang, S., & Young, K. M. M. (2014). White matter plasticity in adulthood. *Neuroscience, 276*, 148–160. doi:10.1016/j.neuroscience.2013.10.018

Weaver, C. M., Gordon, C. M., Janz, K. F., Kalkwarf, H. J., Lappe, J. M., Lewis, R., . . . Zemel, B. S. (2016). The National Osteoporosis Foundation's position statement on peak bone mass development and lifestyle factors: a systematic review and implementation recommendations. *Osteoporosis International, 27*, 1281–1386. doi:10.1007/s00198-015-3440-3

Weerdesteyn, V., Nienhuis, B., Geurts, A. C. H., & Duysens, J. (2007). Age-related deficits in early response characteristics of obstacle avoidance under time pressure. *Journals of Gerontology Series A: Biological Sciences & Medical Sciences, 62A*, 1042–1047.

Welmer, A. K., Rizzuto, D., Laukka, E. J., Johnell, K., & Fratiglioni, L. (2016). Cognitive and physical function in relation to the risk of injurious falls in older adults: A population-based study. *Journals of Gerontology Series A: Biological Sciences and Medical Sciences, 68*, glw141. doi:10.1093/gerona/glw141

Weststrate, N. M., & Glück, J. (2017). Hard-earned wisdom: Exploratory processing of difficult life experience is positively associated with wisdom. *Developmental Psychology, 53*, 800–814. doi:10.1037/dev0000286

Wettstein, M., & Wahl, H.-W. (2016). Hearing. In S. K. Whitbourne (Ed.), *The encyclopedia of adulthood and aging* (pp. 1–5). Hoboken, NJ: John Wiley. doi:10.1002/9781118521373.wbeaa202

White, J., Greene, G., Kivimaki, M., & Batty, G. D. (2018). Association between changes in lifestyle and all-cause mortality: The Health and Lifestyle Survey. *Journal of Epidemiology and Community Health, 72*, 711–714. doi:10.1136/jech-2017-210363

Whitney, C. R. (1997, August 5). Jeanne Calment, world's elder, dies at 122. *New York Times.*

Windle, G., Hughes, D., Linck, P., Russell, I., & Woods, B. (2010). Is exercise effective in promoting mental well-being in older age? A systematic review. *Aging & Mental Health, 14*, 652–669. doi:10.1080/13607861003713232

Wirdefeldt, K., Adami, H.-O., Cole, P., Trichopoulos, D., & Mandel, J. (2011). Epidemiology and etiology of Parkinson's disease: A review of the evidence. *European Journal of Epidemiology, 26*(Suppl. 1), S1–S58. doi:10.1007/s10654-011-9581-6

Wiseman, F. K., Al-Janabi, T., Hardy, J., Karmiloff-Smith, A., Nizetic, D., Tybulewicz, V. L. J., . . . Strydom, A. (2015). A genetic cause of Alzheimer disease: Mechanistic insights from Down syndrome. *Nature Reviews. Neuroscience, 16*, 564–574. doi:10.1038/nrn3983

Withers, M., Moran, R., Nicassio, P., Weisman, M. H., & Karpouzas, G. A. (2015). Perspectives of vulnerable US Hispanics with rheumatoid arthritis on depression: Awareness, barriers to disclosure, and treatment options. *Arthritis Care & Research, 67*, 484–492. doi:10.1002/acr.22462

Witte, A. V., Kerti, L., Hermannstädter, H. M., Fiebach, J. B., Schreiber, S. J., Schuchardt, J. P., . . . Flöel, A. (2014). Long-chain omega-3 fatty acids improve brain function and structure in older adults. *Cerebral Cortex, 24*, 3059–3068. doi:10.1093/cercor/bht163

Woodside, J. V, McGrath, A. J., Lyner, N., & McKinley, M. C. (2015). Carotenoids and health in older people. *Maturitas, 80*, 63–68. doi:10.1016/j.maturitas.2014.10.012

World Health Organization. (2012). *Dementia: A public health priority.* Retrieved from http://www.alzheimer.ca/en/sk/Get-involved/Raise-your-voice/~/media/WHO_ADI_dementia_report_final.ashx

Wright, N. C., Saag, K. G., Dawson-Hughes, B., Khosla, S., & Siris, E. S. (2017). The impact of the new National Bone Health Alliance (NBHA) diagnostic criteria on the prevalence of osteoporosis in the USA. *Osteoporosis International, 28*, 1225–1232. doi:10.1007/s00198-016-3865-3

Wu, M., Kumar, A., & Yang, S. (2016). Development and aging of superficial white matter myelin from young adulthood to old age: Mapping by vertex-based surface statistics (VBSS). *Human Brain Mapping, 37*, 1759–1769. doi:10.1002/hbm.23134

Wynn, M. J., & Carpenter, B. D. (2018). Discourse features among providers, patients, and companions and their effect on outcomes of dementia diagnosis disclosure. *Journals of Gerontology Series B: Psychological Sciences & Social Sciences.* Advance online publication. doi:10.1093/geronb/gbx154

Xu, J. (2016). Mortality among centenarians in the United States, 2000-2014. *NCHS Data Brief, 233*, 1–8. Retrieved from http://www.ncbi.nlm.nih.gov/pubmed/26828422

Xu, W., Yu, J.-T., Tan, M.-S., & Tan, L. (2015). Cognitive reserve and Alzheimer's disease. *Molecular Neurobiology, 51*, 187–208. doi:10.1007/s12035-014-8720-y

Yorgason, J. B., Draper, T. W., Bronson, H., Nielson, M., Babcock, K., Jones, K., . . . Howard, M. (2018). Biological, psychological, and social predictors of longevity among Utah centenarians. *The International Journal of Aging and Human Development.* Advance online publication. doi:10.1177/0091415018757211

Zacher, H., & Staudinger, U. M. (2018). Wisdom and well-being. In E. Diener, S. Oishi, & L. Tay (Eds.), *Handbook of well-being.* Salt Lake City, UT: DEF. doi:DOI:nobascholar.com

Chapter 18

AARP. (2002). *The grandparent study: 2002 report.* Washington, DC: Author.

AARP. (2008). *Update on the aged 55+ worker: 2007.* Washington, DC: Author.

Abu-Raiya, H., Pargament, K. I., Krause, N., & Ironson, G. (2015). Robust links between religious/spiritual struggles, psychological distress, and well-being in a national sample of American adults. *American Journal of Orthopsychiatry, 85*, 565–575. doi:10.1037/ort0000084

Acierno, R., Hernandez, M. A., Amstadter, A. B., Resnick, H. S., Steve, K., Muzzy, W., & Kilpatrick, D. G. (2010). Prevalence and correlates of emotional, physical, sexual, and financial abuse and potential neglect in the United States: The National Elder Mistreatment Study. *American Journal of Public Health, 100*, 292–297. doi:10.2105/ajph.2009.163089

Adams, G. A., Prescher, J., Beehr, T. A., & Lepisto, L. (2002). Applying work-role attachment theory to retirement decision-making. *International Journal of Aging & Human Development, 54*, 125–137. doi:10.2190/JRUQ-XQ2N-UP0A-M432

Adams, K. B., Leibbrandt, S., & Moon, H. (2011). A critical review of the literature on social and leisure activity and wellbeing in later life. *Ageing & Society, 31*, 683–712. doi:10.1017/s0144686x10001091

Adams, K. B., Sanders, S., & Auth, E. A. (2004). Loneliness and depression in independent living retirement communities: Risk and resilience factors. *Aging & Mental Health, 8*, 475–485. doi:10.1080/1360786041001725054

Adams, R. G. (2017). Friendship during the later years. In C. L. Shehan (Ed.), *The Blackwell encyclopedia of sociology* (pp. 1–2). Oxford, England: John Wiley. doi:10.1002/9781405165518.wbeosf069.pub2

Adams, R. G., Blieszner, R., & De Vries, B. (2000). Definitions of friendship in the third age: Age, gender, and study location effects. *Journal of Aging Studies, 14*, 117.

Adams, R. G., & Taylor, E. M. (2015). Friendship and happiness in the third age. In M. Demir (Ed.), *Friendship and happiness* (pp. 155–169). Dordrecht: Springer Netherlands. doi:10.1007/978-94-017-9603-3_9

Addo, F. R., & Lichter, D. T. (2013). Marriage, marital history, and Black-White wealth differentials among older women. *Journal of Marriage and Family, 75*, 342–362. doi:10.1111/jomf.12007

Agrigoroaei, S., Lee-Attardo, A., & Lachman, M. E. (2017). Stress and subjective age: Those with greater financial stress look older. *Research on Aging, 17*, 1075–1099. doi:10.1177/0164027516658502

Anderberg, P., & Berglund, A. L. (2010). Elderly persons' experiences of striving to receive care on their own terms in nursing homes. *International Journal of Nursing Practice, 16*, 64–68. doi:10.1111/j.1440-172X.2009.01808.x

Andonian, L., & MacRae, A. (2011). Well older adults within an urban context: Strategies to create and maintain social participation. *British Journal of Occupational Therapy, 74*, 2–11. doi:10.4276/03080221 1X12947686093486

Andrews-Hanna, J. R., Smallwood, J., & Spreng, R. N. (2014). The default network and self-generated thought: Component processes, dynamic control, and clinical relevance. *Annals of the New York Academy of Sciences, 1316*, 29–52. doi:10.1111/nyas.12360

Antonucci, T. C., Akiyama, H., & Takahashi, K. (2004). Attachment and close relationships across the life span. *Attachment & Human Development, 6*, 353–370. doi:10.1080/1461673042000303136

Atchley, R. C. (1989). A continuity theory of normal aging. *The Gerontologist, 29*, 183–190. doi:10.1093/geront/29.2.183

Atchley, R. C. (2016). Aging, religion, and spirituality. In C. L. Shehan (Ed.), *The Blackwell encyclopedia of sociology* (pp. 1–3). Oxford, England: John Wiley. doi:10.1002/9781405165518.wbeoss220 .pub2

Ayalon, L., Lev, S., Green, O., & Nevo, U. (2016). A systematic review and meta-analysis of interventions designed to prevent or stop elder maltreatment. *Age and Ageing, 45*, 216–227. doi:10.1093/ageing/afv193

Ball, M. M., Whittington, F. J., Perkins, M. M., Patterson, V. L., Hollingworth, C., King, S. V, & Combs, B. L. (2000). Quality of life in assisted living facilities: Viewpoints of residents. *Journal of Applied Gerontology, 19*, 304–325.

Barbosa, L. M., Monteiro, B., & Murta, S. G. (2016). Retirement adjustment predictors—A systematic review. *Work, Aging and Retirement, 2*, 262–280.

Barboza, G. E. (2016). Elder maltreatment. In C. A. Cuevas & C. M. Rennison (Eds.), *The Wiley handbook on the psychology of violence* (pp. 324–352). Chichester, England: John Wiley. doi:10.1002/9781118303092.ch17

Barer, B. M. (2001). The "grands and greats" of very old black grandmothers. *Journal of Aging Studies, 15*, 1.

Bauer, M., Haesler, E., & Fetherstonhaugh, D. (2016). Let's talk about sex: Older people's views on the recognition of sexuality and sexual health in the health-care setting. *Health Expectations, 19*, 1237–1250. doi:10.1111/hex.12418

Bauer, M., McAuliffe, L., & Nay, R. (2007). Sexuality, health care and the older person: An overview of the literature. *International Journal of Older People Nursing, 2*, 63–68.

Bedford, V. H., & Avioli, P. S. (2016). Sibling ties. In S. K. Whitbourne (Ed.), *The encyclopedia of adulthood and aging* (pp. 1–5). Hoboken, NJ: John Wiley. doi:10.1002/9781118521373. wbeaa241

Bell, S., Reissing, E. D., Henry, L. A., & VanZuylen, H. (2017). Sexual activity after 60: A systematic review of associated factors. *Sexual Medicine Reviews, 5*, 52–80. doi:10.1016/j.sxmr.2016.03.001

Bengtson, V. L., & DeLiema, M. (2016). Theories of aging and social gerontology: Explaining how social factors influence well-being in later life. In M. H. Meyer & E. A. Daniele (Eds.), *Gerontology: Changes, challenges, and solutions* (Vol. 2, pp. 25–56). Santa Barbara, CA: ABC-CLIO.

Bengtson, V. L., Silverstein, M., Putney, N. M., & Harris, S. C. (2015). Does religiousness increase with age? Age changes and generational differences over 35 years. *Journal for the Scientific Study of Religion, 54*, 363–379. doi:10.1111/jssr.12183

Bergland, A., Nicolaisen, M., & Thorsen, K. (2014). Predictors of subjective age in people aged 40–79 years: A five-year follow-up study. The impact of mastery, mental and physical health. *Aging & Mental Health, 18*, 653–661. doi:10.1080/13607863.2013.869545

Bishop, B. J. (2008). Stress and depression among older residents in religious monasteries: Do friends and God matter? *International Journal of Aging & Human Development, 67*, 1–23.

Blieszner, R., & Ogletree, A. M. (2018). We get by with a little help from our friends: Aging together in tandem, and meeting the challenges of older age. *Generations, 137*, 949–963.

Böckerman, P., Ilmakunnas, P., Böckerman, P., & Ilmakunnas, P. (2017). *Do good working conditions make you work longer? Evidence on retirement decisions using linked survey and register data* (No. 10964). Retrieved from https://econpapers.repec.org/paper/ izaizaizadps/dp10964.htm

Bogg, T., & Roberts, B. W. (2013). The case for conscientiousness: Evidence and implications for a personality trait marker of health and longevity. *Annals of Behavioral Medicine, 45*, 278–288. doi:10.1007/s12160-012-9454-6

Boswell, G. H., Kahana, E., & Dilworth-Anderson, P. (2006). Spirituality and healthy lifestyle behaviors: Stress counter-balancing effects on the well-being of older adults. *Journal of Religion and Health, 45*, 587–602. doi:10.1007/s10943-006-9060-7

Bowling, A., & Gabriel, Z. (2004). An integrational model of quality of life in older age: Results from the ESRC/MRC HSRC Quality of Life Survey in Britain. *Social Indicators Research, 69*, 1–36. doi:10.1023/ B:SOCI.0000032656.01524.07

Breheny, M., & Griffiths, Z. (2017). "I had a good time when I was young": Interpreting descriptions of continuity among older people. *Journal of Aging Studies, 41*, 36–43. doi:10.1016/J.JAGING.2017.03.003

Brown, S. L., Bulanda, J. R., & Lee, G. R. (2012). Transitions into and out of cohabitation in later life. *Journal of Marriage and the Family, 74*, 774–793. doi:10.1111/j.1741-3737.2012.00994.x

Brown, S. L., & Kawamura, S. (2010). Relationship quality among cohabitors and marrieds in older adulthood. *Social Science Research, 39*, 777–786. doi:10.1016/j. ssresearch.2010.04.010

Brown, S. L., & Wright, M. R. (2016). Older adults' attitudes toward cohabitation: Two decades of change. *Journals of Gerontology Series B: Psychological Sciences and Social Sciences, 71*, 755–764. doi:10.1093/geronb/gbv053

Butler, R. N. (1963). The life review: An interpretation of reminiscence in the aged. *Psychiatry: Interpersonal and Biological Processes, 26*, 65–76.

Butler, R. N. (1974). Successful aging and the role of the life review. *Journal of the American Geriatrics Society, 22*, 529–535. Retrieved from http://www.ncbi.nlm.nih.gov/ pubmed/4420325

Butler, S. S., & Eckart, D. (2007). Civic engagement among older adults in a rural community: A case study of the senior companion program. *Journal of Community Practice, 15*, 77.

Caldwell, J. T., Lee, H., & Cagney, K. A. (2018). Disablement in context: Neighborhood characteristics and their association with frailty onset among older adults. *Journals of Gerontology Series B: Psychological Sciences and Social Sciences*. Advance online publication. doi:10.1093/geronb/gbx123

Calvo, E., Haverstick, K., & Sass, S. A. (2009). Gradual retirement, sense of control, and retirees' happiness. *Research on Aging, 31*, 112–135.

Carstensen, L. L., Fung, H. H., & Charles, S. T. (2003). Socioemotional selectivity theory and the regulation of emotion in the second half of life. *Motivation and Emotion, 27*, 103–123. doi:10.1023/A:1024569803230

Carstensen, L. L., & Mikels, J. A. (2005). At the intersection of emotion and cognition: Aging and the positivity effect. *Current Directions in Psychological Science, 14*, 117–121. doi:10.1111/j.0963-7214.2005.00348.x

Carstensen, L. L., Turan, B., Scheibe, S., Ram, N., Ersner-Hershfield, H., . . . Nesselroade, J. R. (2011). Emotional experience improves with age: Evidence based on over 10 years of experience sampling. *Psychology and Aging, 26*, 21–33. doi:10.1037/a0021285

Chapman, B., Duberstein, P., Tindle, H. A., Sink, K. M., Robbins, J., Tancredi, D. J., & Franks, P. (2012). Personality predicts cognitive function over 7 years in older persons. *American Journal of Geriatric Psychiatry, 20*, 612–621. doi:10.1097/ JGP.0b013e31822cc9cb

Chappell, N., Gee, E., McDonald, L., & Stones, M. (2003). *Aging in contemporary Canada.* Toronto: Pearson Education Canada.

Chen, R., & Dong, X. (2017). Risk factors of elder abuse. In *Elder abuse* (pp. 93–107). Cham, Switzerland: Springer International. doi:10.1007/978-3-319-47504-2_5

Cherry, K. E., Walker, E. J., Brown, J. S., Volaufova, J., LaMotte, L. R., . . . Frisard, M. I. (2013). Social engagement and health in younger, older, and oldest-old adults in the Louisiana Healthy Aging study. *Journal of Applied Gerontology, 32*, 51–75. doi:10.1177/0733464811409034

Clarke, P., & Gallagher, N. A. (2013). Optimizing mobility in later life: The role of the urban built environment for older adults aging in place. *Journal of Urban Health: Bulletin of the New York Academy of Medicine, 90,* 997–1009. doi:10.1007/s11524-013-9800-4

Clarke, P., Morenoff, J., Debbink, M., Golberstein, E., Elliott, M. R., & Lantz, P. M. (2014). Cumulative exposure to neighborhood context: Consequences for health transitions over the adult life course. *Research on Aging, 36,* 115–142. doi:10.1177/0164027512470702

Cohn, D., & Passel, J. S. (2018). *Record 64 million Americans live in multigenerational households | Pew Research Center.* Retrieved April 23, 2018, from http://www.pewresearch.org/fact-tank/2018/04/05/a-record-64-million-americans-live-in-multigenerational-households

Coleman, M., & Ganong, L. (2008). Normative beliefs about sharing housing with an older family member. *International Journal of Aging & Human Development, 66,* 49–72. Retrieved from http://www.ncbi.nlm.nih.gov/pubmed/18429483

Coleman, P. G., Ivani-Chalian, C., & Robinson, M. (2004). Religious attitudes among British older people: Stability and change in a 20-year longitudinal study. *Ageing & Society, 24,* 167–188.

Cooper, C., Selwood, A., & Livingston, G. (2008). The prevalence of elder abuse and neglect: A systematic review. *Age & Ageing, 37,* 151–160. doi:10.1093/ageing/afm194

Cox, K. S., Wilt, J., Olson, B., & McAdams, D. P. (2010). Generativity, the Big Five, and psychosocial adaptation in midlife adults. *Journal of Personality, 78,* 1185–1208. doi:10.1111/j.1467-6494.2010.00647.x

Cuddy, A. J. C., Fiske, S. T., Kwan, V. S. Y., Glick, P., Demoulin, S., . . . Ziegler, R. (2009). Stereotype content model across cultures: Towards universal similarities and some differences. *British Journal of Social Psychology, 48,* 1–33. doi:10.1348/014466608X314935

Cully, J. A., LaVoie, D., & Gfeller, J. D. (2001). Reminiscence, personality, and psychological functioning in older adults. *The Gerontologist, 41,* 89–95.

Damman, M., Henkens, K., & Kalmijn, M. (2015). Missing work after retirement: The role of life histories in the retirement adjustment process. *The Gerontologist, 55,* 802–813. doi:10.1093/geront/gnt169

Dandy, K., & Bollman, R. D. (2008). Seniors in rural Canada. *Rural and Small Town Canada Analysis Bulletin, 7*(8). Retrieved from http://globalag.igc.org/ruralaging/world/2008/ruralcanada.pdf

Darbonne, A., Uchino, B. N., & Ong, A. D. (2012). What mediates links between age and well-being? A test of social support and interpersonal conflict as potential interpersonal pathways. *Journal of Happiness Studies, 14,* 951–963. doi:10.1007/s10902-012-9363-1

Davies, E. M. M., Van der Heijden, B. I. J. M., & Flynn, M. (2017). Job satisfaction, retirement attitude and intended retirement age: A conditional process analysis across workers' level of household income. *Frontiers in Psychology, 8,* 891. doi:10.3389/fpsyg.2017.00891

Davis, N. L., & Degges-White, S. (2008). Catalysts for developing productive life reviews: A multiple case study. *Adultspan: Theory Research & Practice, 7,* 69–79.

De Vaus, D., Wells, Y., Kendig, H., & Quine, S. (2007). Does gradual retirement have better outcomes than abrupt retirement? Results from an Australian panel study. *Ageing & Society, 27,* 667–682.

Debrot, A., Meuwly, N., Muise, A., Impett, E. A., & Schoebi, D. (2017). More than just sex. *Personality and Social Psychology Bulletin, 43,* 287–299. doi:10.1177/0146167216684124

DeLamater, J. (2012). Sexual expression in later life: A review and synthesis. *Journal of Sex Research, 49,* 125–141. doi:10.1080/00224499.2011.603168

DeLamater, J., & Koepsel, E. (2015). Relationships and sexual expression in later life: A biopsychosocial perspective. *Sexual and Relationship Therapy, 30,* 37–59. doi:10.1080/14681994.2014.939506

DeLiema, M., & Bengtson, V. L. (2017). Activity theory, disengagement theory, and successful aging. In N. A. Pachana (Ed.), *Encyclopedia of geropsychology* (pp. 15–20). Singapore: Springer Singapore. doi:10.1007/978-981-287-082-7_102

DeLiema, M., Yonashiro-Cho, J., Gassoumis, Z. D., Yon, Y., & Conrad, K. J. (2018). Using latent class analysis to identify profiles of elder abuse perpetrators. *Journals of Gerontology Series B: Psychological Sciences and Social Sciences, 73,* e49–e58. doi:10.1093/geronb/gbx023

Demiray, B., Mischler, M., & Martin, M. (2018). Reminiscence in everyday conversations: A naturalistic observation study of older adults. *Journals of Gerontology Series B: Psychological Sciences and Social Sciences.* Advance online publication. doi:10.1093/geronb/gbx141

DeNavas-Walt, C., & Proctor, B. D. (2014). Income and poverty in the United States: 2013. Retrieved from http://www.census.gov/hhes/www/poverty/data/incpovhlth/2013/

Dezutter, J., Toussaint, L., & Leijssen, M. (2014). Forgiveness, ego-integrity, and depressive symptoms in community-dwelling and residential elderly adults. *Journals of Gerontology Series B: Psychological Sciences and Social Sciences, 71,* 786–797. https://doi.org/10.1093/geronb/gbu146

Dong, X., & Simon, M. A. (2008). Is greater social support a protective factor against elder mistreatment? *Gerontology, 54,* 381–388. doi:10.1159/000143228

Doskoch, P. (2011). Many men 75 and older consider sex important and remain sexually active. *Perspectives on Sexual and Reproductive Health, 43,* 67–68. doi:10.1363/4306711

Dykstra, P. A., & Fokkema, T. (2010). Relationships between parents and their adult children: A West European typology of late-life families. *Ageing and Society, 31,* 37–59. doi:10.1017/S0144686X10001108

English, T., & Carstensen, L. L. (2014). Selective narrowing of social networks across adulthood is associated with improved emotional experience in daily life. *International Journal of Behavioral Development, 38,* 195–202. doi:10.1177/0165025413515404

English, T., & Carstensen, L. L. (2016). Socioemotional selectivity theory. In N. Pachana (Ed.), *Encyclopedia of geropsychology* (pp. 1–6). New York, NY: Springer. doi:10.1007/978-981-287-080-3_110-1

Erikson, E. H. (1950). *Childhood and society.* New York, NY: Norton.

Erikson, E. H. (1982). *The life cycle completed.* New York, NY: Norton.

Fehr, R. (2012). Is retirement always stressful? The potential impact of creativity. *American Psychologist, 67,* 76–77. doi:10.1037/a0026574

Feldman, D. C., & Beehr, T. A. (2011). A three-phase model of retirement decision making. *The American Psychologist, 66,* 193–203. doi:10.1037/a0022153

Fields, N. L., & Dabelko-Schoeny, H. (2016). Aging in place. In *The encyclopedia of adulthood and aging* (pp. 1–5). Hoboken, NJ: John Wiley. doi:10.1002/9781118521373.wbeaa106

Fingerman, K. L., & Charles, S. T. (2010). It takes two to tango: Why older people have the best relationships. *Current Directions in Psychological Science, 19,* 172–176. doi:10.1177/0963721410370297

Fonda, S. J., Clipp, E. C., & Maddox, G. L. (2002). Patterns in functioning among residents of an affordable assisted living housing facility. *The Gerontologist, 42,* 178.

Freak-Poli, R., Kirkman, M., De Castro Lima, G., Direk, N., Franco, O. H., & Tiemeier, H. (2017). Sexual activity and physical tenderness in older adults: Cross-sectional prevalence and associated characteristics. *Journal of Sexual Medicine, 14,* 918–927. doi:10.1016/j.jsxm.2017.05.010

Freund, A. M., & Smith, J. (1999). Methodological comment: Temporal stability of older person's spontaneous self-definition. *Experimental Aging Research, 25,* 95.

Galek, K., Flannelly, K. J., Ellison, C. G., Silton, N. R., & Jankowski, K. R. B. (2015). Religion, meaning and purpose, and mental health. *Psychology of Religion and Spirituality, 7,* 1–12. doi:10.1037/a0037887.

Gans, D., & Silverstein, M. (2006). Norms of filial responsibility for aging parents across time and generations. *Journal of Marriage & Family, 68,* 961–976.

Geurts, T., Van Tilburg, T. G., & Poortman, A. R. (2012). The grandparent–grandchild relationship in childhood and adulthood: A matter of continuation? *Personal Relationships, 19,* 267–278. doi:10.1111/j.1475-6811.2011.01354.x

George, L. K., Ellison, C. G., & Larson, D. B. (2002). Explaining the relationships between religious involvement and health. *Psychological Inquiry, 13,* 190–200. https://doi.org/10.1207/S15327965PLI1303_04

Gillespie, B. J., Lever, J., Frederick, D., & Royce, T. (2015). Close adult friendships, gender, and the life cycle. *Journal of Social and Personal Relationships, 32,* 709–736. doi:10.1177/0265407514546977

Gilligan, M., Karraker, A., & Jasper, A. (2018). Linked lives and cumulative inequality: A multigenerational family life course framework. *Journal of Family Theory & Review, 10,* 111–125. doi:10.1111/jftr.12244

Glaser, K., Stuchbury, R., Tomassini, C., & Askham, J. (2008). The long-term consequences of partnership dissolution for support in later life in the United Kingdom. *Ageing & Society, 28*, 329–351. doi:10.1017/S0144686X07006642

Glass, T. A., Mendes De Leon, C. F., Bassuk, S. S., & Berkman, L. F. (2006). Social engagement and depressive symptoms in late life. *Journal of Aging & Health, 16*, 604–628.

Goldsen, J., Bryan, A. E. B., Kim, H. J., Muraco, A., Jen, S., & Fredriksen-Goldsen, K. I. (2017). Who says I do: The changing context of marriage and health and quality of life for LGBT older adults. *The Gerontologist, 57*(Suppl. 1), S50–S62. doi:10.1093/geront/gnw174

Gonzales, A. M. (2007). Determinants of parent-child coresidence among older Mexican parents: The salience of cultural values. *Sociological Perspectives, 50*, 561–577.

Goodwin, R. D., & Friedman, H. S. (2006). Health status and the five-factor personality traits in a nationally representative sample. *Journal of Health Psychology, 11*, 643–654. doi:10.1177/1359105306066610

Gopinath, B., Liew, G., Burlutsky, G., McMahon, C. M., & Mitchell, P. (2017). Visual and hearing impairment and retirement in older adults: A population-based cohort study. *Maturitas, 100*, 77–81. doi:10.1016/j.maturitas.2017.03.318

Graham, E. K., & Lachman, M. E. (2012). Personality stability is associated with better cognitive performance in adulthood: Are the stable more able? *Journals of Gerontology Series B: Psychological Sciences and Social Sciences, 67*, 545–554. doi:10.1093/geronb/gbr149

Green, M., & Elliott, M. (2010). Religion, health, and psychological well-being. *Journal of Religion and Health, 49*, 149–163. doi:10.1007/s10943-009-9242-1

Grotz, C., Matharan, F., Amieva, H., Pérès, K., Laberon, S., . . . Letenneur, L. (2017). Psychological transition and adjustment processes related to retirement: Influence on cognitive functioning. *Aging & Mental Health, 21*, 1310–1316. doi:10.1080/13607863.2016.1220920

Grundy, E., & Henretta, J. C. (2006). Between elderly parents and adult children: A new look at the intergenerational care provided by the "sandwich generation." *Ageing & Society, 26*, 707–722.

Hagestad, G. O. (2018). Interdependent lives and relationships in changing times: A life-course view of families and aging. In R. Settersten (Ed.), *Lives in time and place and invitation to the life course* (pp. 135–159). New York, NY: Routledge. doi:10.4324/9781315224206-6

Hao, Y. (2008). Productive activities and psychological well-being among older adults. *Journals of Gerontology Series B: Psychological Sciences and Social Sciences, 63*, S64–S72.

Hatch, L. R., & Bulcroft, K. (2004). Does long-term marriage bring less frequent disagreements? Five explanatory frameworks. *Journal of Family Issues, 25*, 465–495. doi:10.1177/0192513X03257766

Hayward, R. D., & Krause, N. (2013). Changes in church-based social support relationships during older adulthood. *The Journals of Gerontology Series B: Psychological Sciences and Social Sciences, 68*, 85–96. doi:10.1093/geronb/gbs100

Hearn, S., Saulnier, G., Strayer, J., Glenham, M., Koopman, R., & Marcia, J. E. (2011). Between integrity and despair: Toward construct validation of Erikson's eighth stage. *Journal of Adult Development, 19*, 1–20. https://doi.org/10.1007/s10804-011-9126-y

Heckhausen, J., & Brim, O. G. (1997). Perceived problems for self and others: Self-protection by social downgrading throughout adulthood. *Psychology and Aging, 12*, 610–619. Retrieved from http://www.ncbi.nlm.nih.gov/pubmed/9416630

Henry, N. J. M., Berg, C. A., Smith, T. W., & Florsheim, P. (2007). Positive and negative characteristics of marital interaction and their association with marital satisfaction in middle-aged and older couples. *Psychology and Aging, 22*, 428–441.

Heybroek, L., Haynes, M., & Baxter, J., D. (2015). Life satisfaction and retirement in Australia: A longitudinal approach. *Work, Aging and Retirement, 1*, 166–180. doi:10.1093/workar/wav006

Hinterlong, J. E., Morrow-Howell, N., & Rozario, P. A. (2007). Productive engagement and late life physical and mental health: Findings from a nationally representative panel study. *Research on Aging, 29*, 348–370. doi:10.1177/0164027507300806

Holden, C. A., Collins, V. R., Handelsman, D. J., Jolley, D., & Pitts, M. (2014). Healthy aging in a cross-sectional study of Australian men: What has sex got to do with it? *The Aging Male, 17*, 25–29. doi:10.3109/13685538.2013.843167

Homan, K. J., & Boyatzis, C. J. (2010). Religiosity, sense of meaning, and health behavior in older adults. *International Journal for the Psychology of Religion, 20*, 173–186. doi:10.1080/10508619.2010.481225

Howe, C., Matthews, L. R., & Heard, R. (2010). Work to retirement: A snapshot of psychological health in a multicultural Australia population. *Work: Journal of Prevention, Assessment & Rehabilitation, 36*, 119–127.

Huang, C.-S. (2013). Undergraduate students' knowledge about aging and attitudes toward older adults in east and west: A socio-economic and cultural exploration. *International Journal of Aging and Human Development, 77*, 59–76. doi:10.2190/AG.77.1.d

Hughes, M. L., Geraci, L., & De Forrest, R. L. (2013). Aging 5 years in 5 minutes: The effect of taking a memory test on older adults' subjective age. *Psychological Science, 24*, 2481–2488. doi:10.1177/0956797613494853

Huo, M., Kim, K., Zarit, S. H., & Fingerman, K. L. (2017). Support grandparents give to their adult grandchildren. *The Journals of Gerontology Series B: Psychological Sciences and Social Sciences, 73*, 1006–1015. doi:10.1093/geronb/gbw208

Huxhold, O., Fiori, K. L., & Windsor, T. D. (2013). The dynamic interplay of social network characteristics, subjective well-being, and health: The costs and benefits of socioemotional selectivity. *Psychology and Aging, 28*, 3–16. doi:10.1037/a0030170

Huyck, M. H., & Gutmann, D. L. (2006). Men and their wives: Why are some married men vulnerable at midlife? In V. H. Bedford & B. Formaniak Turner (Eds.), *Men in relationships: A new look from a life course perspective* (pp. 27–50). New York, NY: Springer.

Hyde, Z. Z., Flicker, L., Hankey, G. J., Almeida, O. P., McCaul, K. A., Chubb, S. A. P. A. P., & Yeap, B. B. (2010). Prevalence of sexual activity and associated factors in men aged 75 to 95 years. *Annals of Internal Medicine, 153*, 693–702. doi:10.7326/0003-4819-153-11-201012070-00002

Ikeda, A., Kawachi, I., Iso, H., Iwasaki, M., Inoue, M., & Tsugane, S. (2013). Social support and cancer incidence and mortality: The JPHC study cohort II. *Cancer Causes & Control, 24*, 847–860. doi:10.1007/s10552-013-0147-7

Jackson, S. L., & Hafemeister, T. L. (2016). Theory-based models enhancing the understanding of four types of elder maltreatment. *International Review of Victimology, 22*, 289–320. doi:10.1177/0269758016630887

James, J. B., & Zarrett, N. (2006). Ego integrity in the lives of older women. *Journal of Adult Development, 13*, 61–75. Retrieved from 10.1007/s10804-006-9003-2

Jenkins, K. R., Pienta, A. M., & Horgas, A. L. (2002). Activity and health-related quality of life in continuing care retirement communities. *Research on Aging, 24*, 124.

Jeste, D. V., & Oswald, A. J. (2014). Individual and societal wisdom: Explaining the paradox of human aging and high well-being. *Psychiatry: Interpersonal and Biological Processes, 4*, 317–330.

Johannesen, M., & LoGiudice, D. (2013). Elder abuse: A systematic review of risk factors in community-dwelling elders. *Age and Ageing, 42*, 292–298. doi:10.1093/ageing/afs195

Johnson, K. J., & Mutchler, J. E. (2014). The emergence of a positive gerontology: From disengagement to social involvement. *The Gerontologist, 54*, 93–100. doi:10.1093/geront/gnt099

Joshi, S., Mooney, S. J., Rundle, A. G., Quinn, J. W., Beard, J. R., & Cerdá, M. (2017). Pathways from neighborhood poverty to depression among older adults. *Health & Place, 43*, 138–143. doi:10.1016/J.HEALTHPLACE.2016.12.003

Kandler, C., Kornadt, A. E., Hagemeyer, B., & Neyer, F. J. (2015). Patterns and sources of personality development in old age. *Journal of Personality and Social Psychology, 109*, 175–191. doi:10.1037/pspp0000028

Kemp, E. A., & Kemp, J. E. (2002). *Older couples: New romances: Finding & keeping love in later life.* Berkeley, CA: Celestial Arts.

Keyes, C. L. M., & Reitzes, D. C. (2007). The role of religious identity in the mental health of older working and retired adults. *Aging & Mental Health, 11*, 434–443. doi:10.1080/13607860601086371

Kim, J. E., & Moen, P. (2001). Is retirement good or bad for subjective well-being? *Current Directions in Psychological Science, 10*, 83–86. doi:10.1111/1467-8721.00121

Kim, J. E., & Moen, P. (2002). Retirement transitions, gender, and psychological well-being: A life-course, ecological model. *Journals of Gerontology Series B: Psychological Sciences and Social Sciences, 3*, P212–P222.

King, A. C., Salvo, D., Banda, J. A., Ahn, D. K., Chapman, J. E., . . . Frank, L. D. (2017). Preserving older adults' routine outdoor activities in contrasting neighborhood environments through a physical activity intervention. *Preventive Medicine, 96*, 87–93. doi:10.1016/J.YPMED.2016.12.049

King, D. B., Cappeliez, P., Canham, S. L., & O'Rourke, N. (2018). Functions of reminiscence in later life: Predicting change in the physical and mental health of older adults over time. *Aging & Mental Health*. Advance online publication. doi:10.1080/13607863.2017.1396581

King, V., & Scott, M. E. (2005). A comparison of cohabiting relationships among older and younger adults. *Journal of Marriage & Family, 67*, 271–285.

Ko, K. J., Berg, C. A., Butner, J., Uchino, B. N., & Smith, T. W. (2007). Profiles of successful aging in middle-aged and older adult married couples. *Psychology and Aging, 22*, 705–718.

Kornadt, A. E., Hess, T. M., Voss, P., & Rothermund, K. (2018). Subjective age across the life span: A differentiated, longitudinal approach. *Journals of Gerontology Series B: Psychological Sciences and Social Sciences, 73*, 767–777 . doi:10.1093/geronb/gbw072

Kornadt, A. E., & Rothermund, K. (2012). Internalization of age stereotypes into the self-concept via future self-views: A general model and domain-specific differences. *Psychology and Aging, 27*, 164–172. doi:10.1037/a0025110

Korte, J., Drossaert, C. H. C., Westerhof, G. J., & Bohlmeijer, E. T. (2014). Life review in groups? An explorative analysis of social processes that facilitate or hinder the effectiveness of life review. *Aging & Mental Health, 18*, 376–384. doi:10.1080/13607863.2013.837140

Kotter-Grühn, D., Kornadt, A. E., & Stephan, Y. (2016). Looking beyond chronological age: Current knowledge and future directions in the study of subjective age. *Gerontology, 62*, 86–93. doi:10.1159/000438671

Krause, N. (2005). God-mediated control and psychological well-being in late life. *Research on Aging, 27*, 136–164. doi:10.1177/0164027504270475

Krause, N. (2007). Longitudinal study of social support and meaning in life. *Psychology and Aging, 22*, 456–469. doi:10.1037/0882-7974.22.3.456

Kulik, L. (2002). Marital equality and the quality of long-term marriage in later life. *Ageing & Society, 22*, 459.

Lachs, M. S., & Han, S. D. (2015). Age-associated financial vulnerability: An emerging public health issue. *Annals of Internal Medicine, 163*, 877. doi:10.7326/M15-0882

Lang, F. R., Featherman, D. L., & Nesselroade, J. R. (1997). Social self-efficacy and short-term variability in social relationships: The MacArthur successful aging studies. *Psychology and Aging, 12*, 657–666.

Lang, F. R., & Fingerman, K. L. (2004). *Growing together: Personal relationships across the lifespan*. New York, NY: Cambridge University Press.

Laumann, E. O., Leitsch, S. A., & Waite, L. J. (2008). Elder mistreatment in the United States: Prevalence estimates from a nationally representative study. *Journals of Gerontology Series B: Psychological Sciences and Social Sciences, 63*, S248–S254.

Lawrence, A. R., & Schigelone, A. R. S. (2002). Reciprocity beyond dyadic relationships: Aging-related communal coping. *Research on Aging, 24*, 684–704. doi:10.1177/016402702237187

Lee, D. M., Nazroo, J., O'Connor, D. B., Blake, M., & Pendleton, N. (2016). Sexual health and well-being among older men and women in England: Findings from the English Longitudinal Study of Ageing. *Archives of Sexual Behavior, 45*, 133–144. doi:10.1007/s10508-014-0465-1

Lee, E. K. O. (2007). Religion and spirituality as predictors of well-being among Chinese American and Korean American older adults. *Journal of Religion, Spirituality & Aging, 19*, 77–100. doi:10.1300/J496v19n03_06

Lee, E. K. O., & Sharpe, T. (2007). Understanding religious/spiritual coping and support resources among African American older adults: A mixed-method approach. *Journal of Religion, Spirituality & Aging, 19*, 55–75. doi:10.1300/J496v19n03_05

Lee, J. E., Zarit, S. H., Rovine, M. J., Birditt, K. S., & Fingerman, K. L. (2011). Middle-aged couples' exchanges of support with aging parents: Patterns and association with marital satisfaction. *Gerontology, 58*, 88–96. doi:10.1159/000324512

Lee, S., & Shaw, L. (2008). *From work to retirement: Tracking changes in women's poverty status*. Washington, DC: AARP. Retrieved from http://www.aarp.org/research/assistance/lowincome/inb156_poverty.html

Levin, J. S., & Taylor, R. J. (1994). Race and gender differences in religiosity among older adults: Findings from four national surveys. *Journal of Gerontology, 49*, S137.

Li, T., Fok, H. K., & Fung, H. H. (2011). Is reciprocity always beneficial? Age differences in the association between support balance and life satisfaction. *Aging & Mental Health, 15*, 541–547. doi:10.1080/13607863.2010.551340

Lin, I.-F. (2008). Consequences of parental divorce for adult children's support of their frail parents. *Journal of Marriage & Family, 70*, 113–128. doi:10.1111/j.1741-3737.2007.00465.x

Litwin, H. (2003). Social predictors of physical activity in later life: The contribution of social-network type. *Journal of Aging and Physical Activity, 11*, 389–406.

Lowenstein, A., & Doron, I. (2008). Times of transition: Elder abuse and neglect in Israel. *Journal of Elder Abuse & Neglect, 20*, 181–206.

Lucas, R. E., & Donnellan, M. B. (2011). Personality development across the life span: Longitudinal analyses with a national sample from Germany. *Journal of Personality & Social Psychology, 101*, 847–861. doi:10.1037/a0024298

Luchetti, M., Terracciano, A., Stephan, Y., & Sutin, A. R. (2015). Personality and cognitive decline in older adults: Data from a longitudinal sample and meta-analysis. *Journals of Gerontology Series B: Psychological Sciences and Social Sciences, 71*, 591–601. doi:10.1093/geronb/gbu184

Luo, B., Zhou, K., Jin, E. J., Newman, A., & Liang, J. (2013). Ageism among college students: A comparative study between U.S. and China. *Journal of Cross-Cultural Gerontology, 28*, 49–63. doi:10.1007/s10823-013-9186-5

Madero-Cabib, I., & Fasang, A. E. (2016). Gendered work–family life courses and financial well-being in retirement. *Advances in Life Course Research, 27*, 43–60. doi:10.1016/J.ALCR.2015.11.003

Markus, H. R., & Kitayama, S. (2010). Cultures and selves: A cycle of mutual constitution. *Perspectives on Psychological Science, 5*, 420–430. doi:10.1177/1745691610375557

Marsh, H. W., Nagengast, B., & Morin, A. J. S. (2012). Measurement invariance of big-five factors over the life span: ESEM tests of gender, age, plasticity, maturity, and La Dolce Vita effects. *Developmental Psychology, 49*, 1194–1218. doi:10.1037/a002691310.1037/a0026913.supp

McAuliffe, L., Bauer, M., & Nay, R. (2007). Barriers to the expression of sexuality in the older person: The role of the health professional. *International Journal of Older People Nursing, 2*, 69–75.

McBride, D. E., & Parry, J. A. (2016). *Women's rights in the USA: Policy debates and gender roles*. New York, NY: Routledge

McCoy, A., Rauer, A., & Sabey, A. (2017). The meta marriage: Links between older couples' relationship narratives and marital satisfaction. *Family Process, 56*, 900–914. doi:10.1111/famp.12217

McCrae, R. R., Terracciano, A., & The Personality Profiles of Cultures Project. (2005). Universal features of personality traits from the observer's perspective: Data from 50 cultures. *Journal of Personality and Social Psychology, 88*, 547–561.

McDonald, L., & Robb, A. L. (2004). The economic legacy of divorce and separation for women in old age. *Canadian Journal on Aging, 23*, S83–S97.

McLaughlin, D., Adams, J. O. N., Vagenas, D., & Dobson, A. (2011). Factors which enhance or inhibit social support: A mixed-methods analysis of social networks in older women. *Ageing & Society, 31*, 18–33. doi:10.1017/s0144686x10000668

Meier, L. L., Orth, U., Denissen, J. J. A., & Kühnel, A. (2011). Age differences in instability, contingency, and level of self-esteem across the life span. *Journal of Research in Personality, 45*, 604–612. doi:10.1016/j.jrp.2011.08.008

Melchiorre, M. G., Penhale, B., & Lamura, G. (2014). Understanding elder abuse in Italy: Perception and prevalence, types and risk factors from a review of the literature. *Educational Gerontology, 40*, 909–931. doi:10.1080/03601277.2014.912839

Menec, V. H., Shooshtari, S., Nowicki, S., & Fournier, S. (2010). Does the relationship between neighborhood socioeconomic status and health outcomes persist into very old age? A population-based study. *Journal of Aging & Health, 22*, 27–47. doi:10.1177/0898264309349029

Mock, S. E., & Eibach, R. P. (2011). Aging attitudes moderate the effect of subjective age on psychological well-being: Evidence from a 10-year longitudinal study. *Psychology and Aging, 26*, 979–986.

Morin, R., & Fry, R. (2012). *More Americans worry about financing retirement*. Retrieved from http://www.pewsocialtrends .org/2012/10/22/more-americans-worry- about-financing-retirement/

Mortimore, E., Haselow, D., Dolan, M., Hawkes, W. G., Langenberg, P., Zimmerman, S., & Magaziner, J. (2008). Amount of social contact and hip fracture mortality. *Journal of the American Geriatrics Society, 56*, 1069–1074.

Mõttus, R., Luciano, M., Starr, J. M., Pollard, M. C., & Deary. I. J. (2013). Personality traits and inflammation in men and women in their early 70s: The Lothian birth cohort 1936 study of healthy aging. *Psychosomatic Medicine, 75*, 11–19. doi:10.1097/ PSY.0b013e31827576cc

Muratore, A. M., & Earl, J. K. (2015). Improving retirement outcomes: The role of resources, pre-retirement planning and transition characteristics. *Ageing and Society, 35*, 2100–2140. doi:10.1017/S0144686X14000841

Myers, S. A., & Kennedy-Lightsey, C. D. (2014). Communication in adult sibling relationships. In L. H. Turner & R. West (Eds.), *The SAGE handbook of family communication* (p. 504). Thousand Oaks, CA: Sage.

Newman, D. A., Jeon, G., & Hulin, C. L. (2012). *Retirement attitudes: Considering etiology, measurement, attitude-behavior relationships, and attitudinal ambivalence* (M. Wang, Ed.). Oxford, UK: Oxford University Press. doi:10.1093/oxfordhb/ 9780199746521.013.0090

Nguyen, A. W., Chatters, L. M., Taylor, R. J., & Mouzon, D. M. (2016). Social support from family and friends and subjective well-being of older African Americans. *Journal of Happiness Studies, 17*, 959–979. doi:10.1007/ s10902-015-9626-8

Nicolosi, A., Buvat, J., Glasser, D. B., Hartmann, U., Laumann & E. W., & Gingell, C. (2006). Sexual behaviour, sexual dysfunctions and related help seeking patterns in middle-aged and elderly Europeans: The global study of sexual attitudes and behaviors. *World Journal of Urology, 24*, 423–428.

Nilsson, C. J., Lund, R., & Avlund, K. (2008). Cohabitation status and onset of disability among older Danes. *Journal of Aging & Health, 20*, 235–253.

O'Brien, E. L., Hess, T. M., Kornadt, A. E., Rothermund, K., Fung, H., & Voss, P. (2017). Context influences on the subjective experience of aging: The impact of culture and domains of functioning. *The Gerontologist, 57*(Suppl. 2), S127–S137. doi:10.1093/geront/gnx015

O'Rourke, N., Cappeliez, P., & Claxton, A. (2011). Functions of reminiscence and the psychological well-being of young-old and older adults over time. *Aging & Mental Health, 15*, 272–281. doi:10.1080/13607861003713281

O'Rourke, N., King, D. B., & Cappeliez, P. (2017). Reminiscence functions over time: Consistency of self functions and variation of prosocial functions. *Memory, 25*, 403–411. doi:10.1080/09658211.2016.1179331

Orth, U. (2017). The lifespan development of self-esteem. In J. Specht (Ed.), *Personality development across the lifespan* (pp. 181– 195). New York, NY: Elsevier. doi:10.1016/ B978-0-12-804674-6.00012-0

Ortman, J. M., Velkoff, V. A., & Hogan, H. (2014). *An aging nation: The older population in the United States*. Retrieved from https://www .census.gov/prod/2014pubs/p25-1140.pdf

Palacios-Ceña, D., Carrasco-Garrido, P., Hernández-Barrera, V., Alonso-Blanco, C., Jiménez-Garcia, R., & Fernández-de-las-Peñas, C. (2012). Sexual behaviors among older adults in Spain: Results from a population-based national sexual health survey. *Journal of Sexual Medicine, 9*, 121–129. doi:10.1111/j.1743-6109.2011.02511.x

Pew Forum on Religious and Public Life. (2008). U.S. religious landscape survey. *Religious affiliation: Diverse and dynamic*. Washington, DC: Author.

Pew Research Center. (2009). *Growing old in America: Expectations vs. reality*. Retrieved from http://www.pewsocialtrends. org/2009/06/29/growing-old-in-america-expectations-vs-reality/

Pew Research Center. (2016). *The gender gap in religion around the world*. Retrieved from http://www.pewforum.org/2016/03/22/the-gender-gap-in-religion-around-the-world/

Pickering, C. E. Z., Nurenberg, K., & Schiamberg, L. (2017). Recognizing and responding to the "toxic" work environment: Worker safety, patient safety, and abuse/neglect in nursing homes. *Qualitative Health Research, 27*, 1870–1881. doi:10.1177/1049732317723889

Pinquart, M., & Forstmeier, S. (2012). Effects of reminiscence interventions on psychosocial outcomes: A meta-analysis. *Aging & Mental Health, 16*, 541–558. doi:10.1080/13607863.2 011.651434

Pinquart, M., & Schindler, I. (2007). Changes of life satisfaction in the transition to retirement: A latent-class approach. *Psychology & Aging, 22*, 442–455. doi:10.1037/0882-7974.22.3.442

Podnieks, E., Anetzberger, G. J., Wilson, S. J., Teaster, P. B., & Wangmo, T. (2010). WorldView environmental scan on elder abuse. *Journal of Elder Abuse & Neglect, 22*, 164–179. doi:10.1080/08946560903445974

Postigo, J. M. L., & Honrubia, R. L. (2010). The co-residence of elderly people with their children and grandchildren. *Educational Gerontology, 36*, 330–349. doi:10.1080/03601270903212351

Prebble, S. C., Addis, D. R., & Tippett, L. J. (2013). Autobiographical memory and sense of self. *Psychological Bulletin, 139*, 815–840. doi:10.1037/a0030146

Pushkar, D., Chaikelson, J., Conway, M., Etezadi, J., Giannopoulus, C., Li, K., & Wrosch, C. (2010). Testing continuity and activity variables as predictors of positive and negative affect in retirement. *Journals of Gerontology Series B: Psychological Sciences and Social Sciences, 65B*, 42–49. doi:10.1093/geronb/gbp079

Quine, S., Wells, Y., de Vaus, D., & Kendig, H. (2007). When choice in retirement decisions is missing: Qualitative and quantitative findings of impact on well-being. *Australasian Journal on Ageing, 26*, 173–179.

Rasheed, M. N., & Rasheed, J. M. (2003). Rural African American older adults and the Black helping tradition. *Journal of Gerontological Social Work, 41*, 137–150.

Ready, R. E., Carvalho, J. O., & Åkerstedt, A. M. (2012). Evaluative organization of the self-concept in younger, midlife, and older adults. *Research on Aging, 34*, 56–79. doi:10.1177/0164027511415244

Reed, T. D., & Neville, H. A. (2014). The influence of religiosity and spirituality on psychological well-being among Black women. *Journal of Black Psychology, 40*, 384–401. doi:10.1177/0095798413490956

Reitz, A. K., & Staudinger, U. M. (2017). Getting older, getting better? Toward understanding positive personality development across adulthood. In J. Specht (Ed.), *Personality development across the lifespan* (pp. 219– 241). New York, NY: Elsevier. doi:10.1016/ B978-0-12-804674-6.00014-4

Reitzes, D. C., & Mutran, E. J. (2004). The transition to retirement: Stages and factors that influence retirement adjustment. *International Journal of Aging & Human Development, 59*, 63–84.

Richardson, V., & Kilty, K. M. (1991). Adjustment to retirement: Continuity vs. discontinuity. *International Journal of Aging & Human Development, 33*, 151–169.

Roberto, K. A. (2016). The complexities of elder abuse. *American Psychologist, 71*, 302–311. doi:10.1037/a0040259

Robles, T. F., Menkin, J. A., Robles, T. F., & Menkin, J. A. (2015). Social relationships and health in older adulthood. In R. A. Scott & M. C. Buchmann (Eds.), *Emerging trends in the social and behavioral sciences* (pp. 1–15). Hoboken, NJ: John Wiley. doi:10.1002/9781118900772.etrds0310

Ronneberg, C. R., Miller, E. A., Dugan, E., & Porell, F. (2016). The protective effects of religiosity on depression: A 2-year prospective study. *The Gerontologist, 56*, 421–431. doi:10.1093/ geront/gnu073

Salguero, A., Martinez-Garcia, R., Molinero, O., & Márquez, S. (2011). Physical activity, quality of life and symptoms of depression in community-dwelling and institutionalized older adults. *Archives of Gerontology and Geriatrics, 53*, 152–157. doi:10.1016/j .archger.2010.10.005

Samanez-Larkin, G. R., & Knutson, B. (2015). Decision making in the ageing brain: Changes in affective and motivational circuits. *Nature Reviews: Neuroscience, 16*, 278–289. doi:10.1038/nrn3917

Sanford, A. M., Orrell, M., Tolson, D., Abbatecola, A. M., Arai, H., . . . Vellas, B. (2015). An international definition for "nursing home." *Journal of the American Medical Directors Association, 16*, 181–184. doi:10.1016/j .jamda.2014.12.013

Scafato, E., Galluzzo, L., Gandin, C., Ghirini, S., Baldereschi, M., . . . Farchi, G. (2008). Marital and cohabitation status as predictors of mortality: A 10-year follow-up of an Italian elderly cohort. *Social Science & Medicine, 67*, 1456–1464.

Schafer, M. H., & Koltai, J. (2015). Does embeddedness protect? Personal network density and vulnerability to mistreatment among older American adults. *Journals of Gerontology Series B: Psychological Sciences and Social Sciences, 70*, 597–606.

Scherger, S., Nazroo, J., & Higgs, P. (2011). Leisure activities and retirement: Do structures of inequality change in old age? *Ageing & Society, 31*, 146–172. doi:10.1017/ s0144686x10000577

Segel-Karpas, D., Ayalon, L., & Lachman, M. E. (2018). Loneliness and depressive symptoms: The moderating role of the transition into retirement. *Aging & Mental Health, 22,* 135–140. doi:10.1080/13607863.2016.1226770

Seiger Cronfalk, B., Ternestedt, B.-M., & Norberg, A. (2017). Being a close family member of a person with dementia living in a nursing home. *Journal of Clinical Nursing, 26,* 3519–3528. doi:10.1111/jocn.13718

Shaw, B. A. (2005). Anticipated support from neighbors and physical functioning during later life. *Research on Aging, 27,* 503–525. doi:10.1177/0164027505277884

Shaw, B. A., Krause, N., Liang, J., & Bennett, J. (2007). Tracking changes in social relations throughout late life. *Journals of Gerontology Series B: Psychological Sciences & Social Sciences, 62B,* S90–S99.

Sheehan, N. W., & Petrovic, K. (2008). Grandparents and their adult grandchildren: Recurring themes from the literature. *Marriage & Family Review, 44,* 99–124.

Sheldon, K. M., & Kasser, T. (2001). Getting older, getting better? Personal strivings and psychological maturity across the life span. *Developmental Psychology, 37,* 491–501.

Shelton, A. (2007). *Social Security: Basic data.* Washington, DC: AARP.

Shelton, A. (2013). *Social Security: Still lifting many older Americans out of poverty.* Retrieved from http://blog.aarp.org/2013/07/01/social-security-still-lifting-many-older-americans-out-of-poverty/

Shinan-Altman, S., & Werner, P. (2018). Subjective age and its correlates among middle-aged and older adults. *International Journal of Aging and Human Development.* Advance online publication. doi:10.1177/0091415017752941

Siguaw, J. A., Sheng, X., & Simpson, P. M. (2018). Biopsychosocial and retirement factors influencing satisfaction with life. *International Journal of Aging and Human Development.* Advance online publication. doi:10.1177/0091415016685833

Simpson, D. B., Cloud, D. S., Newman, J. L., & Fuqua, D. R. (2008). Sex and gender differences in religiousness and spirituality. *Journal of Psychology & Theology, 36,* 42–52.

Sims, T., Hogan, C. L., & Carstensen, L. L. (2015). Selectivity as an emotion regulation strategy: Lessons from older adults. *Current Opinion in Psychology, 3,* 80–84. doi:10.1016/j.copsyc.2015.02.012

Smith, J., & Freund, A. M. (2002). The dynamics of possible selves in old age. *Journals of Gerontology Series B: Psychological & Social Sciences, 57B,* P492.

Social Security Administration. (2007). *Social Security: A brief history.* Washington, DC: Author. Retrieved from http://www.ssa.gov/history/pdf/2007historybooklet.pdf

Social Security Administration. (2008). *The future of Social Security.* Washington, DC: Author.

Social Security Administration. (2014). *Social Security basic facts.* Retrieved from http://www.ssa.gov/news/press/basicfact.html

Social Security Administration. (2015a). *Social Security is important to African Americans.* Retrieved from http://www.ssa.gov/news/press/factsheets/africanamer.htm

Social Security Administration. (2015b). *Social Security is important to women.* Retrieved April 8, 2015, from http://www.ssa.gov/news/press/factsheets/women-alt.pdf

Social Security Administration. (2016). *Fact sheet—Social Security: Social Security is important to women.* Retrieved April 22, 2018, from https://www.ssa.gov/news/press/factsheets/ss-customer/women-ret.pdf

Social Security Administration. (2018). *Life expectancy.* Retrieved from http://www.ssa.gov/planners/lifeexpectancy.html

Sooryanarayana, R., Choo, W. Y., & Hairi, N. N. (2013). A review on the prevalence and measurement of elder abuse in the community. *Trauma, Violence & Abuse, 14,* 316–325. doi:10.1177/1524838013495963

Soto, C. J. (2015). Is happiness good for your personality? Concurrent and prospective relations of the Big Five with subjective well-being. *Journal of Personality, 83,* 45–55. doi:10.1111/jopy.12081

Spitze, G. D., & Trent, K. (2018). Changes in individual sibling relationships in response to life events. *Journal of Family Issues, 39,* 503–526. doi:10.1177/0192513X16653431

Spreng, R. N., Cassidy, B. N., Darboh, B. S., DuPre, E., Lockrow, A. W., Setton, R., & Turner, G. R. (2017). Financial exploitation is associated with structural and functional brain differences in healthy older adults. *Journals of Gerontology Series A, 72,* 1365–1368. doi:10.1093/gerona/glx051

Spreng, R. N., Karlawish, J., & Marson, D. C. (2016). Cognitive, social, and neural determinants of diminished decision-making and financial exploitation risk in aging and dementia: A review and new model. *Journal of Elder Abuse & Neglect, 28,* 320–344. doi:10.1080/08946566.2016.1237918

Stephan, Y., Caudroit, J., Jaconelli, A., & Terracciano, A. (2014). Subjective age and cognitive functioning: a 10-year prospective study. *American Journal of Geriatric Psychiatry, 22,* 1180–1187. https://doi.org/10.1016/j.jagp.2013.03.007

Stephan, Y., Chalabaev, A., Kotter-Grühn, D., & Jaconelli, A. (2013). "Feeling younger, being stronger": An experimental study of subjective age and physical functioning among older adults. *Journals of Gerontology Series B: Psychological Sciences and Social Sciences, 68,* 1–7. doi:10.1093/geronb/gbs037

Stephan, Y., Sutin, A. R., Canada, B., & Terracciano, A. (2017). Personality and frailty: Evidence from four samples. *Journal of Research in Personality, 66,* 46–53. doi:10.1016/J.JRP.2016.12.006

Stepler, R. (2016). *Smaller share of women ages 65 and older are living alone | Pew Research Center.* Retrieved April 21, 2018, from http://www.pewsocialtrends.org/2016/02/18/smaller-share-of-women-ages-65-and-older-are-living-alone/

Stepler, R. (2017). *Number of cohabiting Americans rises, especially among those 50+ | Pew Research Center.* Retrieved March 16, 2018, from http://www.pewresearch.org/fact-tank/2017/04/06/number-of-u-s-adults-cohabiting-with-a-partner-continues-to-rise-especially-among-those-50-and-older/

Story, T. N., Berg, C. A., Smith, T. W., Beveridge, R., Henry, N. J. M., & Pearce, G. (2007). Age, marital satisfaction, and optimism as predictors of positive sentiment override in middle-aged and older married couples. *Psychology and Aging, 22,* 719–727.

Stroope, S., Cohen, I. F. A., Tom, J. C., Franzen, A. B., Valasik, M. A., & Markides, K. S. (2017). Neighborhood perception and self-rated health among Mexican American older adults. *Geriatrics & Gerontology International, 17,* 2559–2564. doi:10.1111/ggi.13089

Syme, M. L., Klonoff, E. A., Macera, C. A., & Brodine, S. K. (2013). Predicting sexual decline and dissatisfaction among older adults: The role of partnered and individual physical and mental health factors. *Journals of Gerontology Series B: Psychological Sciences and Social Sciences, 68,* 323–332. doi:10.1093/geronb/gbs087

Tan, S. C., & Barber, S. J. (2018). Confucian values as a buffer against age-based stereotype threat for Chinese older adults. *Journals of Gerontology Series B: Psychological Sciences and Social Sciences.* Advance online publication. doi:10.1093/geronb/gby049

Tan, R. S. (2011). *Aging men's health: A case-based approach.* New York, NY: Thieme.

Tang, F. (2008). Socioeconomic disparities in voluntary organization involvement among older adults. *Nonprofit & Voluntary Sector Quarterly, 37,* 57–75.

Taylor, A., & Gosney, M. A. (2011). Sexuality in older age: Essential considerations for healthcare professionals. *Age and Ageing, 40,* 538–543. doi:10.1093/ageing/afr049

Taylor, S. E. (2011). Social support: A review. In H. S. Friedman (Ed.), *The Oxford handbook of health psychology* (p. 936). Oxford, UK: Oxford University Press.

Thiele, D. M., & Whelan, T. A. (2008). The relationship between grandparent satisfaction, meaning, and generativity. *International Journal of Aging & Human Development, 66,* 21–48.

Thomas, P. A. (2010). Is it better to give or to receive? Social support and the well-being of older adults. *The Journals of Gerontology Series B: Psychological Sciences and Social Sciences, 65B,* 351–357. doi:10.1093/geronb/gbp113

Thompson, W. K., Charo, L., Vahia, I. V, Depp, C., Allison, M., & Jeste, D. V. (2011). Association between higher levels of sexual function, activity, and satisfaction and self-rated successful aging in older postmenopausal women. *Journal of the American Geriatrics Society, 59,* 1503–1508. doi:10.1111/j.1532-5415.2011.03495.x

Uddin, L. Q. (2015). Salience processing and insular cortical function and dysfunction. *Nature Reviews Neuroscience, 16,* 55–61. doi:10.1038/nrn3857

U.S. Bureau of the Census. (2017a). Age and sex of all people, family members and unrelated individuals iterated by income-to-poverty ratio and race. Retrieved April 22, 2018, from https://www.census.gov/data/tables/time-series/demo/income-poverty/cps-pov/pov-34.html

U.S. Bureau of the Census. (2017b). Selected characteristics of people 15 years and over, by total money income, work experience, race, Hispanic origin, and sex. Retrieved April 22, 2018, from https://www.census.gov/data/tables/time-series/demo/income-poverty/cps-pinc/pinc-01.html

U.S. Department of Health and Human Services. (2018). Federal Register: Annual update of the HHS Poverty Guidelines 2018. Retrieved April 22, 2018, from https://www.federalregister.gov/documents/2018/01/18/2018-00814/annual-update-of-the-hhs-poverty-guidelines

U.S. Federal Reserve. (2018). *Report on the economic well-being of U.S. households in 2016—May 2017.* Retrieved April 20, 2018, from https://www.federalreserve.gov/publications/2017-economic-well-being-of-us-households-in-2016-retirement.htm

Uchino, B. N. (2006). Social support and health: A review of physiological processes potentially underlying links to disease outcomes. *Journal of Behavioral Medicine, 29,* 377–387. doi:10.1007/s10865-006-9056-5

Vaillant, G. E. (1994). "Successful aging" and psychosocial well-being: Evidence from a 45-year study. In E. H. Thompson Jr. (Ed.), *Older men's lives* (pp. 22–41). Thousand Oaks, CA: Sage.

Vaillant, G. E. (2004). Positive aging. In P. A. Linley & S. Joseph (Eds.), *Positive psychology in practice* (pp. 561–578). Hoboken, NJ: John Wiley.

van Bilsen, P. M. A., Hamers, J. P. H., Groot, W., & Spreeuwenberg, C. (2008). Sheltered housing compared to independent housing in the community. *Scandinavian Journal of Caring Sciences, 22,* 265–274. doi:10.1111/j.1471-6712.2007.00529.x

Van Cauwenberg, J., Cerin, E., Timperio, A., Salmon, J., Deforche, B., & Veitch, J. (2017). Is the association between park proximity and recreational physical activity among mid-older aged adults moderated by park quality and neighborhood conditions? *International Journal of Environmental Research and Public Health, 14,* 192. doi:10.3390/ijerph14020192

van Solinge, H., & Henkens, K. (2008). Adjustment to and satisfaction with retirement: Two of a kind? *Psychology and Aging, 23,* 422–434.

Verma, S. (2003). *Retirement coverage of women and minorities: Analysis from SIPP 1998 data.* Washington, DC: AARP. Retrieved from http://www.aarp.org/research/financial/pensions/aresearch-import-350-DD92.html

Waldinger, R. J., & Schulz, M. S. (2010). What's love got to do with it? Social functioning, perceived health, and daily happiness in married octogenarians. *Psychology and Aging, 25,* 422–431. doi:10.1037/a0019087

Wang, M. (2007). Profiling retirees in the retirement transition and adjustment process: Examining the longitudinal change patterns of retirees' psychological well-being. *Journal of Applied Psychology, 92,* 455–474. Retrieved from mw@pdx.edu

Wang, M., Henkens, K., & van Solinge, H. (2011). A review of theoretical and empirical advancements. *The American Psychologist, 66,* 204–213. doi:10.1037/a0022414

Webster, J. D., Bohlmeijer, E. T., & Westerhof, G. J. (2010). Mapping the future of reminiscence: A conceptual guide for research and practice. *Research on Aging, 32,* 527–564. doi:10.1177/0164027510364122

Weiss, A., Costa, P. T., Jr., Karuza, J., Duberstein, P. R., Friedman, B., & McCrae, R. R. (2005). Cross-sectional age differences in personality among Medicare patients aged 65 to 100. *Psychology and Aging, 20,* 182–185. doi:10.1037/0882-7974.20.1.182

Weiss, D., & Lang, F. R. (2012). "They" are old but "I" feel younger: Age-group dissociation as a self-protective strategy in old age. *Psychology and Aging, 27,* 153–163. doi:10.1037/a0024887

Westerhof, G. J. (2015). Life review and life-story work. In S. K. Whitbourne (Ed.), *The encyclopedia of adulthood and aging* (pp. 1–5). Hoboken, NJ: John Wiley. doi:10.1002/9781118521373.wbeaa209

Westerhof, G. J., & Bohlmeijer, E. T. (2014). Celebrating fifty years of research and applications in reminiscence and life review: State of the art and new directions. *Journal of Aging Studies, 29,* 107–114. doi:10.1016/j.jaging.2014.02.003

Westerhof, G. J., Bohlmeijer, E., & Webster, J. D. (2010). Reminiscence and mental health: A review of recent progress in theory, research and interventions. *Ageing & Society, 30,* 697–721.

Willson, A. E., & Etherington, N. (2016). Poverty, income and wealth across the life course. In M. Harrington Meyer & E. A. Daniele (Eds.), *Gerontology: Changes, challenges, and solutions* (pp. 137–160). Santa Barbara, CA: ABC-CLIO.

Windsor, T. D., Anstey, K. J., & Rodgers, B. (2008). Volunteering and psychological well-being among young-old adults: How much is too much? *The Gerontologist, 48,* 59–70.

Wink, P., & Dillon, M. (2002). Spiritual development across the adult life course: Findings from a longitudinal study. *Journal of Adult Development, 9,* 79–94. doi:10.1023/A:1013833419122

Wink, P., Dillon, M., & Prettyman, A. (2007). Religion as moderator of the sense of control-health connection: Gender differences. *Journal of Religion, Spirituality & Aging, 19,* 21–41.

Wöhrmann, A. M., Fasbender, U., & Deller, J. (2017). Does more respect from leaders postpone the desire to retire? Understanding the mechanisms of retirement decision-making. *Frontiers in Psychology, 8,* 1400. doi:10.3389/fpsyg.2017.01400

Wortman, J., Lucas, R. E., & Donnellan, M. B. (2012). Stability and change in the Big Five personality domains: Evidence from a longitudinal study of Australians. *Psychology and Aging, 27,* 867–874. doi:10.1037/a002932210.1037/a0029322.supp

Wright, M. R., & Brown, S. L. (2017). Psychological well-being among older adults: The role of partnership status. *Journal of Marriage and Family, 79,* 833–849. doi:10.1111/jomf.12375

Wrzus, C., Hänel, M., Wagner, J., & Neyer, F. J. (2013). Social network changes and life events across the life span: A meta-analysis. *Psychological Bulletin, 139,* 53–80. doi:10.1037/a0028601

Wu, Y. T., Prina, A. M., Jones, A. P., Barnes, L. E., Matthews, F. E., Brayne, C., & Medical Research Council Cognitive Function and Ageing Study. (2015). Community environment, cognitive impairment and dementia in later life: Results from the cognitive function and ageing study. *Age and Ageing, 44,* 1005–1011. doi:10.1093/ageing/afv137

Wu, Z., & Schimmele, C. M. (2007). Uncoupling in late life. *Generations, 31,* 41–46.

Yeung, D. Y., & Zhou, X. (2017). Planning for retirement: Longitudinal effect on retirement resources and post-retirement well-being. *Frontiers in Psychology, 8,* 1300. doi:10.3389/fpsyg.2017.01300

Ysseldyk, R., Haslam, S. A., & Haslam, C. (2013). Abide with me: Religious group identification among older adults promotes health and well-being by maintaining multiple group memberships. *Aging & Mental Health, 17,* 869–879. doi:10.1080/13607863.2013.799120

Zacher, H., & Kirby, G. (2015). Remaining time. In S. K. Whitbourne (Ed.), *The encyclopedia of adulthood and aging* (pp. 1–5). Hoboken, NJ: John Wiley. doi:10.1002/9781118521373.wbeaa059

Zhan, M., & Pandey, S. (2002). Postsecondary education and the well-being of women in retirement. *Social Work Research, 26,* 171.

Zhang, X., Xing, C., Guan, Y., Song, X., Melloy, R., Wang, F., & Jin, X. (2016). Attitudes toward older adults: A matter of cultural values or personal values? *Psychology and Aging, 31,* 89–100. doi:10.1037/pag0000068

Zimmer, Z., Jagger, C., Chiu, C. T., Ofstedal, M. B., Rojo, F., & Saito, Y. (2016). Spirituality, religiosity, aging and health in global perspective: A review. *SSM—Population Health, 2,* 373–381. doi:10.1016/J.SSMPH.2016.04.009

Chapter 19

Achté, K., Fagerström, R., Pentikäinen, J., & Farberow, N. L. (1989). Themes of death and violence in lullabies of different countries. *OMEGA—Journal of Death and Dying, 20,* 193–204. doi:10.2190/A7YP-TJ3C-M9C1-JY45

Administration on Aging. (2014). *A profile of older Americans: 2014.* Retrieved from http://www.aoa.acl.gov/Aging_Statistics/Profile/index.aspx

Adolfsson, A. (2011). Meta-analysis to obtain a scale of psychological reaction after perinatal loss: Focus on miscarriage. *Psychology Research and Behavior Management, 4,* 29–39. doi:10.2147/PRBM.S17330

Alberts, A., Elkind, D., & Ginsberg, S. (2007). The personal fable and risk-taking in early adolescence. *Journal of Youth & Adolescence, 36,* 71–76.

American Academy of Pediatrics (1992). American Academy of Pediatrics AAP Task Force on Infant Positioning and SIDS: Positioning and SIDS. *Pediatrics, 89,* 1120–1126.

Astuti, R., & Harris, P. (2008). Understanding mortality and the life of the ancestors in rural Madagascar. *Cognitive Science: A Multidisciplinary Journal, 32,* 713–740. doi:10.1080/03640210802066907

Avelin, P., Rådestad, I., Säflund, K., Wredling, R., & Erlandsson, K. (2013). Parental grief and relationships after the loss of a stillborn baby. *Midwifery, 29,* 668–673. doi:10.1016/j.midw.2012.06.007

Bajanowski, T., & Vennemann, M. (2017). Sudden infant death syndrome (SIDS). In M. M. Houck (Ed.), *Forensic pathology* (p. 259). London, UK: Elsevier.

Balk, E. M. (2009). Adolescent development: The backstory to adolescent encounters with death and bereavement. In E. M. Balk & C. Corr (Eds.), *Adolescent encounters with death, bereavement, and coping* (pp. 3–20). New York, NY: Springer.

Ballesteros, C. (2017). Racism might have spared Black and Latino communities from opioid epidemic, drug abuse expert says. *Newsweek*. Retrieved from http://www.newsweek.com/racism-opiod-epidemic-blacks-latinos-trump-704370

Barrett, H. C., & Behne, T. (2005). Children's understanding of death as the cessation of agency: A test using sleep versus death. *Cognition, 96*, 93–108. doi:10.1016/j.cognition.2004.05.004

Bates, A. T., & Kearney, J. A. (2015). Understanding death with limited experience in life: dying children's and adolescents' understanding of their own terminal illness and death. *Current Opinion in Supportive and Palliative Care, 9*, 40–45. doi:10.1097/SPC.0000000000000118

Bender, A., Jox, R. J., Grill, E., Straube, A., & Lulé, D. (2015). Persistent vegetative state and minimally conscious state: A systematic review and meta-analysis of diagnostic procedures. *Deutsches Ärzteblatt International, 112*, 235–242. doi:10.3238/arztebl.2015.0235

Bennett, K. M., Hughes, G. M., & Smith, P. T. O. (2005). Psychological response to later life widowhood: Coping and the effects of gender. *OMEGA—Journal of Death & Dying, 51*, 33–52.

Bergman, N. J. (2015). Proposal for mechanisms of protection of supine sleep against sudden infant death syndrome: An integrated mechanism review. *Pediatric Research, 77*, 10–19. doi:10.1038/pr.2014.140

Bering, J. M., & Bjorklund, D. F. (2004). The natural emergence of reasoning about the afterlife as a developmental regularity. *Developmental Psychology, 40*, 217–233. doi:10.1037/0012-1649.40.2.217

Bettelheim, B. (1977). *The uses of enchantment—The meaning and importance of fairy tales*. New York, NY: Vintage.

Blair, P. S., Sidebotham, P., Berry, P. J., Evans, M., & Fleming, P. J. (2006). Major epidemiological changes in sudden infant death syndrome: A 20-year population-based study in the UK. *Lancet, 367*, 314–319. doi:10.1016/S0140-6736(06)67968-3

Bluebond-Langner, M. (1989). Worlds of dying children and their well siblings. *Death Studies, 13*, 1–16. doi:10.1080/07481188908252274

Bonanno, G. A., Wortman, C. B., & Nesse, R. M. (2004). Prospective patterns of resilience and maladjustment during widowhood. *Psychology and Aging, 19*, 260–271. doi:10.1037/0882-7974.19.2.260

Bonoti, F., Leondari, A., & Mastora, A. (2013). Exploring children's understanding of death: Through drawings and the death concept questionnaire. *Death Studies, 37*, 47–60. doi:10.1080/07481187.2011.623216

Bratt, A. S., Stenström, U., & Rennemark, M. (2018). Exploring the most important negative life events in older adults bereaved of child, spouse, or both. *OMEGA—Journal of Death and Dying, 76*, 227–236. doi:10.1177/0030222816642453

Brenn, T., & Ytterstad, E. (2016). Increased risk of death immediately after losing a spouse: Cause-specific mortality following widowhood in Norway. *Preventive Medicine, 89*, 251–256. doi:10.1016/j.ypmed.2016.06.019

Brent, D. A., Melhem, N. M., Masten, A. S., Porta, G., & Payne, M. W. (2012). Longitudinal effects of parental bereavement on adolescent developmental competence. *Journal of Clinical Child and Adolescent Psychology, 41*, 778–791. doi:10.1080/15374416.2012.717871

Brent, S. B., Lin, C., Speece, M. W., Dong, Q., & Yang, C. (1996). The development of the concept of death among Chinese and U.S. children 3–17 years of age: From binary to "fuzzy" concepts? *OMEGA—Journal of Death and Dying, 33*, 67–83. doi:10.2190/27L7-G7Q1-DY5Q-J9F3

Brison, K. J. (1995). You will never forget: Narrative, bereavement, and worldview among Kwanga women. *Ethos, 23*, 474–488. doi:10.1525/eth.1995.23.4.02a00060

Brisson, C. D., Hsieh, Y.-T., Kim, D., Jin, A. Y., & Andrew, R. D. (2014). Brainstem neurons survive the identical ischemic stress that kills higher neurons: Insight to the persistent vegetative state. *PLoS ONE, 9*, e96585. doi:10.1371/journal.pone.0096585

Buglass, E. (2010). Grief and bereavement theories. *Nursing Standard, 24*, 44–47. Retrieved from http://cat.inist.fr/?aModele=afficheN&cpsidt=22958713

Cacciatore, J. (2010). The unique experiences of women and their families after the death of a baby. *Social Work in Health Care, 49*, 134–148. doi:10.1080/00981380903158078

Candy, B., Holman, A., Leurent, B., Davis, S., & Jones, L. (2011). Hospice care delivered at home, in nursing homes and in dedicated hospice facilities: A systematic review of quantitative and qualitative evidence. *International Journal of Nursing Studies, 48*, 121–133. doi:10.1016/j.ijnurstu.2010.08.003

Cao, H., Mills-Koonce, W. R., Wood, C., & Fine, M. A. (2016). Identity transformation during the transition to parenthood among same-sex couples: An ecological, stress-strategy-adaptation perspective. *Journal of Family Theory & Review, 8*, 30–59. doi:10.1111/jftr.12124

Carlin, R. F., & Moon, R. Y. (2017). Risk factors, protective factors, and current recommendations to reduce sudden infant death syndrome. *JAMA Pediatrics, 171*, 175. doi:10.1001/jamapediatrics.2016.3345

Carr, D. (2004). The desire to date and remarry among older widows and widowers. *Journal of Marriage and Family, 66*, 1051–1068.

Centers for Disease Control and Prevention. (2017). *Data overview | Drug overdose | CDC injury center*. Retrieved April 26, 2018, from https://www.cdc.gov/drugoverdose/data/index.html

Centers for Disease Control and Prevention. (2018). *Opioid overdoses treated in emergency departments | VitalSigns | CDC*. Retrieved April 26, 2018, from https://www.cdc.gov/vitalsigns/opioid-overdoses/index.html

Central Intelligence Agency. (2018). *The world factbook*. Washington, DC: Author.

Chasteen, A. L., & Madey, S. F. (2003). Belief in a just world and the perceived injustice of dying young or old. *OMEGA—Journal of Death and Dying, 47*, 313–326. doi:10.2190/W7H7-TE9E-1FWN-B8XD

Cheek, C. (2010). Passing over: Identity transition in widows. *International Journal of Aging & Human Development, 70*, 345–364. doi:10.2190/AG.70.4.d

Chopik, W. J. (2017). Death across the lifespan: Age differences in death-related thoughts and anxiety. *Death Studies, 41*, 69–77. doi:10.1080/07481187.2016.1206997

Christ, G. H., Siegel, K., & Christ, A. E. (2002). Adolescent grief. *JAMA, 288*, 1269. doi:10.1001/jama.288.10.1269

Cicirelli, V. G. (2002). *Older adults' views on death. Older adults' views on death*. New York, NY: Springer.

Coelho, A., de Brito, M., & Barbosa, A. (2018). Caregiver anticipatory grief. *Current Opinion in Supportive and Palliative Care, 12*, 52–57. doi:10.1097/SPC.0000000000000321

Cohen, R. (1967). *The Kanuri of Bornu*. New York, NY: Holt, Rinehart and Winston.

Cohen-Mansfield, J., Skornick-Bouchbinder, M., & Brill, S. (2017). Trajectories of end of life: A systematic review. *Journals of Gerontology Series B: Psychological Sciences and Social Sciences, 27*, 998. doi:10.1093/geronb/gbx093

Collins, J. W., Papacek, E., Schulte, N. F., & Drolet, A. (2001). Differing postneonatal mortality rates of Mexican-American infants with United-States-born and Mexico-born mothers in Chicago. *Ethnicity & Disease, 11*, 606–613.

Colson, E. R., Willinger, M., Rybin, D., Heeren, T., Smith, L. A., Lister, G., & Corwin, M. J. (2013). Trends and factors associated with infant bed sharing, 1993–2010. *JAMA Pediatrics, 167*, 1032. doi:10.1001/jamapediatrics.2013.2560

Connor, S. R. (2018). *Hospice and palliative care*. New York, NY: Taylor & Francis.

Corr, C. (2010b). Children, development, and encounters with death, bereavement and coping. In E. D. Balk & C. A. Corr (Eds.), *Children's encounters with death, bereavement, and coping* (pp. 3–20). New York, NY: Springer.

Corr, C. A. (2010a). Children's emerging awareness and understanding of loss and death. In E. D. Balk, & C. A. Corr (Eds.), *Children's encounters with death, bereavement, and coping* (pp. 21–38). New York, NY: Springer.

Corr, C. A., Corr, D. M., & Doka, K. J. (2019). *Death and dying, life and living* (8th ed.) Belmont, CA: Cengage.

Cotton, C. R., & Range, L. M. (2010). Children's death concepts: Relationship to cognitive functioning, age, experience with death, fear of death, and hopelessness. *Journal of Clinical Child Psychology*. Retrieved from http://www.tandfonline.com/doi/abs/10.1207/s15374424jccp1902_3

Counts, D. A., & Counts, D. R. (1985). I'm not dead yet? Aging and death: Processes and experiences in Kalia. In D. A. Counts & D. R. Counts (Eds.), *Aging and its transformations* (pp. 131–156). Langham, MD: University of America Press.

Curlin, F. A., Nwodim, C., Vance, J. L., Chin, M. H., & Lantos, J. D. (2008). To die, to sleep: US physicians' religious and other objections to physician-assisted suicide, terminal sedation, and withdrawal of life support. *American Journal of Hospice & Palliative Care, 25,* 112–120. doi:10.1177/1049909107310141

De Vries, B., Lana, R. D., & Falck, V. T. (1994). Parental bereavement over the life course: A theoretical intersection and empirical review. *OMEGA—Journal of Death and Dying, 29,* 47–69. doi:10.2190/XG2G-G77D-27FL-BCoT

Decker, C., Phillips, C. R., & Haase, J. E. (2004). Information needs of adolescents with cancer. *Journal of Pediatric Oncology Nursing, 21,* 327–334. Retrieved from http://jpo.sagepub.com/content/21/6/327.short

Dennis, D. (2008). *Living, dying, grieving.* Sudbury, MA: Jones & Bartlett.

Doka, K. J. (2015). The awareness of mortality: Continuing Kastenbaum's developmental legacy. *OMEGA—Journal of Death and Dying, 70,* 67–78. doi:10.2190/OM.70.1.g

Dopp, A. R., & Cain, A. C. (2012). The role of peer relationships in parental bereavement during childhood and adolescence. *Death Studies, 36,* 41–60. doi:10.1080/07481187.2011.573175

Dunsmore, J., & Quine, S. (1996). Information, support, and decision-making needs and preferences of adolescents with cancer. *Journal of Psychosocial Oncology, 13,* 39–56. doi:10.1300/J077V13N04_03

Egeland, M., Zunszain, P. A., & Pariante, C. M. (2015). Molecular mechanisms in the regulation of adult neurogenesis during stress. *Nature Reviews Neuroscience, 16,* 189–200. doi:10.1038/nrn3855

Elwert, F., & Christakis, N. A. (2008). The effect of widowhood on mortality by the causes of death of both spouses. *American Journal of Public Health, 98,* 2092–2098.

Enck, G. E. (2003). *The dying process* (Vol. 1). Thousand Oaks, CA: Sage.

Erikson, E. H. (1959). *Identity and the life cycle* (Vol. 1). New York, NY: Norton.

Erikson, E. H. (1982). *The life cycle completed.* New York, NY: Norton.

Erlangsen, A., Jeune, B., Bille-Brahe, U., & Vaupel, J. W. (2004). Loss of partner and suicide risks among oldest old: A population-based register study. *Age & Ageing, 33,* 378–383. Retrieved from 10.1093/ageing/afh128

Evans, A., Bagnall, R. D., Duflou, J., & Semsarian, C. (2013). Postmortem review and genetic analysis in sudden infant death syndrome: An 11-year review. *Human Pathology, 44,* 1730–1736. doi:10.1016/j.humpath.2013.01.024

Evans, W. J., Morley, J. E., Argilés, J., Bales, C., Baracos, V., Guttridge, D., . . . Anker, S. D. (2008). Cachexia: A new definition. *Clinical Nutrition, 27,* 793–799. doi:10.1016/j.clnu.2008.06.013

Fagundes, C. P., Murdock, K. W., LeRoy, A., Baameur, F., Thayer, J. F., & Heijnen, C. (2018). Spousal bereavement is associated with more pronounced ex vivo cytokine production and lower heart rate variability: Mechanisms underlying cardiovascular

risk? *Psychoneuroendocrinology, 93,* 65–71. doi:10.1016/j.psyneuen.2018.04.010

Field, N. P., Gal-Oz, E., & Bonanno, G. A. (2003). Continuing bonds and adjustment at 5 years after the death of a spouse. *Journal of Consulting and Clinical Psychology, 71,* 110–117. doi:10.1037/0022-006x.71.1.110

Filiano, J. J., & Kinney, H. C. (1994). A perspective on neuropathologic findings in victims of the sudden infant death syndrome: The triple-risk model. *Neonatology, 65,* 194–197. doi:10.1159/000244052

Fine, S. (2015). Supreme Court rules Canadians have right to doctor-assisted suicide. *The Globe and Mail.* Retrieved from http://www.theglobeandmail.com/news/national/supreme-court-rules-on-doctor-assisted-suicide/article22828437/

Finley, E. P., Garcia, A., Rosen, K., McGeary, D., Pugh, M. J., & Potter, J. S. (2017). Evaluating the impact of prescription drug monitoring program implementation: A scoping review. *BMC Health Services Research, 17,* 420. doi:10.1186/s12913-017-2354-5

Freed, P. J., Yanagihara, T. K., Hirsch, J., & Mann, J. J. (2009). Neural mechanisms of grief regulation. *Biological Psychiatry, 66,* 33–40. doi:10.1016/j.biopsych.2009.01.019

Gaab, E. M., Owens, G. R., & Macleod, R. D. (2013). Caregivers' estimations of their children's perceptions of death as a biological concept. *Death Studies, 37,* 693–703. Retrieved from 10.1080/07481187.2012.692454

Gavrin, J., & Chapman, C. R. (1995). Clinical management of dying patients. *Western Journal of Medicine, 163,* 268–277.

Gerritsen, L., Wang, H.-X., Reynolds, C. A., Fratiglioni, L., Gatz, M., & Pedersen, N. L. (2017). Influence of negative life events and widowhood on risk for dementia. *American Journal of Geriatric Psychiatry, 25,* 766–778. doi:10.1016/j.jagp.2017.02.009

Gray, R. E. (1989). Adolescents' perceptions of social support after the death of a parent. *Journal of Psychosocial Oncology, 7,* 127–144. doi:10.1300/J077v07n03_09

Greydanus, D. E., & Pratt, H. D. (2016). Caring for the dying adolescent. *International Journal of Child and Adolescent Health, 9,* 281–289.

Grosse, C., & Grosse, A. (2015). Assisted suicide: Models of legal regulation in selected European countries and the case law of the European Court of Human Rights. *Medicine, Science, and the Law, 55,* 246–258. doi:10.1177/0025802414540636

Guiaux, M., van Tilburg, T., & van Groenou, M. B. (2007). Changes in contact and support exchange in personal networks after widowhood. *Personal Relationships, 14,* 457–473.

Guo, Q., & Jacelon, C. S. (2014). An integrative review of dignity in end-of-life care. *Palliative Medicine, 28,* 931–940. doi:10.1177/0269216314528399

Gutierrez, I. T. (2009). *Understanding death in cultural context: A study of Mexican children and their families.* Retrieved from https://www.ideals.illinois.edu/handle/2142/72102

Gutiérrez, I. T., Rosengren, K. S., & Miller, P. J. (2014). Children's understanding of death: toward a contextualized and integrated

account: VI. Mexican American immigrants in the Centerville region: teachers, children, and parents. *Monographs of the Society for Research in Child Development, 79,* 97–112. doi:10.1111/mono.12081

Ha, J. H. (2010). The effects of positive and negative support from children on widowed older adults' psychological adjustment: A longitudinal analysis. *The Gerontologist, 50,* 471–481.

Hallberg, I. R. (2013). Death and dying from old people's point of view: A literature review. *Aging Clinical and Experimental Research, 16,* 87–103. doi:10.1007/BF03324537

Harris, P., & Gimenez, M. (2005). Children's acceptance of conflicting testimony: The case of death. *Journal of Cognition and Culture, 5,* 143–164. doi:10.1163/1568537054068606

Harvard Medical School ad Hoc Committee. (1968). A definition of irreversible coma. *JAMA, 205,* 337. doi:10.1001/jama.1968.03140320031009

Hebert, R. S., Dang, Q., & Schulz, R. (2006). Preparedness for the death of a loved one and mental health in bereaved caregivers of patients with dementia: Findings from the REACH study. *Journal of Palliative Medicine, 9,* 683–693. doi:10.1089/jpm.2006.9.683

Hoffman, K. M., Trawalter, S., Axt, J. R., & Oliver, M. N. (2016). Racial bias in pain assessment and treatment recommendations, and false beliefs about biological differences between Blacks and Whites. *Proceedings of the National Academy of Sciences of the United States of America, 113,* 4296–4301. doi:10.1073/pnas.1516047113

Horowitz, M. M. (1967). *Morne-Paysan: Peasant village in Martinique.* New York, NY: Holt, Rinehart and Winston.

Howarth, R. (2011). Concepts and controversies in grief and loss. *Journal of Mental Health Counseling, 33,* 4–10. doi:10.17744/mehc.33.1.900m56162888u737

Hoyert, D. L. (2012). *75 years of mortality in the United States, 1935–2010.* Hyattsville, MD: National Center for Health Statistics.

Hunter, S. B., & Smith, D. E. (2008). Predictors of children's understandings of death: Age, cognitive ability, death experience and maternal communicative competence. *OMEGA—Journal of Death and Dying, 57,* 143–162. doi:10.2190/OM.57.2.b

Infurna, F. J., & Luthar, S. S. (2017a). Parents' adjustment following the death of their child: Resilience is multidimensional and differs across outcomes examined. *Journal of Research in Personality, 68,* 38–53. doi:10.1016/j.jrp.2017.04.004

Infurna, F. J., & Luthar, S. S. (2017b). The multidimensional nature of resilience to spousal loss. *Journal of Personality and Social Psychology, 112,* 926–947. doi:10.1037/pspp0000095

Jacobs, S., Perez, J., Cheng, Y. I., Sill, A., Wang, J., & Lyon, M. E. (2015). Adolescent end of life preferences and congruence with their parents' preferences: Results of a survey of adolescents with cancer. *Pediatric Blood & Cancer, 62,* 710–714. doi:10.1002/pbc.25358

Jadhav, A., & Weir, D. (2017). Widowhood and depression in a cross-national perspective: Evidence from the United States, Europe,

Korea, and China. *Journals of Gerontology Series B: Psychological Sciences and Social Sciences, 1,* 316–326. doi:10.1093/geronb/gbx021

Jay, S. M., Green, V., Johnson, S., Caldwell, S., & Nitschke, R. (1987). Differences in death concepts between children wither cancer and physically healthy children. *Journal of Clinical Child Psychology, 16,* 301–306. doi:10.1207/s15374424jccp1604_2

Jecker, N. S. (2006). Euthanasia. In R. Schulz (Ed.), *The encyclopedia of aging* (4th ed., pp. 392–394). New York, NY: Springer.

Jecker, N. S. (2011). Medical futility and the death of a child. *Journal of Bioethical Inquiry, 8,* 133–139. doi:10.1007/s11673-011-9288-0

Jozefowski, J. T. (1999). *The Phoenix phenomenon: Rising from the ashes of grief.* Northvale, NJ: Jason Aronson.

Judd, D. (2014). *Give sorrow words: Working with a dying child.* London, England: Karmac.

Kastenbaum, R. J. (2012). *Death, society, and human experience.* New York, NY: Routledge.

Katz, J. (2017). Drug deaths in America are rising faster than ever. *New York Times.* Retrieved April 26, 2018, from https://www.nytimes.com/interactive/2017/06/05/upshot/opioid-epidemic-drug-overdose-deaths-are-rising-faster-than-ever.html

Keesee, N. J., Currier, J. M., & Neimeyer, R. A. (2008). Predictors of grief following the death of one's child: The contribution of finding meaning. *Journal of Clinical Psychology, 64,* 1145–1163. doi:10.1002/jclp.20502

Kenyon, B. L. (2001). Current research in children's conceptions of death: A critical review. *OMEGA—Journal of Death and Dying, 43,* 63–91. doi:10.2190/0X2B-B1N9-A579-DVK1

Khan, A. (2014). For young and old, it's wise to have a living will to state health-care wishes. *U.S. News & World Report.* Retrieved from http://health.usnews.com/health-news/health-wellness/articles/2014/12/19/why-you-need-a-living-will-even-at-age-18

Kochanek, K. D., Murphy, S. L., Xu, J., & Arias, E. (2017). Mortality in the United States, 2016 key findings data from the National Vital Statistics System. *NCHS Data Brief, 293.* Retrieved from https://www.cdc.gov/nchs/data/databriefs/db293.pdf

Kolodny, A., Courtwright, D. T., Hwang, C. S., Kreiner, P., Eadie, J. L., Clark, T. W., & Alexander, G. C. (2015). The prescription opioid and heroin crisis: A public health approach to an epidemic of addiction. *Annual Review of Public Health, 36,* 559–574. doi:10.1146/annurev-publhealth-031914-122957

Kowalski, S. D., & Bondmass, M. D. (2008). Physiological and psychological symptoms of grief in widows. *Research in Nursing & Health, 31,* 23–30. Retrieved from 10.1002/nur.20228

Krause, N., Pargament, K. I., & Ironson, G. (2016). In the shadow of death: Religious hope as a moderator of the effects of age on death anxiety. *Journals of Gerontology Series B: Psychological Sciences and Social Sciences, 22,* gbw039. doi:10.1093/geronb/gbw039

Kübler-Ross, E. (1969). *On death and dying.* New York, NY: Collier/Macmillan.

Lamers, E. P. (1995). Children, death, and fairy tales. *OMEGA—Journal of Death and Dying, 31,* 151–167. doi:10.2190/HXV5-WWE4-N1HH-4JEG

Laureys, S., Celesia, G. G., Cohadon, F., Lavrijsen, J., León-Carrión, J., Sannita, W. G., . . . Dolce, G. (2010). Unresponsive wakefulness syndrome: A new name for the vegetative state or apallic syndrome. *BMC Medicine, 8,* 68. doi:10.1186/1741-7015-8-68

Lazar, A., & Torney-Purta, J. (1991). The development of the subconcepts of death in young children: A short-term longitudinal study. *Child Development, 62,* 1321–1333. doi:10.1111/j.1467-8624.1991.tb01608.x

Legare, C. H., Evans, E. M., Rosengren, K. S., & Harris, P. L. (2012). The coexistence of natural and supernatural explanations across cultures and development. *Child Development, 83,* 779–793. doi:10.1111/j.1467-8624.2012.01743.x

Leming, M., & Dickinson, G. (2016). *Understanding dying, death, and bereavement.* Belmont, CA: Cengage Learning.

Lichtenthal, W. G., Currier, J. M., Neimeyer, R. A., & Keesee, N. J. (2010). Sense and significance: A mixed methods examination of meaning making after the loss of one's child. *Journal of Clinical Psychology, 66,* 791–812. doi:10.1002/jclp.20700

Lichter, I., & Hunt, E. (1990). The last 48 hours of life. *Journal of Palliative Care, 6,* 7–15. Retrieved from http://www.ncbi.nlm.nih.gov/pubmed/1704917

Lund, D. A., & Caserta, M. S. (2001). When the unexpected happens: Husbands coping with the deaths of their wives. In D. A. Lund (Ed.), *Men coping with grief* (pp. 147–167). Amityville, NY: Baywood.

Lunney, J. R., Lynn, J., Foley, D. J., Lipson, S., & Guralnik, J. M. (2003). Patterns of functional decline at the end of life. *JAMA, 289,* 2387. doi:10.1001/jama.289.18.2387

Maciejewski, P. K., Zhang, B., Block, S. D., & Prigerson, H. G. (2007). An empirical examination of the stage theory of grief. *JAMA, 297,* 716–723. doi:10.1001/jama.297.7.716

Mallon, B. (2008). *Death, dying and grief: Working with adult bereavement.* Thousand Oaks, CA: Sage.

Marks, N. F., Jun, H., & Song, J. (2007). Death of parents and adult psychological and physical well-being: A prospective U.S. national study. *Journal of Family Issues, 28,* 1611–1638. doi:10.1177/0192513X07302728

Martins, S. S., Santaella-Tenorio, J., Marshall, B. D. L., Maldonado, A., & Cerdá, M. (2015). Racial/ethnic differences in trends in heroin use and heroin-related risk behaviors among nonmedical prescription opioid users. *Drug and Alcohol Dependence, 151,* 278–283. doi:10.1016/j.drugalcdep.2015.03.020

Masten, A. S., Narayan, A. J., Silverman, W. K., & Osofsky, J. D. (2015). Children in war and disaster. In M. Bornstein & T. Leventhal (Eds.), *Handbook of child psychology and developmental science* (pp. 1–42). Hoboken, NJ: John Wiley. doi:10.1002/9781118963418.childpsy418

Mathers, C. D., Stevens, G. A., Boerma, T., White, R. A., & Tobias, M. I. (2014). Causes of international increases in older age life expectancy. *The Lancet, 385,* 540–548. doi:10.1016/S0140-6736(14)60569-9

Matusow, H., Rosenblum, A., & Parrino, M. (2018). Prescription drug monitoring program utilization among 15 US opioid treatment programs. *Journal of Substance Abuse Treatment, 85,* 17–20. doi:10.1016/J.JSAT.2017.11.009

McAdams, D. P. (2014). The life narrative at midlife. *New Directions for Child and Adolescent Development, 2014,* 57–69. doi:10.1002/cad.20067

McMahan, J. (2001). Brain death, cortical death and persistent vegetative state. In H. Kuhse & R. Singer (Eds.), *A companion to bioethics* (pp. 250–260). New York, NY: Blackwell.

McNamara, B., & Rosenwax, L. (2010). Which carers of family members at the end of life need more support from health services and why? *Social Science & Medicine, 70,* 1035–1041. doi:10.1016/j.socscimed.2009.11.029

Meshot, C. M., & Leitner, L. M. (1992). Adolescent mourning and parental death. *OMEGA—Journal of Death and Dying, 26,* 287–299. doi:10.2190/CHE4-F4ND-QY8C-J2Y5

Miller, P. J., & Rosengren, K. S. (2014). Children's understanding of death: Toward a contextualized and integrated account: VII. Final thoughts. *Monographs of the Society for Research in Child Development, 79,* 113–124. doi:10.1111/mono.12082

Mills, S. (2012). Sounds to soothe the soul: music and bereavement in a traditional South Korean death ritual. *Mortality, 17,* 145–157. doi:10.1080/13576275.2012.675231

Mirescu, C., & Gould, E. (2006). Stress and adult neurogenesis. *Hippocampus, 16,* 233–238. doi:10.1002/hipo.20155

Moon, J. R., Kondo, N., Glymour, M. M., & Subramanian, S. V. (2011). Widowhood and mortality: A meta-analysis. *PLoS ONE, 6,* e23465. doi:10.1371/journal.pone.0023465

Moon, R. Y., & Task Force on Sudden Infant Death Syndrome. (2016). SIDS and other sleep-related infant deaths: Evidence base for 2016 updated recommendations for a safe infant sleeping environment. *Pediatrics, 138,* e20162940. doi:10.1542/peds.2016-2940

Moos, N. L. (1994). An integrative model of grief. *Death Studies, 19,* 337–364. Retrieved from http://eric.ed.gov/?id=EJ511322

Naef, R., Ward, R., Mahrer-Imhof, R., & Grande, G. (2013). Characteristics of the bereavement experience of older persons after spousal loss: An integrative review. *International Journal of Nursing Studies, 50,* 1108–1121. doi:10.1016/j.ijnurstu.2012.11.026

National Institute of Aging. (2011). *Global health and aging.* Retrieved from https://www.nia.nih.gov/research/publication/global-health-and-aging/preface

Nelson, J. M., & Nelson, T. C. (2014). Advance directives: Empowering patients at the end of life. *The Nurse Practitioner, 39,* 34–40. doi:10.1097/01.NPR.0000454979.98327.89

Nguyen, S. P., & Rosengren, K. S. (2004). Parental reports of children's biological knowledge and misconceptions. *International Journal of Behavioral Development, 28,* 411–420. doi:10.1080/01650250444000108

Noppe, I. C., & Noppe, L. D. (2004). Adolescent experiences with death: Letting go of immortality. *Journal of Mental Health Counseling, 26,* 146–167. doi:10.17744/mehc.26.2.py2tk0kmay1ukc3v

O'Connor, M. F. (2012). Immunological and neuroimaging biomarkers of complicated grief. *Dialogues in Clinical Neuroscience, 14,* 141–148. Retrieved from http://www.ncbi.nlm.nih.gov/pubmed/22754286

O'Connor, M. F., Wellisch, D. K., Stanton, A. L., Eisenberger, N. I., Irwin, M. R., & Lieberman, M. D. (2008). Craving love? Enduring grief activates brain's reward center. *NeuroImage, 42,* 969–972. doi:10.1016/j.neuroimage.2008.04.256

Office for National Statistics. (2014). *Death registrations summary tables, England and Wales, 2013.* Retrieved from http://www.ons.gov.uk/ons/rel/vsob1/death-reg-sum-tables/2013/sty-mortality-rates-by-age.html

O'Halloran, C. M., & Altmaier, E. M. (1996). Awareness of death among children: Does a life-threatening illness alter the process of discovery? *Journal of Counseling & Development, 74,* 259–262. doi:10.1002/j.1556-6676.1996.tb01862.x

Ollove, M. (2015). *More states consider "death with dignity" laws.* Retrieved from http://www.pewtrusts.org/en/research-and-analysis/blogs/stateline/2015/3/09/more-states-consider-death-with-dignity-laws

Ollove, M. (2018). Aid-in-dying gains momentum as erstwhile opponents change their minds. Retrieved April 26, 2018, from http://www.pewtrusts.org/en/research-and-analysis/blogs/stateline/2018/03/09/aid-in-dying-gains-momentum-as-erstwhile-opponents-change-their-minds

Onrust, S. A., & Cuijpers, P. (2006). Mood and anxiety disorders in widowhood: A systematic review. *Aging & Mental Health, 10,* 327–334. Retrieved from 10.1080/13607860600638529

Opie, I., & Opie, P. (1969). *Children's games in street and playground: Chasing, catching, seeking, hunting, racing, dueling, exerting, daring, guessing, acting, and pretending.* Oxford, England: Oxford University Press.

Oregon Public Health Division. (2017). *Oregon Death With Dignity Act: 2015 data summary.* Retrieved from https://public.health.oregon.gov/ProviderPartnerResources/EvaluationResearch/DeathwithDignityAct/Documents/year18.pdf

Panagiotaki, G., Hopkins, M., Nobes, G., Ward, E., & Griffiths, D. (2018). Children's and adults' understanding of death: Cognitive, parental, and experiential influences. *Journal of Experimental Child Psychology, 166,* 96–115. doi:10.1016/J.JECP.2017.07.014

Panagiotaki, G., Nobes, G., Ashraf, A., & Aubby, H. (2015). British and Pakistani children's understanding of death: Cultural and developmental influences. *British Journal of Developmental Psychology, 33,* 31–44. doi:10.1111/BJDP.12064

Parks, S. E., Erck Lambert, A. B., & Shapiro-Mendoza, C. K. (2017). Racial and ethnic trends in sudden unexpected infant deaths: United States, 1995–2013. *Pediatrics, 139*(6). Retrieved from http://pediatrics.aappublications.org/content/early/2017/05/11/peds.2016-3844

Peskin, S. M. (2017, June 20). The symptoms of dying. *New York Times.* Retrieved from https://mobile.nytimes.com/2017/06/20/well/live/the-symptoms-of-dying.html

Pew Research Center. (2009). *End-of-life decisions: How Americans cope.* Retrieved from http://www.pewsocialtrends.org/2009/08/20/end-of-life-decisions-how-americans-cope/

Pew Research Center. (2013). *Views on end-of-life medical treatments.* Retrieved from http://www.pewforum.org/2013/11/21/views-on-end-of-life-medical-treatments/

Pousset, G., Bilsen, J., De Wilde, J., Benoit, Y., Verlooy, J., Bomans, A., . . . Mortier, F. (2009). Attitudes of adolescent cancer survivors toward end-of-life decisions for minors. *Pediatrics, 124,* e1142–e1148.

Powers, S. M., Bisconti, T. L., & Bergeman, C. S. (2014). Trajectories of social support and well-being across the first two years of widowhood. *Death Studies, 38,* 499–509. doi:10.1080/07481187.2013.846436

Radwany, S., Albanese, T., Clough, L., Sims, L., Mason, H., & Jahangiri, S. (2009). End-of-life decision making and emotional burden: Placing family meetings in context. *American Journal of Hospice & Palliative Care, 26,* 376–383. doi:10.1177/1049909109338515

Rao, J. K., Anderson, L. A., Lin, F.-C., & Laux, J. P. (2014). Completion of advance directives among U.S. consumers. *American Journal of Preventive Medicine, 46,* 65–70. doi:10.1016/j.amepre.2013.09.008

Renaud, S. J., Engarhos, P., Schleifer, M., & Talwar, V. (2015). Children's earliest experiences with death: Circumstances, conversations, explanations, and parental satisfaction. *Infant and Child Development, 24,* 157–174. doi:10.1002/icd.1889

Renz, M., Reichmuth, O., Bueche, D., Traichel, B., Mao, M. S., Cerny, T., & Strasser, F. (2018). Fear, pain, denial, and spiritual experiences in dying processes. *American Journal of Hospice and Palliative Medicine, 35,* 478–491. doi:10.1177/1049909117725271

Robin, L., & Omar, H. (2014). Adolescent bereavement. In J. Merrick, A. Tenenbaum, & H. A. Omar (Eds.), *School, adolescence, and health issues* (pp. 97–108). Hauppauge, NY: Nova Science.

Robinson, G. E. (2014). Pregnancy loss. *Best Practice & Research, Clinical Obstetrics & Gynaecology, 28,* 169–178. doi:10.1016/j.bpobgyn.2013.08.012

Rogers, C. H., Floyd, F. J., Seltzer, M. M., Greenberg, J., & Hong, J. (2008). Long-term effects of the death of a child on parents' adjustment in midlife. *Journal of Family Psychology, 22,* 203–211. doi:10.1037/0893-3200.22.2.203

Rosenblatt, P. C. (2008). Grief across cultures: A review and research agenda. In M. S. Stroebe, R. O. Hansson, H. Schut, W. Stroebe, & E. Van den Blink (Eds.), *Handbook of bereavement research and practice: Advances in theory and intervention* (pp. 207–222). Washington, DC: American Psychological Association.

Rosnick, C. B., Small, B. J., & Burton, A. M. (2010). The effect of spousal bereavement on cognitive functioning in a sample of older adults. *Aging, Neuropsychology & Cognition, 17,* 257–269. doi:10.1080/13825580903042692

Rossi Ferrario, S., Cardillo, V., Vicario, F., Balzarini, E., & Zotti, A. M. (2004). Advanced cancer

at home: Caregiving and bereavement. *Palliative Medicine, 18,* 129–136. doi:10.1191/0269216304pm8700a

Russac, R. J., Gatliff, C., Reece, M., & Spottswood, D. (2007). Death anxiety across the adult years: An examination of age and gender effects. *Death Studies, 31,* 549–561. doi:10.1080/07481180701356936

Saavedra Pérez, H. C., Ikram, M. A., Direk, N., Prigerson, H. G., Freak-Poli, R., Verhaaren, B. F. J., . . . Tiemeier, H. (2015). Cognition, structural brain changes and complicated grief: A population-based study. *Psychological Medicine, 45,* 1389–1399. doi:10.1017/S0033291714002499

Saldinger, A., Porterfield, K., & Cain, A. C. (2014). Meeting the needs of parentally bereaved children: A framework for child-centered parenting. *Psychiatry, 67,* 331–352.

Sasson, I., & Umberson, D. J. (2014). Widowhood and depression: New light on gender differences, selection, and psychological adjustment. *Journals of Gerontology Series B: Psychological Sciences and Social Sciences, 69,* 135–145. doi:10.1093/geronb/gbt058

Schoenfeld, T. J., & Gould, E. (2013). Differential effects of stress and glucocorticoids on adult neurogenesis. In C. Belzung & P. Wigmore (Eds.), *Neurogenesis and neural plasticity* (pp. 139–164). Heidelberg, Germany: Springer. doi:10.1007/7854_2012_233

Schonfeld, D. J., & Smilansky, S. (1989). A cross-cultural comparison of Israeli and American children's death concepts. *Death Studies, 13,* 593–604. doi:10.1080/07481188908252335

Seth, P., Scholl, L., Rudd, R. A., & Bacon, S. (2018). Overdose deaths involving opioids, cocaine, and psychostimulants—United States, 2015–2016. *MMWR. Morbidity and Mortality Weekly Report, 67,* 349–358. doi:10.15585/mmwr.mm6712a1

Shapiro-Mendoza, C. K., Colson, E. R., Willinger, M., Rybin, D. V., Camperlengo, L., & Corwin, M. J. (2014). Trends in infant bedding use: National Infant Sleep Position Study, 1993–2010. *Pediatrics, 135,* 10–17.

Shear, K., Frank, E., Houck, P. R., & Reynolds, C. F. (2005). Treatment of complicated grief. *JAMA, 293,* 2601. doi:10.1001/jama.293.21.2601

Siegel, K., & Weinstein, L. (2008). Anticipatory grief reconsidered. *Journal of Psychosocial Oncology, 1,* 61–73. doi:10.1300/J077v01n02_04

Singhal, A., Tien, Y.-Y., & Hsia, R. Y. (2016). Racial-ethnic disparities in opioid prescriptions at emergency department visits for conditions commonly associated with prescription drug abuse. *PLoS ONE, 11,* e0159224. doi:10.1371/journal.pone.0159224

Slaughter, V. (2005). Young children's understanding of death. *Australian Psychologist, 40,* 179–186.

Slaughter, V., & Griffiths, M. (2007). Death understanding and fear of death in young children. *Clinical Child Psychology and Psychiatry, 12,* 525–535. doi:10.1177/1359104507080980

Song, J., Floyd, F. J., Seltzer, M. M., Greenberg, J. S., & Hong, J. (2010). Long-term effects of child death on parents' health related quality of life: A dyadic analysis. *Family Relations, 59,* 269–282. doi:10.1111/j.1741-3729.2010.00601.x

Speece, M. W., & Brent, S. B. (1984). Children's understanding of death: A review of three components of a death concept. *Child Development, 55,* 1671.

Spinelli, J., Collins-Praino, L., Van Den Heuvel, C., & Byard, R. W. (2017). Evolution and significance of the triple risk model in sudden infant death syndrome. *Journal of Paediatrics and Child Health, 53,* 112–115. doi:10.1111/jpc.13429

Stevens, M. M., & Dunsmore, J. C. (1996). Adolescents who are living with a life-threatening illness. In C. A. Corr & D. E. Balk (Eds.), *Handbook of adolescent death and bereavement* (pp. 107–135). New York, NY: Springer.

Stevens, M. M., Rytmeister, R. J., Protor, M. T., & Bolster, P. (2010). Children living with life-threatening or life-limiting illnesses: A dispatch from the front lines. In E. Balk & C. A. Corr (Eds.), *Children's encounters with death, bereavement, and coping* (pp. 147–166). New York, NY: Springer.

Stikkelbroek, Y., Bodden, D. H. M., Reitz, E., Vollebergh, W. A. M., & van Baar, A. L. (2016). Mental health of adolescents before and after the death of a parent or sibling. *European Child & Adolescent Psychiatry, 25,* 49–59. doi:10.1007/s00787-015-0695-3

Stokes, J. (2009). Resilience and bereaved children. *Bereavement Care, 28,* 9–17. doi:10.1080/02682620902746078

Stroebe, M., & Schut, H. (2010). The dual process model of coping with bereavement: A decade on. *OMEGA—Journal of Death and Dying, 61,* 273–289. doi:10.2190/OM.61.4.b

Stroebe, M., & Schut, H. (2016). Overload: A missing link in the dual process model? *OMEGA—Journal of Death and Dying, 74,* 96–109. doi:10.1177/0030222816666540

Stroebe, M., Schut, H., & Boerner, K. (2010). Continuing bonds in adaptation to bereavement: Toward theoretical integration. *Clinical Psychology Review, 30,* 259–268. doi:10.1016/j.cpr.2009.11.007

Stroebe, M., Schut, H., & Boerner, K. (2017). Cautioning health-care professionals. *OMEGA—Journal of Death and Dying, 74,* 455–473. doi:10.1177/0030222817691870

Subramanian, S. V., Elwert, F., & Christakis, N. (2008). Widowhood and mortality among the elderly: The modifying role of neighborhood concentration of widowed individuals. *Social Science & Medicine, 66,* 873–884.

Sweeting, H. N., & Gilhooly, M. L. M. (1990). Anticipatory grief: A review. *Social Science & Medicine, 30,* 1073–1080. doi:10.1016/0277-9536(90)90293-2

Swift, A. (2016). *Euthanasia still acceptable to solid majority in U.S.* Retrieved from http://www.gallup.com/poll/193082/euthanasia-acceptable-solid-majority.aspx

Tang, S., & Chow, A. Y. M. (2017). How do risk factors affect bereavement outcomes in later life? An exploration of the mediating role of dual process coping. *Psychiatry Research, 255,* 297–303. doi:10.1016/j.psychres.2017.06.001

Task Force on Sudden Infant Death Syndrome. (2016). SIDS and other sleep-related infant deaths: Updated 2016 recommendations for a safe infant sleeping environment. *Pediatrics, 138,* e20162938. doi:10.1542/peds.2016-2938

Teitelbaum, J., & Shemie, S. (2016). Brain death. In M. M. Smith, G. G. Citerio, & W. A. I. Kofke (Eds.), *Oxford textbook of neurocritical care* (pp. 390–398). Oxford, UK: Oxford University Press. doi:10.1093/med/9780198739555.003.0029

Theunissen, J. M. J., Hoogerbrugge, P. M., van Achterberg, T., Prins, J. B., Vernooij-Dassen, M. J. F. J., & van den Ende, C. H. M. (2007). Symptoms in the palliative phase of children with cancer. *Pediatric Blood & Cancer, 49,* 160–165. doi:10.1002/pbc.21042

Trevino, K. M., Litz, B., Papa, A., Maciejewski, P. K., Lichtenthal, W., Healy, C., & Prigerson, H. G. (2018). Bereavement challenges and their relationship to physical and psychological adjustment to loss. *Journal of Palliative Medicine, 21,* 479–488. doi:10.1089/jpm.2017.0386

Tyson-Rawson, K. J. (1996). Adolescent responses to the death of a parent. In C. Corr & E. M. Balk (Eds.), *Handbook of adolescent death and bereavement* (pp. 155–172). New York, NY: Springer.

Ubelacker, S. (2017). *Canada's opioid crisis is burdening the health care system, report warns—National | Globalnews.ca.* Retrieved April 26, 2018, from https://globalnews.ca/news/3743705/canadas-opioid-crisis-is-burdening-the-health-care-system-report-warns/

Umberson, D. (2003). *Death of a parent: Transition to a new adult identity.* Cambridge, UK: Cambridge University Press.

U.S. Department of Health and Human Services. (2018). *About the US opioid epidemic | HHS.gov.* Retrieved April 26, 2018, from https://www.hhs.gov/opioids/about-the-epidemic/

van der Maas, P. (1991). Euthanasia and other medical decisions concerning the end of life. *The Lancet, 338,* 669–674. doi:10.1016/0140-6736(91)91241-L

Ward, L., Mathias, J. L., & Hitchings, S. E. (2007). Relationships between bereavement and cognitive functioning in older adults. *Gerontology, 53,* 362–372.

Weitzen, S., Teno, J. M., Fennell, M., & Mor, V. (2003). Factors associated with site of death: A national study of where people die. *Medical Care, 41,* 323–335. doi:10.1097/01.MLR.0000044913.37084.27

Weitzner, M. A., Haley, W. E., & Chen, H. (2000). The family caregiver of the older cancer patient. *Hematology/Oncology Clinics of North America, 14,* 269–281. doi:10.1016/S0889-8588(05)70288-4

Wheeler, I. (2001). Parental bereavement: The crisis of meaning. *Death Studies, 25,* 51–66. doi:10.1080/07481801750058627

Whitbourne, S. K. (2007). *Adult development and aging: Biopsychosocial perspectives.* New York, NY: John Wiley.

Wijngaards-de Meij, L., Stroebe, M., Schut, H., Stroebe, W., van den Bout, J., van der Heijden, P. G. M., & Dijkstra, I. (2008). Parents grieving the loss of their child: Interdependence in coping. *British Journal of Clinical Psychology, 47,* 31–42. doi:10.1348/014466507x216152

Wolfelt, A. (2013). *Healing the bereaved child.* New York, NY: Routledge.

Woodgate, R. L. (2006). Living in a world without closure: Reality for parents who have experienced the death of a child. *Journal of Palliative Care, 22,* 75–82.

Wright, P. M., & Hogan, N. S. (2008). Grief theories and models: Applications to hospice nursing practice. *Journal of Hospice & Palliative Nursing, 10,* 350–356.

Zaitchik, D., Iqbal, Y., & Carey, S. (2014). The effect of executive function on biological reasoning in young children: An individual differences study. *Child Development, 85,* 160–175. doi:10.1111/cdev.12145

NAME INDEX

SUBJECT INDEX